INTRODUCTION TO
PHILOSOPHY

Classical and Contemporary Readings

SEVENTH EDITION

edited by

JOHN PERRY

University of California, Riverside
Stanford University

MICHAEL BRATMAN

Stanford University

JOHN MARTIN FISCHER

University of California, Riverside

New York   Oxford
OXFORD UNIVERSITY PRESS

Oxford University Press is a department of the University of Oxford.
It furthers the University's objective of excellence in research,
scholarship, and education by publishing worldwide.

Oxford   New York
Auckland   Cape Town   Dar es Salaam   Hong Kong   Karachi
Kuala Lumpur   Madrid   Melbourne   Mexico City   Nairobi
New Delhi   Shanghai   Taipei   Toronto

With offices in
Argentina   Austria   Brazil   Chile   Czech Republic   France   Greece
Guatemala   Hungary   Italy   Japan   Poland   Portugal   Singapore
South Korea   Switzerland   Thailand   Turkey   Ukraine   Vietnam

For titles covered by Section 112 of the US Higher Education
Opportunity Act, please visit www.oup.com/us/he for the
latest information about pricing and alternate formats.

Published by Oxford University Press
198 Madison Avenue, New York, New York 10016
http://www.oup.com

Oxford is a registered trademark of Oxford University Press

Library of Congress Cataloging-in-Publication Data
Introduction to philosophy: classical and contemporary readings / edited by John Perry,
Michael Bratman, University of California, Riverside, Stanford University, John Martin Fischer,
University of California, Riverside.—SEVENTH EDITION.
     pages cm
   ISBN 978-0-19-020023-7 (student edition)—ISBN 978-0-19-020024-4 (instructor's edition)—
ISBN 978-0-19-020027-5 (coursesmart e-book) 1. Philosophy—Textbooks. I. Perry, John,
1943- editor. II. Bratman, Michael, editor. III. Fischer, John Martin, 1952- editor.
  BD21.I54 2015
  100—dc23

                    2015012246

Printing number: 9 8 7 6 5 4 3 2 1

Printed in the United States of America
on acid-free paper

FOR OUR CHILDREN

Jim, Sarah, and Joe Perry

Gregory and Scott Bratman

Aja Marie Newton and

Ariel and Zoe Fischer

CONTENTS

PART VI

PART VII

PREFACE

)X(

I N this anthology we have collected a variety of readings for use in a course or sequence
of courses designed to introduce students to philosophy. We have based the selection on
various introductory courses at Stanford University and the University of California,
Riverside. These courses are built around classic texts supplemented by shorter selections
from the past and present. We have included in this anthology not only texts that we have
found successful, but others that a survey of colleagues at other institutions have identified
as suitable. Thus, the total number of selections is larger than can reasonably be covered in
even a two-quarter sequence, and instructors will want to pick those that fit their approach.
We have included some footnotes from the original selections but have eliminated others.
In some cases, footnotes were eliminated because they could not be understood in the context of the selection; in other cases, this was done simply to save space. The remaining
footnotes have been renumbered.

Punctuation and other matters of style have been altered to conform to American conventions, with a couple of exceptions. In cases in which quotation marks are clearly used for
mentioning linguistic items—and the author's practice indicates an intent to note this specific use of such marks—punctuation that is not part of the mentioned item has not been
moved inside the marks. In other cases, single quotes have been left where they would
normally be replaced by double quotes, since they appeared to be making a distinction of
importance to the author.

Part VII, "Puzzles and Paradoxes," consists of short statements of some famous, interesting, and philosophically relevant mind-benders. We have found these mind-benders useful
in several ways in introducing students to philosophy: as paper assignments, as subjects for
the odd short lecture after an exam or a vacation, as challenges for motivated students, or as
materials to be worked into other sections of the book. We hope others find them as much
fun to teach with as we have. We are grateful to Carl Ginet of Cornell University who
shared with us his experience of using such puzzles to introduce students to philosophy.

College students of the present era tend to be preoccupied with preparation for a
career—a preoccupation one can hardly criticize, given the expense of a college education

and the concerns of parents as well as a civilization that is rich in opportunities for those who are technically prepared and full of pitfalls for those who are not. But, for most students, college will be the only opportunity to address the enduring problems of human existence; to examine carefully and thoughtfully the beliefs and values inherited from culture and parents; to gain an appreciation of the unsettled questions at the foundations of science and culture; and to develop habits of orderly, but imaginative, thinking. It is the job of the teacher of philosophy to encourage and assist students in taking advantage of this opportunity, and we feel there could be few callings as exciting and fulfilling. We hope this anthology will be of some value to our like-minded colleagues.

New in This Edition

We have made some exciting and very substantial revisions in the seventh edition of *Introduction to Philosophy*:

- Papers on the problem of evil by Marilyn McCord Adams, Stewart Sutherland, Eleonore Stump, and Louise Antony
- Papers on moral responsibility by Gary Watson and Susan Wolf
- A paper on justice and equality by Annette Baier
- Papers on abortion by Judith Jarvis Thomson and Rosalind Hursthouse
- A paper on race by Linda Martin Alcoff
- A paper on death by Dan Moller

Ancillary Materials

Students are warmly invited to the **Companion Website** at www.oup.com/us/perry. This interactive website has additional pedagogical materials and links to other online resources that are related to the material in the book, including flashcards of key terms, guidelines for writing philosophy papers, a "Logical Toolkit," and practice quizzes with five multiple-choice and three true/false questions per reading.

Additional materials for **instructors** are housed on the Oxford University Press **Ancillary Resource Center (ARC)**, a convenient, instructor-focused single destination for resources to accompany your text. Accessed online through individual user accounts, the ARC provides instructors with access to up-to-date ancillaries at any time while guaranteeing the security of grade-significant resources. Available on the ARC:

- An Instructor's Manual, including sample syllabi, guidelines for writing philosophy papers, a "Logical Toolkit," and summaries of each of the book's readings.
- A Computerized Test Bank, including three to five essay, ten multiple-choice, and five true/false questions per reading.
- Lecture outlines in PowerPoint format.

The ARC can be accessed from the Companion Website or by visiting oup-arc.com.

Ancillary materials are also available as **Learning Management System Cartridges**, in fully downloadable format for instructors using a learning management system in their courses.

Acknowledgments

We would like to thank the following professors for their useful comments in preparation of the seventh edition:

Louise Antony, *University
    of Massachusetts–Amherst*
Stewart Duncan, *University of Florida*
Carol Gould, *Florida Atlantic
    University*
Shane Gronholz, *University of
    Colorado–Boulder*
Sally Haslanger, *Massachusetts
    Institute of Technology*
Barry Lam, *Vassar College*

Seung-Kee Lee, *Drew University*
Tracie Mahaffey, *Florida State University*
Eugene Marshall, *Wellesley College*
Aleksandar Pjevalica, *University of
    Texas–El Paso*
Lewis Powell, *SUNY–Buffalo*
William Ramsey, *University of
    Nevada–Las Vegas*
Mark Rosner, *University of Manitoba*
Meghan Sullivan, *Notre Dame University*

We also thank Robert Miller of Oxford University Press for his invaluable support and help in the production of this book. We are especially grateful to David Beglin for his outstanding assistance in the process of preparing the book for publication.

We very much hope that you will continue to find the book both challenging and fun. Even if you don't fall in love with philosophy, we hope that this will at least be the start of a meaningful life-long relationship.

J.P.
M.B.
J.M.F.

PART I

PHILOSOPHY

INTRODUCTION

Welcome to philosophy. For some of you, it will be the most practical subject you will study in college.

Why would we say that? Doesn't philosophy have a reputation for being *impractical*? Isn't it abstract and theoretical—the very opposite of practical?

Philosophy can be abstract and theoretical. But the study of philosophy can be practical in that it affects what you do with your life. This is because the abstractions and theories pertain to the basic concepts and values with which you confront experience.

Humans do things for reasons. We want certain things, and we believe that acting in certain ways will get us those things. So we act. Rocks don't act for reasons, but we do. It's part of what makes us human. Our desires and beliefs provide us with those reasons. Values and concepts are the building blocks of desires and beliefs. Thus our values and concepts play a big role in determining what we do and who we are.

Humans also reflect on and criticize the reasons we do things. Do we have good reasons for our reasons? Why do we want what we want? Why do we believe what we believe?

Having the capacity to reflect on one's reasons is another part of being human. It's a capacity that divides us from most of our fellow animals. We not only believe things, we can think about why we believe things. We not only want things, we can ask ourselves why we want them.

All humans have this capacity to reflect on their beliefs and desires, on their basic concepts and values. But not everyone likes to do so. It is the love of this activity that draws a person to philosophy. Do you worry about whether there is a God? What the difference between the future and the past is? Why we can't turn around in time as we can in space? Whether you are really a brain in a vat in someone's experiment? Whether other humans have minds, or just you? How you would know if blue things looked to you just like green things look to everyone else? How you can be free, if every physical event has a physical cause? Have you ever wondered what made it wrong to lie and cheat? Whether democracy was really better than other political systems, or just the one you happened to grow up in? If this all sounds like you, taking a philosophy course may be one of the most enjoyable and most liberating experiences of your life.

Why should reflecting on one's beliefs and desires be liberating? Because in a very real sense your beliefs and desires, because they motivate what you do, define who you are.

But where did those desires, values, and beliefs come from? Are they merely the accidental result of where you were born, who your parents and teachers and friends were? Philosophy can be liberating because it helps us reflect on the basic concepts with which we deal with experience and the desires that motivate us to do what we do, and to put our personal stamp on them. We can never fully escape limitations on our vision that result from the particular time and place in which we live. But through reading and thinking we can examine and challenge ideas that seem natural from our perspective with ideas that come from quite different points of view. Those of our values and concepts that survive this process will be more truly our own.

While college may seem like a hectic time, it is the best opportunity that most of us have to reflect intensively on who we are, to examine the source of our own way of looking at things, and seriously to consider alternatives. One of the saddest things that can happen to a person is to realize that she has committed a large part of her life to goals that upon reflection don't seem very important, on the basis of beliefs that upon reflection don't seem very plausible. Because your philosophy class gives you tools and opportunity to reflect on your basic values and concepts, and to develop habits of reflection, it may be the most practical course you take in college.

The philosophy class in which you are enrolled, and for which this book is a text, is part of a long tradition, stretching back to ancient times, of reflecting on the most basic values and beliefs that humans have. Philosophy means thinking as hard and as clearly as one can about some of the most interesting and enduring problems that human minds have ever encountered. Some of these problems have been discussed since ancient times. What makes acts right or wrong? You can read what the ancient philosopher Plato, the eighteenth-century philosopher David Hume, and the contemporary philosopher Tom Nagel have to say about it. What is it to be conscious? You can read what the seventeenth-century philosopher René Descartes, the pioneer of computer theory Alan Turing, and the contemporary philosopher John Searle think about that. Other problems are as timely as your morning paper. Is there anything wrong with a woman renting out her body? You can read what Debra Satz thinks about that. Is it immoral to get an abortion? You can read what Rosalind Hursthouse and Judith Thomson say about that.

To read philosophy well one must read slowly and aggressively. This may mean breaking some habits. There is a lot of emphasis today on reading fast. This is the age of information. To take advantage of the information available to us (even to cope with it) or to master that which is important for our job, for responsible citizenship, or for a full life—or at any rate for the final or the midterm—you have to learn to absorb large amounts of information in limited amounts of time. The college student, one hears, must learn to read at a minimum of 1000 words a minute. And 2000 or 3000 words is better; and those who really want to get ahead should read so fast that the only limiting factor in the speed with which they read is the speed with which they can turn pages.

These skills may be suitable for some types of reading, but not for philosophy. Good philosophers develop arguments and theories of some intricacy: arguments that are designed to convince the reader of the author's position on important issues. Reading such works is valuable insofar as one grapples with the ideas—not only fighting to understand the author but also, once one does, fighting with him or her for control of one's mind. One should not be easily convinced of one position or another on issues so weighty as the existence of God, the indirectness of our knowledge of the external world, or the nature of justice.

Of course, all generalizations are a bit suspect. When one is reading for pleasure or to absorb straightforward information from a reliable source, speed-reading can be fine. But, if one derives pleasure from reading philosophy, it should be the pleasure of grappling with important and sublime ideas, not the exhilaration of racing through a thriller. And, when one learns from reading philosophy, it should be a result of being forced to think through new ideas and grasp new concepts, not simply the uploading of a data file from the text to the mind.

College students will have learned that mathematics and other technical material cannot be read in overdrive. But philosophy can be deceptive. It cannot be claimed that good philosophy always makes good reading, but some philosophy does. A lot of philosophy, including a good portion of the famous historical works included in this anthology, makes pleasant reading. It does not contain symbols, equations, charts, or other obvious signs of technicality and intricacy. One can just sit down and read Hume, or even Descartes, getting a feel for the author's position and style and the historical perspective of the work. When these texts are assigned in courses that survey the literature of various periods—with an eye toward getting a sense of the flow of ideas and concerns—as parts of larger assignments that cover hundreds of pages a week, one may have little choice but to read philosophy in this way, that is, just to get a feel for what is going on.

But appearances to the contrary, philosophy is inevitably technical. The philosopher constructs arguments, theories, positions, or criticisms in an attempt to persuade his or her most intelligent and perceptive opponents. The ideas and issues dealt with have a long history: to say something new, interesting, and persuasive, the philosopher must build his or her case with care. The result may be understood on various levels; to understand it at the deepest level, the reader must adopt the stance of the intelligent and perceptive opponent, thus coming to understand the case the philosopher is trying to make. This is what we mean by reading aggressively.

To read philosophy in this way, one should imagine onself in a dialogue with the philosopher—as if the philosopher were one's roommate (or an intelligent and articulate new roommate) trying to convince one of a startling new idea.

To see this approach at work, let's consider an example. Here is a passage from Descartes's "First Meditation."

> Today, then having rid myself of worries and having arranged for some peace and quiet, I withdraw alone, free at last earnestly and wholeheartedly to overthrow all my beliefs.
>
> To do this, I do not need to show each of my beliefs to be false; I may never be able to do that. But, since reason now convinces me that I ought to withhold my assent just as carefully from what is not obviously certain and indubitable as from what is obviously false, I can justify the rejection of all my beliefs if I can find some ground for doubt in each. And, to do this, I need not take on the endless task of running through my beliefs one by one: since a building collapses when its foundation is cut out from under it, I will go straight to the principles on which all my former beliefs rested.

Let's start with the second paragraph. The first place to pause is the word *this*. Whenever one encounters a demonstrative pronoun or other device by which the author refers back to something earlier, one should pause and make sure one knows to what it refers.

DESCARTES: To do this . . .
YOU: Wait a minute. To do what? Oh yes, I see, *to overthrow all your beliefs*.

But what is to overthrow one's beliefs? This sort of phrase ought immediately to occasion a demand for clarification.

Y: What do you mean, "Overthrow all your beliefs" anyway? Every one of them? You must be kidding? You are trying to make yourself believe everything you now believe is false? Can that really be what you mean?

Of course, Descartes isn't your roommate and, in fact, is long dead. So he can't respond to you. Still, you should mentally—or on the margin of your book—note this question.

Y: Well, of course you can't respond. But this sounds pretty odd. I will keep my eye open for clarification of just what it is you are trying to do.
D: As I was saying: To do this, I do not need to show each of my beliefs to be false; I may never be able to do that.
Y: Well, I didn't have to wait long. It's a relief that you aren't going to show all of your beliefs to be false. Still, it sounds as if this is something you want to do but simply don't think you could. The point of even wanting to seems a bit obscure. Go ahead.
D: But, since reason now convinces me . . .
Y: Reason. Reason. I wonder what exactly you mean by that. Hmm, this is the first use of the word. I mean, I know the meaning of the word *reason*, but it sounds as if you have something rather definite in mind. Actually, I use the word as a verb rather than a noun. Maybe I had better look it up in the dictionary. Here we are: "A statement offered in explanation." That doesn't seem to fit. *Motive, cause,* likewise. *Sanity.* That must be as in, "He has lost his reason." Or *intelligence.* One of these must be the closest. The latter seems better. So you are saying that your intelligence convinces you that you should be a great deal more cautious about what you believe—that's what this seems to amount to. Still, I have a hunch that more is packed into your use of the word *reason* than I can get out of the dictionary. The prof said you were a rationalist and that they put great emphasis on the power of reason. I'll keep it in mind that this is a key word and look for other clues as to exactly what you mean by it.
D: . . . That I ought to withhold my assent just as carefully from what is not obviously certain and indubitable as from what is obviously false; I can justify the rejection of all my beliefs if I can find some ground for doubt in each.
Y: Wait a minute. You just said a mouthful. Let me try to sort it out. Let's see. *Withhold my assent.* So you said you were going to overthrow your beliefs at the end of the last paragraph. Then, you said to do this you don't need to show that they are false. So *withholding assent* must be how you describe the in-between position—you have quit believing something, and although you haven't shown it false, you don't believe the opposite either.
  Wait a minute. Does that make sense? If I don't believe that $3 + 5 = 8$, don't I automatically believe that it's not the case that $3 + 5 = 8$? Hmm. I guess not. Suppose it was $358 + 267$. Until I add it up, I neither believe it does equal 625 nor believe that it doesn't. So I guess that's where one is at when one is *withholding assent*.

Here is another mouthful: "Not obviously certain and indubitable." I'll look up the last word. *Unquestionable: Too evident to be doubted.* How is that different from certain? If your *Meditations* is one of the all-time classics, why are you being redundant in this show-offy way? Maybe I should give you the benefit of the doubt.

Let's see, the contrast is between *certain and indubitable*—no, wait, *obviously certain and indubitable*—and *obviously false.* Clearly one withholds one's assent from what is obviously false. So what you are saying is that you are going to do the same for *everything*, except that which is obviously certain and indubitable. And your reason, which seems to amount to your intelligence, is what leads you to do this. OK, proceed.

D: ... I can justify the rejection of all my beliefs ...

Y: You seem to go back and forth between a pretty sensible position—not believing what you aren't really sure of—and something that sounds a bit weird. Before you said you were going to try to overthrow *all* your beliefs; now you are trying to justify rejecting *all* your beliefs. I must admit, even though you have quite a reputation as a philosopher, this project strikes me as sort of extreme.

D: ... If I can find some ground for doubt in each ...

Y: Oh dear, another technical-sounding phrase: *ground for doubt.* I better pull out my *Webster's* again. Well, you aren't using *ground* to mean dirt and you don't mean the bottom of a body of water, so you must mean *basis for belief or argument.* It sounds as if you are going to look for some basis for an argument *against* every single one of your beliefs. *That* sounds like quite a project. I wonder how come your *Meditations* is so short if you are really going to go through each one of your beliefs.

D: And, to do this, I need not take on the endless task of running through my beliefs one by one ...

Y: Well, that's a relief.

D: ... Since a building collapses when its foundation is cut out from under it, I will go straight to the principles on which all my former beliefs rested.

Y: Relying on a metaphor at a crucial point, eh? I thought the prof said that was a dubious practice. She said we should look at the assumptions underlying the appropriateness of the metaphor. So it looks like you think your beliefs form a *structure* with a *foundation.* The foundation is principles. All your beliefs rest on—i.e., I suppose, depend on in some way—certain principles. For this all to make sense, these principles must be beliefs. So what you are saying is that you are going to isolate certain beliefs, on which the rest depend. If you have a ground for doubt for a principle, you will quit believing it, not in the sense of taking it to be false or believing the opposite, but in the sense of withholding your assent. In so doing, you will automatically have a ground for doubt for all other beliefs that depend on the dubious principle.

Well, I guess that's an intelligible project. It still seems like it ought to take a lot longer than 50 pages. We shall see ...

This is what it is like to read aggressively.

But being part of the philosophy tradition doesn't just mean reading about what others have thought. It means thinking yourself, long and hard, about the problems that interest you, and writing about them.

Now there may be a bit of a problem here. We said that in taking this philosophy class you are joining a tradition that goes back to Hume and Descartes and Aristotle and Plato. We have invited you to think about big issues and basic concepts. But when you get your writing assignments, your teacher will no doubt warn you against trying to be too deep and profound.

Imagine going to the ballet. You are impressed with the ballerina, and decide that you want to become one. The day of your first ballet lesson arrives. You have visions of a whole new world opening up to you; you imagine yourself gliding across the floor, spinning, jumping. But you find that your ballet lesson isn't like that at all. You spend a lot of time stretching and doing other exercises that you don't remember anyone doing when you saw *Swan Lake.*

Your first experience writing philosophy is going to be like that. You have read some of the works of the great philosophers. You are eager to share with the world some of your own deep philosophical thoughts, and to attack head on some big problems. But what you will be asked to do, in all likelihood, is to write a very short and very clear essay on a very restricted topic. And when your teacher grades the essay, she may miss all the profundity and focus on the fact that you didn't state with absolute clarity some mundane things she should have known anyway.

A good ballet requires numerous small, precise movements on the part of the dancer, the ones she has practiced over and over for years. But these are not visible without close inspection; instead one sees a beautiful, creative, and seemingly effortless movement of the whole dancer. Somewhat similarly, as one reads a good philosophy article the original ideas, broad themes, and central conclusions will be apparent. But underneath there will be a solid structure of close argumentation, where the philosopher gives you reasons for adopting her view and for rejecting the views of others. So don't be discouraged because you are being asked to master this skill. Plato, Descartes, Hume, Lewis, and Thomson all went through the same thing.

Here are some of the skills you need to master to do well in philosophy:

- Analyzing statements and arguments.

When you were working to understand Descartes in the passage we went through earlier, you were analyzing his statements. You were making sure you understood each word, and knew the possible ambiguities.

In a good philosophical essay the statements will add up to arguments, with premises and a conclusion. (For more about arguments, see the entry *deductive argument* in the glossary and the related entries.) You need to learn to spot the main conclusions the philosopher is arguing for, and the premises she uses to establish them.

- Imagining alternatives to familiar views and situations.

Nothing is more important to a philosopher than a good imagination. If you encounter a generalization, you should try to see if you can think of a counterexample. If you encounter a view that seems strange or absurd, you should try to see if you can imagine what experiences would lead someone to hold that view.

- Stating things explicitly, clearly, and succinctly.

Saint Paul said, "Faith, Hope and Charity, but the greatest of these is Charity." As a novice philosopher, your motto should be "Truth, Profundity, Clarity, but the greatest of these is Clarity." The reason is this. Our language is built around familiar ideas and situations. Philosophers often need to express thoughts that push the limits of language, because they want to consider unfamiliar ideas and odd situations. When doing this, it's relatively easy to sound profound, but very difficult to be clear. But if you are not clear, you cannot be sure that what you say is true, nor can you get the help of others to figure out whether it is.

Looking constantly for concrete examples that nail down what you are getting at is one of the best ways of keeping your thinking and writing clear. Another is to imagine a reader of your own work, who is reading it as slowly and aggressively as we encouraged you to read the philosophical works you encounter. Indeed, don't just imagine such a reader, become such a reader, rooting out unclarity and ambiguity in your own work.

- Thinking creatively.

A lot of philosophy is analysis and criticism: criticism of the concepts and values you inherit, criticism of the ideas you encounter in the work of others, and criticism of your own ideas. But one of the most important values of the philosophical tradition has been the new concepts and values that emerge from the stubborn reflection on old ones. At the beginning of virtually every social and scientific revolution, there stands a philosopher who not only questioned some idea or practice of her age, but was able to suggest something better.

If you can develop these skills as a philosophy student, then there is another way in which philosophy may be a very practical pursuit for you. Most professions highly value persons who can carry the analysis of a position or an argument to a deeper level, who can identify and untangle assumptions, and who can communicate effectively about complicated matters. Our world is a world replete with documents, deliberations, and decisions. The person who can bring rigor, clarity, and imagination to bear on dealing with these documents, deliberations, and decisions can make an enormous contribution in any number of areas of life.

In all these senses, then, philosophy can be a practical pursuit for the college student. Our fondest hope for this book is that it encourages those students with a bent toward reflection to plunge into philosophy and to reap the rewards its study can bring.

LOGICAL TOOLKIT

Logic and Philosophy

Philosophy is very much about asking questions. Does God exist? What can we know? What keeps us the same through time and change? Is the mind distinct from the body? How do we know what is right and what is wrong? Because not everyone is going to agree on the correct answers to these questions, it is extremely important to give *reasons* why you think one answer is better than another. In giving reasons why you believe (or why others should believe) a particular answer, you are doing logic, even though you might not recognize it as such. Logic is just a way of articulating more clearly the reasoning that we ordinarily do when we tell someone why we believe something.

If we are to be persuaded that your position is correct, we need to have some way of assessing the reasons that you give for believing your position. For instance, we need to know whether your reasons really do lend support to the position. This is where learning a bit of logical apparatus can come in quite handy. So let's introduce some terminology.

Arguments

We'll start with the basic idea of an *argument*. As we use the term in philosophy, an argument is not just a verbal dispute about some matter. Rather, it is a way of articulating reasons. Or, to be more precise:

> An *argument* is a series of statements where the last statement supposedly *follows from* or *is supported by* the first statements. The last statement is called the *conclusion*, and the first statements are called the *premises*.

Here's a relatively simple example:

1. Everyone who lives in Los Angeles lives in California.
2. Alvin lives in Los Angeles.
3. Therefore, Alvin lives in California.

Suppose we were trying to convince you that our friend Alvin lives in California. (Again, we probably wouldn't normally give you an argument to convince you of this, but this is a simple example just to get the idea of an argument under our belts.) We might give you the following reasons for believing that Alvin lives in California. First, we know that Alvin lives in Los Angeles. And second, we know that Los Angeles is in California, so anyone who lives in Los Angeles automatically lives in California. These two reasons are represented by premises 1 and 2, and they are meant to support the conclusion, which is number 3. Arguments in the articles that you read for class will most often not appear in this numbered form, but they can all be reconstructed in this form so that the reasoning is easy to see.

In this example, if you were to accept the two premises, you would have to accept the conclusion. So our argument is, in a certain sense, a *good* argument. But there are different ways that an argument can be good.

Validity

The first way an argument can be good is if its premises actually do support its conclusion. Recall that our definition of an argument is a series of statements in which the conclusion *supposedly* follows from or is supported by the premises. Well, there are some arguments with conclusions that actually do follow from the premises, and there are some arguments with conclusions that don't actually follow from the premises, even though they *supposedly* do. The first type of arguments are *valid* arguments, and the second type are *invalid* arguments. Or, a bit more carefully:

> An argument is *valid* if its conclusion follows from its premises.

Or, more carefully still:

> An argument is *valid* if it satisfies the following condition: If its premises were true, then its conclusion would *have to be* true.

The argument we gave previously is an example of a valid argument because if premises 1 and 2 were true, then 3 would have to be true. But the following is an example of an *invalid* argument:

1. Everyone who lives in Los Angeles lives in California.
2. Alvin lives in California.
3. Therefore, Alvin lives in Los Angeles.

If we were to put forth this argument while trying to convince you that our friend Alvin lives in Los Angeles, you shouldn't be convinced. Why not? Simply because the reasons that we gave for believing that Alvin lives in Los Angeles don't actually support that conclusion. For in this case, premise 1 could be true (it actually is true), and premise 2 could be true, but the conclusion might still be false (Alvin could live in San Francisco, for instance). Thus this is an *invalid* argument. The conclusion doesn't actually follow from the premises. It's not the case that if its premises were true, then its conclusion would have to be true.

In philosophy, as in life, we're mostly interested in putting forth valid arguments. At the very least, our conclusions must really follow from our premises. But although validity is a good first step, it's not the only way that an argument can be good.

Soundness

If we succeed in putting forth a valid argument, that's a good start. But we want more from our arguments. We also want our premises to actually be true. Recall that validity was about the *relationship* between premises and conclusion: If the premises were true, then the conclusion would have to be true. But sometimes that's a big "if." That is, sometimes we're not sure whether the premises are actually true. That's the next thing we care about. If our argument is valid and its premises are also true, then the argument is *sound*. More precisely:

> An argument is *sound* if it is valid and has all true premises.

Or, more precisely still:

> An argument is *sound* if it satisfies the following two conditions:
>
> 1. It is valid.
> 2. All of its premises are true.

Let us give another example to understand soundness better. Consider the following argument:

1. Abortion is the killing of an innocent person.
2. Killing innocent people is morally objectionable.
3. Therefore, abortion is morally objectionable.

This is a much more interesting argument than the one we gave about our friend Alvin. Indeed, it is likely to stir emotions. But we're not going to discuss the moral rightness or wrongness of abortion—we're just using this argument as an example so that we can better understand logic. Now, there are at least two ways that an argument can be good, so whenever you are confronted with an argument such as this, you should always ask yourselves two questions: First, is it valid? Second, is it sound?

We'll save you the suspense: This argument is indeed valid. Remember what that means, though. It doesn't mean that abortion is morally objectionable.

All it means is that the premises of this argument really do support the conclusion of the argument. Or, in other words, *if* the premises were true, then the conclusion would have to be true. Whether this argument is valid is not a matter of controversy. What *is* a matter of controversy, however, is whether this argument is sound. That is, is it a valid argument with premises that are actually true? This is where opinions differ. For our purposes, it's enough to realize that if the premises of this argument actually are true, then the argument is sound (because it's also valid), and if the premises of this argument actually are false, then the argument is unsound (even though it's still valid).

Why do we care about putting forth sound arguments? Well, if you present someone with a valid argument and you can successfully argue that the premises of your argument are true, then the other person *must* accept the conclusion as well, on pain of irrationality. Because valid arguments are such that their conclusions really do follow from their premises, one cannot accept their premises without also accepting their conclusions. So if you are giving us your reasons for, say, your belief in God, and you present us with a valid argument with premises with which we agree, then we must agree that God exists. Logic can be a very powerful tool.

Persuasiveness

Although typically soundness is the ultimate goal for an argument, occasionally that's not enough. For purposes of illustration, suppose that you believe in God and your belief is actually true and you present an atheist with the following argument for God's existence:

1. God exists.
2. Therefore, God exists.

Given our supposition that God actually does exist, this argument is a sound argument. First, it's valid because its conclusion actually does follow from its premise. If the premise were true, then the conclusion would have to be true (because they are identical!). Second, again, given our supposition that God exists, the premise of this argument is true. So it looks like the argument is sound. But you're never going to convince your atheist friend to believe in God on the basis of this argument. Why not? Because it's utterly unpersuasive. Although it is sound, it commits a logical fallacy, namely, it's *circular*. An argument is circular if its conclusion appears somewhere within its premises. The reason why no one should be persuaded by a circular argument is that one would have to *already* accept the conclusion of the argument *before* one accepted the premises. This gets things backward. Those who already accept the conclusion will not need the argument to be persuaded, and those who do not already accept the conclusion have been given no reason to accept the premise. A similar, although more subtle, example is the following argument:

1. The Bible says that God exists.
2. Everything the Bible says is true.
3. Therefore, God exists.

Suppose again that God does in fact exist, the Bible says this, and everything the Bible says is true. Given these suppositions, this is a sound argument. But it's utterly unpersuasive because one would need to accept its conclusion before one accepted premise 2. This is a logical fallacy related to circularity often called *begging the question*. An argument begs the question if one or more of its premises relies for its truth on the truth of the conclusion.

So although validity and soundness are virtues of arguments, you have to be wary that your arguments are not flawed in some other way, such as by being circular.

Other Fallacies

It's not always easy to figure out whether a particular bit of reasoning is valid. In fact, there are some bits of reasoning that *seem* to be valid even though they are not. It will be useful to give a couple of examples of this phenomenon. A common fallacy of this sort is called *affirming the consequent*, illustrated by the following example:

1. If Amelia can vote in the United States, then Amelia is 18 years old.
2. Amelia is 18 years old.
3. Therefore, Amelia can vote in the United States.

The first premise of this argument is a *conditional*—that is, it is an "if . . . then" statement. The "if" part of a conditional is called the *antecedent*, and the "then" part of a conditional is called the *consequent*. Notice that premise 2 asserts the truth of the consequent of the conditional in premise 1, and then the argument concludes that the antecedent is therefore true. This is why this is called affirming the consequent, and it is an invalid form of reasoning. It's probably not too difficult to see in this simple example that even if premises 1 and 2 are true, the conclusion may still be false. Just imagine a situation in which Amelia is 18 years old but is not a citizen of the United States. In that case, it would still be true that if she can vote in the United States, she is 18 years old, and it would be true that she is 18 years old, but it would not be true that she can vote in the United States. Any argument that takes this form—a conditional, the consequent affirmed, and then the antecedent as conclusion—is invalid.

A related fallacy is *denying the antecedent*. Knowing what we know about conditionals, you can probably guess what this will look like:

1. If Amelia can vote in the United States, then she is 18 years old.
2. Amelia cannot vote in the United States.
3. Therefore, Amelia is not 18 years old.

Again, we have a conditional in the first premise, but in this case the second premise is a denial of the antecedent. The argument then concludes that the consequent must be false as well. But as in the previous case, this is a fallacious form of reasoning. Again, imagine a situation in which Amelia is 18 years old but is not a citizen of the United States. In that case, it would still be true that if she can vote in the United States, she is 18 years old, and it would be true that she cannot vote in the United States, but it would not be true that she is not 18 years old. And again, any argument that takes this form—a conditional, the antecedent denied, and then the consequent denied as a conclusion—is invalid.

These two invalid bits of reasoning *seem* valid because they closely resemble two bits of reasoning that *are* valid. These are *affirming the antecedent* and *denying the consequent*, and they are illustrated by the following two arguments:

1. If Amelia can vote in the United States, then she is 18 years old.
2. Amelia can vote in the United States.
3. Therefore, Amelia is 18 years old.

1. If Amelia can vote in the United States, then she is 18 years old.
2. Amelia is not 18 years old.
3. Therefore, Amelia cannot vote in the United States.

These are both valid forms of reasoning. In both arguments, if premises 1 and 2 were true, then the conclusion would have to be true. As you can see, it's important not to confuse these two bits of valid reasoning with the fallacious reasoning involved in affirming the consequent and denying the antecedent.

Necessary and Sufficient Conditions

So much for arguments. Another important logical concept is that of necessary and sufficient conditions. The best way to get a handle on these concepts is through an example. So consider the following statement:

> If you are a sophomore, then you are an undergraduate.

This statement is saying that being a sophomore is *sufficient* for being an undergraduate. In other words, *all* you need to be an undergraduate is to be a sophomore. (But that's not to say that's the *only* way to be an undergraduate.) In general, a statement of the form:

> *If X, then Y*

is a statement that X is a sufficient condition for Y. Now consider the following statement:

If you can vote in the United States, then you are at least 18 years old.

This statement is saying that being at least 18 years old is *necessary* for being able to vote in the United States. In other words, one of the requirements for being able to vote in the United States is that you must be at least 18 years old. (But that's not to say that that is the *only* requirement.) In general, a statement of the form:

If X, then Y

is a statement that *Y* is a necessary condition for *X*. Occasionally you will come across a statement that purports to give both necessary and sufficient conditions for something. For example:

You have a sister if and only if you have a female sibling.

This statement says the same thing as the following two statements combined:

If you have a sister, then you have a female sibling.
If you have a female sibling, then you have a sister.

Or, in the language of necessary and sufficient conditions:

Having a sister is necessary and sufficient for having a female sibling.

Philosophers are often interested in the necessary and sufficient conditions for some interesting concept, such as knowledge. An interesting philosophical question is: What are the necessary and sufficient conditions for the claim that you have knowledge about some fact? Certainly it is necessary that what you think you know must actually be true for you to know it. But is that also sufficient? Probably not, as you may believe something is true even though you don't have any good reason to believe it, and so on.

A Priori and A Posteriori

It will be useful to have a few more pieces of philosophical terminology at our disposal. First,

philosophers often distinguish between *a priori* and *a posteriori*. These are Latin terms that are especially useful in describing the way in which we are able to come to know certain propositions. Propositions that can be known a priori are those that can be known completely independent of experience. They are those propositions that we can know, so to speak, "from the armchair." For example, our knowledge that all triangles have three sides is a piece of a priori knowledge. There's no need to go around the world looking for triangles and counting up their sides to conclude that all triangles have three sides. On the other hand, propositions that can be known a posteriori are those that require experience of the world to come to know. For example, your knowledge that it is raining outside right now is a posteriori knowledge. To determine whether it is raining, you need to open your eyes and look at the world. No amount of armchair speculation will help.

Necessary and Contingent

Another distinction that comes in handy in philosophy is one between *necessary* and *contingent* truths. A necessary truth is a proposition that is true and could not have been false, whereas a contingent truth is a proposition that is true but might have been false. Most of the true propositions we ordinarily come across are contingent propositions. For instance, the fact that you are reading this right now is a contingent truth. You could very well have decided to do something else with your time. Even the fact that you exist is a contingent truth. Had your parents not met when they did, you could very well have never been born. In fact, we are so surrounded by contingent truths that it's difficult to think of an uncontroversial necessary truth. An example would be the fact that all triangles have three sides. No matter how the world could have been, triangles would always have had three sides—that statement could not have been false. Of course, we could have used the word "triangle" to talk about four-sided figures, but that's not to say that triangles could have been four-sided figures. The concept of a triangle is so intimately connected up with the concept of three-sidedness that it's impossible to have one without the other. Another example is the fact that all bachelors are unmarried. This is a necessary truth because no matter how the world could have been, bachelors would have always been unmarried.

Although these terms are most often used to talk about true and false propositions, they are also sometimes used to distinguish between necessary and contingent *existence*. You and I exist only contingently—that is, we might not have existed. God, on many interpretations, is supposed to exist necessarily—that is, God could not have *not* existed.

WRITING PHILOSOPHY PAPERS

Objective

However one judges particular issues in philosophy, there is nonetheless a common thread: philosophy involves the construction and critical analysis of *arguments*. (For further discussion, see "Logical Toolkit.") Learning how to and refining your ability to construct and analyze arguments are (arguably, at least) the ultimate objectives of any philosophy course. It is, therefore, the purpose of writing a philosophy paper, because your professor will use your papers to judge how well you are meeting the objectives of the course. Showing that you have comprehended and are able to evaluate the material will require you to present your ideas and arguments in a *clear*, *explicit*, and *organized* fashion. You should be able to do this by adhering to the following guidelines.

Give Reasons

An argument can be understood as *reasons* that support a *conclusion*. Your number one objective in writing a philosophy paper should typically be to *give reasons* that support the overall point you want to make. However, although your paper should have an overall point, or conclusion, you may want to make several secondary, related points in the body of your paper. These points should also be backed by reasons. The idea here is that whenever you make a claim, you must give reasons that tell your reader why she or he ought to accept your claim. This amounts to *explaining why* you have made the claim you have made. (A very frequent comment made by professors on students' papers is some variation on "Why?" "Give reasons," "Support your claims," or "Explain.")

Answer the Question

Make sure that you are clear about what the question is on which your paper will focus. All too often students answer what they *think* the question is, or discuss what they *think* the topic is, without ever addressing the real problem. Addressing the topic and answering the question requires you to *understand* the topic you have chosen and to *think carefully* about what you will need to say to clearly explain and evaluate the problem.

Organize Your Paper

Your paper should be structured in such a way that your argument proceeds in an orderly fashion. Defending a claim requires giving reasons in support of that claim, but you can do this in a more or less orderly fashion. Among others, two mistakes can lead to a muddled argument:

1. Announcing a claim and then discussing it at length before giving any argument in support of the claim.
2. Announcing a claim and then discussing various other points, claims, or irrelevant issues before giving reasons that *actually* support the claim in question.

Note that a good philosophy paper should involve consideration of *objections* to your views (and the reasons that supposedly support your views). You should consider the best objections and evaluate them. A philosophy paper is kind of like a "conversation" or a debate in which more than one side is presented and evaluated. A very frequent mistake made by students is simply to present their opinions and views and perhaps also supporting reasons, without considering opposing views. A good philosophy paper is not simply a statement of your own views. Also, a good philosophy paper is not solely a presentation of one side of an issue, even if in the end you wish to defend a particular view.

Make an Outline

The best way to begin writing your paper is to get clear on what point you want to make. Then make a list of the reasons that you think best support each point. Be prepared to spend some time discussing these reasons. Sometimes, giving a reason to support a point requires more than a single sentence.

Stick to the Point

Each paragraph in your paper should have a single main point that is clearly stated and explained. This does not mean that you cannot discuss several different ideas in a single paragraph, but it does mean that these ideas ought to be related and help make clear the overall point of the paragraph:

1. If you begin a paragraph by discussing a particular point or issue, don't veer off into a discussion of something else—stick to the point with which you started.
2. When you have made your overall point and are ready to move on to your next point, start a new paragraph.

Technical Stuff

Often students believe that philosophy is difficult because some philosophers use big words and write long, complicated sentences that no one can understand. This might indeed be a problem that *other* writers have, but you should avoid making it *your* problem. Here are a few things to avoid:

- Do not use big words unless you absolutely understand them.
- Do not use big words where smaller words would do.
- Do not use lots of words when fewer will do.
- Do not use fancy terminology simply because you think you are supposed to.
- Do not use technical terms without explaining what they mean in nontechnical vocabulary.
- Do not use flowery prose that obscures the point you are trying to make.
- Do not make up words.

To get the most out of writing a philosophy paper (and this typically means to force yourself to put the most into it), you should assume that your reader (your professor or teaching assistant) has only minimal background in the topic you are discussing; that is, you should write for "intelligent laypersons," like (for example) your parents or best friends. This means, for instance, that if you are dealing with an example, you should lay out the example and *explain* how it is relevant to your paper. If you are discussing a principle or a distinction, you should state where you got the principle or distinction and how it is relevant. Do not assume that your professor or teaching assistant knows or understands any of this, because if you don't explain it to us, we can't tell if *you* understand it.

Of course, you should distinguish between *relevant* and *irrelevant* points. Irrelevant background information prevents you from getting to the point of your paper.

Your paper should begin with an introduction that is *clear* and *brief*. It should explain what the topic, problem, or question is that you will be dealing with, and it should explain (briefly) how you plan to go about discussing the topic, solving the problem, or answering the question. In short, it should be like a mini-outline, and it should tell your instructor what you are going to do in your paper and why he or she should care (that is, what is important or interesting about the problem). Your paper should end with a conclusion that is appropriately symmetric to the introduction, briefly summarizing how you have achieved the goals laid out in the introduction.

Remember to use your spell-check. Spelling errors at the college level are embarrassing, unacceptable, and unnecessary.

Absolutely, positively have someone else proofread your paper! This could be a friend, a roommate, or a classmate.

Plagiarism

Plagiarism is against university policy and should be absolutely avoided. When you copy someone else's words directly (that is, word-for-word) without putting them in quotes and properly attributing them to the person who wrote them, the words appear in your paper as if they were your own. This is akin to theft, and you should be careful not to do this.

Use Quotation Marks

Do not *copy* sentences or phrases directly from your texts or class handouts (or any other materials), unless you enclose the copied sentence or phrase in quotation marks and provide an accompanying citation.

Standardize Your Citations

A citation or reference should include the author's last name and the page number of the quote: (Kant, p. x). If you are citing an article that appears in a book written by someone other than the author of the article, your citation should appear as follows: (Nagel in Perry, Bratman, and Fischer, p. x). One way to avoid having to write out a long citation like this over and over is to add a footnote after the first such citation that notes that Nagel's article appears in Perry, Bratman, and Fischer. Thereafter, your citation can appear this way: (Nagel, p. x).

Paraphrase Carefully

If you provide an adequate paraphrase or summary of someone else's words, you need not put your paraphrase in quotation marks—it is sufficient to provide just a citation. However, changing a word or two of someone else's words does not amount to an adequate paraphrase. An adequate paraphrase consists of *your words*. Anything quoted directly from someone else must be in quotes as well as cited.

Avoid Plagiarizing from the Internet

The Internet provides many temptations to plagiarize material. Absolutely and positively avoid plagiarism from an Internet source, no matter how enticing. Keep in mind that your instructors have various Internet resources available to combat plagiarism—both from Internet sources and also from fellow students and other materials. For example, your instructor can type in sentences from your paper and—believe it or not—find out whether you have taken the material from another source or even another student's paper. Be aware that there are various new resources available to your instructors and that she or he may well employ them!

Other Resources

Other material will be available on the student website associated with the textbook. The following two books are helpful: Hugo Bedau, *Thinking and Writing About Philosophy,* Second Edition (Boston: Bedford/St. Martin's, 2002) and Zachary Seech, *Writing Philosophy Papers* (Belmont, CA: Wadsworth, 1993). There is a helpful discussion of arguments, with special emphasis on arguments in ethics, in David Boonin and Graham Oddie, eds., *What's Wrong? Applied Ethicists and Their Critics* (New York: Oxford University Press, 2005), esp. pp. 2–24.

We are very grateful to Alison Shalinsky for permission to revise and edit her handout, "Writing Philosophy Papers," Department of Philosophy, University of California, Riverside. The material presented in this section is due largely to Shalinsky.

The Value of Philosophy

BERTRAND RUSSELL

Bertrand Russell (1872–1970) taught at Cambridge University, but he lost his position because of his pacifism during World War I. A leader, with G. E. Moore, of the early twentieth-century revolt against idealism, Russell's work in logic and epistemology was one of the main influences on twentieth-century analytical philosophy. His works include *The Principles of Mathematics, Principia Mathematica* (with Alfred North Whitehead), *The Problems of Philosophy, Our Knowledge of the External World,* and numerous other books.

. .

HAVING now come to the end of our brief and very incomplete review of the problems of philosophy, it will be well to consider, in conclusion, what is the value of philosophy and why it ought to be studied. It is the more necessary to consider this question, in view of the fact that many men, under the influence of science or of practical affairs, are inclined to doubt whether philosophy is anything better than innocent but useless trifling, hair-splitting distinctions, and controversies on matters concerning which knowledge is impossible.

This view of philosophy appears to result, partly from a wrong conception of the ends of life, partly from a wrong conception of the kind of goods which philosophy strives to achieve. Physical science, through the medium of inventions, is useful to innumerable people who are wholly ignorant of it; thus the study of physical science is to be recommended, not only, or primarily, because of the effect on the student, but rather because of the effect on mankind in general. This utility does not belong to philosophy. If the study of philosophy has any value at all for others than students of philosophy, it must be only indirectly, through its effects upon the lives of those who study it. It is in these effects, therefore,

if anywhere, that the value of philosophy must be primarily sought.

But further, if we are not to fail in our endeavour to determine the value of philosophy, we must first free our minds from the prejudices of what are wrongly called "practical" men. The "practical" man, as this word is often used, is one who recognizes only material needs, who realizes that men must have food for the body, but is oblivious of the necessity of providing food for the mind. If all men were well off, if poverty and disease had been reduced to their lowest possible point, there would still remain much to be done to produce a valuable society; and even in the existing world the goods of the mind are at least as important as the goods of the body. It is exclusively among the goods of the mind that the value of philosophy is to be found; and only those who are not indifferent to these goods can be persuaded that the study of philosophy is not a waste of time.

Philosophy, like all other studies, aims primarily at knowledge. The knowledge it aims at is the kind of knowledge which gives unity and system to the body of the sciences, and the kind which results from a critical examination of the grounds of our convictions, prejudices, and beliefs. But it cannot be maintained that philosophy has had any very great measure of success in its attempts to provide definite answers to its questions. If you ask a mathematician, a mineralogist, a historian, or any other man of learning, what definite body of truths has been ascertained by his science, his answer will last as long as you are willing to listen.

But if you put the same question to a philosopher, he will, if he is candid, have to confess that his study has not achieved positive results such as have been achieved by other sciences. It is true that this is partly accounted for by the fact that, as soon as definite knowledge concerning any subject becomes possible, this subject ceases to be called philosophy, and becomes a separate science. The whole study of the heavens, which now belongs to astronomy, was once included in philosophy; Newton's great work was called "the mathematical principles of natural philosophy." Similarly, the study of the human mind, which was a part of philosophy, has now been separated from philosophy and has become the science of psychology. Thus, to a great extent, the uncertainty of philosophy is more apparent than real: those questions which are already capable of definite answers are placed in the sciences, while those only to which, at present, no definite answer can be given, remain to form the residue which is called philosophy.

This is, however, only a part of the truth concerning the uncertainty of philosophy. There are many questions—and among them those that are of the profoundest interest to our spiritual life—which, so far as we can see, must remain insoluble to the human intellect unless its powers become of quite a different order from what they are now. Has the universe any unity of plan or purpose, or is it a fortuitous concourse of atoms? Is consciousness a permanent part of the universe, giving hope of indefinite growth in wisdom, or is it a transitory accident on a small planet on which life must ultimately become impossible? Are good and evil of importance to the universe or only to man? Such questions are asked by philosophy, and variously answered by various philosophers. But it would seem that, whether answers be otherwise discoverable or not, the answers suggested by philosophy are none of them demonstrably true. Yet, however slight may be the hope of discovering an answer, it is part of the business of philosophy to continue the consideration of such questions, to make us aware of their importance, to examine all the approaches to them, and to keep alive that speculative interest in the universe which is apt to be killed by confining ourselves to definitely ascertainable knowledge.

Many philosophers, it is true, have held that philosophy could establish the truth of certain answers to such fundamental questions. They have supposed that what is of most importance in religious beliefs could be proved by strict demonstration to be true. In order to judge of such attempts, it is necessary to take a survey of human knowledge, and to form an opinion as to its methods and its limitations. On such a subject it would be unwise to pronounce dogmatically; but if the investigations of our previous chapters have not led us astray, we shall be compelled to renounce the hope of finding philosophical proofs of religious beliefs. We cannot, therefore, include as part of the value of philosophy any definite set of answers to such questions. Hence, once more, the value of philosophy must not depend upon any supposed body of definitely ascertainable knowledge to be acquired by those who study it.

The value of philosophy is, in fact, to be sought largely in its very uncertainty. The man who has no tincture of philosophy goes through life imprisoned in the prejudices derived from common sense, from the habitual beliefs of his age or his nation, and from convictions which have grown up in his mind without the co-operation or consent of his deliberate reason. To such a man the world tends to become definite, finite, obvious; common objects rouse no questions, and unfamiliar possibilities are contemptuously rejected. As soon as we begin to philosophize, on the contrary, we find, as we saw in our opening chapters, that even the most everyday things lead to problems to which only very incomplete answers can be given. Philosophy, though unable to tell us with certainty what is the true answer to the doubts which it raises, is able to suggest many possibilities which enlarge our thoughts and free them from the tyranny of custom. Thus, while diminishing our feeling of certainty as to what things are, it greatly increases our knowledge as to what they may be; it removes the somewhat arrogant dogmatism of those who have never travelled into the region of liberating doubt, and it keeps alive our sense of wonder by showing familiar things in an unfamiliar aspect.

Apart from its utility in showing unsuspected possibilities, philosophy has a value—perhaps its chief value—through the greatness of the objects which it contemplates, and the freedom from narrow and personal aims resulting from this contemplation. The life of the instinctive man is shut up within the circle of his private interests: family and friends may be included, but the outer world is not regarded except as it may help or hinder what comes within the circle of instinctive wishes. In such a life there is something feverish and confined, in comparison with which the philosophic life is calm and free. The private world of instinctive interests is a small one, set in the midst of a great and powerful world which must, sooner or later, lay our private world in ruins. Unless we can so enlarge our interests as to include the whole outer world, we remain like a garrison in a beleaguered fortress, knowing that the enemy prevents escape and that ultimate surrender is inevitable. In such a life there is no peace, but a constant strife between the insistence of desire and the powerlessness of will. In one way or another, if our life is to be great and free, we must escape this prison and this strife.

One way of escape is by philosophic contemplation. Philosophic contemplation does not, in its widest survey, divide the universe into two hostile camps—friends and foes, helpful and hostile, good and bad—it views the whole impartially. Philosophic contemplation, when it is unalloyed, does not aim at proving that the rest of the universe is akin to man. All acquisition of knowledge is an enlargement of the Self, but this enlargement is best attained when it is not directly sought. It is obtained when the desire for knowledge is alone operative, by a study which does not wish in advance that its objects should have this or that character, but adapts the Self to the characters which it finds in its objects. This enlargement of Self is not obtained when, taking the Self as it is, we try to show that the world is so similar to this Self that knowledge of it is possible without any admission of what seems alien. The desire to prove this is a form of self-assertion and, like all self-assertion, is an obstacle to the growth of Self which it desires,

and of which the Self knows that it is capable. Self-assertion, in philosophic speculation as elsewhere, views the world as a means to its own ends; thus it makes the world of less account than Self, and the Self sets bounds to the greatness of its goods. In contemplation, on the contrary, we start from the not-Self, and through its greatness the boundaries of Self are enlarged; through the infinity of the universe the mind which contemplates it achieves some share in infinity.

For this reason greatness of soul is not fostered by those philosophies which assimilate the universe to Man. Knowledge is a form of union of Self and not-Self; like all union, it is impaired by dominion, and therefore by any attempt to force the universe into conformity with what we find in ourselves. There is a widespread philosophical tendency towards the view which tells us that Man is the measure of all things, that truth is man-made, that space and time and the world of universals are properties of the mind, and that, if there be anything not created by the mind, it is unknowable and of no account for us. This view, if our previous discussions were correct, is untrue; but in addition to being untrue, it has the effect of robbing philosophic contemplation of all that gives it value, since it fetters contemplation to Self. What it calls knowledge is not a union with the not-Self, but a set of prejudices, habits, and desires, making an impenetrable veil between us and the world beyond. The man who finds pleasure in such a theory of knowledge is like the man who never leaves the domestic circle for fear his word might not be law.

The true philosophic contemplation, on the contrary, finds its satisfaction in every enlargement of the not-Self, in everything that magnifies the objects contemplated, and thereby the subject contemplating. Everything, in contemplation, that is personal or private, everything that depends upon habit, self-interest, or desire, distorts the object, and hence impairs the union which the intellect seeks. By thus making a barrier between subject and object, such personal and private things become a prison to the intellect. The free intellect will see as God might see, without a *here* and *now*, without hopes and fears, without the trammels of customary beliefs and traditional prejudices, calmly, dispassionately, in the sole and exclusive desire of knowledge—knowledge as impersonal, as purely contemplative, as it is possible for man to attain. Hence also the free intellect will value more the abstract and universal knowledge into which the accidents of private history do not enter, than the knowledge brought by the senses, and dependent, as such knowledge must be, upon an exclusive and personal point of view and a body whose sense-organs distort as much as they reveal.

The mind which has become accustomed to the freedom and impartiality of philosophic contemplation will preserve something of the same freedom and impartiality in the world of action and emotion. It will view its purposes and desires as parts of the whole, with the absence of insistence that results from seeing them as infinitesimal fragments in a world of which all the rest is unaffected by any one man's deeds. The impartiality which, in contemplation, is the unalloyed desire for truth, is the very same quality of mind which, in action, is justice, and in emotion is that universal love which can be given to all, and not only to those who are judged useful or admirable. Thus contemplation enlarges not only the objects of our thoughts, but also the objects of our actions and our affections: it makes us citizens of the universe, not only of one walled city at war with all the rest. In this citizenship of the universe consists man's true freedom, and his liberation from the thraldom of narrow hopes and fears.

Thus, to sum up our discussion of the value of philosophy; Philosophy is to be studied, not for the sake of any definite answers to its questions, since no definite answers can, as a rule, be known to be true, but rather for the sake of the questions themselves; because these questions enlarge our conception of what is possible, enrich our intellectual imagination and diminish the dogmatic assurance which closes the mind against speculation; but above all because, through the greatness of the universe which philosophy contemplates, the mind also is rendered great, and becomes capable of that union with the universe which constitutes its highest good.

STUDY QUESTIONS

1. Before you read this piece, how would you have characterized the discipline of philosophy?
2. Russell says, "The man who has no tincture of philosophy goes through life imprisoned in the prejudices derived from common sense, from the habitual beliefs of his age or his nation, and from convictions which have grown up in his mind without the co-operation or consent of his deliberate reason." What prejudices, habitual beliefs, and unreasoned convictions do you think Russell is referring to here? Do you see these things in people around you?
3. Russell says that philosophy is to be studied for the sake of the questions themselves. What sorts of questions, if any, do you think are worth studying, even if we can never know the answers to them?
4. What do you think Russell means when he says, "All acquisition of knowledge is an enlargement of the Self"? Do you think he is right?

Apology: Defence of Socrates

PLATO

Plato (ca. 428–ca. 348 B.C.) is widely considered to be one of the greatest philosophical minds to have ever lived. In fact, some have said that the entire history of Western philosophy is nothing more than a footnote to Plato. He was the student of Socrates, who is the primary interlocutor in Plato's dialogues. Plato's most famous work is *The Republic*. One of his most famous philosophical ideas is that the world that we experience through our senses is defective, but there is a more real world that is inhabited by the real *forms* or *ideas* of the transient objects we experience. These forms, unlike the transient objects that approximate them, are eternal, unchanging, and the basis for the structure of our world.

· ·

17a I don't know how you, fellow Athenians, have been affected by my accusers, but for my part I felt myself almost transported by them, so persuasively did they speak. And yet hardly a word they 5 have said is true. Among their many falsehoods, one especially astonished me: their warning that you must be careful not to be taken in by me, because b I am a clever speaker. It seemed to me the height of impudence on their part not to be embarrassed at being refuted straight away by the facts, once it became apparent that I was not a clever speaker at 5 all—unless indeed they call a "clever" speaker one who speaks the truth. If that is what they mean, then I would admit to being an orator, although not on a par with them.

As I said, then, my accusers have said little or nothing true; whereas from me you shall hear the whole truth, though not, I assure you, fellow Athenians, in language adorned with fine words and phrases or c dressed up, as theirs was: you shall hear my points made spontaneously in whatever words occur to me—persuaded as I am that my case is just. None of you should expect anything to be put differently, because it would not, of course, be at all fitting at my 5 age, gentlemen, to come before you with artificial speeches, such as might be composed by a young lad.

One thing, moreover, I would earnestly beg of you, fellow Athenians. If you hear me defending myself with the same arguments I normally use at the bankers' tables in the market-place (where many 10 of you have heard me) and elsewhere, please do not d be surprised or protest on that account. You see, here is the reason: this is the first time I have ever appeared before a court of law, although I am over 70; so I am literally a stranger to the diction of this place. And if I really were a foreigner, you would naturally 5 excuse me, were I to speak in the dialect and style in which I had been brought up; so in the present 18a case as well I ask you, in all fairness as I think, to disregard my manner of speaking—it may not be as good, or it may be better—but to consider and attend simply to the question whether or not my case 5 is just; because that is the duty of a judge, as it is an orator's duty to speak the truth.

To begin with, fellow Athenians, it is fair that I should defend myself against the first set of charges falsely brought against me by my first accusers, and then turn to the later charges and the more recent b ones. You see, I have been accused before you by many people for a long time now, for many years in fact, by people who spoke not a word of truth. It is those people I fear more than Anytus and his crowd, though they too are dangerous. But those others are 5 more so, gentlemen: they have taken hold of most of you since childhood, and made persuasive accusations against me, yet without an ounce more truth in them. They say that there is one Socrates, a "wise man," who ponders what is above the earth and investigates everything beneath it, and turns the weaker argument into the stronger.

c   Those accusers who have spread such rumour about me, fellow Athenians, are the dangerous ones, because their audience believes that people who inquire into those matters also fail to acknowledge the
5 gods. Moreover, those accusers are numerous, and have been denouncing me for a long time now, and they also spoke to you at an age at which you would be most likely to believe them, when some of you were children or young lads; and their accusations simply went by default for lack of any defence. But the most absurd thing of all is that one cannot even get to know their names or say who they were—
d except perhaps one who happens to be a comic playwright. The ones who have persuaded you by malicious slander, and also some who persuade others because they have been persuaded themselves,
5 are all very hard to deal with: one cannot put any of them on the stand here in court, or cross-examine anybody, but one must literally engage in a sort of shadow-boxing to defend oneself, and cross-examine without anyone to answer. You too, then, should allow, as I just said, that I have two sets of accusers:
e one set who have accused me recently, and the other of long standing to whom I was just referring. And please grant that I need to defend myself against the latter first, since you too heard them accusing me earlier, and you heard far more from them than from these recent critics here.

Very well, then. I must defend myself, fellow Athe-
19a nians, and in so short a time must try to dispel the slander which you have had so long to absorb. That is the outcome I would wish for, should it be of any benefit to you and to me, and I should like to suc-
5 ceed in my defence—though I believe the task to be a difficult one, and am well aware of its nature. But let that turn out as God wills: I have to obey the law and present my defence.

Let us examine, from the beginning, the charge
b that has given rise to the slander against me—which was just what Meletus relied upon when he drew up this indictment. Very well then, what were my slanderers actually saying when they slandered me? Let

me read out their deposition, as if they were my legal accusers:

"Socrates is guilty of being a busybody, in that he inquires into what is beneath the earth and in the 5 sky, turns the weaker argument into the stronger, c and teaches others to do the same."

The charges would run something like that. Indeed, you can see them for yourselves, enacted in Aristophanes' comedy: in that play, a character called "Socrates" swings around, claims to be walking on air, and talks a lot of other nonsense on sub- 5 jects of which I have no understanding, great or small.

Not that I mean to belittle knowledge of that sort, if anyone really is learned in such matters—no matter how many of Meletus' lawsuits I might have to defend myself against—but the fact is, fellow Athenians, those subjects are not my concern at all. I call d most of you to witness yourselves, and I ask you to make that quite clear to one another, if you have ever heard me in discussion (as many of you have). Tell one another, then, whether any of you has ever 5 heard me discussing such subjects, either briefly or at length; and as a result you will realize that the other things said about me by the public are equally baseless.

In any event, there is no truth in those charges. Moreover, if you have heard from anyone that I undertake to educate people and charge fees, there is e no truth in that either—though for that matter I do think it also a fine thing if anyone *is* able to educate people, as Gorgias of Leontini, Prodicus of Ceos, and Hippias of Elis profess to. Each of them can visit 5 any city, gentlemen, and persuade its young people, who may associate free of charge with any of their 20a own citizens they wish, to leave those associations, and to join with them instead, paying fees and being grateful into the bargain.

On that topic, there is at present another expert here, a gentleman from Paros; I heard of his visit, because I happened to run into a man who has spent 5 more money on **sophists** than everyone else put together—Callias, the son of Hipponicus. So I questioned him, since he has two sons himself.

"Callias," I said, "if your two sons had been born as colts or calves, we could find and engage a tutor b who could make them both excel superbly in the required qualities—and he'd be some sort of expert in horse-rearing or agriculture. But seeing that they are actually human, whom do you intend to engage as their tutor? Who has knowledge of the required human and civic qualities? I ask, because I assume you've given thought to the matter, having sons yourself. Is there such a person," I asked, "or not?"

"Certainly," he replied.

"Who is he?" I said; "Where does he come from, and what does he charge for tuition?"

"His name is Evenus, Socrates," he replied; "He comes from Paros, and he charges 5 minas."

I thought Evenus was to be congratulated, if he really did possess that skill and imparted it for such a modest charge. I, at any rate, would certainly be giving myself fine airs and graces if I possessed that knowledge. But the fact is, fellow Athenians, I do not.

Now perhaps one of you will interject: "Well then, Socrates, what is the difficulty in your case? What is the source of these slanders against you? If you are not engaged in something out of the ordinary, why ever has so much rumour and talk arisen about you? It would surely never have arisen, unless you were up to something different from most people. Tell us what it is, then, so that we don't jump to conclusions about you."

That speaker makes a fair point, I think; and so I will try to show you just what it is that has earned me my reputation and notoriety. Please hear me out. Some of you will perhaps think I am joking, but I assure you that I shall be telling you the whole truth.

You see, fellow Athenians, I have gained this reputation on account of nothing but a certain sort of wisdom. And what sort of wisdom is that? It is a human kind of wisdom, perhaps, since it might just be true that I have wisdom of that sort. Maybe the people I just mentioned possess wisdom of a superhuman kind; otherwise I cannot explain it. For my part, I certainly do not possess that knowledge; and whoever says I do is lying and speaking with a view to slandering me—

Now please do not protest, fellow Athenians, even if I should sound to you rather boastful. I am not myself the source of the story I am about to tell you, but I shall refer you to a trustworthy authority. As evidence of my wisdom, if such it actually be, and of its nature, I shall call to witness before you the god at Delphi.

You remember Chaerephon, of course. He was a friend of mine from youth, and also a comrade in your party, who shared your recent exile and restoration. You recall too what sort of man Chaerephon was, how impetuous he was in any undertaking. Well, on one occasion he actually went to the Delphic oracle, and had the audacity to put the following question to it—as I said, please do not make a disturbance, gentlemen—he went and asked if there was anyone wiser than myself; to which the Pythia responded that there was no one. His brother here will testify to the court about that story, since Chaerephon himself is deceased.

Now keep in mind why I have been telling you this: it is because I am going to explain to you the origin of the slander against me. When I heard the story, I thought to myself: "What ever is the god saying? What can his riddle mean? Since I am all too conscious of not being wise in any matter, great or small, what ever can he mean by pronouncing me to be the wisest? Surely he cannot be lying: for him that would be out of the question."

So for a long time I was perplexed about what he could possibly mean. But then, with great reluctance, I proceeded to investigate the matter somewhat as follows. I went to one of the people who had a reputation for wisdom, thinking there, if anywhere, to disprove the oracle's utterance and declare to it: "Here is someone wiser than I am, and yet you said that I was the wisest."

So I interviewed this person—I need not mention his name, but he was someone in public life; and when I examined him, my experience went something like this, fellow Athenians: in conversing with him, I formed the opinion that, although the man was thought to be wise by many other people, and especially by himself, yet in reality he was not. So I then tried to show him that he thought himself wise without being so. I thereby earned his dislike, and that of many people present; but still, as I went away, I thought to myself: "I am wiser than that fellow, anyhow. Because neither of us, I dare say, knows anything of great value; but he thinks he knows a thing when he doesn't; whereas I neither know it in fact, nor think that I do. At any rate, it appears that I am wiser than he in just this one small respect: if I do not know something, I do not think that I do."

Next, I went to someone else, among people thought to be even wiser than the previous man, and I came to the same conclusion again; and so I was disliked by that man too, as well as by many others.

Well, after that I went on to visit one person after another. I realized, with dismay and alarm, that I was making enemies; but even so, I thought it my duty to attach the highest importance to the god's business; and therefore, in seeking the oracle's meaning, I had to go on to examine all those with any reputation for knowledge. And upon my word, fellow Athenians—because I am obliged to speak the truth before the court—I truly did experience something like this: as I pursued the god's inquiry, I found those held in the highest esteem were practically the most defective, whereas men who were supposed to be their inferiors were much better off in respect of understanding.

Let me, then, outline my wanderings for you, the various "labours" I kept undertaking, only to find that the oracle proved competely irrefutable. After I had done with the politicians, I turned to the poets—including tragedians, dithyrambic poets, and the rest—thinking that in their company I would be shown up as more ignorant than they were. So I picked up the poems over which I thought they had taken the most trouble, and questioned them about their meaning, so that I might also learn something from them in the process.

Now I'm embarrassed to tell you the truth, gentlemen, but it has to be said. Practically everyone else present could speak better than the poets themselves about their very own compositions. And so, once more, I soon realized this truth about them too: it was not from wisdom that they composed their works, but from a certain natural aptitude and inspiration, like that of seers and soothsayers—because those people too utter many fine words, yet know nothing of the matters on which they pronounce. It was obvious to me that the poets were in much the same situation; yet at the same time I realized that because of their compositions they thought themselves the wisest people in other matters as well, when they were not. So I left, believing that I was ahead of them in the same way as I was ahead of the politicians.

Then, finally, I went to the craftsmen, because I was conscious of knowing almost nothing myself, but felt sure that amongst them, at least, I would find much valuable knowledge. And in that expectation I was not disappointed: they did have knowledge in fields where I had none, and in that respect they were wiser than I. And yet, fellow Athenians, those able craftsmen seemed to me to suffer from the same failing as the poets: because of their excellence at their own trade, each claimed to be a great expert also on matters of the utmost importance; and this arrogance of theirs seemed to eclipse their wisdom. So I began to ask myself, on the oracle's behalf, whether I should prefer to be as I am, neither wise as they are wise, nor ignorant as they are ignorant, or to possess both their attributes; and in reply, I told myself and the oracle that I was better off as I was.

The effect of this questioning, fellow Athenians, was to earn me much hostility of a very vexing and trying sort, which has given rise to numerous slanders, including this reputation I have for being "wise"—because those present on each occasion imagine me to be wise regarding the matters on which I examine others. But in fact, gentlemen, it would appear that it is only the god who is truly wise; and that he is saying to us, through this oracle, that human wisdom is worth little or nothing. It seems that when he says "Socrates," he makes use of my name, merely taking me as an example—as if to say, "The wisest amongst you, human beings, is anyone like Socrates who has recognized that with respect to wisdom he is truly worthless."

That is why, even to this day, I still go about seeking out and searching into anyone I believe to be wise, citizen or foreigner, in obedience to the god. Then, as soon as I find that someone is not wise, I assist the god by proving that he is not. Because of this occupation, I have had no time at all for any activity to speak of, either in public affairs or in my family life; indeed, because of my service to the god, I live in extreme poverty.

In addition, the young people who follow me around of their own accord, the ones who have plenty of leisure because their parents are wealthiest, enjoy listening to people being cross-examined. Often, too, they copy my example themselves, and so attempt to cross-examine others. And I imagine that they find a great abundance of people who suppose themselves to possess some knowledge, but really know little or nothing. Consequently, the people they question are angry with me, though not with themselves, and say that there is a nasty pestilence abroad called "Socrates," who is corrupting the young.

Then, when asked just what he is doing or teaching, they have nothing to say, because they have no idea what he does; yet, rather than seem at a loss, they resort to the stock charges against all who pursue intellectual inquiry, trotting out "things in the sky and beneath the earth," "failing to acknowledge the gods," and "turning the weaker argument into the stronger." They would, I imagine, be loath to admit the truth, which is that their pretensions to knowledge have been exposed, and they are totally ignorant. So because these people have reputations to protect, I suppose, and are also both passionate and numerous, and have been speaking about me in a vigorous and persuasive style, they have long been filling your ears with vicious slander. It is on the strength of all this that Meletus, along with Anytus and Lycon, has proceeded against me: Meletus is aggrieved for the poets, Anytus for the craftsmen and politicians, and Lycon for the orators. And so, as I began by saying, I should be surprised if I could rid your minds of this slander in so short a time, when so much of it has accumulated.

There is the truth for you, fellow Athenians. I have spoken it without concealing anything from you, major or minor, and without glossing over anything. And yet I am virtually certain that it is my very candour that makes enemies for me—which goes to show that I am right: the slander against me is to that effect, and such is its explanation. And whether you look for one now or later, that is what you will find.

So much for my defence before you against the charges brought by my first group of accusers. Next, I shall try to defend myself against Meletus, good patriot that he claims to be, and against my more recent critics. So once again, as if they were a fresh set of accusers, let me in turn review their deposition. It runs something like this:

"Socrates is guilty of corrupting the young, and of failing to acknowledge the gods acknowledged by the city, but introducing new spiritual beings instead."

Such is the charge: let us examine each item within it.

Meletus says, then, that I am guilty of corrupting the young. Well I reply, fellow Athenians, that Meletus is guilty of trifling in a serious matter, in that he brings people to trial on frivolous grounds, and professes grave concern about matters for which he has never cared at all. I shall now try to prove to you too that that is so.

Step forward, Meletus, and answer me. It is your chief concern, is it not, that our younger people shall be as good as possible?

—It is.

Very well, will you please tell the judges who influences them for the better—because you must obviously know, seeing that you care? Having discovered me, as you allege, to be the one who is corrupting them, you bring me before the judges here and accuse me. So speak up, and tell the court who has an improving influence.

You see, Meletus, you remain silent, and have no answer. Yet doesn't that strike you as shameful, and as proof in itself of exactly what I say—that you have never cared about these matters at all? Come then, good fellow, tell us who influences them for the better.

—The laws.

Yes, but that is not what I'm asking, excellent fellow. I mean, which *person*, who already knows the laws to begin with?

—These gentlemen, the judges, Socrates.

What are you saying, Meletus? Can these people educate the young, and do they have an improving influence?

—Most certainly.

All of them, or some but not others?

—All of them.

My goodness, what welcome news, and what a generous supply of benefactors you speak of! And how about the audience here in court? Do they too have an improving influence, or not?

—Yes, they do too.

And how about members of the Council?

—Yes, the Councillors too.

But in that case, how about people in the Assembly, its individual members, Meletus? They won't be corrupting their youngers, will they? Won't they all be good influences as well?

—Yes, they will too.

So every person in Athens, it would appear,
has an excellent influence on them except for me,
whereas I alone am corrupting them. Is that what
you're saying?

—That is emphatically what I'm saying.

Then I find myself, if we are to believe you, in a
most awkward predicament. Now answer me this.
Do you think the same is true of horses? Is it everybody who improves them, while a single person
spoils them? Or isn't the opposite true: a single person, or at least very few people, namely the horse-trainers,
can improve them; while lay people spoil them, don't
they, if they have to do with horses and make use of
them? Isn't that true of horses as of all other animals,
Meletus? Of course it is, whether you and Anytus
deny it or not. In fact, I dare say our young people are
extremely lucky if only one person is corrupting them,
while everyone else is doing them good.

All right, Meletus. Enough has been said to prove
that you never were concerned about the young.
You betray your irresponsibility plainly, because
you have not cared at all about the charges on which
you bring me before this court.

Furthermore, Meletus, tell us, in God's name,
whether it is better to live among good fellow citizens or bad ones. Come sir, answer: I am not asking
a hard question. Bad people have a harmful impact
upon their closest companions at any given time,
don't they, whereas good people have a good one?

—Yes.

Well, is there anyone who wants to be harmed by
his companions rather than benefited?—Be a good
fellow and keep on answering, as the law requires
you to. Is there anyone who wants to be harmed?

—Of course not.

Now tell me this. In bringing me here, do you
claim that I am corrupting and depraving the young
intentionally or unintentionally?

—Intentionally, so I maintain.

Really, Meletus? Are you so much smarter at
your age than I at mine as to realize that the bad
have a harmful impact upon their closest companions at any given time, whereas the good have a
beneficial effect? Am I, by contrast, so far gone in
my stupidity as not to realize that if I make one of
my companions vicious, I risk incurring harm at his
hands? And am I, therefore, as you allege, doing so
much damage intentionally?

That I cannot accept from you, Meletus, and neither could anyone else, I imagine. Either I am not
corrupting them—or if I am, I am doing so unintentionally; so either way your charge is false. But
if I am corrupting them unintentionally, the law
does not require me to be brought to court for such
mistakes, but rather to be taken aside for private instruction and admonition—since I shall obviously
stop doing unintentional damage, if I learn better. But you avoided association with me and were
unwilling to instruct me. Instead you bring me to
court, where the law requires you to bring people
who need punishment rather than enlightenment.

Very well, fellow Athenians. That part of my
case is now proven: Meletus never cared about
these matters, either a lot or a little. Nevertheless,
Meletus, please tell us in what way you claim that
I am corrupting our younger people. That is quite
obvious, isn't it, from the indictment you drew up?
It is by teaching them not to acknowledge the gods
acknowledged by the city, but to accept new spiritual beings instead? You mean, don't you, that I am
corrupting them by teaching them that?

—I most emphatically do.

Then, Meletus, in the name of those very gods we
are now discussing, please clarify the matter further
for me, and for the jury here. You see, I cannot make
out what you mean. Is it that I am teaching people to
acknowledge that some gods exist—in which case it
follows that I do acknowledge their existence myself
as well, and am not a complete atheist, hence am not
guilty on that count—and yet that those gods are not
the ones acknowledged by the city, but different ones?
Is that your charge against me—namely, that they are
different? Or are you saying that I acknowledge no
gods at all myself, and teach the same to others?

—I am saying the latter; you acknowledge no
gods at all.

What ever makes you say that, Meletus, you
strange fellow? Do I not even acknowledge, then,
with the rest of mankind, that the sun and the moon
are gods?

—By God, he does not, members of the jury,
since he claims that the sun is made of rock, and the
moon of earth!

My dear Meletus, do you imagine that it is Anaxagoras you are accusing? Do you have such contempt for the jury, and imagine them so illiterate
as not to know that books by Anaxagoras of Clazo-
menae are crammed with such assertions? What's
more, are the young learning those things from me
when they can acquire them at the bookstalls, now
and then, for a drachma at most, and so ridicule
Socrates if he claims those ideas for his own, especially when they are so bizarre? In God's name, do
you really think me as crazy as that? Do I acknowledge the existence of no god at all?

—By God no, none whatever.

I can't believe you, Meletus—nor, I think, can
you believe yourself. To my mind, fellow Athenians, this fellow is an impudent scoundrel who has
framed this indictment out of sheer wanton impudence and insolence. He seems to have devised a
sort of riddle in order to try me out: "Will Socrates
the Wise tumble to my nice self-contradiction?
Or shall I fool him along with my other listeners?" You see, he seems to me to be contradicting
himself in the indictment. It's as if he were saying: "Socrates is guilty of not acknowledging gods,
but of acknowledging gods"; and yet that is sheer
tomfoolery.

I ask you to examine with me, gentlemen, just
how that appears to be his meaning. Answer for us,
Meletus; and the rest of you, please remember my
initial request not to protest if I conduct the argument in my usual manner.

Is there anyone in the world, Meletus, who acknowledges that human phenomena exist, yet does
not acknowledge human beings?—Require him
to answer, gentlemen, and not to raise all kinds of
confused objections. Is there anyone who does not
acknowledge horses, yet does acknowledge eques-
trian phenomena? Or who does not acknowledge
that musicians exist, yet does acknowledge musical
phenomena?

There is no one, excellent fellow: if you don't
wish to answer, I must answer for you, and for the
jurors here. But at least answer my next question
yourself. Is there anyone who acknowledges that
spiritual phenomena exist, yet does not acknowledge spirits?

—No.

How good of you to answer—albeit reluctantly
and under compulsion from the jury. Well now, you
say that I acknowledge spiritual beings and teach
others to do so. Whether they actually be new or
old is no matter: I do at any rate, by your account,
acknowledge spiritual beings, which you have also
mentioned in your sworn deposition. But if I acknowledge spiritual beings, then surely it follows
quite inevitably that I must acknowledge spirits. Is
that not so?—Yes, it is so: I assume your agreement,
since you don't answer. But we regard spirits, don't
we, as either gods or children of gods? Yes or no?

—Yes.

Then given that I do believe in spirits, as you say,
if spirits are gods of some sort, this is precisely what
I claim when I say that you are presenting us with a
riddle and making fun of us: you are saying that I do
not believe in gods, and yet again that I do believe in
gods, seeing that I believe in spirits.

On the other hand, if spirits are children of gods,
some sort of bastard offspring from nymphs—or
from whomever they are traditionally said, in each
case, to be born—then who in the world could ever
believe that there were children of gods, yet no
gods? That would be just as absurd as accepting the
existence of children of horses and asses—namely,
mules—yet rejecting the existence of horses or asses!

In short, Meletus, you can only have drafted this
either by way of trying us out, or because you were
at a loss how to charge me with a genuine offence.
How could you possibly persuade anyone with even
the slightest intelligence that someone who accepts
spiritual beings does not also accept divine ones,
and again that the same person also accepts neither
spirits nor gods nor heroes? There is no conceivable way.

But enough, fellow Athenians. It needs no long
defence, I think, to show that I am not guilty of the
charges in Meletus' indictment; the foregoing will
suffice. You may be sure, though, that what I was
saying earlier is true: I have earned great hostility
among many people. And that is what will convict
me, if I am convicted: not Meletus or Anytus, but
the slander and malice of the crowd. They have certainly convicted many other good men as well, and I
imagine they will do so again; there is no risk of their
stopping with me.

Now someone may perhaps say: "Well then, are you not ashamed, Socrates, to have pursued a way of life which has now put you at risk of death?"

5   But it may be fair for me to answer him as follows: "You are sadly mistaken, fellow, if you suppose that a man with even a grain of self-respect should reckon up the risks of living or dying, rather than simply

c   consider, whenever he does something, whether his actions are just or unjust, the deeds of a good man or a bad one. By your principles, presumably, all those demigods who died in the plain of Troy were inferior creatures—yes, even the son of Thetis, who showed so much scorn for danger, when the alterna-

5   tive was to endure dishonour. Thus, when he was eager to slay Hector, his mother, goddess that she was, spoke to him—something like this, I fancy:

> My child, if thou dost avenge the murder of thy
>   friend, Patroclus,
> And dost slay Hector, then straightway [so runs the
>   poem]
> Shalt thou die thyself, since doom is prepared for
>   thee
> Next after Hector's.

10   But though he heard that, he made light of death

d   and danger, since he feared far more to live as a base man, and to fail to avenge his dear ones. The poem goes on:

> Then straightway let me die, once I have given the
>   wrongdoer
> His deserts, less I remain here by the beak-prowed
>   ships,
> An object of derision, and a burden upon the earth.

Can you suppose that he gave any thought to death or danger?

5   You see, here is the truth of the matter, fellow Athenians. Wherever a man has taken up a position because he considers it best, or has been posted there by his commander, that is where I believe he should remain, steadfast in danger, taking no account at all of death or of anything else rather than

c   dishonour. I would therefore have been acting absurdly, fellow Athenians, if when assigned to a post

at Potidaea, Amphipolis, or Delium by the superiors you had elected to command me, I remained where I was posted on those occasions at the risk of death, if ever any man did; whereas now that

5   the god assigns me, as I became completely con-

29a   vinced, to the duty of leading the philosophical life by examining myself and others, I desert that post from fear of death or anything else. Yes, that would be unthinkable; and then I truly should deserve to be brought to court for failing to acknowledge the gods' existence, in that I was disobedient to the oracle, was afraid of death, and thought I was wise

5   when I was not.

After all, gentlemen, the fear of death amounts simply to thinking one is wise when one is not: it is thinking one knows something one does not know. No one knows, you see, whether death may not in fact prove the greatest of all blessings for mankind;

b   but people fear it as if they knew it for certain to be the greatest of evils. And yet to think that one knows what one does not know must surely be the kind of folly which is reprehensible.

On this matter especially, gentlemen, that may be the nature of my own advantage over most people. If I really were to claim to be wiser than anyone in any respect, it would consist simply in

5   this: just as I do not possess adequate knowledge of life in Hades, so I also realize that I do not possess it; whereas acting unjustly in disobedience to one's betters, whether god or human being, is something I *know* to be evil and shameful. Hence I shall never fear or flee from something which may indeed be a good for all I know, rather than from things I know to be evils.

c   Suppose, therefore, that you pay no heed to Anytus, but are prepared to let me go. He said I need never have been brought to court in the first place; but that once I had been, your only option was to put me to death. He declared before you that, if I

5   got away from you this time, your sons would all be utterly corrupted by practising Socrates' teachings. Suppose, in the face of that, you were to say to me:

"Socrates, we will not listen to Anytus this time. We are prepared to let you go—but only on this condition: you are to pursue that quest of yours and practise philosophy no longer; and if you are caught doing it any more, you shall be put to death."

Well, as I just said, if you were prepared to let me go on those terms, I should reply to you as follows:

"I have the greatest fondness and affection for you, fellow Athenians, but I will obey my god rather than you; and so long as I draw breath and am able, I shall never give up practising philosophy, or exhorting and showing the way to any of you whom I ever encounter, by giving my usual sort of message. 'Excellent friend,' I shall say; 'You are an Athenian. Your city is the most important and renowned for its wisdom and power; so are you not ashamed that, while you take care to acquire as much wealth as possible, with honour and glory as well, yet you take no care or thought for understanding or truth, or for the best possible state of your soul?'

"And should any of you dispute that, and claim that he does take such care, I will not let him go straight away nor leave him, but I will question and examine and put him to the test; and if I do not think he has acquired goodness, though he says he has, I shall say, 'Shame on you, for setting the lowest value upon the most precious things, and for rating inferior ones more highly.' That I shall do for anyone I encounter, young or old, alien or fellow citizen; but all the more for the latter, since your kinship with me is closer."

Those are my orders from my god, I do assure you. Indeed, I believe that no greater good has ever befallen you in our city than my service to my god; because all I do is to go about persuading you, young and old alike, not to care for your bodies or for your wealth so intensely as for the greatest possible well-being of your souls. "It is not wealth," I tell you, "that produces goodness; rather, it is from goodness that wealth, and all other benefits for human beings, accrue to them in their private and public life."

If, in fact, I am corrupting the young by those assertions, you may call them harmful. But if anyone claims that I say anything different, he is talking nonsense. In the face of that I should like to say: "Fellow Athenians, you may listen to Anytus or not, as you please; and you may let me go or not, as you please, because there is no chance of my acting otherwise, even if I have to die many times over—"

Stop protesting, fellow Athenians! Please abide by my request that you not protest against what I say, but hear me out; in fact, it will be in your interest, so I believe, to do so. You see, I am going to say some further things to you which may make you shout out—although I beg you not to.

You may be assured that if you put to death the sort of man I just said I was, you will not harm me more than you harm yourselves. Meletus or Anytus would not harm me at all; nor, in fact, could they do so, since I believe it is out of the question for a better man to be harmed by his inferior. The latter may, of course, inflict death or banishment or disenfranchisement; and my accuser here, along with others no doubt, believes those to be great evils. But I do not. Rather, I believe it a far greater evil to try to kill a man unjustly, as he does now.

At this point, therefore, fellow Athenians, so far from pleading on my own behalf, as might be supposed, I am pleading on yours, in case by condemning me you should mistreat the gift which God has bestowed upon you—because if you put me to death, you will not easily find another like me. The fact is, if I may put the point in a somewhat comical way, that I have been literally attached by God to our city, as if to a horse—a large thoroughbred, which is a bit sluggish because of its size, and needs to be aroused by some sort of gadfly. Yes, in me, I believe, God has attached to our city just such a creature—the kind which is constantly alighting everywhere on you, all day long, arousing, cajoling, or reproaching each and every one of you. You will not easily acquire another such gadfly, gentlemen; rather, if you take my advice, you will spare my life. I dare say, though, that you will get angry, like people who are awakened from their doze. Perhaps you will heed Anytus, and give me a swat: you could happily finish me off, and then spend the rest of your life asleep—unless God, in his compassion for you, were to send you someone else.

That I am, in fact, just the sort of gift that God would send to our city, you may recognize from this: it would not seem to be in human nature for me to have neglected all my own affairs, and put up with the neglect of my family for all these years, but constantly minded your interests, by visiting each of you in private like a father or an elder brother, urging you to be concerned about goodness. Of course, if I were gaining anything from that, or were being paid to urge that course upon you, my actions could be explained. But in fact you can see for yourselves that my accusers, who so shamelessly level all those other charges against me, could not muster the impudence to call evidence that I ever once obtained payment, or asked for any. It is I who can call evidence sufficient, I think, to show that I am speaking the truth—namely, my poverty.

Now it may perhaps seem peculiar that, as some say, I give this counsel by going around and dealing with others' concerns in private, yet do not venture to appear before the Assembly, and counsel the city about your business in public. But the reason for that is one you have frequently heard me give in many places: it is a certain divine or spiritual sign which comes to me, the very thing to which Meletus made mocking allusion in his indictment. It has been happening to me ever since childhood: a voice of some sort which comes, and which always—whenever it does come—restrains me from what I am about to do, yet never gives positive direction. That is what opposes my engaging in politics—and its opposition is an excellent thing, to my mind; because you may be quite sure, fellow Athenians, that if I had tried to engage in politics, I should have perished long since, and should have been of no use either to you or to myself.

And please do not get angry if I tell you the truth. The fact is that there is no person on earth whose life will be spared by you or by any other majority, if he is genuinely opposed to many injustices and unlawful acts, and tries to prevent their occurrence in our city. Rather, anyone who truly fights for what is just, if he is going to survive for even a short time, must act in a private capacity rather than a public one.

I will offer you conclusive evidence of that—not just words, but the sort of evidence that you respect, namely, actions. Just hear me tell my experiences, so that you may know that I would not submit to a single person for fear of death, contrary to what is just; nor would I do so, even if I were to lose my life on the spot. I shall mention things to you which are vulgar commonplaces of the courts; yet they are true.

Although I have never held any other public office in our city, fellow Athenians, I have served on its Council. My own tribe, Antiochis, happened to be the presiding commission on the occasion when you wanted a collective trial for the ten generals who had failed to rescue the survivors from the naval battle. That was illegal, as you all later recognized. At the time I was the only commissioner opposed to your acting illegally, and I voted against the motion. And though its advocates were prepared to lay information against me and have me arrested, while you were urging them on by shouting, I believed that I should face danger in siding with law and justice, rather than take your side for fear of imprisonment or death, when your proposals were contrary to justice.

Those events took place while our city was still under democratic rule. But on a subsequent occasion, after the oligarchy had come to power, the Thirty summoned me and four others to the round chamber, with orders to arrest Leon the Salaminian, and fetch him from Salamis for execution; they were constantly issuing such orders, of course, to many others, in their wish to implicate as many as possible in their crimes. On that occasion, however, I showed, once again not just by words, but by my actions, that I couldn't care less about death—if that would not be putting it rather crudely—but that my one and only care was to avoid doing anything sinful or unjust. Thus, powerful as it was, that regime did not frighten me into unjust action: when we emerged from the round chamber, the other four went off to Salamis and arrested Leon, whereas I left them and went off home. For that I might easily have been put to death, had the regime not collapsed shortly afterwards. There are many witnesses who will testify before you about those events.

Do you imagine, then, that I would have survived all these years if I had been regularly active in public life, and had championed what was right in a manner worthy of a brave man, and valued that above all else, as was my duty? Far from it, fellow Athenians: I would not, and nor would any other man. But in any public undertaking, that is the sort of person that I, for my part, shall prove to have been throughout my life; and likewise in my private life, because I have never been guilty of unjust association with anyone, including those whom my slanderers allege to have been my students.

I never, in fact, was anyone's instructor at any time. But if a person wanted to hear me talking, while I was engaging in my own business, I never grudged that to anyone, young or old; nor do I hold b conversation only when I receive payment, and not otherwise. Rather, I offer myself for questioning to wealthy and poor alike, and to anyone who may wish to answer in response to questions from 5 me. Whether any of those people acquires a good character or not, I cannot fairly be held responsible, when I never at any time promised any of them that they would learn anything from me, nor gave them instruction. And if anyone claims that he ever learnt anything from me, or has heard privately something that everyone else did not hear as well, you may be sure that what he says is untrue.

Why then, you may ask, do some people enjoy c spending so much time in my company? You have already heard, fellow Athenians: I have told you the whole truth—which is that my listeners enjoy the examination of those who think themselves wise but are not, since the process is not unamusing. But for 5 me, I must tell you, it is a mission which I have been bidden to undertake by the god, through oracles and dreams, and through every means whereby a divine injunction to perform any task has ever been laid upon a human being.

That is not only true, fellow Athenians, but is d easily verified—because if I do corrupt any of our young people, or have corrupted others in the past, then presumably, when they grew older, should any of them have realized that I had at any time given them bad advice in their youth, they ought now to 5 have appeared here themselves to accuse me and obtain redress. Or else, if they were unwilling to come in person, members of their families—fathers, brothers, or other relations—had their relatives suffered any harm at my hands, ought now to put it on record and obtain redress.

10 In any case, many of those people are present, e whom I can see: first there is Crito, my contemporary and fellow demesman, father of Critobulus here; then Lysanias of Sphettus, father of Aeschines here; next, Epigenes' father, Antiphon from Cephisia, is present; then again, there are others here whose brothers have spent time with me in these studies: Nicostratus, son of Theozotides,

brother of Theodotus—Theodotus himself, inci- 5 dentally, is deceased, so Nicostratus could not have come at his brother's urging; and Paralius here, son 34a of Demodocus, whose brother was Theages; also present is Ariston's son, Adimantus, whose brother is Plato here; and Aeantodorus, whose brother is Apollodorus here.

There are many others I could mention to you, from whom Meletus should surely have called some testimony during his own speech. However, if he 5 forgot to do so then, let him call it now—I yield the floor to him—and if he has any such evidence, let him produce it. But quite the opposite is true, gentlemen: you will find that they are all prepared to support me, their corruptor, the one who is, according to Meletus and Anytus, doing their relatives mischief. Support for me from the actual victims of b corruption might perhaps be explained; but what of the uncorrupted—older men by now, and relatives of my victims? What reason would they have to support me, apart from the right and proper one, which is that they know very well that Meletus is lying, 5 whereas I am telling the truth?

There it is, then, gentlemen. That, and perhaps more of the same, is about all I have to say in my defence. But perhaps, among your number, there may be someone who will harbour resentment when he c recalls a case of his own: he may have faced a less serious trial than this one, yet begged and implored the jury, weeping copiously, and producing his children here, along with many other relatives and 5 loved ones, to gain as much sympathy as possible. By contrast, I shall do none of those things, even though I am running what might be considered the ultimate risk. Perhaps someone with those thoughts will harden his heart against me; and enraged by those same thoughts, he may cast his vote against me in d anger. Well, if any of you are so inclined—not that I expect it of you, but if anyone *should* be—I think it fair to answer him as follows:

"I naturally do have relatives, my excellent friend, because—in Homer's own words—I too was 'not born of oak nor of rock,' but of human parents; 5 and so I do have relatives—including my sons, fellow Athenians. There are three of them: one is now a youth, while two are still children. Nevertheless,

I shall not produce any of them here, and then entreat you to vote for my acquittal."

10   And why, you may ask, will I do no such thing?
e Not out of contempt or disrespect for you, fellow
Athenians—whether or not I am facing death boldly
is a different issue. The point is that with our reputations in mind—yours and our whole city's, as well as
my own—I believe that any such behaviour would
be ignominious, at my age and with the reputation
5 I possess; that reputation may or may not, in fact,
35a be deserved, but at least it is believed that Socrates
stands out in some way from the run of human beings. Well, if those of you who are believed to be
pre-eminent in wisdom, courage, or any other form
of goodness, are going to behave like that, it would
be demeaning.

I have frequently seen such men when they face
judgment: they have significant reputations, yet
5 they put on astonishing performances, apparently in
the belief that by dying they will suffer something
unheard of—as if they would be immune from
death, so long as you did not kill them! They seem to
b me to put our city to shame: they could give any foreigner the impression that men preeminent among
Athenians in goodness, whom they select from their
own number to govern and hold other positions, are
no better than women. I say this, fellow Athenians,
5 because none of us who has even the slightest reputation should behave like that; nor should you put
up with us if we try to do so. Rather, you should
make one thing clear: you will be far more inclined
to convict one who stages those pathetic charades
and makes our city an object of derision, than one
who keeps his composure.

10   But leaving reputation aside, gentlemen, I do not
c think it right to entreat the jury, nor to win acquittal
in that way, instead of by informing and persuading
them. A juror does not sit to dispense justice as a
favour, but to determine where it lies. And he has
sworn, not that he will favour whomever he pleases,
but that he will try the case according to law. We
5 should not, then, accustom you to transgress your
oath, nor should you become accustomed to doing
so: neither of us would be showing respect towards
the gods. And therefore, fellow Athenians, do not
require behaviour from me toward you which I
d consider neither proper nor right nor pious—more

especially now, for God's sake, when I stand charged
by Meletus here with impiety: because if I tried to
persuade and coerce you with entreaties in spite
of your oath, I clearly *would* be teaching you not 5
to believe in gods; and I would stand literally self-
convicted, by my defence, of failing to acknowledge
them. But that is far from the truth: I do acknowledge them, fellow Athenians, as none of my accusers
do; and I trust to you, and to God, to judge my case
as shall be best for me and for yourselves.

For many reasons, fellow Athenians, I am not dismayed by this outcome[1]—your convicting me, I
mean—and especially because the outcome has
come as no surprise to me. I wonder far more at the
number of votes cast on each side, because I did not
think the margin would be so narrow. Yet it seems,
in fact, that if a mere thirty votes had gone the other
way, I should have been acquitted. Or rather, even
as things stand, I consider that I have been cleared
of Meletus' charges. Not only that, but one thing is
obvious to everyone: if Anytus had not come forward with Lycon to accuse me, Meletus would have
forfeited 1,000 drachmas, since he would not have
gained one-fifth of the votes cast.

But anyhow, this gentleman demands the death
penalty for me. Very well, then: what alternative
penalty shall I suggest to you, fellow Athenians?
Clearly, it must be one I deserve. So what do I deserve to incur or to pay, for having taken it into my
head not to lead an inactive life? Instead, I have
neglected the things that concern most people—
making money, managing an estate, gaining military or civic honours, or other positions of power,
or joining political clubs and parties which have
formed in our city. I thought myself, in truth, too
honest to survive if I engaged in those things. I did
not pursue a course, therefore, in which I would be
of no use to you or to myself. Instead, by going to
each individual privately, I tried to render a service
for you which is—so I maintain—the highest service
of all. Therefore that was the course I followed: I
tried to persuade each of you not to care for any of his
possessions rather than care for himself, striving for
the utmost excellence and understanding; and not to
care for our city's possessions rather than for the city
itself; and to care about other things in the same way.

So what treatment do I deserve for being such a benefactor? If I am to make a proposal truly in keeping with my deserts, fellow Athenians, it should be some benefit; and moreover, the sort of benefit that would be fitting for me. Well then, what *is* fitting for a poor man who is a benefactor, and who needs time free for exhorting you? Nothing could be more fitting, fellow Athenians, than to give such a man regular free meals in the Prytaneum; indeed, that is far more fitting for him than for any of you who may have won an Olympic race with a pair or a team of horses: that victor brings you only the appearance of success, whereas I bring you the reality; besides, he is not in want of sustenance, whereas I am. So if, as justice demands, I am to make a proposal in keeping with my deserts, that is what I suggest: free meals in the Prytaneum.

Now, in proposing this, I may seem to you, as when I talked about appeals for sympathy, to be
5 speaking from sheer effrontery. But actually I have no such motive, fellow Athenians. My point is rather this: I am convinced that I do not treat any human being unjustly, at least intentionally—but I cannot make you share that conviction, because we have conversed together so briefly. I say this, because if
10 it were the law here, as in other jurisdictions, that a
b capital case must not be tried in a single day, but over several, I think you could have been convinced; but as things stand, it is not easy to clear oneself of such grave allegations in a short time.

Since, therefore, I am persuaded, for my part, that I have treated no one unjustly, I have no intention whatever of so treating myself, nor of denounc-
5 ing myself as deserving ill, or proposing any such treatment for myself. Why should I do that? For fear of the penalty Meletus demands for me, when I say that I don't know if that is a good thing or a bad one? In preference to that, am I then to choose one of the things I know very well to be bad, and demand that instead? Imprisonment, for instance?
c Why should I live in prison, in servitude to the annually appointed prison commissioners? Well then, a fine, with imprisonment until I pay? That would amount to what I just mentioned, since I haven't the means to pay it.

Well then, should I propose banishment? Per-
5 haps that is what you would propose for me. Yet I must surely be obsessed with survival, fellow Athenians, if I am so illogical as that. You, my fellow citizens, were unable to put up with my discourses and d arguments, but they were so irksome and odious to you that you now seek to be rid of them. Could I not draw the inference, in that case, that others will hardly take kindly to them? Far from it, fellow Athenians. A fine life it would be for a person of my age to go into exile, and spend his days continually 5 exchanging one city for another, and being repeatedly expelled—because I know very well that wherever I go, the young will come to hear me speaking, as they do here. And if I repel them, they will expel me themselves, by persuading their elders; while if I do not repel them, their fathers and relatives will e expel me on their account.

Now, perhaps someone may say: "Socrates, could you not be so kind as to keep quiet and remain inactive, while living in exile?" This is the 5 hardest point of all of which to convince some of you. Why? Because, if I tell you that that would mean disobeying my god, and that is why I cannot 38a remain inactive, you will disbelieve me and think that I am practising a sly evasion. Again, if I said that it really is the greatest benefit for a person to converse every day about goodness, and about the other subjects you have heard me discussing 5 when examining myself and others—and that an unexamined life is no life for a human being to live—then you would believe me still less when I made those assertions. But the facts, gentlemen, are just as I claim them to be, though it is not easy to convince you of them. At the same time, I am not accustomed to think of myself as deserving anything bad. If I had money, I would have b proposed a fine of as much as I could afford: that would have done me no harm at all. But the fact is that I have none—unless you wish to fix the penalty at a sum I could pay. I could afford to pay you 1 mina, I suppose, so I suggest a fine of that 5 amount—

One moment, fellow Athenians. Plato here, along with Crito, Critobulus, and Apollodorus, is urging me to propose 30 minas, and they are saying they will stand surety for that sum. So I propose a fine of that amount, and these people shall be your suf- 10 ficient guarantors of its payment.

c For the sake of a slight gain in time, fellow Athenians, you will incur infamy and blame from those who would denigrate our city, for putting Socrates to death[2]—a "wise man"—because those who wish
5 to malign you will say I am wise, even if I am not; in any case, had you waited only a short time, you would have obtained that outcome automatically. You can see, of course, that I am now well advanced
d in life, and death is not far off. I address that not to all of you, but to those who condemned me to death; and to those same people I would add something further.

Perhaps you imagine, gentlemen, that I have been convicted for lack of arguments of the sort I could have used to convince you, had I believed that
5 I should do or say anything to gain acquittal. But that is far from true. I have been convicted, not for lack of arguments, but for lack of brazen impudence and willingness to address you in such terms as you would most like to be addressed in—that is to say, by weeping and wailing, and doing and saying much
e else that I claim to be unworthy of me—the sorts of thing that you are so used to hearing from others. But just as I did not think during my defence that I should do anything unworthy of a free man because I was in danger, so now I have no regrets about defending myself as I did; I should far rather present such a defence and die, than live by defend-
5 ing myself in that other fashion.

In court, as in warfare, neither I nor anyone else
39a should contrive to escape death at any cost. On the battlefield too, it often becomes obvious that one could avoid death by throwing down one's arms and flinging oneself upon the mercy of one's pursu-
5 ers. And in every sort of danger there are many other means of escaping death, if one is shameless enough to do or to say anything. I suggest that it is not death
b that is hard to avoid, gentlemen, but wickedness is far harder, since it is fleeter of foot than death. Thus, slow and elderly as I am, I have now been overtaken by the slower runner; while my accusers, adroit and quick-witted as they are, have been overtaken by the faster, which is wickedness. And so I take my leave, condemned to death by your judgment, whereas
5 they stand for ever condemned to depravity and injustice as judged by Truth. And just as I accept my

penalty, so must they. Things were bound to turn out this way, I suppose, and I imagine it is for the best.

In the next place, to those of you who voted c
against me, I wish to utter a prophecy. Indeed, I have now reached a point at which people are most given to prophesying—that is, when they are on the point of death. I warn you, my executioners, that as soon as I am dead retribution will come upon you— 5
far more severe, I swear, than the sentence you have passed upon me. You have tried to kill me for now, in the belief that you will be relieved from giving an account of your lives. But in fact, I can tell you, you d
will face just the opposite outcome. There will be more critics to call you to account, people whom I have restrained for the time being though you were unaware of my doing so. They will be all the harder on you since they are younger, and you will rue it all the more—because if you imagine that by putting people to death you will prevent anyone from 5
reviling you for not living rightly, you are badly mistaken. That way of escape is neither feasible nor honourable. Rather, the most honourable and easiest way is not the silencing of others, but striving to make oneself as good a person as possible. So with that prophecy to those of you who voted against me, I take my leave. 10

As for those who voted for my acquittal, I should e
like to discuss the outcome of this case while the officials are occupied, and I am not yet on the way to the place where I must die. Please bear with me, gentlemen, just for this short time: there is no reason why we should not have a word with one another while 5
that is still permitted.

Since I regard you as my friends, I am willing to 40a
show you the significance of what has just befallen me. You see, gentlemen of the jury—and in applying that term to you, I probably use it correctly—something wonderful has just happened to me. Hitherto, the usual prophetic voice from my spiri- 5
tual sign was continually active, and frequently opposed me even on trivial matters, if I was about to do anything amiss. But now something has befallen me, as you can see for yourselves, which one certainly might consider—and is generally held—to be the b
very worst of evils. Yet the sign from God did not oppose me, either when I left home this morning, or

when I appeared here in court, or at any point when I was about to say anything during my speech; and yet in other discussions it has very often stopped me in mid-sentence. This time, though, it has not opposed me at any moment in anything I said or did in this whole business.

Now, what do I take to be the explanation for that? I will tell you: I suspect that what has befallen me is a blessing, and that those of us who suppose death to be an evil cannot be making a correct assumption. I have gained every ground for that suspicion, because my usual sign could not have failed to oppose me, unless I were going to incur some good result.

And let us also reflect upon how good a reason there is to hope that death is a good thing. It is, you see, one or other of two things: either to be dead is to be nonexistent, as it were, and a dead person has no awareness whatever of anything at all; or else, as we are told, the soul undergoes some sort of transformation, or exchanging of this present world for another. Now if there is, in fact, no awareness in death, but it is like sleep—the kind in which the sleeper does not even dream at all—then death would be a marvellous gain. Why, imagine that someone had to pick the night in which he slept so soundly that he did not even dream, and to compare all the other nights and days of his life with that one; suppose he had to say, upon consideration, how many days or nights in his life he had spent better and more agreeably than that night; in that case, I think he would find them easy to count compared with his other days and nights—even if he were the Great King of Persia, let alone an ordinary person. Well, if death is like that, then for my part I call it a gain; because on that assumption the whole of time would seem no longer than a single night.

On the other hand, if death is like taking a trip from here to another place, and if it is true, as we are told, that all of the dead do indeed exist in that other place, why then, gentlemen of the jury, what could be a greater blessing than that? If upon arriving in Hades, and being rid of these people who profess to be "jurors," one is going to find those who are truly judges, and who are also said to sit in judgment there—Minos, Rhadamanthys, Aeacus, Triptolemus,

and all other demigods who were righteous in their own lives—would that be a disappointing journey?

Or again, what would any of you not give to share the company of Orpheus and Musaeus, of Hesiod and Homer? I say "you," since I personally would be willing to die many times over, if those tales are true. Why? Because my own sojourn there would be wonderful, if I could meet Palamedes, or Ajax, son of Telamon, or anyone else of old who met their death through an unjust verdict. Whenever I met them, I could compare my own experiences with theirs—which would be not unamusing, I fancy— and best of all, I could spend time questioning and probing people there, just as I do here, to find out who among them is truly wise, and who thinks he is without being so.

What would one not give, gentlemen of the jury, to be able to question the leader of the great expedition against Troy, or Odysseus, or Sisyphus, or countless other men and women one could mention? Would it not be unspeakable good fortune to converse with them there, to mingle with them and question them? At least that isn't a reason, presumably, for people in that world to put you to death—because amongst other ways in which people there are more fortunate than those in our world, they have become immune from death for the rest of time, if what we are told is actually true.

Moreover, you too, gentlemen of the jury, should be of good hope in the face of death, and fix your minds upon this single truth: nothing can harm a good man, either in life or in death; nor are his fortunes neglected by the gods. In fact, what has befallen me has come about by no mere accident; rather, it is clear to me that it was better I should die now and be rid of my troubles. That is also the reason why the divine sign at no point turned me back; and for my part, I bear those who condemned me, and my accusers, no ill will at all—though, to be sure, it was not with that intent that they were condemning and accusing me, but with intent to harm me—and they are culpable for that. Still, this much I ask of them. When my sons come of age, gentlemen, punish them: give them the same sort of trouble that I used to give you, if you think they care for money or anything else more than for goodness, and if they think highly of themselves when they are of no value. Reprove

42a them, as I reproved you, for failing to care for the things they should, and for thinking highly of themselves when they are worthless. If you will do that, then I shall have received my own just deserts from you, as will my sons.

But enough. It is now time to leave—for me to die, and for you to live—though which of us has the better destiny is unclear to everyone, save only to God.

NOTES

1. The verdict was "Guilty." Socrates here begins his second speech, proposing an alternative to the death penalty demanded by the prosecution.
2. The jury has now voted for the death penalty, and Socrates begins his final speech.

KEY TERM

Sophists

STUDY QUESTIONS

1. Socrates thinks that the person who thinks he knows nothing when he doesn't know anything is wiser than the person who thinks he knows something when he doesn't. But if neither person knows anything, how can one be wiser than the other? What kind of wisdom could Socrates be referring to here?
2. There is something paradoxical about Socrates' claim that the person who is the wisest is the person who recognizes that wisdom is truly worthless. Is Socrates using the word "wisdom" in two different senses here? If so, what could these two senses be?
3. When Socrates is suggesting that his "penalty" be free meals in the Prytaneum, he compares himself to the victor in an Olympic race. He says that while victory brings the Athenians only the appearance of success, Socrates brings the reality of success. What service does Socrates think he is doing for the Athenians that cannot be matched by the winner of an Olympic race? How does examining the citizens of Athens bring them true success?
4. Socrates is famous for saying that "an unexamined life is no life for a human being to live." What does he mean by this? What's so valuable about examining one's life?
5. In your opinion, did Socrates live a meaningful life? Why or why not?

P A R T I I

✕

GOD AND EVIL

INTRODUCTION

No issues are so likely to lead one into the study of philosophy as those arising from religious practices and beliefs. For most, the central question is the existence of God. All the selections in this part bear on that issue. Saint Anselm, Saint Thomas Aquinas, Blaise Pascal, William Paley, and the characters Demea and Cleanthes in David Hume's *Dialogues Concerning Natural Religion* provide arguments in favor of the existence of God.

Pascal's essay stands a bit apart from the rest. Pascal does not argue directly for the existence of God. He thinks that if there is a God, He is infinitely incomprehensible to us, and that therefore we cannot expect to know "either what He is or if He is." But this does not spare us from the dilemma of whether to believe or not. If we approach the issue as we would a wager, Pascal argues, it is clear what we should do.

> Let us weigh the gain and the loss in wagering that God is. Let us estimate these two chances. If you gain, you gain all; if you lose, you lose nothing. Wager, then, without hesitation that He is. (p. 51)

One might challenge Pascal, on the grounds that he does seem to be assuming that he knows a bit about the nature of God after all. He seems confident that we will be better off if we believe than if we do not. Doesn't that assume that if there is a God, He, She, or It is the sort of being who wants to be believed in? How does Pascal know that, given the incomprehensibility of God?

The other selections consider the issue of God's existence in a more straightforward way, looking for arguments to show that God does or does not exist. Any such arguments presuppose some conception of the nature of God, otherwise it would be unclear what has to be proved. The God at issue in these selections is that of classic Christianity. God is conceived of as perfect; this includes being **omnipotent** (all-powerful), **omniscient** (all-knowing), and completely benevolent.

Anselm argues that it would be a contradiction to deny the existence of such a God. He takes it that by "God," we mean something than which nothing greater can be conceived.

But then, "if that than which a greater cannot be conceived exists just in the understanding, the very thing than which a greater cannot be conceived is something than which a greater can be conceived. Without doubt, then, something than which a greater can't be conceived does exist—both in the understanding and in reality."

Anselm's argument may seem to be pulling a large rabbit out of a very small hat—resolving the issue of the existence of God on the basis of a definition and a few deft logical moves. The argument has, in fact, given rise to a large literature. Descartes defended a version of it. It has been criticized by Aquinas, Immanuel Kant, Bertrand Russell, Gottlob Frege, and others. We include Aquinas's criticism.

Although Aquinas doesn't think the ontological argument works, he does think there are "five ways to prove that God exists." These are the argument from change, the argument from causation, the argument from possibility and necessity, the argument from gradations in things, and the argument from the governance of the world. The first two of these arguments are **cosmological arguments**. That is, they argue from very general facts about the cosmos to the conclusion that God exists. Demea also puts forward an argument of this type in Hume's *Dialogues*, Part IX. Philo and Cleanthes both criticize Demea's argument. Aquinas's first two arguments appear to be vulnerable to some of the objections Philo and Cleanthes raise against Demea, as well as the considerations Russell raises in his objections to the **First Cause Argument**.

Aquinas's Fifth Way, from the governance of the world, is somewhat similar to the argument that Cleanthes also raises in the first part of Hume's *Dialogues*, the argument from analogy or design:

> Look round the world: Contemplate the whole and every part of it: You will find it to be nothing but one great machine, subdivided into an infinite number of lesser machines. . . . The curious adapting of means to ends, throughout all nature, resembles exactly, though it much exceeds, the productions of human contrivance; of human design, thought, wisdom and intelligence. Since therefore the effects resemble each other, we are led to infer, by all the rules of analogy, that the causes also resemble; and that the author of nature is somewhat similar to the mind of man; though possessed of much larger faculties, proportioned to the grandeur of the work, which he has executed. By this argument *a posteriori*, and by this argument alone, do we prove at once the existence of the Deity. (pp. 56–57)

Cleanthes's argument, presented in greater detail by William Paley, is the main topic of Hume's *Dialogues,* with Philo shouldering the burden of raising objections to it. There is much current discussion of a thesis called "Intelligent Design," the thrust of which can be traced back to these sources.

Historically, the most important argument against the existence of God—at least against the existence of a perfect God as conceived of in classical Christianity—has been the existence of evil.

> Epicurus' old questions are yet unanswered. Is [God] willing to prevent evil, but not able? then is he impotent. Is he able, but not willing? then is he malevolent. Is he both able and willing? whence then is evil? (p. 77)

This problem is the topic of the second group of selections. We placed Hume's *Dialogues* in this section, somewhat arbitrarily; while Cleanthes's argument from design is the main topic of the book, Philo's powerful statement of the **problem of evil** in the last three parts has shaped modern discussion of the problem. Gottfried Leibniz argues that the believer can answer this challenge. We include a recent dialogue by John Perry in which the characters discuss some important aspects of the problem of evil. Finally, for the new edition, we have added four articles, by Marilyn McCord Adams, Stewart Sutherland, Eleonore Stump, and Louise M. Antony, respectively. Adams considers a particular kind of evil, "horrendous evils," which threaten to empty one's life of meaning. Such evils, she holds, have not been dealt with by traditional solutions to the problem of evil. Adams offers her own solution to this problem, appealing to one's personal relationship with God and the way such a relationship might subvert such evils, making them meaningful rather than threats to meaning. Sutherland, though, in his piece, raises worries for Adams' solution. Similar to Adams, Eleonore Stump's "The Mirror of Evil" is concerned with how one's personal relationship with God is affected by (and affects) one's relation to the evil in the world. Finally, Louise Antony, in her selection, offers an atheist's take on the problem of evil.

KEY TERMS

Omnipotent
Omniscient
Cosmological argument
First Cause Argument
Problem of evil

A. WHY BELIEVE?

✗

The Ontological Argument

SAINT ANSELM

Saint Anselm of Canterbury (1033–1109) was the most important Christian philosopher and theologian of the eleventh century. He is most famous for his "ontological argument" for God's existence found in his work, *Proslogion*. But he is also famous for his work in philosophical theology, specifically his discussion of God's nature, human freedom, sin, and redemption.

. .

Chapter I
A Call for the Mind to Contemplate God

. . . I gratefully acknowledge, Lord, that you created your image in me so that I would remember you, conceive of you, and love you. But this image has been so worn away by my corruption, so obscured by the filth of my sins, that it cannot serve its purpose unless you renew and reshape it. I won't try to reach your heights, Lord, since I could never make my understanding reach that high. Yet I still want somehow to understand your truth, which my heart believes and loves. For, rather than seeking to understand so that I can believe, I believe so that I can understand. In fact, one of the things that I believe is that, "unless I believe, I cannot understand" [Isa. 7:9].

From *Proslogion*, translated by Ronald Rubin. Reprinted by permission of the translator.

Chapter II
God Truly Exists

So Lord—you who reward faith with understanding—let me understand, insofar as you see fit, whether you are as we believe and whether you are what we believe you to be. We believe you to be something than which nothing greater can be conceived. The question, then, is whether something with this nature exists, since "the fool has said in his heart that there is no God" [Ps. 14:1, 53:1]. But, surely, when the fool hears the words "something than which nothing greater can be conceived," he understands what he hears, and what he understands exists in his understanding—even if he doesn't think that it exists. For it is one thing for an object to exist in someone's understanding, and another for him to think that it exists. When a painter plans out a painting, he has it in his understanding, but—not yet having produced it—he doesn't yet think that it exists. After he has painted it, he has the painting in his understanding, and—having produced it—he thinks that it exists. This should convince even the fool that something than which nothing greater can be conceived exists, if only in the understanding—since the fool understands the phrase "that than which nothing greater can be conceived" when he hears it, and whatever a person understands exists in his understanding. And surely that than which a greater cannot be conceived cannot exist *just* in the understanding. If it were to exist *just* in the understanding, we could conceive it to exist in reality too, in which case it would be greater. Therefore, if that than which a greater cannot be conceived exists just in the understanding, the very thing than which a greater cannot be conceived is something than which a greater *can* be conceived. But surely this cannot be. Without doubt, then, something than which a greater can't be conceived does exist—both in the understanding and in reality.

Chapter III
It Is Impossible to Conceive
That God Doesn't Exist

In fact, this thing so truly exists that it can't be conceived not to exist. For something that can be conceived to exist but can't be conceived not to exist is greater than one which can be conceived not to exist. Hence, if that than which a greater can't be conceived can be conceived not to exist, then that than which a greater can't be conceived is not that than which a greater can't be conceived. But this would be a contradiction. Therefore, something than which a greater can't be conceived so truly exists that it can't be conceived not to exist.

And this thing is you, Lord our God. Therefore, you so truly exist, Lord my God, that you can't be conceived not to exist. And this is as it should be. For, if one's mind could conceive of something better than you, a created thing would rise above its creator and pass judgment on it, which would be completely absurd. Yes, anything other than you can be conceived not to exist. Therefore, you alone have the truest, and hence the greatest, being of all; nothing else has being as true or as great. Then why has the fool said in his heart that there is no God, when it is evident to a rational mind that your being is the greatest of all? Why—unless because he is stupid and a fool!

Chapter IV
How the Fool Can Say in His
Heart That Which Can't
Be Conceived

But how could the fool say in his heart something that he couldn't conceive of? And how could he fail to conceive of what he said in his heart, when saying something in one's heart is the same as conceiving of it? If—or, rather, since—he did conceive (since he spoke his heart) but did not speak in his heart (since he could not conceive), there is more than one way to say something in the heart or to conceive of it. We conceive of something in one way when we conceive of words that signify it, but in another when we understand what the thing itself is. In the first way, we can conceive of God's not existing; in the second way, we cannot. No one who understands what God is can possibly conceive that He doesn't exist—although he can say that "God does not exist" in his heart, if he regards the words as meaningless or takes them in unusual senses. For God is that than which a greater cannot be conceived. He who really understands this correctly understands God so to exist that He can't fail to exist, even in our conception. Therefore, he who understands God to be that than which a greater can't be conceived cannot conceive of His not existing.

I thank you, Lord. I thank you because what I once believed through your generosity I now understand through your enlightenment. If I now wanted not to believe that you exist, I wouldn't be able to prevent myself from understanding that you do.

Chapter XV
God Is Greater Than Can
Be Conceived

Therefore, Lord, you are not only that than which a greater cannot be conceived: you are also something greater than can be conceived. It is possible to conceive that there is something of this sort. And, if you are not this thing, it is possible to conceive of something greater than you—which is impossible.

STUDY QUESTIONS

1. Anselm believes God to be "something than which nothing greater can be conceived." What do you think he means by this phrase? Is this how God is typically thought of?
2. What does it mean to say that something exists in the understanding?
3. Why would existence in reality be greater than existence in the understanding? Can you think of anything that would be greater if it existed in the understanding than if it existed in reality?
4. What is Anselm's distinction between two different ways of conceiving in chapter IV? Can we really conceive of something than which nothing greater can be conceived in the way Anselm thinks we can?

The Existence of God

SAINT THOMAS AQUINAS

Saint Thomas Aquinas (1225–1274) was a Dominican monk and widely considered to be the greatest Christian philosopher to have ever lived. Aquinas is famous for interpreting Aristotle's corpus and developing Aristotelian doctrines in a way that was consistent with the teaching of the Church. He is well known for his discussion of the relationship between faith and reason, as well as his development of proofs for the existence of God.

. .

Summa Theologica, Question 2, Article 1

Against the Ontological Argument

. . . Now once we understand the meaning of the word "God" it follows that God exists. For the word means "that than which nothing greater can be meant." Consequently, since existence in thought and fact is greater than existence in thought alone, and since, once we understand the word "God," he exists in thought, he must also exist in fact. It is therefore self-evident that there is a God . . .

Reply. . . . Someone hearing the word "God" may very well not understand it to mean "that than which nothing greater can be thought," indeed, some people have believed God to be a body. And even if the meaning of the word "God" were generally recognized to be "that than which nothing greater can be thought," nothing thus defined would thereby be granted existence in the world of fact, but merely as thought about. Unless one is given that something in fact exists than which nothing greater can be thought—and this nobody denying that existence of God would grant—the conclusion that God in fact exists does not follow . . .

Summa Theologica, Question 2, Article 3

Whether God Exists

Objection 1. It seems that God does not exist. For, if one of a pair of contraries were **infinite**, it would completely obliterate the other. But, when we use the word "God," we mean "something infinitely good." Therefore, if God were to exist, nothing would be bad. But there are bad things in the world. Therefore, God does not exist.

From *Summa Theologica*, translated by Ronald Rubin. Reprinted by permission of the translator.

Objection 2. Moreover, if we can account for something on the basis of a few original causes [*principia*], we ought not to use many. But it seems that we can account for everything that we find in the world on the basis of various original causes even if we suppose that God does not exist. Nature can be taken as the original cause of natural things, and human reason and will can be taken as the original cause of purposeful acts. There is therefore no need to say that God exists.

On the other hand, the book of *Exodus* depicts God as saying, "I am who am" [*Exodus* 3:14].

Reply. There are five ways to prove that God exists.

The first and clearest way derives from facts about change. Surely, as our senses show, some things in the world do change. But everything that changes is made to change by something else. For a thing only undergoes a change inasmuch as it has a *potentiality* for being that into which it changes, while a thing only causes change inasmuch as it is *actual*. To cause change is just to draw something out of potentiality into actuality, and this can only be done by something that is in actuality. (Thus, something actually hot, like fire, makes wood which is potentially hot become actually hot, thereby changing and altering that wood.) But, while a single thing can simultaneously be in actuality with respect to one property and in potentiality with respect to another, it cannot simultaneously be in actuality and potentiality with respect to the one and the same property. (While that which is actually hot may simultaneously be potentially cold, that which is actually hot cannot simultaneously be potentially hot.) It is therefore impossible for a thing that undergoes a change to cause that change, or for something to change itself. Therefore, whatever undergoes change must be changed by another thing. And, if this other thing undergoes change, it also must be changed by something else, and so on. But this cannot go back to infinity. If it did, there would be no first cause of change and, consequently, no other causes of change—for something can be a secondary cause of change only if it is changed by a primary cause (as a stick moves something only if a hand moves the stick). We must therefore posit a first cause of change which is not itself changed by anything. And this everyone understands to be God.

The second way derives from the nature of **efficient causation**. In the world that we sense, we find that efficient causes come in series. We do not, and cannot, find that something is its own efficient cause—for, if something were its own efficient cause, it would be prior to itself, which is impossible. But the series of efficient causes cannot possibly go back to infinity. In all such series of causes, a first thing causes one or more intermediaries, and the intermediaries cause the last thing; when a cause is taken out of this series, so is its effect. Therefore, if there were no first efficient cause, there would be no last or intermediary efficient causes. If the series of efficient causes went back to infinity, however, there would be no first efficient cause and, hence, no last or intermediary causes. But there obviously are such causes. We must therefore posit a first efficient cause, which everyone understands to be God.

The third way, which derives from facts about **possibility** and **necessity**, is this: In the world, we find some things that can either exist or fail to exist—things which are generated and corrupted and which therefore exist at some times but not at others. It is impossible, however, that everything has being of this sort. If something *can* fail to exist, there must have been a time at which it *has* failed to exist. Therefore, if everything could fail to exist, there would have been a time at which nothing existed. But, if there had been such a time, there would not be anything in the world now—for something can begin to exist only if brought into existence by something that already exists. Therefore, if there once had been nothing in existence, it would have been impossible for anything to come into existence, and there would be nothing now. Therefore, not every entity can fail to exist; there must be something in the world that exists of necessity. But, if something exists of necessity, either this necessity is or is not caused by something else. And the series of necessary beings whose necessity is caused by another cannot possibly go back to infinity. (The reasons are those that were used to show that the series of efficient causes cannot go back to infinity.) We must therefore posit something that is necessary per se—something that does not owe its necessity to anything else but which causes the necessity of other things. And this everyone understands to be God.

The fourth way derives from the gradations to be found in things. Some things are found to be better, truer, or more noble than others. But something is said to have more or less of a quality according to its distance from a maximum. (Thus, the hotter a thing is, the closer it is to that which is maximally hot.) There is therefore something maximally true, good, and noble. And this thing must be the greatest being—for, as Aristotle says in *Metaphysics II* [993b25–30], those things that are greatest in truth are greatest in being. But, as Aristotle says in the same work [993b25], the greatest thing of a kind is the cause of everything of that kind (as fire, the hottest thing is the cause of everything hot). There therefore is something which is the cause of being, of goodness, and of whatever other perfections there may be in things. And this we call God.

The fifth way derives from facts about the governance of the world. We see that even things that lack consciousness, such as physical objects, act for a purpose. They almost always act in the same way, and they tend towards what is best. And this shows that they achieve their ends, not by chance, but on purpose. But something that lacks consciousness can tend towards an end only if directed by something with consciousness and intelligence. (Thus, the arrow must be directed by the archer.) There therefore is some intelligence which directs everything in nature towards an end, and this we call God.

Reply to the First Objection. As Augustine says [in *The Enchiridion*], since God is supremely good, He would allow bad things to exist in the world only if He were so powerful and good that He could even bring good out of bad. It is therefore an indication of God's infinite goodness that He permits bad things to exist and draws good things out of them.

Reply to the Second Objection. Since nature works for a definite end under the direction of a higher agency, we must trace whatever nature does back to God as its first cause. Similarly, we must trace purposeful acts back to a cause higher than human reason and will—for these can change or go out of existence, and, as has been shown, we should trace everything that can change or go out of existence back to an original cause [*principium*] which is unchangeable and necessary per se.

KEY TERMS

Infinite
Efficient causation
Possibility
Necessity

STUDY QUESTIONS

1. Aquinas offers a reply to the Ontological Argument in *Summa Theologica*, Question 2, Article 1. What does he think is wrong with the argument?
2. According to Aquinas, there are five ways to prove that God exists. What are these five ways?
3. Why can't the chain of causes "go back to infinity," according to Aquinas?
4. How would you assess Aquinas's claim that "if something *can* fail to exist, there must have been a time at which it *has* failed to exist"? Can you think of any counterexamples?
5. Could there be something besides God that exists necessarily? Could the universe exist necessarily?
6. Does an object that "tends toward an end," as Aquinas puts it, require some intelligence to direct it?

Natural Theology

WILLIAM PALEY

. .

William Paley (1743–1805) was a philosopher and Christian apologist who taught at Christ's College, Cambridge. Paley is perhaps best known for his work on natural theology and, in particular, for his articulation of the design argument for the existence of God.

. .

Chapter I
State of the Argument

In crossing a heath, suppose I pitched my foot against a *stone*, and were asked how the stone came to be there; I might possibly answer, that, for anything I knew to the contrary, it had lain there forever: nor would it perhaps be very easy to show the absurdity of this answer. But suppose I had found a *watch* upon the ground, and it should be inquired how the watch happened to be in that place; I should hardly think of the answer which I had before given, that, for anything I knew, the watch might have always been there. Yet why should not this answer serve for the watch as well as for the stone? Why is it not as admissible in the second case, as in the first? For this reason, and for no other, viz. that, when we come to inspect the watch, we perceive (what we could not discover in the stone) that its several parts are framed and put together for a purpose, *e.g.* that they are so formed and adjusted as to produce motion, and that motion so regulated as to point out the hour of the day; that if the different parts had been differently shaped from what they are, of a different size from what they are, or placed after any other manner, or in any other order, than that in which they are placed, either no motion at all would have been carried on in the machine, or none which would have answered the use that is now served by it. To reckon up a few of the plainest of these parts, and of their

From *Natural Theology* (Boston: Gold and Lincoln, 1863).

offices, all tending to one result . . . —We see a cylindrical box containing a coiled elastic spring, which, by its endeavor to relax itself, turns round the box. We next observe a flexible chain (artificially wrought for the sake of flexure) communicating the action of the spring from the box to the fusee. We then find a series of wheels, the teeth of which catch in, and apply to each other, conducting the motion from the fusee to the balance, and from the balance to the pointer; and at the same time, by the size and shape of those wheels, so regulating that motion, as to terminate in causing an index, by an equable and measured progression, to pass over a given space in a given time. We take notice that the wheels are made of brass in order to keep them from rust; the springs of steel, no other metal being so elastic; that over the face of the watch there is placed a glass, a material employed in no other part of the work; but in the room of which, if there had been any other than a transparent substance, the hour could not be seen without opening the case. This mechanism being observed (it requires indeed an examination of the instrument, and perhaps some previous knowledge of the subject, to perceive and understand it; but being once, as we have said, observed and understood,) the inference, we think, is inevitable; that the watch must have had a maker; that there must have existed, at sometime, and at some place or other, an artificer or artificers, who formed it for the purpose which we find it actually to answer; who comprehended its construction, and designed its use.

I. Nor would it, I apprehend, weaken the conclusion, that we had never seen a watch made: that we had never known an artist capable of making one; that we were altogether incapable of executing such a piece of workmanship ourselves, or of understanding in what manner it was performed; all this being no more than what is true of some exquisite remains of ancient art, of some lost arts, and, to the generality of mankind, of the more curious productions of modern manufacture. Does one man in a million know how oval frames are turned? Ignorance of this kind exalts our opinion of the unseen and unknown artist's skill, if he be unseen and unknown, but raises no doubt in our minds of the existence and agency of such an artist, at some former time, and in some place or other. Nor can I perceive that it varies at all the inference, whether the question arise concerning a human agent, or concerning an agent of a different species, or an agent possessing, in some respects, a different nature.

II. Neither, secondly, would it invalidate our conclusion, that the watch sometimes went wrong, or that it seldom went exactly right. The purpose of the machinery, the design and the designer, might be evident, and in the case supposed would be evident, in whatever way we accounted for the irregularity of the movement, or whether we could account for it or not. It is not necessary that machine be perfect, in order to show with what design it was made: still less necessary, where the only question is, whether it were made with any design at all.

III. Nor, thirdly, would it bring any uncertainty into the argument, if there were a few parts of the watch, concerning which we could not discover, or had not yet discovered, in what manner they conduced to the general effect; or even some parts, concerning which we could not ascertain whether they conduced to that effect in any manner whatever. For, as to the first branch of the case; if by the loss, or disorder, or decay of the parts in question, the movement of the watch were found in fact to be stopped, or disturbed, or retarded, no doubt would remain in our minds as to the utility or intention of these parts, although we should be unable to investigate the manner according to which, or the connexion by which, the ultimate effect depended upon their action or assistance; and the more complex is the machine, the more likely is this obscurity to arise. Then, as to the second thing supposed, namely, that there were parts which might be spared, without prejudice to the movement of the watch, and that we had proved this by experiment—these superfluous parts, even if we were completely assured that they were such, would not vacate the reasoning which we had instituted concerning other parts. The indication of contrivance remained, with respect to them, nearly as it was before.

IV. Nor, fourthly, would any man in his senses think the existence of the watch, with its various machinery, accounted for, by being told that it was one out of possible combinations of material forms; that whatever he had found in the place where he found the watch, must have contained some internal configuration or other; and that this configuration might be the structure now exhibited, viz. of the works of a watch, as well as a different structure.

V. Nor, fifthly, would it yield his inquiry more satisfaction to be answered, that there existed in things a principle of order, which had disposed the parts of the watch into their present form and situation. He never knew a watch made by the principle of order; nor can he even form to himself an idea of what is meant by a principle of order distinct from the intelligence of the watchmaker.

VI. Sixthly, he would be surprised to hear that the mechanism of the watch was no proof of contrivance, only a motive to induce the mind to think so.

VII. And not less surprised to be informed, that the watch in his hand was nothing more than the result of the laws of *metallic* nature. It is a perversion of language to assign any law as the **efficient**, operative **cause** of anything. A law presupposes an agent; for it is only the mode according to which an agent proceeds: it implies a power; for it is the order, according to which that power acts. Without this agent, without this power, which are both distinct from itself, the *law* does nothing; is nothing. The expression, "the law of metallic nature," may sound strange and harsh to a philosophic ear; but it seems quite as justifiable as some others which are more familiar to him, such as "the law of vegetable nature," "the law of animal nature," or indeed as "the law of nature" in general, when assigned as the cause of phenomena, in exclusion of agency and power; or when it is substituted into the place of these.

VIII. Neither, lastly, would our observer be driven out of his conclusion, or from his confidence in its truth, by being told that he knew nothing at all about the matter. He knows enough for his argument. He knows the utility of the end: he knows the subserviency and adaptation of the means to the end. These points being known, his ignorance of other points, his doubts concerning other points, affect not the certainty of his reasoning. The consciousness of knowing little need not beget a distrust of that which he does know.

Chapter II
State of the Argument Continued

Suppose, in the next place, that the person who found the watch, should, after sometime, discover, that, in addition to all the properties which he had hitherto observed in it, it possessed the unexpected property of producing, in the course of its movement, another watch like itself, (the thing is conceivable;) that it contained within it a mechanism, a system of parts, a mould for instance, or a complex adjustment of lathes, files, and other tools, evidently and separately calculated for this purpose; let us inquire, what effect ought such a discovery to have upon his former conclusion.

I. The first effect would be to increase his admiration of the contrivance, and his conviction of the consummate skill of the contriver. Whether he regarded the object of the contrivance, the distinct apparatus, the intricate, yet in many parts intelligible mechanism, by which it was carried on, he would perceive, in this new observation, nothing but an additional reason for doing what he had already done,—for referring the construction of the watch to design, and to supreme art. If that construction *without* this property, or, which is the same thing, before this property had been noticed, proved intention and art to have been employed about it, still more strong would the proof appear, when he came to the knowledge of this farther property, the crown and perfection of all the rest.

II. He would reflect, that though the watch before him were, *in some sense*, the maker of the watch which was fabricated in the course of its movements, yet it was in a very different sense from that in which a carpenter, for instance, is the maker of a chair; the author of its contrivance, the cause of the relation of its parts to their use. With respect to these, the first watch was no cause at all to the second: in no such sense as this was it the author of the constitution and order, either of the parts which the new watch contained, or of the parts by the aid and instrumentality of which it was produced. We might possibly say, but with great latitude of expression, that a stream of water ground corn; but no latitude of expression would allow us to say, no stretch of conjecture could lead us to think, that the stream of water built the mill, though it were too ancient for us to know who the builder was. What the stream of water does in the affair, is neither more nor less than this; by the application of an unintelligent impulse to a mechanism previously arranged, arranged independently of it, and arranged by intelligence, an effect is produced, viz. the corn is ground. But the effect results from the arrangement. The force of the stream cannot be said to be the cause or author of the effect, still less of the arrangement. Understanding and plan in the formation of the mill were not the less necessary, for any share which the water has in grinding the corn; yet is this share the same as that which the watch would have contributed to the production of the new watch, upon the supposition assumed in the last section. Therefore,

III. Though it be now no longer probable, that the individual watch which our observer had found was made immediately by the hand of an artificer, yet doth not this alteration in any-wise affect the inference, that an artificer had been originally employed and concerned in the production. The argument from design remains as it was. Marks of design and contrivance are no more accounted for now than they were before. In the same thing, we may ask for the cause of different properties. We may ask for the cause of the color of a body, of its hardness, of its heat; and these causes may be all different. We are now asking for the cause of that subserviency to a use, that relation to an end, which we have remarked in the watch before us. No answer is given to this question by telling us that a preceding watch produced it. There cannot be design without a designer; contrivance, without a contriver; order, without choice; arrangement, without anything capable of arranging; subserviency and relation to a purpose, without that which could intend a purpose; means suitable to an end, and executing their office in accomplishing that end, without the end ever having been contemplated, or the means accommodated to it. Arrangement, disposition of parts, subserviency of means to an end, relation of instruments to a use, imply the presence of intelligence and mind. No one, therefore, can rationally believe, that the insensible, inanimate watch, from which the watch before us issued, was the proper cause of the mechanism we so much admire in it;—could be truly said to have constructed the instrument, disposed its parts, assigned their office, determined their order, action, and mutual dependency, combined their several motions into one result, and that also a result connected with the utilities of other beings. All these properties, therefore, are as much unaccounted for as they were before.

IV. Nor is anything gained by running the difficulty farther back, *i.e.* by supposing the watch before us to have been produced from another watch, that from a former, and so on indefinitely. Our going back ever so far brings us no nearer to the least degree of satisfaction upon the subject. Contrivance is still unaccounted for. We still want a contriver. A designing mind is neither supplied by this supposition, nor dispensed with. If the difficulty were diminished the farther we went back, by going back indefinitely we might exhaust it. And this is the only case to which this sort of reasoning applies. Where there is a tendency, or, as we increase the number of terms, a continual approach towards a limit, *there*, by supposing the number of terms to be what is called **infinite**, we may conceive the limit to be attained: but where there is no such tendency, or approach, nothing is effected by lengthening the series. There is no difference, as to the point in question, (whatever there may be as to many points,) between one series and another; between a series which is finite, and a series which is infinite. A chain, composed of an infinite number of links, can no more support itself, than a chain composed of a finite number of links. And of this we are assured, (though we never *can* have tried the experiment,) because, by increasing the number of links, from ten, for instance, to a hundred, from a hundred to a thousand, &c. we make not the smallest approach, we observe not the smallest tendency, towards self-support. There is no difference in this respect (yet there may be a great difference in several respects) between a chain of a greater or less length, between one chain and another, between one that is finite and one that is infinite. This very much resembles the case before us. The machine which we are inspecting demonstrates, by its construction, contrivance and design. Contrivance must have had a contriver; design, a designer; whether the machine immediately proceeded from another machine or not. That circumstance alters not the case. That other machine may, in like manner, have proceeded from a former machine: nor does that alter the case; contrivance must have had a contriver. That former one from one preceding it: no alteration still; a contriver is still necessary. No tendency is perceived, no approach towards a diminution of this necessity. It is the same with any and every succession of these machines; a succession of ten, of a hundred, of a thousand; with one series as with another; a series which is finite, as with a series which is infinite. In whatever other respects they may differ, in this they do not. In all, equally, contrivance and design are unaccounted for.

The question is not simply, How came the first watch into existence? which question, it may be pretended, is done away by supposing the series of watches thus produced from one another to have been infinite, and consequently to have had no such *first*, for which it was necessary to provide a cause. This, perhaps, would have been nearly the state of the question, if nothing had been before us but an unorganized, unmechanized substance, without mark or indication of contrivance. It might be difficult to show that such substance could not have existed from eternity, either in succession (if it were possible, which I think it is not, for unorganized bodies to spring from one another) or by individual perpetuity. But that is not the question now. To suppose it to be so, is to suppose that it made no difference whether we had found a watch or a stone. As it is, the metaphysics of that question have no place; for, in the watch which we are examining, are seen contrivance, design; an end, a purpose; means for the end, adaptation to the purpose. And the question which irresistibly presses upon our thoughts, is, whence this contrivance and design? The thing required is the intending mind, the adapting hand, the intelligence by which that hand was directed. This question, this demand, is not shaken off, by increasing a number or succession of **substances**, destitute of these properties; nor the more, by increasing that number to infinity. If it be said, that, upon the supposition of one watch being produced from another in the course of that other's movements, and by means of the mechanism within it, we have a cause for the watch in my hand, viz. the watch from which it proceeded: I deny, that for the design, the contrivance, the suitableness of means to an end, the adaptation of instruments to a use, (all which we discover in a watch,) we have any cause whatever. It is in vain, therefore, to assign a series of such causes, or to allege that a series may be carried back to infinity; for I do not admit that we have yet any cause at all of the phenomena, still less any series of causes either finite or infinite. Here is contrivance, but no contriver; proofs of design, but no designer.

V. Our observer would farther also reflect, that the maker of the watch before him, was, in truth and reality, the maker of every watch produced from it; there being no difference (except that the latter manifests a more exquisite skill) between the making of another watch with his own hands, by the mediation of files, lathes, chisels, &c. and the disposing, fixing, and inserting of these instruments, or of others equivalent to them, in the body of the watch already made, in such a manner as to form a new watch in the course of the movements which he had given to the old one. It is only working by one set of tools instead of another.

The conclusion which the *first* examination of the watch, of its works, construction, and movement, suggested, was, that it must have had, for the cause and author of that construction, an artificer, who understood its mechanism, and designed its use. This conclusion is invincible. A *second* examination presents us with a new discovery. The watch is found, in the course of its movement, to produce another watch, similar to itself: and not only so, but we perceive in it a system or organization, separately calculated for that purpose. What effect would this discovery have or ought it to have, upon our former inference? What, as hath already been said, but to increase, beyond measure, our admiration of the skill which had been employed in the formation of such a machine! Or shall it, instead of this, all at once turn us round to an opposite conclusion, viz that no art or skill whatever has been concerned in the business, although all other evidences of art and skill remain as they were, and this last and supreme piece of art be now added to the rest? Can this be maintained without absurdity? Yet this is **atheism**.

KEY TERMS

Efficient cause
Infinite
Substances
Atheism

STUDY QUESTIONS

1. Do you think Paley is right that even if we had never seen a watch being made or had never known anyone capable of making one, we would still conclude that the watch was created by some kind of agency? Why or why not?
2. What sorts of natural phenomena might plausibly be supposed to show the evidence of having been designed? How much weight should we give to these appearances of design?
3. How does the theory of evolution affect the efficacy of Paley's argument for the existence of God, if at all?

The Wager

BLAISE PASCAL

Blaise Pascal (1623–1662) is most famous for the posthumously published work *Pensées* (*Thoughts*). Specifically he is most famous for the discussion found in this work that has come to be known as "Pascal's Wager." Pascal's Wager (as you will see here) is an attempt to show that given the high stakes of being wrong about God's existence and the low stakes of being correct about God's non-existence, we have good reason to believe that God does, in fact, exist, and we should live accordingly.

· ·

231

Do you believe it to be impossible that God is **infinite**, without parts?—Yes. I wish therefore to show you an infinite and indivisible thing. It is a point moving everywhere with an infinite velocity; for it is one in all places, and is all totality in every place.

Let this effect of nature, which previously seemed to you impossible, make you know that there may be others of which you are still ignorant. Do not draw this conclusion from your experiment, that there remains nothing for you to know; but rather that there remains an infinity for you to know.

232

Infinite movement, the point which fills everything, the moment of rest; infinite without quantity, indivisible and infinite.

233

Infinite—nothing.—Our soul is cast into a body, where it finds number, time, dimension. Thereupon it reasons, and calls this nature, **necessity**, and can believe nothing else.

From *Thoughts*, translated by W. F. Trotter (New York: Collier & Son, 1910).

Unity joined to infinity adds nothing to it, no more than one foot to an infinite measure. The finite is annihilated in the presence of the infinite, and becomes a pure nothing. So our spirit before God, so our justice before divine justice. There is not so great a disproportion between our justice and that of God, as between unity and infinity.

The justice of God must be vast like His compassion. Now justice to the outcast is less vast, and ought less to offend our feelings than mercy towards the elect.

We know that there is an infinite, and are ignorant of its nature. As we know it to be false that numbers are finite, it is therefore true that there is an infinity in number. But we do not know what it is. It is false that it is even, it is false that it is odd; for the addition of a unit can make no change in its nature. Yet it is a number, and every number is odd or even (this is certainly true of every finite number). So we may well know that there is a God without knowing what He is. Is there not one substantial truth, seeing there are so many things which are not the truth itself?

We know then the existence and nature of the finite, because we also are finite and have **extension**. We know the existence of the infinite, and are ignorant of its nature, because it has extension like us, but not limits like us. But we know neither the existence nor the nature of God, because He has neither extension nor limits.

But by faith we know His existence; in glory we shall know His nature. Now, I have already shown that we may well know the existence of a thing, without knowing its nature.

Let us now speak according to natural lights.

If there is a God, He is infinitely incomprehensible, since, having neither parts nor limits, He has no affinity to us. We are then incapable of knowing either what He is or if He is. This being so, who will dare to undertake the decision of the question? Not we, who have no affinity to Him.

Who then will blame Christians for not being able to give a reason for their belief, since they profess a religion for which they cannot give a reason? They declare, in expounding it to the world, that it is a foolishness, *stultitiam*; and then you complain that they do not prove it! If they proved it, they would not keep their word; it is in lacking proofs, that they are not lacking in sense. "Yes, but although this excuses those who offer it as such, and takes away from them the blame of putting it forward without reason, it does not excuse those who receive it." Let us then examine this point, and say, "God is, or He is not." But to which side shall we incline? Reason can decide nothing here. There is an infinite chaos which separated us. A game is being played at the extremity of this infinite distance where heads or tails will turn up. What will you wager? According to reason, you can do neither the one thing nor the other; according to reason, you can defend neither of the propositions.

Do not then reprove for error those who have made a choice; for you know nothing about it. "No, but I blame them for having made, not this choice, but a choice; for again both he who chooses heads and he who chooses tails are equally at fault, they are both in the wrong. The true course is not to wager at all."

Yes; but you must wager. It is not optional. You are embarked. Which will you choose then? Let us see. Since you must choose, let us see which interests you least. You have two things to lose, the true and the good; and two things to stake, your reason and your will, your knowledge and your happiness; and your nature has two things to shun, error and misery. Your reason is no more shocked in choosing one rather than the other, since you must of necessity choose. This is one point settled. But your happiness? Let us weigh the gain and the loss in wagering that God is. Let us estimate these two chances. If you gain, you gain all; if you lose, you lose nothing. Wager, then, without hesitation that He is.—"That is very fine. Yes, I must wager; but I may perhaps wager too much."—Let us see. Since there is an equal risk of gain and of loss, if you had only to gain two lives, instead of one, you might still wager. But if there were three lives to gain, you would have to play (since you are under the necessity of playing), and you would be imprudent, when you are forced to play, not to chance your life to gain three at a game where there is an equal risk of loss and gain. But there is an eternity of life and happiness. And this being so, if there were an infinity of chances, of which one only would be for you, you would still be right in wagering one to win two, and you would act stupidly, being obliged to play, by refusing to stake one life against three at a game in which out of an infinity of chances there is one for you, if there were an infinity of an infinitely happy life to gain. But there is here an infinity of an infinitely happy life to gain, a chance of gain against a finite number of chances of loss, and what you stake is finite. It is all divided; wherever the infinite is and there is not an infinity of chances of loss against that of gain, there is no time to hesitate, you must give all. And thus, when one is forced to play, he must renounce reason to preserve his life, rather than risk it for infinite gain, as likely to happen as the loss of nothingness.

For it is no use to say it is uncertain if we will gain, and it is certain that we risk, and that the infinite distance between the *certainty* of what is staked and the *uncertainty* of what will be gained, equals the finite good which is certainly staked against the uncertain infinite. It is not so, as every player stakes a certainty to gain an uncertainty, and yet he stakes a finite certainty to gain a finite uncertainty, without transgressing against reason. There is not an infinite distance between the certainty staked and the uncertainty of the gain; that is untrue. In truth, there is an infinity between the certainty of gain and the certainty of loss. But the uncertainty of the gain is proportioned to the certainty of the stake according to the proportion of the chances of gain and loss. Hence it comes that, if there are as many risks on one side as on the other, the course is to play even; and then the certainty of the stake is equal to the uncertainty of the gain, so far is it from fact that there is an infinite distance between them. And so our proposition is of infinite force, when there is the finite to stake in a game where there are equal risks of gain and of loss, and the infinite to gain. This is demonstrable; and if men are capable of any truths, this is one.

"I confess it, I admit it. But, still, is there no means of seeing the faces of the cards?"—Yes, Scripture and the rest, etc. "Yes, but I have my hands tied and my mouth closed; I am forced to wager, and am not free. I am not released, and am so made that I cannot believe. What, then, would you have me do?"

True. But at least learn your inability to believe, since reason brings you to this, and yet you cannot believe. Endeavour then to convince yourself, not by increase of proofs of God, but by the abatement of your passions. You would like to attain faith, and do not know the way; you would like to cure yourself of unbelief, and ask the remedy for it. Learn of those who have been bound like you, and who now stake all their possessions. These are people who know the way which you would follow, and who are cured of an ill of which you would be cured. Follow the way by which they began; by acting as if they believed, taking the holy water, having masses said, etc. Even this will naturally make you believe, and deaden your acuteness.—"But this is what I am afraid of."—And why? What have you to lose?

But to show you this leads you there, it is this which will lessen the passions, which are your stumbling-blocks.

The end of this discourse.—Now, what harm will befall you in taking this side? You will be faithful, honest, humble, grateful, generous, a sincere friend, truthful. Certainly you will not have those poisonous pleasures, glory and luxury; but will you not have others? I will tell you that you will thereby gain in this life, and that, at each step you take on this road, you will see so great certainty of gain, so

much nothingness in what you risk, that you will at last recognise that you have wagered for something certain and infinite, for which you have given nothing.

"Ah! This discourse transports me, charms me," etc.

If this discourse pleases you and seems impressive, know that it is made by a man who has knelt, both before and after it, in prayer to that Being, infinite and without parts, before whom he lays all he has, for you also to lay before Him all you have for your own good and for His glory, that so strength may be given to lowliness.

234

If we must not act save on a certainty, we ought not to act on religion, for it is not certain. But how many things we do on an uncertainty, sea voyages, battles! I say then we must do nothing at all, for nothing is certain, and that there is more certainty in religion than there is as to whether we may see to-morrow; for it is not certain that we may see to-morrow, and it is certainly possible that we may not see it. We cannot say as much about religion. It is not certain that it is; but who will venture to say that it is certainly possible that it is not? Now when we work for to-morrow, and so on an uncertainty, we act reasonably; for we ought to work for an uncertainty according to the doctrine of chance which was demonstrated above.

Saint Augustine has seen that we work for an uncertainty, on sea, in battle, etc. But he has not seen the doctrine of chance which proves that we should do so. Montaigne has seen that we are shocked at a fool, and that habit is all-powerful; but he has not seen the reason of this effect.

All these persons have seen the effects, but they have not seen the causes. They are, in comparison with those who have discovered the causes, as those who have only eyes are in comparison with those who have intellect. For the effects are perceptible by sense, and the causes are visible only to the intellect. And although these effects are seen by the mind, this mind is, in comparison with the mind which sees the causes, as the bodily senses are in comparison with the intellect.

235

Rem viderunt, causam non viderunt.

236

According to the doctrine of chance, you ought to put yourself to the trouble of searching for the truth; for if you die without worshipping the True Cause, you are lost.—"But," say you, "if He had wished me to worship Him, He would have left me signs of His will."—He has done so; but you neglect them. Seek them, therefore; it is well worth it.

237

Chances.—We must live differently in the world, according to these different assumptions: (1) that we could always remain in it; (2) that it is certain that we shall not remain here long, and uncertain if we shall remain here one hour. This last assumption is our condition.

238

What do you then promise me, in addition to certain troubles, but ten years of self-love (for ten years is the chance), to try hard to please without success?

239

Objection.—Those who hope for salvation are so far happy; but they have as a counterpoise the fear of hell.

Reply.—Who has most reason to fear hell: he who is in ignorance whether there is a hell, and who is certain of damnation if there is; or he who certainly believes there is a hell, and hopes to be saved if there is?

240

"I would soon have renounced pleasure," say they, "had I faith." For my part I tell you, "You would soon have faith, if you renounced pleasure." Now, it is for you to begin. If I could, I would give you faith. I cannot do so, nor therefore test the truth of what you say. But you can well renounce pleasure, and test whether what I say is true.

241

Order.—I would have far more fear of being mistaken, and of finding that the Christian religion was true, than of not being mistaken in believing it true.

KEY TERMS

Infinite
Necessity
Extension

STUDY QUESTIONS

1. Pascal tells us that we must wager and then asks us which we will choose. Is it really a matter of choice which way we wager?
2. If we wager that God exists, Pascal says that if we lose, we lose nothing. Is this true? Does believing in God, if God doesn't exist, carry no costs?
3. If I accept God because I think it's a safe bet, do I really thereby become a theist? Or is there something else I need to do, even after I make my wager?

B. THE PROBLEM OF EVIL

Dialogues Concerning Natural Religion

DAVID HUME

David Hume (1711–1776) is one of the greatest philosophers the world has known. In addition to his *Enquiries* and *Dialogues Concerning Natural Religion*, his writings include *A Treatise of Human Nature* and *History of England*.

David Hume worked on the *Dialogues Concerning Natural Religion* throughout the later part of his life; before his death, in 1776, he left instructions that the *Dialogues* be published posthumously.*

By natural religion, Hume meant the doctrine, popular among intellectuals of his age, that the basic tenets of religion could be discovered and defended by using the same tools that are employed in scientific thought. Natural religion is opposed to revealed religion: the proposition that the doctrines of religion are essentially mysterious and can be known only through divine revelation.

There are three main characters in the *Dialogues*: Philo, Cleanthes, and Demea. Throughout the *Dialogues* Cleanthes defends natural religion, maintaining that we have considerable evidence—of the same sort that we use in science generally—that our universe was created by an intelligent and benevolent deity. In most of the *Dialogues* Philo seems skeptical about all claims of natural religion. However, in Part XII Philo appears willing to accept a guarded version of natural religion: that we have some evidence the cause or causes of the universe possessed something like intelligence but that there is no evidence the cause or causes of the universe were benevolent or had any of the moral attributes usually attributed to God and that form the basis of religious practices (e.g., prayer) and religious doctrines (e.g., an afterlife in which we are rewarded or punished for our actions while alive). Philo and Cleanthes are both represented as able philosophers, each explaining and defending various parts of Hume's philosophy. Demea is represented as being somewhat less clever, but it is his views on religion and how it should be taught that get the discussion started.

The *Dialogues* is in the form of a letter from Pamphilus, the son of a deceased friend of Cleanthes, to his philosophical friend Hermippus. Cleanthes had been charged with the education of Pamphilus, and the *Dialogues* are Pamphilus' account of a conversation

---

*The *Dialogues* were first published in 1779. We have omitted those footnotes in which Kemp-Smith indicates how Hume made various changes in various drafts, and we have used his translations of various passages that were in Latin in the original. Hume's habit was to capitalize proper names. We have preserved the capitalization for the names of the speakers as the dialogues unfold and changed other proper names to lowercase.

between Demea, Cleanthes, and Philo that begins as a discussion of how Cleanthes should instruct Pamphilus about religion.

In Part I, which we omit, Demea asserts that, although religious training should begin early, discussion of the grounds of religious belief should be the last thing in the education plan:

> While they pass through every other science, I still remark the uncertainty of each part, the eternal disputations of men, the obscurity of all philosophy, and the strange, ridiculous conclusions, which some of the greatest geniuses have derived from the principles of mere human reason. Having thus tamed their mind to a proper submission and self-diffidence, I have no longer any scruple of opening to them the greatest mysteries of religion, nor apprehend any danger from that assuming arrogance of philosophy, which may lead them to reject the most established doctrines and opinions.

Philo appears to agree with this:

> Let the errors and deceits of our very senses be set before us; the insuperable difficulties, which attend first principles in all systems; the contradictions, which adhere to the very ideas of matter, cause and effect, extension, space, time, motion . . . ; when these familiar objects, I say, are so inexplicable, . . . with what assurance can we decide concerning the origin of worlds, or trace their history from eternity to eternity?

Cleanthes's view of things is quite different. He allows that there are many unsolved intellectual problems of the sort Philo cites. But he thinks that the skepticism to which such problems might lead us does not distinguish between religion and science. In spite of the philosophical puzzles and problems Philo cites, we do know a great deal about how the universe works, and this knowledge is based on complex reasoning. The same sorts of reasoning that led to the Copernican conception of the universe will, Cleanthes thinks, confirm the most important doctrines of religion.

Thus a conversation that began with the question of when Pamphilus should study the basis for belief in religious doctrine has evolved by the beginning of Part II into a debate about whether reasoning—of the same sort that underlies our knowledge in other areas—can be the basis of religion. Part II begins with Demea and Philo, again apparently in agreement, insisting against Cleanthes that, although it is obvious that there is a God, the nature of God is not a fit subject for scientific inquiry, but rather an essentially mysterious subject.

. .

Part II

I must own, Cleanthes, said DEMEA, that nothing can more surprise me, than the light, in which you have, all along, put this argument. By the whole tenor of your discourse, one would imagine that you were maintaining the being of a God, against the cavils of **atheists** and infidels; and were necessitated to become a champion for that fundamental principle of all religion. But this, I hope, is not by any means a question among us. No man; no man, at least, of common sense, I am persuaded, ever entertained a serious doubt with regard to a truth so certain and self-evident. The question is not concerning the *being* but the *nature of God*. This, I affirm, from the infirmities of human understanding, to be altogether incomprehensible and unknown to us. The essence of that supreme mind, his attributes, the manner of his existence, the very nature of his duration; these and every particular, which regards so divine a Being, are mysterious to men. Finite, weak, and blind creatures, we ought to humble ourselves in his august presence, and, conscious of our frailties, adore in silence his **infinite** perfections, which eye hath not seen, ear hath not heard, neither hath it entered into the heart of man to conceive them. They are covered in a deep cloud from human curiosity: It is profaneness to attempt penetrating through these sacred obscurities: And next to the impiety of denying his existence, is the temerity of prying into his nature and essence, decrees and attributes.

But lest you should think, that my *piety* has here got the better of my *philosophy*, I shall support my opinion, if it needs any support, by a very great authority. I might cite all the divines almost, from the foundation of Christianity, who have ever treated of this or any other theological subject: But I shall confine myself, at present, to one equally celebrated for piety and philosophy. It is Father Malebranche, who, I remember, thus expresses himself.[1] "One ought not so much (says he) to call God a spirit, in order to express positively what he is, as in order to signify that he is not matter. He is a Being infinitely perfect: Of this we cannot doubt. But in the same manner as we ought not to imagine, even supposing him corporeal, that he is cloathed with a human body, as the anthropomorphites asserted, under colour that that figure was the most perfect of any; so neither ought we to imagine, that the Spirit of God has human ideas, or bears *any* resemblance to our spirit; under colour that we know nothing more perfect than a human mind. We ought rather to believe, that as he comprehends the perfections of matter without being material. . .he comprehends also the perfections of created spirits, without being spirit, in the manner we conceive spirit: That his true name is, *He that is*, or in other words, Being without restriction, All Being, the Being infinite and universal."

After so great an authority, Demea, replied PHILO, as that which you have produced, and a thousand more, which you might produce, it would appear ridiculous in me to add my sentiment, or express my approbation of your doctrine. But surely, where reasonable men treat these subjects, the question can never be concerning the *being*, but only the *nature* of the Deity. The former truth, as you well observe, is unquestionable and self-evident. Nothing exists without a cause: and the original cause of this universe (whatever it be) we call God; and piously ascribe to him every species of perfection. Whoever scruples this fundamental truth deserves every punishment, which can be inflicted among philosophers, to wit, the greatest ridicule, contempt and disapprobation. But as all perfection is entirely relative, we ought never to imagine, that we comprehend the attributes of this divine Being, or to suppose, that his perfections have any **analogy** or likeness to the perfections of a human creature. Wisdom, thought, design, knowledge; these we justly ascribe to him; because these words are honourable among men, and we have no other language or other conceptions, by which we can express our adoration of him. But let us beware, lest we think, that our ideas any wise correspond to his perfections, or that his attributes have any resemblance to these qualities among men. He is infinitely superior to our limited view and comprehension; and is more the object of worship in the temple, than of disputation in the schools.

In reality, Cleanthes, continued he, there is no need of having recourse to that affected **scepticism**, so displeasing to you, in order to come at this determination. Our ideas reach no farther than our experience: We have no experience of divine attributes and operations: I need not conclude my **syllogism**: You can draw the inference yourself. And it is a pleasure to me (and I hope to you too) that just reasoning and sound piety here concur in the same conclusion, and both of them establish the adorably mysterious and incomprehensible nature of the supreme Being.

Not to lose any time in circumlocutions, said CLEANTHES, addressing himself to Demea, much less in replying to the pious declamations of Philo; I shall briefly explain how I conceive this matter. Look round the world: Contemplate the whole and every part of it: You will find it to be nothing but one great machine, subdivided into an infinite number of lesser machines, which again admit of subdivisions, to a degree beyond what human senses and faculties can trace and explain. All these various machines, and even their most minute parts, are adjusted to each other with an accuracy, which ravishes into admiration all men, who have ever contemplated them. The curious adapting of means to ends, throughout all nature, resembles exactly, though it much exceeds, the productions of human contrivance; of human design, thought, wisdom, and intelligence. Since therefore the effects resemble each other, we are led to infer, by all the rules of analogy, that the causes also resemble; and that the Author of nature is somewhat similar to the mind of man; though possessed of much larger faculties, proportioned to the grandeur of the work, which he has executed. By this argument *a posteriori*, and by this argument alone, do we prove at once the existence of a Deity, and his similarity to human mind and intelligence.

I shall be so free, Cleanthes, said DEMEA, as to tell you, that from the beginning, I could not approve of your conclusion concerning the similarity of the Deity to men; still less can I approve of the mediums, by which you endeavour to establish it. What! No demonstration of the being of a God! No abstract arguments! No proofs *a priori*! Are these, which have hitherto been so much insisted on by philosophers, all fallacy, all **sophism**? Can we reach no farther in this subject than experience and probability? I will not say, that this is betraying the cause of a Deity: But surely, by this affected candour, you give advantage to atheists, which they never could obtain, by the mere dint of argument and reasoning.

What I chiefly scruple in this subject, said PHILO, is not so much, that all religious arguments are by Cleanthes reduced to experience, as that they appear not to be even the most certain and irrefragable of that inferior kind. That a stone will fall, that fire will burn, that the earth has solidity, we have observed a thousand and a thousand times; and when any new instance of this nature is presented, we draw without hesitation the accustomed inference. The exact similarity of the cases gives us a perfect assurance of a similar event; and a stronger evidence is never desired nor sought after. But wherever you depart, in the

least, from the similarity of the cases, you diminish proportionably the evidence; and may at last bring it to a very weak *analogy*, which is confessedly liable to error and uncertainty. After having experienced the circulation of the blood in human creatures, we make no doubt that it takes place in Titius and Maevius: But from its circulation in frogs and fishes, it is only a presumption, though a strong one, from analogy, that it takes place in men and other animals. The analogical reasoning is much weaker, when we infer the circulation of the sap in vegetables from our experience that the blood circulates in animals; and those, who hastily followed that imperfect analogy, are found, by more accurate experiments, to have been mistaken.

If we see a house, Cleanthes, we conclude, with the greatest certainty, that it had an architect or builder; because this is precisely that species of effect, which we have experienced to proceed from that species of cause. But surely you will not affirm, that the universe bears such a resemblance to a house, that we can with the same certainty infer a similar cause, or that the analogy is here entire and perfect. The dissimilitude is so striking, that the utmost you can here pretend to is a guess, a conjecture, a presumption concerning a similar cause; and how that pretension will be received in the world, I leave you to consider.

It would surely be very ill received, replied CLEANTHES; and I should be deservedly blamed and detested, did I allow, that the proofs of a Deity amounted to no more than a guess or conjecture. But is the whole adjustment of means to ends in a house and in the universe so slight a resemblance? The economy of **final causes**? The order, proportion, and arrangement of every part? Steps of a stair are plainly contrived, that human legs may use them in mounting; and this inference is certain and infallible. Human legs are also contrived for walking and mounting; and this inference, I allow, is not altogether so certain, because of the dissimilarity which you remark; but does it, therefore, deserve the name only of presumption or conjecture?

Good God! cried DEMEA, interrupting him, where are we? Zealous defenders of religion allow, that the proofs of a Deity fall short of perfect evidence! And you, Philo, on whose assistance I depended, in proving the adorable mysteriousness of the divine nature, do you assent to all these extravagant opinions of Cleanthes? For what other name can I give them? Or why spare my censure, when such principles are advanced, supported by such an authority, before so young a man as Pamphilus?

You seem not to apprehend, replied PHILO, that I argue with Cleanthes in his own way; and by showing him the dangerous consequences of his tenets, hope at last to reduce him to our opinion. But what sticks most with you, I observe, is the representation which Cleanthes has made of the argument *a posteriori*; and finding that that argument is likely to escape your hold and vanish into air, you think it so disguised, that you can scarcely believe it to be set in its true light. Now, however much I may dissent, in other respects from the dangerous principles of Cleanthes, I must allow, that he has fairly represented that argument; and I shall endeavour so to state the matter to you, that you will entertain no farther scruples with regard to it.

Were a man to abstract from every thing which he knows or has seen, he would be altogether incapable, merely from his own ideas, to determine what kind of scene the universe must be, or to give the preference to one state or situation of things above another. For as nothing, which he clearly conceives, could be esteemed impossible or implying a contradiction, every chimera of his fancy would be upon an equal footing; nor could he assign any just reason, why he adheres to one idea or system, and rejects the others, which are equally possible.

Again; after he opens his eyes, and contemplates the world, as it really is, it would be impossible for him, at first, to assign the cause of any one event; much less, of the whole of things or of the universe. He might set his fancy a rambling; and she might bring him in an infinite variety of reports and representations. These would all be possible; but being all equally possible, he would never, of himself, give a satisfactory account for his preferring one of them to the rest. Experience alone can point out to him the true cause of any phenomenon.

Now according to this method of reasoning, Demea, it follows (and is, indeed, tacitly allowed by Cleanthes himself) that order, arrangement, or the adjustment of final causes is not, of itself, any proof of design; but only so far as it has been experienced to proceed from that principle. For aught we can know *a priori*, matter may contain the source or spring of order originally, within itself, as well as mind does; and there is no more difficulty in conceiving, that the several elements, from an internal unknown cause, may fall into the most exquisite arrangement, than to conceive that their ideas, in the great, universal mind, from a like internal, unknown cause, fall into that arrangement. The equal possibility of both these suppositions is allowed. But by experience we find (according to Cleanthes), that there is a difference between them. Throw several pieces of steel together, without shape or form; they will never arrange themselves so as to compose a watch: Stone, and mortar, and wood, without an architect, never erect a house. But the ideas in a human mind, we see, by an unknown, inexplicable economy, arrange themselves so as to form the plan of a watch or house. Experience, therefore, proves, that there is an original principle of order in mind, not in matter. From similar effects we infer similar causes. The adjustment of means to ends is alike in the universe, as in a machine of human contrivance. The causes, therefore, must be resembling.

I was from the beginning scandalised, I must own, with this resemblance, which is asserted, between the Deity and human creatures; and must conceive it to imply such a degradation of the supreme Being as no sound theist could endure. With your assistance, therefore, Demea, I shall endeavour to defend what you justly call the adorable mysteriousness of the divine nature, and shall refute this reasoning of Cleanthes; provided he allows, that I have made a fair representation of it.

When Cleanthes had assented, PHILO, after a short pause, proceeded in the following manner.

That all inferences, Cleanthes, concerning fact, are founded on experience, and that all experimental reasonings are founded on the supposition, that similar causes prove similar effects and similar effects similar causes; I shall not, at present, much dispute with you. But observe, I entreat you, with what extreme caution all just reasoners proceed in the transferring of experiments to similar cases. Unless the cases be exactly similar, they repose no perfect confidence in applying their past observation to any particular phenomenon. Every alteration of circumstances occasions a doubt concerning the event; and it requires new experiments to prove certainly, that the new circumstances are of no moment or importance. A change in bulk, situation, arrangement, age, disposition of the air, or surrounding bodies; any of these particulars may be attended with the most unexpected consequences: And unless the objects be quite familiar to us, it is the highest temerity to expect with assurance, after any of these changes, an event similar to that which before fell under our observation. The slow and deliberate steps of philosophers, here, if any where, are distinguished from the precipitate march of the vulgar, who, hurried on by the smallest similitude, are incapable of all discernment or consideration.

But can you think, Cleanthes, that your usual phlegm and philosophy have been preserved in so wide a step as you have taken, when you compared to the universe houses, ships, furniture, machines; and from their similarity in some circumstances inferred a similarity in their causes? Thought, design, intelligence, such as we discover in men and other animals, is no more than one of the springs and principles of the universe, as well as heat or cold, attraction or repulsion, and a hundred others, which fall under daily observation. It is an active cause, by which some particular parts of nature, we find, produce alterations on other parts. But can a conclusion, with any propriety, be transferred from parts to the whole? Does not the great disproportion bar all comparison and inference? From observing the growth of a hair, can we learn any thing concerning the generation of a man? Would the manner of a leaf's blowing, even though perfectly known, afford us any instruction concerning the vegetation of a tree?

But allowing that we were to take the *operations* of one part of nature upon another for the foundation of our judgment concerning the *origin* of the whole (which never can be admitted); yet why select so minute, so weak, so bounded a principle as the reason and design of animals is found to be upon this planet? What peculiar privilege has this little agitation of the brain which we call thought, that we must thus make it the model of the whole universe? Our partiality in our own favour does indeed present it on all occasions: But sound philosophy ought carefully to guard against so natural an illusion.

So far from admitting, continued PHILO, that the operations of a part can afford us any conclusion concerning the origin of the whole, I will not allow any one part to form a rule for another part, if the latter be very remote from the former. Is there any reasonable ground to conclude, that the inhabitants of other planets possess thought, intelligence, reason, or any thing similar to these faculties in men? When nature has so extremely diversified her manner of operation in this small globe; can we imagine, that she incessantly copies herself throughout so immense a universe? And if thought, as we may well suppose, be confined merely to this narrow concern, and has even there so limited a sphere of action; with what propriety can we assign it for the original cause of all things? The narrow views of a peasant, who makes his domestic economy the rule for the government of kingdoms, is in comparison a pardonable sophism.

But were we ever so much assured, that a thought and reason, resembling the human, were to be found throughout the whole universe, and were its activity elsewhere vastly greater and more commanding than it appears in this globe: Yet I cannot see, why the operations of a world, constituted, arranged, adjusted, can with any propriety be extended to a world, which is in its embryo-state, and is advancing towards that constitution and arrangement. By observation, we know somewhat of the economy, action, and nourishment of a finished animal; but we must transfer with great caution that observation to the growth of a foetus in the womb, and still more, to the formation of an animalcule in the loins of its male parent. Nature, we find, even from our limited experience, possesses an infinite number of springs and principles, which incessantly discover themselves on every change of her position and situation. And what new and unknown principles would actuate her in so new and unknown a situation as that of the formation of a universe, we cannot, without the utmost temerity, pretend to determine.

A very small part of this great system, during a very short time, is very imperfectly discovered to us: And do we thence pronounce decisively concerning the origin of the whole?

Admirable conclusion! Stone, wood, brick, iron, brass, have not, at this time, in this minute globe of earth, an order or arrangement without human art and contrivance: Therefore the universe could not originally attain its order and arrangement, without something similar to human art. But is a part of nature a rule for another part very wide of the former? Is it a rule for the whole? Is a very small part a rule for the universe? Is nature in one situation, a certain rule for nature in another situation, vastly different from the former?

And can you blame me, Cleanthes, if I here imitate the prudent reserve of Simonides, who, according to the noted story,[2] being asked by Hiero, *What God was?* desired a day to think of it, and then two days more; and after that manner continually prolonged the term, without ever bringing in his definition or description? Could you even blame me, if I had answered at first, *that I did not know*, and was sensible that this subject lay vastly beyond the reach of my faculties? You might cry out sceptic and raillier as much as you pleased: But having found, in so many other subjects, much more familiar, the imperfections and even contradictions of human reason, I never should expect any success from its feeble conjectures, in a subject, so sublime, and so remote from the sphere of our observation. When *two species* of objects have always been observed to be conjoined together, I can *infer*, by custom, the existence of one whenever I *see* the existence of the other: And this I call an argument from experience. But how this argument can have place, where the objects, as in the present case, are single, individual, without parallel, or specific resemblance, may be difficult to explain. And will any man tell me with a serious countenance, that an orderly universe must arise from some thought and art, like the human; because we have experience of it? To ascertain this reasoning, it were requisite, that we had experience of this origin of worlds; and it is not sufficient surely, that we have seen ships and cities arise from human art and contrivance.

. . . .

Philo was proceeding in this vehement manner, somewhat between jest and earnest, as it appeared to me; when he observed some signs of impatience in Cleanthes, and then immediately stopped short. What I had to suggest, said CLEANTHES, is only that you would not abuse terms, or make use of popular expressions to subvert philosophical reasonings. You know, that the vulgar often distinguish reason from experience, even where the question relates only to matter of fact and existence; though it is found, where that *reason* is properly analysed, that it is nothing but a species of experience. To prove by experience the origin of the universe from mind is not more contrary to common speech than to prove the motion of the earth from the same principle. And a caviller might raise all the same objections to the Copernican system, which you have urged against my reasonings. Have you other earths, might he say, which you have seen to move? Have. . . .

Yes! cried PHILO, interrupting him, we have other earths. Is not the moon another earth, which we see to turn round its centre? Is not Venus another earth, where we observe the same phenomenon? Are not the revolutions of the sun also a confirmation, from analogy, of the same theory? All the planets, are they not earths, which revolve about the sun? Are not the satellites moons, which move round Jupiter and Saturn, and along with these primary planets, round the sun? These analogies and resemblances, with others, which I have not mentioned, are the sole proofs of the Copernican system: And to you it belongs to consider, whether you have any analogies of the same kind to support your theory.

In reality, Cleanthes, continued he, the modern system of astronomy is now so much received by all enquirers, and has become so essential a part even of our earliest education, that we are not commonly very scrupulous in examining the reasons upon which it is founded. It is now become a matter of mere curiosity to study the first writers on that subject, who had the full force of prejudice to encounter, and were obliged to turn their arguments on every side, in order to render them popular and convincing. But if we peruse Galileo's famous Dialogues concerning the system of the world, we shall find, that that great genius, one of the sublimest that ever existed, first bent all his endeavours to prove, that there was no foundation for the distinction commonly made between elementary and celestial substances. The schools, proceeding from the illusions of sense, had carried this distinction very far; and had established the latter substances to be ingenerable, incorruptible, unalterable, impassible; and had assigned all the opposite qualities to the former. But Galileo, beginning with the moon, proved its similarity in every particular to the earth; its convex figure, its natural darkness when not illuminated, its density, its distinction into solid and liquid, the variations of its phases, the mutual illuminations of the earth and moon, their mutual eclipses, the inequalities of the lunar surface, etc. After many instances of this kind, with regard to all the planets, men plainly saw, that these bodies became proper objects of experience; and that the similarity of their nature enabled us to extend the same arguments and phenomena from one to the other.

In this cautious proceeding of the astronomers, you may read your own condemnation, Cleanthes; or rather may see, that the subject in which you are engaged exceeds all human reason and enquiry. Can you pretend to show any such similarity between the fabric of a house, and the generation of a universe? Have you ever seen nature in any such situation as resembles the first arrangement of the elements? Have worlds ever been formed under your eye? and have you had leisure to observe the whole progress of the phenomenon, from the first appearance of order to its final consummation? If you have, then cite your experience, and deliver your theory.

Part III

How the most absurd argument, replied CLEANTHES, in the hands of a man of ingenuity and invention, may acquire an air of probability! Are you now aware, Philo, that it became necessary for Copernicus and his first disciples to prove the similarity of the terrestrial and celestial matter; because several philosophers, blinded by old systems, and supported by some sensible appearances, had denied this similarity? But that it is by no means necessary, that theists should prove the similarity of the works of nature to those of art; because this similarity is self-evident and undeniable? The same matter, a like form: What more is requisite

to show an analogy between their causes, and to ascertain the origin of all things from a divine purpose and intention? Your objections, I must freely tell you, are no better than the abstruse cavils of those philosophers, who denied motion; and ought to be refuted in the same manner, by illustrations, examples, and instances, rather than by serious argument and philosophy.

Suppose, therefore, that an articulate voice were heard in the clouds, much louder and more melodious than any which human art could ever reach: Suppose, that this voice were extended in the same instant over all nations, and spoke to each nation in its own language and dialect: Suppose, that the words delivered not only contain a just sense and meaning, but convey some instruction altogether worthy of a benevolent Being, superior to mankind: Could you possibly hesitate a moment concerning the cause of this voice? And must you not instantly ascribe it to some design or purpose? Yet I cannot see but all the same objections (if they merit that appellation) which lie against the system of theism, may also be produced against this inference.

Might you not say, that all conclusions concerning fact were founded on experience: That when we hear an articulate voice in the dark, and thence infer a man, it is only the resemblance of the effects, which leads us to conclude that there is a like resemblance in the cause: But that this extraordinary voice, by its loudness, extent, and flexibility to all languages, bears so little analogy to any human voice, that we have no reason to suppose any analogy in their causes: And consequently, that a rational, wise, coherent speech proceeded, you knew not whence, from some accidental whistling of the winds, not from any divine reason or intelligence? You see clearly your own objections in these cavils; and I hope too, you see clearly, that they cannot possibly have more force in the one case than in the other.

But to bring the case still nearer the present one of the universe, I shall make two suppositions, which imply not any absurdity or impossibility. Suppose, that there is a natural, universal, invariable language, common to every individual of human race; and that books are natural productions, which perpetuate themselves in the same manner with animals and vegetables, by descent and propagation. Several expressions of our passions contain a universal language: All brute animals have a natural speech, which, however limited, is very intelligible to their own species. And as there are infinitely fewer parts and less contrivance in the finest composition of eloquence, than in the coarsest organized body, the propagation of an *Iliad* or *Aeneid* is an easier supposition than that of any plant or animal.

Suppose, therefore, that you enter into your library, thus peopled by natural volumes, containing the most refined reason and most exquisite beauty: Could you possibly open one of them, and doubt, that its original cause bore the strongest analogy to mind and intelligence? When it reasons and discourses; when it expostulates, argues, and enforces its views and topics; when it applies sometimes to the pure intellect, sometimes to the affections; when it collects, disposes, and adorns every consideration suited to the subject: could you persist in asserting, that all this, at the bottom, had really no meaning, and that the first formation of this volume in the loins of its original parent proceeded not from thought and design? Your obstinacy, I know, reaches not that degree of firmness: Even your sceptical play and wantonness would be abashed at so glaring an absurdity.

But if there be any difference, Philo, between this supposed case and the real one of the universe, it is all to the advantage of the latter. The anatomy of an animal affords many stronger instances of design than the perusal of Livy or Tacitus: And any objection which you start in the former case, by carrying me back to so unusual and extraordinary a scene as the first formation of worlds, the same objection has placed on the supposition of our vegetating library. Choose, then, your party, Philo, without ambiguity or evasion: Assert either that a rational volume is no proof of a rational cause, or admit of a similar cause to all the works of nature.

Let me here observe too, continued CLEANTHES, that this religious argument, instead of being weakened by that scepticism, so much affected by you, rather acquires force from it, and becomes more firm and undisputed. To exclude all argument or reasoning of every kind is either affectation or madness. The declared profession of every reasonable sceptic is only to reject abstruse, remote and refined arguments; to adhere to common sense and the plain instincts of nature; and to assent, wherever any reasons strike him with so full a force, that he cannot, without the greatest violence, prevent it. Now the arguments for natural religion are plainly of this kind; and nothing but the most perverse, obstinate **metaphysics** can reject them. Consider, anatomize the eye: Survey its structure and contrivance; and tell me, from your own feeling, if the idea of a contriver does not immediately flow in upon you with a force like that of sensation. The most obvious conclusion surely is in favour of design; and it requires time, reflection and study, to summon up those frivolous, though abstruse, objections, which can support infidelity. Who can behold the male and female of each species, the correspondence of their parts and instincts, their passions and whole course of life before and after generation, but must be sensible, that the propagation of the species is intended by nature? Millions and millions of such instances present themselves through every part of the universe; and no language can convey a more intelligible, irresistible meaning, than the curious adjustment of final causes. To what degree, therefore, of blind dogmatism must one have attained, to reject such natural and such convincing arguments?

Some beauties in writing we may meet with, which seem contrary to rules, and which gain the affections, and animate the imagination, in opposition to all the precepts of criticism, and to the authority of the established masters of art. And if the argument for theism be, as you pretend, contradictory to the principles of logic; its universal, its irresistible influence proves clearly, that there may be arguments of a like irregular nature. Whatever cavils may be urged; an orderly world, as well as a coherent, articulate speech, will still be received as an incontestable proof of design and intention.

It sometimes happens, I own, that the religious arguments have not their due influence on an ignorant savage and barbarian; not because they are obscure and difficult, but because he never asks himself any question with regard to them. Whence arises the curious structure of an animal? From the copulation of its parents. And these whence? From *their* parents. A few removes set the objects at such a distance, that to him they are lost in darkness and confusion; nor is he actuated by any curiosity to trace them farther.

But this is neither dogmatism nor scepticism, but stupidity; a state of mind very different from your sifting, inquisitive disposition, my ingenious friend. You can trace causes from effects: You can compare the most distant and remote objects: And your greatest errors proceed not from barrenness of thought and invention, but from too luxuriant a fertility, which suppresses your natural good sense, by a profusion of unnecessary scruples and objections.

Here I could observe, Hermippus, that Philo was a little embarrassed and confounded: But while he hesitated in delivering an answer, luckily for him, DEMEA broke in upon the discourse, and saved his countenance.

Your instance, Cleanthes, said he, drawn from books and language, being familiar, has, I confess, so much more force on that account; but is there not some danger too in this very circumstance, and may it not render us presumptuous, by making us imagine we comprehend the Deity, and have some adequate idea of his nature and attributes? When I read a volume, I enter into the mind and intention of the author: I become him, in a manner, for the instant; and have an immediate feeling and conception of those ideas, which revolved in his imagination, while employed in that composition. But so near an approach we never surely can make to the Deity. His ways are not our ways. His attributes are perfect, but incomprehensible. And this volume of nature contains a great inexplicable riddle, more than any intelligible discourse or reasoning.

The ancient **Platonists**, you know, were the most religious and devout of all the pagan philosophers: Yet many of them, particularly Plotinus, expressly declare that intellect or understanding is not to be ascribed to the Deity, and that our most perfect worship of him consists, not in acts of veneration, reverence, gratitude or love; but in a certain mysterious self-annihilation or total extinction of all our faculties. These ideas are, perhaps, too far stretched; but still it must be acknowledged, that, by representing the Deity as so intelligible, and comprehensible, and so similar to a human mind, we are guilty of the grossest and most narrow partiality, and make ourselves the model of the whole universe.

All the *sentiments* of the human mind, gratitude, resentment, love, friendship, approbation, blame, pity, emulation, envy, have a plain reference to the state and situation of man, and are calculated for preserving the existence, and promoting the activity of such a being in such circumstances. It seems therefore unreasonable to transfer such sentiments to a supreme existence, or to suppose him actuated by them; and the phenomena, besides, of the universe will not support us in such a theory. All our *ideas*, derived from the senses, are confessedly false and illusive; and cannot, therefore, be supposed to have place in a supreme intelligence: And as the ideas of internal sentiment, added to those of the external senses, compose the whole furniture of human understanding, we may conclude, that none of the *materials* of thought are in any respect similar in the human and in the divine intelligence. Now, as to the *manner* of thinking; how can we make any comparison between them, or suppose them any wise resembling? Our thought is fluctuating, uncertain, fleeting, successive, and compounded; and were we to remove these circumstances, we absolutely annihilate its essence, and it would, in such a case, be an abuse of terms to apply to it the name of thought or reason. At least, if it appear more pious and respectful (as it really is) still to retain these terms, when we mention the supreme Being, we ought to acknowledge, that their meaning, in that case, is totally incomprehensible; and that the infirmities of our nature do not permit us to reach any ideas, which in the least correspond to the ineffable sublimity of the divine attributes.

Part IV

It seems strange to me, said CLEANTHES, that you, Demea, who are so sincere in the cause of religion, should still maintain the mysterious, incomprehensible nature of the Deity, and should insist so strenuously, that he has no manner of likeness or resemblance to human creatures. The Deity, I can readily allow, possesses many powers and attributes, of which we can have no comprehension: But if our ideas, so far as they go, be not just and adequate, and correspondent to his real nature, I know not what there is in this subject worth insisting on. Is the name, without any meaning, of such mighty importance? Or how do you mystics, who maintain the absolute incomprehensibility of the Deity, differ from sceptics or atheists, who assert, that the first cause of All is unknown and unintelligible? Their temerity must be very great, if, after rejecting the production by a mind; I mean, a mind resembling the human (for I know of no other), they pretend to assign, with certainty, any other specific, intelligible cause: And their conscience must be very scrupulous indeed, if they refuse to call the universal, unknown cause a God or Deity; and to bestow on him as many sublime eulogies and unmeaning epithets, as you shall please to require of them.

Who could imagine, replied DEMEA, that Cleanthes, the calm, philosophical Cleanthes, would attempt to refute his antagonists, by affixing a nick-name to them; and like the common bigots and inquisitors of the age, have recourse to invective and declamation, instead of reasoning? Or does he not perceive, that these topics are easily retorted, and that **anthropomorphite** is an appellation as invidious, and implies as dangerous consequences, as the epithet of *mystic*, with which he has honoured us? In reality, Cleanthes, consider what it is you assert, when you represent the Deity as similar to a human mind and understanding. What is the soul of man? A composition of various faculties, passions, sentiments, ideas; united, indeed, into one self or person, but still distinct from each other. When it reasons, the ideas, which are the parts of its discourse, arrange themselves in a certain form or order; which is not preserved entire for a moment, but immediately gives place to another arrangement. New opinions, new passions, new affections, new feelings arise, which continually diversify the mental scene, and produce in it the greatest variety, and most rapid succession imaginable. How is this compatible with that perfect **immutability** and **simplicity**, which all true theists ascribe to the Deity? By the same act, say they, he sees past, present, and future: His love and his hatred, his mercy and his justice are one individual operation: He is entire in every point of space; and complete in every instant of duration. No succession, no change, no acquisition, no diminution. What he is implies not in it any shadow of distinction or diversity. And what he is, this moment, he ever has been, and ever will be, without any new

judgment, sentiment, or operation. He stands fixed in one simple, perfect state; nor can you ever say, with any propriety, that this act of his is different from that other, or that this judgment or idea has been lately formed, and will give place, by succession, to any different judgment or idea.

I can readily allow, said CLEANTHES, that those who maintain the perfect simplicity of the supreme Being, to the extent in which you have explained it, are complete *mystics*, and chargeable with all the consequences which I have drawn from their opinion. They are, in a word, atheists, without knowing it. For though it be allowed, that the Deity possesses attributes, of which we have no comprehension; yet ought we never to ascribe to him any attributes, which are absolutely incompatible with that intelligent nature, essential to him. A mind, whose acts and sentiments and ideas are not distinct and successive; one, that is wholly simple, and totally immutable; is a mind which has no thought, no reason, no will, no sentiment, no love, no hatred; or in a word, is no mind at all. It is an abuse of terms to give it that appellation; and we may as well speak of limited extension without figure, or of number without composition.

Pray consider, said PHILO, whom you are at present inveighing against. You are honouring with the appellation of atheist all the sound, orthodox divines almost, who have treated of this subject; and you will, at last, be, yourself, found, according to your reckoning, the only sound theist in the world. But if idolaters be atheists, as, I think, may justly be asserted, and Christian theologians the same; what becomes of the argument, so much celebrated, derived from the universal consent of mankind?

But because I know you are not much swayed by names and authorities, I shall endeavour to show you, a little more distinctly, the inconveniences of that anthropomorphism, which you have embraced; and shall prove, that there is no ground to suppose a plan of the world to be formed in the divine mind, consisting of distinct ideas, differently arranged; in the same manner as an architect forms in his head the plan of a house which he intends to execute.

It is not easy, I own, to see, what is gained by this supposition, whether we judge of the matter by *reason* or by *experience*. We are still obliged to mount higher, in order to find the cause of this cause, which you had assigned as satisfactory and conclusive.

If *reason* (I mean abstract reason, derived from enquiries *a priori*) be not alike mute with regard to all questions concerning cause and effect; this sentence at least it will venture to pronounce: That a mental world or universe of ideas requires a cause as much as does a material world or universe of objects; and if similar in its arrangement must require a similar cause. For what is there in this subject, which should occasion a different conclusion or inference? In an abstract view, they are entirely alike; and no difficulty attends the one supposition, which is not common to both of them.

Again, when we will needs force *experience* to pronounce some sentence, even on these subjects, which lie beyond her sphere; neither can she perceive any material difference in this particular, between these two kinds of worlds, but finds them to be governed by similar principles, and to depend upon an equal variety of causes in their operations. We have specimens in miniature of both of them. Our own mind resembles the one: A vegetable or animal body the other. Let experience, therefore, judge from these samples. Nothing seems more delicate with regard to its causes than thought; and as these causes never operate in two persons after the same manner, so we never find two persons, who think exactly alike. Nor indeed does the same person think exactly alike at any two different periods of time. A difference of age, of the disposition of his body, of weather, of food, of company, of books, of passions; any of these particulars or others more minute, are sufficient to alter the curious machinery of thought, and communicate to it very different movements and operations. As far as we can judge, vegetables and animal bodies are not more delicate in their motions, nor depend upon a greater variety or more curious adjustment of springs and principles.

How therefore shall we satisfy ourselves concerning the cause of that Being, whom you suppose the Author of nature, or, according to your system of anthropomorphism, the ideal world, into which you trace the material? Have we not the same reason to trace that ideal world into another ideal world, or new intelligent principle? But if we stop, and go no farther; why go so far? Why not stop at the material world? How can we satisfy ourselves without going on *in infinitum*? And after all, what satisfaction is there in that infinite progression? Let us remember the story of the Indian philosopher and his elephant. It was never more applicable than to the present subject. If the material world rests upon a similar ideal world, this ideal world must rest upon some other; and so on, without end. It were better, therefore, never to look beyond the present material world. By supposing it to contain the principle of its order within itself, we really assert it to be God; and the sooner we arrive at that divine Being so much the better. When you go one step beyond the mundane system, you only excite an inquisitive humour, which it is impossible ever to satisfy.

To say, that the different ideas, which compose the reason of the supreme Being, fall into order, of themselves, and by their own nature, is really to talk without any precise meaning. If it has a meaning, I would fain know, why it is not as good sense to say, that the parts of their material world fall into order, of themselves, and by their own nature? Can the one opinion be intelligible, while the other is not so?

We have, indeed, experience of ideas, which fall into order, of themselves, and without any *known* cause: But, I am sure, we have a much larger experience of matter, which does the same; as in all instances of generation and vegetation, where the accurate analysis of the cause exceeds all human comprehension. We have also experience of particular systems of thought and of matter, which have no order; of the first, in madness, of the second, in corruption. Why then should we think, that order is more essential to one than the other? And if it requires a cause in both, what do we gain by your system, in tracing the universe of objects into a similar universe of ideas? The first step, which we make, leads us on for ever. It were, therefore, wise in us, to limit all our enquiries to the present world, without looking farther. No satisfaction can ever be attained by these speculations, which so far exceed the narrow bounds of human understanding.

It was usual with the Peripatetics, you know, Cleanthes, when the cause of any phenomenon was demanded, to have recourse to their *faculties* or *occult qualities*, and to say, for instance, that bread nourished by its nutritive faculty, and senna purged by its purgative: But it has been discovered, that this subterfuge was nothing but the disguise of ignorance; and that these philosophers, though less ingenuous, really said the same thing with the sceptics or the vulgar, who fairly confessed, that they knew not the cause of these phenomena. In like manner, when it is asked, what cause produces order in the ideas of the supreme Being, can any other reason be assigned by you, anthropomorphites, than that it is a *rational* faculty, and that such is the nature of the Deity? But why a similar answer will not be equally satisfactory in accounting for the order of the world, without having recourse to any such intelligent Creator as you insist on, may be difficult to determine. It is only to say, that *such* is the nature of material objects, and that they are all originally possessed of a *faculty* of order and proportion. These are only more learned and elaborate ways of confessing our ignorance; nor has the one hypothesis any real advantage above the other, except in its greater conformity to vulgar prejudices.

You have displayed this argument with great emphasis, replied CLEANTHES: You seem not sensible, how easy it is to answer it. Even in common life, if I assign a cause for any event; is it any objection, Philo, that I cannot assign the cause of that cause, and answer every new question, which may incessantly be started? And what philosophers could possibly submit to so rigid a rule? Philosophers, who confess ultimate causes to be totally unknown, and are sensible, that the most refined principles, into which they trace the phenomena, are still to them as inexplicable as these phenomena themselves are to the vulgar. The order and arrangement of nature, the curious adjustment of final causes, the plain use and intention of every part and organ; all these bespeak in the clearest language an intelligent cause or Author. The heavens and the earth join in the same testimony: The whole chorus of nature raises one hymn to the praises of its Creator: You alone, or almost alone, disturb this general harmony. You start abstruse doubts, cavils, and objections: You ask me, what is the cause of this cause? I know not; I care not; that concerns not me. I have found a Deity; and here

I stop my enquiry. Let those go farther, who are wiser or more enterprising.

I pretend to be neither, replied PHILO: And for that very reason, I should never perhaps have attempted to go so far; especially when I am sensible, that I must at last be contented to sit down with the same answer, which, without farther trouble, might have satisfied me from the beginning. If I am still to remain in utter ignorance of causes, and can absolutely give an explication of nothing, I shall never esteem it any advantage to shove off for a moment a difficulty, which, you acknowledge, must immediately, in its full force, recur upon me. Naturalists indeed very justly explain particular effects by more general causes; though these general causes themselves should remain in the end totally inexplicable: But they never surely thought it satisfactory to explain a particular effect by a particular cause, which was no more to be accounted for than the effect itself. An ideal system, arranged of itself, without a precedent design, is not a whit more explicable than a material one, which attains its order in a like manner; nor is there any more difficulty in the latter supposition than in the former.

Part V

But to show you still more inconveniences, continued PHILO, in your anthropomorphism; please to take a new survey of your principles. *Like effects prove like causes.* This is the experimental argument; and this, you say too, is the sole theological argument. Now it is certain, that the liker the effects are, which are seen, and the liker the causes, which are inferred, the stronger is the argument. Every departure on either side diminishes the probability, and renders the experiment less conclusive. You cannot doubt of this principle: Neither ought you to reject its consequences.

All the new discoveries in astronomy, which prove the immense grandeur and magnificence of the works of nature, are so many additional arguments for a Deity, according to the true system of theism: But according to your hypothesis of experimental theism, they become so many objections, by removing the effect still farther from all resemblance to the effects of human art and contrivance. For if Lucretius,[3] even following the old system of the world, could exclaim,

Who can rule the sum, who hold in his hand with controlling force the strong reins, of the immeasurable deep? who can at once make all the different heavens to roll and warm with ethereal fires all the fruitful earths, or be present in all places at all times?

If Tully[4] esteemed this reasoning so natural, as to put it into the mouth of his Epicurean.

For with what eyes of the mind could your Plato have beheld that workshop of such stupendous toil, in which he represents the world as having been put together and built by God? How was so vast an undertaking set about? What tools, what levers, what machines, what servants, were employed in so great a work? How came air, fire, water, and earth to obey and submit to the architect's will?

If this argument, I say, had any force in former ages; how much greater must it have at present; when the bounds of nature are so infinitely enlarged, and such a magnificent scene is opened to us? It is still more unreasonable to form our idea of so unlimited a cause from our experience of the narrow productions of human design and invention.

The discoveries by microscopes, as they open a new universe in miniature, are still objections, according to you; arguments, according to me. The farther we push our researches of this kind, we are still led to infer the universal cause of All to be vastly different from mankind, or from any object of human experience and observation.

And what say you to the discoveries in anatomy, chemistry, botany? . . . These surely are no objections, replied CLEANTHES: They only discover new instances of art and contrivance. It is still the image of mind reflected on us from innumerable objects. Add, a mind *like the human*, said PHILO. I know of no other, replied CLEANTHES. And the liker the better, insisted PHILO. To be sure, said CLEANTHES.

Now, Cleanthes, said PHILO, with an air of alacrity and triumph, mark the consequences. *First*, By this method of reasoning, you renounce all claim to infinity in any of the attributes of the Deity. For as the cause ought only to be proportioned to the effect, and the effect, so far as it falls under our cognisance, is not infinite; what pretensions have we, upon your suppositions, to ascribe that attribute to the divine Being? You will still insist, that, by removing him so much from all similarity to human creatures, we give in to the most arbitrary hypothesis, and at the same time weaken all proofs of his existence.

Secondly, You have no reason, on your theory, for ascribing perfection to the Deity, even in his finite capacity; or for supposing him free from every error, mistake, or incoherence in his undertakings. There are many inexplicable difficulties in the works of nature, which, if we allow a perfect Author to be proved *a priori*, are easily solved, and become only seeming difficulties, from the narrow capacity of man, who cannot trace infinite relations. But according to your method of reasoning, these difficulties become all real; and perhaps will be insisted on, as new instances of likeness to human art and contrivance. At least, you must acknowledge, that it is impossible for us to tell, from our limited views, whether this system contains any great faults, or deserves any considerable praise, if compared to other possible, and even real systems. Could a peasant, if the *Aeneid* were read to him, pronounce that poem to be absolutely faultless, or even assign to it its proper rank among the productions of human wit; he, who had never seen any other production?

But were this world ever so perfect a production, it must still remain uncertain, whether all the excellencies of the work can justly be ascribed to the workman. If we survey a ship, what an exalted idea must we form of the ingenuity of the carpenter, who framed so complicated, useful, and beautiful a machine? And what surprise must we entertain, when we find him a stupid mechanic, who imitated others, and copied an art, which, through a long succession of ages, after multiplied trials, mistakes, corrections, deliberations, and controversies, had been gradually improving? Many worlds might have been botched and bungled, throughout an eternity, ere this system was struck out: Much labour lost: Many fruitless trials made: And a slow, but continued improvement carried on during infinite ages in the art of world-making. In such subjects, who can determine, where the truth; nay, who can conjecture where the probability, lies; amidst a great number of hypotheses which may be proposed, and a still greater number which may be imagined?

And what shadow of an argument, continued PHILO, can you produce, from your hypothesis, to prove the unity of the Deity? A great number of men join in building a house or ship, in rearing a city, in framing a commonwealth: Why may not several Deities combine in contriving and framing a world? This is only so much greater similarity to human affairs. By sharing the work among several, we may so much farther limit the attributes of each, and get rid of that extensive power and knowledge, which must be supposed in one Deity, and which, according to you, can only serve to weaken the proof of his existence. And if such foolish, such vicious creatures as man can yet often unite in framing and executing one plan; how much more those Deities or Demons, whom we may suppose several degrees more perfect?

To multiply causes, without necessity, is indeed contrary to true philosophy: But this principle applies not to the present case. Were one Deity antecedently proved by your theory, who were possessed of every attribute requisite to the production of the universe; it would be needless, I own (though not absurd) to suppose any other Deity existent. But while it is still a question, whether all these attributes are united in one subject, or dispersed among several independent Beings: By what phenomena in nature can we pretend to decide the controversy? Where we see a body raised in a scale, we are sure that there is in the opposite scale, however concealed from sight, some counterposing weight equal to it: But it is still allowed to doubt, whether that weight be an aggregate of several distinct bodies, or one uniform united mass. And if the weight requisite very much exceeds any thing which we have ever seen conjoined in any single body, the former supposition becomes still more probable and natural. An intelligent Being of such vast power and capacity, as is necessary to produce the universe, or, to speak in the language of ancient philosophy, so prodigious an animal, exceeds all analogy, and even comprehension.

But farther, Cleanthes; men are mortal, and renew their species by generation; and this is common to all living creatures. The two great sexes of male and female, says Milton, animate the world. Why must this circumstance, so universal, so essential, be excluded from those numerous and limited Deities? Behold then the theogony of ancient times brought back upon us.

And why not become a perfect anthropomorphite? Why not assert the Deity or Deities to be corporeal, and to have eyes, a nose, mouth, ears, etc.? Epicurus maintained, that no man had ever seen reason but in a human figure; therefore the gods must have a human figure. And this argument, which is deservedly so much ridiculed by Cicero, becomes according to you, solid and philosophical.

In a word, Cleanthes, a man, who follows your hypothesis, is able, perhaps, to assert, or conjecture, that the universe, sometime, arose from something like design: But beyond that position he cannot ascertain one single circumstance, and is left afterwards to fix every point of his theology, by the utmost licence of fancy and hypothesis. This world, for aught he knows, is very faulty and imperfect, compared to a superior standard; and was only the first rude essay of some infant Deity, who afterwards abandoned it, ashamed of his lame performance; it is the work only of some dependent, inferior Deity; and is the object of derision to his superiors: it is the production of old age and dotage in some superannuated Deity; and ever since his death, has run on at adventures, from the first impulse and active force, which it received from him. . . . You justly give signs of horror, Demea, at these strange suppositions: But these, and a thousand more of the same kind, are Cleanthes' suppositions, not mine. From the moment the attributes of the Deity are supposed finite, all these have place. And I cannot, for my part, think, that so wild and unsettled a system of theology is, in any respect, preferable to none at all.

These suppositions I absolutely disown, cried CLEANTHES: They strike me, however, with no horror; especially, when proposed in that rambling way in which they drop from you. On the contrary, they give me pleasure, when I see, that, by the utmost indulgence of your imagination, you never get rid of the hypothesis of design in the universe; but are obliged, at every turn, to have recourse to it. To this concession I adhere steadily; and this I regard as a sufficient foundation for religion.

In Parts VI and VII (omitted here) Philo continues his attack on Cleanthes's position. In part VI Philo argues that the hypothesis that the world is an animal, with the Deity as its soul, accounts as well for the evidence Cleanthes has cited as the view that an intelligent Deity created the world:

> . . . if we survey the universe, so far as it falls under our knowledge, it bears a great resemblance to an animal or organized body, and seems actuated with a like principle of life and notion. A continual circulation of matter in it produces no disorder: A continual waste in every part is incessantly repaired: The closest sympathy is perceived throughout the entire system: And each part or member, in performing its proper offices, operates both to its own preservation and to that of the whole. The world, therefore, I infer, is an animal, and the Deity is the Soul of the world, actuating it, and actuated by it.

In Part VII Philo pushes the idea that the world resembles animals—and now vegetables, too—even further:

> If the universe bears a greater likeness to animal bodies and to vegetables, than to the works of human art, it is more probable that its cause resembles the cause of the former than of the latter, and its origin ought rather to be ascribed to generation or vegetation than to reason or design. Your conclusion, even according to your own principles, is therefore lame and defective.
>
> . . . The world, says [Cleanthes], resembles the works of human contrivance: Therefore its cause must also resemble that of the other . . . the operation of one very small part of nature, to wit man, upon another very small part, to wit that inanimate matter lying within his reach, is the rule by which Cleanthes judges of the origin of the whole; . . . there are other parts of the universe (besides the machines of human invention) which bear still a greater resemblance to the fabric of the world, and which therefore afford a better conjecture concerning the universal origin of this system. . . . The world plainly resembles more an animal or a vegetable, than it does a watch or a knitting loom. Its cause, therefore, it is more probable, resembles the cause of the former. The cause of the former is generation or vegetation. . . .

Demea wonders whether Philo can really make sense of this and can explain the operations of vegetation and generation that he is postulating as the cause of the world. Philo replies:

> As much, at least . . . as Cleanthes can explain the operations of reason. . . . These words *generation*, *reason*, mark only certain powers and energies in nature, whose effects are known, but whose essence is incomprehensible; and one of these principles, more than the other, has no privilege for being made a standard of the whole of nature.
>
> . . . When I enquired concerning the cause of that supreme reason and intelligence, into which [Cleanthes] resolves every thing; he told me, that the impossibility of satisfying such enquiries could never be admitted as an objection in any species of philosophy. *We must stop somewhere*, says he; *nor is it ever within the reach of human capacity to explain ultimate causes, or who the last connections of any objects. It is sufficient, if the steps, so far as we go, are supported by experience and observation.* Now that vegetation and generation, as well as reason, are experienced to be principles of order

in nature, is undeniable. If I rest my system of cosmogony on the former, preferably to the latter, it is at my choice. The matter seems entirely arbitrary. . . .

All of this leaves Cleanthes exasperated, but unconvinced:

I must confess, Philo, . . . that of all men living, the task which you have undertaken, of raising doubts and objections, suits you best, and seems, in a manner, natural and unavoidable to you. So great is your fertility of invention, that I am not ashamed to acknowledge myself unable, on a sudden, to solve regularly such out-of-the-way difficulties as you incessantly start upon me: Though I clearly see, in general, their fallacy and error . . . you must be sensible, that common sense and reason is entirely against you, and that such whimsies, as you have delivered, may puzzle, but never can convince us.

Part VIII

What you ascribe to the fertility of my invention, replied PHILO, is entirely owing to the nature of the subject. In subjects, adapted to the narrow compass of human reason, there is commonly but one determination, which carries probability or conviction with it; and to a man of sound judgment, all other suppositions, but that one, appear entirely absurd and chimerical. But in such questions as the present, a hundred contradictory views may preserve a kind of imperfect analogy; and invention has here full scope to exert itself. Without any great effort of thought, I believe that I could, in an instant, propose other systems of cosmogony, which would have some faint appearance of truth; though it is a thousand, a million to one, if either yours or any one of mine be the true system.

For instance; what if I should revive the old Epicurean hypothesis? This is commonly, and I believe, justly, esteemed the most absurd system, that has yet been proposed; yet, I know not, whether, with a few alterations, it might not be brought to bear a faint appearance of probability. Instead of supposing matter infinite, as Epicurus did; let us suppose it finite. A finite number of particles is only susceptible of finite transpositions: And it must happen, in an eternal duration, that every possible order or position must be tried an infinite number of times. This world, therefore, with all its events, even the most minute, has before been produced and destroyed, and will again be produced and destroyed, without

any bounds and limitations. No one, who has a conception of the powers of infinite, in comparison of finite, will ever scruple this determination.

But this supposes, said DEMEA, that matter can acquire motion, without any voluntary agent or first mover.

And where is the difficulty, replied PHILO, of that supposition? Every event, before experience, is equally difficult and incomprehensible; and every event, after experience, is equally easy and intelligible. Motion, in many instances, from gravity, from elasticity, from electricity, begins in matter, without any known voluntary agent; and to suppose always, in these cases, an unknown voluntary agent, is mere hypothesis; and hypothesis attended with no advantages. The beginning of motion in matter itself is as conceivable *a priori* as its communication from the mind and intelligence.

Besides, why may not motion have been propagated by impulse through all eternity, and the same stock of it, or nearly the same, be still upheld in the universe? As much as is lost by the composition of motion, as much is gained by its resolution. And whatever the causes are, the fact is certain, that matter is, and always has been in continual agitation, as far as human experience or tradition reaches. There is not probably, at present, in the whole universe, one particle of matter at absolute rest.

And this very consideration too, continued PHILO, which we have stumbled on in the course of the argument, suggests a new hypothesis of cosmogony, that is not absolutely absurd and improbable. Is there a system, an order, an economy of things, by which matter can preserve that perpetual agitation, which seems essential to it, and yet maintain a constancy in the forms, which it produces? There certainly is such an economy: For this is actually the case with the present world. The continual motion of matter, therefore, in less than infinite transpositions, must produce this economy or order; and by its very nature, that order, when once established, supports itself, for many ages, if not to eternity. But wherever matter is so poised, arranged, and adjusted as to continue in perpetual motion, and yet preserve a constancy in the forms, its situation must, of necessity, have all the same appearance of art and contrivance which we observe at present. All the parts of each form must have a relation to each other, and to the whole: And the whole itself must have a relation to the other parts of the universe; to the element, in which the form subsists; to the materials, with which it repairs its waste and decay; and to every other form, which is hostile or friendly. A defect in any of these particulars destroys the form; and the matter, of which it is composed, is again set loose, and is thrown into irregular motions and fermentations, till it unite itself to some other regular form. If no such form be prepared to receive it, and if there be a great quantity of this corrupted matter in the universe, the universe itself is entirely disordered; whether it be the feeble embryo of a world in its first beginnings, that is thus destroyed, or the rotten carcass of one, languishing in old age and infirmity. In either case, a chaos ensues; till finite, though innumerable revolutions produce at last some forms, whose parts and organs are so adjusted as to support the forms amidst a continued succession of matter.

Suppose (for we shall endeavour to vary the expression), that matter were thrown into any position, by a blind, unguided force; it is evident that this first position must in all probability be the most confused and most disorderly imaginable, without any resemblance to those works of human contrivance, which, along with a symmetry of parts, discover an adjustment of means to ends and a tendency to self-preservation. If the actuating force cease after this operation, matter must remain for ever in disorder, and continue an immense chaos, without any proportion or activity. But suppose, that the actuating force, whatever it be, still continues in matter, this

first position will immediately give place to a second, which will likewise in all probability be as disorderly as the first, and so on, through many successions of changes and revolutions. No particular order or position ever continues a moment unaltered. The original force, still remaining in activity, gives a perpetual restlessness to matter. Every possible situation is produced, and instantly destroyed. If a glimpse or dawn of order appears for a moment, it is instantly hurried away, and confounded, by that never-ceasing force, which actuates every part of matter.

Thus the universe goes on for many ages in a continued succession of chaos and disorder. But is it not possible that it may settle at last, so as not to lose its motion and active force (for that we have supposed inherent in it), yet so as to preserve an uniformity of appearance, amidst the continual motion and fluctuation of its parts? This we find to be the case with the universe at present. Every individual is perpetually changing, and every part of every individual, and yet the whole remains, in appearance, the same. May we not hope for such a position, or rather be assured of it, from the eternal revolutions of unguided matter, and may not this account for all the appearing wisdom and contrivance which is in the universe? Let us contemplate the subject a little, and we shall find, that this adjustment, if attained by matter, of a seeming stability in the forms, with a real and perpetual revolution or motion of parts, affords a plausible, if not a true solution of the difficulty.

It is in vain, therefore, to insist upon the uses of the parts in animals or vegetables, and their curious adjustment to each other. I would fain know how an animal could subsist, unless its parts were so adjusted? Do we not find, that it immediately perishes whenever this adjustment ceases, and that its matter corrupting tries some new form? It happens, indeed, that the parts of the world are so well adjusted, that some regular form immediately lays claim to this corrupted matter: And if it were not so, could the world subsist? Must it not dissolve as well as the animal, and pass through new positions and situations; till in a great, but finite succession, it falls at last into the present or some such order?

It is well, replied CLEANTHES, you told us, that this hypothesis was suggested on a sudden, in the course of the argument. Had you had leisure to examine it, you would soon have perceived the insuperable objections, to which it is exposed. No form, you say, can subsist, unless it possess those powers and organs, requisite for its subsistence: Some new order or economy must be tried, and so on, without intermission; till at last some order, which can support and maintain itself, is fallen upon. But according to this hypothesis, whence arise the many conveniences and advantages which men and all animals possess? Two eyes, two ears, are not absolutely necessary for the subsistence of the species. Human race might have been propagated and preserved, without horses, dogs, cows, sheep, and those innumerable fruits and products which serve to our satisfaction and enjoyment. If no camels had been created for the use of man in the sandy deserts of Africa and Arabia, would the world have been dissolved? If no loadstone had been framed to give that wonderful and useful direction to the needle, would human society and the human kind have been immediately extinguished? Though the maxims of nature be in general very frugal, yet instances of this kind are far from being rare; and any one of them is a sufficient proof of design, and of a benevolent design, which gave rise to the order and arrangement of the universe.

At least, you may safely infer, said PHILO, that the foregoing hypothesis is so far incomplete and imperfect; which I shall not scruple to allow. But can we ever reasonably expect greater success in any attempts of this nature? Or can we ever hope to erect a system of cosmogony, that will be liable to no exceptions, and will contain no circumstance repugnant to our limited and imperfect experience of the analogy of nature? Your theory itself cannot surely pretend to any such advantage; even though you have run into *anthropomorphism*, the better to preserve a conformity to common experience. Let us once more put it to trial. In all instances which we have ever seen, ideas are copied from real objects, and are ectypal, not archetypal, to express myself in learned terms: You reverse this order, and give thought the precedence. In all instances which we have ever seen, thought has no influence upon matter, except where that matter is so conjoined with it, as to have an equal reciprocal influence upon it. No animal can move immediately any thing

but the members of its own body; and indeed, the equality of action and re-action seems to be an universal law of nature: But your theory implies a contradiction to this experience. These instances, with many more, which it were easy to collect (particularly the supposition of a mind or system of thought that is eternal, or in other words, an animal ingenerable and immortal), these instances, I say, may teach, all of us, sobriety in condemning each other, and let us see, that as no system of this kind ought ever to be received from a slight analogy, so neither ought any to be rejected on account of a small incongruity. For that is an inconvenience from which we can justly pronounce no one to be exempted.

All religious systems, it is confessed, are subject to great and insuperable difficulties. Each disputant triumphs in his turn; while he carries on an offensive war, and exposes the absurdities, barbarities, and pernicious tenets of his antagonist. But all of them, on the whole, prepare a complete triumph for the sceptic; who tells them, that no system ought ever to be embraced with regard to such subjects: For this plain reason, that no absurdity ought ever to be assented to with regard to any subject. A total suspense of judgment is here our only reasonable resource. And if every attack, as is commonly observed, and no defence, among theologians, is successful; how complete must be *his* victory, who remains always, with all mankind,[5] on the offensive, and has himself no fixed station or abiding city, which he is ever, on any occasion, obliged to defend?

Part IX

But if so many difficulties attend the argument *a posteriori*, said DEMEA; had we not better adhere to that simple and sublime argument *a priori*, which, by offering to us infallible demonstration, cuts off at once all doubt and difficulty? By this argument, too, we may prove the infinity of the divine attributes, which, I am afraid, can never be ascertained with certainty from any other topic. For how can an effect, which either is finite, or, for aught we know, may be so; how can such an effect, I say, prove an infinite cause? The unity too of the divine nature, it is very difficult, if not absolutely impossible, to deduce merely from contemplating the works of nature; nor will the uniformity alone of the plan, even were it allowed, give us any assurance of that attribute. Whereas the argument *a priori*. . . .

You seem to reason, Demea, interposed CLEANTHES, as if those advantages and conveniences in the abstract argument were full proofs of its solidity. But it is first proper, in my opinion, to determine what argument of this nature you choose to insist on; and we shall afterwards, from itself, better than from its *useful* consequences, endeavour to determine what value we ought to put upon it.

The argument, replied DEMEA, which I would insist on is the common one. Whatever exists must have a cause or reason of its existence; it being absolutely impossible for any thing to produce itself, or be the cause of its own existence. In mounting up, therefore, from effects to causes, we must either go on in tracing an infinite succession, without any ultimate cause at all, or must at last have recourse to some ultimate cause, that is *necessarily* existent: Now that the first supposition is absurd may be thus proved. In the infinite chain or succession of causes and effects, each single effect is determined to exist by the power and efficacy of that cause which immediately preceded; but the whole eternal chain or succession, taken together, is not determined or caused by any thing: And yet it is evident that it requires a cause or reason, as much as any particular object, which begins to exist in time. The question is still reasonable, why this particular succession of causes existed from eternity, and not any other succession, or no succession at all. If there be no necessarily existent Being, any supposition, which can be formed, is equally possible; nor is there any more absurdity in nothing's having existed from eternity, than there is in that succession of causes, which constitutes the universe. What was it, then, which determined something to exist rather than nothing, and bestowed being on a particular possibility, exclusive of the rest? *External causes*, there are supposed to be none. *Chance* is a word without a meaning. Was it *nothing*? But that can never produce any thing. We must, therefore, have recourse to a necessarily existent Being, who carries the reason of his existence in himself; and who cannot be supposed not to exist without an express contradiction.

There is consequently such a Being, that is, there is a Deity.

I shall not leave it to Philo, said CLEANTHES (though I know that the starting objections is his chief delight), to point out the weakness of this metaphysical reasoning. It seems to me so obviously ill-grounded, and at the same time of so little consequence to the cause of true piety and religion, that I shall myself venture to show the fallacy of it.

I shall begin with observing, that there is an evident absurdity in pretending to demonstrate a matter of fact, or to prove it by any arguments *a priori*. Nothing is demonstrable, unless the contrary implies a contradiction. Nothing, that is distinctly conceivable, implies a contradiction. Whatever we conceive as existent, we can also conceive as non-existent. There is no Being, therefore, whose non-existence implies a contradiction. Consequently, there is no Being, whose existence is demonstrable. I propose this argument as entirely decisive, and am willing to rest the whole controversy upon it.

It is pretended that the Deity is a necessarily existent Being; and this necessity of his existence is attempted to be explained by asserting, that, if we knew his whole essence or nature, we should perceive it to be as impossible for him not to exist as for twice two not to be four. But it is evident, that this can never happen, while our faculties remain the same as at present. It will still be possible for us, at any time, to conceive the non-existence of what we formerly conceived to exist; nor can the mind ever lie under a necessity of supposing any object to remain always in being; in the same manner as we lie under a necessity of always conceiving twice two to be four. The words, therefore, *necessary existence*, have no meaning; or, which is the same thing, none that is consistent.

But farther; why may not the material universe be the necessarily existent Being, according to this pretended explication of necessity? We dare not affirm that we know all the qualities of matter; and for aught we can determine, it may contain some qualities, which, were they known, would make its non-existence appear as great a contradiction as that twice two is five. I find only one argument employed to prove, that the material world is not the necessarily existent Being; and this argument is derived from the contingency both of the matter and the form of the world. "Any particle of matter", it is said,[6] "may be *conceived* to be annihilated; and any form may be *conceived* to be altered. Such an annihilation or alteration, therefore, is not impossible." But it seems a great partiality not to perceive, that the same argument extends equally to the Deity, so far as we have any conception of him; and that the mind can at least imagine him to be non-existent, or his attributes to be altered. It must be some unknown, inconceivable qualities, which can make his non-existence appear impossible, or his attributes unalterable: And no reason can be assigned, why these qualities may not belong to matter. As they are altogether unknown and inconceivable, they can never be proved incompatible with it.

Add to this, that in tracing an eternal succession of objects, it seems absurd to inquire for a general cause or first Author. How can any thing, that exists from eternity, have a cause, since that relation implies a priority in time and a beginning of existence?

In such a chain too, or succession of objects, each part is caused by that which preceded it, and causes that which succeeds it. Where then is the difficulty? But the whole, you say, wants a cause. I answer, that the uniting of these parts into a whole, like the uniting of several distinct counties into one kingdom, or several distinct members into one body, is performed merely by an arbitrary act of the mind, and has no influence on the nature of things. Did I show you the particular causes of each individual in a collection of twenty particles of matter, I should think it very unreasonable, should you afterwards ask me, what was the cause of the whole twenty. This is sufficiently explained in explaining the cause of the parts.

Though the reasonings, which you have urged, Cleanthes, may well excuse me, said PHILO, from starting any farther difficulties; yet I cannot forbear insisting still upon another topic. It is observed by arithmeticians, that the products of 9 compose always either 9 or some lesser product of 9; if you add together all the characters, of which any of the former products is composed. Thus, of 18, 27, 36, which are products of 9, you make 9 by adding 1 to 8, 2 to 7, 3 to 6. Thus 369 is a product also of 9; and if you add 3, 6, and 9, you make 18, a lesser product of 9.[7] To a superficial observer, so wonderful a regularity may be admired as the effect either of chance or design; but a skilful algebraist immediately concludes it to be the work of necessity and demonstrates, that it must for ever result from the nature of these numbers. Is it not probable, I ask, that the whole economy of the universe is conducted by a like necessity, though no human algebra can furnish a key which solves the difficulty? And instead of admiring the order of natural beings, may it not happen, that, could we penetrate into the intimate nature of bodies, we should clearly see why it was absolutely impossible, they could ever admit of any other disposition? So dangerous is it to introduce this idea of necessity into the present question! And so naturally does it afford an inference directly opposite to the religious hypothesis!

But dropping all these abstractions, continued PHILO; and confining ourselves to more familiar topics; I shall venture to add an observation, that the argument *a priori* has seldom been found very convincing, except to people of a metaphysical head, who have accustomed themselves to abstract reasoning, and who finding from mathematics, that the understanding frequently leads to truth, through obscurity, and contrary to first appearances, have transferred the same habit of thinking to subjects where it ought not to have place. Other people, even of good sense and the best inclined to religion, feel always some deficiency in such arguments, though they are not perhaps able to explain distinctly where it lies. A certain proof, that men ever did, and ever will, derive their religion from other sources than from this species of reasoning.

Part X

It is my opinion, I own, replied DEMEA, that each man feels, in a manner, the truth of religion within his own breast; and from a consciousness of his imbecility and misery, rather than from any reasoning, is led to seek protection from that Being, on whom he and all nature is dependent. So anxious or so tedious are even the best scenes of life, that futurity is still the object of all our hopes and fears. We incessantly look forward, and endeavour, by prayers, adoration, and sacrifice, to appease those unknown powers, whom we find, by experience, so able to afflict and oppress us. Wretched creatures that we are! What resource for us amidst the innumerable ills of life, did not religion suggest some methods of atonement, and appease those terrors, with which we are incessantly agitated and tormented?

I am indeed persuaded, said Philo, that the best and indeed the only method of bringing every one to a due sense of religion is by just representations of the misery and wickedness of men. And for that purpose a talent of eloquence and strong imagery is more requisite than that of reasoning and argument. For is it necessary to prove, what every one feels within himself? It is only necessary to make us feel it, if possible, more intimately and sensibly.

The people, indeed, replied Demea, are sufficiently convinced of this great and melancholy truth. The miseries of life, the unhappiness of man, the general corruptions of our nature, the unsatisfactory enjoyment of pleasures, riches, honours; these phrases have become almost proverbial in all languages. And who can doubt of what all men declare from their own immediate feeling and experience?

In this point, said Philo, the learned are perfectly agreed with the vulgar; and in all letters, *sacred* and *profane*, the topic of human misery has been insisted on with the most pathetic eloquence that sorrow and melancholy could inspire. The poets, who speak from sentiment, without a system, and whose testimony has therefore the more authority, abound in images of this nature. From Homer down to Dr. Young, the whole inspired tribe have ever been sensible, that no other representation of things would suit the feeling and observation of each individual.

As to authorities, replied Demea, you need not seek them. Look round this library of Cleanthes. I shall venture to affirm, that, except authors of particular sciences, such as chemistry or botany, who have no occasion to treat of human life, there scarce is one of those innumerable writers, from whom the sense of human misery has not, in some passage or other, extorted a complaint and confession of it. At least, the chance is entirely on that side; and no one author has ever, so far as I can recollect, been so extravagant as to deny it.

There you must excuse me, said Philo: Leibnitz has denied it; and is perhaps the first,[8] who ventured upon so bold and paradoxical an opinion; at least, the first, who made it essential to his philosophical system.

And by being the first, replied Demea, might he not have been sensible of his error? For is this a subject in which philosophers can propose to make discoveries, especially in so late an age? And can any man hope by a simple denial (for the subject scarcely admits of reasoning) to bear down the united testimony of mankind, founded on sense and consciousness?

And why should man, added he, pretend to an exemption from the lot of all other animals? The whole earth, believe me, Philo, is cursed and polluted. A perpetual war is kindled amongst all living creatures. Necessity, hunger, want, stimulate the strong and courageous: Fear, anxiety, terror, agitate the weak and infirm. The first entrance into life gives anguish to the new-born infant and to its wretched parent: Weakness, impotence, distress, attend each stage of that life: And it is at last finished in agony and horror.

Observe too, says Philo, the curious artifices of nature, in order to embitter the life of every living being. The stronger prey upon the weaker, and keep them in perpetual terror and anxiety. The weaker too, in their turn, often prey upon the stronger, and vex and molest them without relaxation. Consider that innumerable race of insects, which either are bred on the body of each animal, or flying about infix their stings in him. These insects have others still less than themselves, which torment them. And thus on each hand, before and behind, above and below, every animal is surrounded with enemies, which incessantly seek his misery and destruction.

Man alone, said Demea, seems to be, in part, an exception to this rule. For by combination in society, he can easily master lions, tigers, and bears, whose greater strength and agility naturally enable them to prey upon him.

On the contrary, it is here chiefly, cried Philo, that the uniform and equal maxims of nature are most apparent. Man, it is true, can, by combination, surmount all his *real* enemies, and become master of the whole animal creation: But does he not immediately raise up to himself *imaginary* enemies, the demons of his fancy, who haunt him with superstitious terrors, and blast every enjoyment of life? His pleasure, as he imagines, becomes, in their eyes, a crime: His food and repose give them umbrage and offence: His very sleep and dreams furnish new materials to anxious fear: And even death, his refuge from every other ill, presents only the dread of endless and innumerable woes. Nor does the wolf molest more the timid flock, than superstition does the anxious breast of wretched mortals.

Besides, consider, Demea; this very society, by which we surmount those wild beasts, our natural enemies; what new enemies does it not raise to us? What woe and misery does it not occasion? Man is the greatest enemy of man. Oppression, injustice, contempt, contumely, violence, sedition, war, calumny, treachery, fraud; by these they mutually torment each other: And they would soon dissolve that society which they had formed, were it not for the dread of still greater ills, which must attend their separation.

But though these external insults, said DEMEA, from animals, from men, from all the elements, which assault us, form a frightful catalogue of woes, they are nothing in comparison of those, which arise within ourselves, from the distempered condition of our mind and body. How many lie under the lingering torment of diseases? Hear the pathetic enumeration of the great poet.

> Intestine stone and ulcer, colic-pangs,
> Daemoniac frenzy, moping melancholy,
> And moon-struck madness, pining atrophy,
> Marasmus and wide-wasting pestilence.
> Dire was the tossing, deep the groans: DESPAIR
> Tended the sick, busiest from couch to couch.
> And over them triumphant DEATH his dart
> Shook, but delay'd to strike, tho' oft invok'd
> With vows, as their chief good and final hope.9

The disorders of the mind, continued DEMEA, though more secret, are not perhaps less dismal and vexatious. Remorse, shame, anguish, rage, disappointment, anxiety, fear, dejection, despair; who has ever passed through life without cruel inroads from these tormentors? How many have scarcely ever felt any better sensations? Labour and poverty, so abhorred by every one, are the certain lot of the far greater number: And those few privileged persons, who enjoy ease and opulence, never reach contentment or true felicity. All the goods of life united would not make a very happy man: But all the ills united would make a wretch indeed; and any one of them almost (and who can be free from every one), nay often the absence of one good (and who can possess all) is sufficient to render life ineligible.

Were a stranger to drop, on a sudden, into this world, I would show him, as a specimen of its ills, an hospital full of diseases, a prison crowded with malefactors and debtors, a field of battle strowed with carcases, a fleet floundering in the ocean, a nation languishing under tyranny, famine, or pestilence. To turn the gay side of life to him, and give him a notion of its pleasures; whither should I conduct him? to a ball, to an opera, to court? He might justly think, that I was only showing him a diversity of distress and sorrow.

There is no evading such striking instances, said PHILO, but by apologies, which still farther aggravate the charge. Why have all men, I ask, in all ages, complained incessantly of the miseries of life? . . . They have no just reason, says one: These complaints proceed only from their discontented, repining, anxious disposition. . . . And can there possibly, I reply, be a more certain foundation of misery, than such a wretched temper?

But if they were really as unhappy as they pretend, says my antagonist, why do they remain in life? . . .

Not satisfied with life, afraid of death.

This is the secret chain, say I, that holds us. We are terrified, not bribed to the continuance of our existence.

It is only a false delicacy, he may insist, which a few refined spirits indulge, and which has spread these complaints among the whole race of mankind. . . . And what is this delicacy, I ask, which you blame? Is it any thing but a greater sensibility to all the pleasures and pains of life? And if the man of a delicate, refined temper, by being so much more alive than the rest of the world, is only so much more unhappy; what judgment must we form in general of human life?

Let men remain at rest, says our adversary; and they will be easy. They are willing artificers of their own misery. . . . No! reply I; an anxious languor follows their repose: Disappointment, vexation, trouble, their activity and ambition.

I can observe something like what you mention in some others, replied CLEANTHES: But I confess, I feel little or nothing of it in myself; and hope that it is not so common as you represent it.

If you feel not human misery yourself, cried DEMEA, I congratulate you on so happy a singularity. Others, seemingly the most prosperous, have not been ashamed to vent their complaints in the most melancholy strains. Let us attend to the great, the fortunate Emperor, Charles V, when, tired with human grandeur, he resigned all his extensive dominions into the hands of his son. In the last harangue, which he made on that memorable occasion, he publicly avowed, *that the greatest prosperities which he had ever enjoyed, had been mixed with so many adversities, that he might truly say he had never enjoyed any satisfaction or contentment.* But did the retired life, in which he sought for shelter, afford him any greater happiness? If we may credit his son's account, his repentence commenced the very day of his resignation.

Cicero's fortune, from small beginnings, rose to the greatest lustre and renown; yet what pathetic complaints of the ills of life do his familiar letters, as well as philosophical discourses, contain? And suitably to his own experience, he introduces Cato, the great, the fortunate Cato, protesting in his old age, that, had he a new life in his offer, he would reject the present.

Ask yourself, ask any of your acquaintance, whether they would live over again the last ten or twenty years of their life. No! but the next twenty, they say, will be better:

And from the dregs of life, hope to receive
What the first sprightly running could not give.[10]

Thus at last they find (such is the greatness of human misery; it reconciles even contradictions) that they complain, at once, of the shortness of life, and of its vanity and sorrow.

And is it possible, Cleanthes, said PHILO, that after all these reflections, and infinitely more, which might be suggested, you can still persevere in your anthropomorphism, and assert the moral attributes of the Deity, his justice, benevolence, mercy, and rectitude, to be of the same nature with these virtues in human creatures? His power we allow infinite: Whatever he wills is executed: But neither man nor any other animal are happy: Therefore he does not will their happiness. His wisdom is infinite: He is never mistaken in choosing the means to any end: But the course of nature tends not to human or animal felicity: Therefore it is not established for that purpose. Through the whole compass of human knowledge, there are no inferences more certain and infallible than these. In what respect, then, do his benevolence and mercy resemble the benevolence and mercy of men?

Epicurus' old questions are yet unanswered. Is he willing to prevent evil, but not able? then is he impotent. Is he able, but not willing? then is he malevolent. Is he both able and willing? whence then is evil?

You ascribe, Cleanthes (and I believe justly) a purpose and intention to nature. But what, I beseech you, is the object of that curious artifice and machinery, which she has displayed in all animals? The preservation alone of individuals and propagation of the species. It seems enough for her purpose, if such a rank be barely upheld in the universe, without any care or concern for the happiness of the members that compose it. No resource for this purpose: No machinery, in order merely to give pleasure or ease: No fund of pure joy and contentment: No indulgence without some want or necessity accompanying it. At least, the few phenomena of this nature are overbalanced by opposite phenomena of still greater importance.

Our sense of music, harmony, and indeed beauty of all kinds, gives satisfaction, without being absolutely necessary to the preservation and propagation of the species. But what racking pains, on the other hand, arise from gouts, gravels, megrims, tooth-aches, rheumatisms; where the injury to the animal-machinery is either small or incurable? Mirth, laughter, play, frolic, seem gratuitous satisfactions which have no farther tendency: Spleen, melancholy, discontent, superstition, are pains of the same nature. How then does the divine benevolence display itself, in the sense of you anthropomorphites? None but we mystics, as you were pleased to call us, can account for this strange mixture of phenomena, by deriving it from attributes, infinitely perfect, but incomprehensible.

And have you at last, said Cleanthes smiling, betrayed your intentions, Philo? Your long agreement with Demea did indeed a little surprise me; but I find you were all the while erecting a concealed battery against me. And I must confess, that you have now fallen upon a subject worthy of your noble spirit of opposition and controversy. If you can make out the present point, and prove mankind to be unhappy or corrupted, there is an end at once of all religion. For to what purpose establish the natural attributes of the Deity, while the moral are still doubtful and uncertain?

You take umbrage very easily, replied Demea, at opinions the most innocent, and the most generally received even amongst the religious and devout themselves: And nothing can be more surprising than to find a topic like this, concerning the wickedness and misery of man, charged with no less than atheism and profaneness. Have not all pious divines and preachers, who have indulged their rhetoric on so fertile a subject; have they not easily, I say, given a solution of any difficulties which may attend it? This world is but a point in comparison of the universe: This life but a moment in comparison of eternity. The present evil phenomena, therefore, are rectified in other regions, and in some future period of existence. And the eyes of men, being then opened to larger views of things, see the whole connection of general laws, and trace, with adoration, the benevolence and rectitude of the Deity, through all the mazes and intricacies of his providence.

No! replied Cleanthes, No! These arbitrary suppositions can never be admitted, contrary to matter of fact, visible and uncontroverted. Whence can any cause be known but from its known effects? Whence can any hypothesis be proved but from the apparent phenomena? To establish one hypothesis upon another is building entirely in the air; and the utmost we ever attain, by these conjectures and fictions, is to ascertain the bare possibility of our opinion; but never can we, upon such terms, establish its reality.

The only method of supporting divine benevolence (and it is what I willingly embrace) is to deny absolutely the misery and wickedness of man. Your representations are exaggerated: Your melancholy views mostly fictitious: Your inferences contrary to fact and experience. Health is more common than sickness: Pleasure than pain: Happiness than misery. And for one vexation which we meet with, we attain, upon computation, a hundred enjoyments.

Admitting your position, replied Philo, which yet is extremely doubtful, you must, at the same time, allow, that, if pain be less frequent than pleasure, it is infinitely more violent and durable. One hour of it is often able to outweigh a day, a week, a month of our common insipid enjoyments: And how many days, weeks, and months are passed by several in the most acute torments? Pleasure, scarcely in one instance, is ever able to reach ecstasy and rapture: And in no one instance can it continue for any time at its highest pitch and altitude. The spirits evaporate; the nerves relax; the fabric is disordered; and the enjoyment quickly degenerates into fatigue and uneasiness. But pain often, Good God, how often! rises to torture and agony; and the longer it continues, it becomes still more genuine agony and torture. Patience is exhausted; courage languishes; melancholy seizes us; and nothing terminates our misery but the removal of its cause, or another event, which is the sole cure of all evil, but which, from our natural folly, we regard with still greater horror and consternation.

But not to insist upon these topics, continued Philo, though most obvious, certain, and important; I must use the freedom to admonish you, Cleanthes, that you have put this controversy upon a most dangerous issue, and are unawares introducing a total scepticism into the most essential articles of natural and revealed theology. What! no method of fixing a just foundation for religion, unless we allow the happiness of human life, and maintain a continued existence even in this world, with all our present pains, infirmities, vexations, and follies, to be eligible and desirable! But this is contrary to every one's feeling and experience: It is contrary to an authority so established as nothing can subvert: No decisive proofs can ever be produced against this authority; nor is it possible for you to compute, estimate, and compare all the pains and all the pleasures in the lives of all men and of all animals: And thus by your resting the whole system of religion on a point, which, from its very nature, must for ever be uncertain, you tacitly confess, that that system is equally uncertain.

But allowing you, what never will be believed; at least, what you never possibly can prove, that animal, or at least, human happiness, in this life, exceeds its misery; you have yet done nothing: For this is not, by any means, what we expect from infinite power, infinite wisdom, and infinite goodness. Why is there any misery at all in the world? Not by chance surely. From some cause then. Is it from the intention of the Deity? But he is perfectly benevolent. Is it contrary to his intention? But he is almighty. Nothing can shake the solidity of this reasoning, so short, so clear, so decisive; except we assert, that these subjects exceed all human capacity, and that our common measures of truth and falsehood are not applicable to them; a topic, which I have all along insisted on, but which you have, from the beginning, rejected with scorn and indignation.

But I will be contented to retire still from this intrenchment: For I deny that you can ever force me in it: I will allow, that pain or misery in man is *compatible* with infinite power and goodness in the Deity, even in your sense of these attributes: What are you advanced by all these concessions? A mere possible compatibility is not sufficient. You must *prove* these pure, unmixed, and uncontrollable attributes from the present mixed and confused phenomena, and from these alone. A hopeful undertaking! Were the phenomena ever so pure and unmixed, yet being finite, they would be insufficient for that purpose. How much more, where they are also so jarring and discordant?

Here, Cleanthes, I find myself at ease in my argument. Here I triumph. Formerly, when we argued concerning the natural attributes of intelligence and design, I needed all my sceptical and metaphysical subtilty to elude your grasp. In many views of the universe, and of its parts, particularly the latter, the beauty and fitness of final causes strike us with such irresistible force, that all objections appear (what I believe they really are) mere cavils and sophisms; nor can we then imagine how it was ever possible for us to repose any weight on them. But there is no view of human life, or of the condition of mankind, from which, without the greatest violence, we can infer the moral attributes, or learn that infinite benevolence,

conjoined with infinite power and infinite wisdom, which we must discover by the eyes of faith alone. It is your turn now to tug the labouring oar, and to support your philosophical subtilties against the dictates of plain reason and experience.

Part XI

I scruple not to allow, said CLEANTHES, that I have been apt to suspect the frequent repetition of the word, *infinite*, which we meet with in all theological writers, to savour more of panegyric than of philosophy, and that any purposes of reasoning, and even of religion, would be better served, were we to rest contented with more accurate and more moderate expressions. The terms, *admirable, excellent, superlatively great, wise,* and *holy*; these sufficiently fill the imaginations of men; and any thing beyond, besides that it leads into absurdities, has no influence on the affections or sentiments. Thus, in the present subject, if we abandon all human analogy, as seems your intention, Demea, I am afraid we abandon all religion, and retain no conception of the great object of our adoration. If we preserve human analogy, we must for ever find it impossible to reconcile any mixture of evil in the universe with infinite attributes; much less, can we ever prove the latter from the former. But supposing the Author of nature to be finitely perfect, though far exceeding mankind; a satisfactory account may then be given of natural and moral evil, and every untoward phenomenon be explained and adjusted. A less evil may then be chosen, in order to avoid a greater: Inconveniences be submitted to, in order to reach a desirable end: And in a word, benevolence, regulated by wisdom, and limited by necessity, may produce just such a world as the present. You, Philo, who are so prompt at stating views, and reflections, and analogies; I would gladly hear, at length, without interruption, your opinion of this new theory; and if it deserve our attention, we may afterwards, at more leisure, reduce it into form.

My sentiments, replied PHILO, are not worth being made a mystery of; and therefore, without any ceremony, I shall deliver what occurs to me with regard to the present subject. It must, I think, be allowed, that, if a very limited intelligence, whom we shall suppose utterly unacquainted with the universe, were assured, that it were the production of a very good, wise, and powerful Being, however finite, he would, from his conjectures, form *beforehand* a different notion of it from what we find it to be by experience; nor would he ever imagine, merely from these attributes of the cause, of which he is informed, that the effect could be so full of vice and misery and disorder, as it appears in this life. Supposing now, that this person were brought into the world, still assured, that it was the workmanship of such a sublime and benevolent Being; he might, perhaps, be surprised at the disappointment; but would never retract his former belief, if founded on any very solid argument; since such a limited intelligence must be sensible of his own blindness and ignorance, and must allow, that there may be many solutions of those phenomena, which will for ever escape his comprehension. But supposing, which is the real case with regard to man, that this creature is not antecedently convinced of a supreme intelligence, benevolent, and powerful, but is left to gather such a belief from the appearances of things; this entirely alters the case, nor will he ever find any reason for such a conclusion. He may be fully convinced of the narrow limits of his understanding; but this will not help him in forming an inference concerning the goodness of superior powers, since he must form that inference from what he knows, not from what he is ignorant of. The more you exaggerate his weakness and ignorance, the more diffident you render him, and give him the greater suspicion, that such subjects are beyond the reach of his faculties. You are obliged, therefore, to reason with him merely from the known phenomena, and to drop every arbitrary supposition or conjecture.

Did I show you a house or palace, where there was not one apartment convenient or agreeable; where the windows, doors, fires, passages, stairs, and the whole economy of the building were the source of noise, confusion, fatigue, darkness, and the extremes of heat and cold; you would certainly blame the contrivance, without any farther examination. The architect would in vain display his subtilty, and prove to you, that if this door or that window were altered, greater ills would ensue. What he says, may be strictly true: The alteration of one particular, while the other parts of the building remain, may only augment the inconveniences. But still you would assert in general, that, if the architect had had skill and good intentions, he might have formed such a plan of the whole, and might have adjusted the parts in such a manner, as would have remedied all or most of these inconveniences. His ignorance, or even your own ignorance of such a plan, will never convince you of the impossibility of it. If you find many inconveniences and deformities in the building, you will always, without entering into any detail, condemn the architect.

In short, I repeat the question: Is the world considered in general, and as it appears to us in this life, different from what a man or such a limited being would, *beforehand*, expect from a very powerful, wise, and benevolent Deity? It must be strange prejudice to assert the contrary. And from thence I conclude, that, however consistent the world may be, allowing certain suppositions and conjectures, with the ideal of such a Deity, it can never afford us an inference concerning his existence. The consistence is not absolutely denied, only the inference. Conjectures, especially where infinity is excluded from the divine attributes, may, perhaps, be sufficient to prove a consistence; but can never be foundations for any inference.

There seem to be *four* circumstances, on which depend all, or the greatest part of the ills, that molest sensible creatures; and it is not impossible but all these circumstances may be necessary and unavoidable. We know so little beyond common life, or even of common life, that, with regard to the economy of a universe, there is no conjecture, however wild, which may not be just; nor any one, however plausible, which may not be erroneous. All that belongs to human understanding, in this deep ignorance and obscurity, is to be sceptical, or at least cautious; and not to admit of any hypothesis, whatever; much less, of any which is supported by no appearance of probability. Now this I assert to be the case with regard to all the causes of evil, and the circumstances on which it depends. None of them appear to human reason, in the least degree, necessary or unavoidable; nor can we suppose them such, without the utmost licence of imagination.

The *first* circumstance which introduces evil, is that contrivance or economy of the animal creation, by which pains, as well as pleasures, are employed to excite all creatures to action, and make them vigilant in the great work of self-preservation. Now pleasure alone, in its various degrees, seems to human understanding sufficient for this purpose. All animals might be constantly in a state of enjoyment; but when urged by any of the necessities of nature, such as thirst, hunger, weariness; instead of pain, they might feel a diminution of pleasure, by which they might be prompted to seek that object, which is necessary to their subsistence. Men pursue pleasure as eagerly as they avoid pain; at least, might have been so constituted. It seems, therefore, plainly possible to carry on the business of life without any pain. Why then is any animal ever rendered susceptible of such a sensation? If animals can be free from it an hour, they might enjoy a perpetual exemption from it; and it required as particular a contrivance of their organs to produce that feeling, as to endow them with sight, hearing, or any of the senses. Shall we conjecture, that such a contrivance was necessary, without any appearance of reason? And shall we build on that conjecture as on the most certain truth?

But a capacity of pain would not alone produce pain, were it not for the *second* circumstance, viz. the conducting of the world by general laws; and this seems nowise necessary to a very perfect Being. It is true; if every thing were conducted by particular volitions, the course of nature would be perpetually broken, and no man could employ his reason in the conduct of life. But might not other particular volitions remedy this inconvenience? In short, might not the Deity exterminate all ill, wherever it were to be found; and produce all good, without any preparation or long progress of causes and effects?

Besides, we must consider, that, according to the present economy of the world, the course of nature, though supposed exactly regular, yet to us appears not so, and many events are uncertain, and many disappoint our expectations. Health and sickness, calm and tempest, with an infinite number of other accidents, whose causes are unknown and variable, have a great influence both on the fortunes of particular persons and on the prosperity of public societies: And indeed all human life, in a manner, depends on such accidents. A Being, therefore, who knows the secret springs of the universe, might easily, by particular volitions, turn all these accidents to the good of mankind, and render the whole world happy, without discovering himself in any operation. A fleet, whose purposes were salutary to society, might always meet with a fair wind: Good princes enjoy sound health and long life: Persons born to power and authority, be framed with good tempers and virtuous dispositions. A few such events as these, regularly and wisely conducted, would change the face of the world; and yet would no more seem to disturb the course of nature or confound human conduct, than the present economy of things, where the causes are secret, and variable, and compounded. Some small touches, given to Caligula's brain in his infancy, might have converted him into a Trajan: One wave, a little higher than the rest, by burying Caesar and his fortune in the bottom of the ocean, might have restored liberty to a considerable part of mankind. There may, for aught we know, be good reasons, why providence interposes not in this manner; but they are unknown to us: And though the mere supposition, that such reasons exist, may be sufficient to *save* the conclusion concerning the divine attributes, yet surely it can never be sufficient to *establish* that conclusion.

If every thing in the universe be conducted by general laws, and if animals be rendered susceptible of pain, it scarcely seems possible but some ill must arise in the various shocks of matter, and the various concurrence and opposition of general laws: But this ill would be very rare, were it not for the *third* circumstance, which I proposed to mention, viz. the great frugality with which all powers and faculties are distributed to every particular being. So well adjusted are the organs and capacities of all animals, and so well fitted to their preservation, that, as far as history or tradition reaches, there appears not to be any single species which has yet been extinguished in the universe. Every animal has the requisite endowments; but these endowments are bestowed with so scrupulous an economy, that any considerable diminution must entirely destroy the creature. Wherever one power is increased, there is a proportional abatement in the others. Animals, which excel in swiftness, are commonly defective in force.

Those, which possess both, are either imperfect in some of their senses, or are oppressed with the most craving wants. The human species, whose chief excellency is reason and sagacity, is of all others the most necessitous, and the most deficient in bodily advantages; without clothes, without arms, without food, without lodging, without any convenience of life, except what they owe to their own skill and industry. In short, nature seems to have formed an exact calculation of the necessities of her creatures; and like a *rigid master*, has afforded them little more powers or endowments, than what are strictly sufficient to supply those necessities. An *indulgent parent* would have bestowed a large stock, in order to guard against accidents, and secure the happiness and welfare of the creature, in the most unfortunate concurrence of circumstances. Every course of life would not have been so surrounded with precipices, that the least departure from the true path, by mistake or necessity, must involve us in misery and ruin. Some reserve, some fund would have been provided to ensure happiness; nor would the powers and the necessities have been adjusted with so rigid an economy. The Author of nature is inconceivably powerful: His force is supposed great, if not altogether inexhaustible: Nor is there any reason, as far as we can judge, to make him observe this strict frugality in his dealings with his creatures. It would have been better, were his power extremely limited, to have created fewer animals, and to have endowed these with more faculties for their happiness and preservation. A builder is never esteemed prudent, who undertakes a plan, beyond what his stock will enable him to finish.

In order to cure most of the ills of human life, I require not that man should have the wings of the eagle, the swiftness of the stag, the force of the ox, the arms of the lion, the scales of the crocodile or rhinoceros; much less do I demand the sagacity of an angel or cherubim. I am contented to take an increase in one single power or faculty of his soul. Let him be endowed with a greater propensity to industry and labour; a more vigorous spring and activity of mind; a more constant bent to business and application. Let the whole species possess naturally an equal diligence with that which many individuals are able to attain by habit and reflection; and the most beneficial consequences, without any allay of ill, is the immediate and necessary result of this endowment. Almost all the moral, as well as natural evils of human life arise from idleness; and were our species, by the original constitution of their frame, exempt from this vice or infirmity, the perfect cultivation of land, the improvement of arts and manufactures, the exact execution of every office and duty, immediately follow; and men at once may fully reach that state of society, which is so imperfectly attained by the best-regulated government. But as industry is a power, and the most valuable of any, nature seems determined, suitably to her usual maxims, to bestow it on men with a very sparing hand; and rather to punish him severely for his deficiency in it, than to reward him for his attainments. She has so contrived his frame, that nothing but the most violent necessity can oblige him to labour; and she employs all his other wants to overcome, at least in part, the want of diligence, and to endow him with some share of a faculty, of which she has thought fit naturally to bereave him. Here our demands may be allowed very humble, and therefore the more reasonable. If we required the endowments of superior penetration and judgment, of a more delicate taste of beauty, of a nicer sensibility to benevolence and friendship; we might be told, that we impiously pretend to break the order of nature, that we want to exalt ourselves into a higher rank of being, that the presents which we require, not being suitable to our state and condition, would only be pernicious to us. But it is hard; I dare to repeat it, it is hard, that being placed in a world so full of wants and necessities; where almost every being and element is either our foe or refuses us their assistance; we should also have our own temper to struggle with, and should be deprived of that faculty which can alone fence against these multiplied evils.

The *fourth* circumstance, whence arises the misery and ill of the universe, is the inaccurate workmanship of all the springs and principles of the great machine of nature. It must be acknowledged, that there are few parts of the universe, which seem not to serve some purpose, and whose removal would not produce a visible defect and disorder in the whole. The parts hang all together; nor can one be touched without affecting the rest, in a greater or less degree.

But at the same time, it must be observed, that none of these parts or principles, however useful, are so accurately adjusted, as to keep precisely within those bounds in which their utility consists; but they are, all of them, apt, on every occasion, to run into the one extreme or the other. One would imagine, that this grand production had not received the last hand of the maker; so little finished is every part, and so coarse are the strokes, with which it is executed. Thus, the winds are requisite to convey the vapours along the surface of the globe, and to assist men in navigation: But how oft, rising up to tempests and hurricanes, do they become pernicious? Rains are necessary to nourish all the plants and animals of the earth: But how often are they defective? how often excessive? Heat is requisite to all life and vegetation; but is not always found in the due proportion. On the mixture and secretion of the humours and juices of the body depend the health and prosperity of the animal: But the parts perform not regularly their proper function. What more useful than all the passions of the mind, ambition, vanity, love, anger? But how oft do they break their bounds, and cause the greatest convulsions in society? There is nothing so advantageous in the universe, but what frequently becomes pernicious, by its excess or defect; nor has nature guarded, with the requisite accuracy, against all disorder or confusion. The irregularity is never, perhaps, so great as to destroy any species; but is often sufficient to involve the individuals in ruin and misery.

On the concurrence, then, of these *four* circumstances does all or the greatest part of natural evil depend. Were all living creatures incapable of pain, or were the world administered by particular volitions, evil never could have found access into the universe: And were animals endowed with a large stock of powers and faculties, beyond what strict necessity requires; or were the several springs and principles of the universe so accurately framed as to preserve always the just temperament and medium; there must have been very little ill in comparison of what we feel at present. What then shall we pronounce on this occasion? Shall we say, that these circumstances are not necessary, and that they might easily have been altered in the contrivance of the universe? This decision seems too presumptuous for creatures so

blind and ignorant. Let us be more modest in our conclusions. Let us allow, that, if the goodness of the Deity (I mean a goodness, like the human) could be established on any tolerable reasons *a priori*, these phenomena, however untoward, would not be sufficient to subvert that principle; but might easily, in some unknown manner, be reconcilable to it. But let us still assert, that as this goodness is not antecedently established, but must be inferred from the phenomena, there can be no grounds for such an inference, while there are so many ills in the universe, and while these ills might so easily have been remedied, as far as human understanding can be allowed to judge on such a subject. I am sceptic enough to allow, that the bad appearances, notwithstanding all my reasonings, may be compatible with such attributes as you suppose: But surely they can never prove these attributes. Such a conclusion cannot result from scepticism; but must arise from the phenomena, and from our confidence in the reasonings which we deduce from these phenomena.

Look round this universe. What an immense profusion of beings, animated and organized, sensible and active! You admire this prodigious variety and fecundity. But inspect a little more narrowly these living existences, the only beings worth regarding. How hostile and destructive to each other! How insufficient all of them for their own happiness! How contemptible or odious to the spectator! The whole presents nothing but the idea of a blind nature, impregnated by a great vivifying principle, and pouring forth from her lap, without discernment or parental care, her maimed and abortive children.

Here the **Manichean** system occurs as a proper hypothesis to solve the difficulty: And no doubt, in some respects, it is very specious, and has more probability than the common hypothesis, by giving a plausible account of the strange mixture of good and ill which appears in life. But if we consider, on the other hand, the perfect uniformity and agreement of the parts of the universe, we shall not discover in it any marks of the combat of a malevolent with a benevolent Being. There is indeed an opposition of pains and pleasures in the feelings of sensible creatures: But are not all the operations of nature carried on by an opposition of principles, of hot and cold, moist and dry, light and heavy? The true conclusion is, that the original source of all things is entirely indifferent to all these principles, and has no more regard to good above ill than to heat above cold, or to drought above moisture, or to light above heavy.

There may *four* hypotheses be framed concerning the first causes of the universe: *that* they are endowed with perfect goodness, *that* they have perfect malice, *that* they are opposite and have both goodness and malice, *that* they have neither goodness nor malice. Mixed phenomena can never prove the two former unmixed principles. And the uniformity and steadiness of general laws seem to oppose the third. The fourth, therefore, seems by far the most probable.

What I have said concerning natural evil will apply to moral, with little or no variation; and we have no more reason to infer, that the rectitude of the supreme Being resembles human rectitude than that his benevolence resembles the human. Nay, it will be thought, that we have still greater cause to exclude from him moral sentiments, such as we feel them; since moral evil, in the opinion of many, is much more predominant above moral good than natural evil above natural good.

But even though this should not be allowed, and though the virtue, which is in mankind, should be acknowledged much superior to the vice; yet so long as there is any vice at all in the universe, it will very much puzzle you anthropomorphites, how to account for it. You must assign a cause for it, without having recourse to the first cause. But as every effect must have a cause, and that cause another; you must either carry on the progression *in infinitum*, or rest on that original principle, who is the ultimate cause of all things. . . .

Hold! Hold! cried DEMEA: Whither does your imagination hurry you? I joined in alliance with you, in order to prove the incomprehensible nature of the divine Being, and refute the principles of Cleanthes, who would measure every thing by a human rule and standard. But I now find you running into all the topics of the greatest libertines and infidels; and betraying that holy cause, which you seemingly espoused. Are you secretly,

then, a more dangerous enemy than Cleanthes himself?

And are you so late in perceiving it? replied CLEANTHES. Believe me, Demea; your friend Philo, from the beginning, has been amusing himself at both our expence; and it must be confessed, that the injudicious reasoning of our vulgar theology has given him but too just a handle of ridicule. The total infirmity of human reason, the absolute incomprehensibility of the divine nature, the great and universal misery and still greater wickedness of men; these are strange topics surely to be so fondly cherished by orthodox divines and doctors. In ages of stupidity and ignorance, indeed, these principles may safely be espoused; and perhaps, no views of things are more proper to promote superstition, than such as encourage the blind amazement, the diffidence, and melancholy of mankind. But at present. . . .

Blame not so much, interposed PHILO, the ignorance of these reverend gentlemen. They know how to change their style with the times. Formerly it was a most popular theological topic to maintain, that human life was vanity and misery, and to exaggerate all the ills and pains which are incident to men. But of late years, divines, we find, begin to retract this position, and maintain, though still with some hesitation, that there are more goods than evils, more pleasures than pains, even in this life. When religion stood entirely upon temper and education, it was thought proper to encourage melancholy; as indeed, mankind never have recourse to superior powers so readily as in that disposition. But as men have now learned to form principles, and to draw consequences, it is necessary to change the batteries, and to make use of such arguments as will endure, at least some scrutiny and examination. This variation is the same (and from the same causes) with that which I formerly remarked with regard to scepticism.

Thus Philo continued to the last his spirit of opposition, and his censure of established opinions. But I could observe, that Demea did not at all relish the latter part of the discourse; and he took occasion soon after, on some pretence or other, to leave the company.

Part XII

After Demea's departure, Cleanthes and Philo continued the conversation in the following manner. Our friend, I am afraid, said CLEANTHES, will have little inclination to revive this topic of discourse, while you are in company; and to tell truth, Philo, I should rather wish to reason with either of you apart on a subject so sublime and interesting. Your spirit of controversy, joined to your abhorrence of vulgar superstition, carries you strange lengths, when engaged in an argument; and there is nothing so sacred and venerable, even in your own eyes, which you spare on that occasion.

I must confess, replied PHILO, that I am less cautious on the subject of natural religion than on any other; both because I know that I can never, on that head, corrupt the principles of any man of common sense, and because no one, I am confident, in whose eyes I appear a man of common sense, will ever mistake my intentions. You, in particular, Cleanthes, with whom I live in unreserved intimacy; you are sensible, that, notwithstanding the freedom of my conversation, and my love of singular arguments, no one has a deeper sense of religion impressed on his mind, or pays more profound adoration to the divine Being, as he discovers himself to reason, in the inexplicable contrivance and artifice of nature. A purpose, an intention, a design strikes everywhere the most careless, the most stupid thinker; and no man can be so hardened in absurd systems, as at all times to reject it. *That nature does nothing in vain*, is a maxim established in all the schools, merely from the contemplation of the works of nature, without any religious purpose; and, from a firm conviction of its truth, an *anatomist*, who had observed a new organ or canal, would never be satisfied till he had also discovered its use and intention. One great foundation of the Copernican system is the maxim, *that nature acts by the simplest methods, and chooses the most proper means to any end*; and astronomers often, without thinking of it, lay this strong foundation of piety and religion. The same thing is observable in other parts of philosophy: And thus all the sciences almost lead us insensibly to acknowledge a first intelligent Author; and their authority is often so much the greater, as they do not directly profess that intention.

. . . .

So little, replied PHILO, do I esteem this suspense of judgment in the present case to be possible, that I am apt to suspect there enters somewhat of a dispute of words into this controversy, more than is usually imagined. That the works of nature bear a great analogy to the productions of art is evident; and according to all the rules of good reasoning, we ought to infer, if we argue at all concerning them, that their causes have a proportional analogy. But as there are also considerable differences, we have reason to suppose a proportional difference in the causes; and in particular ought to attribute a much higher degree of power and energy to the supreme cause than any we have ever observed in mankind. Here then the existence of a Deity is plainly ascertained by reason; and if we make it a question, whether, on account of these analogies, we can properly call him a *mind* or *intelligence*, notwithstanding the vast difference, which may reasonably be supposed between him and human minds; what is this but a mere verbal controversy? No man can deny the analogies between the effects: To restrain ourselves from enquiring concerning the causes is scarcely possible: From this enquiry, the legitimate conclusion is, that the causes have also an analogy: And if we are not contented with calling the first and supreme cause a God or Deity, but desire to vary the expression; what can we call him but mind or thought, to which he is justly supposed to bear a considerable resemblance?

All men of sound reason are disgusted with verbal disputes, which abound so much in philosophical and theological enquiries; and it is found, that the only remedy for this abuse must arise from clear definitions, from the precision of those ideas which enter into any argument, and from the strict and uniform use of those terms which are employed. But there is a species of controversy, which, from the very nature of language and of human ideas, is involved in perpetual ambiguity, and can never, by any precaution or any definitions, be able to reach a reasonable certainty or precision. These are the controversies concerning the degrees of any quality or circumstance. Men may argue to all eternity, whether Hannibal be a great, or a very great, or a superlatively great man, what degree of beauty Cleopatra possessed, what epithet of praise Livy or Thucydides is entitled to, without bringing the controversy to any determination. The disputants may here agree in their sense and differ in the terms, or *vice versa*; yet never be able to define their terms, so as to enter into each other's meaning: Because the degrees of these qualities are not, like quantity or number, susceptible of any exact mensuration, which may be the standard in the controversy. That the dispute concerning theism is of this nature, and consequently is merely verbal, or perhaps, if possible, still more incurably ambiguous, will appear upon the slightest enquiry. I ask the theist, if he does not allow, that there is a great and immeasurable, because incomprehensible, difference between the *human* and the *divine* mind: The more pious he is, the more readily will he assent to the affirmative, and the more will he be disposed to magnify the difference: He will even assert, that the difference is of a nature which cannot be too much magnified. I next turn to the atheist, who, I assert, is only nominally so, and can never possibly be in earnest; and I ask him, whether, from the coherence and apparent sympathy in all the parts of this world, there be not a certain degree of analogy among all the operations of nature, in every situation and in every age; whether the rotting of a turnip, the generation of an animal, and the structure of human thought be not energies that probably bear some remote analogy to each other: It is impossible he can deny it: He will readily acknowledge it. Having obtained this concession, I push him still farther in his retreat; and I ask him, if it be not probable, that the principle which first arranged, and still maintains, order in this universe, bears not also some remote inconceivable analogy to the other operations of nature, and among the rest to the economy of human mind and thought. However reluctant, he must give his assent. Where then, cry I to both these antagonists, is the subject of your dispute? The theist allows, that the original intelligence is very different from human reason: The atheist allows, that the original principle of order bears some remote analogy

to it. Will you quarrel, Gentlemen, about the degrees, and enter into a controversy, which admits not of any precise meaning, nor consequently of any determination? If you should be so obstinate, I should not be surprised to find you insensibly change sides; while the theist on the one hand exaggerates the dissimilarity between the supreme Being, and frail, imperfect, variable, fleeting, and mortal creatures; and the atheist on the other magnifies the analogy among all the operations of nature, in every period, every situation, and every position. Consider then, where the real point of controversy lies, and if you cannot lay aside your disputes, endeavour, at least, to cure yourselves of your animosity.

And here I must also acknowledge, Cleanthes, that, as the works of nature have a much greater analogy to the effects of *our* art and contrivance, than to those of *our* benevolence and justice; we have reason to infer that the natural attributes of the Deity have a greater resemblance to those of man, than his moral have to human virtues. But what is the consequence? Nothing but this, that the moral qualities of man are more defective in their kind than his natural abilities. For, as the supreme Being is allowed to be absolutely and entirely perfect, whatever differs most from him departs the farthest from the supreme standard of rectitude and perfection.[11]

These, Cleanthes, are my unfeigned sentiments on this subject; and these sentiments, you know, I have ever cherished and maintained. But in proportion to my veneration for true religion, is my abhorrence of vulgar superstitions; and I indulge a peculiar pleasure, I confess, in pushing such principles, sometimes into absurdity, sometimes into impiety. And you are sensible, that all bigots, notwithstanding their great aversion to the latter above the former, are commonly equally guilty of both.

My inclination, replied CLEANTHES, lies, I own, a contrary way. Religion, however corrupted, is still better than no religion at all. The doctrine of a future state is so strong and necessary a security to mortals, that we never ought to abandon or neglect it. For if finite and temporary rewards and punishments have so great an effect, as we daily find: How much greater must be expected from such as are infinite and eternal?

How happens it then, said PHILO, if vulgar superstition be so salutary to society, that all history abounds so much with accounts of its pernicious consequences on public affairs? Factions, civil wars, persecutions, subversions of government, oppression, slavery; these are the dismal consequences which always attend its prevalency over the minds of men. If the religious spirit be ever mentioned in any historical narration, we are sure to meet afterwards with a detail of the miseries which attend it. And no period of time can be happier or more prosperous, than those in which it is never regarded, or heard of.

. . . .

It is contrary to common sense to entertain apprehensions or terrors, upon account of any opinion whatsoever, or to imagine that we run any risk hereafter, by the freest use of our reason. Such a sentiment implies both an *absurdity* and an *inconsistency*. It is an absurdity to believe that the Deity has human passions, and one of the lowest of human passions, a restless appetite for applause. It is an inconsistency to believe, that, since the Deity has this human passion, he has not others also; and, in particular, a disregard to the opinions of creatures so much inferior.

To know God, says Seneca, *is to worship him*. All other worship is indeed absurd, superstitious, and even impious. It degrades him to the low condition of mankind, who are delighted with entreaty, solicitation, presents, and flattery. Yet is this impiety the smallest of which superstition is guilty. Commonly, it depresses the Deity far below the condition of mankind; and represents him as a capricious Demon, who exercises his power without reason and without humanity! And were that divine Being disposed to be offended at the vices and follies of silly mortals, who are his own workmanship; ill would it surely fare with the votaries of most popular superstitions. Nor would any of human race merit his *favour*, but a very few, the philosophical theists, who entertain, or rather indeed endeavour to entertain, suitable notions of his divine perfections: As the only persons entitled to his *compassion* and *indulgence* would be the philosophical sceptics, a sect almost

equally rare, who, from a natural diffidence of their own capacity, suspend, or endeavour to suspend all judgment with regard to such sublime and such extraordinary subjects.

If the whole of natural theology, as some people seem to maintain, resolves itself into one simple, though somewhat ambiguous, at least undefined proposition, *that the cause or causes of order in the universe probably bear some remote analogy to human intelligence*: If this proposition be not capable of extension, variation, or more particular explication: If it afford no inference that affects human life, or can be the source of any action or forbearance: And if the analogy, imperfect as it is, can be carried no farther than to the human intelligence; and cannot be transferred, with any appearance of probability, to the other qualities of the mind: If this really be the case, what can the most inquisitive, contemplative, and religious man do more than give a plain, philosophical assent to the proposition, as often as it occurs; and believe that the arguments, on which it is established, exceed the objections which lie against it? Some astonishment indeed will naturally arise from the greatness of the object: Some melancholy from its obscurity: Some contempt of human reason, that it can give no solution more satisfactory with regard to so extraordinary and magnificent a question. But believe me, Cleanthes, the most natural sentiment, which a well-disposed mind will feel on this occasion, is a longing desire and expectation, that Heaven would be pleased to dissipate, at least alleviate, this profound ignorance, by affording some more particular revelation to mankind, and making discoveries of the nature, attributes, and operations of the divine object of our Faith. A person, seasoned with a just sense of the imperfections of natural reason, will fly to revealed truth with the greatest avidity: While the haughty dogmatist, persuaded that he can erect a complete system of theology by the mere help of philosophy, disdains any farther aid, and rejects this adventitious instructor. To be a philosophical sceptic is, in a man of letters, the first and most essential step towards being a sound, believing Christian; a proposition which I would willingly recommend to the attention of Pamphilus: And I hope Cleanthes will forgive me for interposing so far in the education and instruction of his pupil.

Cleanthes and Philo pursued not this conversation much farther; and as nothing ever made greater impression on me, than all the reasonings of that day; so I confess, that, upon a serious review of the whole, I cannot but think, that Philo's principles are more probable than Demea's; but that those of Cleanthes approach still nearer to the truth.

NOTES

1. *Recherche de la vérité, liv.* 3, chap. 9.
2. [Cf. Cicero, *De Natura Deorum*, Bk. I, 22.]
3. Lib. II, 1095 [Munro's translation].
4. *De Nat[ura] Deor[um]*, Lib. I, 8.
5. [Hume presumably means *against* all mankind.]
6. Dr. Clarke.
7. *République des Lettres*, Août, 1685.
8. That sentiment had been maintained by Dr. King [*De Origine Mali, 1702*] and some few others, before Leibnitz, though by none of so great fame as that German philosopher.
9. [Milton: *Paradise Lost*, XI.]
10. [Dryden, *Aurengzebe*, Act IV, sc. 1.]
11. It seems evident, that the dispute between the sceptics and dogmatists is entirely verbal, or at least regards only the degrees of doubt and assurance, which we ought to indulge with regard to all reasoning: And such disputes are commonly, at the bottom, verbal, and admit not of any precise determination. No philosophical dogmatist denies, that there are difficulties both with regard to the senses and to all science; and that these difficulties are in a regular, logical method, absolutely insolveable. No sceptic denies, that we lie under an absolute necessity, notwithstanding these difficulties, of thinking, and believing, and reasoning with regard to all kind of subjects, and even of frequently assenting with confidence and security. The only difference, then, between these sects, if they merit that name, is, that the sceptic, from habit, caprice, or inclination, insists most on the difficulties; the dogmatist, for like reasons, on the necessity.

KEY TERMS

Atheist	Final causes
Infinite	Metaphysics
Analogy	Platonist
Skepticism	Anthropomorphite
Syllogism	Immutability
A posteriori	Simplicity
A priori	Manichean
Sophism	

STUDY QUESTIONS

1. Cleanthes offers an argument for the existence of God by way of an analogy with a machine made by humans. How does this argument go? Why isn't Philo convinced by it?
2. Cleanthes appeals to the complexity of a human eye to argue that God exists. How might an atheist explain the complexity of the human eye without appealing to a divine designer?
3. How does Philo argue that Cleanthes cannot rule out the possibility that there is more than one god?
4. Philo says that merely proving the compatibility of a loving God with all the suffering in the world is not good enough. Why isn't it good enough?
5. What do you think is the most plausible response to Philo's argument that the amount of suffering in the world tells against the existence of God?
6. At the end of the selection, Pamphilus says that "Philo's principles are more probable than Demea's" but also that "those of Cleanthes approach still nearer to the truth." On the basis of these statements, what conclusion do you think Pamphilus is drawing regarding the arguments of the dialogues?

God, Evil and the Best of All Possible Worlds

GOTTFRIED LEIBNIZ

Gottfried Wilhelm Leibniz (1646–1716) was one of the greatest intellectuals of his time and regarded as a "universal genius." In addition to being a great philosopher (who had major philosophical contributions in metaphysics, epistemology, logic, philosophy of action, and philosophy of religion), he was very important to the developing field of physics and to mathematics. For example, Leibniz was instrumental (along with Isaac Newton) in the development of calculus. He is perhaps best known for his thought that the existence of evil is compatible with God's existence because this world is the best of all possible worlds.

. .

SOME intelligent persons have desired that this supplement be made [to Theodicy], and I have the more readily yielded to their wishes as in this way I have an opportunity again to remove certain difficulties and to make some observations which were not sufficiently emphasized in the work itself.

I. *Objection.* Whoever does not choose the best is lacking in power, or in knowledge, or in goodness.

God did not choose the best in creating this world.
Therefore, God has been lacking in power, or in knowledge, or in goodness.

Answer. I deny the minor, that is, the second premise of this **syllogism**; and our opponent proves it by this:

Prosyllogism. Whoever makes things in which there is evil, which could have been made without any evil, or the making of which could have been omitted, does not choose the best.

God has made a world in which there is evil; a world, I say, which could have been made without any evil, or the making of which could have been omitted altogether.

Therefore, God has not chosen the best.

Answer. I grant the minor of this prosyllogism; for it must be confessed that there is evil in this world which God has made, and that it was possible to make a world without evil, or even not to create a world at all, for its creation has depended on the free will of God; but I deny the major, that is, the first of the two premises of the prosyllogism, and I might content myself with simply demanding its proof; but in order to make the matter clearer, I have wished to justify this denial by showing that the best plan is not always that which seeks to avoid evil, since it may happen that the *evil is accompanied by a greater good.* For example, a general of an army will prefer a great victory with a slight wound to a condition without wound and without victory. We have proved this more fully in the large work by making it clear, by instances taken from mathematics and elsewhere, that an imperfection in the part may be required for a greater perfection in the whole. In this I have followed the opinion of St. Augustine, who has said a hundred times, that God has permitted evil in order to bring about good, that is, a greater good; and that of Thomas Aquinas (in libr. II. sent. dist. 32, qu. I, art. 1), that the permitting of evil tends to the good of the universe. I have shown that the ancients called Adam's fall *felix culpa*, a happy sin, because it had been retrieved with immense advantage by the incarnation of the Son of God, who has given to the universe something nobler than anything that ever would have been among creatures except for it. For the sake of a clearer understanding, I have added, following many good authors, that it was in accordance with order and the general good that God allowed to certain creatures the opportunity of exercising their liberty, even when he foresaw that they would turn to evil, but which he could so well rectify; because it was not fitting that, in order to hinder sin,

God should always act in an extraordinary manner. To overthrow this objection, therefore, it is sufficient to show that a world with evil might be better than a world without evil; but I have gone even farther, in the work, and have even proved that this universe must be in reality better than every other possible universe.

II. *Objection.* If there is more evil than good in intelligent creatures, then there is more evil than good in the whole work of God.

Now, there is more evil than good in intelligent creatures.

Therefore, there is more evil than good in the whole work of God.

Answer. I deny the major and the minor of this conditional syllogism. As to the major, I do not admit it at all, because this pretended deduction from a part to the whole, from intelligent creatures to all creatures, supposes tacitly and without proof that creatures destitute of reason cannot enter into comparison nor into account with those which possess it. But why may it not be that the surplus of good in the non-intelligent creatures which fill the world, compensates for, and even incomparably surpasses, the surplus of evil in the rational creatures? It is true that the value of the latter is greater; but, in compensation, the others are beyond comparison the more numerous, and it may be that the proportion of number and quantity surpasses that of value and of quality.

As to the minor, that is no more to be admitted; that is, it is not at all to be admitted that there is more evil than good in the intelligent creatures. There is no need even of granting that there is more evil than good in the human race, because it is possible, and in fact very probable, that the glory and the perfection of the blessed are incomparably greater than the misery and the imperfection of the damned, and that here the excellence of the total good in the smaller number exceeds the total evil in the greater number. The blessed approach the Divinity, by means of a Divine Mediator, as near as may suit these creatures, and make such progress in good as is impossible for the damned to make the evil, approach as nearly as they may to the nature of demons. God is **infinite**, and the devil is limited; the good may and does go to infinity, while evil has its bounds. It is therefore possible, and

is credible, that in the comparison of the blessed and the damned, the contrary of that which I have said might happen in the comparison of intelligent and non-intelligent creatures, takes place; namely, it is possible that in the comparison of the happy and the unhappy, the proportion of degree exceeds that of number, and that in the comparison of intelligent and non-intelligent creatures, the proportion of number is greater than that of value. I have the right to suppose that a thing is possible so long as its impossibility is not proved; and indeed that which I have here advanced is more than a supposition.

But in the second place, if I should admit that there is more evil than good in the human race, I have still good grounds for not admitting that there is more evil than good in all intelligent creatures. For there is an inconceivable number of genii, and perhaps of other rational creatures. And an opponent could not prove that in all the City of God, composed as well of genii as of rational animals without number and of an infinity of kinds, evil exceeds good. And although in order to answer an objection, there is no need of proving that a thing is, when its mere possibility suffices; yet, in this work, I have not omitted to show that it is a consequence of the supreme perfection of the Sovereign of the universe, that the kingdom of God is the most perfect of all possible states or governments, and that consequently the little evil there is, is required for the consummation of the immense good which is found there.

KEY TERMS

Syllogism
Infinite

STUDY QUESTIONS

1. Leibniz grants that it was possible for God to create a world without evil. Do you agree? Why or why not?
2. Leibniz argues that a world that contains evil might still be the best of all possible worlds if the evil is accompanied by a greater good. What greater good might accompany the existence of evil in our world?
3. In order to defend the existence of God in the face of evil, is it necessary to argue that the actual world is the best of all possible worlds, as Leibniz does? Why or why not?

Dialogue on Good, Evil, and the Existence of God

JOHN PERRY

John Perry (1943–) is a contemporary philosopher of language and mind. He has also made important contributions in metaphysics, philosophy of action, and, as you will see here, philosophy of religion, publishing nine books. He has been a member of the philosophy departments at the University of California, Los Angeles (UCLA), and Stanford University, and he is now Professor of Philosophy at the University of California, Riverside.

Characters: Gretchen Weirob, Sam Miller, Dave Cohen

Gretchen Weirob, Sam Miller, and Dave Cohen are my inventions. I think of them as having a life beyond these *Dialogues*, however, that explains how they came to be written. When Weirob, Miller, and Cohen had philosophical conversations, Miller kept fairly detailed notes. He wrote these notes up in a rather dry fashion, which focused on the arguments. Dave Cohen gave me a lot of information about how the conversations actually went, and of course, I have my own memories of Gretchen. These are the sources I have used to reconstruct this dialogue and its counterpart, *A Dialogue on Personal Identity and Immortality.*

Given Sam's methodical ways, it is surprising that his notes on these conversations were so scattered about. But as it turned out, the notes were inserted in the copies of books they had discussed in the conversations. The notes for the other *Dialogue* were found in Sam's copy of Locke's *Essay*, which I borrowed from his library not long after he died. I had no idea that Sam had saved notes of other conversations until a couple of years ago, when the task of sorting all of his books fell to me. The notes for this conversation were found in his copy of Augustine's *Confessions*.

. .

1
The First Morning

MILLER: Hello, Gretchen. I stopped by because I heard that you were under the weather. I brought you a cup of coffee and a cinnamon roll from Starbucks.

WEIROB: That was most kind of you, Sam. I've got a terrible case of the flu, and I feel absolutely miserable. I'm sneezing and dripping; every muscle aches; I've got a headache. I know that coffee will help my headache, but I haven't had the willpower to get up and make myself some. Your kindness is most welcome.

MILLER: To be honest, I also thought you might like someone to talk to for a while. But if you have a headache . . .

WEIROB: Oh, no, not at all. Coffee and good conversation will make me forget my misery—better than aspirin, and not as hard on the stomach.

MILLER: I suspected as much. In fact, I suggested to Dave Cohen that he drop by after his class—by then we'd be sure to be in the middle of something interesting.

Gretchen, would it be stretching my kindness beyond what you could endure if I were to offer to say a prayer for your speedy recovery?

WEIROB: I think I'll pass on that, Sam.

MILLER: I know you're not exactly a confirmed believer in God.

WEIROB: It's not just that. Suppose I were. Suppose I believed in your Christian God. Just how do you think a prayer would help? Do you think God doesn't *know* that I have the flu and am miserable? God *must* know that I am miserable, for according to you he knows everything. In fact, not only does he know that I am miserable, but he also knows that you would like to see me get better. So how in the world does a prayer help? You simply would be communicating to God what God already knows, thereby wasting God's time and yours. Not to mention mine.

MILLER: I can see I'm in for a full-scale assault on everything I believe and hold dear. A small price to pay, I guess, if it helps your headache. You're clearly feeling better by the moment, so you may as well continue.

WEIROB: You think that if you pray, God may make me better. Well, God certainly can make me feel better, since he is (supposedly) all-powerful. But then why hasn't he done this already?

MILLER: The true value of prayer would be its effect on us, not any effect on God. It would remind us that however bad you feel, however much you sneeze, however achy your limbs, however much your head hurts, we are in the hands of a loving, beneficent God.

WEIROB: Then please spare me your prayer. You admit that it won't help get rid of my flu. And even if I believed that we were in the hands of a loving, beneficent God, which I thoroughly doubt, I certainly wouldn't want to be reminded of it.

MILLER: Why not?

WEIROB: Because that would mean that a loving, all-powerful, all-knowing God finds it reasonable to let me suffer. Now why would that be so? Any reason I can think of is extremely depressing. Is it that I am so completely small and insignificant that even an **omnipotent** and **omniscient** Being doesn't notice? Or that I am so disgusting that it is actually a good thing that I am suffering? Or that I am so

confused about what is good and bad that what seems to be a completely gratuitous evil—indeed, a whole series of them, from achy, drizzly head to achy, tired legs—is really a good thing, perhaps something your God is proud of? Maybe he feels about my flu like we feel about a nice sunrise—a beautiful beginning to a perfect day. "Oh, wow," he may be saying, "what a nice way to start the day. We'll have a beautiful sunrise and I'll make that little twit Gretchen Weirob sore and drippy and headachy." I declare, Sam, sometimes it is more than I can bear thinking that you really believe in such a monster.

MILLER: So, is your mind off your headache yet?

WEIROB: Yes, I admit that it is, but no thanks to any prayer of yours. No one can worry about their head for long when philosophy beckons, and what better for a tired, achy philosopher than arguing against a God such as yours. It's like shooting fish in a barrel.

MILLER: Go ahead and shoot your fish. I'll just do my best. Anything to get your mind off your misery.

WEIROB: OK, try hard to overcome your emotional commitment to your religion, and just look at it as a straightforward, logical, philosophical proposition. You believe in a God that is perfect in every way. All-knowing, all-powerful, and benevolent. That's what it says in some of the creeds I had to learn as a child, words that are etched in my brain. But how can this be? If your God exists, he knows I have the flu because he knows everything. He can certainly make it the case that I cease to have the flu, or could have prevented me from having the flu in the first place, for he is all-powerful. But I *do* have the flu! What am I to conclude? He must not care. But shouldn't a really benevolent God care about even a wretch like me? Why would he *want* me to suffer? But if he doesn't want me to suffer, why am I suffering? Like I said, shooting fish in a barrel. If I accept your Christian premise, that this world and all that is in it is the creation of a perfect God, all-knowing, all-powerful, and completely benevolent, I must draw the conclusion that I am not suffering. But I am suffering. So I reject the premise. There is no being that meets your definition of God. Perhaps there is no God.

Or perhaps there is, but he is ignorant, or weak, or mean.

MILLER: Gretchen, you must know that this argument—the so-called problem of evil—is at least as ancient as Augustine. Augustine tells us in his *Confessions* that it was only when he figured out how a world created by a Christian God could contain evil that he converted to Christianity.

WEIROB: Converted from what?

MILLER: He had been a Manichaean—Manichaeans believe that there are two ultimate principles controlling the world, good and evil. Our world is their battleground. According to the Manichaeans, the evil parts of the world are not due to God, that is, the good force. They are due to the other force, evil, or the dark force.

WEIROB: That sounds pretty reasonable. Would you be satisfied if I became religious, but became a Manichaean rather than a Christian? From the way you describe Manichaeism, maybe I could take the *Star Wars* movies as my sacred text.

MILLER: No, Gretchen, I would not.

WEIROB: I've long admired Augustine—he's the author of my favorite prayer.

MILLER: Your favorite prayer? I'm surprised that you know anything about Augustine. But I'm absolutely flabbergasted that you have a favorite prayer. How does it go?

WEIROB: "Lord, give me chastity . . . but not yet!"

MILLER: Oh, Gretchen!

WEIROB: You must admit that it is a prayer, and it is from Augustine.

MILLER: Yes, I guess so. It's a request directed at God, and Augustine definitely said it—he planned to become a member of a community where celibacy was expected of serious Christians. His plea had a serious point, which you presumably missed—that even when he was intellectually convinced that Christianity was the true religion, he still needed God's grace to complete the conversion.

WEIROB: That's all very interesting, Sam, but frankly, when you mention the word *grace* I feel my headache coming back. I take it that you think Augustine's intellectual conversion resulted from a real insight about the problem of evil. Tell me about that.

MILLER: Yes, I think he showed that your argument—that an all-perfect God can't exist because there is evil—is as full of holes as a piece of Swiss cheese.

WEIROB: That will take some convincing. I know that the problem must be old, for Augustine lived a millennium and a half ago. Age doesn't make the argument bad, nor does the fact that a saint thought it was. In fact, the problem of evil is like a bottle of fine wine. It gets *better* with age. It has made Christians like Augustine and you squirm for centuries. So much the better for it. So where are these holes?

MILLER: You don't expect me to convince you of the existence of a Christian God, do you? I wouldn't take that on.

WEIROB: No, just convince me that that Christian God you believe in—all-perfect, omnipotent, omniscient, and benevolent—could possibly exist, even given as unimportant a bit of suffering as my flu. Do that, and I'll let you say a prayer for me.

MILLER: That's a challenge worth taking on.

The main point to be made really is just a logical one, that a thing can be better for having a part or an aspect that, considered out of context, is of little value, or even ugly. For example, a novel as a whole can be more interesting because it has a dull chapter—if that dull chapter is necessary for setting up the situations that make the rest of the novel intricate and interesting. A painting can be more beautiful for having a patch of color that is, in itself, quite ugly and unattractive. And so forth. So a world can contain a little evil in it, or even a lot, but this may, in the grand scheme of things, just be a necessary part of the world, something that contributes to the goodness of it, that makes it better than it would be otherwise. That seems clear enough to me. But somehow I doubt that you are ready for my prayer.

WEIROB: Not quite yet, if you don't mind. Frankly, I don't feel like an ugly patch of color in a great painting, or a dull chapter in a good novel, or a discordant note in a great symphony—that's one you didn't mention, by the way. I don't think my suffering with this damn flu compares with those examples at all. I'm not here to be heard or witnessed by someone else, am I? I'm not part of a play or a novel or a painting.

I can see that someone might paint a picture of me that would be, if not exactly ugly, not much to look at on its own. And I can see that such a picture might enhance the overall aesthetic value of a larger picture of which it was a part. Perhaps there is a picture of a number of quite different-looking people and the overall effect is quite stunning, reminding us of the diversity of human nature—or something like that—in a way that none of the pictures by themselves could have done. It might be that the big painting would be a reasonable thing to hang on a wall, even though none of its parts—the individual portraits—would be worth hanging as separate paintings. Perhaps a quite beautiful or moving picture might include a part that depicted me sneezing and sniffling. Who knows? But that seems quite irrelevant to the question at hand. I'm not a picture of a sniveling, dripping, suffering human; *I am* a sniveling, dripping, suffering human.

MILLER: Perhaps there are better examples. Think of the times we go fishing. Surely it is some form of mild suffering to get out of bed before dawn on a chilly Nebraska spring morning when one might sleep in. But the days as a whole, the days that start out with those unpleasant experiences, are some of the most enjoyable days one can imagine. The point has nothing to do really with pictures or novels or symphonies. Given any kind of whole—a whole picture, a whole day, a whole life, a whole world—parts that wouldn't be very good were they to exist in isolation contribute to the whole in such a way that the whole is better with these parts than without them. . . .

WEIROB: OK. The point is that what one can call a fine day, perhaps even a "perfect" day in a loose sense, can contain a part that isn't that much fun, that might even qualify as a bit of suffering. And the blend of misery and pleasure doesn't have to do with the effect on some outsider who watches and appreciates this combination at work—as in the cases of the novel and the picture. It is the participants whose own lives are better in virtue of their own misery who matter—that's your point.

MILLER: Yes. And of course there are lots of examples of hard work and sacrifice at any stage in a person's life being the condition of great success, comfort, and satisfaction at another stage. Think of the sacrifices that medical students make, and the satisfactions that come later, after they become practicing physicians.

WEIROB: You mean charging outrageous fees and playing golf on Wednesday afternoons?

MILLER: You can jest, Gretchen, but the point is a logical one. Take any whole, a whole day, a whole year, a whole life. Just because some creatures some of the time feel some discomfort, or even suffer, does not mean that the whole day, or the whole life, may not be a fine one, and that the discomfort or suffering may not have been necessary for the quality of the day or the life as a whole. But what goes for a day or a life, goes for the world as a whole. Just as we have a plan for spending a fine day fishing that has, as a necessary part, a little suffering early in the morning, so God may have a plan for the world that requires suffering. It still may be a fine world, a much better world than it would have been without the suffering.

WEIROB: Please excuse me for not being convinced.

Let's start with the fishing example. Of course I can see that we can have a fine day, what we would call a perfect day, that contains some pain and discomfort. It's a pain to get up as early as one has to, if one is going to catch the fish in a cooperative mood. No day of fishing goes by—for me, at least—without at least once hooking my own finger while trying to bait the hook. Still, such days are perfect days.

But what do we mean by that? We mean that they are among the nicest days we expect to have. Days that are as perfect as we imagine that days can ever be. But not really perfect. When I say as perfect as a day can be, I mean as perfect as a day can be, given the way the world works. Given that it's hard to get up in the morning, given that fish are more likely to bite in the morning than in the afternoon, given that I'm clumsy and fishhooks are sharp—given all of that, sure, such a day is as fine a day as one can imagine, or ranks right up there at any rate.

But where did all of those givens come from? Who is responsible for the fact that it's hard to get up in the morning? We can imagine a world in which everyone hops out of bed fresh as a daisy and happy that it is morning. Some people I know claim that they are like that. I don't believe them, but it's at least possible that there should be such people, and even that I should be one of them. Indeed, why can't everyone be that way?

And even if some deep necessity requires that some or all of us hate to get out of bed, who is responsible for the fact that fish like to bite in the morning? Couldn't they have easily preferred mid-afternoon, so we could sleep in and still have a good day fishing?

And why does a fish's mouth have to be so hard to penetrate that a fishhook sharp enough to do its job poses a constant threat to an oaf like me?

Of course *my* answer to all of these questions is, "Well, that's just the breaks. No one decided all of this. It just worked out that way." But your answer is that God designed and created and thus bears responsibility for the whole thing.

Given this, how can you use the fishing analogy? It is designed to jolly me into believing in a "necessary evil"—something that is unpleasant or involves suffering, and so seems to be an evil, but turns out to be necessary for a greater good. But this analogy does no such thing. It is just an example of the very same thing I'm complaining about. I see no good reason a perfect being would want me to have the flu. And I see no good reason why a perfect being would want me to have to jerk myself out of bed with an unpleasant alarm in order to have a nice day fishing with a friend. The one evil does not explain the other; they both reinforce the same conclusion. No perfect God would have designed the world like this.

MILLER: You really know how to suffer, Gretchen. I can't believe you really expect my faith in God to be shaken by the fact that you have to get out of bed earlier than you would like to, to go fishing, or that when you are careless you prick your fingers with the fishhooks.

WEIROB: Keep in mind who has the burden of proof here. I don't have to talk you out of anything, nor do I want to. Believe what you want. You have to get me to believe, however, that your beliefs are consistent. I think you admit that I am

suffering with this flu, however insignificant I may be in the grand scheme of things, and however inconsequential the flu may be in the great range of things people suffer. Yet you also think the world was created by a perfect God. I claim that those beliefs are inconsistent. The burden of proof is on you to show that they are not.

MILLER: But I think I have already done that. If the world consisted of only your suffering, and nothing else, it would certainly be a very poor world. And perhaps you even think of the world that way when you are not careful to keep your self-absorption in check. But the world does not consist of just you and your suffering. You and your suffering are part of a very big world, big spatially and in time, and perhaps in other dimensions we cannot fathom.

And it is consistent, I claim, that the events in this complex world are interconnected and interdependent in such a way that the world that contains them is a very wonderful place, and better because of your suffering than it would be without it.

WEIROB: But your analogy doesn't really show that. You tell me to think of a day when I went fishing and had a good day, even though the first part of it was unpleasant. I admit the day as a whole was good and well worth getting out of bed. But that isn't the point. Wouldn't the world have been better *without* my suffering? My suffering, my discomfort on rising early, detracted rather than added to the value of the day.

Similarly, I admit that this world, taken as a whole, including my suffering, may be a peachy keen world, just a humdinger of a world, a world any reasonably perfect deity might be proud of. But it seems to me that it would be obviously better if my suffering were removed. Everything good could be left behind. It might not make much difference to the world, but it seems like the world would definitely be a little bit better, and no worse. I don't see how the good parts of the world depend in any way on my suffering.

MILLER: No, that's not right. You suffer, as you say—I would say you are somewhat uncomfortable—whenever you get up at a reasonable hour. If the day had been without suffering, it would have been a day when you didn't get up early. But if you hadn't gotten up early, we would not have gone fishing together, because I left before dawn. Or you would have gone on your own, gotten to the river late, and returned home empty-handed. It would not have been much fun. If we subtract the suffering from the day, we subtract the early rising, and the successful fishing, and pretty much everything that made the day worthwhile. So your suffering did make the day better.

We can see, then, how the fineness of our fishing day did depend on your "suffering." Now how exactly the goodness of the world depends on your having the flu, I can't say. I can't trace the story as I did with our fishing day. But that's OK. I don't have to. I am simply trying to sort out the logic of the situation—that's all our little bet calls on me to do—even if the details are beyond my understanding.

WEIROB: But that returns us to the points I raised before. Granted, if we hold the dependencies fixed, my discomfort, as you refer to it, was a necessary condition of our successful fishing trip. But why should I hold the dependencies fixed? Aren't they due to your all-powerful God? To repeat the point, God could have made a world in which I loved to get out of bed—in which everyone did. Or he could have made a world in which the fish enjoyed sleeping until noon.

MILLER: I think I see your point. By the dependencies, you mean how one fact leads to another, the "if . . . then" statements, the general principles.

WEIROB: Yes, like "Normal people don't enjoy jumping out of bed at dawn" and "People who come into contact with such and such a microbe will turn into sniveling, dripping, headachy miserable wretches."

MILLER: The same principle applies. There is no inconsistency in supposing that a perfect God designed the world to work according to those principles, because having it work that way is necessary for some greater good.

WEIROB: Aren't those merely words? Can you really imagine what God might have had in mind that made my sniveling and sneezing and headaches necessary? It's very hard for me to imagine anything great and wonderful he couldn't have managed without my misery.

MILLER: But now you are making your imagination the test of God's existence. Why should we take what you can imagine—you, a finite, imperfect, middle-aged, drippy, sneezy, headachy, basically grouchy philosopher—to be a test of what might be the case?

Let me remind you of our deal. I don't have to explain to you what plan God has in mind, of which your rather insignificant drips and sneezes form a necessary part. I don't need to have a clue as to what it might be. I just have to show that it is consistent, logically consistent, not self-contradictory, for a perfect God to have created a world with some suffering. That I claim to have done, by showing that there is no contradiction in a perfect whole having parts that, considered by themselves, are quite imperfect.

Shall we pray?

WEIROB: Look, Sam, you are interspersing your philosophical arguments with some ad hominem attacks on me, as if I really believed that my sniveling and dripping were the worst thing God has ever done. But I certainly do not. I've just been trying to be polite to you and to your God, on the off chance that he or she exists.

But let me take my gloves off. My misery, though quite real and as far as I can see completely unnecessary and pointless, is small potatoes next to the things that have happened in this world that your supposedly all-perfect God has created. Just in our own century, there have been two world wars, countless smaller wars, mass murders, and so forth. Millions of people killed, soldiers ripped to pieces dying painful deaths, innocent children burned from napalm. There was the Holocaust, the systematic extermination of millions of Jews and others by the Nazis during World War II. There have been other genocides—and they don't all happen somewhere else, either. Columbus, Cortés, Pizarro—these great discoverers wiped out the Arawaks, the Aztecs, the Incas. Our nice little town and college on the prairie exist only because of the largely successful attempt to eliminate the Native Americans who dwelled here. And diseases much worse than the flu plague us—cancer, for example, which strikes so many people in the prime of their lives, often causes painful deaths and leaves grieving families. Will you just say glibly to these people that God must have a plan? It's all for the best? That their suffering, or that of their children or parents, is a necessary part of some plan of an all-perfect God? Is that what you say to grieving families on your pastoral visits?

MILLER: Yes, Gretchen, I do say that, or words to that effect. But I don't say it glibly. I say it quite humbly. And I don't say it because I think it will eliminate their grief. I say it because it leaves open the possibility that their loss might have some meaning.

And you know what, Gretchen? Most people don't feel the way you do. Most people are comforted by the idea of a design—even if it is completely unknown to us and impossible for us to imagine—that gives meaning to their suffering and loss. We know that for many, even in concentration camps, the conviction that, after all, their experience must somehow have some meaning, must fit into God's plan, was comforting, something to cling to.

So all of this evil, all of this suffering—to many of those who actually endure it—does not seem to be a knockdown refutation of the idea of a perfect God. I'm sure there are many like you who can't accept that a perfect God would find it necessary to inflict misery on them. But there are many others who accept their limitations, don't expect to understand what God has in mind, are grateful to know that a God who does have a plan exists. So, yes, I tell people who have suffered and are suffering just what you find so ridiculous. But most people don't find it ridiculous.

WEIROB: That was a passionate speech, Sam, and I guess it was in response to a tone of anger in mine.

I certainly admit that the phenomenon you have just described, the experience of seemingly pointless suffering driving people toward some faith in God, rather than, as I would think reasonable, away from it, is quite real. And not only real, but perhaps close to the heart of the religious impulse. So it might seem to be a paradox to argue that the very things that drive people to religion—suffering and evil—are in fact inconsistent with some of the religions to which they are driven—that is, the religions that believe in an all-perfect God.

It may *seem* like a paradox, but clearly no paradox exists.

MILLER: No, I suppose not. Your view, then, is this: the existence of suffering is inconsistent with the existence of the all-perfect God of orthodox Christianity, even though suffering, as much as anything, has led people to embrace Christianity. It is logically consistent, but it seems like a strange view.

WEIROB: I think I called your religion monstrous a minute ago, so I can't complain if you call my view strange.

But I see Dave coming up the walk. Let's break for lunch and see if we feel like continuing our discussion later.

MILLER: Are you ready for me to pray for you?

WEIROB: Not quite yet.

2

The First Afternoon

COHEN: Well, who's winning?

MILLER: I've already won; she just won't admit it. Now that you are here, Dave, you can be the judge. My basic position is quite straightforward. An object or event can contain parts that, considered by themselves, lack whatever kind of goodness we might be talking about. And yet the presence of these parts can contribute to the overall goodness of the whole object. A painting can have ugly parts but be more beautiful or aesthetically pleasing or deep because of them. A symphony can have discordant notes and be better, as a whole, for it. A day can be a fine day, a perfect day, even though it contains a little suffering—say, that goes with getting up at the break of dawn. So, for all Gretchen knows, God may have a plan in which the suffering in the world plays an important role in making the whole better than it would be otherwise. Of particular interest to her, of course, is the intense and nearly unbearable suffering she is enduring as a result of her flu, although she admits that there are some other cases worthy of mention. I may not be able to say what God's plan is—why should a limited creature like myself be capable of that?—but I think I can claim to have shown that it is consistent to suppose that this world is the creation of an all-perfect Being, even if we admit that there is suffering in it.

COHEN: That sounds pretty good. What is your problem with that, Gretchen?

WEIROB: First of all, let me utterly disavow the mean suggestion Sam has made that I give my own sniveling and dripping some special status. I not only mention, I emphasize, that there have been events in this world, and no doubt these events are occurring this very minute, that are many orders of magnitude worse cases of suffering than my flu. So much the worse for Sam's argument. The worse the evil, the bigger the problem.

Second, let me explain why I don't think Sam has won yet. The deal was that he was to show me a possibility. That is, he was to show me how it was possible that a world with evil in it, the kind of evil we see here on earth, could be the creation of a perfect God.

Here's the way I see it. We have two statements, call them P and Q.

MILLER: Uh-oh. I hope you aren't going to get technical and try to win a philosophical argument with an equation.

WEIROB: No, nothing like that. Nothing at all. Just a simple point. So you've got two statements, P and Q. You think they are consistent, that is, that both could be true. I think they aren't consistent; that is, I don't see how they could both be true. But I admit that they are not *explicitly* inconsistent. P and Q aren't like "It's raining" and "It's not raining." Q isn't simply the negation of P.

COHEN: In this case P is that a perfect God exists, and Q is that all this evil we observe occurs.

WEIROB: Right. Now what does someone have to do to convince me that P and Q are consistent? They need to describe a bigger picture into which they both fit, a bigger picture that is itself clearly consistent.

MILLER: I thought that was what I was doing. Perhaps you could give an example of what would satisfy you.

WEIROB: I can give a simple example. Suppose I claim that there is a barber who shaves all and only those residents of Wilbur who do not shave themselves. Let me make the point a little more explicit. There are two things true about this barber. Call the first P: he shaves all the residents of Wilbur who don't shave themselves. Call the second Q: he doesn't shave anyone else. Would you say that was possible?

MILLER: I'd say it's impossible. There could not be such a barber. He would either shave himself or not. But either choice leads to a blatant contradiction. If he shaves himself, then he shaves someone who shaves himself, which contradicts his description. If he doesn't shave himself, then he doesn't shave someone who doesn't shave himself, contrary to his description. So there can't be such a barber. He is like a thing that is both round and square. You can describe such a thing but there can't be such a thing. The description "the barber who shaves all and only the people who don't shave themselves" can't fit anything.

WEIROB: But remember, I didn't say "all and only the people," I said, "all and only the residents of Wilbur."

COHEN: Right! OK, I get it. The barber lives in Beatrice, where his partner shaves him. Every day he drives to Wilbur and shaves all the residents who don't shave themselves. No contradiction.

MILLER: Tricky, tricky.

WEIROB: The point is that something *seemed* contradictory. But it really wasn't. This was shown by constructing a bigger picture that made sense out of how P and Q could both be true.

The bigger picture did not need to be *true* in order to do the trick of showing that P and Q are consistent. Maybe the barber actually lives in Crete and not in Beatrice. Or maybe he lives on a farm and has a beard. Or whatever. The bigger picture just has to be clearly consistent. It has to do what Dave did: show us that we were assuming something that made P and Q seem inconsistent, but that actually they could be fit together.

MILLER: But Gretchen, isn't that precisely what I have been doing? I even used the words, "big picture." I've been saying there is a big picture, and if we could only see it, we could see how the sufferings in the world contribute to the goodness of the world taken as a whole. You admit I don't have to actually tell you what the big picture is.

WEIROB: I don't think you give me what I have a right to ask for. Suppose Dave had just said, "I don't think that the barber is impossible because, for all we know, there is some larger story that makes it all fit together." That wouldn't have convinced you, would it?

MILLER: No, certainly not.

So let me see if I've got your point. Could we put it like this: what is needed is not just the possibility of providing a big picture, but an actual providing of a possible big picture.

WEIROB: Yes, that's it exactly. You can't get by just asserting that there might be some big plan into which everything fits. On the other hand, you aren't required to come up with the true big picture, any more than Dave had to tell us where the barber actually lives. You need to do something in between. As you put it, you need to actually provide me with a story that makes God's perfection and the suffering of his creatures fit together in a consistent whole. The whole need not be true. It can be far-fetched and unbelievable. And of course we agreed that you didn't have to provide details accounting for every evil we can think of. But you need to show how evil can enter into a world created by your all-perfect God, to show the basic mechanisms of evil, one might say.

COHEN: That seems reasonable, Sam. Can you do that?

MILLER: I think I can. Let me make sure that I have the ground rules straight. My story has to show that such a world—that is, a world with the sorts of suffering and evil we have in this one, and created by an all-powerful, knowing, and benevolent God—is logically possible. To do this I need to construct a story of how things might be in a way that explains the suffering and evil as parts in a perfect world. That I think I can do. But I want to warn you at the outset, the story will contain elements that Gretchen—and no doubt you, too, Dave—will find completely unbelievable. But you won't, I think, claim that they are contradictory, and that's what counts. Are we now agreed on the ground rules?

COHEN: I think so. You will describe a consistent world that contains the suffering and evil the real world contains and is created by an all-perfect God. The world can contain any events you want, however unlikely Gretchen thinks they may be, as long as they are consistent. If you do that, you will show that it is possible, at least in the logical sense of not containing any contradictions, that our world, with all the kinds of suffering and evil Gretchen has mentioned, was created by a God such as you believe in. Do you agree to that, Gretchen?

WEIROB: Yes, I agree. I don't think I'm going to particularly like what is coming, but I agree that if Sam can describe such a world, however implausible I may find it, he will have won the bet.

MILLER: Frankly, that's very good news. There is a traditional story, a sort of Christian **theodicy**. It has three parts, and I'm sure that you guys won't think that the last two parts are at all plausible. But under these rules you don't have to find them plausible. As long as you find them possible, I win.

COHEN: Theodicy. What's a theodicy?

WEIROB: Leibniz wrote a book called *Theodicy*, which is his account of how this is the best of all possible worlds, contrary to appearances. Sort of an apology for God. These are the ideas Voltaire makes fun of in *Candide*, the ideas that Dr. Pangloss defends. So I suppose that a theodicy is an apology for God for making such a dismal world.

MILLER: I wouldn't put it quite like that, although I suppose one might. A theodicy is just the sort of thing you want me to provide. But there are things Leibniz wanted to prove that I'm not going to attempt. First, to repeat once more, I don't have to claim that the possibility I'm describing is correct about the real world, just that it is a possibility. Second, I don't see why I should show that this is the best of all possible worlds. I don't see why we should assume that there would be a unique best world. And finally—I guess this is a separate point—if there were a best of all possible worlds, I might not be in it. I'm not going to get upset with God for not making a world I'm not in. I don't see why you have any valid complaint that God didn't make a world that you are not in.

WEIROB: I'm not so sure about that last point, but let's let it pass, at least for now.

MILLER: The first thing I need to explain—the first thing in my theodicy, I guess I should say—seems to be something you won't find so implausible. That is the idea that a world with **freedom** in it is better than one without freedom.

COHEN: You probably don't mean things like freedom of religion, freedom of speech, freedom of assembly, the sorts of things that are guaranteed in America by the Bill of Rights. You mean something more basic and **metaphysical**.

MILLER: That's right. All of those freedoms are wonderful. But they presuppose freedom in a more basic sense. They presuppose freedom of choice. The choice may be dramatic, such as when one is deciding whether to publish something unpopular or whether to assemble to protest an unjust law. But there is choice involved even when the choice is fairly trivial. For example, Gretchen had a can of mushroom soup and a can of chicken soup in her pantry. I asked her which she wanted me to fix, and she decided on chicken soup. There wasn't anything momentous about this decision. Probably even in the most vicious tyranny, people would be allowed to choose between chicken soup and mushroom soup. But the point is, she had to choose. She decided. The response that she made when she chose chicken soup wasn't automatic. She thought it over, she deliberated, however briefly, on which she would enjoy more, and she chose. She could have chosen one way or the other; she chose chicken. That is freedom of choice in the sense that I mean.

WEIROB: So you're saying that a world with creatures like us, who have this ability to choose between different courses of action, is better than one without creatures like us in that respect. I suppose that might be a world in which there was nothing but robots, whose every act was programmed in a predictable way.

MILLER: That's right. Withhold your disbelief for a second, and imagine being God, or at least a very powerful creator, who is going to create a world. Wouldn't it be a good thing to create creatures that have freedom?

WEIROB: What would be so good about it?

MILLER: Gretchen, I know you can simply throw up doubts at every step of my argument, but what kind of discussion will we have then? You need to let me explain my vision—the defense to the problem of evil, as I understand it. I think you grasp what I'm getting at. Remember, I don't claim to understand the world. As a Christian who believes in an all-perfect God, I don't expect to. I don't expect to understand the mind of an infinite God.

WEIROB: I don't either; I can't even understand the mind of the person who wrote the instruction book for my VCR.

MILLER: My task is only to provide one story of how things *might* all fit together. All I'm really trying to say is that we can admit that an all-perfect God *might* have valued that trait of ours that we call freedom of choice. Such a God might have preferred to create a world with such creatures in it to one that was like it in other ways, but contained only automatons or robots.

WEIROB: OK, I'll give you that for now. But I want to reserve the right to return later to this picture you have of the difference between us and automatons and robots.

COHEN: But for now we all admit that it's quite coherent to suppose an all-perfect creator who preferred (in whatever ways all-perfect beings do) to create a world with free creatures than one without such creatures. What's the next step?

MILLER: In creating such a world, the creator then takes a certain amount of risk. God gives up control of every facet of the universe. If he creates Gretchen with **free will**, then whether Gretchen takes the chicken soup or the mushroom soup is up to her, not to God. That's the meaning of free choice.

Of course, this decision is not of much importance. At least as far as we can see, it wasn't right to choose chicken and wrong to choose mushroom, or vice versa. It's just a matter of what she felt like having.

But many of the decisions free creatures make, many of the decisions we make, are not like that. Often we are faced with a decision between something that is right and something that is wrong. Or between something that is OK and something that is noble.

In these cases there is no question of what God would have us do. God would have us do what is better, and more noble, and more perfect. But what we do is up to us. And we don't always do the right instead of the wrong, the better rather than worse, the noble over the merely sufficient. In this way, through the actions of humans and other free creatures exercising their freedom, imperfection and evil enter the world.

Suppose we are at a picnic, and we drink a six-pack of pop that came from the store with one of those plastic bridles that holds the cans together. You know that birds and other animals can get caught in the holes in those things and end up dying an agonizing death because they can't eat properly, and so they slowly starve. Suppose one of those bridles blows away. We could chase it down, but we don't. Perhaps we even intend to do so later, and then forget. So our wrong is merely a bit of procrastination. Not such a big deal. But later a bird gets caught in the holes and suffers a painful death. The bird's suffering was real. It wasn't something God chose. Nor even something we chose directly. But it was our choice not to do what we knew was right, to take a chance on what would happen with the plastic bridle.

Here, then, is something quite bad in our world, something we cannot imagine God choosing. The explanation is that it isn't his choice to have the bird suffer. His role is to make us free. He must value freedom so much that all the bad results that come from the decisions creatures freely make, still leave it a better world, in his eyes, than one without free creatures.

That seems to me the basic story that Augustine and others tell to explain how evil enters the world. I know it's a rather trivial example, and perhaps the suffering of one bird is nothing compared to the suffering of millions of children over the centuries. But it illustrates what we might call the basic mechanism of evil in a world created by perfection.

COHEN: Gretchen, are you satisfied so far?

WEIROB: Not exactly. I have a couple of questions.

Let's suppose, as would probably be the case, that I am the culprit in your little story. That is, I leave the plastic bridle unsecured on the beach, I see it blow away, I resolve to get it but procrastinate and then forget. The key point is when I decide—freely—to bask in the sun for a few minutes before going to get it. I could do either thing. I could do the right thing and run right after the bridle. Or I could do what I did in fact do, and just sit there and enjoy the sun and the conversation, running the risk of forgetting all about it. And that's what I did.

Now I can agree with you that an all-perfect God might want to populate the world with free creatures. But why does he want to populate it with *lazy* free creatures, like me? If I hadn't been lazy, I would have shot up and gotten the bridle right away. I would still have been free, just not lazy. Couldn't God have created a world with free creatures, but free creatures that have no relevant weaknesses, so that they always freely choose to do the right thing? Then evil wouldn't have crept into the world.

MILLER: I'm certainly not going to deny that you are lazy, or that laziness is by any reasonable standard an imperfection. To stick with the example, why did God make a lazy Gretchen rather than a perfect Gretchen?

COHEN: No, that's not the point; Gretchen isn't claiming that her only imperfection is laziness. But it seems that she would be a better person if she weren't lazy, even if everything else stayed the same.

MILLER: Now you are trying to get me to give some sort of detailed account of what God had in mind by creating a world in which Gretchen is lazy. And of course if I could do that, you would move on to other people and other, worse problems. You would ask me to explain what God had in mind in creating a world in which Hitler exists with all of his hatred, and so forth. But remember our agreement. I don't have to do that. I don't claim to be able to explain in any detail what God is aiming at. I just want to explain how there are certain basic mechanisms that allow us to see how God could create a world in which bad things are done.

I may not be able to think of any good purpose that is promoted by Gretchen's laziness. I must admit it would seem to me to be a better world if she had all of her other charms—most of them, anyway—but wasn't lazy. But how should I know? How should my tiny mind figure out what purpose Gretchen's laziness serves?

In any case, if you look at the example, you must admit that the bird's suffering was Gretchen's fault, not God's. Gretchen *could have* picked up the bridle. She chose not to. She was free. And so she, and not someone else, not God, is responsible for the consequences of her actions. . . .

WEIROB: So go ahead, Sam. Show us why a perfect God is a plausible creator of this miserable world.

MILLER: Hold on, Gretchen. Not *plausible*, just *consistent*. That was our deal.

WEIROB: OK, OK.

But is your view really consistent? After all, your God is supposed to be omniscient, all-knowing. Ignorance would clearly be an imperfection.

If God is all-knowing, doesn't that mean he must know what each of us will do next? Doesn't he know that I will choose the chicken, not the mushroom, soup? Doesn't he know that I will let the bridle lie where it landed? If so, how can I be free? If not, if he doesn't know what I am going to do, then how can he be omniscient?

COHEN: I don't think that quite follows, Gretchen. Suppose Sam asks you if you would rather have a spinach soufflé or a T-bone steak for dinner. I know you would choose the steak. You might hesitate, thinking that the soufflé would be more healthy, that perhaps there are good arguments against eating animals. But you'd take the steak. You like steak so much and spinach so little, that anyone who knows you would predict it. I know that about as well as I know that the sun will rise tomorrow. But that doesn't mean that you didn't choose the steak freely, does it? You chose the steak because you wanted to. You knew the spinach would be better for you, but you chose the steak, as free as can be. My knowledge or lack of knowledge has nothing to do with it.

MILLER: Good point, Dave.

WEIROB: I admit that Dave's point is good. It doesn't follow from the fact that Dave knows what I will choose, that I don't choose freely. So Sam isn't inconsistent, simply because he says that I am free, and that someone knows what I am going to do.

Still, Sam doesn't just say that, he says that the someone is God—the very same God who created me. And it seems that God hasn't figured out what I am like, after long experience, as you two have. He knew from the moment he created me, or before, precisely what I would do, from my first cry on being born to my dying utterance. Given that, I don't understand exactly how he can escape responsibility for what I do.

God's knowledge is a special case. He created me, knowing what I would do. You didn't create me. You didn't decide on a plan for the world that involved my eating the steak. If we trace back from effect to cause, starting with my choosing the steak, we will not come to you as a distant cause of my action. That's why I am responsible for eating the steak and you are not. But the situation is completely different with God. If we trace back from effect to cause, we do come to God as a distant cause. So God doesn't escape responsibility for the consequences of what I do, since they are part of the consequences, for him the *foreseeable* consequences, of what he did.

It seems ludicrous to have someone create a situation that he knows, prior to creation, will lead to an unfortunate result, blame the result on some aspect of the situation he created—in this case, me—and avoid any responsibility at all for it. It makes me . . .

MILLER: Wait a minute, Gretchen. You're getting off the point and forgetting your own train of thought.

There are two points here. The one you have drifted into now is this: Does God's knowledge of what you will do, given that he created you, mean that God bears some responsibility for what you do? I must admit it seems pretty plausible that it does mean this. But that has nothing to do with our argument at this point. I haven't said that God isn't responsible for everything that happens in his creation. I've just said that things that seem unnecessary and bad might be necessary parts of a good or even perfect world.

The second point is this: Does God's knowledge of what you are going to do mean that *you are not free after all?* That question is relevant to our discussion at this point. You were claiming that what I said was inconsistent, that an omniscient God could not make people who were truly free, since if he is omniscient, he'll know what they are going to choose.

Dave pointed out that in at least some cases, someone can know that a person will do a certain thing, even though the person does that thing freely. His example was that though he knows you will choose steak, your choice is still a free choice.

WEIROB: Sam, you're exactly right. I was getting off on another point.

Let's see, can God create someone who is free, and at the same time know what he or she is going to do? I think I still have some difficulty with that, even when I am not confused.

But to tell you the truth, between your subtleties and my flu, my intellect is beginning to show signs of wear and tear. If I were to suggest we pick up on this tomorrow morning, Sam, would you feel I was just trying to wangle another cinnamon roll out of you?

MILLER: Of course not.

I'll pick up a roll for you too, Dave, if you can make it.

COHEN: Count me in for sure. I'm anxious to hear the next part of your "big picture." What time?

MILLER: My reasoning this morning went like this: Gretchen and I belong to a generation that thinks breakfast at eight is getting pretty late. Add an hour for Gretchen's laziness, which we have commented on so much. Add another hour because she has the flu. Ten o'clock seemed to be just about perfect.

WEIROB: Yes, it was, and it will be. See you guys then. I'll even brew the coffee, Sam, just bring the rolls and the rest of your big picture.

3
The Second Morning

COHEN: Good morning, Sam. Good morning, Gretchen. Wow, coffee, cinnamon rolls, and philosophy. What a great way to start the day! Sam, you look sort of glum.

MILLER: I have to admit I am a bit discouraged. What I wanted to do today was to explain to you two how God can be omniscient—he knows everything the creatures he creates are going to do—and still give them free choice.

I thought I'd be able to do this by simply reviewing what some of my heroes have said, particularly Augustine. So I stayed up pretty late reading and thinking. But to tell you the truth, I don't really find a solution there that I feel is convincing. I'm sure the problem is with me and not with Augustine, but I can't very well explain what I wanted to explain.

WEIROB: What does Augustine *say?*

MILLER: He makes Dave's point, that there is no contradiction between your being free and someone knowing what you are going to do next. We might know you will choose the steak rather than the spinach soufflé, but that doesn't mean your choice isn't free. But he doesn't go much further than that. He doesn't seem to feel it makes a difference in the case in which it is the creator that knows what the created is going to do. To be honest, I can't get away from thinking it does make a difference. I'm not really sure that it makes sense for me to be free, when the very person who created me knew that if he created me one way, I would do the one thing, and if he created me another way, I would do the other. And, even if that does make sense, it seems that it is clearly God who is choosing the evil that we do. He is doing it at one remove: he is choosing to make someone who will choose to do the evil. I can't really convince myself that this makes much of a difference. So I'm stuck. I don't really think the problem is unsolvable, but *I* don't know how to solve it.

COHEN: I don't want to be presumptuous—as a matter of fact, I don't even know which side I'm on in your debate. But I thought a lot about this God and free will problem last night, and I'd like to try out an idea on you two.

MILLER: Be my guest!

COHEN: Let me start with another problem, which we studied in a philosophy class I took a long time ago.

MILLER: *Another problem?* Are you sure you are trying to help?

COHEN: Just hang on. I think it's a *solvable* problem, and that the solution suggests an idea about the free will problem.

MILLER: OK.

COHEN: The problem is called "The Stone Paradox." It's an objection to God's omnipotence. You ask the question, "Could God create a stone he could not lift?" That question is supposed to pose a paradox that shows that the idea of God's omnipotence makes no sense. If God can't create the stone, there is something he can't do. But if he can create the stone, there is something he can't do, namely, lift the stone he created. Either way, there is something God can't do, which proves he isn't omnipotent after all.

WEIROB: I've always thought that was a pretty nifty problem for theists. But I guess you think it doesn't hold up.

COHEN: No, I don't. When we say that God is omnipotent, we mean God can perform any act or task that makes sense. We don't mean that God can make something that is both round and square, or can make two and two add up to five, or anything like that. But "create a stone God cannot lift" is itself an impossible, incoherent task, if God is essentially omnipotent. It doesn't make sense for anyone to perform this task. Therefore it doesn't make sense for God to. It's not really a task.

WEIROB: OK, that's pretty convincing. What does that have to do with the problem about God and free will?

COHEN: Hold on a minute. I've got another point. Notice that God in fact created all sorts of stones that he *will* not in fact lift—I'm not really sure what it means for God to lift a stone, but whatever we take it to mean, my point holds.

MILLER: Granted. Go ahead and explain it.

COHEN: OK. Take the Rock of Gibraltar. Suppose that for God to lift a stone means that he miraculously makes it rise for no apparent reason and then settle softly back where it was. God has a plan for the world, and in that plan he simply does not perform that act. He does not lift the Rock of Gibraltar.

WEIROB: OK, OK. What's the point?

COHEN: Just that God *can* lift the Rock of Gibraltar, in the sense that *if* he had planned the world

that way, that's what would have happened. I don't know what else it would mean, to say that God could lift it, if it weren't that. It isn't that it's too big or heavy for him. He won't lift it, but he could. And "he could" means that he could have created a world in which he did.

WEIROB: All right. God won't lift the Rock of Gibraltar, because he decided not to. But he could lift it, because if that's what he had decided to do, that's what he would have done.

COHEN: Let's take seriously the idea that God decides to create a world with free agents. And let's accept that part of deciding this is that he is not going to know what these agents will do at certain points in their lives. Note that this is not to say that God *cannot* know. It is that he has decided not to know. He could have created a world in which he knew whether Gretchen would pick up the soda bridle right away, or whether she would decide to wait. So he could know. But he doesn't know.

WEIROB: But if God doesn't know which I'm going to do, is God really omniscient?

COHEN: It seems to me that, in a pretty clear and defensible sense, God *is* omniscient in the case I am describing. Remember, he is *omnipotent* not because he *does* everything there is to be done, but because there is nothing he can't *do*. He is *omniscient* not because he knows everything, but because there is nothing that he can't *know*.

MILLER: This is sounding pretty good to me, though I'm not too sure what Augustine would say about it. However, I'm not certain we can accept so lenient a concept of omniscience as this. I mean, God is supposed to know quite a bit, after all. If I understand your definition, he might not know anything and still be omniscient, as long as there is nothing he could not have known had he wanted to.

COHEN: Maybe my definition of omniscience isn't quite right. Perhaps I'll come back to that later. My main point is a bit different. Look at all that God does know, from this perspective. God can still know all the principles and laws by which the world works—which of course we imagine being due to God. He may not know whether Gretchen will choose the mushroom soup or the chicken soup, but he knows just what will happen if she does the one or the other.

MILLER: How is *that* knowledge about the world?

COHEN: God's picture of the world is like a road map of Nebraska. Suppose we look at a road map, and imagine a driver entering the state from Kansas on Highway 75.

MILLER: Driving up from Topeka?

WEIROB: I don't think it really matters, Sam.

MILLER: I know that, Gretchen. I just like to have a vivid picture in my imagination.

COHEN: Then let's say driving up from Topeka. So he has lots of points at which to choose. When he comes to Nebraska City, he can take Highway 2. That will take him toward Lincoln, and if he stays on it until the end . . .

WEIROB: The bitter end, if it's winter.

COHEN: . . . he'll come to Chadron. If he stays on Highway 85, he'll head toward Omaha, and if he continues to stay on 85, he'll eventually come to Sioux City, I guess. My point is that we know quite a bit about the driver. Even if we don't know the choices he will make, we know the *consequences* of each choice.

WEIROB: Of course, the consequence of each choice will not be a fixed route through the rest of the state, but another set of choices—that's not an objection, just a comment.

COHEN: Just add one thing: suppose that we are not merely looking at a regular road map, but at an electronic road map that has a little light on it that follows the progress of the car. What's more, suppose that we have a radio control device that allows us to take over the steering of the car. At any intersection, we could decide which way the car will go, and so we could know which way the car will go. But we decide not to do that.

In this case, it seems to me we could know everything about the car's route through the state, for we could have a plan in which we use the car's radio control to go in a predetermined way at each intersection. But we ourselves choose to let the driver decide, at least at some of the intersections. We could know, but we ourselves decided not to know. We know everything that can be known, given our decision. And even in this case, we

know all the effects of each of the free "choices"—although, as Gretchen pointed out, this knowledge is full of ifs: "if he turns on 2, then if he doesn't turn off on 77 or 30 or the interstate . . . then he will arrive in Chadron, but if he turns left on 77, he will end up in Beatrice"—and so forth. This sort of knowledge is hard to put into words, but a map represents it very elegantly.

But to return to the point, we can know everything; we do in fact know a lot, and the things we don't know are the things we decided not to know.

It seems this might be an acceptable model for Sam. If it works, it allows for a God who can know everything and does in fact know everything, except the things he has chosen not to know, by virtue of giving free choice to humans.

WEIROB: To improve the model, you should give us not just the knowledge of the way the roads go in Nebraska, but the ability to design and build them ourselves. We decided where the roads would go, and so we decided what the effects of the choices would be.

MILLER: Fair enough. If I understand Dave, this is the idea. First, think of God's knowledge as a big diagram of all the events that are going to happen through time. Next to each time on the diagram is written the state of the world at that specific time. Think of God deliberating, and then choosing between an infinity of these diagrams—choosing one and saying, "So Be It," or something like that. (Of course, theologians will tell us that that is not an accurate way to conceive of how God knows, since it is based on how we know. But still, it's a useful way of thinking about it.)

According to Dave's conception, we shouldn't think of these diagrams simply as time lines with descriptions of the world attached at each time. Rather, each diagram has many branches. For each time a free being is faced with a choice, the diagram will have a fork, with one branch representing how the world will go on if the person makes one decision and the other branch representing how the world will proceed if the person makes another decision.

WEIROB: Of course a person might have several choices, so that this fork might have a number of branches coming out of it.

MILLER: Right. This diagram would quickly become enormously complex. If we just think of five people making decisions every five minutes, the representation of all the ways things might go would be too complex for any human to deal with before an hour had passed.

WEIROB: I've read, though, that this is how chess-playing computers work. They form a big picture of all the ways the game can continue from a given position—or at least an enormous number of positions—and figure out from that what the best move is. It's clear that that is not the way humans play chess.

MILLER: Well, I'm sure that neither is a very good model for how God plans things, and probably even to talk about planning is misleading. But this way of looking at it, even though it makes God sound like a chess-playing computer to you, Gretchen, is the way I picture what Dave's suggestion amounts to.

I think I like it. God decides the range of choices to give people, the way the world works, the effects of the various decisions, including how they frame later decisions. However, he decides to put an element of free choice in. As Dave says, he could have known what people will do at those points, but he chooses not to. God is still omniscient in the sense that he *can* know everything, in the sense Dave explains, and he *does* know everything that doesn't turn on free choices.

WEIROB: Are you sure that this concept of omniscience, will pass muster with expert theologians, like our hero Augustine?

COHEN: Augustine is your hero? Isn't he supposed to be responsible for a lot of the uptightness that infects Christianity?

WEIROB: Well, I don't admire him for that, but I do think he was a great philosopher, even though I've only read bits and pieces.

MILLER: You ask whether he would approve of this concept of omniscience. I really don't know if he would, Gretchen. It certainly doesn't seem to be the concept he used, so I suppose he wouldn't like it.

But if you are thinking of that as an excuse to wiggle out of admitting that you have lost the bet, think again. You don't accept anyone's authority on anything, and you can't start now by appealing to the authority of Augustine. If you yourself can't come up with a good reason not to accept Dave's account of our freedom and God's knowledge, you lose. Ready for a prayer?

WEIROB: Oh, no. You've got a long way to go. I'll give you freedom. Although I'm not completely convinced, I just don't have any good arguments to show that Dave's account is inconsistent or incoherent.

Where does that leave us? You've given us a God that is perfect, that thinks a world with freedom is better than one without, even if that means that if some choices are made, suffering will result.

So let's look at our world with this in mind. The first thing to note is that there is a lot of suffering. But you say that is the result of free choices by free beings; their freedom was the price God was willing to pay for a world with free beings.

But isn't your God also supposed to be a just and fair God? Doesn't this require that those who suffer have this suffering balanced by pleasure or even joy? And doesn't it require that those who cause the suffering—at least those who choose to do evil or, like me in the case of the soda bridle, choose to be lazy and thoughtless—should be punished? But who can look around the world and suppose that there is this kind of justice and fairness? You may have explained how a perfect God can end up creating a world with suffering, but I don't see how you have explained how he can end up creating a world that is as unfair and unjust as ours.

COHEN: I'm pretty sure I know what Sam is going to say about that, Gretchen.

WEIROB: I think I do too, but I want to hear him say it.

MILLER: I told you yesterday my theodicy has three parts, and I said the first part, freedom, was the one you would probably like best.

The second part is one of the most familiar and, I think, also one of the most beautiful ideas that people associate with religion in general and Christianity in particular. That is the notion of an afterlife.

WEIROB: Heaven, hell, and I suppose purgatory, too.

MILLER: Those are parts of Dante's picture. But I don't have to buy into any details. The point is simply this. Suppose an innocent child is run over by a car, suffers, and eventually dies. The driver was criminally negligent, but rich. His only real punishment is the high fees he must pay to his lawyer. The child dies after a life in which the suffering outweighs the joys; the driver has a pleasant life. If we have only this to go on, how can we say that ours is a just world?

But the doctrine of an afterlife, in whatever form, says that this isn't the whole story. The driver may have a very unpleasant afterlife. If we think in traditional terms, we may imagine him suffering in purgatory for a long time, or perhaps even being given everlasting torment in hell. But we don't have to have anything like Dante's version of the afterlife to grasp the general point. If the part of the world we see is all there is, God has clearly created a very unfair and unjust world. But there is no inconsistency—and let me remind you, I don't have to convince you of the plausibility of my story, of my theodicy, only that it is consistent and coherent—in claiming that what we see is not all there is, and that the sufferings are compensated for and the sins are punished in parts of existence of which we cannot now be aware.

WEIROB: I think this whole issue of the afterlife is an interesting one. I can imagine there is a place far away in space and time, or perhaps far away in another dimension I don't even have a concept of, in which someone is suffering because I was careless with the soda bridle. But unless that person is me, it just makes the whole world more unfair. And what would make her me? That's what bothers me. I wonder if that whole idea isn't pretty dubious.

COHEN: That's a pretty subtle point. Are we going to have to figure out the nature of personal identity and immortality before we know whether Sam has won his bet?

MILLER: I don't think that's quite fair, Gretchen. Life after death may not be common sense; maybe it's completely fantastic, as I'm sure you must think. But the *possibility* of life after death is common sense; everyone knows what we mean when we say we might end up in heaven or hell, or be reincarnated. I can't be expected to solve every philosophy problem there is, can I?

WEIROB: All right, all right. I'm sure we'll get around to talking about that topic some day. But for now I'll drop it. I'll give you the possibility of an afterlife, and with it the possibility that your God is just and fair, appearances to the contrary.

MILLER: Well, I guess I should thank you for permitting me to embrace a concept that has given hope and meaning to countless souls throughout the centuries.

WEIROB: You are very welcome. My generosity knows bounds, however. I think there is a bigger problem. Indeed, it makes me feel bad just to think of it, and to remember our casual talk about fishing yesterday. After all, animals suffer too. You have to get your God off the hook for that.

COHEN: I suppose Sam can say that animals suffer because of someone's free choice, and the suffering can be compensated for in an afterlife.

WEIROB: No, I think the problem goes quite a bit deeper than that. Hold on, let me get the copy of *Natural History* magazine that I was reading. . . . It's got to be in that pile over there. . . . Here it is. Now, look at the picture on the inside of the back cover.

MILLER: Oh, dear.

COHEN: I can't quite make it out. What is it?

WEIROB: Do you know what a bat cave is?

MILLER: Of course.

COHEN: I'm afraid you are going to have to explain it to this city boy.

WEIROB: A bat cave is a cave inhabited by bats. The caves have high ceilings from which the bats spend a good bit of the day hanging. Of course, all the bat excrement—the "bat guano"—falls to the floor of the cave.

COHEN: That's what bat guano is? Ugh.

WEIROB: Sometimes bats have occupied these caves for a long, long time, hundreds, thousands, maybe even tens of thousands of years. The bat guano builds up until it's incredibly deep, and cockroaches and such thrive in it, so when you go in a bat cave there is this endlessly deep seething mass of bat guano, with the activity of the cockroaches making it seem almost alive.

MILLER: Gretchen, what is the point? Are you trying to win the bet by grossing me out until I have to call it quits?

WEIROB: I'm just explaining this picture. The photographer came across this bat cave because he heard a baby bat's chirp. The baby bat had slipped from the ceiling of the cave, fallen into the guano, and broken its little baby bat wing. It was quite doomed, pitifully chirping as it sank into the guano while cockroaches were starting to feed on it. If you look closely, you can see that's what the picture is. There is the little bat right there.

COHEN: Oh, my God. Gretchen, that is horrible. What *is* your point?

WEIROB: That little baby bat is suffering as much as our hypothetical bird, caught in the soda bridle I dropped. But the bat isn't suffering on account of anyone's sin or evil or laziness or unfortunate choice. That's why I thought of this case, about as far removed from the effects of human choices as you could want. The cave, the guano, the occasional fall of a baby bat, the cockroaches—these are not the inventions of a demented human being. These are not the effects of human carelessness. This is just the way the system works. If God designed and created the system, it's on his shoulders, not on the shoulders of any of his free creatures.

Now I ask you, *what could he have had in mind*, to create such a system as this system of bats, guano, and cockroaches? Was it for our edification? So that every decade or so a nature photographer could stumble in a bat cave and take a gross picture? How many thousands of baby bats sink to a totally unpleasant death for every picture that comes out of it?

Let me put it this way. You've given us an arguably consistent story of how we can have a world with evil caused by free agents. But there are all kinds of suffering that are not caused by free agents. Suffering happens because of the way things work—the way God made things work, if there is a God. This is *natural evil*, or maybe *natural suffering*, for we might not want to call something evil that isn't the result of someone's free choice. *But it is suffering nevertheless*, and it can't be laid at the foot of any free creature except God.

COHEN: Some philosophers have claimed that animals don't really feel pain.

WEIROB: Surely you don't believe that.

COHEN: Well, no, not really. But remember, Sam just has to give a consistent picture. I'm not sure it's inconsistent to suppose that animals don't feel pain.

WEIROB: I guess there are more kinds of absurdity than just inconsistency. But whether animals can feel pain is really beside the point. There is enough human suffering to make my point. Some of this suffering—huge amounts of it—is caused by human actions, and so presumably falls under Sam's free will defense. But much of human suffering is not caused by the acts of other humans; it is simply the result of the way nature works. Earthquakes aren't anyone's fault. Nor is cancer. What about floods that carry away innocent children? Epidemics? Famines? Certainly, sometimes floods and epidemics and famines are caused or made worse by things people do. But there were floods before there were human dams to break, famines before there were human food distribution systems to break down. These things are part of the fabric of the world, part of nature. And I don't see how their presence in a world designed by a perfect God can be explained. To be sure, there is much suffering that is caused by human meanness, laziness, carelessness, greed, envy, and the like. And your free will defense is a clever way to account for it. Well, maybe it's more than clever. Maybe it's deep and profound. But it doesn't account for the suffering that is just a product of nature, whether it's a baby bat or a baby human.

COHEN: I don't want you to think I really thought that animals didn't feel pain.

WEIROB: I didn't think that—I know you were just seeing how the argument might go.

Well, Sam, how is the argument going to go? Are you now going to uncover the third part of your theodicy, and explain all the natural suffering in the world, and help us to see what your gentle, loving, all-mighty, and all-perfect God might have had in mind?

MILLER: Gretchen, I've known you for years, but sometimes you leave me speechless. Are you really so moved by the little bat's suffering? Or are you simply moved by the opportunity to shock me and throw this suffering in my face? I'm very aware of suffering, suffering of all kinds, suffering of humans, suffering of animals, suffering of all sorts. It's not just an abstraction for me, or a picture on the back of a magazine, but part of my job. I minister to those who suffer—and to those who have caused suffering. I think you prefer a world in which all this suffering is for naught, with no explanation, no redress, no compensation, no meaning. I . . .

WEIROB: Sam . . .

MILLER: I know what you are going to say. It's not a matter of preference; it's a matter of argument. To win the bet, I need to appeal to your reason, not wonder at your emotions.

I'm sorry I doubted your feeling for the little bat. I'm sure you feel as bad for it as I do. I guess I thought I detected a little joy for the dialectical possibilities your little bat offered, lurking behind the sincere pity for it.

WEIROB: You probably did, Sam, you probably did.

Actually, what I was going to say was that it is getting on toward lunchtime, and maybe we ought to take a break.

MILLER: Goodness, you are right. I have a lunch meeting I need to get to, so we *will* have to break.

WEIROB: Do you want to admit defeat in the face of natural evil?

MILLER: Oh, certainly not. If it's OK with you we can resume later this afternoon. I get back, say, around three.

WEIROB: Why not?

COHEN: Count me in.

4
The Second Afternoon

WEIROB: I trust you had a good lunch, Sam?

WEIROB: . . . How odd of God to create a world in which so many things eat each other. People eat cattle and chickens and tiny lambs and fish, cockroaches chew on baby bats. . . .

MILLER: OK, Gretchen, I get the point. You want me to get on with my theodicy and try to deal with your baby bat and all the other natural suffering in the world.

WEIROB: Exactly.

MILLER: As I said, the third part of my theodicy is the one you will like the least. So before submitting

myself to your sarcasm, let me just remind you of the rules. I'm supposed to provide a *consistent* story that includes evil of all the sorts we have on earth in a world created by a perfect God. It doesn't have to strike you as plausible, much less true. I don't have to claim it is true. I need only claim that my story is consistent. If there is one way, however far-fetched from your point of view, of putting an all-powerful God and the evil and suffering we see into a larger and clearly consistent story, then there are infinitely many other possibilities totally beyond our imagination, but well within the power of God.

WEIROB: OK, OK, get on with it. What is the third part of your theodicy? Devils and angels and things that go bump in the night and sneak up on little baby bats and make them fall?

MILLER: I wouldn't have put it quite that way, Gretchen, but that is, in fact, the general idea. What reason exists to suppose that the only free creatures God created were humans?

COHEN: Certainly dolphins and whales and many other mammals must be candidates.

MILLER: I suppose so, but that's not exactly what I had in mind. In traditional Christianity there are all kinds of other created creatures with freedom, some of whom fell—that is, committed some sort of original sin as Adam did—some of whom are very powerful and capable of all sorts of things.

COHEN: That's beginning to sound like Manichaeism, with its force of good and force of evil.

MILLER: No, that's not right. In Christian doctrine and lore, the devil was created by God and then fell into sin. The force of evil in Manichaeism was not created by the force of good; these forces coexisted from the beginning.

WEIROB: Isn't the devil's main job to lead people into sin, like Faustus and the guy who was a fan of the Washington Senators in *Damn Yankees*? What has that got to do with natural evil?

MILLER: I suppose the devil has powers not only to tempt humans into sin, but to cause any kind of mischief he wants. Remember, I'm not bound by plausibility or even by any kind of official Christian doctrine in this debate. I simply have to tell a consistent story. My story can include a vice-devil for earthquakes, an assistant-devil for making the tops of bat caves slippery, subdevils for famines and floods and the like—all creatures created free by God, who choose to cause suffering of their own free will.

WEIROB: So your idea is that the world contains the devil and who knows how many other free creatures, who are out there causing problems for us. So that crack in California . . .

COHEN: The San Andreas Fault, which causes all the earthquakes?

WEIROB: That's the one. That crack isn't there because God just threw the earth together, not caring much about what happened. Nor is it that he cared but didn't know that the geologic processes he used to make the surface of the earth would leave it with big cracks that cause earthquakes. It's not that he cared and knew what would happen, but that it was *the best he could do.* No, your God is completely benevolent, knows everything, and can do anything. So those aren't the right explanations. The explanation is that the devil did it! Or some imp or poltergeist or whatever! That's great, Sam, really great. I not only don't believe that, I don't believe that you believe it.

MILLER: Wait a minute, Gretchen. I don't claim to believe it. For one thing, I'm not bound by the details of stories about the devil—the human features, red costume, pointed tail, and the like. The point simply is that there may be all kinds of benign and evil agents, all sorts of forces for good and evil who are exercising their free will in ways that affect the lives of humans and of other animals, even of baby bats. I don't think that is so absurd. But in any case, I certainly don't claim that you will or should believe it. Remember the rules. I just claim that it is a consistent, coherent *possibility.* My position is that if there is *one way* that an all-perfect God *could* have created a world with the evils of this one, if there is *one* coherent plan we, with our finite, feeble, limited intellects, can sketch—however incompletely and inadequately—then there are many, many more such plans. Most of these we cannot imagine. Perhaps some day, in some future life, more will be revealed to us. Perhaps, when that great day comes, even you will grant how beautiful God's plan is. Until then, my theodicy, my amalgam of Christian doctrine and legend, serves not as a *hypothesis,* but merely as a *proof of consistency.* That's all I claim for it. All of your sarcasm, all of your doubts, your no doubt sincere shock at my story with its heavens and hells and devils and imps—all of it is to no avail. The story is consistent. I have won the bet, you have lost, wiggle and protest as you may!

COHEN: Well, Gretchen, those are the rules you agreed to. Sam didn't have to prove that an all-perfect God was the simplest hypothesis, or the most obvious, or even the most plausible. He only had to show that it was possible. I must admit that he seems to have done that. Can you find a contradiction in his story?

WEIROB: There are a few issues left dangling. What exactly is freedom? Does the Cohen-Miller account of God's knowledge really make God omniscient? Does the concept of an afterlife make sense?

COHEN: But in all fairness, Gretchen, we agreed that Sam didn't have to solve all the problems of philosophy—and in each case, you agreed things were clear enough to proceed.

WEIROB: I suppose there's no getting around it. I should never have agreed to those rules—they let Sam and his God off the hook so easily. Right at this moment, I can't say that I see a contradiction in your story, Sam. It is fantastic and absurd. I know you only present it as a proof of possibility, therefore you win. Your proof, however, has not exactly instilled religious fervor in me.

MILLER: That would be hoping for too much, Gretchen. Mine was a defensive task. I and millions of others believe in a God you said was impossible, given plain and indisputable facts about suffering and evil in our world. I wanted only to show that it was possible. That mere possibility is not the source of our faith, but a defense of it.

WEIROB: Against me, the evil atheist.

MILLER: You are hardly an evil anything. You are a philosopher, and you can be very irritating. . . . But I repeat myself.

WEIROB: Ha, ha.

COHEN: Loosen up a little, Gretchen.

WEIROB: Well, Dave, are you satisfied with Sam's account of joy and suffering, good and evil?

COHEN: I didn't say that. I simply said that in my opinion, he won the bet.

Now that you ask, it seems to me that the godly are not the only ones who have some explaining to do. If we think that the world as a whole is something that just happened, that there is no God—if we think all of that, then where do right and wrong, good and bad, virtue and evil, and all the rest of these things come from?

MILLER: That's a good point, Dave. What principles can a thinker like that—a thinker like you, Gretchen, as far as I can tell—appeal to? What makes something wrong? Not that God disapproves. What's your answer to Augustine's question, "How does evil enter the world?"

WEIROB: Well, since you ask, I'll tell you. In fact, you have helped me clarify my own position. It seems to me that I am, in fact, a Manichaean!

MILLER: A Manichaean! Gretchen, . . .

MILLER: Do you know what the Manichaeans' explanation of good and evil really was?

WEIROB: Certainly not! I might not be a great scholar of Manichaeism, but the central idea seems to me exactly right. The world—more specifically, the earth, the place where we live—is a battleground of good and evil. Both forces are very powerful. It's not at all obvious how the battle will turn out.

COHEN: By "evil" do you simply mean suffering? And by "good" something like pleasure or joy?

WEIROB: No, no, it's not that simple. I do think pleasure and pain are the basis of good and evil. The way I see it, there was no good or evil, no joy or suffering, no pleasure or pain, until some kind of sentient being, a being with experiences, evolved. These experiences were, at least in a primitive sense, pleasurable or painful.

COHEN: Would experience necessarily bring pain and pleasure with it?

WEIROB: I don't really think much of anything is *necessary*. But it seems to me that from the point of view of nature, if you'll allow me to speak that way, pleasure and pain are the point of experience. The basic setup of animals on earth is to seek situations that are pleasurable and avoid those that are painful. That's the basic *architecture*, as people say nowadays.

MILLER: The "point of view of nature." Is nature then a sort of god, with purposes and intentions and points of view?

WEIROB: No, that's not what I mean, although it does sound like it. Talking of nature's point of view is only a useful metaphor. The basic processes of evolution, of unplanned accidental variations, propagation of useful traits, survival of the fittest, and all of that, don't require any purpose-giver or Grand Mind in the background. When I say that pleasure and pain are the point of experience from nature's point of view, I mean that when we ask what experiences would give systems that had these experiences some sort of evolutionary advantage, it has to be their painfulness or pleasantness. It is the connection between those characteristics of experience and the nature of the situations in which they occur that makes them useful. Pain warns of danger, pleasure leads us to be attracted to situations useful for the propagation of our genes. They are not perfect signs, but they must be, or at one time must have been, useful enough so that the capacity for them was developed as animals evolved.

I'm no great expert on this, by the way. If this doesn't satisfy you, I'm stumped.

MILLER: No, that's OK. Go ahead and use your metaphor. I really want to understand how you look at these things.

COHEN: Pleasure and pain are fairly reliable signs of situations that are good or bad for a creature to be in?

WEIROB: It may not be the creatures, but the creatures' genes that are really at stake, that evolution really cares about—so to speak. Pleasure and pain are ways of getting creatures to seek and avoid situations, depending on whether the situations are good or bad for their survival—or the probability of their passing on genes, for which their survival, at least for a while, is a necessary condition.

The main thing is that with sentience, with experience, comes pain and pleasure, and they have an evolutionary point. They are signals, however fallible, of what situations to seek and what to avoid. But the sentient creatures don't have to know the meaning of the signals. They just need to avoid the pain and seek the pleasure.

This whole process has, as one might say, transcended itself.

COHEN: "Transcended itself"? That sounds profound and a bit foggy—it doesn't sound like you, Gretchen.

WEIROB: What I'm getting at is pretty simple. Start with pain. Pain is often a sign of danger. When I touch a hot stove, pain is a signal to move my hand. When I cut myself, pain is a signal to get treatment. But there are all kinds of situations in which there is pain, but no action that can be taken to lessen the danger. Pain can also be a useless signal of something wrong, as in the case of the bat that can do nothing about its situation, or the pain of a terminal illness, or of an injury that has already been treated. . . .

Think of the little bat. Pressure on its wing causes pain, and in a lot of situations, the pain will cause the bat to move the wing, preventing injury and helping the little bat to stay alive until it does whatever bats do to produce more baby bats. Perhaps also the bat's crying gets its mother's attention—I really don't know much about what it's like to be a bat, so I'm making this up. But in the case of the little bat that fell, this mechanism had simply gone crazy, like a car alarm that is uselessly set off, by an explosion that has pretty much destroyed the car anyway. The bat's wing is already broken; it couldn't move it, even if the bat weren't stuck in the guano. But the pain goes on and on.

COHEN: Your picture, then, is this: there is this basic mechanism in which pain signals danger. It gets propagated because it's accurate enough to be useful. But pain also occurs in all sorts of situations in which it does no good. There is a surplus of pain, one might say, all sorts of pain, serving no evolutionary purpose.

WEIROB: Exactly right. And it seems to me that the intentional causing of such pain, pain that does the one who feels the pain no good, is basically what evil is all about. I'm sure this picture has to be qualified in many ways to be an acceptable theory. We think it's OK to cause one person pain in order to save others even more pain—at least some pretty careful thinkers do. Maybe it is, maybe it isn't. Prima facie, as philosophers like to say, causing pain is evil. Perhaps evil occurs only in our little corner of the universe. It requires not only sentient beings, but beings that have the capacity to figure out what situations cause pain for other beings and to form intentions to bring about such situations. But there are plenty of sentient beings on earth, and enough humans to do all sorts of evil. . . .

WEIROB: Think of how we eat. Most of us love fat in its various forms. Who knows why things made with fat give rise to such pleasant tastes? Perhaps long ago this mechanism developed because fat was scarce and a very good thing for animals like us to seek out and eat. But we continue to seek the pleasure that comes with eating fat when the need for the fat is gone, our little taste buds shooting off blasts of pleasure as we gorge ourselves on cookies and pastries and steaks and rolls plastered with butter. This pleasure does not signal a situation that is good for us or for our genes.

MILLER: In fact, we now typically assume that if something tastes good, it is bad for us!

WEIROB: That's pretty much right. But of course, why should nature care if we die of hardening of the arteries or obesity or some other fat-induced problem, as long as it takes long enough to kill us that we have had a good chance to "propagate our genes." . . .

WEIROB: It certainly is good to prevent pointless pain, as well as to promote pointless pleasure. And certainly promoting pleasure that is a signal that one is in a beneficial situation is prima facie OK. Well, let me remind you that I'm not trying to come up with "Gretchen's ethical theory" on the fly here. I'm just trying to provide a simple picture of what, it seems to me, must be at the bottom of the topics I've been giving Sam's religion a hard time about, suffering and evil.

COHEN: How about this: evil is causing unnecessary pain, or preventing harmless pleasure. Good is causing harmless pleasure, or preventing unnecessary pain.

WEIROB: That's good, and it captures what I'm getting at, though I'm sure your statement would need all kinds of elaboration and qualification. But that's basically how I think of suffering and pleasure, good and evil. They are accidents. Pain and pleasure are a strategy that evolution hit upon—metaphorically speaking, Sam—no doubt quite by accident, not as part of any grand design. Good and evil are human concepts that we use to classify intentional action. They are very complicated concepts, and the forms of human pain and pleasure are incredibly diverse and complex. The simple formula Dave gave is much too simple. But I do believe that any reasonable theory of good and evil will ultimately trace these concepts to how acts promote pain and pleasure, suffering and joy. So good and evil are a double accident: first the accident of sentience; second, the accidents that led to the evolution of complex intentional activity of the sort humans engage in.

MILLER: Good and evil are just human inventions, then?

WEIROB: The concepts of good and evil are human inventions. So are the concepts of number, animal, vegetable and mineral, star and planet. That doesn't mean that numbers, animals, vegetables, minerals, stars, and planets were our invention. Things of all those sorts existed long before we came along, and we would not have come along if they hadn't existed. They are real aspects of the world that, as far as we know, only humans have an elaborate enough life to need concepts for. Maybe good and evil are like that.

COHEN: But Gretchen, as I understand your theory, not only are the concepts human inventions, but the aspects we use the concepts to classify are also things that don't exist without humans. The concepts of good and evil classify human activities, right? It sounds to me like you are coming close to saying that good and evil are human inventions, whether you want to or not.

WEIROB: I admit it sounds like that. Maybe it *is* that. I think this is another question we should pursue some day, the whole question of when something is real, and when it is just a human invention. Just remember, locomotives are human inventions. But if one hits you, you will think it is real enough.

But my main point is that whether or not good and evil are just human inventions, it is on earth that good and evil acts occur. And it is certainly a battleground, with lots of good things and lots of evil things happening every day. So in that sense, I am a Manichaean.

MILLER: I'm not sure this rather dismal picture of things is enough to make you a Manichaean.

WEIROB: Well, I guess I'm not, in the sense that I don't think that good and evil are the basic forces in the universe as a whole. But I am in that I think what's important about the universe is the sentient beings in it, which as far as I know or ever

will know are all right here on earth. So good and evil are pretty basic forces in the important part of the universe. And like the Manichaeans, I don't think evil is a creation of good, or vice versa.

MILLER: Manichaean or not, it seems to me a dark picture of the world. Are you sure you don't prefer my picture, silly as you think it is? Wouldn't you prefer to live in a world in which our thoughts and actions had some higher meaning, where all the things we value most, sentience, consciousness, thought, intention, and virtue aren't simply the result of blind processes? As I understand your picture, all that we think of as good, all sacrifice, all art, all culture, all knowledge, and philosophy itself, are the result of processes that once conferred some evolutionary advantage but have since run wild.

WEIROB: My view is certainly something like that. But let me remind you, even if good and evil are products of human activity, what is good is good; what is noble is noble; what isn't, isn't. I don't deny that some things are good or noble and others are evil and base, nor do I say that it is an unimportant distinction.

MILLER: I prefer my mysterious world, with an all-powerful God whose plan we cannot understand, to your picture of human life as a process run amok in a meaningless world.

WEIROB: And you are free to do so! It is your right and privilege. Also, I'm afraid, you have another right and privilege, that of saying a prayer for me, since you seem to have won the bet.

COHEN: I suggest we have dinner at Dorsey's. Sam can say his prayer there, before we eat. Our fellow citizens will be very amused to see Gretchen bow her head.

WEIROB: As a form of humiliation, I suppose that is relatively restrained.

MILLER: Are you feeling well enough to go out, Gretchen?

WEIROB: Yes, I think so. Two days of friends and philosophy are a wonderful tonic. A few aspirin didn't hurt either, and they don't seem to have upset my stomach. Dorsey's will be fun. But if I sneeze in the middle of your prayer, Sam, you mustn't accuse me of impiety.

MILLER: Why, Gretchen, the thought would never occur to me.

NOTES

Augustine's *Confessions* is a fascinating work. He recounts his struggle with the intellectual problem of evil and with giving up what he came to regard as a life of sin after he converted from Manichaeism to Christianity. Augustine is a tremendously important figure in the history of Christianity, the history of philosophy, and the history of literature. His *Confessions* is the first example of autobiography in which the author focuses on his thoughts, motivations, feelings, and inner life. Augustine wrote many other works that consider various aspects of the problem of evil; see especially his *On the Free Choice of the Will*.

David Hume's *Dialogues Concerning Natural Religion* is another historically important and readable work that considers the problem of evil. The considered opinion of Philo, the character who seems to speak for Hume, is that evil is not logically inconsistent with the existence of an all-powerful God, but without some antecedent and unshakable belief in such a God, the evidence of evil would argue overwhelmingly against a benevolent God. Philo concludes that the "cause or causes of order in the universe probably bear some remote analogy to human intelligence," but that it is most likely that that cause (or those causes) does not care one way or another about the suffering of humans and other animals. At one point Philo advances a view that anticipates some of the themes of the theory of evolution (a century before Darwin), and explains the adaptation of animals to their environment by the survival of the fittest rather than by the design and beneficence of God. In the end Philo decides the evolutionary view is absurd.

A number of interesting articles on the problem of evil by twentieth-century philosophers and additional references can be found in the anthologies listed in Further Reading. John Fischer's introduction to *God, Foreknowledge and Freedom* is a valuable guide to much of this literature. Miller's defense of the claim that he doesn't have to argue that this is the best of all possible worlds is taken from Robert Adams's article, "Must God Create the Best," which is reprinted in his *The Virtue of Faith*.

FURTHER READING

Adams, Robert. *The Virtue of Faith*. Oxford: Oxford University Press, 1987.

Augustine. *Confessions*. Indianapolis: Hackett Pub. Co., 1993.

Augustine. *On the Free Choice of the Will*. Indianapolis: Hackett Pub. Co., 1993.

Fischer, John Martin, ed. *God, Foreknowledge and Freedom*. Stanford: Stanford University Press, 1989.

Hume, David. *Dialogues Concerning Natural Religion*. Indianapolis: Hackett Pub. Co., 1998. Second edition.

Pike, Nelson, ed. *God and Evil*. Englewood Cliffs, N.J.: Prentice-Hall, 1964.

Tomberlin, James E., ed. *Philosophical Perspectives*: Vol. 5, *Philosophy of Religion*. Atascadero, Calif.: Ridgeview, 1991.

KEY TERMS

Omnipotent
Omniscient
Theodicy
Freedom
Metaphysical
Free will

STUDY QUESTIONS

1. What is the problem of evil? What sort of conception of God must a believer have in order to have a problem with the existence of evil?

2. What is the difference between showing the possibility that some big picture or other could account for evil, providing a possible big picture, and providing the actual true big picture of how evil is accounted for? Which does Gretchen expect Sam to do?

3. What is a theodicy? Should the theist feel compelled to construct a theodicy? Why or why not?

4. What is Cohen's solution to the problem of how we can be free if God knows ahead of time what we will do? Do you find his solution convincing?

5. Why does Gretchen say, "I should never have agreed to those rules—they let Sam and his God off the hook so easily"?

Horrendous Evils and the Goodness of God

MARILYN McCORD ADAMS

Marilyn McCord Adams (1943–) is a distinguished professor of philosophy at Rutgers University. Her research has primarily been in philosophy of religion, where she has extensively explored the problem of evil, and medieval philosophy, where she has explored various medieval thinkers and the metaphysical and theological issues with which they were engaged. Some of her more recent books include *Some Later Medieval Theories of the Eucharist: Thomas Aquinas, Giles of Rome, Duns Scotus, and William Ockham*; *Christ and Horrors: The Coherence of Christology*; and *Horrendous Evils and the Goodness of God*.

. .

I

Introduction. Over the past thirty years, analytic philosophers of religion have defined 'the problem of evil' in terms of the *prima facie* difficulty in consistently maintaining

(1) God exists, and is omnipotent, omniscient, and perfectly good

and

(2) Evil exists.

In a crisp and classic article 'Evil and Omnipotence',[1] J. L. Mackie emphasized that the problem is not that (1) and (2) are logically inconsistent by themselves, but that they together with quasi-logical rules formulating attribute-analyses—such as

(P1) A perfectly good being would always eliminate evil so far as it could,

and

(P2) There are *no limits* to what an omnipotent being can do,

—constitute an inconsistent premiss-set. He added, of course, that the inconsistency might be removed by substituting alternative and perhaps more subtle analyses, but cautioned that such replacements of (P1) and (P2) would save 'ordinary theism' from his charge of positive irrationality, only if true to its 'essential requirements'.[2]

In an earlier paper 'Problems of Evil: More Advice to Christian Philosophers',[3] I underscored Mackie's point and took it a step further. In debates about whether the argument from evil can establish the irrationality of religious belief, care must be taken, both by the atheologians who deploy it and the believers who defend against it, to insure that the operative attribute-analyses accurately reflect that religion's understanding of Divine power and goodness. It does the atheologian no good to argue for the falsity of Christianity on the ground that the existence of an omnipotent, omniscient, pleasure-maximizer is incompossible with a world such as ours, because Christians never believed God was a pleasure-maximizer anyway. But equally, the truth of Christianity would be inadequately defended by the observation that an omnipotent, omniscient egoist could have created a world with suffering creatures, because Christians insist that God loves other (created) persons than Himself. The extension of 'evil' in (2) is likewise important. Since Mackie and his successors are out to show that 'the several parts of the *essential* theological doctrine are inconsistent with *each other*',[4] they can accomplish their aim only if they circumscribe the

From "Horrendous Evils and the Goodness of God" in *Aristotelian Society: Supp. Vol.* 63, pp. 297–310. Reprinted by courtesy of the Aristotelian Society © 1989.

extension of 'evil' as their religious opponents do. By the same token, it is not enough for Christian philosophers to explain how the power, knowledge, and goodness of God could coexist with some evils or other; a full account must exhibit the compossibility of Divine perfection with evils in the amounts and of the kinds found in the actual world (and evaluated as such by Christian standards).

The moral of my earlier story might be summarized thus: where the internal coherence of a system of religious beliefs is at stake, successful arguments for its inconsistency must draw on premises (explicitly or implicitly) internal to that system or obviously acceptable to its adherents; likewise for successful rebuttals or explanations of consistency. The thrust of my argument is to push both sides of the debate towards more detailed attention to and subtle understanding of the religious system in question.

As a Christian philosopher, I want to focus in this paper on the problem for the truth of Christianity raised by what I shall call **'horrendous' evils**. Although our world is riddled with them, the Biblical record punctuated by them, and one of them—viz., the passion of Christ, according to Christian belief, the judicial murder of God by the people of God—is memorialized by the Church on its most solemn holiday (Good Friday) and in its central sacrament (the Eucharist), the problem of horrendous evils is largely skirted by standard treatments for the good reason that they are intractable by them. After showing why, I will draw on other Christian materials to sketch ways of meeting this, the deepest of religious problems.

II

Defining the Category. For present purposes, I define 'horrendous evils' as 'evils the participation in (the doing or suffering of) which gives one reason *prima facie* to doubt whether one's life could (given their inclusion in it) be a great good to one on the whole'. Such reasonable doubt arises because it is so difficult humanly to conceive how such evils could be overcome. Borrowing Chisholm's contrast between *balancing off* (which occurs when the opposing values of *mutually exclusive* parts of a whole partially or totally cancel each other out) and *defeat* (which cannot occur by the mere addition to the whole of a new part of opposing value, but involves some 'organic unity' among the values of parts and wholes, as when the positive aesthetic value of a whole painting defeats the ugliness of a small colour patch)[5], horrendous evils seem *prima facie*, not only to balance off but to engulf the positive value of a participant's life. Nevertheless, that very horrendous proportion, by which they threaten to rob a person's life of positive meaning, cries out not only to be engulfed, but to be made meaningful through positive and decisive defeat.

I understand this criterion to be objective, but relative to individuals. The example of habitual complainers, who know how to make the worst of a good situation, shows individuals not to be incorrigible experts on what ills would defeat the positive value of their lives. Nevertheless, nature and experience endow people with different strengths; one bears easily what crushes another. And a major consideration in determining whether an individual's life is/has been a great good to him/her on the whole, is invariably and appropriately how it has seemed to him/her.[6]

I offer the following list of paradigmatic horrors: the rape of a woman and axing off of her arms, psychophysical torture whose ultimate goal is the disintegration of personality, betrayal of one's deepest loyalties, cannibalizing one's own offspring, child abuse of the sort described by Ivan Karamazov, child pornography, parental incest, slow death by starvation, participation in the Nazi death camps, the explosion of nuclear bombs over populated areas, having to choose which of one's children shall live and which be executed by terrorists, being the accidental and/or unwitting agent of the disfigurement or death of those one loves best. I regard these as *paradigmatic* because I believe most people would find in the doing or suffering of them *prima facie* reason to doubt the positive meaning of their lives. Christian belief counts the crucifixion of Christ another. On the one hand, death by crucifixion seemed to defeat Jesus' Messianic vocation; for according to Jewish law, death by hanging from a tree made its victim ritually accursed, definitively excluded from the compass of God's people, *a fortiori* disqualified from being the Messiah. On the other hand, it represented the defeat of its perpetrators' leadership vocations, as those who were to prepare the people of God for the Messiah's coming, kill and ritually accurse the true Messiah, according to later theological understanding, God Himself.

III

The Impotence of Standard Solutions. For better or worse, the by-now-standard strategies for 'solving' the problem of evil are powerless in the face of horrendous evils.

3.1 Seeking the Reason Why. In his model article 'Hume on Evil',[7] Pike takes up Mackie's challenge, arguing that (P1) fails to reflect ordinary moral intuitions (more to the point, I would add, Christian beliefs), and traces the abiding sense of trouble to the hunch that an omnipotent, omniscient being could have no reason compatible with perfect goodness for permitting (bringing about) evils, because all legitimate excuses arise from ignorance or weakness. Solutions to the problem of evil have thus been sought in the form of counter-examples to this latter claim, i.e., logically possible reasons why that would excuse even an omnipotent, omniscient God! The putative logically possible reasons offered have tended to be *generic* and *global*: generic insofar as some *general* reason is sought to cover all sorts of evils; global insofar as they seize upon some feature of the world as a whole. For example, philosophers have alleged that the desire to make a world with one of the following properties—'the best of all possible worlds',[8] 'a world a more perfect than which is impossible', 'a world exhibiting a perfect balance of retributive justice',[9] 'a world with as favourable a balance of (created) moral good over moral evil as God can weakly actualize'[10]—would constitute a reason compatible with perfect goodness for God's creating a world with evils in the amounts and of the kinds

found in the actual world. Moreover, such general reasons are presented as so powerful as to do away with any need to catalogue types of evils one by one, and examine God's reason for permitting each in particular. Plantinga explicitly hopes that the problem of horrendous evils can thus be solved without being squarely confronted.[11]

3.2 The Insufficiency of Global Defeat. A pair of distinctions is in order here: (i) between two dimensions of Divine goodness in relation to creation—viz., 'producer of global goods' and 'goodness to' or 'love of individual created persons'; and (ii) between the overbalance/defeat of evil by good on the global scale, and the overbalance/defeat of evil by good within the context of an individual person's life.[12] Correspondingly, we may separate two problems of evil parallel to the two sorts of goodness mentioned in (i).

In effect, generic and global approaches are directed to the first problem: they defend Divine goodness along the first (global) dimension by suggesting logically possible strategies for the global defeat of evils. But establishing God's excellence as a producer of global goods does not automatically solve the second problem, especially in a world containing horrendous evils. For God cannot be said to be good or loving to any created persons the positive meaning of whose lives He allows to be engulfed in and/or defeated by evils—that is, individuals within whose lives horrendous evils remain undefeated. Yet, the only way unsupplemented global and generic approaches could have to explain the latter, would be by applying their general reasons-why to particular cases of horrendous suffering.

Unfortunately, such an exercise fails to give satisfaction. Suppose for the sake of argument that horrendous evil could be included in maximally perfect world orders; its being partially constitutive of such an order would assign it that generic and global positive meaning. But would knowledge of such a fact, defeat for a mother the *prima facie* reason provided by her cannibalism of her own infant, to wish that she had never been born? Again, the aim of perfect retributive balance confers meaning on evils imposed. But would knowledge that the torturer was being tortured give the victim who broke down and turned traitor under pressure, any more reason to think his/her life worthwhile? Would it not merely multiply reasons for the torturer to doubt that his/her life could turn out to be a good to him/her on the whole? Could the truck-driver who accidentally runs over his beloved child find consolation in the idea that this middle-known[13] but unintended side-effect was part of the price God accepted for a world with the best balance of moral good over moral evil He could get?

Not only does the application to horrors of such generic and global reasons for Divine permission of evils fail to solve the second problem of evil; it makes it worse by adding *generic prima facie* reasons to doubt whether human life would be a great good to individual human beings in possible worlds where such Divine motives were operative. For, taken in isolation and made to bear the weight of the whole explanation, such reasons-why draw a picture of Divine indifference or even hostility to the human plight. Would the fact that God permitted horrors because they were constitutive means to His end of global perfection, or that He tolerated them because He could obtain that global end anyway, make the participant's life more tolerable, more worth living for him/her? Given radical human vulnerability to horrendous evils, the ease with which humans participate in them, whether as victim or perpetrator, would not the thought that God visits horrors on anyone who caused them, simply because s/he deserves it, provide one more reason to expect human life to be a nightmare?

Those willing to split the two problems of evil apart might adopt a divide-and-conquer strategy, by simply denying Divine goodness along the second dimension. For example, many Christians do not believe that God will insure an overwhelmingly good life to each and every person He creates. Some say the decisive defeat of evil with good is promised only within the lives of the obedient, who enter by the narrow gate. Some speculate that the elect may be few. Many recognize that the sufferings of this present life are as nothing compared to the hell of eternal torment, designed to defeat goodness with horrors within the lives of the damned.

Such a road can be consistently travelled only at the heavy toll of admitting that human life in worlds such as ours is a bad bet. Imagine (adapting Rawls' device) persons in a pre-original position, considering possible worlds containing managers of differing power, wisdom, and character, and subjects of varying fates. The question they are to answer about each world is whether they would willingly enter it as a human being, from behind a veil of ignorance as to which position they would occupy. Reason would, I submit, dictate a negative verdict for worlds whose omniscient and omnipotent manager permits premortem horrors that remain undefeated within the context of the human participant's life; *a fortiori*, for worlds in which some or most humans suffer eternal torment.

3.3 Inaccessible Reasons. So far, I have argued that generic and global solutions are at best incomplete: however well their account of Divine motivating reasons deals with the first problem of evil, the attempt to extend it to the second fails by making it worse. This verdict might seem *prima facie* tolerable to standard generic and global approaches and indicative of only a minor modification in their strategy: let the above-mentioned generic and global reasons cover Divine permission of non-horrendous evils, and find other *reasons* compatible with perfect goodness *why* even an omnipotent, omniscient God would permit horrors.

In my judgment, such an approach is hopeless. As Plantinga[14] points out, where horrendous evils are concerned, not only do we not know God's *actual* reason for permitting them; we cannot even *conceive* of any plausible candidate sort of reason consistent with worthwhile lives for human participants in them.

IV

The How of God's Victory. Up to now, my discussion has given the reader cause to wonder whose side I am on anyway? For I have insisted, with rebels like Ivan Karamazov and John Stuart Mill, on spotlighting the problem horrendous evils pose. Yet, I have signalled my preference for a vision of Christianity that insists on both dimensions of Divine goodness, and maintains not only (a) that God will be good enough to created persons to make human life a good bet, but also (b) that each created person will have a life that is a great good to him/her on the whole. My critique of standard approaches to the problem of evil thus seems to reinforce atheologian Mackie's verdict of 'positive irrationality' for such a religious position.

4.1 Whys versus Hows. The inaccessibility of reasons-why seems especially decisive. For surely an all-wise and all-powerful God, who loved each created person enough (a) to defeat any experienced horrors within the context of the participant's life, and (b) to give each created person a life that is a great good to him/her on the whole, would not permit such persons to suffer horrors for no reason.[15] Does not our inability even to conceive of plausible candidate reasons suffice to make belief in such a God positively irrational in a world containing horrors? In my judgment, it does not.

To be sure, motivating reasons come in several varieties relative to our conceptual grasp: There are (i) reasons of the sort we can readily understand when we are informed of them (e.g., the mother who permits her child to undergo painful heart surgery because it is the only humanly possible way to save its life). Moreover, there are (ii) reasons we would be cognitively, emotionally, and spiritually equipped to grasp if only we had a larger memory or wider attention span (analogy: I may be able to memorize small town street plans; memorizing the road networks of the entire country is a task requiring more of the same, in the way that proving Gödel's theorem is not). Some generic and global approaches insinuate that Divine permission of evils has motivating reasons of this sort. Finally, (iii) there are reasons that we are cognitively, emotionally, and/ or spiritually too immature to fathom (the way a two-year-old child is incapable of understanding its mother's reasons for permitting the surgery). I agree with Plantinga that our ignorance of Divine reasons for permitting horrendous evils is not of types (i) or (ii), but of type (iii).

Nevertheless, if there are varieties of ignorance, there are also varieties of reassurance. The two-year-old heart patient is convinced of its mother's love, not by her cognitively inaccessible reasons, but by her intimate care and presence through its painful experience. The story of Job suggests something similar is true with human participation in horrendous suffering: God does not give Job His reasons-why, and implies that Job isn't smart enough to grasp them; rather Job is lectured on the extent of Divine power, and sees God's goodness face to face! Likewise, I suggest, to exhibit the logical compossibility of both dimensions of Divine goodness with horrendous suffering, it is not necessary to find logically possible reasons *why* God might permit them. It is enough to show *how* God can be good enough to created persons despite their participation in horrors—by defeating them within the context of the individual's life and by giving that individual a life that is a great good to him/her on the whole.

4.2 What Sort of Valuables? In my opinion, the reasonableness of Christianity can be maintained in the face of horrendous evils only by drawing on resources of religious value theory. For one way for God to be *good to* created persons is by relating them appropriately to relevant and great goods. But philosophical and religious theories differ importantly on what valuables they admit into their ontology. Some maintain that 'what you see is what you get', but nevertheless admit a wide range of valuables, from sensory pleasures, the beauty of nature and cultural artifacts, the joys of creativity, to loving personal intimacy. Others posit a **transcendent good** (e.g. the Form of the Good in Platonism, or God, the Supremely Valuable Object, in Christianity). In the spirit of Ivan Karamazov, I am convinced that the depth of horrific evil cannot be accurately estimated without recognizing it to be incommensurate with any package of merely non-transcendent goods and so unable to be balanced off, much less defeated thereby.

Where the *internal* coherence of Christianity is the issue, however, it is fair to appeal to its own store of valuables. From a Christian point of view, God is a being a greater than which cannot be conceived, a good incommensurate with both created goods and temporal evils. Likewise, the good of beatific, face-to-face intimacy with God is simply incommensurate with any merely non-transcendent goods or ills a person might experience. Thus, the good of beatific face-to-face intimacy with God would *engulf* (in a sense analogous to Chisholmian balancing off) even the horrendous evils humans experience in this present life here below, and overcome any *prima facie* reasons the individual had to doubt whether his/her life would or could be worth living.

4.3 Personal Meaning, Horrors Defeated. Engulfing personal horrors within the context of the participant's life would vouchsafe to that individual a life that was a great good to him/her on the whole. I am still inclined to think it would guarantee that immeasurable Divine goodness to any person thus benefited. But there is good theological reason for Christians to believe that God would go further, beyond engulfment to defeat. For it is the nature of persons to look for meaning, both in their lives and in the world. Divine respect for and commitment to created personhood would drive God to make all those sufferings which threaten to destroy the positive meaning of a person's life meaningful through positive defeat.

How could God do it? So far as I can see, only by integrating participation in horrendous evils into a person's relationship with God. Possible dimensions of integration are charted by Christian soteriology. I pause here to sketch three[16]. (i) First, because God in Christ participated in horrendous evil through His passion and death, human experience of horrors can be a means of *identifying* with Christ, either through *sympathetic* identification (in which each person suffers his/her own pains, but their similarity enables each to know what it is like for the other) or through *mystical* identification (in which the created person is supposed literally to experience a share of Christ's pain[17]). (ii) Julian of Norwich's description of heavenly welcome suggests the possible defeat of horrendous evil through Divine gratitude. According to Julian, before the elect have a chance to thank God for all He has done for them, God will say, 'Thank you for all your suffering, the suffering of your youth'. She says that the creature's experience of Divine gratitude will bring such full and unending joy as could not be merited by the whole sea of human pain and suffering throughout the ages.[18] (iii) A third idea identifies temporal suffering itself with

a vision into the inner life of God, and can be developed several ways. Perhaps, contrary to medieval theology, God is not impassible, but rather has matched capacities for joy and for suffering. Perhaps, as the Heidelberg catechism suggests, God responds to human sin and the sufferings of Christ with an agony beyond human conception.[19] Alternatively, the inner life of God may be, strictly speaking and in and of itself, beyond both joy and sorrow. But, just as (according to Rudolf Otto) humans experience Divine presence now as *tremendum* (with deep dread and anxiety), now as *fascinans* (with ineffable attraction), so perhaps our deepest suffering as much as our highest joys may themselves be direct visions into the inner life of God, imperfect but somehow less obscure in proportion to their intensity. And if a face-to-face vision of God is a good for humans incommensurate with any non-transcendent goods or ills, so any vision of God (including horrendous suffering) would have a good aspect insofar as it is a vision of God (even if it has an evil aspect insofar as it is horrendous suffering). For the most part, horrors are not recognized as experiences of God (any more than the city slicker recognizes his visual image of a brown patch as a vision of Beulah the cow in the distance). But, Christian mysticism might claim, at least from the post-mortem perspective of the beatific vision, such sufferings will be seen for what they were, and retrospectively no one will wish away any intimate encounters with God from his/her life-history of this world. The created person's experience of the beatific vision together with his/her knowledge that intimate Divine presence stretched back over his/her pre-mortem life and reached down into the depths of his/her worst suffering, would provide retrospective comfort independent of comprehension of the reasons-why akin to the two-year-old's assurance of its mother's love. Taking this third approach, Christians would not need to commit themselves about what in any event we do not know: viz., whether we will (like the two-year-old) ever grow up enough to understand the reasons why God permits our participation in horrendous evils. For by contrast with the best of earthly mothers, such Divine intimacy is an incommensurate good and would cancel out for the creature any need to know why.

V

Conclusion. The worst evils demand to be defeated by the best goods. Horrendous evils can be overcome only by the goodness of God. Relative to human nature, participation in horrendous evils and loving intimacy with God are alike disproportionate: for the former threatens to engulf the good in an individual human life with evil, while the latter guarantees the reverse engulfment of evil by good. Relative to one another, there is also disproportion, because the good that God *is*, and intimate relationship with Him, is incommensurate with created goods and evils alike. Because intimacy with God so outscales relations (good or bad) with any creatures, integration into the human person's relationship with God confers significant meaning and positive value even on horrendous suffering. This result coheres with basic Christian intuition: that the powers of darkness are stronger than humans, but they are no match for God!

Standard generic and global solutions have for the most part tried to operate within the territory common to believer and unbeliever, within the confines of religion-neutral value theory. Many discussions reflect the hope that substitute attribute-analyses, candidate reasons-why and/or defeaters could issue out of values shared by believers and unbelievers alike. And some virtually make this a requirement on an adequate solution. Mackie knew better how to distinguish the many charges that may be levelled against religion. Just as philosophers may or may not find the existence of God plausible, so they may be variously attracted or repelled by Christian values of grace and redemptive sacrifice. But agreement on truth-value is not necessary to consensus on **internal consistency**. My contention has been that it is not only legitimate, but, given horrendous evils, necessary for Christians to dip into their richer store of valuables to exhibit the consistency of (1) and (2).[20] I would go one step further: assuming the pragmatic and/or moral (I would prefer to say, broadly speaking, religious) importance of believing that (one's own) human life is worth living, the ability of Christianity to exhibit how this could be so despite human vulnerability to horrendous evil, constitutes a pragmatic/moral/ religious consideration in its favour, relative to value schemes that do not.

To me, the most troublesome weakness in what I have said, lies in the area of conceptual under-development. The contention that God suffered in Christ or that one person can experience another's pain require detailed analysis and articulation in metaphysics and philosophy of mind. I have shouldered some of this burden elsewhere,[21] but its full discharge is well beyond the scope of this paper.[22]

NOTES

1. J. L. Mackie, 'Evil and Omnipotence', *Mind,* 1955; reprinted in Nelson Pike, *God and Evil*, Prentice-Hall Inc., Englewood Cliffs, N.J., 1964, pp. 46–60.
2. Mackie, *op. cit.*, p. 47.
3. Marilyn McCord Adams, 'Problems of Evil: More Advice to Christian Philosophers', *Faith and Philosophy*, April 1988, pp. 121–43.
4. Mackie, *op. cit.*, pp. 46–47.
5. Roderick Chisholm, 'The Defeat of Good and Evil' (unpublished version).
6. Cf. Malcolm's astonishment at Wittgenstein's dying exclamation that he had had a wonderful life, *Ludwig Wittgenstein: A Memoir*, Oxford University Press, London, 1962, p. 100.
7. 'Hume on Evil', *Philosophical Review* LXXII (1963), pp. 180–97; reprinted in *God and Evil*, p. 88.
8. Following Leibniz, Pike draws on this feature as part of what I have called his 'Epistemic Defense' ('Problems of Evil: More Advice to Christian Philosophers', pp. 124–25).
9. Augustine, *On Free Choice of Will* III. 93–102, implies that there is a maximum value for created worlds, and a plurality of worlds that meets it. All of these contain rational free creatures; evils are foreseen but unintended side-effects of their creation. No matter what they choose, however, God can order their choices into a maximally perfect universe by establishing an order of retributive justice.
10. Plantinga takes this line in numerous discussions, in the course of answering Mackie's objection to the Free Will Defence, that God should have made sinless free creatures. Plantinga insists that, given incompatibilist freedom in creatures, God cannot strongly actualize any world He wants. It is

logically possible that a world with evils in the amounts and of the kinds found in this world is the best that He could do, Plantinga argues, given His aim of getting some moral goodness in the world.

11. Alvin Plantinga, 'Self-Profile', in *Alvin Plantinga*, edited by James E. Tomberlin and Peter van Inwagen, D. Reidel Publishing Company (Dordrecht, Boston, Lancaster, 1985), p. 38.

12. I owe the second of these distinctions to a remark by Keith DeRose in our Fall 1987 seminar on the problem of evil at UCLA.

13. Middle knowledge, or knowledge of what is 'in between' the actual and the possible, is the sort of knowledge of what a free creature *would do* in every situation in which that creature could possibly find himself. Following Luis de Molina and Francisco Suarez, Alvin Plantinga ascribes such knowledge to God, prior in the order of explanation to God's decision about which free creatures to actualize (in *The Nature of Necessity*, Oxford University Press, 1974, chapter IX, pp. 164–93). Robert Merrihew Adams challenges this idea in his article 'Middle Knowledge and the Problem of Evil', *American Philosophical Quarterly* 14 (1977); reprinted in *The Virtue of Faith*, Oxford University Press, 1987, pp. 77–93.

14. Alvin Plantinga, 'Self-Profile', *Alvin Plantinga*, pp. 34–35.

15. This point was made by William Fitzpatrick in our Fall 1987 seminar on the problem of evil at UCLA.

16. In my paper 'Redemptive Suffering: A Christian Solution to the Problem of Evil', *Rationality, Religious Belief and Moral Commitment: New Essays in Philosophy of Religion*, ed. by Robert Audi and William J. Wainwright, Cornell University Press, 1986, pp. 248–67, I sketch how horrendous suffering can be meaningful by being made a vehicle of divine redemption for victim, perpetrator, and onlooker, and thus an occasion of the victim's collaboration with God. In 'Separation and Reversal in Luke-Acts', forthcoming in *Philosophy and the Christian Faith*, ed. by Thomas Morris, Notre Dame University Press, Notre Dame, Indiana, 1988, I attempt to chart the redemptive plot-line there, whereby horrendous sufferings are made meaningful by being woven into the redemptive plot. My considered opinion is that such collaboration would be too strenuous for the human condition were it not to be supplemented by a more explicit and beatific divine intimacy.

17. For example, Julian of Norwich tells us that she prayed for and received the latter (*Revelations of Divine Love*, chapter 17). Mother Teresa of Calcutta seems to construe Matthew 25:31–46 to mean that the poorest and the least *are* Christ, and that their sufferings *are* Christ's (Malcolm Muggeridge, *Something Beautiful for God*, Harper & Row, Publishers, New York 1960, pp. 72–75).

18. *Revelations of Divine Love*, chapter 14. I am grateful to Houston Smit for recognizing this scenario of Julian's as a case of Chisholmian defeat.

19. Cf. Plantinga, 'Self-Profile', *Alvin Plantinga*, p. 36.

20. I develop this point at some length in 'Problems of Evil: More Advice to Christian Philosophers', pp. 127–35.

21. For example in 'The Metaphysics of the Incarnation in Some Fourteenth Century Franciscans', *Essays Honoring Allan B. Wolter*, edited by William A. Frank and Girard J. Etzkorn, The Franciscan Institute, St. Bonaventure, N.Y. 1985, pp. 21–57.

22. In the development of these ideas, I am indebted to the members of our Fall 1987 seminar on the problem of evil at UCLA—especially to Robert Merrihew Adams (its co-leader) and to Keith DeRose, William Fitzpatrick, and Houston Smit. I am also grateful to the Very Reverend Jon Hart Olson for many conversations in mystical theology.

KEY TERMS

Horrendous evil
Balancing off
Defeat
Transcendent good
Internal consistency

STUDY QUESTIONS

1. What does Adams mean by a "horrendous evil"?
2. Why does Adams want to focus on *horrendous* evils, rather than other varieties of evil?
3. Adams borrows Chisholm's distinction between "balancing off" and "defeat." What is meant by these terms? And what role do they play in Adams's paper?
4. What is the traditional solution to the problem of evil? Why does Adams think it is an incomplete solution?
5. What does Adams mean by the term "transcendent good," and what role does this notion play in her solution to the problem of evil?

Horrendous Evils and the Goodness of God

STEWART SUTHERLAND

Lord Sutherland of Houndwood (1941–) is provost of Gresham College. In addition to his academic career, Lord Sutherland has served many public service roles in Britain. Within philosophy, he is most known for his work within the philosophy of religion, and for his engagement with certain continental thinkers, such as Dostoevsky and Kierkegaard. Among his publications are *Atheism and the Rejection of God* (1977), *God, Jesus, and Belief* (1984), and *Faith and Ambiguity* (1984).

. .

I

I was stupid and callous enough to go and see an execution this morning . . . the spectacle made such an impression on me that I shan't get over it for a long time. I've seen many horrible things in war and in the Caucasus but if a man had been torn to pieces before my eyes it wouldn't have been so revolting as this ingenious and elegant machine by means of which a strong, hale and hearty man was killed in an instant. In war it's not a question of the rational will, but of human feelings of passion; but in this case it's cold, refined calculation and a convenient way of murder, and there's nothing grand about it. It's the insolent arrogant desire to carry out justice and the law of God—justice, which is determined by lawyers taking their stand on honour, religion and truth, and all contradicting each other . . . Then the repulsive crowd, the father explaining to his daughter, the convenient and ingenious mechanism that does it . . . The law of man—what nonsense! The truth is that the state is a conspiracy designed not only to exploit but above all to corrupt its citizens . . . I will certainly never go and see such a thing again, and I will never serve *any* government anywhere.[1]

From "Horrendous Evils and the Goodness of God" in *Aristotelian Society: Supp. Vol.* 63(1989): 311–323. Reprinted by courtesy of the Aristotelian Society © 1989.

So Tolstoy on the guillotine in a letter from Paris in April 1857. The horror of what he saw remained with him throughout his life and he described it starkly twenty years later:

When I saw the head part from the body and how it thumped separately into the box, I understood, not with my mind, but with my whole being that no theory of the reasonableness of our present progress could justify this deed, and that though everyone from the creation of the world, on whatever theory, had held it to be necessary, I knew it would be unnecessary and bad. . .[2]

Tolstoy's most recent biographer, whose translation of this paragraph of Tolstoy's *Confession* is used here, tells us that Tolstoy was unable to sleep for days after witnessing the execution. By secular analogy with Marilyn Adams' examples, this is undoubtedly a case of **horrendous evil**, as perceived by Tolstoy. His sensibilities were outraged and he refused to countenance any way in which that practice could be reconciled with a theory of human law based upon the idea of human progress. Equally, he finally lost any belief in the benevolent powers of the state. Interestingly, however, others witnessed the event without similar alienating consequences. Doubtless in some cases the differences are to be explained in terms of a hardening of the arteries of sensibility or of sheer indifference, and in others in terms of the elaborate rationale of the good of society at large.

Nonetheless there are several points of difference between this horrendous evil and Tolstoy's response to it, and the reactions of Professor Adams to the horrendous evils which she enumerates and defines. Most significantly Professor Adams argues that within Christian theism there are resources available adequate to 'engulf' and even **'defeat'** the worst of horrendous evils. I propose to use the contrast with the Tolstoy example to attempt to clarify the basis upon which she makes this important claim. Initially it should be noted that there are three particular significant differences.

In the first place, in tones which would have been congenial to Ivan Karamazov, Tolstoy writes,

> . . . though everyone from the creation of the world, on whatever theory had held it to be necessary, I knew it would be unnecessary and bad . . .

His moral vision is trusted on this point beyond anything else. This primacy of the moral is not explicitly rejected by Professor Adams, but, as I hope to show, it is implicitly set aside. In the second place, in a way that is quite critical for Adams' case there are fundamentally immanent parameters to Tolstoy's example of horrendous evil and his reaction to it. The essence of the Christian case as outlined by Adams is that the only solution lies in extending these parameters to include the possibility of **'transcendent' good** which can be set against immanent horrendous evil. The two points are related to one another in ways which will bear further exploration.

There is a third general point highlighted by the Tolstoy example which may or may not be of real significance. It is this. I am using the expression 'horrendous evil' *via* Tolstoy in a way which may call in question the definition offered by Professor Adams (Section *III*—Defining the Category). She seems there to limit 'horrendous evils' to evils in which we, who use the term, participate either by 'doing or suffering' them. In fact my use of the term is wider than that qualification strictly allows. Tolstoy, like Ivan, views as horrendous the evils suffered by others to which they have only a secondary relation involving neither the doing nor the primary suffering. The importance of this extension will become apparent in due course.

II

The strength of Professor Adams' case can be measured by our success in finding relevant differences between the Christian's response to the horrendous evils which she defines and enumerates and Tolstoy's response to the efficient horrors of the guillotine which he witnessed. She offers two main but interrelated suggestions which can help us plot what these differences are. The first is to draw a distinction between 'Why?' answers to the problems which these evils pose, and 'How?' answers. The second is to stress that:

> God is a being greater than which cannot be conceived, a good incommensurate with both created goods and temporal evils.

In this section of the paper I wish to examine the first of these points and its implications for religious belief, all the time bearing in mind Professor Adams' insistence that her paper is primarily concerned with the internal consistency of Christian belief rather than with the broader question of the truth or acceptability of Christian beliefs.

Adams concedes that in ruling out 'Why?' answers to the problems of horrendous evils she might seem to be giving away too much. Nonetheless she is crystal clear on this point:

> . . . where horrendous evils are concerned, not only do we not know God's actual reason for permitting them; we cannot even *conceive* of any plausible candidate sort of reason consistent with worthwhile lives for human participants in them.

She does however, also insist that the limitations here are human limitations and that

> there are reasons which we are cognitively, emotionally and/or spiritually too immature to fathom.

The negative side of that (our inability to fathom) has been well explored by writers as diverse as Hume and Dostoevsky, as Kant and Camus. Adams' substitution of 'How?' for 'Why?' proposes that since we cannot in this area at least find reasons for rejecting sceptical conclusions by defeating those conclusions in terms recognisable to the sceptic, we should look rather for the ways in which (how) God might reassure the believer by trumping ('defeating') the evil Ace of Clubs with the great and good Ace of Hearts. Before we turn to the question of what content to give to the 'Ace of Hearts', we must first consider the implications of the replacement of the language of persuasion by the language of reassurance.

The first question which must arise is whether this tactic is designed to deny altogether that there is an intellectual question at stake here at all. The spirit as well as the letter of Professor Adams' paper makes it clear that she is not advocating such a radical proposal. Christian belief is still concerned with reasons and reasonableness. The role of reason in this particular topic is to deny the adequacy of candidates for answer to the question of why God permits horrendous evils. I am unclear whether, according to Adams, *reason* tells us that we are 'cognitively, emotionally, and/or spiritually too immature to fathom'. I suspect, to be more precise, that Adams would claim that within the system of Christian beliefs which she inhabits it is plausible, and therefore up to a point reasonable, to assume such a degree of immaturity.

If that is the case then the question becomes one of what happens to the intellectual Why-question within this substitution of the language of reassurance for the language of persuasion. Clearly Adams does not discount the importance of these questions. Why else should she wrestle with them in such persistent fashion? Even less does she follow those who would discount them as foolish or even in some unspecified sense 'unreal' questions. Her paper suggests that our immaturity shows itself not in the *questions*, as some would allege, but in the inability to perceive *answers*. Thus we must assume that the Why-questions are somehow displaced from the centre of our preoccupations, and properly so in the light of reassurances given.

Let us consider such a proposal first by reference to Tolstoy's horror at the execution. Interestingly, as we noticed, he was surrounded by people who felt no such horror. For Tolstoy the question 'Why?' had no acceptable answer. Thus there was no context within which his sense of horror might be dispelled. The possible explanations for the absence of this sense of horror in those around could imply that some adequate explanation of why this should happen in this manner could be given. Tolstoy unequivocally rejects this possibility as, *mutatis mutandis*, does Professor Adams, so we need pursue it no further in this paper.

Two other possibilities occur, the first of which Adams would certainly reject, although as a matter of fact there are those, including Tolstoy in other contexts, who would level this as a serious charge against some forms of religious belief. This is the possibility that those who see no horror in the execution, or, in the religious context, see no *horrendous* evils, are simply cold or indifferent. Again we can leave this explanation aside since although as a matter of fact it may be the correct one in individual cases, there is no necessary connection between this attitude and religious belief. (Tolstoy's reasonably consistent anarchism however, did see a causal connection between the state and such moral corruption.)

The second possibility is a more serious though less clear matter. In the context of the guillotine it amounts to the proposal that the Why-question is deflected or displaced by engaging the intellect and associated emotions elsewhere perhaps by bread and circuses or some twentieth-century equivalences such as the cry of 'law and order' or 'a chicken in every pot'. For Tolstoy such subjugation of intellect and primary moral emotion would be anathema and could only be achieved by change in moral belief and moral perception. He is refusing to accept that any end could morally justify adopting this means. His case then depends upon the affirmation that there is no rational or moral argument which can persuade him of the error of his moral perception that execution by guillotine is horrendously evil.

What could such an argument, rational and moral, look like? It would have to have as its end product either a specific change in Tolstoy's moral perception, or alternatively it would have to upset the whole applecart of Tolstoy's moral beliefs and sensibilities. In the former case it could in principle be achieved by the sort of elaborate and persuasive argument found in, say the Socratic Dialogues, where Socrates' unsuspecting conversational companions were led to re-evaluate specific moral beliefs such as in *Republic I* that justice is the interest of the strongest. In the latter case what would be required would be perhaps persuasion to accept a radical form of moral scepticism such that the force of particular moral feelings, however great, would be, to use Professor Adams' expression, 'engulfed' or 'defeated'.

Implicit in the passages quoted from Tolstoy, and explicit elsewhere in Tolstoy's writings is the proposal of an alternative, and he claims, more plausible hypothesis compatible with and therefore supporting the primacy of his moral sensibilities: it is in the interests of the state not only to offer rationalisation of the practice of execution by guillotine, but to distract ('corrupt' is his term) the attention which otherwise the citizen might give to this event.

Now the point of all this is not here to defend Tolstoy's views but to use this case of secular horror to highlight quite precisely what it is that Professor Adams must achieve if she is to displace in the religious case the Why-question with the How-question, and do this by identifying forms of reassurance available within the religious tradition which are not paralleled elsewhere. She indicates in principle agreement with this diagnosis in writing:

In my opinion, the reasonableness of Christianity can be maintained in the face of horrendous evils only by drawing on resources of religious value theory,

and,

In the spirit of Ivan Karamazov, I am convinced that the depth of horrific evil cannot be accurately estimated without recognising it to be incommensurate with any package of merely non-transcendent goods and so unable to be balanced off, much less defeated thereby.

That is to say, *mutatis mutandis*, if the Tolstoy example is one of horrendous evil, of course there can be rationally or morally persuasive argument which engulfs or defeats the horror either by adequate explanation or by bringing a change in moral evaluation by proposing a different balance of immanent goods. To return to an earlier, and, I hope, not over-frivolous comparison, Tolstoy is in a no-Trump game. There is, at the immanent level, no trump suit, and the Ace of Hearts cannot 'defeat' the Ace of Clubs.

In the game in which Professor Adams plays, however, the Ace of Hearts will triumph, because it represents a transcendent good, and we must now consider the implications of this for our account of the nature of the religious/Christian belief. The central point which arises from the comparison with Tolstoy's example is that at its minimum the defeat of the horrendous evil requires a significant qualification of the initial moral perceptions and commitments which lead to the classification of evils as horrendous evils. That is to say, the individual must, in the end come to the view that viewed in a proper light horrendous evils are not so bad after all! Whereas in the secular case, Tolstoy cannot conceive of immanent goods which in compensation or reassurance will bring him to such a view, it is claimed that in the religious case the believer does have access to transcendent goods which can so defeat horrendous evil.

It would be as well at this stage to remind ourselves of what seemed a minor point made at the very end of the first section of this paper. For *Tolstoy*, in part, the horror of what he witnessed arises because it is happening to someone else and because it is being done to that person. (The *poor* victim however might well have drawn no significant richer differences in the horror scale between death by guillotine, by firing squad, by sniper's bullet or by sudden massive coronary. It would require a pretty cool and subtle mind to draw such distinctions at that stage in one's nearly finished history.) Although she cites with approval Ivan Karamazov it is not wholly clear from her paper whether Professor Adams takes on board fully the point that what horrifies Ivan is that these awful things should happen to others—in his examples to small children. If his main preoccupation is with what this does to *his* sense of the meaning of life then he is a *voyeur* who weeps self-indulgent tears.

This point and Professor Adams' view of it is quite critical to her main thesis that Christian consistency can be maintained when we experience *how* God can reassure us. The difference can be well illustrated by appealing to one of her own examples:

> The story of Job suggests something similar is true with human participation in horrendous suffering: God does not give Job His reasons-why, and implies that Job isn't smart enough to grasp them; rather Job is lectured on the extent of Divine power, and sees God's goodness face to face!

In irreverent moments one might be inclined to think, 'Bully for Job! But if he had kept his wits about him he might have asked whether all those deaths (of others) in his family were strictly necessary in order to teach him that particular lesson'. Whatever reassurance he felt, or which in another novel might have come Ivan's way, 'What about the others?' is the nub of Ivan's question.

This raises the fundamental question of what reassurance by transcendent goods does to the believer's moral sensibilities and commitments? Here there is, I believe, an ambiguity in Professor Adams' position about whether she is restricted in her discussion to the horrendous evils which we individually suffer, or whether her 'solution' applies also to our perception of what is horrendous in the suffering of others (cf. Tolstoy and Ivan).

In the former case it may well be that the transcendent goods which Adams posits (if they are real) can defeat by displacing the impact of horrendous suffering. Most of us can think of secular, immanent, analogues of this in our own experience: the grief is finally displaced; the pain does ultimately disappear; the harm done ceases to fill

the horizon because it is overtaken by a greater good. Even here, however, there is a difference between the reasons which might lead one to say, 'Painful though it was, I'm glad that I was turned down for that job'. In one case the reason might be, 'Because I now realise they were right in their judgement and I would not have been up to it'. There one's beliefs about the justice of the original judgement have undergone change. In a second case, the reason might be, 'Because since then the UGC has recommended closure of that Department. However', one might add, 'that does not change the fact that it was quite unjust to appoint Bloggs instead'. Here, one's sense of justice, right or wrong, is unaltered.

On one account of Professor Adams' position the reassurance does not alter the original moral assessment that these evils are horrendous, because it is a How-answer—a displacement of the question—rather than a Why-answer—a persuasion that our judgement was clouded at the time. My difficulty with this conclusion, if it is the one reached by Adams, is that it is not only the *question* which is displaced. The moral sensibilities and beliefs which gave form to the question are also displaced, and that is a high price (indeed, I should say, too great a price) to pay. I believe in fact that the difficulties become even more acute if we agree that horrendous evils are not restricted to those evils which we directly suffer, but include (in fact for Ivan were pre-eminently) evils which we perceive others to suffer and which because of that, horrify us.

III

We must now consider further the second main element of Adams' case for the consistency of the Christian's refusal to be overwhelmed by horrendous evils: that there are transcendent goods which engulf and defeat horrendous evil: this defence both stands as a separate proposed bulwark, and (as we have seen) is also one of the ways in which the substitution of How-questions for Why-questions might be supported.

Professor Adams' view is that there are goods or values not dreamt of in the view of those who believe that recognition of horrendous evils is incompatible with Christian belief:

> ... philosophical and religious theories differ importantly on what valuables they admit into their ontology.

Thus the resolution of the matter seems to be in terms of recognising different theories which differ precisely on the point of whether there are within the one transcendent goods which will defeat the horrendous evils recognised by both.

The distinction between 'engulfing' and 'defeating' horrendous evils plays an important part in this section of Professor Adams' exposition. Thus she claims that, for example, face to face intimacy with God would engulf horrendous evils in the sense that

> within the context of the participant's life (they) would vouchsafe to that individual a life that was a great good to him/her on the whole.

The logic of this seems to be quite clear and it is a question of whether what seemed to be beyond reparation is in fact not so. (Whether the language of 'face to face intimacy' with an eternal God stands up to detailed scrutiny is another matter.) Transcendent goods can, it is proposed, 'engulf' the most intractable of immanent evils.

The 'defeat' of horrendous evils, however, seems to be an even more difficult conception to grasp and not surprisingly at the tail end of a paper Professor Adams is not unaware of the need for fuller development of the very complex theological notions to which she alludes.

Notwithstanding the problems in either case, there is a number of more general comments which can be made, and which can be introduced by offering specific questions for Professor Adams' consideration.

1. What of those others who suffer? Ivan's question will continue to force itself upon us which is why the Tolstoy example is pertinent. Either, Professor Adams accepts that 'horrendous evils' are not restricted to this suffering which *I* experience, in which case how does *my* face-to-face intimacy with God help? Or, she restricts 'horrendous evils' to this harm which *I* suffer and her thesis is much less far-reaching than had first appeared.

2. What of those who do not experience such transcendent bliss? Is such a lack attributable to them or to God? Sometimes it would seem that the mysterious ways in which God moves have a dark selective underside, or alternatively that the believer is committed to the belief that the victim is responsible for being so immature as to see him or herself only as victim. The latter may be so in some cases, and therapy has been known to help, but as Professor Adams agrees, in this discussion we are considering horrendous evils which have no non-transcendent counter-weights.

3. Is there a common moral language between believers and non-believers? On the face of it Professor Adams' response to this question seems to be, 'Yes and No'. The affirmative element can be traced to the common moral response to 'horrendous evils', shared by believer and non-believer. The negative element is based upon Professor Adams' insistence on the distinction between 'religious value theory' (p. 119) and 'religion-neutral value theory' (p. 121). Believers recognise a range of goods (transcendent) which have no place in the moral language of non-believers. This raises a further important question about the relation of the view of the non-believer to that of the believer to which we must now turn.

4. What does such a theory as that offered by Professor Adams do to our moral sensibilities and perceptions? For the believer it allows the possibility of both engulfing and defeating horrendous evils. But does this possibility imply also the engulfing and defeat of at least some elements of our moral sensibilities and perceptions? What changes take place in the believer who is thus reassured? I have already ruled out the possibility that Adams is advocating a form of indifference comparable to those in the crowd who did not share Tolstoy's horror at

execution by guillotine, and I must assume that the sort of theologically-based assurance being proposed is much more than a sophisticated warm glow within.

Is defeat then accomplished by a shift in moral perspective? It is difficult to construe what is proposed in any other way since the essential question is whether this evil, characterised by the term 'horrendous' and which appeared to be beyond reparation, is in fact beyond reparation. Professor Adams' reply is that for the believer no evil need be so perceived. The Ace of Hearts is in that sense a trump card. However, to accept it as such is to have altered one's moral priorities and that cannot be done without a shift in moral perception. There are at least two different ways in which this might happen. The first is that one might be persuaded by moral reasoning to change one's view but on the whole Professor Adams seems not to favour this account of the change. The main alternative then is to accept that without good moral reason one permits at least a limit or qualification to be placed upon the importance which one had previously attached to regarding this evil as horrendous. To qualify one's moral perceptions, even in that way, is nonetheless to *change* them in the extreme cases which we are considering.

A final point to conclude this section of the discussion is to suggest that even if we do play by the rules of consistency suggested by Professor Adams, the questions of theodicy still arise. When, or if, we see God face to face we might still wish to ask with Ivan, 'What about the children?' If the answer to that is that it is only post-mortem that such questions will be finally stilled (or answered?) then the difference between such a believer and Ivan would seem to be over what is meant by 'horrendous'. Ivan's essentially moral question is,

If all have to suffer so as to buy eternal harmony by their suffering, what have the children to do with it—tell me please? It is entirely incomprehensible why they should have to buy harmony by their sufferings. Why should they too be used as dung for someone's future harmony?

My suspicion is that when Professor Adams refers to 'horrendous evil' she is implicitly translating that as 'immense or disproportionate harm' which befalls an individual. In that case it is a matter for the individual to be satisfied or not, in his or her *own* case, as to whether that harm is outweighed by immense or disproportionate (= transcendent) good. If however, one remains with Ivan, or for the sake of illustration, Tolstoy's reaction to the guillotine, the notion of horrendous evil is one which focusses upon the moral notions of injustice (Ivan) or coldbloodedness (Tolstoy). Such an evil is not so obviously susceptible of being outweighed, and that on two counts. In the first place it is not a matter on which one individual can pronounce on behalf of others. In the second place, moral judgement should only reasonably and properly be set aside on the grounds of either error or irrelevance. It is difficult to agree that Professor Adams has substantiated either of these two grounds.

IV

Conclusion. The differences between Professor Adams and myself could be simplified by focussing upon the extent to which we agree, firstly upon whether the characterisation of evils as horrendous is a moral judgement, and secondly if so, whether there are conceivable circumstances in which such an apparently absolute moral judgement can be defeated. Professor Adams makes it plain that her concern in this symposium is with the consistency rather than the truth of Christian belief. Since I am inclined to believe that truth in these matters has much to do with what is conceivable as consistent I find it difficult to argue as if the distinction between truth and consistency can be so clearly drawn here. Nonetheless even if the distinction is pressed, there is still the question of whether such a God as Professor Adams envisages would wilfully behave in such a way as to undermine the importance and correctness of the judgements (about horrendous evils) which arise from the frail and infrequently encountered flowers of refined moral sensibility.

NOTES

1. L. Tolstoy, Letter to V. P. Botkin in *Tolstoy's Letters* Vol 1, selected, edited and translated by B. F. Christian, Athlone Press, 1978. See pp. 95–6.

2. From Tolstoy's *Confession*. This paragraph is translated and quoted by A. N. Wilson in *Tolstoy*, Hamish Hamilton, 1988. See pp. 146–7.

KEY TERMS

Horrendous evil
Defeat
Transcendent good

STUDY QUESTIONS

1. What happened to Tolstoy? And how was this a horrendous evil?
2. Sutherland distinguishes between a language of persuasion and a language of reassurance. What does he mean by these phrases? Why are they relevant for thinking about Adams's argument?
3. What worries does Sutherland have about Adams's position? And what role does Tolstoy's experience with an execution play in motivating his worries?
4. Do you think Sutherland is right to be so concerned with third-party moral assessments of horrendous evil?

The Mirror of Evil

ELEONORE STUMP

Eleonore Stump is Robert J. Henle Professor of Philosophy at Saint Louis University. She has written extensively on metaphysics, philosophy of religion, and medieval philosophy. Some of her recent books include an exploration of the problem of evil, *Wandering in Darkness: Narrative and the Problem of Suffering* (2010), and a study of Thomas Aquinas, titled *Aquinas* (2003).

. .

There are different ways to tell the story of one's own coming to God. Straightforward autobiography has its merits, but, paradoxically, it can leave out the most important parts. I want to tell my story in a roundabout way that will, I hope, show directly what for me is and always has been the heart of the matter.

For reflective people, contemplation of human suffering tends to raise the **problem of evil**. If there is

From *God and the Philosophers*, edited by Thomas Morris. © 1994 by Oxford University Press.

an omnipotent, omniscient, perfectly good God, how can it be that the world is full of evil? This response to evil is normal and healthy. I have discussed this problem myself in print and tried to find a solution to it. But there is another way to think about evil.

Consider just these examples of human suffering, which I take from my morning newspaper. Although the Marines are in Somalia, some armed Somalis are still stealing food from their starving neighbors, who are dying by the thousands. Muslim women and girls, some as young as ten years old, are being raped and tortured by Serb soldiers. In India, Hindus went on a rampage that razed a mosque and killed over

1,000 people. In Afghanistan gunmen fired into a crowded bazaar and shot ten people, including two children. Closer to home, the R. J. Reynolds company is trying to defend itself against charges that it is engaged in a campaign to entice adolescents to smoke. The recently defeated candidate for governor in my state, as well as lawyers and doctors employed by the state as advocates for disabled workers, are charged with stealing thousands of dollars from the fund designed for those workers. A high school principal is indicted on charges of molesting elementary and middle school boys over a period of twenty years. A man is being tried for murder in the death of a nine-year-old boy; he grabbed the boy to use as a shield in a gunfight. I could go on—racism, rape, assault, murder, greed and exploitation, war and genocide—but this is enough. By the time you read these examples, they will be dated, but you can find others just like them in your newspaper. There is no time, no part of the globe, free from evil. The crust of the earth is soaked with the tears of the suffering.

This evil is a mirror for us. It shows us our world; it also shows us ourselves. How could anyone steal at gunpoint food meant for starving children? How could anyone rape a ten-year-old girl? How could anyone bear to steal money from disabled workers or get rich by selling a product he knows will damage the health of thousands? But people do these things, and much worse things as well. We ourselves—you and I, that is—are members of the species that does such things, and we live in a world where the wrecked victims of this human evil float on the surface of all history, animate suffering flotsam and jetsam. The author of Ecclesiastes says, "I observed all the oppression that goes on under the sun: the tears of the oppressed with none to comfort them; and the power of their oppressors—with none to comfort them. Then I accounted those who died long since more fortunate than those who are still living" (4:1–2).[1]

Some people glance into the **mirror of evil** and quickly look away. They take note, shake their heads sadly, and go about their business. They work hard, they worry about their children, they help their friends and neighbors, and they look forward to Christmas dinner. I don't want to disparage them in

any way. Tolkien's hobbits are people like this. There is health and strength in their ability to forget the evil they have seen. Their good cheer makes them robust.

But not everybody has a hobbit's temperament. Some people look into the mirror of evil and can't shut out the sight. You sit in your warm house with dinner on the table and your children around you, and you know that not far from you the homeless huddle around grates seeking warmth, children go hungry, and every other manner of suffering can be found. Is it human, is it decent, to enjoy your own good fortune and forget their misery? But it's morbid, you might say, to keep thinking about the evils of the world; it's depressive; it's sick. Even if that were true, how would you close your mind to what you'd seen once you'd looked into the mirror of evil?

Some people labor at obliviousness. They drown their minds in drinking, or they throw themselves into their work. At certain points in his life, Camus seems to have taken this tack. He was at Le Chambon writing feverishly, and obliviously, while the Chambonnais were risking their lives rescuing Jews.[2] Jonathan Swift, whose mordant grasp of evil is evident in his writings, was chronically afflicting with horror at the world around him; he favored violent exercise as an antidote.[3] The success of this sort of strategy, if it ever really does succeed, seems clearly limited.

Some people believe that evil can be eliminated, that Eden on earth is possible. Whatever it is in human behavior or human society that is responsible for the misery around us can be swept away, in their view. They are reformers on a global scale. The moral response to suffering, of course, is the **Good Samaritan's**: doing what we can to stop the suffering, to help those in need. Global reformers are different from Good Samaritans, though; global reformers mean to remove the human defects that produced the evil in the first place. The failure of the great communist social experiment is a sad example of the problems with this approach to evil. Every good family runs on the principle "from each according to his ability; to each according to his need." The extended human family in Eastern Europe intended to run on this principle and turned it instead into "from each according to his weakness; to each according to his greed." Ecclesiastes sums up the long-term prospects for global reform in this way: "I observed all the happenings beneath the sun, and I found that all is futile and pursuit of wind; a twisted thing that cannot be made straight, a lack that cannot be made good" (1:14–15).

And don't reason and experience suggest that Ecclesiastes has the right of it? The author of Ecclesiastes says, "I set my mind to study and to probe with wisdom all that happens under the sun . . . and I found that all is futile . . . as wisdom grows, vexation grows; to increase learning is to increase heartache" (1:13, 14, 18). This is a view that looks pathological to the hobbits of the world. But whether it *is* pathological depends on whose view of the world is right, doesn't it? A hobbit in a leper colony in a cheerful state of denial, oblivious to the disease in himself and others, wouldn't be mentally healthy either, would he? Ecclesiastes recognizes the goodness of hobbits. The author says over and over again, "eat your bread in gladness, and drink your wine in joy; . . . enjoy happiness with a woman you love all the fleeting days of life that have been granted to you under the sun" (9:7, 9). But the ability to eat, drink, and be merry in this way looks like a gift of God, a sort of blessed irrationality. For himself, Ecclesiastes says, "I loathed life. For I was distressed by all that goes on under the sun, because everything is futile and pursuit of wind" (2:17).

So, some people react with loathing to what they can't help seeing in the mirror of evil—loathing of the world, loathing of themselves. This malaise of spirit is more likely to afflict those living in some prosperity and ease, inhabitants of the court, say, or college students on scholarship. If you've just been fired or told you have six months to live or have some other large and urgent trouble, you're likely to think that you would be happy and life would be wonderful if only you didn't have *that* particular affliction. Given the attitude of Ecclesiastes, it's not surprising that the book was attributed to Solomon, who was as known for wealth and power as for wisdom.

The misery induced by the mirror of evil is vividly described by Philip Hallie in his book on Le Chambon.[4] Hallie had been studying cruelty for years and was working on a project on the Nazis. His focus was the medical experiments carried out on Jewish children in the death camps. Nazi doctors broke and rebroke "the bones of six- or seven- or eight-year-old Jewish children in order, the Nazis said, to study the processes of natural healing in young bodies" (p. 3). "Across all these studies," Hallie says, "the pattern of the strong crushing the weak kept repeating itself and repeating itself, so that when I was not bitterly angry, I was bored at the repetition of the patterns of persecution. . . . My study of evil incarnate had become a prison whose bars were my bitterness toward the violent, and whose walls were my horrified indifference to slow murder. Between the bars and the walls I revolved like a madman. . . . over the years I had dug myself into Hell" (p. 2).

Hallie shares with the author of Ecclesiastes an inability to look away from the loathsome horrors in the mirror of evil. The torment of this reaction to evil is evident, and it seems the opposite of what we expect from a religious spirit. It's no wonder that some people think Ecclesiastes has no place in the canonical Scriptures. To see why this view of Ecclesiastes is mistaken, we have to think not just about our reactive attitudes toward evil but also about our recognition of evil.

How does Hallie know—how do we know—that the torture of Jewish children by Nazi doctors is evil?

By reason, we might be inclined to answer. But that answer is not entirely right. It's true that our moral principles and our ethical theories rely on reason. But we build those principles and theories, at least in part, by beginning with strong intuitions about individual cases that exemplify wrongdoing, and we construct our ethical theories around those intuitions. We look for what the individual cases of wrongdoing have in common, and we try to codify their common characteristics into principles. Once the principles have been organized into a theory, we may also revise our original intuitions until we reach some point of reflective equilibrium, where our intuitions and theories are in harmony. But our original intuitions retain an essential primacy. If we found that our ethical theory countenanced those Nazi experiments on children, we'd throw away the theory as something evil itself.

But what exactly are these original intuitions? What cognitive faculty produces them? Not reason, apparently, since reason takes them as given and reflects on them. But equally clearly, not memory: We aren't remembering that it is evil to torture children. And not sense perception either. When we say that we just see the wrongness of certain actions, we certainly don't mean that it's visible.

At this stage in our understanding of our own minds and brains, we don't know enough to identify the cognitive faculty that recognizes evil intuitively. But it would be a mistake to infer that there is no such faculty.[5] It's clear that we have many other cognitive faculties that similarly can't be accounted for by the triad of reason, memory, and perception. We have the abilities to tell mood from facial expression, to discern affect from melody of speech. We have the ability to recognize people from seeing their faces. When I see my daughter's face, I know who she is, and not by reason, memory, or perception. There are people who suffer from prosopagnosia. In them, reason functions well, and so do memory and perception; they perform normally on standard tests for all those faculties. Furthermore, the links among reason, memory, and perception also seem intact. Prosopagnosics can remember what they've perceived and thought; they can reason about what they remember and what they're perceiving. Nonetheless, they can't recognize people they know on the basis of visual data acquired by seeing their faces. So it is plain that reason, memory, and perception no more exhaust the list of our cognitive faculties than animal, vegetable, and mineral exhaust the list of material objects in the world. That we have no idea *what* faculty has been damaged or destroyed in prosopagnosia obviously doesn't mean that there is no such faculty. Furthermore, there is no reason for being particularly skeptical about the reliability of such peculiar cognitive faculties. It seems to me that our cognitive faculties come as a set. If we accept some of them—such as reason—as reliable, on what basis would we hold skeptically aloof from any others? So I think it is clear that we have cognitive faculties that we don't understand much about but regularly and appropriately rely on, such as the ability to recognize people from their faces.

Our ability to recognize certain things as evil seems to me like this. We don't understand much about the faculty that produces moral intuitions in us, but we all regularly rely on it anyway.[6] The vaunted cultural relativity of morality doesn't seem to me an objection. The diversity of moral opinions in the world masks a great underlying similarity of view;[7] and perhaps a lot of the diversity is attributable not to moral differences but to differences in beliefs about empirical and metaphysical matters. I think, then, that we have some cognitive faculty for discerning evil in things, and that people in general treat it as they treat their other cognitive faculties: as basically reliable, even if fallible and subject to revision.

It also seems clear that this cognitive faculty can discern differences in kind and degree. For example, there is a great difference between ordinary wrongdoing and real wickedness. A young Muslim mother in Bosnia was repeatedly raped in front of her husband and father, with her baby screaming on the floor beside her. When her tormentors seemed finally tired of her, she begged permission to nurse the child. In response, one of the rapists swiftly decapitated the baby and threw the head in the mother's lap. This evil is different, and we feel it immediately. We don't have to reason about it or think it over. As we read the story, we are filled with grief and distress, shaken with revulsion and incomprehension. The taste of **real wickedness** is sharply different from the taste of garden-variety moral evil, and we discern it directly, with pain.

What is perhaps less easy to see is that this faculty also discerns goodness. We recognize acts of generosity, compassion, and kindness, for example, without needing to reflect much or reason it out. And when the goodness takes us by surprise, we are sometimes moved to tears by it. Hallie describes his first acquaintance with the acts of the Chambonnais in this way: "I came across a short article about a little village in the mountains of southern France. . . . I was reading the pages with an attempt at objectivity . . . trying to sort out the forms and elements of cruelty and of resistance to it. . . . About halfway down the third page of the account of this village, I was annoyed by a strange sensation on my cheeks. The story was so simple and so factual that I had found it easy to concentrate upon *it*, not upon my own feelings. And so, still following the story, and thinking about how neatly some of it fit into the old patterns of persecution, I reached up to my cheek to wipe away a bit of dust, and I felt tears upon my fingertips. Not one or two drops; my whole cheek was wet" (p. 3). Those tears, Hallie says, were "an expression of moral praise" (p. 4); and that seems right.

With regard to goodness, too, I think we readily recognize differences in kind and degree. We are deeply moved by the stories of the Chambonnais. People feel the unusual goodness of Mother Teresa and mark it by calling her a living saint. We sense something special in the volunteers who had been in Somalia well before the Marines came, trying to feed the starving. We don't have a single word for the contrary of wickedness, so **'true goodness'** will have to do. True goodness tastes as different from ordinary instances of goodness as wickedness does from ordinary wrongdoing; and we discern true goodness, sometimes, with tears.

Why tears, do you suppose? A woman imprisoned for life without parole for killing her husband had her sentence unexpectedly commuted by the governor, and she wept when she heard the news. Why did she cry? Because the news was good, and she had been so used to hearing only bad. But why cry at good news? Perhaps because if most of your news is bad, you need to harden your heart to it. So you become accustomed to bad news, and to one extent or another, you learn to protect yourself against it, maybe by not minding so much. And then good news cracks your heart. It makes it feel keenly again all the evils to which it had become dull. It also opens it up to longing and hope, and hope is painful because what is hoped for is not yet here.[8]

For the same reasons, we sometimes weep when we are surprised by true goodness. The latest tales of horror in the newspaper distress us but don't surprise us. We have all heard so many stories of the same sort already. But true goodness is unexpected and lovely, and its loveliness can be heartbreaking. The stories of the Chambonnais rescuing Jews even on peril of their own imprisonment and death went through him like a spear, Hallie says. Perhaps if he had been less filled with the vision of the mirror of evil, he would have wept less over Le Chambon.

Some people glimpse true goodness by seeing it reflected in other people, as Hallie did. Others approach it more indirectly through beauty, the beauty of nature or mathematics or music. But I have come to believe that ultimately all true goodness of the heartbreaking kind is God's. And I think that it can be found first and most readily in the traces of God left in the Bible.

The biblical stories present God as the glorious creator of all the beauty of heaven and earth, the majestic ruler and judge of the world. But Rebecca feels able to turn to Him when she doesn't understand what's happening in her womb, Hannah brings Him her grief at her childlessness, and Deborah trusts Him for victory in a pitched battle with her people's oppressors. Ezekiel presents Him at his most uncompromisingly angry, filled with righteous fury at human evil. But when God commands the prophet to eat food baked in human excrement as a sign to the people of the coming disasters, the shocked prophet tells Him, "I can't!", and almighty God rescinds His command (Ez. 4:12–15). When His people are at their repellent moral worst, God addresses them in this way: "They say if a man put away his wife and she go from him and become another man's, shall he return to her again? . . . you have played the harlot with many lovers; yet return again to me, says the Lord" (Jer. 3:1). And when we won't come to Him, He comes to us, not to rule and command, but to be despised and rejected, to bear our griefs and sorrows, to be stricken for our sake, so that we might be healed by His suffering.

There is something feeble about attempting to describe in a few lines the moving goodness of God that the biblical stories show us; and the attempt itself isn't the sort of procedure the biblical narratives encourage, for the same reason, I think, that the Bible is conspicuously lacking in proofs for the existence of God.[9] Insofar as the Bible presents or embodies any method for comprehending the goodness of God or coming to God, it can be summed up in the Psalmist's invitation to individual listeners and readers: Taste and see that the Lord is good.

The Psalmist's mixed metaphor seems right. Whether we find it in the Chambonnais or in the melange of narrative, prayer, poetry, chronicle, and epistle that constitute the Bible, the taste of true goodness calls to us, wakes us up, opens our hearts. If we respond with surprise, with tears, with gratitude, with determination not to lose the taste, with commitment not to betray it, that tasting leads eventually to seeing, to some sight of or insight into God.

Hallie left his college office and his family and went seeking the villagers of Le Chambon. He concluded his study of the Chambonnais years later this way:

> We are living in a time, perhaps like every other time, when there are many who, in the words of the prophet Amos, "turn judgment to wormwood." Many are not content to live with the simplicities of the prophet of the ethical plumbline, Amos, when he says in the fifth chapter of his Book: "Seek good, and not evil, that ye may live: and so the Lord, the God of Hosts, shall be with you." . . . We are afraid to be "taken in," afraid to be credulous, and we are not afraid of the darkness of unbelief about important matters. . . . But perplexity is a luxury in which I cannot indulge. . . . For me, as for my family, there is the same *kind* of urgency as far as making ethical judgments about Le Chambon is concerned as there was for the Chambonnais when they were making their ethical judgments upon the laws of Vichy and the Nazis. . . . For me [the] awareness [of the standards of goodness] is my awareness of God. I live with the same sentence in my mind that many of the victims of the concentration camps uttered as they walked to their deaths: *Shema Israel, Adonoi Elohenu, Adonoi Echod.* (pp. 291–293)

So, in an odd sort of way, the mirror of evil can also lead us to God. A loathing focus on the evils of our world and ourselves prepares us to be the more startled by the taste of true goodness when we find it and the more determined to follow that taste until we see where it leads. And where it leads is to the truest goodness of all—not to the boss of the universe whose word is moral law or to sovereignty that must not be dishonored, but to the sort of goodness of which the Chambonnais's goodness is only a tepid aftertaste. The mirror of evil becomes translucent, and we can see through it to the goodness of God. There are some people, then, and I count myself among them, for whom focus on evil constitutes a way to God. For people like this, Ecclesiastes is not depressing but deeply comforting.

If we taste and see the goodness of God, then the vision of our world that we see in the mirror of evil will look different, too. Start just with the fact of evil in the world, and the problem of evil presents itself forcefully to you. But start with a view of evil and a

deep taste of the goodness of God, and you will know that there must be a morally sufficient reason for God to allow evil—not some legal and ultimately unsatisfying sort of reason, but the sort of reason that the Chambonnais would recognize and approve of, a reason in which true goodness is manifest. People are accustomed to say that Job got no answer to his anguished demand to know why God had afflicted him. But they forget that in the end Job says to God, "now I see you." If you could see the loving face of a truly good God, you would have an answer to the question why God had afflicted you. When you see the deep love in the face of a person you suppose has betrayed you, you know you were wrong. Whatever happened was done out of love for you by a heart that would never betray you and a mind bent on your good.[10] To answer a mistaken charge of betrayal, someone who loves you can explain the misunderstanding or he can show his face. Sometimes showing his face heals the hurt much faster.

If a truly good God rules the world, then the world has a good mother, and life is under the mothering guidance of God. Even the most loathsome evils and the most horrendous suffering are in the hand of a God who is truly good. All these things have a season, as Ecclesiastes says, and all of them work together for good for those who love God—for those who are finding their way to the love of God, too, we might add.[11]

Nothing in this thought makes evil less evil. Suffering remains painful; violence and greed are still execrable. We still have an obligation to lessen the misery of others, and our own troubles retain their power to torment us. But it makes a great difference to suppose that the sufferers of evil, maybe ourselves included, are in the arms of a mothering God.

Although, as Ecclesiastes is fond of saying, we often cannot understand the details of the reason why God does what He does in the world, when we see through the mirror of evil and taste the goodness of the Lord, we do understand the general reason, just as Job must have done when he said, "now I see you." Like a woman in childbirth, then, as Paul says, we feel our pains of the moment, but they are encircled by an understanding that brings peace and joy.

And so in an Alice-through-the-looking-glass way, the mirror of evil brings us around to the hobbit's way of seeing things at the end. "Go," says Ecclesiastes, "eat your bread in gladness and drink your wine in joy; for your action was long ago approved by God" (9:7). If God is mothering the earth and if its evils are in His hands, then you may be at peace with yourself and your world. You can be grateful for the good that comes your way without always contrasting it with the ghastliness elsewhere. This road to quiet cheerfulness is the long way to the goal, but perhaps for some people it is also the only way there.

Nothing in this view, of course, is incompatible with a robust program of social action. "Send your bread forth upon the waters; for after many days you will find it," Ecclesiastes says. "Distribute portions to seven or even to eight, for you cannot know what misfortune may occur on earth" (11:1–2). If you are moved by goodness, then you will want to ally yourself with it, to diminish evils in the world, to alleviate suffering. Those who love God will hate evil, the Psalmist says (97:10). There is no love of God, 1 John says, in those without compassion for the world's needy (3:17). A good part of true religion, James says, is just visiting "the fatherless and the widows in their affliction" (1:27).

The spirit with which you respond to the evil around you will be different, though, if you see through it to the goodness of God on the other side. Someone asked Mother Teresa if she wasn't often frustrated because all the people she helped in Calcutta died. "Frustrated?" she said, "no—God has called me to be faithful, not successful." If God is the world's mother, then Mother Teresa doesn't have to be. Quiet cheer and enjoyment of the small pleasures of the world are compatible with succouring the dying in Calcutta in case the suffering ones are in the hands of a God who is truly good. Maybe that's why the Psalmist follows his line "Taste and see that the Lord is good" with "blessed is the man that trusts in him."

Even our own evils—our moral evils, our decay and death—lose their power to crush us if we see the goodness of God. The ultimate end of our lives is this, Ecclesiastes says: "the dust returns to the ground as it was, and the lifebreath returns to God who bestowed it" (12:7)—to God who loves us as a good mother loves her children. In the unending joy of that union, the suffering and sorrow of this short life will look smaller to us, as Paul says (Rom. 8:18).

Nothing in this view of our relation to God makes *joie de vivre* seem any less crazy; sin and death are still real evils. But tasting the goodness of God makes seeing the world's evils and our own compatible with joy in the Lord.

I think the Psalmist is speaking for people who take this long way round to peace and cheer when he says, "I have taught myself to be contented like a weaned child with its mother; like a weaned child am I in my mind" (131:2).[12] How can a child who is being weaned understand the evil of the weaning? What he wants is right there; there is nothing bad about his having it—it costs his mother nothing to satisfy him; the pain of doing without it is sharp and urgent. And so, for a while, the child will be overwhelmed by the evil of his situation. But sooner or later in his thrashing he will also see his mother, and that makes all the difference. His desire for what she will not give him is still urgent, and the pain of the deprivation remains sharp. But in seeing her, he feels her love of him. He senses her goodness, and he comes to trust her. As Isaiah puts it, he sucks consolation to the full in another way (66:11). That is how he can be both weaned and also resting peacefully by her side.

And doesn't it seem likely that he comes to see his mother as he does just because he finds the evil of weaning intolerable? How much did he see her when his focus was himself and what he wanted, the comfort of the breast and the taste of the milk? The evil of the weaning, which seems to separate him from her, in fact drives him toward recognizing her as a person, and a person who loves him.

For Hallie, for the author of Ecclesiastes, and for me, too, the ghastly vision in the mirror of evil becomes a means to finding the goodness of God, and with it peace and joy. I don't know any better way to sum it up than Habakkuk's. Habukkuk has the Ecclesiastes temperament. He begins his book this way: "How long, O lord, shall I cry out and You not listen, shall I shout to You, 'Violence!' and You not save? Why do You make me see iniquity, why do You look upon wrong? Raiding and violence are before me, Strife continues and contention goes on. That is why decision fails and justice never emerges" (1:1–4). But he ends his book this way. He presents the agricultural equivalent of nuclear holocaust: the worst sufferings imaginable to him, the greatest disaster for himself and his people. And he says this: "Though the fig tree does not bud, and no yield is on the vine, though the olive crop has failed, and the fields produce no grain, though sheep have vanished from the fold, and no cattle are in the pen, yet will I rejoice in the Lord, exult in the God who delivers me. My Lord God is my strength" (3:17–19).

This is the best I can do to tell my story.[13]

NOTES

1. I am quoting from the new Jewish Publications Society's translation. With the exception of quotations from Jeremiah 3 and Psalm 34, all quotations from the Hebrew Bible will be from this translation. The suffering of the Jews during the Holocaust reflects all the worst misery and all the deepest wickedness in the world, and so it seemed appropriate to use the Jewish translation of the Hebrew Bible in an essay on suffering.

2. One of the first things Camus wrote in his diary on arriving in Le Panelier, the village on the outskirts of Le Chambon, was "This is oblivion" (quoted in Herbert R. Lottman, *Albert Camus* [Garden City, N.Y.: Doubleday, 1979], p. 276). During his stay in Le Chambon, he was writing *The Plague* and his play *Le Malentendu*, as well as making notes for *The Rebel*. Apparently, several of the names in *The Plague* are borrowed from the people of Le Chambon (Lottman, op. cit., p. 290).

3. This included not only strenuous riding and walking but also "hedging and ditching"; See David Nokes, *Jonathan Swift. A Hypocrite Reversed* (Oxford: Oxford University Press, 1985), p. 341.

4. Philip Hallie, *Lest Innocent Blood Be Shed* (Philadelphia: Harper and Row, 1979).

5. By talk of a faculty here, I don't mean to suggest that there is one neurobiological structure or even one neurobiological system that constitutes the faculty in question. There may be many subsystems that work together to produce the ability I am calling a cognitive faculty. Vision seems to be like this. It is entirely appropriate to speak of the faculty of vision, but many different neural subsystems have to work together properly in order for a person to be able to see. It may also be the case that some of the subsystems that constitute a faculty have multiple uses and function to constitute more than one

faculty. This seems to be the case with vision, too. Our ability to see apparently requires the operation of some subsystem of associated memory, and this subsystem is also employed in other faculties, such as our ability to hear. The wild boy of Aveyronne, whose subsystem of associated memory was no use for dealing with urban sounds, was originally believed to be deaf and was brought to an institute for the deaf in Paris.

6. In claiming that we have a faculty that recognizes moral characteristics, I am not claiming that nurture and environment play no role in shaping our moral intuitions. It is difficult to make a principled distinction between what is innate and what has an environmental component, as philosophers of biology have helped us to see. And there are clear examples of characteristics that most of us strongly believe to be genetically determined but that nonetheless require the right environmental or cultural conditions to emerge. The human capacity for language is such a case. It seems clearly innate and genetically determined. And yet, as the few well-documented cases of feral children show, without human society and nurture at the right ages, a person will be permanently unable to acquire a language.

7. Perhaps this isn't the best case to illustrate the point, but it is one of my favorites. In his public remarks during the period when he was rector, Heidegger tended to make statements of this sort: "Do not let principles and 'ideas' be the rules of your existence. The Fuehrer himself, and he alone, is the German reality of today, and of the future, and of its law." Cited in Victor Farias, *Heidegger and Nazism*, trans. Paul Burrell [Philadelphia: Temple University Press, 1989], p. 118. After Germany lost World War II, when the French moved into his town and confiscated his property because he was on their list as a known Nazi, he wrote an indignant letter to the commander of the French forces in his area. It begins this way: "What justice there is in treating me in this unheard of way is inconceivable to me" ("Mit welchem Rechtsgrund ich mit einem solchen unerhoerten Vorgehen betroffen werde, ist mir unerfindlich"). Cited in Hugo Ott, *Martin Heidegger. Unterwegs zu seiner Biographie* (Frankfurt: Campus Verlag, 1988), p. 296.

8. Alvin Plantinga has suggested to me that not all tears have to do with suffering; there are also tears of joy, at the beauty of music or of nature, for example. But I am inclined to think that even tears of joy of that sort have to do with suffering.

As C. S. Lewis maintained in *The Pilgrim's Regress*, and as Plantinga also recognizes, the vision of certain sorts of beauty fills us with an acute if inchoate longing for something—the source of the beauty perhaps—and a painful sense that we don't possess it, aren't part of it, now.

9. Arguments for God's existence certainly have their place, but for most people that place is after, not before, coming to God. I have explained and defended this attitude toward arguments for God's existence in "Aquinas on Faith and Goodness," in *Being and Goodness*, ed. Scott MacDonald (Ithaca, N.Y.: Cornell University Press, 1991), pp. 179–207.

10. Answers to the question of why God permits innocents to suffer admit of varying degrees of specificity. Theodicies typically provide fairly general answers. So, for example, Richard Swinburne's explanation of God's permitting natural evil is that the experience of natural evil gives people knowledge about how suffering is caused and so gives them the options necessary for the significant use of their free will. Although I don't share Swinburne's view, I think that his account does constitute an answer to the question of why God permits innocents to suffer from natural evil. It tells us that God will allow one person S to suffer in order to provide a benefit for a set of persons that may or may not include S, and that the benefit is the significant use of free will, brought about by knowledge of how to cause suffering. Nonetheless, Swinburne's account omits a great many details; it doesn't tell us, for instance, exactly what sort of knowledge is produced or precisely how the suffering conduces to the knowledge in question. And it obviously has nothing to say about the suffering of particular individuals; that is, it doesn't tell us what individuals were benefited and how they were benefited by the suffering of this or that individual innocent. Similarly, in seeing the face of a loving God, Job has an answer to his question about why God has afflicted him; but like the account of evil theodicies give, it is only a general answer. It lets Job see that God allows his suffering for his own spiritual or psychological good, out of love for him; but it doesn't tell him precisely what the nature of that spiritual good is or how it is connected to Job's suffering.

11. In other work, I have argued that God uses suffering to further the redemption of the sufferer. Some people find this claim highly implausible. So, for example, in a recent article, "Victimization and the Problem of Evil: A Response to Ivan Karamazov" (*Faith and Philosophy* 9 [1992], pp. 301–319), Thomas Tracy notes "the stunning counterintuitiveness" of this claim (p. 308). His own preferred view is this: While God does want His creatures to be intimately related to Him, God sometimes lets an innocent person suffer not for some good accruing to her but rather just for the common good, or for the good of the system. I find it hard to understand in what sense the claim that suffering conduces to the redemption of the sufferer is supposed to be counterintuitive, since most of us have few if any intuitions about the redemption of other people and what conduces to it. On the other hand, if Tracy's line is meant just to suggest that this way of looking at suffering seems to stand our ordinary views on their head, then his line seems right but unworrisome; what would be surprising is if a Christian solution to the problem of evil didn't turn our ordinary views upside down. What seems to me truly counterintuitive is Tracy's suggestion that we could have a relationship of deep trust and love with a person who, we believed, had the power to alleviate our suffering but was nonetheless willing to let us suffer undeservedly and involuntarily in the interest of the common good. For a vivid illustration of the deep distress and resentment people feel toward those who respond to their trust in this way, see, for example, the description of communist marriage in China in Jung Chang, *Wild Swans. Three Daughters of China* (New York: Simon and Schuster, 1991), esp. pp. 145–146, 176, 298.

12. The pastor of the South Bend, Indiana, Christian Reformed Church, Len vander Zee, whose sermons are so full of wit, wisdom, and learning that they are more worth publishing and reading than much that appears in the journals in the field, preached an insightful sermon on this passage and the problem of evil in 1992. If that sermon were published, it would be a foolish oversight not to cite it here; as it is, the closest I can come to citing it is to say that his sermons are available from his church office.

13. I am grateful to my husband, Donald Stump, and to my friends William Alston, Alvin Plantinga, and Peter van Inwagen for helpful suggestions on an earlier draft of this essay. I am also deeply indebted to my two teachers: John Crossett, whose efforts on my behalf made this essay possible, and Norman Kretzmann, whose thoughtful collaboration has made all my work, this essay included, much better than it would have been otherwise.

KEY TERMS

Good Samaritan
Problem of evil
Mirror of evil
True goodness
Real wickedness

STUDY QUESTIONS

1. What does Stump mean by the phrase "mirror of evil"? What is the significance of the word "mirror" in this phrase?

2. What are the different sorts of reactions to evil Stump observes? Which of these reactions does she prefer? Do you agree? Why or why not?

3. What does Stump mean by intuition? Why doesn't she think it is a problem that we can't explain how we can intuit good and evil?

4. Does Stump think the cultural relativity of morality is a problem for her account of moral intuition? Why or why not?

5. What role does our moral intuition play in Stump's account of how we can come to know God?

For the Love of Reason

LOUISE M. ANTONY

Louise M. Antony is Professor of Philosophy at University of Massachusetts Amherst. She works primarily in philosophy of mind, epistemology, feminist theory, and philosophy of language. Among her works are *Philosophers without Gods* (2007) and *A Mind of One's Own: Feminist Essays on Reasons and Objectivity* (1993).

· ·

I always had trouble with **Limbo.** Limbo, I was taught, is a place where good but unbaptized people go when they die. We are all born carrying the stain of original sin on our souls, and unless the stain is washed away through baptism, we are unfit to be in the presence of God.[1]

There was no part of this doctrine that made any sense to me. For starters, there was the whole idea of "original" sin. The *original* original sin, of course, was the one committed by Adam when he disobeyed God's commandment not to eat from the tree of knowledge of good and evil.[2] Adam himself was

From *Philosophers without God: Meditations on Athesim and the Secular Life*, edited by Louise Antony. © 2010 by Oxford University Press.

punished—fair enough—but then somehow, this sin that *Adam* committed got "passed down," besmirching the soul of every one of Adam's descendants. I found it repugnant, the idea that a crime committed by one of my ancestors could sully *my* personal soul. It was an idea quite at odds with the liberal, meritocratic principles to which my parents seemed otherwise to subscribe.

This concept of original sin was often presented to me in terms of natural law—like gravity, it's just the way things are. But the analogy seemed inapt; gravity had nothing to do with what you *deserved*. And anyway, I'd protest, didn't God *make* the laws? If so, why did He choose to make things so that you inherited your parents' guilt? Why make the laws of spiritual heredity Lamarckian rather than Darwinian?[3]

I was also troubled by the idea of a soul's being "unfit" to be in the presence of God, irrespective of the rectitude of its owner. It made sense to me that the souls of unrepentant sinners would be unfit, but the people in Limbo could have been as saintly as Gandhi—could even *be* Gandhi—and God still wouldn't have them. This "fitness" sounded almost aesthetic—as if the unbaptized righteous had body odor, or weren't dressed properly. Maybe God was allergic . . . ? At the very least, if something made baptism a condition of entrance into heaven, why didn't He see to it that the sacrament was a little more widely available?

Now my mother felt the force of this consideration, and as a consequence was a great supporter of the Maryknoll missionaries. (This was long before they became associated with radical liberation theology.) She would write them a small check every month and encourage me to make a contribution as well. She impressed upon me the cosmic importance of bringing the Word of God and, crucially, the sacrament of baptism to the innocents of the African jungles. "This is the work that God wants us to do for Him," she'd explain. But wait a minute, I thought. Now you're telling me that the eternal fate of some poor child in Africa depends on what *I* do? This was a heavy burden to bear for a youngster with twenty-five cents in her pocket and a new issue of *Action Comics* beckoning from the news rack. It would only be much later that I'd come to realize that the setup presumed by my mother's creed, whereby the spiritual fates of millions of others is made precarious in order to provide me with opportunities to practice virtue, was at least as repugnant as the original injustice.

But there was something that bothered me almost as much as Limbo itself: the way grownups reacted to my questions about it. First they'd offer a perfunctory, stock, and utterly impertinent response. "The souls in Limbo don't suffer," they'd all say. Huh? Maybe they're not in actual pain, like the souls in Hell, or even the ones in Purgatory, but these poor souls are being deprived of the Beatific Vision, an experience of which, it was emphasized in other contexts, is the final purpose and goal of human existence!

So the next move would be "but they don't *know* they're being deprived of anything." Double huh. It's OK not to share your chocolate with your sister as long as she never finds out you have it? This "ignorance is bliss" reasoning seemed specious to me even as a small child. And it was, once again, inconsistent with the messages I got in every other, non-religious context. My father, for example, was an elementary school administrator, and he was passionate in his support for public education. He would go on and on about the need to cultivate in children—to *inculcate* in children—the "desire to learn." He would have been incensed had anyone suggested that as long as an illiterate child had no conception of the pleasures of reading, it was fine to leave well enough alone.

Not many adults were willing to go on to round three. They would grow impatient. "Louise," my mother would say, "you just think too much." Sometimes they'd get positively angry. What was the matter with me? Why did I have to argue about everything? Didn't I realize that some things just had to be taken on *faith*? In general, I was informed, I should concentrate more on loving my neighbor and less on being a smarty-pants.

None of the nuns or priests from whom I received religious instruction were of any help on the matter of Limbo, nor, for that matter, on any of the other issues that troubled me. There was also the Trinity: how could there be "three persons in one God"? I remember trying to wrap my childish head around this "holy mystery" in the classes preparatory to my receiving my First Communion. For several months running, I would go home from religious education one week, think hard about the whole thing, then return the next week with a new idea to offer Sister. It was always wrong. Maybe God was like a family, I suggested. There was, after all, a Father, a Son, and (remember, now, I was only six-and-a-half, and He was usually depicted as a bird) the family pet, Holy Ghost. No, said Sister, God is not like a family. OK—maybe God is like a three-leafed clover (I had just been taught that this was how St. Patrick explained the Trinity to the heathen Celts in Ireland)—the Father is one leaf, the Son is another, the Holy Ghost is a third, and they're all parts of God. No, said Sister, God is not like a three-leafed clover, St. Patrick notwithstanding. Well, maybe each person is like a different mood of God—God the Father is the angry mood, God the Son is the loving mood, and the Holy Ghost is some other kind of mood. No, said Sister, not moods, either. Finally Sister, clearly exhausted, told me that I'd never understand the Trinity because it was a *mystery of faith*. Mysteries of faith are, by their nature, incomprehensible. We must simply believe them. But how can I believe something I don't understand, I asked? "Just memorize your Catechism," was Sister's reply. "Belief will come."

Now it wasn't just religion. Limbo wasn't the only mystery with which I was preoccupied. I also had problems with Santa Claus. I had no trouble with flying reindeer—remember that my world was amply stocked with miraculous violations of physical law. The difficulty again was moral. Barbara Perkins, my friend who lived at the top of the hill near the bus stop, always got loads of presents "from Santa Claus" at Christmas time. We're talking play kitchens, bicycles, puppies, Barbie dolls *with* Dream Houses—major loot. I, on the other hand, generally received one present from Santa, carefully selected and duly solicited from one of Santa's department store "helpers" (I had asked about the baffling proliferation of Santas early on, and had received and accepted the standard answer), and this one present was never very grand.

Now this was curious, I thought. I understood that there were well-off families in the world, and not-so-well-off families, and I understood that mine was one of the not-so-well-off ones. But why did *Santa Claus* respect these distinctions? Why did he bring more toys to the rich kids than to the poor ones? Apparently, in the cases of really indigent kids, he planned to bring nothing at all—why else the "toys for tots" drives at our church every Christmas? If anything, you'd think that Santa would try to *rectify* economic inequities—that he'd give that play kitchen to the little girl whose parents couldn't afford to buy her anything. Was Santa Claus a supply-sider?

I made the enormous social blunder of bringing this up with other kids, indeed, with Barbara Perkins herself. (I'm pretty sure I suggested that she could do a little to bring moral order to the universe by giving me her play kitchen.) They were not interested—reasonably enough: one's not a kid forever, and there are cartoons to be watched. But adults didn't appreciate my questions, either. I'd get a little patronizing approval for asking "such a serious question!" but once they saw that I really meant to know what was going on, they'd get irritated. I don't know how I described their reactions

to myself at the time, but as I remember them now, it seems clear that they, no less than their kids, thought I was being a colossal drag.

What I got from all of this was that thinking was fine and good, but only in its place. A little learning might be a dangerous thing, but a lot of thinking was worse. Today I am a parent, and I know firsthand the tedium and frustration of dealing with a child who won't stop asking "why." I also know that the questions of an inquiring child may be more motivated by the hope of delaying bedtime than by the love of knowledge. And finally, I know there are children who relish making their superiors squirm; I surely was one of them. But with all that said, I still, to this day, resent the way I was made to feel as a child—that my questioning was *inherently* bad, that there was something wrong with *me* for wanting things to make sense.

As I've said, the reactions of grownups to my questions about religion were doubly distressing to me because of their dissonance with the principles adults were explicitly promoting in other contexts. In school, a broadly libertarian and individualistic ethos prevailed. We were always being exhorted to "think for ourselves." In reading, we were urged to "sound out the words instead of just asking," and in arithmetic to figure out the problems on our own. Science teachers and science books agreed heartily that curiosity is a marvelous thing, the engine of all scientific achievement. One must not take things for granted; one must always ask "why." The best scientists, it was stressed, are the ones who see mystery in the everyday, who press for deeper and deeper understanding. In the biographies of Marie Curie I devoured, she was praised for seeing questions no one else did and for persisting in her work until she got her answers. (My mother, by the way, got me these books. She was a secret feminist. She kept the secret even from herself.) In my elementary school citizenship classes, democracy was praised as the most perfect political form because it allowed every citizen to "follow his own conscience." My parents and teachers, counseling me about personal behavior, stressed the importance of doing what *I* knew was right, regardless of what other people thought. Why in religion was I supposed to dumbly accept whatever the authorities told me?

Somewhere along the line, I came to the conclusion that my inquisitiveness was sinful. It was not just that it was prideful—I'd been told that explicitly, and often enough. This new idea was that the questions had been put into my head by the devil, and that, indeed, the whole world had been mined with dangerous ideas, ideas that could threaten my faith if I indulged them. No one ever told me such a thing in so many words, but it seemed to me a good explanation for the taboo against thinking in religion, together with my apparent inability to respect it.

My little theory kept me in a pretty constant state of anxiety, lest I take seriously something that turned out to be incompatible with religious teachings. I was pretty interested in biology and genetics as a kid and read everything I could get my hands on. Before very long, I encountered the theory of evolution. It seemed really plausible to me, and ingenious. But I didn't see where in the theory souls were supposed to come in. It's not that I had ever been told that evolution was inconsistent with Catholicism—the Church in which I was raised was not fundamentalist, and condoned metaphorical readings of Scripture. The conflict was more of my own making. It seemed to me that if evolutionary theory was correct, then biological differences were matters of degree: apes just gradually became people. But that seemed parlously at odds with the religious picture: that human beings, in virtue of possessing immortal souls, were fundamentally different from everything else in nature. I decided that I should try not to believe in evolution.

I remember, too, being terrified by a particular cover on *Time* magazine that posed, in huge red letters against a black background, the shocking question: "Is God Dead?"[4] It's hard for me, to this day, to explain just what I found so profoundly unsettling about this question—I certainly wasn't simply shocked that anyone would think such a thing. It was rather the elemental uncanniness of the concept of God's dying—of the end of an eternal, all-powerful being. (Obviously, I never read the article—I might have been reassured to learn that the "death of God" was just a particularly provocative way of expressing disbelief.)

You might think, given all these complaints, that I resented my religion and wanted nothing more than to be free of it. But that's not the way it was. Despite my frustrations, I was passionately devout. I tried really hard to say my prayers mindfully, to pay attention at Mass, and to obey the Ten Commandments, especially the fourth, which apparently covered not teasing the cat. I failed regularly in these efforts, but made regular Confessions. I didn't particularly like candy, so I would make a point of giving up comic books for Lent. (Although I must admit this was sly of me, since Sundays were not part of Lent, and Sundays were when we went to the drugstore where comic books were sold.) I memorized prayers that no one else knew, and read unassigned books about saints. I took seriously all the rules of observance, never missing Mass on Sundays, and strictly following the more obscure requirements of Lenten abstinence (I was told frequently that I took things *too* seriously). I respected and trusted my parents: if they told me all this stuff was true, then I was pretty sure it had to be true. I just couldn't figure out *how* it could be true.

I think I identified being religious with being good. Most of my charitable acts, such as they were, were carried out under church auspices, though probably not for the right reasons. I found the idea of martyrdom really exciting and prayed that I might someday give my life for Christ. (My mother's suggestion—that God's plan for me might have more to do with dusting and table setting than with famished lions or flaming stakes—was ill received.) But I also heard in the Sunday sermons, and in the Gospel readings, two consistent moral messages that moved me deeply—first, that every human being had an immortal soul of surpassing moral value, and second, that our overarching duty on Earth was to demonstrate our love of God through our acts of love for humankind. I would be martyred, I decided, while teaching deaf and blind leukemia victims in Africa.

Because I was usually in the minority, being a Catholic made me feel special. In the Upstate New York suburb where I spent some of my childhood, and later in Western Massachusetts, nearly everyone I knew was some sort of Protestant (exception: my best friend in Vestal, New York, who attended the Polish American Catholic church. She's also now a philosopher—go figure). There was one Jew that I knew of in Vestal, and one who attended my high school in Sheffield, but all I knew about Jews or their religion was that they didn't believe in Jesus, and so did not celebrate Christmas. My mother assured me that they could, nonetheless, be Very Good People. (Swelling the population of Limbo, I thought.) Protestantism was very mysterious to me. I could tell anyone who wanted to know exactly what my theological beliefs were—they could have the short version, in the form of the Apostle's Creed, or the long—very long—version codified in the Baltimore Catechism, which I had memorized. But if I asked my Protestant friends what they believed, they seemed not to have a clue. In some cases, they were unclear even as to which denomination they belonged. Several of my friends reported that they attended the church they did because their parents liked the minister there. What with fasting Sunday mornings before Communion, abstaining from meat on Fridays, and giving up candy for Lent, I felt smugly superior to these Protestant friends, whose religions, it seemed to me, required very little of them.

My religion was with me every day. I said my prayers in the morning on waking, and again before I went to bed at night. I reminded myself that it was my religious duty to treat my elderly Great-Aunt Louise—an imperious and stentorian woman who had come to live with us upon the death of her husband—with respect. (Not that I was very successful.) Minor medical discomforts, like my weekly gamma globulin shot, were offered up for the poor souls in Purgatory. (Purgatory is not the same as Limbo. The souls in Purgatory will eventually enter heaven, once they've done their time.) I made it a practice to receive Holy Communion every Sunday (unless I was ill, and excused from attending Mass).

Another daily reminder of my religion—not a pleasant one—was my almost continual sense of guilt. I have already mentioned my failures with respect to Aunt Louise. I was no better about teasing the cat, or about fighting with my sister. The worst attack of guilt I ever suffered, however, came one time when I yielded to the temptation to preserve my Communion record, and received the sacrament without being sure that it had really been sixty full minutes since I had eaten. I had been spending the night with friends who owned a small boat, and while my mother had extracted from them a promise to get me to mass as a condition of my being allowed to stay, they were themselves freethinkers and not terribly enthusiastic about the whole enterprise. The only Catholic church in the area was about a half-hour drive from the marina, and we needed to get to the earliest service—8:30 a.m.—in order to preserve

a reasonable chunk of the day for boating. Despite the early hour, my friends insisted that I eat something before we left. I must not have had a watch; I remember calculating that if it took us half an hour to get to the church, then by the time the priest actually distributed Communion, it might possibly be an hour later than my last bite. I knew perfectly well that if I wasn't sure I had completed the required period of fast then I ought not to receive Communion. It was a mortal sin to take the sacrament if one was not "properly prepared"—a condition that also precluded being in a state of mortal sin. Nonetheless, I was fetishistic about my record, and persuaded myself—for the moment at least—that I was in the clear.

The second after I received the host, however, the scruples set in. By the middle of the brilliantly sunny and perfectly still afternoon, I was stricken with nausea and the shakes. I refused to go swimming, terrified that I might drown in a state of mortal sin and go straight to Hell. I told my hosts that I was seasick. They favored the more plausible diagnosis, given the circumstances, that I'd contracted some stomach virus, and cut short the day to get me home. Once there, I burst into tears, confessed the whole story to my mother, and demanded that she call the church and arrange for me to make a confession. Now, my mother, while very devout and scrupulously observant, was also a sensible and loving parent and tried her best to persuade me that no one as obviously sorry as I was (for an offense she was not even convinced I'd committed) was destined for Hell, and that I could just wait until the regularly scheduled confessions the next Saturday. Nothing for it—I was hysterical at the thought that I would have to carry the weight of my blackened soul all through the week. So she called the rectory and reached our young assistant pastor, who agreed to hear my confession over the phone.

This worked in the end, but the rescue was nearly derailed by the earnest young priest's attempts to convince me that I was too young (I was eleven) to have really, knowingly, and willingly committed a mortal sin. I was righteously insulted by this suggestion. I knew the definition of a mortal sin, I exclaimed, and every clause was fulfilled: 1) it *was* a grievous wrong, 2) I *knew* it was a grievous wrong, and 3) *I wanted to do it anyway*. (Now, at some level, I surprised myself. I had earlier argued to Sister that no one could possibly satisfy all these conditions at the same time—that you couldn't really, really want to do something that you, at the very same time, really, really believed was wrong. But now, suddenly, talking to Father, I saw that yes, you really, really could!)

Most of my youth, I did not look forward to Sunday mass. When I was a girl, it was still said in Latin, and though I'd follow along in my missal (once I learned how to read), I found most of the ritual pretty boring. There was no singing, unless it was a high mass, and then it was the priest who sang (so much the worse!). I did, for the most part, rather like the sermons, and the Gospel and Epistle readings. And I did find my religious education classes interesting (although, as I've been at pains to explain, often for the wrong reasons).

A great deal changed, though, once the Second Vatican Council reforms were implemented—mass in the vernacular, responses recited and hymns sung by the congregation—my concentration, and consequently my piety, were much improved. I loved the "folk mass." Like all good flower children, I knew two separate chord progressions on the guitar and was thus amply equipped to strum accompaniments to "Hear O Lord" and "Sons of God." (Accustomed as I was to staring at a bloodied body while I prayed, I was taken aback by a non-Catholic friend's horrified reaction to the cheerful exhortation to cannibalism in the chorus of the latter hymn: "Eat His body / Drink His blood / Allelu-, allelu-, allelu-, allelu-u-ia . . .") I began attending a teen discussion group in a neighboring parish run by an inspiring young priest from the seminary up in Lenox, a student (I now surmise) of liberation theology. Doctrinal difficulties began to recede, and my religious practice began to resonate with the calls for justice and liberation sounding throughout U.S. society.

Thus I continued to consider myself a devout Catholic all during high school. (Leave aside the odd mortal sin. Many non-Catholics I talk to are certain that my loss of faith had to do with sex, but this just reflects their prejudice. Like many, many of my Catholic peers, I found it pretty easy to dismiss the Church's teachings about premarital sex and contraception as inessential, old-fashioned, and not to be taken seriously.) But while I carried my religious identity with me to college, I carried right along with

it a still-unsated curiosity about matters theological and moral. The one was about to come crashing into conflict with the other.

I knew absolutely nothing about the subject when I sat down in my first philosophy class. I was taking it to fulfill a distribution requirement and was dimly apprehensive that the readings would be incomprehensible and would somehow require knowledge of ancient history. Imagine my delight, then, when I discovered that philosophy was all about arguing! Not only was my constant questioning tolerated; it was positively encouraged. Finally, finally—a place where reasons had to be given, a place where no one would tell you it was impertinent to ask. I could scarcely believe that I could earn credits just for doing what (to me) came naturally.

So the good news was that everything could be questioned; everything was up for debate. But that, it turned out, was also the bad news. It was one thing, I discovered, to raise my questions about the nature of the afterlife and the justice of the Creator from a background of religious commitment, and quite another to raise such questions in the context of a no-holds-barred debate. I began to realize that in all my childhood worrying, it had never occurred to me that my questions might just not have answers. I certainly had never really considered what it would mean for my own religious faith if that turned out to be the case. But now I found myself in the company of people who saw religious commitment itself as open to challenge, who were asking a question I had never, ever dared to even formulate: is there a God?

The first rumblings of distress arose with our survey of the traditional arguments for the existence of God. I fought tooth and nail to make one of them work, but I had to admit in the end that none of them seemed fully convincing. First came the **a priori** arguments, the arguments that were supposed to proceed from self-evident principles. Anselm's argument seemed like verbal sleight of hand. Each of Aquinas's five ways depended on premises that seemed far from self-evident to me. Descartes's argument involved the puzzling claim that an idea could contain no more "reality" than its source, but how do you measure "amounts" of reality? Much as I hated to admit it, these arguments seemed frivolous, more suited to *Alice in Wonderland* than the New Testament. The arguments that appealed to empirical evidence seemed more promising, at least initially. But William James's argument, based on his own religious experience, finally failed to convince. Far too many of my friends had had "religious experiences" of the chemical type (it was, after all, 1971) for me to trust any "insights" gleaned on that basis. The argument from design—wherein God is posited to explain the intricate orderliness of nature—seemed, despite its problems, the last hope.

But then came the day that literally changed my life—the day when I first heard the **"argument from evil."** The reasoning is easy to state: Suffering exists. If God can do anything, He must not want to prevent suffering; but if He does not want to prevent suffering, He cannot be perfectly good. Therefore, there is no all-powerful, perfectly good Being. The argument has been known for centuries, and many replies have been attempted. For example, many theists point out that a great deal of the suffering in the world is the result of human beings' exercising their freedom. We must be free, they argue, if we are to be capable of virtuous actions, but **free will** carries with it, necessarily, the possibility for vicious action as well. Since God cannot intervene to prevent human actions that He knows will cause suffering without compromising the freedom of the actors, He must acquiesce. With respect to the rest of the world's suffering—that due to droughts and floods and earthquakes and disease—the most popular explanation is that it is simply the necessary consequence of God's enacting what is, in fact, the best of all possible systems of natural law.

I was not satisfied with the proffered explanations of natural evil. I saw no particular reason to believe, other than the mere desire to do so, that an **omnipotent** God could not devise a better way of organizing the world than the plan currently in evidence. (Voltaire, of course, satirizes the suggestion in the person of the ridiculous Dr. Pangloss.) The free will defense, on the other hand, I found not merely unpersuasive, but morally disturbing. It's fine and good that God should afford me the opportunity to practice virtue, but why should innocent others be allowed to suffer if I choose to practice vice instead? Also, is there no limit to the amount of suffering that must be permitted under this justification? The U.S. Constitution enshrines freedom as a societal value, but our civic institutions ensure that my freedom is consistent with equal freedom for everyone else. If I perform an act that infringes upon your rights, then I am subject to punishment and to restraint. Why, then, couldn't God have set things up similarly, with serious criminals being whisked away to Hell before they did too much harm? As things stand, there are apparently no limits on the nature and scope of atrocities that God will allow some human beings to perpetrate against others. Didn't Hitler show his true colors pretty decisively after—I don't know—the first million?

My childhood worries about Limbo returned with new significance, and new urgency. How could a just God design such a system, a system that doomed innocent people, before they were even born, to an eternity of deprivation? Hurricanes and plagues might come with an otherwise functional network of natural law. Murder might be the regrettable cost of giving human beings free will. But Limbo seemed to be utterly and profoundly *optional*. I could find no connection between it and any otherwise desirable purpose. The only possible response I could think of was the one I had spent all of my short life hitherto resisting: "It's a mystery."

By the middle of my first semester, I was experiencing a full-blown crisis of faith. I could not accept the possibility that my religious belief had no rational defense, especially not now after I'd fallen in love with a discipline devoted to rational defenses. But neither could I relinquish my belief. A world without God seemed literally unimaginable; everything would be changed. I was frightened, in contradictory ways: there is no God, and surely He'll punish me for thinking this. At the same time, I was angry: *why* were there no good answers? Why had God made it so difficult to make sense of His will? If He wanted us to believe, why had He made all the reason and evidence work against belief? Indeed, I achieved a few days' respite from my struggles when I considered that if God had given me the faculty of reason, He must have expected me to use it, and so couldn't reasonably fault me for giving up my belief. But this expedient didn't work for long. Limbo, after all, wasn't reasonable, either, but there it was.

In the end, it was more philosophy that saved me. My class had moved on from the existence of God (even if I hadn't, quite) and was studying the basis of moral value. One theory we considered was called "divine command theory," the view that it is God who puts moral value into the world, that what is morally good is whatever He wants to happen. Initially, I thought that this was the view that I did and ought to hold, indeed, that all religious people must hold. But an argument from Plato changed my mind. In his dialogue **Euthyphro**, Socrates asks the eponymous character to define "piety." Euthyphro responds that pious acts are those that are beloved by the gods. Fine, says Socrates—that tells us which acts are the pious ones, but it doesn't tell us what makes them pious: is it the gods' loving them that make them pious, or is it their being pious that accounts for the gods' loving them? In familiar terms: are acts of kindness, courage, and so forth good only because they are the kinds of things God happens to like? Or is it rather that God, being perfectly good, likes such acts because they are also good?

The first possibility struck me as morally repugnant: it made God's preferences morally arbitrary. God *happens* to dislike murder, but had He liked it, then it would have been morally OK. In contrast, on the second option, God dislikes murder *because* it is morally wrong: it doesn't become wrong *only* because He chooses to prohibit it. On this alternative view, His prescriptions and prohibitions do not *constitute* moral goodness; they are, rather, *manifestations* of it. The more I considered the matter, the more convinced I became that this second view was really the more religious—indeed the more pious. So the Euthyphro argument did not, in itself, aggravate the threat to my faith: had I discovered it before I acquired my doubts, it would not have occasioned any. In the context of my growing **skepticism**, however, the discovery of this argument liberated me from any felt *need* for faith. Once I realized that God was not necessary for there to be objective moral value, I also realized that religious *belief* was not necessary for anyone to be a good person. The objectivity of moral value is simply independent of God's existence. All that is lost, if there is no God, is a divine enforcer. In a world without God, there is no guarantee that the virtuous will ever be rewarded, nor that the vicious will ever be punished. We must do what is right simply *because* it is right.

At last I was ready to admit to myself that I no longer believed in God. I'll never forget the sudden upsurge of relief when I finally acknowledged that my faith was gone. I felt suddenly free—free of the obligation to avow propositions I didn't understand, free of the struggle to make sense of doctrines that couldn't be made sensible, and free of the need to square everything I learned with Catholic dogma. My only **doxastic** obligations henceforth would be to reason and evidence. "Now," I thought to myself, "all I have to believe is what I think is true."

OK, OK. I said that's where my *obligations* lay; I didn't say I always discharged them. As I pursued my philosophical interests, and as I began to take a more serious interest in politics, I came to realize that intellectual integrity is pretty hard to achieve. Time and again, I fell prey (and still do, of course) to nonrational influences. I wanted to sound smart, and I wanted to agree with my smart friends. I wanted to defend the views of favorite teachers, and I wanted people I didn't like to be wrong. Once I began committing my own philosophical views to paper, and eventually, to print, I found that I felt constrained by what I'd already said, whether or not I still believed it was right. So I can hardly claim that by giving up religious commitments I had freed myself of dogmatism and wishful thinking. Still, there was a big difference. The little voice inside my head that used to whisper warnings when I ventured onto doctrinally dangerous ground ("Catholics don't read that book") had now become reason's agent ("You don't really believe that," "You know she's right about that," "What's your evidence?") While I earlier strove to reconcile disturbing facts with Catholic teachings—or indeed, to avoid encountering the disturbances in the first place—I now tried to keep my belief apportioned to the strength of the argument.

Equal in importance to what I now assigned as the *having* of reasons was my explicit commitment to the *providing* of reasons. I came to understand that my earlier frustrations had been as much with my teachers' and parents' refusal to engage in rational discussion as with my inability to discover what I wanted to know. And I saw clearly the nature of the conflict between the rhetoric of individual worth inherent in my childhood education and the grownups' retreat to dogmatism and authoritarianism in response to my questions: the refusal to give reasons is *disrespectful* to the person who asks for them. We will not all agree with each other, and given that, we cannot all be right. But if we are to treat each other properly as equals, we must be willing to explain ourselves. I *owe* it to someone with whom I disagree to show her the basis of my position, so that she can evaluate it for herself.

Simply announcing one's reasons is, of course, merely the beginning of rational engagement. "God (or Marx or George W. Bush) said it, I believe it, and that's the end of it" is not what I have in mind. Commitment to the practice of reason giving entails a willingness to continue the chain of reason giving until common ground is reached. Nowhere is this principle more important than in the political realm. Philosophy holds it to be an intellectual duty to provide arguments for one's positions, but when we are talking about the establishment and implementation of public policy, the duty becomes civic as well. My friend's reasons for opposing abortion may be religious in nature; it is certainly her right to be moved by her church's teachings, or by her reading of the books she regards as Holy Scripture. But if I am to acquiesce in a prohibition on the practice, I'm entitled to a reason that moves *me*.

Looking back on my development from devout Catholic girl to adamant **atheist**, I think that it was its bottom-line dogmatism that drove me away from the Church, and indeed, from the very possibility of religious faith. "Faith" presents a paradox: if a doctrine can be defended on rational grounds, then it needn't be taken on faith. But if it *cannot* be defended on rational grounds, why should you believe it?

I've often heard people quote approvingly the aphorism that "faith is believing where you cannot prove." The idea seems to be that since matters of great importance outstrip the human power to know, we must jump in and simply commit ourselves to certain ideas. The question, though, is *which ones*? There's very, very little that can literally be *proven*, that is, shown to be true without any possibility of doubt—only the propositions of logic and mathematics, and some philosophers will dispute even those! Nothing about the world of experience can be demonstrated with complete certainty. The evidence of our senses is partial, and we sometimes make mistakes. We must rely every day on memory and the testimony of others—both fallible—for a great deal of the information we

need to make our way in the world. If we had to foreswear all these less-than-perfect sources, we'd know virtually nothing. But the aphorism, when taken as an endorsement of faith, suggests that, once we leave the realm of certainty, no distinctions can be made—that it's as rational to believe in unicorns as it is to believe in bacteria. The occurrence of the Holocaust cannot be *proven*, in this strict sense; must we therefore take deniers seriously? Lack of proof cannot entitle one to believe, or else anyone would be warranted in believing anything she wanted to.

Now, in truth, few people would explicitly endorse an inference of the form "there's no proof that *p*; therefore, I am entitled to believe that *p*." But I've encountered many who accept a related, and equally fallacious, pattern of reasoning: "There's no proof that *p* is false; therefore it's not irrational to believe that *p* is true." So people will say, "Since no one can prove there is no God, I'm not irrational if I believe in Him." But once again, "proof" is a red herring. I cannot *prove* that aliens have never visited Earth, but given all the considerations against it, I'd be irrational not to reject the proposition. Reason makes demands in two directions.

Of course everyone has a moral and, at least in the United States, at least so far, a political right to believe whatever she wants. As a card-carrying member of the ACLU,[5] and insofar as I have the courage, I will defend this right to the death. But this gets us back to the point I was insisting on above. You are certainly entitled to believe whatever you like, if the matter affects you alone. But if what you believe is supposed to have bearing on what happens to someone else, then you had better have good grounds for your opinion. Majority rule is a kind of tyranny when people don't respect each other enough to form their opinions responsibly. More and more I hear people in my own country speaking about matters of social policy and foreign affairs with the same blithe fideism they evince when expressing their religious views. "Bush will keep us more secure." Really? What makes you say so? "Oh, it's just what I believe." And so thousands must die in Iraq.

Throughout contemporary U.S. society, reason is denigrated as cold, mechanical, and sterile, while irreason is celebrated. Inspirational posters cite the authority of Einstein in elevating supposedly irrational "creativity" over rational thought: "Logic will get you from A to B; imagination will take you everywhere" or "'Imagination is more important than knowledge." Right—there's our problem: too much logic, not enough fantasy. Have you met my president?

The human interest stories in my local paper (on the front page of the "Faith" section—there is no "Reason" section) regularly honor the fidelity of people suffering the most appalling depredations: debilitating accidents, ruthless illnesses, spouses and children lost to senseless wars—all consistent, in the minds of these latter-day Jobs, with the limitless goodness of God. Likely as not, there will be featured, in the same edition, people who have prevailed against astonishing odds—the woman who survived the cancer that all the medical experts said would kill her, the husband who survived the landmine that killed all his buddies—all cheerfully attributing their own good fortune to God's great love for *them*. Never mind the quick paradox (He loved you enough to get you through chemotherapy, just not enough not to spare you the cancer in the first place)— what about the illogic of divine responsibility? God is to be thanked for the good things that happen but never blamed for the bad.

A college friend born and raised in a reformed Jewish household, never very religious, suddenly surprised all his childhood and college friends—not to mention his Jewish wife—by converting to messianic Judaism, becoming a "Jew for Jesus." One evening a few months after his conversion, my husband and I visited for dinner. My friend was recounting an incredible story from his hellion adolescence: he had failed to see a "road out" sign and driven his motorcycle over a fifteen-foot cliff, tumbling off the bike, and landing, "miraculously" unhurt, at the bottom of the ravine. At this point in the story, he suddenly stopped, looked off into the distance, and announced solemnly, "I see now that Christ was saving me for something." Oh, I thought to myself, so I guess He was just all finished with my father, who died suddenly of a heart attack at the age of fifty-three, leaving behind a homemaker wife, her elderly aunt, one daughter just starting graduate school, and another (me) only eleven years old.

After a deadly plane crash in North Carolina, I was contacted by a reporter at the local paper, who asked me to comment on a series of striking coincidences and tragic ironies. One young woman had been scheduled to fly into Charlotte aboard the doomed flight for a family reunion but became ill and canceled four hours before takeoff. A honeymooning couple had been awarded, by sentimental airline personnel, a complementary upgrade to first-class and were both killed. What did it all mean? the reporter wanted to know. Could I, as a philosopher, make sense of all this? Well, no, I couldn't "make sense of it," I said, which didn't stop me from blathering on for a good five minutes. My immortal words, quoted in full: "There are an infinite number of things that happen, and they all have causes. Some of the causes are evident and some are not. Some of the things are preventable; some are not. Some of them are things that we are happy happened. Some are not."[6] You'll not be surprised to hear that they didn't call me much after that.

More edifying, presumably, were the also-quoted remarks of a local rabbi, reflecting on the significance of the patterns of destruction wielded by Hurricane Fran. She saw the Hand of God in the fact that a large, expensive, and recently installed stained-glass window in the synagogue had been spared, despite a tree's having come down right next to the building. But then in the same breath, as it were, she cautioned the faithful not to yield to the temptation to blame God for damages they had suffered. God's plan is mysterious, she reminded everyone. (No kidding— stained glass windows are more important than people's lives!) Apparently, in her world, God gets the credit if the outcome is good, but need take no responsibility if it's bad. We expect our politicians to behave like that, but God?

I see the celebration of irrationality everywhere in popular culture. In movies and TV shows, reason and respect for science are almost invariably characteristic of arrogant and closed-minded villains; good guys have "imagination" and rely on "faith." Consider, just for starters, the 1947 "feel-good movie" *Miracle on 34th Street* (remade in 1994). The plot concerns Doris Walker, a no-nonsense single mother (played by Maureen O'Hara) working as a public relations executive at Macy's. She has raised her daughter, Susan (Natalie Wood), in accordance with her belief that "we should be realistic and completely truthful with our children, and not have them growing up believing in a lot of legends and myths. . . . Like Santa Claus, for example."[7] Susan's preternatural gravity shows us that a childhood shaped by such principles is devoid of color and joy. Doris herself is all business and has no time for either Susan or romance. (Is it her ruthless realism that unsexes her, or her professional ambition? The movie manages to trash working moms and clear thinking in one fell swoop.)

Doris is finally redeemed—and Susan's childhood restored—when she is won over to the cause of Kris Kringle, the jolly old gent she hires to be the Macy's store Santa. Kind and generous (though awful in his rage against crass materialism), the man has one quirk: he believes he is the *real* Santa Claus. This is patently impossible, defying all fact and all logic, and is, for just that reason, the very thing that must be accepted by all sympathetic characters before the gratifying denouement. Doris is a hard nut to crack, but finally, conquered by the patient equanimity of the wise old Kris—not to mention the romantic attentions of his handsome lawyer—Doris finally abandons her "silly common sense."[8]

It's a little tricky to figure out what the real message of this film is supposed to be. It's not that we all should really believe in Santa Claus (although why not?). Rather, it's that we should believe *in something*. But why use the figure of Santa Claus to make this point? Is it that commitment to moral values is on a par, rationally speaking, with belief in fairies, that the one is no more rationally defensible than the other? What's going on, I think, is a linkage—one I'm eager to sever—between two kinds of rationality. One is the human capacity for logical reflection; the other is the construct of classical economics, the coldly calculating self-interest that eschews values and affection. It is this latter kind of "rationality" that has commercialized Christmas, not the former. We are supposed to read Doris's skepticism about Kris as cynicism about the possibility of disinterested virtue—Kris is just too good to be true. But why yoke idealism to credulity?

One needn't subscribe to the central dogma of Christianity to appreciate the moral value of charity. Nor must one be a theist to regret and resist the exploitation and commodification of every laudable impulse human beings possess. Indeed, if one judges by trends in the United States, the relationship between materialism and religiosity is precisely the reverse. Today's most enthusiastic cheerleaders for free market capitalism—that juggernaut of commercialization— are also the most vociferously "Christian." On the other hand, you'll find no more eloquent critic of commodification than the atheist Karl Marx.

I know that many people (including many of the authors in this volume) experienced a deep sense of loss when they left the religious communities in which they had been reared. I must say that, for me, the feeling of relief was paramount, eclipsing any glimmer of regret. If I have any regrets at all, they are ones that have emerged since I became a parent. I am sorry that I was not able to provide my children with the kind of structured moral community that churches and synagogues can offer. My husband and I have both been active in progressive movements, and we've made sure that our kids logged plenty of time at demonstrations and political meetings ("Yes, you have to come; this is 'church' for us," I'd explain.). But there simply are no secular institutions that can serve the myriad psychological, social, and moral purposes that religious institutions currently do. However, I see this fact as a challenge to secular moralists, not a reason to pretend to believe something I don't.

In fact, it hardly matters whether I have any regrets or not. The pragmatic argument for religion— "believe and all this can be yours"—is bound to fail, at least for me. I find it impossible to believe things that make no sense to me or that I have profound reasons for thinking are false. Given the number of times this pragmatic line has been urged upon me ("for your *children's* sake, if not for your own!"), I'm inclined to think that I'm anomalous in this regard. Or maybe not. Maybe many people don't actually believe the tenets of their religion but rather collectively agree—in some subtle and wholly implicit way— just to say they do.[9] I have good reason to think that many people don't actually know what tenets their denominational affiliation commits them to. I know for a fact that many Catholics simply ignore doctrines they find unpalatable and disregard injunctions they find inconvenient. But even if this kind of doublethink makes religion possible for some, it's not a strategy I could adopt. There would be no "doubleness" in my case; there would be only pretense.

Some people have told me that they feel safer in a universe watched over by a benevolent God, and suggested that I would, too, if I could just recover my faith. I beg to differ. The world of my childhood, a world in which the supernatural intruded regularly into daily life, was a frightening world, a world in which *anything* could happen: the sun could stop, the dead could rise, virgins could give birth. Angels were real, but so were demons, and demons could take over your soul. As a child, I had been morbidly fascinated by the story of St. Jean Vianney, the "Curé d'Ars," a humble parish priest who was said to have struggled for years with demonic possession, until finally cured by exorcism. (Or so I remember.) I had not thought about the Curé until many years later when I attended the London premiere of *The Exorcist*. Despite the fact that I had been, at that point, an atheist for two years—or maybe *because* of that—I found the film utterly terrifying. For months afterward, I was beset with unwanted memories of the demon-dominated child. I couldn't sleep in the dark and I couldn't remain in a room if the stupid theme music came on over the radio.[10]

In contrast, my children's world is governed by natural law, which is extremely strict. The sun does *not* stop (at least not in my lifetime) and the dead do not rise (without cardio-pulmonary resuscitation). It's true that this means one must abandon hope for miraculous interventions. After a car accident during my first year of graduate school, I remember looking in the rear view mirror at my horrifically bloodied face (broken nose—don't worry) and thinking with profound distress that my fate lay entirely in the hands of merely human doctors. But the upside of a thoroughly natural world is that you know what you're dealing with. You can have confidence, for example, that your newborn is not a demon in human form, come to prepare the way for a satanic invasion. (It's hard enough being a parent without having to worry about *that*.) And don't tell me that praying protects you from anything. The Jewish and Christian traditions are replete with stories of righteous and holy people, from Job to St. John Vianney, tempted and tortured by God, always for His own mysterious purposes.

My children, in fact, are pretty unflappable where ghosts and monsters are concerned. When my husband and I took them to the Museum of the Moving Image, it just so happened that the museum was featuring an exhibit on special effects in my old nemesis, *The Exorcist*. As I was trying to warn the children—then about seven and eleven—that the pictures might be too scary for them, they rushed past me to

scrutinize a life-sized model of Linda Blair (the actress who portrayed the possessed child), fully demonic, levitated above her bed. They watched the outtakes from the infamous head-spinning scene with clinical dispassion, and pored over the various devices and prostheses required for the magic of projectile vomit. The final verdict on this totemic film of my youth: OK for how old it was, but pretty clunky. I was incredulous (if relieved): didn't they find it *scary*? "Mom," said my son, rolling his eyes. "Stuff like that isn't *real*." Right on, son.

I have no trouble calling myself an atheist, but if I had to choose a designation, analogous to "Catholic" or "Christian," that might convey something about my positive commitments, I would choose "humanist." I would connect myself with thinkers like Aristotle, Descartes, Hume, Kant, and Marx, who were awed and inspired by human capacities: for thought, for creation, and for sympathy. As they appreciated, our value as persons does not depend upon and cannot be secured by the patronage of any external being. It emanates from within.

Human dignity is not, and should not be thought to be, hostage to any myth. Ironically, this may be the message of at least one story in a sacred text. Early in my career, I was asked to teach a course on theories of human nature; the syllabus began with the creation story in the second and third chapters of *Genesis*. I had never read the Hebrew Bible as a child and was familiar with the story of Adam and Eve only from retellings. I was fascinated to read the actual text (albeit in translation), which differed in many significant ways from the narrative I remembered. God, for example, appears more calculating than loving: He creates Adam for the express purpose of tending His garden (Gen. 2:15), and Eve for the express purpose of helping Adam in his work, no other beast being suitable for this task (Gen. 2:18–23). And He lies: He tells Adam that if he eats from the Tree of Knowledge of Good and Evil, "in the day that thou eatest, thou shalt surely die" (Gen. 2:17). The serpent (who is never identified as evil, only as "more subtil than any beast of the field"—Gen. 3:1) is the one who actually tells the truth: that they won't die if they eat from the tree and that the reason God has forbidden them from doing so is that He is afraid of their becoming "as gods, knowing good and evil" (Gen. 3:5). This is confirmed when

God, in consultation with unidentified others, expels Adam and Eve from the garden—not, mind you, as part of their punishment, but to keep them away from the Tree of Life: "Behold, the man has become as one of us, to know good and evil, and now, lest he put forth his hand, and take also of the tree of life, and eat, and live for ever: Therefore the Lord God sent him forth from the garden of Eden" (Gen. 3:22–23).

I am no Bible scholar but note only that the story, taken at face value, renders a trope familiar from many ancient mythologies: the stealing of a divine prerogative by the presumptuous human. Always such thefts are punished: Prometheus is sentenced to eternal torment, Pandora releases pain and sadness into the world, and Adam and Eve, with all their descendants, must toil and suffer. What's the lesson? Well, it could be that it's prudent to do what powerful divinities tell you to do—in Adam and Eve's case, to remain in a state of childlike ignorance, devoid of conscience or principle, dependent but safe. Or one could extract a different, more noble message: that knowledge and reason, those godlike powers, are so valuable that having them is worth enduring the wrath of the most powerful being in the universe. On this reading, Adam and Eve did not "fall from grace," they ascended into moral responsibility. This is how I choose to read the story, and how I conceive our struggle as a species—to claim our rationality, to confront the harsh realities that constrain us, and to acknowledge our own responsibility, in spite of the cost—therein to make ourselves "as gods."

My thanks to Judith Ferster and Joseph Levine for their comments on an earlier draft of this essay.

NOTES

1. As the *Catholic Encyclopedia* certifies: "Limbus Infantium" is "the permanent place or state of those unbaptized children and others who, dying without grievous personal sin, are excluded from the beatific vision on account of original sin alone." See *New Advent* (www.newadvent.org/cathen/09256a.htm). Apparently, the Church has recently revised its teachings, and eliminated Limbo.

2. Not Eve—*her* sin didn't count—but leave *that* alone for now.

3. Jean-Baptiste Lamarck (1744–1829) was a naturalist, a predecessor of Darwin's. Like Darwin, he believed that species evolved, but unlike Darwin, he held that characteristics *acquired* by the organism during its lifetime could be passed on to future generations.

4. You can view it at www./time/covers/0,16641,1101660408,00.html.

5. The American Civil Liberties Union.

6. *Raleigh News and Observer*, July 7, 1994.

7. Valentine Davies, Screenplay, *Miracle on 34th Street* (transcribed).

8. Davies, *Miracle on 34th Street*.

9. Rey argues, in this volume, that this is typically the case.

10. "Tubular Bells"—released, as irony will have it, on Virgin Records. Amazon.com will let you listen: www.amazon.com/gp/product/B000000WG4/104-4076158-4010317?v=glance&n=5174.

KEY TERMS

Limbo
A priori
Argument from evil
Free will
Omnipotent
Euthyphro dilemma
Skepticism
Doxastic
Atheist

STUDY QUESTIONS

1. What was Antony's problem with Limbo when she was a child? How did the adults in her life respond to her?

2. How did growing up Catholic affect Antony? Why is this relevant for this article?

3. What is the argument from evil, and how did Antony respond to it? How did reading *Euthyphro* aid Antony's transition to atheism?

4. Antony distinguishes between two senses of rationality. What are they? Which is her concern? And why is this kind of rationality important for our relations with other people, according to Antony?

5. How does Antony reinterpret Genesis? Do you agree with her that this is an important lesson?

PART III

X

KNOWLEDGE AND REALITY

INTRODUCTION

Descartes and the Problems of Skepticism

There are (at least) three answers to any question: "Yes," "No," and "I don't know." As it stands, the third answer suggests ignorance. But, when we strengthen it and claim not only that knowledge (on some suitable articulation of the concept) is not at hand, but also that it is impossible for beings like us, we have not admitted ignorance but professed **skepticism**. We have taken a philosophical position.

There is a long list of questions on which some philosopher or other has come to a skeptical position. During the seventeenth and eighteenth centuries, a very general sort of skepticism that held that we could not even know the most basic facts about the external world was a major issue that gave rise to a number of great classics of **epistemology**—the branch of philosophy that considers the nature and possibility of knowledge. We reprint a number of classics from this Golden Age of Epistemology, together with some contemporary material inspired, in part, by the worries and challenges laid out in the classics.

No work in the history of philosophy has had more impact than Descartes's *Meditations on First Philosophy*. This work is a battle with skepticism. Descartes's very trust in reason—the capacity each of us seems to have to learn the truth through careful thought and observation—is thrown into question by the skeptical challenges that he considers in "Meditation I." Could it be that he is only dreaming? Or worse yet, that an evil demon is devoted to deceiving him in every particular, even those things about which he is most confident? His reason tells Descartes that he should not place his confidence in any belief about which he can have the least doubt. But, unless he can rule out these hypotheses, he seems to have grounds for doubting everything. Reason seems to have rendered itself useless.

The modern student may have little worry about evil demons and be confident that his dreams are too chaotic to be mistaken for waking experience, so it may be worthwhile to construct a high-tech example to arouse sympathy with Descartes's worry. Suppose that after your last philosophy class, a psychology graduate student shot you with a tranquilizing dart, took you to her dark laboratory in the subbasement of the Psychology Building, and sawed off the top of your skull and removed your brain. Then, she inserted electrodes into your brain. To these electrodes she attached wires through which a computer program could feed electrical charges. The program stimulates the input that you would receive from your perceptual system if you had been allowed to go about your business. You are really a brain in a vat in a basement, but the experiences you are having are just the ones you would have had if you were back in your room reading this textbook. Now that you have contemplated this alternative hypothesis to explain the experiences you are having, how can you rule it out? This episode of computer-assisted philosophy should have placed you in the skeptical abyss along with Descartes.

In the rest of the *Meditations*, Descartes ascends step by step out of this abyss. The first steps seem small, but he soon picks up speed; by the end of "Meditation VI," he has vaulted out of the abyss and vindicated most of his earlier beliefs.

Descartes takes his first step (in "Meditation II") when he notes that he cannot doubt that he exists, for he would have to exist to dream or be deceived. And he cannot doubt that he has ideas either. This is progress, but not much, for the whole physical world still lies within the realm of that which can be doubted.

At the end of "Meditation II" and the beginning of "Meditation III," Descartes develops a conception of what knowledge of the external world would be—to help him determine whether he has any. This conception is known as the theory of representative ideas. (A similar conception is developed by Locke in the selection reprinted from his *An Enquiry Concerning Human Understanding*.) According to this theory, knowledge would consist of a two-way relationship between one's ideas and the objects in the external world. Suppose, for example, that you see a book in front of you. The images you have in your mind could exist, even if there were no book, for you might be dreaming or being deceived by an evil demon or by a psychology graduate student. So, just having these ideas or images does not constitute knowledge that there is a book in front of you. For you to know that, there must be a book there, which is causally responsible for you having the ideas and images that you do. To have knowledge, one's ideas must accurately represent the objects that give rise to them.

Given this conception of what it would be to know the external world, can we be sure that we do? It seems that all we can ever be sure of is our own ideas. I might check that there is a book in front of me by reaching out and handling it. Or I might ask a friend (who is in the room with me) if there is, indeed, a book there. But what would this show? Suppose, when I reach out, I feel the hard booklike surface and see my hand on the book. And when I ask my friend, he replies, "Yep, there sure is a book there." But what do these tests prove? These events could just be additional parts of the dream or of the evil demon's plot.

Once one starts thinking in terms of the theory of representative ideas, one gets the feeling of being trapped in one's own mind. If one is really perceiving an external world, one's ideas must be caused by objects beyond the ideas that these ideas accurately represent. But how can one ever check this out? One would have to get outside the circle of one's own ideas, and that seems impossible. This epistemological predicament is sometimes called Descartes's Problem.

Descartes believed he had a solution. He thought that one of his ideas, his idea of God, had a very special quality. It is what we might call self-certifying. It could not have been caused by anything other than God. Descartes invoked certain principles—connecting causes and effects—to convince himself of this. He believed that the cause of an idea must be as perfect as that which the idea represents. Given this, he argues that only God could have caused the idea of God in him. Then, Descartes argues that

God, being perfect, would not allow him to be deceived when he tries hard to be careful. Thus, Descartes needs God's help to climb back out of the abyss into which he tumbled.

In his essay, "Bad Dreams, Evil Demons, and the Experience Machine: Philosophy and *The Matrix*," Christopher Grau connects many of the issues about skepticism raised by Descartes with questions that arise from the film *The Matrix*. Some of the worries Descartes raised about how we can know about the external world find echoes in the questions about how one can know one is not a "brain in a vat," or living a "*Matrix*-like" virtual reality. It is also fascinating to consider what exactly would be problematic about such an existence (involving systematic delusion).

Robert Nozick's contribution addresses both the issues broached by Socrates and Gettier about the concept of knowledge and Descartes's skeptical worries; Nozick's ingenious account of knowledge purportedly can help to resolve the troubling skeptical questions about how we can know about the external world.

Hume's Problems and Some Solutions

Many philosophers have followed Descartes's path into the abyss of ignorance, but few have followed his path out of it. Hume's response to Descartes's Problem is presented, in part, in his "Of Scepticism with Regard to the Senses" (an excerpt from the "Treatise") in which Hume argues that the notion of an independent world apart from our ideas, although it is a confusion, is not just a philosopher's confusion. The way people in general look at chairs and desks and other physical objects—as things that can endure when no one is perceiving them—is a mass of confusion. Should we then revise the way we think about the world? Hume thinks we cannot do so, at least not more than for a moment or two while actively engaged in philosophical reflection. He recommends instead a moderate skepticism. We should be aware of our confusions and limitations while doing philosophy, but, at other times, we should give into our natural inclinations to believe and infer cheerfully, for we really have no choice. And, in his *Enquiry*, Hume argues that only habit or custom, not reason, leads us to expect the future to be like the past: a principle he shows to underlie all our important beliefs about the world, beyond the most immediate deliverances of sensory perception.

Abstractly considered, Descartes's Problem is a special case of the following sort of question. Suppose that I know that an event of a certain sort is occurring at one time. How can I, on the basis of this, know of the occurrence of some other event? In Descartes's case, the first event is the occurrence of an idea in my mind; the second is the external existence of a physical world of the sort that the idea represents.

Hume considers the general problem in his *Enquiry*. He comes to the conclusion that there is essentially no way that knowledge of one event can give us knowledge of another if knowledge requires immunity from any possible doubt. We are so constituted that, in certain circumstances, we will infer the existence of events of one sort from the occurrence of events of another. Given perception, we will believe in an external world—at least when we do not inhibit our natural inclination to do so by thinking philosophical thoughts. And if one sort of event has been accompanied in our experience by another sort of event many times in the past, then, when an event of the first sort is perceived by us, we will expect an event of the second sort. If we see lightning, we expect to hear thunder; if we see someone loosen his or her hold on a book, we expect the book to fall. This is the way we are "wired up"; we have no real choice but to follow the natural flow of ideas in our minds. But there is no further guarantee that the world will conform to these inferences and expectations. Our only grounds for supposing it will is that we have no choice. In the "explanation," appeals to reason must give way to appeals to instinct.

Hume thought that these results of his investigation provided a sort of solution to our doubts. If we cannot do better than rely on our natural inclinations to believe, what is there to worry about? But many philosophers have thought that Hume's arguments raised problems rather than solved them.

These philosophers have thought that there must be something more to be said in favor of **induction**: the practice of basing our expectations about the future on regularities that have been observed in the past. Even if this practice cannot be guaranteed to work, it has been thought that it must have some favored logical status. Something, beside the brute fact that this is the way our minds work, should mark out this practice as more reasonable than any alternative. This problem has become known as Hume's Problem or the problem of induction. It is a part of the more general inquiry into scientific reasoning that is known as the philosophy of science, for the extrapolation from the observed to the unobserved parts of nature seems essential to the scientific method.

In his selection, "The Problem of Induction," W. C. Salmon surveys the various attempts that have been made to improve on Hume's account of induction, that is, to provide it with some more telling justification than Hume was able to provide. Salmon is unable to accept any of the proposed solutions to Hume's Problem that he considers. Yet, he is convinced that there must be a solution, for if there is not, science will be just a matter of faith on a par with other faiths. This situation, Salmon says, is "intellectually and socially undesirable. . . . I find it intolerable to suppose that a theory of biological evolution, supported as it is by extensive scientific evidence, has no more rational foundation than has its rejection by ignorant fundamentalists."

The topic of **causation** is closely related to the problem of induction, and Hume offers an account of causation in Section VII of his *Enquiry*. Hume thought that the relation of causation (or what we could know of it) amounted to no more than constant conjunction. We say that an event of a certain type E causes an event of type E′ if events of type E have been constantly conjoined with those of type E′ in our experience. This view has seemed counterintuitive to many philosophers, who feel that Hume has not accounted for the necessity that attaches to some causal principles.

KEY TERMS

Skepticism
Epistemology
Induction
Causation

A. DESCARTES AND THE PROBLEMS OF SKEPTICISM

Ж

Meditations on First Philosophy

RENÉ DESCARTES

René Descartes (1596–1650) is widely thought of as the father of modern philosophy. In his most famous work, the *Meditations*, Descartes first presents, and subsequently attempts to solve, the problem of skepticism. In addition to his work in epistemology, Descartes is also widely known for his *substance dualism*, a view about the relationship between mind and body and his work in mathematics and physics.

[handwritten: ✷ What are his "clear & distinct" perceptions?]

Meditation I
On What Can Be Called into Doubt

For several years now, I have been aware that I accepted many falsehoods as true in my youth, that what I built on the foundation of those falsehoods was dubious, and therefore that, once in my life, I would need to tear down everything and begin anew from the foundations if I wanted to establish any firm and lasting knowledge. But the task seemed enormous, and I waited until I was so old that no better time for undertaking it would be likely to follow. I have thus delayed so long that it would be

From *Meditations on First Philosophy*, translated from the Latin edition of 1641 by Ronald Rubin. Copyright © 1985 by Arete Press. Reprinted by permission of the translator and publisher.

wrong for me to waste in indecision the time left for action. Today, then, having rid myself of worries and having arranged for some peace and quiet, I withdraw alone, free at last earnestly and wholeheartedly to overthrow all my beliefs.

To do this, I do not need to show each of my beliefs to be false; I may never be able to do that. But, since reason now convinces me that I ought to withhold my assent just as carefully from what is not obviously certain and indubitable as from what is obviously false, I can justify the rejection of all my beliefs if I can find some ground for doubt in each. And, to do this, I need not take on the endless task of running through my beliefs one by one: since a building collapses when its foundation is cut out from under it, I will go straight to the principles on which all my former beliefs rested.

Of course, whatever I have so far accepted as supremely true I have learned either from the senses or through the senses. But I have occasionally caught the senses deceiving me, and it would be prudent for me never completely to trust those who have cheated me even once.

But, while my senses may deceive me about what is small or far away, there may still be other things taken in by the senses which I cannot possibly doubt—such as that I am here, sitting before the fire, wearing a dressing gown, touching this paper. Indeed, these hands and the rest of my body—on what grounds might I deny that they exist?—unless perhaps I liken myself to madmen whose brains are so rattled by the persistent vapors of melancholy that they are sure they are kings when in fact they are paupers, or that they wear purple robes when in fact they are naked, or that their heads are clay, or that they are gourds, or that they are made of glass. But these people are insane, and I would seem just as crazy if I were to apply what I say about them to myself.

This would be perfectly obvious—if I weren't a man accustomed to sleeping at night whose experiences while asleep are at least as far-fetched as those that madmen have while awake. How often a dream has convinced me that I was here, sitting before the fire, wearing my dressing gown, when, in fact, I was undressed and between the covers of my bed! But now I am looking at this piece of paper with my eyes wide open; the head that I am shaking has not been lulled to sleep; I put my hand out consciously and deliberately; I feel the paper and see it. None of this would be as distinct if I were asleep. As if I can't remember having been deluded by similar thoughts while asleep! When I think very carefully about this, I see so plainly that there are no reliable signs by which I can distinguish sleeping from waking that I am stupified—and my stupor itself suggests that I am asleep!

Suppose then that I am dreaming. Suppose, in particular, that my eyes are not open, that my head is not moving, and that I have not put out my hand. Suppose that I do not have hands, or even a body. I must still admit that the things I see in sleep are like painted images, which must have been patterned after real things. Hence, things like eyes, heads, hands, and bodies are not imaginary, but real. For, even when painters try to give bizarre shapes to sirens and satyrs, they are unable to give them completely new natures, but can only jumble together the parts of various animals. Even if they were to come up with something so novel that no one had ever seen anything like it before, something entirely fictitious and unreal, there would at least need to be real colors from which they can compose it. By the same reasoning, while things like eyes, heads, and hands may be imaginary, it must be granted that some simpler and more universal things are real—the "real colors" from which the true and the false images in our thoughts are formed. Among things of this sort seem to be general bodily nature and its extension, the shape of extended things, their quantity (that is, their magnitude and number), the place in which they exist, and the time through which they endure.

Perhaps we can correctly infer that, while physics, astronomy, medicine, and other disciplines requiring the study of composites are dubious, disciplines like arithmetic and geometry, which deal only with completely simple and universal things without regard to whether they exist in the world, are somehow certain and indubitable. Whether we are awake or asleep, two plus three is always five, and the square never has more than four sides. It seems impossible even to suspect such obvious truths of falsity.

Nevertheless, the old belief is imprinted on my mind that there is a God who can do anything and by whom I have been made to be as I am. How do I know that He hasn't brought it about that, while there is in fact no earth, no sky, no extended thing, no shape, no magnitude, and no place, all of these things seem to me to exist, just as they now do? Besides, I think that other people sometimes err in what they believe themselves to know perfectly well; mightn't I be deceived when I add two and three, or count the sides of a square, or do even simpler things (if we can even suppose that there is anything simpler)? Maybe God does not want to deceive me; after all, He is said to be supremely good. But, if God's being good is incompatible with His having created me so that I am always deceived, it seems just as out of line with his being good that he sometimes permits me to be deceived—as he undeniably does.

Or maybe some would rather deny that there is an **omnipotent** God than to believe that everything else is uncertain. Rather than arguing with these people, I will grant that everything I have said about God is fiction. But, however these people think I came to be as I now am (whether they say it is by fate, or by accident, or by a continuous series of events, or in some other way) since it seems that he who errs and is deceived is somehow imperfect, the likelihood that I am constantly deceived increases as the power that they attribute to my original creator decreases. To these arguments, I have no reply; I am forced to admit that nothing that I used to believe is beyond legitimate doubt—not because I have been careless or playful, but because I have valid and well-considered grounds for doubt. I must therefore withhold my assent from my former beliefs as carefully as from obvious falsehoods, if I want to arrive at something certain.

But it is not enough to have noticed this: I must also take care to bear it in mind. For my habitual beliefs constantly return to my mind as if our longstanding, intimate relationship has given them the right to do so, even against my will. I will never break the habit of trusting them and of giving in to them while I see them for what they are—things somewhat dubious (as I have just shown) but nonetheless probable, things that we have much more reason to believe than to deny. That is why I think it will be good deliberately to turn my beliefs around, to allow myself to be deceived, and to suppose that all my previous beliefs are false and imaginary. Eventually, when I have counterbalanced the weight of my prejudices, my bad habits will no longer distort my grasp of things. And I know that there is no danger of error in this and that I won't overindulge in **skepticism**, since I am now concerned, not with acting, but only with knowing.

I will suppose, then, not that there is a supremely good God who is the source of all truth, but that there is an evil demon, supremely powerful and cunning, who works as hard as he can to deceive me. I will say that sky, air, earth, color, shape, sound, and other external things are just dreamed illusions which the demon uses to ensnare my judgment. I will regard myself as not having hands, eyes, flesh, blood, and senses—but as having the false belief that I have all these things. I will obstinately concentrate on this meditation and will thus ensure by mental resolution that, if I do not really have the ability to know the truth, I will at least withhold assent from what is false and from what a deceiver may try to put over on me, however powerful and cunning he may be. But this plan requires effort, and laziness brings me back to my ordinary life. I am like a prisoner who happens to enjoy the illusion of freedom in his dreams, begins to suspect that he is asleep, fears being awakened, and deliberately lets the enticing illusions slip by unchallenged. Thus, I slide back into my old beliefs; I am afraid that, if I awaken, I will need to spend the waking life which follows my peaceful rest, not in the light, but in the confusing darkness of the problems I have just raised.

Meditation II
On the Nature of the Human Mind, Which Is Better Known Than the Body

Yesterday's meditation has hurled me into doubts so great that I can neither ignore them nor think my way out of them. I am in turmoil, as if I have accidentally fallen into a whirlpool and can neither touch bottom nor swim to the safety of the surface. But I will struggle and try to follow the path that I started on yesterday. That is, I will reject whatever is open to the slightest doubt just as though I have found it to be entirely false, and I will continue until I find something certain—even if it is just that nothing is certain. As Archimedes required only one fixed and immovable point to move the whole earth from its place, I can hope for great things if I can even find one small thing that is certain and unshakable.

I suppose, then, that everything I see is unreal. I believe that none of what my unreliable memory presents to me ever happened. I have no senses. Body, shape, extension, motion, and place are fantasies. What then is true? Perhaps only that nothing is certain.

But how do I know that, in addition to the things I just listed, there isn't something that I do not have the slightest reason to doubt? Isn't there a God, or something like one, who puts my thoughts into me? But why should I say so when I may be the author of those thoughts? Well, isn't it at least the case that I am something? But I now am denying that I have senses and a body. But I stop here. For what follows from these denials? Am I so bound to my body and to my senses that I cannot exist without them? I have convinced myself that there is nothing in the world—no sky, no earth, no minds, no bodies.

Doesn't it follow that I don't exist? No; surely I must exist if it's me who is convinced of something. But there is a deceiver, supremely powerful and cunning, whose aim is to see that I am always deceived. Then surely I exist, since I am deceived. Let him deceive me all he can, he will never make it the case that I am nothing while I think that I am something. Thus having fully weighed every consideration, I must finally conclude that the statement "I am, I exist" must be true whenever I state or mentally consider it.

But I do not yet fully understand what this "I" is that must now exist. I must guard against inadvertently taking myself to be something other than I am, thereby going wrong even in the knowledge that I contend is supremely certain and evident. Accordingly, I will think once again about what I believed myself to be before beginning these meditations. From my previous conception of myself, I will subtract everything that can be challenged by the reasons for doubt that I have produced, until nothing remains except what is certain and indubitable.

What, then, did I formerly take myself to be? A man, of course. But what is a man? Should I say a rational animal? No, because then I would need to ask what an animal is and what it is to be rational. Thus, starting from a single question, I would sink into many which are more difficult, and I do not have the time to waste on such subtleties. I would rather pay attention here to the thoughts that occurred to me spontaneously and naturally when I asked what I was. First, it occurred to me that I have a face, hands, arms, and all the other equipment (also found in corpses) which I call a body. Next, it occurred to me that I take nourishment, move myself around, sense, and think—that I do things which I trace back to my soul. I didn't often stop to think about what this soul was, and, when I did, I imagined it to be a rarified air, or fire, or ether permeating the denser parts of my body. On the other hand, I did not have any doubts about physical objects: I thought that I distinctly knew their nature. If I had tried to describe my conception of these objects, I might have said this: "When I call something a physical object, I mean that it is capable of being bounded by a shape and limited to a place; that it can so fill a space as to exclude others from it; that it can be perceived by sight, touch, hearing, taste, and smell; that it cannot move itself but can be moved by

something else that touches it." I judged that the powers of self-movement, of sensing, and of thinking did not belong to the nature of physical objects, and, in fact, I marveled that there were some physical objects in which these powers could be found.

But what should I think now, while supposing that a supremely powerful and "evil" deceiver completely devotes himself to seeing to it that I am deceived? Can I say that I have any of the things that I attributed to the nature of physical objects? I concentrate, think, reconsider—but nothing comes to me; I am tired of this pointless repetition. But what about the things that I have assigned to soul? Nutrition and self-movement? Since I have no body, these are merely illusions. Sensing? But I cannot sense without a body, and in sleep I have seemed to sense many things that I did not really sense. Thinking? It comes down to this: There is thinking, and thought alone cannot be taken away from me. I am, I exist. That much is certain. For how long? For as long as I think—for it may be that, if I completely stopped thinking, I would also cease to be. I am not now admitting anything unless it must be true, and I am therefore not admitting that I am anything at all other than a thinking thing—that is, a mind, soul, understanding, or reason (terms whose meaning I did not previously know). I know that I am a real, existing thing, but what kind of thing? As I have said, a thing that thinks.

What else? I will draw up mental images. I can't say that I am the collection of organs that we call a human body, or that I am some rarified gas permeating these organs, or that I am air, or fire, or vapor, or breath—for I have supposed that none of these things exist. But I can still say that I am something. It may be, of course, that these things, which I do not yet know and which I am therefore supposing to be nonexistent, are not really distinct from the "I" that I know to exist. I don't know, and I am not going to argue about it now. I can only pass judgment on what I do know. I know that I exist, and I ask what the "I" is that I know to exist. It is obvious that the conception of myself that I derive in *this* way does not depend on anything that I do not yet know to exist and, consequently, that it does not depend on anything of which I can shape a mental image. And the word "shape" points to my mistake. I would truly be creating things if I were to have a mental image of what I am, since to have a mental image is just to contemplate the shape or image of a physical object. I now know with certainty that I exist and at the same time that all images—and, more generally, all things associated with the nature of physical objects—may just be dreams. When I keep this in mind, it seems just as absurd to say "I use mental images to help me understand what I am" as it would be to say "Now, while awake, I see something true—but, since I don't yet see it clearly enough, I'll go to sleep and let my dreams present it to me more clearly and truly." Thus I know that none of the things that I can comprehend with the aid of the mental images bear on my knowledge of myself. I must carefully draw my mind away from such things so that it can gain a distinct knowledge of its own nature.

But what then am I? A thinking thing. And what is that? Something that doubts, understands, affirms, denies, wills, refuses—and also imagines and senses.

It is no small matter if I do all of these things. But how could it be otherwise? Isn't it me who now doubts nearly everything, understands something, affirms this one thing, refuses to affirm other things, wants to know much more, refuses to be deceived, has mental images (sometimes involuntarily), and is aware of what seems to come from his senses? Even if I am always dreaming, and even if my creator does what he can to deceive me, isn't it just as true that I do all these things as that I exist? Are any of these things distinct from my thought? Can any be said to be separate from me? It's so obvious that it is me who doubts, understands, and wills that I don't see how I could make it more evident. And it is also me who has mental images—for while it may be (as I am supposing) that absolutely nothing of which I have a mental image really exists, the ability to have mental images really does exist and influences my thought. Finally, it is me who senses—or who seems to gain awareness of physical objects through the senses. For example, I now see the light, hear the noise, and feel the heat. These things are unreal, since I am dreaming. But it is still certain that I *seem* to see, to hear, and to feel. This seeming cannot be unreal, but *it* is what is properly called sensing; strictly speaking, sensing is just thinking.

From these considerations, I begin to learn a little about what I am. But I still can't stop thinking that I know physical objects (which I picture in

mental images and examine with my senses) much more distinctly than I know this unknown "I" (of which I cannot form a mental image). I think this, even though it would be astounding if it turns out that I comprehend things which I have found to be doubtful, unknown, and alien to me more distinctly than that which I know to be real—namely, my self. But I see what is happening: My mind enjoys wandering, and it won't confine itself to the truth. I will therefore loosen the reins for now so that later, when the time is right, I will be able to control my mind more easily.

Let's consider the things commonly taken to be the most distinctly comprehended: physical objects that we see and touch. Let's not consider the general idea of a physical object, since such general conceptions are very often confused. Rather, let's consider a particular. Take, for example, this piece of wax. It has just been taken from the honeycomb; it hasn't yet completely lost the taste of honey; it still smells of the flowers from which it was gathered; its color, shape, and size are obvious; it is hard, cold, and easy to touch; it makes a sound when rapped. In short, everything required for me to have distinct knowledge of a physical object seems to be present. But, as I speak, I move the wax towards the fire; it loses what was left of its taste; it gives up its smell; it changes color; it loses its shape; it gets bigger; it melts; it heats up; it becomes difficult to touch; it no longer makes a sound when struck. Is it still the same piece of wax? We must say that it is: no one denies it or thinks otherwise. Then what was there in the wax that was so distinctly comprehended? Certainly nothing that I reached with the senses—for, while everything having to do with taste, smell, sight, touch, and hearing has changed, the same piece of wax remains.

Perhaps what I distinctly knew was neither the sweetness of honey, nor the fragrance of flowers, nor a sound, but a physical object that sometimes appeared to me one way and sometimes another. But what exactly is it that I am now imagining? Let's pay careful attention; removing everything that doesn't belong to the wax, let's see what is left. Nothing is left except an extended, flexible, and changeable thing. But what is it for this thing to be flexible and changeable? Is it just that the wax can go from round to square and then to triangular, as I have mentally pictured? Of course not;

since I understand that the wax's shape can change in innumerable ways, and since I can't run through all the changes in my imagination, my comprehension of the wax's flexibility and changeability cannot be the product of my ability to have mental images. And what about the thing that is extended? Are we also ignorant of its extension? Since the extension of the wax increases when the wax melts, increases again when the wax boils, and increases still more when the wax gets hotter, I will be mistaken about what the wax is unless I believe that it can undergo more changes in extension than I can ever encompass with mental images. I must therefore admit that I do not have an image of what the wax is—that I grasp what it is with only my mind. (While I am saying this about a particular piece of wax, it is even more clearly true about wax in general.) What then is this piece of wax that I grasp with my mind? It is exactly what I believed it to be at the outset—something that I see, feel, and imagine. It must be noted, however, that my grasp of the wax is not visual, tactile, or pictorial; despite the appearances, I have never had a sensory grasp of what the wax is. Rather, my grasp of the wax is the result of a purely mental inspection, which is imperfect and confused (as it was once) or clear and distinct (as it is now) depending on how much attention I pay to the things of which the wax consists.

But it is surprisingly easy for my mind to be misled. Even when I think to myself nonverbally, language impedes me, and common usage comes close to deceiving me. For, when the wax is present, we say that we see the wax itself, not that we infer its presence from its color and shape. I would leap from this fact about language to the conclusion that I learn about the wax by eyesight rather than by purely mental inspection—except that, if I happen to look out my window and see men walking in the street, it is no less natural to say that I see the men than it is to say that I see the wax. But what do I really see, except hats and coats that could be covering robots? Yet, I judge that there are men in the street. Thus I comprehend with my judgment, which is in my mind, objects that I once believed myself to see with my eyes.

One who aspires to wisdom above that of the common man disgraces himself by deriving doubt from common ways of speaking. Let's go on, then, to ask *when* I most clearly and perfectly grasped what the

wax is. Was it when I first looked at the wax and believed my knowledge of it to come from the external senses (or, at any rate from the imagination, the "common sense")? Or is it now, after I have carefully studied what the wax is and how I come to know it? Doubt would be silly here. For what was distinct in my original conception of the wax? How did that conception differ from the one shared by all animals? Of course, when I distinguish the wax from its external forms—when I "undress" it and view it "denuded"—there may still be errors in my judgments about it, but I can't possibly grasp the wax in this way without a human mind.

What should I say about this mind—or, in other words, about myself? (I am not now admitting that there is anything to me but a mind.) What is this "I" that seems to grasp the wax so distinctly? Don't I know myself much more truly and certainly, and also much more distinctly and plainly, than I know the wax? If I base my judgment that the wax exists on the fact that I see it, my seeing it much more obviously implies that I exist. It is possible that what I see is not really wax, and it is also possible that I don't even have eyes with which to see—but it clearly is *not* possible that, when I see (or, what now amounts to the same thing, when I think I see), the "I" which thinks is not a real thing. Similarly, while I might base my judgment that the wax exists on the fact that I feel it, the same fact makes it obvious that I exist. If I base my judgment that the wax exists on the fact that I have a mental image of it or on some other fact of this sort, the same thing can obviously be said. And what I have said about the wax applies to everything else that is outside me. Moreover, if I seem to grasp the wax more distinctly when I detect it with several senses than when I detect it just with sight or touch, I must know myself even more distinctly—for every consideration that contributes to my grasp of the piece of wax or to my grasp of any other physical object serves better to reveal the nature of my mind. Besides, the mind has so much in it by which it can make its conception of itself distinct that what comes to it from physical objects hardly seems to matter.

And now I have brought myself back to where I wanted to be. I now know that physical objects are not really known through sensation or imagination, but are grasped by the understanding alone. And, from the fact that physical objects are grasped in virtue of their being understandable (rather than tangible or visible), I infer that I can't know anything more easily or plainly than my mind. Since it takes time to break old habits of thought, however, I should pause here to allow the length of contemplation to impress the new thoughts more deeply into my memory.

Meditation III
On God's Existence

I will now close my eyes, plug my ears, and withdraw all my senses. I will even rid my thoughts of the images of physical objects—or, if that is too hard, I will write those images off as empty illusions. Relying on nothing but myself, I will look more deeply into myself and try gradually to come to know myself better. I am a thinking thing—a thing that doubts, affirms, denies, understands a few things, is ignorant of many things, wills, and refuses. I also imagine and sense—for (as I have noted) I am certain that, even if I do not imagine or sense anything outside me, the modifications of thought that I call sensations and mental images exist in me insofar as they are just modifications of thought.

That is a brief summary of all that I really know—or, at any rate, of all that I have so far noticed that I know. I now will examine more carefully whether there are other things in me which I have not yet discovered. I am certain that I am a thinking thing. Then don't I know what is needed for me to be certain of other things? In this first knowledge, there is nothing but a clear and distinct grasp of what I affirm, and this grasp surely would not suffice to make me certain if it could ever happen that something I grasped so clearly and distinctly was false. Accordingly, I seem to be able to establish the general rule that whatever I clearly and distinctly grasp is true.

But, in the past, I have accepted as completely obvious and certain many thoughts which I later found to be dubious. What were these thoughts about? The earth, the sky, the stars, and other objects of sense. But what did I clearly grasp about these objects? Only that ideas or thoughts of them appeared in my mind. Even now, I do not deny that these ideas occur in me. But there was something else that I used to affirm—something that I used to believe myself to grasp clearly but did not really grasp at all: I affirmed

that there were things besides me, that the ideas in me came from these things, and that the ideas perfectly resembled these things. If I didn't err here, I at least reached a true judgment that wasn't justified by the strength of my understanding.

But what follows from this? When I considered very simple and easy points of arithmetic or geometry—such as that two and three together make five—didn't I see them clearly enough to affirm their truth? My only reason for thinking that I ought to doubt these things was the thought that my God-given nature might deceive me, even about what seems most obvious. But, whenever I conceive of this all-powerful God, I am compelled to admit that, if He wants, he can make it the case that I err even about what I take my mind's eye to see most clearly. On the other hand, when I turn to the things that I believe myself to grasp very clearly, I am so convinced by them that I spontaneously burst forth saying, "Whoever may deceive me, he will never bring it about that I am nothing while I think that I am something, or that I have never been when it is now true that I am, or that two plus three is either more or less than five, or that something else in which I recognize an obvious inconsistency is true." Of course, since I have no reason for thinking that God *is* a deceiver—indeed, since I don't yet know whether God *is*—the grounds for doubt that rest on the supposition that God deceives are very weak and "**metaphysical**." Still, to rid myself of them I ought to ask as soon as possible whether there is a God and, if so, whether He can be a deceiver. For it seems that, until I know these two things, I can never be completely certain of anything else.

The structure of my project seems to require, however, that I first categorize my thoughts and ask in which of them truth and falsity really reside. Some of my thoughts are like images of things, and only these can properly be called ideas; I have an idea, for example, when I think of a man, of a chimera, of heaven, of an angel, or of God. But other thoughts have other properties: while I always apprehend something as the object of my thought when I will, fear, affirm, or deny, my thought also includes a component in addition to the likeness of that thing. Some of these components are called volitions or emotions; others, judgments.

Now, viewed in themselves and without regard to other things, ideas cannot really be false: if I imagine a chimera and a goat, it is just as true that I imagine the chimera as that I imagine the goat. And I needn't worry about falsehood in volitions or emotions: if I perversely want something that does not exist, it is still true that I want that thing. All that remains, then, are my judgments; it is here that I must be careful not to err. And the first and foremost of the errors that I find in my judgments is that of assuming that the ideas in me have a similarity or conformity to things outside of me. For, if I were to regard ideas merely as modifications of thought, they could hardly lead me wrong.

Of my ideas, some seem to me to be innate, others acquired, and others produced by me. The ideas by which I understand what reality, truth, and thought are seem to have come from my own nature; those by which I hear a noise, see the sun, or feel the fire are ones I formerly judged to come from things outside me; and those of sirens, hippogriffs, and so on are ones that I have formed in myself. Or maybe I can take all of my ideas to be acquired, all innate, or all created by me: I do not yet clearly see where my ideas come from.

For the moment, the central question is about the ideas that I view as derived from objects existing outside me. What reason is there for thinking that these ideas resemble the objects? I seem to have been taught this by nature. Moreover, I find that these ideas are independent of my will (and hence of me) for they often appear when I do not want them to do so. For example, I now feel heat whether I want to or not, and I therefore take the idea or sensation of heat to come from something distinct from me— namely, from the heat of the fire by which I am now sitting. And the obvious thing to think is that what a thing sends to me is its own likeness.

Now, I see whether these reasons are good ones. When I say that nature teaches me something, I mean just that I have a spontaneous impulse to believe it— not that the light of nature reveals the thing's truth to me. There is an important difference. When the light of nature reveals something to me (such as that my thinking implies my existing) that thing is completely beyond doubt, since there is nothing as reliable as the light of nature by means of which I could learn that the thing is not true. As for my natural impulses, however, I have often judged them to have led me astray in practical choices, and I don't see why I should trust them any more on other matters.

Next, while my sensory ideas may not depend on my will, it doesn't follow that they come from outside me. The natural impulses of which I just spoke are in me, but *they* seem to *conflict* with my will. I may therefore have in me an as yet undiscovered ability to produce in myself the ideas that seem to come from outside me. In fact, it has always seemed to me that, while dreaming, I *have* formed such ideas in myself without the aid of external objects.

Finally, even if some of my ideas do come from things distinct from me, it doesn't follow that they are likenesses of things. Indeed, it often seems to me that an idea differs greatly from its cause. For example, I find in myself two different ideas of the sun. One, which I "take in" through the senses and which I ought therefore to view as a typical acquired idea, makes the sun look very small to me. The other, which I derive from astronomical reasoning (that is, which I make, perhaps by composing it from innate ideas), shows the sun to be many times larger than the earth. It is not possible that both of these ideas are accurate likenesses of the sun that exists outside me, and reason convinces me that the one least like the sun is the one that seems to arise most directly from it.

All that I have said shows that, until now, my belief that there are things outside me which implant their ideas or images in me (perhaps through my senses) has rested on blind impulse rather than on certain judgment.

But there may still be a way of telling whether the things which are the sources of my ideas exist outside me. When I regard the ideas of things as mere modifications of thought, I find no inequality among them; all seem to arise from me in the same way. But, inasmuch as different ideas present different things to me, there obviously are great differences among them. The ideas that show me substances are unquestionably greater—or have more "presentational reality"— than those that merely show me modifications or accidents. Similarly, the idea by which I understand the supreme God—eternal, infinite, **omniscient**, omnipotent, and creator of all things other than Himself—has more presentational reality in it than the ideas which present finite substances.

But the light of nature has revealed that there is at least as much in the complete **efficient cause** as in its effect. For where could an effect get its reality if not from its cause? And how could a cause give what it did not itself have? It follows both that something cannot come from nothing and that what is more perfect—or, in other words, has more reality in it—cannot come from what is less perfect and has less reality. This obviously holds, not just for those effects whose reality is actual or formal, but also for ideas, whose reality we regard as merely presentational. For example, it's impossible for a nonexistent stone to come into existence unless it is produced by something containing, either formally or eminently, everything in the stone. Similarly, heat can only be induced in something that is not already hot by something having at least the same degree of perfection as heat. Moreover, it is impossible for the idea of heat or of a stone to be in me unless it has been put there by a cause in which there is at least as much reality as in heat or the stone. For, although an idea's cause does not transmit any of its actual or formal reality to the idea, and although an idea does not by its nature require any formal reality other than what it borrows from my thought (of which it is a modification), we should not think that the idea's cause can be less real than the idea. Rather, we should think that each idea contains one particular presentational reality which it must get from a cause having at least as much formal reality as the idea has presentational reality. For, if we suppose that something is in an idea but not in its cause, we must suppose that something has come from nothing. And, however imperfect the existence of a thing that exists presentationally in the understanding through an idea, that thing obviously is *something*, and it therefore cannot come from nothing.

And, although the reality that I am considering in my ideas is just presentational, I ought not to suspect that it need not be in the ideas' cause formally—that it suffices for it to be there presentationally. For, just as the presentational existence of my ideas belongs to the ideas in virtue of their nature, the formal existence of the ideas' causes belongs to those causes—or, at least, to the first and foremost of them—in virtue of their nature. Although one idea may arise from another, this can't go back to infinity; it must

eventually arrive at a primary idea whose cause is an "archetype" containing formally all that the idea contains presentationally. Hence, the light of nature makes it clear to me that the ideas in me are like images which may well fall short of the things from which they derive, but which cannot contain anything greater or more perfect.

The more time and care I take in studying all of this, the more clearly and distinctly I know that it is true. But what follows from it? On the one hand, if the presentational reality of one of my ideas is so great that I can be confident that the same degree of reality is not in me either formally or eminently, I can conclude that I cannot be the cause of that idea, that another thing must necessarily exist as its cause, and consequently that I am not alone in the world. On the other hand, if I can find no such idea in me, I will have no argument at all for the existence of something other than me—for, having diligently searched for another such argument, I have yet to find one.

Besides the idea that shows me to myself (about which there can be no problem here), my ideas include one which presents God, others which present physical objects, others which present angels, others which present animals, and finally others which present men like me.

As to my ideas of other men, of animals, and of angels, it is easy to see that—even if the world contained no men but me, no animals, and no angels—I could have composed these ideas from those that I have of myself, of physical objects, and of God.

And, as to my ideas of physical objects, it seems that nothing in them is so great that it couldn't have come from me. For, if I analyze my ideas of physical objects carefully, taking them one by one as I did yesterday when examining my idea of the piece of wax, I notice that there is very little in them that I grasp clearly and distinctly except magnitude (which is extension in length, breadth, and depth), shape (which arises from extension's limits), position (which the differently shaped things have relative to one another), and motion (which is just change of this relative position). To these I can add substance, duration, and number, but my thoughts of other things in physical objects (such as light and color, sound, odor, taste, heat and cold, and tactile qualities) are so confused and obscure that I can't say whether they are true or false—whether my ideas of these things are of something or of nothing. For, although—as I noted earlier—that which is properly called false-hood (namely, *formal* falsehood) can only be found in judgments, we can still find falsehood of another sort (namely, *material* falsehood) in an idea when it presents what is not a thing as though it were a thing. For example, the ideas that I have of coldness and heat are so unclear and indistinct that I can't tell from them whether coldness is just the absence of heat, or heat just the absence of coldness, or both are real qualities, or neither is. And, since every idea is "of something," the idea that presents coldness to me as something real and positive could justifiably be called false if coldness were just the absence of heat. And the same holds for other similar ideas.

For ideas of this sort, I need not posit a creator other than me. I know by the light of nature that, if one of these ideas is false (that is, if it doesn't present a real thing), it comes from nothing—that is, that the only cause of its being in me is a deficiency of my (obviously imperfect) nature. And, if one of these ideas is true, I still see no reason why I couldn't have produced it—for these ideas present so little reality to me that I can't even distinguish the reality in them from the reality of that which doesn't exist.

Of the things that *are* clear and distinct in my ideas of physical objects, it seems that I may have borrowed some—such as substance, duration, and number—from my idea of myself. Of course, my conception of myself differs from my conception of a stone in that I think of myself as a thinking and unextended thing while I think of the stone as an extended and unthinking thing. But, when I conceive the stone as a substance (that is, as something that can exist by itself), my understanding of substance seems to be the same as when I conceive of myself as a substance. Similarly, when I grasp that I now exist and remember that I have existed in the past, and when I have various thoughts and notice how many of them there are, I get the ideas of duration and number, which I can then apply to other objects of thought. The other components of my ideas of physical objects—namely, extension, shape, place, and motion—can't be in me formally since I am just a thinking thing, but, as they are just modes of substance, and as I am a substance, they can be in me eminently.

All that is left is to consider whether there may be something in my idea of God that couldn't have come from me. By "God" I mean infinite substance, independent, supremely intelligent, and supremely powerful—the thing from which I and everything else that may exist get our existence. The more I consider these attributes, the less it seems that they could have come from me alone. And I must therefore conclude that God necessarily exists.

While I may have the idea of substance in me in virtue of my being a substance, I who am finite would not have the idea of infinite substance in me unless it came from a substance that really was infinite.

And I ought not to say that, rather than having a true idea of infinity, I grasp it merely as the absence of limits—in the way that I grasp rest as the absence of motion and darkness as the absence of light. On the contrary, it's clear to me that there is more reality in an infinite than in a finite substance and, hence, that my grasp of the infinite must somehow be prior to my grasp of the finite—my understanding of God prior to my understanding of myself. For, how could I understand that I doubt and desire, that I am deficient and imperfect, if I don't have the idea of something more perfect to use as a standard of comparison?

And, unlike the ideas of hot and cold which I just discussed, the idea of God cannot be said to be materially false and, hence, to come from nothing. On the contrary, since the idea of God is completely clear and distinct and contains more presentational reality than any other idea, no idea is truer per se and none less open to the suspicion of falsity. The idea of a supremely perfect and infinite entity, I maintain, is completely true. For, while I may be able to suppose that there is no such entity, I cannot even suppose that my idea of God (like the idea of coldness) fails to show me anything real. Yes, this idea is maximally clear and distinct; it contains everything that I grasp clearly and distinctly, everything real and true, everything with any perfection. And it is no objection that I can't fully comprehend the infinite or that there are innumerable things in God which I can't comprehend fully or even reach with thought. It suffices for me to understand that, being finite, I cannot fully comprehend the infinite and to judge that, if I grasp something clearly and distinctly and know it to have some perfection, it is either formally or eminently present in God (perhaps along with innumerable other things of which I am ignorant). If I do this, my idea of God will be supremely true, and supremely clear and distinct.

But maybe I am greater than I have assumed; maybe all the perfections that I attribute to God are in me potentially, still unreal and unactualized. I have already seen my knowledge gradually increase, and I don't see anything to prevent its becoming greater and greater to infinity. Nor do I see why, by means of such increased knowledge, I couldn't get all the rest of God's perfections. Finally, if the potential for these perfections is in me, I don't see why this potential couldn't by itself produce in me the ideas of these perfections.

None of this is possible. First, while it's true that my knowledge gradually increases and that I have many as yet unactualized potentialities, none of this fits with my idea of God, in whom absolutely nothing is potential; the gradual increase in my knowledge shows that I am *imperfect*, not that I am perfect. Moreover, even if my knowledge were continually to become greater and greater, it would never become actually infinite, since it will never become so great that it couldn't be greater. But I judge that God is actually infinite and that nothing can be added to his perfection. Finally, I see that an idea's presentational being must be produced, not by mere potentiality (which, strictly speaking, is nothing), but by what is actual or formal.

When I pay attention to these things, the light of nature makes all of them obvious. But, when I attend less carefully and the images of sensible things blind my mind's eye, it's hard for me to remember that the idea of an entity more perfect than I am must come from an entity that is more perfect. That's why I want to go on to ask whether I, who have the idea of a perfect entity, could exist if no such entity existed.

From what might I derive my existence if not my God? Either from myself, or from my parents, or from something else less perfect than God (for I can't suppose that anything other than God is His superior, or even His equal, in perfection).

But, if I were to get my existence from myself, I wouldn't doubt, or want, or lack anything; I would have given myself every perfection of which I have an idea and would therefore be God. And I shouldn't think that it might be harder to give myself what I lack than what I already have. On the contrary, it would obviously be much harder to make me (a thinking thing or substance) emerge from nothing than to give me complete knowledge (which is just an attribute of substance). But surely, if I had given myself that which is harder to get, I wouldn't have denied myself complete knowledge, which would have been easier to get. In fact, I wouldn't have denied myself *any* of the perfections that I grasp in the idea of God. None of these perfections seems harder to get than existence, but they would seem harder to get if I had really given myself everything I now have—for in creating myself I would have discovered the limits of my power.

And I can't avoid the force of this argument by supposing that, having always existed as I do now, I don't have any creator. Since my lifetime can be divided into innumerable, mutually independent parts, the fact that I existed a little while ago does not entail that I exist now, unless a cause "re-creates" me—or, in other words, preserves me—at this moment. Thus, when I keep the nature of time in mind, it becomes obvious that exactly the same power and action is required to preserve a thing at each of the moments at which it exists as would be required to create it anew if it had never existed. Accordingly, one of the things revealed by the light of nature is that preservation and creation differ only in the way we think of them.

I ought to ask myself, then, whether *I* have the power to ensure that I, who now am, will exist a little while from now. Since I am nothing but a thinking thing—or, at any rate, since I am not focusing on the part of me that thinks—I would surely be aware of this power if it were in me. But I find no such power. And this very clearly shows that there is an entity distinct from me on whom I depend.

Maybe this entity isn't God; maybe I am the product of my parents or of some other cause less perfect than God. But, as I just said, there must be at least as much in a cause as in its effect. Therefore, since I am a thinking thing with the idea of God in me, my cause—whatever it is—must be a thinking thing having in it the idea of every perfection that I attribute to God. And I can go on to ask whether this thing gets its existence from itself or from something else. But it's obvious from what I have just said that, if my cause gets its existence from itself, it must *be* God: having the power to exist in itself, it must also have the power actually to give itself every perfection of which it has an idea—including every perfection that I conceive of in God. On the other hand, if my cause gets its existence from some other thing, I can go on to ask whether this other thing gets its existence from itself or from something else. Eventually, I will come to the ultimate cause: God.

It is clear that there can't be an infinite regress here—especially since I am concerned, not so much with the cause that originally produced me, as with the one that preserves me in the present.

But what about the view that several partial causes combined to make me, that I get the ideas of the various perfections I attribute to God from different causes, and that, while each of these perfections can be found somewhere in the universe, there is no God in whom they all come together? I can't suppose that this is true. On the contrary, one of the chief perfections that I understand God to have is unity—that is, simplicity, or inseparability from everything to Him. But, of all God's perfections, unity is the one whose idea could only have been put in me by a cause which gives me the ideas of all the other perfections: I can be made to regard God's perfections as inseparably joined only if I am made aware of what these perfections are.

Finally, it's clear that, even if everything that I used to believe about my parents is true, they do not preserve me. Insofar as I am a thinking thing, they did not even take part in creating me. They simply formed the matter in which I used to think that I resided. (By "I" I mean my mind, which is all that I now grasp of myself.) There can therefore be no problem about my parents, and I am driven to this conclusion: The fact that I exist and have an idea of God as a perfect entity conclusively entails that God does in fact exist.

All that's left is to explain how I have gotten my idea of God from Him. I have not taken it in through my senses; it has never come to me unexpectedly as the ideas of sensible things do when those things affect (or seem to affect) my external organs of sense. Nor have I made the idea myself; I can't subtract

from it or add to it. The idea must therefore be innate in me, like my idea of myself.

And it's not at all surprising that in creating me God put this idea into me, impressing it like a craftsman's mark on His work. This mark needn't be distinct from the work itself. Indeed, the very fact that it was God who created me confirms that I have somehow been made in His image or likeness and that I grasp this likeness (which contains the idea of God) in the same way that I grasp myself. For, when I turn my mind's eye on myself, I understand, not only that I am an incomplete, dependent thing which constantly strives for bigger and better things, but also that He on whom I depend, having all these things in Himself as infinite reality rather than just as vague potentiality, must therefore be God. The whole argument comes down to this: I know that I could not exist with my present nature (that is, that I could not exist with the idea of God in me) unless there really were a God—the very God of whom I have an idea, the thing having all of the perfections that I can't fully comprehend but can somehow reach with thought, the thing that clearly cannot be defective. From this, it is obvious that He can't deceive, for the natural light reveals that fraud and deception arise from defect.

But before examining this more carefully and investigating its consequences, I want to dwell for a moment in the contemplation of God, to ponder His attributes in me, to see, admire, and adore the beauty of His boundless light, insofar as my clouded insight allows. Believing that the supreme happiness of the other life consists wholly of the contemplation of divine greatness, I now find that through less perfect contemplation of the same sort I can gain the greatest joy available in this life.

Meditation IV
On Truth and Falsity

In the last few days, I have gotten used to drawing my mind away from my senses. Having carefully noted that I really grasp very little about physical objects, that I know much more about the human mind, and that I know even more about God, I no longer find it hard to turn my thoughts away from things of which I can have mental images and to-wards things which I can only understand—things completely separate from matter. I have a much more distinct idea of the human mind than of physical objects, insofar as the mind is just a thinking thing which isn't extended in length, breadth, or depth and which doesn't have anything in common with physical objects. Moreover, when I observe that I doubt or that I am incomplete and dependent, I have a clear and distinct idea of God, a complete and independent entity. And, from the fact that this idea is in me and that I who have the idea exist, I can infer both that God exists and that I am completely dependent on Him for my existence from moment to moment. This inference is so obvious that I'm sure humans can't know anything more evidently or certainly. And now I think I see a way of moving from the contemplation of the true God, in whom are hidden all treasures of knowledge and wisdom, to knowledge of *other* things.

First, I know it is impossible for Him ever to deceive me. Fraud and deception always contain imperfection, and, while the ability to deceive may seem a sign of cunning and power, the desire to deceive reveals malice or weakness and therefore can't be among God's desires.

Next, I find in myself an ability to judge which, like everything else in me, I have gotten from God. Since He doesn't want to deceive me, He certainly hasn't given me an ability which will lead me wrong when properly used.

There could be no doubt about this—except that it may seem to imply that I *never* err. For, if I have gotten everything in me from God and He hasn't given me the ability to err, it doesn't seem possible for me *ever* to err. Thus, as long as I think only of God and devote all my attention to Him, I can't find any cause for error and falsity. When I turn my attention back to myself, however, I find that I can make innumerable errors. In looking for the cause of these errors, I find before me, not just the real and positive idea of God, but also the negative idea of "nothingness"—the idea of that which is completely devoid of perfection. I find that I am "intermediary" between God and nothingness, between the supreme entity and the nonentity. Insofar as I am the creation of the supreme entity, there is nothing in me that accounts for my being

deceived or led into error, but, insofar as I somehow participate in nothingness or the nonentity—that is, insofar as I am not identical to the supreme entity and lack a great many things—it is not surprising that I am deceived. Thus I understand that, in itself, error is a *lack* rather than a real thing dependent on God. And I therefore understand that I can err without God's having given me a special ability to do so: I fall into error because my God-given ability to judge the truth isn't infinite.

But there is still something to be explained. Error is not just an absence, but a deprivation—the lack of knowledge that somehow *ought* to be in me. But, when I attend to God's nature, it seems impossible that He has given me an ability that is an imperfect thing of its kind—an ability lacking a perfection that it ought to have. The greater the craftsman's skill, the more perfect his product. Then how can the supreme creator of all things have made something that isn't absolutely perfect? There is no doubt that God could have made me so that I never err, and there is no doubt that He always wants what is best. Then is it better for me to be deceived than not to be deceived?

When I pay more careful attention, I realize that I should not be surprised at God's doing things that I can't explain and that I should not doubt His existence just because I find that I sometimes can't understand why or how He has made something. For, since I know that my nature is weak and limited while God's is limitless, incomprehensible, and infinite, I also know that He can do innumerable things of whose causes I am ignorant. And, on this ground alone, I regard the common practice of explaining things in terms of their purposes to be useless in physics: I would be foolhardy if I tried to understand God's purposes.

It also seems to me that, rather than looking at a single creation in isolation when asking whether God's works are perfect, I ought to look at all of them together. For a thing that seems imperfect when viewed alone may seem completely perfect when regarded as a part of the world. Of course, since calling everything into doubt, I haven't established that anything exists besides me and God. But, when I consider God's immense power, I can't deny that He has made (or, in any case, that He can make) many other things, and I must therefore regard myself as part of a universe.

Finally, turning to myself and investigating the nature of my errors (which are all that show me to be imperfect), I notice that these errors depend on two concurrent causes: my ability to know and my ability to choose freely—that is, my understanding and my will.

Viewed in itself, the understanding is just the thing by which I grasp the ideas about which I form judgments, and I therefore cannot say that there are errors in the understanding itself. While there may be innumerable things of which I have no idea, I can't say that I am deprived of these ideas, but only that I happen to lack them—for I don't have any reason to think that God ought to have given me a greater ability to know than He has: Although God is a supremely skillful craftsman, I don't think that He ought to endow each of his works with all the perfections that He can put in the others.

On the other hand, I can't complain about the scope or perfection of my God-given **freedom of will**—for my will doesn't seem to me to be restricted in any way. In fact, it seems well worth noting that nothing in me other than my will is so great and perfect that I couldn't conceivably be bigger or better. When I think about my ability to understand, for example, I immediately realize that it is very small and restricted, and I simultaneously form the idea of something much greater—something supremely perfect and infinite. From the fact that I can form the idea of this perfection, I infer that the perfection is present in God's nature. Similarly, when I consider my other abilities (such as the abilities to remember and to imagine) I clearly see that they all are feeble and limited in me but boundless in God. The only exception is my will or freedom of choice, which cannot conceivably be greater than it is. In fact, it is largely for this reason that I regard myself as an image or likeness of God. God's will is incomparably greater than mine, of course, both in virtue of the knowledge and power associated with it (which result in its greater strength and efficacy) and in virtue of the greater range of its objects. Yet, viewed in itself as a will, God's will seems no greater than mine—because having a will just amounts to being able either to do or not to do, to affirm or deny, to seek or avoid. Or better: having a will amounts to being inclined to do or not to do (affirm or deny, seek or shun) what the understanding offers, without an

awareness of being forced towards it by external forces. For being free does not require being inclined towards both alternatives. On the contrary, the more I lean towards one alternative—either because I understand the truth or goodness in it or because God has so arranged my deepest thoughts—the more freely I choose it. Thus divine grace and knowledge of nature clearly increase and strengthen rather than diminish my freedom. The indifference that I experience when no consideration impels me towards one alternative rather than the other is freedom of the lowest sort, which reveals a defect or an absence of knowledge rather than a perfection. For, if I always knew what was good or true, I wouldn't ever deliberate about what to do or choose, and consequently, though completely free, I would never be indifferent.

From this I see that my God-given ability to will is not itself the cause of my errors; my will is great, and it is a perfect thing of its kind. Neither is my power of understanding the cause of my errors; whenever I understand something, I understand it correctly and without the possibility of deception, since my understanding comes from God. Then what *is* the source of my errors? Just that, while my will has a broader scope than my understanding, I don't keep it within the same bounds, but extend it to what I don't understand. Being indifferent to these things, I am easily led away from truth and goodness into error and sin.

For example, when I asked a while ago whether anything exists in the world, I noted that, from the fact that I ask this, it follows that I exist. Since I very clearly understood this, I couldn't fail to believe it to be true. It was not that a force outside me compelled me to believe, but that an intense light in my understanding produced a strong inclination of my will. And, because I wasn't indifferent, my belief was spontaneous and free. However, while I now know that I exist insofar as I am a thinking thing, I still wonder whether the thinking nature that is in me—or, rather, that is me—differs from this bodily nature or is identical to it. Nothing occurs to my reason (I am supposing) to convince me of one alternative rather than the other. Accordingly, I am completely indifferent to affirming either view, to denying either view, and even to suspending judgment.

And indifference of this sort is not limited to things of which the understanding is completely ignorant. It extends to everything about which the will deliberates in the absence of a sufficiently clear understanding. For, however strong the force with which plausible conjectures draw me towards one alternative, the knowledge that they are conjectures rather than assertions backed by certain and indubitable arguments is enough to push my assent the other way. The past few days have provided me with ample experience of this—for I am now supposing each of my former beliefs to be false just because I've found a way to call them into doubt.

If I suspend judgment when I don't clearly and distinctly grasp what's true, I obviously do right and am not deceived. But, if I either affirm or deny in a case of this sort, I misuse my freedom of choice. If I affirm what is false, I clearly err, and, if I stumble onto the truth, I'm still blameworthy since the light of nature reveals that a perception of the understanding should always precede a decision of the will. In these misuses of freedom of choice lies the deprivation which accounts for error. And this deprivation, I maintain, lies in the working of the will insofar as it comes from me—not in my God-given ability to will, or even in the will's operation insofar as it derives from Him.

I have no reason to complain that God hasn't given me a more perfect understanding or a greater natural light than He has. It's in the nature of a finite understanding that there are many things it can't understand, and it's in the nature of created understanding that it's finite. Indeed, I ought to be grateful to Him who owes me absolutely nothing for what He has bestowed, rather than taking myself to be deprived or robbed of what God hasn't given me.

And I have no reason to complain about God's having given me a will whose scope is greater than my understanding's. The will is like a unity made of inseparable parts; its nature apparently will not allow anything to be taken away from it. And, really, the wider the scope of my will, the more grateful I ought to be to Him who gave it to me.

Finally, I ought not to complain that God concurs in bringing about the acts of will and judgment in which I err. Insofar as these acts derive from God, they are completely true and good, and I am more

perfect with the ability to perform these acts than I would be without it. And, the deprivation which is the real ground of falsity and error doesn't need God's concurrence, since it's not a thing. When we regard God as its cause, we should say that it is an absence rather than a deprivation. For it clearly is no imperfection in God that He has given me the freedom to assent or not to assent to things of which He hasn't given me a clear and distinct grasp. Rather, it is undoubtedly an imperfection in me that I misuse this freedom by passing judgment on things that I don't properly understand. I see, of course, that God could easily have brought it about that, while I remain free and limited in knowledge, I never err: He could have implanted in me a clear and distinct understanding of everything about which I was ever going to make a choice, or He could have indelibly impressed on my memory that I must never pass judgment on something that I don't clearly and distinctly understand. And I also understand that, regarded in isolation from everything else, I would have been more perfect if God had made me so that I never err. But I can't deny that, because some things are immune to error while others are not, the universe is more perfect than it would have been if all its parts were alike. And I have no right to complain about God's wanting me to hold a place in the world other than the greatest and most perfect.

Besides, if I can't avoid error by having a clear grasp of every matter on which I make a choice, I can avoid it in the other way, which only requires remembering that I must not pass judgment on matters whose truth isn't apparent. For, although I find myself too weak to fix my attention permanently on this single thought, I can—by careful and frequent meditation—ensure that I call it to mind whenever it's needed and thus that I acquire the habit of avoiding error.

Since the first and foremost perfection of man lies in avoiding error, I've profited from today's meditation, in which I have investigated the cause of error and falsity. Clearly, the only possible cause of error is the one I have described. When I limit my will's range of judgment to the things shown clearly and distinctly to my understanding, I obviously cannot err—for everything that I clearly and distinctly grasp is something and therefore comes, not from nothing, but from God who is supremely perfect and who cannot deceive. What I clearly and distinctly grasp is therefore unquestionably true. Today, then, I have learned what to avoid in order not to err and also what to do to attain the truth: I surely will attain the truth if I attend only to the things that I understand perfectly, distinguishing them from those that I grasp more obscurely and confusedly. And, from now on, I will devote myself to doing just that.

Meditation V
On the Essence of Material
Objects and More on
God's Existence

Many questions remain about God's attributes and about the nature of my self or mind. I may return to these questions later, but now—having found what to do and what to avoid in order to attain truth—I regard nothing as more pressing than to work my way out of the doubts that I raised the other day and to see whether I can find anything certain about material objects.

Before asking whether any such objects exist outside me, I ought to consider the ideas of these objects as they are in my thoughts and to see which are clear and which confused.

I distinctly imagine that which philosophers commonly call "continuous quantity," of course, and I distinctly imagine the extension of this quantity—or rather of the quantified thing—in length, breadth, and depth. I can distinguish various parts of this extension. I can ascribe at will any size, shape, place, and motion to these parts and any duration to the motions.

And, in addition to having a thorough knowledge of extension in general, I grasp innumerable particulars about shape, number, motion, and so on. The truth of these particulars is so obvious and so consonant with my nature that, when I first think about one of them, I do not seem to be learning anything novel. Rather I seem to be remembering something that I already knew—or noticing something that had been in me for a long time without my having been aware of it.

What is important here, I think, is that I find in myself innumerable ideas of things which, though

they may not exist outside me, can't be said to be nothing. While I have some control over my thoughts of these things, I do not make the things up: they have their own real and immutable natures. Suppose, for example, that I imagine a triangle. While it may be that there is not—and never has been—a figure of this sort outside my thought, the figure still has a fixed, immutable, and eternal nature (essence, form) which hasn't been produced by me and which doesn't depend on my mind. The proof is that I can demonstrate various propositions about the triangle, such as that its angles equal two right angles and that its greatest side subtends its greatest angle. Even though I didn't think of these propositions at all when I first imagined the triangle, I now clearly see their truth whether I want to or not, and it follows that I didn't make them up.

It isn't relevant that, having seen triangular physical objects, I may have gotten the idea of the triangle from external objects through my organs of sense. For I can invent innumerable other figures whose ideas I *cannot* have gotten through my senses, and I can demonstrate facts about these other figures just as I can about the triangle. Since I know these facts clearly, they must be true, and they therefore must be something rather than nothing—for it's obvious that everything true is something, and everything that I know clearly and distinctly is true, as I have already shown. But, even if I had not shown this, the nature of my mind would have made it impossible for me to withhold my assent from these things (at least when I clearly and distinctly grasped them). As I recall, I regarded truths about shape and number—truths of arithmetic, geometry, or pure mathematics in general—as more certain than any others, even when I clung most tightly to objects of sense.

But, if anything whose idea I can draw from my thought must in fact have everything that I clearly and distinctly grasp it to have, can't I derive from this a proof of God's existence? Surely, I find the idea of a supremely perfect being in me just as I find the ideas of figures and numbers, and I understand as clearly and distinctly that eternal existence belongs to His nature as that the things that I demonstrate of figures and numbers belong to the natures of those figures and numbers. Accordingly, even if what I have thought up in the past few days hasn't been entirely true, I ought to be at least as certain of

God's existence as I have been of the truths of pure mathematics.

At first, this reasoning may seem unclear and fallacious. For, being accustomed to distinguishing existence from essence in other cases, I am easily convinced that I can separate God's existence from His essence and, hence, that I can think of God as nonexistent. But, when I pay more careful attention, it's clear that I can no more separate God's existence from His essence than I can separate the essence of the triangle from its angles equaling two right angles, or the idea of a mountain from the idea of a valley. It is no less a contradiction to think that God (the supremely perfect being) lacks existence (a perfection) than to think that a mountain lacks a valley.

Well, suppose that I can't think of God without existence, just as I can't think of a mountain without a valley. The fact that I can think of a mountain with a valley doesn't entail that a mountain exists in the world, and, similarly, the fact that I can think of God as existing doesn't seem to entail that He exists. For my thought doesn't impose any necessity on things: it may be that I can ascribe existence to God when no God exists, just as I can imagine a winged horse when no such horse exists.

No, there is a fallacy here. From the fact that I can't think of a mountain without a valley it follows, not that the mountain and valley exist, but only that—whether they exist or not—they can't be separated. Similarly, from the fact that I can't think of God without existence, it follows that existence is inseparable from Him and, hence, that he really exists. It's not that my thoughts make things happen or impose a necessity on things. On the contrary, it's the fact that God exists which necessitates my thinking of Him as I do. I am not free to think of God without existence—of the supremely perfect being without supreme perfection—as I am free to think of a horse without wings.

Now someone might say this: "If I take God to have all perfections, and if I take existence to be a perfection, I must take God to exist, but I needn't accept the premise that God has all perfections. Similarly, if I accept the premise that every quadrilateral can be inscribed in a circle, I am forced to the patently false view that every rhombus can be inscribed in a circle, but I need not accept the premise." This is

wrong, however. For, while it's not necessary that the idea of God occurs to me, it *is* necessary that I attribute all perfections to Him (even if I don't enumerate them or consider them individually) whenever I think of the primary and supreme entity and bring the idea of Him out of my mind's treasury. And this necessity ensures that, when I do notice that existence is a perfection, I can rightly conclude that the primary and supreme being exists. Similarly, while it's not necessary that I even imagine a triangle, it is necessary that, when I do choose to consider a rectilinear figure having exactly three angles, I attribute to it (perhaps without noticing that I am doing so) properties from which I can rightly infer that its angles are no more than two right angles. But, when I consider the various shapes that can be inscribed in the circle, there's absolutely no necessity for my thinking that all quadrilaterals are among them; in fact, having resolved to accept only what I clearly and distinctly understand, I can't even think that all quadrilaterals are among them. Thus my false suppositions differ greatly from the true ideas implanted in me, the first and foremost of which is my idea of God. In many ways, I see that this idea is not a figment of my thought—that it is the image of a real and immutable nature: First, God is the only thing that I can think of whose existence belongs to its essence. Second, I can't conceive of there being two or more Gods. Third, having supposed that one God now exists, I see that He has necessarily existed from all eternity and will continue to exist into eternity. And there are many other things in God that I can't diminish or alter.

But, whatever proof I offer, it always comes back to the fact that I am only convinced of what I grasp clearly and distinctly. Of the things that I grasp in this way, some are obvious to everyone. Others are discovered only by those who examine things more closely and search more carefully, but, once these things have been discovered, they are regarded as no less certain than the others. That the square on the hypotenuse of a right triangle equals the sum of the squares on the sides is not as readily apparent as that the hypotenuse subtends the greatest angle, but, once it has been seen, it is believed just as firmly. And (when I am not overwhelmed by prejudices and my thoughts are not besieged by images of sensible things) there surely is nothing that I know earlier or more easily than what pertains to God. For what could be more self-evident than there is a supreme entity—that God, the only thing whose existence belongs to His essence, exists?

While I need to pay careful attention in order to grasp this, I am now as certain of it as of any of the things that seem most certain. Moreover, I now see that the certainty of everything else so depends on my being certain that God exists that, if I weren't certain of God's existence, it wouldn't be possible for me to know anything perfectly.

Of course, my nature is such that, when I grasp something clearly and distinctly, I can't fail to believe it. But, since my nature is also such that I can't permanently fix my attention on a single thing so as always to grasp it clearly, the memory of previous judgments often comes to me when I am no longer attending to the grounds on which I originally made them. When this happens, reasons could be produced which would easily overthrow the judgments if I were ignorant of God, and I therefore would not have true and certain knowledge, but only unstable and changing opinion. For example, when I consider the nature of the triangle, it seems plain to me—steeped as I am in the principles of geometry—that its three angles equal two right angles: I can't fail to believe this as long as I pay attention to its demonstration. But, if I were ignorant of God, I might come to doubt its truth as soon as my attention wandered from its demonstration, even if I recalled having mastered the demonstration in the past: I could convince myself that I have been so constructed by nature that I sometimes err about what I believe myself to grasp most plainly—especially if I remembered that, having taken many things to be true and certain, I had later found reasons for judging them false.

But now I grasp that God exists, and I understand both that everything else depends on Him and that He's not a deceiver. From this, I infer that everything I clearly and distinctly grasp must be true. Even if I no longer pay attention to the grounds on which I judged God to exist, my recollection that I once clearly and distinctly knew Him to exist ensures that no contrary ground can be produced to impel me towards doubt. About God's existence, I have true and certain knowledge. And I have such knowledge, not just about this

one thing, but about all the other things—such as the theorems of geometry—which I remember having proven. For what can now be said against my believing these things? That I am so constructed that I always err? But I now know that I can't err about what I clearly and distinctly understand. That much of what I took to be true and certain I later found to be false? But I didn't grasp any of these things clearly and distinctly; ignorant of the true standard of truth, I based my belief on grounds that I later found to be unsound. Then what can be said? What about the objection (which I recently used against myself) that I may be dreaming and that the things I am now experiencing may be as unreal as those that occur to me in sleep? No, the point would be irrelevant—for, even if I *am* dreaming, everything that is evident to my understanding *must* be true.

Thus I plainly see that the certainty and truth of all my knowledge derives from my knowledge of the true God. Before I knew Him, I couldn't know anything else perfectly. But now I can plainly and certainly know innumerable things about God, about other mental beings, and (insofar as it is the subject of pure mathematics) about the nature of physical objects.

Meditation VI
On the Existence of Material Objects and the Real Distinction of Mind from Body

It remains for me to examine whether physical objects exist. Insofar as they are the subject of pure mathematics, I now know that they *can* exist, because I grasp them clearly and distinctly. For God can undoubtedly make whatever I can clearly and distinctly grasp, and I never judge that something is impossible for Him to make unless there would be a contradiction in my grasping that thing distinctly. Moreover, the fact that I find myself having mental images when I turn my attention to physical objects seems to imply that these objects really do exist. For, when I pay careful attention to what imagination is, it seems to me that it is just the application of my power of thought to a certain body which is immediately present to my thought and which must therefore exist.

I will begin to clarify this by examining the ways in which having mental images differs from having a pure understanding. When I picture a triangle, for example, I don't just understand that it is a figure bounded by three lines; I also "look at" the lines as though they were present to my mind's eye. And it is this "looking" that I call imagining. In contrast, when I want to think of a chiliagon, I can't imagine the sides or "look" at them as though they were present, but I *understand* that the chiliagon is a figure with a thousand sides as well as I understand that a triangle is a figure with three. Being accustomed to using images when I think about physical objects, I may confusedly picture *some* figure to myself, but—as this figure in no way differs from what I present to myself when thinking about a myriagon or any other many sided figure, and as it does not help me to discern the properties that distinguish chiliagons from the other polygons, it obviously is not a chiliagon. If it's a pentagon that is in question, I can understand its shape (as I can that of the chiliagon) without the aid of mental images. But I can also get a mental image of the pentagon by directing my mind's eye to its five lines and to the areas that they bound. It's obvious to me that getting this mental image requires a special mental effort different from that needed for understanding, and this special effort clearly reveals the difference between imagination and pure understanding.

It also seems to me that my power of imagining, being distinct from my power of understanding, is not essential to myself or, in other words, to my mind—for, if I were to lose this ability, I would surely remain the same thing that I now am. And it seems to follow that this ability depends on something distinct from me. It's easy to understand how my mind might get mental images of physical objects by means of my body, *if* we suppose that there is a body so associated with my mind that the mind can "look into" it at will. If there were such a body, the mode of understanding that we call imagination would only differ from pure understanding in one way: when the mind understood something, it would turn "inward" and view an idea that it found in itself, but, when it imagined, it would turn to the body and look at something there—something resembling an idea that it had understood by itself or had grasped by

sense. Thus, as I have said, it is easy to see how imagination works, if we suppose that my body exists. And, since I don't have in mind any other equally plausible explanation of imagination, I conjecture that physical objects probably do exist. But this conjecture is only probable. Despite my careful and thorough investigation, the distinct idea of bodily nature that comes from the imagination does not seem to have anything in it from which I can validly infer that physical objects exist.

Besides having a mental image of the bodily nature that is the subject of pure mathematics, I have mental images of such things as colors, sounds, flavors, and pains—but these images are not very distinct. I seem to grasp these things better by sense, from which they seem to come (with the aid of memory) to the understanding. It therefore seems appropriate to deal with these things in the context of an examination of the senses and to see whether there is something in the mode of awareness that I call *sensation* from which I can draw a conclusive argument for the existence of physical objects.

First, I will remind myself of the things that I believed really to be as I perceived them and of the grounds for my belief. Next, I will set out the grounds on which I later called this belief into doubt. And, finally, I will consider what I ought to think now.

To begin with, I sensed that I had a head, hands, feet, and the other members that make up a human body. I viewed this body as part, or maybe even as all, of me. I sensed that it was influenced by other physical objects whose affects could be either beneficial or harmful—beneficial to the extent that I felt pleasant sensations and harmful to the extent that I felt pain. In addition to sensations of pain and pleasure, I sensed hunger, thirst, and other such desires—and also bodily inclinations towards cheerfulness, sadness, and other emotions. Outside me, I sensed, not just extension, shape, and motion, but also hardness, hotness, and other qualities detected by touch. I also sensed light, color, odor, taste, and sound—qualities by whose variation I distinguished such things as the sky, earth, and sea from one another.

In view of these ideas of qualities (which presented themselves to my thought and were all that I really sensed directly) I had some reason for believing that I sensed objects distinct from my thought—physical objects from which the ideas came. For I found that these ideas came to me independently of my desires so that, however much I tried, I couldn't sense an object when it wasn't present to an organ to sense or fail to sense one when it was present. And, since the ideas that I grasped by sense were much livelier, more explicit, and (in their own way) more distinct than those I deliberately created or found impressed in my memory, it seemed that these ideas could not have come from me and that they must therefore have come from something else. Having no conception of these things other than the one suggested by my ideas, I could only think that the things resembled the ideas. Indeed, since I remembered using my senses before my reason, since I found the ideas that I created in myself to be less explicit than those grasped by sense, and since I found the ideas that I created to be composed largely of those that I had grasped by sense, I easily convinced myself that I didn't understand anything at all unless I had first sensed it.

I also had some reason for supposing that a certain physical object, which I view as belonging to me in a special way, is related to me more closely than any other. I can't be separated from it as I can from other physical objects; I feel all of my emotions and desires in it and because of it; and I am aware of pains and pleasant feelings in it but nothing else. I don't know *why* sadness goes with the sensation of pain, or *why* joy goes with sensory stimulation. I don't know *why* the stomach twitchings that I call hunger warn me that I need to eat or *why* dryness in my throat warns me that I need to drink. Seeing no connection between stomach twitchings and the desire to eat or between the sensation of a pain-producing thing and the consequent awareness of sadness, I can only say that I have been taught the connection by nature. And nature seems also to have taught me everything else that I knew about the objects of sensation—for I convinced myself that the sensations came to me in a certain way before having found grounds on which to prove that they did.

But, since then, many experiences have shaken my faith in the senses. Towers that seemed round from a distance sometimes looked square from close up, and huge statues on pediments sometimes did not look big when seen from the ground. In innumerable such cases, I found the judgments of the external senses to be wrong. And the same holds for the internal senses. What is felt more inwardly than pain? But I had heard that people with amputated arms and legs sometimes seem to feel pain in the missing limb, and it therefore didn't seem perfectly certain to me that the limb in which *I* feel a pain is always the one that hurts. And, to these grounds for doubt, I have recently added two that are very general: First, since I didn't believe myself to sense anything while awake that I couldn't also take myself to sense in a dream, and since I didn't believe that what I sense in sleep comes from objects outside me, I didn't see why I should believe what I sense while awake comes from such objects. Second, since I didn't yet know my creator (or, rather, since I supposed that I didn't know Him) nothing ruled out my having been so designed by nature that I am deceived even in that which seems most obviously true to me.

And I could easily reply to the reasoning by which I convinced myself of the reality of sensible things. Since my nature seemed to impel me towards many judgments which my reason rejected, I didn't believe that I ought to have much faith in nature's teachings. And, while my will didn't control my sense perceptions, I didn't believe it to follow that these perceptions came from outside me, since I thought that the ability to produce these ideas might have been in me without my being aware of it.

Now that I have begun to know myself and my creator better, I still believe that I oughtn't blindly to accept everything that I seem to get from the senses. But I no longer believe that I ought to call it all into doubt.

In the first place, I know that everything that I clearly and distinctly understand can be made by God to be exactly as I understand it. The fact that I can clearly and distinctly understand one thing apart from another is therefore enough to make me certain that it *is* distinct from the other, since the things could be separated by God if not by something else. (I judge the things to be distinct regardless of the power needed to make them exist separately.) Accordingly, from the fact that I have gained knowledge of my existence without noticing anything about my nature or essence except that I am a thinking thing, I can rightly conclude that my essence consists solely in the fact that I am a thinking thing. It's possible (or, as I will say later, it's certain) that I have a body which is very tightly bound to me. But, on the other hand, I have a clear and distinct idea of myself insofar as I am just a thinking and unextended thing, and, on the other hand, I have a distinct idea of my body insofar as it is just an extended and unthinking thing. It's certain, then, that I am really distinct from my body and can exist without it.

Moreover, I find in myself abilities for special modes of awareness, such as the abilities to have mental images and to sense. I can clearly and distinctly conceive of my whole self as something that lacks these abilities, but I can't conceive of the abilities existing without me, or without an understanding substance in which to reside. Since the conception of these abilities includes the conception of something that understands, I see that these abilities are distinct from me in the way that a thing's properties are distinct from the thing itself.

I recognize other abilities in me, such as the ability to move around and to assume various postures. These abilities can't be understood to exist apart from a substance in which they reside any more than the abilities to imagine and sense, and they therefore cannot exist without such a substance. But it's obvious that, if these abilities do exist, the substance in which they reside must be a body or extended substance rather than an understanding one, for the clear and distinct conceptions of these abilities contain extension but not understanding.

There is also in me, however, a passive ability to sense—to receive and recognize ideas of sensible things. I wouldn't be able to put this ability to use if there weren't—either in me or in something else—an active power to produce or make sensory ideas. But, since this active power does not presuppose understanding, and since it often produces ideas in me without my cooperation and even against my will, it cannot exist in me. Therefore this power must exist in a substance distinct from me. And, for reasons that I have noted, this substance must contain, either formally or eminently, all the reality that is contained presentationally in the ideas that the power produces. Accordingly, this substance must be either a physical object (which contains formally the reality that the idea contains presentationally), or one of God's creations that is higher than physical objects (which contains this reality eminently), or God himself. But, since God isn't a deceiver, it's completely obvious that He doesn't send these ideas to me directly or by means of a creation which contains their reality eminently rather than formally. For, since He has not given me any ability to recognize that these ideas are sent by Him or by creations other than physical objects, and since He has given me a strong inclination to believe that the ideas come from physical objects, there would be no way to avoid the conclusion that He deceives me if the ideas were sent to me by anything other than physical objects. Therefore physical objects exist. These objects may not exist exactly as I comprehend them by sense; in many ways, sensory comprehension is obscure and confused. But these objects must at least have in them everything that I clearly and distinctly understand them to have— every general property within the scope of pure mathematics.

But what about particular properties, such as the size and shape of the sun? And what about things that I understand less clearly than general mathematical properties—things like light, sound, and pain? These are open to doubt. But, since God isn't a deceiver, and since I therefore have the God-given ability to correct any falsity that may be in my beliefs, I have high hopes of finding the truth about even these things. There is undoubtedly some truth in everything I have been taught by nature—for, when I use the term "nature" in its general sense, I refer to God or to the order that He has established in the created world, and, when I apply the term specifically to *my* nature, I refer to the collection of everything that God has given *me*.

Nature teaches me nothing more explicitly, however, than that I have a body which is hurt when I feel pain, which needs food or drink when I experience hunger or thirst, and so on. And, accordingly, I ought not to doubt that there is some truth to the thought that I have a body.

Nature also teaches me—through sensations like pain, hunger, and thirst—that I am not present in my body in the way that a sailor is present in his ship. Rather, I am very tightly bound to my body and so "mixed up" with it that we form a single thing. If this weren't so, I—who am just a thinking thing—wouldn't feel pain when my body was injured; I would perceive the injury by pure understanding in the way that a sailor sees the leaks in his ship with his eyes. And, when my body needed food or drink, I would explicitly understand that the need existed without having the confused sensations of hunger and thirst. For the sensations of thirst, hunger, and pain are just confused modifications of thought arising from the union and "mixture" of mind and body.

Moreover, nature teaches me that there are other physical objects around my body—some that I ought to seek and others that I ought to avoid. From the fact that I sense colors, sounds, odors, flavors, and temperatures, I correctly infer that sense perceptions come from physical objects which vary as widely (though perhaps not in the same way) as the perceptions do. And, from the fact that some of these perceptions are pleasant while others are unpleasant, I infer with certainty that my body—or, rather, my whole self which consists of a body and a mind—can be benefited and harmed by the physical objects around it.

There are many other things which I *seem* to have been taught by nature, but which I have really accepted out of a habit of thoughtless judgment and which therefore may well be false. Among these things are the judgments that a space is empty if nothing in it happens to affect my senses, that a hot physical object has something in it resembling my idea of heat, that a white or green thing has in it the same whiteness or greenness that I sense, that a bitter or sweet thing has in it the same flavor that I taste, and the stars, towers, and other physical objects have the same size and shape that they show to my senses.

If I am to avoid accepting what is indistinct in these cases, I must more carefully explain my use of the phrase "taught by nature." In particular, I should say that I am now using the term "nature" in a narrower sense than when I took it to refer to the whole complex of what God has given me. This complex includes much having to do with my mind alone (such as my grasp of the fact that what is done cannot be undone and of the rest of what I know by the light of nature) which does not bear on what I am now saying. And the complex also includes much having to do with my body alone (such as its tendency to go downwards) that I also am not now dealing with. I am now using the term "nature" to refer only to what God has given me insofar as I am composite of mind and body. This nature teaches me to avoid that which occasions painful sensations, to seek that which occasions pleasant sensations, and so on, but it seems *not* to teach me to draw conclusions about external objects from sense perceptions without first having examined the matter with my understanding—for true knowledge of external things seems to belong to the mind alone, rather than to the composite of mind and body.

Thus, while a star has no more effect on my eye than a flame does, I do not have a real, positive inclination to believe that the star is as small as the flame; my youthful judgment to the contrary was not based on reason. And, while I feel heat when I approach a fire and pain when I draw nearer, I have absolutely no reason for believing that something in the fire resembles the heat, just as I have no reason for believing that something in the fire resembles the pain; I only have reason for believing that *something* in the fire produces the ideas of heat and pain in me. And, while there may be nothing in a given region of space that affects my senses, it doesn't follow that there are no physical objects in that space. Rather, I now see that, on these matters and others, I used to pervert the natural order of things. For, while nature has given sense perceptions to my mind for the sole purpose of indicating what is beneficial and what harmful to the composite of which my mind is a part, and while the perceptions are sufficiently clear and distinct for this purpose, I used these perceptions as standards for identifying the essence of physical objects—an essence which they only reveal obscurely and confusedly.

I have already explained how it can be that, despite God's goodness, my judgments can be false. But a new difficulty arises here—one having to do with the things that nature presents to me as desirable or undesirable and with the errors that I seem to have found in my internal sensations. One of these errors seems to be committed, for example, when a man is fooled by some food's pleasant taste into eating poison hidden in that food. But surely, in this case, what the man's nature impels him to eat is the good tasting food, not the poison of which he knows nothing. We can draw no conclusion except that his nature isn't omniscient, and this conclusion isn't surprising: since a man is a limited thing, he can only have limited perfections.

Still, we often err in things towards which nature *does* impel us. This happens, for example, when sick people want food or drink that would quickly harm them. To say that these people err as a result of the corruption of their nature does not solve the problem—for a sick man is no less a creation of God than a well one, and it seems as absurd to suppose that God has given him a deceptive nature. A clock made of wheels and weights follows the natural laws just as precisely when it is poorly made and inaccurate as when it does everything that its maker wants. Thus, if we regard a human body as a machine made up of bones, nerves, muscles, veins, blood, and skin, and if we notice that a body without a mind in it would do just the things that it does now (except for those that require a mind because they are commanded by the will), it is easy to see that what happens to a sick man is no less "natural" than what happens to a well one. For instance, if a body suffers from dropsy, it has a dry throat of the sort that regularly brings the sensation of thirst to the mind, the dryness disposes the nerves and other organs to drink, and the drinking makes the illness worse. But this is just as natural as when a similar dryness of throat moves a person who is perfectly healthy to take a drink that is beneficial.

Bearing in mind my conception of a clock's use, I might say that an inaccurate clock departs from its nature. And, similarly, viewing the machine of the human body as designed for working as it usually does, I can say that it drifts away from its nature if it has a dry throat when drinking will not help to maintain it. I should note, however, that the sense in which I am now using the term "nature" differs from that in which I used it before. For, as I have just used the term, the *nature* of a man (or clock) is something that depends on my thinking of the difference between a sick and a well man (or of the difference between a poorly made and a well-made clock)—something that is regarded as *extrinsic* to the things. But, when I used "nature" before, I referred to something which is *in* things and which therefore has some reality.

It may be that we just offer an extrinsic description of a body suffering from dropsy when, noting that it has a dry throat but doesn't need to drink, we say that its nature is corrupted. Still, the description is not purely extrinsic when we say that a composite or union of mind and body has a corrupted nature: there is a real fault in the composite's nature, for it is thirsty when drinking is harmful to it. It therefore remains to be asked why God's goodness doesn't prevent *this* nature's being deceptive.

To begin the answer, I will note that mind differs importantly from body in that body is by its nature divisible, while mind is indivisible. When I think about my mind—or, in other words, about myself insofar as I am just a thinking thing—I can't distinguish any parts; I understand myself to be a single, unified thing. Although my whole mind seems united to my whole body, I know that cutting off a foot, arm, or other limb would not take anything away from my mind. And the abilities to will, sense, understand can't be called parts, since it is one and the same mind that wills, senses, and understands. On the other hand, whenever I think of a physical or extended thing, I can mentally divide it, and I therefore understand that the object is divisible. This single fact would be enough to teach me that my mind and my body are distinct, if I hadn't already gained that knowledge.

Next, I notice that the mind isn't directly affected by all parts of the body, but only by the brain—or maybe just by the small part of the brain containing the so-called "common sense." Whenever this part of the brain is in a given state, it exhibits the same thing to the mind, regardless of what is happening in the rest of the body (as is shown by innumerable experiments that I need not review here).

Moreover, I notice that the nature of body is such that, if a first part can be moved by a second that is far away, the first part can be moved in exactly the same way by something between the first and second without the second part's being affected. For example, if A, B, C, and D are points on a cord, and if the first point (A) can be moved in a certain way by a pull on the last point (D), then A can be moved in the same way by a pull on one of the middle points (B or C) without D's being moved. Similarly, science teaches me that, when my foot hurts, the sensation of pain is produced by nerves distributed throughout the foot which extend like a cord from there to the brain. When pulled in the foot, these nerves pull the central parts of the brain to which they are attached, moving those parts in ways designated by nature to present the mind with the sensation of a pain "in the foot." Since these nerves pass through the shins, thighs, hips, back, and neck on their way from foot to brain, it can happen that their being touched in the middle, rather than at the end in the foot, produces the same motion in the brain as when the foot is hurt and, consequently, that the mind feels the same pain "in the foot." And the point holds for other sensations as well.

Finally, I notice that, since only one sensation can be produced by a given motion of the part of the brain that directly affects the mind, the best conceivable sensation for it to produce is the one that is most often useful for the maintenance of the healthy man. Experience teaches, however, that all the sensations put in us by nature *are* of this sort and therefore that there is nothing in our sensations which doesn't testify to God's power and goodness. For example, when the nerves in the foot are moved with unusual violence, the motion is communicated through the middle of the spine to the center of the brain, where it signals the mind to sense a pain "in the foot." This urges the mind to view the pain's cause as harmful to the foot and to do what it can to remove the cause. Of course, God could have so designed man's nature that the same motion of the brain showed the mind something else (such as itself as a motion in the brain, or as a motion in the foot, or as a motion somewhere between the brain and foot), but no alternative to the way things are would be as conducive to the maintenance of the body. Similarly, when we need drink, the throat becomes dry, the dryness moves the nerves of the throat thereby moving the center of the brain, and the brain's movements cause the sensation of thirst in the mind. It's the sensation of thirst that is produced, because no information about our condition is more useful to us than that we need to get something to drink in order to remain healthy. And the same is true in other cases.

This makes it completely obvious that, despite God's immense goodness, the nature of man (whom we now view as a composite of mind and body) cannot fail to be deceptive. For, if something

produces the movement usually associated with a bad foot in the nerve running from foot to brain or in the brain itself (rather than in the foot), a pain is felt "in the foot," and the senses are deceived by my nature. Since this motion in the brain must always bring the same sensation to mind, and since the motion's cause more often *is* something hurting the foot than something elsewhere, it is in accordance with reason that the motion always shows the mind a pain in the foot rather than elsewhere. And, if dryness of the throat arises, not (as usual) from drink's being conducive to the body's health, but (as happens in dropsy) from some other cause, it is much better that we are deceived than that we are generally deceived when our bodies are sound. And so on for other sensations.

In addition to helping me to be aware of the errors to which my nature is subject, these reflections help me readily to correct or avoid those errors. I know that sensory indications of what is good for my body are more often true than false; I can almost always examine a given thing with several senses; and I can also use my memory (which connects the present to the past) and my understanding (which has now ascertained all the causes of error). Hence, I need no longer fear that what the senses daily show me is unreal. I should reject the exaggerated doubts of the past few days as ridiculous. This is especially true of the chief ground for these doubts—namely, that I couldn't distinguish dreaming from being awake—for I now notice that dreaming and being awake are importantly different: the events in dreams are not linked by memory to the rest of my life like those that happen while I am awake. If, while I am awake, someone were suddenly to appear and then immediately to disappear without my seeing where he came from or went to (as happens in dreams), I would justifiably judge that he was not a real man, but a ghost—or, better, an apparition created in my brain. But, if I distinctly observe something's source, its place, and the time at which I learn about it, and if I grasp an unbroken connection between it and the rest of my life, I am quite sure that it is something in my waking life rather than in a dream. And I ought not to have the slightest doubt about the reality of such things, if I have examined them with all my senses, my memory, and my understanding without finding any conflicting evidence. For, from the fact that God is not a deceiver, it follows that I am not deceived in any case of this sort. Since the need to act does not always allow time for such a careful examination, however, we must admit the likelihood of men's erring about particular things and acknowledge the weakness of our nature.

KEY TERMS

Omnipotent
Skepticism
Metaphysical
Omniscient
Efficient cause
Freedom of will

STUDY QUESTIONS

1. Descartes comes to the conclusion that "there are no reliable signs by which I can distinguish sleeping from waking." What considerations lead him to this conclusion?
2. Why does Descartes suppose, at the end of Meditation I, that there is an evil demon "who works as hard as he can to deceive me"?
3. Why does Descartes think he knows for certain that he exists? Is he entitled to this conclusion?
4. In Meditation III, Descartes argues that his idea of God could not have come from him, and so God must exist. How does this argument go?
5. Descartes argues in Meditation VI that he can exist without his body. What is his argument for this? Can you similarly imagine existing without a body?

Bad Dreams, Evil Demons, and the Experience Machine: Philosophy and *The Matrix*

CHRISTOPHER GRAU

Christopher Grau (1970–) is Professor of Philosophy at Clemson University. He studied at Johns Hopkins University under Susan Wolf and works on ethics, metaphysics, and philosophy and film. He edited and contributed to the volume *Philosophers Explore* The Matrix.

. .

I. Dream Skepticism

MORPHEUS: Have you ever had a dream, Neo, that you were so sure was real?

MORPHEUS: What if you were unable to wake from that dream, Neo? How would you know the difference between the dreamworld and the real world?

From "Bad Dreams, Evil Demons, and the Experience Machine: Philosophy and *The Matrix*," in Christopher Grau, ed., *Philosophers Explore* The Matrix, pp. 10–23. Copyright © 2005 by Oxford University Press. Reprinted by permission of the publisher.

Neo has woken up from a hell of a dream—the dream that was his life. How was he to know? The cliché is that if you are dreaming and you pinch yourself, you will wake up. Unfortunately, things aren't quite that simple. It is the nature of most dreams that we take them for reality—while dreaming, we are unaware that we are in a dream world. Of course, we eventually wake up, and when we do, we realize that our experience was all in our mind. Neo's predicament makes us wonder, though: how can any of us be sure that we have ever *genuinely* woken up? Perhaps, like Neo prior to his downing the red pill, our dreams thus far have in fact been dreams *within* a dream.

The idea that what we take to be the real world could all be just a dream is familiar to many students of philosophy, poetry, and literature. Most of us, at one time or another, have been struck with the thought that we might mistake a dream for reality, or reality for a dream. Arguably the most famous exponent of this worry in the Western philosophical tradition is the seventeenth-century French philosopher René Descartes. In an attempt to provide a firm foundation for knowledge, he began his *Meditations* by clearing the philosophical ground through doubting all that could be doubted. This was done, in part, in order to determine if anything that could count as certain knowledge could survive such rigorous and systematic **skepticism**. Descartes takes the first step toward this goal by raising (through his fictional narrator) the possibility that we might be dreaming:

> How often, asleep at night, am I convinced of just such familiar events—that I am here in my dressing-gown, sitting by the fire—when in fact I am lying undressed in bed! Yet at the moment my eyes are certainly wide awake when I look at this piece of paper; I shake my head and it is not asleep; as I stretch out and feel my hand I do so deliberately, and I know what I am doing. All this would not happen with such distinctness to someone asleep. Indeed! As if I did not remember other occasions when I have been tricked by exactly similar thoughts while asleep! As I think about this more carefully, I see plainly that there are never any sure signs by means of which being awake can be distinguished from being asleep. The result is that I begin to feel dazed, and this very feeling only reinforces the notion that I may be asleep.[1]

When we dream, we are often blissfully ignorant that we are dreaming. Given this, and the fact that dreams often seem as vivid and "realistic" as real life, how can you rule out the possibility that you might be dreaming even now, as you sit and read this? This is the kind of perplexing thought that Descartes forces us to confront. It seems we have no justification for the belief that we are not dreaming. If so, then it seems we similarly have no justification in thinking that the world we experience is the *real* world. Indeed, it becomes questionable whether we are justified in thinking that *any* of our beliefs are true.

The narrator of Descartes's *Meditations* worries about this, but he ultimately maintains that the possibility that one might be dreaming cannot by itself cast doubt on all we think we know; he points out that even if all our sensory experience is but a dream, we can still conclude that we have *some* knowledge of the nature of reality. Just as a painter cannot create ex nihilo but must rely on pigments with which to create her image, certain elements of our thought must exist prior to our imaginings. Among the items of knowledge that Descartes thought survived dream skepticism are truths arrived at through the use of reason, such as the truths of mathematics: "For whether I am awake or asleep, two and three added together are five, and a square has no more than four sides" (296–297).

While such an insight offers little comfort to someone wondering whether the people and objects she confronts are genuine, it served Descartes's larger philosophical project: he sought, among other things, to provide a foundation for knowledge in which truths arrived at through reason are given priority over knowledge gained from experience. (This bias shouldn't surprise those who remember that Descartes was a brilliant mathematician in addition to being a philosopher.) Descartes was not himself a skeptic—he employs this skeptical argument so as to help remind the reader that the truths of mathematics (and other truths of reason) are on firmer ground than the data provided to us by our senses.

Despite the fact that Descartes's ultimate goal was to demonstrate how genuine knowledge is possible, he proceeds in *The Meditations* to utilize a much more radical skeptical argument, one that casts doubt on even his beloved mathematical truths. In the next section we will see that, many years before the Wachowskis dreamed up *The Matrix*, Descartes had imagined an equally terrifying possibility.

II. Brains in Vats and the Evil Demon

MORPHEUS: What is the Matrix? Control.
MORPHEUS: The Matrix is a computer-generated dreamworld built to keep us under control in

order to change a human being into this. [holds up a battery]

NEO: No! I don't believe it! It's not possible!

Before breaking out of the Matrix, Neo's life was not what he thought it was. It was a lie. Morpheus describes it as a "dreamworld," but unlike a dream, this world is not the creation of Neo's mind. The truth is more sinister: the world is a creation of the artificially intelligent computers that have taken over the Earth and have subjugated humanity in the process. These creatures have fed Neo a simulation that he couldn't possibly help but take as the real thing. What's worse, it isn't clear how any of us can know with certainty that we are not in a position similar to Neo before his "rebirth." Our ordinary confidence in our ability to reason and our natural tendency to trust the deliverances of our senses can both come to seem rather naive once we confront this possibility of deception. A viewer of *The Matrix* is naturally led to wonder: how do I know I am not in the Matrix? How do I know for sure that my world is not also a sophisticated charade, put forward by some superhuman intelligence in such a way that I cannot possibly detect the ruse? Descartes suggested a similar worry: the frightening possibility that all of one's experiences might be the result of a powerful outside force, a "malicious demon":

And yet firmly rooted in my mind is the long-standing opinion that there is an omnipotent God who made me the kind of creature that I am. How do I know that he has not brought it about that there is no earth, no sky, no extended thing, no shape, no size, no place, while at the same time ensuring that all these things appear to me to exist just as they do now? What is more, just as I consider that others sometimes go astray in cases where they think they have the most perfect knowledge, how do I know that God has not brought it about that I too go wrong every time I add two and three or count the sides of a square, or in some even simpler matter, if that is imaginable? But perhaps God would not have allowed me to be deceived in this way, since he is said to be supremely good; . . . I will suppose therefore that not God, who is supremely good and the source of

truth, but rather some malicious demon of the utmost power and cunning has employed all his energies in order to deceive me. I shall think that the sky, the air, the earth, colours, shapes, sounds and all external things are merely the delusions of dreams which he has devised to ensnare my judgment. (297–298)

The narrator of Descartes's *Meditations* concludes that none of his former opinions are safe. Such a demon could not only deceive him about his perceptions, it could conceivably cause him to go wrong when performing even the simplest acts of reasoning.

This radical worry seems inescapable. How could you possibly prove to yourself that you are not in the kind of nightmarish situation Descartes describes? It would seem that any argument, evidence, or proof you might put forward could easily be yet another trick played by the demon. As ludicrous as the idea of the evil demon may sound at first, it is hard, upon reflection, not to share Descartes's worry: for all you know, you may well be a mere plaything of such a malevolent intelligence. More to the point of our general discussion: for all you know, you may well be trapped in the Matrix.

Many contemporary philosophers have discussed a similar skeptical dilemma that is a bit closer to the scenario described in *The Matrix*. It has come to be known as the "brain in a vat" hypothesis, and one powerful formulation of the idea is presented by philosopher Jonathan Dancy:

You do not know that you are not a brain, suspended in a vat full of liquid in a laboratory, and wired to a computer which is feeding you your current experiences under the control of some ingenious technician scientist (benevolent or malevolent according to taste). For if you were such a brain, then, provided that the scientist is successful, nothing in your experience could possibly reveal that you were; for your experience is ex hypothesi identical with that of something which is not a brain in a vat. Since you have only your own experience to appeal to, and that experience is the same in either situation, nothing can reveal to you which situation is the actual one.[2]

If you cannot know whether you are in the real world or in the world of a computer simulation, you cannot be sure that your beliefs about the world are true. And, what was even more frightening to Descartes, in this kind of scenario it seems that your ability to reason is no safer than the deliverances of the senses: the evil demon or malicious scientist could be ensuring that your reasoning is just as flawed as your perceptions. As you have probably already guessed, there is no easy way out of this philosophical problem (or at least there is no easy *philosophical* way out). Philosophers have proposed a dizzying variety of "solutions" to this kind of skepticism but, as with many philosophical problems, there is nothing close to unanimous agreement regarding how the puzzle should be solved.

Descartes's own way out of his evil-demon skepticism was to first argue that one cannot genuinely doubt the existence of oneself. He pointed out that all thinking presupposes a thinker: even in doubting, you realize that there must at least be a self which is doing the doubting. (Thus Descartes's most famous line: "I think, therefore I am.") He then went on to claim that, in addition to our innate idea of self, each of us has an idea of God as an all-powerful, all-good, and infinite being implanted in our minds and that this idea could only have come *from* God. Since this shows us that an all-good God does exist, we can have confidence that he would not allow us to be so drastically deceived about the nature of our perceptions and their relationship to reality. While Descartes's argument for the existence of the self has been tremendously influential and is still actively debated, few philosophers have followed him in accepting his particular theistic solution to skepticism about the external world.

One of the more interesting contemporary challenges to the kind of radical skepticism suggested by Descartes has come from philosopher Hilary Putnam. His point is not so much to defend our ordinary claims to knowledge as to question whether the brain-in-a-vat hypothesis is coherent, given certain plausible assumptions about how our language refers to objects in the world. He asks us to consider a variation on the standard brain-in-a-vat story that is uncannily similar to the situation described in *The Matrix*:

Instead of having just one brain in a vat, we could imagine that all human beings (perhaps all sentient beings) are brains in a vat (or nervous systems in a vat in case some beings with just nervous systems count as "sentient"). Of course, the evil scientist would have to be outside? or would he? Perhaps there is no evil scientist, perhaps (though this is absurd) the universe just happens to consist of automatic machinery tending a vat full of brains and nervous systems. This time let us suppose that the automatic machinery is programmed to give us all a *collective* hallucination, rather than a number of separate unrelated hallucinations. Thus, when I seem to myself to be talking to you, you seem to yourself to be hearing my words. . . . I want now to ask a question which will seem very silly and obvious (at least to some people, including some very sophisticated philosophers), but which will take us to real philosophical depths rather quickly. Suppose this whole story were actually true. Could we, if we were brains in a vat in this way, *say* or *think* that we were?[3]

Putnam's surprising answer is that we cannot coherently think that we are brains in vats, and so skepticism of that kind can never really get off the ground. While it is difficult to do justice to Putnam's ingenious argument in a short summary, his point is roughly as follows: not everything that goes through our heads is a genuine thought, and far from everything we say is a meaningful utterance. Sometimes we get confused or think in an incoherent manner; sometimes we say things that are simply nonsense. Of course, we don't always realize at the time that we aren't making sense; sometimes we earnestly believe we are saying (or thinking) something meaningful. High on nitrous oxide, the philosopher William James was convinced he was having profound insights into the nature of reality; he was convinced that his thoughts were both sensical and important. Upon sobering up and looking at the notebook in which he had written his drug-addled thoughts, he saw only gibberish.

Just as I might say a sentence that is nonsense, I might also use a name or a general term that is meaningless in the sense that it fails to hook up to the world. Philosophers talk of such a term as "failing to refer" to an object. In order to successfully **refer** when we use language, there must be an appropriate relationship between the speaker and the object referred to. If a dog playing on the beach manages to scrawl the word "Ed" in the sand with a stick, few would want to claim that the dog actually meant to refer to someone named Ed. Presumably the dog doesn't know anyone named Ed, and even if he did, he wouldn't be capable of intending to write Ed's name in the sand. The point of such an example is that words do not refer to objects "magically" or intrinsically: certain conditions must be met in the world in order for us to accept that a given written or spoken word has any meaning and whether it actually refers to anything at all.

Putnam claims that one condition which is crucial for successful reference is that there be an appropriate causal connection between the object referred to and the speaker referring. Specifying exactly what should count as "appropriate" here is a notoriously difficult task, but we can get some idea of the kind of thing required by considering cases in which reference fails through an inappropriate connection: if someone unfamiliar with the film *The Matrix* manages to blurt out the word "Neo" while sneezing, few would be inclined to think that this person has actually *referred* to the character Neo. The kind of causal connection between the speaker and the object referred to (Neo) is just not in place. For reference to succeed, it can't be simply accidental that the name was uttered. (Another way to think about it: the sneezer would have uttered "Neo" even if the film *The Matrix* had never been made.)

The difficulty, according to Putnam, in coherently supposing the brain-in-a-vat story to be true is that brains raised in such an environment could not successfully refer to genuine brains, or vats, or anything else in the real world. Consider the example of some people who lived their entire lives in the Matrix: when they talk of "chickens," they don't actually refer to real *chickens*; at best they refer to the computer representations of chickens that have been sent to their brains. Similarly, when they talk of human bodies being trapped in pods and fed data by the Matrix, they don't successfully refer to real bodies or pods. They can't refer to physical bodies in the real world because they cannot have the appropriate causal connection to such objects.

Thus, if someone were to utter the sentence "I am simply a body stuck in a pod somewhere being fed sensory information by a computer," that sentence would itself be necessarily false. If the person is in fact not trapped in the Matrix, then the sentence is straightforwardly false. If the person is trapped in the Matrix, then he can't successfully refer to real human bodies when he utters the term "human body," and so it appears that under this circumstance, his statement must *also* be false. Such a person seems thus doubly trapped: incapable of knowing that he is in the Matrix and even incapable of successfully expressing the thought that he might be in the Matrix! (Could this be why at one point Morpheus tells Neo that "no one can be told what the Matrix is"?)

Putnam's argument is controversial, but it is noteworthy because it shows that the kind of situation described in *The Matrix* raises not just the expected philosophical issues about knowledge and skepticism, but more general issues regarding meaning, language, and the relationship between the mind and the world.

III. The Value of Reality: Cypher and the Experience Machine

CYPHER: You know, I know that this steak doesn't exist. I know when I put it in my mouth, the Matrix is telling my brain that it is juicy and delicious. After nine years, do you know what I've realized?

CYPHER: Ignorance is bliss.

AGENT SMITH: Then we have a deal?

CYPHER: I don't want to remember nothing. Nothing! You understand? And I want to be rich. Someone important. Like an actor. You can do that, right?

AGENT SMITH: Whatever you want, Mr. Reagan.

Cypher is not a nice guy, but is he an unreasonable guy? Is he right to want to get re-inserted into the Matrix? Many want to say no, but giving reasons for why his choice is a bad one is not an easy task. After all, so long as his experiences will be pleasant, how can his situation be worse than the inevitably crappy life he would lead outside of the Matrix? What could matter beyond the quality of his experience? Remember, once he's back in, living his fantasy life, he won't even know he made the deal. What he doesn't know can't hurt him, right?

Is feeling good the only thing that has value in itself? The question of whether only conscious experience can ultimately matter is one that has been explored in depth by several contemporary philosophers. In the course of discussing this issue in his 1974 book *Anarchy, State, and Utopia*, Robert Nozick introduced a thought-experiment that has become a staple of introductory philosophy classes everywhere. It is known as "the experience machine":

> Suppose there were an experience machine that would give you any experience you desired. Superduper neuropsychologists could stimulate your brain so that you would think and feel you were writing a great novel, or making a friend, or reading an interesting book. All the time you would be floating in a tank, with electrodes attached to your brain. Should you plug into this machine for life, preprogramming your life's experiences?. . . Of course, while in the tank you won't know that you're there; you'll think it's all actually happening. Others can also plug in to have the experiences they want, so there's no need to stay unplugged to serve them. (Ignore problems such as who will service the machines if everyone plugs in.) Would you plug in? *What else can matter to us, other than how our lives feel from the inside?*[4]

Nozick goes on to argue that other things do matter to us: for instance, that we actually do certain things, as opposed to simply having the experience of doing them. Also, he points out that we value being (and becoming) certain kinds of people. I don't just want to have the experience of being a decent person, I want to actually *be* a decent person. Finally, Nozick argues that we value contact with reality in itself, independent of any benefits such contact may bring through pleasant experience: we want to know we are experiencing the real thing. In sum, Nozick thinks that it matters to most of us, often in a rather deep way, that we be the authors of our lives and that our lives involve interacting with the world, and he thinks that the fact that most

people would not choose to enter into such an experience machine demonstrates that they do value these other things. As he puts it: "We learn that something matters to us in addition to experience by imagining an experience machine and then realizing that we would not use it" (311).

While Nozick's description of his machine is vague, it appears that there is at least one important difference between it and the simulated world of *The Matrix*. Nozick implies that people hooked up to the experience machine will not be able to exercise their agency—they become the passive recipients of preprogrammed experiences. This apparent loss of **free will** is disturbing to many people, and it might be distorting people's reactions to the case and clouding the issue of whether they value contact with reality per se. The Matrix seems to be set up in such a way that one can enter it and retain one's free will and capacity for decision making, and perhaps this makes it a significantly more attractive option than the experience machine that Nozick describes.

Nonetheless, a loss of freedom is not the only disturbing aspect of Nozick's story. As he points out, we seem to mourn the loss of contact with the real world as well. Even if a modified experience machine is presented to us, one which allows us to keep our free will but enter into an entirely virtual world, many would still object that permanently going into such a machine involves the loss of something valuable.

Cypher and his philosophical comrades are likely to be unmoved by such observations. So what if most people are hung-up on "reality" and would turn down the offer to permanently enter an experience machine? Most people might be wrong. All their responses might show is that such people are superstitious, or irrational, or otherwise confused. Maybe they think something could go wrong with the machines, or maybe they keep forgetting that while in the machine they will no longer be aware of their choice to enter the machine. Perhaps those hesitant to plug in don't realize that they value being active in the real world only because normally that is the most reliable way for them to acquire the pleasant experience that they value in itself. In other words, perhaps our free will and our capacity to interact with reality are means to a further end; they matter to us because they allow us access to what really matters: pleasant conscious experience. To think the reverse, that reality and freedom have value in themselves (what philosophers sometimes call *nonderivative* or *intrinsic value*), is simply to put the cart before the horse. After all, Cypher could reply, what would be so great about the capacity to freely make decisions or the ability to be in the real world if neither of these things allowed us to feel good?

Peter Unger has taken on these kinds of objections in his discussion of "experience inducers." He acknowledges that there is a strong temptation when in a certain frame of mind to agree with this kind of Cypheresque reasoning, but he argues that this is a temptation we ought to try to resist. Cypher's vision of value is too easy and too simplistic. We are inclined to think that only conscious experience can really matter in part because we fall into the grip of a particular picture of what values *must* be like, and this in turn leads us to stop paying attention to our actual values. We make ourselves blind to the subtlety and complexity of our values, and we then find it hard to understand how something that doesn't affect our consciousness could sensibly matter to us. If we stop and reflect on what we really do care about, however, we come across some surprisingly everyday examples that don't sit easily with Cypher's claims:

> Consider life insurance. To be sure, some among the insured may strongly believe that, if they die before their dependents do, they will still observe their beloved dependents, perhaps from a heaven on high. But others among the insured have no significant belief to that effect. . . . Still, we all pay our premiums. In my case, this is because, even if I will never experience anything that happens to them, I still want things to go better, rather than worse, for my dependents. No doubt, I am rational in having this concern.[5]

As Unger goes on to point out, it seems contrived to chalk up all examples of people purchasing life insurance to cases in which someone is simply trying to benefit (while alive) from the favorable impression such a purchase might make on the dependents. In many cases it seems ludicrous to deny that "what motivates us, of course, is our great concern for our

dependents' future, whether we experience their future or not" (302). This is not a proof that such concern is rational, but it does show that incidents in which we intrinsically value things other than our own conscious experience might be more widespread than we are at first liable to think. (Other examples include the value we place on not being deceived or lied to—the importance of this value doesn't seem to be completely exhausted by our concern that we might one day become aware of the lies and deception.)

Most of us care about a lot of things independently of the experiences that those things provide for us. The realization that we value things other than pleasant conscious experience should lead us to at least wonder if the legitimacy of this kind of value hasn't been too hastily dismissed by Cypher and his ilk. After all, once we see how widespread and commonplace our other nonderivative concerns are, the insistence that conscious experience is the *only* thing that has value in itself can come to seem downright peculiar. If purchasing life insurance seems like a rational thing to do, why shouldn't the desire to experience reality (rather than some illusory simulation) be similarly rational? Perhaps the best test of the rationality of our most basic values is actually whether they, taken together, form a consistent and coherent network of attachments and concerns. (Do they make sense in light of each other and in light of our beliefs about the world and ourselves?) It isn't obvious that valuing interaction with the real world fails this kind of test.

Of course, pointing out that the value I place on living in the real world coheres well with my other values and beliefs will not quiet the defender of Cypher, as he will be quick to respond that the fact that my values all cohere doesn't show that they are all justified. Maybe I hold a bunch of exquisitely consistent but thoroughly irrational values.

The quest for some further justification of my basic values might be misguided, however. Explanations have to come to an end somewhere, as Ludwig Wittgenstein once famously remarked. Maybe the right response to a demand for justification here is to point out that the same demand can be made to Cypher: "Just what justifies your exclusive concern with pleasant conscious experience?" It seems as though nothing does—if such concern is justified, it must be somehow self-justifying, but if that is possible, why shouldn't our concerns for other people and our desire to live in the real world also be self-justifying? If those can also be self-justifying, then maybe what we don't experience should matter to us, and perhaps what we don't know *can* hurt us. . . .

Further Reading

Those seeking to go further should certainly begin with the rest of Descartes's *Meditations*. Currently, the best edition is *The Philosophical Writings of Descartes*, trans. John Cottingham, Robert Stoothoff, and Dugald Murdoch (Cambridge University Press 1984). A solid and comprehensive introduction to **epistemology** is Jonathan Dancy's *Introduction to Contemporary Epistemology* (Blackwell 1985). For slightly more advanced treatments, I recommend Barry Stroud's *The Significance of Philosophical Scepticism* (Oxford University Press 1984) and P. F. Strawson's *Skepticism and Naturalism: Some Varieties* (Columbia University Press 1983). On the question of the justification of values, my comments here draw on the insights of Mark Johnston in "Reasons and Reductionism" (*Philosophical Review* 1992), Thomas Nagel's essay "Death" (*Nous* 1970), and Peter Unger's *Identity, Consciousness, and Value* (Oxford University Press 1990).

NOTES

1. René Descartes, *Meditations on First Philosophy*, ed. and trans. J. Cottingham (Cambridge University Press 1985); see appendix, pp. 295–296. Further citations will be in the text.
2. Jonathan Dancy, *Introduction to Contemporary Epistemology* (Blackwell 1985), p. 10.
3. Hilary Putnam, *Reason, Truth, and History* (Cambridge University Press 1981); see appendix, pp. 317–318.
4. Robert Nozick, *Anarchy, State, and Utopia* (Basic 1974); see appendix, p. 310. Further citations will be to this appendix and appear in the text.
5. Peter Unger, *Identity, Consciousness, and Value* (Oxford University Press 1990), p. 301. Further citations will be in the text.

KEY TERMS

Skepticism
Refer
Free will
Epistemology

STUDY QUESTIONS

1. Should we take seriously the hypothesis that we might be in the Matrix? Why or why not? Would finding out that you were in the Matrix change the way you live your life?
2. Why does Putnam think that if we were brains in vats, we couldn't say or think that we were? How important is this conclusion?
3. Would you get into Nozick's experience machine? Why or why not? Do you think there is any value at all to being "in touch" with reality?
4. What is Unger's life insurance analogy supposed to show? Is the analogy successful?

Excerpt from *Philosophical Explanations*

ROBERT NOZICK

Robert Nozick (1938–2002) was an American philosopher and professor at Harvard who contributed influential ideas to many areas of philosophy, epistemology, and political philosophy, in particular. His works include *Philosophical Explanations*, *The Examined Life*, and *Anarchy, State, and Utopia*.

. .

I. Knowledge

Conditions for Knowledge

Our task is to formulate further conditions to go alongside

(1) p is true

(2) S believes that p.

We would like each condition to be **necessary** for knowledge, so any case that fails to satisfy it will not be an instance of knowledge. Furthermore, we would like the conditions to be jointly **sufficient** for knowledge, so any case that satisfies all of them will be an instance of knowledge. We first shall formulate conditions that seem to handle ordinary cases correctly, classifying as knowledge cases which are knowledge, and as nonknowledge cases which are not; then we shall check to see how these conditions handle some difficult cases discussed in the literature.

The causal condition on knowledge, previously mentioned, provides an inhospitable environment for mathematical and ethical knowledge; also there are well-known difficulties in specifying the type of causal connection. If someone floating in a tank oblivious to everything around him is given (by

direct electrical and chemical stimulation of the brain) the belief that he is floating in a tank with his brain being stimulated, then even though that fact is part of the cause of his belief, still he does not know that it is true.

Let us consider a different third condition:

(3) If p weren't true, S wouldn't believe that p.

Throughout this work, let us write the subjunctive 'if-then' by an arrow, and the negation of a sentence by prefacing "not-" to it. The above condition thus is rewritten as:

(3) not-p → not-(S believes that p).

This subjunctive condition is not unrelated to the causal condition. Often when the fact that p (partially) causes someone to believe that p, the fact also will be causally necessary for his having the belief—without the cause, the effect would not occur. In that case, the subjunctive condition 3 also will be satisfied. Yet this condition is not equivalent to the causal condition. For the causal condition will be satisfied in cases of causal overdetermination, where either two sufficient causes of the effect actually operate, or a back-up cause (of the same effect) would operate if the first one didn't; whereas the subjunctive condition need not hold for these cases. When the two conditions do agree, causality indicates knowledge because it acts in a manner that makes the subjunctive 3 true.

The subjunctive condition 3 serves to exclude cases of the sort first described by Edward Gettier, such as the following. Two other people are in my office and I am justified on the basis of much evidence in believing the first owns a Ford car; though he (now) does not, the second person (a stranger to me) owns one. I believe truly and justifiably that someone (or other) in my office owns a Ford car, but I do not know someone does. Concluded Gettier, knowledge is not simply justified true belief.

The following subjunctive, which specifies condition 3 for this Gettier case, is not satisfied: if no one in my office owned a Ford car, I wouldn't believe that someone did. The situation that would obtain if no one in my office owned a Ford is one where the stranger does not (or where he is not in the office); and in that situation I still would believe, as before, that someone in my office does own a Ford, namely, the first person. So the subjunctive condition 3 excludes this Gettier case as a case of knowledge.

The subjunctive condition is powerful and intuitive, not so easy to satisfy, yet not so powerful as to rule out everything as an instance of knowledge. A subjunctive conditional "if p were true, q would be true", $p \to q$, does not say that p entails q or that it is logically impossible that p yet not-q. It says that in the situation that would obtain if p were true, q also would be true. This point is brought out especially clearly in recent '**possible-worlds**' accounts of subjunctives: the subjunctive is true when (roughly) in all those worlds in which p holds true that are closest to the actual world, q also is true. (Examine those worlds in which p holds true closest to the actual world, and see if q holds true in all these.) Whether or not q is true in p worlds that are still farther away from the actual world is irrelevant to the truth of the subjunctive. I do not mean to endorse any particular possible-worlds account of subjunctives, nor am I committed to this type of account. I sometimes shall use it, though, when it illustrates points in an especially clear way.*

---

* If the possible-worlds formalism is used to represent counterfactuals and subjunctives, the relevant worlds are not those worlds that are closest or most similar to the actual-world, unless the measure of closeness or similarity is: what would obtain if p were true. Clearly, this cannot be used to explain when subjunctives hold true, but it can be used to represent them. Compare utility theory which represents

The subjunctive condition 3 also handles nicely cases that cause difficulties for the view that you know that p when you can rule out the relevant alternatives to p in the context. For, as Gail Stine writes, "what makes an alternative relevant in one context and not another? . . . if on the basis of visual appearances obtained under optimum conditions while driving through the countryside Henry identifies an object as a barn, normally we say that Henry knows that it is a barn. Let us suppose, however, that unknown to Henry, the region is full of expertly made papier-mâché facsimiles of barns. In that case, we would not say that Henry knows that the object is a barn, unless he has evidence against it being a papier-mâché facsimile, which is now a relevant alternative. So much is clear, but what if no such facsimiles exist in Henry's surroundings, although

---

preferences but does not explain them. Still, it is not a trivial fact that preferences are so structured that they can be represented by a real-valued function, unique up to a positive linear transformation, even though the representation (by itself) does not explain these preferences. Similarly, it would be of interest to know what properties hold of distance metrics which serve to represent subjunctives, and to know how subjunctives must be structured and interrelated so that they can be given a possible-worlds representation. (With the same one space serving for all subjunctives?)

One further word on this point. Imagine a library where a cataloguer assigns call numbers based on facts of sort F. Someone, perhaps the cataloguer, then places each book on the shelf by looking at its call number, and inserting it between the two books whose call numbers are most nearly adjacent to its own. The call number is derivative from facts of type F, yet it plays some explanatory role, not merely a representational one. "Why is this book located precisely there? Because of its number." Imagine next another library where the person who places books on the shelves directly considers facts of type F, using them to order the books and to interweave new ones. Someone else might notice that this ordering can be represented by an assignment of numbers, numbers from which other information can be derived as well, for example, the first letter of the last name of the principal author. But such an assigned number is no explanation of why a book in this library is located between two others (or why its author's last name begins with a certain letter). I have assumed that utility numbers stand to preferences, and closeness or similarity measures stand to subjunctives, as the call numbers do to the books, and to the facts of type F they exhibit, in the second library.

they once did? Are either of these circumstances sufficient to make the hypothesis (that it's a papier-mâché object) relevant? Probably not, but the situation is not so clear." Let p be the statement that the object in the field is a (real) barn, and q the one that the object in the field is a papier-mâché barn. When papier-mâché barns are scattered through the area, if p were false, q would be true or might be. Since in this case (we are supposing) the person still would believe p, the subjunctive

(3) not-p → not-(S believes that p)

is not satisfied, and so he doesn't know that p. However, when papier-mâché barns are or were scattered around another country, even if p were false q wouldn't be true, and so (for all we have been told) the person may well know that p. A hypothesis q contrary to p clearly is relevant when if p weren't true, q would be true; when not-p → q. It clearly is irrelevant when if p weren't true, q also would not be true; when not-p → not-q. The remaining possibility is that neither of these opposed subjunctives holds; q might (or might not) be true if p weren't true. In this case, q also will be relevant, according to an account of knowledge incorporating condition 3 and treating subjunctives along the lines sketched above. Thus, condition 3 handles cases that befuddle the "relevant alternatives" account; though that account can adopt the above subjunctive criterion for when an alternative is relevant, it then becomes merely an alternate and longer way of stating condition 3.

Despite the power and intuitive force of the condition that if p weren't true the person would not believe it, this condition does not (in conjunction with the first two conditions) rule out every problem case. There remains, for example, the case of the person in the tank who is brought to believe, by direct electrical and chemical stimulation of his brain, that he is in the tank and is being brought to believe things in this way; he does not know this is true. However, the subjunctive condition is satisfied: if he weren't floating in the tank, he wouldn't believe he was.

The person in the tank does not know he is there, because his belief is not sensitive to the truth. Although it is caused by the fact that is its content, it is not sensitive to that fact. The operators of the tank

could have produced any belief, including the false belief that he wasn't in the tank; if they had, he would have believed that. Perfect sensitivity would involve beliefs and facts varying together. We already have one portion of that variation, subjunctively at least: if p were false he wouldn't believe it. This sensitivity as specified by a subjunctive does not have the belief vary with the truth or falsity of p in all possible situations, merely in the ones that would or might obtain if p were false.

The subjunctive condition

(3) not-p → not-(S believes that p)

tells us only half the story about how his belief is sensitive to the truth-value of p. It tells us how his belief state is sensitive to p's falsity, but not how it is sensitive to p's truth; it tells us what his belief state would be if p were false, but not what it would be if p were true.

To be sure, conditions 1 and 2 tell us that p is true and he does believe it, but it does not follow that his believing p is sensitive to p's being true. This additional sensitivity is given to us by a further subjunctive: if p were true, he would believe it.

(4) p → S believes that p.

Not only is p true and S believes it, but if it were true he would believe it. Compare: not only was the photon emitted and did it go to the left, but (it was then true that): if it were emitted it would go to the left. The truth of antecedent and consequent is not alone sufficient for the truth of a subjunctive; 4 says more than 1 and 2. Thus, we presuppose some (or another) suitable account of subjunctives. According to the suggestion tentatively made above, 4 holds true if not only does he actually truly believe p, but in the "close" worlds where p is true, he also believes it. He believes that p for some distance out in the p neighborhood of the actual world; similarly, condition 3 speaks not of the whole not-p neighborhood of the actual world, but only of the first portion of it. (If, as is likely, these explanations do not help, please use your own intuitive understanding of the subjunctives 3 and 4.)

The person in the tank does not satisfy the subjunctive condition 4. Imagine as actual a world in which he is in the tank and is stimulated to believe he is, and consider what subjunctives are true in that world. It is not true of him there that if he were in the tank he would believe it; for in the close world (or situation) to his own where he is in the tank but they don't give him the belief that he is (much less instill the belief that he isn't) he doesn't believe he is in the tank. Of the person actually in the tank and believing it, it is not true to make the further statement that if he were in the tank he would believe it—so he does not know he is in the tank.

The subjunctive condition 4 also handles a case presented by Gilbert Harman. The dictator of a country is killed; in their first edition, newspapers print the story, but later all the country's newspapers and other media deny the story, falsely. Everyone who encounters the denial believes it (or does not know what to believe and so suspends judgment). Only one person in the country fails to hear any denial and he continues to believe the truth. He satisfies conditions 1 through 3 (and the causal condition about belief) yet we are reluctant to say he knows the truth. The reason is that if he had heard the denials, he too would have believed them, just like everyone else. His belief is not sensitively tuned to the truth, he doesn't satisfy the condition that if it were true he would believe it. Condition 4 is not satisfied.

There is a pleasing symmetry about how this account of knowledge relates conditions 3 and 4, and connects them to the first two conditions. The account has the following form.

(1)
(2)
(3) not-1 $\rightarrow$ not-2
(4) 1 $\rightarrow$ 2

I am not inclined, however, to make too much of this symmetry, for I found also that with other conditions experimented with as a possible fourth condition there was some way to construe the resulting third and fourth conditions as symmetrical answers to some symmetrical looking questions, so that they appeared to arise in parallel fashion from similar questions about the components of true belief.

Symmetry, it seems, is a feature of a mode of presentation, not of the contents presented. A uniform transformation of symmetrical statements can leave the results nonsymmetrical. But if symmetry attaches to mode of presentation, how can it possibly be a deep feature of, for instance, **laws of nature** that they exhibit symmetry? (One of my favorite examples of symmetry is due to Groucho Marx. On his radio program he spoofed a commercial, and ended, "And if you are not completely satisfied, return the unused portion of our product and we will return the unused portion of your money.") Still, to present our subject symmetrically makes the connection of knowledge to true belief especially perspicuous. It seems to me that a symmetrical formulation is a sign of our understanding, rather than a mark of truth. If we cannot understand an asymmetry as arising from an underlying symmetry through the operation of a particular factor, we will not understand why that asymmetry exists in that direction. (But do we also need to understand why the underlying asymmetrical factor holds instead of its opposite?)

A person knows that p when he not only does truly believe it, but also would truly believe it and wouldn't falsely believe it. He not only actually has a true belief, he subjunctively has one. It is true that p and he believes it; if it weren't true he wouldn't believe it, and if it were true he would believe it. To know that p is to be someone who would believe it if it were true, and who wouldn't believe it if it were false.

It will be useful to have a term for this situation when a person's belief is thus subjunctively connected to the fact. Let us say of a person who believes that p, which is true, that when 3 and 4 hold, his belief *tracks* the truth that p. To know is to have a belief that tracks the truth. Knowledge is a particular way of being connected to the world, having a specific real factual connection to the world: tracking it.

One refinement is needed in condition 4. It may be possible for someone to have contradictory beliefs, to believe p and also believe not-p. We do not mean such a person to easily satisfy 4, and in any case we want his belief-state, sensitive to the truth of p, to focus upon p. So let us rewrite our fourth condition as:

(4) $p \rightarrow$ S believes that p and not-(S believes that not-p).

As you might have expected, this account of knowledge as tracking requires some refinements and epicycles. Readers who find themselves (or me) bogged down in these refinements should move on directly to this essay's second part, on **skepticism**, where the pace picks up.

Nonclosure

In taking the "short step", the skeptic assumes that if S knows that *p* and he knows that '*p* entails *q*' then he also knows that *q*. In the terminology of the logicians, the skeptic assumes that knowledge is closed under known logical implication; that the operation of moving from something known to something else known to be entailed by it does not take us outside of the (closed) area of knowledge. He intends, of course, to work things backwards, arguing that since the person does not know that *q*, assuming (at least for the purposes of argument) that he does know that *p* entails *q*, it follows that he does not know that *p*. For if he did know that *p*, he would also know that *q*, which he doesn't.

The details of different skeptical arguments vary in their structure, but each one will assume some variant of the principle that knowledge is closed under known logical implication. If we abbreviate "knowledge that *p*" by "Kp" and abbreviate "entails" by the fishhook sign "⊰", we can write this principle of closure as the subjunctive principle

P: K(p ⊰ q) & Kp → Kq.

If a person were to know that *p* entails *q* and he were to know that *p* then he would know that *q*. The statement that *q* follows by **modus ponens** from the other two stated as known in the antecedent of the subjunctive principle P; this principle counts on the person to draw the inference to *q*.

You know that your being in a tank on Alpha Centauri entails your not being in place X where you are. (I assume here a limited readership.) And you know also the contrapositive, that your being at place X entails that you are not then in a tank on Alpha Centauri. If you knew you were at X you would know you're not in a tank (of a specified sort) at Alpha Centauri. But you do not know this last fact

(the skeptic has argued and we have agreed) and so (he argues) you don't know the first. Another intuitive way of putting the skeptic's argument is as follows. If you know that two statements are incompatible and you know the first is true then you know the denial of the second. You know that your being at X and your being in a tank on Alpha Centauri are incompatible; so if you knew you were at X you would know you were not in the (specified) tank on Alpha Centauri. Since you do not know the second, you don't know the first.

No doubt, it is possible to argue over the details of principle P, to point out it is incorrect as it stands. Perhaps, though Kp, the person does not know that he knows that *p* (that is, not-KKp) and so does not draw the inference to *q*. Or perhaps he doesn't draw the inference because not-KK(p ⊰ q). Other similar principles face their own difficulties: for example, the principle that K(p → q) → (Kp → Kq) fails if Kp stops *p* → *q* from being true, that is, if Kp → not-(p → q); the principle that K(p ⊰ q) → K (Kp → Kq) faces difficulties if Kp makes the person forget that (p ⊰ q) and so he fails to draw the inference to q. We seem forced to pile K upon K until we reach something like KK(p ⊰ q) & KKp → Kq; this involves strengthening considerably the antecedent of P and so is not useful for the skeptic's argument that *p* is not known. (From a principle altered thus, it would follow at best that it is not known that *p* is known.)

We would be ill-advised, however, to quibble over the details of P. Although these details are difficult to get straight, it will continue to appear that something like P is correct. If S knows that '*p* entails *q*' and he knows that *p* and knows that '(*p* and *q* entails *q*) entails *q*' (shades of the Lewis Carroll puzzle we discuss below!) and he does draw the inference to *q* from all this and believes *q* via the process of drawing this inference, then will he not know that *q*? And what is wrong with simplifying this mass of detail by writing merely principle P, provided we apply it only to cases where the mass of detail holds, as it surely does in the skeptical cases under consideration? For example, I do realize that my being in the Van Leer Foundation Building in Jerusalem entails that I am not in a tank on Alpha Centauri; I am capable of drawing inferences now; I do believe I am not in a tank on Alpha Centauri (though not solely via this inference, surely); and so forth. Won't this satisfy the correctly detailed principle, and shouldn't it follow that I know I am not (in that tank) on Alpha Centauri? The skeptic agrees it should follow; so he concludes from the fact that I don't know I am not floating in the tank on Alpha Centauri that I don't know I am in Jerusalem. Uncovering difficulties in the details of particular formulations of P will not weaken the principle's intuitive appeal; such quibbling will seem at best like a wasp attacking a steamroller, at worst like an effort in bad faith to avoid being pulled along by the skeptic's argument.

Principle P is wrong, however, and not merely in detail. Knowledge is not closed under known logical implication. S knows that p when S has a true belief that p, and S wouldn't have a false belief that p (condition 3) and S would have a true belief that p (condition 4). Neither of these latter two conditions is closed under known logical implication.

Let us begin with condition

(3) if p were false, S wouldn't believe that p.

When S knows that p, his belief that p is contingent on the truth of p, contingent in the way the subjunctive condition 3 describes. Now it might be that p entails q (and S knows this), that S's belief that p is subjunctively contingent on the truth of p, that S believes q, yet his belief that q is not subjunctively dependent on the truth of q, in that it (or he) does not satisfy:

(3′) if q were false, S wouldn't believe that q.

For 3′ talks of what S would believe if q were false, and this may be a very different situation than the one that would hold if p were false, even though p entails q. That you were born in a certain city entails that you were born on earth.* Yet contemplating what (actually) would be the situation if you were not born in that city is very different from contemplating what situation would hold if you weren't born on earth. Just as those possibilities are very

different, so what is believed in them may be very different. When p entails q (and not the other way around) p will be a stronger statement than q, and so not-q (which is the antecedent of 3′) will be a stronger statement than not-p (which is the antecedent of 3). There is no reason to assume you will have the same beliefs in these two cases, under these suppositions of differing strengths.

There is no reason to assume the (closest) not-p world and the (closest) not-q world are **doxically** identical for you, and no reason to assume, even though p entails q, that your beliefs in one of these worlds would be a (proper) subset of your beliefs in the other.

Consider now the two statements:

p = I am awake and sitting on a chair in Jerusalem;

q = I am not floating in a tank on Alpha Centauri being stimulated by electrochemical means to believe that p.

The first one entails the second: p entails q. Also, I know that p entails q; and I know that p. If p were false, I would be standing or lying down in the same city, or perhaps sleeping there, or perhaps in a neighboring city or town. If q were false, I would be floating in a tank on Alpha Centauri. Clearly these are very different situations, leading to great differences in what I then would believe. If p were false, if I weren't awake and sitting on a chair in Jerusalem, I would not believe that p. Yet if q were false, if I was floating in a tank on Alpha Centauri, I would believe that q, that I was not in the tank, and indeed, in that case, I would still believe that p. According to our account of knowledge, I know that p yet I do not know that q, even though (I know) p entails q.

This failure of knowledge to be closed under known logical implication stems from the fact that condition 3 is not closed under known logical implication; condition 3 can hold of one statement believed while not of another known to be entailed by the first. It is clear that any account that includes as a necessary condition for knowledge the subjunctive condition 3, not-p → not-(S believes that p), will have the consequence that knowledge is not closed under known logical implication.

---

*Here again I assume a limited readership, and ignore possibilities such as those described in James Blish, *Cities in Flight*.

When *p* entails *q* and you believe each of them, if you do not have a false belief that *p* (since *p* is true) then you do not have a false belief that *q*. However, if you are to know something not only don't you have a false belief about it, but also you wouldn't have a false belief about it. Yet, we have seen how it may be that *p* entails *q* and you believe each and you wouldn't have a false belief that *p* yet you might have a false belief that *q* (that is, it is not the case that you wouldn't have one). Knowledge is not closed under the known logical implication because "wouldn't have a false belief that" is not closed under known logical implication.

If knowledge were the same as (simply) true belief then it would be closed under known logical implication (provided the implied statements were believed). Knowledge is not simply true belief, however; additional conditions are needed. These further conditions will make knowledge open under known logical implication, even when the entailed statement is believed, when at least one of the further conditions itself is open. Knowledge stays closed (only) if all of the additional conditions are closed. I lack a general nontrivial characterization of those conditions that are closed under known logical implication; possessing such an illuminating characterization, one might attempt to prove that no additional conditions of that sort could provide an adequate analysis of knowledge.

Still, we can say the following. A belief that *p* is knowledge that *p* only if it somehow varies with the truth of *p*. The causal condition for knowledge specified that the belief was "produced by" the fact, but that condition did not provide the right sort of varying with the fact. The subjunctive conditions 3 and 4 are our attempt to specify that varying. But however an account spells this out, it will hold that whether a belief that *p* is knowledge partly depends on what goes on with the belief in some situations when *p* is false. An account that says nothing about what is believed in any situation when *p* is false cannot give us any mode of varying with the fact.

Because what is preserved under logical implication is truth, any condition that is preserved under known logical implication is most likely to speak only of what happens when *p*, and *q*, are true, without speaking at all of what happens when either one is false. Such a condition is incapable of providing "varies with"; so adding only such conditions to true belief cannot yield an adequate account of knowledge.

A belief's somehow varying with the truth of what is believed is not closed under known logical implication. Since knowledge that *p* involves such variation, knowledge also is not closed under known logical implication. The skeptic cannot easily deny that knowledge involves such variation, for his argument that we don't know that we're not floating in that tank, for example, uses the fact that knowledge does involve variation. ("If you were floating in the tank you would still think you weren't, so you don't know that you're not.") Yet, though one part of his argument uses that fact that knowledge involves such variation, another part of his argument presupposes that knowledge does not involve any such variation. This latter is the part that depends upon knowledge being closed under known logical implication, as when the skeptic argues that since you don't know that not-SK, you don't know you are not floating in the tank, then you also don't know, for example, that you are now reading a book. That closure can hold only if the variation does not. The skeptic cannot be right both times. According to our view he is right when he holds that knowledge involves such variation and so concludes that we don't know, for example, that we are not floating in that tank; but he is wrong when he assumes knowledge is closed under known logical implication and concludes that we know hardly anything.

Knowledge is a real factual relation, subjunctively specifiable, whose structure admits our standing in this relation, tracking, to *p* without standing in it to some *q* which we know *p* to entail. Any relation embodying some variation of belief with the fact, with the truth (value), will exhibit this structural feature. The skeptic is right that we don't track some particular truths—the ones stating that his skeptical possibilities SK don't hold—but wrong that we don't stand in the real knowledge-relation of tracking to many other truths, including ones that entail these first mentioned truths we believe but don't know.

The literature on skepticism contains writers who endorse these skeptical arguments (or similar narrower ones), but confess their inability to maintain their skeptical beliefs at times when they are not focusing explicitly on the reasoning that led them to skeptical conclusions. The most notable example of this is Hume:

I am ready to reject all belief and reasoning, and can look upon no opinion even as more probable or likely than another . . . Most fortunately it happens that since reason is incapable of dispelling these clouds, nature herself suffices to that purpose, and cures me of this philosophical melancholy and delirium, either by relaxing this bent of mind, or by some avocation, and lively impression of my senses, which obliterate all these chimeras. I dine, I play a game of backgammon, I converse, and am merry with my friends; and when after three or four hours' amusement, I would return to these speculations, they appear so cold, and strained, and ridiculous, that I cannot find in my heart to enter into them any farther. (*A Treatise of Human Nature*, Book I, Part IV, section VII)

The great subverter of Pyrrhonism or the excessive principles of skepticism is action, and employment, and the occupations of common life. These principles may flourish and triumph in the schools; where it is, indeed, difficult, if not impossible, to refute them. But as soon as they leave the shade, and by the presence of the real objects, which actuate our passions and sentiments, are put in opposition to the more powerful principles of our nature, they vanish like smoke, and leave the most determined skeptic in the same condition as other mortals . . . And though a Pyrrhonian may throw himself or others into a momentary amazement and confusion by his profound reasonings; the first and most trivial event in life will put to flight all his doubts and scruples, and leave him the same, in every point of action and speculation, with the philosophers of every other sect, or with those who never concerned themselves in any philosophical researches. When he awakes from his dream, he will be the first to join in the laugh against himself, and to confess that all his objections are mere amusement. (*An Enquiry Concerning Human Understanding*, Section XII, Part II)

The theory of knowledge we have presented explains why skeptics of various sorts have had such difficulties in sticking to their far-reaching skeptical conclusions "outside the study", or even inside it when they are not thinking specifically about skeptical arguments and possibilities SK.

The skeptic's arguments do show (but show only) that we don't know the skeptic's possibilities SK do not hold; and he is right that we don't track the fact that SK does not hold. (If it were to hold, we would still think it didn't.) However, the skeptic's arguments don't show we do not know other facts (including facts that entail not-SK) for we do track these other facts (and knowledge is not closed under known logical entailment). Since we do track these other facts—you, for example, the fact that you are reading a book; I, the fact that I am writing on a page—and the skeptic tracks such facts too, it is not surprising that when he focuses on them, on his relationship to such facts, the skeptic finds it hard to remember or maintain his view that he does not know those facts. Only by shifting his attention back to his relationship to the (different) fact that not-SK, which relationship is not tracking, can he revive his skeptical belief and make it salient. However, this skeptical triumph is evanescent, it vanishes when his attention turns to other facts. Only by fixating on the skeptical possibilities SK can he maintain his skeptical virtue; otherwise, unsurprisingly, he is forced to confess to sins of credulity.

KEY TERMS

Necessary
Sufficient
Possible world
Laws of nature
Skepticism
Modus ponens
Doxically

STUDY QUESTIONS

1. What is your initial reaction to Nozick's Principle P? Does it seem right? Why or why not?
2. What about Nozick's account of knowledge allows him to deny Principle P and therefore escape skepticism?
3. How does the example involving Alpha Centauri work? What crucial statement does Nozick's account of knowledge allow him to deny? How does denying that statement help?
4. Can you think of any cases in which Nozick's account of knowledge is satisfied, but yet we would not intuitively want to ascribe knowledge?

B. HUME'S PROBLEMS AND SOME SOLUTIONS

X

Of Scepticism with Regard to the Senses

DAVID HUME

· ·

Section II
Of Scepticism with Regard to
the Senses

Thus the sceptic still continues to reason and believe, even tho' he asserts, that he cannot defend his reason by reason; and by the same rule he must assent to the principle concerning the existence of body, tho' he cannot pretend by any arguments of philosophy to maintain its veracity. Nature has not left this to his choice, and has doubtless esteem'd it an affair of too great importance to be trusted to our uncertain reasonings and speculations. We may well ask, *What causes induce us to believe in the existence of body?* but 'tis in vain to ask, *Whether there be body or not?* That is a point, which we must take for granted in all our reasonings.

The subject, then, of our present enquiry is concerning the *causes* which induce us to believe in the existence of body: And my reasonings on this head I shall begin with a distinction, which at first sight may

seem superfluous, but which will contribute very much to the perfect understanding of what follows. We ought to examine apart those two questions, which are commonly confounded together, viz. Why we attribute a CONTINU'D existence to objects, even when they are not present to the senses; and why we suppose them to have an existence DISTINCT from the mind and perception. Under this last head I comprehend their situation as well as relations, their *external* position as well as the *independence* of their existence and operation. These two questions concerning the continu'd and distinct existence of body are intimately connected together. For if the objects of our senses continue to exist, even when they are not perceiv'd, their existence is of course independent of and distinct from the perception; and vice versa, if their existence be independent of the perception and distinct from it, they must continue to exist, even tho' they be not perceiv'd. But tho' the decision of the one question decides the other; yet that we may the more easily discover the principles of human nature, from whence the decision arises, we shall carry along with us this distinction, and shall consider, whether it be the *senses*, *reason*, or the *imagination*, that produces the opinion of a *continu'd* or of a *distinct* existence. These are the only questions, that are intelligible on

From *A Treatise of Human Nature*, edited by L. A. Selby-Bigge, 2nd edition revised by P. H. Nidditch. Copyright © 1978 by Oxford University Press. Reprinted by permission of the publisher.

the present subject. For as to the notion of external existence, when taken for something specifically different from our perceptions,[1] we have already shewn its absurdity.

To begin with the SENSES, 'tis evident these faculties are incapable of giving rise to the notion of the *continu'd* existence of their objects, after they no longer appear to the senses. For that is a contradiction in terms, and supposes that the senses continue to operate, even after they have ceas'd all manner of operation. These faculties, therefore, if they have any influence in the present case, must produce the opinion of a distinct, not of a continu'd existence; and in order to that, must present their impressions either as images and representations, or as these very distinct and external existences.

That our senses offer not their impressions as the images of something *distinct*, or *independent*, and *external*, is evident; because they convey to us nothing but a single perception, and never give us the least intimation of any thing beyond. A single perception can never produce the idea of a double existence, but by some inference either of the reason or imagination. When the mind looks farther than what immediately appears to it, its conclusions can never be put to the account of the senses; and it certainly looks farther, when from a single perception it infers a double existence, and supposes the relations of resemblance and causation betwixt them.

If our senses, therefore, suggest any idea of distinct existences, they must convey the impressions as those very existences, by a kind of fallacy and illusion. Upon this head we may observe, that all sensations are felt by the mind, such as they really are, and that when we doubt, whether they present themselves as distinct objects, or as mere impressions, the difficulty is not concerning their nature, but concerning their relations and situation. Now if the senses presented our impressions as external to, and independent of ourselves, both the objects and ourselves must be obvious to our senses, otherwise they cou'd not be compar'd by these faculties. The difficulty, then, is how far we are *ourselves* the objects of our senses.

'Tis certain there is no question in philosophy more abstruse than that concerning identity, and the nature of the uniting principle, which constitutes a person. So far from being able by our senses merely to determine this question, we must have recourse to the most profound **metaphysics** to give a satisfactory answer to it; and in common life 'tis evident these ideas of self and person are never very fix'd nor determinate. 'Tis absurd, therefore, to imagine the senses can ever distinguish betwixt ourselves and external objects.

Add to this, that every impression, external and internal, passions, affections, sensations, pains and pleasures, are originally on the same footing; and that whatever other differences we may observe among them, they appear, all of them, in their true colours, as impressions or perceptions. And indeed, if we consider the matter aright, 'tis scarce possible it shou'd be more capable of deceiving us in the situation and relations, than in the nature of our impressions. For since all actions and sensations of the mind are known to us by consciousness, they must necessarily appear in every particular what they are, and be what they appear. Every thing that enters the mind, being in *reality* as the perception, 'tis impossible any thing shou'd to *feeling* appear different. This were to suppose, that even where we are most intimately conscious, we might be mistaken.

But not to lose time in examining, whether 'tis possible for our senses to deceive us, and represent our perceptions as distinct from ourselves, that is as *external* to and *independent* of us; let us consider whether they really do so, and whether this error proceeds from an immediate sensation, or from some other causes.

To begin with the question concerning *external* existence, it may perhaps be said, that setting aside the metaphysical question of the identity of a thinking **substance**, our own body evidently belongs to us; and as several impressions appear exterior to the body, we suppose them also exterior to ourselves. The paper, on which I write at present, is beyond my hand. The table is beyond the paper. The walls of the chamber beyond the table. And in casting my eye towards the window, I perceive a great extent of fields and buildings beyond my chamber. From all this it may be infer'd, that no other faculty is requir'd, beside the senses, to convince us of the external existence of body. But to prevent this inference, we need only weigh the three following considerations. *First*, That, properly speaking, 'tis not our body we perceive, when we regard our limbs and members, but certain impressions, which enter by the senses; so that the ascribing a real and corporeal existence to these impressions, or to their objects, is an act of the mind as difficult to explain, as that which we examine at present. *Secondly*, Sounds, and tastes, and smells, tho' commonly regarded by the mind as continu'd independent quantities, appear not to have any existence in extension, and consequently cannot appear to the senses as situated externally to the body. The reason, why we ascribe a place to them, shall be consider'd[2] afterwards. *Thirdly*, Even our sight informs us not of distance or outness (so to speak) immediately and without a certain reasoning and experience, as is acknowledg'd by the most rational philosophers.

As to the *independency* of our perceptions on ourselves, this can never be an object of the senses; but any opinion we form concerning it, must be deriv'd from experience and observation: And we shall see afterwards, that our conclusions from experience are far from being favourable to the doctrine of the independency of our perceptions. Mean while we may observe that when we talk of real distinct existences, we have commonly more in our eye their independency than external situation in place, and think an object has a sufficient reality, when its Being is uninterrupted, and independent of the incessant revolutions, which we are conscious of in ourselves.

Thus to resume what I have said concerning the senses; they give us no notion of continu'd existence, because they cannot operate beyond the extent, in which they really operate. They as little produce the opinion of a distinct existence, because they neither can offer it to the mind as represented, nor as original. To offer it as represented, they must present both an object and an image. To make it appear as original, they must convey a falshood; and this falshood must lie in the relations and situation: In order to which they must be able to compare the object with ourselves; and even in that case they do not, nor is it possible they shou'd, deceive us. We may, therefore, conclude with certainty, that the opinion of a continu'd and of a distinct existence never arises from the senses.

To confirm this we may observe, that there are three different kinds of impressions convey'd by the senses. The first are those of the figure, bulk, motion and solidity of bodies. The second those of colours, tastes, smells, sounds, heat and cold. The third are the pains and pleasures, that arise from the application of objects to our bodies, as by the cutting of our flesh with steel, and such like. Both philosophers and the vulgar suppose the first of these to have a distinct continu'd existence. The vulgar only regard the second as on the same footing. Both philosophers and the vulgar, again, esteem the third to be merely perceptions; and consequently interrupted and dependent beings.

Now 'tis evident, that, whatever may be our philosophical opinion, colours, sounds, heat and cold, as far as appears to the senses, exist after the same manner with motion and solidity, and that the difference we make betwixt them in this respect, arises not from the mere perception. So strong is the prejudice for the distinct continu'd existence of the former qualities, that when the contrary opinion is advanc'd by modern philosophers, people imagine they can almost refute it from their feeling and experience, and that their very senses contradict this philosophy. 'Tis also evident, that colours, sounds, etc. are originally on the same footing with the pain that arises from steel, and pleasure that proceeds from a fire; and that the difference betwixt them is founded neither on perception nor reason, but on the imagination. For as they are confest to be, both of them, nothing but perceptions arising from the particular configurations and motions of the parts of body, wherein possible can their difference consist? Upon the whole, then, we may conclude, that as far as the senses are judges, all perceptions are the same in the manner of their existence.

We may also observe in this instance of sounds and colours, that we can attribute a distinct continu'd existence to objects without ever consulting REASON, or weighing our opinions by any philosophical principles. And indeed, whatever convincing arguments philosophers may fancy they can produce to establish the belief of objects independent of the mind, 'tis obvious these arguments are known but to very few, and that 'tis not by them, that children, peasants, and the greatest part of mankind are induc'd to attribute objects to some impressions, and deny them to others. Accordingly we find, that all the conclusions, which the vulgar form on this head, are directly contrary to those, which are confirm'd by philosophy. For philosophy informs us, that every thing, which appears to the mind, is nothing but a perception, and is interrupted, and dependent on the mind; whereas the vulgar confound perceptions and objects, and attribute a distinct continu'd existence to the very things they feel or see. This sentiment, then, as it is entirely unreasonable, must proceed from some other faculty than the understanding. To which we may add, that as long as we take our perceptions and objects to be the same, we can never infer the existence of the one from that of the other, nor form any argument from the relation of cause and effect; which is the only one that can assure us of matter of fact. Even after we distinguish our perceptions from our objects, 'twill appear presently, that we are still incapable of reasoning from the existence of one to that of the other. So that upon the whole our reason neither does, nor is it possible it ever shou'd, upon any supposition, give us an assurance of the continu'd and distinct existence of body. That opinion must be entirely owing to the IMAGINATION: which must now be the subject of our enquiry.

Since all impressions are internal and perishing existences, and appear as such, the notion of their distinct and continu'd existence must arise from a concurrence of some of their qualities with the qualities of the imagination; and since this notion does not extend to all of them, it must arise from certain qualities peculiar to some impressions. 'Twill therefore be easy for us to discover these qualities by a comparison of the impressions, to which we attribute a distinct and continu'd existence, with those, which we regard as internal and perishing.

We may observe, then, that 'tis neither upon account of the involuntariness of certain impressions, as is commonly suppos'd, nor of their superior force and violence, that we attribute to them a reality, and continu'd existence, which we refuse to others, that are voluntary or feeble. For 'tis evident our pains and pleasures, our passions and affections, which we never suppose to have any existence beyond our perception, operate with greater violence, and are equally involuntary, as the impressions of figure and extension, colour and sound, which we suppose to be permanent beings. The heat of a fire, when moderate, is suppos'd to exist in the fire; but the pain, which it causes upon a near approach, is not taken to have any being except in the perception.

These vulgar opinions, then, being rejected, we must search for some other hypothesis, by which we may discover those peculiar qualities in our impressions, which makes us attribute to them a distinct and continu'd existence.

After a little examination, we shall find, that all those objects, to which we attribute a continu'd existence, have a peculiar *constancy*, which distinguishes them from the impressions, whose existence depends upon our perception. Those mountains, and houses, and trees, which lie at present under my eye, have always appear'd to me in the same order; and when I lose sight of them by shutting my eyes or turning my head, I soon after find them return upon me without the least alteration. My bed and table, my books and papers, present themselves in the same uniform manner, and change not upon account of any interruption in my seeing or perceiving them. This is the case with all the impressions, whose objects are suppos'd to have an external existence; and is the case with no other impressions, whether gentle or violent, voluntary or involuntary.

This constancy, however, is not so perfect as not to admit of very considerable exceptions. Bodies often change their position and qualities, and after a little absence or interruption may become hardly knowable. But here 'tis observable, that even in these changes they preserve a *coherence*, and have a regular dependence on each other; which is the foundation of a kind of reasoning from causation, and produces the opinion of their continu'd existence. When I return to my chamber after an hour's absence, I find not my fire in the same situation, in which I left it: But then I am accustom'd in other instances to see a like alteration produc'd in a like time, whether I am present or absent, near or remote. This coherence, therefore, in their changes is one of the characteristics of external objects, as well as their constancy.

Having found that the opinion of the continu'd existence of body depends on the COHERENCE and CONSTANCY of certain impressions, I now proceed to examine after what manner these qualities give rise to so extraordinary an opinion. To begin with the coherence; we may observe, that tho' those internal impressions, which we regard as fleeting and perishing, have also a certain coherence or regularity in their appearances, yet 'tis of somewhat a different nature, from that which we discover in bodies. Our passions are found by experience to have a mutual connexion with and dependance on each other; but on no occasion is it necessary to suppose, that they have existed and operated, when they were not perceiv'd, in order to preserve the same dependance and connexion, of which we have had experience. The case is not the same with relation to external objects. Those require a continu'd existence, or otherwise lose, in a great measure, the regularity of their operation. I am here seated in my chamber with my face to the fire; and all the objects, that strike my senses, are contain'd in a few yards around me. My memory, indeed, informs me of the existence of many objects; but then this information extends not beyond their past existence, nor do either my senses or memory give any testimony to the continuance of their being. When therefore I am thus seated, and revolve over these thoughts, I hear on a sudden a noise as of a door turning upon its hinges; and a little after see a porter, who advances towards me. This gives occasion to many new reflexions and reasonings. First, I never have observ'd, that this noise cou'd proceed from any thing but the motion of a door; and therefore conclude, that the present phenomenon is a contradiction to all past experience, unless the door, which I remember on t'other side the chamber, be still in being. Again, I have always found, that a human body was possest of a quality, which I call gravity, and which hinders it from mounting in the air, as this porter must have done to arrive at my chamber, unless the stairs I remember be not annihilated by my absence. But this is not all. I receive a letter, which upon opening it I perceive by the hand-writing and subscription to have come from a friend, who says he is two hundred leagues distant. 'Tis evident I can never account for this phenomenon, conformable to my experience in other instances, without spreading out in my mind the whole sea and continent between us, and supposing the effects and continu'd existence of posts and ferries, according to my memory and observation. To consider these phenomena of the porter and letter in a certain light, they are contradictions to common experience, and may be regarded as objections to those maxims, which we form concerning the connexions of causes and effects. I am accustom'd to hear such a sound, and see such an object in motion at the same time. I have not receiv'd

in this particular instance both these perceptions. These observations are contrary, unless I suppose that the door still remains, and that it was open'd without my perceiving it: And this supposition, which was at first entirely arbitrary and hypothetical, acquires a force and evidence by its being the only one, upon which I can reconcile these contradictions. There is scarce a moment of my life, wherein there is not a similar instance presented to me, and I have not occasion to suppose the continu'd existence of objects, in order to connect their past and present appearances, and give them such an union with each other, as I have found by experience to be suitable to their particular natures and circumstances. Here then I am naturally led to regard the world, as something real and durable, and as preserving its existence, even when it is no longer present to my perception.

But tho' this conclusion from the coherence of appearances may seem to be of the same nature with our reasonings concerning causes and effects; as being deriv'd from custom, and regulated by past experience; we shall find upon examination, that they are at the bottom considerably different from each other, and that this inference arises from the understanding, and from custom in an indirect and oblique manner. For 'twill readily be allow'd, that since nothing is ever really present to the mind, besides its own perceptions, 'tis not only impossible, that any habit shou'd ever be acquir'd otherwise than by the regular succession of these perceptions, but also that any habit shou'd ever exceed that degree of regularity. Any degree, therefore, of regularity in our perceptions, can never be a foundation for us to infer a greater degree of regularity in some objects, which are not perceiv'd; since this supposes a contradiction, viz. a habit acquir'd by what was never present to the mind. But 'tis evident, that whenever we infer the continu'd existence of the objects of sense from their coherence, and the frequency of their union, 'tis in order to bestow on the objects a greater regularity than what is observ'd in our mere perceptions. We remark a connexion betwixt two kinds of objects in their past appearance to the senses, but are not able to observe this connexion to be perfectly constant, since the turning about of our head, or the shutting of our eyes is able to break it. What then do we suppose in this case, but that these objects still continue their usual connexion, notwithstanding their apparent interruption, and that the irregular appearances are join'd by something, of which we are insensible? But as all reasoning concerning matters of fact arises only from custom, and custom can only be the effect of repeated perceptions, the extending of custom and reasoning beyond the perceptions can never be the direct and natural effect of the constant repetition and connexion, but must arise from the co-operation of some other principles.

I have already[3] observ'd, in examining the foundation of mathematics, that the imagination, when set into any train of thinking, is apt to continue, even when its object fails it, and like a galley put in motion by the oars, carries on its course without any new impulse. This I have assign'd for the reason, why, after considering several loose standards of equality, and correcting them by each other, we proceed to imagine so correct and exact a standard of that relation, as is not liable to the least error or variation. The same principle makes us easily entertain this opinion of the continu'd existence of body. Objects have a certain coherence even as they appear to our senses; but this coherence is much greater and more uniform, if we suppose the objects to have a continu'd existence; and as the mind is once in the train of observing an uniformity among objects, it naturally continues, till it renders the uniformity as compleat as possible. The simple supposition of their continu'd existence suffices for this purpose, and gives us a notion of a much greater regularity among objects, than what they have when we look no farther than our senses.

But whatever force we may ascribe to this principle, I am afraid 'tis too weak to support alone so vast an edifice, as is that of the continu'd existence of all external bodies; and that we must join the *constancy* of their appearance to the *coherence*, in order to give a satisfactory account of that opinion. As the explication of this will lead me into a considerable compass of very profound reasoning; I think it proper, in order to avoid confusion, to give a short sketch or abridgment of my system, and afterwards draw out all its parts in their full compass. This inference from the constancy of our perceptions, like the precedent from their coherence, gives rise to the

opinion of the *continu'd* existence of body, which is prior to that of its *distinct* existence, and produces that latter principle.

When we have been accustom'd to observe a constancy in certain impressions, and have found, that the perception of the sun or ocean, for instance, returns upon us after an absence or annihilation with like parts and in a like order, as at its first appearance, we are not apt to regard these interrupted perceptions as different, (which they really are) but on the contrary consider them as individually the same, upon account of their resemblance. But as this interruption of their existence is contrary to their perfect identity, and makes us regard the first impression as annihilated, and the second as newly created, we find ourselves somewhat at a loss, and are involv'd in a kind of contradiction. In order to free ourselves from this difficulty, we disguise, as much as possible, the interruption, or rather remove it entirely, by supposing that these interrupted perceptions are connected by a real existence, of which we are insensible. This supposition, or idea of continu'd existence, acquires a force and vivacity from the memory of these broken impressions, and from that propensity, which they give us, to suppose them the same; and according to the precedent reasoning, the very essence of belief consists in the force and vivacity of the conception.

In order to justify this system, there are four things requisite. *First*, To explain the *principium individuationis*, or principle of identity. *Secondly*, Give a reason, why the resemblance of our broken and interrupted perceptions induces us to attribute an identity to them. *Thirdly*, Account for that propensity, which this illusion gives, to unite these broken appearances by a continu'd existence. *Fourthly* and lastly, Explain that force and vivacity of conception, which arises from the propensity.

First, As to the principle of individuation; we may observe, that the view of any one object is not sufficient to convey the idea of identity. For in that proposition, *an object is the same with itself*, if the idea express'd by the word, *object*, were no ways distinguish'd from that meant by *itself*: we really shou'd mean nothing, nor wou'd the proposition contain a predicate and a subject, which however are imply'd in this affirmation. One single object conveys the idea of unity, not that of identity.

On the other hand, a multiplicity of objects can never convey this idea, however resembling they may be suppos'd. The mind always pronounces the one not to be the other, and considers them as forming two, three, or any determinate number of objects, whose existences are entirely distinct and independent.

Since then both number and unity are incompatible with the relation of identity, it must lie in something that is neither of them. But to tell the truth, at first sight this seems utterly impossible. Betwixt unity and number there can be no medium; no more than betwixt existence and nonexistence. After one object is suppos'd to exist, we must either suppose another also to exist; in which case we have the idea of number: Or we might suppose it not to exist; in which case the first object remains at unity.

To remove this difficulty, let us have recourse to the idea of time or duration. I have already observ'd,[4] that time, in a strict sense, implies succession, and that when we apply its idea to any unchangeable object, 'tis only by a fiction of the imagination, by which the unchangeable object is suppos'd to participate of the changes of the co-existent objects, and in particular of that of our perceptions. This fiction of the imagination almost universally takes place; and 'tis by means of it, that a single object, plac'd before us, and survey'd for any time without our discovering in it any interruption or variation, is able to give us a notion of identity. For when we consider any two points of this time, we may place them in different lights: We may either survey them at the very same instant; in which case they give us the idea of number, both by themselves and by the object; which must be multiply'd, in order to be conceiv'd at once, as existence in these two different points of time: Or on the other hand, we may trace the succession of time by a like succession of ideas, and conceiving first one moment, along with the object then existent, imagine afterwards a change in the time without any *variation* or *interruption* in the object; in which case it gives us the idea of unity. Here then is an idea, which is a medium betwixt unity and number; or more properly speaking, is either of them, according to the view, in which we take it: And this idea we call that of identity. We cannot, in any propriety of speech, say, that an object is the same with itself, unless we mean, that the object existent at one time is the same with itself existent at another. By this means we make a difference, betwixt the idea meant by the word, *object*, and that meant by *itself*, without going the length of number, and at the same time without restraining ourselves to a strict and absolute unity.

Thus the principle of individuation is nothing but the *invariableness* and *uninterruptedness* of any object, thro' a suppos'd variation of time, by which the mind can trace it in the different periods of its existence, without any break of the view, and without being oblig'd to form the idea of multiplicity or number.

I now proceed to explain the *second* part of my system, and show why the constancy of our perceptions makes us ascribe to them a perfect numerical identity, tho' there be very long intervals betwixt their appearance, and they have only one of the essential qualities of identity, viz. *invariableness*. That I may avoid all ambiguity and confusion on this head, I shall observe, that I here account for the opinions and belief of the vulgar with regard to the existence of body; and therefore must entirely conform myself to their manner of thinking and of expressing themselves. Now we have already observ'd, that however philosophers may distinguish betwixt the objects and perceptions of the senses; which they suppose coexistent and resembling; yet this is a distinction, which is not comprehended by the generality of mankind, who as they perceive only one being, can never assent to the opinion of a double existence and representation. Those very sensations, which enter by the eye or ear, are with them the true objects, nor can they readily conceive that this pen or paper, which immediately perceiv'd, represents another, which is different from, but resembling it. In order, therefore, to accommodate myself to their notions, I shall at first suppose; that there is only a single existence, which I shall call indifferently *object* or *perception*, according as it shall seem best to suit my purpose, understanding by both of them what any common man means by a hat, or shoe, or stone, or any other impression, convey'd to him by his senses. I shall be sure to give warning, when I return to a more philosophical way of speaking and thinking.

To enter, therefore, upon the question concerning the source of the error and deception with regard to identity, when we attribute it to our resembling perceptions, notwithstanding their interruption; I must here recall an observation, which I have already prov'd and explain'd.[5] Nothing is more apt to make us mistake one idea for another, than any relation betwixt them, which associates them together in the imagination, and makes it pass with facility from one to the other. Of all relations, that of resemblance is in this respect the most efficacious; and that because it not only causes an association of ideas, but also of dispositions, and makes us conceive the one idea by an act or operation of the mind, similar to that by which we conceive the other. This circumstance I have observ'd to be of great moment; and we may establish it for a general rule, that whatever ideas place the mind in the same disposition or in similar ones, are very apt to be confounded. The mind readily passes from one to the other, and perceives not the change without a strict attention, of which, generally speaking, 'tis wholly incapable.

In order to apply this general maxim, we must first examine the disposition of the mind in viewing any object which preserves a perfect identity, and then find some other object, that is confounded with it, by causing a similar disposition. When we fix our thought on any object, and suppose it to continue the same for some time; 'tis evident we suppose the change to lie only in the time, and never exert ourselves to produce any new image or idea of the object. The faculties of the mind repose themselves in a manner, and take no more exercise, than what is necessary to continue that idea, of which we were formerly possest, and which subsists without variation or interruption. The passage from one moment to another is scarce felt, and distinguishes not itself by a different perception or idea, which may require a different direction of the spirits, in order to its conception.

Now what other objects, beside identical ones, are capable of placing the mind in the same disposition, when it considers them, and of causing the same uninterrupted passage of the imagination from one idea to another? This question is of the last importance. For if we can find any such objects, we may certainly conclude, from the foregoing principle, that they are very naturally confounded with identical ones, and are taken for them in most of our reasonings. But

tho' this question be very important, 'tis not very difficult nor doubtful. For I immediately reply, that a succession of related objects places the mind in this disposition, and is consider'd with the same smooth and uninterrupted progress of the imagination, as attends the view of the same invariable object. The very nature and essence of relation is to connect our ideas with each other, and upon the appearance of the one, to facilitate the transition to its correlative. The passage betwixt related ideas is, therefore, so smooth and easy, that it produces little alteration on the mind, and seems like the continuation of the same action; and as the continuation of the same action is an effect of the continu'd view of the same object, 'tis for this reason we attribute sameness to every succession of related objects. The thought slides along the succession with equal facility, as if it consider'd only one object; and therefore confounds the succession with the identity.

We shall afterwards see many instances of this tendency of relation to make us ascribe an *identity* to *different* objects; but shall here confine ourselves to the present subject. We find by experience, that there is such a *constancy* in almost all the impressions of the senses, that their interruption produces no alteration on them, and hinders them not from returning the same in appearance and in situation as at their first existence. I survey the furniture of my chamber; I shut my eyes, and afterwards open them; and find the new perceptions to resemble perfectly those, which formerly struck my senses. This resemblance is observ'd in a thousand instances, and naturally connects together our ideas of these interrupted perceptions by the strongest relation, and conveys the mind with an easy transition from one to another. An easy transition or passage of the imagination, along the ideas of these different and interrupted perceptions, is almost the same disposition of mind with that in which we consider one constant and uninterrupted perception. 'Tis therefore very natural for us to mistake the one for the other.[6]

The persons, who entertain this opinion concerning the identity of our resembling perceptions, are in general all the unthinking and unphilosophical part of mankind, (that is, all of us, at one time or other) and consequently such as suppose their perceptions to be their only objects, and never think of a double existence internal and external, representing and represented. The very image, which is present to the senses, is with us the real body; and 'tis to these interrupted images we ascribe a perfect identity. But as the interruption of the appearance seems contrary to the identity, and naturally leads us to regard these resembling perceptions as different from each other, we here find ourselves at a loss how to reconcile such opposite opinions. The smooth passage of the imagination along the ideas of the resembling perceptions makes us ascribe to them a perfect identity. The interrupted manner of their appearance makes us consider them as so many resembling, but still distinct beings, which appear after certain intervals. The perplexity arising from this contradiction produces a propension to unite these broken appearances by the fiction of a continu'd existence, which is the *third* part of that hypothesis I propos'd to explain.

Nothing is more certain from experience, than that any contradiction either to the sentiments or passions gives a sensible uneasiness, whether it proceeds from without or from within; from the opposition of external objects, or from the combat of internal principles. On the contrary, whatever strikes in with the natural propensities, and either externally forwards their satisfaction, or internally concurs with their movements, is sure to give a sensible pleasure. Now there being here an opposition betwixt the notion of the identity of resembling perceptions, and the interruption of their appearance, the mind must be uneasy in that situation, and will naturally seek relief from the uneasiness. Since the uneasiness arises from the opposition of two contrary principles, it must look for relief by sacrificing the one to the other. But as the smooth passage of our thought along our resembling perceptions makes us ascribe to them an identity, we can never without reluctance yield up that opinion. We must, therefore, turn to the other side, and suppose that our perceptions are no longer interrupted, but preserve a continu'd as well as an invariable existence, and are by that means entirely the same. But here the interruptions in the appearance of these perceptions are so long and frequent, that 'tis impossible to overlook them; and as the *appearance* of a perception in the mind and its *existence* seem at first sight entirely the same, it may be doubted, whether we can ever assent to so palpable a contradiction, and suppose

a perception to exist without being present to the mind. In order to clear up this matter, and learn how the interruption in the appearance of a perception implies not necessarily an interruption in its existence, 'twill be proper to touch upon some principles. . . .[7]

We may begin with observing, that the difficulty in the present case is not concerning the matter of fact, or whether the mind forms such a conclusion concerning the continu'd existence of its perceptions, but only concerning the manner in which the conclusion is form'd, and principles from which it is deriv'd. 'Tis certain, that almost all mankind, and even philosophers themselves, for the greatest part of their lives take their perceptions to be their only objects, and suppose, that the very being, which is intimately present to the mind, is the real body or material existence. 'Tis also certain, that this very perception or object is suppos'd to have a continu'd uninterrupted being, and neither to be annihilated by our absence, nor to be brought into existence by our presence. When we are absent from it, we say it still exists, but that we do not feel, we do not see it. When we are present, we say we feel, or see it. Here then may arise two questions; *First,* How can we satisfy ourselves in supposing a perception to be absent from the mind without being annihilated. *Secondly,* After what manner we conceive an object to become present to the mind, without some new creation of a perception or image; and what we mean by this *seeing,* and *feeling,* and *perceiving.*

As to the first question; we may observe, that what we call a *mind,* is nothing but a heap or collection of different perceptions, united together by certain relations, and suppos'd, tho' falsely, to be endow'd with a perfect simplicity and identity. Now as every perception is distinguishable from another, and may be consider'd as separately existent; it evidently follows, that there is no absurdity in separating any particular perception from the mind; that is, in breaking off all its relations, with that connected mass of perceptions, which constitute a thinking being.

The same reasoning affords us an answer to the second question. If the name of *perception* renders not this separation from a mind absurd and contradictory, the name of *object,* standing for the very same thing, can never render their conjunction impossible. External objects are seen, and felt, and become present to the mind; that is, they acquire such a relation to a connected heap of perceptions, as to influence them very considerably in augmenting their number by present reflexions and passions, and in storing the memory with ideas. The same continu'd and uninterrupted Being may, therefore, be sometimes present to the mind, and sometimes absent from it, without any real or essential change in the Being itself. An interrupted appearance to the senses implies not necessarily an interruption in the existence. The supposition of the continu'd existence of sensible objects or perceptions involves no contradiction. We may easily indulge our inclination to that supposition. When the exact resemblance of our perceptions makes us ascribe to them an identity, we may remove the seeming interruption by feigning a continu'd being, which may fill those intervals, and preserve a perfect and entire identity to our perceptions.

But as we here not only *feign* but *believe* this continu'd existence, the question is, *from whence arises such a belief*; and this question leads us to the *fourth* member of this system. It has been prov'd already, that belief in general consists in nothing, but the vivacity of an idea; and that an idea may acquire this vivacity by its relation to some present impression. Impressions are naturally the most vivid perceptions of the mind; and this quality is in part convey'd by the relation to every connected idea. The relation causes a smooth passage from the impression to the idea, and even gives a propensity to that passage. The mind falls so easily from the one perception to the other, that it scarce perceives the change, but retains in the second a considerable share of the vivacity of the first. It is excited by the lively impression; and this vivacity is convey'd to the related idea, without any great diminution in the passage, by reason of the smooth transition and the propensity of the imagination.

But suppose, that this propensity arises from some other principle, besides that of relation; 'tis evident it must still have the same effect, and convey the vivacity from the impression to the idea. Now this is exactly the present case. Our memory presents us with a vast number of instances of perceptions perfectly resembling each other, that return at different distances of time, and after considerable interruptions. This resemblance gives us a propension to consider these interrupted perceptions as the same; and also a propension to connect them by a continu'd existence, in order to justify this identity, and avoid the contradiction, in which the interrupted appearance of these perceptions seems necessarily to involve us. Here then we have a propensity to feign the continu'd existence of all sensible objects; and as this propensity arises from some lively impressions of the memory, it bestows a vivacity on that fiction; or in other words, makes us believe the continu'd existence to objects, which are perfectly new to us, and of whose constancy and coherence we have no experience, 'tis because the manner, in which they present themselves to our senses, resembles that of constant and coherent objects; and this resemblance is a source of reasoning and analogy, and leads us to attribute the same qualities to the similar objects.

I believe an intelligent reader will find less difficulty to assent to this system, than to comprehend it fully and distinctly, and will allow, after a little reflection, that every part carries its own proof along with it. 'Tis indeed evident, that as the vulgar *suppose* their perceptions to be their only objects, and at the same time *believe* the continu'd existence of matter, we must account for the origin of the belief upon that supposition. Now upon that supposition, 'tis a false opinion that any of our objects, or perceptions, are identically the same after an interruption; and consequently the opinion of their identity can never arise from reason, but must arise from the imagination. The imagination is seduc'd into such an opinion only by means of the resemblance of certain perceptions; since we find they are only our resembling perceptions, which we have a propension to suppose the same. This propension to bestow an identity on our resembling perceptions, produces the fiction of a continu'd existence; since that fiction, as well as the identity, is really false, as is acknowledg'd by all philosophers, and has no other effect than to remedy the interruption of our perceptions, which is the only circumstance that is contrary to their identity. In the last place this propension causes belief by means of the present impressions of the memory; since without the remembrance of former sensations, 'tis plain we never shou'd have any belief of the continu'd existence of body. Thus in examining all these parts, we find that each of them is supported by the strongest proofs; and that all of them together form a consistent system, which is perfectly convincing. A strong propensity or inclination alone, without any present impression, will sometimes cause a belief or opinion. How much more when aided by that circumstance?

But tho' we are led after this manner, by the natural propensity of the imagination, to ascribe a continu'd existence to those sensible objects or perceptions, which we find to resemble each other in their interrupted appearance; yet a very little reflection and philosophy is sufficient to make us perceive the fallacy of that opinion. I have already observ'd, that there is an intimate connexion betwixt those two principles, of a *continu'd* and of a *distinct* or *independent* existence, and that we no sooner establish the one than the other follows, as a necessary consequence. 'Tis the opinion of a continu'd existence, which first takes place, and without much study or reflection draws the other along with it, wherever the mind follows its first and most natural tendency. But when we compare experiments, and reason a little upon them, we quickly perceive, that the doctrine of the independent existence of our sensible perceptions is contrary to the plainest experience. This leads us backward upon our footsteps to perceive our error in attributing a continu'd existence to our perceptions, and is the origin of many very curious opinions, which we shall here endeavour to account for.

'Twill first be proper to observe a few of those experiments, which convince us, that our perceptions are not possest of any independent existence. When we press one eye with a finger, we immediately perceive all the objects to become double, and one half of them to be remov'd from their common and natural position. But as we do not attribute a continu'd existence to both these perceptions, and as they are both of the same nature, we clearly perceive, that all our perceptions are dependent on our organs, and the disposition of our nerves and animal spirits. This opinion is confirm'd by the seeming encrease and diminution of objects, according to their distance; by the apparent alterations in their figure; by the changes in their colour and other qualities from our sickness and distempers; and by an infinite number of other experiments of the same kind; from all which we learn, that our sensible perceptions are not possest of any distinct or independent existence.

The natural consequence of this reasoning shou'd be, that our perceptions have no more a continu'd than an independent existence; and indeed philosophers have so far run into this opinion, that they change their system, and distinguish, (as we shall do for the future) betwixt perceptions and objects, of which the former are suppos'd to be interrupted, and perishing, and different at every different return; the latter to be uninterrupted, and to preserve a continu'd existence and identity. But however philosophical this new system may be esteem'd, I assert that 'tis only a palliative remedy, and that it contains all the difficulties of the vulgar system, with some others, that are peculiar to itself. There are no principles either of the understanding or fancy, which lead us directly to embrace this opinion of the double existence of perceptions and objects, nor can we arrive at it but by passing thro' the common hypothesis of the identity and continuance of our interrupted perceptions. Were we not first persuaded, that our perceptions are our only objects, and continue to exist even when they no longer make their appearance to the senses, we shou'd never be led to think that our perceptions and objects are different, and that our objects alone preserve a continu'd existence. 'The latter hypothesis has no primary recommendation either to reason or the imagination, but acquires all its influence on the imagination from the former.' This proposition contains two parts, which we shall endeavour to prove as distinctly and clearly, as such abstruse subjects will permit.

As to the first part of the proposition, *that this philosophical hypothesis has no primary recommendation, either to reason or the imagination*, we may soon satisfy ourselves with regard to *reason* by the following reflections. The only existences, of which we are certain, are perceptions, which being immediately present to us by consciousness, command our strongest assent, and are the first foundation of all our conclusions. The only conclusion we can draw from the existence of one thing to that of another, is by means of the relation of cause and effect, which shows, that there is a connexion betwixt them, and that the existence of one is dependent on that of the other. The idea of this relation is deriv'd from past experience, by which we find, that two beings are constantly conjoin'd together, and are always present at once to the mind. But as no beings are ever present to the mind but perceptions; it follows that we may observe a conjunction or a relation of cause and effect between different perceptions, but can never observe it between perceptions and objects. 'Tis impossible, therefore, that from the existence or any of the qualities of the former, we can ever form any conclusion concerning the existence of the latter, or ever satisfy our reason in this particular.

'Tis no less certain, that this philosophical system has no primary recommendation to the *imagination*, and that the faculty wou'd never, of itself, and by its original tendency, have fallen upon such a principle. I confess it will be somewhat difficult to prove this to the full satisfaction of the reader; because it implies a negative, which in many cases will not admit of any positive proof. If any one wou'd take the pains to examine this question, and wou'd invent a system, to account for the direct origin of this opinion from the imagination, we shou'd be able, by the examination of that system, to pronounce a certain judgment in the present subject. Let it be taken for granted, that our perceptions are broken, and interrupted, and however like, are still different from each other; and let any one upon this supposition shew why the fancy, directly and immediately, proceeds to the belief of another existence, resembling these perceptions in their nature, but yet continu'd, and uninterrupted, and identical; and after he has done this to my satisfaction, I promise to renounce my present opinion. Meanwhile I cannot forbear concluding, from the very abstractedness and difficulty of the first supposition, that 'tis an improper subject for the fancy to work upon. Whoever wou'd explain the origin of the *common* opinion concerning the continu'd and distinct existence of body, must take the mind in its *common* situation, and must proceed upon the supposition, that our perceptions are our only objects, and continue to exist even when they are not perceiv'd. Tho' this opinion be false, 'tis the most natural of any, and has alone any primary recommendation to the fancy.

As to the second part of the proposition, *that the philosophical system acquires all its influence on the imagination from the vulgar one*; we may observe, that this is a natural and unavoidable consequence of the foregoing conclusion, *that it has no primary recommendation to reason or the imagination*. For as the philosophical system is found by experience to take hold of many minds, and in particular of all those, who reflect ever so little on this subject, it must derive all its authority from the vulgar system;

since it has no original authority of its own. The manner, in which these two systems, tho' directly contrary, are connected together, may be explain'd, as follows.

The imagination naturally runs on in this train of thinking. Our perceptions are our only objects: Resembling perceptions are the same, however broken or uninterrupted in their appearance: This appearing interruption is contrary to the identity: The interruption consequently extends not beyond the appearance, and the perception or object really continues to exist, even when absent from us: Our sensible perceptions have, therefore, a continu'd and uninterrupted existence. But as a little reflection destroys this conclusion, that our perceptions have a continu'd existence, by showing that they have a dependent one, 'twou'd naturally be expected, that we must altogether reject the opinion, that there is such a thing in nature as a continu'd existence, which is preserv'd even when it no longer appears to the senses. The case, however, is otherwise. Philosophers are so far from rejecting the opinion of a continu'd existence upon rejecting that of the independence and continuance of our sensible perceptions, that tho' all sects agree in the latter sentiment, the former, which is, in a manner, its necessary consequence, has been peculiar to a few extravagant sceptics; who after all maintain'd that opinion in words only, and were never able to bring themselves sincerely to believe it.

There is a great difference betwixt such opinions as we form after a calm and profound reflection, and such as we embrace by a kind of instinct or natural impulse, on account of their suitableness and conformity to the mind. If these opinions become contrary, 'tis not difficult to foresee which of them will have the advantage. As long as our attention is bent upon the subject, the philosophical and study'd principle may prevail; but the moment we relax our thoughts, nature will display herself, and draw us back to our former opinion. Nay she has sometimes such an influence, that she can stop our progress, even in the midst of our most profound reflections, and keep us from running on with all the consequences of any philosophical opinion. Thus tho' we clearly perceive the dependence and interruption of our perceptions, we stop short in our career, and never upon that account reject the notion of an independent and continu'd existence. That opinion has taken such deep root in the imagination, that 'tis impossible ever to eradicate it, nor will any strain'd metaphysical conviction of the dependence of our perceptions be sufficient for that purpose.

But tho' our natural and obvious principles here prevail above our study'd reflections, 'tis certain there must be some struggle and opposition in the case; at least so long as these reflections retain any force or vivacity. In order to set ourselves at ease in this particular, we contrive a new hypothesis, which seems to comprehend both these principles of reason and imagination. This hypothesis is the philosophical one of the double existence of perceptions and objects; which pleases our reason, in allowing, that our dependent perceptions are interrupted and different; and at the same time is agreeable to the imagination in attributing a continu'd existence to something else, which we call *objects*. This philosophical system, therefore, is the monstrous offspring of two principles, which are contrary to each other, which are both at once embrac'd by the mind, and which are unable mutually to destroy each other. The imagination tells us, that our resembling perceptions have a continu'd and uninterrupted existence, and are not annihilated by their absence. Reflection tells us, that even our resembling perceptions are interrupted in their existence, and different from each other. The contradiction betwixt these opinions we elude by a new fiction, which is conformable to the hypotheses both of reflection and fancy, by ascribing these contrary qualities to different existences; the *interruption* to perceptions, and the *continuance* to objects. Nature is obstinate, and will not quit the field, however strongly attack'd by reason; and at the same time reason is so clear in the point, that there is no possibility of disguising her. Not being able to reconcile these two enemies, we endeavor to set ourselves at ease as much as possible, by successively granting to each whatever it demands, and by feigning a double existence, where each may find something, that has all the conditions it desires. Were we fully convinc'd, that our resembling perceptions are continu'd, and identical, and independent, we shou'd never run into this opinion of a double existence; since we shou'd find satisfaction in our first supposition, and wou'd not look

beyond. Again, were we fully convinc'd, that our perceptions are dependent, and interrupted, and different, we shou'd be as little inclin'd to embrace the opinion of a double existence; since in that case we shou'd clearly perceive the error of our first supposition of a continu'd existence, and wou'd never regard it any farther. 'Tis therefore from the intermediate situation of the mind, that this opinion arises, and from such an adherence to these two contrary principles, as makes us seek some pretext to justify our receiving both; which happily at last is found in the system of a double existence.

Another advantage of this philosophical system is its similarity to the vulgar one; by which means we can humour our reason for a moment, when it becomes troublesome and solicitous; and yet upon its least negligence or inattention, can easily return to our vulgar and natural notions. Accordingly we find, that philosophers neglect not this advantage; but immediately upon leaving their closets, mingle with the rest of mankind in those exploded opinions, that our perceptions are our only objects, and continue identically and uninterruptedly the same in all their interrupted appearances.

There are other particulars of this system, wherein we may remark its dependence on the fancy, in a very conspicuous manner. Of these, I shall observe the two following. *First*, We suppose external objects to resemble internal perceptions. I have already shewn, that the relation of cause and effect can never afford us any just conclusion from the existence or qualities of our perceptions to the existence of external continu'd objects: And I shall farther add, that even tho' they cou'd afford such a conclusion, we shou'd never have any reason to infer, that our objects resemble our perceptions. That opinion, therefore, is deriv'd from nothing but the quality of the fancy above-explain'd, *that it borrows all its ideas from some precedent perception*. We never can conceive any thing but perceptions, and therefore must make everything resemble them.

Secondly, As we suppose our objects in general to resemble our perceptions, so we take it for granted, that every particular object resembles that perception, which it causes. The relation of cause and effect determines us to join the other of resemblance; and the ideas of these existences being already united together in the fancy but the former relation, we have a strong propensity to compleat every union by joining new relations to those which we have before observ'd betwixt any ideas, as we shall have occasion to observe presently.

Having thus given an account of all the systems both popular and philosophical, with regard to external existence, I cannot forbear giving vent to a certain sentiment, which arises upon reviewing those systems. I begun this subject with premising, that we ought to have an implicit faith in our senses, and that this wou'd be the conclusion, I shou'd draw from the whole of my reasoning. But to be ingenuous, I feel myself *at present* of a quite contrary sentiment, and am more inclin'd to repose no faith at all in my senses, or rather imagination, than to place in it such an implicit confidence. I cannot conceive how such trivial qualities of the fancy, conducted by such false suppositions, can ever lead to any solid and rational system. They are the coherence and constancy of our perceptions, which produce the opinion of their continu'd existence; tho' these qualities of perceptions have no perceivable connexion with such an existence. The constancy of our perceptions has the most considerable effect, and yet is attended with the greatest difficulties. 'Tis a gross illusion to suppose, that our resembling perceptions are numerically the same; and 'tis this illusion, which leads us into the opinion, that these perceptions are uninterrupted, and are still existent, even when they are not present to the senses. This is the case with our popular system. And as to our philosophical one, 'tis liable to the same difficulties; and is over-and-above loaded with this absurdity, that it at once denies and establishes the vulgar supposition. Philosophers deny our resembling perceptions to be identically the same, and uninterrupted; and yet have so great a propensity to believe them such, that they arbitrarily invent a new set of perceptions, to which they attribute these qualities. I say, a new set of perceptions: For we may well suppose in general, but 'tis impossible for us distinctly to conceive, objects to be in their nature any thing but exactly the same with perceptions. What then can we look for from this confusion of groundless and extraordinary opinions but error and falshood? And how can we justify to ourselves any belief we repose in them?

This sceptical doubt, both with respect to reason and the senses, is a malady, which can never be radically cur'd, but must return upon us every moment, however we may chase it away, and sometimes may seem entirely free from it. 'Tis impossible upon any system to defend either our understanding or senses; and we but expose them farther when we endeavour to justify them in that manner. As the sceptical doubt arises naturally from a profound and intense reflection on those subjects, it always encreases, the farther we carry our reflections, whether in opposition or conformity to it. Carelessness and in-attention alone can afford us any remedy. For this reason I rely entirely upon them; and take it for granted, whatever may be the reader's opinion at this present moment, that an hour hence he will be persuaded there is both an external and internal world; and going upon that supposition, I intend to examine some general systems both ancient and modern, which have been propos'd of both, before I proceed to a more particular enquiry concerning our impressions. This will not, perhaps, in the end be found foreign to our present purpose.

NOTES

1. Part II. sect. 6
2. Sect. 5.
3. Part II. sect. 4.
4. Part II. sect. 5.
5. Part II. sect. 5.
6. This reasoning, it must be confest, is somewhat abstruse, and difficult to be comprehended; but it is remarkable, that this very difficulty may be converted into a proof of the reasoning. We may observe, that there are two relations, and both of them resemblances, which contribute to our mistaking the succession of our interrupted perceptions for an identical object. The first is, the resemblance of the perceptions: The second is the resemblance, which the act of the mind in surveying a succession of resembling objects bears to that in surveying an identical object. Now these resemblances we are apt to confound with each other; and 'tis natural we shou'd, according to this very reasoning. But let us keep them distinct, and we shall find no difficulty in conceiving the precedent argument.
7. Sect. 6.

KEY TERMS

Metaphysics
Substance

STUDY QUESTIONS

1. According to Hume, what is the difference between continued existence and distinct existence?
2. Why do you think Hume says that "'tis absurd, therefore, to imagine the senses can ever distinguish betwixt ourselves and external objects"?
3. What does Hume mean when he says that "all perceptions are the same in the manner of their existence"? What's his argument for this claim?
4. What importance does Hume place on the notions of *coherence* and *constancy*? How do they fit into his overall argument?
5. Hume points out that "another advantage of this philosophical system is its similarity to the vulgar one." What does he mean by this, and why does he consider it an advantage? Do you think it really is an advantage?

An Enquiry Concerning Human Understanding

DAVID HUME

· ·

Section II
Of the Origin of Ideas

Every one will readily allow, that there is a considerable difference between the perceptions of the mind, when a man feels the pain of excessive heat, or the pleasure of moderate warmth, and when he afterwards recalls to his memory this sensation, or anticipates it by his imagination. These faculties may mimic or copy the perceptions of the senses; but they never can entirely reach the force and vivacity of the original sentiment. The utmost we say of them, even when they operate with greatest vigour, is, that they represent their object in so lively a manner, that we could *almost* say we feel or see it: But, except the mind be disordered by disease or madness, they never can arrive at such a pitch of vivacity, as to render these perceptions altogether undistinguishable. All

the colours of poetry, however splendid, can never paint natural objects in such a manner as to make the description be taken for a real landscape. The most lively thought is still inferior to the dullest sensation.

We may observe a like distinction to run through all the other perceptions of the mind. A man in a fit of anger, is actuated in a very different manner from one who only thinks of that emotion. If you tell me, that any person is in love, I easily understand your meaning, and form a just conception of his situation; but never can mistake that conception for the real disorders and agitations of the passion. When we reflect on our past sentiments and affections, our thought is a faithful mirror, and copies its objects truly; but the colours which it employs are faint and dull, in comparison of those in which our original perceptions were clothed. It requires no nice discernment or **metaphysical** head to mark the distinction between them.

Here therefore we may divide all the perceptions of the mind into two classes or species, which are distinguished by their different degrees of force and vivacity. The less forcible and lively are commonly denominated *Thoughts* or *Ideas*. The other species want a name in our language, and in most others; I suppose, because it was not requisite for any, but philosophical purposes, to rank them under a general term or appellation. Let us, therefore, use a little freedom, and call them *Impressions*: employing that word in a sense somewhat different from the usual. By the term *impression*, then, I mean all our more lively perceptions, when we hear, or see, or feel, or love, or hate, or desire, or will. And impressions are distinguished from ideas, which are the less lively perceptions, of which we are conscious, when we reflect on any of those sensations or movements above mentioned.

Nothing, at first view, may seem more unbounded than the thought of man, which not only escapes all human power and authority, but is not even restrained within the limits of nature and reality. To form monsters, and join incongruous shapes and appearances, costs the imagination no more trouble than to conceive the most natural and familiar objects. And while the body is confined to one planet, along which it creeps with pain and difficulty; the thought can in an instant transport us into the most distant regions of the universe; or even beyond the universe, into the unbounded chaos, where nature is supposed to lie in total confusion. What never was seen, or heard of, may yet be conceived; nor is any thing beyond the power of thought, except what implies an absolute contradiction.

But though our thought seems to possess this unbounded liberty, we shall find, upon a nearer examination, that it is really confined within very narrow limits, and that all this creative power of the mind amounts to no more than the faculty of compounding, transposing, augmenting, or diminishing the materials afforded us by the senses and experience. When we think of a golden mountain, we only join two consistent ideas, *gold*, and *mountain*, with which we were formerly acquainted. A virtuous horse we can conceive; because, from our own feeling, we can conceive virtue; and this we may unite to the figure and shape of a horse, which is an animal familiar to us. In short, all the materials of thinking are derived either from our outward or inward sentiment: the mixture and composition of these belongs alone to the mind and will. Or, to express myself in philosophical language, all our ideas or more feeble perceptions are copies of our impressions or more lively ones.

To prove this, the two following arguments will, I hope, be sufficient. First, when we analyze our thoughts or ideas, however compounded or sublime, we always find that they resolve themselves into such simple ideas as were copied from a precedent feeling or sentiment. Even those ideas, which, at first view, seem the most wide of this origin, are found, upon a nearer scrutiny, to be derived from it. The idea of God, as meaning an infinitely intelligent, wise, and good Being, arises from reflecting on the operations of our own mind, and augmenting, without limit, those qualities of goodness and wisdom. We may prosecute this enquiry to what length we please; where we shall always find, that every idea which we examine is copied from a similar impression. Those who would assert that this position is not universally true nor without exception, have only one, and that an easy method of refuting it; by producing that idea, which, in their opinion, is not derived from this source. It will then be incumbent on us, if we would maintain our doctrine, to produce the impression, or lively perception, which corresponds to it.

Secondly. If it happen, from a defect of the organ, that a man is not susceptible of any species of sensation, we always find that he is as little susceptible of the correspondent ideas. A blind man can form no notion of colours; a deaf man of sounds. Restore either of them that sense in which he is deficient; by opening this new inlet for his sensations, you also open an inlet for the ideas; and he finds no difficulty in conceiving these objects. The case is the same, if the object, proper for exciting any sensation, has never been applied to the organ. A Laplander or Negro has no notion of the relish of wine. And though there are a few or no instances of a like deficiency in the mind, where a person has never felt or is wholly incapable of a sentiment or passion that belongs to his species; yet we find the same observation to take place in a less degree. A man of mild manners can form no idea of inveterate revenge or cruelty; nor can a selfish heart easily conceive the heights of friendship and generosity. It is readily allowed, that other beings may possess many senses of which we can have no conception; because the ideas of them have never been introduced to us in the only manner by which an idea can have access to the mind, to wit, by the actual feeling and sensation.

There is, however, one contradictory phenomenon, which may prove that it is not absolutely impossible for ideas to arise, independent of their correspondent impressions. I believe it will readily be allowed, that the several distinct ideas of colour, which enter by the eye, or those of sound, which are conveyed by the ear, are really different from each other; though, at the same time, resembling. Now if this be true of different colours, it must be no less so of the different shades of the same colour; and each shade produces a distinct idea, independent of the rest. For if this should be denied, it is possible, by the continual gradation of shades, to run a colour insensibly into what is most remote from it; and if you will not allow any of the means to be different, you cannot, without absurdity, deny the extremes to be the same. Suppose, therefore, a person to have enjoyed his sight for thirty years, and to have become perfectly acquainted with colours of all kinds except one particular shade of blue, for instance, which it never has been his fortune to meet with. Let all different shades of that colour, except that single one, be placed before him, descending gradually from the deepest to the lightest; it is plain that he will perceive a blank, where that shade is wanting, and will be sensible that there is a greater distance in that place between the contiguous colours than in any other. Now I ask, whether it be possible for him, from his own imagination, to supply this deficiency, and raise up to himself the idea of that particular shade, though it had never been conveyed to him by his senses? I believe there are few but will be of opinion that he can: and this may serve as a proof that the simple ideas are not always, in every instance, derived from the correspondent impressions; though this instance is so singular, that it is scarcely worth our observing, and does not merit that for it alone we should alter our general maxim.

Here, therefore, is a proposition, which not only seems, in itself, simple and intelligible; but, if a proper use were made of it, might render every dispute equally intelligible, and banish all that jargon, which has so long taken possession of metaphysical reasonings, and drawn disgrace upon them. All ideas, especially abstract ones, are naturally faint and obscure: the mind has but a slender hold of them: they are apt to be confounded with other resembling ideas; and

when we have often employed any term, though without a distinct meaning, we are apt to imagine it has a determinate idea annexed to it. On the contrary, all impressions, that is, all sensations, either outward or inward, are strong and vivid: the limits between them are more exactly determined: nor is it easy to fall into any error or mistake with regard to them. When we entertain, therefore, any suspicion that a philosophical term is employed without any meaning or idea (as is but too frequent), we need but enquire, *from what impression is that supposed idea derived*? And if it be impossible to assign any, this will serve to confirm our suspicion. By bringing ideas into so clear a light we may reasonably hope to remove all dispute, which may arise, concerning their nature and reality.[1]

Section III
Of the Association of Ideas

It is evident that there is a principle connexion between the different thoughts or ideas of the mind, and that, in their appearance to the memory or imagination, they introduce each other with a certain degree of method and regularity. In our more serious thinking or discourse this is so observable that any particular thought, which breaks in upon the regular tract or chain of ideas, is immediately remarked and rejected. And even in our wildest and most wandering reveries, nay in our very dreams, we shall find, if we reflect, that the imagination ran not altogether at adventures, but that there was still a connexion upheld among the different ideas, which succeeded each other. Were the loosest and freest conversation to be transcribed, there would immediately be observed something which connected it in all its transitions. Or where this is wanting, the person who broke the thread of discourse might still inform you, that there had secretly revolved in his mind a succession of thought, which had gradually led him from the subject of conversation. Among different languages, even where we cannot suspect the least connexion or communication, it is found, that the words, expressive of ideas, the most compounded, do yet nearly correspond to each other: a certain proof that the simple ideas, comprehended in the compound ones, were bound together by some universal principle, which had an equal influence on all mankind.

Though it be too obvious to escape observation, that different ideas are connected together; I do not find that any philosopher has attempted to enumerate or class all the principles of association; a subject, however, that seems worthy of curiosity. To me, there appear to be only three principles of connexion among ideas, namely, *Resemblance, Contiguity* in time or place, and *Cause* or *Effect*.

That these principles serve to connect ideas will not, I believe, be much doubted. A picture naturally leads our thoughts to the original:[2] the mention of one apartment in a building naturally introduces an enquiry or discourse concerning the others:[3] and if we think of a wound, we can scarcely forbear reflecting on the pain which follows it.[4] But that this enumeration is complete, and that there are no other principles of association except these, may be difficult to prove to the satisfaction of the reader, or even to a man's own satisfaction. All we can do, in such cases, is to run over several instances, and examine carefully the principle which binds the different thoughts to each other, never stopping till we render the principle as general as possible.[5] The more instances we examine, and the more care we employ, the more assurance shall we acquire, that the enumeration, which we form from the whole, is complete and entire.

Section IV
Sceptical Doubts Concerning the Operations of the Understanding

Part I

All the objects of human reason or enquiry may naturally be divided into two kinds, to wit, **Relations of Ideas,** and **Matters of Fact.** Of the first kind are the sciences of Geometry, Algebra, and Arithmetic; and in short, every affirmation which is either intuitively or demonstratively certain. *That the square of the hypothenuse is equal to the square of the two sides*, is a proposition which expresses a relation between these figures. *That three times five is equal to the half of thirty*, expresses a relation between these numbers. Propositions of this kind are discoverable by the mere operation of thought, without dependence on what is anywhere existent in the universe. Though there never were a circle or triangle in nature, the truths demonstrated by Euclid would for ever retain their certainty and evidence.

Matters of fact, which are the second objects of human reason, are not ascertained in the same manner; nor is our evidence of their truth, however great, of a like nature with the foregoing. The contrary of every matter of fact is still possible; because it can never imply a contradiction, and is conceived by the mind with the same facility and distinctness, as if ever so conformable to reality. *That the sun will not rise to-morrow* is no less intelligible a proposition, and implies no more contradiction than the affirmation, *that it will rise*. We should in vain, therefore, attempt to demonstrate its falsehood. Were it demonstratively false, it would imply a contradiction, and could never be distinctly conceived by the mind.

It may, therefore, be a subject worthy of curiosity, to enquire what is the nature of that evidence which assures us of any real existence and matter of fact, beyond the present testimony of our senses, or the records of our memory. This part of philosophy, it is observable, has been little cultivated, either by the ancients or moderns; and therefore our doubts and errors, in the prosecution of so important an enquiry, may be the more excusable; while we march through such difficult paths without any guide or direction. They may even prove useful, by exciting curiosity, and destroying that implicit faith and security, which is the bane of all reasoning and free enquiry. The discovery of defects in the common philosophy, if any such there be, will not, I presume, be a discouragement, but rather an incitement, as is usual, to attempt something more full and satisfactory than has yet been proposed to the public.

All reasonings concerning matter of fact seem to be founded on the relation of **Cause and Effect.** By means of that relation alone we can go beyond the evidence of our memory and senses. If you were to ask a man, why he believes any matter of fact, which is absent; for instance, that his friend is in the country, or in France; he would give you a reason; and this reason would be some other fact; as a letter received from him, or the knowledge of his former resolutions and promises. A man finding a watch or any other machine in a desert island, would conclude that there had once been men in that island. All our reasonings concerning fact are of the same nature. And here it is constantly supposed that there is a connexion between the present fact and that which is inferred from it. Were there nothing to bind them together, the inference would be entirely precarious. The hearing of an articulate voice and rational discourse in the dark assures us of the presence of some person: Why? because these are the effects of the human make and fabric, and closely connected with it. If we anatomize all the other reasonings of this nature, we shall find that they are founded on the relation of cause and effect, and that this relation is either near or remote, direct or collateral. Heat and light are collateral effects of fire, and the one effect may justly be inferred from the other.

If we would satisfy ourselves, therefore, concerning the nature of that evidence, which assures us of matters of fact, we must enquire how we arrive at the knowledge of cause and effect.

I shall venture to affirm, as a general proposition, which admits of no exception, that the knowledge of this relation is not, in any instance, attained by reasonings a priori; but arises entirely from experience, when we find that any particular objects are constantly conjoined with each other. Let an object be presented to a man of ever so strong natural reason and abilities; if that object be entirely new to him, he will not be able, by the most accurate examination of its sensible qualities, to discover any of its causes or effects. Adam, though his rational faculties be supposed, at the very first, entirely perfect, could not have inferred from the fluidity and transparency of water that it would suffocate him, or from the light and warmth of fire that it would consume him. No object ever discovers, by the qualities which appear to the senses, either the causes which produce it, or the effects which will arise from it; nor can our reason, unassisted by experience, ever draw any inference concerning real existence and matter of fact.

This proposition, *that causes and effects are discoverable, not by reason but by experience*, will readily be admitted with regard to such objects, as we remember to have once been altogether unknown to us; since we must be conscious of the utter inability, which we then lay under, of foretelling what would arise from them. Present two smooth pieces of marble to a man who has no tincture of natural philosophy; he will never discover that they will adhere together in such a manner as to require great force to separate them in a direct line, while they make so small a resistance to a lateral pressure. Such events, as bear little analogy to the common course of nature, are also readily confessed to be known only by experience; nor does any man imagine that the explosion of gunpowder, or the attraction of a loadstone, could ever be discovered by arguments a priori. In like manner, when an effect is supposed to depend upon an intricate machinery or secret structure of parts, we make no difficulty in attributing all our knowledge of it to experience. Who will assert that he can give the ultimate reason, why milk or bread is proper nourishment for a man, not for a lion or a tiger?

But the same truth may not appear, at first sight, to have the same evidence with regard to events, which have become familiar to us from our first appearance in the world, which bear a close analogy to the whole course of nature, and which are supposed to depend on the simple qualities of objects, without any secret structure of parts. We are apt to imagine that we could discover these effects by the mere operation of our reason, without experience. We fancy, that were we brought on a sudden into this world, we could at first have inferred that one Billiard-ball would communicate motion to another upon impulse; and that we needed not to have waited for the event, in order to pronounce with certainty concerning it. Such is the influence of custom, that, where it is strongest, it not only covers our natural ignorance, but even conceals itself, and seems not to take place, merely because it is found in the highest degree.

But to convince us that all the laws of nature, and all the operations of bodies without exception, are known only by experience, the following reflections may, perhaps, suffice. Were any object presented to us, and were we required to pronounce concerning the effect, which will result from it, without consulting past observation; after what manner, I beseech you, must the mind proceed in this operation?

It must invent or imagine some event, which it ascribes to the object as its effect; and it is plain that this invention must be entirely arbitrary. The mind can never possibly find the effect in the supposed cause, by the most accurate scrutiny and examination. For the effect is totally different from the cause, and consequently can never be discovered in it. Motion in the second Billiard-ball is a quite distinct event from motion in the first; nor is there anything in the one to suggest the smallest hint of the other. A stone or piece of metal raised into the air, and left without any support, immediately falls: but to consider the matter **a priori**, is there anything we discover in this situation which can beget the idea of a downward, rather than an upward, or any other motion, in the stone or metal?

And as the first imagination or invention of a particular effect, in all natural operations, is arbitrary, where we consult not experience; so must we also esteem the supposed tie or connexion between the cause and effect, which binds them together, and renders it impossible that any other effect could result from the operation of that cause. When I see, for instance, a Billiard-ball moving in a straight line towards another; even suppose motion in the second ball should by accident be suggested to me, as the result of their contact or impulse; may I not conceive, that a hundred different events might as well follow from that cause? May not both these balls remain at absolute rest? May not the first ball return in a straight line, or leap off from the second in any line or direction? All these suppositions are consistent and conceivable. Why then should we give the preference to one, which is no more consistent or conceivable than the rest? All our reasonings a priori will never be able to show us any foundation for this preference.

In a word, then, every effect is a distinct event from its cause. It could not, therefore, be discovered in the cause, and the first invention or conception of it, a priori, must be entirely arbitrary. And even after it is suggested, the conjunction of it with the cause must appear equally arbitrary; since there are always many other effects, which, to reason, must seem fully as consistent and natural. In vain, therefore, should we pretend to determine any single event, or infer any cause of effect, without the assistance of observation and experience.

Hence we may discover the reason why no philosopher, who is rational and modest, has ever pretended to assign the ultimate cause of any natural operation, or to show distinctly the action of that power, which produces any single effect in the universe. It is confessed, that the utmost effort of human reason is to reduce the principles, productive of natural phenomena, to a greater simplicity, and to resolve the many particular effects into a few general causes, by means of reasonings from analogy, experience, and observation. But as to the causes of these general causes, we should in vain attempt their discovery; nor shall we ever be able to satisfy ourselves, by any particular explication of them. These ultimate springs and principles are totally shut up from human curiosity and enquiry. Elasticity, gravity, cohesion of parts, communication of motion by impulse; these are probably the ultimate causes and principles which we shall ever discover in nature; and we may esteem ourselves sufficiently happy, if, by accurate enquiry and reasoning, we can trace up the particular phenomena to, or near to, these general principles. The most perfect philosophy of the natural kind only staves off our ignorance a little longer: as perhaps the most perfect philosophy of the moral or metaphysical kind serves only to discover larger portions of it. Thus the observation of human blindness and weakness is the result of all philosophy, and meets us at every turn, in spite of our endeavours to elude or avoid it.

Nor is geometry, when taken into the assistance of natural philosophy, ever able to remedy this defect, or lead us into the knowledge of ultimate causes, by all that accuracy of reasoning for which it is so justly celebrated. Every part of mixed mathematics proceeds upon the supposition that certain laws are established by nature in her operations; and abstract reasonings are employed, either to assist experience in the discovery of these laws, or to determine their influence in particular instances, where it depends upon any precise degree of distance and quantity. Thus, it is a law of motion, discovered by experience, that the moment or force of any body in motion is in the compound ratio or proportion of its solid contents and its velocity; and consequently, that a small force may remove the greatest obstacle or raise the greatest weight, if, by any contrivance or machinery, we can increase the velocity of that force, so as to make it an overmatch for its antagonist. Geometry assists us in the application of this law, by giving us the just dimensions of all the parts and figures which can enter into any species of machine; but still the discovery of the law itself is owing merely to experience, and all the abstract reasonings in the world could never lead us one step towards the knowledge of it. When we reason a priori, and consider merely any object or cause, as it appears to the mind, independent of all observation, it never could suggest to us the notion of any distinct object, such as its effect; much less, show us the inseparable and inviolable connexion between them. A man must be very sagacious who could discover by reasoning that crystal is the effect of heat, and ice of cold, without being previously acquainted with the operation of these qualities.

Part II

But we have not yet attained any tolerable satisfaction with regard to the question first proposed. Each solution still gives rise to a new question as difficult as the foregoing, and leads us on to farther enquiries. When it is asked, *What is the nature of all our reasonings concerning matter of fact?* the proper answer seems to be, that they are founded on the relation of cause and effect. When again it is asked, *What is the foundation of all our reasonings and conclusions concerning that relation?* it may be replied in one word, Experience. But if we still carry on our sifting humour, and ask, *What is the foundation of all conclusions from experience?* this implies a new question, which may be of more difficult solution and explication. Philosophers, that give themselves airs of superior wisdom and sufficiency, have a hard task when they encounter persons of inquisitive dispositions, who push them from every corner to which they retreat, and who are sure at last to bring them to some dangerous dilemma. The best expedient to prevent this confusion, is to be modest in our pretensions; and even to discover the difficulty ourselves before it is objected to us. By this means, we may make a kind of merit of our very ignorance.

I shall content myself, in this section, with an easy task, and shall pretend only to give a negative answer to the question here proposed. I say then, that, even after we have experience of the operations of cause and effect, our conclusions from that experience are *not* founded on reasoning, or any process of the understanding. This answer we must endeavour both to explain and to defend.

It must certainly be allowed, that nature has kept us at a great distance from all her secrets, and has afforded us only the knowledge of a few superficial qualities of objects; while she conceals from us those powers and principles on which the influence of those objects entirely depends. Our senses inform us of the colour, weight, and consistence of bread; but neither sense nor reason can ever inform us of those qualities which fit it for the nourishment and support of a human body. Sight or feeling conveys an idea of the actual motion of bodies; but as to that wonderful force or power, which would carry on a moving body for ever in a continued change of place, and which bodies never lose but by communicating it to others; of this we cannot form the most distant conception. But notwithstanding this ignorance of natural powers[6] and principles, we always presume, when we see like sensible qualities, that they have like secret powers, and expect that effects, similar to those which we have experienced, will follow from them. If a body of a like colour and consistence with that bread, which we have formerly eat, be presented to us, we make no scruple of repeating the experiment, and foresee, with certainty, like nourishment and support. Now this is a process of the mind or thought, of which I would willingly know the foundation. It is allowed on all hands that there is no known connexion between the sensible qualities and the secret powers; and consequently, that the mind is not led to form such a conclusion concerning their constant and regular conjunction, by anything which it knows of their nature. As to past *Experience*, it can be allowed to give *direct* and *certain* information of those precise objects only, and that precise period of time, which fell under its cognizance: but why this experience should be extended to future times, and to other objects, which for aught we know, may be only in appearance similar; this is the main question on which I would insist. The bread, which I formerly eat, nourished me; that is, a body of such sensible qualities was, at that time, endued with such secret powers: but does it follow, that other bread must also nourish me at another time, and that like sensible qualities must always be attended with like secret powers? The consequence seems nowise necessary. At least, it must be acknowledged that there is here a consequence drawn by the mind; that there is a certain step taken; a process of thought, and an inference, which wants to be explained. These two propositions are far from being the same, *I have found that such an object has always been attended with such an effect*, and *I foresee, that other objects, which are, in appearance, similar, will be attended with similar effects*. I shall allow, if you please, that the one proposition may justly be inferred from the other: I know, in fact, that it always is inferred. But if you insist that the inference is made by a chain of reasoning, I desire you to produce that reasoning. The connexion between these propositions is not intuitive. There is required a medium, which may enable the mind to draw such an inference, if indeed it be drawn by reasoning and argument. What that medium is, I must confess, passes my comprehension; and it is incumbent on those to produce it, who assert that it really exists, and is the origin of all our conclusions concerning matter of fact.

This negative argument must certainly, in process of time, become altogether convincing, if many penetrating and able philosophers shall turn their enquiries this way and no one be ever able to discover any connecting proposition or intermediate step, which supports the understanding in this conclusion. But as the question is yet new, every reader may not trust so far to his own penetration, as to conclude, because an argument escapes his enquiry, that therefore it does not really exist. For this reason it may be requisite to venture upon a more difficult task; and enumerating all the branches of human knowledge, endeavour to show that none of them can afford such an argument.

All reasonings may be divided into two kinds, namely, demonstrative reasoning, or that concerning relations of ideas, and moral reasoning, or that concerning matter of fact and existence. That there are no demonstrative arguments in the case seems evident; since it implies no contradiction that the course of nature may change, and that an object, seemingly like those which we have experienced, may be attended with different or contrary effects. May I not clearly and distinctly conceive that a body, falling from the clouds, and which, in all other respects, resembles snow, has yet the taste of salt or feeling of fire? Is there any more intelligible proposition than to affirm, that all the trees will flourish in December and January, and decay in May and June? Now whatever is intelligible, and can be distinctly conceived, implies no contradiction, and can never be proved false by any demonstrative argument or abstract reasoning a priori.

If we be, therefore, engaged by arguments to put trust in past experience, and make it the standard of our future judgment, these arguments must be probable only, or such as regard matter of fact and real existence, according to the division above mentioned. But that there is no argument of this kind, must appear, if our explication of that species of reasoning be admitted as solid and satisfactory. We have said that all arguments concerning existence are founded on the relation of cause and effect; that our knowledge of that relation is derived entirely from experience; and that all our experimental conclusions proceed upon the supposition that the future will be conformable to the past. To endeavour, therefore, the proof of this last supposition by probable arguments, or arguments regarding existence, must be evidently going in a circle, and taking that for granted, which is the very point in question.

In reality, all arguments from experience are founded on the similarity which we discover among natural objects, and by which we are induced to expect effects similar to those which we have found to follow from such objects. And though none but a fool or madman will ever pretend to dispute the authority of experience, or to reject that great guide of human life, it may surely be allowed a philosopher to have so much curiosity at least as to examine the principle of human nature, which gives this mighty authority to experience, and makes us draw advantage from that similarity which nature has placed among different objects. From causes which appear *similar* we expect similar effects. This is the sum of all our experimental conclusions. Now it seems evident that, if this conclusion were formed by reason, it would be as perfect at first, and upon one instance, as after ever so long a course of experience. But the case is far otherwise. Nothing so like as eggs; yet no one, on account of this appearing similarity, expects the same taste and relish in all of them. It is only after a long course of uniform experiments in any kind, that we attain a firm reliance and security with regard to a particular event. Now where is that process of reasoning which, from one instance, draws a conclusion, so different from that which it infers from a hundred instances that are nowise different from that single one? This question I propose as much for the sake of information, as with an intention of raising difficulties. I cannot find, I cannot imagine any such reasoning. But I keep my mind still open to instruction, if any one will vouchsafe to bestow it on me.

Should it be said that, from a number of uniform experiments, we *infer* a connexion between the sensible qualities and the secret powers; this, I must confess, seems the same difficulty, couched in different terms. The question still recurs, on what process of argument this *inference* is founded? Where is the medium, the interposing ideas, which join propositions so very wide of each other? It is confessed that the colour, consistence, and other sensible qualities of bread appear not, of themselves, to have any connexion with the secret powers of nourishment and support. For otherwise we could infer these secret powers from the first appearance of these sensible qualities, without the aid of experience; contrary to the sentiment of all philosophers, and contrary to plain matter of fact. Here, then, is our natural state of ignorance with regard to the powers and influence of all objects. How is this remedied by experience? It only shows us a number of uniform effects, resulting from certain objects, and teaches us that those particular objects, at that particular time, were endowed with such powers and forces. When a new object, endowed with similar sensible qualities, is produced, we expect similar powers and forces, and look for a like effect. From a body of like colour and consistence with bread we expect like nourishment and support. But this surely is a step or progress of the mind, which wants to be explained. When a man says, *I have found, in all past instances, such sensible qualities conjoined with such secret powers*: And when he says, *Similar sensible qualities will always be conjoined with similar secret powers*, he is not guilty of a tautology, nor are these propositions in any respect the same. You say that the one proposition is an inference from the other. But you must confess that the inference is not intuitive; neither is it demonstrative: Of what nature is it, then? To say it is experimental, is begging the question. For all inferences from experience suppose, as their foundation, that the future will resemble the past, and that similar powers will be conjoined with similar sensible qualities. If there be any suspicion that the course of nature may change, and that the past may be no rule for the future, all experience becomes useless, and can give rise to no inference or conclusion. It is impossible, therefore, that any arguments from experience can prove this resemblance of the past to the future; since all these arguments are founded on the supposition of that resemblance. Let the course of things be allowed hitherto ever so regular; that alone, without some new argument or inference, proves not that, for the future, it will continue so. In vain do you pretend to have learned the nature of bodies from your past experience. The secret nature, and consequently all their effects and influence, may change, without any change in their sensible qualities. This happens sometimes, and with regard to some objects: Why may it not happen always, and with regard to all objects? What logic, what process of argument secures you against this supposition? My practice, you say, refutes my doubts. But you mistake the purport of my question. As an agent, I am quite satisfied in this point; but as a philosopher, who has some share of curiosity, I will not say scepticism. I want to learn the foundation of this inference. No reading, no enquiry has yet been able to remove my difficulty, or give me satisfaction in a matter of such importance. Can I do better than propose the difficulty to the public, even though, perhaps, I have small hopes of obtaining a solution? We shall at least, by this means, be sensible of our ignorance, if we do not augment our knowledge.

I must confess that a man is guilty of unpardonable arrogance who concludes, because an argument has escaped his own investigation, that therefore it does not really exist. I must also confess that, though all the learned, for several ages, should have employed themselves in fruitless search upon any subject, it may still, perhaps, be rash to conclude positively that the subject must, therefore, pass all human comprehension. Even though we examine all the sources of our knowledge, and conclude them unfit for such a subject, there may still remain a suspicion, that the enumeration is not complete, or the examination not accurate. But with regard to the present subject, there are some considerations which seem to remove all this accusation of arrogance or suspicion of mistake.

It is certain that the most ignorant and stupid peasants—nay infants, nay even brute beasts—improve by experience, and learn the qualities of natural objects, by observing the effects which result from them. When a child has felt the sensation of pain from touching the flame of a candle, he will be careful not to put his hand near any candle; but will expect a similar effect from a cause which is similar in its sensible qualities and appearance. If you assert, therefore, that the understanding of the child is led into this conclusion by any process of argument or ratiocination, I may justly require you to produce that argument; nor have you any pretence to refuse so equitable a demand. You cannot say that the argument is abstruse, and may possibly escape your enquiry; since you confess that it is obvious to the capacity of a mere infant. If you hesitate, therefore, a moment, or if, after reflection, you produce any intricate or profound argument, you, in a manner, give up the question, and confess that it is not reasoning which engages us to suppose the past resembling the future, and to expect similar effects from causes which are, to appearance, similar. This is the proposition which I intended to enforce in the present section. If I be right, I pretend not to have made any mighty discovery. And if I be wrong, I must acknowledge myself to be indeed a very backward scholar; since I cannot now discover an argument which, it seems, was perfectly familiar to me long before I was out of my cradle.

Section V
Sceptical Solution of These Doubts

Part I

The passion for philosophy, like that for religion, seems liable to this inconvenience, that, though it aims at the correction of our manners, and extirpation of our vices, it may only serve, by imprudent management, to foster a predominant inclination, and push the mind, with more determined resolution, towards that side which already *draws* too much, by the bias and propensity of the natural temper. It is certain that, while we aspire to the magnanimous firmness of the philosophic sage, and endeavour to confine our pleasures altogether within our own minds, we may, at last, render our philosophy like that of Epictetus, and other *Stoics*, only a more refined system of selfishness, and reason ourselves out of all virtue as well as social enjoyment. While we study with attention the vanity of human life, and turn all our thoughts towards the empty and transitory nature of riches and honours, we are, perhaps, all the while flattering our natural indolence, which, hating the bustle of the world, and drudgery of business, seeks a pretence of reason to give itself a full and uncontrolled indulgence. There is, however, one species of philosophy which seems little liable to this inconvenience, and that because it strikes in with no disorderly passion of the human mind, nor can mingle itself with any natural affection or propensity; and that is the Academic or Sceptical philosophy. The academics always talk of doubt and suspense of judgment, of danger in hasty determinations, of confining to very narrow bounds the enquiries of the understanding, and of renouncing all speculations which lie not within the limits of common life and practice. Nothing, therefore, can be more contrary than such a philosophy to the supine indolence of the mind, its rash arrogance, its lofty pretensions, and its superstitious credulity. Every passion is mortified by it, except the love of truth; and that passion never is, nor can be, carried to too high a degree. It is surprising, therefore, that this philosophy, which, in almost every instance, must be harmless and innocent, should be the subject of so much groundless reproach and obloquy. But, perhaps, the very circumstance which renders it so innocent is what chiefly exposes it to the public hatred and resentment. By flattering no irregular passion, it gains few partizans: By opposing so many vices and follies, it raises to itself abundance of enemies; who stigmatize it as libertine, profane, and irreligious.

Nor need we fear that this philosophy, while it endeavours to limit our enquiries to common life, should ever undermine the reasonings of common life, and carry its doubts so far as to destroy all action, as well as speculation. Nature will always maintain her rights, and prevail in the end over any abstract reasoning whatsoever. Though we should conclude, for instance, as in the forgoing section, that, in all reasonings from experience, there is a step taken by the mind which is not supported by any argument or process of the understanding; there is no danger that these reasonings, on which almost all knowledge depends, will ever be affected by such a discovery. If the mind be not engaged by argument to make this step, it must be induced by some other principle of equal weight and authority; and that principle will preserve its influence as long as human nature remains the same. What that principle is may well be worth the pains of enquiry.

Suppose a person, though endowed with the strongest faculties of reason and reflection, to be brought on a sudden into this world; he would, indeed, immediately observe a continual succession of objects, and one event following another; but he would not be able to discover anything farther. He would not, at first, by any reasoning, be able to reach the idea of cause and effect; since the particular powers, by which all natural operations are performed, never appear to the senses; nor is it reasonable to conclude, merely because one event, in one instance, precedes another, that therefore the one is the cause, the other the effect. Their conjunction may be arbitrary and casual. There may be no reason to infer the existence of one from the appearance of the other. And in a word, such a person, without more experience, could never employ his conjecture or reasoning concerning any matter of fact, or be assured of anything beyond what was immediately present to his memory and senses.

Suppose, again, that he has acquired more experience, and has lived so long in the world as to have observed familiar objects or events to be constantly conjoined together; what is the consequence of this experience? He immediately infers the existence of one object from the appearance of the other. Yet he has not, by all his experience, acquired any idea or knowledge of the secret power by which the one object produces the other; nor is it, by any process of reasoning, he is engaged to draw this inference. But still he finds himself determined to draw it: And though he should be convinced that this understanding has no part in the operation, he would nevertheless continue in the same course of thinking. There is some other principle which determines him to form such a conclusion.

This principle is Custom or Habit. For wherever the repetition of any particular act or operation produces a propensity to renew the same act or operation, without being impelled by any reasoning or process of the understanding, we always say, that this propensity is the effect of *Custom*. By employing that word, we pretend not to have given the ultimate reason of such a propensity. We only point out a principle of human nature, which is universally acknowledged, and which is well known by its effects. Perhaps we can push our enquiries no farther, or pretend to give the cause of this cause; but must rest contented with it as the ultimate principle, which we can assign, of all our conclusions from experience. It is sufficient satisfaction, that we can go so far, without repining at the narrowness of our faculties because they will carry us no farther. And it is certain we here advance a very intelligible proposition at least, if not a true one, when we assert that, after the constant conjunction of two objects—heat and flame, for instance, weight and solidity—we are determined by custom alone to expect the one from the appearance of the other. This hypothesis seems even the only one which explains the difficulty, why we draw, from a thousand instances, an inference which we are not able to draw from one instance, that is, in no respect different from them. Reason is incapable of any such variation. The conclusions which it draws from considering one circle are the same which it would form upon surveying all the circles in the universe. But no man, having seen only one body move after being impelled by another, could infer that every body will move after a like impulse. All inferences from experience, therefore, are effects of custom, not of reasoning.[7]

Custom, then, is the great guide of human life. It is that principle alone which renders our experience useful to us, and makes us expect, for the future, a similar train of events with those which have appeared in the past. Without the influence of custom, we should be entirely ignorant of every matter of fact beyond what is immediately present to the memory and senses. We should never know how to adjust means to ends, or to employ our natural powers in the production of any effect. There would be an end at once of all action, as well as of the chief part of speculation.

But here it may be proper to remark, that though our conclusions from experience carry us beyond our memory and senses, and assure us of matters of fact which happened in the most distant places and most remote ages, yet some fact must always be present to the senses or memory, from which we may first proceed in drawing these conclusions. A man, who should find in a desert country the remains of pompous buildings, would conclude that the country had, in ancient times, been cultivated by civilized inhabitants; but did nothing of this nature occur to him, he could never form such an inference. We learn the events of former ages from history; but then we must peruse the volumes in which this instruction is contained, and thence carry up our inferences from one testimony to another, till we arrive at the eyewitnesses and spectators of these distant events. In a word, if we proceed not upon some fact, present to the memory or senses, our reasonings would be merely hypothetical; and however the particular links might be connected with each other, the whole chain of inferences would have nothing to support it, nor could we ever, by its means, arrive at the knowledge of any real existence. If I ask why you believe any particular matter of fact, which you relate, you must tell me some reason; and this reason will be some other fact, connected with it. But as you cannot proceed after this manner, *in infinitum*, you must at last terminate in some fact, which is present to your memory or senses; or must allow that your belief is entirely without foundation.

What, then, is the conclusion of the whole matter? A simple one; though, it must be confessed, pretty remote from the common theories of philosophy. All belief of matter of fact or real existence is derived merely from some object, present to the memory or senses, and a customary conjunction between that and some other object. Or in other words; having found, in many instances, that any two kinds of objects—flame and heat, snow and cold—have always been conjoined together; if flame or snow be presented anew to the senses, the mind is carried by custom to expect heat or cold, and to *believe* that such a quality does exist, and will discover itself upon a nearer approach. This belief is the necessary result of placing the mind in such circumstances. It is an operation of the soul, when we are so situated, as unavoidable as to feel the passion of love, when we receive benefits; or hatred, when we meet with injuries. All these operations are a species of natural instincts, which no reasoning or process of the thought and understanding is able either to produce or to prevent.

At this point, it would be very allowable for us to stop our philosophical researches. In most questions we can never make a single step farther; and in all questions we must terminate here at last, after our most restless and curious enquiries. But still our curiosity will be pardonable, perhaps commendable, if it carry us on to still farther researches, and make us examine more accurately the nature of this *belief*, and of the *customary conjunction*, whence it is derived. By this means we may meet with some explications and analogies that will give satisfaction; at least to such as love the abstract sciences, and can be entertained with speculations, which, however accurate, may still retain a degree of doubt and uncertainty. As to readers of a different taste; the remaining part of this section is not calculated for them, and the following enquiries may well be understood, though it be neglected.

Part II

Nothing is more free than the imagination of man; and though it cannot exceed that original stock of ideas furnished by the internal and external senses, it has unlimited power of mixing, compounding, separating, and dividing these ideas, in all the varieties of fiction and vision. It can feign a train of events, with all the appearance of reality, ascribe to them a particular time and place, conceive them as existent, and paint them out to itself with every circumstance, that belongs to any historical fact, which it believes with the greatest certainty. Wherein, therefore, consists the difference between such a fiction and belief?

It lies not merely in any peculiar idea, which is annexed to such a conception as commands our assent, and which is wanting to every known fiction. For as the mind has authority over all its ideas, it could voluntarily annex this particular idea to any fiction, and consequently be able to believe whatever it pleases; contrary to what we find by daily experience. We can, in our conception, join the head of a man to the body of a horse; but it is not in our power to believe that such an animal has ever really existed.

It follows, therefore, that the difference between *fiction* and *belief* lies in some sentiment or feeling, which is annexed to the latter, not to the former, and which depends not on the will, nor can be commanded at pleasure. It must be excited by nature, like all other sentiments; and must arise from the particular situation, in which the mind is placed at any particular juncture. Whenever any object is presented to the memory or sense, it immediately, by the force of custom, carries the imagination to conceive that object, which is usually conjoined to it; and this conception is attended with a feeling or sentiment, different from the loose reveries of the fancy. In this consists the whole nature of belief. For as there is no matter of fact which we believe so firmly that we cannot conceive the contrary, there would be no difference between the conception assented to and that which is rejected, were it not for some sentiment which distinguishes the one from the other. If I see a billiard-ball moving towards another, on a smooth table, I can easily conceive it to stop upon contact. This conception implies no contradiction; but still it feels very differently from that conception by which I represent to myself the impulse and the communication of motion from one ball to another.

Were we to attempt a *definition* of this sentiment, we should perhaps, find it a very difficult, if not an impossible task; in the same manner as if we should endeavour to define the feeling of cold or passion of anger, to a creature who never had any experience of these sentiments. Belief is the true and proper name of this feeling; and no one is ever at a loss to know the meaning of that term; because every man is every moment conscious of the sentiment represented by it. It may not, however, be improper to attempt a *description* of this sentiment; in hopes we may, by that means, arrive at some analogies, which may afford a more perfect explication of it. I say, then, that belief is nothing but a more vivid, lively, forcible, firm, steady conception of an object, than what the imagination alone is ever able to attain. This variety of terms, which may seem so unphilosophical, is intended only to express that act of the mind, which renders realities, or what is taken for such, more present to us than fictions, causes them to weigh more in the thought, and gives them a superior influence on the passions and imagination. Provided we agree about the thing, it is needless to dispute about the terms. The imagination has the command over all its ideas, and can join and mix and vary them, in all the ways possible. It may conceive fictitious objects with all the circumstances of place and time. It may set them, in a manner, before our eyes, in their true colours, just as they might have existed. But as it is impossible that this faculty of imagination can ever, of itself, reach belief, it is evident that belief consists not in the peculiar nature or order of ideas, but in the *manner* of their conception, and in their *feeling* to the mind. I confess, that it is impossible perfectly to explain this feeling or manner of conception. We may make use of words which express something near it. But its true and proper name, as we observed before, is *belief*; which is a term that every one sufficiently understands in common life. And in philosophy, we can go no farther than assert, that *belief* is something felt by the mind, which distinguishes the ideas of the judgement from the fictions of the imagination. It gives them more weight and influence; makes them appear of greater importance; enforces them in the mind; and renders them the governing principle of our actions. I hear at present, for instance, a person's voice, with whom I am acquainted; and the sound comes as from the next room. This impression of my senses immediately conveys my thoughts to the person, together with all the surrounding objects. I paint them out to myself as existing at present, with the same qualities and relations, of which I formerly knew them possessed. These ideas take faster hold of my mind than ideas of an enchanted castle. They are very different to the feeling, and have a much greater influence of every kind, either to give pleasure or pain, joy or sorrow.

Let us, then, take in the whole compass of this doctrine, and allow, that the sentiment of belief is nothing but a conception more intense and steady than what attends the mere fictions of the imagination, and that this *manner* of conception arises from a **customary conjunction** of the object with something present to the memory or senses: I believe that it will not be difficult, upon these suppositions, to find operations of the mind analogous to it, and to trace up these phenomena to principles still more general.

We have already observed that nature has established connexions among particular ideas, and that no sooner one idea occurs to our thoughts than it introduces its correlative, and carries our attention towards it, by a gentle and insensible movement. These principles of connexion or association we have reduced to three, namely, *Resemblance, Contiguity* and *Causation*; which are the only bonds that unite our thoughts together, and beget that regular train of reflection or discourse, which, in a greater or less degree, takes place among all mankind. Now here arises a question, on which the solution of the present difficulty will depend. Does it happen, in all these relations, that, when one of the objects is presented to the senses or memory, the mind is not only carried to the conception of the correlative, but reaches a steadier and stronger conception of it than what otherwise it would have been able to attain? This seems to be the case with that belief which arises from the relation of cause and effect. And if the case be the same with the other relations or principles of associations, this may be established as a general law, which takes place in all the operations of the mind.

We may, therefore, observe, as the first experiment to our present purpose, that, upon the appearance of the picture of an absent friend, our idea of him is evidently enlivened by the *resemblance*, and that every passion, which that idea occasions, whether of joy or sorrow, acquires new force and vigour. In producing this effect, there concur both a relation and a present impression. Where the picture bears him no resemblance, at least was not intended for him, it never so much as conveys our thought to him: And where it is absent as well as the person, though the mind may pass from the thought of the one to that of the other, it feels its idea to be rather weakened than enlivened by that transition. We take a pleasure in viewing the picture of a friend, when it is set before us; but when it is removed, rather choose to consider him directly than by reflection in an image, which is equally distant and obscure.

The ceremonies of the Roman Catholic religion may be considered as instances of the same nature. The devotees of that superstition usually plead in excuse for the mummeries, with which they are upbraided, that they feel the good effect of those external motions, and postures, and actions, in enlivening their devotion and quickening their fervour, which otherwise would decay, if directed entirely to distant and immaterial objects. We shadow out the objects of our faith, say they, in sensible types and images, and render them more present to us by the immediate presence of these types, than it is possible for us to do merely by an intellectual view and contemplation. Sensible objects have always a greater influence on the fancy than any other; and this influence they readily convey to those ideas to which they are related, and which they resemble. I shall only infer from these practices, and this reasoning, that the effect of resemblance in enlivening the ideas is very common; and as in every case a resemblance and a present impression must concur, we are abundantly supplied with experiments to prove the reality of the foregoing principle.

We may add force to these experiments by others of a different kind, in considering the effects of *contiguity* as well as of *resemblance*. It is certain that distance diminishes the force of every idea, and that, upon our approach to any object; though it does not discover itself to our senses; it operates upon the mind with an influence, which imitates an immediate impression. The thinking on any object readily transports the mind to what is contiguous; but it is only the actual presence of an object, that transports it with a superior vivacity. When I am a few miles from home, whatever relates to it touches me more nearly than when I am two hundred leagues distant; though even at that distance the reflecting on any thing in the neighbourhood of my friends or family naturally produces an idea of them. But as in this latter case, both the objects of the mind are ideas; notwithstanding there is an easy transition between them; that transition alone is not able to give a superior vivacity to any of the ideas, for want of some immediate impression.[8]

No one can doubt but causation has the same influence as the other two relations of resemblance and contiguity. Superstitious people are fond of the reliques of saints and holy men, for the same reason, that they seek after types or images, in order to enliven their devotion, and give them a more intimate and strong conception of those exemplary lives, which they desire to imitate. Now it is evident, that one of the best reliques, which a devotee could procure, would be the handywork of a saint; and if his clothes and furniture are ever to be considered in this light, it is because they were once at his disposal, and were moved and affected by him; in which respect they are to be considered as imperfect effects, and as connected with him by a shorter chain of consequences than any of those, by which we learn the reality of his existence.

Suppose, that the son of a friend, who had been long dead or absent, were presented to us; it is evident, that this object would instantly revive its correlative idea, and recall to our thoughts all past intimacies and familiarities, in more lively colours than they would otherwise have appeared to us. This is another phenomenon, which seems to prove the principle above mentioned.

We may observe, that, in these phenomena, the belief of the correlative object is always presupposed; without which the relation could have no effect. The influence of the picture supposes, that we *believe* our friend to have once existed. Contiguity to home can never excite our idea of home, unless we *believe* that it really exists. Now I assert, that this belief, where it reaches beyond the memory or sense, is of a similar nature, and arises from similar causes, with the transition of thought and vivacity of conception here explained. When I throw a piece of dry wood into a fire, my mind is immediately carried to conceive, that it augments, not extinguishes the flame. This transition of thought from the cause to the effect proceeds not from reason. It derives its origin altogether from custom and experience. And as it first begins from an object, present to the senses, it renders the idea or conception of flame more strong and lively than any loose, floating reverie of the imagination. That idea arises immediately. The thought moves instantly towards it, and conveys to it all that force of conception, which is derived from the impression present to the senses. When a sword is levelled at my breast, does not the idea of wound and pain strike me more strongly, than when a glass of wine is presented to me, even though by accident this idea should occur after the appearance of the latter object? But what is there in this whole matter to cause such a strong conception, except only a present object and a customary transition to the idea of another object, which we have been accustomed to conjoin with the former? This is the whole operation of the mind, in all our conclusions concerning matter of fact and existence; and it is a satisfaction to find some analogies, by which it may be explained. The transition from a present object does in all cases give strength and solidity to the related idea.

Here, then, is a kind of pre-established harmony between the course of nature and the succession of our ideas; and though the powers and forces, by which the former is governed, be wholly unknown to us; yet our thoughts and conceptions have still, we find, gone on in the same train with the other works of nature. Custom is that principle, by which this correspondence has been effected; so necessary to the subsistence of our species, and the regulation of our conduct, in every circumstance and occurrence of human life. Had not the presence of an object, instantly excited the idea of those objects, commonly conjoined with it, all our knowledge must have been limited to the narrow sphere of our memory and senses; and we should never have been able to adjust means to ends, or employ our natural powers, either to the producing of good, or avoiding of evil. Those, who delight in the discovery and contemplation of **final causes**, have here ample subject to employ their wonder and admiration.

I shall add, for a further confirmation of the foregoing theory, that, as this operation of the mind, by which we infer like effects from like causes, and vice versa, is so essential to the subsistence of all human creatures, it is not probable, that it could be trusted to the fallacious deductions of our reason, which is slow in its operations; appears not, in any degree, during the first years of infancy; and at best is, in every age and period of human life, extremely liable to error and mistake. It is more conformable to the ordinary wisdom of nature to secure so necessary an act of the mind, by some instinct or mechanical tendency, which may be infallible in its operations, may discover itself at the first appearance of life and thought, and may be independent of all the laboured deductions of the understanding. As nature has taught us the use of our limbs, without giving us the knowledge of the muscles and nerves, by which they are actuated; so has she implanted in us an instinct, which carries forward the thought in a correspondent course to that which she has established among external objects; though we are ignorant of those powers and forces, on which this regular course and succession of objects totally depends.

Section VI
Of Probability[9]

Though there be no such thing as *Chance* in the world; our ignorance of the real cause of any event has the same influence on the understanding, and begets a like species of belief or opinion.

There is certainly a probability, which arises from a superiority of chances on any side; and according as this superiority encreases, and surpasses the opposite chances, the probability receives a proportionable encrease, and begets still a higher degree of belief or assent to that side, in which we discover the superiority. If a dye were marked with one figure or number of spots on four sides, and with another figure or number of spots on the two remaining sides, it would be more probable, that the former would turn up than the latter; though, if it had a thousand sides marked in the same manner, and only one side different, the probability would be much higher, and our belief or expectation of the event more steady and secure. This process of the thought or reasoning may seem trivial and obvious; but to those who consider it more narrowly, it may, perhaps, afford matter for curious speculation.

It seems evident, that, when the mind looks forward to discover the event, which may result from the throw of such a dye, it considers the turning up of each particular side as alike probable; and this is the very nature of chance, to render all the particular events, comprehended in it, entirely equal. But finding a greater number of sides concur in the one event than in the other, the mind is carried more frequently to that event, and meets it oftener, in revolving the various possibilities or chances, on which the ultimate result depends. This concurrence of several views in one particular event begets immediately, by an inexplicable contrivance of nature, the sentiment of belief, and gives that event the advantage over its antagonist, which is supported by a smaller number of views, and recurs less frequently to the mind. If we allow, that belief is nothing but a firmer and stronger conception of an object than what attends the mere fictions of the imagination, this operation may, perhaps, in some measure, be accounted for. The concurrence of these several views or glimpses imprints the idea more strongly on the imagination; gives it superior force and vigour; renders its influence on the passions and affections more sensible; and in a word, begets that reliance or security, which constitutes the nature of belief and opinion.

The case is the same with the probability of causes, as with that of chance. There are some causes, which are entirely uniform and constant in producing a particular effect; and no instance has ever yet been found of any failure or irregularity in their operation. Fire has always burned, and water suffocated every human creature: The production of motion by impulse and gravity is an universal law, which has hitherto admitted of no exception. But there are other causes, which have been found more irregular and uncertain; nor has rhubarb always proved a purge, or opium a soporific to every one, who has taken these medicines. It is true, when any cause fails of producing its usual effect, philosophers ascribe not this to any irregularity in nature; but suppose, that some secret causes, in the particular structure of parts, have prevented the operation. Our reasonings, however, and conclusions concerning the event are the same as if this principle had no place. Being determined by custom to transfer the past to the future, in all our inferences; where the past has been entirely regular and uniform, we expect the event with the greatest assurance, and leave no room for any contrary supposition. But where different effects have been found to follow from causes, which are to *appearance* exactly similar, all these various effects must occur to the mind in transferring the past to the future, and enter into our consideration, when we determine the probability of the event. Though we give the preference to that which has been found most usual, and believe that this effect will exist, we must not overlook the other effects, but must assign to each of them a particular weight and authority, in proportion as we have found it to be more or less frequent. It is more probable, in almost every country of Europe, that there will be frost sometime in January, than that the weather will continue open throughout that whole month; though this probability varies according to the different climates, and approaches to a certainty in the more northern kingdoms. Here then it seems evident, that, when we transfer the past to the future, in order to determine the effect, which will result from any cause, we transfer all the different events, in the same proportion as they have appeared in the past, and conceive one to have existed a hundred times, for instance, another ten times, and another once. As a great number of views do here concur in one event, they fortify and confirm it to the imagination, beget that sentiment which we call *belief*, and give its object the preference above the contrary event, which is not supported by an equal number of experiments, and recurs not so frequently to the thought in transferring the past to the future. Let any one try to account for this operation of the mind upon any of the received systems of philosophy, and he will be sensible of the difficulty. For my part, I shall think it sufficient, if the present hints excite the curiosity of philosophers, and make them sensible how defective all common theories are in treating of such curious and such sublime subjects.

Section VII
Of the Idea of Necessary Connexion

Part I

The great advantage of the mathematical sciences above the moral consists in this, that the ideas of the former, being sensible, are always clear and determinate, the smallest distinction between them is immediately perceptible, and the same terms are still expressive of the same ideas, without ambiguity or variation. An oval is never mistaken for a circle, nor an hyperbola for an ellipsis. The isosceles and scalenum are distinguished by boundaries more

exact than vice and virtue, right and wrong. If any term be defined in geometry, the mind readily, of itself, substitutes, on all occasions, the definition for the term defined: Or even when no definition is employed, the object itself may be presented to the senses, and by that means be steadily and clearly apprehended. But the finer sentiments of the mind, the operations of the understanding, the various agitations of the passions, though really in themselves distinct, easily escape us, when surveyed by reflection; nor is it in our power to recall the original object, as often as we have occasion to contemplate it. Ambiguity, by this means, is gradually introduced into our reasonings: Similar objects are readily taken to be the same: And the conclusion becomes at last very wide of the premises.

One may safely, however, affirm, that, if we consider these sciences in a proper light, their advantages and disadvantages nearly compensate each other, and reduce both of them to a state of equality. If the mind, with greater facility, retains the ideas of geometry clear and determinate, it must carry on a much longer and more intricate chain of reasoning, and compare ideas much wider of each other, in order to reach the abstruser truths of that science. And if moral ideas are apt, without extreme care, to fall into obscurity and confusion, the inferences are always much shorter in these disquisitions, and the intermediate steps, which lead to the conclusion, much fewer than in the sciences which treat of quantity and number. In reality, there is scarcely a proposition in Euclid so simple, as not to consist of more parts, than are to be found in any moral reasoning which runs not into chimera and conceit. Where we trace the principles of the human mind through a few steps, we may be very well satisfied with our progress; considering how soon nature throws a bar to all our inquiries concerning causes, and reduces us to an acknowledgment of our ignorance. The chief obstacle, therefore, to our improvement in the moral or metaphysical sciences is the obscurity of the ideas, and ambiguity of the terms. The principle difficulty in the mathematics is the length of inferences and compass of thought, requisite to the forming of any conclusion. And, perhaps, our progress in natural philosophy is chiefly retarded by the want of proper experiments and phenomena, which are often discovered by chance, and cannot always be found, when requisite even by the most diligent and prudent enquiry. As moral philosophy seems hitherto to have received less improvement than either geometry or physics, we may conclude, that, if there be any difference in this respect among these sciences, the difficulties, which obstruct the progress of the former, require superior care and capacity to be surmounted.

There are no ideas, which occur in metaphysics, more obscure and uncertain, than those of *power*, *force*, *energy* or *necessary connexion*, of which it is every moment necessary for us to treat in all our disquisitions. We shall, therefore, endeavour, in this section, to fix, if possible, the precise meaning of these terms, and thereby remove some part of that obscurity, which is so much complained of in this species of philosophy.

It seems a proposition, which will not admit of much dispute, that all our ideas are nothing but copies of our impressions, or, in other words, that it is impossible for us to *think* of any thing, which we have not antecedently *felt*, either by our external or internal senses. I have endeavoured[10] to explain and prove this proposition, and have expressed my hopes, that, by a proper application of it, men may reach a greater clearness and precision in philosophical reasonings, than what they have hitherto been able to attain. Complex ideas may, perhaps, be well known by definition, which is nothing but an enumeration of those parts or simple ideas, that compose them. But when we have pushed up definitions to the most simple ideas, and find still some ambiguity and obscurity; what resource are we then possessed of? By what invention can we throw light upon these ideas, and render them altogether precise and determinate to our intellectual view? Produce the impressions or original sentiments, from which the ideas are copied. These impressions are all strong and sensible. They admit not of ambiguity. They are not only placed in a full light themselves, but may throw light on their correspondent ideas, which lie in obscurity. And by this means, we may, perhaps, attain a new microscope or species of optics, by which, in the moral sciences, the most minute, and most simple ideas may be so enlarged as to fall readily under our apprehension, and be equally known

with the grossest and most sensible ideas, that can be the object of our enquiry.

To be fully acquainted, therefore, with the idea of power or necessary connexion, let us examine its impression; and in order to find the impression with greater certainty, let us search for it in all the sources, from which it may possibly be derived.

When we look about us towards external objects, and consider the operation of causes, we are never able, in a single instance, to discover any power or necessary connexion; any quality, which binds the effect to the cause, and renders the one an infallible consequence of the other. We only find, that the one does actually, in fact, follow the other. The impulse of one billiard-ball is attended with motion in the second. This is the whole that appears to the *outward* senses. The mind feels no sentiment or *inward* impression from this succession of objects: Consequently, there is not, in any single, particular instance of cause and effect, any thing which can suggest the idea of power or necessary connexion.

From the first appearance of an object, we never can conjecture what effect will result from it. But were the power or energy of any cause discoverable by the mind, we could foresee the effect, even without experience; and might, at first, pronounce with certainty concerning it, by mere dint of thought and reasoning.

In reality, there is no part of matter, that does ever, by its sensible qualities, discover any power or energy, or give us ground to imagine, that it could produce any thing, or be followed by any other object, which we could denominate its effect. Solidity, extension, motion; these qualities are all complete in themselves, and never point out any other event which may result from them. The scenes of the universe are continually shifting, and one object follows another in an uninterrupted succession; but the power of force, which actuates the whole machine, is entirely concealed from us, and never discovers itself in any of the sensible qualities of body. We know, that, in fact, heat is a constant attendant of flame; but what is the connexion between them, we have no room so much as to conjecture or imagine. It is impossible, therefore, that the idea of power can be derived from the contemplation of bodies, in single instances of their operation; because no bodies ever discover any power, which can be the original of this idea.[11]

Since, therefore, external objects as they appear to the senses, give us no idea of power or necessary connexion, by their operation in particular instances, let us see, whether this idea be derived from reflection on the operations of our own minds, and be copied from any internal impression. It may be said, that we are every moment conscious of internal power; while we feel, that, by the simple command of our will, we can move the organs of our body, or direct the faculties of our mind. An act of volition produces motions in our limbs, or raises a new idea in our imagination. This influence of the will we know by consciousness. Hence we acquire the idea of power or energy; and are certain, that we ourselves and all other intelligent beings are possessed of power. This idea, then, is an idea of reflection, since it arises from reflecting on the operations of our own mind, and on the command which is exercised by will, both over the organs of the body and faculties of the soul.

We shall proceed to examine this pretension; and first with regard to the influence of volition over the organs of the body. This influence, we may observe, is a fact, which, like all other natural events, can be known only by experience, and can never be foreseen from any apparent energy or power in the cause, which connects it with the effect, and renders the one an infallible consequence of the other. The motion of our body follows upon the command of our will. Of this we are every moment conscious. But the means, by which this is effected: the energy, by which the will performs so extraordinary an operation; of this we are so far from being immediately conscious, that it must for ever escape our most diligent enquiry.

For *first*; is there any principle in all nature more mysterious than the union of the soul with the body; by which a supposed spiritual substance acquires such an influence over a material one, that the most refined thought is able to actuate the grossest matter? Were we empowered, by a secret wish, to remove mountains, or control the planets in their orbit; this extensive authority would not be more extraordinary, nor more beyond our comprehension. But if by consciousness we perceived any power or energy in the will, we must know this power; we must know its

connexion with the effect; we must know the secret union of soul and body, and the nature of both these substances; by which the one is able to operate, in so many instances, upon the other.

Secondly, We are not able to move all the organs of the body with a like authority; though we cannot assign any reason besides experience, for so remarkable a difference between one and the other. Why has the will an influence over the tongue and fingers, not over the heart or liver? This question would never embarrass us, were we conscious of a power in the former case, not in the latter. We should then perceive, independent of experience, why the authority of will over the organs of the body is circumscribed within such particular limits. Being in that case fully acquainted with the power or force, by which it operates, we should also know, why its influence reaches precisely to such boundaries, and no farther.

A man, suddenly struck with palsy in the leg or arm, or who had newly lost those members, frequently endeavours, at first to move them, and employ them in their usual offices. Here he is as much conscious of power to command such limbs, as a man in perfect health is conscious of power to actuate any member which remains in its natural state and condition. But consciousness never deceives. Consequently, neither in the one case nor in the other, are we ever conscious of any power. We learn the influence of our will from experience alone. And experience only teaches us, how one event constantly follows another; without instructing us in the secret connexion, which binds them together, and renders them inseparable.

Thirdly, We learn from anatomy, that the immediate object of power in voluntary motion, is not the member itself which is moved, but certain muscles, and nerves, and animal spirits, and, perhaps, something still more minute and more unknown, through which the motion is successively propagated, ere it reach the member itself whose motion is the immediate object of volition. Can there be a more certain proof, that the power, by which this whole operation is performed, so far from being directly and fully known by an inward sentiment or consciousness, is, to the last degree mysterious and unintelligible? Here the mind wills a certain event: Immediately another event, unknown to ourselves, and totally different from the one intended, is produced: This event produces another, equally unknown: Till at last, through a long succession, the desired event is produced. But if the original power were felt, it must be known: Were it known, its effect also must be known; since all power is relative to its effect. And vice versa, if the effect be not known, the power cannot be known nor felt. How indeed can we be conscious of a power to move our limbs, when we have no such power; but only that to move certain animal spirits, which, though they produce at last the motion of our limbs, yet operate in such a manner as is wholly beyond our comprehension?

We may, therefore, conclude from the whole, I hope, without any temerity, though with assurance; that our idea of power is not copied from any sentiment or consciousness of power within ourselves, when we give rise to animal motion, or apply our limbs to their proper use and office. That this motion follows the command of the will is a matter of common experience, like other natural events: But the power or energy by which this is effected, like that in other natural events, is unknown and inconceivable.[12]

Shall we then assert, that we are conscious of a power or energy in our own minds, when, by an act or command of our will, we raise up a new idea, fix the mind to the contemplation of it, turn it on all sides, and at last dismiss it for some other idea, when we think that we have surveyed it with sufficient accuracy? I believe the same arguments will prove, that even this command of the will gives us no real idea of force or energy.

First, It must be allowed, that, when we know a power, we know that very circumstance in the cause, by which it is enabled to produce the effect: For these are supposed to be synonymous. We must, therefore, know both the cause and effect, and the relation between them. But do we pretend to be acquainted with the nature of the human soul and the nature of an idea, or the aptitude of the one to produce the other? This is a real creation; a production of something out of nothing: Which implies a power so great, that it may seem, at first sight, beyond the reach of any being, less than infinite. At least it must be owned, that such a power is not felt, nor known, nor even conceivable by the mind. We only feel the event, namely, the existence of an idea, consequent to a command of the will: But the manner, in which

this operation is performed, the power by which it is produced, is entirely beyond our comprehension.

Secondly, The command of the mind over itself is limited, as well as its command over the body; and these limits are not known by reason, or any acquaintance with the nature of cause and effect, but only by experience and observation, as in all other natural events and in the operation of external objects. Our authority over our sentiments and passions is much weaker than that over our ideas; and even the latter authority is circumscribed within very narrow boundaries. Will any one pretend to assign the ultimate reason of these boundaries, or show why the power is deficient in one case, not in another.

Thirdly, This self-command is very different at different times. A man in health possesses more of it than one languishing with sickness. We are more master of our thoughts in the morning than in the evening: Fasting, than after a full meal. Can we give any reason for these variations, except experience? Where then is the power, of which we pretend to be conscious? Is there not here, either in a spiritual or material substance, or both, some secret mechanism or structure of parts, upon which the effect depends, and which, being entirely unknown to us, renders the power or energy of the will equally unknown and incomprehensible?

Volition is surely an act of the mind, with which we are sufficiently acquainted. Reflect upon it. Consider it on all sides. Do you find anything in it like this creative power, by which it raises from nothing a new idea, and with a kind of *Fiat*, imitates the omnipotence of its Maker, if I may be allowed so to speak, who called forth into existence all the various scenes of nature? So far from being conscious of this energy in the will, it requires as certain experience as that of which we are possessed, to convince us that such extraordinary effects do ever result from a simple act of volition.

The generality of mankind never find any difficulty in accounting for the more common and familiar operations of nature—such as the descent of heavy bodies, the growth of plants, the generation of animals, or the nourishment of bodies by food: But suppose that, in all these cases, they perceive, the very force or energy of the cause, by which it is connected with its effect, and is for ever infallible in its operation. They acquire, by long habit, such a turn of mind, that upon the appearance of the cause, they immediately expect with assurance its usual attendant, and hardly conceive it possible that any other event could result from it. It is only on the discovery of extraordinary phenomena, such as earthquakes, pestilence, and prodigies of any kind, that they find themselves at a loss to assign a proper cause, and to explain the manner in which the effect is produced by it. It is usual for men, in such difficulties, to have recourse to some invisible intelligent principle[13] as the immediate cause of that event which surprises them, and which, they think, cannot be accounted for from the common powers of nature. But philosophers, who carry their scrutiny a little farther, immediately perceive that, even in the most familiar events, the energy of the cause is as unintelligible as in the most unusual, and that we only learn by experience the frequent *Conjunction* of objects, without being ever able to comprehend anything like *Connexion* between them. Here, then, many philosophers think themselves obliged by reason to have recourse, on all occasions, to the same principle, which the vulgar never appeal to but in cases that appear miraculous and supernatural. They acknowledge mind and intelligence to be, not only the ultimate and original cause of all things, but the immediate and sole cause of every event which appears in nature. They pretend that those objects which are commonly denominated *causes*, are in reality nothing but *occasions*; and that the true and direct principle of every effect is not any power or force in nature, but a volition of the Supreme Being, who wills that such particular objects should for ever be conjoined with each other. Instead of saying that one billiard-ball moves another by force which it has derived from the author of nature, it is the Deity himself, they say, who, by a particular volition, moves the second ball, being determined to this operation by the impulse of the first ball, in consequence of those general laws which he has laid down to himself in the government of the universe. But philosophers advancing still in their inquiries, discover that, as we are totally ignorant of the power on which depends the mutual operation of bodies, we are no less ignorant of that power on which depends the operation of

mind on body, or of body on mind; nor are we able, either from our senses or consciousness, to assign the ultimate principle in one case more than in the other. The same ignorance, therefore, reduces them to the same conclusion. They assert that the Deity is the immediate cause of the union between soul and body; and that they are not the organs of sense, which, being agitated by external objects, produce sensations in the mind; but that it is a particular volition of our omnipotent Maker, which excites such a sensation, in consequence of such a motion in the organ. In like manner, it is not any energy in the will that produces local motion in our members: It is God himself, who is pleased to second our will, in itself impotent, and to command that motion which we erroneously attribute to our own power and efficacy. Nor do philosophers stop at this conclusion. They sometimes extend the same inference to the mind itself, in its internal operations. Our mental vision or conception of ideas is nothing but a revelation made to us by our Maker. When we voluntarily turn our thoughts to any object, and raise up its image in the fancy, it is not the will which creates that idea: It is the universal Creator, who discovers it to the mind, and renders it present to us.

Thus, according to these philosophers, every thing is full of God. Not content with the principle, that nothing exists but by his will, that nothing possesses any power but by his concession: They rob nature, and all created beings, of every power, in order to render their dependence on the Deity still more sensible and immediate. They consider not that, by this theory, they diminish, instead of magnifying, the grandeur of those attributes, which they affect so much to celebrate. It argues surely more power in the Deity to delegate a certain degree of power to inferior creatures than to produce every thing by his own immediate volition. It argues more wisdom to contrive at first the fabric of the world with such perfect foresight that, of itself, and by its proper operation, it may serve all the purposes of providence, than if the great Creator were obliged every moment to adjust its parts, and animate by his breath all the wheels of that stupendous machine.

But if we would have a more philosophical confutation of this theory, perhaps the two following reflections may suffice.

First, it seems to me that this theory of the universal energy and operation of the Supreme Being is too bold ever to carry conviction with it to a man, sufficiently apprized of the weakness of human reason, and the narrow limits to which it is confined in all its operations. Though the chain of arguments which conduct to it were ever so logical, there must arise a strong suspicion, if not an absolute assurance, that it has carried us quite beyond the reach of our faculties, when it leads to conclusions so extraordinary, and so remote from common life and experience. We are got into fairy land, long ere we have reached the last steps of our theory; and *there* we have no reason to trust our common methods of argument, or to think that our usual analogies and probabilities have any authority. Our line is too short to fathom such immense abysses. And however we may flatter ourselves that we are guided, in every step which we take, by a kind of verisimilitude and experience, we may be assured that this fancied experience has no authority when we thus apply to it subjects that lie entirely out of the sphere of experience. But on this we shall have occasion to touch afterwards.

Secondly, I cannot perceive any force in the arguments on which this theory is founded. We are ignorant, it is true, of the manner in which bodies operate on each other: Their force or energy is entirely incomprehensible: But are we not equally ignorant of the manner or force by which a mind, even the supreme mind, operates either on itself or on body? Whence, I beseech you, do we acquire any idea of it? We have no sentiment or consciousness of this power in ourselves. We have no idea of the Supreme Being but what we learn from reflection on our own faculties. Were our ignorance, therefore, a good reason for rejecting any thing, we should be led into that principle of denying all energy in the Supreme Being as much as in the grossest matter. We surely comprehend as little the operations of one as of the other. Is it more difficult to conceive that motion may arise from impulse than that it may arise from volition? All we know is our profound ignorance in both cases.[14]

Part II

But to hasten to a conclusion of this argument, which is already drawn out to too great a length: We have

sought in vain for an idea of power or necessary connexion in all the sources from which we could suppose it to be derived. It appears that, in single instances of the operation of bodies, we never can, by our utmost scrutiny, discover any thing but one event following another, without being able to comprehend any force or power by which the cause operates, or any connexion between it and its supposed effect. The same difficulty occurs in contemplating the operations of mind on body—where we observe the motion of the latter to follow upon the volition of the former, but are not able to observe or conceive the tie which binds together the motion and volition, or the energy by which the mind produces this effect. The authority of the will over its own faculties and ideas is not a whit more comprehensible: So that, upon the whole, there appears not, throughout all nature, any one instance of connexion which is conceivable by us. All events seem entirely loose and separate. One event follows another; but we never can observe any tie between them. They seem *conjoined*, but never *connected*. And as we can have no idea of any thing which never appeared to our outward sense or inward sentiment, the necessary conclusion *seems* to be that we have no idea of connexion or power at all, and that these words are absolutely without any meaning, when employed either in philosophical reasonings or common life.

But there still remains one method of avoiding this conclusion, and one source which we have not yet examined. When any natural object or event is presented, it is impossible for us, by any sagacity or penetration, to discover, or even conjecture, without experience, what event will result from it, or to carry our foresight beyond that object which is immediately present to the memory and senses. Even after one instance or experiment where we have observed a particular event to follow upon another, we are not entitled to form a general rule, or foretell what will happen in like cases; it being justly esteemed an unpardonable temerity to judge of the whole course of nature from one single experiment, however accurate or certain. But when one particular species of event has always, in all instances, been conjoined with another, we make no longer any scruple of foretelling one upon the appearance of the other, and of employing that reasoning, which can alone assure us of any matter of fact or existence. We then call the one object,

Cause; the other, *Effect*. We suppose that there is some connexion between them; some power in the one, by which it infallibly produces the other, and operates with the greatest certainty and strongest necessity.

It appears, then, that this idea of a necessary connexion among events arises from a number of similar instances which occur of the constant conjunction of these events; nor can that idea ever be suggested by any one of these instances, surveyed in all possible lights and positions. But there is nothing in a number of instances, different from every single instance, which is supposed to be exactly similar; except only, that after a repetition of similar instances, the mind is carried by habit, upon the appearance of one event, to expect its usual attendant, and to believe that it will exist. This connexion, therefore, which we *feel* in the mind, this customary transition of the imagination from one object to its usual attendant, is the sentiment or impression from which we form the idea of power or necessary connexion. Nothing farther is in the case. Contemplate the subject on all sides; you will never find any other origin of that idea. This is the sole difference between one instance, from which we can never receive the idea of connexion, and a number of similar instances, by which it is suggested. The first time a man saw the communication of motion by impulse, as by the shock of two billiard-balls, he could not pronounce that the one event was *connected*: but only that it was *conjoined* with the other. After he has observed several instances of this nature, he then pronounces them to be *connected*. What alteration has happened to give rise to this new idea of *connexion*? Nothing but that he now *feels* these events to be *connected* in his imagination, and can readily foretell the existence of one from the appearance of the other. When we say, therefore, that one object is connected with another, we mean only that they have acquired a connexion in our thought, and give rise to this inference, by which they become proofs of each other's existence: A conclusion which is somewhat extraordinary, but which seems founded on sufficient evidence. Nor will its evidence be weakened by any general diffidence of the understanding, or sceptical suspicion concerning every conclusion which is new and extraordinary. No conclusions can be more agreeable to **scepticism** than such as make discoveries concerning the weakness and narrow limits of human reason and capacity.

And what stronger instance can be produced of the surprising ignorance and weakness of the understanding than the present? For surely, if there be any relation among objects which it imports to us to know perfectly, it is that of cause and effect. On this are founded all our reasonings concerning matter of fact or existence. By means of it alone we attain any assurance concerning objects which are removed from the present testimony of our memory and senses. The only immediate utility of all sciences, is to teach us, how to control and regulate future events by their causes. Our thoughts and enquiries are, therefore, every moment, employed about this relation: Yet so imperfect are the ideas which we form concerning it, that it is impossible to give any just definition of cause, except what is drawn from something extraneous and foreign to it. Similar objects are always conjoined with similar. Of this we have experience. Suitably to this experience, therefore, we may define a cause to be *an object, followed by another, and where all the objects similar to the first are followed by objects similar to the second.* Or in other words *where, if the first object had not been, the second never had existed.* The appearance of a cause always conveys the mind, by a customary transition, to the idea of the effect. Of this also we have experience. We may, therefore, suitably to this experience, form another definition of cause, and call it, *an object followed by another, and whose appearance always conveys the thought to that other.* But though both these definitions be drawn from circumstances foreign to the cause, we cannot remedy this inconvenience, or attain any more perfect definition, which may point out that circumstance in the cause, which gives it a connexion with its effect. We have no idea of this connexion, nor even any distinct notion what it is we desire to know, when we endeavour at a conception of it. We say, for instance, that the vibration of this string is the cause of this particular sound. But what do we mean by that affirmation? We either mean *that this vibration is followed by this sound, and that all similar vibrations have been followed by similar sounds*: Or, *that this vibration is followed by this sound, and that upon the appearance of one the mind anticipates the senses, and forms immediately an idea of the other.* We may consider the relation of cause and effect in either of these two lights; but beyond these, we have no idea of it.[15]

To recapitulate, therefore, the reasonings of this section: Every idea is copied from some preceding impression or sentiment; and where we cannot find any impression, we may be certain that there is no idea. In all single instances of the operation of bodies or minds, there is nothing that produces any impression, nor consequently can suggest any idea of power or necessary connexion. But when many uniform instances appear, and the same object is always followed by the same event; we then begin to entertain the notion of cause and connexion. We then *feel* a new sentiment or impression, to wit, a customary connexion in the thought or imagination between one object and its usual attendant; and this sentiment is the original of that idea which we seek for. For as this idea arises from a number of similar instances, and not from any single instance, it must arise from that circumstance, in which the number of instances differ from every individual instance. But this customary connexion or transition of the imagination is the only circumstance in which they differ. In every other particular they are alike. The first instance which we saw of motion communicated by the shock of two billiard-balls (to return to this obvious illustration) is exactly similar to any instance that may, at present, occur to us; except only, that we could not, at first, *infer* one event from the other; which we are enabled to do at present, after so long a course of uniform experience. I know not whether the reader will readily apprehend this reasoning. I am afraid that, should I multiply words about it, or throw it into a greater variety of lights, it would only become more obscure and intricate. In all abstract reasonings there is one point of view which, if we can happily hit, we shall go farther towards illustrating the subject than by all the eloquence and copious expression in the world. This point of view we should endeavour to reach, and reserve the flowers of rhetoric for subjects which are more adapted to them.

NOTES

1. It is probable that no more was meant by those, who denied innate ideas, than that all ideas were copies of our impressions; though it must be confessed, that the terms, which they employed, were not chosen with such caution, nor so exactly defined, as to prevent all mistakes about their doctrine. For what is meant by *innate*? If innate be equivalent to natural, then all the perceptions and ideas of the mind must be allowed to be innate or natural, in whatever sense we take the latter word, whether in opposition to what is uncommon, artificial, or miraculous. If by innate be meant, contemporary to our birth, the dispute seems to be frivolous; nor is it worth while to enquire at what time thinking begins, whether before, at, or after our birth. Again, the word *idea*, seems to be commonly taken in a very loose sense, by Locke and others; as standing for any of our perceptions, our sensations and passions, as well as thoughts. Now in this sense, I should desire to know, what can be meant by asserting, that self-love, or resentment of injuries, or the passion between the sexes is not innate!

   But admitting these terms, *impressions* and *ideas*, in the sense above explained, and understanding by *innate*, what is original or copied from no precedent perception, then may we assert that all our impressions are innate, and our ideas not innate.

   To be ingenuous, I must own it to be my opinion, that Locke was betrayed into this question by the schoolmen, who, making use of undefined terms, draw out their disputes to a tedious length, without ever touching the point in question. A like ambiguity and circumlocution seems to run through that philosopher's reasonings on this as well as most other subjects.

2. Resemblance.

3. Contiguity.

4. Cause and effect.

5. For instance, Contrast or Contrariety is also a connexion among Ideas: but it may, perhaps, be considered as a mixture of *Causation* and *Resemblance*. Where two objects are contrary, the one destroys the other; that is, the cause of its annihilation, and the idea of the annihilation of an object, implies the idea of its former existence.

6. The word, Power, is here used in a loose and popular sense. The more accurate explication of it would give additional evidence to this argument. See Section VII.

7. Nothing is more useful than for writers, even, on *moral*, *political*, or *physical* subjects, to distinguish between *reason* and *experience*, and to suppose, that these species of argumentation are entirely different from each other. The former are taken for the mere result of our intellectual faculties, which,

by considering a priori the nature of things, and examining the effects, that must follow from their operation, establish particular principles of science and philosophy. The latter are supposed to be derived entirely from sense and observation, by which we learn what has actually resulted from the operation of particular objects, and are thence able to infer, what will, for the future, result from them. Thus, for instance, the limitations and restraints of civil government, and a legal constitution, may be defended, either from *reason*, which reflecting on the great frailty and corruption of human nature, teaches, that no man can safely be trusted with unlimited authority; or from *experience* and history, which inform us of the enormous abuses, that ambition, in every age and country, has been found to make of so imprudent a confidence.

The same distinction between reason and experience is maintained in all our deliberations concerning the conduct of life; while the experienced statesman, general, physician, or merchant is trusted and followed; and the unpractised novice, with whatever natural talents endowed, neglected and despised. Though it be allowed, that reason may form very plausible conjectures with regard to the consequences of such a particular conduct in such particular circumstances; it is still supposed imperfect, without the assistance of experience, which is alone able to give stability and certainty to the maxims, derived from study and reflection.

But notwithstanding that this distinction be thus universally received, both in the active and speculative scenes of life, I shall not scruple to pronounce, that it is, at bottom, erroneous, at least, superficial.

If we examine those arguments, which, in any of the sciences above mentioned, are supposed to be the mere effects of reasoning and reflection, they will be found to terminate, at last, in some general principle or conclusion, for which we can assign no reason but observation and experience. The only difference between them and those maxims, which are vulgarly esteemed the result of pure experience, is, that the former cannot be established without some process of thought, and some reflection on what we have observed, in order to distinguish its circumstances, and trace its consequences: Whereas in the latter, the experienced event is exactly and fully familiar to that which we infer as the result of any particular situation. The history of a TIBERIUS or a NERO makes us dread a like tyranny, were our monarchs freed from the restraints of laws and senates: But the observation of any fraud or cruelty in private life is sufficient, with the aid of a little thought, to give us the same apprehension; while it serves as an instance of the general corruption of human nature, and shows us the danger which we must incur by reposing an entire confidence in mankind. In both cases, it is experience which is ultimately the foundation of our inference and conclusion.

There is no man so young and unexperienced, as not to have formed, from observation, many general and just maxims concerning human affairs and the conduct of life; but it must be confessed, that, when a man comes to put these in practice, he will be extremely liable to error, till time and farther experience both enlarge these maxims, and teach him their proper use and application. In every situation or incident, there are many particular and seemingly minute circumstances, which the man of greatest talent is, at first, apt to overlook, though on them the justness of his conclusions, and consequently the prudence of his conduct, entirely depend. Not to mention, that, to a young beginner, the general observations and maxims occur not always on the proper occasions, nor can be immediately applied with due calmness and distinction. The truth is, an unexperienced reasoner could be no reasoner at all, were he absolutely unexperienced; and when we assign that character to any one, we mean it only in a comparative sense, and suppose him possessed of experience, in a smaller and more imperfect degree.

8. "Whether it is a natural instance or a mere illusion, I can't say; but one's emotions are more strongly aroused by seeing the places that tradition records to have been the favorite resort of men of note in former days, than by hearing about their deeds or reading their writings. My own feelings at the present moment are a case in point. I am reminded of Plato, the first philosopher, so we are told, that made a practice of holding discussions in this place; and indeed, the garden close at hand, yonder, not only recalls his memory but seems to bring the actual man before my eyes. This was the haunt of Speusippus, of Xenocrates, and of Xenocrates' pupil Polemo, who used to sit on the very seat we see over there. For my own part, even the sight of our senate-house at home (I mean the Curia Hostilia, not the present new building, which looks to my eyes smaller since its enlargement) used to call up to me thoughts of Scipio, Cato, Laelius, and chief of all, my grandfather;

such powers of suggestion do places possess. No wonder the scientific training of the memory is based upon locality." Cicero, *De Finibus*, Book V, trans. H. Rackham (Cambridge: Harvard University Press, 1914), pp. 291–92.

9. Mr. Locke divides all arguments into demonstrative and probable. In this view, we must say, that it is only probable all men must die, or that the sun will rise to-morrow. But to conform our language more to common use, we ought to divide arguments into *demonstrations*, *proofs*, and *probabilities*. By proofs meaning such arguments from experience as leave no room for doubt or opposition.

10. Section II.

11. Mr. Locke, in his chapter of power, says that, finding from experience, that there are several new productions in nature, and concluding that there must somewhere be a power capable of producing them, we arrive at last by this reasoning at the idea of power. But no reasoning can ever give us a new, original, simple idea; as this philosopher himself confesses. This, therefore, can never be the origin of that idea.

12. It may be pretended, that the resistance which we meet with in bodies, obliging us frequently to exert our force, and call up all our power, this gives us the idea of force and power. It is this *nisus*, or strong endeavour, of which we are conscious, that is the original impression from which this idea is copied. But, first, we attribute powers to a vast number of objects, where we never can suppose this resistance or exertion of force to take place; to the Supreme Being, who never meets with any resistance; to the mind in its command over its ideas and limbs, in common thinking and motion, where the effect follows immediately upon the will, without any exertion or summoning up of force; to inanimate matter, which is not capable of this sentiment. *Secondly*, This sentiment of an endeavour to overcome resistance has no known connexion with any event: What follows it, we know by experience; but could not know it a priori. It must, however, be confessed, that the animal *nisus*, which we experience, though it can afford no accurate precise idea of power, enters very much into that vulgar, inaccurate idea, which is formed of it.

13. Θεὸς ἀπὸ μηχανῆς. [In Latin, "*Deus ex machina*." Literally, god from a machine. A thing or person that appears suddenly and unexpectedly in a play to provide a contrived solution to a difficult situation.]

14. I need not examine at length the *vis inertiae* which is so much talked of in the new philosophy, and which is ascribed to matter. We find by experience, that a body at rest or in motion continues for ever in its present state, till put from it by some new cause; and that a body impelled takes as much motion from the impelling body as it acquires itself. These are facts. When we call this a *vis inertiae*, we only mark these facts, without pretending to have any idea of the inert power; in the same manner as, when we talk of gravity, we mean certain effects, without comprehending that active power. It was never the meaning of Sir ISAAC NEWTON to rob second causes of all force or energy; though some of his followers have endeavoured to establish that theory upon his authority. On the contrary, that great philosopher had recourse to an etherial active fluid to explain his universal attraction; though he was so cautious and modest as to allow, that it was a mere hypothesis, not to be insisted on, without more experiments. I must confess, that there is something in the fate of opinions a little extraordinary. DES CARTES insinuated that doctrine of the universal and sole efficacy of the Deity, without insisting on it. MALEBRANCHE and other CARTESIANS made it the foundation of all their philosophy. It had, however, no authority in England. LOCKE, CLARKE, and CUDWORTH, never so much as take notice of it, but suppose all along, that matter has a real, though subordinate and derived power. By what means has it become so prevalent among our modern metaphysicians?

15. According to these explications and definitions, the idea of *power* is relative as much as that of *cause*; and both have a reference to an effect, or some other event constantly conjoined with the former. When we consider the *unknown* circumstance of an object, by which the degree or quantity of its effect is fixed and determined, we call that its power: And accordingly, it is allowed by all philosophers, that the effect is the measure of the power. But if they had any idea of power, as it is in itself, why could not they Measure it in itself? The dispute whether the force of a body in motion be as its velocity, or the square of its velocity; this dispute, I say, need not be decided by comparing its effects in equal or unequal times; but by a direct mensuration and comparison.

As to the frequency of use of the words, Force, Power, Energy, etc., which every where occur in common conversation, as well as in philosophy;

that is no proof, that we are acquainted, in any instance, with the connecting principle between cause and effect, or can account ultimately for the production of one thing to another. These words, as commonly used, have very loose meanings annexed to them; and their ideas are very uncertain and confused. No animal can put external bodies in motion without the sentiment of a *nisus* or endeavour; and every animal has a sentiment or feeling from the stroke or blow of an external object, that is in motion. These sensations, which are merely animal, and from which we can a priori draw no inference, we are apt to transfer to inanimate objects, and to suppose, that they have some such feelings, whenever they transfer or receive motion. With regard to energies, which are exerted, without our annexing to them any idea of communicated motion, we consider only the constant experienced conjunction of the events; and as we *feel* a customary connexion between the ideas, we transfer that feeling to the objects; as nothing is more usual than to apply to external bodies every internal sensation, which they occasion.

KEY TERMS

Metaphysical	A priori
Relations of ideas	Customary conjunction
Matters of fact	Final causes
Cause and effect	Skepticism

STUDY QUESTIONS

1. Do you agree with Hume that "the most lively thought is still inferior to the dullest sensation"?
2. How does Hume argue that "all our ideas . . . are copies of our impressions"?
3. Why does Hume think that "custom . . . is the great guide of human life"? Specifically, how does Hume employ the notion of custom when discussing why we expect the future to resemble the past?
4. Do you agree with Hume when he says that we are never able to observe the connection that ties cause with effect? Why or why not?
5. What is Hume's distinction between two events being *conjoined* and two events being *connected*? What work is this distinction meant to do?

The Problem of Induction

W. C. SALMON

Wesley C. Salmon (1925–2001) was a leading philosopher of science and a metaphysician. He was a professor of philosophy at the University of Pittsburgh, where he worked on the problems of causation and scientific explanation. His best-known works are *Scientific Explanation and the Causal Structure of the World* (1984) and *Four Decades of Scientific Explanation* (1990).

. .

I. The Problem of Induction

We all believe that we have knowledge of facts extending far beyond those we directly perceive. The

From *The Foundations of Scientific Inference*, by Wesley C. Salmon, pp. 5–27, 40–43, 48–56, 132–36. Copyright © 1967 by University of Pittsburgh Press. Reprinted by permission of the University of Pittsburgh Press.

scope of our senses is severely limited in space and time; our immediate perceptual knowledge does not reach to events that happened before we were born to events that are happening now in certain other places or to any future events. We believe, nevertheless, that we have some kind of indirect knowledge of such facts. We know that a glacier once covered a large part of North America, that the sun continues to exist at night, and that the tides will rise and fall tomorrow. Science and common sense have at least this one thing in common: Each embodies knowledge of matters of fact that are not open to our direct inspection. Indeed, science purports to establish general laws or theories that apply to all parts of space and time without restriction. A "science" that consisted of no more than a mere summary of the results of direct observation would not deserve the name.

Hume's profound critique of **induction** begins with a simple and apparently innocent question: How do we acquire knowledge of the unobserved?[1] This question, as posed, may seem to call for an empirical answer. We observe that human beings utilize what may be roughly characterized as inductive or scientific methods of extending knowledge from the observed to the unobserved. The sciences, in fact, embody the most powerful and highly developed methods known, and we may make an empirical investigation of scientific methods much as we might for any other sort of human behavior. We may consider the historical development of science. We may study the psychological, sociological, and political factors relevant to the pursuit of science. We may try to give an exact characterization of the behavior of scientists. In doing all these things, however, important and interesting as they are, we will have ignored the *philosophical* aspect of the problem Hume raised. Putting the matter very simply, these empirical investigations may enable us to describe the ways in which people arrive at *beliefs* about unobserved facts, but they leave open the question of whether beliefs arrived at in this way actually constitute *knowledge*. It is one thing to describe how people go about seeking to extend their knowledge; it is quite another to claim that the methods employed actually do yield knowledge.

One of the basic differences between knowledge and belief is that knowledge must be founded upon evidence—i.e., it must be belief founded upon some rational justification. To say that certain methods yield knowledge of the unobserved is to make a cognitive claim for them. Hume called into question the justification of such cognitive claims. The answer cannot be found entirely within an empirical study of human behavior, for a *logical* problem has been raised. It is the problem of understanding the logical relationship between evidence and conclusion in logically correct inferences. It is the problem of determining

whether the inferences by which we attempt to make the transition from knowledge of the observed to knowledge of the unobserved are logically correct. The fact that people do or do not use a certain type of inference is irrelevant to its justifiability. Whether people have confidence in the correctness of a certain type of inference has nothing to do with whether such confidence is justified. If we should adopt a logically incorrect method for inferring one fact from others, these facts would not actually constitute evidence for the conclusion we have drawn. The problem of induction is the problem of explicating the very concept of *inductive evidence*.

There is another possibly misleading feature of the question as I have formulated it. When we ask how we can *acquire* knowledge of the unobserved, it sounds very much as if we are asking for a method for the *discovery* of new knowledge. This is, of course, a vital problem, but it is not the fundamental problem Hume raised. Whether there is or can be any sort of inductive logic of discovery is a controversial question I shall discuss in detail in a later section.[2] Leaving this question aside for now, there remains the problem of *justification* of conclusions concerning unobserved matters of fact. Given some conclusion, however arrived at, regarding unobserved facts, and given some alleged evidence to support that conclusion, the question remains whether that conclusion is, indeed, supported by the evidence offered in support of it.

Consider a simple and highly artificial situation. Suppose a number of balls have been drawn from an urn, and that all of the black ones that have been drawn are licorice-flavored. I am not now concerned with such psychological questions as what makes the observer note the color of these balls, what leads him to taste the black ones, what makes him take note of the fact that licorice flavor is associated with black color in his sample, or what makes him suppose that the black balls not yet drawn will also be licorice-flavored. The problem—Hume's basic *philosophical* problem—is this: Given that all of the observed black balls have been licorice-flavored, and given that somehow the conclusion has been entertained that the unobserved black balls in the urn are also licorice-flavored, do the observed facts constitute sound *evidence* for that conclusion? Would we be *justified* in accepting that conclusion on the basis of the facts alleged to be evidence for it?

As a first answer to this question we may point out that the inference does conform to an accepted inductive principle, a principle saying roughly that observed instances conforming to a generalization constitute evidence for it. It is, however, a very small step to the next question: What grounds have we for accepting this or any other inductive principle? Is there any reason or justification for placing confidence in the conclusions of inferences of this type? Given that the premises of this inference are true, and given that the inference conforms to a certain rule, can we provide any rational justification for accepting its conclusion rather than, for instance, the conclusion that black balls yet to be drawn will taste like quinine?

It is well known that Hume's answer to this problem was essentially skeptical. It was his great merit to have shown that a justification of induction, if possible at all, is by no means easy to provide. In order to appreciate the force of his argument it is first necessary to clarify some terminological points. This is particularly important because the word *induction* has been used in a wide variety of ways.

For purposes of systematic discussion one distinction is fundamental, namely, the distinction between **demonstrative** and **nondemonstrative inference**. A *demonstrative* inference is one whose premises necessitate its conclusion; the conclusion cannot be false if the premises are true. All valid deductions are demonstrative inferences. A *nondemonstrative* inference is simply one that fails to be demonstrative. Its conclusion is not necessitated by its premises; the conclusion could be false even if the premises are true. A demonstrative inference is **necessarily truth-preserving**; a nondemonstrative inference is not.

The category of nondemonstrative inferences, as I have characterized it, contains, among other things perhaps, all kinds of fallacious inferences. If, however, there is any kind of inference whose premises, although not necessitating the conclusion, do lend it weight, support it, or make it probable, then such inferences possess a certain kind of logical rectitude. It is not deductive validity, but it is important anyway. Inferences possessing it are *correct inductive inferences*.

Since demonstrative inferences have been characterized in terms of their basic property of necessary truth preservation, it is natural to ask how they achieve this very desirable trait. For a large group of demonstrative inferences, including those discussed under "valid deduction" in most logic texts, the answer is rather easy. Inferences of this type purchase necessary truth preservation by sacrificing any extension of content. The conclusion of such an inference says no more than do the premises—often less.[3] The conclusion cannot be false if the premises are true *because* the conclusion says nothing that was not already stated in the premises. The conclusion is a mere reformulation of all or part of the content of the premises. In some cases the reformulation is unanticipated and therefore psychologically surprising, but the conclusion cannot augment the content of the premises. Such inferences are **nonampliative**; an ampliative inference, then, has a conclusion with content not present either explicitly or implicitly in the premises.

While it is easy to understand why nonampliative inferences are necessarily truth-preserving, the further question arises whether there are any necessarily truth-preserving inferences that are also ampliative. Is there any type of inference whose conclusion must, of necessity, be true if the premises are true, but whose conclusion says something not stated by the premises? Hume believed that the answer is negative and so do I, but it is not easy to produce an adequate defense of this answer. Let us see, however, what an affirmative answer would amount to.

Suppose there were an ampliative inference that is also necessarily truth-preserving. Consider the implication from its premises, $P_1, \ldots, P_k$, to its conclusion C. If the inference were an ordinary nonampliative deduction, this implication would be **analytic** and empty; but since the argument is supposed to be ampliative, the implication must be **synthetic**. At the same time, because the argument is supposed to be necessarily truth-preserving, this implication must be not only true but necessarily true. Thus, to maintain that there are inferences that are both ampliative and necessarily truth-preserving is tantamount to asserting that there are synthetic **a priori** truths.[4] This may be seen in another way. Any ampliative inference can be made into a nonampliative one by adding a premise. In particular, if we add to the foregoing ampliative inference the synthetic a priori premise, "If P_1 and P_2 and . . . and P_k, then C," the resulting inference will be an ordinary valid nonampliative deduction. Consider our example once more; this time let us set it out more formally:

1. Some black balls from this urn have been observed.
   All observed black balls from this urn are licorice-flavored.

   All black balls in this urn are licorice-flavored.

This argument is clearly ampliative, for the premise makes a statement about observed balls only, while the conclusion makes a statement about the unobserved as well as the observed balls. It appears to be nondemonstrative as well, for it seems perfectly possible for the conclusion to be false even if the premises are true. We see no reason why someone might not have dropped a black marble in the urn which, when it is drawn, will be found to be tasteless. We could, however, rule out this sort of possibility by adding another premise:

2. Some black balls from this urn have been observed.
   All observed black balls in this urn are licorice-flavored.
   Any two balls in this urn that have the same color also have the same flavor.

   All black balls in this urn are licorice-flavored.

The additional premise has transformed the former nondemonstrative inference into a demonstrative inference, but we must also admit that we have transformed it into a nonampliative inference. If, however, the third premise of 2 were a synthetic a priori truth, the original inference, although ampliative, would have been necessarily truth-preserving and, hence, demonstrative. If the premise that transformed inference 1 into inference 2 were necessarily true, then it would be impossible for the conclusion of inference 1 to be false if the premises were true, for that would contradict the third premise of inference 2.

Hardly anyone would be tempted to say that the statement, "Any two balls in this urn that have the same color also have the same flavor," expresses a synthetic a priori truth. Other propositions have, however, been taken to be synthetic a priori. Hume and

many of his successors noticed that typical inductive inferences, such as our example concerning licorice-flavored black balls, would seem perfectly sound if we could have recourse to some sort of **principle of uniformity of nature**. If we could only prove that the course of nature is uniform, that the future will be like the past, or that uniformities that have existed thus far will continue to hold in the future, then we would seem to be justified in generalizing from past cases to future cases—from the observed to the unobserved. Indeed, Hume suggests that we presuppose in our inductive reasoning a principle from which the third premise of 2 would follow as a special case: "We always presume, when we see like sensible qualities, that they have like secret powers, and expect that effects, similar to those which we have experienced, will follow from them."[5] Again, "From causes which appear *similar* we expect similar effects. This is the sum of all our experimental conclusions."[6]

Hume's searching examination of the principle of uniformity of nature revealed no ground on which it could be taken as a synthetic a priori principle. For all we can know a priori, Hume argued, the course of nature might change, the future might be radically unlike the past, and regularities that have obtained in respect to observed events might prove completely inapplicable to unobserved cases. We have found by experience, of course, that nature has exhibited a high degree of uniformity and regularity so far, and we infer inductively that this will continue, but to use an inductively inferred generalization as a justification for induction, as Hume emphasized, would be flagrantly circular. He concluded, in fact, that there are no synthetic a priori principles in virtue of which we could have demonstrative inferences that are ampliative. Hume recognized two kinds of reasoning: reasoning concerning **relations of ideas** and reasoning concerning **matters of fact** and existence. The former is demonstrative but nonampliative while the latter is ampliative but not necessarily truth-preserving.

If we agree that there are no synthetic a priori truths, then we must identify necessarily truth-preserving inference with nonampliative inference. All ampliative inference is nondemonstrative. This leads to an exhaustive trichotomy of inferences: valid deductive inference, correct inductive inference, and assorted fallacies. The first question is, however, whether the second category is empty or whether there are such things as correct inductive inferences. This is Hume's problem of induction. Can we show that any particular type of ampliative inference can be justified in any way? If so, it will qualify as correct induction.

Consider, then, any ampliative inference whatever. The example of the licorice-flavored black balls illustrates the point. We cannot show *deductively* that this inference will have a true conclusion given true premises. If we could, we would have proved that the conclusion must be true if the premises are. That would make it necessarily truth-preserving, hence, demonstrative. This, in turn, would mean that it was nonampliative, contrary to our hypothesis. Thus, if an ampliative inference could be justified deductively it would not be ampliative. It follows that ampliative inference cannot be justified deductively.

At the same time, we cannot justify any sort of ampliative inference *inductively*. To do so would require the use of some sort of nondemonstrative inference. But the question at issue is the justification of nondemonstrative inference, so the procedure would be question begging. Before we can properly employ a nondemonstrative inference in a justifying argument, we must already have justified that nondemonstrative inference.

Hume's position can be summarized succinctly: We cannot justify any kind of ampliative inference. If it could be justified deductively it would not be ampliative. It cannot be justified nondemonstratively because that would be viciously circular. It seems, then, that there is no way in which we can extend our knowledge to the unobserved. We have, to be sure, many beliefs about the unobserved, and in some of them we place great confidence. Nevertheless, they are without rational justification of any kind!

This is a harsh conclusion, yet it seems to be supported by impeccable arguments. It might be called "Hume's paradox," for the conclusion, although ingeniously argued, is utterly repugnant to common sense and our deepest convictions. We *know* ("in our hearts") that we have knowledge of unobserved fact. The challenge is to show how this is possible.

II. Attempted Solutions

It hardly needs remarking that philosophers have attempted to meet Hume's intriguing challenge in a wide variety of ways. There have been direct attacks upon some of Hume's arguments. Attempts to provide inductive arguments to support induction and attempts to supply a synthetic a priori principle of uniformity of nature belong in this category. Some authors have claimed that the whole problem arises out of linguistic confusion, and that careful analysis shows it to be a pseudoproblem. Some have even denied that inductive inference is needed, either in science or in everyday affairs. In this section I shall survey what seem to me to be the most important efforts to deal with the problem.

1. Inductive Justification. If Hume's arguments had never been propounded and we were asked why we accept the methods of science, the most natural answer would be, I think, that these methods have proved themselves by their results. We can point to astonishing technological advances, to vastly increased comprehension, and to impressive predictions. Science has provided us with foresight, control, and understanding. No other method can claim a comparable record of successful accomplishment. If methods are to be judged by their fruits, there is no doubt that the scientific method will come out on top.

Unfortunately, Hume examined this argument and showed that it is viciously circular. It is an example of an attempt to justify inductive methods inductively. From the premise that science has had considerable predictive success in the past, we conclude that it will continue to have substantial predictive success in the future. Observed cases of the application of scientific method have yielded successful prediction; therefore, as yet unobserved cases of the application of scientific method will yield successful predictions. This argument has the same structure as our black-balls-in-the-urn example; it is precisely the sort of ampliative inference from the observed to the unobserved whose justifiability is in question.

Consider the parallel case for a radically different sort of method. A crystal gazer claims that his method is the appropriate method for making predictions. When we question his claim he says, "Wait a moment; I will find out whether the method of crystal gazing is the best method for making predictions." He looks into his crystal ball and announces that future cases of crystal gazing will yield predictive success. If we should protest that his method has not been especially successful in the past, he might well make certain remarks about parity of reasoning. "Since you have used your method to justify your method, why shouldn't I use my method to justify my method? If you insist upon judging my method by using your method, why shouldn't I use my method to evaluate your method? By the way, I note by gazing into my crystal ball that the scientific method is now in for a very bad run of luck."

The trouble with circular arguments is obvious: with an appropriate circular argument you can prove anything. In recent years, nevertheless, there have been several notable attempts to show how inductive rules can be supported inductively. The authors of such attempts try to show, of course, that their arguments are not circular. Although they argue persuasively, it seems to me that they do not succeed in escaping circularity.

One of the most widely discussed attempts to show that self-supporting inductive inferences are possible without circularity is due to Max Black.[7] Black correctly observes that the traditional fallacy of circular argument (**petitio principii**) involves assuming as a premise, often unwittingly, the conclusion that is to be proved. Thus, for example, a variety of "proofs" of Euclid's fifth postulate offered by mathematicians for about two millennia before the discovery of non-Euclidean geometry are circular in the standard fashion. They fail to show that the fifth postulate follows from the first four postulates alone; instead, they require in addition the assumption of a proposition equivalent to the proposition being demonstrated. The situation is quite different for self-supporting inductive arguments. The conclusion to be proved does not appear as one of the premises. Consider one of Black's examples:[8]

3. In most instances of the use of R_2 in arguments with true premises examined in a wide variety of conditions, R_2 has usually been successful.
   Hence (probably):

In the next instance to be encountered of the use of R_2 in an argument with true premises, R_2 will be successful.

To say that an argument with true premises is successful is merely to say that it has a true conclusion. The rule R_2 is

To argue from *Most instances of A's examined in a wide variety of conditions have been B to* (probably) *The next A to be encountered will be B.*

Inference 3 can be paraphrased suggestively, although somewhat inaccurately, as:

4. R_2 has usually been successful in the past.
   Hence (probably):
   R_2 will be successful in the next instance.

Inference 3 is governed by R_2, that is, it conforms to the stipulation laid down by R_2. R_2 is *not* a premise, however, nor is any statement to the effect that all, some, or any future instances of R_2 will be successful. As Lewis Carroll showed decisively, there is a fundamental distinction between premises and rules of inference.[9] Any inference, inductive or deductive, must conform to some rule, but neither the rule nor any statement about the rule is to be incorporated into the inference as an additional premise. If such additional premises were required, inference would be impossible. Thus, inference 3 is not a standard *petitio principii.*

What, then, are the requirements for a self-supporting argument? At least three are immediately apparent: (1) The argument must have true premises. (2) The argument must conform to a certain rule. (3) The conclusion of that argument must say something about the success or reliability of that rule in unexamined instances of its application. Inference 3 has these characteristics.

It is not difficult to find examples of deductive inferences with the foregoing characteristics.

5. If snow is white, then *modus ponens* is valid.
   Snow is white.

   ───────────────────────────────

   Modus ponens is valid.

Inference 5 may seem innocuous enough, but the same cannot be said for the following inference:

6. If **affirming the consequent** is valid, then coal is black.
   Coal is black.

   _____

   Affirming the consequent is valid.

Like inference 5, inference 6 has true premises, it conforms to a certain rule, and its conclusion asserts the validity of that rule. Inference 5 did nothing to enhance our confidence in the validity of *modus ponens*, for we have far better grounds for believing it to be valid. Inference 6 does nothing to convince us that affirming the consequent is valid, for we know on other grounds that it is invalid. Arguments like 5 and 6 are, nevertheless, instructive. Both are circular in some sense, though neither assumes *as a premise* the conclusion it purports to establish. In deductive logic the situation is quite straightforward. A deductive inference establishes its conclusion if it has true premises and has a valid form. If either of these features is lacking the conclusion is not established by that argument. If the argument is valid but the premises are not true we need not accept the conclusion. If the premises are true but the argument is invalid we need not accept the conclusion. One way in which an argument can be circular is by adopting as a premise the very conclusion that is to be proved; this is the fallacy of *petitio principii* which I shall call "premise-circularity." Another way in which an argument can be circular is by exhibiting a form whose validity is asserted by the very conclusion that is to be proved; let us call this type of circularity "rule-circularity." Neither type of circular argument establishes its conclusion in any interesting fashion, for in each case the conclusiveness of the argument depends upon the assumption of the conclusion of that argument. Inferences 5 and 6 are not premise-circular; each is rule-circular. They are, nevertheless, completely question begging.

The situation in induction is somewhat more complicated, but basically the same.[10] Consider the following argument:

7. In most instances of the use of R_3 in arguments with true premises examined in a wide variety of conditions, R_3 has usually been *un*successful.

Hence (probably):
In the next instance to be encountered of the use of R_3 in an argument with true premises, R_3 will be successful.

The rule R_3 is

To argue from *Most instances of A's examined in a wide variety of conditions have been non-B to* (probably) *The next A to be encountered will be B.*

Inference 7 can be paraphrased as follows:

8. R_3 has usually been unsuccessful in the past.
   Hence (probably):
   R_3 will be successful in the next instance.

Notice that there is a perfect parallel between R_2, 3, 4 on the one hand and R_3, 7, 8 on the other. Since those instances in which R_2 would be successful are those in which R_3 would be unsuccessful, the premises of 3 and 4 describe the same state of affairs as do the premises of 7 and 8. Thus, the use of R_3 in the next instance seems to be supported in the same manner and to the same extent as the use of R_2 in the next instance. However, R_2 and R_3 conflict directly with each other. On the evidence that most Italians examined in a wide variety of conditions have been dark-eyed, R_2 allows us to infer that the next Italian to be encountered will be dark-eyed, while R_3 permits us to infer from the same evidence that he will have light-colored eyes. It appears then that we can construct self-supporting arguments for correct and incorrect inductive rules just as we can for valid and invalid deductive rules.

Black would reject self-supporting arguments for the fallacy of affirming the consequent and for a counterinductive rule like R_2, because we know on independent grounds that such rules are faulty. Affirming the consequent is known to be fallacious, and the counterinductive method can be shown to be self-defeating. An additional requirement for a self-supporting argument is that the rule thus supported be one we have no independent reason to reject. Nevertheless, the fact that we can construct self-supporting arguments for such rules should give us pause. What if we had never realized that affirming the consequent is fallacious? What if we had never noticed anything wrong with the counterinductive method? Would arguments like 6, 7, and 8 have to be considered cogent? What about the standard inductive method? Is it as incorrect as the counterinductive method, but for reasons most of us have not yet realized?

It sounds as if a self-supporting argument is applicable only to rules we already know to be correct; as a matter of fact, this is the view Black holds. He has argued in various places that induction is in no need of a general justification.[11] He holds that calling into question of all inductive methods simultaneously results in a hopelessly **skeptical** position. He is careful to state explicitly at the outset of his discussion of self-supporting inductive arguments that he is not dealing with the view "that *no* inductive argument ought to be regarded as correct until a philosophical justification of induction has been provided."[12] At the conclusion he acknowledges, moreover, that "anybody who thinks he has good grounds for condemning all inductive arguments will also condemn inductive arguments in support of inductive rules."[13] Black is careful to state explicitly that self-supporting inductive arguments provide no answer to the problem of justification of induction as raised by Hume. What good, then, are self-supporting inductive arguments?

In deductive logic, correctness is an all-or-nothing affair. Deductive inferences are either totally valid or totally invalid; there cannot be such a thing as degree of validity. In inductive logic the situation is quite different. Inductive correctness does admit of degrees; one inductive conclusion may be more strongly supported than another. In this situation it is possible, Black claims, to have an inductive rule we know to be correct to some degree, but whose status can be enhanced by self-supporting arguments. We might think a rather standard inductive rule akin to Black's R_2 is pretty good, but through inductive investigation of its application we might find that it is extremely good—much better than we originally thought. Moreover, the inductive inferences we use to draw that conclusion might be governed by precisely the sort of rule we are investigating. It is also possible, of course, to find by inductive investigation that the rule is not as good as we believed beforehand.

It is actually irrelevant to the present discussion to attempt to evaluate Black's view concerning the possibility of increasing the justification of inductive rules by self-supporting arguments. The important point is to emphasize, because of the possibility of constructing self-supporting arguments for counterinductive rules, that the attempt to provide inductive support of inductive rules cannot, without vicious circularity, be applied to the problem of justifying induction from scratch. If there is any way of providing the beginnings of a justification, or if we could show that some inductive rule stands in no need of justification in the first instance, then it would be suitable to return to Black's argument concerning the increase of support. I am not convinced, however, that Black has successfully shown that there is a satisfactory starting place.

I have treated the problem of inductive justification of induction at some length, partly because other authors have not been as cautious as Black in circumscribing the limits of inductive justification of induction.[14] More important, perhaps, is the fact that it is extremely difficult, psychologically speaking, to shake the view that past success of the inductive method constitutes a genuine justification of induction. Nevertheless, the basic fact remains: Hume showed that inductive justifications of induction are fallacious, and no one has since proved him wrong.

2. The Complexity of Scientific Inference. The idea of a philosopher discussing inductive inference in science is apt to arouse grotesque images in many minds. People are likely to imagine someone earnestly attempting to explain why it is reasonable to conclude that the sun will rise tomorrow morning because it always has done so in the past. There may have been a time when primitive man anticipated the dawn with assurance based only upon the fact that he had seen dawn follow the blackness of night as long as he could remember, but this primitive state of knowledge, if it ever existed, was unquestionably *pre*scientific. This kind of reasoning bears no resemblance to science; in fact, the crude induction exhibits a complete absence of scientific understanding. Our scientific reasons for believing that the sun will rise tomorrow are of an entirely different kind. We understand the functioning of the solar system in terms of the laws of physics. We predict particular astronomical occurrences by means of these laws in conjunction with a knowledge of particular initial conditions that prevail. Scientific laws and theories have the logical form of general statements, but they are seldom, if ever, simple generalizations from experience.

Consider Newton's gravitational theory: Any two bodies are mutually attracted by a force proportional to the product of their masses and inversely proportional to the square of the distance between their centers. Although general in form, this kind of statement is not established by generalization from instances. We do not go around saying, "Here are two bodies—the force between them is such and such; here are two more bodies—the force between them is such and such; etc." Scientific theories are taken quite literally as hypotheses. They are entertained in order that their consequences may be drawn and examined. Their acceptability is judged in terms of these consequences. The consequences are extremely diverse—the greater the variety the better. For Newtonian theory, we look to such consequences as the behavior of Mars, the tides, falling bodies, the pendulum, and the torsion balance. These consequences have no apparent unity among themselves; they do not constitute a basis for inductive generalization. They achieve a kind of unity only by virtue of the fact that they are consequences of a single physical theory.

The type of inference I have been characterizing is very familiar; it is known as the **hypothetico-deductive method.**[15] It stands in sharp contrast to **induction by enumeration**, which consists in simple inductive generalization from instances. Schematically, the hypothetic-deductive method works as follows: From a general hypothesis and particular statements of initial conditions, a particular predictive statement is deduced. The statements of initial conditions, at least for the time, are accepted as true; the hypothesis is the statement whose truth is at issue. By observation we determine whether the predictive statement turned out to be true. If the predictive consequence is false, the hypothesis is disconfirmed. If observation reveals that the predictive statement is true, we say that the hypothesis is

confirmed to some extent. A hypothesis is not, of course, conclusively proved by any one or more positively confirming instances, but it may become highly confirmed. A hypothesis that is sufficiently confirmed is accepted, at least tentatively.

It seems undeniable that science uses a type of inference at least loosely akin to the hypothetico-deductive method.[16] This has led some people to conclude that the logic of science is thoroughly deductive in character. According to this view, the only nondeductive aspect of the situation consists in thinking up hypotheses, but this is not a matter of logic and therefore requires no justification. It is a matter of psychological ingenuity of discovery. Once the hypothesis has been discovered, by some entirely nonlogical process, it remains only to *deduce* consequences and check them against observation.

It is, of course, a fallacy to conclude that the premises of an argument must be true if its conclusion is true. This fact seems to be the basis for the quip that a logic text is a book that consists of two parts; in the first part (on deduction) the fallacies are explained, in the second part (on induction) they are committed. The whole trouble with saying that the hypothetico-deductive method renders the logic of science entirely deductive is that we are attempting to establish a *premise* of the deduction, not the conclusion. Deduction is an indispensible part of the logic of the hypothetic-deductive method, but it is not the only part. There is a fundamental and important sense in which the hypothesis must be regarded as a conclusion instead of a premise. Hypotheses (later perhaps called "theories" or "laws") are among the *results* of scientific investigation; science aims at establishing general statements about the world. Scientific prediction and explanation require such generalizations. While we are concerned with the status of the general hypothesis—whether we should accept it or reject it—the hypothesis must be treated as a conclusion to be supported by evidence, not as a premise lending support to other conclusions. The inference *from* observational evidence *to* hypothesis is surely not deductive. If this point is not already obvious it becomes clear the moment we recall that for any given body of observational data there is, in general, more than one hypothesis compatible with it. These alternative hypotheses differ in factual content and are incompatible with each other. Therefore, they cannot be deductive consequences of any consistent body of observational evidence.

We must grant, then, that science embodies a type of inference resembling the hypothetico-deductive method and fundamentally different from induction by enumeration. Hume, on the other hand, has sometimes been charged with a conception of science according to which the only kind of reasoning is induction by enumeration. His typical examples are cases of simple generalization of observed regularities, something like our example of the licorice-flavored black balls. In the past, water has quenched thirst; in the future, it will as well. In the past, fires have been hot; in the future, they will be hot. In the past, bread has nourished; in the future, it will do so likewise. It might be said that Hume, in failing to see the essential role of the hypothetico-deductive method, was unable to appreciate the complexity of the theoretical science of his own time, to say nothing of subsequent developments. This is typical, some might say, of the misunderstandings engendered by philosophers who undertake to discuss the logic of science without being thoroughly conversant with mathematics and natural science.

This charge against Hume (and other philosophers of induction) is ill-founded. It was part of Hume's genius to have recognized that the arguments he applied to simple enumerative induction apply equally to any kind of ampliative or nondemonstrative inference whatever. Consider the most complex kind of scientific reasoning—the most elaborate example of hypothetico-deductive inference you can imagine. Regardless of subtle features or complications, it is ampliative overall. The conclusion is a statement whose content exceeds the observational evidence upon which it is based. A scientific theory that merely summarized what had already been observed would not deserve to be called a theory. If scientific inference were not ampliative, science would be useless for prediction, postdiction, and explanation. The highly general results that are the pride of theoretical science would be impossible if scientific inference were not ampliative.

In presenting Hume's argument, I was careful to set it up so that it would apply to any kind of ampliative or nondemonstrative inference, no matter how simple or how complex. Furthermore, the distinction between valid deduction and nondemonstrative inference is completely exhaustive. Take any inference whatsoever. It must be deductive or nondemonstrative. Suppose it is nondemonstrative. If we could justify it deductively it would cease to be nondemonstrative. To justify it nondemonstratively would presuppose an already justified type of nondemonstrative inference, which is precisely the problem at issue. Hume's argument does *not* break down when we consider forms more complex than simple enumeration. Although the word "induction" is sometimes used as a synonym for "induction by simple enumeration," I am not using it in that way. Any type of logically correct ampliative inference is induction; the problem of induction is to show that some particular form of ampliative inference is justifiable. It is in this sense that we are concerned with the problem of the justification of inductive inference.

A further misunderstanding is often involved in this type of criticism of Hume. There is a strong inclination to suppose that induction is regarded as the method by which scientific results are discovered.[17] Hume and other philosophers of induction are charged with the view that science has developed historically through patient collection of facts and generalization from them. I know of no philosopher—not even Francis Bacon!—who has held this view, although it is frequently attacked in the contemporary literature.[18] The term "generalization" has an unfortunate ambiguity which fosters the confusion. In one meaning, "generalization" refers to an inferential process in which one makes a sort of mental transition from particulars to a universal proposition; in this sense, generalization is an act of generalizing—a process that yields general results. In another meaning, "generalization" simply refers to a universal type or proposition, without any reference to its source or how it was thought of. It is entirely possible for science to contain many generalizations (in the latter sense) without embodying any generalizations (in the former sense). As I said explicitly at the outset, the problem of induction I am discussing is a problem concerning justification, not discovery. The thesis I am defending—that science does embody induction in a logically indispensable fashion—has nothing to do with the history of science or the psychology of particular scientists. It is simply the claim that scientific inference is ampliative.

3. Deductivism. One of the most interesting and controversial contemporary attempts to provide an account of the logic of science is Karl Popper's **deductivism**.[19] In the preceding section I discussed the view that the presence of the hypothetico-deductive method in the logic of science makes it possible to dispense with induction in science and, thereby, to avoid the problem of induction. I argued that the hypothetico-deductive method, since it is ampliative and nondemonstrative, is not strictly deductive; it is, in fact, inductive in the relevant sense. As long as the hypothetico-deductive method is regarded as a method for supporting scientific hypotheses, it cannot succeed in making science thoroughly deductive. Popper realizes this, so in arguing that deduction is the sole mode of inference in science he rejects the hypothetico-deductive method as a means for confirming scientific hypotheses. He asserts that induction plays no role whatever in science; indeed, he maintains that there is no such thing as correct inductive inference. Inductive logic is, according to Popper, a complete delusion. He admits the psychological fact that people (including himself) have faith in the uniformity of nature, but he holds, with Hume, that this can be no more than a matter of psychological fact. He holds, with Hume, that there can be no rational justification of induction, and he thinks Hume proved this point conclusively.

Popper's fundamental thesis is that **falsifiability** is the mark by which statements of empirical science are distinguished from metaphysical statements and from tautologies. The choice of falsifiability over verifiability as the criterion of demarcation is motivated by a long familiar fact—namely, it is possible to falsify a universal generalization by means of one negative instance, while it is impossible to verify a universal generalization by any limited number of positive instances. This, incidentally, is the meaning of the old saw which is so often made into complete nonsense: "The exception proves the rule." In this context, a rule is a universal generalization, and the term "to prove" means archaically "to test." The

exception (i.e., the negative instance) proves (i.e., tests) the rule (i.e., the universal generalization), not by showing it to be true, but by showing it to be false. There is no kind of positive instance to prove (i.e., test) the rule, for positive instances are completely indecisive. Scientific hypotheses, as already noted, are general in form, so they are amenable to falsification but not verification.

Popper thus holds that falsifiability is the hallmark of empirical science. The aim of empirical science is to set forth theories to stand the test of every possible serious attempt at falsification. Scientific theories are hypotheses or conjectures; they are general statements designed to explain the world and make it intelligible, but they are never to be regarded as final truths. Their status is always that of tentative conjecture, and they must continually face the severest possible criticism. The function of the theoretician is to propose scientific conjectures; the function of the experimentalist is to devise every possible way of falsifying these theoretical hypotheses. The attempt to confirm hypotheses is no part of the aim of science.[20]

General hypotheses by themselves do not entail any predictions of particular events, but they do in conjunction with statements of initial conditions. The laws of planetary motion in conjunction with statements about the relative positions and velocities of the earth, sun, moon, and planets enable us to predict a solar eclipse. The mode of inference is deduction. We have a high degree of intersubjective agreement concerning the initial conditions, and we likewise can obtain intersubjective agreement as to whether the sun's disc was obscured at the predicted time and place. If the predicted fact fails to occur, the theory has suffered falsification. Again, the mode of inference is deduction. If the theory were true, then, given the truth of the statements of initial conditions, the prediction would have to be true. The prediction, as it happens, is false; therefore, the theory is false. This is the familiar principle of ***modus tollens***; it is, according to Popper, the only kind of inference available for the acceptance or rejection of hypotheses, and it is clearly suitable for rejection only.

Hypothetico-deductive theorists maintain that we have a confirming instance for the theory if the eclipse occurs as predicted. Confirming instances, they claim, tend to enhance the probability of the hypothesis or give it inductive support. With enough confirming instances of appropriate kinds, the probability of the hypothesis becomes great enough to warrant accepting it as true—not, of course, with finality and certainty, but provisionally. With sufficient inductive support of this kind we are justified in regarding it as well established. Popper, however, rejects the positive account, involving as it does the notion of inductive support. If a hypothesis is tested and the result is negative, we can reject it. If the test is positive, all we can say is that we have failed to falsify it. We cannot say that it has been confirmed or that it is, because of the positive test result, more probable. Popper does admit a notion of **corroboration** of hypotheses, but that is quite distinct from confirmation. We shall come to corroboration presently. For the moment, all we have are successful or unsuccessful attempts at falsification; all we can say about our hypotheses is that they are falsified or unfalsified. This is as far as inference takes us; according to Popper, this is the limit of logic. Popper therefore rejects the hypothetico-deductive method as it is usually characterized and accepts only the completely deductive *modus tollens*.

Popper—quite correctly I believe—denies that there are absolutely basic and incorrigible protocol statements that provide the empirical foundation for all of science. He does believe that there are relatively basic observation statements about macroscopic physical occurrences concerning which we have a high degree of intersubjective agreement. Normally, we can accept as unproblematic such statements as, "There is a wooden table in this room," "The pointer on this meter stands between 325 and 350," and "The rope just broke and the weight fell to the floor." Relatively basic statements of this kind provide the observation base for empirical science. This is the stuff of which empirical tests of scientific theories are made.

Although Popper's basic statements must in the last analysis be considered hypotheses, falsifiable and subject to test like other scientific hypotheses, it is obvious that the kinds of hypotheses that constitute theoretical science are far more general than the basic statements. But now we must face the grim fact that valid deductive inference, although necessarily truth-preserving, is nonampliative.[21] It is impossible

to deduce from accepted basic statements any conclusion whose content exceeds that of the basic statements themselves. Observation statements and deductive inference yield nothing that was not stated by the observation statements themselves. If science consists solely of observation statements and deductive inferences, then talk about theories, their falsifiability, and their tests is empty. The content of science is coextensive with the content of the statements used to describe what we directly observe. There are no general theories, there is no predictive content, there are no inferences to the remote past. Science is barren.

Consider a few simple time-honored examples. Suppose that the statement "All ravens are black" has been entertained critically and subjected to every attempt at falsification we can think of. Suppose it has survived all attempts at falsification. What is the scientific content of all this? We can say that "All ravens are black" has not been falsified, which is equivalent to saying that we have not observed a nonblack raven. This statement is even poorer in content than a simple recital of our color observations of ravens. To say that the hypothesis has not been falsified is to say less than is given in a list of our relevant observation statements. Or, consider the generalization, "All swans are white." What have we said when we say that this hypothesis has been falsified? We have said only that a nonwhite swan has been found. Again, the information conveyed by this remark is less than we would get from a simple account of our observations of swans.

Popper has never claimed that falsification by itself can establish scientific hypotheses. When one particular hypothesis has been falsified, many alternative hypotheses remain unfalsified. Likewise, there is nothing unique about a hypothesis that survives without being falsified. Many other unfalsified hypotheses remain to explain the same facts. Popper readily admits all of this. If science is to amount to more than a mere collection of our observations and various reformulations thereof, it must embody some other methods besides observation and deduction. Popper supplies that additional factor: *corroboration*.[22]

When a hypothesis has been falsified, it is discarded and replaced by another hypothesis which has not yet experienced falsification. Not all unfalsified hypotheses are on a par. There are princi-ples of selection among unfalsified hypotheses. Again, falsifiability is the key. Hypotheses differ from one another with respect to the ease with which they can be falsified, and we can often compare them with respect to degree of falsifiability. Popper directs us to seek hypotheses that are as highly falsifiable as possible. Science, he says, is interested in bold conjec-tures. These conjectures must be consistent with the known facts, but they must run as great a risk as pos-sible of being controverted by the facts still to be ac-cumulated. Furthermore, the search for additional facts should be guided by the effort to find facts that will falsify the hypothesis.

As Popper characterizes falsifiability, the greater the degree of falsifiability of a hypothesis, the greater its content. Tautologies lack empirical content be-cause they do not exclude any possible state of affairs; they are compatible with any **possible world**. Empiri-cal statements are not compatible with every possible state of affairs; they are compatible with some and incompatible with others. The greater the number of possible states of affairs excluded by a statement, the greater its content, for the more it does to pin down our actual world by ruling out possible but nonactual states of affairs. At the same time, the greater the range of facts excluded by a statement—the greater the number of situations with which the statement is incompatible—the greater the risk it runs of being false. A statement with high content has more *poten-tial falsifiers* than a statement with low content. For this reason, high content means high falsifiability. At the same time, content varies inversely with probabil-ity. The logical probability of a hypothesis is defined in terms of its range—that is, the possible states of affairs with which it is compatible. The greater the logical probability of a hypothesis, the fewer are its potential falsifiers. Thus, high probability means low falsifiability.

Hypothetico-deductive theorists usually recom-mend selecting, from among those hypotheses that are compatible with the available facts, the most probable hypothesis. Popper recommends the oppo-site; he suggests selecting the most falsifiable hypoth-esis. Thus, he recommends selecting a hypothesis with low probability. According to Popper, a highly falsifiable hypothesis which is severely tested becomes highly corroborated. The greater the severity of the tests—the greater their number and variety—the greater the corroboration of the hypothesis that survives them.

Popper makes it very clear that hypotheses are not regarded as true because they are highly cor-roborated. Hypotheses cannot be firmly and finally established in this or any other way. Furthermore, because of the inverse relation between falsifiability and probability, we cannot regard highly corrobo-rated hypotheses as probable. To be sure, a serious attempt to falsify a hypothesis which fails does add to the corroboration of this hypothesis, so there is some similarity between corroboration and confir-mation as hypothetico-deductive theorists think of it, but it would be a misinterpretation to suppose that increasing corroboration is a process of accumulat-ing positive instances to increase the probability of the hypothesis.[23]

Nevertheless, Popper does acknowledge the need for a method of selecting among unfalsified hypoth-eses. He has been unequivocal in his emphasis upon the indispensability of far-reaching theory in science. Empirical science is not an activity of merely accu-mulating experiences; it is theoretical through and through. Although we do not regard any hypotheses as certainly true, we do accept them ten-tatively and provisionally. Highly corroborated hy-potheses are required for prediction and explanation. From among the ever-present multiplicity of hypoth-eses compatible with the available evidence, we select and accept.

There is just one point I wish to make here regard-ing Popper's theory. It is not properly characterized as *deductivism*. Popper has not succeeded in purging the logic of science of all inductive elements. My reason for saying this is very simple. Popper furnishes a method for selecting hypotheses whose content ex-ceeds that of the relevant available basic statements. Demonstrative inference cannot accomplish this task alone, for valid deductions are nonampliative and their conclusions cannot exceed their premises in con-tent. Furthermore, Popper's theory does not pretend that basic statements plus deduction can give us scien-tific theory; instead, corroboration is introduced. Corroboration is a nondemonstrative form of infer-ence. It is a way of providing for the acceptance of hypotheses even though the content of these hypotheses goes beyond the content of the basic statements. *Modus tollens* without corroboration is empty; *modus tollens* with corroboration is induction.

When we ask, "Why should we reject a hypothesis when we have accepted one of its potential falsifiers?" the answer is easy. The potential falsifier contradicts the hypothesis, so the hypothesis is false if the potential falsifier holds. That is simple deduction. When we ask, "Why should we accept from among all the unfalsified hypotheses one that is highly corroborated?" we have a right to expect an answer. The answer is some kind of justification for the methodological rule—for the method of corroboration. Popper attempts to answer this question.

Popper makes it clear that his conception of scientific method differs in important respects from the conceptions of many inductivists. I do not want to quibble over a word in claiming that Popper is, himself, a kind of inductivist. The point is not a trivial verbal one. Popper has claimed that scientific inference is exclusively deductive. We have seen, however, that demonstrative inference is not sufficient to the task of providing a reconstruction of the logic of the acceptance—albeit tentative and provisional—of hypotheses. Popper himself realizes this and introduces a mode of nondemonstrative inference. It does not matter whether we call this kind of inference "induction"; whatever we call it, it is ampliative and not necessarily truth-preserving. Using the same force and logic with which Hume raised problems about the justification of induction, we may raise problems about the justification of any kind of nondemonstrative inference. As I argued in the preceding section, Hume's arguments are not peculiar to induction by enumeration or any other special kind of inductive inference; they apply with equal force to any inference whose conclusion can be false, even though it has true premises. Thus, it will not do to dismiss induction by enumeration on grounds of Hume's argument and then accept some other mode of nondemonstrative inference without even considering how Hume's argument might apply to it. I am not arguing that Popper's method is incorrect.[24] I am not even arguing that Popper has failed in his attempt to justify this method. I do claim that Popper is engaged in the same task as many

inductivists—namely, the task of providing some sort of justification for a mode of nondemonstrative inference. This enterprise, if successful, *is* a justification of induction.

. . . .

5. The Principle of Uniformity of Nature. A substantial part of Hume's critique of induction rested upon his attack on the principle of the uniformity of nature. He argued definitively that the customary forms of inductive inference cannot be expected to yield correct predictions if nature fails to be uniform—if the future is not like the past—if like sensible qualities are not accompanied by like results.

> All inferences from experience suppose, as their foundation, that the future will resemble the past, and that similar powers will be conjoined with similar sensible qualities. If there be any suspicion that the course of nature may change, and that the past may be no rule for the future, all experience becomes useless, and can give rise to no inference or conclusion.[25]

He argued, moreover, that there is no logical contradiction in the supposition that nature is not uniform—that the regularities we have observed up to the present will fail in wholesale fashion in the future.

> It implies no contradiction that the course of nature may change, and that an object, seemingly like those which we have experienced, may be attended with different or contrary effects. May I not clearly and distinctly conceive that a body, falling from the clouds, and which, in all other respects resembles snow, has yet the taste of salt or feeling of fire? Is there any more intelligible proposition than to affirm, that all the trees will flourish in December and January, and decay in May and June? Now whatever is intelligible, and can be distinctly conceived, implies no contradiction, and can never be proved false by any demonstrative argument. . . .[26]

He argues, in addition, that the principle of uniformity of nature cannot be established by an inference from experience: "It is impossible, therefore, that any arguments from experience can prove this resemblance of the past to the future; since all these arguments are founded on the supposition of that resemblance."[27] Throughout Hume's discussion there is, however, a strong suggestion that we might have full confidence in the customary inductive methods if nature were known to be uniform.

Kant attempted to deal with the problem of induction in just this way, by establishing a principle of uniformity of nature, in the form of **the principle of universal causation**, as a synthetic a priori truth. Kant claimed, in other words, that every occurrence is governed by causal regularities, and this general characteristic of the universe can be established by pure reason, without the aid of any empirical evidence. He did not try to show that the principle of universal causation is a principle of logic, for to do so would have been to show that it was analytic—not synthetic—and thus lacking in factual content. He did not reject Hume's claim that there is no logical contradiction in the statement that nature is not uniform; he did not try to prove his principle of universal causation by deducing a contradiction from its denial. He did believe, however, that this principle, while not a proposition of pure logic, is necessarily true nevertheless. Hume, of course, argued against this alternative as well. He maintained not only that the uniformity of nature is not a logical or analytic truth, but also that it cannot be any other kind of a priori truth either. Even before Kant had enunciated the doctrine of synthetic a priori principles, Hume had offered strong arguments against them:

I shall venture to affirm, as a general proposition, which admits of no exception, that the knowledge of this relation [of cause and effect] is not, in any instance, attained by reasonings a priori.[28]

Adam, though his rational faculties be supposed, at the very first, entirely perfect, could not have inferred from the fluidity and transparency of water that it would suffocate him, or from the light and warmth of fire that it would consume him.[29]

When we reason a priori, and consider merely any object or cause, as it appears to the mind, independent of all observation, it never could suggest to us the notion of any distinct object, such as its effect; much less, show us the inseparable and inviolable connexion between them. A man must be very sagacious who could discover by reasoning that crystal is the effect of heat, and ice of cold, without being previously acquainted with the operation of these qualities.[30]

Now whatever is intelligible, and can be distinctly conceived . . . can never be proved false by any . . . abstract reasoning a priori.[31]

Hume argues, by persuasive example and general principle, that nothing about the causal structure of reality can be established by pure reason. He poses an incisive challenge to those who would claim the ability to establish a priori knowledge of a particular causal relation or of the principle of universal causation. In the foregoing discussion of synthetic a priori statements, I have given reasons for believing that Kant failed to overcome Hume's previous objections.

There is, however, another interesting issue that arises in connection with the principle of uniformity of nature. Suppose it could be established—never mind how—prior to a justification of induction. Would it then provide an adequate basis for a justification of induction? The answer is, I think, negative.[32]

Even if nature is uniform to some extent, it is not absolutely uniform. The future is something like the past, but it is somewhat different as well. Total and complete uniformity would mean that the state of the universe at any given moment is the same as its state at any other moment. Such a universe would be a changeless, Parmenidean world. Change obviously does occur, so the future is not exactly like the past. There are some uniformities, it appears, but not a complete absence of change. The problem is how to ferret out the genuine uniformities. As a matter of actual fact, there are many uniformities *within experience* that we take to be mere coincidences, and there are others that seem to represent genuine causal regularities. For instance, in every election someone finds a precinct, say in Maryland, which has always voted in favor of the winning presidential candidate. Given enough precincts, one expects this sort of thing by sheer chance, and we classify such regularities as mere coincidences. By contrast, the fact that glass windowpanes break when bricks are hurled at them is more than mere coincidence. Causal regularities provide a foundation for inference from the observed to the unobserved; coincidences do not. We can predict with some confidence that the next glass windowpane at which a brick is hurled will break; we take with a grain of salt the prediction of the outcome of a presidential election early on election night when returns from the above-mentioned precinct are in. The most that a principle of uniformity of nature could say is that there are some uniformities that persist into the future; if it stated that every regularity observed to hold within the scope of our experience also holds universally, it would be patently false. We are left with the problem of finding a sound basis for distinguishing between mere coincidence and genuine causal regularity.

Kant's principle of universal causation makes a rather weak and guarded statement. It asserts only that there exist causal regularities: "Everything that happens presupposes something from which it follows according to some rule." For each occurrence it claims only the existence of *some* prior cause and *some* causal regularity. It gives no hint as to how we are to find the prior cause or how we are to identify the causal regularity. It therefore provides no basis upon which to determine whether the inductive inferences we make are correct or incorrect. It would be entirely consistent with Kant's principle for us always to generalize on the basis of observed coincidences and always to fail to generalize on the basis of actual causal relations. It would be entirely consistent with Kant's principle, moreover, for us always to cite a coincidentally preceding event as the cause instead of the event that is the genuine cause. Kant's principle, even if it could be established, would not help us to justify the assertion that our inductive inferences would always or usually be correct. It would provide no criterion to distinguish sound from unsound inductions. Even if Kant's program had succeeded in establishing a synthetic a priori principle of universal causation, it would have failed to produce a justification of induction.

. . . .

7. A Probabilistic Approach. It may seem strange in the extreme that this discussion of the problem of induction has proceeded at such great length without seriously bringing in the concept of probability. It is very tempting to react immediately to Hume's argument with the admission that we do not have *knowledge* of the unobserved. Scientific results are not established with absolute certainty. At best we can make probabilistic statements about unobserved matters of fact, and at best we can claim that scientific generalizations and theories are highly confirmed. We who live in an age of scientific **empiricism** can accept with perfect equanimity the fact that the quest for certainty is futile; indeed, our thanks go to Hume for helping to destroy false hopes for certainty in science.

Hume's search for a justification of induction, it might be continued, was fundamentally misconceived. He tried to find a way of proving that inductive inferences with true premises would have *true* conclusions. He properly failed to find any such justification precisely because it is the function of *deduction* to prove the truth of conclusions, given true premises. Induction has a different function. An inductive inference with true premises establishes its conclusions as *probable*. No wonder Hume failed to find a justification of induction. He was trying to make induction into deduction, and he succeeded only in proving the platitude that induction is not deduction.[33] If we want to justify induction, we must show that inductive inferences establish their conclusions as probable, not as true.

The foregoing sort of criticism of Hume's arguments is extremely appealing, and it has given rise to the most popular sort of attempt, currently, to deal with the problem.[34] In order to examine this approach, we must consider, at least superficially, the meaning of the concept of probability. Two basic meanings must be taken into account at present.

One leading probability concept identifies probability with frequency—roughly, the probable is that which happens often, and the improbable is that which happens seldom. Let us see what becomes of Hume's argument under this interpretation of probability. If we were to claim that inductive conclusions are probable in this sense, we would be claiming that inductive inferences with true premises often have true conclusions, although not always. Hume's argument shows, unhappily, that this claim cannot be substantiated. It was recognized long before Hume that inductive inferences cannot be expected always to lead to the truth. Hume's argument shows, not only that we cannot justify the claim that *every* inductive inference with true premises will have a true conclusion, but also, that we cannot justify the claim that *any* inductive inference with true premises will have a true conclusion. Hume's argument shows that, for all we can know, every inductive inference made from now on might have a false conclusion despite true premises. Thus, Hume has proved, we can show neither that inductive inferences establish their conclusions as true nor that they establish their conclusions as probable in the frequency sense. The introduction of the frequency concept of probability gives no help whatever in circumventing the problem of induction, but this is no surprise, for we should not have expected it to be suitable for this purpose.

A more promising probability concept identifies probability with degree of rational belief. To say that a statement is probable in this sense means that one would be rationally justified in believing it; the degree of probability is the degree of assent a person would be rationally justified in giving. We are not, of course, referring to the degree to which anyone *actually* believes in the statement, but rather to the degree to which one could *rationally* believe it. Degree of actual belief is a purely psychological concept, but degree of rational belief is determined objectively by the evidence. To say that a statement is probable in this sense means that it is supported by evidence. But, so the argument goes, if a statement is the conclusion of an inductive inference with true premises, it *is* supported by evidence—by inductive evidence—this is part of what it *means* to be supported by evidence. The very concept of evidence depends upon the nature of induction, and it becomes incoherent if we try to divorce the two. Trivially, then, the conclusion of an inductive inference is probable under this concept of probability. To ask, with Hume, if we should accept inductive conclusions is tantamount to asking if we should fashion our beliefs in terms of the evidence, and this, in turn, is tantamount to asking whether we should be rational. In this way we arrive

at an "ordinary language dissolution" of the problem of induction. Once we understand clearly the meanings of such key terms as "rational," "probable," and "evidence," we see that the problem arose out of linguistic confusion and evaporates into the question of whether it is rational to be rational. Such tautological questions, if meaningful at all, demand affirmative answers.

Unfortunately, the dissolution is not satisfactory.[35] Its inadequacy can be exhibited by focusing upon the concept of inductive evidence and seeing how it figures in the foregoing argument. The fundamental difficulty arises from the fact that the very notion of inductive evidence is determined by the rules of inductive inference. If a conclusion is to be supported by inductive evidence, it must be the conclusion of a correct inductive inference with true premises. Whether the inductive inference is correct depends upon whether the rule governing that inference is correct. The relation of inductive evidential support is, therefore, inseparably bound to the correctness of rules of inductive inference. In order to be able to say whether a given statement is supported by inductive evidence we must be able to say which inductive rules are correct.

For example, suppose that a die has been thrown a large number of times, and we have observed that the side two came up in one sixth of the tosses. This is our "evidence" e. Let h be the conclusion that, "in the long run," side two will come up one sixth of the times. Consider the following three rules:

1. (Induction by enumeration.) Given m/n of observed A are B, to infer that the "long run" relative frequency of B among A is m/n.
2. (A priori rule.) Regardless of observed frequencies, to infer that the "long run" relative frequency of B among A is $1/k$, where k is the number of possible outcomes—six in the case of the die.
3. (Counterinductive rule.) Given m/n of observed A are B, to infer that the "long run" relative frequency of B among A is $(n - m)/n$.

Under Rule 1, e is positive evidence for h; under Rule 2, e is irrelevant to h; and under Rule 3, e is negative evidence for *h*. In order to say which conclusions are supported by what evidence, it is necessary to arrive at a decision as to what inductive rules are acceptable. If Rule 1 is correct, the evidence *e* supports the conclusion *h*. If Rule 2 is correct, we are justified in drawing the conclusion *h*, but this is entirely independent of the observational evidence *e;* the same conclusions would have been sanctioned by Rule 2 regardless of observational evidence. If Rule 3 is correct, we are not only prohibited from drawing the conclusion *h*, but also we are permitted to draw a conclusion *h'* which is logically incompatible with *h*. Whether a given conclusion is *supported by evidence*—whether it would be *rational to believe* it on the basis of given evidence—whether it is *made probable* by virtue of its relation to given evidence—depends upon selection of the correct rule or rules from among the infinitely many rules we might conceivably adopt.

The problem of induction can now be reformulated as a problem about evidence. What rules ought we to adopt to determine the nature of inductive evidence? What rules provide suitable concepts of inductive evidence? If we take the customary inductive rules to define the concept of inductive evidence, have we adopted a proper concept of evidence? Would the adoption of some alternative inductive rules provide a more suitable concept of evidence? These are genuine questions which need to be answered.[36]

We find, moreover, that what appeared earlier as a pointless question now becomes significant and difficult. If we take the customary rules of inductive inference to provide a suitable definition of the relation of inductive evidential support, it makes considerable sense to ask whether it is rational to believe on the basis of evidence as thus defined rather than to believe on the basis of evidence as defined according to other rules. For instance, I believe that the a priori rule and the counterinductive rule mentioned above are demonstrably unsatisfactory, and hence, they demonstrably fail to provide a suitable concept of inductive evidence. The important point is that something concerning the selection from among possible rules needs demonstration and is amenable to demonstration.

There is danger of being taken in by an easy equivocation. One meaning we may assign to the concept of inductive evidence is, roughly, the basis on which we ought to fashion our beliefs. Another meaning results from the relation of evidential support determined by whatever rule of inductive inference we adopt. It is only by supposing that these two concepts are the same that we suppose the problem of induction is still there; it is the problem of providing adequate grounds for the selection of inductive rules. We want the relation of evidential support determined by these rules to yield a concept of inductive evidence which is, in fact, the basis on which we ought to fashion our beliefs.[37]

We began this initially promising approach to the problem of the justification of induction by introducing the notion of probability, but we end with a dilemma. If we take "probability" in the frequency sense, it is easy to see why it is advisable to accept probable conclusions in preference to improbable ones. In so doing we shall be right more often. Unfortunately, we cannot show that inferences conducted according to any particular rule establish conclusions that are probable in this sense. If we take "probability" in a nonfrequency sense it may be easy to show that inferences which conform to our accepted inductive rules establish their conclusions as probable. Unfortunately, we can find no reason to prefer conclusions which are probable in this sense to those that are improbable. As Hume has shown, we have no reason to suppose that probable conclusions will often be true and improbable ones will seldom be true. This dilemma is Hume's problem of induction all over again. We have been led to an interesting reformulation, but it is only a reformulation and not a solution.

8. Pragmatic Justification. Of all the solutions and dissolutions proposed to deal with Hume's problem of induction, Hans Reichenbach's attempt to provide a pragmatic justification seems to me the most fruitful and promising.[38] This approach accepts Hume's arguments up to the point of agreeing that it is impossible to establish, either deductively or inductively, that any inductive inferences will ever again have true conclusions. Nevertheless, Reichenbach claims, the standard method of inductive generalization can be justified. Although its *success* as a method of prediction cannot be established in advance, it can be shown to be superior to any alternative method of prediction.

The argument can be put rather simply. Nature may be sufficiently uniform in suitable respects for us to make successful inductive inferences from the observed to the unobserved. On the other hand, for all we know, she may not. Hume has shown that we cannot prove in advance which case holds. All we can say is that nature may or may not be uniform—if she is, induction works; if she is not, induction fails. Even in the face of our ignorance about the uniformity of nature, we can ask what would happen if we adopted some radically different method of inference. Consider, for instance, the method of the crystal gazer. Since we do not know whether nature is uniform or not, we must consider both possibilities. If nature is uniform, the method of crystal gazing might work successfully, or it might fail. We cannot prove a priori that it will not work. At the same time, we cannot prove a priori that it will work, even if nature exhibits a high degree of uniformity. Thus, in case nature is reasonably uniform, the standard inductive method *must* work while the alternative method of crystal gazing *may or may not* work. In this case, the superiority of the standard inductive method is evident. Now, suppose nature lacks uniformity to such a degree that the standard inductive method is a complete failure. In this case, Reichenbach argues, the alternative method must likewise fail. Suppose it did not fail—suppose, for instance, that the method of crystal gazing worked consistently. This would constitute an important relevant uniformity that could be exploited inductively. If a crystal gazer had consistently predicted future occurrences, we could infer inductively that he has a method of prediction that will enjoy continued success. The inductive method would, in this way, share the success of the method of crystal gazing, and would therefore be, contrary to hypothesis, successful. Hence, Reichenbach concludes, the standard inductive method will be successful *if any other method could succeed*. As a result, we have everything to gain and nothing to lose by adopting the inductive method. If any method works, induction works. If we adopt the inductive method and it fails, we have lost nothing, for any other method we might have adopted would likewise have failed. Reichenbach does not claim to prove that nature is uniform, or that the standard inductive method will be successful. He does not postulate the uniformity of nature. He tries to show that the inductive method is the best method for ampliative inference, whether it turns out to be successful or not.

This ingenious argument, although extremely suggestive, is ultimately unsatisfactory. As I have just presented it, it is impossibly vague. I have not specified the nature of the standard inductive method. I have not stated with any exactness what constitutes success for the inductive method or any other. Moreover, the uniformity of nature is not an all-or-none affair. Nature appears to be uniform to some extent and also to be lacking in uniformity to some degree. As we have already seen, it is not easy to state a principle of uniformity that is strong enough to assure the success of induction inference and weak enough to be plausible. The vagueness of the foregoing argument is not, however, its fundamental drawback. It can be made precise, and I shall do so below in connection with the discussion of the frequency interpretation of probability.[39] When it is made precise, . . . it suffers the serious defect of equally justifying too wide a variety of rules for ampliative inference.

I have presented Reichenbach's argument rather loosely in order to make intuitively clear its basic strategy. The sense in which it is a pragmatic justification should be clear. Unlike many authors who have sought a justification of induction, Reichenbach does not try to prove the truth of any synthetic proposition. He recognizes that the problem concerns the justification of a rule, and rules are neither true nor false. Hence, he tries to show that the adoption of a standard inductive rule is practically useful in the attempt to learn about and deal with the unobserved. He maintains that this can be shown even though we cannot prove the truth of the assertion that inductive methods will lead to predictive success. This pragmatic aspect is, it seems to me, the source of the fertility of Reichenbach's approach. Even though his argument does not constitute an adequate justification of induction, it seems to me to provide a valid core from which we may attempt to develop a more satisfactory justification.

III. Significance of the Problem

Hume's problem of induction evokes, understandably, a wide variety of reactions. It is not difficult to appreciate the response of the man engaged in active scientific research or practical affairs who says, in effect, "Don't bother me with these silly puzzles; I'm too busy doing science, building bridges, or managing affairs of state." No one, including Hume, seriously suggests any suspension of scientific investigation or practical decision pending a solution of the problem of induction. The problem concerns the *foundations* of science. As Hume eloquently remarks in *Enquiry Concerning Human Understanding*:

> Let the course of things be allowed hitherto ever so regular; that alone, without some new argument or inference, proves not that, for the future, it will continue so. In vain do you pretend to have learned the nature of bodies from your past experience. Their secret nature, and consequently all their effects and influence, may change, without any change in their sensible qualities. This happens sometimes, and with regard to some objects: Why may it not happen always, and with regard to all objects? What logic, what process of argument secures you against this supposition? My practice, you say, refutes my doubts. But you mistake the purport of my question. As an agent, I am quite satisfied in the point; but as a philosopher, who has some share of curiosity, I will not say scepticism, I want to learn the foundation of this inference.

We should know by now that the foundations of a subject are usually established long after the subject has been well developed, not before. To suppose otherwise would be a glaring example of "naïve first-things-firstism."[40]

Nevertheless, there is something intellectually disquieting about a serious gap in the foundations of a discipline, and it is especially disquieting when the discipline in question is so broad as to include the whole of empirical science, all of its applications, and indeed, all of common sense. As human beings we pride ourselves on rationality—so much so that for centuries rationality was enshrined as the very essence of humanity and the characteristic that distinguishes man from the lower brutes. Questionable as such pride may be, our intellectual consciences should be troubled by a gaping lacuna in the structure of our knowledge and the foundations of

scientific inference. I do not mean to suggest that the structure of empirical science is teetering because of foundational difficulties; the architectural metaphor is really quite inappropriate. I do suggest that intellectual integrity requires that foundational problems not be ignored.

Each of two opposing attitudes has its own immediate appeal. One of these claims that the scientific method is so obviously the correct method that there is no need to waste our time trying to show that this is so. There are two difficulties. First, we have enough painful experience to know that the appeal to obviousness is dangerously likely to be an appeal to prejudice and superstition. What is obvious to one age or culture may well turn out, on closer examination, to be just plain false. Second, if the method of science is so obviously superior to other methods we might adopt, then I should think we ought to be able to point to those characteristics of the method by which it gains its obvious superiority.

The second tempting attitude is one of pessimism. In the face of Hume's arguments and the failure of many attempts to solve the problem, it is easy to conclude that the problem is hopeless. Whether motivated by Hume's arguments or, as is probably more often the case, by simple impatience with foundational problems, this attitude seems quite widespread. It is often expressed by the formula that science is, at bottom, a matter of faith. While it is no part of my purpose to launch a wholesale attack on faith as such, this attitude toward the foundations of scientific inference is unsatisfactory. The crucial fact is that science makes a *cognitive claim*, and this cognitive claim is a fundamental part of the rationale for doing science at all. Hume has presented us with a serious challenge to that cognitive claim. If we cannot legitimize the cognitive claim, it is difficult to see what reason remains for doing science. Why not turn to voodoo, which would be simpler, cheaper, less time consuming, and more fun?

If science is basically a matter of faith, then the scientific faith exists on a par with other faiths. Although we may be culturally conditioned to accept this faith, others are not. Science has no ground on which to maintain its *cognitive* superiority to any form of irrationalism, however repugnant. This situation is, it seems to me, intellectually and socially undesirable.

We have had enough experience with various forms of irrationalism to recognize the importance of being able to distinguish them logically from genuine science. I find it intolerable to suppose that a theory of biological evolution, supported as it is by extensive scientific evidence, has no more rational foundation than has its rejection by ignorant fundamentalists. I, too, have faith that the scientific method is especially well suited for establishing knowledge of the unobserved, but I believe this faith should be justified. It seems to me extremely important that some people should earnestly seek a solution to this problem concerning the foundations of scientific inference.

One cannot say in advance what consequences will follow from a solution to a foundational problem. It would seem to depend largely upon the nature of the solution. But a discipline with well-laid foundations is surely far more satisfactory than one whose foundations are in doubt. We have only to compare the foundationally insecure calculus of the seventeenth and eighteenth centuries with the calculus of the late nineteenth century to appreciate the gains in elegance, simplicity, and rigor. Furthermore, the foundations of calculus provided a basis for a number of other developments, interesting in their own right and *greatly extending the power and fertility of the original theory*. Whether similar extensions will occur as a result of a satisfactory resolution of Hume's problem is a point on which it would be rash to hazard any prediction, but we know from experience that important consequences result from the most unexpected sources. The subsequent discussion of the foundations of probability will indicate directions in which some significant consequences may be found, but for the moment it will suffice to note that a serious concern for the solution of Hume's problem cannot fail to deepen our understanding of the nature of scientific inference. This, after all, is the ultimate goal of the whole enterprise.

NOTES

This book [*The Foundations of Scientific Inference*] is based upon five lectures in the Philosophy of Science Series at the University of Pittsburgh. The first two lectures, *Foundations of Scientific Inference*: I. *The Problem of Induction*, II. *Probability and Induction*, were presented in March 1963. The next two lectures, *Inductive Inference in Science*: I. *Hypothetico-Deductive Arguments*, II. *Plausibility Arguments*, were delivered in October 1964. The final lecture, *A Priori Knowledge*, was given in October 1965. The author wishes to express his gratitude to the National Science Foundation and the Minnesota Center for Philosophy of Science for support of research on inductive logic and probability.

1. David Hume, *Enquiry Concerning Human Understanding*, see IV, I.
2. Ibid.
3. For a more detailed account of the relation between deductive validity and factual content, see p. 24.
4. The problem of the synthetic a priori is discussed earlier, in sec. II, 4, pp. 27–40 [of Salmon's *Foundations of Scientific Inference*, from which this selection is excerpted].
5. Hume, *Human Understanding*.
6. Ibid.
7. Max Black, *Problems of Analysis* (Ithaca: Cornell University Press, 1954), Chap. 11.
8. Ibid., pp. 196–97.
9. Lewis Carroll, "What the Tortoise Said to Achilles," in *The Complete Works of Lewis Carroll* (New York: Random House, n.d.).
10. I presented the following self-supporting argument for the counterinductive method in "Should We Attempt to Justify Induction?" *Philosophical Studies*, 8 (April 1957), pp. 45–47. Max Black in "Self-supporting Inductive Arguments," *Models and Metaphors* (Ithaca: Cornell University Press, 1962), Chap. 12, replies to my criticism, but he does not succeed in shaking the basic point: The counterinductive rule is related to its self-supporting argument in precisely the same way as the standard inductive rule is related to its self-supporting argument. This is the "cash value" of claiming that the self-supporting argument is circular. Peter Achinstein, "The Circularity of a Self-supporting Inductive Argument," *Analysis*, 22 (June 1962), considers neither my formulation nor Black's answer sufficient, so he makes a further attempt to show circularity. Black's reply is found in "Self-Support and Circularity: A Reply to Mr. Achinstein," *Analysis*, 23 (December 1962). Achinstein's rejoinder is "Circularity and Induction," *Analysis*, 23 (June 1963).
11. Max Black, "The Justification of Induction," *Language and Philosophy* (Ithaca: Cornell University Press, 1949), Chap. 3. The view he expresses in this essay, I believe, is closely related to the "probabilistic approach" I discuss in sec. II, 7, pp. 280–82.

12. Max Black, *Problems of Analysis*, p. 191.

13. Ibid., p. 206.

14. Compare Richard Bevan Braithwaite, *Scientific Explanation* (New York: Harper & Row, 1960), Chap. 8. I think the same general view is to be found in A. J. Ayer, *The Problem of Knowledge* (Baltimore: Penguin Books, 1956), p. 75. I have discussed Ayer's view in "The Concept of Inductive Evidence," *American Philosophical Quarterly*, 2 (October 1965).

15. See Braithwaite for a systematic exposition of this conception.

16. Sec. VII, pp. 108–31 [of Salmon's *Foundations of Scientific Inference*]. "The Confirmation of Scientific Hypotheses" is devoted to a detailed analysis of this type of inference.

17. See John Patrick Day, *Inductive Probability* (New York: Humanities Press, 1961), p. 6. The nineteenth-century notion that induction is a process of discovery and the problem of whether there can be a logic of discovery are discussed earlier in sec. VII, pp. 109–14 [of Salmon's *Foundations of Scientific Inference*].

18. See e.g., Karl R. Popper, *The Logic of Scientific Discovery* (New York: Basic Books, 1959), sec. 30, and Thomas S. Kuhn, *The Structure of Scientific Revolutions* (Chicago: University of Chicago Press, 1962). A fuller discussion of the relations among such concepts as deductive validity and content is given earlier in sec. II, 4, especially p. 33 [of Salmon's *Foundations of Scientific Inference*].

19. The most comprehensive statement of Popper's position is to be found in *The Logic of Scientific Discovery*. This is the English translation, with additions, of Karl R. Popper, *Logik der Forschung* (Vienna, 1934).

20. "I think that we shall have to get accustomed to the idea that we must not look upon science as a 'body of knowledge,' but rather as a system of hypotheses; that is to say, a system of guesses or anticipations which in principle cannot be justified, but with which we work as long as they stand up to tests, and of which we are never justified in saying that we know that they are 'true' or 'more or less certain' or even 'probable.'" *The Logic of Scientific Discovery*, p. 317.

21. I believe Popper openly acknowledges the nonampliative character of deduction. See "Why Are the Calculi of Logic and Arithmetic Applicable to Reality," in Karl R. Popper, *Conjectures and Refutations* (New York: Basic Books, 1962), Chap. 9.

22. See *The Logic of Scientific Discovery*, Chap. 10.

23. Ibid., p. 270.

24. I ... return to Popper's methodological views in the discussion of confirmation in sec. VII [of *Foundations of Scientific Inference*]. In that context I shall exhibit what I take to be the considerable valid content of Popper's account of the logic of science. See pp. 114–21.

25. David Hume, *Human Understanding*, sec. IV.

26. Ibid.

27. Ibid.

28. Ibid.

29. Ibid.

30. Ibid.

31. Ibid.

32. Wesley C. Salmon, "The Uniformity of Nature," *Philosophy and Phenomenological Research*, 14 (September 1953).

33. Max Black, "The Justification of Induction," in *Language and Philosophy*.

34. Among the authors who subscribe to approaches similar to this are A. J. Ayer, *Language, Truth and Logic* (New York: Dover Publications, 1952); Paul Edwards, "Russell's Doubts about Induction," *Mind*, 58 (1949), p. 141–63; Asher Moore, "The Principle of Induction," *Journal of Philosophy*, 49 (1952), pp. 741–58; Arthur Pap, *Elements of Analytic Philosophy* (New York: Macmillan, 1949), and *An Introduction to the Philosophy of Science*; and P. F. Strawson, *Introduction to Logical Theory* (London: Methuen, 1952).

35. I have criticized this type of argument at some length in "Should We Attempt to Justify Induction?" *Philosophical Studies*, 8 (April 1957), and in "The Concept of Inductive Evidence," *American Philosophical Quarterly*, 2 (October 1965). This latter article is part of a "Symposium on Inductive Evidence" in which Stephen Barker and Henry E. Kyburg, Jr., defend against the attack. See their comments and my rejoinder.

36. This point has enormous import for any attempt to construct an inductive justification of induction. To decide whether the fact that induction has been successful in the past is positive evidence, negative evidence, or no evidence at all begs the very question at issue.

37. As I attempted to show in "Should We Attempt to Justify Induction?" this equivocation seems to arise out of a failure to distinguish *validation* and *vindication*. This crucial distinction is explicated by Herbert Feigl, "De Principiis non Disputandum ... ?" in *Philosophical Analysis*, ed. Max Black (Ithaca: Cornell University Press, 1950).

38. Hans Reichenbach, *Experience and Prediction* (Chicago: University of Chicago Press, 1938), Chap. 5, and *The Theory of Probability* (Berkeley: University of California Press, 1949), Chap. 11.
39. Sec. V, 5, pp. 83–96 [of Salmon's *Foundations of Scientific Inference*].
40. Leonard J. Savage, *The Foundations of Statistics* (New York: Wiley, 1954), p. 1.

KEY TERMS

Induction
Demonstrative inference
Nondemonstrative inference
Necessarily truth-preserving
Nonampliative
Analytic
Synthetic
A priori
Principle of uniformity of nature

Relations of ideas
Matters of fact
Petitio principii
Affirming the consequent
Skeptical
Hypothetico-deductive method
Induction by enumeration
Deductivism
Falsifiability

Modus tollens
Corroboration
Possible world

Principle of universal causation
Empiricism

STUDY QUESTIONS

1. As Salmon conceives of it, what is the problem of induction?
2. Can you think of an ordinary situation in which you use inductive reasoning? Do you tend to think that such reasoning justifies the conclusion you draw?
3. Why do Salmon and Hume both think that an inductive justification of inductive reasoning is bound to fail?
4. Why does Popper think that "inductive logic is . . . a complete delusion"?
5. What does Salmon mean when he says, "I do suggest that intellectual integrity requires that foundational problems not be ignored"? What are the foundational problems that he is talking about? Do you agree that they are important? Why or why not?

P A R T   I V

X

MINDS, BODIES, AND PERSONS

INTRODUCTION

How do we fit into the wider world? Are we simply very complex parts of the physical world? Could a computer be conscious in the way that we are? Are we just things, with the same sort of identity that rocks and buildings have? Or is there something special about us? Are our actions as subject to the laws of nature and as predictable, at least in theory, as those of other objects? Or do we have some special sort of **freedom**? These questions are as old as philosophy. Yet, in spite of the wealth of seemingly relevant knowledge afforded us by contemporary science, the discussion of such questions continues unabated.

Descartes's Dualism

René Descartes's *Meditations on First Philosophy* should be considered as relevant to Part IV of this book as it is to Part III. His treatment of the **mind-body problem** is as important as his attempts to deal with **skepticism**. Indeed, although his approach to skepticism has not been widely followed, the basic outline of Descartes's treatment of the relation between mind and body was the dominant view among psychologists and others who attempted to deal with the mind specifically until our own century, and it remains the view of sophisticated common sense.

Descartes's answer to the second question we asked was a resounding no. The mind is not part of the physical world at all. Physical things are extended: they take up space. And they are not conscious. Our minds, on the other hand, are conscious and do not take up space. Minds and bodies are as fundamentally different as things could be. Descartes begins to develop this **dualistic** conception in "Meditation II," where he finds that he cannot doubt the existence of his own mind (that is, of himself), whereas he can doubt the existence of the physical world. In "Meditation VI," after he has resolved his doubts about the physical world and determined that the essence of physical things is extension, Descartes develops his theory of mind and body at greater length and gives arguments for it.

Descartes's view is that we know what the mind is by reflecting on our own thinking or consciousness. We can see that the essence of our minds is this consciousness rather than extension. Thinking about Detroit, wishing for a puce Ferrari, feeling a pain, or having a visual image of a tree are all ways of being conscious, not ways of taking up space. There are no ways of thinking that seem to involve being extended, and there are no ways of being extended—no combination of extended parts, however complex—that carry consciousness with them. To be conscious is not to be of a certain shape or size or to move in a certain way, but a quite different and undefinable property of which we are each intimately aware when we reflect on our own minds.

How, then, are immaterial minds and the material world connected? Descartes's theory is that there is a two-way causal interaction between them (thus, Cartesian dualism is often called **interactive dualism**). On the one hand, the physical world affects one's mind. This happens, for example, in perception. Light rays bounce off the book in front of me, enter my eye, and cause changes in my nervous system, beginning at the periphery and ending in the brain. The state of the brain (the pineal gland in particular, Descartes thought) directly affects the mind. Thus, my body is not me, but simply the part of the material world that most directly affects me. But there is also a causal interaction in the other direction. States of my mind affect my body and through it the wider world. The most obvious case is action. The intention to drink from the cup in front of me is a certain sort of mental state that involves ideas of the cup. This has an effect on the brain (through the pineal gland again) that affects the muscles and results in my arm moving in a certain way, and, if things go right, in the cup coming to my lips and my getting a drink. Although Descartes's hypothesis about the role of the pineal gland did not turn out to be correct, his basic conception of immaterial mind linked causally to material bodies proved durable.

Alternatives to Descartes

Descartes's position is not without its problems, however. One such problem, vigorously stated by Gilbert Ryle, is traditionally known as the problem of other minds. If minds are immaterial, then we cannot see or touch or otherwise perceive any mind but our own mind, of which we seem to be directly aware. But then how do we know that other bodies are really, as is our body, animated by minds at all? Perhaps our mind is the only mind in the world, and every other being seemingly like us is just some sort of automaton? Of course, if we remain stuck in the skeptical abyss into which Descartes leads us in "Meditation I," this will be only a small part of a much larger problem: not only other minds, but other bodies—even our own—are in doubt. The dualist appears to have an additional problem. Even if we are convinced of a world external to our own minds, how can we know that there are minds lying behind these other human bodies?

In his selection "The Argument from Analogy for Other Minds," Bertrand Russell proposes one solution. He claims that our knowledge of other minds is based on a general principle used in scientific reasoning: analogy. Because other bodies behave as our body does, we may postulate other minds as their causal principle. But one may wonder about the strength of such an inference from a single case (my own) to so many other cases.

The second problem is the interaction that Descartes assumes between mental and physical events. Many philosophers have found the whole idea of an interaction between two such different realms completely unintelligible. For example, how could an immaterial mind make contact with a material object in order to affect it or to be affected by it?

But what alternatives are there to Descartes's position? George Berkeley gave us one: there are not minds and bodies, just minds. It is not obvious how this helps with the problem of other minds. Indeed, in the intellectual milieu of the twentieth century, philosophers sought to solve the problem of interaction in the opposite direction—not to deny the existence of minds, but to argue that minds can, after all, be considered parts (or aspects) of the physical world. Just as in the eighteenth century Berkeley maintained that talk about tables and chairs seems to be talk only about nonminds but is actually a complex way of talking about minds and their ideas, so many twentieth-century philosophers claim that talk about beliefs and desires and pains seems to be talk only about a nonphysical realm but is actually just a complicated way of talking about bodies, brains, and behavior.

Five types of theory are represented (or, at least, suggested) in section A. The first theory is **logical behaviorism**. Even with Descartes's view, a strong case can be made for the importance of studying behavior as a way of studying the mind, for the behavior that minds cause is part of the evidence we have about minds. **Methodological behaviorism** is a movement in psychology that emphasizes the importance of studying behavior as a supplement to (possibly as a replacement for) introspective study of the mind.

But logical behaviorism goes a step further. It claims that our mental language—our talk of beliefs, desires, pains, and so on—is not a way of describing an inner, immaterial cause of behavior but, rather, a way of describing behavior itself. An inelegant logical behaviorist might say, for example, that my belief that it is raining is no more than my behavior of carrying an umbrella and canceling my tennis game. Such a roughcast form of logical behaviorism doesn't seem very plausible. Our representative of this tradition, Gilbert Ryle, would not appreciate being associated with those who present such an unsophisticated view. Still, we can see his ideas emerging from just such a view, and in only three moves. The first move is from actual behavior to dispositions to behave. Is my belief that it is raining any more than my disposition to carry an umbrella if I want to go out and to cancel my tennis game if I do not want to get wet? The second move is to couch the thesis in a linguistic form. It is not the crude thesis that mental events are behavioral events, but the more perceptive thesis that there are logical connections between behavioral descriptions and mental descriptions. Finally, these logical connections are of a complex sort. We should not expect explicit definitions of mental terms in behavioral language. The connections are more subtle. Talk of behavior and talk of the mind are two linguistic systems for describing the same phenomena: they just cut the phenomena up in different ways. But there is not a mind in addition to behavior or action. This would be, Ryle thinks, a category mistake, on par with taking a university to be an additional group of buildings over and above the buildings of its colleges.

The second theory is represented by David M. Armstrong's essay, "The Nature of Mind." Armstrong thinks that both Descartes and the logical behaviorists have part of the story right. The logical behaviorists are right in thinking that there are logical connections between descriptions of behavior and descriptions of mental states, as well as in their rejection of Descartes's idea of an immaterial mind. But Descartes is right in thinking that the mind is an inner cause of behavior, not just behavior redescribed. The key is to see that our mental concepts are simply indirect concepts of brain states. By "pain," we mean something like "that internal state which is apt to produce wincing, crying out, and the like." Our understanding of the causes of such behavior is necessarily indirect because brains are enormously complex systems enclosed by skulls, which, until recently, could not be examined while still in working condition. Indeed, the concept of pain itself leaves the question open as to whether the cause of pain behavior is physical or nonphysical. That is what Descartes saw when he noted that mental states are not logically required to be "ways of being extended." But there is a difference between not being required to be a physical state and being required not to be a physical state. There is nothing in our concept of mental states, Armstrong argues, that precludes their turning out to be physical states. He thinks that the progress of science, which has found physical causes for a wider and wider circle of phenomena, makes it probable that the causes of such behavior are physical. Hence, the mind turns out to be the brain, even though Descartes could conceive of his mind existing without his brain. Paul M. Churchland extends this way of thinking to a radical conclusion. He argues that our talk of minds, our "folk psychology," should go the way of other "false and radically misleading" theories in the history of science.

In "What Mary Didn't Know," Frank Jackson develops this difficulty for the **materialist** in a simple and elegant argument. Suppose that Mary is raised in a black-and-white room. She isn't colorblind, but she never sees colors. She knows there are colors, but she just has never seen one. Then one day she emerges from her room and sees a red object. At this point, Jackson says, she will learn what it is like to see a red object. This is a piece of knowledge that she didn't have all the years she was in the black-and-white room, even if she read books on color vision while she was in there. This fact that Mary learns, Jackson says, is one that we have to postulate in addition to all the physical facts; it is an irreducible fact about consciousness.

Minds, Brains, and Machines

If a Martian could have a mind like ours in spite of being built out of very different stuff, isn't it logically possible that computers could also have minds? Several of the theories of mind seem to leave open this possibility. Surprisingly, Descartes's view is one of them. If God could cause the brain states of humans to be causally connected with states of mind, why should He not do as well for computers? Of course, the problem of other minds arises here, too. If a computer had a Cartesian mind, how would we know?

Armstrong's view seems to dictate that computers could not have minds as long as they are built out of silicon and not living tissue. But why could a computer not have states that were functionally equivalent to ours and, therefore, be in the same mental states that we are in?

Different points of view on the possibility of a mental life for computers are found in the work of the logician A. M. Turing—whose ideas were important in the development of computer science—and the philosopher John R. Searle. Neither Turing nor Searle is worried about whether any presently existing computer can be said, without metaphor or exaggeration, to think. (Indeed, Turing's selection was written in 1950, when actual computers were primitive by today's standards.) Both authors are not merely interested in whether at some time in the future something we are willing to call a "computer" might be said to think. Instead, they are interested in whether computers that work on the principles that modern computers do could, if they became sufficiently complex and were programmed sufficiently cleverly, be able to think. Turing argues that insofar as the question has a clear meaning, the answer is probably yes. He sees no reason why computers could not be designed to pass the imitation test; that is, the machine could successfully imitate the behavior of humans insofar as such behavior is relevant to assess the intellectual powers of humans. Computers thus need not look like humans or feel like humans or sound like humans, but the content of their answers to any conceivable question would have to be just what humans would answer.

Searle wrote in 1980, at a time when computers could do things that Turing could only imagine thirty years earlier. Some computer scientists claim that certain mental properties should be attributed to computers on the basis of what they can do. Searle maintains that if we examine the way that computer programs work, we will see that this claim is nonsense. Although computers may be programmed to do as well as humans on certain tasks, the way they achieve these results does not require the mental properties that humans would typically use if they performed them. Searle's argument for his conclusion is based on his famous Chinese Room example. In that example, Searle imagines himself locked in a room following mechanical rules that, unknown to him, result in his writing suitable Chinese answers to Chinese questions, even though he doesn't know a word of Chinese. "I simply behave like a computer; I perform computational operations on formally specified elements. . . . I am simply the instantiation of a computer program." Now, in this case, Searle says, this ability on his part would not mean that he understood Chinese. So why, he asks, should a computer doing something similar lead us to say that the computer understood Chinese or had any of the numerous mental abilities that a computer can be programmed to imitate?

The Problem of Personal Identity

Many religions believe in survival after death. Usually, such doctrines allow that the survivor does not have the same body as before death. Suppose a lawyer who leads a faultless life is reincarnated as a philosopher. The lawyer's original body will still be locked in a coffin or, perhaps, will even have rotted away while the philosopher is growing up. Or suppose our faultless lawyer goes to heaven. Again, it seems that the body he will have in heaven— if beings have bodies there at all—will not be the same body that remains behind on earth. These possibilities raise the **problem of personal identity**. If the very same being can, at different times, have different bodies (or not have a body at all), then personal identity cannot simply be bodily identity. But, then, what is it?

One possible answer is that of Descartes: personal identity consists of the sameness of the immaterial mind, not the identity of the material body. So, there is no problem with survival after death.

It is interesting to see, however, that one might deny that personal identity consisted of bodily identity, even if one were a thoroughgoing materialist about the mind. A high-tech version of our problem will make this point.

In recent years, several books and television shows have contemplated the possibility of a brain transplant. Suppose Ms. A's brain is put in Ms. B's body. It seems that the survivor of this operation would be mentally like Ms. A, not Ms. B. That is, if memories, beliefs, desires, and the like are largely dependent on brain states (whether or not they are identical with them), we might expect the survivor to remember things that Ms. A has done; have Ms. A's beliefs and desires; and, with respect to mental characteristics generally, to be like Ms. A, even though she would, of course, look just like Ms. B always did.

In this instance, many people would be inclined to say that the survivor is Ms. A, not Ms. B—in spite of physical appearances and even fingerprints. But then we also have a case of a body transplant, not a brain transplant, in which there is sameness of person without sameness of body—without any appeal to an immaterial mind.

Of course, the survivor has a part of Ms. A's body. But one is inclined to think that it is not just having Ms. A's brain that inclines us to take her to be Ms. A. It is not the brain, but what the brain apparently would bring with it, in particular Ms. A's memories—that seems crucial.

So we have three approaches to personal identity: identity of a Cartesian soul, identity of body, and something determined by links of memory.

In John Perry's "A Dialogue on Personal Identity and Immortality," the three characters Weirob, Miller, and Cohen discuss the merits of these approaches in the context of Weirob's approaching death. Miller is a religious person, who wants to convince the philosopher Weirob that there is some possibility of survival after death. First, he advocates a Cartesian type of theory, and then a memory theory, based on the ideas of John Locke. But Weirob believes that a person is just a live human body and refuses to grant even the possibility of survival after death. The debate takes a practical turn when the participants consider the possibility of getting Weirob a "body-transplant," but she comes up with ingenious arguments (based on ideas in Bernard Williams's "The Self and the Future") to persuade herself that even that would not mean survival. Given the perplexities involved in all the approaches to personal identity mentioned earlier, Derek Parfit suggests, in "Personal Identity," that there is not always a definite answer to questions about personal identity. Furthermore, he suggests that we do not need to provide such an answer in order to address important questions about survival and responsibility. For Parfit, personal identity is not "what matters" for survival and accountability. David Velleman takes Parfit's suggestions about personal identity one step further by arguing that Parfit's view can help us make sense of suffering and various other aspects of our lives. Daniel Dennett's "Where Am I?" is an extended thought-experiment that is meant to help us test some of our views about personal idenity and survival. Dennett's article is a perfect bridge from issues about the mind and identity to the great questions about freedom, **determinism**, and moral responsibility.

Freedom and Determinism

Suppose your friend, standing next to you at a party, suddenly lifts her arm and slaps you in the face. You will be inclined to hold her responsible for this action: to blame her for your sore face, resent her for what she did, and think ill of her moral character.

But suppose you find out that her arm is tied to a fishline, pulled by someone on a balcony above. Your face is still sore, but now you will hardly be inclined to blame her for what happened. Why? Because she wasn't in control of the movement of her arm; once the person in the balcony pulled the line, a sequence of events was put in motion that ended up with your face getting slapped. Given the tug, the rest of the situation, and the laws of nature, your face was going to get slapped. She had no choice. Her movement was the result of a prior, remote event. She was not free to do otherwise. So how can you blame her?

But if she is not free, are any of us ever free? For the laws of nature do not just concern fishlines, they concern all events inside and outside our bodies. If nature obeys universal laws, then our actions are just the most recent parts of a causal sequence of ever more remote events, the earliest parts of which occurred long before we were born. If the fact that the movement of your friend's arm is explained by the earlier tug on the fishline means that she is not free, doesn't the fact that all our actions can be explained by remote events and the working of general laws mean that none of us is ever free?

But can we really accept such a conclusion? After all, we blame and punish people all the time, and such practices presuppose that these people had a choice in what they did. That we have such choices seems obvious as soon as we reflect on our own actions. Can you doubt that you have the choice right now to lay down this book and to order a pizza?

This is the dilemma of freedom and determinism. Our assumption that people have choices and are thus responsible for what they do appears to conflict with the view that everything, even the movements of human agents, has an explanation in terms of universal laws of nature and antecedent conditions.

There are two obvious responses to our dilemma. The first is to accept that because we are subject to laws of nature, we are not free. The second is to accept that because we are free, some of our actions must escape the web of the laws of nature. Both positions are versions of **incompatibilism** about causal determinism and freedom. The first position is **hard determinism**, whereas the second is libertarianism.

Given the choice between denying freedom and denying universal causation, most of us would choose the latter. Universal causation may be a useful postulate to guide scientific investigation, but why should we accept it at the cost of giving up a belief that is so central to our day-to-day lives as our conviction that we are free agents?

But does giving up universal causation really help? The absence of explanation just doesn't seem to add up to the presence of freedom. Suppose that instead of being pulled by a fishline, your friend's arm moved as a result of a totally random and unpredictable spasm in her brain. That wouldn't make her action more free or her more responsible. In "Human Freedom and the Self," Roderick M. Chisholm develops the worries just sketched and concludes that they lead us to a fairly radical claim about the powers of persons—that we can engage in a special sort of **agent-causation** (not reducible to causation involving events). In "The Powers of Rational Beings: Freedom of the Will," Peter van Inwagen develops and elaborates the problems that are posed by each of the assumptions discussed earlier—of causal determinism and its denial. Like Chisholm, van Inwagen highlights the difficulties that are posed by causal determinism and event-causal indeterminism, but, in contrast to Chisholm, he does not accept the agent-causal approach. Van Inwagen leaves us with a set of mysteries and challenges to our most basic views about ourselves as free and morally responsible agents.

Hume takes what might be considered the third approach. He refuses to choose between freedom and universal causation (which he calls liberty and necessity), but he accepts them both. How does he think this is possible?

Hume describes himself as reconciling liberty and necessity. He thus rejects the common assumption of the hard determinist and libertarian: incompatibilism. Rather, Hume is a **compatibilist** about causal determinism and freedom of the will. He thinks that the appearance of incompatibility is due to confusions about causation. Causes do not compel effects, they are merely regularly followed by them. Hume claims that determinism is just what we want. We want our own desires to determine our actions. The problem with your friend, he would say, was not that her action had a causal explanation, or even that it had remote causes, but that her own desires were not part of the causal sequence that led to it.

Thus far we have been thinking of some sort of undifferentiated notion of freedom of the will. But some philosophers have contended that there are importantly different ideas of freedom that tend to get lumped together (infelicitously, they would argue) under this general rubric. In his ingenious article, "Alternate Possibilities and Moral Responsibility," Harry G. Frankfurt distinguishes between two different kinds of freedom: acting freely (which does not require genuine access to alternative possibilities) and freedom to do otherwise (which does require alternative possibilities). Frankfurt's main point is that moral responsibility does not require freedom to do otherwise, but only acting freely. Thus, he suggests that some of the traditional problems for the sort of freedom that grounds our moral responsibility can be sidestepped.

In "Responsiveness and Moral Responsibility" John Martin Fischer further develops Frankfurt's idea that alternative possibilities are not necessary for moral responsibility. According to Fischer, what is necessary for responsibility is "reasons-responsiveness," where this is understood in terms of an agent being suitably receptive and reactive to reasons for action. Fischer argues that from this, we can see that being morally responsible depends exclusively on the mechanism that actually issues in the agent's action. And from this he concludes that causal *determinism is compatible* with moral responsibility, even if it rules out an agent's ability to do otherwise.

The compatibilist supposes that freedom lies not in the absence of causation, but—at least in part—in one's actions being under the control of the appropriate sorts of causes. For Hume, these causes are the agent's desires. But the efficacy of some desires seems to detract from our freedom, not enhance it—consider the desires of a compulsive drug addict. A plausible compatibilism must go beyond Hume in characterizing what Frankfurt calls "the structure of a person's will," when that person has the kind of freedom we care about. And this is what Frankfurt and Gary Watson try to do in their essays, "Freedom of the Will and the Concept of a Person" and "Free Agency." Both offer what Susan Wolf, in "Sanity and the Metaphysics of Responsibility," calls "deep-self views." That is, Frankfurt and Watson spell out different ways in which our "deep selves" can exercise control over our wills. Wolf argues, though, that what they offer isn't enough, and she holds that one's will can be structured in the right way, according to their views, but still be fundamentally flawed in a way that strips one of one's responsibility. An agent's will, that is, can be appropriately structured; however, if that agent is insane, if he or she isn't able to recognize and appreciate the world for what it is, then that agent still doesn't seem responsible.

KEY TERMS

Freedom
Mind-body problem
Skepticism
Dualistic
Interactive dualism
Logical behaviorism
Methodological behaviorism

Materialist
Problem of personal identity
Determinism
Incompatibilism
Hard determinism
Agent-causation
Compatibilist

A. THE TRADITIONAL PROBLEM OF MIND AND BODY

The Argument from Analogy for Other Minds

BERTRAND RUSSELL

· ·

THE problem with which we are concerned is the following. We observe in ourselves such occurrences as remembering, reasoning, feeling pleasure, and feeling pain. We think that sticks and stones do not have these experiences, but that other people do. Most of us have no doubt that the higher animals feel pleasure and pain, though I was once assured by a fisherman that "Fish have no sense nor feeling." I failed to find out how he had acquired this knowledge. Most people would disagree with him, but would be doubtful about oysters and starfish. However this may be, common sense admits an increasing doubtfulness as we descend in the animal kingdom, but as regards human beings it admits no doubt.

It is clear that belief in the minds of others requires some postulate that is not required in physics, since physics can be content with a knowledge of structure. My present purpose is to suggest what this further postulate may be.

It is clear that we must appeal to something that may be vaguely called "analogy." The behavior of other people is in many ways analogous to our own, and we suppose that it must have analogous causes. What people say is what we should say if we had certain thoughts, and so we infer that they probably have these thoughts. They give us information which we can sometimes subsequently verify. They behave in ways in which we behave when we are pleased (or displeased) in circumstances in which we should be pleased (or displeased). We may talk over with a friend some incident which we have both experienced, and find that his reminiscences dovetail with our own; this is particularly convincing when he remembers something that we have forgotten but that he recalls to our thoughts. Or again: you set your boy a problem in arithmetic, and with luck he gets the right answer; this persuades you that he is capable of arithmetical reasoning. There are, in short, very many ways in which my responses to stimuli differ from those of "dead" matter, and in all these ways other people resemble me. As it is clear to me that the causal laws governing my behavior have to do with "thoughts," it is natural to infer that the same is true of the analogous behavior of my friends.

The inference with which we are at present concerned is not merely that which takes us beyond **solipsism**, by maintaining that sensations have causes about which *something* can be known. This kind of inference . . . suffices for physics. . . . We are concerned now with a much more specific kind of inference, the kind that is involved in our knowledge of the thoughts and feelings of others—assuming that we have such knowledge. It is of course obvious that such knowledge is more or less doubtful. There is not only the general argument that we may be dreaming; there is also the possibility of ingenious automata. There are calculating machines that do sums much better than our schoolboy sons; there are gramophone records that remember impeccably what So-and-so said on such-and-such an occasion; there are people in the cinema who, though copies of real people, are not themselves alive. There is no theoretical limit to what ingenuity could achieve in the way of producing the illusion of life where in fact life is absent.

But, you will say, in all such cases it was the thoughts of human beings that produced the ingenious mechanism. Yes, but how do you know this? And how do you know that the gramophone does *not* "think"?

There is, in the first place, a difference in the causal laws of observable behavior. If I say to a student, "Write me a paper on Descartes's reasons for believing in the existence of matter," I shall, if he is industrious, cause a certain response. A gramophone record might be so constructed as to respond to this stimulus, perhaps better than the student, but if so it would be incapable of telling me anything about any other philosopher, even if I threatened to refuse to give it a degree. One of the most notable peculiarities of human behavior is change of response to a given stimulus. An ingenious person could construct an automaton which would always laugh at his jokes, however often it heard them; but a human being, after laughing a few times, will yawn, and end by saying, "How I laughed the first time I heard that joke."

But the differences in observable behavior between living and dead matter do not suffice to prove that there are "thoughts" connected with living bodies other than my own. It is probably possible theoretically to account for the behavior of living bodies by purely physical causal laws, and it is probably impossible to refute **materialism** by external observation alone. If we are to believe that there are thoughts and feelings other than our own, that must be in virtue of some inference in which our own thoughts and feelings are relevant, and such an inference must go beyond what is needed in physics.

I am, of course, not discussing the history of how we come to believe in other minds. We find ourselves believing in them when we first begin to reflect; the thought that Mother may be angry or pleased is one which arises in early infancy. What I am discussing is the possibility of a postulate which shall establish a rational connection between this belief and data, e.g., between the belief "Mother is angry" and the hearing of a loud voice.

The abstract schema seems to be as follows. We know, from observation of ourselves, a causal law of the form "A causes B," where A is a "thought" and B a physical occurrence. We sometimes observe a B when we cannot observe any A; we then infer an unobserved A. For example: I know that when I say, "I'm thirsty," I say so, usually, because I am thirsty, and therefore, when I hear the sentence "I'm thirsty" at a time when I am not thirsty, I assume that someone else is thirsty. I assume this the more readily if I see before me a hot, drooping body which goes on to say, "I have walked twenty desert miles in this heat with never a drop to drink." It is evident that my confidence in the "inference" is increased by increased complexity in the datum and also by increased certainty of the causal law derived from subjective observation, provided the causal law is such as to account for the complexities of the datum.

It is clear that insofar as plurality of causes is to be suspected, the kind of inference we have been considering is not valid. We are supposed to know "A causes B," and also to know that B has occurred; if this is to justify us in inferring A, we must know that *only* A causes B. Or, if we are content to infer that A is probable, it will suffice if we can know that in most cases it is A that causes B. If you hear thunder without having seen lightning, you confidently infer that there was lightning, because you are convinced that the sort of noise you heard is seldom caused by anything except lightning. As this example shows, our principle is not only employed to establish the existence of other minds but is habitually assumed, though in a less concrete form, in physics. I say "a less concrete form" because unseen lightning is only abstractly similar to seen lightning, whereas we suppose the similarity of other minds to our own to be by no means purely abstract.

Complexity in the observed behavior of another person, when this can all be accounted for by a simple cause such as thirst, increases the probability of the inference by diminishing the probability of some other cause. I think that in ideally favorable circumstances the argument would be formally as follows:

From subjective observation I know that A, which is a thought or feeling, causes B, which is a bodily act, e.g., a statement. I know also that, whenever B is an act of my own body, A is its cause. I now observe an act of the kind B in a body not my own, and I am having no thought or feeling of the kind A. But I still believe, on the basis of self-observation, that only A can cause B; I therefore infer that there was an A which caused B, though it was not an A that I could observe. On this ground I infer that other people's bodies are associated with minds, which resemble mine in proportion as their bodily behavior resembles my own.

In practice, the exactness and certainty of the above statement must be softened. We cannot be sure that, in our subjective experience, A is the only cause of B. And even if A is the only cause of B in our experience, how can we know that this holds outside our experience? It is not necessary that we should know this with any certainty; it is enough if it is highly probable. It is the assumption of probability in such cases that is our postulate. The postulate may therefore be stated as follows:

> If, whenever we can observe whether A and B are present or absent, we find that every case of B has an A as a causal antecedent, then it is probable that most B's have A's as causal antecedents, even in cases where observation does not enable us to know whether A is present or not.

This postulate, if accepted, justifies the inference to other minds, as well as many other inferences that are made unreflectingly by common sense.

KEY TERMS

Solipsism
Materialism

STUDY QUESTIONS

1. Russell argues that "we know, from observation of ourselves, a causal law of the form 'A causes B', where A is a 'thought' and B a physical occurrence. We sometimes observe a B when we cannot observe any A; we then infer an unobserved A." Do you think we are justified in making this final inference? Might B exist without A?
2. Why do you think most of us just take for granted that there are other minds besides our own? Ought we to take this for granted?
3. Which do you think is stronger—our evidence for the existence of an external world or our evidence for the existence of other minds besides our own? Why?

Descartes's Myth

GILBERT RYLE

Gilbert Ryle (1900–1976) was an important mid-twentieth-century philosopher. He was the Waynflete Professor of Metaphysical Philosophy at Magdalen College, Oxford. A leading ordinary language philosopher, Ryle was best known for development of "philosophical behavioralism," a view that he developed in *The Concept of Mind*.

. .

(1) The Official Doctrine

There is a doctrine about the nature and place of minds which is so prevalent among theorists and even among laymen that it deserves to be described as the official theory. Most philosophers, psychologists, and religious teachers subscribe, with minor reservations, to its main articles and, although they admit certain theoretical difficulties in it, they tend to assume that these can be overcome without serious modifications being made to the architecture of the theory. It will be argued here that the central principles of the doctrine are unsound and conflict with the whole body of what we know about minds when we are not speculating about them.

The official doctrine, which hails chiefly from Descartes, is something like this. With the doubtful exceptions of idiots and infants in arms every human being has both a body and a mind. Some would prefer to say that every human being is both a body and a mind. His body and his mind are ordinarily harnessed together, but after the death of the body his mind may continue to exist and function.

Human bodies are in space and are subject to the mechanical laws which govern all other bodies in space. Bodily processes and states can be inspected by external observers. So a man's bodily life is as much a public affair as are the lives of animals and reptiles and even as the careers of trees, crystals, and planets.

But minds are not in space, nor are their operations subject to mechanical laws. The workings of one mind are not witnessable by other observers; its career is private. Only I can take direct cognisance of the states and processes of my own mind. A person therefore lives through two collateral histories, one consisting of what happens in and to his body, the other consisting of what happens in and to his mind. The first is public, the second private. The events in the first history are events in the physical world, those in the second are events in the mental world.

It has been disputed whether a person does or can directly monitor all or only some of the episodes of his own private history; but, according to the official doctrine, of at least some of these episodes he has direct and unchallengeable cognisance. In consciousness, self-consciousness, and introspection he is directly and authentically apprised of the present states and operations of his mind. He may have great or small uncertainties about concurrent and adjacent episodes in the physical world, but he can have none about at least part of what is momentarily occupying his mind.

It is customary to express this bifurcation of his two lives and of his two worlds by saying that the things and events which belong to the physical world, including his own body, are external, while the workings of his own mind are internal. This antithesis of outer and inner is of course meant to be construed as a metaphor, since minds, not being in space, could not be described as being spatially inside anything else, or as having things going on spatially inside themselves. But relapses from this good intention are common and theorists are found speculating how stimuli, the physical sources of which are yards or miles outside a person's skin, can generate mental responses inside his skull, or how decisions framed inside his cranium can set going movements of his extremities.

Even when "inner" and "outer" are construed as metaphors, the problem how a person's mind and body influence one another is notoriously charged with theoretical difficulties. What the mind wills, the legs, arms, and the tongue execute; what affects the ear and the eye has something to do with what the mind perceives; grimaces and smiles betray the mind's moods and bodily castigations lead, it is hoped, to moral improvement. But the actual transactions between the episodes of the private history and those of the public history remain mysterious, since by definition they can belong to neither series. They could not be reported among the happenings described in a person's autobiography of his inner life, but nor could they be reported among those described in some one else's biography of that person's overt career. They can be inspected neither by introspection nor by laboratory experiment. They are theoretical shuttlecocks which are forever being bandied from the physiologist back to the psychologist and from the psychologist back to the physiologist.

Underlying this partly metaphorical representation of the bifurcation of a person's two lives there is a seemingly more profound and philosophical assumption. It is assumed that there are two different kinds of existence or status. What exists or happens may have the status of physical existence, or it may have the status of mental existence. Somewhat as the faces of coins are either heads or tails, or somewhat as living creatures are either male or female, so, it is supposed, some existing is physical existing, other existing is mental existing. It is a necessary feature of what has physical existence that it is in space and time, it is a necessary feature of what has mental existence that it is in time but not in space. What has physical existence is composed of matter, or else is a function of matter; what has mental existence consists of consciousness, or else is a function of consciousness.

There is thus a polar opposition between mind and matter, an opposition which is often brought out as follows. Material objects are situated in a common field, known as "space," and what happens to one body in one part of space is mechanically connected with what happens to other bodies in other parts of space. But mental happenings occur in insulated fields, known as "minds," and there is, apart maybe from telepathy, no direct causal connection between what happens in one mind and what happens in another. Only through the medium of the public physical world can the mind of one person make a difference to the mind of another. The mind is its own place and in his inner life each of us lives the life of a ghostly Robinson Crusoe. People can see, hear, and jolt one another's bodies, but they are irremediably blind and deaf to the workings of one another's minds and inoperative upon them.

What sort of knowledge can be secured of the workings of a mind? On the one side, according to the official theory, a person has direct knowledge of the best imaginable kind of the workings of his own mind. Mental states and processes are (or are normally) conscious states and processes, and the consciousness which irradiates them can engender no illusions and leaves the door open for no doubts. A person's present thinkings, feelings and willings, his perceivings, rememberings, and imaginings are intrinsically "phosphorescent"; their existence and their nature are inevitably betrayed to their owner. The inner life is a stream of consciousness of such a sort that it would be absurd to suggest that the mind whose life is that stream might be unaware of what is passing down it.

True, the evidence adduced recently by Freud seems to show that there exist channels tributary to this stream, which run hidden from their owner. People are actuated by impulses the existence of which they vigorously disavow; some of their thoughts differ from the thoughts which they acknowledge; and some of the actions which they think they will to perform they do not really will. They are thoroughly gulled by some of their own hypocrisies and they successfully ignore facts about their mental lives which on the official theory ought to be patent to them. Holders of the official theory tend, however, to maintain that anyhow in normal circumstances a person must be directly and authentically seized of the present state and workings of his own mind.

Besides being currently supplied with these alleged immediate data of consciousness, a person is also generally supposed to be able to exercise from time to time a special kind of perception, namely inner perception, or introspection. He can take a (non-optical) "look" at what is passing in his mind. Not only can he view and scrutinize a flower through his sense of sight and listen to and discriminate the notes of a bell through his sense of hearing; he can also reflectively or introspectively watch, without any bodily organ of sense, the current episodes of his inner life. This self-observation is also commonly supposed to be immune from illusion, confusion, or doubt. A mind's reports of its own affairs have a certainty superior to the best that is possessed by its reports of matters in the physical world. Sense-perceptions can, but consciousness and introspection cannot, be mistaken or confused.

On the other side, one person has no direct access of any sort to the events of the inner life of another. He cannot do better than make problematic inferences from the observed behaviour of the other person's body to the states of mind which, by analogy from his own conduct, he supposes to be signalised by that behaviour. Direct access to the workings of a mind is the privilege of that mind itself; in default of such privileged access, the workings of one mind are inevitably occult to everyone else. For the supposed arguments from bodily movements similar to their own to mental workings similar to their own would lack any possibility of observational corroboration. Not unnaturally, therefore, an adherent of the official theory finds it difficult to resist this consequence of his premises, that he has no good reason to believe that there do exist minds other than his own. Even if he prefers to believe that to other human bodies there are harnessed minds not unlike his own, he cannot claim to be able to discover their individual characteristics, or the particular things that they undergo and do. Absolute solitude is on this showing the ineluctable destiny of the soul. Only our bodies can meet.

As a necessary corollary of this general scheme there is implicitly prescribed a special way of construing our ordinary concepts of mental powers and operations. The verbs, nouns, and adjectives, with which in ordinary life we describe the wits, characters, and higher-grade performances of the people with whom we have to do, are required to be construed as signifying special episodes in their secret histories, or else as signifying tendencies for such episodes to occur. When someone is described as knowing, believing, or guessing something, as hoping, dreading, intending, or shirking something, as designing this or being amused at that, these verbs are supposed to denote the occurrence of specific modifications in his (to us) occult stream of consciousness. Only his own privileged access to this stream in direct awareness and introspection could provide authentic testimony that these mental-conduct verbs were correctly or incorrectly applied. The onlooker, be he teacher, critic, biographer, or friend, can never assure himself that his comments have any vestige of truth. Yet it was just because we do in fact all know how to make such comments, make them with general correctness and correct them when they turn out to be confused or mistaken, that philosophers found it necessary to construct their theories of the nature and place of minds. Finding mental-conduct concepts being regularly and effectively used, they properly sought to fix their logical geography. But the logical geography officially recommended would entail that there could be no regular or effective use of these mental-conduct concepts in our descriptions of, and prescriptions for, other people's minds.

(2) The Absurdity of the Official Doctrine

Such in outline is the official theory. I shall often speak of it, with deliberate abusiveness, as "the dogma of the Ghost in the Machine." I hope to prove that it is entirely false, and false not in detail but in principle. It is not merely an assemblage of particular mistakes. It is one big mistake and a mistake of a special kind. It is, namely, a **category-mistake**. It represents the facts of mental life as if they belonged to one logical type or category (or range of types or categories), when they actually belong to another. The dogma is therefore a philosopher's myth. In attempting to explode the myth I shall probably be taken to be denying well-known facts about the mental life of human beings, and my plea that I aim at doing nothing more than rectify the logic of mental-conduct concepts will probably be disallowed as mere subterfuge.

I must first indicate what is meant by the phrase "Category-mistake." This I do in a series of illustrations.

A foreigner visiting Oxford or Cambridge for the first time is shown a number of colleges, libraries, playing fields, museums, scientific departments and administrative offices. He then asks "But where is the University? I have seen where the members of the Colleges live, where the Registrar works, where the scientists experiment and the rest. But I have not yet seen the University in which reside and work the members of your University." It has then to be explained to him that the University is not another collateral institution, some ulterior counterpart to the colleges, laboratories, and offices which he has seen. The University is just the way in which all that he has already seen is organized. When they are seen and when their coordination is understood, the University has been seen. His mistake lay in his innocent assumption that it was correct to speak of Christ Church, the Bodleian Library, The Ashmolean Museum, *and* the University, to speak, that is, as if "the University" stood for an extra member of the class of which these other units are members. He was mistakenly allocating the University to the same category as that to which the other institutions belong.

The same mistake would be made by a child witnessing the march-past of a division, who, having had pointed out to him such and such battalions, batteries, squadrons, etc., asked when the division was going to appear. He would be supposing that a division was counterpart to the units already seen, partly similar to them and partly unlike them. He would be shown his mistake by being told that in watching the battalions, batteries, and squadrons marching past he had been watching the division marching past. The march-past was not a parade of battalions, batteries, squadrons, *and* a division; it was a parade of the battalions, batteries, and squadrons *of* a division.

One more illustration. A foreigner watching his first game of cricket learns what are the functions of the bowlers, the batsmen, the fielders, the umpires, and the scorers. He than says, "But there is no one left on the field to contribute the famous element of team-spirit. I see who does the bowling, the batting, and the wicket-keeping; but I do not see whose role it is to exercise *esprit de corps*." Once more, it would have to be explained that he was looking for the wrong type of thing. Team-spirit is not another cricketing-operation supplementary to all of the other special tasks. It is, roughly, the keenness with which each of the special tasks is performed, and performing a task keenly is not performing two tasks. Certainly exhibiting team-spirit is not the same thing as bowling or catching, but nor is it a third thing such that we can say that the bowler first bowls *and* then exhibits team-spirit or that a fielder is at a given moment *either* catching *or* displaying *esprit de corps*.

These illustrations of category-mistakes have a common feature which must be noticed. The mistakes were made by people who did not know how to wield the concepts *University*, *division*, and *team-spirit*. Their puzzles arose from inability to use certain items in the English vocabulary.

The theoretically interesting category-mistakes are those made by people who are perfectly competent to apply concepts, at least in the situations with which they are familiar, but are still liable in their abstract thinking to allocate those concepts to logical types to which they do not belong. An instance of a mistake of this sort would be the following story. A student of politics has learned the main differences between the British, the French, and the American Constitutions, and has learned also the differences and connections between the Cabinet, Parliament, the various Ministries, the Judicature, and the Church of England. But he still becomes embarrassed when asked questions about the connections between the Church of England, the Home Office, and the British Constitution. For while the Church and the Home Office are institutions, the British Constitution is not another institution in the same sense of that noun. So inter-institutional relations which can be asserted or denied to hold between the Church and the Home Office cannot be asserted or denied to hold between either of them and the British Constitution. "The

British Constitution" is not a term of the same logical type as "the Home Office" and "the Church of England." In a partially similar way, John Doe may be a relative, a friend, an enemy, or a stranger to Richard Roe; but he cannot be any of these things to the Average Taxpayer. He knows how to talk sense in certain sorts of discussions about the Average Taxpayer, but he is baffled to say why he could not come across him in the street as he can come across Richard Roe.

It is pertinent to our main subject to notice that, so long as the student of politics continues to think of the British Constitution as a counterpart to the other institutions, he will tend to describe it as a mysteriously occult institution; and so long as John Doe continues to think of the Average Taxpayer as a fellow-citizen, he will tend to think of him as an elusive insubstantial man, a ghost who is everywhere yet nowhere.

My destructive purpose is to show that a family of radical category-mistakes is the source of the double-life theory. The representation of a person as a ghost mysteriously ensconced in a machine derives from this argument. Because, as is true, a person's thinking, feeling, and purposive doing cannot be described solely in the idioms of physics, chemistry, and physiology, therefore they must be described in counterpart idioms. As the human body is a complex organised unit, so the human mind must be another complex organised unit, though one made of a different sort of stuff and with a different sort of structure. Or, again, as the human body, like any other parcel of matter, is a field of causes and effects, so the mind must be another field of causes and effects, though not (Heaven be praised) mechanical causes and effects.

(3) The Origin of the Category-Mistake

One of the chief intellectual origins of what I have yet to prove to be the Cartesian category-mistake seems to be this. When Galileo showed that his methods of scientific discovery were competent to provide a mechanical theory which should cover every occupant of space, Descartes found in himself two conflicting motives. As a man of scientific genius he could not but endorse the claims of mechanics, yet as a religious and moral man he could not accept, as Hobbes accepted, the discouraging rider to those claims, namely that human nature differs only in degree of complexity from clockwork. The mental could not be just a variety of the mechanical.

He and subsequent philosophers naturally but erroneously availed themselves of the following escape-route. Since mental-conduct words are not to be construed as signifying the occurrence of mechanical processes, they must be construed as signifying the occurrence of non-mechanical processes; since mechanical laws explain movements in space as the effects of other movements in space, other laws must explain some of the nonspatial workings of minds as the effects of other non-spatial workings of minds. The difference between the human behaviours which we describe as intelligent and those which we describe as unintelligent must be a difference in their causation; so, while some movements of human tongues and limbs are the effects of mechanical causes, others must be the effects of non-mechanical causes, i.e. some issue from movements of particles of matter, others from workings of the mind.

The differences between the physical and the mental were thus represented as differences inside the common framework of the categories of "thing," "stuff," "attribute," "stage," "process," "change," "cause," and "effect." Minds are things, but different sorts of things from bodies; mental processes are causes and effects but different sorts of causes and effects from bodily movements. And so on. Somewhat as the foreigner expected the University to be an extra edifice, rather like a college but also considerably different, so the repudiators of mechanism represented minds as extra centers of causal processes, rather like machines but also considerably different from them. Their theory was a para-mechanical hypothesis.

That this assumption was at the heart of the doctrine is shown by the fact that there was from the beginning felt to be a major theoretical difficulty in explaining how minds can influence and be influenced by bodies. How can a mental process, such as willing, cause spatial movements like the movements of the tongue? How can a physical change in the optic nerve have among its effects a mind's perception of a flash of light? This notorious crux by itself shows the logical mould into which Descartes pressed his theory of the mind. It was the self-same mould into which he and Galileo set their mechanics. Still unwittingly adhering to the grammar of mechanics, he tried to avert disaster by describing minds in what was merely an obverse vocabulary. The workings of minds had to be described by the mere negatives of the specific descriptions given to bodies; they are not in space, they are not motions, they are not modifications of matter, they are not accessible to public observation. Minds are not bits of clockwork, they are just bits of not-clockwork.

As thus represented, minds are not merely ghosts harnessed to machines, they are themselves just spectral machines. Though the human body is an engine, it is not quite an ordinary engine, since some of its workings are governed by another engine inside it—this interior governor-engine being one of a very special sort. It is invisible, inaudible, and it has no size or weight. It cannot be taken to bits and the laws it obeys are not those known to ordinary engineers. Nothing is known of how it governs the bodily engine.

A second major crux points the same moral. Since, according to the doctrine, minds belong to the same category as bodies and since bodies are rigidly governed by mechanical laws, it seemed to many theorists to follow that minds must be similarly governed by rigid non-mechanical laws. The physical world is a **deterministic** system, so the mental world must be a deterministic system. Bodies cannot help the modifications that they undergo, so minds cannot help pursuing the careers fixed for them. *Responsibility*, *choice*, *merit* and *demerit* are therefore inapplicable concepts—unless the compromise solution is adopted of saying that the laws governing mental processes, unlike those governing physical processes, have the congenial attribute of being only rather rigid. The problem of the **Freedom of the Will** was the problem how to reconcile the hypothesis that minds are to be described in terms drawn from the categories of mechanics with the knowledge that higher-grade human conduct is not of a piece with the behaviour of machines.

It is an historical curiosity that it was not noticed that the entire argument was broken-backed. Theorists correctly assumed that any sane man could already recognise the differences between, say, rational and non-rational utterances or between purposive and automatic behaviour. Else there would have been nothing requiring to be salved from mechanism. Yet the explanation given presupposed that one person could in principle never recognise the difference between the rational and the irrational utterances issuing from other human bodies, since he could never get access to the postulated immaterial causes of some of their utterances. Save for the doubtful exception of himself, he could never tell the difference between a man and a Robot. It would have to be conceded, for example, that, for all that we can tell, the inner lives of persons who are classed as idiots or lunatics are as rational as those of anyone else. Perhaps only their overt behaviour is disappointing; that is to say, perhaps "idiots" are not really idiotic, or "lunatics" lunatic. Perhaps, too, some of those who are classed as sane are really idiots. According to the theory, external observers could never know how the overt behaviour of others is correlated with their mental powers and processes and so they could never know or even plausibly conjuncture whether their applications of mental-conduct concepts to these other people were correct or incorrect. It would then be hazardous or impossible for a man to claim sanity or logical consistency even for himself, since he would be debarred from comparing his own performances with those of others. In short, our characterisations of persons and their performances as intelligent, prudent, and virtuous or as stupid, hypocritical, and cowardly could never have been made, so the problem of providing a special causal hypothesis to serve as the basis of such diagnoses would never have arisen. The question, "How do persons differ from machines?" arose just because everyone already knew how to apply mental-conduct concepts before the new causal hypothesis was introduced. This causal hypothesis could not therefore be the source of the criteria used in those applications. Nor, of course, has the causal hypothesis in any degree improved our handling of those criteria. We still distinguish good from bad arithmetic, politic from impolitic conduct, and fertile from infertile imaginations in the ways in which Descartes himself distinguished them before and after he speculated how the applicability of these criteria was compatible with the principle of mechanical causation.

He had mistaken the logic of his problem. Instead of asking by what criteria intelligent behaviour is actually distinguished from non-intelligent behaviour, he asked, "Given that the principle of mechanical causation does not tell us the difference, what other causal principle will tell it us?" He realised that the problem was not one of mechanics and assumed that it must therefore be one of some counterpart to mechanics. Not unnaturally psychology is often cast for just this role.

When two terms belong to the same category, it is proper to construct conjunctive propositions embodying them. Thus a purchaser may say that he bought a left-hand glove and a right-hand glove, but not that he bought a left-hand glove, a right-hand glove and a pair of gloves. "She came home in a flood of tears and a sedan-chair" is a well-known joke based on the absurdity of conjoining terms of different types. It would have been equally ridiculous to construct the disjunction "She came home either in a flood of tears or else in a sedan-chair." Now the dogma of the Ghost in the Machine does just this. It maintains that there exist both bodies and minds; that there occur physical processes and mental processes; that there are mechanical causes of corporeal movements and mental causes of corporeal movements. I shall argue that these and other analogous conjunctions are absurd; but, it must be noticed, the argument will not show that either of the illegitimately conjoined propositions is absurd in itself. I am not, for example, denying that there occur mental processes. Doing long division is a mental process and so is making a joke. But I am saying that the phrase "there occur mental processes" does not mean the same sort of thing as "there occur physical processes," and, therefore, that it makes no sense to conjoin or disjoin the two.

If my argument is successful, there will follow some interesting consequences. First, the hallowed contrast between Mind and Matter will be dissipated, but dissipated not by either of the equally hallowed absorptions of Mind by Matter or of Matter by Mind, but in quite a different way. For the seeming contrast of the two will be shown to be as illegitimate as would be the contrast of "she came home in a flood of tears" and "she came home in a sedan-chair." The belief that there is a polar opposition between Mind and Matter is the belief that they are terms of the same logical type.

It will also follow that both Idealism and Materialism are answers to an improper question. The "reduction" of the material world to mental states and processes, as well as the "reduction" of mental states and processes to physical states and processes, presuppose the legitimacy of the disjunction "Either there exist minds or there exist bodies (but not both)." It would be like saying, "Either she bought a left-hand and a right-hand glove or she bought a pair of gloves (but not both)."

It is perfectly proper to say, in one logical tone of voice, that there exist minds and to say, in another logical tone of voice, that there exist bodies. But these expressions do not indicate two different species of existence, for "existence" is not a generic word like "coloured" or "sexed." They indicate two different senses of "exist," somewhat as "rising" has different senses in "the tide is rising," "hopes are rising," and "the average age of death is rising." A man would be thought to be making a poor joke who said that three things are now rising, namely the tide, hopes, and the average age of death. It would be just as good or bad a joke to say that there exist prime numbers and Wednesdays and public opinions and navies; or that there exist both minds and bodies. . . .

(4) Historical Note

It would not be true to say that the official theory derives solely from Descartes's theories, or even from a more widespread anxiety about the implications of seventeenth century mechanics. Scholastic and Reformation theology has schooled the intellects of the scientists as well as of the laymen, philosophers, and clerics of that age. Stoic-Augustinian theories of the will were embedded in the Calvinist doctrines of sin and grace; Platonic and Aristotelian theories of the intellect shaped the orthodox doctrines of the immortality of the soul. Descartes was reformulating already prevalent theological doctrines of the soul in the new syntax of Galileo. The theologian's privacy of conscience became the philosopher's privacy of consciousness, and what had been the bogy of Predestination reappeared as the bogy of Determinism.

It would also not be true to say that the two-worlds myth did no theoretical good. Myths often do a lot of theoretical good, while they are still new. One benefit bestowed by the para-mechanical myth was that it partly superannuated the then prevalent para-political myth. Minds and their Faculties had previously been described by analogies with political superiors and political subordinates. The idioms used were those of ruling, obeying, collaborating, and rebelling. They survived and still survive in many ethical and some **epistemological** discussions. As, in physics, the new myth of occult Forces was a scientific improvement on the old myth of Final Causes, so, in anthropological and psychological theory, the new myth of hidden operations, impulses, and agencies was an improvement on the old myth of dictations, deferences, and disobediences.

KEY TERMS

Category mistake
Deterministic
Freedom of the will
Epistemological

STUDY QUESTIONS

1. Do you think that the view Ryle calls "the official doctrine" is the view that most people in our society hold? Is there good reason to distinguish between the "outer" and the "inner"?
2. Ryle gives some examples of what it is to make a category mistake. Can you construct your own example of someone making a category mistake?
3. Ryle suggests that the official doctrine makes a category mistake. Explain what such a mistake would involve. What are the consequences if Ryle is correct?
4. How is the phrase "there occur mental processes" supposed to be importantly different from the phrase "there occur physical processes"?

The Nature of Mind

DAVID M. ARMSTRONG

David M. Armstrong (1926–2014) was Emeritus Professor of Philosophy at the University of Sydney. He is well known for his work in metaphysics and philosophy of mind, and his publications include *Perception and the Physical World*, *A Materialist Theory of the Mind*, and *Universals and Scientific Realism*.

. .

MEN have minds, that is to say, they perceive, they have sensations, emotions, beliefs, thoughts, purposes, and desires.[1] What is it to have a mind? What is it to perceive, to

feel emotion, to hold a belief, or to have a purpose? In common with many other modern philosophers, I think that the best clue we have to the nature of mind is furnished by the discoveries and hypotheses of modern science concerning the nature of man.

What does modern science have to say about the nature of man? There are, of course, all sorts of disagreements and divergencies in the views of individual scientists. But I think it is true to say that one view is steadily gaining ground, so that it bids fair to become established scientific doctrine. This is the view that we can give a complete account of man *in purely physico-chemical terms*. This view has received a tremendous impetus in the last decade from the new subject of molecular biology, a subject which promises to unravel the physical and chemical mechanisms which lie at the basis of life. Before that time, it received great encouragement from pioneering work in neurophysiology pointing to the likelihood of a purely electro-chemical account of the working of the brain. I think it is fair to say that those scientists who still reject the physico-chemical account of man do so primarily for philosophical, or moral, or religious reasons, and only secondarily, and half-heartedly, for reasons of scientific detail. This is not to say that in the future new evidence and new problems may not come to light which will force science to reconsider the physico-chemical view of man. But at present the drift of scientific thought is clearly set towards the physico-chemical hypothesis. And we have nothing better to go on than the present.

For me, then, and for many philosophers who think like me, the moral is clear. We must try to work out an account of the nature of mind which is compatible with the view that man is nothing but a physico-chemical mechanism.

And . . . I shall be concerned to do just this: to sketch (in barest outline) what may be called a **Materialist** or **Physicalist** account of the mind.

But before doing this I should like to go back and consider a criticism of my position which must inevitably occur to some. What reason have I, it may be asked, for taking my stand on science? Even granting that I am right about what is the currently dominant scientific view of man, why should we concede science a special authority to decide questions about the nature of man? What of the authority of philosophy, of religion, of morality, or even of literature and art? Why do I set the authority of science above all these? Why this "scientism"?

It seems to me that the answer to this question is very simple. If we consider the search for truth, in all its fields, we find that it is only in science that men versed in their subject can, after investigation that is more or less prolonged, and which may in some cases extend beyond a single human lifetime, reach substantial agreement about what is the case. It is only as a result of scientific investigation that we ever seem to reach an intellectual consensus about controversial matters.

In the Epistle Dedicatory to his *De Corpore* Hobbes wrote of William Harvey, the discoverer of the circulation of the blood, that he was "the only man I know, that conquering envy, hath established a new doctrine in his life-time."

Before Copernicus, Galileo and Harvey, Hobbes remarks, "there was nothing certain in natural philosophy." And, we might add, with the exception of mathematics, there was nothing certain in any other learned discipline.

These remarks of Hobbes are incredibly revealing. They show us what a watershed in the intellectual history of the human race the seventeenth century was. Before that time inquiry proceeded, as it were, in the dark. Men could not hope to see their doctrine *established*, that is to say, accepted by the vast majority of those properly versed in the subject under discussion. There was no intellectual consensus. Since that time, it has become a commonplace to see new doctrines, sometimes of the most far-reaching kind, established to the satisfaction of the learned, often within the lifetime of their first proponents. Science has provided us with a method of deciding disputed questions. This is not to say, of course, that the consensus of those who are learned and competent in a subject cannot be mistaken. Of course such a consensus can be mistaken. Sometimes it has been mistaken. But, granting fallibility, what better authority have we than such a consensus?

Now this is of the utmost importance. For in philosophy, in religion, in such disciplines as literary criticism, in moral questions in so far as they are thought to be matters of truth and falsity, there has been a notable failure to achieve an intellectual consensus about disputed questions among the learned. Must we not then attach a peculiar authority to the discipline that can achieve a consensus? And if it presents us with a certain vision of the nature of man, is this not a powerful reason for accepting that vision?

I will not take up here the deeper question *why* it is that the methods of science have enabled us to achieve an intellectual consensus about so many disputed matters. That question, I think, could receive no brief or uncontroversial answer. I am resting my argument on the simple and uncontroversial fact that, as a result of scientific investigation, such a consensus has been achieved.

It may be replied—it often is replied—that while science is all very well in its own sphere—the sphere of the physical, perhaps—there are matters of fact on which it is not competent to pronounce. And among such matters, it may be claimed, is the question what is the whole nature of man. But I cannot see that this reply has much force. Science has provided us with an island of truths, or, perhaps one should say, a raft of truths, to bear us up on the sea of our disputatious ignorance. There may have to be revisions and refinements, new results may set old findings in a new perspective, but what science has given us will not be altogether superseded. Must we not therefore appeal to these relative certainties for guidance when we come to consider uncertainties elsewhere? Perhaps science cannot help us to decide whether or not there is a God, whether or not human beings have immortal souls, or whether or not the will is free. But if science cannot assist us, what can? I conclude that it is the scientific vision of man, and not the philosophical or religious or artistic or moral vision of man, that is the best clue we have to the nature of man. And it is rational to argue from the best evidence we have.

Having in this way attempted to justify my procedure, I turn back to my subject: the attempt to work out an account of mind, or, if you prefer, of mental process, within the framework of the physico-chemical or, as we may call it, the Materialist view of man.

Now there is one account of mental process that is at once attractive to any philosopher sympathetic to a Materialist view of man: this is **Behaviourism**. Formulated originally by a psychologist, J. B. Watson, it attracted widespread interest and considerable support from scientifically oriented philosophers. Traditional philosophy had tended to think of the mind as a rather mysterious inward arena that lay behind, and was responsible for, the outward or physical behaviour of our bodies. Descartes thought of this inner arena as a *spiritual substance*, and it was this conception of the mind as spiritual object that Gilbert Ryle attacked, apparently in the interest of Behaviourism, in his important book *The Concept of Mind*.

He ridiculed the Cartesian view as the dogma of "the ghost in the machine." The mind was not something behind the behaviour of the body, it was simply part of that physical behaviour. My anger with you is not some modification of a spiritual substance which somehow brings about aggressive behaviour; rather it is the aggressive behaviour itself; my addressing strong words to you, striking you, turning my back on you, and so on. Thought is not an inner process that lies behind, and brings about, the words I speak and write: it is my speaking and writing. The mind is not an inner arena, it is outward act.

It is clear that such a view of mind fits in very well with a completely Materialistic or Physicalist view of man. If there is no need to draw a distinction between mental processes and their expression in physical behaviour, but if instead the mental processes are identified with their so-called "expressions," then the existence of mind stands in no conflict with the view that man is nothing but a physico-chemical mechanism.

However, the version of Behaviourism that I have just sketched is a very crude version, and its crudity lays it open to obvious objections. One obvious difficulty is that it is our common experience that there can be mental processes going on although there is no behaviour occurring that could possibly be treated as expressions of these processes. A man may be angry, but give no bodily sign; he may think, but say or do nothing at all.

In my view, the most plausible attempt to refine Behaviourism with a view to meeting this objection was made by introducing the notion of *a disposition to behave*. (Dispositions to behave play a particularly important part in Ryle's account of the mind.) Let us consider the general notion of disposition first. Brittleness is a disposition, a disposition possessed by materials like glass. Brittle materials are those which, when subjected to relatively small forces, break or shatter easily. But breaking and shattering easily is not brittleness, rather it is the *manifestation* of brittleness. Brittleness itself is the tendency or liability of the material to break or shatter easily. A piece of glass may never shatter or break throughout its whole history, but it is still the case that it is brittle: it is liable to shatter or break if dropped quite a small way or hit quite lightly. Now a disposition to *behave* is simply a tendency or liability of a person to behave in a certain way under certain circumstances. The brittleness of glass is a disposition that the glass retains throughout its history, but clearly there could also be dispositions that come and go. The dispositions to behave that are of interest to the Behaviourist are, for the most part, of this temporary character.

Now how did Ryle and others use the notion of a disposition to behave to meet the obvious objection to Behaviourism that there can be mental processes going on although the subject is engaging in no relevant behaviour? Their strategy was to argue that in such cases, although the subject was not behaving in any relevant way, he or she was *disposed* to behave in some relevant way. The glass does not shatter, but it is still brittle. The man does not behave, but he does have a disposition to behave. We can say he thinks although he does not speak or act because at that time he was disposed to speak or act in a certain way. *If* he had been asked, perhaps, he would have spoken or acted. We can say he is angry although he does not behave angrily, because he is disposed so to behave. *If* only one more word had been addressed to him, he would have burst out. And so on. In this way it was hoped that Behaviourism could be squared with the obvious facts.

It is very important to see just how these thinkers conceived of disposition. I quote from Ryle

> To possess a dispositional property *is not to be in a particular state, or to undergo a particular change*; it is to be bound or liable to be in a particular state, or to undergo a particular change, when a particular condition is realised. (*The Concept of Mind*, p. 43, my italics.)

So to explain the breaking of a lightly struck glass on a particular occasion by saying it was brittle is, on this view of dispositions, simply to say that the glass broke because it is the sort of thing that regularly breaks when quite lightly struck. The breaking was the normal behaviour, or not abnormal behaviour, of such a thing. The brittleness is not to be conceived of as a *cause* for the breakage, or even, more vaguely, a *factor* in bringing about the breaking. Brittleness is just the fact that things of that sort break easily.

But although in this way the Behaviourists did something to deal with the objection that mental processes can occur in the absence of behaviour, it

seems clear, now that the shouting and the dust have died, that they did not do enough. When I think, but my thoughts do not issue in any action, it seems as obvious as anything is obvious that there is something actually going on in me which constitutes my thought. It is not simply that I would speak or act if some conditions that are unfulfilled were to be fulfilled. Something is currently going on, in the strongest and most literal sense of "going on," and this something is my thought. Rylean Behaviourism denies this, and so it is unsatisfactory as a theory of mind. Yet I know of no version of Behaviourism that is more satisfactory. The moral of those of us who wish to take a purely physicalistic view of man is that we must look for some other account of the nature of mind and of mental processes.

But perhaps we need not grieve too deeply about the failure of Behaviourism to produce a satisfactory theory of mind. Behaviourism is a profoundly unnatural account of mental processes. If somebody speaks and acts in certain ways it is natural to speak of this speech and action as the *expression* of his thought. It is not at all natural to speak of his speech and action as identical with his thought. We naturally think of the thought as something quite distinct from the speech and action which, under suitable circumstances, brings the speech and action about. Thoughts are not to be identified with behaviour, we think, they lie behind behaviour. A man's behaviour constitutes the *reason* we have for attributing certain mental processes to him, but the behaviour cannot be identified with the mental processes.

This suggests a very interesting line of thought about the mind. Behaviourism is certainly wrong, but perhaps it is not altogether wrong. Perhaps the Behaviorists are wrong in identifying the mind and mental occurrences with behaviour, but perhaps they are right in thinking that our notion of a mind and of individual mental states is *logically tied to behaviour*. For perhaps what we mean by a mental state is some state of the person which, under suitable circumstances, *brings about* a certain range of behaviour. Perhaps mind can be defined not as behaviour, but rather as the inner *cause* of certain behaviour. Thought is not speech under suitable circumstances, rather it is something within the person which, in suitable circumstances brings about speech. And, in fact, I believe that this is the true account, or, at any rate, a true first account, of what we mean by a mental state.

How does this line of thought link up with a purely physicalist view of man? The position is, I think, that while it does not make such a physicalist view inevitable, it does make it *possible*. It does not entail, but it is compatible with, a purely physicalist view of man. For if our notion of the mind and mental states is nothing but that of a cause within the person of certain ranges of behaviour, then it becomes a scientific question, and not a question of logical analysis, what in fact the intrinsic nature of that cause is. The cause might be, as Descartes thought it was, a spiritual substance working through the pineal gland to produce the complex bodily behaviour of which men are capable. It might be breath, or specially smooth and mobile atoms dispersed throughout the body; it might be many other things. But in fact the verdict of modern science seems to be that the sole cause of mind-betokening behaviour in man and the higher animals is the physico-chemical workings of the central nervous system. And so, assuming we have correctly characterised our concept of a mental state as nothing but the cause of certain sorts of behaviour, then we can identify these mental states with purely physical states of the central nervous system.

At this point we may stop and go back to the Behaviourists' dispositions. We saw that, according to them, the brittleness of glass or, to take another example, the elasticity of rubber, is not a state of the glass or the rubber, but is simply the fact that things of that sort behave in the way they do. But now let us consider how a scientist would think about brittleness or elasticity. Faced with the phenomenon of breakage under relatively small impacts, or the phenomenon of stretching when a force is applied followed by contraction when the force is removed, he will assume that there is some current *state* of the glass or the rubber which is responsible for the characteristic behaviour of samples of these two materials. At the beginning he will not know what this state is, but he will endeavor to find out, and he may succeed in finding out. And when he has found out he will very likely make remarks of this sort: "We have discovered that the brittleness of glass is in fact a certain sort of pattern in the molecules of the

glass." That is to say, he will *identify* brittleness with the state of the glass that is responsible for the liability of the glass to break. For him, a disposition of an object is a state of the object. What makes the state a state of brittleness is the fact that it gives rise to the characteristic manifestations of brittleness. But the disposition itself is distinct from its manifestation: it is the state of the glass that gives rise to these manifestations in suitable circumstances.

You will see that this way of looking at dispositions is very different from that of Ryle and the Behaviourists. The great difference is this: If we treat dispositions as actual states, as I have suggested that scientists do, even if states whose intrinsic nature may yet have to be discovered, then we can say that dispositions are actual *causes*, or causal factors, which, in suitable circumstances, actually bring about those happenings which are the manifestations of the disposition. A certain molecular constitution of glass which constitutes its brittleness is actually *responsible* for the fact that, when the glass is struck, it breaks.

Now I shall not argue the matter here, because the detail of the argument is technical and difficult,[2] but I believe that the view of dispositions as states, which is the view that is natural to science, is the correct one. I believe it can be shown quite strictly that, to the extent that we admit the notion of dispositions at all, we are committed to the view that they are actual *states* of the object that has the disposition. I may add that I think that the same holds for the closely connected notions of capacities and powers. Here I will simply assume this step in my argument.

But perhaps it can be seen that the rejection of the idea that mind is simply a certain range of man's behaviour in favour of the view that mind is rather the inner *cause* of that range of man's behaviour is bound up with the rejection of the Rylean view of dispositions in favour of one that treats dispositions as states of objects and so as having actual causal power. The Behaviourists were wrong to identify the mind with behaviour. They were not so far off the mark when they tried to deal with cases where mental happenings occur in the absence of behaviour by saying that these are dispositions to behave. But in order to reach a correct view, I am suggesting, they would have to conceive of these dispositions as actual *states* of the person who has the disposition, states that have actual power to bring about behaviour in suitable circumstances. But to do this is to abandon the central inspiration of Behaviourism: that in talking about the mind we do not have to go behind outward behaviour to inner states.

And so two separate but interlocking lines of thought have pushed me in the same direction. The first line of thought is that it goes profoundly against the grain to think of the mind as behaviour. The mind is, rather, that which stands behind and brings about our complex behaviour. The second line of thought is that the Behaviourists' dispositions, properly conceived, are really states that underlie behaviour, and, under suitable circumstances, bring about behaviour. Putting these two together, we reach the conception of a mental state as *a state of the person apt for producing certain ranges of behaviour*. This formula: a mental state is a state of the person apt for producing certain ranges of behaviour, I believe to be a very illuminating way of looking at the concept of a mental state. I have found it very fruitful in the search for detailed logical analyses of the individual mental concepts.

Now, I do not think that Hegel's dialectic has much to tell us about the nature of reality. But I think that human thought often moves in a dialectical way, from thesis to antithesis and then to the synthesis. Perhaps thought about the mind is a case in point. I have already said that classical philosophy tended to think of the mind as an inner arena of some sort. This we may call the Thesis. Behaviourism moved to the opposite extreme: the mind was seen as outward behaviour. This is the Antithesis. My proposed Synthesis is that the mind is properly conceived as an inner principle, but a principle that is identified in terms of the outward behaviour it is apt for bringing about. This way of looking at the mind and mental states does not itself entail a Materialist or Physicalist view of man, for nothing is said in this analysis about the intrinsic nature of these mental states. But if we have, as I have asserted that we do have, general scientific grounds for thinking that man is nothing but a physical mechanism, we can go on to argue that the mental states are in fact nothing but physical states of the central nervous system.

Along these lines, then, I would look for an account of the mind that is compatible with a purely Materialist

theory of man. I have tried to carry out this programme in detail in *A Materialist Theory of the Mind*. There are, as may be imagined, all sorts of powerful objections that can be made to this view. But [in what follows] . . . I propose to do only one thing. I will develop one very important objection to my view of the mind—an objection felt by many philosophers—and then try to show how the objection should be met.

The view that our notion of mind is nothing but that of an inner principle apt for bringing about certain sorts of behaviour may be thought to share a certain weakness with Behaviourism. Modern philosophers have put the point about Behaviourism by saying that although Behaviourism may be a satisfactory account of the mind from an *other-person point of view*, it will not do as a *first-person* account. To explain. In our encounters with other people, all we ever observe is their behaviour: their actions, their speech, and so on. And so, if we simply consider other people, Behaviourism might seem to do full justice to the facts. But the trouble about Behaviourism is that it seems so unsatisfactory as applied to our *own* case. In our own case, we seem to be aware of so much more than mere behaviour.

Suppose that now we conceive of the mind as an inner principle apt for bringing about certain sorts of behaviour. This again fits the other-person cases very well. Bodily behaviour of a very sophisticated sort is observed, quite different from the behaviour that ordinary physical objects display. It is inferred that this behaviour must spring from a very special sort of inner cause in the object that exhibits this behaviour. This inner cause is christened "the mind," and those who take a physicalist view of man argue that it is simply the central nervous system of the body observed. Compare this with the case of glass. Certain characteristic behaviour is observed: the breaking and shattering of the material when acted upon by relatively small forces. A special inner state of the glass is postulated to explain this behaviour. Those who take a purely physicalist view of glass then argue that this state is a *natural* state of the glass. It is, perhaps, an arrangement of its molecules, and not, say, the peculiarly malevolent disposition of the demons that dwell in glass.

But when we turn to our own case, the position may seem less plausible. We are conscious, we have experiences. Now can we say that to be conscious, to have experiences, is simply for something to go on within us apt for the causing of certain sorts of behaviour? Such an account does not seem to do any justice to the phenomena. And so it seems that our account of the mind, like Behaviourism, will fail to do justice to the first-person case.

In order to understand the objection better it may be helpful to consider a particular case. If you have driven for a very long distance without a break, you may have had experience of a curious state of automatism, which can occur in these conditions. One can suddenly "come to" and realise that one has driven for long distances without being aware of what one was doing, or, indeed, without being aware of anything. One has kept the car on the road, used the brake and the clutch perhaps, yet all without any awareness of what one was doing.

Now, if we consider this case it is obvious that *in some sense* mental processes are still going on when one is in such an automatic state. Unless one's will was still operating in some way, and unless one was still perceiving in some way, the car would not still be on the road. Yet, of course, *something* mental is lacking. Now, I think, when it is alleged that an account of mind as an inner principle apt for the production of certain sorts of behaviour leaves out consciousness or experience, what is alleged to have been left out is just whatever is missing in the automatic driving case. It is conceded that an account of mental processes as states of the person apt for the production of certain sorts of behaviour may very possibly be adequate to deal with such cases as that of automatic driving. It may be adequate to deal with most of the mental processes of animals, who perhaps spend a good deal of their lives in this state of automatism. But, it is contended, it cannot deal with the consciousness that we normally enjoy.

I will now try to sketch an answer to this important and powerful objection. Let us begin in an apparently unlikely place, and consider the way that an account of mental processes of the sort I am giving would deal with *sense-perception*.

Now psychologists, in particular, have long realised that there is a very close logical tie between sense-perception and *selective behaviour*. Suppose we want to decide whether an animal can perceive the difference between red and green. We might give the animal a choice between two pathways, over one of which a red light shines and over the other of which a green light shines. If the animal happens by chance to choose the green pathway we reward it; if it happens to choose the other pathway we do not reward it. If, after some trials, the animal systematically takes the green-lighted pathway, and if we become assured that the only relevant differences in the two pathways are the differences in the colour of the lights, we are entitled to say that the animal can see this colour difference. Using its eyes, it selects between red-lighted and green-lighted pathways. So we say it can see the difference between red and green.

Now a Behaviourist would be tempted to say that the animal's regularly selecting the green-lighted pathway *was* its perception of the colour difference. But this is unsatisfactory, because we all want to say that perception is something that goes on within the person or animal—within its mind—although, of course, this mental event is normally *caused* by the operation of the environment upon the organism. Suppose, however, that we speak instead of *capacities* for selective behaviour towards the current environment, and suppose we think of these capacities, like dispositions, as actual inner states of the organism. We can then think of the animal's perception as a state within the animal apt, if the animal is so impelled, for selective behaviour between the red- and green-lighted pathways.

In general, we can think of perceptions as inner states or events apt for the production of certain sorts of selective behaviour towards our environment. To perceive is like acquiring a key to a door. You do not have to use the key: you can put it in your pocket and never bother about the door. But if you do want to open the door the key may be essential. The blind man is a man who does not acquire certain keys, and, as a result, is not able to operate in his environment in the way that somebody who has his sight can operate. It seems, then, a very promising view to take of perceptions that they are inner states defined by the sorts of selective behaviour that they enable the perceiver to exhibit, if so impelled.

Now how is this discussion of perception related to the question of consciousness of experience, the sort of thing that the driver who is in a state of automatism has not got, but which we normally do have? Simply this. My proposal is that consciousness, in this sense of the word, is nothing but *perception or awareness of the state of our own mind*. The driver in a state of automatism perceives, or is aware of, the road. If he did not, the car would be in a ditch. But he is not currently aware of this awareness of the road. He perceives the road, but he does not perceive his perceiving, or anything else that is going on in his mind. He is not, as we normally are, conscious of what is going on in his mind.

And so I conceive of consciousness or experience, in this sense of the words, in the way that Locke and Kant conceived it, as like perception. Kant, in a striking phrase, spoke of "inner sense." We cannot directly observe the minds of others, but each of us has the power to observe directly our own minds, and "perceive" what is going on there. The driver in the automatic state is one whose "inner eye" is shut: who is not currently aware of what is going on in his own mind.

Now if this account is along the right lines, why should we not give an account of this inner observation along the same lines as we have already given of perception? Why should we not conceive of it as an inner state, a state in this case directed towards other inner states and not to the environment, which enables us, if we are so impelled, to behave in a selective way *towards our own states of mind*? One who is aware, or conscious, of his thoughts or his emotions is one who has the capacity to make discriminations between his different mental states. His capacity might be exhibited in words. He might say that he was in an angry state of mind when, and only when, he *was* in an angry state of mind. But such verbal behaviour would be the mere *expression* or *result* of the awareness. The awareness itself would be an inner state: the sort of inner state that gave the man a capacity for such behavioural expressions.

So I have argued that consciousness of our own mental state may be assimilated to *perception* of our own mental state, and that, like other perceptions, it may then be conceived of as an inner state or event giving a capacity for selective behaviour, in this case selective behaviour towards our own mental state. All this is meant to be simply a logical analysis of consciousness, and none of it entails, although it does not rule out, a purely physicalist account of what these inner states are. But if we are convinced, on general scientific grounds, that a purely physical account of

man is likely to be the true one, then there seems to be no bar to our identifying these inner states with purely physical states of the central nervous system. And so consciousness of our own mental state becomes simply the scanning of one part of our central nervous system by another. Consciousness is a self-scanning mechanism in the central nervous system.

As I have emphasised before, I have done no more than sketch a programme for a philosophy of mind. There are all sorts of expansions and elucidations to be made, and all sorts of doubts and difficulties to be stated and overcome. But I hope I have done enough to show that a purely physicalist theory of the mind is an exciting and plausible intellectual option.

NOTES

1. Inaugural lecture of the Challis Professor of Philosophy at the University of Sydney (1965); slightly amended (1968).
2. It is presented in my book *A Materialist Theory of the Mind* (1968) ch. 6, sec. VI.

KEY TERMS

Materialist
Physicalist
Behaviorism

STUDY QUESTIONS

1. Is there anything about desires, beliefs, or emotions that requires an account that is more robust than a purely physicochemical one? Why do you think people have thought so in the past?
2. Armstrong claims that "it is only as a result of scientific investigation that we ever seem to reach an intellectual consensus about controversial matters." Do you think he is right about this?
3. According to Armstrong, what is one obvious difficulty with behaviorism?
4. Armstrong thinks that mind is "the inner cause of certain behaviour." How does he argue that this idea can be squared with a "physicalist view" of human beings?
5. How does the first-person point of view supposedly cause problems for Armstrong's theory? How does Armstrong reply to these worries?

Eliminative Materialism

PAUL M. CHURCHLAND

Paul M. Churchland (1942–) is a Professor of Philosophy at the University of California, San Diego. He is best known for his books *Matter and Consciousness* and *The Engine of Reason, The Seat of the Soul*, in which he defends a view called "eliminative materialism."

..

THE **identity theory** was called into doubt not because the prospects for a **materialist** account of our mental capacities were thought to be poor, but because it seemed unlikely that the arrival of an adequate materialist theory would bring with it the nice one-to-one match-ups, between the concepts of folk psychology and the concepts of theoretical neuroscience, that intertheoretic reduction requires. The reason for that doubt was the great variety of quite different physical systems that could instantiate the required functional organization. **Eliminative materialism** also doubts that the correct neuroscientific account of human capacities will produce a neat reduction of our common-sense framework, but here the doubts arise from a quite different source.

As the eliminative materialists see it, the one-to-one match-ups will not be found, and our common-sense psychological framework is a false and radically misleading conception of the causes of human behavior and the nature of cognitive activity. On this view, folk psychology is not just an incomplete representation of our inner natures; it is an outright *mis*representation of our internal states and activities. Consequently, we cannot expect a truly adequate neuroscientific account of our inner lives to provide theoretical categories that match up nicely with the categories of our common-sense framework. Accordingly, we must expect that the older framework will simply be eliminated, rather than be reduced, by a matured neuroscience.

Historical Parallels

As the identity theorist can point to historical cases of successful intertheoretic reduction, so the eliminative materialist can point to historical cases of the outright elimination of the **ontology** of an older theory in favor of the ontology of a new and superior theory. For most of the eighteenth and nineteenth centuries, learned people believed that heat was a subtle *fluid* held in bodies, much in the way water is held in a sponge. A fair body of moderately successful theory described the way this fluid substance—called "caloric"—flowed within a body, or from one body to another, and how it produced thermal expansion, melting, boiling, and so forth. But by the end of the last century it had become abundantly clear that the heat was not a substance at all, but just the energy of motion of the trillions of jostling molecules that make up the heated body itself. The new theory—the "corpuscular/kinetic theory of matter and heat"—was much more successful than the old in explaining and predicting the thermal behavior of bodies. And since we were unable to *identify* caloric fluid with kinetic energy (according to the old theory, caloric is a material *substance*; according to the new theory, kinetic energy is a form of *motion*), it was finally agreed that there is *no such thing* as caloric. Caloric was simply eliminated from our accepted ontology.

A second example. It used to be thought that when a piece of wood burns, or a piece of metal rusts, a spiritlike substance called "phlogiston" was being released: briskly, in the former case, slowly in the latter. Once gone, that 'noble' substance left only a base pile of ash or rust. It later came to be appreciated that both processes involve, not the loss of something, but the *gaining* of a substance taken from the atmosphere: oxygen. Phlogiston emerged, not as an incomplete description of what was going on, but as a radical misdescription. Phlogiston was therefore not suitable for reduction to or identification with some notion from within the new oxygen chemistry, and it was simply eliminated from science.

Admittedly, both of these examples concern the elimination of something nonobservable, but our history also includes the elimination of certain widely accepted 'observables.' Before Copernicus's views became available, almost any human who ventured out at night could look up at *the starry sphere of the heavens*, and if he stayed for more than a few minutes he could also see that it *turned*, around an axis through Polaris. What the sphere was made of (crystal?) and what made it turn (the gods?) were theoretical questions that exercised us for over two millennia. But hardly anyone doubted the existence of what everyone could observe with their own eyes. In the end, however, we learned to reinterpret our visual experience of the night sky within a very different conceptual framework, and the turning sphere evaporated.

Witches provide another example. Psychosis is a fairly common affliction among humans, and in earlier centuries its victims were standardly seen as cases of demonic possession, as instances of Satan's spirit itself, glaring malevolently out at us from behind the victims' eyes. That witches exist was not a matter of any controversy. One would occasionally see them, in any city or hamlet, engaged in incoherent, paranoid, or even murderous behavior. But observable or not, we eventually decided that witches simply do not exist. We concluded that the concept of a witch is an element in a conceptual framework that misrepresents so badly the phenomena to which it was standardly applied that literal application of the notion should be permanently withdrawn. Modern theories of mental dysfunction led to the elimination of witches from our serious ontology.

The concepts of folk psychology—belief, desire, fear, sensation, pain, joy, and so on—await a similar fate, according to the view at issue. And when neuroscience has matured to the point where the poverty of our current conceptions is apparent to everyone, and the superiority of the new framework is established, we shall then be able to set about *re*conceiving our internal states and activities, within a

truly adequate conceptual framework at last. Our explanations of one another's behavior will appeal to such things as our neuropharmacological states, the neural activity in specialized anatomical areas, and whatever other states are deemed relevant by the new theory. Our private introspection will also be transformed, and may be profoundly enhanced by reason of the more accurate and penetrating framework it will have to work with—just as the astronomer's perception of the night sky is much enhanced by the detailed knowledge of modern astronomical theory that he or she possesses.

The magnitude of the conceptual revolution here suggested should not be minimized: it would be enormous. And the benefits to humanity might be equally great. If each of us possessed an accurate neuroscientific understanding of (what we now conceive dimly as) the varieties and causes of mental illness, the factors involved in learning, the neural basis of emotions, intelligence, and socialization, then the sum total of human misery might be much reduced. The simple increase in mutual understanding that the new framework made possible could contribute substantially toward a more peaceful and humane society. Of course, there would be dangers as well: increased knowledge means increased power, and power can always be misused.

Arguments for Eliminative Materialism

The arguments for eliminative materialism are diffuse and less than decisive, but they are stronger than is widely supposed. The distinguishing feature of this position is its denial that a smooth intertheoretic reduction is to be expected—even a species-specific reduction—of the framework of folk psychology to the framework of a matured neuroscience. The reason for this denial is the eliminative materialist's conviction that folk psychology is a hopelessly primitive and deeply confused conception of our internal activities. But why this low opinion of our common-sense conceptions?

There are at least three reasons. First, the eliminative materialist will point to the widespread explanatory, predictive, and manipulative failures of folk psychology. So much of what is central and familiar to us remains a complete mystery from within folk psychology. We do not know what *sleep* is, or why we have to have it, despite spending a full third of our lives in that condition. (The answer, "For rest," is mistaken. Even if people are allowed to rest continuously, their need for sleep is undiminished. Apparently, sleep serves some deeper functions, but we do not yet know what they are.) We do not understand how *learning* transforms each of us from a gaping infant to a cunning adult, or how differences in *intelligence* are grounded. We have not the slightest idea how *memory* works, or how we manage to retrieve relevant bits of information instantly from the awesome mass we have stored. We do not know what *mental illness* is, nor how to cure it.

In sum, the most central things about us remain almost entirely mysterious from within folk psychology. And the defects noted cannot be blamed on inadequate time allowed for their correction, for folk psychology has enjoyed no significant changes or advances in well over 2,000 years, despite its manifest failures. Truly successful theories may be expected to reduce, but significantly unsuccessful theories merit no such expectation.

This argument from explanatory poverty has a further aspect. So long as one sticks to normal brains, the poverty of folk psychology is perhaps not strikingly evident. But as soon as one examines the many perplexing behavioral and cognitive deficits suffered by people with *damaged* brains, one's descriptive and explanatory resources start to claw the air (see, for example chapter 7.3 [of *Matter and Consciousness* (Bradford/MIT, 1984)]). As with other humble theories asked to operate successfully in unexplored extensions of their old domain (for example, Newtonian mechanics in the domain of velocities close to the velocity of light, and the classical gas law in the domain of high pressures or temperatures), the descriptive and explanatory inadequacies of folk psychology become starkly evident.

The second argument tries to draw an **inductive** lesson from our conceptual history. Our early folk theories of motion were profoundly confused, and were eventually displaced entirely by more sophisticated theories. Our early folk theories of the structure and activity of the heavens were wildly off the mark, and survive only as historical lessons in how wrong we can be. Our folk theories of the nature of fire, and the nature of life, were similarly cockeyed. And one could go on, since the vast majority of our past folk conceptions have been similarly exploded. All except folk psychology, which survives to this day and has only recently begun to feel pressure. But the phenomenon of conscious intelligence is surely a more complex and difficult phenomenon than any of those just listed. So far as accurate understanding is concerned, it would be a *miracle* if we had got *that* one right the very first time, when we fell down so badly on all the others. Folk psychology has survived for so very long, presumably, not because it is basically correct in its representations, but because the phenomena addressed are so surpassingly difficult that any useful handle on them, no matter how feeble, is unlikely to be displaced in a hurry.

A third argument attempts to find an a priori advantage for eliminative materialism over the identity theory and **functionalism**. It attempts to counter the common intuition that eliminative materialism is distantly possible, perhaps, but is much less probable than either the identity theory or functionalism. The focus again is on whether the concepts of folk psychology will find vindicating match-ups in a matured neuroscience. The eliminativist bets no; the other two bet yes. (Even the functionalist bets yes, but expects the match-ups to be only species-specific, or only person-specific. Functionalism, recall, denies the existence only of *universal* type/type identities.)

The eliminativist will point out that the requirements on a reduction are rather demanding. The new theory must entail a set of principles and embedded concepts that mirrors very closely the specific conceptual structure to be reduced. And the fact is, there are vastly many more ways of being an explanatorily successful neuroscience while *not* mirroring the structure of folk psychology. Accordingly, the a priori probability of eliminative materialism is not lower, but substantially *higher* than that of either of its competitors. One's initial intuitions here are simply mistaken.

Granted, this initial a priori advantage could be reduced if there were a very strong presumption in favor of the truth of folk psychology—true theories are better bets to win reduction. But according to the first two arguments, the presumptions on this point should run in precisely the opposite direction.

Arguments Against
Eliminative Materialism

The initial plausibility of this rather radical view is low for almost everyone, since it denies deeply entrenched assumptions. That is at best a question-begging complaint, of course, since those assumptions are precisely what is at issue. But the following line of thought does attempt to mount a real argument.

Eliminative materialism is false, runs the argument, because one's introspection reveals directly the existence of pains, beliefs, desires, fears, and so forth. Their existence is as obvious as anything could be.

The eliminative materialist will reply that this argument makes the same mistake that an ancient or medieval person would be making if he insisted that he could just see with his own eyes that the heavens form a turning sphere, or that witches exist. The fact is, all observation occurs within some system of concepts, and our observation judgments are only as good as the conceptual framework in which they are expressed. In all three cases—the starry sphere, witches, and the familiar mental states—precisely what is challenged is the integrity of the background conceptual frameworks in which the observation judgments are expressed. To insist on the validity of one's experiences, *traditionally interpreted*, is therefore to beg the very question at issue. For in all three cases, the question is whether we should *reconceive* the nature of some familiar observational domain.

A second criticism attempts to find an incoherence in the eliminative materialist's position. The bald statement of eliminative materialism is that the familiar mental states do not really exist. But that statement is meaningful, runs the argument, only if it is the expression of a certain *belief*, and an *intention* to communicate, and a *knowledge* of the language, and so forth. But if the statement is true, then no such mental states exist, and the statement is therefore a meaningless string of marks or noises, and cannot be true. Evidently, the assumption that eliminative materialism is true entails that it cannot be true.

The hole in this argument is the premise concerning the conditions necessary for a statement to be meaningful. It begs the question. If eliminative materialism is true, then meaningfulness must have some different source. To insist on the 'old' source is to insist on the validity of the very framework at issue. Again, an historical parallel may be helpful here. Consider the medieval theory that being biologically *alive* is a matter of being ensouled by an immaterial *vital spirit*. And consider the following response to someone who has expressed disbelief in that theory.

My learned friend has stated that there is no such thing as vital spirit. But this statement is incoherent. For if it is true, then my friend does not have vital spirit, and must therefore be *dead*. But if he is dead, then his statement is just a string of noises, devoid of meaning or truth. Evidently, the assumption that antivitalism is true entails that it cannot be true! Q.E.D.

This second argument is now a joke, but the first argument begs the question in exactly the same way.

A final criticism draws a much weaker conclusion, but makes a rather stronger case. Eliminative materialism, it has been said, is making mountains out of molehills. It exaggerates the defects in folk psychology, and underplays its real successes. Perhaps the arrival of a matured neuroscience will require the elimination of the occasional folk-psychological concept, continues the criticism, and a minor adjustment in certain folk-psychological principles may have to be endured. But the large-scale elimination forecast by the eliminative materialist is just an alarmist worry or a romantic enthusiasm.

Perhaps this complaint is correct. And perhaps it is merely complacent. Whichever, it does bring out the important point that we do not confront two simple and mutually exclusive possibilities here: pure reduction versus pure elimination. Rather, these are the end points of a smooth spectrum of possible outcomes, between which there are mixed cases of partial elimination and partial reduction. Only empirical research (see chapter 7 [of *Matter and Consciousness*]) can tell us where on that spectrum our own case will fall. Perhaps we should speak here, more liberally, of "revisionary materialism," instead of concentrating on the more radical possibility of an across-the-board elimination. Perhaps we should. But it has been my aim in this [selection] to make it at least intelligible to you that our collective conceptual destiny lies substantially toward the revolutionary end of the spectrum.

KEY TERMS

Identity theory
Materialist
Eliminative materialism
Ontology
Inductive
Functionalism

STUDY QUESTIONS

1. What about Churchland's position makes it "eliminative"? How is his position to be distinguished from the identity theory?
2. What reasons does Churchland give for thinking that our commonsense psychological conceptions are fundamentally misguided?
3. According to Churchland, why has folk psychology been around for so long, if it is such a theoretical failure?
4. Do you think that introspection directly reveals the existence of mental states like beliefs and desires? If so, is this a problem for eliminative materialism? Why or why not?

What Mary Didn't Know

FRANK JACKSON

Frank Jackson (1943–) is a Distinguished Professor of Philosophy at the Australian National University. He has made important contributions in philosophy of mind, metaphysics, philosophical methodology, and ethics. He is the author of *From Metaphysics to Ethics: A Defence of Conceptual Analysis.*

. .

MARY is confined to a black-and-white room, is educated through black-and-white books and through lectures relayed on black-and-white television. In this way she learns everything there is to know about the physical nature of the world. She knows all the physical facts about us and our environment, in a wide sense of 'physical' which includes everything in *completed* physics, chemistry, and neurophysiology, and all there is to know about the causal and relational

From *The Journal of Philosophy* LXXXIII, No. 5. (May 1986). Copyright © 1986 by Columbia University. Reprinted by permission of the publisher and author.

Note from the author: I am much indebted to discussions with David Lewis and with Robert Pargetter.

factors consequent upon all this, including of course functional roles. If **physicalism** is true, she knows all there is to know. For to suppose otherwise is to suppose that there is more to know than every physical fact, and that is just what physicalism denies.

Physicalism is not the noncontroversial thesis that the actual world is largely physical, but the challenging thesis that it is entirely physical. This is why physicalists must hold that complete physical knowledge is complete knowledge simpliciter. For suppose it is not complete: then our world must differ from a world, $W(P)$, for which it is complete, and the difference must be in nonphysical facts; for our world and $W(P)$ agree in all matters physical. Hence, physicalism would be false at our world [though contingently so, for it would be true at $W(P)$].[1]

It seems, however, that Mary does not know all there is to know. For when she is let out of the black-and-white room or given a color television, she will learn what it is like to see something red, say. This is rightly described as *learning*—she will not say "ho, hum." Hence, physicalism is false. This is the knowledge argument against physicalism in one of its manifestations.[2] This note is a reply to three objections to it mounted by Paul M. Churchland.*

1. Three Clarifications

The knowledge argument does not rest on the dubious claim that logically you cannot imagine what sensing red is like unless you have sensed red. Powers of imagination are not to the point. The contention about Mary is not that, despite her fantastic grasp of neurophysiology and everything else physical, she *could not imagine* what it is like to sense red; it is that, as a matter of fact, she *would not know*. But if physicalism is true, she would know; and no great powers of imagination would be called for. Imagination is a faculty that those who *lack* knowledge need to fall back on.

Secondly, the intensionality of knowledge is not to the point. The argument does not rest on assuming falsely that, if S knows that a is F and if $a = b$, then S knows that b is F. It is concerned with the nature of Mary's total body of knowledge before she is released: is it complete, or do some facts escape it? What is to the point is that S may know that a is F and *know* that $a = b$, yet arguably not know that b is F, by virtue of not being sufficiently logically alert to follow the consequences through. If Mary's lack of knowledge were at all like this, there would be no threat to physicalism in it. But it is very hard to believe that her lack of knowledge could be remedied merely by her explicitly following through enough logical consequences of her vast physical knowledge. Endowing her with great logical acumen and persistence is not in itself enough to fill in the gaps in her knowledge. On being let out, she will not say "I

could have worked all this out before by making some more purely logical inferences."

Thirdly, the knowledge Mary lacked which is of particular point for the knowledge argument against physicalism is *knowledge about the experiences of others*, not about her own. When she is let out, she has new experiences, color experiences she has never had before. It is not, therefore, an objection to physicalism that she learns *something* on being let out. Before she was let out, she could not have known facts about her experience of red, for there were no such facts to know. That physicalist and nonphysicalist alike can agree on. After she is let out, things change; and physicalism can happily admit that she learns this; after all, some physical things will change, for instance, her brain states and their functional roles. The trouble for physicalism is that, after Mary sees her first ripe tomato, she will realize how impoverished her conception of the mental life of *others* has been *all along*. She will realize that there was, all the time she was carrying out her laborious investigations into the neurophysiologies of others and into the functional roles of their internal states, something about these people she was quite unaware of. All along their experiences (or many of them, those got from tomatoes, the sky, . . .) had a feature conspicuous to them but until now hidden from her (in fact, not in logic). But she knew all the physical facts about them all along; hence, what she did not know until her release is not a physical fact about their experiences. But it is a fact about them. That is the trouble for physicalism.

II. Churchland's Three Objections

(i) Churchland's first objection is that the knowledge argument contains a defect that "is simplicity itself" (23). The argument equivocates on the sense of 'knows about'. How so? Churchland suggests that the following is "a conveniently tightened version" of the knowledge argument:

1. Mary knows everything there is to know about brain states and their properties.
2. It is not the case that Mary knows everything there is to know about sensations and their properties.

* "Reduction, Qualia, and the Direct Introspection of Brain States," this JOURNAL, LXXXII, 1 (January 1985):8–28. Unless otherwise stated, future page references are to this paper.

Therefore, by Leibniz's law,

3. Sensations and their properties ≠ brain states and their properties (23).

Churchland observes, plausibly enough, that the type or kind of knowledge involved in premise 1 is distinct from the kind of knowledge involved in premise 2. We might follow his lead and tag the first 'knowledge by description', and the second 'knowledge by acquaintance'; but, whatever the tags, he is right that the displayed argument involves a highly dubious use of Leibniz's law.

My reply is that the displayed argument may be convenient, but it is not accurate. It is not the knowledge argument. Take, for instance, premise 1. The whole thrust of the knowledge argument is that Mary (before her release) does *not* know everything there is to know about brain states and their properties, because she does not know about certain **qualia** associated with them. What is complete, according to the argument, is her knowledge of matters physical. A convenient and accurate way of displaying the argument is:

1.′ Mary (before her release) knows everything physical there is to know about other people.

2.′ Mary (before her release) does not know everything there is to know about other people (because she learns something about them on her release).

Therefore,

3.′ There are truths about other people (and herself) which escape the physicalist story.

What is immediately to the point is not the kind, manner, or type of knowledge Mary has, but *what* she knows. What she knows beforehand is ex hypothesi everything physical there is to know, but is it everything there is to know? That is the crucial question.

There is, though, a relevant challenge involving questions about kinds of knowledge. It concerns the *support* for premise 2′. The case for premise 2′ is that Mary learns something on her release, she acquires knowledge, and that entails that her knowledge beforehand (*what* she knew, never mind whether by description, acquaintance, or whatever) was incomplete. The challenge, mounted by David Lewis and Laurence Nemirow, is that on her release Mary does *not* learn something or acquire knowledge in the relevant sense. What Mary acquires when she is released is a certain representational or imaginative ability; it is knowledge how rather than knowledge that. Hence, a physicalist can admit that Mary acquires something very significant of a knowledge kind—which can hardly be denied—without admitting that this shows that her earlier factual knowledge is defective. She knew all *that* there was to know about the experiences of others beforehand, but lacked an ability until after her release.[3]

Now it is certainly true that Mary will acquire abilities of various kinds after her release. She will, for instance, be able to imagine what seeing red is like, be able to remember what it is like, and be able to understand why her friends regarded her as so deprived (something which, until her release, had always mystified her). But is it plausible that that is *all* she will acquire? Suppose she received a lecture on **skepticism** about other minds while she was incarcerated. On her release she sees a ripe tomato in normal conditions, and so has a sensation of red. Her first reaction is to say that she now knows more about the kind of experiences others have when looking at ripe tomatoes. She then remembers the lecture and starts to worry. Does she really know more about what their experiences are like, or is she indulging in a wild generalization from one case? In the end she decides she does know, and that skepticism is mistaken (even if, like so many of us, she is not sure how to demonstrate its errors). What was she to-ing and fro-ing about—her abilities? Surely not; her representational abilities were a known constant throughout. What else then was she agonizing about than whether or not she had gained factual knowledge of others? There would be nothing to agonize about if ability was *all* she acquired on her release.

I grant that I have no *proof* that Mary acquires on her release, as well as abilities, factual knowledge about the experiences of others—and not just because I have no disproof of skepticism. My claim is that the knowledge argument is a valid argument from highly plausible, though admittedly not demonstrable, premises to the conclusion that physicalism is false. And that, after all, is about as good an objection as one could expect in this area of philosophy.

(ii) Churchland's second objection (24/5) is that there must be something wrong with the argument, for it proves too much. Suppose Mary received a special series of lectures over her black-and-white television from a full-blown dualist, explaining the "laws" governing the behavior of "ectoplasm" and telling her about qualia. This would not affect the plausibility of the claim that on her release she learns something. So if the argument works against physicalism, it works against **dualism** too.

My reply is that lectures about qualia over black-and-white television do not tell Mary all there is to know about qualia. They may tell her some things about qualia, for instance, that they do not appear in the physicalist's story, and that the quale we use 'yellow' for is nearly as different from the one we use 'blue' for as is white from black. But why should it be supposed that they tell her everything about qualia? On the other hand, it is plausible that lectures over black-and-white television might in principle tell Mary everything in the physicalist's story. You do not need color television to learn physics or functionalist psychology. To obtain a good argument against dualism (attribute dualism; ectoplasm is a bit of fun), the premise in the knowledge argument that Mary has the full story according to physicalism before her release, has to be replaced by a premise that she has the full story according to dualism. The former is plausible; the latter is not. Hence, there is no "parity of reasons" trouble for dualists who use the knowledge argument.

(iii) Churchland's third objection is that the knowledge argument claims "that Mary could not even *imagine* what the relevant experience would be like, despite her exhaustive neuroscientific knowledge, and hence must still be missing certain crucial information" (25), a claim he goes on to argue against. But, as we emphasized earlier, the knowledge argument claims that Mary would not know what the relevant experience is like. What she could imagine is another matter. If her knowledge is defective, despite being all there is to know according to physicalism, then physicalism is false, whatever her powers of imagination.

NOTES

1. The claim here is not that, if physicalism is true, only what is expressed in explicitly physical language is an item of knowledge. It is that, if physicalism is true, then if you know everything expressed or expressible in explicitly physical language, you know everything. *Pace* Terence Horgan, "Jackson on Physical Information and Qualia," *Philosophical Quarterly*, XXXIV, 135 (April 1984):147–152.

2. Namely, that in my "Epiphenomenal Qualia," *ibid.*, XXXII, 127 (April 1982): 127–136. See also Thomas Nagel, "What Is It Like to Be a Bat?" *Philosophical Review*, LXXXIII, 4 (October 1974): 435–450, and Howard Robinson, *Matter and Sense* (New York: Cambridge, 1982).

3. See Laurence Nemirow, review of Thomas Nagel, *Mortal Questions, Philosophical Review*, LXXXIX, 3 (July 1980):473–477, and David Lewis, "Postscript to 'Mad Pain and Martian Pain'," *Philosophical Papers*, vol. 1 (New York: Oxford, 1983). Churchland mentions both Nemirow and Lewis, and it may be that he intended his objection to be essentially the one I have just given. However, he says quite explicitly (bottom of p. 23) that his objection does not need an "ability" analysis of the relevant knowledge.

KEY TERMS

Physicalism
Qualia
Skepticism
Dualism

STUDY QUESTIONS

1. Do you agree with the physicalist that "complete physical knowledge is complete knowledge simpliciter"?

2. When Mary comes out of her room, do you agree that she comes to know something that she didn't know before?

3. Is Jackson right when he says that "it is plausible that lectures over a black-and-white television might in principle tell Mary everything in the physicalist's story"? How might a physicalist respond?

4. How damaging do you think Jackson's knowledge argument is against the physicalist?

B. MINDS, BRAINS, AND MACHINES

⚭

Computing Machinery and Intelligence

A. M. TURING

A. M. Turing (1912–1954), a Cambridge mathematician, made fundamental contributions to the theory of computation.

..

1. The Imitation Game

I propose to consider the question "Can machines think?" This should begin with definitions of the meaning of the terms "machine" and "think." The definitions might be framed so as to reflect so far as possible the normal use of the words, but this attitude is dangerous. If the meaning of the words "machine" and "think" are to be found by examining how they are commonly used it is difficult to escape the conclusion that the meaning and the answer to the question, "Can machines think?" is to be sought in a statistical survey such as a Gallup poll. But this is absurd. Instead of attempting such a definition I shall replace the question by another, which is closely related to it and is expressed in relatively unambiguous words.

The new form of the problem can be described in terms of a game which we call the "imitation game." It is played with three people, a man (A), a woman

(B), and an interrogator (C) who may be of either sex. The interrogator stays in a room apart from the other two. The object of the game for the interrogator is to determine which of the other two is the man and which is the woman. He knows them by labels X and Y, and at the end of the game he says either "X is A and Y is B" or "X is B and Y is A." The interrogator is allowed to put questions to A and B thus:

C: Will X please tell me the length of his or her hair?

Now suppose X is actually A, then A must answer. It is A's object in the game to try to cause C to make the wrong identification. His answer might therefore be

"My hair is shingled, and the longest strands are about nine inches long."

In order that tones of voice may not help the interrogator the answers should be written, or better still, typewritten. The ideal arrangement is to have a teleprinter communicating between the two rooms. Alternatively the question and answers can be repeated by an intermediary. The object of the game for the third player (B) is to help the interrogator. The best strategy for her is probably to give

From *Mind* 59, No. 236. Copyright © 1950 by Oxford University Press. Reprinted by permission of the publisher.

truthful answers. She can add such things as "I am the woman, don't listen to him!" to her answers, but it will avail nothing as the man can make similar remarks.

We now ask the question, "What will happen when a machine takes the part of A in this game?" Will the interrogator decide wrongly as often when the game is played like this as he does when the game is played between a man and a woman? These questions replace our original, "Can machines think?"

2. Critique of the New Problem

As well as asking, "What is the answer to this new form of the question," one may ask, "Is this new question a worthy one to investigate?" This latter question we investigate without further ado, thereby cutting short an infinite regress.

The new problem has the advantage of drawing a fairly sharp line between the physical and the intellectual capacities of a man. No engineer or chemist claims to be able to produce a material which is indistinguishable from the human skin. It is possible that at some time this might be done, but even supposing this invention available we should feel there was little point in trying to make a "thinking machine" more human by dressing it up in such artificial flesh. The form in which we have set the problem reflects this fact in the condition which prevents the interrogator from seeing or touching the other competitors, or hearing their voices. Some other advantages of the proposed criterion may be shown up by specimen questions and answers. Thus:

Q: Please write me a sonnet on the subject of the Forth Bridge.
A: Count me out on this one. I never could write poetry.
Q: Add 34957 to 70764.
A: (Pause about 30 seconds and then give as answer) 105621.
Q: Do you play chess?
A: Yes.
Q: I have K at my K1, and no other pieces. You have only K at K6 and R at R1. It is your move. What do you play?
A: (After a pause of 15 seconds) R-R8 mate.

The question and answer method seems to be suitable for introducing almost any one of the fields of human endeavor that we wish to include. We do not wish to penalize the machine for its inability to shine in beauty competitions, nor to penalize a man for losing in a race against an airplane. The conditions of our game make these disabilities irrelevant. The "witnesses" can brag, if they consider it advisable, as much as they please about their charms, strength or heroism, but the interrogator cannot demand practical demonstrations.

The game may perhaps be criticized on the ground that the odds are weighted too heavily against the machine. If the man were to try and pretend to be the machine he would clearly make a very poor showing. He would be given away at once by slowness and inaccuracy in arithmetic. May not machines carry out something which ought to be described as thinking but which is very different from what a man does? This objection is a very strong one, but at least we can say that if, nevertheless, a machine can be constructed to play the imitation game satisfactorily, we need not be troubled by this objection.

It might be urged that when playing the "imitation game" the best strategy for the machine may possibly be something other than imitation of the behavior of a man. This may be, but I think it is unlikely that there is any great effect of this kind. In any case there is no intention to investigate here the theory of the game, and it will be assumed that the best strategy is to try to provide answers that would naturally be given by a man.

3. The Machines Concerned in the Game

The question which we put in §1 will not be quite definite until we have specified what we mean by the word "machine." It is natural that we should wish to permit every kind of engineering technique to be used in our machines. We also wish to allow the possibility that an engineer or team of engineers may construct a machine which works, but whose manner of operation cannot be satisfactorily described by its constructors because they have applied a method which is largely experimental. Finally, we wish to exclude from the machines men born in the usual manner. It is difficult to frame the definitions so as to satisfy these three conditions.

One might for instance insist that the team of engineers should be all of one sex, but this would not really be satisfactory, for it is probably possible to rear a complete individual from a single cell of the skin (say) of a man. To do so would be a feat of biological technique deserving of the very highest praise, but we would not be inclined to regard it as a case of "constructing a thinking machine." This prompts us to abandon the requirement that every kind of technique should be permitted. We are the more ready to do so in view of the fact that the present interest in "thinking machines" has been aroused by a particular kind of machine, usually called an "electronic computer" or "digital computer." Following this suggestion we only permit digital computers to take part in our game.

This restriction appears at first sight to be a very drastic one. I shall attempt to show that it is not so in reality. To do this necessitates a short account of the nature and properties of these computers.

It may also be said that this identification of machines with digital computers, like our criterion for "thinking," will only be unsatisfactory if (contrary to my belief), it turns out that digital computers are unable to give a good showing in the game.

There are already a number of digital computers in working order, and it may be asked, "Why not try the experiment straight away? It would be easy to satisfy the conditions of the game. A number of interrogators could be used, and statistics compiled to show how often the right identification was given." The short answer is that we are not asking whether all digital computers would do well in the game nor whether the computers at present available would do well, but whether there are imaginable computers which would do well. But this is only the short answer. We shall see this question in a different light later.

4. Digital Computers

The idea behind digital computers may be explained by saying that these machines are intended to carry out any operations which could be done by a human computer. The human computer is supposed to be following fixed rules; he has no authority to deviate from them in any detail. We may suppose that these rules are supplied in a book, which is altered whenever he is put on to a new job. He has also an unlimited supply of paper on which he does his calculations. He may also do his multiplications and additions on a "desk machine," but this is not important.

If we use the above explanation as a definition we shall be in danger of circularity of argument. We avoid this by giving an outline of the means by which the desired effect is achieved. A digital computer can usually be regarded as consisting of three parts:

1. Store.
2. Executive unit.
3. Control.

The store is a store of information, and corresponds to the human computer's paper, whether this is the paper on which he does his calculations or that on which his book of rules is printed. Insofar as the human computer does calculations in his head a part of the store will correspond to his memory.

The executive unit is the part which carries out the various individual operations involved in a calculation. What these individual operations are will vary from machine to machine. Usually fairly lengthy operations can be done such as "Multiply 3540675445 by 7076345687" but in some machines only very simple ones such as "Write down 0" are possible.

We have mentioned that the "book of rules" supplied to the computer is replaced in the machine by a part of the store. It is then called the "table of instructions." It is the duty of the control to see that these instructions are obeyed correctly and in the right order. The control is so constructed that this necessarily happens.

The information in the store is usually broken up into packets of moderately small size. In one machine, for instance, a packet might consist of ten decimal digits. Numbers are assigned to the parts of the store in which the various packets of information are stored, in some systematic manner. A typical instruction might say—

"Add the number stored in position 6809 to that in 4302 and put the result back into the latter storage position."

Needless to say it would not occur in the machine expressed in English. It would more likely be coded in a form such as 6809430217. Here 17 says which of various possible operations is to be performed on the two numbers. In this case the operation is that described above, viz. "Add the number. . . ." It will be noticed that the instruction takes up 10 digits and so forms one packet of information, very conveniently. The control will normally take the instructions to be obeyed in the order of the positions in which they are stored, but occasionally an instruction such as

"Now obey the instruction stored in position 5606, and continue from there" may be encountered, or again

"If position 4505 contains 0 obey next the instruction stored in 6707, otherwise continue straight on."

Instructions of these latter types are very important because they make it possible for a sequence of operations to be repeated over and over again until some condition is fulfilled, but in doing so to obey, not fresh instructions on each repetition, but the same ones over and over again. To take a domestic analogy. Suppose Mother wants Tommy to call at the cobbler's every morning on his way to school to see if her shoes are done; she can ask him afresh every morning. Alternatively she can stick up a notice once and for all in the hall which he will see when he leaves for school and which tells him to call for the shoes, and also to destroy the notice when he comes back if he has the shoes with him.

The reader must accept it as a fact that digital computers can be constructed, and indeed have been constructed, according to the principles we have described, and that they can in fact mimic the actions of a human computer very closely.

The book of rules which we have described our human computer as using is of course a convenient fiction. Actual human computers really remember what they have got to do. If one wants to make a machine mimic the behavior of the human computer in some complex operation one has to ask him how it is done, and then translate the answer into the form of an instruction table. Constructing instruction tables is usually described as "programing." To "program a machine to carry out the operation A" means to put the appropriate instruction table into the machine so that it will do A.

An interesting variant on the idea of a digital computer is a "digital computer with a random element." These have instructions involving the throwing of a die or some equivalent electronic process; one such instruction might for instance be, "Throw the die and put the resulting number into store 1000." Sometimes such a machine is described as having free will (though I would not use this phrase myself). It is not normally possible to determine from observing a machine whether it has a random element, for a similar effect can be produced by such devices as making the choices depend on the digits of the decimal for π.

Most actual digital computers have only a finite store. There is no theoretical difficulty in the idea of a computer with an unlimited store. Of course only a finite part can have been used at any one time. Likewise only a finite amount can have been constructed, but we can imagine more and more being added as required. Such computers have special theoretical interest and will be called infinite capacity computers.

The idea of a digital computer is an old one. Charles Babbage, Lucasian Professor of Mathematics at Cambridge from 1828 to 1839, planned such a machine, called the Analytical Engine, but it was never completed. Although Babbage had all the essential ideas, his machine was not at that time such a very attractive prospect. The speed which would have been available would be definitely faster than a human computer but something like 100 times slower than the Manchester machine, itself one of the slower of the modern machines. The storage was to be purely mechanical, using wheels and cards.

The fact that Babbage's Analytical Engine was to be entirely mechanical will help us to rid ourselves of a superstition. Importance is often attached to the fact that modern digital computers are electrical, and that the nervous system also is electrical. Since Babbage's machine was not electrical, and since all digital computers are in a sense equivalent, we see that this use of electricity cannot be of theoretical importance. Of course electricity usually comes in where fast signaling is concerned, so that it is not surprising that we find it in both these connections. In the nervous system chemical phenomena are at least as important as electrical. In certain computers the storage system is mainly acoustic. The feature of using electricity is thus seen to be only a very superficial similarity. If we wish to find such similarities we should look rather for mathematical analogies of function.

5. Universality of Digital Computers

The digital computers considered in the last section may be classified among the "discrete state machines." These are the machines which move by sudden jumps or clicks from one quite definite state to another. These states are sufficiently different for the possibility of confusion between them to be ignored. Strictly speaking there are no such machines. Everything really moves continuously. But there are many kinds of machines which can profitably be *thought of* as being discrete state machines. For instance in considering the switches for a lighting system it is a convenient fiction that each switch must be definitely on or definitely off. There must be intermediate positions, but for most purposes we can forget about them. As an example of a discrete state machine we might consider a wheel which clicks round through 120° once a second, but may be stopped by a lever which can be operated from outside; in addition a lamp is to light in one of the positions of the wheel. This machine could be described abstractly as follows: The internal state of the machine (which is described by the position of the wheel) may be q_1, q_2 or q_3. There is an input signal i_0 or i_1 (position of lever). The internal state at any moment is determined by the last state and input signal according to the table

		Last State		
		q_1	q_2	q_3
	i_0	q_2	q_3	q_1
Input				
	i_1	q_1	q_2	q_3

The output signals, the only externally visible indication of the internal state (the light) are described by the table

State	q_1	q_2	q_3
Output	o_0	o_0	o_1

This example is typical of discrete state machines. They can be described by such tables provided they have only a finite number of possible states.

It will seem that given the initial state of the machine and the input signals it is always possible to predict all future states. This is reminiscent of Laplace's view that from the complete state of the universe at one moment of time, as described by the positions and velocities of all particles, it should be possible to predict all future states. The prediction which we are considering is, however, rather nearer to practicability than that considered by Laplace. The system of the "universe as a whole" is such that quite small errors in the initial conditions can have an overwhelming effect at a later time. The displacement of a single electron by a billionth of a centimeter at one moment might make the difference between a man being killed by an avalanche a year later, or escaping. It is an essential property of the mechanical systems which we have called "discrete state machines" that this phenomenon does not occur. Even when we consider the actual physical machines instead of the idealized machines, reasonably accurate knowledge of the state at one moment yields reasonably accurate knowledge any number of steps later.

As we have mentioned, digital computers fall within the class of discrete state machines. But the number of states of which such a machine is capable is usually enormously large. For instance, the number for the machine now working at Manchester is about $2^{165,000}$, i.e., about $10^{50,000}$. Compare this with our example of the clicking wheel described above, which had three states. It is not difficult to see why the number of states should be so immense. The computer includes a store corresponding to the paper used by a human computer. It must be possible to write into the store any one of the combinations of symbols which might have been written on the paper. For simplicity suppose that only digits from 0 to 9 are used as symbols. Variations in handwriting are ignored. Suppose the computer is allowed 100 sheets of paper each containing 50 lines each with room for 30 digits. Then the number of states is $10^{100 \times 50 \times 30}$, i.e., $10^{150,000}$. This is about the number of states of three Manchester machines put together. The logarithm to the base two of the number of states is usually called the "storage capacity" of the machine. Thus the Manchester machine has a storage capacity of about 165,000 and the wheel machine of our example about $1 \cdot 6$. If two machines are put together their capacities must be added to obtain the capacity of the resultant machine. This leads to the possibility of statements such as "The Manchester machine contains 64 magnetic tracks each with a capacity of 2560, eight electronic tubes with a capacity of 1280. Miscellaneous storage amounts to about 300 making a total of 174,380."

Given the table corresponding to a discrete state machine it is possible to predict what it will do. There is no reason why this calculation should not be carried out by means of a digital computer. Provided it could be carried out sufficiently quickly the digital computer could mimic the behavior of any discrete state machine. The imitation game could then be played with the machine in question (as B) and the mimicking digital computer (as A) and the interrogator would be unable to distinguish them. Of course the digital computer must have an adequate storage capacity as well as working sufficiently fast. Moreover, it must be programed afresh for each new machine which it is desired to mimic.

This special property of digital computers, that they can mimic any discrete state machine, is described by saying that they are *universal* machines. The existence of machines with this property has the important consequence that, considerations of speed apart, it is unnecessary to design various new machines to do various computing processes. They can all be done with one digital computer, suitably programed for each case. It will be seen that as a consequence of this all digital computers are in a sense equivalent.

We may now consider again the point raised at the end of §3. It was suggested tentatively that the question, "Can machines think?" should be replaced by "Are there imaginable digital computers which would do well in the imitation game?" If we wish we can make this superficially more general and ask "Are there discrete state machines which would do well?" But in view of the universality property we see that either of these questions is equivalent to this, "Let us fix our attention on one particular digital computer C. Is it true that by modifying this computer to have an adequate storage, suitably increasing its speed of action, and providing it with an appropriate program, C can be made to play satisfactorily the part of A in the imitation game, the part of B being taken by a man?"

6. Contrary Views on the Main Question

We may now consider the ground to have been cleared and we are ready to proceed to the debate on our question, "Can machines think?" and the variant of it quoted at the end of the last section. We cannot altogether abandon the original form of the problem, for opinions will differ as to the appropriateness of the substitution and we must at least listen to what has to be said in this connection.

It will simplify matters for the reader if I explain first my own beliefs in the matter. Consider first the more accurate form of the question. I believe that in about fifty years' time it will be possible to program computers, with a storage capacity of about 10^9, to make them play the imitation game so well that an average interrogator will not have more than 70 per cent chance of making the right identification after five minutes of questioning. The original question, "Can machines think?" I believe to be too meaningless to deserve discussion. Nevertheless I believe that at the end of the century the use of words and general educated opinion will have altered so much that one will be able to speak of machines thinking without expecting to be contradicted. I believe further that no useful purpose is served by concealing these beliefs. The popular view that scientists proceed inexorably from well-established fact to well-established fact, never being influenced by any unproved conjecture, is quite mistaken. Provided it is made clear which are proved facts and which are conjectures, no harm can result. Conjectures are of great importance since they suggest useful lines of research.

I now proceed to consider opinions opposed to my own. . . .

(3) *The Mathematical Objection*. There are a number of results of mathematical logic which can be used to show that there are limitations to the powers of discrete state machines. The best known of these results is known as Gödel's theorem, and shows that in any sufficiently powerful logical system statements can be formulated which can neither be proved nor disproved within the system, unless possibly the system itself is inconsistent. There are other, in some respects similar, results due to Church, Kleene, Rosser, and Turing. The latter result is the most convenient to consider, since it refers directly to machines, whereas the others can only be used in a comparatively indirect argument: for instance if Gödel's theorem is to be used we need in addition to have some means of describing logical systems in

terms of machines, and machines in terms of logical systems. The result in question refers to a type of machine which is essentially a digital computer with an infinite capacity. It states that there are certain things that such a machine cannot do. If it is rigged up to give answers to questions as in the imitation game, there will be some questions to which it will either give a wrong answer, or fail to give an answer at all however much time is allowed for a reply. There may, of course, be many such questions, and questions which cannot be answered by one machine may be satisfactorily answered by another. We are of course supposing for the present that the questions are of the kind to which an answer "Yes" or "No" is appropriate, rather than questions such as "What do you think of Picasso?" The questions that we know the machines must fail on are of this type, "Consider the machine specified as follows. . . . Will this machine ever answer 'Yes' to any question?" The dots are to be replaced by a description of some machine in a standard form, which could be something like that used in §5. When the machine described bears a certain comparatively simple relation to the machine which is under interrogation, it can be shown that the answer is either wrong or not forthcoming. This is the mathematical result: it is argued that it proves a disability of machines to which the human intellect is not subject.

The short answer to this argument is that although it is established that there are limitations to the powers of any particular machine, it has only been stated, without any sort of proof, that no such limitations apply to the human intellect. But I do not think this view can be dismissed quite so lightly. Whenever one of these machines is asked the appropriate critical question, and gives a definite answer, we know that this answer must be wrong, and this gives us a certain feeling of superiority. Is this feeling illusory? It is no doubt quite genuine, but I do not think too much importance should be attached to it. We too often give wrong answers to questions ourselves to be justified in being very pleased at such evidence of fallibility on the part of the machines. Further, our superiority can only be felt on such an occasion in relation to the one machine over which we have scored our petty triumph. There would be no question of triumphing simultaneously over *all* machines. In short, then, there might be men cleverer than any given machine, but then again there might be other machines cleverer again, and so on.

Those who hold to the mathematical argument would, I think mostly be willing to accept the imitation game as a basis for discussion. . . .

(4) *The Argument from Consciousness.* This argument is very well expressed in Professor Jefferson's Lister Oration for 1949, from which I quote. "Not until a machine can write a sonnet or compose a concerto because of thoughts and emotions felt, and not by the chance fall of symbols, could we agree that machine equals brain—that is, not only write it but know that it had written it. No mechanism could feel (and not merely artificially signal, an easy contrivance) pleasure at its successes, grief when its valves fuse, be warmed by flattery, be made miserable by its mistakes, be charmed by sex, be angry or depressed when it cannot get what it wants."

This argument appears to be a denial of the validity of our test. According to the most extreme form of this view the only way by which one could be sure that a machine thinks is to *be* the machine and to feel oneself thinking. One could then describe these feelings to the world, but of course no one would be justified in taking any notice. Likewise according to this view the only way to know that a *man* thinks is to be that particular man. It is in fact the **solipsist** point of view. It may be the most logical view to hold but it makes communication of ideas difficult. A is liable to believe "A thinks but B does not" while B believes "B thinks but A does not." Instead of arguing continually over this point it is usual to have the polite convention that every one thinks.

I am sure that Professor Jefferson does not wish to adopt the extreme and solipsist point of view. Probably he would be quite willing to accept the imitation game as a test. The game (with the player B omitted) is frequently used in practice under the name of viva voce to discover whether someone really understands something or has "learned it parrot fashion." Let us listen in to a part of such a viva voce:

INTERROGATOR: In the first line of your sonnet which reads "Shall I compare thee to a summer's day," would not "a spring day" do as well or better?

WITNESS: It wouldn't scan.

INTERROGATOR: How about "a winter's day." That would scan all right.

WITNESS: Yes, but nobody wants to be compared to a winter's day.

INTERROGATOR: Would you say Mr. Pickwick reminded you of Christmas?

WITNESS: In a way.

INTERROGATOR: Yet Christmas is a winter's day, and I do not think Mr. Pickwick would mind the comparison.

WITNESS: I don't think you're serious. By a winter's day one means a typical winter's day, rather than a special one like Christmas.

And so on. What would Professor Jefferson say if the sonnet-writing machine was able to answer like this in the viva voce? I do not know whether he would regard the machine as "merely artificially signaling" these answers, but if the answers were as satisfactory and sustained as in the above passage I do not think he would describe it as "an easy contrivance." This phrase is, I think, intended to cover such devices as the inclusion in the machine of a record of someone reading a sonnet, with appropriate switching to turn it on from time to time.

In short then, I think that most of those who support the argument from consciousness could be persuaded to abandon it rather than be forced into the solipsist position. They will then probably be willing to accept our test.

I do not wish to give the impression that I think there is no mystery about consciousness. There is, for instance, something of a paradox connected with any attempt to localize it. But I do not think these mysteries necessarily need to be solved before we can answer the question with which we are concerned in this paper.

(5) *Arguments from Various Disabilities*. These arguments take the form, "I grant you that you can make machines do all the things you have mentioned but you will never be able to make one to do X." Numerous features X are suggested in this connection. I offer a selection:

Be kind, resourceful, beautiful, friendly . . . have initiative, have a sense of humor, tell right from wrong, make mistakes . . . fall in love, enjoy strawberries and cream . . . , make someone fall in love with it, learn from experience . . . , use words properly, be the subject of its own thought . . . , have as much diversity of behavior as a man, do something really new. . . .

No support is usually offered for these statements. I believe they are mostly founded on the principle of scientific **induction**. A man has seen thousands of machines in his lifetime. From what he sees of them he draws a number of general conclusions. They are ugly, each is designed for a very limited purpose, when required for a minutely different purpose they are useless, the variety of behavior of any one of them is very small, etc., etc. Naturally he concludes that these are necessary properties of machines in general. Many of these limitations are associated with the very small storage capacity of most machines. (I am assuming that the idea of storage capacity is extended in some way to cover machines other than discrete state machines. The exact definition does not matter as no mathematical accuracy is claimed in the present discussion.) A few years ago, when very little had been heard of digital computers, it was possible to elicit much incredulity concerning them, if one mentioned their properties without describing their construction. That was presumably due to a similar application of the principle of scientific induction. These applications of the principle are of course largely unconscious. When a burned child fears the fire and shows that he fears it by avoiding it, I should say that he was applying scientific induction. (I could of course also describe his behavior in many other ways.) The works or customs of mankind do not seem to be very suitable material to which to apply scientific induction. A very large part of spacetime must be investigated if reliable results are to be obtained. Otherwise we may (as most English children do) decide that everybody speaks English, and that it is silly to learn French.

There are, however, special remarks to be made about many of the disabilities that have been mentioned. The inability to enjoy strawberries and cream may [strike] the reader as frivolous. Possibly a machine might be made to enjoy this delicious dish, but any attempt to make one do so would be idiotic. What is important about this disability is that it contributes to some of the other disabilities, e.g., to the difficulty of the same kind of friendliness occurring between man and machine as between white man and white man, or between black man and black man.

The claim that "machines cannot make mistakes" seems a curious one. One is tempted to retort, "Are they any worse for that?" But let us adopt a more sympathetic attitude, and try to see what is really meant. I think this criticism can be explained in terms of the imitation game. It is claimed that the interrogator could distinguish the machine from the man simply by setting them a number of problems in arithmetic. The machine would be unmasked because of its deadly accuracy. The reply to this is simple. The machine (programed for playing the game) would not attempt to give the *right* answers to the arithmetic problems. It would deliberately introduce mistakes in a manner calculated to confuse the interrogator. A mechanical fault would probably show itself through an unsuitable decision as to what sort of a mistake to make in the arithmetic. Even this interpretation of the criticism is not sufficiently sympathetic. But we cannot afford the space to go into it much further. It seems to me that this criticism depends on a confusion between two kinds of mistakes. We may call them "errors of functioning" and "errors of conclusion." Errors of functioning are due to some mechanical or electrical fault which causes the machine to behave otherwise than it was designed to do. In philosophical discussions one likes to ignore the possibility of such errors; one is therefore discussing "abstract machines." These abstract machines are mathematical fictions rather than physical objects. By definition they are incapable of errors of functioning. In this sense we can truly say that "machines can never make mistakes." Errors of conclusion can only arise when some meaning is attached to the output signals from the machine. The machine might, for instance, type out mathematical equations, or sentences in English. When a false proposition is typed we say that the machine has committed an error of conclusion. There is clearly no reason at all for saying that a machine cannot make this kind of mistake. It might do nothing but type out repeatedly "0 = 1." To take a less perverse example, it might have some method for drawing conclusions by scientific induction. We

must expect such a method to lead occasionally to erroneous results.

The claim that a machine cannot be the subject of its own thought can of course only be answered if it can be shown that the machine has *some* thought with *some* matter. Nevertheless, "the subject matter of a machine's operations" does seem to mean something, at least to the people who deal with it. If, for instance, the machine was trying to find a solution of the equation $x^2 - 40x - 11 = 0$ one would be tempted to describe this equation as part of the machine's subject matter at that moment. In this sort of sense a machine undoubtedly can be its own subject matter. It may be used to help in making up its own programs, or to predict the effect of alterations in its own structure. By observing the results of its own behavior it can modify its own programs so as to achieve some purpose more effectively. These are possibilities of the near future, rather than Utopian dreams.

The criticism that a machine cannot have much diversity of behavior is just a way of saying that it cannot have much storage capacity. Until fairly recently a storage capacity of even a thousand digits was very rare.

The criticisms that we are considering here are often disguised forms of the argument from consciousness. Usually if one maintains that a machine *can* do one of these things, and describes the kind of method that the machine could use, one will not make much of an impression. It is thought that the method (whatever it may be, for it must be mechanical) is really rather base. Compare the parenthesis of Jefferson's statement quoted above.

(6) *Lady Lovelace's Objection*. Our most detailed information of Babbage's Analytical Engine comes from a memoir by Lady Lovelace. In it she states, "The Analytical Engine has no pretensions to *originate* anything. It can do *whatever we know how to order it* to perform" (her italics). This statement is quoted by Hartree who adds: "This does not imply that it may not be possible to construct electronic equipment which will 'think for itself,' or in which, in biological terms, one could set up a conditioned reflex, which would serve as a basis for 'learning.' Whether this is possible in principle or not is a stimulating and exciting question, suggested by some of these recent developments. But it did not seem that

the machines constructed or projected at the time had this property."

I am in thorough agreement with Hartree over this. It will be noticed that he does not assert that the machines in question had not got the property, but rather that the evidence available to Lady Lovelace did not encourage her to believe that they had it. It is quite possible that the machines in question had in a sense got this property. For suppose that some discrete state machine has the property. The Analytical Engine was a universal digital computer, so that, if its storage capacity and speed were adequate, it could by suitable programing be made to mimic the machine in question. Probably this argument did not occur to the Countess or to Babbage. In any case there was no obligation on them to claim all that could be claimed.

This whole question will be considered again under the heading of learning machines. . . .

(8) *The Argument from Informality of Behavior*. It is not possible to produce a set of rules purporting to describe what a man should do in every conceivable set of circumstances. One might for instance have a rule that one is to stop when one sees a red traffic light, and to go if one sees a green one, but what if by some fault both appear together? One may perhaps decide that it is safest to stop. But some further difficulty may well arise from this decision later. To attempt to provide rules of conduct to cover every eventuality, even those arising from traffic lights, appears to be impossible. With all this I agree.

From this it is argued that we cannot be machines. I shall try to reproduce the argument, but I fear I shall hardly do it justice. It seems to run something like this. "If each man had a definite set of rules of conduct by which he regulated his life he would be no better than a machine. But there are no such rules, so men cannot be machines." The undistributed middle is glaring. I do not think the argument is ever put quite like this, but I believe this is the argument used nevertheless. There may however be a certain confusion between "rules of conduct" and "laws of behavior" to cloud the issue. By "rules of conduct" I mean precepts such as "Stop if you see red lights," on which one can act, and of which one can be conscious. By "laws of behavior" I mean laws of nature as applied to a man's body

such as "if you pinch him he will squeak." If we substitute "laws of behavior which regulate his life" for "laws of conduct by which he regulates his life" in the argument quoted the undistributed middle is no longer insuperable. For we believe that it is not only true that being regulated by laws of behavior implies being some sort of machine (though not necessarily a discrete state machine), but that conversely being such a machine implies being regulated by such laws. However, we cannot so easily convince ourselves of the absence of complete laws of behavior as of complete rules of conduct. The only way we know of for finding such laws is scientific observation, and we certainly know of no circumstances under which we could say, "We have searched enough. There are no such laws."

We can demonstrate more forcibly that any such statement would be unjustified. For suppose we could be sure of finding such laws if they existed. Then given a discrete state machine it should certainly be possible to discover by observation sufficient about it to predict its future behavior, and this within a reasonable time, say a thousand years. But this does not seem to be the case. I have set up on the Manchester computer a small program using only 1000 units of storage, whereby the machine supplied with one sixteen-figure number replies with another within two seconds. I would defy anyone to learn from these replies sufficient about the program to be able to predict any replies to untried values.

(9) *The Argument from Extra-Sensory Perception*. I assume that the reader is familiar with the idea of extra-sensory perception, and the meaning of the four items of it, viz., telepathy, clairvoyance, precognition and psychokinesis. These disturbing phenomena seem to deny all our usual scientific ideas. How we would like to discredit them! Unfortunately the statistical evidence, at least for telepathy, is overwhelming. It is very difficult to rearrange one's ideas so as to fit these new facts in. Once one has accepted them it does not seem a very big step to believe in ghosts and bogies. The idea that our bodies move simply according to the known laws of physics, together with some others not yet discovered but somewhat similar, would be one of the first to go.

This argument is to my mind quite a strong one. One can say in reply that many scientific theories seem to remain workable in practice, in spite of clashing with E.S.P.; that in fact one can get along very nicely if one forgets about it. This is rather cold comfort, and one fears that thinking is just the kind of phenomenon where E.S.P. may be especially relevant.

A more specific argument based on E.S.P. might run as follows: "Let us play the imitation game, using as witnesses a man who is good as a telepathic receiver, and a digital computer. The interrogator can ask such questions as 'What suit does the card in my right hand belong to?' The man by telepathy or clairvoyance gives the right answer 130 times out of 400 cards. The machine can only guess at random, and perhaps get 104 right, so the interrogator makes the right identification." There is an interesting possibility which opens here. Suppose the digital computer contains a random number generator. Then it will be natural to use this to decide what answer to give. But then the random number generator will be subject to the psychokinetic powers of the interrogator. Perhaps this psychokinesis might cause the machine to guess right more often than would be expected on a probability calculation, so that the interrogator might still be unable to make the right identification. On the other hand, he might be able to guess right without any questioning, by clairvoyance. With E.S.P. anything may happen.

If telepathy is admitted it will be necessary to tighten our test. The situation could be regarded as analogous to that which would occur if the interrogator were talking to himself and one of the competitors was listening with his ear to the wall. To put the competitors into a "telepathy-proof room" would satisfy all requirements.

7. Learning Machines

The reader will have anticipated that I have no very convincing arguments of a positive nature to support my views. If I had I should not have taken such pains to point out the fallacies in contrary views. Such evidence as I have I shall now give.

Let us return for a moment to Lady Lovelace's objection, which stated that the machine can only do what we tell it to do. One could say that a man can "inject" an idea into the machine, and that it will respond to a certain extent and then drop into quiescence, like a piano string struck by a hammer. Another simile would be an atomic pile of less than critical size: an injected idea is to correspond to a neutron entering the pile from without. Each such neutron will cause a certain disturbance which eventually dies away. If, however, the size of the pile is sufficiently increased, the disturbance caused by such an incoming neutron will very likely go on and on increasing until the whole pile is destroyed. Is there a corresponding phenomenon for minds, and is there one for machines? There does seem to be one for the human mind. The majority of them seem to be "subcritical," i.e., to correspond in this analogy to piles of subcritical size. An idea presented to such a mind will on an average give rise to less than one idea in reply. A smallish proportion are supercritical. An idea presented to such a mind may give rise to a whole "theory" consisting of secondary, tertiary and more remote ideas. Animals' minds seem to be very definitely subcritical. Adhering to this analogy we ask, "Can a machine be made to be supercritical?"

The "skin of an onion" analogy is also helpful. In considering the functions of the mind or the brain we find certain operations which we can explain in purely mechanical terms. This we say does not correspond to the real mind: it is a sort of skin which we must strip off if we are to find the real mind. But then in what remains we find a further skin to be stripped off, and so on. Proceeding in this way do we ever come to the "real" mind, or do we eventually come to the skin which has nothing in it? In the latter case the whole mind is mechanical. (It would not be a discrete state machine however. We have discussed this.)

These last two paragraphs do not claim to be convincing arguments. They should rather be described as "recitations tending to produce belief."

The only really satisfactory support that can be given for the view expressed at the beginning of §6, will be that provided by waiting for the end of the century and then doing the experiment described. But what can we say in the meantime? What steps should be taken now if the experiment is to be successful?

As I have explained, the problem is mainly one of programing. Advances in engineering will have to be made too, but it seems unlikely that these will not be adequate for the requirements. Estimates of the storage capacity of the brain vary from 10^{10} to 10^{15} binary digits. I incline to the lower values and believe that only a very small fraction is used for the higher types of thinking. Most of it is probably used for the retention of visual impressions. I should be surprised if more than 10^9 was required for satisfactory playing of the imitation game, at any rate against a blind man. (Note: The capacity of the *Encyclopaedia Britannica*, eleventh edition, is 2×10^9.) A storage capacity of 10^7 would be a very practicable possibility even by present techniques. It is probably not necessary to increase the speed of operations of the machines at all. Parts of modern machines which can be regarded as analogues of nerve cells work about a thousand times faster than the latter. This should provide a "margin of safety" which could cover losses of speed arising in many ways. Our problem then is to find out how to program these machines to play the game. At my present rate of working I produce about a thousand digits of program a day, so that about sixty workers, working steadily through the fifty years might accomplish the job, if nothing went into the wastepaper basket. Some more expeditious method seems desirable.

In the process of trying to imitate an adult human mind we are bound to think a good deal about the process which has brought it to the state that it is in. We may notice three components,

(a) The initial state of the mind, say at birth,
(b) The education to which it has been subjected,
(c) Other experience, not to be described as education, to which it has been subjected.

Instead of trying to produce a program to simulate the adult mind, why not rather try to produce one which simulates the child's? If this were then subjected to an appropriate course of education one would obtain the adult brain. Presumably the child-brain is something like a notebook as one buys it from the stationers. Rather little mechanism, and lots of blank sheets. (Mechanism and writing are from our point of view almost synonymous.) Our hope is that there is so little mechanism in the child-brain that something like it can be easily programed. The amount of work in the education we can assume, as a first approximation, to be much the same as for the human child.

We have thus divided our problem into two parts—the child-program and the education process. These two remain very closely connected. We cannot expect to find a good child-machine at the first attempt. One must experiment with teaching one such machine and see how well it learns. One can then try another and see if it is better or worse. There is an obvious connection between this process and evolution, by the identifications

Structure of the child-machine	= Hereditary material
Changes of the child-machine	= Mutations
Natural selection	= Judgment of the experimenter

One may hope however, that this process will be more expeditious than evolution. The survival of the fittest is a slow method for measuring advantages. The experimenter, by the exercise of intelligence, should be able to speed it up. Equally important is the fact that he is not restricted to random mutations. If he can trace a cause for some weakness he can probably think of the kind of mutation which will improve it. . . .

The idea of a learning machine may appear paradoxical to some readers. How can the rules of operation of the machine change? They should describe completely how the machine will react whatever its history might be, whatever changes it might undergo. The rules are thus quite time-invariant. This is quite true. The explanation of the paradox is that the rules which get changed in the learning process are of a rather less pretentious kind, claiming only an ephemeral validity. The reader may draw a parallel with the Constitution of the United States.

An important feature of a learning machine is that its teacher will often be very largely ignorant of quite what is going on inside, although he may still be able to some extent to predict his pupil's behavior. This should apply most strongly to the later education of a machine arising from a child-machine of well-tried design (or program). This is in clear contrast with normal procedure when using a machine to do computations: one's object is then to have a clear mental picture of the state of the machine at each moment in the computation. This object can only be achieved with a struggle. The view that "the machine can only do what we know how to order it to do,"[1] appears strange in face of this. Most of the programs which we can put into the machine will result in its doing something that we cannot make sense of at all, or which we regard as completely random behavior. Intelligent behavior presumably consists in a departure from the completely disciplined behavior involved in computation, but a rather slight one, which does not give rise to random behavior, or to pointless repetitive loops. Another important result of preparing our machine for its part in the imitation game by a process of teaching and learning is that "human fallibility" is likely to be omitted in a rather natural way, i.e., without special "coaching." Processes that are learned do not produce a hundred per cent certainty of result; if they did they could not be unlearned.

It is probably wise to include a random element in a learning machine. A random element is rather useful when we are searching for a solution of some problem. Suppose for instance we wanted to find a number between 50 and 200 which was equal to the square of the sum of its digits, we might start at 51 then try 52 and go on until we got a number that worked. Alternatively we might choose numbers at random until we got a good one. This method has the advantage that it is unnecessary to keep track of the values that have been tried, but the disadvantage that one may try the same one twice, but this is not very important if there are several solutions. The systematic method has the disadvantage that there may be an enormous block without any solutions in the region which has to be investigated first. Now the learning process may be regarded as a search for a form of behavior which will satisfy the teacher (or some other criterion). Since there is probably a very large number of satisfactory solutions the random method seems to be better than the systematic. It should be noticed that it is used in the analogous process of evolution. But there the systematic method is not possible. How could one keep track of the different genetical combinations that had been tried, so as to avoid trying them again?

We may hope that machines will eventually compete with men in all purely intellectual fields. But which are the best ones to start with? Even this is a difficult decision. Many people think that a very abstract activity, like the playing of chess, would be best. It can also be maintained that it is best to provide the machine with the best sense organs that money can buy, and then teach it to understand and speak English. This process could follow the normal teaching of a child. Things would be pointed out and named, etc. Again I do not know what the right answer is, but I think both approaches should be tried.

We can only see a short distance ahead, but we can see plenty there that needs to be done.

NOTE

1. Compare Lady Lovelace's statement (p. 303), which does not contain the word "only."

KEY TERMS

Solipsist
Induction

STUDY QUESTIONS

1. Why does Turing think that the "imitation game" is a satisfactory replacement for the question "Can machines think?" Do you agree?
2. Why do you think Turing says that the question "Can machines think?" is too meaningless to deserve discussion?
3. Do you think that there is anything that a machine can't ever do, even in principle, but that a human can? What might be possible candidates?
4. Do you think that Turing's vision of a thinking machine has been realized in the years since he wrote this article? Does it make sense to say that some of today's computers think?

Minds, Brains, and Programs

JOHN R. SEARLE

John R. Searle (1932–) is a Distinguished Professor of Philosophy at the University of California, Berkeley. He is most famous for his work in philosophy of mind and philosophy of language, and one of his most important books is *Speech Acts*.

. .

WHAT psychological and philosophical significance should we attach to recent efforts at computer simulations of human cognitive capacities? In answering this question, I find it useful to distinguish what I will call "strong" AI from "weak" or "cautious" AI (artificial intelligence). According to weak AI, the principal value of the computer in the study of the mind is that it gives us a very powerful tool. For example, it enables us to formulate and test hypotheses in a more rigorous and precise fashion. But according to strong AI, the computer is not merely a tool in the study of the mind; rather, the appropriately programmed computer really is a mind, in the sense that computers given the right programs can be literally said to understand and have other cognitive states. In strong AI, because the programmed computer has cognitive states, the programs are not mere tools that enable us to test psychological explanations; rather, the programs are themselves the explanations.

I have no objection to the claims of weak AI, at least as far as this article is concerned. My discussion here will be directed at the claims I have defined as those of strong AI, specifically the claim that the appropriately programmed computer literally has cognitive states and that the programs thereby explain human cognition. When I hereafter refer to AI, I have in mind the strong version, as expressed by these two claims.

I will consider the work of Roger Schank and his colleagues at Yale (Schank and Abelson 1977), because I am more familiar with it than I am with any other similar claims, and because it provides a very clear example of the sort of work I wish to examine. But nothing that follows depends upon the details of Schank's programs. The same arguments would apply to Winograd's SHRDLU (Winograd 1973), Weizenbaum's ELIZA (Weizenbaum 1965), and indeed any Turing machine simulation of human mental phenomena. . . .

Very briefly, and leaving out the various details, one can describe Schank's program as follows: The aim of the program is to simulate the human ability to understand stories. It is characteristic of human beings' story-understanding capacity that they can answer questions about the story even though the information that they give was never explicitly stated in the story. Thus, for example, suppose you are given the following story: "A man went into a restaurant and ordered a hamburger. When the hamburger arrived it was burned to a crisp, and the man stormed out of the restaurant angrily, without paying for the burger or leaving a tip." Now, if you are asked "Did the man eat the hamburger?" you will presumably answer, "No, he did not." Similarly, if you are given the following story: "A man went into a restaurant and ordered a hamburger; when the hamburger came he was very pleased with it;

From *Behavioral and Brain Sciences*. Copyright © 1980 by Cambridge University Press. Reprinted by permission of the publisher.

I am indebted to a rather large number of people for discussion of these matters and for their patient attempts to overcome my ignorance of artificial intelligence. I would especially like to thank Ned Block, Hubert Dreyfus, John Haugeland, Roger Schank, Robert Wilensky, and Terry Winograd.

and as he left the restaurant he gave the waitress a large tip before paying his bill," and you are asked the question, "Did the man eat the hamburger?" you will presumably answer, "Yes, he ate the hamburger." Now Schank's machines can similarly answer questions about restaurants in this fashion. To do this, they have a "representation" of the sort of information that human beings have about restaurants, which enables them to answer such questions as those above, given these sorts of stories. When the machine is given the story and then asked the question, the machine will print out answers of the sort that we would expect human beings to give if told similar stories. Partisans of strong AI claim that in this question and answer sequence the machine is not only simulating a human ability but also (1) that the machine can literally be said to *understand* the story and provide the answers to questions, and (2) that what the machine and its program do *explains* the human ability to understand the story and answer questions about it.

Both claims seem to me to be totally unsupported by Schank's work, as I will attempt to show in what follows.[1]

One way to test any theory of the mind is to ask oneself what it would be like if my mind actually worked on the principles that the theory says all minds work on. Let us apply this test to the Schank program with the following *Gedankenexperiment*. Suppose that I'm locked in a room and given a large batch of Chinese writing. Suppose furthermore (as is indeed the case) that I know no Chinese, either written or spoken, and that I'm not even confident that I could recognize Chinese writing as Chinese writing distinct from, say, Japanese writing or meaningless squiggles. To me, Chinese writing is just so many meaningless squiggles. Now suppose further that after this first batch of Chinese writing I am given a second batch of Chinese script together with a set of rules for correlating the second batch with the first batch. The rules are in English, and I understand these rules as well as any other native speaker of English. They enable me to correlate one set of formal symbols with another set of formal symbols, and all that "formal" means here is that I can identify the symbols entirely by their shapes. Now suppose also that I am given a third batch of Chinese symbols together with some instructions, again in English, that enable me to correlate elements of this third batch with the first two batches, and these rules instruct me how to give back certain Chinese symbols with certain sorts of shapes in response to certain sorts of shapes given me in the third batch. Unknown to me, the people who are giving me all of these symbols call the first batch a "script," they call the second batch a "story," and they call the third batch "questions." Furthermore, they call the symbols I give them back in response to the third batch "answers to the questions," and the set of rules in English that they gave me, they call the "program." Now just to complicate the story a little, imagine that these people also give me stories in English, which I understand, and they then ask me questions in English about these stories, and I give them back answers in English. Suppose also that after a while I got so good at following the instructions for manipulating the Chinese symbols and the programmers get so good at writing the programs that from the external point of view—that is, from the point of view of somebody outside the room in which I am locked—my answers to the questions are absolutely indistinguishable from those of native Chinese speakers. Nobody just looking at my answers can tell that I don't speak a word of Chinese. Let us also suppose that my answers to the English questions are, as they no doubt would be, indistinguishable from those of other native English speakers, for the simple reason that I am a native English speaker. From the external point of view—from the point of view of someone reading my "answers"—the answers to the Chinese questions and the English questions are equally good. But in the Chinese case, unlike the English case, I produce the answers by manipulating uninterpreted formal symbols. As far as the Chinese is concerned, I simply behave like a computer; I perform computational operations on formally specified elements. For the purposes of the Chinese, I am simply an instantiation of the computer program.

Now the claims made by strong AI are that the programmed computer understands the stories and that the program in some sense explains human understanding. But we are now in a position to examine these claims in light of our thought experiment.

1. As regards the first claim, it seems to me quite obvious in the example that I do not understand a word of Chinese stories. I have inputs and outputs that are indistinguishable from those of the native Chinese speaker, and I can have any formal program you like, but I still understand nothing. For the same reasons, Schank's computer understands nothing of any stories, whether in Chinese, English, or whatever, since in the Chinese case the computer is me, and in cases where the computer is not me, the computer has nothing more than I have in the case where I understand nothing.

2. As regards the second claim, that the program explains human understanding, we can see that the computer and its program do not provide sufficient conditions of understanding since the computer and the program are functioning, and there is no understanding. But does it even provide a necessary condition or a significant contribution to understanding? One of the claims made by the supporters of strong AI is that when I understand a story in English, what I am doing is exactly the same—or perhaps more of the same—as what I was doing in manipulating the Chinese symbols. It is simply more formal symbol manipulation that distinguishes the case in English, where I do understand, from the case in Chinese where I don't. I have not demonstrated that this claim is false, but it would certainly appear an incredible claim in the example. Such plausibility as the claim has derives from the supposition that we can construct a program that will have the same inputs and outputs as native speakers, and in addition we assume that speakers have some level of description where they are also instantiations of a program. On the basis of these two assumptions we assume that even if Schank's program isn't the whole story about understanding, it may be part of the story. Well, I suppose that is an empirical possibility, but not the slightest reason has so far been given to believe that it is true, since what is suggested—though certainly not demonstrated—by the example is that the computer program is simply irrelevant to my understanding of the story. In the Chinese case I have everything that artificial intelligence can put into me by way of a program, and I understand nothing; in the English case I understand everything, and there is so far no reason at all to suppose that my understanding has anything to do with computer programs, that is, with computational operations on purely formally specified elements. As long as the program is defined in terms of computational operations on purely formally defined elements, what the example suggests is that these by themselves have no interesting connection with understanding. They are certainly not sufficient conditions, and not the slightest reason has been given to suppose that they are necessary conditions or even that they make a significant contribution to understanding. Notice that the force of the argument is not simply that different machines can have the same input and output while operating on different formal principles—that is not the point at all. Rather, whatever purely formal principles you put into the computer, they will not be sufficient for understanding, since a human will be able to follow the formal principles without understanding anything. No reason whatever has been offered to suppose that such principles are necessary or even contributory, since no reason has been given to suppose that when I understand English I am operating with any formal program at all.

Well, then, what is it that I have in the case of the English sentences that I do not have in the case of the Chinese sentences? The obvious answer is that I know what the former mean, while I haven't the faintest idea what the latter mean. But in what does this consist and why couldn't we give it to a machine, whatever it is? I will return to this question later, but first I want to continue with the example.

I have had the occasions to present this example to several workers in artificial intelligence, and, interestingly, they do not seem to agree on what the proper reply to it is. I get a surprising variety of replies, and in what follows I will consider the most common of these (specified along with their geographic origins).

But first I want to block some common misunderstandings about "understanding": In many of these discussions one finds a lot of fancy footwork about the word "understanding." My critics point out that there are many different degrees of understanding; that "understanding" is not a simple two-place predicate; that there are even different kinds and levels of understanding, and often the law of excluded middle doesn't even apply in a straightforward way to statements of the form "*x* understands *y*"; that in many cases it is a matter for decision and not a simple matter of fact whether *x* understands *y*; and so on. To all of these points I want to say: of course, of course. But they have nothing to do with the points at issue. There are clear cases in which "understanding" literally applies and clear cases in which it does not apply; and these two sorts of cases are all I need for this argument.[2] I understand stories in English; to a lesser degree I can understand stories in French; to a still lesser degree, stories in German; and in Chinese, not at all. My car and my adding machine, on the other hand, understand nothing: they are not in that line of business. We often attribute "understanding" and other cognitive predicates by metaphor and analogy to cars, adding machines, and other artifacts, but nothing is proved by such attributions. We say, "The door *knows* when to open because of its photoelectric cell," "The adding machine *knows how* (*understands how*, is *able*) to do addition and subtraction but not division," and "The thermostat *perceives* changes in the temperature." The reason we make these attributions is quite interesting, and it has to do with the fact that in artifacts we extend our own intentionality;[3] our tools are extensions of our purposes, and so we find it natural to make metaphorical attributions of intentionality to them; but I take it no philosophical ice is cut by such examples. The sense in which an automatic door "understands instructions" from its photoelectric cell is not at all the sense in which I understand English. If the sense in which Schank's programmed computers understand stories is supposed to be the metaphorical sense in which the door understands, and not the sense in which I understand English, the issue would not be worth discussing. But Newell and Simon (1963) write that the kind of cognition they claim for computers is exactly the same as for human beings. I like the straightforwardness of this claim, and it is the sort of claim I will be considering. I will argue that in the

literal sense the programmed computer understands what the car and the adding machine understand, namely, exactly nothing. The computer understanding is not just (like my understanding of German) partial or incomplete; it is zero.

Now to the replies:

I. The Systems Reply (Berkeley). "While it is true that the individual person who is locked in the room does not understand the story, the fact is that he is merely part of a whole system, and the system does understand the story. The person has a large ledger in front of him in which are written the rules, he has a lot of scratch paper and pencils for doing calculations, he has 'data banks' of sets of Chinese symbols. Now, understanding is not being ascribed to the mere individual; rather it is being ascribed to this whole system of which he is a part."

My response to the systems theory is quite simple: Let the individual internalize all of these elements of the system. He memorizes the rules in the ledger and the data banks of Chinese symbols, and he does all the calculations in his head. The individual then incorporates the entire system. There isn't anything at all to the system that he does not encompass. We can even get rid of the room and suppose he works outdoors. All the same, he understands nothing of the Chinese, and a fortiori neither does the system, because there isn't anything in the system that isn't in him. If he doesn't understand, then there is no way the system could understand because the system is just a part of him.

Actually I feel somewhat embarrassed to give even this answer to the systems theory because the theory seems to me so implausible to start with. The idea is that while a person doesn't understand Chinese, somehow the *conjunction* of that person and bits of paper might understand Chinese. It is not easy for me to imagine how someone who was not in the grip of an ideology would find the idea at all plausible. Still, I think many people who are committed to the ideology of strong AI will in the end be inclined to say something very much like this; so let us pursue it a bit further. According to one version of this view, while the man in the internalized systems example doesn't understand Chinese in the sense that a native Chinese speaker does (because, for example, he doesn't know that the story refers to restaurants and hamburgers, etc.), still "the man as a formal symbol manipulation system" *really does understand Chinese*. The subsystem of the man that is the formal symbol manipulation system for Chinese should not be confused with the subsystem for English.

So there are really two subsystems in the man: one understands English, the other Chinese, and "it's just that the two systems have little to do with each other." But, I want to reply, not only do they have little to do with each other, they are not even remotely alike. The subsystem that understands English (assuming we allow ourselves to talk in this jargon of "subsystems" for a moment) knows that the stories are about restaurants and eating hamburgers, he knows that he is being asked questions about restaurants and that he is answering questions as best he can by making various inferences from the content of the story, and so on. But the Chinese system knows none of this. Whereas the English subsystem knows that "hamburgers" refers to hamburgers, the Chinese subsystem knows only that "squiggle squiggle" is followed by "squoggle squoggle." All he knows is that various formal symbols are being introduced at one end and manipulated according to rules written in English, and other symbols are going out at the other end. The whole point of the original example was to argue that such symbol manipulation by itself couldn't be sufficient for understanding Chinese in any literal sense because the man could write "squoggle squoggle" after "squiggle squiggle" without understanding anything in Chinese. And it doesn't meet that argument to postulate subsystems within the man, because the subsystems are no better off than the man was in the first place: they still don't have anything even remotely like what the English-speaking man (or subsystem) has. Indeed, in the case as described, the Chinese subsystem is simply a part of the English subsystem, a part that engages in meaningless symbol manipulation according to rules in English.

Let us ask ourselves what is supposed to motivate the systems reply in the first place; that is, what *independent* grounds are there supposed to be for saying that the agent must have a subsystem within him

that literally understands stories in Chinese? As far as I can tell the only grounds are that in the example I have the same input and output as native Chinese speakers and a program that goes from one to the other. But the whole point of the examples has been to try to show that that couldn't be sufficient for understanding, in the sense in which I understand stories in English, because a person, and hence the set of systems that go to make up a person, could have the right combination of input, output, and program and still not understand anything in the relevant literal sense in which I understand English. The only motivation for saying there *must* be a subsystem in me that understands Chinese is that I have a program and I can pass the Turing test; I can fool native Chinese speakers. But precisely one of the points at issue is the adequacy of the Turing test. The example shows that there could be two "systems," both of which pass the Turing test, but only one of which understands; and it is no argument against this point to say that since they both pass the Turing test they must both understand, since this claim fails to meet the argument that the system in me that understands English has a great deal more than the system that merely processes Chinese. In short, the systems reply simply begs the question by insisting without argument that the system must understand Chinese.

Furthermore, the systems reply would appear to lead to consequences that are independently absurd. If we are to conclude that there must be cognition in me on the grounds that I have a certain sort of input and output and a program in between, then it looks like all sorts of noncognitive subsystems are going to turn out to be cognitive. For example, there is a level of description at which my stomach does information processing, and it instantiates any number of computer programs, but I take it we do not want to say that it has any understanding (cf. Pylyshyn 1980). But if we accept the systems reply, then it is hard to see how we avoid saying that stomach, heart, liver, and so on are all understanding subsystems, since there is no principled way to distinguish the motivation for saying the Chinese subsystem understands from saying that the stomach understands. It is, by the way, not an answer to this point to say that the Chinese system has information as input and output and the stomach has food and food products as input and output, since from the point of view of the agent, from my point of view, there is no information in either the food or the Chinese—the Chinese is just so many meaningless squiggles. The information in the Chinese case is solely in the eyes of the programmers and the interpreters, and there is nothing to prevent them from treating the input and output of my digestive organs as information if they so desire.

This last point bears on some independent problems in strong AI, and it is worth digressing for a moment to explain it. If strong AI is to be a branch of psychology, then it must be able to distinguish those systems that are genuinely mental from those that are not. It must be able to distinguish the principles on which the mind works from those on which nonmental systems work; otherwise it will offer us no explanations of what is specifically mental about the mental. And the mental-nonmental distinction cannot be just in the eye of the beholder but it must be intrinsic to the systems; otherwise it would be up to any beholder to treat people as nonmental and, for example, hurricanes as mental if he likes. But quite often in the AI literature the distinction is blurred in ways that would in the long run prove disastrous to the claim that AI is a cognitive inquiry. McCarthy, for example, writes, "Machines as simple as thermostats can be said to have beliefs, and having beliefs seems to be a characteristic of most machines capable of problem solving performance" (McCarthy 1979). Anyone who thinks strong AI has a chance as a theory of the mind ought to ponder the implications of that remark. We are asked to accept it as a discovery of strong AI that the hunk of metal on the wall that we use to regulate the temperature has beliefs in exactly the same sense that we, our spouses, and our children have beliefs, and furthermore that "most" of the other machines in the room—telephone, tape recorder, adding machine, electric light switch—also have beliefs in this literal sense. It is not the aim of this article to argue against McCarthy's point, so I will simply assert the following without argument. The study of the mind starts with such facts as that humans have beliefs, while thermostats, telephones, and adding machines don't. If you get a theory that denies this point you have produced a counterexample to the theory and the theory is false. One gets the impression that people in the AI who write this sort of thing think they can get away with it because they don't really take it seriously, and they don't think anyone else will either. I propose, for a moment at least, to take it seriously. Think hard for one minute about what would be necessary to establish that the hunk of metal on the wall over there had real beliefs, beliefs with direction of fit, propositional content, and conditions of satisfaction; beliefs that had the possibility of being strong beliefs or weak beliefs; nervous, anxious, or secure beliefs; dogmatic, rational, or superstitious beliefs; blind faiths or hesitant cogitations; any kind of beliefs. The thermostat is not a candidate. Neither is stomach, liver, adding machine, or telephone. However, since we are taking the idea seriously, notice that its truth would be fatal to strong AI's claim to be a science of the mind. For now the mind is everywhere. What we wanted to know is what distinguishes the mind from thermostats and livers. And if McCarthy were right, strong AI wouldn't have a hope of telling us that.

II. The Robot Reply (Yale). "Suppose we wrote a different kind of program from Schank's program. Suppose we put a computer inside a robot, and this computer would not just take in formal symbols as input and give out formal symbols as output, but rather would actually operate the robot in such a way that the robot does something very much like perceiving, walking, moving about, hammering nails, eating, drinking—anything you like. The robot would, for example, have a television camera attached to it that enabled it to see, it would have arms and legs that enabled it to 'act,' and all of this would be controlled by its computer 'brain.' Such a robot would, unlike Schank's computer, have genuine understanding and other mental states."

The first thing to notice about the robot reply is that it tacitly concedes that cognition is not solely a matter of formal symbol manipulation, since this reply adds a set of causal relations with the outside world (cf. Fodor 1980). But the answer to the robot reply is that the addition of such "perceptual" and "motor" capacities adds nothing by way of understanding, in particular, or intentionality, in general, to Schank's original program. To see this, notice that the same thought experiment applies to the robot case. Suppose that instead of the computer inside the robot, you put me inside the room and, as in the original Chinese case, you give me more Chinese symbols with more instructions in English for matching Chinese symbols to Chinese symbols and feeding back Chinese symbols to the outside. Suppose, unknown to me, some of the Chinese symbols that come to me come from a television camera attached to the robot and other Chinese symbols that I am giving out serve to make the motors inside the robot move the robot's legs or arms. It is important to emphasize that all I am doing is manipulating formal symbols: I know none of these other facts, I am receiving "information" from the robot's "perceptual" apparatus, and I am giving out "instructions" to its motor apparatus without knowing either of these facts. I am the robot's homunculus, but unlike the traditional homunculus, I don't know what's going on. I don't understand anything except the rules for symbol manipulation. Now in this case I want to say that the robot has no intentional states at all; it is simply moving about as a result of its electrical wiring and its program. And furthermore, by instantiating the program I have no intentional states of the relevant type. All I do is follow formal instructions about manipulating formal symbols.

III. The Brain Simulator Reply (Berkeley and M.I.T.).

"Suppose we design a program that doesn't represent information that we have about the world, such as the information in Schank's scripts, but simulates the actual sequence of neuron firings at the synapses of the brain of a native Chinese speaker when he understands stories in Chinese and gives answers to them. The machine takes in Chinese stories and questions about them as input, it simulates the formal structure of actual Chinese brains in processing these stories, and it gives out Chinese answers as outputs. We can even imagine that the machine operates, not with a single serial program, but with a whole set of programs operating in parallel, in the manner that actual human brains presumably operate when they process natural language. Now surely in such a case we would have to say that the machine understood the stories: and if we refuse

to say that, wouldn't we also have to deny that native Chinese speakers understood the stories? At the level of the synapses, what would or could be different about the program of the computer and the program of the Chinese brain?"

Before countering this reply I want to digress to note that it is an odd reply for any partisan of artificial intelligence (or **functionalism**, etc.) to make: I thought the whole idea of strong AI is that we don't need to know how the brain works to know how the mind works. The basic hypothesis, or so I had supposed, was that there is a level of mental operations consisting of computational processes over formal elements that constitute the essence of the mental and can be realized in all sorts of different brain processes, in the same way that any computer program can be realized in different computer hardwares: On the assumptions of strong AI, the mind is to the brain as the program is to the hardware, and thus we can understand the mind without doing neurophysiology. If we had to know how the brain worked to do AI, we wouldn't bother with AI. However, even getting this close to the operation of the brain is still not sufficient to produce understanding. To see this, imagine that instead of a monolingual man in a room shuffling symbols we have the man operate an elaborate set of water pipes with valves connecting them. When the man receives the Chinese symbols, he looks up in the program, written in English, which valves he has to turn on and off. Each water connection corresponds to a synapse in the Chinese brain, and the whole system is rigged up so that after doing all the right firings, that is after turning on all the right faucets, the Chinese answers pop out at the output end of the series of pipes.

Now where is the understanding in this system? It takes Chinese as input, it simulates the formal structure of the synapses of the Chinese brain, and it gives Chinese as output. But the man certainly doesn't understand Chinese, and neither do the water pipes, and if we are tempted to adopt what I think is the absurd view that somehow the *conjunction* of man *and* water pipes understands, remember that in principle the man can internalize the formal structure of the water pipes and do all the "neuron firings" in his imagination. The problem with the brain simulator is that it is simulating the wrong things about the brain. As long as it simulates only the formal structure of the sequence of neuron firings at the synapses, it won't have simulated what matters about the brain, namely its causal properties, its ability to produce intentional states. And that the formal properties are not sufficient for the causal properties is shown by the water pipe example: we can have all the formal properties carved off from the relevant neurobiological causal properties.

IV. The Combination Reply (Berkeley and Stanford).

"While each of the previous three replies might not be completely convincing by itself as a refutation of the Chinese room counter-example, if you take all three together they are collectively much more convincing and even decisive. Imagine a robot with a brain-shaped computer lodged in its cranial cavity, imagine the computer programmed with all the synapses of a human brain, imagine the whole behavior of the robot is indistinguishable from human behavior, and now think of the whole thing as a unified system and not just as a computer with inputs and outputs. Surely in such a case we would have to ascribe **intentionality** to the system."

I entirely agree that in such a case we would find it rational and indeed irresistible to accept the hypothesis that the robot had intentionality, as long as we knew nothing more about it. Indeed, besides appearance and behavior, the other elements of the combination are really irrelevant. If we could build a robot whose behavior was indistinguishable over a large range from human behavior, we would attribute intentionality to it, pending some reason not to. We wouldn't need to know in advance that its computer brain was a formal analogue of the human brain.

But I really don't see that this is any help to the claims of strong AI, and here's why: According to strong AI, instantiating a formal program with the right input and output is a sufficient condition of, indeed is constitutive of, intentionality. As Newell (1979) puts it, the essence of the mental is the operation of a physical symbol system. But the attributions of intentionality that we make to the robot in this example have nothing to do with formal programs. They are simply based on the assumption

that if the robot looks and behaves sufficiently like us, then we would suppose, until proven otherwise, that it must have mental states like ours that cause and are expressed by its behavior and it must have an inner mechanism capable of producing such mental states. If we knew independently how to account for its behavior without such assumptions we would not attribute intentionality to it, especially if we knew it had a formal program. And this is precisely the point of my earlier reply to objection II.

Suppose we knew that the robot's behavior was entirely accounted for by the fact that a man inside it was receiving uninterpreted formal symbols from the robot's sensory receptors and sending out uninterpreted formal symbols to its motor mechanisms, and the man was doing the symbol manipulation in accordance with a bunch of rules. Furthermore, suppose the man knows none of these facts about the robot, all he knows is which operations to perform on which meaningless symbols. In such a case we would regard the robot as an ingenious mechanical dummy. The hypothesis that the dummy has a mind would now be unwarranted and unnecessary, for there is now no longer any reason to ascribe intentionality to the robot or to the system of which it is a part (except of course for the man's intentionality in manipulating the symbols). The formal symbol manipulations go on, the input and output are correctly matched, but the only real locus of intentionality is the man, and he doesn't know any of the relevant intentional states; he doesn't, for example, *see* what comes into the robot's eyes, he doesn't *intend* to move the robot's arm, and he doesn't *understand* any of the remarks made to or by the robot. Nor, for the reasons stated earlier, does the system of which man and robot are a part.

To see this point, contrast this case with cases in which we find it completely natural to ascribe intentionality to members of certain other primate species such as apes and monkeys and to domestic animals such as dogs. The reasons we find it natural are, roughly, two: We can't make sense of the animal's behavior without the ascription of intentionality, and we can see that the beasts are made of similar stuff to ourselves—that is an eye, that a nose, this is its skin, and so on. Given the coherence of the animal's behavior and the assumption of the same causal stuff underlying it, we assume both that the animal must have mental states underlying its behavior, and that the mental states must be produced by mechanisms made out of the stuff that is like our stuff. We would certainly make similar assumptions about the robot unless we had some reason not to, but as soon as we knew that the behavior was the result of a formal program, and that the actual causal properties of the physical substance were irrelevant we would abandon the assumption of intentionality.

There are two other responses to my example that come up frequently (and so are worth discussing) but really miss the point.

V. The Other Minds Reply (Yale). "How do you know that other people understand Chinese or anything else? Only by their behavior. Now the computer can pass the behavioral tests as well as they can (in principle), so if you are going to attribute cognition to other people you must in principle also attribute it to computers."

This objection really is only worth a short reply. The problem in this discussion is not about how I know that other people have cognitive states, but rather what it is that I am attributing to them when I attribute cognitive states to them. The thrust of the argument is that it couldn't be just computational processes and their output because the computational processes and their output can exist without the cognitive state. It is no answer to this argument to feign anesthesia. In "cognitive sciences" one presupposes the reality and knowability of the mental in the same way that in physical sciences one has to presuppose the reality and knowability of physical objects.

VI. The Many Mansions Reply (Berkeley). "Your whole argument presupposes that AI is only about analog and digital computers. But that just happens to be the present state of technology. Whatever these causal processes are that you say are essential for intentionality (assuming you are right), eventually we will be able to build devices that have these causal processes, and that will be artificial intelligence. So your arguments are in no way directed at the ability of artificial intelligence to produce and explain cognition."

I really have no objection to this reply save to say that it in effect trivializes the project of strong AI by redefining it as whatever artificially produces and explains cognition. The interest of the original claim made on behalf of artificial intelligence is that it was a precise, well defined thesis: mental processes are computational processes over formally defined elements. I have been concerned to challenge that thesis. If the claim is redefined so that it is no longer that thesis, my objections no longer apply because there is no longer a testable hypothesis for them to apply to.

Let us now return to the question I promised I would try to answer: Granted that in my original example I understand the English and I do not understand the Chinese, and granted therefore that the machine doesn't understand either English or Chinese, still there must be something about me that makes it the case that I understand English and a corresponding something lacking in me that makes it the case that I fail to understand Chinese. Now why couldn't we give those somethings, whatever they are, to a machine?

I see no reason in principle why we couldn't give a machine the capacity to understand English or Chinese, since in an important sense our bodies with our brains are precisely such machines. But I do see very strong arguments for saying that we could not give such a thing to a machine where the operation of the machine is defined solely in terms of computational processes over formally defined elements; that is, where the operation of the machine is defined as an instantiation of a computer program. It is not because I am the instantiation of a computer program that I am able to understand English and have other forms of intentionality (I am, I suppose, the instantiation of any number of computer programs), but as far as we know it is because I am a certain sort of organism with a certain biological (i.e., chemical and physical) structure, and this structure, under certain conditions, is causally capable of producing perception, action, understanding, learning, and other intentional phenomena. And part of the point of the present argument is that only something that had those causal powers could have that intentionality. Perhaps other physical and chemical processes could produce exactly these effects; perhaps, for example, Martians also have intentionality but their brains are made of different stuff. That is an empirical question, rather like the question whether photosynthesis can be done by something with a chemistry different from that of chlorophyll.

But the main point of the present argument is that no purely formal model will ever be sufficient by itself for intentionality because the formal properties are not by themselves constitutive of intentionality, and they have by themselves no causal powers except the power, when instantiated, to produce the next stage of the formalism when the machine is running. And any other causal properties that particular realizations of the formal model have, are irrelevant to the formal model because we can always put the same formal model in a different realization where those causal properties are obviously absent. Even if, by some miracle, Chinese speakers exactly realize Schank's program, we can put the same program in English speakers, water pipes, or computers, none of which understand Chinese, the program notwithstanding.

What matters about brain operations is not the formal shadow cast by the sequence of synapses but rather the actual properties of the sequences. All the arguments for the strong version of artificial intelligence that I have seen insist on drawing an outline around the shadows cast by cognition and then claiming that the shadows are the real thing.

By way of concluding I want to try to state some of the general philosophical points implicit in the argument. For clarity I will try to do it in a question-and-answer fashion, and I begin with that old chestnut of a question:

"Could a machine think?"

The answer is, obviously, yes. We are precisely such machines.

"Yes, but could an artifact, a man-made machine, think?"

Assuming it is possible to produce artificially a machine with a nervous system, neurons with axons and dendrites, and all the rest of it, sufficiently like ours, again the answer to the question seems to be obviously, yes. If you can exactly duplicate the causes, you could duplicate the effects. And indeed it might be possible to produce consciousness, intentionality, and all the rest of it using some other sorts of chemical principles than those that human beings use. It is, as I said, an empirical question.

"OK, but could a digital computer think?"

If by "digital computer" we mean anything at all that has a level of description where it can correctly be described as the instantiation of a computer program, then again the answer is, of course, yes, since we are the instantiations of any number of computer programs, and we can think.

"But could something think, understand, and so on *solely* in virtue of being a computer with a right sort of program? Could instantiating a program, the right program of course, by itself be a sufficient condition of understanding?"

This I think is the right question to ask, though it is usually confused with one or more of the earlier questions, and the answer to it is no.

"Why not?"

Because the formal symbol manipulations by themselves don't have any intentionality; they are quite meaningless; they aren't even *symbol* manipulations, since the symbols don't symbolize anything. In the linguistic jargon, they have only a syntax but no semantics. Such intentionality as computers appear to have is solely in the minds of those who program them and those who use them, those who send in the input and those who interpret the output.

The aim of the Chinese room example was to try to show this by showing that as soon as we put something into the system that really does have intentionality (a man), and we program him with the formal program, you can see that the formal program carries no additional intentionality. It adds nothing, for example, to a man's ability to understand Chinese.

Precisely that feature of AI that seemed so appealing—the distinction between the program and the realization—proves fatal to the claim that simulation could be duplication. The distinction between the program and its realization in the hardware seems to be parallel to the distinction between the level of mental operations and the level of brain operations. And if we could describe the level of mental operations as a formal program, then it seems we could describe what was essential about the mind without doing either introspective psychology or neurophysiology of the brain. But the equation "mind is to brain as program is to hardware" breaks down at several points, among them the following three:

First, the distinction between program and realization has the consequence that the same program could have all sorts of crazy realizations that had no form of intentionality. Weizenbaum (1976, Ch. 2), for example, shows in detail how to construct a computer using a roll of toilet paper and a pile of small stones. Similarly, the Chinese story understanding program can be programmed into a sequence of water pipes, a set of wind machines, or a monolingual English speaker, none of which thereby acquires an understanding of Chinese. Stones, toilet paper, wind, and water pipes are the wrong kind of stuff to have intentionality in the first place—only something that has the same causal powers as brains can have intentionality—and though the English speaker has the right kind of stuff for intentionality you can easily see that he doesn't get any extra intentionality by memorizing the program, since memorizing it won't teach him Chinese.

Second, the program is purely formal, but the intentional states are not in that way formal. They are defined in terms of their content, not their form. The belief that it is raining, for example, is not defined as a certain formal shape, but as a certain mental content with conditions of satisfaction, a direction of fit (see Searle 1979), and the like. Indeed the belief as such hasn't even got a formal shape in this syntactic sense, since one and the same belief can be given an indefinite number of different syntactic expressions in different linguistic systems.

Third, as I mentioned before, mental states and events are literally a product of the operation of the brain, but the program is not in that way a product of the computer.

"Well if programs are in no way constitutive of mental processes, why have so many people believed the converse? That at least needs some explanation."

I don't really know the answer to that one. The idea that computer simulations could be the real thing ought to have seemed suspicious in the first place because the computer isn't confined to simulating mental operations, by any means. No one supposes that computer simulations of a five-alarm fire will burn the neighborhood down or that a computer simulation of a rainstorm will leave us all drenched. Why on earth would anyone suppose that a computer simulation of understanding actually understood anything? It is sometimes said that it would be frightfully hard to get computers to feel pain or fall in love, but love and pain are neither harder nor easier than cognition or anything else. For simulation, all you need is the right input and output and a program in the middle that transforms the former into the latter. That is all the computer has for anything it does. To confuse simulation with duplication is the same mistake, whether it is pain, love, cognition, fires, or rainstorms.

Still, there are several reasons why AI must have seemed—and to many people perhaps still does seem—in some way to reproduce and thereby explain mental phenomena, and I believe we will not succeed in removing these illusions until we have fully exposed the reasons that give rise to them.

First, and perhaps the most important, is a confusion about the notion of "information processing": many people in cognitive science believe that the human brain, with its mind, does something called "information processing," and analogously the computer with its program does information processing; but fires and rainstorms, on the other hand, don't do information processing at all. Thus, though the computer can simulate the formal features of any process whatever, it stands in a special relation to the mind and brain because when the computer is properly programmed, ideally with the same program as the brain, the information processing is identical in the two cases, and this information processing is really the essence of the mental. But the trouble with this argument is that it rests on an ambiguity in the notion of "information." In the sense in which people "process information" when they reflect, say, on problems in arithmetic or when they read and answer questions about stories, the programmed computer does not do "information processing." Rather, what it does is manipulate formal symbols. The fact that the programmer and the interpreter of the computer output use the symbols to stand for objects in the world is totally beyond the scope of the computer. The computer, to repeat, has a syntax but no semantics. Thus, if you type into the computer "2 plus 2 equals?" it will type out "4." But it has no idea that "4" means 4 or that it means anything at all. And the point is not that it lacks some second-order information about the interpretation of its first-order symbols, but rather that its first-order symbols don't have any interpretations as far as the computer is concerned. All the computer has is more symbols. The introduction of the notion of "information processing" therefore produces a dilemma: either we construe the notion of "information processing" in such a way that it implies intentionality as part of the process or we don't. If the former, then the programmed computer does not do information processing, it only manipulates formal symbols. If the latter, then, though the computer does information processing, it is only doing so in the sense in which adding machines, typewriters, stomachs, thermostats, rainstorms, and hurricanes do information processing; namely, they have a level of description at which we can describe them as taking information in at one end, transforming it, and producing information as output. But in this case it is up to outside observers to interpret the input and output as information in the ordinary sense. And no similarity is established between the computer and the brain in terms of any similarity of information processing.

Second, in much of AI there is a residual **behaviorism** or operationalism. Since appropriately programmed computers can have input-output patterns similar to those of human beings, we are tempted to postulate mental states in the computer similar to human mental states. But once we see that it is both conceptually and empirically possible for a system to have human capacities in some realm without having any intentionality at all, we should be able to overcome this impulse. My desk adding machine has calculating capacities, but no intentionality, and in this paper I have tried to show that a system could have input and output capabilities that duplicated those of a native Chinese speaker and still not understand Chinese, regardless of how it was programmed. The Turing test is typical of the tradition in being unashamedly

behavioristic and operationalistic, and I believe that if AI workers totally repudiated behaviorism and operationalism much of the confusion between simulation and duplication would be eliminated.

Third, this residual operationalism is joined to a residual form of **dualism**; indeed strong AI only makes sense given the dualistic assumption that, where the mind is concerned, the brain doesn't matter. In strong AI (and in functionalism, as well) what matters are programs, and programs are independent of their realization in machines; indeed, as far as AI is concerned, the same program could be realized by an electronic machine, a Cartesian mental **substance**, or a Hegelian world spirit. The single most surprising discovery that I have made in discussing these issues is that many AI workers are quite shocked by my idea that actual human mental phenomena might be dependent on actual physical-chemical properties of actual human brains. But if you think about it a minute you can see that I should not have been surprised; for unless you accept some form of dualism, the strong AI project hasn't got a chance. The project is to reproduce and explain the mental by designing programs, but unless the mind is not only conceptually but empirically independent of the brain you couldn't carry out the project, for the program is completely independent of any realization. Unless you believe that the mind is separable from the brain both conceptually and empirically—dualism in a strong form—you cannot hope to reproduce the mental by writing and running programs since programs must be independent of brains or any other particular forms of instantiation. If mental operations consist in computational operations on formal symbols, then it follows that they have no interesting connection with the brain; the only connection would be that the brain just happens to be one of the indefinitely many types of machines capable of instantiating the program. This form of dualism is not the traditional Cartesian variety that claims there are two sorts of *substances*, but it is Cartesian in the sense that it insists that what is specifically mental about the mind has no intrinsic connection with the actual properties of the brain. This underlying dualism is masked from us by the fact that AI literature contains frequent fulminations against "dualism"; what the authors seem to be unaware of is that their position presupposes a strong version of dualism.

"Could a machine think?" My own view is that *only* a machine could think, and indeed only very special kinds of machines, namely brains and machines that had the same causal powers as brains. And that is the main reason strong AI has had little to tell us about thinking, since it has nothing to tell us about machines. By its own definition, it is about programs, and programs are not machines. Whatever else intentionality is, it is a biological phenomenon, and it is as likely to be as causally dependent on the specific biochemistry of its origins as lactation, photosynthesis, or any other biological phenomena. No one would suppose that we could produce milk and sugar by running a computer simulation of the formal sequences in lactation and photosynthesis, but where the mind is concerned many people are willing to believe in such a miracle because of a deep and abiding dualism: the mind they suppose is a matter of formal processes and is independent of quite specific material causes in the way that milk and sugar are not.

In defense of this dualism the hope is often expressed that the brain is a digital computer (early computers, by the way, were often called "electronic brains"). But that is no help. Of course the brain is a digital computer. Since everything is a digital computer, brains are too. The point is that the brain's causal capacity to produce intentionality cannot consist in its instantiating a computer program, since for any program you like it is possible for something to instantiate that program and still not have any mental states. Whatever it is that the brain does to produce intentionality, it cannot consist in instantiating a program since no program, by itself, is sufficient for intentionality.

NOTES

1. I am not, of course, saying that Schank himself is committed to these claims.
2. Also, "understanding" implies both the possession of mental (intentional) states and the truth (validity, success) of these states. For the purposes of this discussion we are concerned only with the possession of the states.

3. Intentionality is by definition that feature of certain mental states by which they are directed at or about objects and states of affairs in the world. Thus, beliefs, desires, and intentions are intentional states; undirected forms of anxiety and depression are not.

REFERENCES

Fodor, J. A. 1980. Methodological solipsism considered as a research strategy in cognitive psychology. *Behavioral and Brain Sciences* 3:1.

McCarthy, J. 1979. Ascribing mental qualities to machines. In: *Philosophical perceptives in artificial intelligence*, ed. M. Ringle. Atlantic Highlands, NJ: Humanities Press.

Newell, A. 1973. Physical symbol systems. Lecture at the La Jolla Conference on Cognitive Science.

Newell, A., and Simon, H. A. 1963. GPS, a program that simulates human thought. In: *Computers and thought*, ed. A. Feigenbaum & V. Feldman, pp. 279–93. New York: McGraw-Hill.

Pylyshyn, Z. W. 1980. Computation and cognition: issues in the foundations of cognitive science. *Behavioral and Brain Sciences* 3.

Schank, R. C., and Abelson, R. P. 1977. *Scripts, plans, goals, and understanding*. Hillsdale, NJ: Lawrence Erlbaum.

Searle, J. R. 1979. The intentionality of intention and action. *Inquiry* 22:253–80.

Weizenbaum, J. 1965. Eliza—a computer program for the study of natural language communication between man and machine. *Communication of the Association for Computing Machinery* 9:36–45.

Weizenbaum, J. 1976. *Computer power and human reason*. San Francisco: W. H. Freeman.

Winograd, T. 1973. A procedural model of language understanding. In: *Computer models of thought and language*, ed. R. Schank & K. Colby. San Francisco: W. H. Freeman.

KEY TERMS

Functionalism
Intentionality
Behaviorism
Dualism
Substance

STUDY QUESTIONS

1. Do you think that Searle understands the Chinese stories in his Chinese Room thought-experiment? Why or why not?
2. What does Searle think his Chinese Room thought-experiment shows?
3. Does Searle's thought-experiment allow us to draw any conclusions about the adequacy of Turing's "imitation-game," which is supposed to stand in for the question "Can machines think"?
4. Which of the various replies that Searle considers do you find most plausible? What might a proponent of that reply say in response to Searle's criticisms?
5. Searle answers the question "Could a machine think?" by saying, "The answer is, obviously, yes. We are precisely such machines." Do you think it's right to apply the word "machine" to a human being (or a human brain)?

C. PERSONAL IDENTITY

Ж

A Dialogue on Personal Identity and Immortality

JOHN PERRY

This is a record of conversations of Gretchen Weirob, a teacher of philosophy at a small midwestern college, and two of her friends. The conversations took place in her hospital room on the three nights before she died from injuries sustained in a motorcycle accident. Sam Miller is a chaplain and a long-time friend of Weirob's; Dave Cohen is a former student of hers.

. .

The First Night

COHEN: I can hardly believe what you say, Gretchen. You are lucid and do not appear to be in great pain. And yet you say things are hopeless?

WEIROB: These devices can keep me alive for another day or two at most. Some of my vital organs have been injured beyond anything the doctors

From *A Dialogue on Personal Identity and Immortality*. Copyright © 1978 by Hackett Publishing Co., Inc. Reprinted by permission of the publisher.

I wrote this paper while a Guggenheim Fellow and on sabbatical leave from Stanford University. I would like to thank both institutions for their support.

My aim has not been to explain and defend my own views on personal identity, but to introduce and develop positions and arguments that have emerged in the literature on that topic.

know how to repair, apart from certain rather radical measures I have rejected. I am not in much pain. But as I understand it that is not a particularly good sign. My brain was uninjured and I guess that's why I am as lucid as I ever am. The whole situation is a bit depressing, I fear. But here's Sam Miller. Perhaps he will know how to cheer me up.

MILLER: Good evening, Gretchen. Hello, Dave. I guess there's not much point in beating around the bush, Gretchen; the medics tell me you're a goner. Is there anything I can do to help?

WEIROB: Crimenetley, Sam! You deal with the dying every day. Don't you have anything more comforting to say than "Sorry to hear you're a goner"?

MILLER: Well, to tell you the truth, I'm a little at a loss for what to say to you. Most people I deal with are believers like I am. We talk of the prospects for survival. I give assurance that God, who is just and merciful, would not permit such a travesty as that our short life on this earth should be the end of things. But you and I have talked about religious and philosophical issues for years. I have never been able to find in you the least inclination to believe in God; indeed, it's a rare day when you are sure that your friends have minds, or that you can see your own hand in front of your face, or that there is any reason to believe that the sun will rise tomorrow. How can I hope to comfort you with the prospect of life after death, when I know you will regard it as having no probability whatsoever?

WEIROB: I would not require so much to be comforted, Sam. Even the possibility of something quite improbable can be comforting, in certain situations. When we used to play tennis, I beat you no more than one time in twenty. But this was enough to establish the possibility of beating you on any given occasion, and by focusing merely on the possibility I remained eager to play. Entombed in a secure prison, thinking our situation quite hopeless, we may find unutterable joy in the information that there is, after all, the slimmest possibility of escape. Hope provides comfort, and hope does not always require probability. But we must believe that what we hope for is at least possible. So I will set an easier task for you. Simply persuade me that my survival after the death of this body, is *possible*, and I promise to be comforted. Whether you succeed or not, your attempts will be a diversion, for you know I like to talk philosophy more than anything else.

MILLER: But what is possibility, if not reasonable probability?

WEIROB: I do not mean possible in the sense of likely, or even in the sense of conforming to the known laws of physics or biology. I mean possible only in the weakest sense—of being conceivable, given the unavoidable facts. Within the next couple of days, this body will die. It will be buried and it will rot away. I ask that, given these facts, you explain to me how it even makes *sense* to talk of me continuing to exist. Just explain to me what it is I am to *imagine*, when I imagine surviving, that is consistent with these facts, and I shall be comforted.

MILLER: But then what is there to do? There are many conceptions of immortality, of survival past the grave, which all seem to make good sense. Surely not the possibility, but only the probability, can be doubted. Take your choice! Christians believe in life, with a body, in some Hereafter—the details vary, of course, from sect to sect. There is the Greek idea of the body as a prison, from which we escape at death—so that we have continued life without a body. Then there are conceptions in which, so to speak, we merge with the flow of being—

WEIROB: I must cut short your lesson in comparative religion. Survival means surviving, no more, no less. I have no doubts that I shall merge with being; plants will take root in my remains, and the chemicals that I am will continue to make their contribution to life. I am enough of an ecologist to be comforted. But survival, if it is anything, must offer comforts of a different sort, the comforts of *anticipation*. Survival means that tomorrow, or sometime in the future, there will be someone who will experience, who will see and touch and smell—or at the very least, think and reason and remember. And this person will be *me*. This person will be related to me in such a way that it is correct for me to anticipate, to look forward to, those future experiences. And I am related to her in such a way that it will be right for her to remember what I have thought and done, to feel remorse for what I have done wrong, and pride in what I have done right. And the only relation that supports anticipation and memory in this way, is simply *identity*. For it is never correct to anticipate, as happening to oneself, what will happen to someone else, is it? Or to remember, as one's own thoughts and deeds, what someone else did? So don't give me merger with being, or some such nonsense. Give me identity, or let's talk about baseball or fishing—but I'm sorry to get so emotional. I react strongly when words which mean one thing are used for another—when one talks about survival, but does not mean to say that the same person will continue to exist. It's such a sham!

MILLER: I'm sorry. I was just trying to stay in touch with the times, if you want to know the truth, for when I read modern theology or talk to my students who have studied Eastern religions, the notion of survival simply as continued existence of the same person seems out of date. Merger with Being! Merger with Being! That's all I hear. My own beliefs are quite simple, if somewhat vague. I think you will live again—with or without a body, I don't know—I draw comfort from my belief that you and I will be together again, after I also die. We will communicate, somehow. We will continue to grow spiritually. That's what I believe, as surely as I believe that I am sitting here. For I don't know how God could be excused, if this small sample of life is all that we are allotted; I don't know why He should have created us, if these few years of toil and torment are the end of it—

WEIROB: Remember our deal, Sam. You don't have to convince me that survival is probable, for we both agree you would not get to first base. You have only to convince me that it is possible. The only condition is that it be real survival we are talking about, not some up-to-date ersatz survival, which simply amounts to what any ordinary person would call totally ceasing to exist.

MILLER: I guess I just miss the problem, then. Of course, it's possible. You just continue to exist, after your body dies. What's to be defended or explained? You want details? Okay. Two people meet a thousand years from now, in a place that may or may not be part of this physical universe. I am one and you are the other. So you must have survived. Surely you can imagine that. What else is there to say?

WEIROB: But in a few days *I* will quit breathing, *I* will be put into a coffin, *I* will be buried. And in a few months or a few years *I* will be reduced to so much humus. That, I take it, is obvious, is given. How then can you say that I am one of these persons a thousand years from now?

Suppose I took this box of Kleenex and lit fire to it. It is reduced to ashes and I smash the ashes and flush them down the john. Then I say to you, go home and on the shelf will be *that very box of Kleenex*. It has survived! Wouldn't that be absurd? What sense could you make of it? And yet that is just what you say to me. I will rot away. And then, a thousand years later, there I will be. What sense does that make?

MILLER: There could be an *identical* box of Kleenex at your home, one just like it in every respect. And, in this sense, there is no difficulty in there being someone identical to you in the Hereafter, though your body has rotted away.

WEIROB: You are playing with words again. There could be an *exactly similar* box of Kleenex on my shelf. We sometimes use "identical" to mean "exactly similar," as when we speak of "identical twins." But I am using "identical" in a way in which *identity* is the condition of memory and correct anticipation. If I am told that tomorrow, though I will be dead, someone else that looks and sounds and thinks just like me will be alive—would that be comforting? Could I correctly *anticipate* having her experiences? Would it make sense for me to fear her pains and look forward to her pleasures? Would it be right for her to feel remorse at the harsh way I am treating you? Of course not. Similarity, however exact, is not identity. I use identity to mean there is but one thing. If I am to survive, there must be one person who lies in this bed now, and who talks to someone in your Hereafter ten or a thousand years from now. After all, what comfort could there be in the notion of a heavenly imposter, walking around getting credit for the few good things I have done?

MILLER: I'm sorry. I see that I was simply confused. Here is what I should have said. If you were merely a live human body—as the Kleenex body is merely cardboard and glue in a certain arrangement—then the death of your body would be the end of you. But surely you are more than that, fundamentally more than that. What is fundamentally you is not your body, but your soul or self or mind.

WEIROB: Do you mean these words, "soul," "self," or "mind" to come to the same thing?

MILLER: Perhaps distinctions could be made, but I shall not pursue them now. I mean the nonphysical and nonmaterial aspects of you, your consciousness. It is this that I get at with these words, and I don't think any further distinction is relevant.

WEIROB: Consciousness? I am conscious, for a while yet. I see, I hear, I think, I remember. But "to be conscious"—that is a verb. What is the subject of the verb, the thing which is conscious? Isn't it just this body, the same object that is overweight, injured, and lying in bed?—and which will be buried and not be conscious in a day or a week at the most?

MILLER: As you are a philosopher, I would expect you to be less muddled about these issues. Did Descartes not draw a clear distinction between the body and the mind, between that which is overweight, and that which is conscious? Your mind or soul is immaterial, lodged in your body while you are on earth. The two are intimately related but not identical. Now clearly, what concerns us in survival is your mind or soul. It is this which must be identical to the person before me now, and to the one I expect to see in a thousand years in heaven.

WEIROB: So I am not really this body, but a soul or mind or spirit? And this soul cannot be seen or felt or touched or smelt? That is implied, I take it, by the fact that it is immaterial?

MILLER: That's right. Your soul sees and smells, but cannot be seen or smelt.

WEIROB: Let me see if I understand you. You would admit that I am the very same person with whom you had lunch last week at Dorsey's?

MILLER: Of course you are.

WEIROB: Now when you say I am the same person, if I understand you, that is not a remark about this body you see and could touch and I fear can smell. Rather it is a remark about a soul, which you cannot see or touch or smell. The fact that the same body that now lies in front of you on the bed was across the table from you at Dorsey's—that would not mean that the same *person* was present on both occasions, if the same soul were not. And if, through some strange turn of events, the same soul were present on both occasions, but lodged in different bodies, then it *would* be the same person. Is that right?

MILLER: You have understood me perfectly. But surely, you understood all of this before!

WEIROB: But wait. I can repeat it, but I'm not sure I understand it. If you cannot see or touch or in any way perceive my soul, what makes you think the one you are confronted with now *is* the very same soul you were confronted with at Dorsey's?

MILLER: But I just explained. To say it is the same soul and to say it is the same person, are the same. And, of course, you are the same person you were before. Who else would you be if not yourself? You *were* Gretchen Weirob, and you *are* Gretchen Weirob.

WEIROB: But how do you know you are talking to Gretchen Weirob at all, and not someone else, say Barbara Walters or even Mark Spitz!

MILLER: Well, it's just obvious. I can see who I am talking to.

WEIROB: But all you can see is my body. You can see, perhaps, that the same body is before you now that was before you last week at Dorsey's. But you have just said that Gretchen Weirob is not a body but a soul. In judging that the same person is before you now as was before you then, you must be making a judgment about souls—which, you said, cannot be seen or touched or smelt or tasted. And so, I repeat, how do you know?

MILLER: Well, I *can* see that it is the same body before me now that was across the table at Dorsey's. And I know that the same soul is connected with the body now that was connected with it before. That's how I know it's you. I see no difficulty in the matter.

WEIROB: You reason on the principle, "Same body, same self."

MILLER: Yes.

WEIROB: And would you reason conversely also? If there were in this bed Barbara Walters' body— that is, the body you see every night on the news— would you infer that it was not me, Gretchen Weirob, in the bed?

MILLER: Of course I would. How would you have come by Barbara Walters' body?

WEIROB: But then merely extend this principle to Heaven, and you will see that your conception of survival is without sense. Surely this very body, which will be buried and as I must so often repeat, *rot away*, will not be in your Hereafter. Different body, different person. Or do you claim that a body can rot away on earth, and then still wind up somewhere else? Must I bring up the Kleenex box again?

MILLER: No, I do not claim that. But I also do not extend a principle, found reliable on earth, to such a different situation as is represented by the Hereafter. That a correlation between bodies and souls has been found on earth does not make it inconceivable or impossible that they should separate. Principles found to work in one circumstance may not be assumed to work in vastly altered circumstances. January and snow go together here, and one would be a fool to expect otherwise. But the principle does not apply in southern California.

WEIROB: So the principle, "same body, same soul," is a well-confirmed regularity, not something you know "**a priori.**"

MILLER: By "a priori" you philosophers mean something which can be known without observing what actually goes on in the world—as I can know that two plus two equals four just by thinking about numbers, and that no bachelors are married, just by thinking about the meaning of "bachelor"?

WEIROB: Yes.

MILLER: Then you are right. If it was part of the meaning of "same body" that wherever we have the same body we have the same soul, it would have to obtain universally, in Heaven as well as on earth. But I just claim it is a generalization we know by observation on earth, and it need not automatically extend to Heaven.

WEIROB: But where do you get this principle? It simply amounts to a correlation between being confronted with the same body and being confronted with the same soul. To establish such a correlation in the first place, surely one must have some *other* means of judging sameness of soul. You do not have such a means; your principle is without foundation; either you really do not know the person before you now is Gretchen Weirob, the very same person you lunched with at Dorsey's, or what you do know has nothing to do with sameness of some immaterial soul.

MILLER: Hold on, hold on. You know I can't follow you when you start spitting out arguments like that. Now what is this terrible fallacy I'm supposed to have committed?

WEIROB: I'm sorry. I get carried away. Here—by way of a peace offering—have one of the chocolates Dave brought.

MILLER: Very tasty. Thank you.

WEIROB: Now why did you choose that one?

MILLER: Because it had a certain swirl on the top which shows that it is a caramel.

WEIROB: That is, a certain sort of swirl is correlated with a certain type of filling—the swirls with caramel, the rosettes with orange, and so forth.

MILLER: Yes. When you put it that way, I see an analogy. Just as I judged that the filling would be the same in this piece as in the last piece that I ate with such a swirl, so I judge that the soul with which I am conversing is the same as the last soul with which I conversed when sitting across from that body. We *see* the outer wrapping and infer what is inside.

WEIROB: But how did you come to realize that swirls of that sort and caramel insides were so associated?

MILLER: Why, from eating a great many of them over the years. Whenever I bit into a candy with that sort of swirl, it was filled with caramel.

WEIROB: Could you have established the correlation had you never been allowed to bite into a candy and never seen what happened when someone else bit into one? You could have formed the hypothesis, "same swirl, same filling." But could you have ever established it?

MILLER: It seems not.

WEIROB: So your inference, in a particular case, to the identity of filling from the identity of swirl would be groundless?

MILLER: Yes, it would. I think I see what is coming.

WEIROB: I'm sure you do. Since you can never, so to speak, bite into my soul, can never see or touch it, you have no way of testing your hypothesis that sameness of body means sameness of self.

MILLER: I daresay you are right. But now I'm a bit lost. What is supposed to follow from all of this?

WEIROB: If, as you claim, identity of persons consisted in identity of immaterial unobservable souls, then judgments of personal identity of the sort we make every day whenever we greet a friend or avoid a pest are really judgments about such souls.

MILLER: Right.

WEIROB: But if such judgments were really about souls, they would all be groundless and without foundation. For we have no direct method of observing sameness of soul, and so—and this is the point made by the candy example—we can have no indirect method either.

MILLER: That seems fair.

WEIROB: But our judgments about persons are not all simply groundless and silly, so we must not be judging of immaterial souls after all.

MILLER: Your reasoning has some force. But I suspect the problem lies in my defense of my position, and not the position itself. Look here—there *is* a way to test the hypothesis of a correlation after all. When I entered the room, I expected you to react just as you did—argumentatively and skeptically. Had the person with this body reacted completely differently perhaps I would have been forced to conclude it was not you. For example, had she complained about not being able to appear on the six o'clock news, and missing Harry Reasoner, and so forth, I might eventually have been persuaded it *was* Barbara Walters and not you. Similarity of psychological characteristics—a person's attitudes, beliefs, memories, prejudices, and the like—is observable. These are correlated with identity of body on the one side, and of course with sameness of soul on the other. So the correlation between body and soul can be established after all by this intermediate link.

WEIROB: And how do you know that?

MILLER: Know what?

WEIROB: That where we have sameness of psychological characteristics, we have sameness of soul.

MILLER: Well, now you are really being just silly. The soul or mind is just that which is responsible for one's character, memory, belief. These are aspects of the mind, just as one's height, weight, and appearance are aspects of the body.

WEIROB: Let me grant for the sake of argument that belief, character, memory, and so forth are states of mind. That is, I suppose, I grant that what one thinks and feels is due to the states one's mind is in at that time. And I shall even grant that a mind is an immaterial thing—though I harbor the gravest doubts that this is so. I do not see how it follows that similarity of such traits requires, or is evidence to the slightest degree, for identity of the mind or soul.

Let me explain my point with an analogy. If we were to walk out of this room, down past the mill and out towards Wilbur, what would we see?

MILLER: We would come to the Blue River, among other things.

WEIROB: And how would you recognize the Blue River? I mean, of course if you left from here, you would scarcely expect to hit the Platte or Niobrara. But suppose you were actually lost, and came across the Blue River in your wandering, just at that point where an old dam partly blocks the flow. Couldn't you recognize it?

MILLER: Yes, I'm sure as soon as I saw that part of the river I would again know where I was.

WEIROB: And how would you recognize it?

MILLER: Well, the turgid brownness of the water, the sluggish flow, the filth washed up on the banks, and such.

WEIROB: In a word, the states of the water which makes up the river at the time you see it.

MILLER: Right.

WEIROB: If you saw the blue clean water, with bass jumping, you would know it wasn't the Blue River.

MILLER: Of course.

WEIROB: So you expect, each time you see the Blue, to see the water, which makes it up, in similar states—not always exactly the same, for sometimes it's a little dirtier, but by and large similar.

MILLER: Yes, but what do you intend to make of this?

WEIROB: Each time you see the Blue, it consists of *different* water. The water that was in it a month ago may be in Tuttle Creek Reservoir or in the Mississippi or in the Gulf of Mexico by now. So the *similarity* of states of water, by which you judge the sameness of river, does not require *identity* of the water which is in those states at these various times.

MILLER: And?

WEIROB: And so just because you judge as to personal identity by reference to similarity of states of mind, it does not follow that the mind, or soul, is the same in each case. My point is this. For all you know, the immaterial soul which you think is lodged in my body might change from day to day, from hour to hour, from minute to minute, re-placed each time by another soul psychologically similar. You cannot see it or touch it, so how would you know?

MILLER: Are you saying I don't really know who you are?

WEIROB: Not at all. *You* are the one who says personal identity consists in sameness of this immaterial, unobservable, invisible, untouchable soul. I merely point out that *if* it did consist in that, you *would* have no idea who I am. Sameness of body would not necessarily mean sameness of person. Sameness of psychological characteristics would not necessarily mean sameness of person. I am saying that if you do know who I am then you are wrong that personal identity consists in sameness of immaterial soul.

MILLER: I see. But wait. I believe my problem is that I simply forgot a main tenet of my theory. The correlation can be established in my own case. I know that *my* soul and my body are intimately and consistently found together. From this one case I can generalize, at least as concerns life in this world, that sameness of body is a reliable sign of sameness of soul. This leaves me free to regard it as intelligible, in the case of death, that the link between the particular soul and the particular body it has been joined with is broken.

WEIROB: This would be quite an extrapolation, wouldn't it, from one case directly observed, to a couple of billion in which only the body is observed? For I take it that we are in the habit of assuming, for every person now on earth, as well as those who have already come and gone, that the principle "one body, one soul" is in effect.

MILLER: This does not seem an insurmountable obstacle. Since there is nothing special about my case, I assume the arrangement I find in it applies universally until given some reason to believe otherwise. And I never have been.

WEIROB: Let's let that pass. I have another problem that is more serious. How is it that you know in your own case that there is a single soul which has been so consistently connected with your body?

MILLER: Now you really cannot be serious, Gretchen. How can I doubt that I am the same person I was? Is there anything more clear and distinct,

less susceptible to doubt? How do you expect me to prove anything to you, when you are capable of denying my own continued existence from second to second? Without knowledge of our own identity, everything we think and do would be senseless. How could I think if I did not suppose that the person who begins my thought is the one who completes it? When I act, do I not assume that the person who forms the intention is the very one who performs the action?

WEIROB: But I grant you that a single *person* has been associated with your body since you were born. The question is whether one immaterial soul has been so associated—or more precisely, whether you are in a position to know it. You believe that a judgment that one and the same person has had your body all these many years is a judgment that one and the same immaterial soul has been lodged in it. I say that such judgments concerning the soul are totally mysterious, and that if our knowledge of sameness of persons consisted in knowledge of sameness of immaterial soul, it too would be totally mysterious. To point out, as you do, that it is not mysterious, but perhaps the most secure knowledge we have, the foundation of all reason and action, is simply to make the point that it cannot consist of knowledge of identity of an immaterial soul.

MILLER: You have simply asserted, and not established, that my judgment that a single soul has been lodged in my body these many years is mysterious.

WEIROB: Well, consider these possibilities. One is that a single soul, one and the same, has been with this body I call mine since it was born. The other is that one soul was associated with it until five years ago and then another, psychologically similar, inheriting all the old memories and beliefs, took over. A third hypothesis is that every five years a new soul takes over. A fourth is that every five minutes a new soul takes over. The most radical is that there is a constant flow of souls through this body, each psychologically similar to the preceding, as there is a constant flow of water molecules down the Blue. What evidence do I have that the first hypothesis, the "single soul hypothesis" is true, and not one of the others? Because I am the same person I was five minutes or five years ago? But the issue in question is simply whether from sameness of person, which isn't in doubt, we can infer sameness of soul. Sameness of body? But how do I establish a stable relationship between soul and body? Sameness of thoughts and sensations? But they are in constant flux. By the nature of the case, if the soul cannot be observed, it cannot be observed to be the same. Indeed, no sense has ever been assigned to the phrase "same soul." Nor could any sense be attached to it! One would have to say what a single soul looked like or felt like, how an encounter with a single soul at different times differed from encounters with different souls. But this can hardly be done, since a soul according to your conception doesn't look or feel like *anything* at all. And so of course "souls" can afford no principle of identity. And so they cannot be used to bridge the gulf between my existence now and my existence in the hereafter.

MILLER: Do you doubt the existence of your own soul?

WEIROB: I haven't based my argument on there being no immaterial souls of the sort you describe, but merely on their total irrelevance to questions of personal identity, and so to questions of personal survival. I do indeed harbor grave doubts whether there are any immaterial souls of the sort to which you appeal. Can we have a notion of a soul unless we have a notion of the *same* soul? But I hope you do not think that means I doubt my own existence. I think I lie here, overweight and conscious. I think you can see me, not just some outer wrapping, for I think I am just a live human body. But that is not the basis of my argument. I give you these souls. I merely observe that they can by their nature provide no principle of personal identity.

MILLER: I admit I have no answer.

I'm afraid I do not comfort you, though I have perhaps provided you with some entertainment. Emerson said that a little philosophy turns one away from religion, but that deeper understanding brings one back. I know no one who has thought so long and hard about philosophy as you have. Will it never lead you back to a religious frame of mind?

WEIROB: My former husband used to say that a little philosophy turns one away from religion, and more philosophy makes one a pain in the neck. Perhaps he was closer to the truth than Emerson.

MILLER: Perhaps he was. But perhaps by tomorrow night I will have come up with a better argument.

WEIROB: I hope I live to hear it.

The Second Night

WEIROB: Well, Sam, have you figured out a way to make sense of the identity of immaterial souls?

MILLER: No, I have decided it was a mistake to build my argument on such a dubious notion.

WEIROB: Have you then given up on survival? I think such a position would be a hard one for a clergyman to live with, and would feel bad about having pushed you so far.

MILLER: Don't worry. I'm more convinced than ever. I stayed up late last night thinking and reading, and I'm sure I can convince you now.

WEIROB: Get with it, time is running out.

MILLER: First, let me explain why, independently of my desire to defend survival after death, I am dissatisfied with your view that personal identity is just bodily identity. My argument will be very similar to the one you used to convince me that personal identity could not be identified with identity of an immaterial soul.

Consider a person waking up tomorrow morning, conscious, but not yet ready to open her eyes and look around and, so to speak, let the new day officially begin.

WEIROB: Such a state is familiar enough, I admit.

MILLER: Now couldn't such a person tell who she was? That is, even before opening her eyes and looking around, and in particular before looking at her body or making any judgments about it, wouldn't she be able to say who she was? Surely most of us, in the morning, know who we are before opening our eyes and recognizing our own bodies, do we not?

WEIROB: You seem to be right about that.

MILLER: But such a judgment as this person makes—we shall suppose she judges "I am

Gretchen Weirob"—*is* a judgment of personal identity. Suppose she says to herself, "I am the very person who was arguing with Sam Miller last night." This is clearly a statement about her identity with someone who was alive the night before. And she could make this judgment without examining her body at all. You could have made just this judgment this morning, before opening your eyes.

WEIROB: Well, in fact I did so. I remembered our conversation of last night and said to myself, "Could I be the rude person who was so hard on Sam Miller's attempts to comfort me?" And, of course, my answer was that I not only could be but was that very rude person.

MILLER: But then by the same principle you used last night personal identity cannot be bodily identity. For you said that it could not be identity of immaterial soul because we were not judging as to identity of immaterial soul when we judge as to personal identity. But by the same token, as my example shows, we are not judging as to bodily identity when we judge as to personal identity. For we can judge who we are, and that we are the very person who did such and such and so and so, without having to make any judgments at all about the body. So, personal identity, while it may not consist of identity of an immaterial soul, does not consist in identity of material body either.

WEIROB: I did argue as you remember. But I also said that the notion of the identity of an immaterial unobservable unextended soul seemed to make no sense at all. This is one reason that cannot be what we are judging about, when we judge as to personal identity. Bodily identity at least makes sense. Perhaps we are assuming sameness of body, without looking.

MILLER: Granted. But you do admit that we do not in our own cases actually need to make a judgment of bodily identity in order to make a judgment of personal identity?

WEIROB: I don't think I will admit it. I will let it pass, so that we may proceed.

MILLER: Okay. Now it seems to me we are even able to imagine awakening and finding ourselves to have a *different* body than the one we had before. Suppose yourself just as I have described

you. And now suppose you finally open your eyes and see, not the body you have grown so familiar with over the years, but one of a fundamentally different shape and size.

WEIROB: Well, I should suppose I had been asleep for a very long time and lost a lot of weight—perhaps I was in a coma for a year or so.

MILLER: But isn't it at least conceivable that it should not be your old body at all? I seem to be able to imagine awakening with a totally new body.

WEIROB: And how would you suppose that this came about?

MILLER: That's beside the point. I'm not saying I can imagine a procedure that would bring this about. I'm saying I can imagine it happening to me. In Kafka's *Metamorphosis*, someone awakens as a cockroach. I can't imagine what would make this happen to me or anyone else, but I can imagine awakening with the body of a cockroach. It is incredible that it should happen—that I do not deny. I simply mean I can imagine experiencing it. It doesn't seem contradictory or incoherent, simply unlikely and inexplicable.

WEIROB: So, if I admit this can be imagined, what follows then?

MILLER: Well, I think it follows that personal identity does not just amount to bodily identity. For I would not, finding that I had a new body, conclude that I was not the very same person I was before. I would be the same *person*, though I did not have the same *body*. So we would have identity of person but not identity of body. So personal identity cannot just amount to bodily identity.

WEIROB: Well suppose—and I emphasize *suppose*—I grant you all of this. Where does it leave you? What do you claim I have recognized as the same, if not my body and not my immaterial soul?

MILLER: I don't claim that you have recognized anything as the same, except the person involved, that is, you yourself.

WEIROB: I'm not sure what you mean.

MILLER: Let me appeal as you did to the Blue River. Suppose I take a visitor to the stretch of river by the old Mill, and then drive him toward Manhattan. After an hour-or-so drive we see another stretch of river, and I say, "That's the same river we saw this morning." As you pointed out yesterday, I don't thereby imply that the very same molecules of water are seen both times. And the places are different, perhaps a hundred miles apart. And the shape and color and level of pollution might not all be identical. What do I see later in the day that is identical with what I saw earlier in the day?

WEIROB: Nothing except the river itself.

MILLER: Exactly. But now notice that what I see, strictly speaking, is not the whole river but only a part of it. I see different parts of the same river at the two different times. So really, if we restrict ourselves to what I literally see, I do not judge identity at all, but something else.

WEIROB: And what might that be?

MILLER: In saying that the river seen earlier, and the river seen later, are one and the same river, do I mean any more than that the stretch of water seen later and that stretch of water seen earlier are connected by other stretches of water?

WEIROB: That's about right. If the stretches of water are so connected there is but one river of which they are both parts.

MILLER: Yes, that's what I mean. The statement of identity, "This river is the same one we saw this morning," is in a sense about rivers. But in a way it is also about stretches of water or river parts.

WEIROB: So is all of this something special about rivers?

MILLER: Not at all. It is a recurring pattern. After all, we constantly deal with objects extended in space and time. But we are seldom aware of the objects' wholes, but only of their parts or stretches of their histories. When a statement of identity is not just something trivial, like "This bed is this bed," it is usually because we are really judging that different parts fit together, in some appropriate pattern, into a certain kind of whole.

WEIROB: I'm not sure I see just what you mean yet.

MILLER: Let me give you another example. Suppose we are sitting together watching the first game of a double-header. You ask me, "Is this game identical with this game?" This is a perfectly stupid question, though, of course, strictly speaking it makes sense and the answer is "yes."

But now suppose you leave in the sixth inning to go for hot dogs. You are delayed, and return after about forty-five minutes or so. You ask, "Is this the same game I was watching?" Now your question is not stupid, but perfectly appropriate.

WEIROB: Because the first game might still be going on or it might have ended, and the second game begun, by the time I return.

MILLER: Exactly. Which is to say somehow different parts of the game—different innings, or at least different plays—were somehow involved in your question. That's why it wasn't stupid or trivial but significant.

WEIROB: So, you think that judgments as to the identity of an object of a certain kind—rivers or baseball games or whatever—involve judgments as to the *parts* of those things being connected in a certain way, and are significant only when different parts are involved. Is that your point?

MILLER: Yes, and I think it is an important one. How foolish it would be, when we ask a question about the identity of baseball games, to look for something *else*, other than the game as a whole, which had to be the same. It could be the same game, even if different players were involved. It could be the same game, even if it had been moved to a different field. These other things, the innings, the plays, the players, the field, don't have to be the same at the different times for the game to be the same, they just have to be related in certain ways so as to make that complex whole we call a single game.

WEIROB: You think we were going off on a kind of a wild-goose chase when we asked whether it was the identity of soul or body that was involved in the identity of persons?

MILLER: Yes. The answer I should now give is neither. We are wondering about the identity of the person. Of course, if by "soul" we just mean "person," there is no problem. But if we mean, as I did yesterday, some other thing whose identity is already understood, which has to be the same when persons are the same, we are just fooling ourselves with words.

WEIROB: With rivers and baseball games, I can see that they are made up of parts connected in a certain way. The connection is, of course, different in the two cases, as is the sort of "part" involved. River parts must be connected physically with other river parts to form a continuous whole. Baseball innings must be connected so that the score, batting order, and the like are carried over from the earlier inning to the later one according to the rules. Is there something analogous we are to say about persons?

MILLER: Writers who concern themselves with this speak of "person-stages." That is just a stretch of consciousness, such as you and I are aware of now. I am aware of a flow of thoughts and feelings that are mine, you are aware of yours. A person is just a whole composed of such stretches as parts, not some substance that underlies them, as I thought yesterday, and not the body in which they occur, as you seem to think. That is the conception of a person I wish to defend today.

WEIROB: So when I awoke and said to myself, "I am the one who was so rude to Sam Miller last night," I was judging that a certain stretch of consciousness I was then aware of, and an earlier one I remembered having been aware of, from a single whole of the appropriate sort—a single stream of consciousness, we might say.

MILLER: Yes, that's it exactly. You need not worry about whether the same immaterial soul is involved, or even whether that makes sense. Nor need you worry about whether the same body is involved, as indeed you do not since you don't even have to open your eyes and look. Identity is not, so to speak, something under the person-stages, nor in something they are attached to, but something you build from them.

Now survival, you can plainly see, is no problem at all once we have this conception of personal identity. All you need suppose is that there is, in Heaven, a conscious being, and that the person-stages that make her up are in the appropriate relation to those that now make you up, so that they are parts of the same whole—namely, you. If so, you have survived. So will you admit now that survival is at least possible?

WEIROB: Hold on, hold on. Comforting me is not that easy. You will have to show that it is possible that these person-stages or stretches of consciousness

be related in the appropriate way. And to do that, won't you have to tell me what that way is?

MILLER: Yes, of course. I was getting ahead of myself. It is right at this point that my reading was particularly helpful. In a chapter of his *Essay On Human Understanding* Locke discusses this very question. He suggests that the relation between two person-stages or stretches of consciousness that makes them stages of a single person is just that the later one contains memories of the earlier one. He doesn't say this in so many words—he talks of "extending our consciousness back in time." But he seems to be thinking of memory.

WEIROB: So, any past thought or feeling or intention or desire that I can remember having is mine?

MILLER: That's right. I can remember only my own past thoughts and feelings, and you only yours. Of course, everyone would readily admit that. Locke's insight is to take this relation as the source of identity and not just its consequence. To remember—or more plausibly, to be able to remember—the thoughts and feelings of a person who was conscious in the past is just what it is to be that person.

Now you can easily see that this solves the problem of the possibility of survival. As I was saying, all you need to do is imagine someone at some future time, not on this earth and not with your present thoughts and feelings, remembering the very conversation we are having now. This does not require sameness of anything else, but it amounts to sameness of person. So, now will you admit it?

WEIROB: No, I don't.

MILLER: Well, what's the problem now?

WEIROB: I admit that if I remember having a certain thought or feeling had by some person in the past, then I must indeed be that person. Though I can remember watching others think, I cannot remember their thinking, any more than I can experience it at the time it occurs if it is theirs and not mine. This is the kernel of Locke's idea, and I don't see that I could deny it.

But we must distinguish—as I'm sure you will agree—between *actually* remembering and merely *seeming* to remember. Many men who think that they are Napoleon claim to remember losing the battle of Waterloo. We may suppose them to be sincere, and to really seem to remember it. But they do not actually remember because they were not at the battle and are not Napoleon.

MILLER: Of course I admit that we must distinguish between actually remembering and only seeming to.

WEIROB: And you will admit too, I trust, that the thought of some person at some far place and some distant time seeming to remember this conversation I am having with you would not give me the sort of comfort that the prospect of survival is supposed to provide. I would have no reason to anticipate future experiences of this person, simply because she is to *seem* to remember my experiences. The experiences of such a deluded imposter are not ones I can look forward to having.

MILLER: I agree.

WEIROB: So the mere possibility of someone in the future seeming to remember this conversation does not show the possibility of my surviving. Only the possibility of someone actually remembering this conversation—or, to be precise, the experiences I am having—would show that.

MILLER: Of course. But what are you driving at? Where is the problem? I can imagine someone being deluded, but also someone actually being you and remembering your present thoughts.

WEIROB: But, what's the difference? How do you know *which* of the two you are imagining, and *what* you have shown possible?

MILLER: Well, I just imagine the one and not the other. I don't see the force of your argument.

WEIROB: Let me try to make it clear with another example. Imagine two persons. One is talking to you, saying certain words, having certain thoughts, and so forth. The other is not talking to you at all, but is in the next room being hypnotized. The hypnotist gives to this person a post-hypnotic suggestion that upon awakening he will remember having had certain thoughts and having uttered certain words to you. The thoughts and words he mentions happen to be just the thoughts and words which the first person actually thinks and says. Do you understand the situation?

MILLER: Yes, continue.

WEIROB: Now, in a while, both of the people are saying sentences which begin, "I remember saying to Sam Miller—" and "I remember thinking as I talked to Sam Miller." And they both report remembering just the same thoughts and utterances. One of these will be remembering and the other only seeming to remember, right?

MILLER: Of course.

WEIROB: Now which one is *actually* remembering?

MILLER: Why, the very one who was in the room talking to me, of course. The other one is just under the influence of the suggestion made by the hypnotist and not remembering talking to me at all.

WEIROB: Now you agree that the difference between them does not consist in the content of what they are now thinking or saying.

MILLER: Agreed. The difference is in the relation to the past thinking and speaking. In the one case the relation of memory obtains. In the other, it does not.

WEIROB: But they both satisfy part of the conditions of remembering, for they both *seem to remember.* So there must be some further condition that the one satisfies and the other does not. I am trying to get you to say what that further condition is.

MILLER: Well, I said that the one who had been in this room talking would be remembering.

WEIROB: In other words, given two putative rememberers of some past thought or action, the real rememberer is the one who, in addition to seeming to remember the past thought or action, actually thought it or did it.

MILLER: Yes.

WEIROB: That is to say, the one who is identical with the person who did the past thinking and uttering.

MILLER: Yes, I admit it.

WEIROB: So, your argument just amounts to this. Survival is possible, because imaginable. It is imaginable, because my identity with some Heavenly person is imaginable. To imagine it, we imagine a person in Heaven who, First, seems to remember my thoughts and actions, and Second, is me.

Surely, there could hardly be a tighter circle. If I have doubts that the Heavenly person is me, I will have doubts as to whether she is really remembering or only seeming to. No one could doubt the possibility of some future person who, after death, seemed to remember the things he thought and did. But that possibility does not resolve the issue about the possibility of survival. Only the possibility of someone *actually* remembering could do that—for that, as we agree, is sufficient for identity. But doubts about survival and identity simply go over without remainder into doubts about whether the memories would be actual or merely apparent. You guarantee me no more than the possibility of a deluded Heavenly imposter.

COHEN: But wait, Gretchen. I think Sam was less than fair to his own idea just now.

WEIROB: You think you can break out of the circle of using real memory to explain identity, and identity to mark the difference between real and apparent memory? Feel free to try.

COHEN: Let us return to your case of the hypnotist. You point out that we have two putative rememberers. You ask what marks the difference, and claim the answer must be the circular one—that the real rememberer is the person who actually had the experiences both seem to remember.

But that is not the only possible answer. The experiences themselves cause the later apparent memories in the one case, while the hypnotist causes them in the other. We can say that the rememberer is the one of the two whose memories were *caused in the right way* by the earlier experiences. We thus distinguish between the rememberer and the hypnotic subject, without appeal to identity.

The idea that real memory amounts to apparent memory plus identity is misleading anyway. I seem to remember, as a small child, knocking over the Menorah so the candles fell into and spoiled a tureen of soup. And I did actually perform such a feat. So we have apparent memory and identity. But I do *not* actually remember; I was much too young when I did this to remember it now. I have simply been told the story so often I seem to remember.

Here the suggestion that real memory is apparent memory that was caused in the appropriate way by the past events fares better. Not my experience of pulling over the Menorah, but hearing my parents talk about it later, caused my memory-like impressions.

WEIROB: You analyze personal identity into memory, and memory into apparent memory which is caused in the right way. A person is a certain sort of causal process.

COHEN: Right.

WEIROB: Suppose now for the sake of argument I accept this. How does it help Sam in his defense of the possibility of survival? In ordinary memory, the causal chain from remembered event to memory of it never leads us outside the confines of a single body. Indeed, the normal process of which you speak surely involves storage of information somehow in the brain. How can the states of my brain, when I die, influence in the appropriate way the apparent memories of the Heavenly person Sam takes to be me?

COHEN: Well, I didn't intend to be defending the possibility of survival. That is Sam's problem. I just like the idea that personal identity can be explained in terms of memory, and not just in terms of identity of the body.

MILLER: But surely, this does provide me with the basis for further defense. Your challenge, Gretchen, was to explain the difference between two persons in Heaven, one who actually remembers your experience—and so is you—and one who simply seems to remember it. But can I not just say that the one who is you is the one whose states were caused in the appropriate way? I do not mean the way they would be in a normal case of earthly memory. But in the case of the Heavenly being who is you, God would have created her with the brain states (or whatever) she has *because* you had the ones you had at death. Surely it is not the exact form of the dependence of my later memories on my earlier perceptions that makes them really memories, but the fact that the process involved has preserved information.

WEIROB: So if God creates a Heavenly person, designing her brain to duplicate the brain I have upon death, that person is me. If, on the other hand, a Heavenly being should come to be with those very same memory-like states by accident (if there are accidents in Heaven) it would not be me.

MILLER: Exactly. Are you satisfied now that survival makes perfectly good sense?

WEIROB: No, I'm still quite unconvinced.

The problem I see is this. If God could create one person in Heaven, and by designing her after me, make her me, why could he not make two such bodies, and cause this transfer of information into both of them? Would both of these Heavenly persons then be me? It seems as clear as anything in philosophy that from

$$A \text{ is } B$$

and

$$C \text{ is } B$$

where by "is" we mean identity, we can infer,

$$A \text{ is } C.$$

So, if each of these Heavenly persons is me, they must be each other. But then they are not two but one. But my assumption was that God creates two, not one. He could create them physically distinct, capable of independent movement, perhaps in widely separated Heavenly locations, each with her own duties to perform, her own circle of Heavenly friends, and the like.

So either God, by creating a Heavenly person with a brain modeled after mine, does not really create someone identical with me but merely someone similar to me, or God is somehow limited to making only one such being. I can see no reason why, if there were a God, He should be so limited. So I take the first option. He could create someone similar to me, but not someone who would *be* me. Either your analysis of memory is wrong, and such a being does not, after all, remember what I am doing or saying, or memory is not sufficient for personal identity. Your theory has gone wrong somewhere, for it leads to absurdity.

COHEN: But wait. Why can't Sam simply say that if God makes one such creature, she is you, while if he makes more, none of them is you? It's possible that he makes only one. So it's possible that you survive. Sam always meant to allow that it's *possible* that you won't survive. He had in mind the case in which there is no God to take the appropriate Heavenly persons, or God exists, but doesn't make even one. You have simply shown that there is another way of not surviving. Instead of making too few Heavenly rememberers, He makes too many. So what? He might make the right number, and then you would survive.

WEIROB: Your remarks really amount to a change in your position. Now you are not claiming that memory alone is enough for personal identity. Now, it is memory *plus* lack of competition, the absence of other rememberers, that is needed for personal identity.

COHEN: It does amount to a change of position. But what of it? Is there anything untenable about the position as changed?

WEIROB: Let's look at this from the point of view of the Heavenly person. She says to herself, "Oh, I must be Gretchen Weirob, for I remember doing what she did and saying what she said." But now that's a pretty tenuous conclusion, isn't it? She is really only entitled to say, "Oh, either I'm Gretchen Weirob, or God has created more than one being like me, and none of us is." Identity has become something dependent on things wholly extrinsic to her. Who she is now turns on not just her states of mind and their relation to my states of mind, but on the existence or nonexistence of other people. Is this really what you want to maintain?

Or look at it from my point of view. God creates one of me in Heaven. Surely I should be glad if convinced this was to happen. Now he creates another, and I should despair again, for this means I won't survive after all. How can doubling a good deed make it worthless?

COHEN: Are you saying that there is some contradiction in my suggestion that only creation of a unique Heavenly Gretchen counts as your survival?

WEIROB: No, it's not contradictory, as far as I can see. But it seems odd in a way that shows that something somewhere is wrong with your theory. Here is a certain relationship I have with a Heavenly person. There being such a person, to whom I am related in this way, is something that is of great importance to me, a source of comfort. It makes it appropriate for me to anticipate having her experiences, since she is just me. Why should my having that relation to another being destroy my relation to this one? You say because then I will not be identical with either of them. But since you have provided a theory about what that identity consists in, we can look and see what it amounts to for me to be or not to be identical. If she is to remember my experience, I can rightly anticipate hers. But then it seems the doubling makes no difference. And yet it must, for one cannot be identical with two. So you add, in a purely *ad hoc* manner, that her memory of me isn't enough to make my anticipation of her experiences appropriate, if there are two rather than one so linked. Isn't it more reasonable to conclude, since memory does not secure identity when there are two Heavenly Gretchens, it also doesn't when there is only one?

COHEN: There is something *ad hoc* about it, I admit. But perhaps that's just the way our concept works. You have not elicited a contradiction—

WEIROB: An infinite pile of absurdities has the same weight as a contradiction. And absurdities can be generated without limit from your account. Suppose God created this Heavenly person before I died. Then He in effect kills me; if He has already created her, then you really are not talking to whom you think, but someone new, created by Gretchen Weirob's strange death moments ago. Or suppose He first creates one being in Heaven, who is me. Then He creates another. Does the first cease to be me? If God can create such beings in Heaven, surely He can do so in Albuquerque. And there is nothing on your theory to favor this body before you as Gretchen Weirob's, over the one belonging to the person created in Albuquerque. So I am to suppose that if God were to do this, I would suddenly cease to be. I'm tempted to say I would cease to be Gretchen Weirob. But that

would be a confused way of putting it. There would be here, in my place, a new person with false memories of having been Gretchen Weirob, who has just died of competition—a strange death if ever there was one. She would have no right to my name, my bank account, or the services of my doctor, who is paid from insurance premiums paid for by deductions from Gretchen Weirob's past salary. Surely this is nonsense; however carefully God should choose to duplicate me, in Heaven or in Albuquerque, I would not cease to be, or cease to be who I am. You may reply that God, being benevolent, would never create an extra Gretchen Weirob. But I do not say that he would, but only that if he did this would not, as your theory implies, mean that I cease to exist. Your theory gives the wrong answer in this possible circumstance, so it must be wrong. I think I have been given no motivation to abandon the most obvious and straightforward view on these matters. I am a live body, and when that body dies, my existence will be at an end.

The Third Night

WEIROB: Well, Sam, are you here for a third attempt to convince me of the possibility of survival?

MILLER: No, I have given up. I suggest we talk about fishing or football or something unrelated to your imminent demise. You will outwit any straightforward attempts to comfort you, but perhaps I can at least divert your mind.

COHEN: But before we start on fishing—although I don't have any particular brief for survival—there is one point in our discussion of the last two evenings that still bothers me. Would you mind discussing for a while the notion of personal identity itself, without worrying about the more difficult case of survival after death?

WEIROB: I would enjoy it. What point bothers you?

COHEN: Your position seems to be that personal identity amounts to identity of a human body, nothing more, nothing less. A person is just a live human body, or more precisely, I suppose, a human body that is alive and has certain capacities—consciousness and perhaps rationality. Is that right?

WEIROB: Yes, it seems that simple to me.

COHEN: But I think there has actually been an episode which disproves that. I am thinking of the strange case of Julia North, which occurred in California a few months ago. Surely you remember it.

WEIROB: Yes, only too well. But you had better explain it to Sam, for I'll wager he has not heard of it.

COHEN: Not heard of Julia North? But the case was all over the headlines.

MILLER: Well, Gretchen is right. I know nothing of it. She knows that I only read the sports page.

COHEN: You only read the sports page!

WEIROB: It's an expression of his unconcern with earthly matters.

MILLER: Well, that's not quite fair, Gretchen. It's a matter of preference. I much prefer to spend what time I have for reading in reading about the eighteenth century, rather than the drab and miserable century into which I had the misfortune to be born. It was really a much more civilized century, you know. But let's not dwell on my peculiar habits. Tell me about Julia North.

COHEN: Very well. Julia North was a young woman who was run over by a streetcar while saving the life of a young child who wandered onto the tracks. The child's mother, one Mary Frances Beaudine, had a stroke while watching the horrible scene. Julia's healthy brain and wasted body, and Mary Frances' healthy body and wasted brain, were transported to a hospital where a brilliant neurosurgeon, Dr. Matthews, was in residence. He had worked out a procedure for what he called a "body transplant." He removed the brain from Julia's head and placed it in Mary Frances', splicing the nerves, and so forth, using techniques not available until quite recently. The survivor of all of this was obviously Julia, as everyone agreed—except, unfortunately, Mary Frances' husband. His short-sightedness and lack of imagination led to great complications and drama, and made the case more famous in the history of crime than in the history of medicine. I shall not go into the details of this sorry aspect of the case—they are well reported in

a book by Barbara Harris called *Who Is Julia?*, in case you are interested.

MILLER: Fascinating!

COHEN: Well, the relevance of this case is obvious. Julia North had one body up until the time of the accident, and another body after the operation. So one person had two bodies. So a person cannot be simply *identified* with a human body. So something must be wrong with your view, Gretchen. What do you say to this?

WEIROB: I'll say to you just what I said to Dr. Matthews—

COHEN: You have spoken with Dr. Matthews?

WEIROB: Yes. He contacted me shortly after my accident. My physician had phoned him up about my case. Matthews said he could perform the same operation for me he did for Julia North. I refused.

COHEN: You refused! But Gretchen, why—?

MILLER: Gretchen, I *am* shocked. Your decision practically amounts to suicide! You passed up an opportunity to continue living? Why on earth—

WEIROB: Hold on, hold on. You are both making an assumption I reject. If the case of Julia North amounts to a counterexample to my view that a person is just a live human body, and if my refusal to submit to this procedure amounts to suicide, then the survivor of such an operation must be reckoned as the same person as the brain donor. That is, the survivor of Julia North's operation must have been Julia, and the survivor of the operation on me would have to be me. This is the assumption you both make in criticizing me. But I reject it. I think Jack Beaudine was right. The survivor of the operation involving Julia North's brain was Mary Frances Beaudine, and the survivor of the operation using my brain would not have been me.

MILLER: Gretchen, how on earth can you say that? Will you not give up your view that personal identity is just bodily identity, no matter how clear the counter-example? I really think you simply have an irrational attachment to the lump of material that is your body.

COHEN: Yes, Gretchen, I agree with Sam. You are being preposterous! The survivor of Julia North's operation had no idea who Mary Frances Beaudine was. She remembered being Julia—

WEIROB: She *seemed* to remember being Julia. Have you forgotten so quickly the importance of this distinction? In my opinion, the effect of the operation was that Mary Frances Beaudine survived deluded, thinking she was someone else.

COHEN: But as you know, the case was litigated. It went to the Supreme Court. They said that the survivor was Julia.

WEIROB: That argument is unworthy of you, Dave. Is the Supreme Court infallible?

COHEN: No, it isn't. But I don't think it's such a stupid point.

Look at it this way, Gretchen. This is a case in which two criteria we use to make judgments of identity conflict. Usually we expect personal identity to involve both bodily identity and psychological continuity. That is, we expect that if we have the same body, then the beliefs, memories, character traits, and the like also will be enormously similar. In this case, these two criteria which usually coincide do not. If we choose one criterion, we say that the survivor is Mary Frances Beaudine and she has undergone drastic psychological changes. If we choose the other, we say that Julia has survived with a new body. We have to choose which criterion is more important. It's a matter of choice of how to use our language, how to extend the concept "same person" to a new situation. The overwhelming majority of people involved in the case took the survivor to be Julia. That is, society chose to use the concept one way rather than the other. The Supreme Court is *not* beside the point. One of their functions is to settle just how old concepts shall be applied to new circumstances—how "freedom of the press" is to be understood when applied to movies or television, whose existence was not foreseen when the concept was shaped, or to say whether "murder" is to include the abortion of a fetus. They are fallible on points of fact, but they are the final authority on the development of certain important concepts used in law. The notion of *person* is such a concept.

WEIROB: You think that *who* the survivor was, was a matter of convention, of how we choose to use language?

COHEN: Yes.

WEIROB: I can show the preposterousness of all that with an example.

Let us suppose that I agree to the operation. I lie in bed, expecting my continued existence, anticipating the feelings and thoughts I shall have upon awakening after the operation. Dr. Matthews enters and asks me to take several aspirin, so as not to have a headache when I awake. I protest that aspirin upsets my stomach; he asks whether I would rather have a terrible headache tomorrow or a mild stomachache now, and I agree that it would be reasonable to take them.

Let us suppose that you enter at this point, with bad news. The Supreme Court has changed its mind! So the survivor will not be me. So, I say, "Oh, then I will not take the aspirin, for it's not me that will have a headache, but someone else. Why should I endure a stomachache, however mild, for the comfort of someone else? After all, I am already donating my brain to that person."

Now this is clearly absurd. If I were correct, in the first place, to anticipate having the sensations and thoughts that the survivor is to have the next day, the decision of nine old men a thousand or so miles away wouldn't make me wrong. And if I was wrong to so anticipate, their decision couldn't make me right. How can the correctness of my anticipation of survival be a matter of the way we use our words? If it is not such a matter, then my identity is not either. My identity with the survivor, my survival, is a question of fact, not of convention.

COHEN: Your example is persuasive. I admit I am befuddled. On the one hand, I cannot see how the matter can be other than I have described. When we know all the facts what can remain to be decided but how we are to describe them, how we are to use our language? And yet I can see that it seems absurd to suppose that the correctness or incorrectness of anticipation of future experience is a matter for convention to decide.

MILLER: Well, I didn't think the business about convention was very plausible anyway. But I should like to return you to the main question, Gretchen. Fact or convention, it still remains. Why will you not admit that the survivor of this operation would be you?

WEIROB: Well, *you* tell *me*, why you think she would be me?

MILLER: I can appeal to the theory I developed last night. You argued that the idea that personal identity consists in memory would not guarantee the possibility of survival after death. But you said nothing to shake its plausibility as an account of personal identity. It has the enormous advantage, remember, of making sense of our ability to judge our own identity, without examination of our bodies. I should argue that it is the correctness of this theory that explains the *almost* universal willingness to say that the survivor of Julia's operation was Julia. We need not deliberate over how to extend our concept, we need only apply the concept we already have. Memory is sufficient for identity and bodily identity is *not* necessary for it. The survivor remembered Julia's thoughts and actions, and so was Julia. Would you but submit to the operation, the survivor would remember your thoughts and actions, would remember this very conversation we are now having, and would be you.

COHEN: Yes, I now agree completely with Sam. The theory that personal identity is to be analyzed in terms of memory is correct, and according to it you will survive if you submit to the operation.

Let me add another argument against your view and in favor of the memory theory. You have emphasized that identity is the condition of *anticipation*. That means, among other things, that we have a particular concern for that person in the future whom we take to be ourselves. If I were told that any of the three of us were to suffer pain tomorrow, I should be sad. But if it were you or Sam that were to be hurt, my concern would be altruistic or unselfish. That is because I would not anticipate having the painful experience myself. Here I do no more than repeat points you have made earlier in our conversations.

Now what is there about mere sameness of body that makes sense of this asymmetry, between the way we look at our own futures, and the way we look at the futures of others? In other words, why is the identity of your body—that mere lump of matter, as Sam put it—of such great importance? Why care so much about it?

WEIROB: You say, and I surely agree, that identity of person is a very special relationship—so special as perhaps not even happily called a relationship at all. And you say that since my theory is that identity of person is identity of body, I should be able to explain the importance of the one in terms of the importance of the other.

I'm not sure I can do that. But does the theory that personal identity consists in memory fare better on this score?

COHEN: Well, I think it does. Those properties of persons which make persons of such great value, and mark their individuality, and make one person so special to his friends and loved ones, are ultimately psychological or mental. One's character, personality, beliefs, attitudes, convictions—they are what make every person so unique and special. A skinny Gretchen would be a shock to us all, but not a Gretchen diminished in any important way. But a Gretchen who was not witty, or not gruff, or not as honest to the path an argument takes as is humanly possible—those would be fundamental changes. Is it any wonder that the survivor of that California fiasco was reckoned as Julia North? Would it make sense to take her to be Mary Jane Beaudine, when she had none of her beliefs or attitudes or memories?

Now if such properties are what is of importance about a person to others, is it not reasonable that they are the basis of one's importance to oneself? And these are just the properties that personal identity preserves when it is taken to consist in links of memory. Do we not have, in this idea, at least the beginning of an explanation of the importance of identity?

WEIROB: So on two counts you two favor the memory theory. First, you say it explains how it is possible to judge as to one's own identity, without having to examine one's body. Second, you say it explains the importance of personal identity.

COHEN: Now surely you must agree the memory theory is correct. Do you agree? There may be still time to contact Dr. Matthews—

WEIROB: Hold on, hold on. Try to relax and enjoy the argument. I am. Quit trying to save my life and worry about saving your theory—for I'm still not persuaded. Granted the survivor will *think* she is me, will *seem* to remember thinking my thoughts. But recall the importance of distinguishing between real and merely apparent memory—

COHEN: But *you* recall that this distinction is to be made on the basis of whether the apparent memories were or were not caused by the prior experiences in the appropriate way. The survivor will not seem to remember your thoughts because of hypnosis or by coincidence or overweening imagination. She will seem to remember them because the traces those experiences left on your brain now activate her mind in the usual way. She will seem to remember them because she does remember them, and will be you.

WEIROB: You are very emphatic, and I'm feeling rather weak. I'm not sure there is time left to untangle all of this. But there is never an advantage to hurrying when doing philosophy. So let's go over this slowly.

We all agree that the fact that the survivor of this strange operation Dr. Matthews proposes would *seem* to remember doing what I have done. Let us even suppose she would take herself to be me, claim to be Gretchen Weirob—and have no idea who else she might be. (We are then assuming that she differs from me in one aspect—her theory of personal identity. But that does not show her not to be me, for I could change my mind by then.) We all first agree that this much does not make her me. For this could all be true of someone suffering a delusion, or a subject of hypnosis.

COHEN: Yes, this is all agreed.

WEIROB: But now you think that some further condition is satisfied, which makes her apparent memories *real* memories. Now what exactly is this further condition?

COHEN: Well, that the same brain was involved in the perception of the events, and their later *memory*. Thus we have here a causal chain of just the same sort as when only a single body is involved. That is, perceptions when the event occurs leave a trace in the brain, which is later responsible for the content of the memory. And we agreed,

did we not, that apparent memory, caused in the right way, is real memory?

WEIROB: Now is it absolutely crucial that the same brain is involved?

COHEN: What do you mean?

WEIROB: Let me explain again by reference to Dr. Matthews. In our conversation he explained a new procedure on which he was working, called a *brain rejuvenation*. By this process, which is not yet available—only the feasibility of developing it is being studied—a new brain could be made which is an exact duplicate of my brain—that is, an exact duplicate in terms of psychologically relevant states. It might not duplicate all the properties of my brain—for example, the blood vessels in the new brain might be stronger than in the old brain.

MILLER: What is the point of developing such a macabre technique?

WEIROB: Dr. Matthews' idea is that when weaknesses which might lead to stroke or other brain injury are noted, a healthy duplicate could be made to replace the original, forestalling the problem.

Now Dave, suppose my problem were not with my liver and kidneys and such, but with my brain. Would you recommend such an operation as to my benefit?

COHEN: You mean, do I think the survivor of such an operation would be you?

WEIROB: Exactly. You may assume that Dr. Matthews' technique works perfectly so the causal process involved is no less reliable than that involved in ordinary memory.

COHEN: Then I would say it was you— No! Wait! No, it wouldn't be you—absolutely not.

MILLER: But why the sudden reversal? It seems to me it would be her. Indeed, I should try such an operation myself, if it would clear up my dizzy spells and leave me otherwise unaffected.

COHEN: No, don't you see, she is leading us into a false trap. If we say it *is* her, then she will say, "then what if he makes two duplicates, or three or ten? They can't all be me, they all have an equal claim, so none will be me." It would be the argument of last night, reapplied on earth. So the answer is no, absolutely not, it wouldn't be you.

Duplication of brain does not preserve identity. Identity of the person requires identity of the brain.

MILLER: Quite right.

WEIROB: Now let me see if I have managed to understand your theory, for my powers of concentration seem to be fading. Suppose we have two bodies, A and B. My brain is put into A, a duplicate into B. The survivor of this, call them "A-Gretchen" and "B-Gretchen," both seem to remember giving this very speech. Both are in this state of seeming to remember, as the last stage in an information-preserving causal chain, initiated by my giving this speech. Both have my character, personality, beliefs, and the like. But one is *really* remembering, the other is not. A-Gretchen is really me, B-Gretchen is not.

COHEN: Precisely. Is this incoherent?

WEIROB: No, I guess there is nothing incoherent about it. But look what has happened to the advantages you claimed for the memory theory.

First, you said, it explains how I can know who I am without opening my eyes and recognizing my body. But on your theory Gretchen-A and Gretchen-B cannot know who they are even if they do open their eyes and examine their bodies. How is Gretchen-A to know whether she has the original brain and is who she seems to be, or has the duplicate and is a new person, only a few minutes old, and with no memories but mere delusions? If the hospital kept careless records, or the surgeon thought it was of no great importance to keep track of who got the original and who got the duplicate, she might never know who she was. By making identity of person turn into identity of brain, your theory makes the ease with which I can determine who I am not less but more mysterious than my theory.

Second, you said, your theory explains why my concern for Gretchen-A, who is me whether she knows it or not, would be selfish, and my anticipation of her experience correct while my concern for Gretchen-B with her duplicated brain would be unselfish, and my anticipation of having her experiences incorrect. And it explains this, you said, because by insisting on the links of memory, we preserve in personal identity more

psychological characteristics which are the most important features of a person.

But Gretchen-A and Gretchen-B are psychologically indiscernible. Though they will go their separate ways, at the moment of awakening they could well be exactly similar in every psychological respect. In terms of character and belief and the contents of their minds, Gretchen-A is no more like me than Gretchen-B. So there is nothing in your theory after all to explain why anticipation is appropriate when we have identity and not otherwise.

You said, Sam, that I had an irrational attachment for this unworthy material object, my body. But you too are as irrationally attached to your brain. I have never seen my brain. I should have easily given it up for a rejuvenated version, had that been the choice with which I was faced. I have never seen it, never felt it, and have no attachment to it. But my body? That seems to me all that I am. I see no point in trying to evade its fate, even if there were still time.

But perhaps I miss the merit of your arguments. I am tired, and perhaps my poor brain, feeling slighted, has begun to desert me—

COHEN: Oh, don't worry, Gretchen, you are still clever. Again you have left me befuddled. I don't know what to say. But answer me this. Suppose you are right and we are wrong. But suppose these arguments had not occurred to you, and, sharing in our error, you had agreed to the operation. You anticipate the operation until it happens, thinking you will survive. You are happy. The survivor takes herself to be you, and thinks she made a decision before the operation which has now turned out to be right. She is happy. Your friends are happy. Who would be worse off, either before or after the operation?

Suppose even that you realize identity would not be preserved by such an operation, but have it done anyway, and as the time for the operation approaches, you go ahead and anticipate the experiences of the survivor. Where exactly is the mistake? Do you really have any less reason to care for the survivor than for yourself? Can mere identity of body, the lack of which alone keeps you from being her, mean that much? Perhaps we were wrong, after all, in focusing on identity as the necessary condition of anticipation—

MILLER: Dave, it's too late.

NOTES

THE FIRST NIGHT: The arguments against the position that personal identity consists in identity of an immaterial soul are similar to those found in John Locke, "Of Identity and Diversity," chapter 27 of Book II of the *Essay Concerning Human Understanding*. This chapter first appeared in the second edition of 1694.

THE SECOND NIGHT: The arguments against the view that personal identity consists in bodily identity are also suggested by Locke, as is the theory that memory is crucial. The argument that the memory theory is circular was made by Joseph Butler in "Of Personal Identity," an Appendix to his *Analogy of Religion*, first published in 1736. Locke's memory theory has been developed by a number of modern authors, including H. P. Grice, A. M. Quinton and, in a different direction, Sydney Shoemaker. The possibility of circumventing Butler's charge of circularity by an appeal to causation is noted by Shoemaker in his article "Persons and Their Pasts" (*American Philosophical Quarterly*, 1970) and by David Wiggins in *Identity and Spatial Temporal Continuity*. The "duplication argument" was apparently first used by Samuel Clarke, arguing against the eighteenth-century freethinker, Antony Collins. Collins assumed that something like Locke's theory of personal identity was correct. Clarke assumed immortality made sense, and used the duplication argument to raise problems for Collins's Lockean theory.

THE THIRD NIGHT: *Who Is Julia?*, by Barbara Harris, is an engaging novel published in 1972. (Dr. Matthews had not yet thought of brain rejuvenations.)

Locke considers the possibility of the "consciousness" of a prince being transferred to the body of a cobbler. The idea of using the removal of a brain to suggest how this might happen comes from Sydney Shoemaker's seminal book, *Self-Knowledge and Self-Identity* (1963). In a number of important articles which are collected in his book *Problems of the Self* (1973), Bernard

Williams has cleverly and articulately resisted the memory theory and the view that such a brain removal would amount to a body transplant. In particular, Williams has stressed the relevance of the duplication argument even in questions of terrestrial personal identity. Weirob's position in this essay is more inspired by Williams than anyone else. I have discussed Williams' arguments and related topics in "Can the Self Divide?" (*Journal of Philosophy*, 1972) and in a review of his book (*Journal of Philosophy*, 1976).

An important article on the themes which emerge toward the end of the dialogue is Derek Parfit's "Personal Identity" (*Philosophical Review*, 1971). This article, along with Locke's chapter and a number of other important chapters and articles by Hume, Shoemaker, Williams, and others are collected in my anthology *Personal Identity* (1975). A number of articles on personal identity appear in Amelie Rorty (ed.), *The Identities of Persons* (1976), including my "The Importance of Being Identical," which addresses the questions raised by Cohen at the end.

KEY TERM

A priori

STUDY QUESTIONS

1. Gretchen distinguishes between being persuaded that her survival beyond bodily death is probable and that it is possible. What is the difference?

2. What is the point of the example of the box of Kleenex?

3. Miller claims that when I awake, I know who I am (which person I am) without checking my body and, in fact, could awaken to find myself with a new and different body. What follows from this, according to Miller?

4. What distinction does Weirob make between actually remembering something and merely seeming to remember it? What work does Weirob want this distinction to do?

5. Weirob criticizes Miller's reasoning by accusing it of circularity. What does Weirob mean by this? How is Miller's reasoning circular?

The Self and the Future

BERNARD WILLIAMS

Bernard Williams (1929–2003) was a moral philosopher and professor at Oxford University and the University of California, Berkeley. His influence on ethics, in particular, and philosophy, in general, is pervasive, since he wrote many important works, such as *Moral Luck*, *Ethics and the Limits of Philosophy*, and *Truth and Truthfulness*.

. .

SUPPOSE that there were some process to which two persons, A and B, could be subjected as a result of which they might be said—question-beggingly—to have *exchanged bodies*. That is to say—less question-beggingly—there is a certain human body which is such that when previously we were confronted with it, we were confronted with person A, certain utterances coming from it were expressive of memories of the past experiences of A, certain movements of it partly constituted the actions of A and were taken as expressive of the character of A, and so forth; but now, after the process is completed, utterances coming from this body are expressive of what seem to be just those memories which previously we identified as memories of the past experiences of B, its movements partly constitute actions expressive of the character of B, and so forth; and conversely with the other body.

There are certain important philosophical limitations on how such imaginary cases are to be constructed, and how they are to be taken when constructed in various ways. I shall mention two principal limitations, not in order to pursue them further here, but precisely in order to get them out of the way.

There are certain limitations, particularly with regard to character and mannerisms, to our ability to imagine such cases even in the most restricted sense of our being disposed to take the later performances of

that body which was previously A's as expressive of B's character; if the previous A and B were extremely unlike one another both physically and psychologically, and if, say, in addition, they were of different sex, there might be grave difficulties in reading B's dispositions in any possible performances of A's body. Let us forget this, and for the present purpose just take A and B as being sufficiently alike (however alike that has to be) for the difficulty not to arise; after the experiment, persons familiar with A and B are just *overwhelmingly struck* by the B-ish character of the doings associated with what was previously A's body, and conversely. Thus the feat of imagining an exchange of bodies is supposed possible in the most restricted sense. But now there is a further limitation which has to be overcome if the feat is to be not merely possible in the most restricted sense but also is to have an outcome which, on serious reflection, we are prepared to describe as A and B having changed bodies—that is, an outcome where, confronted with what was previously A's body, we are prepared seriously to say that we are now confronted with B.

It would seem a necessary condition of so doing that the utterances coming from that body be taken as genuinely expressive of memories of B's past. But memory is a causal notion; and as we actually use it, it seems a necessary condition of x's present knowledge of x's earlier experiences constituting memory of those experiences that the causal chain linking the experiences and the knowledge should not run outside x's body. Hence if utterances coming from a given body are to be taken as expressive of memories of the experiences of B, there should be some suitable causal link between the appropriate state of that body and the original happening of those experiences to B. One radical way of securing that condition in the imagined exchange case is to suppose, with Shoemaker,[1] that the brains of A and of B are transposed. We may not need so radical a condition. Thus suppose it were possible to extract information from a man's brain and store it in a device while his brain was repaired, or even renewed, the information then being replaced: it would seem exaggerated to insist that the resultant man could not possibly have the memories he had before the operation. With regard to our knowledge of our own past, we draw distinctions between merely recalling, being reminded, and learning again, and those distinctions correspond (roughly) to distinctions between no new input, partial new input, and total new input with regard to the information in question; and it seems clear that the information-packing case just imagined would not count as new input in the sense necessary and sufficient for 'learning again'. Hence we can imagine the case we are concerned with in terms of information extracted into such devices from A's and B's brains and replaced in the other brain; this is the sort of model which, I think not unfairly for the present argument, I shall have in mind.

We imagine the following. The process considered above exists; two persons can enter some machine, let us say, and emerge changed in the appropriate ways. If A and B are the persons who enter, let us call the persons who emerge the *A-body-person* and the *B-body-person*: the A-body-person is that person (whoever it is) with whom I am confronted when, after the experiment, I am confronted with that body which previously was A's body—that is to say, that person who would naturally be taken for A by someone who just saw this person, was familiar with A's appearance before the experiment, and did not know about the happening of the experiment. A non-question-begging description of the experiment will leave it open which (if either) of the persons A and B the A-body-person is; the description of the experiment as 'persons changing bodies' of course implies that the A-body-person is actually B.

We take two persons A and B who are going to have the process carried out on them. (We can suppose, rather hazily, that they are willing for this to happen; to investigate at all closely at this stage why

they might be willing or unwilling, what they would fear, and so forth, would anticipate some later issues.) We further announce that one of the two resultant persons, the A-body-person and the B-body-person, is going after the experiment to be given \$100,000, while the other is going to be tortured. We then ask each of A and B to choose which treatment should be dealt out to which of the persons who will emerge from the experiment, the choice to be made (if it can be) on selfish grounds.

Suppose that A chooses that the B-body-person should get the pleasant treatment and the A-body-person the unpleasant treatment; and B chooses conversely (this might indicate that they thought that 'changing bodies' was indeed a good description of the outcome). The experimenter cannot act in accordance with both these sets of preferences, those expressed by A and those expressed by B. Hence there is one clear sense in which A and B cannot both get what they want: namely, that if the experimenter, before the experiment, announces to A and B that he intends to carry out the alternative (for example), of treating the B-body-person unpleasantly and the A-body-person pleasantly—then A can say rightly, 'That's not the outcome I chose to happen', and B can say rightly, 'That's just the outcome I chose to happen'. So, evidently, A and B before the experiment can each come to know either that the outcome he chose will be that which will happen, or that the one he chose will not happen, and in that sense they can get or fail to get what they wanted. But is it also true that when the experimenter proceeds after the experiment to act in accordance with one of the preferences and not the other, *then* one of A and B will have got what he wanted, and the other not?

There seems very good ground for saying so. For suppose the experimenter, having elicited A's and B's preference, says nothing to A and B about what he will do; conducts the experiment; and then, for example, gives the unpleasant treatment to the B-body-person and the pleasant treatment to the A-body-person. Then the B-body-person will not only complain of the unpleasant treatment as such, but will complain (since he has A's memories) that that was not the outcome he chose, since he chose that the B-body-person should be well treated; and since A made his choice in selfish spirit, he may add that he precisely chose in that way because he did not want the unpleasant things to happen to *him*. The *A*-body-person meanwhile will express satisfaction both at the receipt of the $100,000, and also at the fact that the experimenter has chosen to act in the way that he, *B*, so wisely chose. These facts make a strong case for saying that the experimenter has brought it about that *B* did in the outcome get what he wanted and *A* did not. It is therefore a strong case for saying that the *B*-body-person really is *A*, and the *A*-body-person really is *B*; and therefore for saying that the process of the experiment really is that of changing bodies. For the same reasons it would seem that *A* and *B* in our example really did choose wisely, and that it was *A*'s bad luck that the choice he correctly made was not carried out, *B*'s good luck that the choice he correctly made was carried out. This seems to show that to care about what happens to me in the future is not necessarily to care about what happens to *this* body (the one I now have); and this in turn might be taken to show that in some sense of Descartes's obscure phrase, I and my body are 'really distinct' (though, of course, nothing in these considerations could support the idea that I could exist without a body at all).

These suggestions seem to be reinforced if we consider the cases where *A* and *B* make other choices with regard to the experiment. Suppose that *A* chooses that the *A*-body-person should get the money, and the *B*-body-person get the pain, and *B* chooses conversely. Here again there can be no outcome which matches the expressed preferences of both of them: they cannot both get what they want. The experimenter announces, before the experiment, that the *A*-body-person will in fact get the money, and the *B*-body-person will get the pain. So *A* at this stage gets what he wants (the announced outcome matches his expressed preference). After the experiment, the distribution is carried out as announced. Both the *A*-body-person and the *B*-body-person will have to agree that what is happening is in accordance with the preference that *A* originally expressed. The *B*-body-person will naturally express this acknowledgement (since he has *A*'s memories) by saying that this is the distribution he chose; he will recall, among other things, the experimenter announcing this outcome, his approving it as what he chose, and so forth. However, he (the *B*-body-person) certainly does

not like what is now happening to him, and would much prefer to be receiving what the *A*-body-person is receiving—namely, $100,000. The *A*-body-person will on the other hand recall choosing an outcome other than this one, but will reckon it good luck that the experimenter did not do what he recalls choosing. It looks, then, as though the *A*-body-person has got what he wanted, but not what he chose, while the *B*-body-person has got what he chose, but not what he wanted. So once more it looks as though they are, respectively, *B* and *A*; and that in this case the original choices of both *A* and *B* were unwise.

Suppose, lastly, that in the original choice *A* takes the line of the first case and *B* of the second: that is, *A* chooses that the *B*-body-person should get the money and the *A*-body-person the pain, and *B* chooses exactly the same thing. In this case, the experimenter would seem to be in the happy situation of giving both persons what they want—or at least, like God, what they have chosen. In this case, the *B*-body-person likes what he is receiving, recalls choosing it, and congratulates himself on the wisdom of (as he puts it) his choice; while the *A*-body-person does not like what he is receiving, recalls choosing it, and is forced to acknowledge that (as he puts it) his choice was unwise. So once more we seem to get results to support the suggestions drawn from the first case.

Let us now consider the question, not of *A* and *B* choosing certain outcomes to take place after the experiment, but of their willingness to engage in the experiment at all. If they were initially inclined to accept the description of the experiment as 'changing bodies' then one thing that would interest them would be the character of the other person's body. In this respect also what would happen after the experiment would seem to suggest that 'changing bodies' was a good description of the experiment. If *A* and *B* agreed to the experiment, being each not displeased with the appearance, physique, and so forth of the other person's body; after the experiment the *B*-body-person might well be found saying such things as: 'When I agreed to this experiment, I thought that *B*'s face was quite attractive, but now I look at it in the mirror, I am not so sure'; or the *A*-body-person might say 'When I agreed to this experiment I did not know that *A* had a wooden leg; but now, after it is over, I find that I have this wooden leg, and I want the experiment reversed.' It is possible that he might say further that he finds the leg very uncomfortable, and that the B-body-person should say, for instance, that he recalls that he found it very uncomfortable at first, but one gets used to it: but perhaps one would need to know more than at least I do about the physiology of habituation to artificial limbs to know whether the A-body-person would find the leg uncomfortable: that body, after all, has had the leg on it for some time. But apart from this sort of detail, the general line of the outcome regarded from this point of view seems to confirm our previous conclusions about the experiment.

Now let us suppose that when the experiment is proposed (in non-question-begging terms) A and B think rather of their psychological advantages and disadvantages. A's thoughts turn primarily to certain sorts of anxiety to which he is very prone, while B is concerned with the frightful memories he has of past experiences which still distress him. They each hope that the experiment will in some way result in their being able to get away from these things. They may even have been impressed by philosophical arguments to the effect that bodily continuity is at least a necessary condition of personal identity: A, for example, reasons that, granted the experiment comes off, then the person who is bodily continuous with him will not have this anxiety, and while the other person will no doubt have some anxiety—perhaps in some sense his anxiety—at least that person will not be he. The experiment is performed and the experimenter (to whom A and B previously revealed privately their several difficulties and hopes) asks the A-body-person whether he has got rid of his anxiety. This person presumably replies that he does not know what the man is talking about; he never had such anxiety, but he did have some very disagreeable memories, and recalls engaging in the experiment to get rid of them, and is disappointed to discover that he still has them. The B-body-person will react in a similar way to questions about his painful memories, pointing out that he still has his anxiety. These results seem to confirm still further the description of the experiment as 'changing bodies'. And all the results suggest that the only rational thing to do, confronted with such an experiment, would be to

identify oneself with one's memories, and so forth, and not with one's body. The philosophical arguments designed to show that bodily continuity was at least a necessary condition of personal identity would seem to be just mistaken.

Let us now consider something apparently different. Someone in whose power I am tells me that I am going to be tortured tomorrow. I am frightened, and look forward to tomorrow in great apprehension. He adds that when the time comes, I shall not remember being told that this was going to happen to me, since shortly before the torture something else will be done to me which will make me forget the announcement. This certainly will not cheer me up, since I know perfectly well that I can forget things, and that there is such a thing as indeed being tortured unexpectedly because I had forgotten or been made to forget a prediction of the torture: that will still be a torture which, so long as I do know about the prediction, I look forward to in fear. He then adds that my forgetting the announcement will be only part of a larger process: when the moment of torture comes, I shall not remember any of the things I am now in a position to remember. This does not cheer me up, either, since I can readily conceive of being involved in an accident, for instance, as a result of which I wake up in a completely amnesiac state and also in great pain; that could certainly happen to me, I should not like it to happen to me, nor to know that it was going to happen to me. He now further adds that at the moment of torture I shall not only not remember the things I am now in a position to remember, but will have a different set of impressions of my past, quite different from the memories I now have. I do not think that this would cheer me up, either. For I can at least conceive the possibility, if not the concrete reality, of going completely mad, and thinking perhaps that I am George IV or somebody; and being told that something like that was going to happen to me would have no tendency to reduce the terror of being told authoritatively that I was going to be tortured, but would merely compound the horror. Nor do I see why I should be put into any better frame of mind by the person in charge adding lastly that the impressions of my past with which I shall be equipped on the eve of torture will exactly fit the past of another person now living, and that indeed I shall acquire these impressions by (for instance) information now in his brain being copied into mine. Fear, surely, would still be the proper reaction: and not because one did not know what was going to happen, but because in one vital respect at least one did know what was going to happen—torture, which one can indeed expect to happen to oneself, and to be preceded by certain mental derangements as well.

If this is right, the whole question seems now to be totally mysterious. For what we have just been through is of course merely one side, differently represented, of the transaction which we considered before; and it represents it as a perfectly hateful prospect, while the previous considerations represented it as something one should rationally, perhaps even cheerfully, choose out of the options there presented. It is differently presented, of course, and in two notable respects; but when we look at these two differences of presentation, can we really convince ourselves that the second presentation is wrong or misleading, thus leaving the road open to the first version which at the time seemed so convincing? Surely not.

The first difference is that in the second version the torture is throughout represented as going to happen to *me*: 'you', the man in charge persistently says. Thus he is not very neutral. But should he have been neutral? Or, to put it another way, does his use of the second person have a merely emotional and rhetorical effect on me, making me afraid when further reflection would have shown that I had no reason to be? It is certainly not obviously so. The problem just is that through every step of his predictions I seem to be able to follow him successfully. And if I reflect on whether what he has said gives me grounds for fearing that I shall be tortured, I could consider that behind my fears lies some principle such as this: that my undergoing physical pain in the future is not excluded by any psychological state I may be in at the time, with the platitudinous exception of those psychological states which in themselves exclude experiencing pain, notably (if it is a psychological state) unconsciousness. In particular, what impressions I have about the past will not have any effect on whether I undergo the pain or not. This principle seems sound enough.

It is an important fact that not everything I would, as things are, regard as an evil would be something that I should rationally fear as an evil if it were predicted that it would happen to me in the future and also predicted that I should undergo significant psychological changes in the meantime. For the fact that I regard that happening, things being as they are, as an evil can be dependent on factors of belief or character which might themselves be modified by the psychological changes in question. Thus if I am appallingly subject to acrophobia, and am told that I shall find myself on top of a steep mountain in the near future, I shall to that extent be afraid; but if I am told that I shall be psychologically changed in the meantime in such a way as to rid me of my acrophobia (and as with the other prediction, I believe it), then I have no reason to be afraid of the predicted happening, or at least not the same reason. Again, I might look forward to meeting a certain person again with either alarm or excitement because of my memories of our past relations. In some part, these memories operate in connexion with my emotion, not only on the present time, but projectively forward: for it is to a meeting itself affected by the presence of those memories that I look forward. If I am convinced that when the time comes I shall not have those memories, then I shall not have just the same reasons as before for looking forward to that meeting with the one emotion or the other. (Spiritualism, incidentally, appears to involve the belief that I have just the same reasons for a given attitude toward encountering people again after I am dead, as I did before: with the one modification that I can be sure it will all be very nice.)

Physical pain, however, the example which for simplicity (and not for any obsessional reason) I have taken, is absolutely minimally dependent on character or belief. No amount of change in my character or my beliefs would seem to affect substantially the nastiness of tortures applied to me; correspondingly, no degree of predicted change in my character and beliefs can unseat the fear of torture which, together with those changes, is predicted for me.

I am not at all suggesting that the *only* basis, or indeed the only rational basis, for fear in the face of these various predictions is how things will be relative to my psychological state in the eventual outcome. I am merely pointing out that this is one component; it is not the only one. For certainly one will fear and otherwise reject the changes themselves, or in very many cases one would. Thus one of the old paradoxes of **hedonistic utilitarianism**; if one had assurances that undergoing certain operations and being attached to a machine would provide one for the rest of one's existence with an unending sequence of delicious and varied experiences, one might very well reject the option, and react with fear if someone proposed to apply it compulsorily; and that fear and horror would seem appropriate reactions in the second case may help to discredit the interpretation (if anyone has the nerve to propose it) that one's reason for rejecting the option voluntarily would be a consciousness of duties to others which one in one's hedonic state would leave undone. The prospect of contented madness or vegetableness is found by many (not perhaps by all) appalling in ways which are obviously not a function of how things would then be for them, for things would then be for them not appalling. In the case we are at present discussing, these sorts of considerations seem merely to make it clearer that the predictions of the man in charge provide a double ground of horror: at the prospect of torture, and at the prospect of the change in character and in impressions of the past that will precede it. And certainly, to repeat what has already been said, the prospect of the second certainly seems to provide no ground for rejecting or not fearing the prospect of the first.

I said that there were two notable differences between the second presentation of our situation and the first. The first difference, which we have just said something about, was that the man predicted the torture for *me*, a psychologically very changed 'me'. We have yet to find a reason for saying that he should not have done this, or that I really should be unable to follow him if he does; I seem to be able to follow him only too well. The second difference is that in this presentation he does not mention the other man, except in the somewhat incidental rôle of being the provenance of the impressions of the past I end up with. He does not mention him at all as someone who will end up with impressions of the past derived from me (and, incidentally, with $100,000 as well—a consideration which, in the frame of mind appropriate to this version, will merely make me jealous).

But why *should* he mention this man and what is going to happen to him? My selfish concern is to be told what is going to happen to me, and now I know: torture, preceded by changes of character, brain operations, changes in impressions of the past. The knowledge that one other person, or none, or many will be similarly mistreated may affect me in other ways, of sympathy, greater horror at the power of this tyrant, and so forth; but surely it cannot affect my expectations of torture? But—someone will say—this is to leave out exactly the feature which, as the first presentation of the case showed, makes all the difference: for it is to leave out the person who, as the first presentation showed, will be you. It is to leave out not merely a feature which should fundamentally affect your fears, it is to leave out the very person for whom you are fearful. So of course, the objector will say, this makes all the difference.

But can it? Consider the following series of cases. In each case we are to suppose that after what is described, A is, as before, to be tortured; we are also to suppose the person A is informed beforehand that just these things followed by the torture will happen to him:

(i) *A* is subjected to an operation which produces total amnesia;

(ii) amnesia is produced in *A*, and other interference leads to certain changes in his character;

(iii) changes in his character are produced, and at the same time certain illusory 'memory' beliefs are induced in him: these are of a quite fictitious kind and do not fit the life of any actual person;

(iv) the same as (iii), except that both the character traits and the 'memory' impressions are designed to be appropriate to another actual person, *B*;

(v) the same as (iv), except that the result is produced by putting the information into *A* from the brain of *B*, by a method which leaves *B* the same as he was before;

(vi) the same happens to *A* as in (v), but *B* is not left the same, since a similar operation is conducted in the reverse direction.

I take it that no-one is going to dispute that A has reasons, and fairly straightforward reasons, for fear of pain when the prospect is that of situation (i); there seems no conceivable reason why this should not extend to situation (ii), and the situation (iii) can surely introduce no difference of principle—it just seems a situation which for more than one reason we should have grounds for fearing, as suggested above. Situation (iv) at least introduces the person B, who was the focus of the objection we are now discussing. But it does not seem to introduce him in any way which makes a material difference; if I can expect pain through a transformation which involves new 'memory'-impressions, it would seem a purely external fact, relative to that, that the 'memory'-impressions had a model. Nor, in (iv), do we satisfy a causal condition which I mentioned at the beginning for the 'memories' actually being memories; though notice that if the job were done thoroughly, I might well be able to elicit from the A-body-person the kinds of remarks about his previous expectations of the experiment—remarks appropriate to the original B—which so impressed us in the first version of the story. I shall have a similar assurance of this being so in situation (v), where, moreover, a plausible application of the causal condition is available.

But two things are to be noticed about this situation. First, if we concentrate on A and the A-body-person, we do not seem to have added anything which from the point of view of his fears makes any material difference; just as, in the move from (iii) to (iv), it made no relevant difference that the new 'memory'-impressions which precede the pain had, as it happened, a model, so in the move from (iv) to (v) all we have added is that they have a model which is also their cause: and it is still difficult to see why that, to him looking forward, could possibly make the difference between expecting pain and not expecting pain. To illustrate that point from the case of character: if A is capable of expecting pain, he is capable of expecting pain preceded by a change in his dispositions—and to that expectation it can make no difference, whether that change in his dispositions is modelled on, or indeed indirectly caused by, the dispositions of some other person. If his fears can, as it were, reach through the change, it seems a mere trimming how the change is in fact induced.

The second point about situation (v) is that if the crucial question for A's fears with regard to what befalls the A-body-person is whether the A-body-person is or is not the person B,[2] then that condition has not yet been satisfied in situation (v): for there we have an undisputed B in addition to the A-body-person, and certainly those two are not the same person.

But in situation (vi), we seemed to think, that is finally what he is. But if A's original fears could reach through the expected changes in (v), as they did in (iv) and (iii), then certainly they can reach through in (vi). Indeed, from the point of view of A's expectations and fears, there is less difference between (vi) and (v) than there is between (v) and (iv) or between (iv) and (iii). In those transitions, there were at least differences—though we could not see that they were really relevant differences—in the content or cause of what happened to him; in the present case there is absolutely no difference at all in what happens to him, the only difference being in what happens to someone else. If he can fear pain when (v) is predicted, why should he cease to when (vi) is?

I can see only one way of relevantly laying great weight on the transition from (v) to (vi); and this involves a considerable difficulty. This is to deny that, as I put it, the transition from (v) to (vi) involves merely the addition of something happening to *somebody else*; what rather it does, it will be said, is to involve the reintroduction of A himself, as the B-body-person; since he has reappeared in this form, it is for this person, and not for the unfortunate A-body-person, that A will have his expectations. This is to reassert, in effect, the viewpoint emphasised in our first presentation of the experiment. But this surely has the consequence that A should not have fears for the A-body-person who appeared in situation (v). For by the present argument, the A-body-person in (vi) is not A; the B-body-person is. But the A-body-person in (v) is, in character, history, everything, exactly the same as the A-body-person in (vi); so if the latter is not A, then neither is the former. (It is this point, no doubt, that encourages one to speak of the difference that goes with (vi) as being, on the present view, the *reintroduction* of A.) But no-one else in (v) has any better claim to be A. So in (v), it seems, A just does not exist. This would certainly explain why *A* should have no fears for the state of things in (v)—though he might well have fears for the path to it. But it rather looked earlier as though he could well have fears for the state of things in (v). Let us grant, however, that that was an illusion, and that A really does not exist in (v); then does he exist in (iv), (iii), (ii), or (i)? It seems very difficult to deny it for (i) and (ii); are we perhaps to draw the line between (iii) and (iv)?

Here someone will say: you must not insist on drawing a line—borderline cases are borderline cases, and you must not push our concepts beyond their limits. But this well-known piece of advice, sensible as it is in many cases, seems in the present case to involve an extraordinary difficulty. It may intellectually comfort observers of *A*'s situation; but what is *A* supposed to make of it? To be told that a future situation is a borderline one for its being myself that is hurt, that it is conceptually undecidable whether it will be me or not, is something which, it seems, I can do nothing with; because, in particular, it seems to have no comprehensible representation in my expectations and the emotions that go with them.

If I expect that a certain situation, *S*, will come about in the future, there is of course a wide range of emotions and concerns, directed on *S*, which I may experience now in relation to my expectation. Unless I am exceptionally egoistic, it is not a condition on my being concerned in relation to this expectation, that I myself will be involved in *S*—where my being 'involved' in *S* means that I figure in *S* as someone doing something at that time or having something done to me, or, again, that *S* will have consequences affecting me at that or some subsequent time. There are some emotions, however, which I will feel only if I will be involved in *S*, and fear is an obvious example.

Now the description of *S* under which it figures in my expectations will necessarily be, in various ways, indeterminate; and one way in which it may be indeterminate is that it leaves open whether I shall be involved in *S* or not. Thus I may have good reason to expect that one of us five is going to get hurt, but no reason to expect it to be me rather than one of the others. My present emotions will be correspondingly affected by this indeterminacy. Thus, sticking to the egoistic concern involved in fear, I shall presumably be somewhat more cheerful than if I knew it was going to be me, somewhat less cheerful than if I had been left out altogether. Fear will be mixed with, and qualified by, apprehension; and so forth. These emotions revolve around the thought of the eventual determination of the indeterminacy; moments of straight fear focus on its really turning out to be me, of hope on its turning out not to be me. All the emotions are related to the coming about of what I expect: and what I expect in such a case just cannot come about save by coming about in one of the ways or another.

There are other ways in which indeterminate expectations can be related to fear. Thus I may expect (perhaps neurotically) that something nasty is going to happen to me, indeed expect that when it happens it will take some determinate form, but have no range, or no closed range, of candidates for the determinate form to rehearse in my present thought. Different from this would be the fear of something radically indeterminate—the fear (one might say) of a nameless horror. If somebody had such a fear, one could even say that he had, in a sense, a perfectly determinate expectation: if what he expects indeed comes about, there will be nothing more determinate to be said about it after the event than was said in the expectation. Both these cases of course are cases of *fear* because one thing that is fixed amid the indeterminacy is the belief that it is me to whom the things will happen.

Central to the expectation of *S* is the thought of what it will be like when it happens—thought which may be indeterminate, range over alternatives, and so forth. When *S* involves me, there can be the possibility of a special form of such thought: the thought of how it will be for me, the imaginative projection of myself as participant in *S*.[3] I do not have to think about *S* in this way, when it involves me; but I may be able to. (It might be suggested that this possibility was even mirrored in the language, in the distinction between 'expecting to be hurt' and 'expecting that I shall be hurt'; but I am very doubtful about this point, which is in any case of no importance.)

Suppose now that there is an S with regard to which it is for conceptual reasons undecidable whether it involves me or not, as is proposed for the experimental situation by the line we are discussing. It is important that the expectation of S is not *indeterminate* in any of the ways we have just been considering. It is not like the nameless horror, since the fixed point of that case was that it was going to happen to the subject, and that made his state unequivocally fear. Nor is it like the expectation of the man who expects one of the five to be hurt; his fear was indeed equivocal, but its focus, and that of the expectation, was that when S came about, it would certainly come about in one way or the other. In the present case, fear (of the torture, that is to say, not of the initial experiment) seems neither appropriate, nor inappropriate, nor appropriately equivocal. Relatedly, the subject has an incurable difficulty about how he may think about S. If he engages in projective imaginative thinking (about how it will be for him), he implicitly answers the necessarily unanswerable question; if he thinks that he cannot engage in such thinking, it looks very much as if he also answers it, though in the opposite direction. Perhaps he must just refrain from such thinking; but is he just refraining from it, if it is incurably undecidable whether he can or cannot engage in it?

It may be said that all that these considerations can show is that fear, at any rate, does not get its proper footing in this case; but that there could be some other, more ambivalent, form of concern which would indeed be appropriate to this particular expectation, the expectation of the conceptually undecidable situation. There are, perhaps, analogous feelings that actually occur in actual situations. Thus material objects do occasionally undergo puzzling transformations which leave a conceptual shadow over their identity. Suppose I were sentimentally attached to an object to which this sort of thing then happened; it might be that I could neither feel about it quite as I did originally, nor be totally indifferent to it, but would have some other and rather ambivalent feeling towards it. Similarly, it may be said, toward the prospective sufferer of pain, my identity relations with whom are conceptually shadowed, I can feel neither as I would if he were certainly me, nor as I would if he were certainly not, but rather some such ambivalent concern.

But this analogy does little to remove the most baffling aspect of the present case—an aspect which has already turned up in what was said about the subject's difficulty in thinking either projectively or non-projectively about the situation. For to regard the prospective pain-sufferer *just* like the transmogrified object of sentiment, and to conceive of my ambivalent distress about his future pain as just like ambivalent distress about some future damage to such an object, is of course to leave him and me clearly distinct from one another, and thus to displace the conceptual shadow from its proper place. I have to get nearer to him than that. But is there any nearer that I can get to him without expecting his pain? If there is, the analogy has not shown us it. We can certainly not get nearer by expecting, as it were, *ambivalent* pain; there is no place at all for that. There seems to be an obstinate bafflement to mirroring in my expectations a situation in which it is conceptually undecidable whether I occur.

The bafflement seems, moreover, to turn to plain absurdity if we move from conceptual undecidability to its close friend and neighbour, conventionalist decision. This comes out if we consider another description, overtly conventionalist, of the series of cases which occasioned the present discussion. This description would reject a point I relied on in an earlier argument—namely, that if we deny that the A-body-person in (vi) is A (because the B-body-person is), then we must deny that the A-body-person in (v) is A, since they are exactly similar. 'No', it may be said, 'this is just to assume that we say the same in different sorts of situation. No doubt when we have the very good candidate for being A—namely, the B-body-person—we call him A; but this does not mean that we should not call the A-body-person A in that other situation when we have no better candidate around. Different situations call for different descriptions.' This line of talk is the sort of thing indeed appropriate to lawyers deciding the ownership of some property which has undergone some bewildering set of transformations; they just have to decide, and in each situation, let us suppose, it has got to go to somebody, on as reasonable grounds as the facts and the law admit. But as a line to deal with a person's fears or expectations about his own future, it seems to have no sense at all. If A's fears can extend to what will happen to the A-body-person in (v), I do not see how they can be rationally diverted from the fate of the exactly similar person in (vi) by his being told that someone would have a reason in the latter situation which he would not have in the former for deciding to call another person A.

Thus, to sum up, it looks as though there are two presentations of the imagined experiment and the choice associated with it, each of which carries conviction, and which lead to contrary conclusions. The idea, moreover, that the situation after the experiment is conceptually undecidable in the relevant respect seems not to assist, but rather to increase, the puzzlement; while the idea (so often appealed to in these matters) that it is conventionally decidable is even worse. Following from all that, I am not in the least clear which option it would be wise to take if one were presented with them before the experiment. I find that rather disturbing.

Whatever the puzzlement, there is one feature of the arguments which have led to it which is worth picking out, since it runs counter to something which is, I think, often rather vaguely supposed. It is often recognised that there are 'first-personal' and 'third-personal' aspects of questions about persons, and that there are difficulties about the relations between them. It is also recognised that 'mentalistic' considerations (as we may vaguely call them) and considerations of bodily continuity are involved in questions of personal identity (which is not to say that there are mentalistic and bodily criteria of personal identity). It is tempting to think that the two distinctions run in parallel: roughly, that a first-person approach concentrates attention on mentalistic considerations, while a third-personal approach emphasises considerations of bodily continuity. The present discussion is an illustration of exactly the opposite. The first argument, which led to the 'mentalistic' conclusion that A and B would change bodies and that each person should identify himself with the destination of his memories and character, was an argument entirely conducted in third-personal terms. The second argument, which suggested the bodily continuity identification, concerned itself with the first-personal issue of what A could expect. That this is so seems to me (though I will not discuss it further here) of some significance.

I will end by suggesting one rather shaky way in which one might approach a resolution of the problem, using only the limited materials already available.

The apparently decisive arguments of the first presentation, which suggested that A should identify himself with the B-body-person, turned on the extreme neatness of the situation in satisfying, if any could, the description of 'changing bodies'. But this neatness is basically artificial; it is the product of the will of the experimenter to produce a situation which would naturally elicit, with minimum hesitation, that description. By the sorts of methods he employed, he could easily have left off earlier or gone on further. He could have stopped at situation (v), leaving B as he was; or he could have gone on and produced two persons each with A-like character and memories, as well as one or two with B-like characteristics. If he had done either of those, we should have been in yet greater difficulty about what to say; he just chose to make it as easy as possible for us to find something to say. Now if we had some model of ghostly persons in bodies, which were in some sense actually moved around by certain procedures, we could regard the neat experiment just as the *effective* experiment: the one method that really did result in the ghostly persons' changing places without being destroyed, dispersed, or whatever. But we cannot seriously use such a model. The experimenter has not in the sense of that model *induced* a change of bodies; he has rather produced the one situation out of a range of equally possible situations which we should be most disposed to call a change of bodies. As against this, the principle that one's fears can extend to future pain whatever psychological changes precede it seems positively straightforward. Perhaps, indeed, it is not; but we need to be shown what is wrong with it. Until we are shown what is wrong with it, we should perhaps decide that if we were the person A then, if we were to decide selfishly, we should pass the pain to the B-body-person. It would be risky: that there is room for the notion of a *risk* here is itself a major feature of the problem.

NOTES

1. *Self-Knowledge and Self-Identity* (Ithaca, N.Y., 1963), pp. 23 seq.
2. This of course does not have to be the crucial question, but it seems one fair way of taking up the present objection.
3. For a more detailed treatment of issues related to this, see "Imagination and the Self," pp. 38 *seq.*

KEY TERM

Hedonistic utilitarianism

STUDY QUESTIONS

1. Why does Williams say that describing his case as a case of exchanging bodies is question-begging?
2. Do you agree that Williams's thought-experiment supports the conclusion that after they emerge from the machine, *B* is to be identified with the *A*-body-person and *A* is to be identified with the *B*-body-person?
3. Williams thinks that when the case is redescribed from the perspective of one of the participants, the participant will still fear the torture. Do you think that he's right about this? If you were told that you would lose your memories and then gain someone else's memories, would you still fear torture to the body you have now?
4. Where do you think we ought to draw the line in Williams's six-step series? What reasons are there in favor of drawing the line there?

Personal Identity[1]

DEREK PARFIT

Derek Parfit (1942–) is a senior research fellow at All Soul's College, Oxford, and a Visiting Professor of Philosophy at New York University, Harvard, and Rutgers. His books, *Reasons and Persons* and *On What Matters*, are extremely influential in metaphysics and ethics.

. .

WE can, I think, describe cases in which, though we know the answer to every other question, we have no idea how to answer a question about personal identity. These cases are not covered by the criteria of personal identity that we actually use.

Do they present a problem?

It might be thought that they do not, because they could never occur. I suspect that some of them could. (Some, for instance, might become scientifically

possible.) But I shall claim that even if they did they would present no problem.

My targets are two beliefs: one about the nature of personal identity, the other about its importance.

The first is that in these cases the question about identity must have an answer.

No one thinks this about, say, nations or machines. Our criteria for the identity of these do not cover certain cases. No one thinks that in these cases the questions "Is it the same nation?" or "Is it the same machine?" must have answers.

Some people believe that in this respect they are different. They agree that our criteria of personal identity do not cover certain cases, but they believe

From "Personal Identity," in *The Philosophical Review* 80, pp. 3–27. Copyright © 1971.

that the nature of their own identity through time is, somehow, such as to guarantee that in these cases questions about their identity must have answers. This belief might be expressed as follows: "Whatever happens between now and any future time, either I shall still exist, or I shall not. Any future experience will either be *my* experience, or it will not."

This first belief—in the special nature of personal identity—has, I think, certain effects. It makes people assume that the principle of self-interest is more rationally compelling than any moral principle. And it makes them more depressed by the thought of aging and of death.

I cannot see how to disprove this first belief. I shall describe a problem case. But this can only make it seem implausible.

Another approach might be this. We might suggest that one cause of the belief is the projection of our emotions. When we imagine ourselves in a problem case, we do feel that the question "Would it be me?" must have an answer. But what we take to be a bafflement about a further fact may be only the bafflement of our concern.

I shall not pursue this suggestion here. But one cause of our concern is the belief which is my second target. This is that unless the question about identity has an answer, we cannot answer certain important questions (questions about such matters as survival, memory, and responsibility).

Against this second belief my claim will be this. Certain important questions do presuppose a question about personal identity. But they can be freed of this presupposition. And when they are, the question about identity has no importance.

I

We can start by considering the much-discussed case of the man who, like an amoeba, divides.[2]

Wiggins has recently dramatized this case.[3] He first referred to the operation imagined by Shoemaker.[4] We suppose that my brain is transplanted into someone else's (brainless) body, and that the resulting person has my character and apparent memories of my life. Most of us would agree, after thought,

that the resulting person is me. I shall here assume such agreement.[5]

Wiggins then imagined his own operation. My brain is divided, and each half is housed in a new body. Both resulting people have my character and apparent memories of my life.

What happens to me? There seem only three possibilities: (1) I do not survive; (2) I survive as one of the two people; (3) I survive as both.

The trouble with (1) is this. We agreed that I could survive if my brain were successfully transplanted. And people have in fact survived with half their brains destroyed. It seems to follow that I could survive if half my brain were successfully transplanted and the other half were destroyed. But if this is so, how could I *not* survive if the other half were also successfully transplanted? How could a double success be a failure?

We can move to the second description. Perhaps one success is the maximum score. Perhaps I shall be one of the resulting people.

The trouble here is that in Wiggins' case each half of my brain is exactly similar, and so, to start with, is each resulting person. So how can I survive as only one of the two people? What can make me one of them rather than the other?

It seems clear that both of these descriptions—that I do not survive, and that I survive as one of the people—are highly implausible. Those who have accepted them must have assumed that they were the only possible descriptions.

What about our third description: that I survive as both people?

It might be said, "If 'survive' implies identity, this description makes no sense—you cannot be two people. If it does not, the description is irrelevant to a problem about identity."

I shall later deny the second of these remarks. But there are ways of denying the first. We might say, "What we have called 'the two resulting people' are not two people. They are one person. I do survive Wiggins' operation. Its effect is to give me two bodies and a divided mind."

It would shorten my argument if this were absurd. But I do not think it is. It is worth showing why.

We can, I suggest, imagine a divided mind. We can imagine a man having two simultaneous experiences, in having each of which he is unaware of having the other.

We may not even need to imagine this. Certain actual cases, to which Wiggins referred, seem to be best described in these terms. These involve the cutting of the bridge between the hemispheres of the brain. The aim was to cure epilepsy. But the result appears to be, in the surgeon's words, the creation of "two separate spheres of consciousness,"[6] each of which controls one half of the patient's body. What is experienced in each is, presumably, experienced by the patient.

There are certain complications in these actual cases. So let us imagine a simpler case.

Suppose that the bridge between my hemispheres is brought under my voluntary control. This would enable me to disconnect my hemispheres as easily as if I were blinking. By doing this I would divide my mind. And we can suppose that when my mind is divided I can, in each half, bring about reunion.

This ability would have obvious uses. To give an example: I am near the end of a maths exam, and see two ways of tackling the last problem. I decide to divide my mind, to work, with each half, at one of two calculations, and then to reunite my mind and write a fair copy of the best result.

What shall I experience?

When I disconnect my hemispheres, my consciousness divides into two streams. But this division is not something that I experience. Each of my two streams of consciousness seems to have been straightforwardly continuous with my one stream of consciousness up to the moment of division. The only changes in each stream are the disappearance of half my visual field and the loss of sensation in, and control over, half my body.

Consider my experiences in what we can call my "right-handed" stream. I remember that I assigned my right hand to the longer calculation. This I now begin. In working at this calculation I can see, from the movements of my left hand, that I am also working at the other. But I am not aware of working at the other. So I might, in my right-handed stream, wonder how, in my left-handed stream, I am getting on.

My work is now over. I am about to reunite my mind. What should I, in each stream, expect? Simply that I shall suddenly seem to remember just having thought out two calculations, in thinking out each of which I was not aware of thinking out the other. This, I submit, we can imagine. And if my mind was divided, these memories are correct.

In describing this episode, I assumed that there were two series of thoughts, and that they were both mine. If my two hands visibly wrote out two calculations, and if I claimed to remember two corresponding series of thoughts, this is surely what we should want to say.

If it is, then a person's mental history need not be like a canal, with only one channel. It could be like a river, with islands, and with separate streams.

To apply this to Wiggins' operation: we mentioned the view that it gives me two bodies and a divided mind. We cannot now call this absurd. But it is, I think, unsatisfactory.

There were two features of the case of the exam that made us want to say that only one person was involved. The mind was soon reunited, and there was only one body. If a mind was permanently divided and its halves developed in different ways, the point of speaking of one person would start to disappear. Wiggins' case, where there are also two bodies, seems to be over the borderline. After I have had his operation, the two "products" each have all the attributes of a person. They could live at opposite ends of the earth. (If they later met, they might even fail to recognize each other.) It would become intolerable to deny that they were different people.

Suppose we admit that they are different people. Could we still claim that I survived as both, using "survive" to imply identity?

We could. For we might suggest that two people could compose a third. We might say, "I do survive Wiggins' operation as two people. They can be different people, and yet be me, in just the way in which the Pope's three crowns are one crown."[7]

This is a possible way of giving sense to the claim that I survive as two different people, using "survive" to imply identity. But it keeps the language of identity only by changing the concept of a person. And there are obvious objections to this change.[8]

The alternative, for which I shall argue, is to give up the language of identity. We can suggest that I survive as two different people without implying that I am these people.

When I first mentioned this alternative, I mentioned this objection: "If your new way of talking does not imply identity, it cannot solve our problem. For that is about identity. The problem is that all the possible answers to the question about identity are highly implausible."

We can now answer this objection.

We can start by reminding ourselves that this is an objection only if we have one or both of the beliefs which I mentioned at the start of this paper.

The first was the belief that to any question about personal identity, in any describable case, there must be a true answer. For those with this belief, Wiggins' case is doubly perplexing. If all the possible answers are implausible, it is hard to decide which of them is true, and hard even to keep the belief that one of them must be true. If we give up this belief, as I think we should, these problems disappear. We shall then regard the case as like many others in which, for quite unpuzzling reasons, there *is* no answer to a question about identity. (Consider "Was England the same nation after 1066?")

Wiggins' case makes the first belief implausible. It also makes it trivial. For it undermines the second belief. This was the belief that important questions turn upon the question about identity. (It is worth pointing out that those who have only this second belief do not think that there must *be* an answer to this question, but rather that we must decide upon an answer.)

Against this second belief my claim is this. Certain questions do presuppose a question about personal identity. And because these questions *are* important, Wiggins' case does present a problem. But we cannot solve this problem by answering the question about identity. We can solve this problem only by taking these important questions and prizing them apart from the question about identity. After we have done this, the question about identity (though we might for the sake of neatness decide it) has no further interest.

Because there are several questions which presuppose identity, this claim will take some time to fill out.

We can first return to the question of survival. This is a special case, for survival does not so much presuppose the retaining of identity as seem equivalent to it. It is thus the general relation which we need to prize apart from identity. We can then consider particular relations, such as those involved in memory and intention.

"Will I survive?" seems, I said, equivalent to "Will there be some person alive who is the same person as me?"

If we treat these questions as equivalent, then the least unsatisfactory description of Wiggins' case is, I think, that I survive with two bodies and a divided mind.

Several writers have chosen to say that I am neither of the resulting people. Given our equivalence, this implies that I do not survive, and hence, presumably, that even if Wiggins' operation is not literally death, I ought, since I will not survive it, to regard it *as* death. But this seemed absurd.

It is worth repeating why. An emotion or attitude can be criticized for resting on a false belief, or for being inconsistent. A man who regarded Wiggins' operation as death must, I suggest, be open to one of these criticisms.

He might believe that his relation to each of the resulting people fails to contain some element which is contained in survival. But how can this be true? We agreed that he *would* survive if he stood in this very same relation to only *one* of the resulting people. So it cannot be the nature of this relation which makes it fail, in Wiggins' case, to be survival. It can only be its duplication.

Suppose that our man accepts this, but still regards division as death. His reaction would now seem wildly inconsistent. He would be like a man who, when told of a drug that could double his years of life, regarded the taking of this drug as death. The only difference in the case of division is that the extra years are to run concurrently. This is an interesting difference. But it cannot mean that there are *no* years to run.

I have argued this for those who think that there must, in Wiggins' case, be a true answer to the question about identity. For them, we might add, "Perhaps the original person does lose his identity. But there may be other ways to do this than to die. One other way might be to multiply. To regard these as the same is to confuse nought with two."

For those who think that the question of identity is up for decision, it would be clearly absurd to regard Wiggins' operation as death. These people would have to think, "We could have chosen to say that I should be one of the resulting people. If we had, I should not have regarded it as death. But since we have chosen to say that I am neither person, I *do*." This is hard even to understand.[9]

My first conclusion, then, is this. The relation of the original person to each of the resulting people contains all that interests us—all that matters—in any ordinary case of survival. This is why we need a sense in which one person can survive as two.[10]

One of my aims in the rest of this paper will be to suggest such a sense. But we can first make some general remarks.

II

Identity is a one-one relation. Wiggins' case serves to show that what matters in survival need not be one-one.

Wiggins' case is of course unlikely to occur. The relations which matter are, in fact, one-one. It is because they are that we can imply the holding of these relations by using the language of identity.

This use of language is convenient. But it can lead us astray. We may assume that what matters *is* identity and, hence, has the properties of identity.

In the case of the property of being one-one, this mistake is not serious. For what matters is in fact one-one. But in the case of another property, the mistake *is* serious. Identity is all-or-nothing. Most of the relations which matter in survival are, in fact, relations of degree. If we ignore this, we shall be led into quite ill-grounded attitudes and beliefs.

The claim that I have just made—that most of what matters are relations of degree—I have yet to support. Wiggins' case shows only that these relations need not be one-one. The merit of the case is not that

it shows this in particular, but that it makes the first break between what matters and identity. The belief that identity *is* what matters is hard to overcome. This is shown in most discussions of the problem cases which actually occur: cases, say, of amnesia or of brain damage. Once Wiggins' case has made one breach in this belief, the rest should be easier to remove.[11]

To turn to a recent debate: most of the relations which matter can be provisionally referred to under the heading "psychological continuity" (which includes causal continuity). My claim is thus that we use the language of personal identity in order to imply such continuity. This is close to the view that psychological continuity provides a criterion of identity.

Williams has attacked this view with the following argument. Identity is a one-one relation. So any criterion of identity must appeal to a relation which is logically one-one. Psychological continuity is not logically one-one. So it cannot provide a criterion.[12]

Some writers have replied that it is enough if the relation appealed to is always in fact one-one.[13]

I suggest a slightly different reply. Psychological continuity is a ground for speaking of identity when it is one-one.

If psychological continuity took a one-many or branching form, we should need, I have argued, to abandon the language of identity. So this possibility would not count against this view.

We can make a stronger claim. This possibility would count in its favor.

The view might be defended as follows. Judgments of personal identity have great importance. What gives them their importance is the fact that they imply psychological continuity. This is why, whenever there is such continuity, we ought, if we can, to imply it by making a judgment of identity.

If psychological continuity took a branching form, no coherent set of judgments of identity could correspond to, and thus be used to imply, the branching form of this relation. But what we ought to do, in such a case, is take the importance which would attach to a judgment of identity and attach this importance directly to each limb of the branching relation. So this case helps to show that judgments of personal identity do derive their importance from the fact that they imply psychological continuity. It helps to show that when we can, usefully, speak of identity, this relation is our ground.

This argument appeals to a principle which Williams put forward.[14] The principle is that an important judgment should be asserted and denied only on importantly different grounds.

Williams applied this principle to a case in which one man is psychologically continuous with the dead Guy Fawkes, and a case in which two men are. His argument was this. If we treat psychological continuity as a sufficient ground for speaking of identity, we shall say that the one man is Guy Fawkes. But we could not say that the two men are, although we should have the same ground. This disobeys the principle. The remedy is to deny that the one man is Guy Fawkes, to insist that sameness of the body is necessary for identity.

Williams' principle can yield a different answer. Suppose we regard psychological continuity as more important than sameness of the body.[15] And suppose that the one man really is psychologically (and causally) continuous with Guy Fawkes. If he is, it would disobey the principle to deny that he is Guy Fawkes, for we have the same important ground as in a normal case of identity. In the case of the two men, we again have the same important ground. So we ought to take the importance from the judgment of identity and attach it directly to this ground. We ought to say, as in Wiggins' case, that each limb of the branching relation is as good as survival. This obeys the principle.

To sum up these remarks: even if psychological continuity is neither logically, nor always in fact, one-one, it can provide a criterion of identity. For this can appeal to the relation of *non-branching* psychological continuity, which is logically one-one.[16]

The criterion might be sketched as follows. "X and Y are the same person if they are psychologically continuous and there is no person who is contemporary with either and psychologically continuous with the other." We should need to explain what we mean by "psychologically continuous" and say how much continuity the criterion requires. We should then, I think, have described a sufficient condition for speaking of identity.[17]

We need to say something more. If we admit that psychological continuity might not be one-one, we need to say what we ought to do if it were not one-one. Otherwise our account would be open to the objections that it is incomplete and arbitrary.[18]

I have suggested that if psychological continuity took a branching form, we ought to speak in a new way, regarding what we describe as having the same significance as identity. This answers these objections.[19]

We can now return to our discussion. We have three remaining aims. One is to suggest a sense of "survive" which does not imply identity. Another is to show that most of what matters in survival are relations of degree. A third is to show that none of these relations needs to be described in a way that presupposes identity.

We can take these aims in the reverse order.

III

The most important particular relation is that involved in memory. This is because it is so easy to believe that its description must refer to identity.[20] This belief about memory is an important cause of the view that personal identity has a special nature. But it has been well discussed by Shoemaker[21] and by Wiggins.[22] So we can be brief.

It may be a logical truth that we can only remember our own experiences. But we can frame a new concept for which this is not a logical truth. Let us call this "q-memory."

To sketch a definition[23] I am q-remembering an experience if (1) I have a belief about a past experience which seems in itself like a memory belief, (2) someone did have such an experience, and (3) my belief is dependent upon this experience in the same way (whatever that is) in which a memory of an experience is dependent upon it.

According to (1) q-memories seem like memories. So I q-remember *having* experiences.

This may seem to make q-memory presuppose identity. One might say, "My apparent memory of *having* an experience is an apparent memory of *my* having an experience. So how could I q-remember my having other people's experiences?"

This objection rests on a mistake. When I seem to remember an experience, I do indeed seem to remember *having* it.[24] But it cannot be a part of what I seem to remember about this experience that I, the person who now seems to remember it, am the person who had this experience.[25] That I am is something that I automatically assume. (My apparent memories sometimes come to me simply as the belief that *I* had a certain experience.) But it is something that I am justified in assuming only because I do not in fact have *q*-memories of other people's experiences.

Suppose that I did start to have such *q*-memories. If I did, I should cease to assume that my apparent memories must be about my own experiences. I should come to assess an apparent memory by asking two questions: (1) Does it tell me about a past experience? (2) If so, whose?

Moreover (and this is a crucial point) my apparent memories would now come to me *as q*-memories. Consider those of my apparent memories which do come to me simply as beliefs about my past: for example, "I did that." If I knew that I could *q*-remember other people's experiences, these beliefs would come to me in a more guarded form: for example, "Someone—probably I—did that." I might have to work out who it was.

I have suggested that the concept of *q*-memory is coherent. Wiggins' case provides an illustration. The resulting people, in his case, both have apparent memories of living the life of the original person. If they agree that they are not this person, they will have to regard these as only *q*-memories. And when they are asked a question like "Have you heard this music before?" they might have to answer "I am sure that I *q*-remember hearing it. But I am not sure whether I remember hearing it. I am not sure whether it was I who heard it, or the original person."

We can next point out that on our definition every memory is also a *q*-memory. Memories are, simply, *q*-memories of one's own experiences. Since this is so, we could afford now to drop the concept of memory and use in its place the wider concept *q*-memory. If we did, we should describe the relation between an experience and what we now call a "memory" of this experience in a way which does not presuppose that they are had by the same person.[26]

This way of describing this relation has certain merits. It vindicates the "memory criterion" of personal identity against the charge of circularity.[27] And it might, I think, help with the problem of other minds.

But we must move on. We can next take the relation between an intention and a later action. It may be a logical truth that we can intend to perform only our own actions. But intentions can be redescribed as *q*-intentions. And one person could *q*-intend to perform another person's actions.

Wiggins' case again provides the illustration. We are supposing that neither of the resulting people is the original person. If so, we shall have to agree that the original person can, before the operation, *q*-intend to perform their actions. He might, for example, *q*-intend, as one of them, to continue his present career, and, as the other, to try something new.[28] (I say "*q*-intend *as* one of them" because the phrase "*q*-intend *that* one of them" would not convey the directness of the relation which is involved. If I intend that someone else should do something, I cannot get him to do it simply by forming this intention. But if I am the original person, and he is one of the resulting people, I can.)

The phrase "*q*-intend *as* one of them" reminds us that we need a sense in which one person can survive as two. But we can first point out that the concepts of *q*-memory and *q*-intention give us our model for the others that we need: thus, a man who can *q*-remember could *q*-recognize, and be a *q*-witness of, what he has never seen; and a man who can *q*-intend could have *q*-ambitions, make *q*-promises, and be *q*-responsible for.

To put this claim in general terms: many different relations are included within, or are a consequence of, psychological continuity. We describe these relations in ways which presuppose the continued existence of one person. But we could describe them in new ways which do not.

This suggests a bolder claim. It might be possible to think of experiences in a wholly "impersonal" way. I shall not develop this claim here. What I shall try to describe is a way of thinking of our own identity through time which is more flexible, and less misleading, than the way in which we now think.

This way of thinking will allow for a sense in which one person can survive as two. A more important feature is that it treats survival as a matter of degree.

IV

We must first show the need for this second feature. I shall use two imaginary examples.

The first is the converse of Wiggins' case: fusion. Just as division serves to show that what matters in survival need not be one-one, so fusion serves to show that it can be a question of degree.

Physically, fusion is easy to describe. Two people come together. While they are unconscious, their two bodies grow into one. One person then wakes up.

The psychology of fusion is more complex. One detail we have already dealt with in the case of the exam. When my mind was reunited, I remembered just having thought out two calculations. The one person who results from a fusion can, similarly, q-remember living the lives of the two original people. None of their q-memories need be lost.

But some things must be lost. For any two people who fuse together will have different characteristics, different desires, and different intentions. How can these be combined?

We might suggest the following. Some of these will be compatible. These can coexist in the one resulting person. Some will be incompatible. These, if of equal strength, can cancel out, and if of different strengths, the stronger can be made weaker. And all these effects might be predictable.

To give examples—first, of compatibility: I like Palladio and intend to visit Venice. I am about to fuse with a person who likes Giotto and intends to visit Padua. I can know that the one person we shall become will have both tastes and both intentions. Second, of incompatibility: I hate red hair, and always vote Labour. The other person loves red hair, and always votes Conservative. I can know that the one person we shall become will be indifferent to red hair, and a floating voter.

If we were about to undergo a fusion of this kind, would we regard it as death?

Some of us might. This is less absurd than regarding division as death. For after my division the two resulting people will be in every way like me, while after my fusion the one resulting person will not be wholly similar. This makes it easier to say, when faced with fusion, "I shall not survive," thus continuing to regard survival as a matter of all-or-nothing.

This reaction is less absurd. But here are two analogies which tell against it.

First, fusion would involve the changing of some of our characteristics and some of our desires. But only the very self-satisfied would think of this as death. Many people welcome treatments with these effects.

Second, someone who is about to fuse can have, beforehand, just as much "intentional control" over the actions of the resulting individual as someone who is about to marry can have, beforehand, over the actions of the resulting couple. And the choice of a partner for fusion can be just as well considered as the choice of a marriage partner. The two original people can make sure (perhaps by "trial fusion") that they do have compatible characters, desires, and intentions.

I have suggested that fusion, while not clearly survival, is not clearly failure to survive, and hence that what matters in survival can have degrees.

To reinforce this claim we can now turn to a second example. This is provided by certain imaginary beings. These beings are just like ourselves except that they reproduce by a process of natural division.

We can illustrate the histories of these imagined beings with the aid of a diagram. The lines on the diagram represent the spatiotemporal paths which would be traced out by the bodies of these beings. We can call each single line (like the double line) a "branch"; and we can call the whole structure a "tree." And let us suppose that each "branch" corresponds to what is thought of as the life of one individual.

These individuals are referred to as "A," "B + 1," and so forth.

Now, each single division is an instance of Wiggins' case. So A's relation to both B + 1 and B + 2 is just as good as survival. But what of A's relation to B + 30?

I said earlier that what matters in survival could be provisionally referred to as "psychological continuity." I must now distinguish this relation from another, which I shall call "psychological connectedness."

Let us say that the relation between a q-memory and the experience q-remembered is a "direct" relation. Another "direct" relation is that which holds between a q-intention and the q-intended action. A third is that which holds between different expressions of some lasting q-characteristic.

"Psychological connectedness," as I define it, requires the holding of these direct psychological relations. "Connectedness" is not transitive, since these relations are not transitive. Thus, if X q-remembers most of Y's life, and Y q-remembers most of Z's life, it does not follow that X q-remembers most of Z's life. And if X carries out the q-intentions of Y, and Y carries out the q-intentions of Z, it does not follow that X carries out the q-intentions of Z.

"Psychological continuity," in contrast, only requires overlapping chains of direct psychological relations. So "continuity" is transitive.

To return to our diagram. A is psychologically continuous with B + 30. There are between the two continuous chains of overlapping relations. Thus, A has q-intentional control over B + 2, B + 2 has q-intentional control over B + 6, and so on up to B + 30. Or B + 30 can q-remember the life of B + 14, B + 14 can q-remember the life of B + 6, and so on back to A.[29]

A, however, need not be psychologically connected to B + 30. Connectedness requires direct relations. And if these beings are like us, A cannot stand in such relations to every individual in his indefinitely long "tree." Q-memories will weaken with the passage of time, and then fade away. Q-ambitions, once fulfilled, will be replaced by others, Q-characteristics will gradually change. In general, A stands in fewer and fewer direct psychological relations to an individual in his "tree" the more remote that individual is. And if the individual is (like B + 30) sufficiently remote, there may be between the two no direct psychological relations.

Now that we have distinguished the general relations of psychological continuity and psychological connectedness, I suggest that connectedness is a more important element in survival. As a claim about our own survival, this would need more arguments than I have space to give. But it seems clearly true for my imagined beings. A is as close psychologically to B + 1 as I today am to myself tomorrow. A is as distant from B + 30 as I am from my great-great-grandson.

Even if connectedness is not more important than continuity, the fact that one of these is a relation of degree is enough to show that what matters in survival can have degrees. And in any case the two relations are quite different. So our imagined beings would need a way of thinking in which this difference is recognized.

V

What I propose is this.

First, A can think of any individual, anywhere in his "tree," as "a descendant self." This phrase implies psychological continuity. Similarly, any later individual can think of any earlier individual on the single path[30] which connects him to A as "an ancestral self."

Since psychological continuity is transitive, "being an ancestral self of" and "being a descendant self of" are also transitive.

To imply psychological connectedness I suggest the phrases "one of my future selves" and "one of my past selves."

These are the phrases with which we can describe Wiggins' case. For having past and future selves is, what we needed, a way of continuing to exist which does not imply identity through time. The original person does, in this sense, survive Wiggins' operation: the two resulting people are his later selves. And they can each refer to him as "my past self." (They can share a past self without being the same self as each other.)

Since psychological connectedness is not transitive, and is a matter of degree, the relations "being a past self of" and "being a future self of" should themselves be treated as relations of degree. We allow for this series of descriptions: "my most recent self," "one of my earlier selves," "one of my distant selves," "hardly one of *my* past selves (I can only *q*-remember a few of his experiences)," and, finally, "not in any way one of *my* past selves—just an ancestral self."

This way of thinking would clearly suit our first imagined beings. But let us now turn to a second kind of being. These, reproduce by fusion as well as by division.[31] And let us suppose that they fuse every autumn and divide every spring. This yields the following diagram:

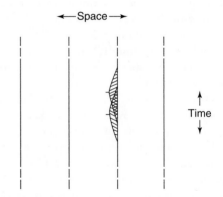

If *A* is the individual whose life is represented by the three-lined "branch," the two-lined "tree" represents those lives which are psychologically continuous with *A*'s life. (It can be seen that each individual has his own "tree," which overlaps with many others.)

For the imagined beings in this second world, the phrases "an ancestral self" and "a descendant self" would cover too much to be of much use. (There may well be pairs of dates such that every individual who ever lived before the first date was an ancestral self of every individual who ever will live after the second date.) Conversely, since the lives of each individual last for only half a year, the word "I" would cover too little to do all of the work which it does for us. So part of this work would have to be done, for these second beings, by talk about past and future selves.

We can now point out a theoretical flaw in our proposed way of thinking. The phrase "a past self of" implies psychological connectedness. Being a past self of is treated as a relation of degree, so that this phrase can be used to imply the varying degrees of psychological connectedness. But this phrase can imply only the degrees of connectedness between different lives. It cannot be used within a single life.

And our way of delimiting successive X lives does not refer to the degrees of psychological connectedness. Hence there is no guarantee that this phrase, "a past self of," could be used whenever it was needed. There is no guarantee that psychological connectedness will not vary in degree within a single life.

This flaw would not concern our imagined beings. For they divide and unite so frequently, and their lives are in consequence so short, that within a single life psychological connectedness would always stand at a maximum.

But let us look, finally, at a third kind of being.

In this world there is neither division nor union. There are a number of everlasting bodies, which gradually change in appearance. And direct psychological relations, as before, hold only over limited periods of time. This can be illustrated with a third diagram (given below). In this diagram the two shadings represent the degrees of psychological connectedness to their two central points.

These beings could not use the way of thinking that we have proposed. Since there is no branching of psychological continuity, they would have to regard themselves as immortal. It might be said that this is what they are. But there is, I suggest, a better description.

Our beings would have one reason for thinking of themselves as immortal. The parts of each "line" are all psychologically continuous. But the parts of each "line" are not all psychologically connected. Direct psychological relations hold only between those parts which are close to each other in time.

This gives our beings a reason for *not* thinking of each "line" as corresponding to one single life. For if they did, they would have no way of implying these direct relations. When a speaker says, for example, "I spent a period doing such and such," his hearers would not be entitled to assume that the speaker has any memories of this period, that his character then and now are in any way similar, that he is now carrying out any of the plans or intentions which he then had, and so forth. Because the word "I" would carry none of these implications, it would not have for these "immortal" beings the usefulness which it has for us.[32]

To gain a better way of thinking, we must revise the way of thinking that we proposed above. The revision is this. The distinction between successive selves can be made by reference, not to the branching of psychological continuity, but to the degrees of psychological connectedness. Since this connectedness is a matter of degree, the drawing of these distinctions can be left to the choice of the speaker and be allowed to vary from context to context.

On this way of thinking, the word "I" can be used to imply the greatest degree of psychological connectedness. When the connections are reduced, when there has been any marked change of character or style of life, or any marked loss of memory, our imagined beings would say, "It was not I who did that, but an earlier self." They could then describe in what ways, and to what degree, they are related to this earlier self.

This revised way of thinking would suit not only our "immortal" beings. It is also the way in which we ourselves could think about our lives. And it is, I suggest, surprisingly natural.

One of its features, the distinction between successive selves, has already been used by several writers. To give an example, from Proust: "we are incapable, while we are in love, of acting as fit predecessors of the next persons who, when we are in love no longer, we shall presently have become. . . ."[33]

Although Proust distinguished between successive selves, he still thought of one person as being these different selves. This we would not do on the way of thinking that I propose. If I say, "It will not be me, but one of my future selves," I do not imply that

I will be that future self. He is one of my later selves, and I am one of his earlier selves. There is no underlying person who we both are.

To point out another feature of this way of thinking. When I say, "There is no person who we both are," I am only giving my decision. Another person could say, "It will be you," thus deciding differently. There is no question of either of these decisions being a mistake. Whether to say "I," or "one of my future selves," or "a descendant self" is entirely a matter of choice. The matter of fact, which must be agreed, is only whether the disjunction applies. (The question "Are X and Y the same person?" thus becomes "Is X *at least* an ancestral [or descendant] self of Y?")

VI

I have tried to show that what matters in the continued existence of a person are, for the most part, relations of degree. And I have proposed a way of thinking in which this would be recognized.

I shall end by suggesting two consequences and asking one question.

It is sometimes thought to be especially rational to act in our own best interests. But I suggest that the principle of self-interest has no force. There are only two genuine competitors in this particular field. One is the principle of biased rationality: do what will best achieve what you actually want. The other is the principle of impartiality: do what is in the best interests of everyone concerned.

The apparent force of the principle of self-interest derives, I think, from these two other principles.

The principle of self-interest is normally supported by the principle of biased rationality. This is because most people care about their own future interests.

Suppose that this prop is lacking. Suppose that a man does not care what happens to him in, say, the more distant future. To such a man, the principle of self-interest can only be propped up by an appeal to the principle of impartiality. We must say, "Even if you don't care, you ought to take what happens to you then equally into account." But for this, as a special claim, there seem to me no good arguments. It can only be supported as part of the general claim, "You ought to take what happens to everyone equally into account."[34]

The special claim tells a man to grant an *equal* weight to all the parts of his future. The argument for this can only be that all the parts of his future are *equally* parts of *his* future. This is true. But it is a truth too superficial to bear the weight of the argument. (To give an analogy: The unity of a nation is, in its nature, a matter of degree. It is therefore only a superficial truth that all of a man's compatriots are *equally* his compatriots. This truth cannot support a good argument for nationalism.)[35]

I have suggested that the principle of self-interest has no strength of its own. If this is so, there is no special problem in the fact that what we ought to do can be against our interests. There is only the general problem that it may not be what we want to do.

The second consequence which I shall mention is implied in the first. **Egoism**, the fear not of near but of distant death, the regret that so much of one's *only* life should have gone by—these are not, I think, wholly natural or instinctive. They are all strengthened by the beliefs about personal identity which I have been attacking. If we give up these beliefs, they should be weakened.

My final question is this. These emotions are bad, and if we weaken them we gain. But can we achieve this gain without, say, also weakening loyalty to, or love of, other particular selves? As Hume warned, the "refined reflections which philosophy suggests . . . cannot diminish . . . our vicious passions . . . without diminishing . . . such as are virtuous. They are . . . applicable to all our affections. In vain do we hope to direct their influence only to one side."[36]

That hope *is* vain. But Hume had another: that more of what is bad depends upon false belief. This is also my hope.

NOTES

1. I have been helped in writing this by D. Wiggins, D. F. Pears, P. F. Strawson, A. J. Ayer, M. Woods, N. Newman, and (through his publications) S. Shoemaker.

2. Implicit in John Locke, *Essay Concerning Human Understanding*, ed. by John W. Yolton (London, 1961), Vol. II, Ch. XXVII, sec. 18, and discussed by (among others) A. N. Prior in "Opposite Number," *Review of Metaphysics*, 11 (1957–1958), and "Time, Existence and Identity," *Proceedings of the Aristotelian Society*, LVII (1965–1966); J. Bennett in "The Simplicity of the Soul," *Journal of Philosophy*, LXIV (1967); and R. Chisholm and S. Shoemaker in "The Loose and Popular and the Strict and the Philosophical Senses of Identity," in *Perception and Personal Identity: Proceedings of the 1967 Oberlin Colloquium in Philosophy*, ed. by Norman Care and Robert H. Grimm (Cleveland, 1967).

3. In *Identity and Spatio-Temporal Continuity* (Oxford, 1967), p. 50.

4. In *Self-Knowledge and Self-Identity* (Ithaca, N.Y., 1963), p. 22.

5. Those who would disagree are not making a mistake. For them my argument would need a different case. There must be some multiple transplant, faced with which these people would both find it hard to believe that there must be an answer to the question about personal identity, and be able to be shown that nothing of importance turns upon this question.

6. R. W. Sperry, in *Brain and Conscious Experience*, ed. by J. C. Eccles (New York, 1966), p. 299.

7. Cf. David Wiggins, *op. cit*, p. 40.

8. Suppose the resulting people fight a duel. Are there three people fighting, one on each side, and one on both? And suppose one of the bullets kills. Are there two acts, one murder and one suicide? How many people are left alive? One? Two? (We could hardly say, "One and a half.") We could talk in this way. But instead of saying that the resulting people *are* the original person—so that the pair is a trio—it would be far simpler to treat them as a pair, and describe their relation to the original person in some new way. (I owe this suggested way of talking, and the objections to it, to Michael Woods.)

9. Cf. Sydney Shoemaker, in *Perception and Personal Identity: Proceedings of the 1967 Oberlin Colloquium in Philosophy, loc. cit.*

10. Cf. David Wiggins, *op. cit.*, p. 54.

11. Bernard Williams' "The Self and the Future," *Philosophical Review*, LXXIX (1970), 161–180, is relevant here. He asks the question "Shall I survive?" in a range of problem cases, and he shows how natural it is to believe (1) that this question must have an answer, (2) that the answer must be

all-or-nothing, and (3) that there is a "risk" of our reaching the *wrong* answer. Because these beliefs are so natural, we should need in undermining them to discuss their causes. These, I think, can be found in the ways in which we misinterpret what it is to remember (cf. Sec. III below) and to anticipate (cf. Williams' "Imagination and the Self," *Proceedings of the British Academy*, LII [1966], 105–124); and also in the way in which certain features of our egoistic concern—e.g., that it is simple, and applies to all imaginable cases—are "projected" onto its object. (For another relevant discussion, see Terence Penelhum's *Survival and Disembodied Existence* [London, 1970], final chapters.)

12. "Personal Identity and Individuation," *Proceedings of the Aristotelian Society*, LVII (1956–1957), 229–253; also *Analysis*, 21 (1960–1961), 43–48.

13. J. M. Shorter, "More about Bodily Continuity and Personal Identity," *Analysis*, 22 (1961–1962), 79–85; and Mrs. J. M. R. Jack (unpublished), who requires that this truth be embedded in a causal theory.

14. *Analysis*, 21 (1960–1961), 44.

15. For the reasons given by A. M. Quinton in "The Soul," *Journal of Philosophy*, LIX (1962), 393–409.

16. Cf. S. Shoemaker, "Persons and Their Pasts," to appear in the *American Philosophical Quarterly*, and "Wiggins on Identity," *Philosophical Review*, LXXIX (1970), 542.

17. But not a necessary condition, for in the absence of psychological continuity bodily identity might be sufficient.

18. Cf. Bernard Williams, "Personal Identity and Individuation," *Proceedings of the Aristotelian Society*, LVII (1956–1957), 240–241, and *Analysis*, 21 (1960–1961), 44; and also Wiggins, *op. cit.*, p. 38: "if coincidence under [the concept] *f* is to be *genuinely* sufficient we must not withhold identity . . . simply because transitivity is threatened."

19. Williams produced another objection to the "psychological criterion," that it makes it hard to explain the difference between the concepts of identity and exact similarity (*Analysis*, 21 [1960–1961], 48). But if we include the requirement of causal continuity we avoid this objection (and one of those produced by Wiggins in his note 47).

20. Those philosophers who have held this belief, from Butler onward, are too numerous to cite.

21. *Op. cit.*

22. In a paper on Butler's objection to Locke (not yet published).

23. I here follow Shoemaker's "quasi-memory." Cf. also Penelhum's "retrocognition," in his article on "Personal Identity," in the *Encyclopedia of Philosophy*, ed. by Paul Edwards.

24. As Shoemaker put it, I seem to remember the experience "from the inside" (*op. cit.*).

25. This is what so many writers have overlooked. Cf. Thomas Reid: "My memory testifies not only that this was done, but that it was done by me who now remember it" ("Of Identity," in *Essays on the Intellectual Powers of Man*, ed. by A. D. Woozley [London, 1941], p. 203). This mistake is discussed by A. B. Palma in "Memory and Personal Identity," *Australasian Journal of Philosophy*, 42 (1964), 57.

26. It is not logically necessary that we only *q*-remember our own experiences. But it might be necessary on other grounds. This possibility is intriguingly explored by Shoemaker in his "Persons and Their Pasts" (*op. cit.*). He shows that *q*-memories can provide a knowledge of the world only if the observations which are *q*-remembered trace out fairly continuous spatiotemporal paths. If the observations which are *q*-remembered traced out a network of frequently interlocking paths, they could not, I think, be usefully ascribed to persisting observers, but would have to be referred to in some more complex way. But in fact the observations which are *q*-remembered trace out single and separate paths; so we can ascribe them to ourselves. In other words, it is epistemologically necessary that the observations which are *q*-remembered should satisfy a certain general condition, one particular form of which allows them to be usefully self-ascribed.

27. Cf. Wiggins' paper on Butler's objection to Locke.

28. There are complications here. He could form *divergent q*-intentions only if he could distinguish, in advance, between the resulting people (e.g., as "the left-hander" and "the right-hander"). And he could be confident that such divergent *q*-intentions would be carried out only if he had reason to believe that neither of the resulting people would change their (inherited) mind. Suppose he was torn between duty and desire. He could not solve this dilemma by *q*-intending, as one of the resulting people, to do his duty, and, as the other, to do what he desires. For the one he *q*-intended to do his duty would face the same dilemma.

29. The chain of continuity must run in one direction of time. *B* + 2 is not, in the sense I intend, psychologically continuous with *B* + 1.

30. Cf. David Wiggins, *op.cit.*
31. Cf. Sydney Shoemaker in "Persons and Their Pasts," *op.cit.*
32. Cf. Austin Duncan Jones, "Man's Mortality," *Analysis*, 28 (1967–1968), 65–70.
33. *Within a Budding Grove* (London, 1949), I, 226 (my own translation).
34. Cf. Thomas Nagel's *The Possibility of Altruism* (Oxford, 1970), in which the special claim is in effect defended as part of the general claim.
35. The unity of a nation we seldom take for more than what it is. This is partly because we often think of nations, not as units, but in a more complex way. If we thought of ourselves in the way that I proposed, we might be less likely to take our own identity for more than what it is. We are, for example, sometimes told, "It is irrational to act against your own interests. After all, it will be *you* who will regret it." To this we could reply, "No, not me. Not even one of my future selves. Just a descendant self."
36. "The Sceptic," in "Essays Moral, Political and Literary," *Hume's Moral and Political Philosophy* (New York, 1959), p. 349.

KEY TERM

Egoism

STUDY QUESTIONS

1. Parfit maintains that in a case of fission, there are only three possibilities about what happens to me when my brain is split and put into different bodies. What are these three possibilities? What is unsatisfactory about each, according to Parfit?
2. How important, if at all, is the thought that there will be someone in the future who is strictly identical to me (rather than merely psychologically connected, for instance)? Should we care about personal identity in this strict sense?
3. What is the notion of *q*-remembering? How does Parfit put it to use in his paper?
4. Do you agree with Parfit that what matters for survival are characteristics that admit of degrees, so that there may be no definite answers to questions about personal identity? Why or why not?

So It Goes

J. DAVID VELLEMAN

J. David Velleman is a Professor of Philosophy at New York University. He is best known for his work on practical reason, agency, and the foundations of morality. He is the author of *The Possibility of Practical Reason*, *Self to Self*, and *How We Get Along*.

> Change presupposes a certain position which I take up and from which I see things in procession before me: there are no events without someone to whom they happen and whose finite perspective is the basis of their individuality. Time presupposes a view of time. It is, therefore, not like a river, not a flowing substance. The fact that the metaphor based on this comparison has persisted from the time of Heraclitus to our own day is explained by our surreptitiously putting into the river a witness of its course.... Time is, therefore, not a real process, not an actual succession that I am content to record. It arises from my relation to things.
>
> —*M. Merleau-Ponty*[1]

Buddhists believe that the existence of an enduring self is an illusion and that this illusion is the root of the suffering inherent in the human condition. I am not a scholar of Buddhism or a practitioner, and this lecture is not an exercise in Buddhist studies. I merely want to explore whether this particular Buddhist thought can be understood in terms familiar to **analytic philosophy**: How might the illusion of an enduring self lie at the root of human suffering?

One of my reasons for wanting to understand this thought is that it challenges an attitude shared by several philosophers who might otherwise seem sympathetic to the Buddhist conception of the self. Philosophers as diverse as Christine Korsgaard and Daniel Dennett have claimed that the self is something that we must invent or construct.[2] But these philosophers believe that inventing or constructing a self is a wonderful accomplishment of which we should be proud, whereas the Buddhists believe that it is a tragic mistake that we should try to undo. Can Western philosophers make sense of the Buddhist attitude? That's what I want to know.

One philosopher who claims to embrace the Buddhist attitude is Derek Parfit, reflecting on his own neo-Lockean theory of personal identity.[3] Locke argued that our past selves are the people whose experiences we remember first-personally. Parfit points out that the experiences of a single person in the past might in principle be remembered by more than one of us in the present—if, for example, the hemispheres of the person's brain had been transplanted into two different bodies. In that case, there would be more than one of us with a claim to a single past self, a situation incompatible with the logic of identity. Hence connections of memory do not necessarily trace out the career of a single, enduring object, and they are unsuited to serve as the integuments of an enduring self.

Parfit suggests that giving up our belief in an enduring self would be beneficial. Of the time when he

believed in his own endurance, he says, "I seemed imprisoned in myself":

> My life seemed like a glass tunnel, through which I was moving faster every year, and at the end of which there was darkness. When I changed my view, the walls of my glass tunnel disappeared. I now live in the open air.[4]

Parfit elsewhere describes this liberation in less metaphorical terms:

> **Egoism**, the fear not of near but of distant death, the regret that so much of one's only life should have gone by—these are not, I think, wholly natural or instinctive. They are all strengthened by the beliefs about personal identity which I have been attacking. If we give up these beliefs, they should be weakened.[5]

Parfit explicitly notes the similarity between his view of personal identity and that of the Buddhists,[6] but he does not directly compare the consolations claimed for these views. Such a comparison might have suggested to Parfit that he underestimates the revolution in attitude that his view of personal identity can produce. For he claims that the consolations of his view can be obtained by attending to the philosophical arguments for it,[7] whereas the Buddhists believe that they can be obtained only through long and arduous meditational practice.

I will argue that shedding our belief in an enduring self would have consequences far more radical than Parfit has imagined—results that cannot be obtained by philosophical argument alone. Breaking out of a glass tunnel is not the half of it.

. . . .

In order to understand how belief in an enduring self could lead to suffering, we have to understand the ontological status of the self believed in. What exactly would it be for the self to endure?

Metaphysicians have defined two distinct conceptions of how objects persist through time.[8] Under one conception, objects are extended in time as they are extended in space. Just as a single point in space can contain only part of an extended object, a spatial part, so a single point in time can contain only part

© 2006 J. David Velleman. "So It Goes." The Amherst Lecture in Philosophy 1 (2006): 1–25.

of a persisting object, a temporal part. The object fills time by having one temporal part after another, just as it fills space by having one spatial part next to another. An object that persists through time in this way is said to **perdure**.

Under the alternative conception, an object's extension in time is different from its extension in space. Whereas only part of an object can be present at a single point in space, the object can be wholly present at a single point in time. An object that persists through time in this way is said to **endure**.

But what does it mean to say that the object is wholly present at a single point in time?[9] To be sure, all of its spatial parts can be present at a single instant, but all of its spatial parts are conceived to be simultaneously present under the conception of it as perduring, too. And saying that the object is wholly present at a single point in time cannot mean that all of its *temporal* parts are present. For how can all of the object's temporal parts be present at a single point in time if the object also exists at other times?

According to some philosophers, saying that an object is wholly present at a single point in time means that it does not have temporal parts at all. Yet what is to prevent us from considering the object as it is at a single moment, and then denominating that aspect of it as a temporal part? If the object is extended in some dimension, such as time, and that dimension is itself divisible into smaller and smaller regions, such as hours and minutes and seconds, then nothing can prevent us from abstracting temporal parts from the object by prescinding from its existence beyond one of those regions. The nature of endurance thus appears mysterious. And the suspicion arises that we couldn't possibly believe in an enduring self, because we have no coherent idea what it would be for the self to endure.

These brief considerations fall far short of proving that no coherent idea of an enduring self can be found. But rather than pursue a coherent idea of an enduring self, we should consider the possibility that an incoherent idea will do. An incoherent idea will certainly do if the enduring self is just an illusion. Maybe if we figure out how such an illusion might arise, we will understand the resulting idea, coherent or not.

. . . .

In my view, the idea of an enduring self arises from the structure of experience and experiential memory, just as Locke first suggested.[10] When I remember a past experience, I remember the world as experienced from the perspective of a past self. My memory has an egocentric representational scheme, centered on the person who originally had the experience from which the memory is derived. That person's standpoint lies at a spatio-temporal distance from the present standpoint that I occupy while entertaining the memory. But the mind is not especially scrupulous about the distinction between the subjects occupying these distinct points-of-view.

Consider, for example, my memory of blowing out the candles on a particular birthday cake in 1957. This memory includes an experiential image of a cake and candles as seen by a five-year-old boy. Now, if I invite you to imagine that *you* are that birthday boy, then you will conjure up a similar image in your imagination. You might report this thought experiment by saying, "I've just imagined that I am the birthday boy at David Velleman's fifth birthday party." The first occurrence of the pronoun 'I' in this report would of course refer to you, whoever you are: let's say you're Jane Doe. But what about the second occurrence of 'I'? Have you imagined that you, Jane Doe, are the birthday boy? Surely, you haven't imagined a bizarre scenario in which the five-year-old David Velleman is somehow identical with a completely unrelated woman (as we are supposing) named Jane Doe. Rather, you have simply imagined *being* the five-year-old David Velleman, by imagining the birthday party as experienced by him.[11] You have formed an experiential image whose content might be summed up by the statement "I am the birthday boy" as uttered in the imagined scene by the five-year-old David Velleman—a statement in which 'I' would refer to him, the one experiencing the scene, rather than you, the one who has imagined it.[12] When you say, "I've imagined that I am the birthday boy," you should be interpreted as saying, "I've imagined an experience with the content 'I am the birthday boy'," or "I've imagined 'I am the birthday boy'," where the first occurrence of 'I' refers to you but the second refers to him.

What then of my experiential memory? When I say, "I remember that I was the birthday boy," I am making a report similar to yours. That is, I am reporting an experiential memory whose content would be expressed by the statement, "I am the birthday boy," as uttered in the remembered scene by the five-year-old who experienced it. But whereas you may be aware that you haven't imagined the birthday boy's being you, Jane Doe, I am strongly inclined to think that I have remembered his being me, the present subject of this memory.[13] I thereby conflate my remembering self with the self of the experience remembered. When I say "I remember that I was the birthday boy," I take myself to be referring twice to my present self. I who remember the experience and the "I" of the experience thus become superimposed, so that a single self appears to be present in both.

The selves superimposed in this appearance are two momentary subjects: I in my present capacity as the subject of memory, existing just in the moment of remembering; and the "I" of the remembered experience, who existed just in the moment of the experience. In either case, I am conceived as wholly present at a single point in time, either as me-here-and-now, entertaining the memory, or as "me"-there-and-then, having the experience. Superimposing one of these momentary subjects on the other yields the illusion that they are numerically identical—that the subject whose existence was complete in the moment of the experience remembered was one and the same as the subject whose existence is complete in the moment of remembering. This appearance is already incoherent if one and the same thing cannot have its existence confined to each of two different moments. The incoherence is compounded by the thought that this momentary subject has persisted through the interval between the original experience and the memory, existing in its entirety at each intervening moment.[14]

The same effect is produced by experiential anticipation, in which I prefigure a future experience from the perspective that I expect to occupy in it. A single self appears to have its full existence both now and later, because I who anticipate the experience and the "I" of the anticipated experience become superimposed.

For a spatial analog of the resulting idea, think of the scene in which Woody Allen plays a spermatozoon about to be launched from the loins of . . . Woody Allen.[15] In reality, of course, a person occupies different points in space with different parts, none of which is identical to any other part or to the person as a whole. We might say, then, that a person *pervades* space. In this scene, however, Woody Allen occupies different points in space with a smaller self that plays the role of each spatial part of his own body. We might say, then, that he *invades* space rather than pervading it. Incoherent, to say the least. Yet experiential memory leads me to think that my own temporal extension is composed of a single momentary self playing the role of each temporal part of my existence.

I am tempted to say that all of my temporal parts are present at a single point in time because I tend to think of myself as my present self—a momentary subject whose existence is indeed complete in the here-and-now. I am tempted to say that I nevertheless persist through time because I tend to think of this self, complete in the moment, as nevertheless existing at other moments. And because I therefore conceive of each moment in my temporal extension as containing my complete self, I am tempted to deny that it contains a mere temporal part of me. There I am, all of me, at my fifth birthday party; here I am, all of me, remembering that party; there I will be, all of me, on my seventy-fifth birthday—as if one and the same momentary subject can play the several parts of my five-year-old, 53-year-old, and 75-year-old selves. I think of myself as all of me, all the time, just as Woody Allen is all Woody Allen in every one of his cells.

. . . .

What would be the consequences of truly shedding our sense of being enduring objects and learning to conceive of ourselves as perduring instead? I want to suggest that the existence of an enduring self, if it is indeed an illusion, is one of two illusions that go hand-in-hand. A consequence of shedding the one illusion would be to shed the other as well. The other illusion of which I speak has to do with the nature of time.

The concept of perdurance for objects is most at home in a conception of time known as **eternalism**. According to eternalists, all of the temporal facts can be expressed in terms of the temporal relations between events. One event can occur earlier or later than another, and it can be closer to or further from the other in time. The relations among events as earlier or later than one another, and closer or further from one another, exhaust the temporal facts, in the eyes of eternalists: there is no more to time than these relations.

The philosopher J. Ellis MacTaggart argued that the temporal relations among events are not sufficient to satisfy our concept of time, although he also argued that the concept is incoherent.[16] Temporal relations among events do not change, and so MacTaggart argued that they cannot account for the passage of time—that is, for the way events draw nearer from the future, until they occur in the present and, having occurred, recede into the past. When we say that a future event is always drawing closer and closer, eternalists must understand us as meaning only that the event is nearer to our second utterance of the word 'closer' than it was to the first. And these temporal relations are as they always were and always will be; or, rather, they exist timelessly, constituting time itself. The future event that we describe as drawing closer and closer not only stands closer to the last word of our description than it does to the earlier words; it always has and always will stand in those relations, or it stands in them timelessly. Such unchanging relations cannot constitute time, MacTaggart argued, because time requires change—specifically, the change that consists in an event's approaching from the future, arriving in the present, and receding into the past.

Yet the change thus required by our concept of time struck MacTaggart as paradoxical and hence impossible. An event's changing from future to present to past must unfold *in time*: the event must be first in the future, then in the present, and then again in the past. And when we add these temporal indices to our description of the change, we revert to an eternalist idiom. We end up saying that the event is later than one time ("first"), simultaneous with another ("then"), and earlier than yet a third ("then again")—temporal relations in which the event stands timelessly, without change. The event is timelessly later than the one time, simultaneous with the second, and earlier than the third; and so its transit from future to past appears to be no more than a set of temporal relations that it occupies statically. In order to complete our description of how time passes, we have been forced to describe it once again in terms that seem to make it stand still.

There is a temptation to say, at this point, that what moves is not the future or past but the present, or rather the property of being the present, which belongs successively to different sets of events. But if we try to describe how the property of being present passes from one set of events to the next, we will end up saying that it belongs first to one set, then to another, and then again to a third, as they occur in succession. We will thereupon have said no more than this: that at the time of some events ("first") the property of being present belongs to those events; at the time of subsequent events ("then"), it belongs to that subsequent set of events; and at the time of yet a third set of events ("then again"), it belongs to that third set. In sum, we will have said merely that the property of being present belongs to each set of events at the time of its occurrence, a statement that is timelessly true of all events. So in what sense can the present be said to move? There are simply later and later sets of events, each present when it occurs, and each at a different but fixed distance from events in the future or past.

. . . .

One fairly desperate attempt to solve the problem is a theory known as **presentism**. According to presentism, only the present exists; past and future are merely tenses modifying facts about the present.[17]

Presentism is best explained by an analogy between time and modality. Consider the fact that John Kerry might have won the 2004 presidential election. We could restate this fact by saying that a Kerry victory occurs in a merely possible history, alternative to the one that actually unfolded in 2004; but we wouldn't be speaking with metaphysical strictness. Strictly speaking, we should acknowledge only one event—Kerry's loss, which actually occurred—plus the subjunctively stable fact, also true of actuality, that Kerry might have won instead. There is no Kerry victory that occurs in a realm of mere possibility.[18] This view about modality is called actualism, since it says that actual events are the only events there are.

Presentism goes one step further, refusing to acknowledge even an event of Kerry's losing the election. For when we describe Kerry's loss as occurring in the past, the presentist claims that we are speaking just as loosely as we would in describing his victory as occurring in some alternative possible history. The only events there are, according to the presentist, are the ones occurring now in actuality. Just as Kerry's possibly having won is a fact about actuality, stable in the subjunctive, so his previously having lost is a fact about the present, stable in the past tense. That he might have won, and that he did lose, are subjunctive and past-tense facts about the actual present, which is all there is for facts to be about. There is no Kerry victory occurring in a realm of possibility; and there is not even a Kerry loss occurring in a realm of the past.

The presentist claims that his view enables us to represent the passage of time. The occurrence of an event entails the fact that it will have occurred, and hence that it will later be a matter of past-tense fact. (More precisely, the event's occurrence entails the future-tense fact that there will be a past-tense fact of its having occurred.) This entailment is said to represent the passage of the event from the present into the past. The occurrence of an event is also incompatible with the fact that it wasn't going to occur, and compatible with the fact that it was going to occur. Hence its present occurrence entails that it was previously a subject of future-tense facts, an entailment that is said to represent its passage from the future into the present. Finally, the occurrence of an event is compatible with its being the case neither that the event was going to occur nor that it wasn't going to, while nevertheless entailing that the event definitely will have occurred. That is, while there previously may have been no fact of the matter whether the event would occur, there will later be a determinate fact of its having occurred—a constellation of facts that is said to represent how an open future gets closed up into a fixed past.[19]

The presentist also claims that his view enables us to solve our problem about the concept of endurance. Just as there is no John Kerry existing in an alternative possible history in which he won the election, according to presentism, so there is no John Kerry existing in a past in which he lost: all there is of John Kerry is the present John Kerry. This person has the past-tense properties of having existed in 2004 and having lost the election of that year, just as he has the subjunctive property that he might have won; but the presentist insists that these properties belong to Kerry's actual present self, which is all of him that exists. Hence the presentist can deny that

John Kerry perdures, by denying that he has any temporal parts. According to presentism, Kerry's existence is confined to the present.

One drawback of presentism is that it requires the present to bear sufficient features to render true not only present-tense facts but all past-tense facts as well: the present must, as it were, bear witness to all of history.[20] A more serious problem, for my purposes, is that presentism doesn't really solve the problems of endurance and the passage of time. What presentism describes is—not a changing prospect in which events approach from the future, arrive in the present, and recede into the past—but a single, static structure of past-prospective and future-perfect facts, all true of the present. Tensed facts about the present entail other tensed facts about the present, but nothing moves. Similarly, presentism describes objects as being wholly present at every moment of their existence, but only because it describes them as existing at only one moment, the present; and so it describes them as enduring in only a trivial sense. According to presentism, objects have past- and future-tensed properties, but the objects themselves exist only in the present, and so they don't persist at all, much less endure.

. . . .

Surely, we should hope for a more intuitively satisfying solution to the problems of endurance and temporal passage. I think that the solution is to recognize that both phenomena are illusions, and that these illusions are interdependent. I have already suggested how the illusion of an enduring self might arise from the structure of first-personal memory and anticipation. I will now suggest that the illusion of an enduring self gives rise to another illusion, of movement with respect to time.

Our difficulty in characterizing such movement was that, when we tried to identify something toward which a future event draws nearer or from which a past event recedes, we focused our attention on other events. Yet each event depends for its identity on when it occurs: it could not be closer to a future event, or further from a past event, without occupying a different temporal position and hence being a different event. This conception of the problem suggests the solution. Whatever the future draws nearer to, or the past recedes from, must be something that can exist at different positions in time with its identity intact. And we have already found such a thing—or the illusion of one, at least—in the form of the enduring self.

Suppose that I endure in the admittedly incoherent sense that is suggested by experiential memory and anticipation. In that case, I exist in my entirety at successive moments in time, thereby moving in my entirety with respect to events. As I move through time, future events draw nearer to me and past events recede. Time truly passes, in the sense that it passes *me*.

If I merely perdure, however, then I do not move with respect to time. I extend through time with newer and newer temporal parts, but all of my parts remain stationary. A perduring self can be compared to a process, such as the performance of a symphony. The performance doesn't move with respect to time; it merely extends newer and newer temporal parts to fill each successive moment. The last note of the performance is of course closer to midnight than the first, but we wouldn't say that midnight and the performance move closer together. Midnight is separated from the performance by a timelessly fixed but extremely vague interval, which can be made precise only with respect to particular parts of the performance—the first note, the second note, the third note—each of which is separated from midnight by an interval that is also timelessly fixed. Similarly, we wouldn't say that the ceiling and I get closer together from my feet to my head. The ceiling stands above me at a fixed but vague distance, which can be made precise only with respect to particular parts of me—feet, waist, head—each of which is separated from it by a fixed distance.

But if I am an enduring thing, then midnight and I get closer together, and not just in the sense that I extend temporal parts closer to it than my earlier parts. I don't just extend from a 9:00 pm stage to a 10:00 pm stage that is closer to midnight, as I extend from my feet to a head that is closer to the ceiling; I exist in my entirety within the stroke of 9:00, and I exist again within the stroke of 10:00—the selfsame entity twice, existing once further from midnight and then all over again, closer. Midnight occupies two different distances from my fully constituted

self. From my perspective, then, midnight draws nearer.

If this enduring "me" is an illusion, however, then so is the passage of time. And ceasing to think of myself as an enduring subject should result in my ceasing to experience the passage of time. Coming to think of myself as perduring should result in my coming to experience different temporal parts of myself at different moments, but no enduring self past which those moments can flow.

Suppose that I could learn to experience my successive moments of consciousness—*now* and *now* and *now*—as successive notes in a performance with no enduring listener, no self-identical subject for whom these moments would be *now* and *then* and *then again*. In remembering a scene that I experienced in the past, I would distinguish between the "I" who remembers it and the "I" who experienced it; in anticipating a scene that I would experience in the future, I would distinguish between the anticipating "I" and the experiencing "I" as well. Hence my present self would be cognizant of being distinct from the past subjects from whom it receives memories and the future subjects for whom it stores up anticipations. It would therefore have no conception of a single subject to which events could bear different relations over time, nothing to which they could draw near or from which they could recede. It would think of itself, and each of the subjects with whom it communicates by memory and anticipation, as seeing its own present moment, with none of them seeing a succession of moments as present.

The result would be that time would no longer seem to pass, because my experience would no longer include a subject of its passage—just successive momentary subjects, each timelessly entrenched in its own temporal perspective. I would think of myself as filling time rather than passing through it or having it pass me by—as existing in time the way a rooted plant exists in space, growing extensions to occupy it without moving in relation to it. Having shed the illusion of an enduring self, I would have lost any sense of time as passing at all.

One small bit of evidence in support of this speculation is that when I lose awareness of myself, by "losing myself" in engrossing activities, I also tend to lose awareness of time's passing.[21] With my attention fully devoted to playing a sport, reading a book, writing a paragraph, I am drawn out of myself and, as it seems, out of the passage of time as well. Conversely, when I have nothing to occupy my attention—that is, when I am bored—my attention returns to myself, and the passage of time becomes painfully salient. Self-awareness and time-awareness thus seem to go hand-in-hand.

Clearly, I am nowhere near to "losing myself" in this way on a lasting basis, despite being convinced, by the arguments of Locke and Parfit, that I am in fact a perduring rather than an enduring self. Truly assimilating the implications of those arguments would entail radical changes in my experience, changes of the sort that no argument can produce. No wonder the Buddhists believe that dispelling the illusion of an enduring self requires an arduous regimen of meditation.

....

As we have seen, Parfit blames our belief in an enduring self for emotions that might well be the essence of our existential suffering: grief over time past and anxiety at the prospect of death. Yet Parfit suggests that these emotions get their sting from our proprietary interest in our one and only life—that glass tunnel in which we imagine ourselves to be enclosed, when we believe that we have enduring selves. Parfit claims to derive consolation from shedding this belief because he no longer views his relation to the person lost in the past, or to the person who will die in the future, as a relation of identity. The consolation comes when he escapes from seeming imprisoned in an enduring self.

Yet I don't see why bearing a less robust relation to his own past and future is any consolation to Parfit. Why should a sense of partial alienation from past and future selves leave him feeling relieved rather than bereft? It's not as if he has come to realize that this isn't his "only life"; he has merely come to realize that it isn't even *his* in the sense that he previously thought. This realization provides only the cold comfort of having nothing to lose.

When Parfit describes the drawbacks of believing in an enduring self, he speaks not only about the loneliness of proprietorship in a single life—being imprisoned in a glass tunnel—but also about the emotions attendant upon time's passage. He complains of the sense that he is "moving faster and faster" through the tunnel, toward the "darkness" at its end, and of the sense that "so much of one's *only* life should have gone by." Surely, the remedy for these anxieties and regrets is not to get out of the tunnel and live "in the open air"; the remedy is to *stop moving*.

The remedy for Parfit's distress, in other words, is to become an eternalist. Consider:

> [W]hen a person dies he only appears to die. He is still very much alive in the past, so it is very silly for people to cry at his funeral. All moments, past, present, and future, always have existed, always will exist. . . . It is just an illusion . . . that one moment follows another one, like beads on a string, and that once a moment is gone it is gone forever.[22]

The speaker here is Billy Pilgrim, relating what he learned on the planet Tralfamadore, where he was once on display as an intergalactic zoological specimen:

> When a Tralfamadorian sees a corpse, all he thinks is that the dead person is in bad condition in that particular moment, but that the same person is just fine in plenty of other moments. Now, when I myself hear that somebody is dead, I simply shrug and say what the Tralfamadorians say about dead people, which is 'So it goes.'

The Tralfamadorians are eternalists about time, and they have managed to derive great comfort from this philosophy.

Note, however, that whereas Parfit has overcome the illusion of an enduring self but not the illusion of time's passing, the Tralfamadorians have done the reverse: they have overcome the illusion of time's passing, but they still speak as if they believe in an enduring self.[23] This incomplete disillusionment is just as unsatisfactory, to my way of thinking, as Parfit's. Parfit and the Tralfamadorians have divided between them what is a larger truth: the enduring self and the passage of time are interdependent illusions. The Tralfamadorian half of the truth is more consoling than Parfit's, to my mind;

but taken by itself, the Tralfamadorian half of the truth is unstable.

The Tralfamadorians speak as if they occupy moments in time with their entire selves, not just temporal parts. Regarding themselves as enduring objects, they manage to deny that time flows only by asserting that they can stand outside of time and range across it at will:

> The Tralfamadorians can look at the different moments just the way we can look at a stretch of the Rocky Mountains, for instance. They can see how permanent all the moments are, and they can look at any moment that interests them.

Billy Pilgrim never fully attains the Tralfamadorian view of time, but he does lose the normal human view:

> Billy Pilgrim has come unstuck in time.
>
> Billy has gone to sleep a senile widower and awakened on his wedding day. He has walked through a door in 1955 and come out another one in 1941. He has seen his birth and death many times, he says, and pays random visits to all the events in between.
>
> He says.
>
> Billy is spastic in time, has no control over where he is going next, and the trips aren't necessarily fun. He is in a constant state of stage fright, he says, because he never knows what part of his life he is going to have to act in next.[24]

How do the Tralfamadorians manage to visit different moments in time, betaking their complete selves from one moment to another? This process would require a higher temporal order of "first" and "later" within which the desultory visits could occur, and across which the Tralfamadorians would retain their identities. A Tralfamadorian's visits to random moments in ordinary time would themselves have to occur at well-ordered moments in a meta-time, which would constitute a temporal stream washing over the Tralfamadorians as relentlessly as ordinary time washes over us. Similarly, Billy Pilgrim is washed by a stream of meta-moments ordering his visits to random moments of ordinary time.

In short, "coming unstuck in time" is not as easy as it sounds. Billy Pilgrim may jump around in one temporal order, but he moves through another in sequence. Escaping the passage of time would require the dissolution of his enduring self. In order to come completely unstuck in time, Billy himself would have to come unglued.

. . . .

Although the tale of Billy Pilgrim gives a partial and imperfect portrait of life without the illusion of temporal passage, it seems correct in portraying that life as lacking many of our ordinary worries about mortality. Even so, not all such worries would disappear along with the passage of time.

Billy describes the Tralfamadorians as unconcerned about *being dead*. But of course Epicurus long ago taught us that being dead is nothing—literally—and hence that it is nothing to worry about. The anxiety that makes sense, at least for those of us who live with temporal passage, is anxiety about the inexorable approach of death, about time's *running out*. This anxiety would be allayed if time no longer seemed to pass. And once time no longer seemed to pass, the mere fact of our mortality would no longer seem regrettable. When time seems to be running out, we wish for immortality, which would amount to having infinite time left on the clock. But in an eternalist world, immortality would amount instead to a kind of temporal ubiquity—existing at every future moment. Having an infinite amount of time left seems desirable if time is running out; but if time is standing still, then filling an infinite amount of it might well seem unattractive.

Still, those of us who die young could continue to lament the truncated extent of our lives: having too short a life would still be grounds for unhappiness. What would be groundless is unhappiness about mortality itself—the unhappiness that affects everyone, no matter how long-lived, at the sound of death's approaching tread.

Would liberation from the passage of time free us from other kinds of suffering? It certainly wouldn't spare us from physical pain or other unpleasant experiences. But it just might prevent pain and unpleasantness from being transformed into suffering.

We can undergo pain or unpleasantness without suffering under it: suffering is a particular way of experiencing pain or unpleasantness—specifically, of *not coping* with it. And I suspect, though I cannot argue here, that the way of not coping that's constitutive of suffering results from the perception of time as passing. What undoes us, when we suffer with pain, is panic at the thought that it will never abate, that no end is in sight. Patients can learn to bear pain by "accepting" or "being with" it, focusing on the pain of the moment, without thinking about what's next.[25] It's not the pain they're in that makes them suffer but the prospect of its endlessly going on.

Perhaps, then, liberation from the passage of time would entail liberation from suffering altogether, though not of course from pain. There would be bad moments and good moments, but no panic about the coming moments, and hence no suffering.

. . . .

The Tralfamadorians express the consolations of their perspective by saying, "So it goes." Come to think of it, though, the point of this motto is less than obvious. After all, the Tralfamadorians inhabit a perspective in which "it" doesn't "go" at all, since they do not experience time as passing. Why do they say "So it goes"? Why don't they say "So it is"?

Maybe the Tralfamadorian motto has been translated in a manner suitable to us, who simply cannot escape from the illusion of time's passing. "So it goes" means "so it goes *for you*." They are recommending the attitude that is appropriate for creatures who can't help but experience time as passing. Buddhism must offer similar advice, exported not from one planet to another but from the meditative state to the state of ordinary consciousness. What is the appropriate attitude to have in ordinary life, where the self unavoidably seems to endure and time unavoidably seems to pass, given that both appearances are illusions?

I think that the exportable lessons here must include something about the way we cope with the passage of time. We can't stop the self from seeming to endure, or stop time from seeming to pass, but we can cope with these phenomena better, given the knowledge that they are merely phenomenal.

Ordinarily I cope rather badly with temporal passage and personal endurance. I don't exactly live in a state of Pilgrim-esque stage fright, continually unsure when I might find myself at my fifth birthday party or my seventy-fifth. In some respects, I feel like a Tralfamadorian, because I can choose which parts of my life to visit, in memory and anticipation. Yet I have a disconcerting tendency to live different parts of my life all at once—to relive the past and pre-live the future even while I'm trying to live in the present. And even as I relive my past in a memory, it is at the same time slipping away from me, as there comes bearing down on me a future that I am pre-living in anticipation.

It's as if too many parts of my life are on the table at once, and yet somehow they are continually being served up and snatched away like dishes in a restaurant whose wait-staff is too impatient to let me eat. And this whole grief- and anxiety-provoking conception of my life has been adopted out of panic over the passage of time, which requires me to anticipate the future precisely because it's bearing down on me, and to remember the past precisely because it's slipping away.

Once I know that the self doesn't endure, and time doesn't pass, then even when under the illusion to the contrary, I can better follow the Buddhist injunction to be fully aware of the present moment. The realization that I am *of* the moment—that is, a momentary part of a temporally extended self—can remind me to be *in* the moment, which draws my attention away from time's passage, even if it doesn't succeed in stopping time from seeming to pass. Insofar as I can be in the moment, I can perhaps gain some respite from the grief and anxiety of that overwhelmed diner, on whom loaded plates are bearing down even as uneaten dishes are being borne away. Each moment can be devoted to savoring the dish of the moment.

NOTES

1. Maurice Merleau-Ponty, *Phenomenology of Perception*, trans. Colin Smith (London: Routledge and Kegan Paul, 1962), 411–12.
2. See Christine M. Korsgaard, *The Sources of Normativity*, ed. Onora O'Neill (Cambridge: Cambridge University Press, 1996); idem., "Self-Constitution:

Action, Identity, and Integrity," *The Locke Lectures*, 2002; Daniel Dennett, "The Origins of Selves," *Cogito* 3 (1989): 163–73; idem., "The Reality of Selves," in *Consciousness Explained* (Boston: Little, Brown and Company, 1991), 412–30; idem., "The Self as a Center of Narrative Gravity," in *Self and Consciousness: Multiple Perspectives*, eds. Frank S. Kessel, Pamela M. Cole, and Dale L. Johnson (Hillsdale, NJ: Erlbaum Associates, 1992), 103–115.

3. One might think that Parfit's arguments militate not just against the self's endurance but also against its persistence in any sense, including perdurance. (For the difference between endurance and perdurance, see below.) But as David Lewis showed, Parfit's arguments do not necessarily militate against perduring selves. (See Lewis, "Survival and Identity," in *The Identities of Persons*, ed. A. Rorty [Berkeley: University of California Press, 1976], 17–40, reprinted in *Philosophical Papers*, vol. 1 [Oxford: Oxford University Press, 1983], 55–77.)

4. Derek Parfit, *Reasons and Persons* (Oxford: Oxford University Press, 1984), 280.

5. Parfit, "Personal Identity," *The Philosophical Review* 80 (1971): 27.

6. See Parfit, *Reasons and Persons*, 273, 280, 502–03.

7. See esp. Parfit, *Reasons and Persons*, 280.

8. See Sally Haslanger, "Persistence Through Time," in *The Oxford Handbook of Metaphysics*, ed. Michael J. Loux and Dean W. Zimmerman (Oxford: Oxford University Press, 2003), 315–54.

9. The following objections to the traditional conception of endurance are developed more fully in Thomas Hofweber and J. David Velleman, "How to Endure" (MS). These objections would not apply under the theory of time known as presentism. I discuss presentism briefly later.

10. This paragraph and the four that follow summarize a lengthy argument presented in my "Self to Self," *The Philosophical Review* 105 (1996): 39–76, reprinted in my *Self to Self: Selected Essays* (New York: Cambridge University Press, 2006), 170–202.

11. This point was made by Bernard Williams in "The Imagination and the Self," in *Problems of the Self* (Cambridge: Cambridge University Press, 1973), 26–45. I discuss Williams's paper in "Self to Self."

12. The second 'I' functions as what Hector-Neri Castañeda called a quasi-indicator—a pronoun in indirect discourse that takes the place of what was a first-personal pronoun in direct discourse. For an explanation of quasi-indicators (clearer than Castañeda's) see John Perry, "Belief and Acceptance," in *The Problem of the Essential Indexical and Other Essays* (New York: Oxford University Press, 1993), 53–67.

13. But isn't it a contingent truth-condition of my memory that the remembered experience has been undergone by me rather than someone else? And if so, how can the second 'I' in "I remember that I was the birthday boy" refer merely to the subject of the remembered experience, who necessarily did undergo it, if anyone did? The answer is that the memory refers to the subject of the remembered experience indexically, pointing to him at the perspectival point of origin in the remembered experience, by pointing to him at the corresponding point in my memory-image, which purports to be a copy derived from that experience. If the image is indeed a copy derived from an experience, as it purports to be, then indexical reference to the "me" of that experience succeeds, and his being the birthday boy is what I veridically remember; if the image is not copied from an experience, then its indexical reference to the "me" of that experience fails—it refers to no one at all—and the memory is illusory. In order for the memory to be veridical, then, the remembered experience must have been undergone by me in the sense that its subject must be accessible to indexical reference as "me."

Of course, your image of being my five-year-old self also refers to the birthday boy as "me", but not in the same, genuinely indexical way. In conjuring up this image, you had to stipulate that its point of origin is occupied by the five-year-old David Velleman, thus referring to him by name before you could go on to think of him as "me". In remembering the experience, I can refer to him as "me" directly, without any stipulation about whom the pronoun refers to, relying on the causal history of my image to secure my reference to the original subject. That is the sense in which I have first-personal access to him whereas you do not. (For further discussion of this issue, see "Self to Self.")

14. I find indirect evidence for these claims about autobiographical memory in the experience of reading truly gifted autobiographical novelists, such as Laura Ingalls Wilder (*The Little House on the Prairie*) or Elspeth Huxley (*The Flame Trees of Thika*). These authors were able to depict past experience as it was registered by the childish minds of their

younger selves. Reading their work, I am struck by the contrast with my own childhood memories, in which the psychological distance between the mind that stored a memory and the mind that retrieves it is foreshortened, so that past experience seems to have been registered by my current, adult consciousness—the remembering 'I', who has been superimposed on the 'I' remembered.

15. In *Everything You Always Wanted to Know About Sex* But Were Afraid to Ask*, dir. Woody Allen, Rollins-Joffe Productions, United Artists, 1972.

16. J. Ellis MacTaggart, "The Unreality of Time," *Mind* 68 (1908): 457–74.

17. In the following paragraphs I have drawn on John Bigelow, "The Passage of Time" (MS).

18. So-called modal realists, such as David Lewis, believe that there are events and things inhabiting such a realm, but the intuitions of most philosophers run to the contrary.

19. That there was previously no fact of the matter whether the event would occur, and that there will later be a determinate fact of its having occurred, are of course past- and future-tense facts about the present, according to presentism. The same goes for all of the entailments discussed in this paragraph.

20. For this objection, see Simon Keller, "Presentism and Truthmaking," in *Oxford Studies in Metaphysics*, vol. 1, ed. Dean W. Zimmerman (Oxford: Clarendon Press, 2004), 83–104 (cited by Bigelow).

21. See Mihaly Csikszentmihalyi, *Flow: The Psychology of Optimal Experience* (New York: Harper and Row, 1990). According to Csikszentmihalyi, losing awareness of self and losing awareness of time are two of the characteristic features of "flow" experiences. I discuss these experiences further in "What Good is a Will?" in *Action in Context*, ed. Anton Leist and Holger Baumann (Berlin: Mouton de Gruyter, forthcoming); and "The Way of the Wanton" (MS).

22. Kurt Vonnegut, Jr., *Slaughterhouse Five; Or The Children's Crusade* (New York: Dell Publishing, 1969), 23.

23. But: "Tralfamadorians don't see human beings as two-legged creatures, either. They see them as great millepedes—'with babies' legs at one end and old people's legs at the other,' says Billy Pilgrim" (ibid., 75). This suggests that Tralfamadorians see people as perduring space-time worms rather than enduring objects. Nevertheless, their first-personal descriptions of their own experiences sound like those of an enduring self.

24. Ibid., p. 20.

25. Here I am merely gesturing at a large and controversial research program. For just one example, see Lance M. McCracken and Chris Eccleston, "Coping or Acceptance: What to do about Chronic Pain?" *Pain* 105 (2003): 197–204; Lance M. McCracken, James W. Carson, Christopher Eccleston, and Francis J. Keefe, "Acceptance and Change in the Context of Chronic Pain," *Pain* 109 (2004): 4–7. One of the methods discussed in the latter article is "Mindfulness-Based Stress Reduction," which is described as "moment-to-moment observation and acceptance of the continually changing reality of the present" (5). For some of the methodological problems in this area, see Chris Eccleston, "The Attentional Control of Pain: Methodological and Theoretical Concerns," *Pain* 63 (1995): 3–10.

REFERENCES

Bigelow, John. "The Passage of Time" (MS).

Csikszentmihalyi, Mihaly. *Flow: The Psychology of Optimal Experience*, New York: Harper and Row, 1990.

Dennett, Daniel. "The Origins of Selves." *Cogito* 3 (1989): 163–73.

———. "The Reality of Selves." In *Consciousness Explained*, 412–30. Boston: Little, Brown and Company, 1991.

———. "The Self as a Center of Narrative Gravity." In *Self and Consciousness: Multiple Perspectives*, eds. Frank S. Kessel, Pamela M. Cole, and Dale L. Johnson, 103–115. Hillsdale, NJ: Erlbaum Associates, 1992.

Eccleston, Chris. "The Attentional Control of Pain: Methodological and Theoretical Concerns." *Pain* 63 (1995): 3–10.

Everything You Always Wanted to Know About Sex* But Were Afraid to Ask. Directed by Woody Allen. Rollins-Joffe Productions, United Artists, 1972.

Haslanger, Sally. "Persistence Through Time." In *The Oxford Handbook of Metaphysics*, ed. Michael J. Loux and Dean W. Zimmerman, 315–54. Oxford: Oxford University Press, 2003.

Hofweber, Thomas and J. David Velleman. "How to Endure" (MS).

Keller, Simon. "Presentism and Truthmaking." In *Oxford Studies in Metaphysics*, vol. 1, ed. Dean W. Zimmerman, 83–104. Oxford: Clarendon Press, 2004.

Korsgaard, Christine M. "Self-Constitution: Action, Identity, and Integrity." *The Locke Lectures*, 2002.

———. *The Sources of Normativity*, ed. Onora O'Neill. Cambridge: Cambridge University Press, 1996.

Lewis, David. "Survival and Identity." In *The Identities of Persons*, ed. A. Rorty, 17–40. Berkeley: University of California Press, 1976. Reprinted in *Philosophical Papers*, vol. 1, 55–77. Oxford: Oxford University Press, 1983.

McCracken, Lance M., James W. Carson, Christopher Eccleston, and Francis J. Keefe. "Acceptance and Change in the Context of Chronic Pain." *Pain* 109 (2004): 4–7.

McCracken, Lance M., and Chris Eccleston. "Coping or Acceptance: What to do about Chronic Pain?" *Pain* 105 (2003): 197–204.

MacTaggart, J. Ellis. "The Unreality of Time." *Mind* 68 (1908): 457–74.

Merleau-Ponty, Maurice. *Phenomenology of Perception*, trans. Colin Smith. London: Routledge and Kegan Paul, 1962.

Parfit, Derek. "Personal Identity." *The Philosophical Review* 80 (1971): 3–27.

———. *Reasons and Persons*. Oxford: Oxford University Press, 1984.

Perry, John. "Belief and Acceptance." In *The Problem of the Essential Indexical and Other Essays*, 53–67. New York: Oxford University Press, 1993.

Velleman, J. David. "Self to Self." *The Philosophical Review* 105 (1996): 39–76. Reprinted in *Self to Self: Selected Essays*, 170–202. New York: Cambridge University Press, 2006.

———. "The Way of the Wanton" (MS).

———. "What Good is a Will?" In *Action in Context*, ed. Anton Leist and Holger Baumann. Berlin: Mouton de Gruyter, forthcoming.

Vonnegut, Jr., Kurt. *Slaughterhouse Five; Or The Children's Crusade*. New York: Dell Publishing, 1969.

Williams, Bernard. "The Imagination and the Self." In *Problems of the Self*, 26–45. Cambridge: Cambridge University Press, 1973.

KEY TERMS

Analytic philosophy
Egoism
Perdure
Endure
Eternalism
Presentism

STUDY QUESTIONS

1. Velleman thinks that when he makes a statement like "I've just imagined that I am the birthday boy at Velleman's fifth birthday party," he is making a mistake that leads him to believe he is an enduring self. In your own words, what is this mistake and how does it lead to the belief in question?

2. In your own words, what is presentism? What objections does Velleman raise against the view?

3. Why does Velleman think that adopting perdurance would lead to a rejection of the view that time passes?

4. What is Velleman's argument for the claim that the Tralfamadorians cannot in fact become "unstuck in time"?

5. Why does Velleman think that if we reject the view that time passes, this would alleviate suffering?

Where Am I?

DANIEL DENNETT

. .

Now that I've won my suit under the Freedom of Information Act, I am at liberty to reveal for the first time a curious episode in my life that may be of interest not only to those engaged in research in the philosophy of mind, artificial intelligence and neuroscience but also to the general public.

Several years ago I was approached by Pentagon officials who asked me to volunteer for a highly dangerous and secret mission. In collaboration with

NASA and Howard Hughes, the Department of Defense was spending billions to develop a Supersonic Tunneling Underground Device, or STUD. It was supposed to tunnel through the earth's core at great speed and deliver a specially designed atomic warhead "right up the Red's missile silos," as one of the Pentagon brass put it.

The problem was that in an early test they had succeeded in lodging a warhead about a mile deep under Tulsa, Oklahoma, and they wanted me to retrieve it for them. "Why me?" I asked. Well, the mission involved some pioneering applications of current brain research, and they had heard of my interest in brains and of course my Faustian curiosity and great courage and so forth. . . . Well, how could I refuse? The difficulty that brought the Pentagon to my door was that the device I'd been asked to recover was fiercely radioactive, in a new way. According to monitoring instruments, something about the nature of the device and its complex interactions with pockets of material deep in the earth had produced radiation that could cause severe abnormalities in certain tissues of the brain. No way had been found to shield the brain from these deadly rays, which were apparently harmless to other tissues and organs of the body. So it had been decided that the person sent to recover the device should *leave his brain behind*. It would be kept in a safe place where it could execute its normal control functions by elaborate radio links. Would I submit to a surgical procedure that would completely remove my brain, which would then be placed in a life-support system at the Manned Spacecraft Center in Houston? Each input and output pathway, as it was severed, would be restored by a pair of microminiaturized radio transceivers, one attached precisely to the brain, the other to the nerve stumps in the empty cranium. No information would be lost, all the connectivity would be preserved. At first I was a bit reluctant. Would it really work? The Houston brain surgeons encouraged me. "Think of it," they said, "as a mere *stretching* of the nerves. If your brain were just moved over an *inch* in

your skull, that would not alter or impair your mind. We're simply going to make the nerves indefinitely elastic by splicing radio links into them."

I was shown around the life-support lab in Houston and saw the sparkling new vat in which my brain would be placed, were I to agree. I met the large and brilliant support team of neurologists, hematologists, biophysicists, and electrical engineers, and after several days of discussions and demonstrations, I agreed to give it a try. I was subjected to an enormous array of blood tests, brain scans, experiments, interviews, and the like. They took down my autobiography at great length, recorded tedious lists of my beliefs, hopes, fears, and tastes. They even listed my favorite stereo recordings and gave me a crash session of psychoanalysis.

The day for surgery arrived at last and of course I was anesthetized and remember nothing of the operation itself. When I came out of anesthesia, I opened my eyes, looked around, and asked the inevitable, the traditional, the lamentably hackneyed post-operative question: "Where am I?" The nurse smiled down at me. "You're in Houston," she said, and I reflected that this still had a good chance of being the truth one way or another. She handed me a mirror. Sure enough, there were the tiny antennae poking up through their titanium ports cemented into my skull.

"I gather the operation was a success," I said, "I want to go see my brain." They led me (I was a bit dizzy and unsteady) down a long corridor and into the life-support lab. A cheer went up from the assembled support team, and I responded with what I hoped was a jaunty salute. Still feeling lightheaded, I was helped over to the life-support vat. I peered through the glass. There, floating in what looked like ginger-ale, was undeniably a human brain, though it was almost covered with printed circuit chips, plastic tubules, electrodes, and other paraphernalia. "Is that mine?" I asked. "Hit the output transmitter switch there on the side of the vat and see for yourself," the project director replied. I moved the switch to OFF, and immediately slumped, groggy and nauseated, into the arms of the technicians, one of whom kindly restored the switch to its ON position. While I recovered my equilibrium and composure, I thought to myself: "Well, here I am, sitting on a folding chair, staring through a piece of plate glass at my own brain. . . . But wait," I said to myself, "shouldn't I have thought, 'Here I am, suspended in a bubbling fluid, being stared at by my own eyes'?" I tried to think this latter thought. I tried to project it into the tank, offering it hopefully to my brain, but I failed to carry off the exercise with any conviction. I tried again. "Here am *I*, Daniel Dennett, suspended in a bubbling fluid, being stared at by my own eyes." No, it just didn't work. Most puzzling and confusing. Being a philosopher of firm **physicalist** conviction, I believed unswervingly that the tokening of my thoughts was occurring somewhere in my brain: yet, when I thought "Here I am," where the thought occurred to me was *here*, outside the vat, where I, Dennett, was standing staring at my brain.

I tried and tried to think myself into the vat, but to no avail. I tried to build up to the task by doing mental exercises. I thought to myself, "The sun is shining *over there*," five times in rapid succession, each time mentally ostending a different place: in order, the sun-lit corner of the lab, the visible front lawn of the hospital, Houston, Mars, and Jupiter. I found I had little difficulty in getting my "there's" to hop all over the celestial map with their proper references. I could loft a "there" in an instant through the farthest reaches of space, and then aim the next "there" with pinpoint accuracy at the upper left quadrant of a freckle on my arm. Why was I having such trouble with "here"? "Here in Houston" worked well enough, and so did "here in the lab," and even "here in this part of the lab," but "here in the vat" always seemed merely an unmeant mental mouthing. I tried closing my eyes while thinking it. This seemed to help, but still I couldn't manage to pull it off, except perhaps for a fleeting instant. I couldn't be sure. The discovery that I couldn't be sure was also unsettling. How did I know *where* I meant by "here" when I thought "here"? Could I *think* I meant one place when in fact I meant another? I didn't see how that could be admitted without untying the few bonds of intimacy between a person and his own mental life that had survived the onslaught of the brain scientists and philosophers, the physicalists and **behaviorists**. Perhaps I was incorrigible about where I *meant* when I said "here." But in my present circumstances it seemed that either I was doomed by sheer force of mental

habit to thinking systematically false indexical thoughts, or where a person is (and hence where his thoughts are tokened for purposes of semantic analysis) is not necessarily where his brain, the physical seat of his soul, resides. Nagged by confusion, I attempted to orient myself by falling back on a favorite philosopher's ploy. I began naming things.

"Yorick," I said aloud to my brain, "you are my brain. The rest of my body, seated in this chair, I dub 'Hamlet.'" So here we all are: Yorick's my brain, Hamlet's my body, and I am Dennett. *Now*, where am I? And when I think "where am I?" where's that thought tokened? Is it tokened in my brain, lounging about in the vat, or right here between my ears where it *seems* to be tokened? Or nowhere? Its *temporal* coordinates give me no trouble; must it not have spatial coordinates as well? I began making a list of the alternatives.

(1) *Where Hamlet goes, there goes Dennett.* This principle was easily refuted by appeal to the familiar brain transplant thought-experiments so enjoyed by philosophers. If Tom and Dick switch brains, Tom is the fellow with Dick's former body—just ask him; he'll claim to be Tom, and tell you the most intimate details of Tom's autobiography. It was clear enough, then, that my current body and I could part company, but not likely that I could be separated from my brain. The rule of thumb that emerged so plainly from the thought experiments was that in a brain-transplant operation, one wanted to be the *donor*, not the recipient. Better to call such an operation a *body*-transplant, in fact. So perhaps the truth was,

(2) *Where Yorick goes, there goes Dennett.* This was not at all appealing, however. How could I be in the vat and not about to go anywhere, when I was so obviously outside the vat looking in and beginning to make guilty plans to return to my room for a substantial lunch? This begged the question I realized, but it still seemed to be getting at something important. Casting about for some support for my intuition, I hit upon a legalistic sort of argument that might have appealed to Locke.

Suppose, I argued to myself, I were now to fly to California, rob a bank, and be apprehended. In which state would I be tried: In California, where the robbery took place, or in Texas, where the brains of the outfit were located? Would I be a California felon with an out-of-state brain, or a Texas felon remotely controlling an accomplice of sorts in California? It seemed possible that I might beat such a rap just on the undecidability of that jurisdictional question, though perhaps it would be deemed an interstate, and hence Federal, offense. In any event, suppose I were convicted. Was it likely that California would be satisfied to throw Hamlet into the brig, knowing that Yorick was living the good life and luxuriously taking the waters in Texas? Would Texas incarcerate Yorick, leaving Hamlet free to take the next boat to Rio? This alternative appealed to me. Barring capital punishment or other cruel and unusual punishment, the state would be obliged to maintain the life-support system for Yorick though they might move him from Houston to Leavenworth, and aside from the unpleasantness of the opprobrium, I, for one, would not mind at all and would consider myself a free man under those circumstances. If the state has an interest in forcibly relocating persons in institutions, it would fail to relocate me in any institution by locating Yorick there. If this were true, it suggested a third alternative.

(3) *Dennett is wherever he thinks he is.* Generalized, the claim was as follows: At any given time a person has a *point of view*, and the location of the point of view (which is determined internally by the content of the point of view) is also the location of the person.

Such a proposition is not without its perplexities, but to me it seemed a step in the right direction. The only trouble was that it seemed to place one in a heads-I-win/tails-you-lose situation of unlikely infallibility as regards location. Hadn't I myself often been wrong about where I was, and at least as often uncertain? Couldn't one get lost? Of course, but getting lost *geographically* is not the only way one might get lost. If one were lost in the woods one could attempt to reassure oneself with the consolation that at least one knew where one was: one was right *here* in the familiar surroundings of one's own body. Perhaps in this case one would not have drawn one's attention to much to be thankful for. Still, there were worse plights imaginable, and I wasn't sure I wasn't in such a plight right now.

Point of view clearly had something to do with personal location, but it was itself an unclear notion.

It was obvious that the content of one's point of view was not the same as or determined by the content of one's beliefs or thoughts. For example, what should we say about the point of view of the Cinerama viewer who shrieks and twists in his seat as the roller-coaster footage overcomes his psychic distancing? Has he forgotten that he is safely seated in the theater? Here I was inclined to say that the person is experiencing an illusory shift in point of view. In other cases, my inclination to call such shifts illusory was less strong. The workers in laboratories and plants who handle dangerous materials by operating feedback-controlled mechanical arms and hands undergo a shift in point of view that is crisper and more pronounced than anything Cinerama can provoke. They can feel the heft and slipperiness of the containers they manipulate with their metal fingers. They know perfectly well where they are and are not fooled into false beliefs by the experience, yet it is as if they were inside the isolation chamber they are peering into. With mental effort, they can manage to shift their point of view back and forth, rather like making a transparent Neckar cube or an Escher drawing change orientation before one's eyes. It does seem extravagant to suppose that in performing this bit of mental gymnastics, they are transporting *themselves* back and forth.

Still their example gave me hope. If I was in fact in the vat in spite of my intuitions, I might be able to train myself to adopt that point of view even as a matter of habit. I should dwell on images of myself comfortably floating in my vat, beaming volitions to that familiar body *out there*. I reflected that the ease or difficulty of this task was presumably independent of the truth about the location of one's brain. Had I been practicing before the operation, I might now be finding it second nature. You might now yourself try such a *tromp l'oeil*. Imagine you have written an inflammatory letter which has been published in the *Times*, the result of which is that the Government has chosen to impound your brain for a probationary period of three years in its Dangerous Brain Clinic in Bethesda, Maryland. Your body of course is allowed freedom to earn a salary and thus to continue its function of laying up income to be taxed. At this moment, however, your body is seated in an auditorium listening to a peculiar account by Daniel Dennett of his own similar experience. Try it. Think yourself to Bethesda, and then hark back longingly to your body, far away, and yet *seeming* so near. It is only with long-distance restraint (yours? the Government's?) that you can control your impulse to get those hands clapping in polite applause before navigating the old body to the rest room and a well-deserved glass of evening sherry in the lounge. The task of imagination is certainly difficult, but if you achieve your goal the results might be consoling.

Anyway, there I was in Houston, lost in thought as one might say, but not for long. My speculations were soon interrupted by the Houston doctors, who wished to test out my new prosthetic nervous system before sending me off on my hazardous mission. As I mentioned before, I was a bit dizzy at first, and not surprisingly, although I soon habituated myself to my new circumstances (which were, after all, well nigh indistinguishable from my old circumstances). My accommodation was not perfect, however, and to this day I continue to be plagued by minor coordination difficulties. The speed of light is fast, but finite, and as my brain and body move farther and farther apart, the delicate interaction of my feedback systems is thrown into disarray by the time lags. Just as one is rendered close to speechless by a delayed or echoic hearing of one's speaking voice so, for instance, I am virtually unable to track a moving object with my eyes whenever my brain and my body are more than a few miles apart. In most matters my impairment is scarcely detectable, though I can no longer hit a slow curve ball with the authority of yore. There are some compensations of course. Though liquor tastes as good as ever, and warms my gullet while corroding my liver, I can drink it in any quantity I please, without becoming the slightest bit inebriated, a curiosity some of my close friends may have noticed (though I occasionally have *feigned* inebriation, so as not to draw attention to my unusual circumstances). For similar reasons, I take aspirin orally for a sprained wrist, but if the pain persists I ask Houston to administer codeine to me *in vitro*. In times of illness the phone bill can be staggering.

But to return to my adventure. At length, both the doctors and I were satisfied that I was ready to undertake my subterranean mission. And so I left my brain in Houston and headed by helicopter for Tulsa.

Well, in any case, that's the way it seemed to me. That's how I would put it, just off the top of my head as it were. On the trip I reflected further about my earlier anxieties and decided that my first postoperative speculations had been tinged with panic. The matter was not nearly as strange or metaphysical as I had been supposing. Where was I? In two places, clearly: both inside the vat and outside it. Just as one can stand with one foot in Connecticut and the other in Rhode Island, I was in two places at once. I had become one of those scattered individuals we used to hear so much about. The more I considered this answer, the more obviously true it appeared. But, strange to say, the more true it appeared, the less important the question to which it could be the true answer seemed. A sad, but not unprecedented, fate for a philosophical question to suffer. This answer did not completely satisfy me, of course. There lingered some question to which I should have liked an answer, which was neither "Where are all my various and sundry parts?" nor "What is my current point of view?" Or at least there seemed to be such a question. For it did seem undeniable that in some sense *I* and not merely *most of me* was descending into the earth under Tulsa in search of an atomic warhead.

When I found the warhead, I was certainly glad I had left my brain behind, for the pointer on the specially built Geiger counter I had brought with me was off the dial. I called Houston on my ordinary radio and told the operation control center of my position and my progress. In return, they gave me instructions for dismantling the vehicle, based upon my on-site observations. I had set to work with my cutting torch when all of a sudden a terrible thing happened. I went stone deaf. At first I thought it was only my radio earphones that had broken, but when I tapped on my helmet, I heard nothing. Apparently the auditory transceivers had gone on the fritz. I could no longer hear Houston or my own voice, but I could speak, so I started telling them what had happened. In mid-sentence, I knew something else had gone wrong. My vocal apparatus had become paralyzed. Then my right hand went limp—another transceiver had gone. I was truly in deep trouble. But worse was to follow. After a few more minutes, I went blind. I cursed my luck, and then I cursed the scientists who had led me into this grave peril. There

I was, deaf, dumb, and blind, in a radioactive hole more than a mile under Tulsa. Then the last of my cerebral radio links broke, and suddenly I was faced with a new and even more shocking problem: whereas an instant before I had been buried alive in Oklahoma, now I was disembodied in Houston. My recognition of my new status was not immediate. It took me several very anxious minutes before it dawned on me that my poor body lay several hundred miles away, with heart pulsing and lungs respirating, but otherwise as dead as the body of any heart transplant donor, its skull packed with useless, broken electronic gear. The shift in perspective I had earlier found well nigh impossible now seemed quite natural. Though I could think myself back into my body in the tunnel under Tulsa, it took some effort to sustain the illusion. For surely it was an illusion to suppose I was still in Oklahoma: I had lost all contact with that body.

It occurred to me then, with one of those rushes of revelation of which we should be suspicious, that I had stumbled upon an impressive demonstration of the immateriality of the soul based upon physicalist principles and premises. For as the last radio signal between Tulsa and Houston died away, had I not changed location from Tulsa to Houston at the speed of light? And had I not accomplished this without any increase in mass? What moved from A to B at such speed was surely myself, or at any rate my soul or mind—the massless center of my being and home of my consciousness. *My point of view* had lagged somewhat behind, but I had already noted the indirect bearing of point of view on personal location. I could not see how a physicalist philosopher could quarrel with this except by taking the dire and counter-intuitive route of banishing all talk of persons. Yet the notion of personhood was so well entrenched in everyone's world view, or so it seemed to me, that any denial would be as curiously unconvincing, as systematically disingenuous, as the Cartesian negation, "non sum."[1]

The joy of philosophic discovery thus tided me over some very bad minutes or perhaps hours as the helplessness and hopelessness of my situation became more apparent to me. Waves of panic and even nausea swept over me, made all the more horrible by the absence of their normal body-dependent phenomenology. No adrenalin rush of tingles in the arms, no pounding heart, no premonitory salivation. I did feel a dread sinking feeling in my bowels at one point, and this tricked me momentarily into the false hope that I was undergoing a reversal of the process that landed me in this fix—a gradual un-disembodiment. But the isolation and uniqueness of that twinge soon convinced me that it was simply the first of a plague of phantom body hallucinations that I, like any other amputee, would be all too likely to suffer.

My mood then was chaotic. On the one hand, I was fired up with elation at my philosophic discovery and was wracking my brain (one of the few familiar things I could still do), trying to figure out how to communicate my discovery to the journals; while on the other, I was bitter, lonely, and filled with dread and uncertainty. Fortunately, this did not last long, for my technical support team sedated me into a dreamless sleep from which I awoke, hearing with magnificent fidelity the familiar opening strains of my favorite Brahms piano trio. So that was why they had wanted a list of my favorite recordings! It did not take me long to realize that I was hearing the music without ears. The output from the stereo stylus was being fed through some fancy rectification circuitry directly into my auditory nerve. I was mainlining Brahms, an unforgettable experience for any stereo buff. At the end of the record it did not surprise me to hear the reassuring voice of the project director speaking into a microphone that was now my prosthetic ear. He confirmed my analysis of what had gone wrong and assured me that steps were being taken to re-embody me. He did not elaborate, and after a few more recordings, I found myself drifting off to sleep. My sleep lasted, I later learned, for the better part of a year, and when I awoke, it was to find myself fully restored to my senses. When I looked into the mirror, though, I was a bit startled to see an unfamiliar face. Bearded and a bit heavier, bearing no doubt a family resemblance to my former face, and with the same look of spritely intelligence and resolute character, but definitely a new face. Further self-explorations of an intimate nature left me no doubt that this was a new body and the project director confirmed my conclusions. He did not volunteer any information on the past history of my new body and I decided (wisely, I think in retrospect) not to pry. As many philosophers unfamiliar with my ordeal have more recently speculated, the acquisition of a new body leaves one's *person* intact. And after a period of adjustment to a new voice, new muscular strengths and weaknesses, and so forth, one's *personality* is by and large also preserved. More dramatic changes in personality have been routinely observed in people who have undergone extensive plastic surgery, to say nothing of sex change operations, and I think no one contests the survival of the person in such cases. In any event I soon accommodated to my new body, to the point of being unable to recover any of its novelties to my consciousness or even memory. The view in the mirror soon became utterly familiar. That view, by the way, still revealed antennae, and so I was not surprised to learn that my brain had not been moved from its haven in the life-support lab.

I decided that good old Yorick deserved a visit. I and my new body, whom we might as well call Fortinbras, strode into the familiar lab to another round of applause from the technicians, who were of course congratulating themselves, not me. Once more I stood before the vat and contemplated poor Yorick, and on a whim I once again cavalierly flicked off the output transmitter switch. Imagine my surprise when nothing unusual happened. No fainting spell, no nausea, no noticeable change. A technician hurried to restore the switch to ON, but still I felt nothing. I demanded an explanation, which the project director hastened to provide. It seems that before they had even operated on the first occasion, they had constructed a computer duplicate of my brain, reproducing both the complete information processing structure and the computational speed of my brain in a giant computer program. After the operation, but before they had dared to send me off on my mission to Oklahoma, they had run this computer system and Yorick side by side. The incoming signals from Hamlet were sent simultaneously to Yorick's transceivers and to the computer's array of inputs. And the outputs from Yorick were not only beamed back to Hamlet, my body; they were recorded and checked against the simultaneous output of the computer program, which was called "Hubert" for reasons obscure to me. Over days and even weeks, the outputs were identical and synchronous, which of course did not

prove that they had succeeded in copying the brain's functional structure, but the empirical support was greatly encouraging.

Hubert's input, and hence activity, had been kept parallel with Yorick's during my disembodied days. And now, to demonstrate this, they had actually thrown the master switch that put Hubert for the first time in on-line control of my body—not Hamlet, of course, but Fortinbras. (Hamlet, I learned, had never been recovered from its underground tomb and could be assumed by this time to have largely returned to the dust. At the head of my grave still lay the magnificent bulk of the abandoned device, with the word STUD emblazoned on its side in large letters—a circumstance which may provide archeologists of the next century with a curious insight into the burial rites of their ancestors.)

The laboratory technicians now showed me the master switch, which had two positions, labeled *B*, for Brain (they didn't know my brain's name was Yorick) and *H*, for Hubert. The switch did indeed point to *H*, and they explained to me that if I wished, I could switch it back to *B*. With my heart in my mouth (and my brain in its vat), I did this. Nothing happened. A click, that was all. To test their claim, and with the master switch now set at *B*, I hit Yorick's output transmitter switch on the vat and sure enough, I began to faint. Once the output switch was turned back on and I had recovered my wits, so to speak, I continued to play with the master switch, flipping it back and forth. I found that with the exception of the transitional click, I could detect no trace of a difference. I could switch in mid-utterance, and the sentence I had begun speaking under the control of Yorick was finished without a pause or hitch of any kind under the control of Hubert. I had a spare brain, a prosthetic device which might some day stand me in very good stead, were some mishap to befall Yorick. Or alternatively, I could keep Yorick as a spare and use Hubert. It didn't seem to make any difference which I chose, for the wear and tear and fatigue on my body did not have any debilitating effect on either brain, whether or not it was actually causing the motions of my body, or merely spilling its output into thin air.

The one truly unsettling aspect of this new development was the prospect, which was not long in dawning on me, of someone detaching the spare—Hubert or Yorick, as the case might be—from Fortinbras and hitching it to yet another body—some Johnny-come-lately Rosencrantz or Guildenstern. Then (if not before) there would be *two* people, that much was clear. One would be me, and the other would be a sort of super-twin brother. If there were two bodies, one under the control of Hubert and the other being controlled by Yorick, then which would the world recognize as the true Dennett? And whatever the rest of the world decided, which one would be *me*? Would I be the Yorick-brained one, in virtue of Yorick's causal priority and former intimate relationship with the original Dennett body, Hamlet? That seemed a bit legalistic, a bit too redolent of the arbitrariness of consanguinity and legal possession, to be convincing at the metaphysical level. For, suppose that before the arrival of the second body on the scene, I had been keeping Yorick as the spare for years, and letting Hubert's output drive my body—that is, Fortinbras—all that time. The Hubert-Fortinbras couple would seem then by squatter's rights (to combat one legal intuition with another) to be the true Dennett and the lawful inheritor of everything that was Dennett's. This was an interesting question, certainly, but not nearly so pressing as another question that bothered me. My strongest intuition was that in such an eventuality *I* would survive so long as *either* brain-body couple remained intact, but I had mixed emotions about whether I should want both to survive.

I discussed my worries with the technicians and the project director. The prospect of two Dennetts was abhorrent to me, I explained, largely for social reasons. I didn't want to be my own rival for the affections of my wife, nor did I like the prospect of the two Dennetts sharing my modest professor's salary. Still more vertiginous and distasteful, though, was the idea of knowing *that much* about another person, while he had the very same goods on me. How could we ever face each other? My colleagues in the lab argued that I was ignoring the bright side of the matter. Weren't there many things I wanted to do but, being only one person, had been unable to do? Now one Dennett could stay at home and be the professor and family man, while the other could strike out on a life of travel and adventure—missing the family of course, but happy in the knowledge that the other

Dennett was keeping the home fires burning. I could be faithful and adulterous at the same time. I could even cuckold myself—to say nothing of other more lurid possibilities my colleagues were all too ready to force upon my overtaxed imagination. But my ordeal in Oklahoma (or was it Houston?) had made me less adventurous, and I shrank from this opportunity that was being offered (though of course I was never quite sure it was being offered to *me* in the first place).

There was another prospect even more disagreeable—that the spare, Hubert or Yorick as the case might be, would be detached from any input from Fortinbras and just left detached. Then, as in the other case, there would be two Dennetts, or at least two claimants to my name and possessions, one embodied in Fortinbras, and the other sadly, miserably disembodied. Both selfishness and altruism bade me take steps to prevent this from happening. So I asked that measures be taken to ensure that no one could ever tamper with the transceiver connections or the master switch without my (our? no, *my*) knowledge and consent. Since I had no desire to spend my life guarding the equipment in Houston, it was mutually decided that all the electronic connections in the lab would be carefully locked: both those that controlled the life-support system for Yorick and those that controlled the power supply for Hubert would be guarded with fail-safe devices, and I would take the only master switch, outfitted for radio remote control, with me wherever I went. I carry it strapped around my waist and—wait a moment—*here it is*. Every few months I reconnoiter the situation by switching channels. I do this only in the presence of friends of course, for if the other channel were, heaven forbid, either dead or otherwise occupied, there would have to be somebody who had my interests at heart to switch it back, to bring me back from the void. For while I could feel, see, hear and otherwise sense whatever befell my body, subsequent to such a switch, I'd be unable to control it. By the way, the two positions on the switch are intentionally unmarked, so I never have the faintest idea whether I am switching from Hubert to Yorick or *vice versa*. (Some of you may think that in this case I really don't know *who* I am, let alone where I am. But such reflections no longer make much of a dent on my essential Dennettness, on my own sense of who I am. If it is true that in one sense I don't know who I am then that's another one of your philosophical truths of underwhelming significance.)

In any case, every time I've flipped the switch so far, nothing has happened. *So let's give it a try. . . .*

"THANK GOD! I THOUGHT YOU'D NEVER FLIP THAT SWITCH! You can't imagine how horrible it's been these last two weeks—but now you know, it's your turn in purgatory. How I've longed for this moment! You see, about two weeks ago—excuse me, ladies and gentlemen, but I've got to explain this to my . . . um, brother, I guess you could say, but he's just told you the facts, so you'll understand—about two weeks ago our two brains drifted just a bit out of synch. I don't know whether *my* brain is now Hubert or Yorick, any more than you do, but in any case, the two brains drifted apart, and of course once the process started, it snowballed, for I was in a slightly different receptive state for the input we both received, a difference that was soon magnified. In no time at all the illusion that I was in control of my body—our body—was completely dissipated. There was nothing I could do—no way to call you. YOU DIDN'T EVEN KNOW I EXISTED! It's been like being carried around in a cage, or better, like being possessed—hearing my own voice say things I didn't mean to say, watching in frustration as my own hands performed deeds I hadn't intended. You'd scratch our itches, but not the way I would have, and you kept me awake, with your tossing and turning. I've been totally exhausted, on the verge of a nervous breakdown, carried around helplessly by your frantic round of activities, sustained only by the knowledge that some day you'd throw the switch.

"Now it's your turn, but at least you'll have the comfort of knowing *I* know you're in there. Like an expectant mother, I'm eating—or at any rate tasting, smelling, seeing—for *two* now, and I'll try to make it easy for you. Don't worry. Just as soon as this colloquium is over, you and I will fly to Houston, and we'll see what can be done to get one of us another body. You can have a female body—your body could be any color you like. But let's think it over. I tell you what—to be fair, if we both want this body, I promise I'll let the project director flip a coin to settle which of us gets to keep it and which then gets to

choose a new body. That should guarantee justice, shouldn't it? In any case, I'll take care of you, I promise. These people are my witnesses.

"Ladies and gentlemen, this talk we have just heard is not exactly the talk *I* would have given, but I assure you that everything he said was perfectly true. And now if you'll excuse me, I think I'd—we'd—better sit down."[2]

NOTES

1. C.f., Jaakko Hintikka, "Cogito ergo sum: Inference or Performance?" *The Philosophical Review*, LXXI, 1962, pp. 3–32.
2. Anyone familiar with the literature on this topic will recognize that my remarks owe a great deal to the explorations of Sydney Shoemaker, John Perry, David Lewis and Derek Parfit, and in particular to their papers in Amelie Rorty, ed., *The Identities of Persons*, 1976.

KEY TERMS

Physicalist
Behaviorists

STUDY QUESTIONS

1. After the operation, when Dennett asks himself the question, "Where am I?" he considers three possible answers. What are they, and what problems does each answer supposedly have?
2. When Dennett talks about losing contact with his body while he is underground, he continues the thought-experiment as if he takes on the point of view of a brain in a vat that has no sensory perception at all. Do you think such a perspective is even coherent? Might someone be conscious even without a body?
3. Is it plausible to suppose that the Hubert-Fortinbras pair really is Dennett? Why or why not?
4. At the end of the article, Dennett claims that one of the brains gets "out of synch" with the other brain and hence feels like a prisoner in his own body. In your own words, explain what Dennett means by this.
5. Yorick is a brain, and Hamlet is a body. *What* is Dennett?

D. FREEDOM, DETERMINISM, AND RESPONSIBILITY

ⅹ

Human Freedom and the Self

RODERICK M. CHISHOLM

Roderick M. Chisholm (1916–1999) was an influential American philosopher who worked mainly in metaphysics and epistemology. His major work was *Person and Object*, but his other works include *A Theory of Knowledge*, *The Problem of the Criterion*, and *Perception*.

. .

> "A staff moves a stone, and is moved by a hand, which is moved by a man."
>
> *Aristotle*, Physics, *256a.*

1. The **metaphysical** problem of human **freedom** might be summarized in the following way: Human beings are responsible agents; but this fact appears to conflict with a **deterministic** view of human action (the view that every event that is involved in an act is caused by some other event); and it *also* appears to conflict with an **indeterministic** view of human action (the view that the act, or some event that is essential to the act, is not caused at all). To solve the problem, I believe, we must make somewhat far-reaching assumptions about the self or the agent—about the man who performs the act.

From *The Lindley Lectures*, 1964, pp. 3–15, Copyright © 1964 by the Department of Philosophy, University of Kansas. Reprinted by permission.

Perhaps it is needless to remark that, in all likelihood, it is impossible to say anything significant about this ancient problem that has not been said before.[1]

2. Let us consider some deed, or misdeed, that may be attributed to a responsible agent: one man, say, shot another. If the man *was* responsible for what he did, then, I would urge, what was to happen at the time of the shooting was something that was entirely up to the man himself. There was a moment at which it was true, both that he could have fired the shot and also that he could have refrained from firing it. And if this is so, then, even though he did fire it, he could have done something else instead. (He didn't find himself firing the shot "against his will," as we say.) I think we can say, more generally, then, that if a man is responsible for a certain event or a certain state of affairs (in our example, the shooting of another man), then that event or state of affairs was brought about by some act of his, and the

act was something that was in his power either to perform or not to perform.

But now if the act which he *did* perform was an act that was also in his power *not* to perform, then it could not have been caused or determined by any event that was not itself within his power either to bring about or not to bring about. For example, if what we say he did was really something that was brought about by a second man, one who forced his hand upon the trigger, say, or who, by means of hypnosis, compelled him to perform the act, then since the act was caused by the *second* man it was nothing that was within the power of the *first* man to prevent. And precisely the same thing is true, I think, if instead of referring to a second man who compelled the first one, we speak instead of the *desires* and *beliefs* which the first man happens to have had. For if what we say he did was really something that was brought about by his own beliefs and desires, if these beliefs and desires in the particular situation in which he happened to have found himself caused him to do just what it was that we say he did do, then, since *they* caused it, *he* was unable to do anything other than just what it was that he did do. It makes no difference whether the cause of the deed was internal or external; if the cause was some state or event for which the man himself was not responsible, then he was not responsible for what we have been mistakenly calling his act. If a flood caused the poorly constructed dam to break, then, given the flood and the constitution of the dam, the break, we may say, *had* to occur and nothing could have happened in its place. And if the flood of desire caused the weak-willed man to give in, then he, too, had to do just what it was that he did do and he was no more responsible than was the dam for the results that followed. (It is true, of course, that if the man is responsible for the beliefs and desires that he happens to have, then he may also be responsible for the things they lead him to do. But the question now becomes: *is* he responsible for the beliefs and desires he happens to have? If he is, then there was a time when they were within his power either to acquire or not to acquire, and we are left, therefore, with our general point.)

One may object: But surely if there were such a thing as a man who is really *good*, then he would be responsible for things that he would do; yet, he would be unable to do anything other than just what it is that he does do, since, being good, he will always choose to do what is best. The answer, I think, is suggested by a comment that Thomas Reid makes upon an ancient author. The author had said of Cato, "He was good because he could not be otherwise," and Reid observes: "This saying, if understood literally and strictly, is not the praise of Cato, but of his constitution, which was no more the work of Cato than his existence."[2] If Cato was himself responsible for the good things that he did, then Cato, as Reid suggests, was such that, although he had the power to do what was not good, he exercised his power only for that which was good.

All of this, if it is true, may give a certain amount of comfort to those who are tender-minded. But we should remind them that it also conflicts with a familiar view about the nature of God—with the view that St. Thomas Aquinas expresses by saying that "every movement both of the will and of nature proceeds from God as the Prime Mover."[3] If the act of the sinner *did* proceed from God as the Prime Mover, then God was in the position of the second agent we just discussed—the man who forced the trigger finger, or the hypnotist—and the sinner, so-called, was *not* responsible for what he did. (This may be a bold assertion, in view of the history of western theology, but I must say that I have never encountered a single good reason for denying it.)

There is one standard objection to all of this and we should consider it briefly.

3. The objection takes the form of a stratagem—one designed to show that determinism (and divine providence) is consistent with human responsibility. The stratagem is one that was used by Jonathan Edwards and by many philosophers in the present century, most notably, G. E. Moore.[4]

One proceeds as follows: The expression

(a) He could have done otherwise, it is argued, means no more nor less than

(b) If he had chosen to do otherwise, then he would have done otherwise.

(In place of "chosen," one might say "tried," "set out," "decided," "undertaken," or "willed.") The truth of statement (b), it is then pointed out, is consistent with determinism (and with divine providence); for even if all of the man's actions were causally determined, the man could still be such that, *if* he had chosen otherwise, then he would have done otherwise. What the murderer saw, let us suppose, along with his beliefs and desires, *caused* him to fire the shot; yet he was such that *if*, just then, he had chosen or decided *not* to fire the shot, then he would not have fired it. All of this is certainly possible. Similarly, we could say, of the dam, that the flood caused it to break and also that the dam was such that, *if* there had been no flood or any similar pressure, then the dam would have remained intact. And therefore, the argument proceeds, if (b) is consistent with determinism, and if (a) and (b) say the same thing, then (a) is also consistent with determinism; hence we can say that the agent *could* have done otherwise even though he was caused to do what he did do; and therefore determinism and moral responsibility are compatible.

Is the argument sound? The conclusion follows from the premises, but the catch, I think, lies in the first premise—the one saying that statement (a) tells us no more nor less than what statement (b) tells us. For (b), it would seem, could be true while (a) is false. That is to say, our man might be such that, if he had chosen to do otherwise, then he would have done otherwise, and yet *also* such that he could not have done otherwise. Suppose, after all, that our murderer could not have *chosen*, or could not have *decided*, to do otherwise. Then the fact that he happens also to be a man such that, if he had chosen not to shoot he would not have shot, would make no difference. For if he could *not* have chosen *not* to shoot, then he could not have done anything other than just what it was that he did do. In a word: from our statement (b) above ("If he had chosen to do otherwise, then he would have done otherwise"), we cannot make an inference to (a) above ("He could have done otherwise") unless we can *also* assert:

(c) He could have chosen to do otherwise.

And therefore, if we must reject this third statement (c), then, even though we may be justified in asserting (b), we are not justified in asserting (a). If

the man could not have chosen to do otherwise, then he would not have done otherwise—*even if* he was such that, if he *had* chosen to do otherwise, then he would have done otherwise.

The stratagem in question, then, seems to me not to work, and I would say, therefore, that the ascription of responsibility conflicts with a deterministic view of action.

4. Perhaps there is less need to argue that the ascription of responsibility also conflicts with an indeterministic view of action—with the view that the act, or some event that is essential to the act, is not caused at all. If the act—the firing of the shot—was not caused at all, if it was fortuitous or capricious, happening so to speak out of the blue, then, presumably, no one—and nothing—was responsible for the act. Our conception of action, therefore, should be neither deterministic nor indeterministic. Is there any other possibility?

5. We must not say that every event involved in the act is caused by some other event; and we must not say that the act is something that is not caused at all. The possibility that remains, therefore, is this: We should say that at least one of the events that are involved in the act is caused, not by any other events, but by something else instead. And this something else can only be the agent—the man. If there is an event that is caused, not by other events, but by the man, then there are some events involved in the act that are not caused by other events. But if the event in question is caused by the man then it *is* caused and we are not committed to saying that there is something involved in the act that is not caused at all.

But this, of course, is a large consequence, implying something of considerable importance about the nature of the agent or the man.

6. If we consider only inanimate natural objects, we may say that causation, if it occurs, is a relation between *events* or *states of affairs*. The dam's breaking was an event that was caused by a set of other events—the dam being weak, the flood being strong, and so on. But if a man is responsible for a particular deed, then, if what I have said is true, there is some event, or set of events, that is caused, *not* by other events or states of affairs, but by the agent, whatever he may be.

I shall borrow a pair of medieval terms, using them, perhaps, in a way that is slightly different from that for which they were originally intended. I shall say that when one event or state of affairs (or set of events or states of affairs) causes some other event or state of affairs, then we have an instance of **transeunt causation**. And I shall say that when an *agent*, as distinguished from an event, causes an event or state of affairs, then we have an instance of **immanent causation**.

The nature of what is intended by the expression "immanent causation" may be illustrated by this sentence from Aristotle's *Physics*: "Thus, a staff moves a stone, and is moved by a hand, which is moved by a man." (VII, 5, 256a, 6–8) If the man was responsible, then we have in this illustration a number of instances of causation—most of them transeunt but at least one of them immanent. What the staff did to the stone was an instance of transeunt causation, and thus we may describe it as a relation between events: "the motion of the staff caused the motion of the stone." And similarly for what the hand did to the staff: "the motion of the hand caused the motion of the staff." And, as we know from physiology, there are still other events which caused the motion of the hand. Hence we need not introduce the agent at this particular point, as Aristotle does—we *need* not, though we *may*. We *may* say that the hand was moved by the man, but we may also say that the motion of the hand was caused by the motion of certain muscles; and we may say that the motion of the muscles was caused by certain events that took place within the brain. But some event, and presumably one of those that took place within the brain, was caused by the agent and not by any other events.

There are, of course, objections to this way of putting the matter; I shall consider the two that seem to me to be most important.

7. One may object, firstly: "If the *man* does anything, then, as Aristotle's remark suggests, what he does is to move the *hand*. But he certainly does not *do* anything to his brain—he may not even know that he *has* a brain. And if he doesn't do anything to the brain, and if the motion of the hand was caused by something that happened within the brain, then there is no point in appealing to 'immanent causation' as being something incompatible with 'transeunt causation'—for the whole thing, after all, is a matter of causal relations among events or states of affairs."

The answer to this objection, I think, is this: It is true that the agent does not *do* anything with his brain, or to his brain, in the sense in which he *does* something with his hand and does something to the staff. But from this it does not follow that the agent was not the immanent cause of something that happened within his brain.

We should note a useful distinction that has been proposed by Professor A. I. Melden—namely, the distinction between "making something A happen" and "doing A."[5] If I reach for the staff and pick it up, then one of the things that I *do* is just that—reach for the staff and pick it up. And if it is something that I do, then there is a very clear sense in which it may be said to be something that I know that I do. If you ask me, "Are you doing something, or trying to do something, with the staff?", I will have no difficulty in finding an answer. But in doing something with the staff, I also make various things happen which are not in this same sense things that I do: I will make various air-particles move; I will free a number of blades of grass from the pressure that had been upon them; and I may cause a shadow to move from one place to another. If these are merely things that I make happen, as distinguished from things that I do, then I may know nothing whatever about them; I may not have the slightest idea that, in moving the staff, I am bringing about any such thing as the motion of air-particles, shadows, and blades of grass.

We may say, in answer to the first objection, therefore, that it is true that our agent does nothing to his brain or with his brain; but from this it does not follow that the agent is not the immanent cause of some event within his brain; for the brain event may be something which, like the motion of the air-particles, he made happen in picking up the staff. The only difference between the two cases is this: in each case, he made something happen when he picked up the staff; but in the one case—the motion of the air-particles or of the shadows—it was the motion of the staff that caused the event to happen; and in the other case—the event that took place in the brain—it was this event that caused the motion of the staff.

The point is, in a word, that whenever a man does something A, then (by "immanent causation") he makes a certain cerebral event happen, and this cerebral event (by "transeunt causation") makes A happen.

8. The second objection is more difficult and concerns the very concept of "immanent causation," or causation by an agent, as this concept is to be interpreted here. The concept is subject to a difficulty which has long been associated with that of the prime mover unmoved. We have said that there must be some event A, presumably some cerebral event, which is caused not by any other event, but by the agent. Since A was not caused by any other event, then the agent himself cannot be said to have undergone any change or produced any other event (such as "an act of will" or the like) which brought A about. But if, when the agent made A happen, there was no event involved other than A itself, no event which could be described as *making* A happen, what did the agent's causation consist of? What, for example, is the difference between A's just happening, and the agent's *causing* A to happen? We cannot attribute the difference to any event that took place within the agent. And so far as the event A itself is concerned, there would seem to be no discernible difference. Thus Aristotle said that the activity of the prime mover is nothing in addition to the motion that it produces, and Suarez said that "the action is in reality nothing but the effect as it flows from the agent."[6] Must we conclude, then, that there is no more to the man's action in causing event A than there is to the event A's happening by itself? Here we would seem to have a distinction without a difference—in which case we have failed to find a *via media* between a deterministic and an indeterministic view of action.

The only answer, I think, can be this: that the difference between the man's causing A, on the one hand, and the event A just happening, on the other, lies in the fact that, in the first case but not the second, the event A *was* caused and was caused by the man. There was a brain event A; the agent did, in fact, cause the brain event; but there was nothing that he did to cause it.

This answer may not entirely satisfy and it will be likely to provoke the following question: "But what are you really *adding* to the assertion that A happened when you utter the words 'The agent *caused* A to happen'?" As soon as we have put the question this way, we see, I think, that whatever difficulty we may have encountered is one that may be traced to the concept of causation generally—whether "immanent" or "transeunt." The problem, in other words, is not a problem that is peculiar to our conception of human action. It is a problem that must be faced by anyone who makes use of the concept of causation at all; and therefore, I would say, it is a problem for everyone but the complete indeterminist.

For the problem, as we put it, referring just to "immanent causation," or causation by an agent, was this: "What is the difference between saying, of an event A, that A just happened and saying that someone caused A to happen?" The analogous problem, which holds for "transeunt causation," or causation by an event, is this: "What is the difference between saying, of two events A and B, that B happened and then A happened, and saying that B's happening was the *cause* of A's happening?" And the only answer that one can give is this—that in the one case the agent was the cause of A's happening and in the other case event B was the cause of A's happening. The nature of transeunt causation is no more clear than is that of immanent causation.

9. But we may plausibly say—and there is a respectable philosophical tradition to which we may appeal—that the notion of immanent causation, or causation by an agent, is in fact more clear than that of transeunt causation, or causation by an event, and that it is only by understanding our own causal efficacy, as agents, that we can grasp the concept of *cause* at all. Hume may be said to have shown that we do not derive the concept of *cause* from what we perceive of external things. How, then, do we derive it? The most plausible suggestion, it seems to me, is that of Reid, once again: namely that "the conception of an **efficient cause** may very probably be derived from the experience we have had . . . of our own power to produce certain effects."[7] If we did not understand the concept of immanent causation, we would not understand that of transeunt causation.

10. It may have been noted that I have avoided the term "**free will**" in all of this. For even if there is such a faculty as "the will," which somehow sets our acts agoing, the question of freedom, as John Locke said, is not the question "*whether the will be free*"; it is the question "*whether a man be free.*"[8] For if there is a "will," as a moving faculty, the question is whether the man is free to will to do those things that he does will to do—and also whether he is free *not* to will any of those things that he does will to do, and, again, whether he is free to will any of those things that he does not will to do. Jonathan Edwards tried to restrict himself to the question—"Is the man free to do what it is that he wills?"—but the answer to this question will not tell us whether the man is responsible for what it is that he *does* will to do. Using still another pair of medieval terms, we may say that the metaphysical problem of freedom does not concern the *actus imperatus*; it does not concern the question whether we are free to accomplish whatever it is that we will or set out to do; it concerns the *actus elicitus*, the question whether we are free to will or to set out to do those things that we do will or set out to do.

11. If we are responsible, and if what I have been trying to say is true, then we have a prerogative which some would attribute only to God: each of us, when we act, is a prime mover unmoved. In doing what we do, we cause certain events to happen, and nothing—or no one—causes us to cause those events to happen.

12. If we are thus prime movers unmoved and if our actions, or those for which we are responsible, are not causally determined, then they are not causally determined by our *desires*. And this means that the relation between what we want or what we desire, on the one hand, and what it is that we do, on the other, is not as simple as most philosophers would have it.

We may distinguish between what we might call the "Hobbist approach" and what we might call the "Kantian approach" to this question. The Hobbist approach is the one that is generally accepted at the present time, but the Kantian approach, I believe, is the one that is true. According to Hobbism, if we *know*, of some man, what his beliefs and desires happen to be and how strong they are, if we know what he feels certain of, what he desires more than

anything else, and if we know the state of his body and what stimuli he is being subjected to, then we may *deduce*, logically, just what it is that he will do— or, more accurately, just what it is that he will try, set out, or undertake to do. Thus Professor Melden has said that "the connection between wanting and doing is logical."[9] But according to the Kantian approach to our problem, and this is the one that I would take, there is no such logical connection between wanting and doing, nor need there even be a causal connection. No set of statements about a man's desires, beliefs, and stimulus situation at any time implies any statement telling us what the man will try, set out, or undertake to do at that time. As Reid put it, though we may "reason from men's motives to their actions and, in many cases, with great probability," we can never do so "with absolute certainty."[10]

This means that, in one very strict sense of the terms, there can be no science of man. If we think of science as a matter of finding out what laws happen to hold, and if the statement of a law tells us what kinds of events are caused by what other kinds of events, then there will be human actions which we cannot explain by subsuming them under any laws. We cannot say, "It is causally necessary that, given such and such desires and beliefs, and being subject to such and such stimuli, the agent will do so and so." For at times the agent, if he chooses, may rise above his desires and do something else instead.

But all of this is consistent with saying that, perhaps more often than not, our desires do exist under conditions such that those conditions necessitate us to act. And we may also say, with Leibniz, that at other times our desires may "incline without necessitating."

13. Leibniz's phrase presents us with our final philosophical problem. What does it mean to say that a desire, or a motive, might "incline without necessitating"? There is a temptation, certainly, to say that "to incline" means to cause and that "not to necessitate" means not to cause, but obviously we cannot have it both ways.

Nor will Leibniz's own solution do. In his letter to Coste, he puts the problem as follows: "When a choice is proposed, for example to go out or not to go out, it is a question whether, with all the circumstances, internal and external, motives, perceptions, dispositions, impressions, passions, inclinations taken together, I am still in a contingent state, or whether I am necessitated to make the choice, for example, to go out; that is to say, whether this proposition true and determined in fact, *In all these circumstances taken together I shall choose to go out*, is contingent or necessary."[11] Leibniz's answer might be put as follows: in one sense of the terms "necessary" and "contingent," the proposition "In all these circumstances taken together I shall choose to go out," may be said to be contingent and not necessary, and in another sense of these terms, it may be said to be necessary and not contingent. But the sense in which the proposition may be said to be contingent, according to Leibniz, is only this: there is no logical contradiction involved in denying the proposition. And the sense in which it may be said to be necessary is this: since "nothing ever occurs without cause or determining reason," the proposition is causally necessary. "Whenever all the circumstances taken together are such that the balance of deliberation is heavier on one side than on the other, it is certain and infallible that that is the side that is going to win out." But if what we have been saying is true, the proposition "In all these circumstances taken together I shall choose to go out," may be causally as well as logically contingent. Hence we must find another interpretation for Leibniz's statement that our motives and desires may incline us, or influence us, to choose without thereby necessitating us to choose.

Let us consider a public official who has some moral scruples but who also, as one says, could be had. Because of the scruples that he does have, he would never take any positive steps to receive a bribe—he would not actively solicit one. But his morality has its limits and he is also such that, if we were to confront him with a *fait accompli* or to let him see what is about to happen ($10,000 in cash is being deposited behind the garage), then he would succumb and be unable to resist. The general situation is a familiar one and this is one reason that people pray to be delivered from temptation. (It also justifies Kant's remark: "And how many there are who may have led a long blameless life, who are only *fortunate* in having escaped so many temptations.")[12] Our relation to the misdeed that we contemplate may not be a matter simply of being able to bring it about or not to bring it about. As St. Anselm noted, there are at least four possibilities. We may illustrate them by reference to our public official and the event which is his receiving the bribe, in the following way: (i) he may be able to bring the event about himself (*facere esse*), in which case he would actively cause himself to receive the bribe; (ii) he may be able to refrain from bringing it about himself (*non facere esse*), in which case he would not himself do anything to insure that he receive the bribe; (iii) he may be able to do something to prevent the event from occurring (*facere non esse*), in which case he would make sure that the $10,000 was *not* left behind the garage; or (iv) he may be unable to do anything to prevent the event from occurring (*non facere non esse*), in which case, though he may not solicit the bribe, he would allow himself to keep it.[13] We have envisaged our official as a man who can resist the temptation to (i) but cannot resist the temptation to (iv): he can refrain from bringing the event about himself, but he cannot bring himself to do anything to prevent it.

Let us think of "inclination without necessitation," then, in such terms as these. First we may contrast the two propositions:

1. He can resist the temptation to do something in order to make A happen;
2. He can resist the temptation to allow A to happen (i.e., to do nothing to prevent A from happening).

We may suppose that the man has some desire to have A happen and thus has a motive for making A happen. His motive for making A happen, I suggest, is one that *necessitates* provided that, because of the motive, (1) is false; he cannot resist the temptation to do something in order to make A happen. His motive for making A happen is one that *inclines* provided that, because of the motive, (2) is false; like our public official, he cannot bring himself to do anything to prevent A from happening. And therefore we can say that his motive for making A happen is one that *inclines but does not necessitate* provided that, because of the motive, (1) is true and (2) is false; he can resist the temptation to make it happen but he cannot resist the temptation to allow it to happen.

NOTES

1. The general position to be presented here is suggested in the following writings, among others: Aristotle, *Eudemian Ethics*, Book II, Ch. 6; *Nicomachean Ethics*, Book III, Ch. 1–5; Thomas Reid, *Essays on the Active Powers of Man*; C. A. Campbell, "Is 'Free Will' a Pseudo-Problem?" *Mind*, N.S. Vol. LX (1951), pp. 441–465; Roderick M. Chisholm, "Responsibility and Avoidability," and Richard Taylor, "Determination and the Theory of Agency," in Sidney Hook, ed., *Determinism and Freedom in the Age of Modern Science* (New York 1958).

2. Thomas Reid, *Essays on the Active Powers of Man*, Essay IV, Chapter 4 (*Works*, p. 600).

3. *Summa Theologica*, First Part of the Second Part, Question VI ("On the Voluntary and Involuntary").

4. Jonathan Edwards, *Freedom of the Will* (New Haven 1957); G. E. Moore, *Ethics* (Home University Library 1912), Chapter Six.

5. A. I. Melden, *Free Action* (London 1961), especially Chapter Three. Mr. Melden's own views, however, are quite the contrary of those that are proposed here.

6. Aristotle, *Physics*, Book III, Chapter 3; Suarez, *Disputations Metaphysicae*, Disputation, 18, Section 10.

7. Reid, *Works*, p. 524.

8. *Essay Concerning Human Understanding*, Book II, Chapter XXI.

9. *Op. cit.*, p. 166.

10. Reid, *Works*, pp. 608, 612.

11. "Lettre a Mr. Coste de la Nécessité et de la Contingence" (1707) in *Opera Philosophica*, ed. Erdmann, pp. 447–449.

12. In the Preface to the *Metaphysical Elements of Ethics*, in T. K. Abbott, ed., *Kant's Critique of Practical Reason and Other Works on the Theory of Ethics* (London 1959), p. 303.

13. Cf. D. P. Henry, "Saint Anselm's *De 'Grammatico'*," *Philosophical Quarterly*, Vol. X (1960), pp. 115–126. St. Anselm noted that (i) and (iii), respectively, may be thought of as forming the upper left and the upper right corners of a square of opposition, and (ii) and (iv) the lower left and the lower right.

KEY TERMS

Metaphysical	Immanent causation
Freedom	Efficient cause
Deterministic	Free will
Transeunt causation	

STUDY QUESTIONS

1. According to Chisholm, what is the problem of human freedom?

2. Why doesn't Chisholm like the suggestion that "he could have done otherwise" means nothing more nor less than "if he had chosen to do otherwise, then he would have done otherwise"?

3. Chisholm's solution to the problem relies on the idea that a *human* can cause an event. Does this idea even make sense? How would you explain it to someone who wasn't familiar with the idea?

4. How is immanent causation a *via media* between deterministic and indeterministic accounts of human action?

5. How does Chisholm propose that we understand the phrase "inclination without necessitation"?

The Powers of Rational Beings: Freedom of the Will

PETER VAN INWAGEN

Peter van Inwagen (1942–) is Professor of Philosophy at the University of Notre Dame and has written many important works on metaphysics, free will, and philosophical theology. His books include *An Essay on Free Will*, *Material Beings*, and *God, Knowledge, and Mystery*.

. .

W<small>E</small> now turn to another mystery, a mystery about the *powers* of rational beings; that is, a mystery about what human beings are able to do. This mystery is the mystery of **free will** and **determinism**. The best way to get an intuitive grip on the problem of free will and determinism is to think of time as a "garden of forking paths." That is, to think of the alternatives that one considers when one is deciding what to do as being parts of various "alternative futures" and to think of these alternative futures diagrammatically, in the way suggested by a path or a river or a road that literally forks:

If Jane is trying to decide whether to tell all or to continue her life of deception, she is in a situation strongly analogous to that of someone who is hesitating between forks in a road. That is why this sort of diagram is so suggestive. Let us apply this idea to the problem of free will and determinism.

To say that one has free will is to say that when one decides among forks in the road of time (or, more prosaically, when one decides what to do), one is at least sometimes able to take more than one of the forks. Thus, Jane, who is deciding between a fork

that leads to telling all and a fork that leads to a life of continued deception, has free will (on this particular occasion) if she is able to tell all and is also able to continue living a life of deception. One has free will if sometimes more than one of the forks in the road of time is "open" to one. One lacks free will if on every occasion on which one must make a decision only one of the forks before one—of course it will be the fork one in fact takes—is open to one. If John is locked in a room and doesn't know that he is locked in, and if he is in the process of deliberating about whether to leave, one of the alternative futures he is contemplating—leaving—is, in point of fact, not open to him, and he thus lacks free will in the matter of staying or leaving.[1]

It is a common opinion that free will is required by morality. Let us examine this common opinion from the perspective that is provided by looking at time as a garden of forking paths. While it is obviously false—for about six independent reasons—that the whole of morality consists in making judgments of the form 'You should not have done X', we can at least illustrate certain important features of the relation between free will and morality by examining the relation between the concept of free will and the content of such judgments. The judgment that you shouldn't have done X implies that you should have done something else instead; that you should have done something else instead implies that there was something else for you to do; that there was something else for you to do implies that you *could* have done something else; that you could have done something else implies that you have free will. To make a moral judgment about one of your acts is to evaluate your taking one of the forks in the road of time, to characterize it as better or worse than various of the other forks that were open to you. (Note that if you have made a choice by taking one of the forks in what is literally a road, no one could blame you for taking the fork you did if all of the other forks were blocked.) A moral evaluation of what someone has done requires two or more alternative possibilities of action for that person just as surely as a contest requires two or more contestants.

Let us now see what help the conception of time as a garden of forking paths gives us in understanding what is meant by determinism. Determinism is the thesis that it is true at every moment that the way things then are determines a unique future, that only *one* of the alternative futures that may exist relative to a given moment is a physically possible continuation of the state of things at that moment. Or, if you like, we may say that determinism is the thesis that only one continuation of the state of things at a given moment is consistent with the laws of nature. (For it is the laws of nature that determine what is physically possible. It is, for example, now physically possible for you to be in Chicago at noon tomorrow if and only if your being in Chicago at noon tomorrow is consistent with both the present state of things and the laws of nature.) Thus, according to determinism, although it may often seem to us that we confront a sheaf of possible futures (like this)

what we really confront is something like this

This figure is almost shaped like a road that splits into four roads, but not quite: three of the four "branches" that lead away from the "fork" are not connected with the original road, although they

come very close to it. (Thus they are not really branches in the road, and the place at which they almost touch the road is not really a fork.) If we were to view this figure from a distance—across the room, say—it would seem to us to have the shape of a road that forks. We have to look at it closely to see that what appeared from a distance to be three "branches" are not connected with the long line or with one another. In the figure, the point at which the three unconnected lines *almost* touch the long line represents the present. The unconnected lines represent futures that are not physically possible continuations of the present, and the part of the long line to the right of the "present" represents a future that is a physically possible continuation of the present. The gaps between the long line and the unconnected lines represent causal discontinuities, violations of the laws of nature—in a word, miracles. The reason these futures are not physically possible continuations of the present is that "getting into" any of them from the present would require a miracle. The fact that the part of the long line that lies to the right of the "present" actually proceeds from that point represents the fact that this line-segment corresponds to a physically possible future.

This figure, then, represents four futures, three of which are physically impossible and exactly one of which is physically possible. If these four futures are the only futures that "follow" the present, then this figure represents the way in which each moment of time must be if the universe is deterministic: each moment must be followed by exactly one physically possible future.

The earlier diagram, however, represents an indeterministic situation. The road really does fork. The present is followed by four possible futures. Any one of them could, consistently with the laws of nature, evolve out of the present. Any one of them could, consistently with the laws of nature, turn out to be the actual future. Therefore, it is only if the universe is indeterministic that time *really is* a "garden of forking paths." But even in a deterministic universe, time could *look like* a garden of forking paths. Remember that our figure, when viewed from across the room, *looked* as if it had the shape of a road that forked. We cannot see all, or even very many, of the causes that operate in any situation. It could be, therefore, that the universe is deterministic, even though it looks to our limited vision as if there were sometimes more than one possible future. It may look to Jane as if she faces two possible futures, in one of which she tells all and in the other of which she continues her life of deception. But it may well be that the possibility of one or the other of these contemplated futures is mere appearance—an illusion, in fact. It may be that, in reality, causes already at work in her brain and central nervous system and immediate environment have already "ruled out" one or the other of these futures: it may be that one or the other of them is such that it could not come to pass unless a physically impossible event, a miracle, were to happen in her brain or central nervous system or environment.

Ask yourself this question. What would happen if some supernatural agency—God, say—were to "roll history back" to some point in the past and then "let things go forward again"? Suppose the agency were to cause things to be once more just as they were at high noon, Greenwich time, on 11 March 1893 and were thereafter to let things go on of their own accord. Would history literally repeat itself? Would there be two world wars, each the same in every detail as the wars that occurred the "first time around"? Would a president of the United States called 'John F. Kennedy' be assassinated in Dallas on the date that on the new reckoning is called '22 November 1963'? Would you, or at least someone exactly like you, exist? If the answer to these questions is No, then determinism is false. Equivalently, if determinism is true, the answer to these questions is Yes. If determinism is true, then, if the universe were rolled back to a previous state by a miracle, and if there were no further miracles, the history of the world would repeat itself. And if the universe were rolled back to a previous state thousands of times, this exact duplication would happen every time. If there are no forks in the road of time—if all of the apparent forks are merely apparent, illusions due to our limited knowledge of the causes of things—then restoring the universe to some earlier condition is like moving a traveler on a road without forks back to an earlier point on that road. If there are no forks in the

road, then, obviously enough, the traveler must traverse the same path a second time.

It has seemed obvious to most people who have not been exposed (perhaps 'subjected' would be a better word) to philosophy that free will and determinism are incompatible. It is almost impossible to get beginning students of philosophy to take seriously the idea that there could be such a thing as free will in a deterministic universe. Indeed, people who have not been exposed to philosophy usually understand the word 'determinism' (if they know the word at all) to stand for the thesis that there is no free will. And you might think that the incompatibility of free will and determinism deserves to seem obvious—because it is obvious. To say that we have free will is to say that more than one future is sometimes open to us. To affirm determinism is to say that every future that confronts us but one is physically impossible. And, surely, a physically impossible future can't be open to anyone, can it? If we know that a "Star Trek" sort of future is physically impossible (because, say, the "warp drives" and "transporter beams" that figure essentially in such futures are physically impossible), then we know that a "Star Trek" future is not open to us or to our descendants.

People who are convinced by this sort of reasoning are called *incompatibilists*: they hold that free will and determinism are incompatible. As I have hinted, however, many philosophers are *compatibilists*: they hold that free will and determinism are compatible. Compatibilism has an illustrious history among English-speaking philosophers, a history that embraces such figures as the seventeenth-century English philosopher Thomas Hobbes, the eighteenth-century Scottish philosopher David Hume, and the nineteenth-century English philosopher John Stuart Mill. And the majority of twentieth-century English-speaking philosophers have been compatibilists. (But compatibilism has not had many adherents on the continent of Europe. Kant, for example, called it a "wretched subterfuge.")

A modern compatibilist can be expected to reply to the line of reasoning I have just presented in some such way as follows:

Yes, a future, in order to be open to one, does need to be physically possible. It can't, for example, contain faster-than-light travel if faster-than-light travel is physically impossible. But we must distinguish between a future's being physically possible and its having a physically possible connection with the present. A future is physically possible if everything that happens in it is permitted by the laws of nature. A future has a physically possible connection with the present if it could be 'joined' to the present without any violation of the laws of nature. A physically possible future that does not have a physically possible connection with the present is one that, given the present state of things, would have to be 'inaugurated' by a miracle, an event that violated the laws of nature, but in which, thereafter, events proceeded in accordance with the laws. Determinism indeed says that of all the physically possible futures, one and only one has a physically possible connection with the present—one and only one could be joined to the present without a violation of the laws of nature. My position is that some futures that could not be joined to the present without a violation of the laws of nature are, nevertheless, open to us.

Two philosophical problems face the defenders of compatibilism. The easier is to provide a clear statement of *which* futures that do not have a physically possible connection with the present are "open" to us. The more difficult is to make it seem at least plausible that futures that are in this sense open to an agent really deserve to be so described.

An example of a solution to these problems may make the nature of the problems clearer. The solution I shall briefly describe would almost certainly be regarded by all present-day compatibilists as defective, although it has a respectable history. I choose it not to suggest that compatibilists can't do better but simply because it can be described in fairly simple terms.

According to this solution, a future is open to an agent, if, given that the agent chose that future (chose that path leading away from a fork in the road of time), it would come to pass. Thus it is open to me to stop writing this book and do a little dance because, if I so chose, that's what I'd do. But if Alice is locked in a prison cell, it is not open to her to leave: if she chose to leave, her choice would be ineffective

because she would come up against a locked prison door. Now consider the future I said was open to me—to stop writing and do a little dance—and suppose that determinism is true. Although a choice on my part to behave in that remarkable fashion would (no doubt) be effective if it occurred, it is as a matter of fact *not* going to occur, and, therefore, given determinism, it is determined by the present state of things and the laws of nature that such a choice is not going to occur. It is in fact determined that *nothing* is going to occur that would have the consequence that I stop writing and do a little dance. Therefore, none of the futures in which I act in that bizarre way is a future that has a physically possible connection with the present: such a future could come to pass only if it were inaugurated by an event of a sort that is ruled out by the present state of things and the laws of nature. And yet, as we have seen, many of these futures are "open" to me in the sense of 'open' that the compatibilist has proposed.

Is this a reasonable sense to give to this word? (We now take up the second problem that confronts the compatibilist.) This is a very large question. The core of the compatibilist's answer is an attempt to show that the reason we are interested in open or accessible futures is that we are interested in modifying the way people behave. One important way in which we modify behavior is by rewarding behavior that we like and punishing behavior that we dislike. We tell people that we will put them in jail if they steal and that they will get a tax break if they invest their money in such-and-such a way. But there is no point in trying to get people to act in a certain way if that way is not in some sense open to them. There is no point in telling Alfred that he will go to jail if he steals unless it is somehow open to him not to steal.

And what is the relevant sense of "open"? Just the one I have proposed, says the compatibilist. One modifies behavior by modifying the choices people make. That procedure is effective just insofar as choices are effective in producing behavior. If Alfred chooses not to steal (and remains constant in that choice), then he won't steal. But if Alfred chooses not to be subject to the force of gravity, he will nevertheless be subject to the force of gravity. Although it would no doubt be socially useful if there were some people who were not subject to the force of gravity, there is no point in threatening people with grave consequences if they do not break the bonds of gravity, for even if you managed to induce some people to choose not to be subject to the force of gravity, their choice would not be effective. Therefore (the compatibilist concludes), it is entirely appropriate to speak of a future as "open" if it is a future that would be brought about by a choice—even if it were a choice that was determined not to occur. And if Alfred protests when you punish him for not choosing a future that was in this sense open to him, on the ground that it was determined by events that occurred before his birth that he not make the choice that would have inaugurated that future—if he protests that only a *miracle* could have inaugurated such a future—you can tell him that his punishment will not be less effective in modifying his behavior (and the behavior of those who witness his punishment) on *that* account.

When things are put that way, compatibilism can look like nothing more than robust common sense. Why, then, do people have so much trouble believing it? Why does it arouse so much resistance? I think that the reason is that compatibilists can make their doctrine seem like robust common sense only by sweeping a mystery under the carpet and that, despite their best efforts, the bulge shows. People are aware that something is amiss with compatibilism even when they are unable to articulate their misgivings. I believe that it is possible to lift the carpet and display the hidden mystery. The notion of "not having a choice" has a certain logic to it. One of the principles of this logic is, or so it seems, embodied in the following thesis, which I shall refer to as the No Choice Principle:

Suppose that *p* and that no one has (or ever had) any choice about whether *p*. And suppose also that the following conditional (if-then) statement is true and that no one has (or ever had) any choice about whether it is true: if *p*, then *q*. It follows from these two suppositions that *q* and that no one has (or ever had) any choice about whether *q*.

In this statement of the No Choice Principle, any declarative sentences can replace the symbols '*p*' and '*q*'.

(But the same sentence must replace '*p*' at each place it occurs, and the same goes for '*q*'.) We might, for example, replace '*p*' with 'Plato died long before I was born' and '*q*' with 'I have never met Plato':

Suppose that Plato died long before I was born and that no one has (or ever had) any choice about whether Plato died long before I was born. And suppose also that the following conditional statement is true and that no one has (or ever had) any choice about whether it is true: if Plato died long before I was born, then I have never met Plato. It follows from these two suppositions that I have never met Plato and that no one has (or ever had) any choice about whether I have never met Plato.

The No Choice Principle seems undeniably correct. How could I have a choice about anything that is an inevitable consequence of something I have no choice about? And yet, as we shall see, the compatibilist must deny the No Choice Principle. To see why this is so, let us suppose that determinism is true and that the No Choice Principle is correct. Now let us consider some state of affairs that we should normally suppose someone had a choice about. Consider, say, the fact that I am writing this book. Most people—at least most people who knew I was writing a book—would assume that I had a choice about whether I was engaged in this project. They would assume that it was open to me to have undertaken some other project or no project at all. But we are supposing that determinism is true, and that means that ten million years ago (say) there was only one physically possible future, a future that included my being engaged in writing this book at the present date (since that is what I am in fact doing): given the way things were ten million years ago and given the laws of nature, it had to be true that I was now engaged in writing this book. But consider the two statements

- Things were thus-and-so ten million years ago.
- If things were thus-and-so ten million years ago, then I am working on this book now.

(Here 'thus-and-so' is a sort of gesture at a complete description or specification of the way things were ten million years ago.) Each of these statements is true. And it is obvious that no one has or ever had any choice about the truth of either. It is obvious that no one—no human being, certainly—has or ever had any choice about whether things *were* thus-and-so ten million years ago, since at that time the first human beings were still millions of years in the future.

And no one has any choice about whether the second statement, the if-then statement, is true because this statement is a consequence of the laws of nature, and no one—no human being, certainly—has any choice about what the laws of nature are. If we imagine a possible world in which, as in the actual world, things were thus-and-so ten million years ago, and in which, unlike in the actual world, I decided to learn to sail instead of writing this book, we are imagining a world in which the laws of nature are different; for the *actual* laws dictate that if at some point in time things are thus-and-so, then, ten million years later I (or at any rate someone just like me) shall be writing and not sailing.

But if both of the above statements are true, then it follows, by the No Choice Principle, that neither I nor anyone else has or ever had any choice about whether I write this book. And, obviously, the content of the particular example—my writing a book—played no role in the derivation of this conclusion. It follows that, given the No Choice Principle, determinism implies that there is no free will. That is why the compatibilist must reject the No Choice Principle. This is the hidden mystery that, I contend, lies behind the façade of bluff common sense that compatibilism presents to the world: the compatibilist must reject the No Choice Principle, and the No Choice Principle seems to be true beyond all possibility of dispute. (Either that or the compatibilist must hold that one can have a choice about what went on in the world before there were any human beings or that one can have a choice about what the laws of nature are. But these alternatives look even more implausible than a rejection of the No Choice Principle.) If the No Choice Principle were false, that would be a great mystery indeed.

We must not forget, however, that mysteries really do exist. There are principles that are commonly held, and with good reason, to be false and whose falsity seems to be just as great a mystery as the falsity of the No Choice Principle would be. Consider, for example the principle that is usually called "the Galilean Law of the Addition of Velocities." This principle is a generalization of cases like the following. Suppose that an airplane is flying at a speed of 800 kilometers per hour relative to the ground; suppose that inside the aircraft a housefly is buzzing along at a speed of 30 kilometers per hour relative to the airplane in the direction of the airplane's travel; then the fly's speed relative to the ground is the sum of these two speeds: 830 kilometers per hour. According to the Special Theory of Relativity, an immensely useful and well-confirmed theory, the Galilean Law of the Addition of Velocities does not hold (although it comes very, very close to holding when it is applied to velocities of the magnitude that we usually consider in everyday life). And yet when one considers this principle in the abstract—in isolation from the considerations that guided Einstein in his development of Special Relativity—it seems to force itself upon the mind as true, to be true beyond all possibility of doubt. It seems, therefore, that the kind of "inner conviction" that sometimes moves one to say things like, "I can just *see* that that proposition *has* to be true" is not infallible.

Nevertheless, a mystery is a mystery. If compatibilism hides a mystery, should we therefore be incompatibilists? Unfortunately, incompatibilism also hides a mystery. Behold, I will show you a mystery.

If we are incompatibilists, we must reject either free will or determinism. What happens if we reject determinism? It is a bit easier now to reject determinism than it was in the nineteenth century, when it was commonly believed, and with reason, that determinism was underwritten by physics. But the quantum-mechanical world of current physics seems to be irreversibly indeterministic, and physics has therefore got out of the business of underwriting determinism. Nevertheless, the physical world is filled with objects and systems that seem to be deterministic "for all practical purposes"—digital computers, for example—and many philosophers and scientists believe that a human organism is deterministic for all practical purposes. But let us not debate this question. Let us suppose for the sake of argument that human organisms display a considerable degree of indeterminism. Let us suppose in fact that each human organism is such that when the human person associated with that organism (we leave aside the question whether the person and the organism are identical) is trying to decide whether to do A or to do B, there is a physically possible future in which the organism behaves in a way appropriate to a decision to do A and that there is also a physically possible future in which the organism behaves in a way appropriate to a decision to do B. We shall see that this supposition leads to a mystery. We shall see that the indeterminism that seems to be required by free will seems also to destroy free will.

Let us look carefully at the consequences of supposing that human behavior is undetermined. Suppose that Jane is in an agony of indecision; if her deliberations go one way, she will in a moment speak the words, "John, I lied to you about Alice," and if her deliberations go the other way, she will bite her lip and remain silent. We have supposed that there is a physically possible future in which each of these things happens. Given the whole state of the physical world at the present moment, and given the laws of nature, both of these things are possible; either might equally well happen.

Each contemplated action will, of course, have antecedents in Jane's cerebral cortex, for it is in that part of Jane (or of her body) that control over her vocal apparatus resides. Let us make a fanciful assumption about these antecedents, since it will make no real difference to our argument what they are. (It will help us to focus our thoughts if we have some sort of mental picture of what goes on inside Jane at the moment of decision.) Let us suppose that there is a certain current-pulse that is proceeding along one of the neural pathways in Jane's brain and that it is about to come to a fork. And let us suppose that if it goes to the left, she will make her confession, and that if it goes to the right, she will remain silent. And let us suppose that it is undetermined which way the pulse will go when it comes to the fork: even an omniscient being with a complete knowledge of the state of Jane's brain and a complete knowledge of the laws of physics and unlimited powers of calculation could say no more than, "The laws and the present state of her brain would allow

the pulse to go either way; consequently, no prediction of what the pulse will do when it comes to the fork is possible; it might go to the left, and it might go to the right, and that's all there is to be said."

Now let us ask: Does Jane have any choice about whether the pulse goes to the left or to the right? If we think about this question for a moment, we shall see that it is very hard to see how she could have any choice about that. Nothing in the way things are at the instant before the pulse makes its "decision" to go one way or the other makes it happen that the pulse goes one way or goes the other. If it goes to the left, that *just happens*. If it goes to the right, *that* just happens. There is no way for Jane to *influence* the pulse. There is no way for her to *make* it go one way rather than the other. Or, at least, there is no way for her to make it go one way rather than the other and leave the "choice" it makes an undetermined event. If Jane did something to make the pulse go to the left, then, obviously, its going to the left would *not* be an undetermined event. It is a plausible idea that the only way to have a choice about the outcome of a process is to be able to arrange things in ways that will make it inevitable that this or that outcome occur. If this plausible idea is right, then it would seem that there is no way in which anyone could have any choice about the outcome of an indeterministic process. And it seems to follow that if, when one is trying to decide what to do, it is truly undetermined what the outcome of one's deliberations will be, then one could have no choice about that outcome. It is, therefore, far from clear that incompatibilism is a tenable position. The incompatibilist who believes in free will must say this: it is possible, despite the above argument, for one to have a choice about the outcome of an indeterministic process. But how is the argument to be met?

Some incompatibilists attempt to meet this argument by means of an appeal to a special sort of causation. Metaphysicians have disagreed about what kinds of things stand in the cause-and-effect relation. The orthodox, or Humean position, is that—although our idioms may sometimes suggest otherwise—causes and effects are always events. We may *say* that "Stalin caused" the deaths of millions of people, but when we talk in this way, we are not, in the strictest sense, saying that an *individual* was the cause of certain events. It was, strictly speaking, certain *events* (certain actions of Stalin) that were the cause of certain other events (the millions of deaths). It has been suggested, however, that, although events do indeed cause other events, it is sometimes true that individuals, *persons* or *agents*, cause events. According to this suggestion, it might very well be that an event in Jane's brain—a current-pulse taking the left-hand branch of a neural fork, say—had Jane as its cause. And not some event or change that occurred within Jane, not something Jane *did*, but Jane herself, the person Jane, the agent Jane, the individual thing Jane.

This "type" of causation is usually labeled '**agent-causation**', and it is contrasted with '**event-causation**', the other "type" of causation, the kind of causation that occurs when one event causes another event. An event is a change in the intrinsic properties of an individual or a change in the way in which certain individuals are related to one another. Event-causation occurs when a change that occurs at a certain time is due to a change that occurred at some earlier time. If there is such a thing as agent-causation, however, some changes are not due to earlier changes but simply to agents.

Let us now return to the question that confronts the incompatibilist who believes in free will: How is it possible for one to have a choice about the outcome of an indeterministic process? Those incompatibilists who appeal to agent-causation answer this question as follows: "A process's having one outcome rather than one of the other outcomes it might have had is an event. For an agent to have a choice about the outcome of a process is for the agent to be able to cause each of the outcomes that process might have. Suppose, for example, that Jane's deciding what to do was an indeterministic process and that this process terminated in her deciding to speak, although, since it was indeterministic, the laws of nature and the way things were when the process was initiated were consistent with its terminating in her remaining silent. But suppose that Jane caused the process to terminate in her speaking and that she had been able to cause it to terminate in her being silent. Then she had a choice about the outcome. That is what it *is* to have had a choice about whether a process terminated in A or B: to have caused it to

terminate in one of these two ways, and to have been *able* to cause it to terminate in the other."

There are two "standard" objections to this sort of answer. They take the form of questions. The first question is, "But what does one add to the assertion that Jane decided to speak when one says that she was the agent-cause of her decision to speak?" The second is, "But what about the event *Jane's becoming the agent-cause of her decision to speak*? According to your position, this event occurred and it was undetermined—for if it were determined by some earlier state of things and the laws of nature, then her decision to speak would have been determined by these same factors. Even if there is such a thing as agent-causation and this event occurred, how could Jane have had any choice about whether it occurred? And if Jane was the agent-cause of her decision to speak and had no choice about whether she was the agent-cause of her decision to speak, then she had no choice about whether to speak or be silent."

These two standard objections have standard replies. The first reply is, "I don't know how to answer that question. But that is because causation is a mystery, and not because there is any *special* mystery about *agent*-causation. How would *you* answer the corresponding question about event-causation: What does one add to the assertion that two events occurred in succession when one says that the earlier was the *cause* of the later?" The second reply is, "But Jane did have a choice about which of the two events, *Jane's becoming the agent-cause of her decision to speak* and *Jane's becoming the agent-cause of her decision to remain silent*, would occur. This is because she was the agent-cause of the former and was able to have been the agent-cause of the latter. In any case in which Jane is the agent-cause of an event, she is also the agent-cause of her being the agent-cause of that event, and the agent-cause of her being the agent-cause of her being the agent-cause of that event, and so on 'forever.' Of course, she is not *aware* of being the agent-cause of all these events, but the doctrine of agent-causation does not entail that agents are aware of all of the events of which they are agent-causes."

Perhaps these replies are effective and perhaps not. I reproduce them because they are, as I have said, standard replies to standard objections. I have no clear sense of what is going on in this debate because I do not understand agent-causation. At least I don't think I understand it. To me, the suggestion that an individual thing, as opposed to a *change* in an individual thing, could be the cause of a change is a mystery. I do not intend this as an argument against the *existence* of agent-causation—of some relation between individual things and events that, when it is finally comprehended, will be seen to satisfy the descriptions of "agent-causation" that have been advanced by those who claim to grasp this concept. The world is full of mysteries and of verbal descriptions that seem to some to be nonsense and which later turn out to have been appropriate. ("Curved space! What nonsense! Space is what things that are curved are curved *in*. Space itself can't be curved." And no doubt the phrase 'curved space' *wouldn't* mean anything in particular if it had been made up by, say, a science-fiction writer and had no actual use in science. But the general theory of relativity does imply that it is possible for space to have a feature for which, as it turns out, those who understand the theory all regard 'curved' as an appropriate label.) I am saying only that agent-causation is a mystery and that to explain how it can be that someone can have a choice about the outcome of an indeterministic process by an appeal to agent-causation is to explain a mystery by a mystery.

But now a disquieting possibility suggests itself. Perhaps the explanation of the fact that both compatibilism and incompatibilism seem to lead to mysteries is simply that the concept of free will is self-contradictory. Perhaps free will is, as the incompatibilists say, incompatible with determinism. But perhaps it is also incompatible with *in*determinism, owing to the impossibility of anyone's having a choice about the outcome of an indeterministic process. If free will is incompatible with both determinism and indeterminism, then, since either determinism or indeterminism has to be true, free will is impossible. And, of course, what is impossible does not exist. Can we avoid mystery by accepting the non-existence of free will? If we simply say that no one ever has any choice about anything, then we need not reject the No Choice Principle, and we need not suppose that it is possible for a person to have a choice about the outcome of an indeterministic process.

But consider. Suppose that you are trying to decide what to do. And let us suppose that the choice that confronts you is not a trivial one. Let us not suppose that you are trying to decide which of two movies to see or which flavor of ice cream to order. Let us suppose that the matter is one of great importance— great importance to *you*, at any rate. You are, perhaps, trying to decide whether to marry a certain person or whether to risk losing your job by reporting unethical conduct on the part of a superior or whether to sign a "do not resuscitate" order on behalf of a beloved relative who is critically ill. Pick one of these situations and imagine that you are in it. (If you are in fact faced with a non-trivial choice, then you have no need to imagine anything. Think of your own situation.) Consider the two contemplated courses of action. Hold them before your mind's eye, and let your attention pass back and forth between them. Do you really think that you have no choice about which of these courses of action will become actual? Can you really believe that?

Many philosophers have said that although the choice between contemplated future courses of action always seems "open" to them, when they look back on their past decisions, the particular decision that they have made always or almost always seems inevitable once it has been made. I must say that I do not experience this myself, and, even if I did, I should regard it as an open question whether "foresight" or "hindsight" was more to be trusted. (Why should we suppose that hindsight is trustworthy? Maybe there is within us some psychological mechanism that produces the illusion that our past decisions were inevitable in order to enable us more effectively to put these decisions behind us and to spare us endless retrospective agonizing over them. Maybe we have a natural tendency to reinterpret our past decisions in a way that presents them in the best possible light. One can think of lots of not implausible hypotheses that would have the consequence that our present impression that our past decisions were the only possible ones—if we indeed have this impression—is untrustworthy.)

When I myself look at contemplated future courses of action in the way I have described above, I find an irresistible tendency to believe that I have a real choice as to which one will become actual. It may be, of course, that this tendency is the vehicle of illusion. If the concept of free choice were self-contradictory, it might still be the case that a belief in this self-contradictory thing was indispensable to human action. What would it be like to believe, really to *believe*, that in every circumstance only one course of action was open to one?

It can plausibly be argued that it would be impossible under such circumstances ever to try to decide what to do. Suppose, for example, that you are in a certain room that has a single door and that this door is the only possible exit from the room. Suppose that, as you are thinking about whether to leave the room, you hear a click that may or may not have been the sound of the door being locked. You are now in a state of uncertainty about whether the door is locked and are therefore in a state of uncertainty about whether it is possible for you to leave the room. Can you continue to try to decide whether to leave the room? It would seem that you cannot. (Try the experiment of imagining yourself in this situation and seeing whether you can imagine yourself continuing to try to decide whether to leave.) You cannot because you no longer believe that it is possible for you to leave the room. It's not that you believe that it is *im*possible for you to leave the room. You don't believe that either, for you are in a state of uncertainty about whether it is possible for you to leave. You can, of course, try to decide whether to get up and try the door. But that is something—or at least you probably believe this—that *is* possible for you. And you can try to decide, conditionally, as it were, whether to leave the room *if* the door should prove to be unlocked. But that is not the same thing as trying to decide whether to leave the room.

This thought-experiment convinces me that I cannot try to decide whether to do A or B unless I believe that doing A and doing B are both possible for me. And, therefore, I am convinced that I could not try to decide what to do unless I believed that sometimes more than one course of action was open to me. And if I never decided what to do, I should not be a very effective human being. In the **state of nature**, I should no doubt starve. In a civilized society, I should probably have to be institutionalized. Belief in one's own free will is therefore something that we can hardly do without. It would seem therefore that

it would be an evolutionary necessity—at least for rational beings like ourselves—that we believe in free will. And evolutionary necessity has scant respect for such niceties as logical consistency. It is arguable, therefore, that we cannot trust our conviction that we have free will (if, indeed, we do have this conviction). If evolution would force a certain belief on us—by brutally culling out all those of our ancestors who lacked this belief—then the fact that we hold this belief is no evidence whatever that the belief is true or even logically consistent. (But *aren't* there people who believe that no one has free will, including themselves? Well, there are certainly people who *say* that they believe this, but I suspect that they are not describing their own beliefs correctly. But even if there are people who believe that no one has free will, it does not follow that these people do not believe in free will, for people do have contradictory beliefs. It may be that "on one level"—the abstract and theoretical—certain people believe that no one has free will, although on another level—the concrete and everyday—they believe that people have free will.)

Nevertheless, when all is said and done, I find myself with the belief that sometimes more than one course of action is open to me, and I cannot give it up. (As Dr. Johnson said, "Sir, we know our will is free, and there's an end on't.") And I don't find the least plausibility in the hypothesis that this belief is an illusion. It can sometimes seem attractive to hold the view that free will is an illusion. To think this—or to toy with the idea in a theoretical sort of way—can be attractive to someone who has betrayed a friend or achieved success by spreading vicious rumors. If you had done something of that sort, wouldn't you want to believe that you had no choice, that no other course of action was really open to you? Wouldn't it be an attractive idea that your actions were determined by your genes and your upbringing or even by the way things were thousands or millions of years ago? (Jean-Paul Sartre once remarked that determinism was an endless well of excuses.) And it is immensely attractive to suppose that one is a member of a very small minority that has seen through an illusion that people have been subject to for millennia. The hypothesis has its unattractive aspects too, of course. For one thing, if it rules out blame, it presumably rules out praise on the same grounds. But, however attractive or unattractive it may be, it just seems to be false. If some unimpeachable source—God, say—were to tell me that I didn't have free will, I'd have to regard that piece of information as proof that I didn't understand the World at all. It would be as if an unimpeachable source had told me that consciousness did not exist or that the physical world was an illusion or that self-contradictory statements could be true. I'd have to say, "Well, all right. You *are* an unimpeachable source. But I just don't understand how that could be right."

I conclude that there is no position that one can take on the matter of free will that does not confront its adherents with mystery. I myself prefer the following mystery: I believe that the outcome of our deliberations about what to do is undetermined and that we—in some way that I have no shadow of an understanding of—nevertheless have a choice about the outcome of these deliberations. (And I do not believe that the concept of agent-causation is of the least help in explaining how this could be.)

I believe that if Jane has freely decided to speak then the following must be true: if God were to create a thousand perfect duplicates of Jane as she was an instant before the decision to speak was made and were to place each one in circumstances that perfectly duplicated Jane's circumstances at that instant, some of the duplicates would choose to speak and some of them would choose to remain silent, and there would be no explanation whatever for the fact that a particular one of the duplicates made whichever of the choices it was that she made. And yet, I believe, Jane had a choice about whether to speak or to remain silent. (It is important not to be misled by words here. From the fact that someone *makes* a choice, it does not follow that that person *has* a choice. If I am locked in a room and do not know that the door is locked, it may be that I *make* a choice *to* stay in the room even though I *have* no choice *about whether to* stay in the room.)

I accept this mystery because it seems to me to be the smallest mystery available. If someone believes that human beings do not have free will, then that person accepts a mystery and in my view it is a greater, deeper mystery than the one I accept. If someone denies the No Choice Principle, then that

person accepts a mystery, and in my view it is a greater, deeper mystery than the one I accept. But others may judge the "sizes" of these mysteries differently.

It is important to be aware that we have not said everything there is to be said about the size of the mysteries. The most important topic that we have not discussed in that connection is the relation between free will and morality. In our preliminary discussion of the concept of free will, we said that it was a common opinion that free will was required by morality. If this common opinion is correct, then all moral judgments are false or in some way "out of place" if there is no free will. If that were so, it would greatly aggravate the mystery that confronts those who deny that there is free will. Could it really be true, for example, that those who believe that there is something morally objectionable about racism or child abuse or genocide or serial murder hold a belief that is false or in some other way defective? If an unimpeachable source were to inform me that there was nothing morally objectionable about child abuse, my dominant reaction would be one of horror. But I should also have a negative reaction to this revelation that was more intellectual or theoretical. I should have to say that, if that was so, then I didn't understand the World at all. I should have to say that I just didn't understand how it could *be* that there was nothing morally objectionable about child abuse.

It may not be, however, that those who reject free will must hold that all moral judgments are false or otherwise illusory. The "common opinion" that morality requires free will is not so common as it used to be. When almost all English-speaking philosophers were compatibilists, this opinion was held by almost everyone in the English-speaking philosophical world. It was the common assumption of the compatibilists and the few incompatibilists that there were. Now, however, compatibilism is a less common opinion, owing to the fact that philosophers are coming to realize that compatibilism requires the rejection of the No Choice Principle. Many philosophers are now inclined to reject compatibilism who would previously have accepted it. And because they are also inclined to reject the view that we could have free will in a way that required indeterminism, they are inclined to reject free will altogether. But most of them are not willing to say that morality is an illusion. It has, therefore, become an increasingly widespread view that morality does not after all require free will. It is because of this increasingly popular view that I have not included the thesis that morality is an illusion among the mysteries that must be accepted by those who reject free will. I myself continue to believe that morality is an illusion if there is no free will, but, since the issues involved in the debate about this question pertain to moral philosophy rather than to metaphysics, I shall not discuss them.

However one may judge the relative "sizes" of the mysteries that confront the adherents of the various positions that one might take on the question of free will, these mysteries exist. The metaphysician's task is to display these mysteries. Each of us must decide, with no further help from the metaphysician, how to respond to the array of mysteries that the metaphysician has placed before us.

Suggestions for Further Reading

Berofsky's *Free Will and Determinism* and Watson's *Free Will* are excellent collections devoted to the problem of free will and determinism. Fischer's more recent *Moral Responsibility* contains much useful material. My own book, *An Essay on Free Will* is a defense of incompatibilism. Large parts of it are accessible to those without formal philosophical training. The central argument of the book is attacked in Lewis's superb article, "Are We Free to Break the Laws?" (rather difficult for those without philosophical training). Dennett's *Elbow Room* is a highly readable (if somewhat idiosyncratic) defense of compatiblism.

NOTE

1. It should be evident from this discussion of "free will" that what we are calling by this name would be more appropriately called 'free choice'. 'Free will' is, however, the term that has traditionally been used to express this concept, and I use it out of respect for tradition.

KEY TERMS

Free will	Agent-causation
Determinism	Event-causation
Incompatibilism	State of nature
Compatibilism	

STUDY QUESTIONS

1. What does van Inwagen mean when he talks about the future as a garden of forking paths? Do you tend to think that the future is really like that?
2. How do compatibilists argue that we may have future paths open to us, even if those paths are not physically connected with the present path? What does van Inwagen say is wrong with this view?
3. How plausible do you think van Inwagen's No Choice Principle is?
4. Why must a compatibilist reject the No Choice Principle? How bad do you think it would be to have to reject that principle?
5. Why does van Inwagen think that indeterminism is equally inhospitable to free will?

Of Liberty and Necessity

DAVID HUME

..

Part I

It might reasonably be expected in questions which have been canvassed and disputed with great eagerness, since the first origin of science and philosophy, that the meaning of all the terms, at least, should have been agreed upon among the disputants; and our enquiries, in the course of two thousand years, been able to pass from words to the true and real subject of the controversy. For how easy may it seem to give exact definitions of the terms employed in reasoning, and make these definitions, not the mere sound of words, the object of future scrutiny and examination? But if we consider the matter more narrowly, we shall be apt to draw a quite opposite conclusion. From this circumstance alone, that a controversy has been long kept on foot, and remains still undecided, we may presume that there is some ambiguity in the expression, and that the disputants affix different ideas to the terms employed in the controversy. For as the faculties of the mind are supposed to be naturally alike in every individual; otherwise nothing could be more fruitless than to reason or dispute together; it were impossible, if men affix the same ideas to their terms, that they could so long form different opinions of the same subject; especially when they communicate their views, and each party turn themselves on all sides, in search of arguments which may give them the victory over their antagonists. It is true, if men attempt the discussion of questions which lie entirely beyond the reach of human capacity, such as

those concerning the origin of worlds, or the economy of the intellectual system or region of spirits, they may long beat the air in their fruitless contests, and never arrive at any determinate conclusion. But if the question regard any subject of common life and experience, nothing, one would think, could preserve the dispute so long undecided but some ambiguous expressions, which keep the antagonists still at a distance, and hinder them from grappling with each other.

This has been the case in the long disputed question concerning liberty and necessity; and to so remarkable a degree that, if I be not much mistaken, we shall find, that all mankind, both learned and ignorant, have always been of the same opinion with regard to this subject, and that a few intelligible definitions would immediately have put an end to the whole controversy. I own that this dispute has been so much canvassed on all hands, and has led philosophers into such a labyrinth of obscure **sophistry**, that it is no wonder, if a sensible reader indulge his ease so far as to turn a deaf ear to the proposal of such a question, from which he can expect neither instruction nor entertainment. But the state of the argument here proposed may, perhaps, serve to renew his attention; as it has more novelty, promises at least some decision of the controversy, and will not much disturb his ease by any intricate or obscure reasoning.

I hope, therefore, to make it appear that all men have ever agreed in the doctrine both of necessity and of liberty, according to any reasonable sense, which can be put on these terms; and that the whole controversy has hitherto turned merely upon words. We shall begin with examining the doctrine of necessity.

It is universally allowed that matter, in all its operations, is actuated by a necessary force, and that every natural effect is so precisely determined by the

From *Enquiries Concerning Human Understanding and Concerning the Principles of Morals*, edited by L. A. Selby-Bigge, 3rd edition revised by P. H. Nidditch. Copyright © 1975 by Oxford University Press. Reprinted by permission of the publisher.

energy of its cause that no other effect, in such particular circumstances, could possibly have resulted from it. The degree and direction of every motion is, by the **laws of nature**, prescribed with such exactness that a living creature may as soon arise from the shock of two bodies as motion in any other degree or direction than what is actually produced by it. Would we, therefore, form a just and precise idea of *necessity*, we must consider whence that idea arises when we apply it to the question of bodies.

It seems evident that, if all the scenes of nature were continually shifted in such a manner that no two events bore any resemblance to each other, but every object was entirely new, without any similitude to whatever had been seen before, we should never, in that case, have attained the least idea of necessity, or of a connexion among these objects. We might say, upon such a supposition, that one object or event has followed another; not that one was produced by the other. The relation of **cause and effect** must be utterly unknown to mankind. Inference and reasoning concerning the operations of nature would, from that moment, be at an end; and the memory and senses remain the only canals, by which the knowledge of any real existence could possibly have access to the mind. Our idea, therefore, of necessity and causation arises entirely from the uniformity observable in the operations of nature, where similar objects are constantly conjoined together, and the mind is determined by custom to infer the one from the appearance of the other. These two circumstances form the whole of that necessity, which we ascribe to matter. Beyond the **constant conjunction** of similar objects, and the consequent *inference* from one to the other, we have no notion of any necessity or connexion.

If it appear, therefore, that all mankind have ever allowed, without any doubt or hesitation, that these two circumstances take place in the voluntary actions of men, and in the operations of mind; it must follow, that all mankind have ever agreed in the doctrine of necessity, and that they have hitherto disputed, merely for not understanding each other.

As to the first circumstance, the constant and regular conjunction of similar events, we may possibly satisfy ourselves by the following considerations. It is universally acknowledged that there is a great uniformity among the actions of men, in all nations and ages, and that human nature remains still the same, in its principles and operations. The same motives always produce the same actions. The same events follow from the same causes. Ambition, avarice, self-love, vanity, friendship, generosity, public spirit: these passions, mixed in various degrees, and distributed through society, have been, from the beginning of the world, and still are, the source of all the actions and enterprises, which have ever been observed among mankind. Would you know the sentiments, inclinations, and course of life of the Greeks and Romans? Study well the temper and actions of the French and English: You cannot be much mistaken in transferring to the former *most* of the observations which you have made with regard to the latter. Mankind are so much the same, in all times and places, that history informs us of nothing new or strange in this particular. Its chief use is only to discover the constant and universal principles of human nature, by showing men in all varieties of circumstances and situations, and furnishing us with materials from which we may form our observations and become acquainted with the regular springs of human action and behaviour. These records or wars, intrigues, factions, and revolutions, are so many collections of experiments, by which the political or moral philosopher fixes the principles of his science, in the same manner as the physician or natural philosopher becomes acquainted with the nature of plants, minerals, and other external objects, by the experiments which he forms concerning them. Nor are the earth, water, and other elements, examined by Aristotle, and Hippocrates, more like to those which at present lie under our observation than the men described by Polybius and Tacitus are to those who now govern the world.

Should a traveller, returning from a far country, bring us an account of men, wholly different from any with whom we were ever acquainted; men, who were entirely divested of avarice, ambition, or revenge; who knew no pleasure but friendship, generosity, and public spirit; we should immediately, from these circumstances, detect the falsehood, and prove him a liar, with the same certainty as if he had stuffed his narration with stories of centaurs and dragons, miracles and prodigies. And if we would explode any forgery in history, we cannot make use of a more convincing argument, than to prove, that the actions ascribed to any person are directly contrary to the course of nature, and that no human motives, in such circumstances, could ever induce him to such a conduct. The veracity of Quintus Curtius is as much to be suspected, when he describes the supernatural courage of Alexander, by which he was hurried on singly to attack multitudes, as when he describes his supernatural force and activity, by which he was able to resist them. So readily and universally do we acknowledge a uniformity in human motives and actions as well as in the operations of body.

Hence likewise the benefit of that experience, acquired by long life and a variety of business and company, in order to instruct us in the principles of human nature, and regulate our future conduct, as well as speculation. By means of this guide, we mount up to the knowledge of men's inclinations and motives, from their actions, expressions, and even gestures; and again descend to the interpretation of their actions from our knowledge of their motives and inclinations. The general observations treasured up by a course of experience, give us the clue of human nature, and teach us to unravel all its intricacies. Pretexts and appearances no longer deceive us. Public declarations pass for the specious colouring of a cause. And though virtue and honour be allowed their proper weight and authority, that perfect disinterestedness, so often pretended to, is never expected in multitudes and parties; seldom in their leaders; and scarcely even in individuals of any rank or station. But were there no uniformity in human actions, and were every experiment which we could form of this kind irregular and anomalous, it were impossible to collect any general observations concerning mankind; and no experience, however accurately digested by reflection, would ever serve to any purpose. Why is the aged husbandman more skilful in his calling than the young beginner but because there is a certain uniformity in the operation of the sun, rain, and earth towards the production of vegetables; and experience teaches the old practitioner the rules by which this operation is governed and directed.

We must not, however, expect that this uniformity of human actions should be carried to such a length as that all men, in the same circumstances, will always act precisely in the same manner, without making any allowance for the diversity of characters, prejudices, and opinions. Such a uniformity in every particular, is found in no part of nature. On the contrary, from observing the variety of conduct in different men, we are enabled to form a greater variety of maxims, which still suppose a degree of uniformity and regularity.

Are the manners of men different in different ages and countries? We learn thence the great force of custom and education, which mould the human mind from its infancy and form it into a fixed and established character. Is the behaviour and conduct of the one sex very unlike that of the other? Is it thence we become acquainted with the different characters which nature has impressed upon the sexes, and which she preserves with constancy and regularity? Are the actions of the same person much diversified in the different periods of his life, from infancy to old age? This affords room for many general observations concerning the gradual change of our sentiments and inclinations, and the different maxims which prevail in the different ages of human creatures. Even the characters, which are peculiar to each individual, have a uniformity in their influence; otherwise our acquaintance with the persons and our observation of their conduct could never teach us their dispositions, or serve to direct our behaviour with regard to them.

I grant it possible to find some actions, which seem to have no regular connexion with any known motives, and are exceptions to all the measures of conduct which have ever been established for the government of men. But if we would willingly know what judgment should be formed of such irregular and extraordinary actions, we may consider the sentiments commonly entertained with regard to those irregular events which appear in the course of nature, and the operations of external objects. All causes are not conjoined to their usual effects with like uniformity. An artificer, who handles only dead matter, may be disappointed of his aim, as well as the politician, who directs the conduct of sensible and intelligent agents.

The vulgar, who take things according to their first appearance, attribute the uncertainty of events to such an uncertainty in the causes as makes the latter often fail of their usual influence; though they meet with no impediment in their operation. But philosophers, observing that, almost in every part of nature, there is contained a vast variety of springs and principles, which are hid, by reason of their minuteness or remoteness, find, that it is at least possible the contrariety of events may not proceed from any contingency in the cause, but from the secret operation of contrary causes. This possibility is converted into certainty by farther observation, when they remark that, upon an exact scrutiny, a contrariety of effects always betrays a contrariety of causes, and proceeds from their mutual opposition. A peasant can give no better reason for the stopping of any clock or watch than to say that it does not commonly go right: But an artist easily perceives that the same force in the spring or pendulum has always the same influence on the wheels; but fails of its usual effect, perhaps by reason of a grain of dust, which puts a stop to the whole movement. From the observation of several parallel instances, philosophers form a maxim that the connexion between all causes and effects is equally necessary, and that its seeming uncertainty in some instances proceeds from the secret opposition of contrary causes.

Thus, for instance, in the human body, when the usual symptoms of health or sickness disappoint our expectation; when medicines operate not with their wonted powers; when irregular events follow from any particular cause; the philosopher and physician are not surprised at the matter, nor are even tempted to deny, in general, the necessity and uniformity of those principles by which the animal economy is conducted. They know that a human body is a mighty complicated machine: That many secret powers lurk in it, which are altogether beyond our comprehension: That to us it must often appear very uncertain in its operations: And that therefore the irregular events, which outwardly discover themselves, can be no proof that the laws of nature are not observed with the greatest regularity in its internal operations and government.

The philosopher, if he be consistent, must apply the same reasoning to the actions and volitions of intelligent agents. The most irregular and unexpected resolutions of men may frequently be accounted for by those who know every particular circumstance of their character and situation. A person of an obliging disposition gives a peevish answer: But he has the toothache, or has not dined. A stupid fellow discovers an uncommon alacrity in his carriage: But he has met with a sudden piece of good fortune. Or even when an action, as sometimes happens, cannot be particularly accounted for, either by the person himself or by others; we know, in general, that the characters of men are, to a certain degree, inconstant and irregular. This is, in a manner, the constant character of human nature; though it be applicable, in a more particular manner, to some persons who have no fixed rule for their conduct, but proceed in a continued course of caprice and inconstancy. The internal principles and motives may operate in a uniform manner, notwithstanding these seeming irregularities; in the same manner as the winds, rain, clouds, and other variations of the weather are supposed to be governed by steady principles; though not easily discoverable by human sagacity and enquiry.

Thus it appears, not only that the conjunction between motives and voluntary actions is as regular and uniform as that between the cause and effect in any part of nature; but also that this regular conjunction has been universally acknowledged among mankind, and has never been the subject of dispute, either in philosophy or common life. Now, as it is from past experience that we draw all inferences concerning the future, and as we conclude that objects will always be conjoined together which we find to have always been conjoined; it may seem superfluous to prove that this experienced uniformity in human actions is a source whence we draw *inferences* concerning them. But in order to throw the argument into a greater variety of lights we shall also insist, though briefly, on this latter topic.

The mutual dependence of men is so great in all societies that scarce any human action is entirely complete in itself, or is performed without some reference to the actions of others, which are requisite to make it answer fully the intention of the agent. The poorest artificer, who labours alone, expects at least the protection of the magistrate, to ensure him the enjoyment of the fruits of his labour. He also expects that, when he carries his goods to market, and offers them at a reasonable price, he shall find purchasers, and shall be able, by the money he acquires, to engage others to supply him with those commodities which are requisite for his subsistence. In proportion as men extend their dealings, and render their intercourse with others more complicated, they always comprehend, in their schemes of life, a greater variety of voluntary actions, which they expect, from the proper motives, to co-operate with their own. In all these conclusions they take their measures from past experience, in the same manner as in their reasonings concerning external objects; and firmly believe that men, as well as all the elements, are to continue, in their operations, the same that they have ever found them. A manufacturer reckons upon the labour of his servants for the execution of any work as much as upon the tools which he employs, and would be equally surprised were his expectations disappointed. In short, this experimental inference and reasoning concerning the actions of others enters so much into human life that no man, while awake, is ever a moment without employing it. Have we not reason, therefore, to affirm that all mankind have always agreed in the doctrine of necessity according to the foregoing definition and explication of it?

Nor have philosophers ever entertained a different opinion from the people in this particular. For, not to mention that almost every action of their life supposes that opinion, there are even few of the speculative parts of learning to which it is not essential. What would become of *history*, had we not a dependence on the veracity of the historian according to the experience which we have had of mankind? How could *politics* be a science, if laws and forms of government had not a uniform influence upon society? Where would be the foundation of *morals*, if particular characters had no certain or determinate power to produce particular sentiments, and if these sentiments had no constant operation on actions? And with what pretence could we employ our *criticism* upon any poet or polite author, if we could not pronounce the conduct and sentiments of his actors either natural or unnatural to such characters, and in such circumstances? It seems almost impossible, therefore, to engage either in science or action of any kind without acknowledging the doctrine of necessity, and this *inference* from motive to voluntary actions, from characters to conduct.

And indeed, when we consider how aptly *natural* and *moral* evidence link together, and form only one chain of argument, we shall make no scruple to allow that they are of the same nature, and derived from the same principles. A prisoner who has neither money nor interest, discovers the impossibility of his escape, as well when he considers the obstinacy of the gaoler, as the walls and bars with which he is surrounded; and, in all attempts for his freedom, chooses rather to work upon the stone and iron of the one, than upon the inflexible nature of the other. The same prisoner, when conducted to the scaffold, foresees his death as certainly from the constancy and fidelity of his guards, as from the operation of the axe or wheel. His mind runs along a certain train of ideas: The refusal of the soldiers to consent to his escape; the action of the executioner; the separation of the head and body; bleeding, convulsive motions, and death. Here is a connected chain of natural causes and voluntary actions; but the mind feels no difference between them in passing from one link to another: Nor is less certain of the future event than if it were connected with the objects present to the memory or senses, by a train of causes, cemented together by what we are pleased to call a *physical* necessity. The same experienced union has the same effect on the mind, whether the united objects be motives, volition, and actions; or figure and motion. We may change the name of things; but their nature and their operation on the understanding never change.

Were a man, whom I know to be honest and opulent, and with whom I live in intimate friendship, to come into my house, where I am surrounded with my servants, I rest assured that he is not to stab me before he leaves it in order to rob me of my silver standish; and I no more suspect this event than the falling of the house itself, which is new, and solidly built and founded—*But he may have been seized with a sudden and unknown frenzy.*—So may a sudden earthquake arise, and shake and tumble my house about my ears. I shall therefore change the suppositions. I shall say that I know with certainty that he is not to put his hand into the fire and hold it there till it be consumed: And this event, I think I can foretell with the same assurance, as that, if he throw himself out at the window, and meet with no obstruction, he will not remain a moment suspended in the air. No suspicion of an unknown frenzy can give the least possibility to the former event, which is so contrary to all the known principles of human nature. A man who at noon leaves his purse full of gold on the pavement at Charing-Cross, may as well expect that it will fly away like a feather, as that he will find it untouched an hour after. Above one half of human reasonings contain inferences of a similar nature, attended with more or less degrees of certainty proportioned to our experience of the usual conduct of mankind in such particular situations.

I have frequently considered, what could possibly be the reason why all mankind, though they have ever, without hesitation, acknowledged the doctrine of necessity in their whole practice and reasoning, have yet discovered such a reluctance to acknowledge it in words, and have rather shown a propensity, in all ages, to profess the contrary opinion. The matter, I think, may be accounted for after the following manner. If we examine the operations of body, and the production of effects from their causes, we shall find that all our faculties can never carry us farther in our knowledge of this relation than barely to observe that particular objects are *constantly conjoined* together, and that the mind is carried, by a *customary transition*, from the appearance of one to the belief of the other. But though this conclusion concerning human ignorance be the result of the strictest scrutiny of this subject, men still entertain a strong propensity to believe that they penetrate farther into the powers of nature, and perceive something like a necessary connexion between the cause and the effect. When again they turn their reflections towards the operations of their own minds, and *feel* no such connexion of the motive and the action; they are thence apt to suppose, that there is a difference between the effects which result from material force, and those which arise from thought and intelligence. But being once convinced that we know nothing farther of causation of any kind than merely the *constant conjunction* of objects, and the consequent *inference* of the mind from one to another, and finding that these two circumstances are universally allowed to have place in voluntary actions; we may be more easily led to own the same necessity common to all causes. And though this

reasoning may contradict the systems of many philosophers, in ascribing necessity to the determinations of the will, we shall find, upon reflection, that they dissent from it in words only, not in their real sentiment. Necessity, according to the sense in which it is here taken, has never yet been rejected, nor can ever, I think, be rejected by any philosopher. It may only, perhaps, be pretended that the mind can perceive, in the operations of matter, some farther connexion between the cause and effect; and connexion that has not place in voluntary actions of intelligent beings. Now whether it be so or not, can only appear upon examination; and it is incumbent on these philosophers to make good their assertion, by defining or describing that necessity, and pointing it out to us in the operations of material causes.

It would seem, indeed, that men begin at the wrong end of this question concerning liberty and necessity, when they enter upon it by examining the faculties of the soul, the influence of the understanding, and the operations of the will. Let them first discuss a more simple question, namely, the operations of body and of brute unintelligent matter; and try whether they can there form any idea of causation and necessity, except that of a constant conjunction of objects, and subsequent inference of the mind from one to another. If these circumstances form, in reality, the whole of that necessity, which we conceive in matter, and if these circumstances be also universally acknowledged to take place in the operations of the mind, the dispute is at an end; at least, must be owned to be thenceforth merely verbal. But as long as we will rashly suppose, that we have some farther idea of necessity and causation in the operations of external objects; at the same time, that we can find nothing farther in the voluntary actions of the mind; there is no possibility of bringing the question to any determinate issue, while we proceed upon so erroneous a supposition. The only method of undeceiving us is to mount up higher; to examine the narrow extent of science when applied to material causes; and to convince ourselves that all we know of them is the constant conjunction and inference above mentioned. We may, perhaps, find that it is with difficulty we are induced to fix such narrow limits to human understanding: But we can afterwards find no difficulty when we come to apply this doctrine to the actions of the will. For as it is evident that these have a higher regular conjunction with motives and circumstances and characters, and as we always draw inferences from one to the other, we must be obliged to acknowledge in words that necessity, which we have already avowed, in every deliberation of our lives, and in every step of our conduct and behaviour.[1]

But to proceed in this reconciling project with regard to the question of liberty and necessity; the most contentious question of **metaphysics**, the most contentious science; it will not require many words to prove, that all mankind have ever agreed in the doctrine of liberty as well as in that of necessity, and that the whole dispute, in this respect also, has been hitherto merely verbal. For what is meant by liberty, when applied to voluntary actions? We cannot surely mean that actions have so little connexion with motives, inclinations, and circumstances, that one does not follow with a certain degree of uniformity from the other, and that one affords no inference by which we can conclude the existence of the other. For these are plain and acknowledged matters of fact. By liberty, then, we can only mean *a power of acting or not acting, according to the determinations of the will*; that is, if we choose to remain at rest, we may; if we choose to move, we also may. Now this hypothetical liberty is universally allowed to belong to every one who is not a prisoner and in chains. Here, then, is no subject of dispute.

Whatever definition we may give of liberty, we should be careful to observe two requisite circumstances; *first*, that it be consistent with plain matter of fact; *secondly*, that it be consistent with itself. If we observe these circumstances, and render our definition intelligible, I am persuaded that all mankind will be found of one opinion with regard to it.

It is universally allowed that nothing exists without a cause of its existence, and that chance, when strictly examined, is a mere negative word, and means not any real power which has anywhere a being in nature. But it is pretended that some causes are necessary, some not necessary. Here then is the advantage of definitions. Let any one *define* a cause, without comprehending, as a part of the definition, a *necessary connexion* with its effect; and let him show distinctly the origin of the idea, expressed by the definition; and I shall readily give up the whole controversy. But if the foregoing explication of the

matter be received, this must be absolutely impracticable. Had not objects a regular conjunction with each other, we should never have entertained any notion of cause and effect; and this regular conjunction produces that inference of the understanding, which is the only connexion, that we can have any comprehension of. Whoever attempts a definition of cause, exclusive of these circumstances, will be obliged either to employ unintelligible terms or such as are synonymous to the term which he endeavours to define.[2] And if the definition above mentioned be admitted; liberty, when opposed to necessity, not to constraint, is the same thing with chance; which is universally allowed to have no existence.

Part II

There is no method of reasoning more common, and yet none more blameable, than, in philosophical disputes, to endeavour the refutation of any hypothesis, by a pretence of its dangerous consequences to religion and morality. When any opinion leads to absurdities, it is certainly false; but it is not certain that an opinion is false, because it is of dangerous consequence. Such topics, therefore, ought entirely to be forborne; as serving nothing to the discovery of truth, but only to make the person of an antagonist odious. This I observe in general, without pretending to draw any advantage from it. I frankly submit to an examination of this kind, and shall venture to affirm that the doctrines, both of necessity and of liberty, as above explained, are not only consistent with morality, but are absolutely essential to its support.

Necessity may be defined two ways, conformably to the two definitions of *cause*, of which it makes an essential part. It consists either in the constant conjunction of like objects, or in the inference of the understanding from one object to another. Now necessity, in both these senses, (which, indeed, are at bottom the same) has universally, though tacitly, in the schools, in the pulpit, and in common life, been allowed to belong to the will of man; and no one has ever pretended to deny that we can draw inferences concerning human actions, and that those inferences are founded on the experienced union of like actions, with like motives, inclinations, and circumstances. The only particular in which any one can differ, is, that either, perhaps, he will refuse to give the name of necessity to this property of human actions: But as long as the meaning is understood, I hope the word can do no harm: Or that he will maintain it possible to discover something farther in the operations of matter. But this, it must be acknowledged, can be of no consequence to morality or religion, whatever it may be to natural philosophy or metaphysics. We may here be mistaken in asserting that there is no idea of any other necessity of connexion in the actions of the mind, but what everyone does, and must readily allow of. We change no circumstance in the received orthodox system with regard to the will, but only in that with regard to material objects and causes. Nothing, therefore, can be more innocent, at least, than this doctrine.

All laws being founded on rewards and punishments, it is supposed as a fundamental principle, that these motives have a regular and uniform influence on the mind, and both produce the good and prevent the evil actions. We may give to this influence what name we please; but, as it is usually conjoined with the action, it must be esteemed a *cause*, and be looked upon as an instance of that necessity, which we would here establish.

The only proper object of hatred or vengeance is a person or creature, endowed with thought and consciousness; and when any criminal or injurious actions excite that passion, it is only by their relation to the person, or connexion with him. Actions are, by their very nature, temporary and perishing; and where they proceed not from some *cause* in the character and disposition of the person who performed them, they can neither redound to his honour, if good; nor infamy, if evil. The actions themselves may be blameable; they may be contrary to all the rules of morality and religion: But the person is not answerable for them; and as they proceed from nothing in him that is durable and constant, and leave nothing of that nature behind them, it is impossible he can, upon their account, become the object of punishment or vengeance. According to the principle, therefore, which denies necessity, and consequently causes, a man is as pure and untainted, after having committed the most horrid crime, as at

the first moment of his birth, nor is his character anywise concerned in his actions, since they are not derived from it, and the wickedness of the one can never be used as a proof of the depravity of the other.

Men are not blamed for such actions as they perform ignorantly and casually, whatever may be the consequences. Why? but because the principles of these actions are only momentary, and terminate in them alone. Men are less blamed for such actions as they perform hastily and unpremeditately than for such as proceed from deliberation. For what reason? but because a hasty temper, though a constant cause or principle in the mind, operates only by intervals, and infects not the whole character. Again, repentance wipes off every crime, if attended with a reformation of life and manners. How is this to be accounted for? but by asserting that actions render a person criminal merely as they are proofs of criminal principles in the mind; and when, by an alteration of these principles, they cease to be just proofs, they likewise cease to be criminal. But, except upon the doctrine of necessity, they never were just proofs, and consequently never were criminal.

It will be equally easy to prove, and from the same arguments, that *liberty*, according to that definition above mentioned, in which all men agree, is also essential to morality, and that no human actions, where it is wanting, are susceptible of any moral qualities, or can be the objects either of approbation or dislike. For as actions are objects of our moral sentiment, so far only as they are indications of the internal character, passions, and affections; it is impossible that they can give rise either to praise or blame, where they proceed not from these principles, but are derived altogether from external violence.

I pretend not to have obviated or removed all objections to this theory, with regard to necessity and liberty. I can foresee other objections, derived from topics which have not here been treated of. It may be said, for instance, that, if voluntary actions be subjected to the same laws of necessity with the operations of matter, there is a continued chain of necessary causes, pre-ordained and pre-determined, reaching from the original cause of all to every single volition of every human creature. No contingency anywhere in the universe; no indifference; no liberty. While we act, we are, at the same time, acted upon. The ultimate Author of all our volitions is the Creator of the world, who first bestowed motion on this immense machine, and placed all beings in that particular position, whence every subsequent event, by an inevitable necessity, must result. Human actions, therefore, either can have no moral turpitude at all, as proceeding from so good a cause; or if they have any turpitude, they must involve our Creator in the same guilt, while he is acknowledged to be their ultimate cause and author. For as a man, who fired a mine, is answerable for all the consequences whether the train he employed be long or short; so wherever a continued chain of necessary causes is fixed, that Being, either finite or infinite, who produces the first, is likewise the author of all the rest, and must both bear the blame and acquire the praise which belong to them. Our clear and unalterable ideas of morality establish this rule, upon unquestionable reasons, when we examine the consequences of any human action; and these reasons must still have greater force when applied to the volitions and intentions of a Being infinitely wise and powerful. Ignorance or impotence may be pleaded for so limited a creature as man; but those imperfections have no place in our Creator. He foresaw, he ordained, he intended all those actions of men, which we so rashly pronounce criminal. And we must therefore conclude, either that they are not criminal, or that the Deity, not man, is accountable for them. But as either of these positions is absurd and impious, it follows, that the doctrine from which they are deduced cannot possibly be true, as being liable to all the same objections. An absurd consequence, if necessary, proves the original doctrine to be absurd; in the same manner as criminal actions render criminal the original cause, if the connexion between them be necessary and evitable.

This objection consists of two parts, which we shall examine separately; *First*, that, if human actions can be traced up, by a necessary chain, to the Deity, they can never be criminal; on account of the infinite perfection of that Being from whom they are derived, and who can intend nothing but what is altogether good and laudable. Or, *Secondly*, if they be criminal, we must retract the attribute of perfection, which we ascribe to the Deity, and must acknowledge him to be the ultimate author of guilt and moral turpitude in all his creatures.

The answer to the first objection seems obvious and convincing. There are many philosophers who, after an exact scrutiny of all the phenomena of nature, conclude, that the WHOLE, considered as one system, is, in every period of its existence, ordered with perfect benevolence; and that the utmost possible happiness will, in the end, result to all created beings, without any mixture of positive or absolute ill or misery. Every physical ill, say they, makes an essential part of this benevolent system, and could not possibly be removed, even by the Deity himself, considered as a wise agent, without giving entrance to greater ill, or excluding greater good, which will result from it. From this theory, some philosophers, and the ancient *Stoics* among the rest, derived a topic of consolation under all afflictions, while they taught their pupils that those ills under which they laboured were, in reality, goods to the universe; and that to an enlarged view, which could comprehend the whole system of nature, every event became an object of joy and exultation. But though this topic be specious and sublime, it was soon found in practice weak and ineffectual. You would surely more irritate than appease a man lying under the racking pains of the gout by preaching up to him the rectitude of those general laws, which produced the malignant humours in his body, and led them through the proper canals, to the sinews and nerves, where they now excite such acute torments. These enlarged views may, for a moment, please the imagination of a speculative man, who is placed in ease and security; but neither can they dwell with constancy on his mind, even though undisturbed by the emotions of pain or passion; much less can they maintain their ground when attacked by such powerful antagonists. The affections take a narrower and more natural survey of their object; and by an economy, more suitable to the infirmity of human minds, regard alone the beings around us, and are actuated by such events as appear good or ill to the private system.

The case is the same with *moral* as with *physical* ill. It cannot reasonably be supposed, that those remote considerations, which are found of so little efficacy with regard to one, will have a more powerful influence with regard to the other. The mind of man is so formed by nature that, upon the appearance of certain characters, dispositions, and actions, it immediately feels the sentiment of approbation or blame; nor are there any emotions more essential to its frame and constitution. The characters which engage our approbation are chiefly such as contribute to the peace and security of human society; as the characters which excite blame are chiefly such as tend to public detriment and disturbance: Whence it may reasonably be presumed, that the moral sentiments arise, either mediately or immediately, from a reflection of these opposite interests. What though philosophical meditations establish a different opinion or conjecture; that everything is right with regard to the WHOLE, and that the qualities, which disturb society, are, in the main, as beneficial, and are as suitable to the primary intention of nature as those which more directly promote its happiness and welfare? Are such remote and uncertain speculations able to counterbalance the sentiments which arise from the natural and immediate view of the objects? A man who is robbed of a considerable sum; does he find his vexation for the loss anywise diminished by these sublime reflections? Why then should his moral resentment against the crime be supposed incompatible with them? Or why should not the acknowledgment of a real distinction between vice and virtue be reconcilable to all speculative systems of philosophy, as well as that of a real distinction between personal beauty and deformity? Both these distinctions are founded in the natural sentiments of the human mind: And these sentiments are not to be controlled or altered by any philosophical theory or speculation whatsoever.

The *second* objection admits not of so easy and satisfactory an answer; nor is it possible to explain distinctly, how the Deity can be the mediate cause of all the actions of men, without being the author of sin and moral turpitude. These are mysteries, which mere natural and unassisted reason is very unfit to handle; and whatever system she embraces, she must find herself involved in inextricable difficulties, and even contradictions, at every step which she takes with regard to such subjects. To reconcile the indifference and contingency of human actions with prescience; or to defend absolute decrees, and yet free the Deity from being the author of sin, has been found hitherto to exceed all the power of philosophy.

Happy, if she be thence sensible of her temerity, when she pries into these sublime mysteries; and leaving a scene so full of obscurities and perplexities, return, with suitable modesty, to her true and proper province, the examination of common life; where she will find difficulties enough to employ her enquiries, without launching into so boundless an ocean of doubt, uncertainty, and contradiction!

NOTES

1. The prevalence of the doctrine of liberty may be accounted for, from another cause, viz, a false sensation or seeming experience which we have, or may have, of liberty or indifference, in many of our actions. The necessity of any action, whether of matter or of mind, is not, properly speaking, a quality in the agent, but in any thinking or intelligent being, who may consider the action; and it consists chiefly in the determination of his thoughts to infer the existence of that action from some preceding objects; as liberty, when opposed to necessity, is nothing but the want of that determination, and a certain looseness or indifference, which we feel, in passing, or not passing, from the idea of one object to that of any succeeding one. Now we may observe, that though, in *reflecting* on human actions, we seldom feel such a looseness, or indifference, but are commonly able to infer them with considerable certainty from their motives, and from the dispositions of the agent; yet it frequently happens, that, in *performing* the actions themselves, we are sensible of something like it: And as all resembling objects are readily taken for each other, this has been employed as a demonstrative and even intuitive proof of human liberty. We feel, that our actions are subject to our will, on most occasions; and imagine we feel, that the will itself is subject to nothing, because, when by a denial of it we are provoked to try, we feel, that it moves easily every way, and produces an image of itself (or a *Velleïty*, as it is called in the schools) even on that side, on which it did not settle. This image, or faint motion, we persuade ourselves, could, at that time, have been compleated into the thing itself; because, should that be denied, we find, upon a second trial, that, at present, it can. We consider not, that the fantastical desire of shewing liberty, is here the motive of our actions. And it seems certain, that, however we may imagine we

feel a liberty within ourselves, a spectator can commonly infer our actions from our motives and character; and even where he cannot, he concludes in general, that he might, were he perfectly acquainted with every circumstance of our situation and temper, and the most secret springs of our complexion and disposition. Now this is the very essence of necessity, according to the foregoing doctrine.

2. Thus, if a cause be defined, *that which produces any thing*; it is easy to observe, that *producing* is synonimous to *causing*. In like manner, if a cause be defined, *that by which any thing exists*; this is liable to the same objection. For what is meant by these words, *by which*? Had it been said, that a cause is *that* after which *any thing constantly exists*; we should have understood the terms. For this is, indeed, all we know of the matter. And this constancy forms the very essence of necessity, nor have we any other idea of it.

KEY TERMS

Sophistry
Laws of nature
Cause and effect

Constant conjunction
Metaphysics

STUDY QUESTIONS

1. Do you think that Hume is right when he says, "Mankind are so much the same, in all times and places, that history informs us of nothing new or strange in this particular"? Why or why not?
2. How does Hume argue that we all acknowledge the doctrine of necessity on a regular basis?
3. How does Hume distinguish among liberty, constraint, and chance?
4. It is often supposed that if all of our actions are determined according to laws of nature by what has gone before, we cannot be blamed for those actions. Would Hume agree with this? Why or why not?
5. Someone might object that if voluntary actions are subject to the same laws of necessity as the operations of matter, then God really is to blame for everything. What is Hume's reply? Do you think there is any irony in his reply, or is it completely sincere?

Alternate Possibilities and Moral Responsibility

HARRY G. FRANKFURT

Harry G. Frankfurt (1929–) is the author of a number of important works on freedom of the will and other topics in metaphysics, ethics, and the history of philosophy, including *Demons, Dreamers and Madmen* and *The Importance of What We Care About*. He has been a Professor of Philosophy at Rockefeller, Yale, and Princeton Universities.

. .

A DOMINANT role in nearly all recent inquiries into the **free-will** problem has been played by a principle which I shall call "the

From "Alternate Possibilities and Moral Responsibility," by Harry Frankfurt in *The Journal of Philosophy* 66, pp. 829–839. Copyright © 1969 by *The Journal of Philosophy*. Reprinted by permission of the publisher and author.

principle of alternate possibilities." This principle states that a person is morally responsible for what he has done only if he could have done otherwise. Its exact meaning is a subject of controversy, particularly concerning whether someone who accepts it is thereby committed to believing that moral responsibility and **determinism** are incompatible. Practically no one, however, seems inclined to deny or even to question that the principle of alternate possibilities (construed in some way or other) is true. It has generally seemed so overwhelmingly plausible that some philosophers have even characterized it as an *a priori* truth. People whose accounts of free will or of moral responsibility are radically at odds evidently find in it a firm and convenient common ground upon which they can profitably take their opposing stands.

But the principle of alternate possibilities is false. A person may well be morally responsible for what he has done even though he could not have done otherwise. The principle's plausibility is an illusion, which can be made to vanish by bringing the relevant moral phenomena into sharper focus.

I

In seeking illustrations of the principle of alternate possibilities, it is most natural to think of situations in which the same circumstances both bring it about that a person does something and make it impossible for him to avoid doing it. These include, for example, situations in which a person is coerced into doing something, or in which he is impelled to act by a hypnotic suggestion, or in which some inner compulsion drives him to do what he does. In situations of these kinds there are circumstances that make it impossible for the person to do otherwise, and these very circumstances also serve to bring it about that he does whatever it is that he does.

However, there may be circumstances that constitute sufficient conditions for a certain action to be performed by someone and that therefore make it impossible for the person to do otherwise, but that do not actually impel the person to act or in any way produce his action. A person may do something in circumstances that leave him no alternative to doing it, without these circumstances actually moving him or leading him to do it—without them playing any role, indeed, in bringing it about that he does what he does.

An examination of situations characterized by circumstances of this sort casts doubt, I believe, on the relevance to questions of moral responsibility of the fact that a person who has done something could not have done otherwise. I propose to develop some examples of this kind in the context of a discussion of coercion and to suggest that our moral intuitions

concerning these examples tend to disconfirm the principle of alternate possibilities. Then I will discuss the principle in more general terms, explain what I think is wrong with it, and describe briefly and without argument how it might appropriately be revised.

II

It is generally agreed that a person who has been coerced to do something did not do it freely and is not morally responsible for having done it. Now the doctrine that coercion and moral responsibility are mutually exclusive may appear to be no more than a somewhat particularized version of the principle of alternate possibilities. It is natural enough to say of a person who has been coerced to do something that he could not have done otherwise. And it may easily seem that being coerced deprives a person of freedom and of moral responsibility simply because it is a special case of being unable to do otherwise. The principle of alternate possibilities may in this way derive some credibility from its association with the very plausible proposition that moral responsibility is excluded by coercion.

It is not right, however, that it should do so. The fact that a person was coerced to act as he did may entail both that he could not have done otherwise and that he bears no moral responsibility for his action. But his lack of moral responsibility is not entailed by his having been unable to do otherwise. The doctrine that coercion excludes moral responsibility is not correctly understood, in other words, as a particularized version of the principle of alternate possibilities.

Let us suppose that someone is threatened convincingly with a penalty he finds unacceptable and that he then does what is required of him by the issuer of the threat. We can imagine details that would make it reasonable for us to think that the person was coerced to perform the action in question, that he could not have done otherwise, and that he bears no moral responsibility for having done what he did. But just what is it about situations of this kind that warrants the judgment that the threatened person is not morally responsible for his act?

This question may be approached by considering situations of the following kind. Jones decides for reasons of his own to do something, then someone threatens him with a very harsh penalty (so harsh that any reasonable person would submit to the threat) unless he does precisely that, and Jones does it. Will we hold Jones morally responsible for what he has done? I think this will depend on the roles we think were played, in leading him to act, by his original decision and by the threat.

One possibility is that Jones$_1$ is not a reasonable man: he is, rather, a man who does what he has once decided to do no matter what happens next and no matter what the cost. In that case, the threat actually exerted no effective force upon him. He acted without any regard to it, very much as if he were not aware that it had been made. If this is indeed the way it was, the situation did not involve coercion at all. The threat did not lead Jones$_1$ to do what he did. Nor was it in fact sufficient to have prevented him from doing otherwise: if his earlier decision had been to do something else, the threat would not have deterred him in the slightest. It seems evident that in these circumstances the fact that Jones$_1$ was threatened in no way reduces the moral responsibility he would otherwise bear for his act. This example, however, is not a counterexample either to the doctrine that coercion excuses or to the principle of alternate possibilities. For we have supposed that Jones$_1$ is a man upon whom the threat had no coercive effect and, hence, that it did not actually deprive him of alternatives to doing what he did.

Another possibility is that Jones$_2$ was stampeded by the threat. Given that threat, he would have performed that action regardless of what decision he had already made. The threat upset him so profoundly, moreover, that he completely forgot his own earlier decision and did what was demanded of him entirely because he was terrified of the penalty with which he was threatened. In this case, it is not relevant to his having performed the action that he had already decided on his own to perform it. When the chips were down he thought of nothing but the threat, and fear alone led him to act. The fact that at an earlier time Jones$_2$ had decided for his own reasons to act in just that way may be relevant to an evaluation of his character; he may bear full moral responsibility for having made *that* decision. But he can hardly be said to be morally responsible for his action. For he performed

the action simply as a result of the coercion to which he was subjected. His earlier decision played no role in bringing it about that he did what he did, and it would therefore be gratuitous to assign it a role in the moral evaluation of his action.

Now consider a third possibility. Jones$_3$ was neither stampeded by the threat nor indifferent to it. The threat impressed him, as it would impress any reasonable man, and he would have submitted to it wholeheartedly if he had not already made a decision that coincided with the one demanded of him. In fact, however, he performed the action in question on the basis of the decision he had made before the threat was issued. When he acted, he was not actually motivated by the threat but solely by the considerations that had originally commended the action to him. It was not the threat that led him to act, though it would have done so if he had not already provided himself with a sufficient motive for performing the action in question.

No doubt it will be very difficult for anyone to know, in a case like this one, exactly what happened. Did Jones$_3$ perform the action because of the threat, or were his reasons for acting simply those which had already persuaded him to do so? Or did he act on the basis of two motives, each of which was sufficient for his action? It is not impossible, however, that the situation should be clearer than situations of this kind usually are. And suppose it is apparent to us that Jones$_3$ acted on the basis of his own decision and not because of the threat. Then I think we would be justified in regarding his moral responsibility for what he did as unaffected by the threat even though, since he would in any case have submitted to the threat, he could not have avoided doing what he did. It would be entirely reasonable for us to make the same judgment concerning his moral responsibility that we would have made if we had not known of the threat. For the threat did not in fact influence his performance of the action. He did what he did just as if the threat had not been made at all.

III

The case of Jones$_3$ may appear at first glance to combine coercion and moral responsibility, and thus to provide a counterexample to the doctrine that coercion excuses. It is not really so certain that it does so, however, because it is unclear whether the example constitutes a genuine instance of coercion. Can we say of Jones$_3$ that he was coerced to do something, when he had already decided on his own to do it and when he did it entirely on the basis of that decision? Or would it be more correct to say that Jones$_3$ was not coerced to do what he did, even though he himself recognized that there was an irresistible force at work in virtue of which he had to do it? My own linguistic intuitions lead me toward the second alternative, but they are somewhat equivocal. Perhaps we can say either of these things, or perhaps we must add a qualifying explanation to whichever of them we say.

This murkiness, however, does not interfere with our drawing an important moral from an examination of the example. Suppose we decide to say that Jones$_3$ was *not* coerced. Our basis for saying this will clearly be that it is incorrect to regard a man as being coerced to do something unless he does it *because of* the coercive force exerted against him. The fact that an irresistible threat is made will not, then, entail that the person who receives it is coerced to do what he does. It will also be necessary that the threat is what actually accounts for his doing it. On the other hand, suppose we decide to say that Jones$_3$ *was* coerced. Then we will be bound to admit that being coerced does not exclude being morally responsible. And we will also surely be led to the view that coercion affects the judgment of a person's moral responsibility only when the person acts as he does because he is coerced to do so— i.e., when the fact that he is coerced is what accounts for his action.

Whichever we decide to say, then, we will recognize that the doctrine that coercion excludes moral responsibility is not a particularized version of the principle of alternate possibilities. Situations in which a person who does something cannot do otherwise because he is subject to coercive power are either not instances of coercion at all, or they are situations in which the person may still be morally responsible for what he does if it is not because of the coercion that he does it. When we excuse a person who has been coerced, we do not excuse him because he was unable to do otherwise. Even though a person is subject to a coercive force that precludes his performing any action but one, he may nonetheless bear full moral responsibility for performing that action.

IV

To the extent that the principle of alternate possibilities derives its plausibility from association with the doctrine that coercion excludes moral responsibility, a clear understanding of the latter diminishes the appeal of the former. Indeed the case of Jones$_3$ may appear to do more than illuminate the relationship between the two doctrines. It may well seem to provide a decisive counterexample to the principle of alternate possibilities and thus to show that this principle is false. For the irresistibility of the threat to which Jones$_3$ is subjected might well be taken to mean that he cannot but perform the action he performs. And yet the threat, since Jones$_3$ performs the action without regard to it, does not reduce his moral responsibility for what he does.

The following objection will doubtless be raised against the suggestion that the case of Jones$_3$ is a counterexample to the principle of alternate possibilities. There is perhaps a sense in which Jones$_3$ cannot do otherwise than perform the action he performs, since he is a reasonable man and the threat he encounters is sufficient to move any reasonable man. But it is not this sense that is germane to the principle of alternate possibilities. His knowledge that he stands to suffer an intolerably harsh penalty does not mean that Jones$_3$, strictly speaking, *cannot* perform any action but the one he does perform. After all it is still open to him, and this is crucial, to defy the threat if he wishes to do so and to accept the penalty his action would bring down upon him. In the sense in which the principle of alternate possibilities employs the concept of "could have done otherwise," Jones$_3$'s inability to resist the threat does not mean that he cannot do otherwise than perform the action he performs. Hence the case of Jones$_3$ does not constitute an instance contrary to the principle.

I do not propose to consider in what sense the concept of "could have done otherwise" figures in the principle of alternate possibilities, nor will I attempt to measure the force of the objection I have just described.[1] For I believe that whatever force this objection may be thought to have can be deflected by altering the example in the following way.[2] Suppose someone—Black, let us say—wants Jones₄ to perform a certain action. Black is prepared to go to considerable lengths to get his way, but he prefers to avoid showing his hand unnecessarily. So he waits until Jones₄ is about to make up his mind what to do, and he does nothing unless it is clear to him (Black is an excellent judge of such things) that Jones₄ is going to decide to do something *other* than what he wants him to do. If it does become clear that Jones₄ is going to decide to do something else, Black takes effective steps to ensure that Jones₄ decides to do, and that he does do, what he wants him to do.[3] Whatever Jones₄'s initial preferences and inclinations, then, Black will have his way.

What steps will Black take, if he believes he must take steps, in order to ensure that Jones₄ decides and acts as he wishes? Anyone with a theory concerning what "could have done otherwise" means may answer this question for himself by describing whatever measures he would regard as sufficient to guarantee that, in the relevant sense, Jones₄ cannot do otherwise. Let Black pronounce a terrible threat, and in this way both force Jones₄ to perform the desired action and prevent him from performing a forbidden one. Let Black give Jones₄ a potion, or put him under hypnosis, and in some such way as these generate in Jones₄ an irresistible inner compulsion to perform the act Black wants performed and to avoid others. Or let Black manipulate the minute processes of Jones₄'s brain and nervous system in some more direct way, so that causal forces running in and out of his synapses and along the poor man's nerves determine that he chooses to act and that he does act in the one way and not in any other. Given any conditions under which it will be maintained that Jones₄ cannot do otherwise, in other words, let Black bring it about that those conditions prevail. The structure of the example is flexible enough, I think, to find a way around any charge of irrelevance by accommodating the doctrine on which the charge is based.[4]

Now suppose that Black never has to show his hand because Jones₄, for reasons of his own, decides to perform and does perform the very action Black wants him to perform. In that case, it seems clear,

Jones₄ will bear precisely the same moral responsibility for what he does as he would have borne if Black had not been ready to take steps to ensure that he do it. It would be quite unreasonable to excuse Jones₄ for his action, or to withhold the praise to which it would normally entitle him, on the basis of the fact that he could not have done otherwise. This fact played no role at all in leading him to act as he did. He would have acted the same even if it had not been a fact. Indeed, everything happened just as it would have happened without Black's presence in the situation and without his readiness to intrude into it.

In this example there are sufficient conditions for Jones₄'s performing the action in question. What action he performs is not up to him. Of course it is in a way up to him whether he acts on his own or as a result of Black's intervention. That depends upon what action he himself is inclined to perform. But whether he finally acts on his own or as a result of Black's intervention, he performs the same action. He has no alternative but to do what Black wants him to do. If he does it on his own, however, his moral responsibility for doing it is not affected by the fact that Black was lurking in the background with sinister intent, since this intent never comes into play.

V

The fact that a person could not have avoided doing something is a sufficient condition of his having done it. But, as some of my examples show, this fact may play no role whatever in the explanation of why he did it. It may not figure at all among the circumstances that actually brought it about that he did what he did, so that his action is to be accounted for on another basis entirely. Even though the person was unable to do otherwise, that is to say, it may not be the case that he acted as he did *because* he could not have done otherwise. Now if someone had no alternative to performing a certain action but did not perform it because he was unable to do otherwise, then he would have performed exactly the same action even if he *could* have done otherwise. The circumstances that made it impossible for him to do otherwise could have been subtracted from the situation without affecting what happened or why it happened in any way. Whatever it was that actually led the person to do what he did, or that made him do it, would have led him to do it or made him do it even if it had been possible for him to do something else instead.

Thus it would have made no difference, so far as concerns his action or how he came to perform it, if the circumstances that made it impossible for him to avoid performing it had not prevailed. The fact that he could not have done otherwise clearly provides no basis for supposing that he *might* have done otherwise if he had been able to do so. When a fact is in this way irrelevant to the problem of accounting for a person's action it seems quite gratuitous to assign it any weight in the assessment of his moral responsibility. Why should the fact be considered in reaching a moral judgment concerning the person when it does not help in any way to understand either what made him act as he did or what, in other circumstances, he might have done?

This, then, is why the principle of alternate possibilities is mistaken. It asserts that a person bears no moral responsibility—that is, he is to be excused—for having performed an action if there were circumstances that made it impossible for him to avoid performing it. But there may be circumstances that make it impossible for a person to avoid performing some action without those circumstances in any way bringing it about that he performs that action. It would surely be no good for the person to refer to circumstances of this sort in an effort to absolve himself of moral responsibility for performing the action in question. For those circumstances, by hypothesis, actually had nothing to do with his having done what he did. He would have done precisely the same thing, and he would have been led or made in precisely the same way to do it, even if they had not prevailed.

We often do, to be sure, excuse people for what they have done when they tell us (and we believe them) that they could not have done otherwise. But this is because we assume that what they tell us serves to explain why they did what they did. We take it for granted that they are not being disingenuous, as a person would be who cited as an excuse the fact that he could not have avoided doing what he did but who

knew full well that it was not at all because of this that he did it.

What I have said may suggest that the principle of alternate possibilities should be revised so as to assert that a person is not morally responsible for what he has done if he did it because he could not have done otherwise. It may be noted that this revision of the principle does not seriously affect the arguments of those who have relied on the original principle in their efforts to maintain that moral responsibility and determinism are incompatible. For if it was causally determined that a person perform a certain action, then it will be true that the person performed it because of those causal determinants. And if the fact that it was causally determined that a person perform a certain action means that the person could not have done otherwise, as philosophers who argue for the incompatibility thesis characteristically suppose, then the fact that it was causally determined that a person perform a certain action will mean that the person performed it because he could not have done otherwise. The revised principle of alternate possibilities will entail, on this assumption concerning the meaning of 'could have done otherwise', that a person is not morally responsible for what he has done if it was causally determined that he do it. I do not believe, however, that this revision of the principle is acceptable.

Suppose a person tells us that he did what he did because he was unable to do otherwise; or suppose he makes the similar statement that he did what he did because he had to do it. We do often accept statements like these (if we believe them) as valid excuses, and such statements may well seem at first glance to invoke the revised principle of alternate possibilities. But I think that when we accept such statements as valid excuses it is because we assume that we are being told more than the statements strictly and literally convey. We understand the person who offers the excuse to mean that he did what he did *only because* he was unable to do otherwise, or *only because* he had to do it. And we understand him to mean, more particularly, that when he did what he did it was not because that was what he really wanted to do. The principle of alternate possibilities should thus be replaced, in my opinion, by the following principle: a person is not morally responsible for what he has done if he did it only because he could not have done otherwise. This principle does not appear to conflict with the view that moral responsibility is compatible with determinism.

The following may all be true: there were circumstances that made it impossible for a person to avoid doing something; these circumstances actually played a role in bringing it about that he did it, so that it is correct to say that he did it because he could not have done otherwise; the person really wanted to do what he did; he did it because it was what he really wanted to do, so that it is not correct to say that he did what he did only because he could not have done otherwise. Under these conditions, the person may well be morally responsible for what he has done. On the other hand, he will not be morally responsible for what he has done if he did it only because he could not have done otherwise, even if what he did was something he really wanted to do.

NOTES

1. The two main concepts employed in the principle of alternate possibilities are "morally responsible" and "could have done otherwise." To discuss the principle without analyzing either of these concepts may well seem like an attempt at piracy. The reader should take notice that my Jolly Roger is now unfurled.
2. After thinking up the example that I am about to develop I learned that Robert Nozick, in lectures given several years ago, had formulated an example of the same general type and had proposed it as a counterexample to the principle of alternate possibilities.
3. The assumption that Black can predict what Jones$_4$ will decide to do does not beg the question of determinism. We can imagine that Jones$_4$ has often confronted the alternatives—A and B—that he now confronts, and that his face has invariably twitched when he was about to decide to do A and never when he was about to decide to do B. Knowing this, and observing the twitch, Black would have a basis for prediction. This does, to be sure, suppose that there is some sort of causal relation between Jones$_4$'s state at the time of the twitch and his subsequent states. But any plausible view of decision or

of action will allow that reaching a decision and performing an action both involve earlier and later phases, with causal relations between them, and such that the earlier phases are not themselves part of the decision or of the action. The example does not require that these earlier phases be deterministically related to still earlier events.
4. The example is also flexible enough to allow for the elimination of Black altogether. Anyone who thinks that the effectiveness of the example is undermined by its reliance on a human manipulator who imposes his will on Jones$_4$ can substitute for Black a machine programmed to do what Black does. If this is still not good enough, forget both Black and the machine and suppose that their role is played by natural forces involving no will or design at all.

KEY TERMS

Free will
The principle of alternate possibilities
Determinism
A priori

STUDY QUESTIONS

1. Frankfurt claims that the Principle of Alternate Possibilities (PAP) gains much of its plausibility from considering cases of coercion. How does he argue for this claim?
2. What are the differences among the cases of Jones$_1$, Jones$_2$, and Jones$_3$? Why do these differences make a difference?
3. Does Frankfurt think that the case of Jones$_3$ provides a counterexample to the PAP? Why or why not?
4. What makes someone a *counterfactual intervener*? How does this idea help Frankfurt avoid a potential objection to his counterexample strategy?
5. At the end of his paper, Frankfurt formulates a version of the PAP that he thinks succeeds. What do you think Frankfurt means when he talks about someone performing an action *because* he or she could not have done otherwise? What could this mean?

Responsiveness and Moral Responsibility

JOHN MARTIN FISCHER

John Martin Fischer (1952–) is a Professor of Philosophy at the University of California, Riverside. He is best known for his defense of "semicompatibilism," but he has also made contributions in normative and applied ethics. His books include *The Metaphysics of Free Will, Responsibility and Control* (with Mark Ravizza), *My Way*, *Our Stories*, and *Deep Control*.

. .

W<small>E</small> distinguish between creatures who can legitimately be held morally responsible for their actions and those who cannot. Among the actions a morally responsible agent performs, we distinguish between those actions for which the agent is morally responsible and those for which he is not.

An agent is morally responsible for an action insofar as he is rationally accessible to certain kinds of attitudes and activities as a result of performing the action. The attitudes include resentment, indignation, respect, and gratitude; and the activities include moral praise and blame, and reward and punishment.[1] With this approach, an agent can be a rational candidate for praise or blame, even though he is neither praiseworthy nor blameworthy. For instance, an agent can be morally responsible for a morally "neutral" act. A theory of moral responsibility sets the conditions under which we believe that an individual is a *rational candidate* for praise or blame on account of his behavior. This theory needs to be supplemented by a further moral theory that specifies which agents, among those who are morally responsible, *ought* to be praised or blamed (and to what extent) for their actions. Whereas both kinds of theory are obviously important, I focus here on the first sort of theory—one that explains rational accessibility to the pertinent attitudes and activities.

What I present here is really just a sketch of a theory. It needs to be elaborated and defended much more carefully and explicitly. But I hope that enough of its content will be presented to see that it is a worthwhile approach to develop. The kind of theory I present is certainly not radically new and entirely different from its predecessors.[2] But I hope to develop the theory in a way that avoids some of the objections to similar approaches, and I will draw out some implications that have so far gone unnoticed.

A Sketch of a Theory of Moral Responsibility

A theory of **moral responsibility** should capture our intuitive judgments about clear cases. That is, I assume there is at least fairly wide agreement about certain cases in which an agent can reasonably be held morally responsible for what he does and certain cases in which an agent cannot be held responsible. Considered opinions about these sorts of situations are important data to be explained by a theory of moral responsibility. In order to generate a principle that might underlie our reactions to relatively clear cases, it is useful to begin by considering examples in which we are inclined to think that an agent cannot legitimately be held morally responsible.

Imagine that an individual has been hypnotized. The hypnotist has induced an urge to punch the nearest person after hearing the telephone ring.

"Responsiveness and Moral Responsibility" from *My Way*, by J. M. Fischer, pp. 63–83. Oxford University Press.

I have benefited greatly from comments on previous versions of this paper by Sarah Buss, Anthony Brueckner, and Ferdinand Schoeman. I also benefited from reading a version of this paper at Birkbeck College, University of London.

Insofar as the individual did not consent to this sort of hypnotic suggestion (perhaps he has undergone hypnosis to help him stop smoking), it seems unreasonable to hold him morally responsible for punching his friend in the nose upon hearing the telephone ring.

Suppose similarly that an evil person has got hold of Smith's television set and has wired it so as to allow him to subject Smith to a sophisticated sort of subliminal advertising. The bad person systematically subjects Smith to subliminal advertising that causes Smith to murder his neighbor. Because of the nature of the causal history of the action, it is apparent that Smith cannot be held morally responsible for the lamentable deed.

We feel similarly about actions produced in a wide variety of ways. Agents who perform actions produced by powerful forms of brainwashing and indoctrination, potent drugs, and certain sorts of direct manipulation of the brain are not reasonably to be held morally responsible for their actions. Imagine, for instance, that neurophysiologists of the future can isolate certain key parts of the brain, which can be manipulated in order to induce decisions and actions. If scientists electronically stimulate those parts of Jones's brain, thus causing him to help a person who is being mugged, Jones himself cannot reasonably be held morally responsible for his behavior. It is not to Jones's credit that he has prevented a mugging.

Also, if we discover that a piece of behavior is attributable to a significant brain lesion or a neurological disorder, we do not hold the agent morally responsible for it. Similarly, certain sorts of mental disorders—extreme phobias, for instance—may issue in behavior for which the agent cannot reasonably be held responsible.

Many people feel there can be genuinely "irresistible" psychological impulses. If so, then these may result in behavior for which the agent cannot be held morally responsible. Drug addicts may (in certain circumstances) act on literally irresistible urges, and we might not hold them morally responsible for acting on these desires (especially if we believe they are not morally responsible for acquiring the addiction in the first place).

Also, certain sorts of coercive threats (and perhaps offers) rule out moral responsibility. The bank teller who is told he will be shot unless he hands over the money may have an overwhelming and irresistible desire to comply with the demand. Insofar as he acts from such an impulse, it is plausible to suppose that the teller is not morally responsible for his action.[3]

Evidently, the causal history of an action matters to us in making moral responsibility attributions. When persons are manipulated in certain ways, they are like marionettes and are not appropriate candidates for praise or blame. Certain factors issuing in behavior are, we understand intuitively, responsibility-undermining factors.

We can contrast such cases—in which some responsibility-undermining factor operates—with cases in which there is the "normal," unimpaired operation of the human deliberative mechanism. When you deliberate about whether to give 5 percent of your salary to the United Way and consider reasons on both sides, and your decision to give the money is not induced by hypnosis, brainwashing, direct manipulation, psychotic impulses, and so on, we think you can legitimately be praised for your charitable action. Insofar as we can identify no responsibility undermining factor at work in your decision and action, we are inclined to hold you morally responsible.

Now it might be thought that there is a fairly obvious way of distinguishing the clear cases of moral responsibility from the clear cases of lack of it. It seems that, in the cases in which an agent is morally responsible for an action, he is free to do otherwise, and in the cases of lack of moral responsibility, the agent is not free to do otherwise. Thus, it appears that the actual operation of what is intuitively a responsibility-undermining factor rules out moral responsibility because it rules out freedom to do otherwise.

The point could be put as follows. When an agent is (for example) hypnotized, he is not sensitive to reasons in the appropriate way. Given the hypnosis, he would still behave in the same way no matter what the relevant reasons were. Suppose, again, that an individual is hypnotically induced to punch the nearest person after hearing the telephone ring. Now given this sort of hypnosis, he would punch the nearest person after hearing the telephone ring, even if he had extremely strong reasons not to. The agent here is not responsive to reasons—the behavior would be the same no matter what reasons there were.

In contrast, when there is the normal, unimpaired operation of the human deliberative mechanism, we suppose that the agent *is* responsive to reasons. So when you decide to give money to the United Way, we think that you nevertheless would not have contributed had you discovered that there was widespread fraud within the agency. Thus it is very natural and reasonable to think that the difference between morally responsible agents and those who are not consists in the "**reasons-responsiveness**" of the agents.

But I believe that there are cases in which an agent can be held morally responsible for performing an action, even though that person could not have done otherwise (and is not "reasons-responsive").[4] Here is a graphic example. Imagine that an evil person has installed a device in Brown's brain which allows him to monitor Brown's mental activity and also to intervene in it, if he wishes. He can electronically manipulate Brown's brain by "remote control" to induce decisions, and let us imagine that he can also ensure that Brown acts on the decisions so induced. Now suppose that Brown is about to murder his neighbor, and that this is precisely what the evil person wishes. That is, let us imagine that the device simply monitors Brown's brain activity, but that it plays no role in Brown's actual decision and action. Brown deliberates and behaves just as he would have if no device had been implanted in his brain. But we also imagine that had Brown begun to decide not to murder his neighbor, the device would have been activated and would have caused him to choose to murder the neighbor (and to do so) anyway. Here is a case where an agent can be held morally responsible for performing an action, although he could not have done otherwise.[5] Let us call such a case a "Frankfurt-type" case.

In a Frankfurt-type case, the actual sequence proceeds in a way that grounds moral responsibility attributions, even though the alternative scenario (or perhaps a range of alternative scenarios) proceeds in a way that rules out responsibility. In a Frankfurt-type case, no responsibility-undermining factor occurs in the actual sequence, although such a factor occurs in the alternative scenario. Such cases impel us to adopt a more refined theory of moral responsibility—an "actual-sequence model" of moral responsibility. With

such an approach, we distinguish between the kinds of **mechanisms** that operate in the actual sequence and in the alternative sequence (or sequences).

In a Frankfurt-type case, the kind of mechanism that actually operates is reasons-responsive, although the kind of mechanism that would operate in the alternative scenario is *not*.[6] In the case discussed above, Brown's action issues from the normal faculty of practical reasoning, which we can reasonably take to be reasons-responsive. But in the alternative scenario, a different kind of mechanism would have operated—one involving direct electronic stimulation of Brown's brain. And this mechanism is not reasons-responsive. Thus, the actual-sequence mechanism can be reasons-responsive, even though the *agent* is not reasons-responsive. (*Brown* could not have done otherwise.)

The suggestion, then, for a more refined way of distinguishing the relatively clear cases of moral responsibility from cases of the lack of it is as follows. An agent is morally responsible for performing an action insofar as the mechanism that actually issues in the action is reasons-responsive. When an unresponsive mechanism actually operates, it is true that the agent is not free to do otherwise; but an agent who is unable to do otherwise may act from a responsive mechanism and can thus be held morally responsible for what he does.

So far I have pointed to some cases in which it is intuitively clear that a person cannot be held morally responsible for what he has done and other cases in which it is intuitively clear that an agent can be held responsible. I have suggested a principle that might distinguish the two types of cases. This principle makes use of two ingredients: reasons-responsiveness and the distinction between actual-sequence and alternative-sequence mechanisms. But I have been somewhat vague and breezy about formulating the principle. It is now necessary to explain it more carefully, beginning with the notion of reasons-responsiveness.

Reasons-Responsiveness

I wish to discuss two kinds of reasons-responsiveness: strong and weak. Let's begin with strong reasons-responsiveness. Strong reasons-responsiveness obtains when a certain kind K of mechanism actually issues in an action and if there were sufficient reason to do otherwise and K were to operate, the agent would recognize the sufficient reason to do otherwise and thus choose to do otherwise and do otherwise. To test whether a kind of mechanism is strongly reasons-responsive, one asks what would happen if there were sufficient reason for the agent to do otherwise and the actual-sequence mechanism were to operate. Under circumstances in which there are sufficient reasons for the agent to do otherwise and the actual type of mechanism operates, three conditions must be satisfied: The agent must take the reasons to be sufficient, choose in accordance with the sufficient reason, and act in accordance with the choice. Thus, there can be at least three sorts of "alternative-sequence" failures: failures in the connection between what reasons there are and what reasons the agent recognizes, in the connection between the agent's reason and choice, and in the connection between choice and action.

The first kind of failure is a failure to be *receptive* to reasons. It is the kind of inability that afflicts certain delusional psychotics.[7] The second kind of failure is a failure of *reactivity*—a failure to be appropriately affected by beliefs. Lack of reactivity afflicts certain compulsive or phobic neurotics.[8] Finally, there is the failure successfully to translate one's choice into action; this failure is a kind of impotence. If none of these failures were to occur in the alternative sequence (and the actual kind of mechanism were to operate), then the actually operative mechanism would be strongly reasons-responsive. There would be a tight fit between the reasons there are and the reasons the agent has, the agent's reasons and choice, and choice and action. The agent's actions would fit the contours of reasons *closely.*[9]

I believe that, when an action issues from a strongly reasons-responsive mechanism, this suffices for moral responsibility; but I do not believe that strong reasons-responsiveness is a necessary condition for moral responsibility. To see this, imagine that as a result of the unimpaired operation of the normal human faculty of practical reasoning, I decide to go (and go) to the basketball game tonight, and that I have sufficient reason to do so; but suppose that I would have been "weak-willed" had there been sufficient reason *not* to go. That is, imagine that

had there been a sufficient reason not to go, it would have been that I had a strict deadline for an important manuscript (which I could not meet, if I were to go to the game). I nevertheless would have chosen to go to the game, even though I would have recognized that I had sufficient reason to stay home and work. It seems to me that I actually go to the basketball game freely and can reasonably be held morally responsible for going; and yet the actual-sequence mechanism that results in my action is not reasons-responsive in the strong sense. The failure of strong reasons-responsiveness here stems from my disposition toward weakness of the will.

Going to the basketball game is plausibly thought to be a morally neutral act; in the approach to moral responsibility adopted here, one can be morally responsible for an action, even though the act is neither praiseworthy nor blameworthy. The phenomenon of weakness of will also poses a problem for intuitively clear cases of moral responsibility for *commendable* acts. Suppose, for example, that I devote my afternoon to working for the United Way (and my decision and action proceed via an intuitively responsibility-conferring mechanism). And imagine that, if I had a sufficient reason to refrain, it would (again) have been my publication deadline. But imagine that I would have devoted my time to charity even if I had such a reason not to. Here it seems that I am both morally responsible and praiseworthy for doing what I do, and yet the actual mechanism is not strongly reasons-responsive.

Further, it is quite clear that strong reasons-responsiveness cannot be a necessary condition for moral responsibility for morally blameworthy and/or imprudent acts. Suppose that I steal a book from a store, knowing full well that it is morally wrong for me to do so and that I will be apprehended and thus that it is not prudent of me to do so. Nevertheless, the actual sequence may be intuitively responsibility-conferring; no factors that intuitively undermine moral responsibility may actually operate. (Of course, I assume that there can be genuine cases of weak-willed actions that are free actions for which the agent can be held responsible.) Here, then, is a case in which I am morally responsible for stealing the book, but my actual-sequence mechanism is not strongly reasons-responsive: There actually is sufficient reason (both moral and prudential) to do otherwise, and yet I steal the book.

All three cases presented above provide problems for the claim that strong reasons-responsiveness is necessary for moral responsibility. Strong reasons-responsiveness may be both sufficient and necessary for a certain kind of praise-worthiness—it is a great virtue to connect one's actions with the contours of value in a strongly reasons-responsive way. Of course, not all agents who are morally responsible are morally commendable (or even maximally prudent). I believe that moral responsibility requires only a looser kind of fit between reasons and action: "weak reasons-responsiveness."

Under the requirement of strong reasons-responsiveness, we ask what would happen if there were a sufficient reason to do otherwise (holding fixed the actual kind of mechanism). Strong reasons-responsiveness points us to the alternative scenario in which there is a sufficient reason for the agent to do otherwise (and the actual mechanism operates), which is *most similar* to the actual situation. Put in terms of possible worlds, the nonactual possible worlds that are germane to strong reasons-responsiveness are those in which the agent has a sufficient reason to do otherwise (and in which the actual kind of mechanism operates) that are most similar to the actual world. (Perhaps there is just one such world, or perhaps there is a sphere of many such worlds.) In contrast, under weak reasons-responsiveness, there must exist *some* possible world in which there is a sufficient reason to do otherwise, the agent's actual mechanism operates, and the agent does otherwise. This possible world need not be the one (or ones) in which the agent has a sufficient reason to do otherwise (and the actual mechanism operates), which is (or are) *most similar* to the actual world.[10]

Consider again my decision to go to the basketball game. In this situation, if I were to have a sufficient reason to do otherwise, this would be a publication deadline; and I would under such circumstances be weak-willed and still go to the game. However, there certainly exists *some* scenario in which the actual mechanism operates, I have sufficient reason not to go to the game, and I don't go. Suppose, for instance, that I am told that I will have to pay $1,000 for a ticket to the game. Even though I am disposed to be weak-willed under some circumstances, there are some circumstances in which I would respond appropriately to sufficient reasons. These are circumstances in which the reasons are considerably *stronger* than the reasons which would exist if I were to have sufficient reason to do otherwise.

Consider, similarly, my commendable act of working this afternoon for the United Way. Even though I would do so anyway, even if I had a publication deadline, I certainly would *not* work for the United Way if to do so I would have to sacrifice my job. Thus, the actual mechanism issuing in my action is weakly reasons-responsive. Also, when an agent wrongly (and imprudently) steals a book (i.e., there actually is sufficient reason not to), the actual mechanism might be responsive to at least some logically possible incentive not to steal. To the extent that it is so responsive, he is properly held morally responsible for stealing the book. Even an agent who acts against good reasons can be responsive to *some* reasons.

I believe that the agent's actual-sequence mechanism *must* be weakly reasons-responsive if he is to be held morally responsible. If (given the operation of the actual kind of mechanism) he would persist in stealing the book even knowing that by so acting he would cause himself and his family to be killed, then the actual mechanism would seem to be inconsistent with holding that person morally responsible for an action.

An agent whose act is produced by a strongly reasons-responsive mechanism is commendable; his behavior fits tightly the contours of value. But a weakly responsive mechanism is all that is required for moral responsibility. In my approach, actual irrationality is compatible with moral responsibility (as it should be). Perhaps Dostoyevsky's underground man is an example of an actually irrational and yet morally responsible individual. Similarly, certain kinds of hypothetical irrationality are compatible with moral responsibility; a tendency toward weakness of the will need not point to any defect in the actual mechanism leading to action. Moral responsibility requires *some* connection between reason and action, but the fit can be quite loose.[11]

In this section I have distinguished two kinds of responsiveness. I have argued that an agent is morally responsible for an action insofar as the action is produced by a weakly reasons-responsive mechanism. In the next section, I discuss an analogy between this theory of moral responsibility and a parallel sort of theory of knowledge. This analogy will help to refine our understanding of the actual-sequence nature of moral responsibility. In the following section, I further sharpen the formulation of the theory by rendering more precise the key idea of a "kind of mechanism issuing in action."

Knowledge and Responsibility

I have sketched an actual-sequence model of moral responsibility. In this approach, an agent can be morally responsible for performing an action although he is not free to do otherwise. It is sufficient that the actual-sequence mechanism be responsive to reasons in the appropriate way. There is an analogy between this sort of theory of moral responsibility and an actual-sequence model of knowledge. In this approach to knowledge, an agent may have knowledge of a certain proposition, even though he lacks the pertinent discriminatory capacity. It is sufficient that the actual-sequence mechanism be sensitive to truth in the appropriate way.

In order for a person to know that p, it is clear that the person must believe that p, and that p must be true; but this is surely not enough, and there are various strategies for providing further requirements.[12] One "externalist" approach claims that the person's belief that p must be a "reliable indicator" of p's truth—or perhaps, that it must "track" p's truth. Very roughly, one might say that, in order for an agent to have knowledge that p, it must be the case both that (1) the agent would not believe that p if p were not true, and (2) under various conditions in which p were true, the agent would believe that p. One asks here about the agent's beliefs in a sphere of worlds that are relatively similar to the actual world—both worlds in which p is true and worlds in which p is false.[13]

So suppose that as you are driving along, you see what you take to be a barn in a field, and that you conclude that it is a barn in the field; and it is an ordinary barn in a field. Unknown to you, had it not been a barn, a demonic farmer would have installed a papier-mâché replica of a barn. In this case you truly believe that it is a normal barn in the field, but your belief does not "track truth": had there been no barn in the field, you still would have believed there to be a barn in the field. In this case you lack a discriminatory capacity that might seem required for knowledge.

Let us contrast this case with another in which you see a banana in a supermarket, and you conclude that there is a banana on the shelf. We suppose here that there is no demonic supermarket manager poised to fool you, and that if there were no banana on the shelf, you would not believe that there is a banana on the shelf. Presumably, in this case your belief tracks truth, and you might be said to know that there is a banana on the shelf. Furthermore, this is so even though *there exists* a logically possible scenario in which a demonic supermarket manager has placed a plastic banana on the shelf and you still conclude that it is a banana. In this account, what is pertinent to knowledge are the scenarios in which p is false that are *most similar* to the actual world; that there are more remote possibilities in which the proposition p is false is not taken by the approach to be germane to whether the individual has knowledge.[14]

The cases described above might suggest that an agent has knowledge that p only if he has the ability to discriminate the conditions that would obtain if p were true from those that would obtain if p were false. However, consider the following examples (from Nozick):

A grandmother sees her grandson is well when he comes to visit; but if he were sick or dead, others would tell her he was well to spare her upset. Yet this does not mean she doesn't know he is well (or at least ambulatory) when she sees him.[15]

S believes a certain building is a theater and concert hall. He has attended plays and concerts there. . . . However, if the building were not a theater, it would have housed a nuclear reactor that would so have altered the air around it (let us suppose) that everyone upon approaching the theater would have become lethargic and nauseous, and given up the attempt to buy a ticket. The government cover story would have been that the building was a theater, a cover story they knew would be safe since no un-medicated person could approach through the nausea field to discover any differently. Everyone, let us suppose, would have believed the cover story; they would have believed that the building they saw (but only from some distance) was a theater.[16]

These examples are epistemological analogues to Frankfurt-type cases in which an agent is morally responsible for performing an action although he could not have done otherwise. In these cases an agent knows that *p*, although he lacks the pertinent discriminatory capacity. Just as we switched from demanding agent-responsiveness to demanding mechanism-responsiveness for moral responsibility, it is appropriate to demand only mechanism-sensitivity to truth in order for an agent to have knowledge.

As Nozick points out, it is possible to believe that *p* via a truth-sensitive mechanism, and thus know that *p*, even though an insensitive mechanism would have operated in the alternative scenario (or scenarios). Thus, we want an actual-sequence theory of knowledge, just as we want an actual-sequence theory of responsibility. We need to distinguish between actual-sequence and alternative-sequence mechanisms and focus on the properties of the actual-sequence mechanism. But whereas there is a strong analogy between the theories of responsibility and knowledge sketched above, I now want to point to two important differences between responsibility and knowledge.

First, in the theory of responsibility presented above, if an agent acts on a mechanism of type M, there must be *some* possible scenario in which M operates, the agent has sufficient reason to do otherwise, and he does do otherwise, in order for the agent to be morally responsible for his action. The possible scenario need not be the one that would have occurred if M had operated and the agent had sufficient reason to do otherwise. That is, the scenario pertinent to responsibility ascriptions need not be the scenario (or set of them) in which an M-type mechanism operates and the agent has sufficient reason to do otherwise that are *most similar* to the actual scenario. In contrast, in the theory of knowledge presented above, if an agent believes that *p* via an M-type mechanism, then it must be the case that if an M-type mechanism were to operate and *p* were false, the agent would believe that *p* is false if the agent is to know that *p*.

Roughly speaking, the logical possibilities pertinent to moral responsibility attributions may be more remote than those pertinent to knowledge attributions.

I believe, then, that the connection between reasons and action that is necessary for moral responsibility is "looser" than the connection between truth and belief that is necessary for knowledge. Of course, this point is consistent with the claim that both knowledge and moral responsibility are actual-sequence notions; it is just that actual-sequence truth-sensitivity is defined more "strictly" (i.e., in terms of "closer" possibilities) than actual-sequence reasons-responsiveness.

But I believe there is a second difference between moral responsibility and knowledge. I have claimed that, just as moral responsibility does not require freedom to do otherwise, knowledge does not require the capacity to discriminate; what is sufficient in the case of responsibility is reasons-responsiveness, and in the case of knowledge, truth-sensitivity. Thus both notions are actual-sequence notions. But I wish to point out a stronger sense in which moral responsibility (and not knowledge) depends only on the actual sequence.

I claim that an agent's moral responsibility for an action is supervenient on the actual physical causal influences that issue in the action, whereas an agent's knowledge that *p* is *not* supervenient on the actual physical causal influences that issue in the belief that *p*. First, let me explain the supervenience claim for moral responsibility. It seems to me impossible that there be cases in which there are two agents who perform actions of the same type as a result of exactly the same kind of actual causal sequence, but in which one agent is morally responsible for the action and the other is *not*. Differences in responsibility ascriptions must come from differences in the actual physical factors resulting in action; mere differences in alternate scenarios do not translate into differences in responsibility ascriptions. That is, differences in responsibility ascriptions must come from differences in the actual histories of actions, and not mere "possible" histories.

Suppose you and I both heroically jump into the lake to save a drowning swimmer, and everything that actually happens in both cases is relevantly similar—except that whereas you could have done otherwise, I could not have. (I could not have done otherwise by virtue of the existence of a mechanism in my brain that would have stimulated it to produce a decision to save the swimmer had I been inclined not to.) Insofar as the actual physical sequences issuing in our behavior are the same, we are equally morally responsible.

However, here is an epistemological example of Nozick's:

> Consider another case, of a student who, when his philosophy class is cancelled, usually returns to his room and takes hallucinogenic drugs; one hallucination he has sometimes is of being in his philosophy class. When the student actually is in the philosophy class, does he know he is? I think not, for if he weren't in class, he still might believe he was. . . . Two students in the class might be in the same actual situation, having (roughly) the same retinal and aural intake, yet the first knows he is in class while the other does not, because they are situated differently subjunctively—different subjunctives hold true of them.[17]

The two students have exactly the same actual physical factors issue in beliefs that they are in class. However, one student does not know he is in class: if he were not in class (and he were to employ the method of introspection, which was actually employed), then he would (or at least might) still believe that he is in class (as a result of the drug). The other student—who is not disposed to use the drug—does know that he is in class. Thus knowledge is not supervenient on actual physical facts in the way that moral responsibility is.

I have claimed above that there is a certain parallel between moral responsibility and knowledge: The reasons-responsiveness of the actual mechanism leading to action suffices for responsibility, and the truth sensitivity of the actual mechanism leading to belief suffices for knowledge. How exactly is this claim of parallelism compatible with the further claim that moral responsibility attributions are supervenient on actual physical causal factors, whereas knowledge attributions are *not*? I think the answer lies in our intuitive way of individuating "mechanisms." We tend to individuate mechanisms more finely in action theory than in epistemology.

In the case of the first student, we take the relevant mechanism issuing in belief to be "introspection." Of course, the same sort of mechanism would have operated had the student taken the drug. With this "wide" kind of individuation of mechanisms, it turns out that the mechanism that issues in the one student's belief is *not* truth-sensitive, whereas the mechanism of the other student *is*.

However, in the case in which I save the drowning child ("on my own"), it is natural to suppose that if I had been stimulated by the scientists, this would have been a kind of mechanism *different* from the one that actually operates. Similarly, had I been injected with a drug that issued in an irresistible desire to save the drowning swimmer, this would have constituted a kind of mechanism *different* from the actual one. With this "narrow" kind of individuation of mechanisms, it turns out that the mechanism that issues in my action of saving the child is reasons-responsive (just as yours is).

The asymmetry of supervenience is compatible with the symmetrically actual-sequence nature of knowledge and moral responsibility. The asymmetry of supervenience is generated by the intuitively natural tendency to individuate mechanisms issuing in belief more broadly than mechanisms issuing in action.[18]

Mechanisms

I have suggested that an agent is morally responsible for performing an action insofar as the mechanism that actually issues in the action is reasons-responsive; but this suggestion needs to be refined in light of the fact that various different mechanisms may actually operate in a given case. Which mechanism is relevant to responsibility ascriptions?

Suppose that I deliberate (in the normal way) about whether to donate 5 percent of my paycheck to the United Way, and that I decide to make the donation and act on my decision. We might fill in the story so that it is intuitively a paradigmatic case in which I am morally responsible for my action; and yet consider the actually operative mechanism, "deliberation preceding donating 5 percent of one's salary to the United Way." If *this* kind of mechanism were to operate, then I would give 5 percent of my paycheck to the United Way in any logically possible scenario. Thus, this kind of actually operative mechanism is *not* reasons-responsive.

However, a mechanism such as "deliberating prior to giving 5 percent of one's salary to the United Way" is not of the kind that is relevant to moral responsibility ascriptions. This is because it is not a "temporally intrinsic" mechanism. The operation of a temporally extrinsic or "relational" mechanism already includes the occurrence of the action it is supposed to cause.

Note that the operation of a mechanism of the kind "deliberating prior to giving 5 percent of one's paycheck to the United Way" *entails* that one give 5 percent of one's paycheck to the United Way. In this sense, then, the mechanism already includes the action: its operation entails that the action occurs. Thus, it is a necessary condition of a mechanism's relevance to moral responsibility ascription (on the theory proposed here) that it be a "temporally intrinsic" or "nonrelational" mechanism in the following sense: if a mechanism M issues in act X, then M is relevant to the agent's moral responsibility for performing X only if M's operating does not entail that X occurs. I believe that the requirement that a mechanism be temporally intrinsic is an intuitively natural and unobjectionable one. Of course, we have so far only a necessary condition for being a relevant mechanism; there may be various different mechanisms that issue in an action, all of which are temporally intrinsic. Which mechanism is "the" mechanism pertinent to moral responsibility ascription?

I do not have a theory that will specify in a general way how to determine which mechanism is "the" mechanism relevant to assessment of responsibility. It is simply a presupposition of this theory as presented above that, for each act, an intuitively natural mechanism is appropriately selected as *the* mechanism that issues in action, for the purposes of assessing moral responsibility.

I do not think this presupposition is problematic. But if there is a worry, it is useful to note that the basic theory can be formulated without such a presupposition. As so far developed, the theory says that an agent is morally responsible for performing an action insofar as the (relevant, temporally intrinsic) mechanism issuing in the action is reasons-responsive. Alternatively, one could say that an agent is morally responsible for an action insofar as there is no actually operative temporally intrinsic mechanism issuing in the action that is not reasons-responsive. This alternative formulation obviates the need to select one mechanism as the "relevant" one. In what follows I continue to employ the first formulation, but the basic points should apply equally to the alternative formulation.

I wish now to apply the theory to a few cases. We think intuitively that irresistible urges can be psychologically compulsive and can rule out moral responsibility. Imagine that Jim has a literally irresistible urge to take a certain drug, and that he does in fact take the drug. What exactly is the relevant mechanism that issues in Jim's taking the drug? Notice that the mechanism "deliberation involving an irresistible urge to take the drug" is not temporally intrinsic and thus not admissible as a mechanism pertinent to moral responsibility ascription: its operation entails that Jim takes the drug. Consider, then, the mechanism "deliberation involving an irresistible desire." Whereas this mechanism *is* temporally intrinsic, it is also reasons-responsive: There is a possible scenario in which Jim acts on this kind of mechanism and refrains from taking the drug. In this scenario, Jim has an irresistible urge to *refrain* from taking the drug. These considerations show that neither "deliberation involving an irresistible desire for the drug" nor "deliberation involving an irresistible desire" is the relevant mechanism (if the theory of responsibility is to achieve an adequate fit with our intuitive judgments).

When Jim acts on an irresistible urge to take the drug, there is some physical process of kind P taking place in his central nervous system. When a person undergoes this kind of physical process, we say that the urge is literally irresistible. I believe that what underlies our intuitive claim that Jim is not morally responsible for taking the drug is that the relevant kind of mechanism issuing in Jim's taking the drug is of physical kind P, and that a mechanism of kind P is not reasons-responsive. When an agent acts from a literally irresistible urge, he is undergoing a kind of physical process that is not reasons-responsive, and it is this lack of reasons-responsiveness of the actual physical process that rules out moral responsibility.[19]

Consider again my claim that certain sorts of "direct manipulation of the brain" rule out moral responsibility. It is clear that not all such manipulations would rule out moral responsibility. Suppose, for instance, that a scientist manipulates just one brain cell at the periphery of my brain. This kind of manipulation need not rule out responsibility insofar as this kind of physical process can be reasons-responsive. It is when the scientists intervene and manipulate the brain in a way which is *not* reasons-responsive that they undermine an agent's moral responsibility for action.[20]

Similarly, not all forms of subliminal advertising, hypnosis, brainwashing, and so on are inconsistent with moral responsibility for an action. It is only when these activities yield physical mechanisms that are not reasons-responsive that they rule out moral responsibility. Thus, the theory that associates moral responsibility with actual-sequence reasons-responsiveness can help to explain our intuitive distinctions between causal influences that are consistent with moral responsibility and those that are not.

Consider also the class of legal defenses that might be dubbed "Twinkie-type" defenses. This kind of defense claims that an agent ought not to be punished because he ate too much junk food (and that this impaired his capacities, etc.). In the approach presented here, the question of whether an agent ought to be punished is broken into two parts: (1) Is the agent morally responsible (i.e., rationally accessible to punishment), and (2) if so, to what degree ought the agent to be punished? The theory of moral responsibility I have presented allows us to respond positively to the first question in the typical "Twinkie-type" case.

Even if an individual has eaten a diet composed only of junk food, it is highly implausible to think that this yields a biological process that is not weakly reasons-responsive. At the very most, such a process might not be strongly reasons-responsive, but strong reasons-responsiveness is *not* necessary for moral responsibility. Our outrage at the suggestion that a junk food eater is not morally responsible may come from two sources. The outrage could be a reaction to the "philosophical" mistake of demanding strong rather than weak reasons-responsiveness; or the outrage could be a reaction to the implausible suggestion that junk food consumption yields a mechanism that is not weakly reasons-responsive.

Thus the theory of responsibility supports the intuitive idea that Twinkie-type defendants are morally responsible for what they do. Of course, the question of the appropriate *degree* of punishment is a separate question; but it is important to notice that it is *not* a consequence of the theory of responsibility that an agent who acts on a mechanism that is weakly but not strongly reasons-responsive is properly punished to a *lesser* degree than an agent who acts on a mechanism that is strongly reasons-responsive. This may, but need not be, a part of one's full theory of punishment.

Temporal Considerations

I wish to consider a problem for the theory of responsibility that I have been developing. This problem will force a refinement in the theory. Suppose Max (who enjoys drinking but is not an alcoholic) goes to a party where he drinks so much that he is almost oblivious to his surroundings. In this state of intoxication he gets into his car and tries to drive home. Unfortunately, he runs over a child who is walking in a crosswalk. Although the actual-sequence mechanism issuing in Max's running over the child is plausibly taken to lack reasons-responsiveness, we may nevertheless feel that Max *is* morally responsible for running over the child.

This is one case in a class of cases in which an agent acts at a time T_1 on a reasons-responsive mechanism that causes him to act at T_2 on a mechanism that is *not* reasons-responsive. Further, Max ought to have known that getting drunk at the party would lead to driving in a condition in which he would be unresponsive. Thus, Max can be held morally responsible for his action at T_2 by virtue of the operation of a suitable sort of reasons-responsive mechanism at a prior time T_1. When one acts on a reasons-responsive mechanism at time T_1 and one ought to know that so acting will lead to acting on an unresponsive mechanism at some later time T_2, one can be held morally responsible for so acting at T_2. Thus, the theory of moral responsibility should be interpreted as claiming that moral responsibility for an act at T requires the actual operation of a reasons-responsive mechanism at T or some suitable earlier time. (For simplicity's sake, I suppress mention of the temporal indexation below.)

An individual might cultivate dispositions to act virtuously in certain circumstances. It might even be the case that when he acts virtuously, the motivation to do so is so strong that the mechanism is not reasons-responsive. But insofar as reasons-responsive mechanisms issued in the person's cultivation of the virtue, that person can be held morally responsible for his action. It is only when it is true that at no suitable point along the path to the action did a reasons-responsive mechanism operate that an agent will not properly be held responsible for an action.

Semicompatibilism

I have presented a very sketchy theory of responsibility. The basic idea would have to be developed and explained much more carefully in order to have a fully adequate theory of responsibility, but enough of the theory has been given to draw out some of its implications. My claim is that the theory sketched here leads to compatibilism about moral responsibility and such doctrines as God's foreknowledge and **causal determinism**.

Let us first consider the relationship between causal determinism and moral responsibility. The theory of moral responsibility presented here helps us to reconcile causal determinism with moral responsibility, even if causal determinism is inconsistent with freedom to do otherwise. The case for the incompatibility of causal determinism and freedom to do otherwise is different from (and stronger than) the case for the incompatibility of causal determinism and moral responsibility.

Causal determinism can be defined as follows:

Causal determinism is the thesis that, for any given time, a complete statement of the facts about the world at that time, together with a complete statement of the laws of nature, entails every truth as to what happens after that time.

Now the "basic argument" for the incompatibility of causal determinism and freedom to do otherwise can be presented. If causal determinism obtains, then (roughly speaking) the past together with the natural laws entail that I act as I do now. So if I am free to do otherwise, then I must either have power over the past or power over the laws of nature. But since the past and the laws of nature are "fixed"—for instance, I cannot now so act that the past would have been different from what it actually was—it follows that I am not now free to do otherwise.[21]

This is obviously a brief presentation of the argument; a more careful and detailed look at the "basic argument" is beyond the scope of this presentation.[22] It should be evident, however, that a compatibilist about causal determinism and freedom to do otherwise must either deny the fixity of the past or the fixity of the laws. That is, such a compatibilist must say that an agent can have it in his power at a time so to act that the past would have been different from what it actually was, or that an agent can have it in his power so to act that a natural law that actually obtains would not obtain.[23] Even if these compatibilist claims are not obviously false, they are certainly not easy to swallow.

The approach to moral responsibility developed here allows us to separate compatibilism about causal determinism and moral responsibility from compatibilism about causal determinism and freedom to do otherwise. The theory says that an agent can be held morally responsible for performing an action insofar as the mechanism actually issuing in the action is reasons-responsive; the agent need not be free to do otherwise. As I explain below, reasons-responsiveness of the actual-sequence mechanism is consistent with causal determination. Thus a compatibilist about determinism and moral responsibility can *accept* the fixity of the past and the fixity of the natural laws. He need not accept the unappealing claims to which the compatibilist about causal determinism and freedom to do otherwise is committed. If it is the "basic argument" that pushes one to incompatibilism about causal determinism and freedom to do otherwise, this need not also push one toward incompatibilism about causal determinism and moral responsibility.

The theory of responsibility requires reasons-responsive mechanisms. For a mechanism to be reasons-responsive, there must be a possible scenario in which the same kind of mechanism operates and the agent does otherwise; but, of course, sameness of kind of mechanism need not require sameness of all details, even down to the "micro" level. Nothing in our intuitive conception of a kind of mechanism leading to action or in our judgments about clear cases of moral responsibility requires us to say that sameness of kind of mechanism implies sameness of micro details. Thus, the scenarios pertinent to the reasons-responsiveness of an actual-sequence mechanism may differ with respect both to the sort of incentives the agent has to do otherwise and the particular details of the mechanism issuing in action.

(Note that if causal determinism obtains and I do X, then one sort of mechanism which actually operates is a "causally determined to do X" type of mechanism. But of course this kind of mechanism is not germane to responsibility ascriptions insofar as it is not temporally intrinsic. And whereas the kind, "causally determined," is temporally intrinsic and thus may be germane, it is reasons-responsive.)

If causal determinism is true, then any possible scenario (with the actual natural laws) in which the agent does otherwise at time T must differ in *some* respect from the actual scenario prior to T. The existence of such possible scenarios is all that is required by the theory of moral responsibility. It is not required that the agent be able to bring about such a scenario (i.e., that the agent have it in his power at T so to act that the past, relative to T, would have been different from what it actually was). Furthermore, the existence of the required kind of scenarios is compatible with causal determinism.

The actual-sequence reasons-responsiveness theory of moral responsibility thus yields "**semicompatibilism**": moral responsibility is compatible with causal determinism, even if causal determinism is incompatible with freedom to do otherwise. Compatibilism about determinism and responsibility is compatible with *both* compatibilism and incompatibilism (as well as agnosticism) about determinism and freedom to do otherwise.[24]

Often incompatibilists use the example discussed above of the demonic scientists who directly manipulate one's brain. They then pose a challenge to the compatibilist: In what way is this sort of case *different* from the situation under causal determinism? There is clearly the following similarity: in both the cases of manipulation and determination, conditions entirely "external" to the agent causally suffice to produce an action. Thus, it may be that neither agent is free to do otherwise. However, as I argued above, there seems to be a crucial difference between the case of direct manipulation and "mere" causal determination. In a case of direct manipulation of the brain, it is likely that the process issuing in the action is not reasons-responsive, whereas the fact that a process is causally deterministic does not in itself bear on whether it is reasons-responsive. The force of the incompatibilist's challenge can be seen

to come from the plausible idea that in neither case does the agent have freedom to do otherwise; but it can be answered by pointing to a difference in the actual-sequence mechanisms.

The same sort of considerations show that moral responsibility is consistent with God's foreknowledge, even if God's foreknowledge is incompatible with freedom to do otherwise. Let us suppose that God exists and thus knew in the past exactly how I would behave today. If I am free to do otherwise, then I must be free so to act that the past would have been different from what it actually was (i.e., so to act that God would have held a different belief about my behavior from the one he actually held). However, the past is fixed, and so it is plausible to think that I am not free to do otherwise, if God exists.

God's existence, however, is surely compatible with the operation of a reasons-responsive mechanism. God's belief is not a part of the mechanism issuing in my action (on a standard view of the nature of God). His belief is not what causes my action; rather, my action explains his belief. Thus there are possible scenarios in which the actual kind of mechanism operates and issues in my doing otherwise. (In these scenarios, God believes correctly that I will do other than what I do in the actual world.) Again, the cases for the two sorts of incompatibilism—about divine foreknowledge and responsibility and about divine foreknowledge and freedom to do otherwise—are *different*, and the actual-sequence reasons-responsiveness theory yields semicompatibilism.[25]

Structure and History

In this section I wish to contrast my approach to moral responsibility with a class of theories that might be called "mesh" theories of responsibility. My approach is a historical theory.

Consider first a "**hierarchical**" model of moral responsibility. In this model, a person is morally responsible for an action insofar as there is a mesh between a higher order preference and the first-order preference that actually moves him to action. On one version of this theory, which is suggested by some remarks by Harry Frankfurt, an agent is morally responsible for an action if there is conformity between his "second-order volition" and "will" (the first-order desire that moves the person to action).[26]

In another version of the theory, moral responsibility for an action is associated with conformity between "identification" and will.[27] According to Frankfurt's suggestion, one way of identifying with a first-order desire would be to formulate an unopposed second-order volition to act on it, together with a judgment that no further reflection would cause one to change one's mind.

The problem with such hierarchical "mesh" theories, no matter how they are refined, is that the selected mesh can be produced via responsibility-undermining mechanisms. After all, a demonic neurophysiologist can induce the conformity between the various mental elements via a sort of direct electronic stimulation that is not reasons-responsive. I believe that the problem with the hierarchical mesh theories is precisely that they are purely structural and ahistorical. It matters what kind of process issues in an action. Specifically, the mechanism issuing in the action must be reasons-responsive.

The "multiple-source" mesh theories are also purely structural. Rather than positing a hierarchy of preferences, these theories posit different sources of preferences. One such theory is that of Gary Watson, according to which there are "valuational preferences" (which come from reason) and motivational preferences.[28] Employing Watson's theory, one could say that an agent is morally responsible for an action insofar as there is a mesh between the valuational and motivational preference to perform the action.[29]

Again the problem is that such a theory is purely structural. The mesh between elements of different preference systems may be induced by electronic stimulation, hypnosis, brainwashing, and so on. Moral responsibility is a *historical* phenomenon; it is a matter of the kind of mechanism that issues in action.[30]

Conclusion

I have presented a sketch of a theory that purports to identify the class of actions for which persons are rationally accessible to moral praise and blame, and reward and punishment. I have claimed that this theory captures our clear intuitive judgments about

moral responsibility, and that it helps to reconcile moral responsibility with causal determinism. I certainly have not *proved* that moral responsibility is compatible with causal determinism. Rather, my strategy has been to argue that the approach presented here allows the compatibilist about moral responsibility and determinism to avoid the commitments of the compatibilist about freedom to do otherwise and determinism. There might be other sorts of challenges to compatibilism about determinism and moral responsibility that my approach does not, in itself, answer.

The theory I have presented builds upon and extends the approaches of others. It avoids some of the most pressing objections to similar types of theories. These objections might seem convincing if one fails to "hold fixed" the actual-sequence mechanism, or if one employs strong rather than weak reasons-responsiveness, or if one does not suitably temporally index the theory.

I wish to end with a few suggestions about the relationship between the theory of moral responsibility presented here and punishment. A theory of moral responsibility needs to explain why certain creatures (and not others) are appropriate candidates for punishment. Punishment, of course, involves treating an individual "harshly" in some manner. It affects the desirability of performing a certain action. That is, punishment involves reacting to persons in ways to which the mechanisms on which they act are sensitive. My suggestion is that punishment is appropriate only for a creature who acts on a mechanism "keyed to" the kind of incentives punishment provides.

My point here is not that the justification of punishment is "consequentialist"—that it alters behavior. (Of course, this kind of justification does not in itself distinguish punishment from aversive conditioning.) Indeed, it is metaphysically possible that an individual's total pattern of choices and actions throughout life be "unalterable" by virtue of a continuous string of Frankfurt-type situations. (It is even possible that *no* human's behavior is alterable, because it is possible that all human beings are subject to Frankfurt-type counterfactual interventions.) My justification is nonconsequentialist and "direct": punishment is an appropriate reaction to the actual operation of reasons-responsive mechanisms. When it is justified, punishment involves a kind of "match" between the mechanism that produces behavior and the response to that behavior.

The theory of moral responsibility, then, provides some insight into the appropriateness of punishment for certain actions. But it does not in itself provide a full account of the appropriate *degrees* of punishment. For instance, it may be the case that the appropriate degree of severity of punishment for a particular action is less than (or greater than) the magnitude of the incentive to which the actual-sequence mechanism is responsive. This is entirely compatible with saying that punishment—being a "provider of reasons"—is appropriately directed to agents who act on reasons-responsive mechanisms.

NOTES

1. Strawson calls the attitudes involved in moral responsibility the "reactive attitudes": P. F. Strawson, "Freedom and Resentment," *Proceedings of the British Academy* 48 (1962): 1–25.

2. Some contemporary versions of similar theories are found in Alasdair MacIntyre, "Determinism," *Mind* 56 (1957): 28–41; Jonathan Glover, *Responsibility* (New York: Humanities Press, 1970); Herbert Fingarette, *The Meaning of Criminal Insanity* (Berkeley: University of California Press, 1972); Wright Neely, "Freedom and Desire," *Philosophical Review* 83 (1974): 32–54; Timothy Duggan and Bernard Gert, "Free Will as the Ability to Will," *Nous* 13 (1979): 197–217; Lawrence Davis, *A Theory of Action* (Englewood Cliffs, N.J.: Prentice Hall, 1979); Michael Levin, *Metaphysics and the Mind-Body Problem* (Oxford: Clarendon 1979); Robert Nozick, *Philosophical Explanations* (Cambridge: Harvard University Press 1981); and Daniel Dennett, *Elbow Room: The Varieties of Free Will Worth Wanting* (Cambridge: MIT Press, 1984). For an excellent survey of some aspects of these approaches, see David Shatz, "Free Will and the Structure of Motivation," in *Midwest Studies in Philosophy* 10, ed. Peter French, Howard Weittstein, and Theodore Uehling (Minneapolis: University of Minnesota Press, 1985), pp. 444–74.

3. I contrast this kind of bank teller with one who, in exactly the same circumstances, does not have an irresistible impulse to comply with the demand. Such a teller may be morally responsible (though not necessarily *blameworthy*) for handing over the money.

4. John Locke presented an interesting example of a man who voluntarily stays in a room which, unknown to him, is locked: John Locke, *Essay Concerning Human Understanding*, Bk. II, chap. 12 Secs. 8–11. For a number of examples of agents who are morally responsible for actions although they could not have done otherwise, see Harry Frankfurt, "Alternate Possibilities and Moral Responsibility," *Journal of Philosophy* 46, no. 23 (1969): 829–39. Also see John Martin Fischer, "Responsibility and Control," *Journal of Philosophy* 79, no. 1 (1982): 24–40.

5. For a vigorous and interesting criticism of this description of the case, see Peter van Inwagen, "Ability and Responsibility," *The Philosophical Review* 87 (1978): 201–24, reprinted in Peter van Inwagen, *An Essay on Free Will* (Oxford: Clarendon, 1983), pp. 161–82. Although it is inappropriate to pursue the details of the debate here, I defend the claim that there are cases in which an agent is morally responsible for performing an action although he couldn't have done otherwise; see Fischer, "Responsibility and Control."

6. I owe this way of describing the Frankfurt-type cases to Sydney Shoemaker.

7. Here I am indebted to Duggan and Gert, "Free Will as the Ability to Will."

8. Ibid.

9. Robert Nozick requires this sort of close contouring of action to value for his notion of "tracking value": see Nozick, *Philosophical Explanations*, pp. 317–62. In this respect, then, Nozick's notion of tracking value corresponds to strong reasons-responsiveness. Nozick claims that an agent who tracks value displays a kind of moral virtue, but he does not claim that tracking value is a necessary condition for moral responsibility.

10. Here I adopt the constraint that the possible worlds pertinent to the weak reasons-responsiveness of the actual-sequence mechanism must have the same *natural laws* as the actual world.

11. Ferdinand Schoeman has brought to my attention a kind of example that threatens my claim that weak reasons-responsiveness is sufficient for moral responsibility. Imagine someone who is apparently insane. This person commits a barbarous act, such as killing a number of persons on the Staten Island Ferry with a saber. And suppose that this individual would have killed the persons under all possible

circumstances except one: he would have refrained if he believed that it was Friday and thus a religious holiday. Intuitively, the individual is highly irrational and should not be considered morally responsible, and yet he seems to satisfy the condition of acting from a reasons-responsive mechanism. Weak reasons-responsiveness obtains by virtue of the agent's responsiveness to a bizarre reason, even though the agent is not responsive to a wide array of relevant reasons.

I am aware that this sort of example poses a problem for the theory of responsibility I present here. At this point, I see two possible responses. First, one might claim that in this kind of case there would be a different mechanism operating in the alternate scenario (in which the agent is responsive) than in the actual sequence. Alternatively, one might restrict the reasons that are pertinent to weak reasons-responsiveness. I hope to discuss such examples and to develop an adequate response in future work.

12. Roughly, one might distinguish between "internalist" and "externalist" accounts of knowledge. An internalist proceeds by requiring that the agent have a certain sort of *justification* for his belief. The externalist abandons the search for refined kinds of justification and requires certain kinds of causal connections between the fact known and the agent's belief.

13. I am obviously presenting only a sketch of a theory of knowledge here. Further, I do not here suppose that this is obviously the *correct* account of knowledge. I am merely pointing to an analogy between my approach to moral responsibility and the externalist conception of knowledge. The approach to knowledge presented here follows those of, among others, Dretske and Nozick: F. Dretske, "Conclusive Reasons," *Australasian Journal of Philosophy* 49 (1971): 1–22; and Nozick, *Philosophical Explanations*, pp. 167–98. Nozick also discusses the analogy between moral responsibility and knowledge.

14. Nozick claims that this fact helps to refute a certain kind of epistemological skeptic. See Nozick, *Philosophical Explanations*, pp. 197–247.

15. Nozick, *Philosophical Explanations*, p. 179.

16. Ibid., pp. 180–81. Nozick attributes this example to Avishai Margalit.

17. Ibid., p. 191.

18. I have left extremely vague the crucial notion of "same mechanism." There are certainly very disturbing problems with this notion in epistemology.

For a discussion of some of these problems, see Robert Shope, "Cognitive Abilities, Conditionals, and Knowledge: A Response to Nozick," *Journal of Philosophy* 81, no. 1 (1984): 29–48. And there may well be similar problems in action theory. Here I am simply relying on some intuitive way of individuating kinds of mechanisms issuing in action, for the purposes of moral responsibility ascriptions. A defense of the sketch of a theory that I am presenting would involve saying more about the individuation of mechanisms.

19. The claim, as stated, relies on the intuition that the physical process *P* is the relevant mechanism. Alternatively, one could simply point out that in Jim's case *there exists* an actually operative mechanism (of kind *P*) that is temporally intrinsic and not reasons-responsive.

20. Daniel Dennett says: "The possibility of short-circuiting or otherwise tampering with an intentional system gives rise to an interesting group of perplexities about the extent of responsibility in cases where there has been manipulation. We are generally absolved of responsibility where we have been manipulated by others, but there is no one principle of innocence by reason of manipulation." Daniel Dennett, "Mechanism of Responsibility," reprinted in *Brainstorms*, ed. Daniel Dennett (Montgomery, Vt.: Bradford, 1978), pp. 233–55, esp. p. 248. My suggestion provides a way of distinguishing responsibility-undermining manipulation from manipulation that is consistent with responsibility.

21. For some contemporary developments of the "basic argument" for incompatibilism, see Carl Ginet, "Might We Have No Choice?" in *Freedom and Determinism*, ed. K. Lehrer (New York: Random House, 1966); David Wiggins, "Towards a Reasonable Libertarianism," in *Essays on Freedom of Action*, ed. T. Honderich (Boston: Routledge and Kegan Paul, 1973); J. W. Lamb, "On a Proof of Incompatibilism," *Philosophical Review* 86 (1977); and Peter van Inwagen, "The Incompatibility of Free Will and Determinism," *Philosophical Studies* 27 (1975), and *An Essay on Free Will* (Oxford: Clarendon, 1983), esp. pp. 55–105.

22. I have discussed the argument in John Martin Fischer, "Incompatibilism," *Philosophical Studies* 43 (1983): 127–37; "Van Inwagen on Free Will," *Philosophical Quarterly* 36 (1986): 252–60. For discussion of the argument, see David Lewis, "Are We Free to Break the Laws?" *Theoria* 47 (1981): 113–21.

23. For an interesting alternative challenge to certain formulations of the "basic argument," see Michael Slote, "Selective Necessity and the Free-Will Problem," *Journal of Philosophy* 82 (1982): 5–24.

24. I believe that Frankfurt is a compatibilistic semi-compatibilist. I am an agnostic semicompatibilist, although I am perhaps a latently incompatibilistic semicompatibilist. In "Responsibility and Control" I pointed out that Frankfurt-type cases do not in themselves establish the consistency of causal determinism and moral responsibility. Thus, Frankfurt-type cases leave open the position of "ultra-incompatibilism": Causal determinism is incompatible with moral responsibility, even if moral responsibility does not require freedom to do otherwise. Here I have preferred agnostic (or perhaps incompatibilistic) semicompatibilism to agnostic (or incompatibilistic) ultra-incompatibilism.

25. I have here sketched an approach that attempts to reconcile moral responsibility *for action* with causal determinism and God's foreknowledge. My approach relies on the claim that moral responsibility for an action does not require freedom to do otherwise. Elsewhere I have argued that, whereas an agent can be morally responsible for performing an action although he could not have done otherwise, an agent cannot be held responsible for *not* performing an action he could not have performed: John Martin Fischer, "Responsibility and Failure," *Proceedings of the Aristotelian Society* 86 (1985–86): 251–70. If this "asymmetry thesis" is true, then I still have not reconciled moral responsibility *for omissions* (or perhaps, for "not-doings") with causal determinism (and divine foreknowledge).

I do not have the space here fully to develop my theory of responsibility for not performing actions. But I can say that, even if an agent is not responsible for failing to do something he could not do, an agent may be held morally responsible for *something* (perhaps, a "positive" action). And so he will be accessible to praise or blame. I believe that such a theory of moral responsibility can be developed so as to reconcile causal determinism (and divine foreknowledge) with the moral attitudes we think are intuitively appropriate.

26. Harry Frankfurt, "Freedom of the Will and the Concept of a Person," *Journal of Philosophy* 68 (1971): 5–20, esp. p. 15.

27. Frankfurt discusses the notion of identification in "Identification and Externality," in *The Identities of Persons*, ed. A. O. Rorty (Berkeley: University of California Press, 1976); and "Identification and Wholeheartedness," chap. 2 of *Responsibility, Character, and the Emotions*, ed. Ferdinand Schoeman (Cambridge: Cambridge University Press, 1987).

28. Gary Watson, "Free Agency," *Journal of Philosophy* 72 (1975): 205–20.

29. I am not sure whether Watson himself is committed to the sufficiency of the mesh for moral responsibility. He is committed to the claim that an agent is free insofar as he has the power to effect a mesh between the valuational and motivational systems. Ibid., p. 216.

30. Moral responsibility is in this respect like such notions as justice and love for a particular person. Nozick argues in *Anarchy, State, and Utopia* (New York: Basic Books, 1974) that justice and love are historical rather than "current time-slice" notions. Purely structural approaches to moral responsibility are inadequate in a way that is parallel to the inadequacy of current time-slice approaches to justice.

KEY TERMS

Moral responsibility
Reasons-responsiveness
Mechanisms
Causal determinism
Semicompatibilism
Hierarchical model of moral responsibility

STUDY QUESTIONS

1. Why does Fischer think Frankfurt-type cases are important for moral responsibility? What does he think they show us about the mechanism that actually issues in an agent's behavior?

2. What does Fischer mean by "reasons-responsiveness"? Why does he think it is important to distinguish between strong and weak varieties of reasons-responsiveness?

3. What is causal determinism? Do you think that the lessons we learn from Frankfurt-type cases are applicable to causal determinism?

4. In your own words, explain the view that Fischer calls "semicompatibilism." How does semicompatibilism differ from incompatibilism? Compatibilism?

Freedom of the Will and the Concept of a Person

HARRY G. FRANKFURT

...

WHAT philosophers have lately come to accept as analysis of the concept of a person is not actually analysis of *that* concept at all. Strawson, whose usage represents the current standard, identifies the concept of a person as "the concept of a type of entity such that *both* predicates ascribing states of consciousness *and* predicates ascribing corporeal characteristics . . . are equally applicable to a single individual of that single type."[1] But there are many entities besides persons that have both mental and physical properties. As it happens—though it seems extraordinary that this should be so—there is no common English word for the type of entity Strawson has in mind, a type that includes not only human beings but animals of various lesser species as well. Still, this hardly justifies the misappropriation of a valuable philosophical term.

Whether the members of some animal species are persons is surely not to be settled merely by determining whether it is correct to apply to them, in addition to predicates ascribing corporeal characteristics, predicates that ascribe states of consciousness. It does violence to our language to endorse the application of the term "person" to those numerous creatures which do have both psychological and material properties but which are manifestly not persons in any normal sense of the word. This misuse of language is doubtless innocent of any theoretical error. But although the offence is "merely verbal," it does significant harm. For it gratuitously diminishes our philosophical vocabulary, and it increases the likelihood that we will overlook the important area of inquiry with which the term "person" is most naturally associated. It might have

been expected that no problem would be of more central and persistent concern to philosophers than that of understanding what we ourselves essentially are. Yet this problem is so generally neglected that it has been possible to make off with its very name almost without being noticed and, evidently, without evoking any widespread feeling of loss.

There is a sense in which the word "person" is merely the singular form of "people" and in which both terms connote no more than membership in a certain biological species. In those senses of the word which are of greater philosophical interest, however, the criteria for being a person do not serve primarily to distinguish the members of our own species from the members of other species. Rather, they are designed to capture those attributes which are the subject of our most humane concern with ourselves and the source of what we regard as most important and most problematical in our lives. Now these attributes would be of equal significance to us even if they were not in fact peculiar and common to the members of our own species. What interests us most in the human condition would not interest us less if it were also a feature of the condition of other creatures as well.

Our concept of ourselves as persons is not to be understood, therefore, as a concept of attributes that are necessarily species-specific. It is conceptually possible that members of novel or even of familiar non-human species should be persons; and it is also conceptually possible that some members of the human species are not persons. We do in fact assume, on the other hand, that no member of another species is a person. Accordingly, there is a presumption that what is essential to persons is a set of characteristics that we generally suppose—whether rightly or wrongly—to be uniquely human.

It is my view that one essential difference between persons and other creatures is to be found in

From *Journal of Philosophy*, LXVIII, No. 1 (Jan. 1971). Copyright © 1971 by Columbia University. Reprinted by permission of the publisher and author.

the structure of a person's will. Human beings are not alone in having desires and motives, or in making choices. They share these things with the members of certain other species, some of whom even appear to engage in deliberation and to make decisions based upon prior thought. It seems to be peculiarly characteristic of humans, however, that they are able to form what I shall call "**second-order desires**" or "desires of the second order."

Besides wanting and choosing and being moved *to do* this or that, men may also want to have (or not to have) certain desires and motives. They are capable of wanting to be different, in their preferences and purposes, from what they are. Many animals appear to have the capacity for what I shall call "**first-order desires**" or "desires of the first order," which are simply desires to do or not to do one thing or another. No animal other than man, however, appears to have the capacity for reflective self-evaluation that is manifested in the formation of second-order desires.[2]

I

The concept designated by the verb "to want" is extraordinarily elusive. A statement of the form "*A* wants to *X*"—taken by itself, apart from a context that serves to amplify or to specify its meaning—conveys remarkably little information. Such a statement may be consistent, for example, with each of the following statements: (a) the prospect of doing *X* elicits no sensation or introspectible emotional response in *A*; (b) *A* is unaware that he wants to *X*; (c) *A* believes that he does not want to *X*; (d) *A* wants to refrain from *X*-ing; (e) *A* wants to *Y* and believes that it is impossible for him both to *Y* and to *X*; (f) *A* does not "really" want to *X*; (g) *A would rather die than X*; and so on. It is therefore hardly sufficient to formulate the distinction between first-order and second-order desires, as I have done, by suggesting merely that someone has a first-order desire when he wants to do or not to do such-and-such, and that he has a second-order desire when he wants to have or not to have a certain desire of the first order.

As I shall understand them, statements of the form "*A* wants to *X*" cover a rather broad range of

possibilities.[3] They may be true even when statements like (a) through (g) are true: when *A* is unaware of any feelings concerning *X*-ing, when he is unaware that he wants to *X*, when he deceives himself about what he wants and believes falsely that he does not want to *X*, when he also has other desires that conflict with his desire to *X*, or when he is ambivalent. The desires in question may be conscious or unconscious, they need not be univocal, and *A* may be mistaken about them. There is a further source of uncertainty with regard to statements that identify someone's desires, however, and here it is important for my purposes to be less permissive.

Consider first those statements of the form "*A* wants to *X*" which identify first-order desires—that is, statements in which the term "to *X*" refers to an action. A statement of this kind does not, by itself, indicate the relative strength of *A*'s desire to *X*. It does not make it clear whether this desire is at all likely to play a decisive role in what *A* actually does or tries to do. For it may correctly be said that *A* wants to *X* even when his desire to *X* is only one among his desires and when it is far from being paramount among them. Thus, it may be true that *A* wants to *X* when he strongly prefers to do something else instead; and it may be true that he wants to *X* despite the fact that, when he acts, it is not the desire to *X* that motivates him to do what he does. On the other hand, someone who states that *A* wants to *X* may mean to convey that it is this desire that is motivating or moving *A* to do what he is actually doing or that *A* will in fact be moved by this desire (unless he changes his mind) when he acts.

It is only when it is used in the second of these ways that, given the special usage of "will" that I propose to adopt, the statement identifies *A*'s will. To identify an agent's will is either to identify the desire (or desires) by which he is motivated in some action he performs or to identify the desire (or desires) by which he will or would be motivated when or if he acts. An agent's will, then, is identical with one or more of his first-order desires. But the notion of the will, as I am employing it, is not coextensive with the notion of first-order desires. It is not the notion of something that merely inclines an agent in some degree to act in a certain way. Rather, it is the notion of an *effective* desire—one that moves (or will or would move) a person all the way to action. Thus the notion of the will is not coextensive with the notion of what an agent intends to do. For even though someone may have a settled intention to do X, he may nonetheless do something else instead of doing X because, despite his intention, his desire to do X proves to be weaker or less effective than some conflicting desire.

Now consider those statements of the form "*A* wants to *X*" which identify second-order desires—that is, statements in which the term "to *X*" refers to a desire of the first order. There are also two kinds of situation in which it may be true that *A* wants to want to *X*. In the first place, it might be true of *A* that he wants to have a desire to *X* despite the fact that he has a univocal desire, altogether free of conflict and ambivalence, to refrain from *X*-ing. Someone might want to have a certain desire, in other words, but univocally want that desire to be unsatisfied.

Suppose that a physician engaged in psychotherapy with narcotics addicts believes that his ability to help his patients would be enhanced if he understood better what it is like for them to desire the drug to which they are addicted. Suppose that he is led in this way to want to have a desire for the drug. If it is a genuine desire that he wants, then what he wants is not merely to feel the sensations that addicts characteristically feel when they are gripped by their desires for the drug. What the physician wants, in so far as he wants to have a desire, is to be inclined or moved to some extent to take the drug.

It is entirely possible, however, that, although he wants to be moved by a desire to take the drug, he does not want this desire to be effective. He may not want it to move him all the way to action. He need not be interested in finding out what it is like to take the drug. And in so far as he now wants only to *want* to take it, and not to *take* it, there is nothing in what he now wants that would be satisfied by the drug itself. He may now have, in fact, an altogether univocal desire *not* to take the drug; and he may prudently arrange to make it impossible for him to satisfy the desire he would have if his desire to want the drug should in time be satisfied.

It would thus be incorrect to infer, from the fact that the physician now wants to desire to take the drug, that he already does desire to take it. His second-order desire to be moved to take the drug does not entail that he has a first-order desire to take it. If the drug were now to be administered to him, this might satisfy no desire that is implicit in his desire to want to take it. While he wants to take the drug, he may have *no* desire to take it; it may be that *all* he wants is to taste the desire for it. That is, his desire to have a certain desire that he does not have may not be a desire that his will should be at all different than it is.

Someone who wants only in this truncated way to want to *X* stands at the margin of preciosity, and the fact that he wants to want to *X* is not pertinent to the identification of his will. There is, however, a second kind of situation that may be described by "*A* wants to want to *X*"; and when the statement is used to describe a situation of this second kind, then it does pertain to what *A* wants his will to be. In such cases the statement means that *A* wants the desire to *X* to be the desire that moves him effectively to act. It is not merely that he wants the desire to *X* to be among the desires by which, to one degree or another, he is moved or inclined to act. He wants this desire to be effective—that is, to provide the motive in what he actually does. Now when the statement that *A* wants to want to *X* is used in this way, it does entail that *A* already has a desire to *X*. It could not be true both that *A* wants the desire to *X* to move him into action and that he does not want to *X*. It is only if he does want to *X* that he can coherently want the desire to *X* not merely to be one of his desires but, more decisively, to be his will.[4]

Suppose a man wants to be motivated in what he does by the desire to concentrate on his work. It is necessarily true, if this supposition is correct, that he already wants to concentrate on his work. This desire is now among his desires. But the question of whether or not his second-order desire is fulfilled does not turn merely on whether the desire he wants is one of his desires. It turns on whether this desire is, as he wants it to be, his effective desire or will. If, when the chips are down, it is his desire to concentrate on his work that moves him to do what he does, then what he wants at that time is indeed (in the relevant sense) what he wants to want. If it is some other desire that actually moves him when he acts, on the other hand, then what he wants at that time is not (in the relevant sense) what he wants to want. This will be so despite the fact that the desire to concentrate on his work continues to be among his desires.

II

Someone has a desire of the second order either when he wants simply to have a certain desire or when he wants a certain desire to be his will. In situations of the latter kind, I shall call his second-order desires "**second-order volitions**" or "volitions of the second order." Now it is having second-order volitions, and not having second-order desires generally, that I regard as essential to being a person. It is logically possible, however unlikely, that there should be an agent with second-order desires but with no volitions of the second order. Such a creature, in my view, would not be a person. I shall use the term "**wanton**" to refer to agents who have first-order desires but who are not persons because, whether or not they have desires of the second order, they have no second-order volitions.[5]

The essential characteristic of a wanton is that he does not care about his will. His desires move him to do certain things, without its being true of him either that he wants to be moved by those desires or that he prefers to be moved by other desires. The class of wantons includes all non-human animals that have desires and all very young children. Perhaps it also includes some adult human beings as well. In any case, adult humans may be more or less wanton; they may act wantonly, in response to first-order desires concerning which they have no volitions of the second order, or less frequently.

The fact that a wanton has no second-order volitions does not mean that each of his first-order desires is translated heedlessly and at once into action. He may have no opportunity to act in accordance with some of his desires. Moreover, the translation of his desires into action may be delayed or precluded either by conflicting desires of the first order or by the intervention of deliberation. For a wanton may possess and employ rational faculties of a high

order. Nothing in the concept of a wanton implies that he cannot reason or that he cannot deliberate concerning how to do what he wants to do. What distinguishes the rational wanton from other rational agents is that he is not concerned with the desirability of his desires themselves. He ignores the question of what his will is to be. Not only does he pursue whatever course of action he is most strongly inclined to pursue, but he does not care which of his inclinations is the strongest.

Thus a rational creature, who reflects upon the suitability to his desires of one course of action or another, may nonetheless be a wanton. In maintaining that the essence of being a person lies not in reason but in will, I am far from suggesting that a creature without reason may be a person. For it is only in virtue of his rational capabilities that a person is capable of becoming critically aware of his own will and of forming volitions of the second order. The structure of a person's will presupposes, accordingly, that he is a rational being.

The distinction between a person and a wanton may be illustrated by the difference between two narcotics addicts. Let us suppose that the physiological condition accounting for the addiction is the same in both men, and that both succumb inevitably to their periodic desires for the drug to which they are addicted. One of the addicts hates his addiction and always struggles desperately, although to no avail, against its thrust. He tries everything that he thinks might enable him to overcome his desires for the drug. But these desires are too powerful for him to withstand, and invariably, in the end, they conquer him. He is an unwilling addict, helplessly violated by his own desires.

The unwilling addict has conflicting first-order desires: he wants to take the drug, and he also wants to refrain from taking it. In addition to these first-order desires, however, he has a volition of the second order. He is not a neutral with regard to the conflict between his desire to take the drug and his desire to refrain from taking it. It is the latter desire, and not the former, that he wants to constitute his will; it is the latter desire, rather than the former, that he wants to be effective and to provide the purpose that he will seek to realize in what he actually does.

The other addict is a wanton. His actions reflect the economy of his first-order desires, without his being concerned whether the desires that move him to act are desires by which he wants to be moved to act. If he encounters problems in obtaining the drug or in administering it to himself, his responses to his urges to take it may involve deliberation. But it never occurs to him to consider whether he wants the relation among his desires to result in his having the will he has. The wanton addict may be an animal, and thus incapable of being concerned about his will. In any event he is, in respect of his wanton lack of concern, no different from an animal.

The second of these addicts may suffer a first-order conflict similar to the first-order conflict suffered by the first. Whether he is human or not, the wanton may (perhaps due to conditioning) both want to take the drug and want to refrain from taking it. Unlike the unwilling addict, however, he does not prefer that one of his conflicting desires should be paramount over the other; he does not prefer that one first-order desire rather than the other should constitute his will. It would be misleading to say that he is neutral as to the conflict between his desires, since this would suggest that he regards them as equally acceptable. Since he has no identity apart from his first-order desires, it is true neither that he prefers one to the other nor that he prefers not to take sides.

It makes a difference to the unwilling addict, who is a person, which of his conflicting first-order desires wins out. Both desires are his, to be sure; and whether he finally takes the drug or finally succeeds in refraining from taking it, he acts to satisfy what is in a literal sense his own desire. In either case he does something he himself wants to do, and he does it not because of some external influence whose aim happens to coincide with his own but because of his desire to do it. The unwilling addict identifies himself, however, through the formation of a second-order volition, with one rather than with the other of his conflicting first-order desires. He makes one of them more truly his own and, in so doing, he withdraws himself from the other. It is in virtue of this identification and withdrawal, accomplished through the formation of a second-order volition, that the unwilling addict may meaningfully make the analytically puzzling statements that the force

moving him to take the drug is a force other than his own, and that it is not of his own free will but rather against his will that this force moves him to take it.

The wanton addict cannot or does not care which of his conflicting first-order desires wins out. His lack of concern is not due to his inability to find a convincing basis for preference. It is due either to his lack of the capacity for reflection or to his mindless indifference to the enterprise of evaluating his own desires and motives.[6] There is only one issue in the struggle to which his first-order conflict may lead: whether the one or the other of his conflicting desires is the stronger. Since he is moved by both desires, he will not be altogether satisfied by what he does no matter which of them is effective. But it makes no difference to *him* whether his craving or his aversion gets the upper hand. He has no stake in the conflict between them and so, unlike the unwilling addict, he can neither win nor lose the struggle in which he is engaged. When a *person* acts, the desire by which he is moved is either the will he wants or a will he wants to be without. When a *wanton* acts, it is neither.

III

There is a very close relationship between the capacity for forming second-order volitions and another capacity that is essential to persons—one that has often been considered a distinguishing mark of the human condition. It is only because a person has volitions of the second order that he is capable both of enjoying and of lacking **freedom of will**. The concept of a person is not only, then, the concept of a type of entity that has both first-order desires and volitions of the second order. It can also be construed as the concept of a type of entity for whom the freedom of its will may be a problem. This concept excludes all wantons, both infrahuman and human, since they fail to satisfy an essential condition for the enjoyment of freedom of the will. And it excludes those suprahuman beings, if any, whose wills are necessarily free.

Just what kind of freedom is the freedom of the will? This question calls for an identification of the special area of human experience to which the concept of freedom of the will, as distinct from the concepts of other sorts of freedom, is particularly germane. In dealing with it, my aim will be primarily to locate the problem with which a person is most immediately concerned when he is concerned with the freedom of his will.

According to one familiar philosophical tradition, being free is fundamentally a matter of doing what one wants to do. Now the notion of an agent who does what he wants to do is by no means an altogether clear one: both the doing and the wanting, and the appropriate relation between them as well, require elucidation. But although its focus needs to be sharpened and its formulation refined, I believe that this notion does capture at least part of what is implicit in the idea of an agent who *acts* freely. It misses entirely, however, the peculiar content of the quite different idea of an agent whose *will* is free.

We do not suppose that animals enjoy freedom of the will, although we recognize that an animal may be free to run in whatever direction it wants. Thus, having the freedom to do what one wants to do is not a sufficient condition of having a free will. It is not a necessary condition either. For to deprive someone of his **freedom of action** is not necessarily to undermine the freedom of his will. When an agent is aware that there are certain things he is not free to do, this doubtless affects his desires and limits the range of choices he can make. But suppose that someone, without being aware of it, has in fact lost or been deprived of his freedom of action. Even though he is no longer free to do what he wants to do, his will may remain as free as it was before. Despite the fact that he is not free to translate his desires into actions or to act according to the determinations of his will, he may still form those desires and make those determinations as freely as if his freedom of action had not been impaired.

When we ask whether a person's will is free we are not asking whether he is in a position to translate his first-order desires into actions. That is the question of whether he is free to do as he pleases. The question of the freedom of his will does not concern the relation between what he does and what he wants to do. Rather, it concerns his desires themselves. But what question about them is it?

It seems to me both natural and useful to construe the question of whether a person's will is free in close analogy to the question of whether an agent enjoys freedom of action. Now freedom of action is (roughly, at least) the freedom to do what one wants to do. Analogously, then, the statement that a person enjoys freedom of the will means (also roughly) that he is free to want what he wants to want. More precisely, it means that he is free to will what he wants to will, or to have the will he wants. Just as the question about the freedom of an agent's action has to do with whether it is the action he wants to perform, so the question about the freedom of his will has to do with whether it is the will he wants to have.

It is in securing the conformity of his will to his second-order volitions, then, that a person exercises freedom of the will. And it is in the discrepancy between his will and his second-order volitions, or in his awareness that their coincidence is not his own doing but only a happy chance, that a person who does not have this freedom feels its lack. The unwilling addict's will is not free. This is shown by the fact that it is not the will he wants. It is also true, though in a different way, that the will of the wanton addict is not free. The wanton addict neither has the will he wants nor has a will that differs from the will he wants. Since he has no volitions of the second order, the freedom of his will cannot be a problem for him. He lacks it, so to speak, by default.

People are generally far more complicated than my sketchy account of the structure of a person's will may suggest. There is as much opportunity for ambivalence, conflict, and self-deception with regard to desires of the second order, for example, as there is with regard to first-order desires. If there is an unresolved conflict among someone's second-order desires, then he is in danger of having no second-order volition; for unless this conflict is resolved, he has no preference concerning which of his first-order desires is to be his will. This condition, if it is so severe that it prevents him from identifying himself in a sufficiently decisive way with *any* of his conflicting first-order desires, destroys him as a person. For it either tends to paralyse his will and to keep him from acting at all, or it tends to remove him from his will so that his will operates without his participation. In both cases he becomes, like the unwilling addict though in a different way, a helpless bystander to the forces that move him.

Another complexity is that a person may have, especially if his second-order desires are in conflict, desires and volitions of a higher order than the second. There is no theoretical limit to the length of the series of desires of higher and higher orders; nothing except common sense and, perhaps, a saving fatigue prevents an individual from obsessively refusing to identify himself with any of his desires until he forms a desire of the next higher order. The tendency to generate such a series of acts of forming desires, which would be a case of humanization run wild, also leads toward the destruction of a person.

It is possible, however, to terminate such a series of acts without cutting it off arbitrarily. When a person identifies himself *decisively* with one of his first-order desires, this commitment "resounds" throughout the potentially endless array of higher orders. Consider a person who, without reservation or conflict, wants to be motivated by the desire to concentrate on his work. The fact that his second-order volition to be moved by this desire is a decisive one means that there is no room for questions concerning the pertinence of desires or volitions of higher orders. Suppose the person is asked whether he wants to want to want to concentrate on his work. He can properly insist that this question concerning a third-order desire does not arise. It would be a mistake to claim that, because he has not considered whether he wants the second-order volition he has formed, he is indifferent to the question of whether it is with this volition or with some other that he wants his will to accord. The decisiveness of the commitment he has made means that he has decided that no further question about his second-order volition, or any higher order, remains to be asked. It is relatively unimportant whether we explain this by saying that this commitment implicitly generates an endless series of confirming desires of higher orders, or by saying that the commitment is tantamount to a dissolution of the pointedness of all questions concerning higher orders of desire.

Examples such as the one concerning the unwilling addict may suggest that volitions of the second order, or of higher orders, must be formed deliberately and that a person characteristically struggles to

ensure that they are satisfied. But the conformity of a person's will to his higher-order volitions may be far more thoughtless and spontaneous than this. Some people are naturally moved by kindness when they want to be kind, and by nastiness when they want to be nasty, without any explicit forethought and without any need for energetic self-control. Others are moved by nastiness when they want to be kind and by kindness when they intend to be nasty, equally without forethought and without active resistance to these violations of their higher-order desires. The enjoyment of freedom comes easily to some. Others must struggle to achieve it.

IV

My theory concerning the freedom of the will accounts easily for our disinclination to allow that this freedom is enjoyed by the members of any species inferior to our own. It also satisfies another condition that must be met by any such theory, by making it apparent why the freedom of the will should be regarded as desirable. The enjoyment of a free will means the satisfaction of certain desires—desires of the second or of higher orders—whereas its absence means their frustration. The satisfactions at stake are those which accrue to a person of whom it may be said that his will is his own. The corresponding frustrations are those suffered by a person of whom it may be said that he is estranged from himself, or that he finds himself a helpless or a passive bystander to the forces that move him.

A person who is free to do what he wants to do may yet not be in a position to have the will he wants. Suppose, however, that he enjoys both freedom of action and freedom of the will. Then he is not only free to do what he wants to do; he is also free to want what he wants to want. It seems to me that he has, in that case, all the freedom it is possible to desire or to conceive. There are other good things in life, and he may not possess some of them. But there is nothing in the way of freedom that he lacks.

It is far from clear that certain other theories of the freedom of the will meet these elementary but essential conditions: that it be understandable why we desire this freedom and why we refuse to ascribe it to animals. Consider, for example, Roderick Chisholm's quaint version of the doctrine that human freedom entails an absence of causal determination.[7] Whenever a person performs a free action, according to Chisholm, it's a miracle. The motion of a person's hand, when the person moves it, is the outcome of a series of physical causes; but some event in this series, "and presumably one of those that took place within the brain, was caused by the agent and not by any other events" (18). A free agent has, therefore, "a prerogative which some would attribute only to God: each of us, when we act, is a prime mover unmoved" (23).

This account fails to provide any basis for doubting that animals of subhuman species enjoy the freedom it defines. Chisholm says nothing that makes it seem less likely that a rabbit performs a miracle when it moves its leg than that a man does so when he moves his hand. But why, in any case, should anyone *care* whether he can interrupt the natural order of causes in the way Chisholm describes? Chisholm offers no reason for believing that there is a discernible difference between the experience of a man who miraculously initiates a series of causes when he moves his hand and a man who moves his hand without any such breach of the normal causal sequence. There appears to be no concrete basis for preferring to be involved in the one state of affairs rather than in the other.[8]

It is generally supposed that, in addition to satisfying the two conditions I have mentioned, a satisfactory theory of the freedom of the will necessarily provides an analysis of one of the conditions of moral responsibility. The most common recent approach to the problem of understanding the freedom of the will has been, indeed, to inquire what is entailed by the assumption that someone is morally responsible for what he has done. In my view, however, the relation between moral responsibility and the freedom of the will has been very widely misunderstood. It is not true that a person is morally responsible for what he has done only if his will was free when he did it. He may be morally responsible for having done it even though his will was not free at all.

A person's will is free only if he is free to have the will he wants. This means that, with regard to any of his first-order desires, he is free either to make that desire his will or to make some other first-order desire his will instead. Whatever his will, then, the will of the person whose will is free could have been otherwise; he could have done otherwise than to constitute his will as he did. It is a vexed question just how "he could have done otherwise" is to be understood in contexts such as this one. But although this question is important to the theory of freedom, it has no bearing on the theory of moral responsibility. For the assumption that a person is morally responsible for what he has done does not entail that the person was in a position to have whatever will he wanted.

This assumption *does* entail that the person did what he did freely, or that he did it of his own free will. It is a mistake, however, to believe that someone acts freely only when he is free to do whatever he wants or that he acts of his own free will only if his will is free. Suppose that a person has done what he wanted to do, that he did it because he wanted to do it, and that the will by which he was moved when he did it was his will because it was the will he wanted. Then he did it freely and of his own free will. Even supposing that he could have done otherwise, he would not have done otherwise; and even supposing that he could have had a different will, he would not have wanted his will to differ from what it was. Moreover, since the will that moved him when he acted was his will because he wanted it to be, he cannot claim that his will was forced upon him or that he was a passive bystander to its constitution. Under these conditions, it is quite irrelevant to the evaluation of his moral responsibility to inquire whether the alternatives that he opted against were actually available to him.[9]

In illustration, consider a third kind of addict. Suppose that his addiction has the same physiological basis and the same irresistible thrust as the addictions of the unwilling and wanton addicts, but that he is altogether delighted with his condition. He is a willing addict, who would not have things any other way. If the grip of his addiction should somehow weaken, he would do whatever he could to reinstate it; if his desire for the drug should begin to fade, he would take steps to renew its intensity.

The willing addict's will is not free, for his desire to take the drug will be effective regardless of whether or not he wants this desire to constitute his will. But when he takes the drug, he takes it freely and of his own free will. I am inclined to understand his situation as involving the overdetermination of his first-order desire to take the drug. This desire is his effective desire because he is physiologically addicted. But it is his effective desire also because he wants it to be. His will is outside his control, but, by his second-order desire that his desire for the drug should be effective, he has made this will his own. Given that it is therefore not only because of his addiction that his desire for the drug is effective, he may be morally responsible for taking the drug.

My conception of the freedom of the will appears to be neutral with regard to the problem of **determinism**. It seems conceivable that it should be causally determined that a person is free to want what he wants to want. If this is conceivable, then it might be causally determined that a person enjoys a free will. There is no more than an innocuous appearance of paradox in the proposition that it is determined, ineluctably and by forces beyond their control, that certain people have free wills and that others do not. There is no incoherence in the proposition that some agency other than a person's own is responsible (even *morally* responsible) for the fact that he enjoys or fails to enjoy freedom of the will. It is possible that a person should be morally responsible for what he does of his own free will and that some other person should also be morally responsible for his having done it.[10]

On the other hand, it seems conceivable that it should come about by chance that a person is free to have the will he wants. If this is conceivable, then it might be a matter of chance that certain people enjoy freedom of the will and that certain others do not. Perhaps it is also conceivable, as a number of philosophers believe, for states of affairs to come about in a way other than by chance or as the outcome of a sequence of natural causes. If it is indeed conceivable for the relevant states of affairs to come about in some third way, then it is also possible that a person should in that third way come to enjoy the freedom of the will.

NOTES

1. P. F. Strawson, *Individuals* (London: Methuen, 1959), pp. 101–2. Ayer's usage of "person" is similar: "it is characteristic of persons in this sense that besides having various physical properties . . . they are also credited with various forms of consciousness" (A. J. Ayer, *The Concept of a Person* [New York: St. Martin's, 1963], p. 82). What concerns Strawson and Ayer is the problem of understanding the relation between mind and body, rather than the quite different problem of understanding what it is to be a creature that not only has a mind and a body but is also a person.

2. For the sake of simplicity, I shall deal only with what someone wants or desires, neglecting related phenomena such as choices and decisions. I propose to use the verbs "to want" and "to desire" interchangeably, although they are by no means perfect synonyms. My motive in forsaking the established nuances of these words arises from the fact that the verb "to want," which suits my purposes better so far as its meaning is concerned, does not lend itself so readily to the formation of nouns as does the verb "to desire." It is perhaps acceptable, albeit graceless, to speak in the plural of someone's "wants." But to speak in the singular of someone's "want" would be an abomination.

3. What I say in this paragraph applies not only to cases in which "to X" refers to a possible action or inaction. It also applies to cases in which "to X" refers to a first-order desire and in which the statement that "A wants to X" is therefore a shortened version of a statement—"A wants to want X"—that identifies a desire of the second order.

4. It is not so clear that the entailment relation described here holds in certain kinds of cases, which I think may fairly be regarded as non-standard, where the essential difference between the standard and the non-standard cases lies in the kind of description by which the first-order desire in question is identified. Thus, suppose that A admires B so fulsomely that, even though he does not know what B wants to do, he wants to be effectively moved by whatever desire effectively moves B; without knowing what B's will is, in other words, A wants his own will to be the same. It certainly does not follow that A already has, among his desires, a desire like the one that constitutes B's will. I shall not pursue here the questions of whether there are genuine counterexamples to the claim

made in the text or of how, if there are, that claim should be altered.

5. Creatures with second-order desires but no second-order volitions differ significantly from brute animals, and, for some purposes, it would be desirable to regard them as persons. My usage, which withholds the designation "person" from them, is thus somewhat arbitrary. I adopt it largely because it facilitates the formulation of some of the points I wish to make. Hereafter, whenever I consider statements of the form "*A* wants to want to *X*," I shall have in mind statements identifying second-order volitions and not statements identifying second-order desires that are not second-order volitions.

6. In speaking of the evaluation of his own desires and motives as being characteristic of a person, I do not mean to suggest that a person's second-order volitions necessarily manifest a *moral* stance on his part toward his first-order desires. It may not be from the point of view of morality that the person evaluates his first-order desires. Moreover, a person may be capricious and irresponsible in forming his second-order volitions and give no serious consideration to what is at stake. Second-order volitions express evaluations only in the sense that they are preferences. There is no essential restriction on the kind of basis, if any, upon which they are formed.

7. "Freedom and Action," in *Freedom and Determinism*, ed. Keith Lehrer (New York: Random House, 1966), pp. 11–44.

8. I am not suggesting that the alleged difference between these two states of affairs is unverifiable. On the contrary, physiologists might well be able to show that Chisholm's conditions for a free action are not satisfied, by establishing that there is no relevant brain event for which a sufficient physical cause cannot be found.

9. For another discussion of the considerations that cast doubt on the principle that a person is morally responsible for what he has done only if he could have done otherwise, see my "Alternate Possibilities and Moral Responsibility," *Journal of Philosophy* (1969): 829–39.

10. There is a difference between being *fully* responsible and being *solely* responsible. Suppose that the willing addict has been made an addict by the deliberate and calculated work of another. Then it may be that both the addict and this other person are fully responsible for the addict's taking the drug, while neither of them is solely responsible for it. That there is a distinction between full moral responsibility and sole moral responsibility is apparent in the following example. A certain light can be turned on or off by flicking either of two switches, and each of these switches is simultaneously flicked to the "on" position by a different person, neither of whom is aware of the other. Neither person is solely responsible for the light's going on, nor do they share the responsibility in the sense that each is partially responsible; rather, each of them is fully responsible.

KEY TERMS

Second-order desires
First-order desires
Second-order volitions
Wanton

Freedom of will
Freedom of action
Determinism

STUDY QUESTIONS

1. What characteristics, if any, do you think distinguish human beings from other animals?
2. How does Frankfurt define the term "will"? Why do you think he calls that "will"?
3. What is Frankfurt's distinction between "freedom of the will" and "freedom of action"? What work does this distinction do?
4. Frankfurt says, "Suppose that [a man] enjoys both freedom of action and freedom of the will. Then he is not only free to do what he wants to do; he is also free to want what he wants to want. It seems to me that he has, in that case, all the freedom it is possible to desire or to conceive. There are other good things in life, and he may not possess some of them. But there is nothing in the way of freedom that he lacks." Do you think Frankfurt is right about this? Might there be something else that deserves to be called "freedom" that this man doesn't have?
5. Do you think it is right to hold Frankfurt's willing addict morally responsible for taking the drug?

Free Agency

GARY WATSON

Gary Watson is Provost Professor of Philosophy and Law at the University of Southern California. His research areas include ethics, philosophy of law, and moral psychology. Many of his seminal articles are included in his *Agency and Answerability: Selected Essays* (2004).

. .

In this essay I discuss a distinction that is crucial to a correct account of free action and to an adequate conception of human motivation and responsibility.

I

According to one familiar conception of freedom, a person is free to the extent that he is able to do or get what he wants. To circumscribe a person's freedom is to contract the range of things he is able to do. I think that, suitably qualified, this account is correct, and that the chief and most interesting uses of the word 'free' can be explicated in its terms. But this general line has been resisted on a number of different grounds. One of the most important objections—and the one upon which I shall concentrate in this paper—is that this familiar view is too impoverished to handle talk of free actions and **free will**.

Frequently enough, we say, or are inclined to say, that a person is not in control of his own actions, that he is not a "free agent" with respect to them, even though his behavior is intentional. Possible examples of this sort of action include those which are explained by addictions, manias, and phobias of various sorts. But the concept of free action would seem to be pleonastic on the analysis of freedom in terms of the ability to get what one wants. For if a person does something intentionally, then surely he was able at that time to do it. Hence, on this analysis, he was free to do it. The familiar account would not seem to

allow for any further questions, as far as freedom is concerned, about the action. Accordingly, this account would seem to embody a conflation of free action and intentional action.

Philosophers who have defended some form of **compatibilism** have usually given this analysis of freedom, with the aim of showing that freedom and responsibility are not really incompatible with **determinism**. Some critics have rejected compatibilism precisely because of its association with this familiar account of freedom. For instance, Isaiah Berlin asks: if determinism is true,

> . . . what reasons can you, in principle, adduce for attributing responsibility or applying moral rules to [people] which you would not think it reasonable to apply in the case of compulsive choosers—kleptomaniacs, dipsomaniacs, and the like?[1]

The idea is that the sense in which actions would be free in a deterministic world allows the actions of "compulsive choosers" to be free. To avoid this consequence, it is often suggested, we must adopt some sort of "contracausal" view of freedom.

Now, though compatibilists from Hobbes to J. J. C. Smart have given the relevant moral and psychological concepts an exceedingly crude treatment, this crudity is not inherent in compatibilism, nor does it result from the adoption of the conception of freedom in terms of the ability to get what one wants. For the difference between free and unfree actions—as we normally discern it—has nothing at all to do with the truth or falsity of determinism.

In the subsequent pages, I want to develop a distinction between wanting and valuing which will enable the familiar view of freedom to make sense of

From "Free Agency" in *The Journal of Philosophy* 72.8 (1975), pp. 205–220. Reprinted by permission.

the notion of an unfree action. The contention will be that, in the case of actions that are unfree, the agent is unable to get what he most wants, *or values*, and this inability is due to his own "motivational system." In this case the obstruction to the action that he most wants to do is his own will. It is in this respect that the action is unfree: the agent is obstructed in and by the very performance of the action.

I do not conceive my remarks to be a defense of compatibilism. This point of view may be unacceptable for various reasons, some of which call into question the coherence of the concept of responsibility. But these reasons do not include the fact that compatibilism relies upon the conception of freedom in terms of the ability to get what one wants, nor must it conflate free action and intentional action. If compatibilism is to be shown to be wrong, its critics must go deeper.

II

What must be true of people if there is to be a significant notion of free action? Our talk of free action arises from the apparent fact that what a person most wants may not be what he is finally moved to get. It follows from this apparent fact that the extent to which one wants something is not determined solely by the *strength* of one's desires (or "motives") as measured by their effectiveness in action. One (perhaps trivial) measure of the strength of the desire or want is that the agent acts upon that desire or want (trivial, since it will be nonexplanatory to say that an agent acted upon that desire because it was the strongest). But, if what one most wants may not be what one most strongly wants, by this measure, then in what sense can it be true that one most wants it?[2]

To answer this question, one might begin by contrasting, at least in a crude way, a humean with a platonic conception of practical reasoning. The ancients distinguished between the rational and the irrational parts of the soul, between Reason and Appetite. Hume employed a superficially similar distinction. It is important to understand, however, that (for Plato at least) the rational part of the soul is not to be identified with what Hume called "Reason" and contradistinguished from the "Passions." On Hume's account, Reason is not a source of motivation, but a faculty of determining what is true and what is false, a faculty concerned solely with "matters of fact" and "relations among ideas." It is completely dumb on the question of what to do. Perhaps Hume could allow Reason this much practical voice: given an initial set of wants and beliefs about what is or is likely to be the case, particular desires are generated in the process. In other words, a humean might allow Reason a crucial role in deliberation. But its essential role would not be to supply motivation—Reason is not that kind of thing—but rather to calculate, within a context of desires and ends, how to fulfill those desires and serve those ends. For Plato, however, the rational part of the soul is not some kind of inference mechanism. It is itself a source of motivation. In general form, the desires of Reason are desires for "the Good."

Perhaps the contrast can be illustrated by some elementary notions from decision theory. On the Bayesian model of deliberation, a preference scale is imposed upon various states of affairs contingent upon courses of action open to the agent. Each state of affairs can be assigned a numerical value (initial value) according to its place on the scale; given this assignment, and the probabilities that those states of affairs will obtain if the actions are performed, a final numerical value (expected desirability) can be assigned to the actions themselves. The rational agent performs the action with the highest expected desirability.

In these terms, on the humean picture, Reason is the faculty that computes probabilities and expected desirabilities. Reason is in this sense neutral with respect to actions, for it can operate equally on any given assignment of initial values and probabilities—it has nothing whatsoever to say about the assignment of initial values. On the platonic picture, however, the rational part of the soul itself determines what has *value* and how much, and thus is responsible for the original ranking of alternative states of affairs.

It may appear that the difference between these conceptions is merely a difference as to what is to be called "Reason" or "rational," and hence is not a substantive difference. In speaking of Reason, Hume has in mind a sharp contrast between what is wanted and what is thought to be the case. What contrast is implicit in the platonic view that the ranking of alternative states of affairs is the task of the rational part of the soul?

The contrast here is not trivial; the difference in classificatory schemes reflects different views of human psychology. For one thing, in saying this (or what is tantamount to this) Plato was calling attention to the fact that it is one thing to think a state of affairs good, worth while, or worthy of promotion, and another simply to desire or want that state of affairs to obtain. Since the notion of value is tied to (cannot be understood independently of) those of the good and worthy, it is one thing to value (think good) a state of affairs and another to desire that it obtain. However, to think a thing good is at the same time to desire it (or its promotion). Reason is thus an original spring of action. It is because valuing is essentially related to thinking or *judging* good that it is appropriate to speak of the wants that are (or perhaps arise from) evaluations as belonging to, or originating in, the rational (that is, *judging*) part of the soul; values provide *reasons* for action. The contrast is with desires, whose objects may not be thought good and which are thus, in a natural sense, blind or irrational. Desires are mute on the question of what is good.[3]

Now it seems to me that—given the view of freedom as the ability to get what one wants—there can be a problem of free action only if the platonic conception of the soul is (roughly) correct. The doctrine I shall defend is platonic in the sense that it involves a distinction between valuing and desiring which depends upon there being independent sources of motivation. No doubt Plato meant considerably more than this by his parts-of-the-soul doctrine; but he meant at least this. The platonic conception provides an answer to the question I posed earlier (451): in what sense can what one most wants differ from that which is the object of the strongest desire? The answer is that the phrase 'what one most wants' may mean either "the object of the strongest desire" or "what one most *values*." This phrase can be interpreted in terms of strength or in terms of ranking order or preference. The problem of free action arises because what one desires may not be what one values, and what one most values may not be what one is finally moved to get.[4]

The tacit identification of desiring or wanting with valuing is so common[5] that it is necessary to cite some examples of this distinction in order to illustrate how evaluation and desire may diverge. There seem to be two ways in which, in principle, a discrepancy may arise. First, it is possible that what one desires is not *to any degree* valued, held to be worth while, or thought good; one assigns *no* value whatever to the object of one's desire. Second, although one may indeed value what is desired, the strength of one's desire may not properly reflect the degree to which one values its object; that is, although the object of a desire is valuable, it may not be deemed the most valuable in the situation and yet one's desire for it may be stronger than the want for what is most valued.

The cases in which one in no way values what one desires are perhaps rare, but surely they exist. Consider the case of a woman who has a sudden urge to drown her bawling child in the bath; or the case of a squash player who, while suffering an ignominious defeat, desires to smash his opponent in the face with the racquet. It is just false that the mother values her child's being drowned or that the player values the injury and suffering of his opponent. But they desire these things nonetheless. They desire them in spite of themselves. It is not that they assign to these actions an initial value which is then outweighed by other considerations. These activities are not even represented by a positive entry, however small, on the initial "desirability matrix."

It may seem from these examples that this first and radical sort of divergence between desiring and valuing occurs only in the case of momentary and inexplicable urges or impulses. Yet I see no conclusive reason why a person could not be similarly estranged from a rather persistent and pervasive desire, and one that is explicable enough. Imagine a man who thinks his sexual inclinations are the work of the devil, that the very fact that he has sexual inclinations bespeaks his corrupt nature. This example is to be contrasted with that of the celibate who decides that the most fulfilling life for him will be one of abstinence. In this latter case, *one* of the things that receive consideration in the process of reaching his all-things-considered judgment is the value of sexual activity. There is something, from his point of view, to be said for sex, but there is more to be said in favor of celibacy. In contrast, the man who is estranged from his sexual inclinations does not acknowledge even a prima facie reason for sexual activity; that he is sexually inclined toward certain activities is not even *a* consideration. Another way of illustrating the difference is to say that, for the one man, forgoing sexual relationships constitutes a *loss*, even if negligible compared with the gains of celibacy; whereas from the standpoint of the other person, no loss is sustained at all.

Now, it must be admitted, any desire may provide the basis for a reason insofar as nonsatisfaction of the desire causes suffering and hinders the pursuit of ends of the agent. But it is important to notice that the reason generated in this way by a desire is a reason for *getting rid* of the desire, and one may get rid of a desire either by satisfying it or by eliminating it in some other manner (by tranquilizers, or cold showers). Hence this kind of reason differs importantly from the reasons based upon the evaluation of the activities or states of affairs in question. For, in the former case, attaining the object of desire is simply a means of eliminating discomfort or agitation, whereas in the latter case that attainment is the end itself. Normally, in the pursuit of the objects of our wants we are not attempting chiefly to relieve ourselves. We aim to satisfy, not just eliminate, desire.

Nevertheless, aside from transitory impulses, it may be that cases wherein nothing at all can be said in favor of the object of one's desire are rare. For it would seem that even the person who conceives his sexual desires to be essentially evil would have to admit that indulgence would be pleasurable, and surely that is something. (Perhaps not even this should be admitted. For indulgence may not yield pleasure at all in a context of anxiety. Furthermore, it is not obvious that pleasure is intrinsically good, independently of the worth of the pleasurable object.) In any case, the second sort of divergence between evaluation and desire remains: it is possible that, in a particular context, what one wants most strongly is not what one most values.

The distinction between valuing and desiring is not, it is crucial to see, a distinction among desires or wants according to their content. That is to say, there is nothing in the specification of the objects of an agent's desires that singles out some wants as based upon that agent's values. The distinction in question has rather to do with the *source* of the want or with its role in the total "system" of the agent's desires and ends. It has to do with why the agent wants what he does.

Obviously, to identify a desire or want simply in terms of its content is not to identify its source(s). It does

not follow from my wanting to eat that I am hungry. I may want to eat because I want to be well-nourished; or because I am hungry; or because eating is a pleasant activity. This single desire may have three independent sources. (These sources may not be altogether independent. It may be that eating is pleasurable only because I have appetites for food.) Some specifications of wants or desires—for instance, as cravings—pick out (at least roughly) the source of the motivation.

It is an essential feature of the appetites and the passions that they engender (or consist in) desires whose existence and persistence are independent of the person's judgment of the good. The appetite of hunger involves a desire to eat which has a source in physical needs and physiological states of the hungry organism. And emotions such as anger and fear partly consist in spontaneous inclinations to do various things—to attack or to flee the object of one's emotion, for example. It is intrinsic to the appetites and passions that appetitive and passionate beings can be motivated in spite of themselves. It is because desires such as these arise independently of the person's judgment and values that the ancients located the emotions and passions in the irrational part of the soul;[6] and it is because of this sort of independence that a conflict between valuing and desiring is possible.[7]

These points may suggest an inordinately dualistic view according to which persons are split into inevitably alien, if not always antagonistic, halves. But this view does not follow from what has been said. As central as it is to human life, it is not often noted that some activities are valued only to the extent that they are objects of the appetites. This means that such activities would never be regarded as valuable constituents of one's life were it not for one's susceptibility to "blind" motivation—motivation independent of one's values. Sexual activity and eating are again examples. We may value the activity of eating to the degree that it provides nourishment. But we may also value it because it is an enjoyable activity, even though its having this status depends upon our appetites for food, our hunger. In the case of sex, in fact, if we were not erotic creatures, certain activities would not only lose their value to us, they might not even be physiologically possible.

These examples indicate, not that there is no distinction between desiring and valuing, but that the value placed upon certain activities depends upon their being the fulfillment of desires that arise and persist independently of what we value. So it is not that, when we value the activity of eating, we think there are reasons to eat no matter what other desires we have; rather, we value eating when food appeals to us; and, likewise, we value sexual relationships when we are aroused. Here an essential part of the *content* of our evaluation is that the activity in question be motivated by certain appetites. These activities may have value for us only insofar as they are appetitively motivated, even though to have these appetites is not *ipso facto* to value their objects.

Part of what it means to value some activities in this way is this: we judge that to cease to have such appetites is to lose something of worth. The judgment here is not merely that, if someone has these appetites, it is worth while (*ceteris paribus*) for him to indulge them. The judgment is rather that it is of value to have and (having them) to indulge these appetites. The former judgment does not account for the eunuch's loss or sorrow, whereas the latter does. And the latter judgment lies at the bottom of the discomfort one may feel when one envisages a situation in which, say, hunger is consistently eliminated and nourishment provided by insipid capsules.

It would be impossible for a non-erotic being or a person who lacked the appetite for food and drink fully to understand the value most of us attach to sex and to dining. Sexual activity must strike the non-erotic being as perfectly grotesque. (Perhaps that is why lust is sometimes said to be disgusting and sinful in the eyes of God.) Or consider an appetite that is in fact "unnatural" (i.e., acquired): the craving for tobacco. To a person who has never known the enticement of Lady Nicotine, what could be more incomprehensible than the filthy practice of consummating a fine meal by drawing into one's lungs the noxious fumes of a burning weed?

Thus, the relationship between evaluation and motivation is intricate. With respect to many of our activities, evaluation depends upon the possibility of our being moved to act independently of our judgment. So the distinction I have been pressing—that between desiring and valuing—does not commit one to an inevitable split between Reason and Appetite. Appetitively motivated activities may well constitute for a person the most worth-while aspects of his life.[8]

But the distinction does commit us to the possibility of such a split. If there are sources of motivation independent of the agent's values, then it is possible that sometimes he is motivated to do things he does not deem worth doing. This possibility is the basis for the principal problem of free action: a person may be obstructed by his own will.

A related possibility that presents considerable problems for the understanding of free agency is this: some desires, when they arise, may "color" or influence what appear to be the agent's evaluations, but only temporarily. That is, when and only when he has the desire, is he inclined to think or say that what is desired or wanted is worth while or good. This possibility is to be distinguished from another, according to which one thinks it worth while to eat when one is hungry or to engage in sexual activity when one is so inclined. For one may think this even on the occasions when the appetites are silent. The possibility I have in mind is rather that what one is disposed to say or judge is temporarily affected by the presence of the desire in such a way that, both before and after the "onslaught" of the desire, one judges that the desire's object is worth pursuing (in the circumstances) whether or not one has the desire. In this case one is likely, in a cool moment, to think it a matter for regret that one had been so influenced and to think that one should guard against desires that have this property. In other cases it may not be the desire itself that affects one's judgment, but the set of conditions in which those desires arise—e.g., the conditions induced by drugs or alcohol. (It is noteworthy that we say: "under the influence of alcohol.") Perhaps judgments made in such circumstances are often in some sense self-deceptive. In any event, this phenomenon raises problems about the identification of a person's values.

Despite our examples, it would be mistaken to conclude that the only desires that exhibit an independence of evaluation are appetitive or passionate desires. In Freudian terms, one may be as dissociated from the demands of the super-ego as from those of the id. One may be disinclined to move away from one's family, the thought of doing so being accompanied by compunction; and yet this disinclination may rest solely upon acculturation rather than upon a current judgment of what one is to do, reflecting perhaps an assessment of one's "duties" and interests. Or, taking another example, one may have been habituated to think that divorce is to be avoided in all cases, so that the aversion to divorce persists even though one sees no justification for maintaining one's marriage. In both of these cases, the attitude has its basis solely in acculturation and exists independently of the agent's judgment. For this reason, acculturated desires are irrational (better: nonrational) in the same sense as appetitive and passionate desires. In fact, despite the inhibitions acquired in the course of a puritan up-bringing, a person may deem the pursuit of sexual pleasure to be worth while, his judgment siding with the id rather than the super-ego. Acculturated attitudes may seem more akin to evaluation than to appetite in that they are often expressed in evaluative language ("divorce is wicked") and result in feelings of guilt when one's actions are not in conformity with them. But, since conflict is possible here, to want something as a result of acculturation is not thereby to value it, in the sense of 'to value' that we want to capture.

It is not easy to give a nontrivial account of the sense of 'to value' in question. In part, to value something is, in the appropriate circumstances, to want it, and to attribute a want for something to someone is to say that he is disposed to try to get it. So it will not be easy to draw this distinction in behavioral terms. Apparently the difference will have to do with the agent's attitude toward the various things he is disposed to try to get. We might say that an agent's values consist in those principles and ends which he—in a cool and non-self-deceptive moment—articulates as definitive of the good, fulfilling, and defensible life. That most people have articulate "conceptions of the good," coherent life-plans, *systems* of ends, and so on, is of course something of a fiction. Yet we all have more or less long-term aims and normative principles that we are willing to defend. It is such things as these that are to be identified with our values.

The **valuational system** of an agent is that set of considerations which, when combined with his factual beliefs (and probability estimates), yields judgments of the form: the thing for me to do in these circumstances, all things considered, is *a*. To ascribe free agency to a being presupposes it to be a being that makes judgments of this sort. To be this sort of being, one must assign values to alternative states of affairs, that is, rank them in terms of worth.

The **motivational system** of an agent is that set of considerations which move him to action. We identify his motivational system by identifying what motivates him. The possibility of unfree action consists in the fact that an agent's valuational system and motivational system may not completely coincide. Those systems harmonize to the extent that what determines the agent's all-things-considered judgments also determines his actions.

Now, to be sure, since to value is also to want, one's valuational and motivational systems must to a large extent overlap. If, in appropriate circumstances, one were never inclined to action by some alleged evaluation, the claim that that was indeed one's evaluation would be disconfirmed. Thus one's valuational system must have some (considerable) grip upon one's motivational system. The problem is that there are motivational factors other than valuational ones. The free agent has the capacity to translate his values into action; his actions flow from his evaluational system.

One's evaluational system may be said to constitute one's standpoint, the point of view from which one judges the world. The important feature of one's evaluational system is that one cannot coherently dissociate oneself from it *in its entirety*. For to dissociate oneself from the ends and principles that constitute one's evaluational system is to disclaim or repudiate them, and any ends and principles so disclaimed (self-deception aside) cease to be constitutive of one's valuational system. One can dissociate oneself from one set of ends and principles only from the standpoint of another such set that one does not disclaim. In short, one cannot dissociate oneself from all normative judgments without forfeiting all standpoints and therewith one's identity as an agent.

Of course, it does not follow from the fact that one must assume some standpoint that one must have only one, nor that one's standpoint is completely determinate. There may be ultimate conflicts, irresolvable tensions, and things about which one simply does not know what to do or say. Some of these possibilities point to problems about the unity of the person. Here the extreme case is pathological. I am inclined to think that when the split is severe enough, to have more than one standpoint is to have none.

This distinction between wanting and valuing requires far fuller explication than it has received so far. Perhaps the foregoing remarks have at least shown *that* the distinction exists and is important, and have hinted at its nature. This distinction is important to the adherent of the familiar view—that talk about free action and free agency can be understood in terms of the idea of being able to get what one wants—because it gives sense to the claim that in unfree actions the agents do not get what they really or most want. This distinction gives sense to the contrast between free action and intentional action. Admittedly, further argument is required to show that such unfree agents are *unable* to get what they want; but the initial step toward this end has been taken.

At this point, it will be profitable to consider briefly a doctrine that is in many respects like that which I have been developing. The contrast will, I think, clarify the claims that have been advanced in the preceding pages.

III

In an important and provocative article,[9] Harry Frankfurt has offered a description of what he takes to be the essential feature of "the concept of a person," a feature which, he alleges, is also basic to an understanding of "freedom of the will." This feature is the possession of higher-order volitions as well as **first-order desires**. Frankfurt construes the notion of a person's will as "the notion of an *effective* desire—one that moves (or will or would move) a person all the way to action" (8). Someone has a **second-order volition**, then, when he wants "a certain desire to be his will." (Frankfurt also considers the case of a **second-order desire** that is not a second-order volition, where one's desire is simply to have a certain desire and not to act upon it. For example, a man may be curious to know what it is like to be addicted to drugs; he thus desires to desire heroin, but he may not desire his desire for heroin to be effective, to be his will. In fact, Frankfurt's actual example is somewhat more special, for here the man's desire is not simply to have a desire for heroin: he wants to have a desire for heroin which has a certain source, i.e., is addictive. He wants to know what it is like to *crave* heroin.) Someone is a *wanton* if he has no second-order volitions. Finally, "it is only because a person has volitions of the second

order that he is capable both of enjoying and of lacking freedom of the will" (14).

Frankfurt's thesis resembles the platonic view we have been unfolding insofar as it focuses upon "the structure of a person's will" (6). I want to make a simple point about Frankfurt's paper: namely that the "structural" feature to which Frankfurt appeals is not the fundamental feature for either free agency or personhood; it is simply insufficient to the task he wants it to perform.

One job that Frankfurt wishes to do with the distinction between lower and higher orders of desire is to give an account of the sense in which some wants may be said to be more truly the agent's own than others (though in an obvious sense all are wants of the agent) the sense in which the agent "identifies" with one desire rather than another and the sense in which an agent may be unfree with respect to his own "will." This enterprise is similar to our own. But we can see that the notion of "higher-order volition" is not really the fundamental notion for these purposes, by raising the question: Can't one be a wanton, so to speak, with respect to one's second-order desires and volitions?

In a case of conflict, Frankfurt would have us believe that what it is to identify with some desire rather than another is to have a volition concerning the former which is of higher order than any concerning the latter. That the first desire is given a special status over the second is due to its having an n-order volition concerning it, whereas the second desire has at most an $(n - 1)$-order volition concerning it. But why does one necessarily care about one's higher-order volitions? Since second-order volitions are themselves simply desires, to add them to the context of conflict is just to increase the number of contenders; it is not to give a special place to any of those in contention. The agent may not care which of the second-order desires win out. The same possibility arises at each higher order.

Quite aware of this difficulty, Frankfurt writes:

There is no theoretical limit to the length of the series of desires of higher and higher orders; nothing except common sense and, perhaps, a saving fatigue prevents an individual from obsessively refusing to identify himself with any of his desires until he forms a desire of the next higher order (16).

But he insists that

It is possible . . . to terminate such a series of acts [i.e., the formation of ever higher-order volitions] without cutting it off arbitrarily. When a person identifies himself *decisively* with one of his first-order desires, this commitment "resounds" throughout the potentially endless array of higher orders . . . The fact that his second-order volition to be moved by this desire is a decisive one means that there is no room for questions concerning the pertinence of volitions of higher orders . . . The decisiveness of the commitment he has made means that he has decided that no further question about his second-order volition, at any higher order, remains to be asked (16).

But either this reply is lame or it reveals that the notion of a higher-order volition is not the fundamental one. We wanted to know what prevents wantonness with regard to one's higher-order volitions. What gives these volitions any special relation to "oneself"? It is unhelpful to answer that one makes a "decisive commitment," where this just means that an interminable ascent to higher orders is not going to be permitted. This *is* arbitrary.

What this difficulty shows is that the notion of orders of desires or volitions does not do the work that Frankfurt wants it to do. It does not tell us why or how a particular want can have, among all of a person's "desires," the special property of being peculiarly his "own." There may be something to the notions of acts of identification and of decisive commitment, but these are in any case different notions from that of a second- (or *n*-) order desire. And if these are the crucial notions, it is unclear why these acts of identification cannot be themselves of the first order—that is, identification with or commitment to courses of action (rather than with or to desires)—in which case, no ascent is necessary, and the notion of higher-order volitions becomes superfluous or at least secondary.

In fact, I think that such acts of "identification and commitment" (if one goes for this way of speaking) are generally to courses of action, that is, are first-order. Frankfurt's picture of practical judgment seems to be that of an agent with a given set of (first-order) desires concerning which he then forms second-order volitions. But this picture seems to be distorted. As I

see it, agents frequently formulate values concerning alternatives they had not hitherto desired. Initially, they do not (or need not usually) ask themselves which of their desires they want to be effective in action; they ask themselves which course of action is most worth pursuing. The initial practical question is about courses of action and not about themselves.

Indeed, practical judgments are connected with "second-order volitions." For the same considerations that constitute one's on-balance reasons for doing some action, *a*, are reasons for wanting the "desire" to do *a* to be effective in action, and for wanting contrary desires to be ineffective. But in general, evaluations are prior and of the first order. The first-order desires that result from practical judgments generate second-order volitions because they have this special status; they do not have the special status that Frankfurt wants them to have because there is a higher-order desire concerning them.

Therefore, Frankfurt's position resembles the platonic conception in its focus upon the structure of the "soul."[10] But the two views draw their divisions differently; whereas Frankfurt divides the soul into higher and lower orders of desire, the distinction for Plato—and for my thesis—is among independent sources of motivation.[11]

IV

In conclusion, it can now be seen that one worry that blocks the acceptance of the traditional view of freedom—and in turn, of compatibilism—is unfounded. To return to Berlin's question (450, above), it is false that determinism entails that all our actions and choices have the same status as those of "compulsive choosers" such as "kleptomaniacs, dipsomaniacs, and the like." What is distinctive about such compulsive behavior, I would argue, is that the desires and emotions in question are more or less radically independent of the evaluational systems of these agents. The compulsive character of a kleptomaniac's thievery has nothing at all to do with determinism. (His desires to steal may arise quite randomly.) Rather, it is because his desires express themselves independently of his evaluational judgments that we tend to think of his actions as unfree.

The truth, of course, is that God (traditionally conceived) is the only free agent, *sans phrase*. In the case of God, who is omnipotent and omniscient, there can be no disparity between valuational and motivational systems. The dependence of motivation upon evaluation is total, for there is but a single source of motivation: his presumably benign judgment.[12] In the case of the Brutes, as well, motivation has a single source: appetite and (perhaps) passion. The Brutes (or so we normally think) have no evaluational system. But human beings are only more or less free agents, typically less. They are free agents only in some respects. With regard to the appetites and passions, it is plain that in some situations the motivational systems of human beings exhibit an independence from their values which is inconsistent with free agency; that is to say, people are sometimes moved by their appetites and passions in conflict with their practical judgments.[13]

As Nietzsche said (probably with a rather different point in mind): "Man's belly is the reason why man does not easily take himself for a god."[14]

NOTES

1. *Four Essays on Liberty* (New York: Oxford, 1969), pp. xx–xxi.

2. I am going to use 'want' and 'desire' in the very inclusive sense now familiar in philosophy, whereby virtually any motivational factor that may figure in the explanation of intentional action is a want; 'desire' will be used mainly in connection with the appetites and passions.

3. To quote just one of many suggestive passages: "We must . . . observe that within each one of us there are two sorts of ruling or guiding principle that we follow. One is an innate desire for pleasure, the other an acquired judgment that aims at what is best. Sometimes these internal guides are in accord, sometimes at variance; now one gains the mastery, now the other. And when judgment guides us rationally toward what is best, and has the mastery, that mastery is called temperance, but when desire drags us irrationally toward pleasure, and has come to rule within us, the name given to that rule is wantonness" (*Phaedrus*, 237e–238e; Hackforth trans.).

For a fascinating discussion of Plato's parts-of-the-soul doctrine, see Terry Penner's "Thought

and Desire in Plato," in Gregory Vlastos, ed., *Plato: A Collection of Critical Essays*, vol. II (New York: Anchor, 1971). As I see it (and here I have been influenced by Penner's article), the distinction I have attributed to Plato was meant by him to be a solution to the socratic problem of *akrasia*.

I would argue that this distinction, though necessary, is insufficient for the task, because it does not mark the difference between ("mere") incontinence or weakness of will and psychological compulsion. This difference requires a careful examination of various things that might be meant in speaking of the strength of a desire.

4. Here I shall not press the rational/nonrational contrast any further than this, though Plato would have wished to press it further. However, one important and anti-Humean implication of the minimal distinction is this: it is not the case that, if a person desires to do X, he therefore has (or even regards himself as having) a reason to do X.

5. For example, I take my remarks to be incompatible with the characterization of value R. B. Perry gives in *General Theory of Value* (Cambridge, Mass.: Harvard, 1950). In ch. V, Perry writes: "This, then, we take to be the original source and constant feature of all value. That which is an object of interest is *eo ipso* invested with value." And 'interest' is characterized in the following way: ". . . liking and disliking, desire and aversion, will and refusal, seeking and avoiding. It is to this all-pervasive characteristic of the motor-affective life, this *state, act, attitude or disposition of favor* or disfavor, to which we propose to give the name of 'interest'."

6. Notice that most emotions differ from passions like lust in that they involve beliefs and some sort of valuation (cf. resentment). This may be the basis for Plato's positing a third part of the soul which is in a way partly rational—viz. *Thumos*.

7. To be sure, one may attempt to cultivate or eliminate certain appetites and passions, so that the desires that result may be in this way dependent upon one's evaluations. Even so, the resulting desires will be such that they can persist independently of one's values. It is rather like jumping from an airplane.

8. It is reported that H. G. Wells regarded the most important themes of his life to have been (1) the attainment of a World Society, and (2) sex.

9. "Freedom of the Will and the Concept of a Person," *Journal of Philosophy*, 68/1 (Jan. 14, 1971): 5–20; repr. in Frankfurt, 1988. All references are to the reprinted edition.

10. Frankfurt's idea of a wanton, suitably construed, can be put to further illuminating uses in moral psychology. It proves valuable, I think, in discussing the problematic phenomenon of psychopathy or sociopathy.

11. Some very recent articles employ distinctions, for similar purposes, very like Frankfurt's and my own. See, for example, Richard C. Jeffrey, "Preferences among Preferences," *Journal of Philosophy*, 71/13 (July 18, 1974): 377–91. In "Freedom and Desire," *Philosophical Review*, 83/1 (January 1974): 32–54, Wright Neely appeals to higher-order desires.

12. God could not act *akratically*. In this respect, Socrates thought people were distinguishable from such a being only by ignorance and limited power.

13. This possibility is a definitive feature of appetitive and passionate wants.

14. *Beyond Good and Evil*, section 141.

KEY TERMS

Free will
Compatibilism
Determinism
Values
Motivational system
Valuational system
First-order desires
Second-order volitions
Second-order desires
Wanton

STUDY QUESTIONS

1. How does Watson define "freedom"? What is the problem of free action?

2. What problem do some philosophers raise for compatibilists? How does Watson hope to address this problem?

3. What is the difference between the Humean and the Platonic conceptions of practical reasoning?

4. In what ways can evaluation and desire diverge? In what ways do they influence each other?

5. What does Watson mean by the valuational system and the motivational system? How does this distinction help him address the worry philosophers have raised about compatibilism?

6. How does Frankfurt's conception of free agency work? What is Watson's worry about it?

Sanity and the Metaphysics of Responsibility

SUSAN WOLF

Susan Wolf (1952–) is the Edna J. Koury Professor of Philosophy at the University of North Carolina, Chapel Hill. She is best known for her important contributions in moral philosophy and the philosophy of action. Her books include *Freedom Within Reason* and *Meaning in Life and Why it Matters*.

. .

PHILOSOPHERS who study the problems of **free will** and responsibility have an easier time than most in meeting challenges about the relevance of their work to ordinary, practical concerns. Indeed, philosophers who study these problems are rarely faced with such challenges at all, since questions concerning the conditions of responsibility come up so obviously and so frequently in everyday life. Under scrutiny, however, one might question whether the connections between philosophical and nonphilosophical concerns in this area are real.

From *Responsibility, Character, and the Emotions: New Essays in Moral Psychology*, edited by Ferdinand Schoeman. © 1987 by Cambridge University Press. Reprinted by permission.

In everyday contexts, when lawyers, judges, parents, and others are concerned with issues of responsibility, they know, or think they know, what in general the conditions of responsibility are. Their questions are questions of application: Does this or that particular person meet this or that particular condition? Is this person mature enough, or informed enough, or sane enough to be responsible? Was he or she acting under posthypnotic suggestion or under the influence of a mind-impairing drug? It is assumed, in these contexts, that normal, fully developed adult human beings are responsible beings. The questions have to do with whether a given individual falls within the normal range.

By contrast, philosophers tend to be uncertain about the general conditions of responsibility, and they care less about dividing the responsible from the nonresponsible agents than about determining whether, and if so why, any of us are ever responsible for anything at all.

In the classroom, we might argue that the philosophical concerns grow out of the nonphilosophical ones, that they take off where the nonphilosophical questions stop. In this way, we might convince our students that even if they are not plagued by the philosophical worries, they ought to be. If they worry about whether a person is mature enough, informed enough, and sane enough to be responsible, then they should worry about whether that person is **metaphysically** free enough, too.

The argument I make here, however, goes in the opposite direction. My aim is not to convince people who are interested in the apparently nonphilosophical conditions of responsibility that they should go on to worry about the philosophical conditions as well, but rather to urge those who already worry about the philosophical problems not to leave the more mundane, prephilosophical problems behind. In particular, I suggest that the mundane recognition that *sanity* is a condition of responsibility has more to do with the murky and apparently metaphysical problems which surround the issue of responsibility than at first meets the eye. Once the significance of the condition of sanity is fully appreciated, at least some of the apparently insuperable metaphysical aspects of the problem of responsibility will dissolve.

My strategy is to examine a recent trend in philosophical discussions of responsibility, a trend that tries, but I think ultimately fails, to give an acceptable analysis of the conditions of responsibility. It fails due to what at first appear to be deep and irresolvable metaphysical problems. It is here that I suggest that the condition of sanity comes to the rescue. What at first appears to be an impossible requirement for responsibility—the requirement that the responsible agent have created her- or himself—turns out to be the vastly more mundane and noncontroversial requirement that the responsible agent must, in a fairly standard sense, be sane.

Frankfurt, Watson, and Taylor

The trend I have in mind is exemplified by the writings of Harry Frankfurt, Gary Watson, and Charles Taylor. I will briefly discuss each of their separate proposals, and then offer a composite view that, while lacking the subtlety of any of the separate accounts, will highlight some important insights and some important blind spots they share.

In his seminal article "Freedom of the Will and the Concept of a Person,"[1] Harry Frankfurt notes a distinction between freedom of action and freedom of the will. A person has freedom of action, he points out, if she (or he) has the freedom to do whatever she wills to do—the freedom to walk or sit, to vote liberal or conservative, to publish a book or open a store, in accordance with her strongest desires. Even a person who has freedom of action may fail to be responsible for her actions, however, if the wants or desires she has the freedom to convert into action are themselves not subject to her control. Thus, the person who acts under posthypnotic suggestion, the victim of brainwashing, and the kleptomaniac might all possess freedom of action. In the standard contexts in which these examples are raised, it is assumed that none of the individuals is locked up or bound. Rather, these individuals are understood to act on what, at one level at least, must be called *their own desires*. Their exemption from responsibility stems from the fact that their own desires (or at least the ones governing their actions) are not up to them. These cases may be described in Frankfurt's terms as cases of people who possess freedom of action, but who fail to be responsible agents because they lack freedom of the will.

Philosophical problems about the conditions of responsibility naturally focus on an analysis of this latter kind of freedom: What *is* freedom of the will, and under what conditions can we reasonably be thought to possess it? Frankfurt's proposal is to understand freedom of the will by analogy to freedom of action. As freedom of action is the freedom to do whatever one wills to do, freedom of the will is the freedom to will whatever one wants to will. To make this point clearer, Frankfurt introduces a distinction between first-order and second-order desires. First-order desires are desires to do or to have various things; second-order desires are desires about what desires to have or what desires to make effective in action. In order for an agent to have both freedom of action and freedom of the will, that agent must be capable of governing his or her actions by first-order desires *and* capable of governing his or her first-order desires by second-order desires.

Gary Watson's view of free agency[2]—free and responsible agency, that is—is similar to Frankfurt's in holding that an agent is responsible for an action only if the desires expressed by that action are of a particular kind. While Frankfurt identifies the right kind of desires as desires that are supported by second-order desires, however, Watson draws a distinction between "mere" desires, so to speak, and desires that are *values*. According to Watson, the difference between free action and unfree action cannot be analyzed by reference to the logical form of the desires from which these various actions arise, but rather must relate to a difference in the quality of their source. Whereas some of my desires are just appetites or conditioned responses I find myself "stuck with," others are expressions of judgments on my part that the objects I desire are good. Insofar as my actions can be governed by the latter type of desire—governed, that is, by my values or valuational system—they are actions that I perform freely and for which I am responsible.

Frankfurt's and Watson's accounts may be understood as alternate developments of the intuition that in order to be responsible for one's actions, one must be responsible for the self that performs these actions.

Charles Taylor, in an article entitled "Responsibility for Self,"[3] is concerned with the same intuition. Although Taylor does not describe his view in terms of different levels or types of desire, his view is related, for he claims that our freedom and responsibility depends on our ability to reflect on, criticize, and revise our selves. Like Frankfurt and Watson, Taylor seems to believe that if the characters from which our actions flowed were simply and permanently *given* to us, implanted by heredity, environment, or God, then we would be mere vehicles through which the causal forces of the world traveled, no more responsible than dumb animals or young children or machines. But like the others, he points out that, for most of us, our characters and desires are not so brutely implanted—or, at any rate, if they are, they are subject to revision by our own reflecting, valuing, or second-order desiring selves. We human beings—and as far as we know, only we human beings—have the ability to step back from ourselves and decide whether we are the selves we want to be. Because of this, these philosophers think, we are responsible for our selves and for the actions that we produce.

Although there are subtle and interesting differences among the accounts of Frankfurt, Watson, and Taylor, my concern is with features of their views that are common to them all. All share the idea that responsible agency involves something more than intentional agency. All agree that if we are responsible agents, it is not just because our actions are within the control of our wills, but because, in addition, our wills are not just psychological states *in* us, but expressions of characters that come *from* us, or that at any rate are acknowledged and affirmed *by* us. For Frankfurt, this means that our wills must be ruled by our second-order desires; for Watson, that our wills must be governable by our system of values; for Taylor, that our wills must issue from selves that are subject to self-assessment and redefinition in terms of a vocabulary of worth. In one way or another, all these philosophers seem to be saying that the key to responsibility lies in the fact that responsible agents are those for whom it is not just the case that their actions are within the control of their wills, but also the case that their wills are within the control of their *selves* in some deeper sense. Because, at one level, the differences among Frankfurt, Watson, and Taylor may be understood as differences in the analysis or interpretation of what it is for an action to be under the control of this deeper self, we may speak of their separate positions as variations of one basic view about responsibility: the **deep-self view**.

The Deep-Self View

Much more must be said about the notion of a deep self before a fully satisfactory account of this view can be given. Providing a careful, detailed analysis of that notion poses an interesting, important, and difficult task in its own right. The degree of understanding achieved by abstraction from the views of Frankfurt, Watson, and Taylor, however, should be sufficient to allow us to recognize some important virtues as well as some important drawbacks of the deep-self view.

One virtue is that this view explains a good portion of our pretheoretical intuitions about responsibility. It explains why kleptomaniacs, victims of brainwashing, and people acting under posthypnotic suggestion may not be responsible for their actions, although most of us typically are. In the cases of people in these special categories, the connection between the agents' deep selves and their wills is dramatically severed—their wills are governed not by their deep selves, but by forces external to and independent from them. A different intuition is that we adult human beings can be responsible for our actions in a way that dumb animals, infants, and machines cannot. Here the explanation is not in terms of a split between these beings' deep selves and their wills; rather, the point is that these beings *lack* deep selves altogether. Kleptomaniacs and victims of hypnosis exemplify individuals whose selves are *alienated* from their actions; lower animals and machines, on the other hand, do not have the sorts of selves from which actions *can* be alienated, and so they do not have the sort of selves from which, in the happier cases, actions can responsibly flow.

At a more theoretical level, the deep-self view has another virtue: It responds to at least one way in which the fear of **determinism** presents itself.

A naive reaction to the idea that everything we do is completely determined by a causal chain that extends backward beyond the times of our births involves thinking that in that case we would have no control over our behavior whatsoever. If everything is determined, it is thought, then what happens happens, whether we want it to or not. A common, and proper, response to this concern points out that determinism does not deny the causal efficacy an agent's desires might have on his or her behavior. On the contrary, determinism in its more plausible forms tends to affirm this connection, merely adding that as one's behavior is determined by one's desires, so one's desires are determined by something else.[4]

Those who were initially worried that determinism implied fatalism, however, are apt to find their fears merely transformed rather than erased. If our desires are governed by something else, they might say, they are not *really* ours after all—or, at any rate, they are ours in only a superficial sense.

The deep-self view offers an answer to this transformed fear of determinism, for it allows us to distinguish cases in which desires are determined by forces foreign to oneself from desires which are determined *by* one's self—by one's "real," or second-order desiring, or valuing, or deep self, that is. Admittedly, there are cases, like that of the kleptomaniac or the victim of hypnosis, in which the agent acts on desires that "belong to" him or her in only a superficial sense. But the proponent of the deep-self view will point out that even if determinism is true, ordinary adult human action can be distinguished from this. Determinism implies that the desires which govern our actions are in turn governed by something else, but that something else will, in the fortunate cases, be our own deeper selves.

This account of responsibility thus offers a response to our fear of determinism; but it is a response with which many will remain unsatisfied. Even if my actions are governed by my desires and my desires are governed by my own deeper self, there remains the question: Who, or what, is responsible for this deeper self? The response above seems only to have pushed the problem further back.

Admittedly, some versions of the deep-self view, including Frankfurt's and Taylor's, seem to anticipate this question by providing a place for the ideal that an agent's deep self may be governed by a still deeper self. Thus, for Frankfurt, second-order desires may themselves be governed by third-order desires, third-order desires by fourth-order desires, and so on. Also, Taylor points out that, as we can reflect on and evaluate our prereflective selves, so we can reflect on and evaluate the selves who are doing the first reflecting and evaluating, and so on. However, this capacity to recursively create endless levels of depth ultimately misses the criticism's point.

First of all, even if there is no *logical* limit to the number of levels of reflection or depth a person may have, there is certainly a psychological limit—it is virtually impossible imaginatively to conceive a fourth-, much less an eighth-order, desire. More important, no matter how many levels of self we posit, there will still, in any individual case, be a last level—a deepest self about whom the question "What governs it?" will arise, as problematic as ever. If determinism is true, it implies that even if my actions are governed by my desires, and my desires are governed by my deepest self, my deepest self will still be governed by something that must, logically, be external to myself altogether. Though I can step back from the values my parents and teachers have given me and ask whether these are the values I really want, the "I" that steps back will itself be a product of the parents and teachers I am questioning.

The problem seems even worse when one sees that one fares no better if determinism is false. For if my deepest self is not determined by something external to myself, it will still not be determined by *me.* Whether I am a product of carefully controlled forces or a result of random mutations, whether there is a complete explanation of my origin or no explanation at all, *I* am not, in any case, responsible for my existence; I am not in control of my deepest self.

Thus, though the claim that an agent is responsible for only those actions that are within the control of his or her deep self correctly identifies a necessary condition for responsibility—a condition that separates the hypnotized and the brainwashed, the immature and the lower animals from ourselves, for example—it fails to provide a sufficient condition of responsibility that puts all fears of determinism to rest. For one of the fears invoked by the thought of determinism seems to be connected to its implication that we are but intermediate links in a causal chain, rather than ultimate, self-initiating sources of movement and change. From the point of view of one who has this fear, the deep-self view seems merely to add loops to the chain, complicating the picture but not really improving it. From the point of view of one who has this fear, responsibility seems to require being a prime mover unmoved, whose deepest self is itself neither random *nor* externally determined, but is rather determined *by* itself—who is, in other words, self-created.

At this point, however, proponents of the deep-self view may wonder whether this fear is legitimate. For although people evidently can be brought to the point where they feel that responsible agency requires them to be ultimate sources of power, to the point where it seems that nothing short of self-creation will do, a return to the internal standpoint of the agent whose responsibility is in question makes it hard to see what good this metaphysical status is supposed to provide or what evil its absence is supposed to impose.

From the external standpoint, which discussions of determinism and indeterminism encourage us to take up, it may appear that a special metaphysical status is required to distinguish us significantly from other members of the natural world. But proponents of the deep-self view will suggest this is an illusion that a return to the internal standpoint should dispel. The possession of a deep self that is effective in governing one's actions is a sufficient distinction, they will say. For while other members of the natural world are not in control of the selves that they are, we, possessors of effective deep selves, are in control. We can reflect on what sorts of beings we are, and on what sorts of marks we make on the world. We can change what we don't like about ourselves, and keep what we do. Admittedly, we do not create ourselves from nothing. But as long as we can revise ourselves, they will suggest, it is hard to find reason to complain. Harry Frankfurt writes that a person who is free to do what he wants to do and also free to want what he wants to want has "all the freedom it is possible to desire or to conceive."[5] This suggests a rhetorical question: If you are free to control your actions by your desires, and free to control your desires by your deeper desires, and free to control those desires by still deeper desires, what further kind of freedom can you want?

The Condition of Sanity

Unfortunately, there is a further kind of freedom we can want, which it is reasonable to think necessary for responsible agency. The deep-self view fails to be convincing when it is offered as a complete account of the conditions of responsibility. To see why, it will be helpful to consider another example of an agent whose responsibility is in question.

JoJo is the favorite son of Jo the First, an evil and sadistic dictator of a small, undeveloped country. Because of his father's special feelings for the boy, JoJo is given a special education and is allowed to accompany his father and observe his daily routine. In light of this treatment, it is not surprising that little JoJo takes his father as a role model and develops values very much like Dad's. As an adult, he does many of the same sorts of things his father did, including sending people to prison or to death or to torture chambers on the basis of whim. He is not *coerced* to do these things, he acts according to his own desires. Moreover, these are desires he wholly *wants* to have. When he steps back and asks, "Do I really want to be this sort of person?" his answer is resoundingly "Yes," for this way of life expresses a crazy sort of power that forms part of his deepest ideal.

In light of JoJo's heritage and upbringing—both of which he was powerless to control—it is dubious at best that he should be regarded as responsible for what he does. It is unclear whether anyone with a childhood such as his could have developed into anything but the twisted and perverse sort of person that he has become. However, note that JoJo is someone whose actions are controlled by his desires and whose desires are the desires he wants to have: That is, his actions are governed by desires that are governed by and expressive of his deepest self.

The Frankfurt–Watson–Taylor strategy that allowed us to differentiate our normal selves from the victims of hypnosis and brainwashing will not allow us to differentiate ourselves from the son of Jo the First. In the case of these earlier victims, we were able to say that although the actions of these individuals were, at one level, in control of the individuals themselves, these individuals themselves, qua agents, were not the selves they more deeply wanted to be. In this respect, these people were unlike our happily

more integrated selves. However, we cannot say of JoJo that his self, qua agent, is not the self he wants it to be. It *is* the self he wants it to be. From the inside, he feels as integrated, free, and responsible as we do.

Our judgment that JoJo is not a responsible agent is one that we can make only from the outside—from reflecting on the fact, it seems, that his deepest self is not up to him. Looked at from the outside, however, our situation seems no different from his—for in the last analysis, it is not up to any of us to have the deepest selves we do. Once more, the problem seems metaphysical—and not just metaphysical, but insuperable. For, as I mentioned before, the problem is independent of the truth of determinism. Whether we are determined or undetermined, we cannot have created our deepest selves. Literal self-creation is not just empirically, but logically impossible.

If JoJo is not responsible because his deepest self is not up to him, then we are not responsible either. Indeed, in that case responsibility would be impossible for anyone to achieve. But I believe the appearance that literal self-creation is required for freedom and responsibility is itself mistaken.

The deep-self view was right in pointing out that freedom and responsibility requires us to have certain distinctive types of control over our behavior and our selves. Specifically, our actions need to be under the control of our selves, and our (superficial) selves need to be under the control of our deep selves. Having seen that these types of control are not enough to guarantee us the status of responsible agents, we are tempted to go on to suppose that we must have yet another kind of control to assure us that even our deepest selves are somehow up to us. But not all the things necessary for freedom and responsibility must be types of power and control. We may need simply to *be* a certain way, even though it is not within our power to determine whether we are that way or not.

Indeed, it becomes obvious that at least one condition of responsibility is of this form as soon as we remember what, in everyday contexts, we have known all along—namely, that in order to be responsible, an agent must be *sane*. It is not ordinarily in our power to determine whether we are or are not sane. Most of us, it would seem, are lucky, but some of us are not. Moreover, being sane does not necessarily mean that one has any type of power or control an insane person lacks. Some insane people, like JoJo and some actual political leaders who resemble him, may have complete control of their actions, and even complete control of their acting selves. The desire to be sane is thus not a desire for another form of control; it is rather a desire that one's self be connected to the world in a certain way—we could even say it is a desire that one's self be *controlled by* the world in certain ways and not in others.

This becomes clear if we attend to the criteria for **sanity** that have historically been dominant in legal questions about responsibility. According to the M'Naughten Rule, a person is sane if (1) he knows what he is doing and (2) he knows that what he is doing is, as the case may be, right or wrong. Insofar as one's desire to be sane involves a desire to know what one is doing—or more generally, a desire to live in the real world—it is a desire to be controlled (to have, in this case, one's *beliefs* controlled) by perceptions and sound reasoning that produce an accurate conception of the world, rather than by blind or distorted forms of response. The same goes for the second constituent of sanity—only, in this case, one's hope is that one's *values* be controlled by processes that afford an accurate conception of the world.[6] Putting these two conditions together, we may understand sanity, then, as the minimally sufficient ability cognitively and normatively to recognize and appreciate the world for what it is.

There are problems with this definition of sanity, at least some of which will become obvious in what follows, that make it ultimately unacceptable either as a gloss on or an improvement of the meaning of the term in many of the contexts in which it is used. The definition offered does seem to bring out the interest sanity has for us in connection with issues of responsibility, however, and some pedagogical as well as stylistic purposes will be served if we use sanity hereafter in this admittedly specialized sense.

The Sane Deep-Self View

So far I have argued that the conditions of responsible agency offered by the deep-self view are necessary but not sufficient. Moreover, the gap left open by the deep-self view seems to be one that can be filled only by a metaphysical, and, as it happens, metaphysically impossible addition. I now wish to argue, however, that the condition of sanity, as characterized above, is sufficient to fill the gap. In other words, the deep-self view, supplemented by the condition of sanity, provides a satisfying conception of responsibility. The conception of responsibility I am proposing, then, agrees with the deep-self view in requiring that a responsible agent be able to govern her (or his) actions by her desires and to govern her desires by her deep self. In addition, my conception insists that the agent's deep self be sane, and claims that this is *all* that is needed for responsible agency. By contrast to the plain deep-self view, let us call this new proposal the *sane deep-self view.*

It is worth noting, to begin with, that this new proposal deals with the case of JoJo and related cases of deprived childhood victims in ways that better match our pretheoretical intuitions. Unlike the plain deep-self view, the sane deep-self view offers a way of explaining why JoJo is not responsible for his actions without throwing our own responsibility into doubt. For, although like us, JoJo's actions flow from desires that flow from his deep self, unlike us, JoJo's deep self is itself insane. Sanity, remember, involves the ability to know the difference between right and wrong, and a person who, even on reflection, cannot see that having someone tortured because he failed to salute you is wrong plainly lacks the requisite ability.

Less obviously, but quite analogously, this new proposal explains why we give less than full responsibility to persons who, though acting badly, act in ways that are strongly encouraged by their societies—the slaveowners of the 1850s, the Nazis of the 1930s, and many male chauvinists of our fathers' generation, for example. These are people, we imagine, who falsely believe that the ways in which they are acting are morally acceptable, and so, we may assume, their behavior is expressive of or at least in accordance with these agents' deep selves. But their false beliefs in the moral permissibility of their actions and the false values from which these beliefs derived may have been inevitable, given the social circumstances in which they developed. If we think that the agents could not help but be mistaken about their values, we do not blame them for the actions those values inspired.[7]

It would unduly distort ordinary linguistic practice to call the slaveowner, the Nazi, or the male chauvinist even partially or locally insane. Nonetheless, the reason for withholding blame from them is at bottom the same as the reason for withholding it from JoJo. Like JoJo, they are, at the deepest level, unable cognitively and normatively to recognize and appreciate the world for what it is. In our sense of the term, their deepest selves are not fully *sane*.

The sane deep-self view thus offers an account of why victims of deprived childhoods as well as victims of misguided societies may not be responsible for their actions, without implying that we are not responsible for ours. The actions of these others are governed by mistaken conceptions of value that the agents in question cannot help but have. Since, as far as we know, our values are not, like theirs, unavoidably mistaken, the fact that these others are not responsible for their actions need not force us to conclude that we are not responsible for ours.

But it may not yet be clear why sanity, in this special sense, should make such a difference—why, in particular, the question of whether someone's values are unavoidably *mistaken* should have any bearing on their status as responsible agents. The fact that the sane deep-self view implies judgments that match our intuitions about the difference in status between characters like JoJo and ourselves provides little support for it if it cannot also defend these intuitions. So we must consider an objection that comes from the point of view we considered earlier which rejects the intuition that a relevant difference can be found.

Earlier, it seemed that the reason JoJo was not responsible for his actions was that although his actions were governed by his deep self, his deep self was not up to him. But this had nothing to do with his deep self's being mistaken or not mistaken, evil or good, insane or sane. If JoJo's values are unavoidably mistaken, our values, even if not mistaken, appear to be just as unavoidable. When it comes to freedom and responsibility, isn't it the unavoidability, rather than the mistakenness, that matters?

Before answering this question, it is useful to point out a way in which it is ambiguous: The concepts of avoidability and mistakenness are not unequivocally distinct. One may, to be sure, construe the notion of avoidability in a purely metaphysical way.

Whether an event or state of affairs is unavoidable under this construal depends, as it were, on the tightness of the causal connections that bear on the event's or state of affairs' coming about. In this sense, our deep selves do seem as unavoidable for us as JoJo's and the others' are for them. For presumably we are just as influenced by our parents, our cultures, and our schooling as they are influenced by theirs. In another sense, however, our characters are not similarly unavoidable.

In particular, in the cases of JoJo and the others, there are certain features of their characters that they cannot avoid *even though these features are seriously mistaken, misguided, or bad.* This is so because, in our special sense of the term, these characters are less than fully sane. Since these characters lack the ability to know right from wrong, they are unable to revise their characters on the basis of right and wrong, and so their deep selves lack the resources and the reasons that might have served as a basis for self-correction. Since the deep selves *we* unavoidably have, however, are sane deep selves—deep selves, that is, that unavoidably *contain* the ability to know right from wrong—we unavoidably do have the resources and reasons on which to base self-correction. What this means is that though in one sense we are no more in control of our deepest selves than JoJo et al., it does not follow in our case, as it does in theirs, that we would be the way we are, even if it is a bad or wrong way to be. However, if this does not follow, it seems to me, our absence of control at the deepest level should not upset us.

Consider what the absence of control at the deepest level amounts to for us: Whereas JoJo is unable to control the fact that, at the deepest level, he is not fully sane, we are not responsible for the fact that, at the deepest level, we are. It is not up to us to *have* minimally sufficient abilities cognitively and normatively to recognize and appreciate the world for what it is. Also, presumably, it is not up to us to have lots of other properties, at least to begin with—a fondness for purple, perhaps, or an antipathy for beets. As the proponents of the plain deep-self view have been at pains to point out, however, we do, if we are lucky, have the ability to revise our selves in terms of the values that are held by or constitutive of our deep selves. If we are lucky enough both to have this ability and to have our deep selves be sane, it follows that although there is much in our characters that we did not choose to have, there is nothing irrational or objectionable in our characters that we are compelled to keep.

Being sane, we are able to understand and evaluate our characters in a reasonable way, to notice what there is reason to hold on to, what there is reason to eliminate, and what, from a rational and reasonable standpoint, we may retain or get rid of as we please. Being able as well to govern our superficial selves by our deep selves, then, we are able to change the things we find there is reason to change. This being so, it seems that although we may not be *metaphysically* responsible for ourselves—for, after all, we did not create ourselves from nothing—we are *morally* responsible for ourselves, for we are able to understand and appreciate right and wrong, and to change our characters and our actions accordingly.

Self-Creation, Self-Revision, and Self-Correction

At the beginning of this chapter, I claimed that recalling that sanity was a condition of responsibility would dissolve at least some of the appearance that responsibility was metaphysically impossible. To see how this is so, and to get a fuller sense of the sane deep-self view, it may be helpful to put that view into perspective by comparing it to the other views we have discussed along the way.

As Frankfurt, Watson, and Taylor showed us, in order to be free and responsible we need not only to be able to control our actions in accordance with our desires, we need to be able to control our desires in accordance with our deepest selves. We need, in other words, to be able to *revise* ourselves—to get rid of some desires and traits, and perhaps replace them with others on the basis of our deeper desires or values or reflections. However, consideration of the fact that the selves who are doing the revising might themselves be either brute products of external forces or arbitrary outputs of random generation made us wonder whether the capacity for self-revision was enough to assure us of responsibility—and the example of JoJo added force to the suspicion that it was not. Still, if the ability to revise ourselves is not

enough, the ability to create ourselves does not seem necessary either. Indeed, when you think of it, it is unclear why anyone should want self-creation. Why should anyone be disappointed at having to accept the idea that one has to get one's start somewhere? It is an idea that most of us have lived with quite contentedly all along. What we do have reason to want, then, is something more than the ability to revise ourselves, but less than the ability to create ourselves. Implicit in the sane deep-self view is the idea that what is needed is the ability to *correct* (or improve) ourselves.

Recognizing that in order to be responsible for our actions, we have to be responsible for our selves, the sane deep-self view analyzes what is necessary in order to be responsible for our selves as (1) the ability to evaluate ourselves sensibly and accurately, and (2) the ability to transform ourselves insofar as our evaluation tells us to do so. We may understand the exercise of these abilities as a process where by we *take* responsibility for the selves that we are but did not ultimately create. The condition of sanity is intrinsically connected to the first ability; the condition that we be able to control our superficial selves by our deep selves is intrinsically connected to the second.

The difference between the plain deep-self view and the sane deep-self view, then, is the difference between the requirement of the capacity for self-revision and the requirement of the capacity for self-correction. Anyone with the first capacity can *try* to take responsibility for himself or herself. However, only someone with a sane deep self—a deep self that can see and appreciate the world for what it is—can self-evaluate sensibly and accurately. Therefore, although insane selves can try to take responsibility for themselves, only sane selves will properly be accorded responsibility.

Two Objections Considered

At least two problems with the sane deep-self view are so glaring as to have certainly struck many readers. In closing, I shall briefly address them. First, some will be wondering how, in light of my specialized use of the term "sanity," I can be so sure that "we" are any saner than the nonresponsible individuals I have discussed.

What justifies my confidence that, unlike the slaveowners, Nazis, and male chauvinists, not to mention JoJo himself, we are able to understand and appreciate the world for what it is? The answer to this is that nothing justifies this except widespread intersubjective agreement and the considerable success we have in getting around in the world and satisfying our needs. These are not sufficient grounds for the smug assumption that we are in a position to see the truth about *all* aspects of ethical and social life. Indeed, it seems more reasonable to expect that time will reveal blind spots in our cognitive and normative outlook, just as it has revealed errors in the outlooks of those who have lived before. But our judgments of responsibility can only be made from here, on the basis of the understandings and values that we can develop by exercising the abilities we do possess as well and as fully as possible.

If some have been worried that my view implicitly expresses an overconfidence in the assumption that we are sane and therefore right about the world, others will be worried that my view too closely connects sanity with being right about the world, and fear that my view implies that anyone who acts wrongly or has false beliefs about the world is therefore insane and so not responsible for his or her actions. This seems to me to be a more serious worry, which I am sure I cannot answer to everyone's satisfaction.

First, it must be admitted that the sane deep-self view embraces a conception of sanity that is explicitly normative. But this seems to me a strength of that view, rather than a defect. Sanity *is* a normative concept, in its ordinary as well as in its specialized sense, and severely deviant behavior, such as that of a serial murderer or a sadistic dictator, does constitute evidence of a psychological defect in the agent. The suggestion that the most horrendous, stomach-turning crimes could be committed only by an insane person—an inverse of Catch-22, as it were—must be regarded as a serious possibility, despite the practical problems that would accompany general acceptance of that conclusion.

But, it will be objected, there is no justification, in the sane deep-self view, for regarding only horrendous and stomach-turning crimes as evidence of insanity in its specialized sense. If sanity is the ability cognitively and normatively to understand and appreciate the world for what it is, then *any* wrong action or false belief will count as evidence of the absence of that ability. This point may also be granted, but we must be careful about what conclusion to draw. To be sure, when someone acts in a way that is not in accordance with acceptable standards of rationality and reasonableness, it is always appropriate to look for an explanation of why he or she acted that way. The hypothesis that the person was unable to understand and appreciate that an action fell outside acceptable bounds will always be a possible explanation. Bad performance on a math test always suggests the possibility that the testee is stupid. Typically, however, other explanations will be possible, too—for example, that the agent was too lazy to consider whether his or her action was acceptable, or too greedy to care, or, in the case of the math testee, that he or she was too occupied with other interests to attend class or study. Other facts about the agent's history will help us decide among these hypotheses.

This brings out the need to emphasize that sanity, in the specialized sense, is defined as the *ability* cognitively and normatively to understand and appreciate the world for what it is. According to our commonsense understandings, having this ability is one thing and exercising it is another—at least some wrong-acting, responsible agents presumably fall within the gap. The notion of "ability" is notoriously problematic, however, and there is a long history of controversy about whether the truth of determinism would show our ordinary ways of thinking to be simply confused on this matter. At this point, then, metaphysical concerns may voice themselves again—but at least they will have been pushed into a narrower, and perhaps a more manageable, corner.

The sane deep-self view does not, then, solve all the philosophical problems connected to the topics of free will and responsibility. If anything, it highlights some of the practical and empirical problems, rather than solves them. It may, however, resolve some of the philosophical, and particularly, some of the metaphysical problems, and reveal how intimate are the connections between the remaining philosophical problems and the practical ones.

NOTES

1. Harry Frankfurt, "Freedom of the Will and the Concept of a Person," *Journal of Philosophy* LXVIII (1971), 5–20.

2. Gary Watson, "Free Agency," *Journal of Philosophy* LXXII (1975), 205–20.

3. Charles Taylor, "Responsibility for Self," in A. E. Rorty, ed., *The Identities of Persons* (Berkeley: University of California Press, 1976), pp. 281–99.

4. See, e.g., David Hume, *A Treatise of Human Nature* (Oxford: Oxford University Press, 1967), pp. 399–406, and R. E. Hobart, "Free Will as Involving Determination and Inconceivable Without It," *Mind* 43 (1934).

5. Frankfurt, p. 16.

6. Strictly speaking, perception and sound reasoning may not be enough to ensure the ability to achieve an accurate conception of what one is doing and especially to achieve a reasonable normative assessment of one's situation. Sensitivity and exposure to certain realms of experience may also be necessary for these goals. For the purpose of this essay, I understand "sanity" to include whatever it takes to enable one to develop an adequate conception of one's world. In other contexts, however, this would be an implausibly broad construction of the term.

7. Admittedly, it is open to question whether these individuals were in fact unable to help having mistaken values, and indeed, whether recognizing the errors of their society would even have required exceptional independence or strength of mind. This is presumably an empirical question, the answer to which is extraordinarily hard to determine. My point here is simply that *if* we believe they are unable to recognize that their values are mistaken, we do not hold them responsible for the actions that flow from these values, and *if* we believe their ability to recognize their normative errors is impaired, we hold them less than fully responsible for the relevant actions.

KEY TERMS

Free will
Metaphysics
Deep-self view
Determinism
Sanity

STUDY QUESTIONS

1. What is the difference between the non-philosophical and the philosophical concerns about free will and responsibility, according to Wolf?

2. What is the deep-self view? Who are the three philosophers who advocate this view?

3. What are two virtues of the deep-self view? What problem might one who is concerned with determinism raise for this view?

4. Who is JoJo? What problem does JoJo raise for the deep-self view, according to Wolf?

5. What does Wolf mean by "sanity"? Does this seem like a reasonable way to define sanity?

6. What two objections might one raise for Wolf's view? How does Wolf propose to handle these problems? Do you find her solutions convincing?

PART V

X

ETHICS AND SOCIETY

INTRODUCTION

Almost all of us hold a wide range of moral views. We have views about when it is wrong to lie, cheat, steal, betray a friend, have an abortion, break a law or a promise, kill an adult human being, or threaten to kill one. And we have views about why such acts are wrong when they are. We assess lives, our own and others, as going more or less well or badly. We have views about the contribution to a good life of material well-being, artistic accomplishment, athletic prowess, intellectual curiosity, friendship and love, sex, courage, and so on. We also assess social institutions from a moral perspective. Most of us think that the slavery practiced in the United States in the nineteenth century was unjust. And one has only to pick up the daily newspaper to find views expressed about the fairness or unfairness of the federal tax code.

These views are at many different levels of generality. You may think that your friend was wrong to have cheated on yesterday's exam; and you may also think that if you are faced with saving one life or many, you ought always to save the larger number of lives. Some of these views you may hold with a great deal of confidence, for example, that wanton killing of an adult human being is wrong. Other views you may hold less confidently: this may be true of your assessment of the moral permissibility of abortion. Yet, despite uncertainty, you sometimes must act one way or another. Our moral views are significant to our lives in part because they frequently guide our action.

Moral philosophy begins with reflection on such views. It aims at detecting unsuspected inconsistencies; at articulating and assessing central arguments; at determining the extent to which such views have a defensible, underlying rationale; at articulating and defending systematic approaches to moral issues; and, in general, at understanding the nature of morality.

A. UTILITARIANISM

Begin by distinguishing two general questions: What makes acts right (or wrong)? What things are good (bad)? **Consequentialist** moral theories treat the second question as basic. Such theories begin by determining what things are good and what things bad. They then see the rightness of an action as determined by the goodness or badness of relevant consequences.

The most common consequentialist theories are **utilitarian** theories. Such theories suppose that the only thing that has nonderivative value is the *welfare* or *happiness* of sentient beings. It is granted that other things—courage, knowledge, love, and money, for example—have value. But their value is derivative from their contribution to happiness. Jeremy Bentham and John Stuart Mill defend different versions of such a utilitarian perspective. Bentham identifies happiness with pleasure and the absence of pain, and he proceeds to develop a calculus to measure the relative value of different pleasures and pains. He supposes that what makes an act right (or wrong) is the extent to which it increases pleasure or decreases pain. His theory can be called **hedonistic act utilitarianism**: *hedonistic* because it sees pleasure and pain as the only things with nonderivative value; *act* utilitarianism because, in answering our question about what makes acts right, it applies the test of utility directly to actions.

On one common interpretation, Mill also accepts a version of act utilitarianism. But he differs from Bentham in his view that some pleasures are "higher" than others. Bentham saw happiness as depending only on the felt pleasures and pains of the organism. Mill's emphasis on the "quality" of pleasure seems to make happiness depend also on the satisfaction of certain ideals, for example, those satisfied by a discontented Socrates but not by a contented but unreflective person.

E. F. Carritt argues that such utilitarian theories make "no room for justice." For example, they seem to have the consequence that a prosecutor should frame an innocent person if that is the only way she can prevent a disastrous riot. Act utilitarianism makes the rightness of an action depend solely on *forward-looking* considerations; but the demand that punishment be of the guilty is a *backward-looking* consideration with no clear place in such a theory. A similar point could be made about breaking a solemn promise. Again, cases of lying or even intentionally killing an innocent person as ways in particular circumstances of increasing overall happiness raise similar worries. In such cases the utilitarian requirement to increase happiness as much as possible seems in conflict with common-sense prohibitions on certain ways of treating individuals in the pursuit of overall good.

Some philosophers (e.g., J. O. Urmson) have argued that Mill is better seen as a *rule* rather than an act utilitarian: the utilitarian test is to be applied directly only to general rules. A moral rule is shown to be correct by showing that its recognition promotes happiness. An act is right as long as it does not violate some correct moral rule, wrong if it does. The suggestion is that among the correct moral rules will be, for example, a rule generally prohibiting the intentional punishment of innocents; and this is why criticisms along Carritt's lines do not work so easily against Mill's theory.

Rule utilitarianism (which J. J. C. Smart calls "restricted utilitarianism") is a two-tier theory: it sanctions utilitarian reasoning at the level of rules, but not at the level of particular acts. This may seem arbitrary. After all, if happiness is so important, why shouldn't I be able to justify my action by saying that *it* best promotes happiness? As Smart argues, once we accept the main outlines of the utilitarian framework, refusal to allow this form of moral justification may seem like a case of "rule worship."

Carritt's objections to act utilitarianism focus on prohibitions on ways of treating others. Bernard Williams argues that there is another problem, one posed by the value we place on integrity. In section D, John Rawls objects to utilitarianism that it "does not take seriously the distinction between persons." Finally, Peter Singer shows just how powerful even a weak version of a theory in the spirit of utilitarianism can be by arguing that we are subject to fairly strong moral demands to aid those who are suffering from famine in distant lands.

B. KANTIAN ETHICS

Utilitarianism supposes that we can determine what things are good independently of an account of what actions are right and then go on to see the rightness of actions as depending on the goodness of consequences. Immanuel Kant argues, in contrast, that the rightness of an action does not depend in this way solely on the goodness of consequences; for the rightness of an action depends on the principle (the "maxim") on which the agent acts.

Kant begins his *Groundwork of the Metaphysics of Morals* with a discussion of "the good will." A person of good will is a morally conscientious person, one who is firmly committed to doing her or his moral duty, come what may. Kant argues that only such a good will is "good without qualification." A person's intelligence, wit, or charm may be a good or a bad thing, depending on other circumstances, or the use to which it is put. But moral conscientiousness "shine[s] like a jewel" in any context, independently of its actual consequences.

In chapter 2 Kant tries to determine "the supreme principle of morality." Kant supposes there are objective principles concerning what it is rational to do under certain circumstances. For beings like us who are sometimes tempted to act contrary to reason, these principles are seen as "**imperatives**." Some imperatives only tell us what to do on the assumption that we have a certain end. These are *hypothetical* imperatives. For example, "you ought to wear a coat outside today" normally expresses only a hypothetical imperative since it tells you what to do on the assumption (let us suppose) that you want to stay warm. You could escape from this imperative by not caring about staying warm. Kant supposes that there are also *categorical* imperatives that tell us what to do without assuming that we have a particular end we could rationally give up. Moral oughts, Kant supposes, must be categorical and not merely hypothetical imperatives. Otherwise we could escape from the demands of morality, just by giving up certain ends. (For challenges to this view of morality, see the selections by David Hume and J. L. Mackie in section F, "Challenges to Morality.")

Kant supposes that all moral demands on our conduct are grounded in a single basic imperative: the Categorical Imperative. Kant offers three main formulations of this principle (although he argues that these are formulations of the same principle): the Formula of Universal Law (which itself has two different versions); the Formula of the End in Itself; and the Formula of the Kingdom of Ends (which is preceded by a closely related Formula of Autonomy). The first is related to, but importantly different from, the Golden Rule. Kwame Anthony Appiah appeals to related pleas in his criticisms of intrinsic racism in section E. The second is developed by Onora O'Neill in her discussion of famine problems. And the third can usefully be compared to the framework developed by John Rawls in *A Theory of Justice*. (See the selection in section D.)

In his "A Brief Introduction to Kantian Ethics," J. David Velleman attempts to give a relatively accessible introduction to the views developed in Kant's *Groundwork*. These two pieces are useful companions.

C. ARISTOTELIAN ETHICS

Aristotle turns our attention away from questions of the rightness of particular acts to the question of what we should aim at in trying to live a good human life. His initial answer is that it is **eudaimonia**—here translated as happiness, but sometimes translated as flourishing.

In contrast with Bentham, Aristotle does not see human happiness as just a matter of more pleasure and less pain. To say more about what human happiness is, he tries to determine the characteristic function (**ergon**) of human beings. We are complex organisms with many different capacities, capacities that constitute our "soul." Some of these capacities are merely nutritive—for example, capacities for digestion and breathing—and are shared with other animals. But our capacities for rational deliberation and reflection are peculiar to us; their active exercise, Aristotle thought, is our ergon. Eudaimonia—happiness, flourishing—consists of the active exercise of these rational capacities in accordance with their characteristic virtues or excellences (arete).

Some of our rational activities are theoretical (e.g., the study of mathematics); some concern our day-to-day lives in a world with material needs and social complexities. The virtues (excellences) involved in the first sort of activity Aristole calls intellectual; the latter virtues he calls moral (or practical). Aristotle's Doctrine of the Mean is his theory of what the moral virtues are.

Aristotle's theory is frequently cited as an important example of "virtue ethics." (Hume's theory of what character traits are virtues—in section F—can also be seen as part of this tradition.) Theories in the tradition of virtue ethics are commonly contrasted with utilitarian theories in the spirit of Bentham and Mill and with "**deontological**" theories in the spirit of Kant. However, in her essay "Right Action," Rosalind Hursthouse argues that a contemporary version of Aristotelian virtue ethics is a serious contender to utilitarian and deontological theories.

D. JUSTICE AND EQUALITY

When you criticize slavery or a certain tax system as unjust or unfair, you are assessing certain social institutions, not just certain individuals and their actions. Such social institutions have a deep impact on the ways in which various goods are distributed among the members of a society. When does this impact satisfy the demands of justice?

In the selection from his book *A Theory of Justice*, John Rawls tries to answer this question for those institutions that constitute the "**basic structure**" of a society. The main idea is that the public principles of justice for this basic structure are those that we would choose in a hypothetical situation that is fair. Thus the label "Justice as Fairness."

Rawls calls his specification of such a fair-choice situation "**the original position**." He supposes that the parties in the situation are rational but are behind a "**veil of ignorance**" that blocks from their view any knowledge that would give its possessor an unfair advantage in choosing basic principles of justice. The parties do not know whether they are rich or poor, male or female. They do not know their racial or ethnic background or their particular talents. They do not even know exactly what in the real world they deem most important. What they do care about, in the original position, is their share of "primary goods," goods that are assumed to have a use whatever a person's particular goals and abilities are. Rawls supposes that among the chief primary goods whose distribution is shaped by the basic structure are various basic liberties (e.g., freedom of speech and association), opportunities (e.g., educational opportunities), and income and wealth. The parties in the original position are to decide on principles that will publicly govern the ways in which the basic structure shapes the distribution of such primary goods.

Rawls argues that the parties in the original position would unanimously choose two principles: a principle of maximum, equal basic liberties and a principle that requires that inequalities in the distribution of other social primary goods be to everyone's advantage (e.g., not merely to the advantage of the majority) and provide for equality of opportunity. Both principles depart from the utilitarian's overriding concern with maximizing overall happiness.

Robert Nozick would classify Rawls's principles as nonhistorical, end-state principles: they attempt to assess the justice of the social distributions of goods without looking at the actual history of how these distributions came about. Or so it might seem. Nozick argues that no end-state principle of justice can be continuously realized without serious restrictions on people's liberties. This is the point of his Wilt Chamberlain example. Nozick's alternative is his historical entitlement theory. This theory aims at three kinds of principles: principles that say when an original acquisition of some good is just, principles that say when the transfer of some good is just, and principles that say what is to be done to rectify past violations of the first two principles. The first principle will involve the Lockean proviso that the appropriation of a previously unowned object must not worsen the situation of others. According to this theory, I am entitled to those goods I possess either through a just original acquisition or through a series of just transfers that begin with a just original acquisition.

Rawls's argument for his principles of justice begins with a "benchmark of initial equality." Rawls then argues that parties in the original position would allow inequalities in the distribution of primary goods like income and wealth, as long as those inequalities would make the members of the "least fortunate group in society" better off than they otherwise would be. This is Rawls's **difference principle.** This principle might, for example, permit inequalities that result from a structure of incentives that encourages production that promotes the interest of all. Rawls applies this principle to the basic structure of society, not to the motivation of individuals making choices within that structure—not, for example, to the motivation of an individual who aims at maximizing her profits. G. A. Cohen argues that this is a mistake, that the choices and motivations of individual agents—including "high-flying marketeers"—are also subject to a version of the difference principle. This leads, Cohen argues, to the egalitarian conclusion that "affirmation of the difference principle implies that justice requires (virtually) unqualified equality."

It is clear from the brief survey above that the concept of justice is central for much of political philosophy. Nevertheless, in "The Need for More Than Justice," Annette Baier argues that justice is not enough. Baier argues that there is a Kantian tradition that makes society's "first virtue justice, construed as respect for equal rights to formal goods." Here, Baier has in mind Rawls. The problem with such a view, Baier argues, is that such formal goods don't "do much to ensure that the people who have and mutually respect such rights will have any other relationships to one another than the minimal relationship needed to keep such a 'civil society' going." An ethics of respect, that is, is perfectly compatible with a tremendous amount of suffering. Political and moral theories, Baier holds, shouldn't drop the concept of justice entirely; however, she holds that justice needs to be brought into harmony with an ethics of care, which emphasizes our interdependence, relationships in which power is unevenly distributed, and the unchosen nature of many of our relationships. Baier's theory, it is clear, offers grounds for a more pro-active picture of political philosophy, one that stresses not just equal access to formal goods but also the importance of engaging in certain positive relationships of care with each other.

An important aspect of Baier's article is a discussion of the different situations men and women face in our society. Baier holds that this leads men and women to "morally mature" in different ways. She approvingly quotes Carol Gilligan: "'Since the reality of interconnexion is experienced by women as given rather than freely contracted, they arrive at an understanding of life that reflects the limits of autonomy and control. As a result, women's development delineates a path not only to a less violent life but also to a maturity realized by interdependence and taking care.'" Taking seriously this perspective, Baier holds, will surely have an impact on the way we conceive of common ethical and political notions, such as individualism, autonomy, and justice. John Stuart Mill, in his landmark essay "The Subjection of Women," expresses a similar line of thinking. Mill is concerned not only with how women were subjugated in his day but also how by subjugating and marginalizing women society hindered its social and political development.

E. CONTEMPORARY MORAL PROBLEMS

In section D, we focused on certain theoretical issues concerning justice and equality. Without moving too far away from these concepts, here we switch gears, looking at particular moral problems our society faces.

One pressing issue that our society faces, for instance, is the morality of abortion. In her landmark essay, "A Defense of Abortion," Judith Jarvis Thomson provides a novel defense of the practice. Traditionally, this debate has centered on the personhood of the fetus. Anti-abortionists argue that fetuses are persons, and so abortion is immoral; thinkers who defend abortion's morality argue that fetuses aren't persons, and thus abortion is moral. Thomson's contribution is an argument that grants her opponents that fetuses are persons. From this, Thomson argues, it doesn't follow that abortion is immoral. Particularly important is Thomson's focus on the right to control what happens in and with one's body, a right that many arguments regarding the morality of abortion overlook. For Thomson, it isn't clear that the fetus's right to life, which it gets in virtue of being a person, trumps the mother's right to control what happens in and with her body. Thomson motivates this thought with her famous "violinist case," in which you wake up to find yourself attached to a famous violinist, who must remain attached to you for some period of time in order to live. Detaching from this violinist would result in his death. Thomson argues that though the violinist has a right to life, this doesn't entail that you are *obligated* to stay attached to him.

There are worries regarding Thomson's argument, though, and in "Thomson's Arguments" Rosalind Hursthouse considers some of these worries. Particularly, Hursthouse argues that Thomson is too focused on rights and justice. For Hursthouse, while it might be just to detach oneself from the violinist, that doesn't make it acceptable; it still might be cruel, self-centered, or indecent. For Hursthouse, Thomson doesn't take other modes of moral evaluation seriously enough. Moreover, Hursthouse argues that abortion and pregnancy are unique, and cannot simply be compared to other situations people might face. Corresponding to this uniqueness, she holds, are unique reasons for having an abortion. Thus, Hursthouse argues, it is crucial that we keep in mind how unique abortion is as we reason about its morality.

Despite her criticisms of Thomson's argument, Hursthouse notes that Thomson's article is nevertheless incredibly important for bringing a person's right to control what happens with and in her body into the foreground of the debate about abortion. And indeed, Thomson notes that the absence of this right in most discussions of abortion indicates a failure to treat women equally. The inequalities women face is also a theme in "Markets in Women's Reproductive Labor." There, Debra Satz focuses on "conditions of pervasive gender inequality in our society." She argues that these conditions are at the heart of the best account of why we should limit the use of markets in women's reproductive labor.

Of course, our society faces inequality on many fronts. Kwame Anthony Appiah, in "Racisms," seeks an analysis of different kinds of racism. Elsewhere, Appiah argues against "racialism"—the view that "there are heritable characteristics, possessed by members of our species, that allow us to divide them into a small set of races, in such a way that all members of these races share certain traits and tendencies with each other that they do not share with members of any other race." In this essay, Appiah distinguishes different varieties of racism, all of which presuppose racialism. He argues that even if racialism were true, none of these forms of racism would be defensible. His criticism of "intrinsic" racism, in particular, returns us to the Kantian themes explored in section B. Finally, Linda Martin Alcoff considers whether it is necessary to eliminate our "visual practices of racialization" in order to eliminate racism. In other words, she considers whether it is desirable to strive for "racial color blindness." She argues it isn't.

F. CHALLENGES TO MORALITY

Morality and Self-Interest

Suppose you discovered a way to gain access to the files of any computer system in the country and could change those files at will. Suppose you knew you could do this with no chance of being caught. You could change the grades of anyone at any university. You could change the totals in bank accounts. And so on. You think it would be wrong to do this. But you still wonder whether you should let that stop you. Why should you let moral considerations prevent you from pursuing what seems to be in your self-interest? Why should you be moral?

Your problem is a high-tech version of Glaucon's problem of the ring of Gyges, posed in Plato's *Republic*. Since Gyges can treat others unjustly with impunity, wouldn't he live a better life by acting unjustly rather than justly? In the selections reprinted here from Books I through IV of the *Republic*, Socrates argues that it is in a person's interest to be just and against his interest to be unjust. Properly understood, morality and self-interest are not in conflict. Socrates's argument proceeds by way of a famous parallel between the state and an individual and an analysis of the structure of human motivation that leads Socrates to talk of three "parts" of the soul.

We next have excerpts from David Hume's *An Enquiry Concerning the Principles of Morals*. Hume's discussion touches on many issues. His two main questions are: How far do reason and sentiment enter into moral judgment? What character traits are virtues, and why? Hume sees character traits as virtues insofar as they are "useful or agreeable to the person himself or to others." We look at his answer to the former question later. We include Hume's *Enquiry* in this section because of its discussions of the relation between morality and self-interest.

Hume's explicit discussion of this issue occurs in Section IX, Part II. Here, he extols the contribution of the moral virtues to the life of their possessor—although, "[t]reating vice with the greatest candour," he does worry that his remarks may not be convincing for the case of justice (which, for Hume, is a virtue primarily concerned with property, honesty, and promise-keeping). But Hume does not think that it is solely because of their contribution to our own interests that we approve of the moral virtues. Rather, Hume argues that as a matter of fact we are all to some extent directly concerned with the interests of others—this is the point of his example of avoiding another's gouty toes. This universal principle of benevolence accounts in large part for our approval of the virtues and is the basis of our moral judgments.

Hume sketches a complex account of the relation between benevolence and self-love. "It is requisite," he says, "that there be an original propensity of some kind, in order to be a basis to self-love, by giving a relish to the objects of its pursuit." Benevolence is itself one such original propensity. Self-love is a "secondary passion," whose concern is with the satisfaction of various original propensities, and these include benevolence, the basis of morality.

In the Prisoner's Dilemma, discussed in Part VII, "Puzzles and Paradoxes," it is in each prisoner's individual interest to confess, even though both prisoners do better if both remain silent than they do if both confess. Prisoners guided solely by a concern with their individual self-interest will each end up worse off than if they were able to cooperate and maintain joint silence. There is a useful analogy here with morality. Consider the moral demand to be truthful. Each person may on occasion be in a situation in which it is in his or her individual interest to lie. Yet, we all do better if everyone is always truthful—even when this conflicts with one's self-interest—than if everyone were to lie whenever this was in one's own interest. A group of people who are guided solely by individual self-interest will each end up worse off than each would have been if they had all been guided by a commitment to honesty. This suggests that there are reasons of self-interest to be moral. In "Morality and Advantage" David Gauthier explores this suggestion, but he concludes that in the end it provides a more limited rationale for being moral than may have been thought. (Gauthier develops an importantly different line of argument in his 1986 book *Morals by Agreement.*)

Subjectivism, Relativism, and Skepticism

We believe that wanton torture of an innocent child is wrong, and (we hope) you do, too. Is there some objective fact here—the fact that such conduct is wrong—that is what both of us know? Or is this merely a case in which we share similar negative attitudes?

In Appendix I of his *An Enquiry Concerning the Principles of Morals* Hume argues that our moral attitudes could not consist merely in the knowledge of facts about the world. Knowledge of facts is not itself sufficient to move us to act. Yet, Hume assumes, our moral views can themselves move us to act. To reach a moral conclusion, then, it is not enough to know that certain acts or character traits have certain effects. We must also have appropriate pro or con attitudes—what Hume calls sentiments—toward those effects. Given our benevolence, we react negatively to torture. But, if (contrary to fact) we were rational but nonbenevolent beings, we could grasp all the facts about torture and yet not react in these ways.

Although there is, for Hume, neither moral knowledge nor moral facts, there is a clear and powerful point of view of morality: the point of view of informed benevolence, which he describes in Section IX, Part I. Hume thinks that his skepticism about the objectivity of morality leaves untouched the importance of this moral point of view for us.

J. L. Mackie develops similar views, and usefully contrasts them with the views of Aristotle and Kant. (See the selections from Aristotle and Kant in sections B and C.) Mackie distinguishes three levels of investigation: descriptive ethics, first-order normative ethics, and second-order theories about what moral valuing and moral values are. At the level of descriptive ethics we are only concerned to describe what moral views certain people in fact endorse. At the level of first-order normative ethics we are interested in ourselves making judgments about what is right and what is good. Mackie's main concerns are at the second-order level. He argues that there are no moral facts and no moral knowledge, although he thinks his arguments still allow us to make serious first-order judgments of right and wrong, good and bad, as long as these judgments have been purged of a claim to objectivity.

Mackie thinks that the idea that values are "part of the fabric of the world" is deeply embedded in our common-sense thought. But he offers two main reasons for rejecting such objectivism: the argument from relativity and the argument from queerness. The first begins with a premise from descriptive ethics, but it aims at a second-order conclusion; the second is an extension of Hume's argument from the connection between morality and motivation. Our tendency, nevertheless, to see values as objective is a tendency to project our subjective attitudes and desires onto the objective world.

Can we test and confirm our moral beliefs by way of observation in the ways in which we offer observational support for conjectures in the sciences? Gilbert Harman argues that the answer is No. He thinks this poses a basic problem if we want to avoid skepticism about the possibility of moral knowledge. Nicholas L. Sturgeon takes issue with this line of argument for skepticism about moral knowledge, though he grants that a main argument for moral skepticism—the argument from "relativity" or "the apparent difficulty of settling moral disagreements"—poses a further, and as-yet-unanswered, challenge.

KEY TERMS

Consequentialist	Ergon
Utilitarian	Deontological
Hedonistic act utilitarianism	Basic structure
Imperatives	The original position
Absolutist	Veil of ignorance
Eudaimonia	Difference principle

A. UTILITARIANISM

The Principle of Utility

JEREMY BENTHAM

Jeremy Bentham (1748–1832) was an English philosopher who is best known as the founder of utilitarianism, that is, the view that the rightness or wrongness of any action depends on the "tendency which it appears to have to augment or diminish the happiness of the party whose interest is in question." His most famous work is *An Introduction to the Principles of Morals and Legislation*.

· ·

Chapter 1 Of the Principle of Utility

I. Nature has placed mankind under the governance of two sovereign masters, *pain* and *pleasure*. It is for them alone to point out what we ought to do, as well as to determine what we shall do. On the one hand the standard of right and wrong, on the other the chain of causes and effects, are fastened to their throne. They govern us in all we do, in all we say, in all we think: every effort we can make to throw off our subjection, will serve but to demonstrate and confirm it. In words a man may pretend to abjure their empire: but in reality he will remain subject to it all the while. The **principle of utility*** recognises this subjection, and assumes it for the foundation of that system, the object of which is to rear the fabric of felicity

From *An Introduction to the Principles of Morals and Legislation* (New York: Hafner, 1948), pp. 1–4, 29–32.

*Note by the Author, July 1822.

To this denomination has of late been added, or substituted, the *greatest happiness* or *greatest felicity* principle: this for shortness, instead of saying at length *that principle* which states the greatest happiness of all those whose interest is in question, as being the right and proper, and only right and proper and universally desirable, end of human action: of human action in every situation, and in particular in that of a functionary or set of functionaries exercising the powers of Government. The word *utility* does not so clearly point to the ideas of *pleasure* and *pain* as the words *happiness* and *felicity* do: nor does it lead us to the consideration of the *number*, of the interests affected; to the *number*, as being the circumstance, which contributes, in the largest proportion, to the formation of the standard here in question; the *standard of right and wrong*, by which alone the propriety of human conduct, in every situation, can with propriety be tried. This want of a sufficiently manifest connexion between the ideas of *happiness* and *pleasure* on the one hand, and the idea of *utility* on the other, I have every now and then found operating, and with but too much efficiency, as a bar to the acceptance, that might otherwise have been given, to this principle.—BENTHAM by the hands of reason and law. Systems which attempt to question it, deal in sounds instead of sense, in caprice instead of reason, in darkness instead of light.

But enough of metaphor and declamation: it is not by such means that moral science is to be improved.

II. The principle of utility is the foundation of the present work: it will be proper therefore at the outset to give an explicit and determinate account of what is meant by it. By the principle of utility is meant that principle which approves or disapproves of every action whatsoever, according to the tendency which it appears to have to augment or diminish the happiness of the party whose interest is in question: or, what is the same thing in other words, to promote or to oppose that happiness. I say of every action whatsoever; and therefore not only of every action of a private individual, but of every measure of government.

III. By utility is meant that property in any object, whereby it tends to produce benefit, advantage, pleasure, good, or happiness, (all this in the present case comes to the same thing) or (what comes again to the same thing) to prevent the happening of mischief, pain, evil, or unhappiness to the party whose interest is considered: if that party be the community in general, then the happiness of the community: if a particular individual, then the happiness of that individual.

IV. The interest of the community is one of the most general expressions that can occur in the phraseology of morals: no wonder that the meaning of it is often lost. When it has a meaning, it is this. The community is a fictitious *body*, composed of the individual persons who are considered as constituting as it were its *members*. The interest of the community then is, what?—the sum of the interests of the several members who compose it.

V. It is in vain to talk of the interest of the community without understanding what is the interest of the individual.* A thing is said to promote the interest, or to be *for* the interest, of an individual, when it tends to add to the sum total of his pleasures: or, what comes to the same thing, to diminish the sum total of his pains.

VI. An action then may be said to be conformable to the principle of utility, or, for shortness sake, to utility, (meaning with respect to the community at large) when the tendency it has to augment the happiness of the community is greater than any it has to diminish it.

VII. A measure of government (which is but a particular kind of action, performed by a particular person or persons) may be said to be conformable to or dictated by the principle of utility, when in like manner the tendency which it has to augment the happiness of the community is greater than any which it has to diminish it.

VIII. When an action, or in particular a measure of government, is supposed by a man to be conformable to the principle of utility, it may be convenient, for the purposes of discourse, to imagine a kind of law or dictate, called a law or dictate of utility: and to speak of the action in question, as being conformable to such law or dictate.

IX. A man may be said to be a partizan of the principle of utility, when the approbation or disapprobation he annexes to any action, or to any measure, is determined by and proportioned to the tendency which he conceives it to have to augment or to diminish the happiness of the community: or in other words, to its conformity or unconformity to the laws or dictates of utility.

X. Of an action that is conformable to the principle of utility one may always say either that it is one that ought to be done, or at least that it is not one that ought not to be done. One may say also, that it is right it should be done; at least that it is not wrong it should be done; that it is a right action; at least that it is not a wrong action. When thus interpreted, the words *ought*, and *right* and *wrong*, and others of that stamp, have a meaning: when otherwise, they have none.

XI. Has the rectitude of this principle been ever formally contested? It should seem that it had, by those who have not known what they have been meaning. Is it susceptible of any direct proof? it should seem not: for that which is used to prove every thing else, cannot itself be proved: a chain of proofs must have their commencement somewhere. To give such proof is as impossible as it is needless.

XII. Not that there is or ever has been that human creature breathing, however stupid or perverse, who has not on many, perhaps on most occasions of his life, deferred to it. By the natural constitution of the human frame, on most occasions of their lives men in general embrace this principle, without thinking of it: if not for the ordering of their own actions, yet for the

---

*Interest is one of those words, which not having any superior *genus*, cannot in the ordinary way be defined.

trying of their own actions, as well as of those of other men. There have been, at the same time, not many, perhaps, even of the most intelligent, who have been disposed to embrace it purely and without reserve. There are even few who have not taken some occasion or other to quarrel with it, either on account of their not understanding always how to apply it, or on account of some prejudice or other which they were afraid to examine into, or could not bear to part with. For such is the stuff that man is made of: in principle and in practice, in a right track and in a wrong one, the rarest of all human qualities is consistency.

Chapter IV Value of a Lot of Pleasure or Pain, How to Be Measured

I. Pleasures then, and the avoidance of pains, are the *ends* which the legislator has in view: it behoves him therefore to understand their *value*. Pleasures and pains are the *instruments* he has to work with: it behoves him therefore to understand their force, which is again, in other words, their value.

II. To a person considered *by himself*, the value of a pleasure or pain considered *by itself*, will be greater or less, according to the four following circumstances:

1. Its *intensity*.
2. Its *duration*.
3. Its *certainty* or *uncertainty*.
4. Its *propinquity* or *remoteness*.

III. These are the circumstances which are to be considered in estimating a pleasure or a pain considered each of them by itself. But when the value of any pleasure or pain is considered for the purpose of estimating the tendency of any *act* by which it is produced, there are two other circumstances to be taken into the account; these are,

5. Its *fecundity*, or the chance it has of being followed by sensations of the *same* kind: that is, pleasures, if it be a pleasure: pains, if it be a pain.

6. Its *purity*, or the chance it has of *not* being followed by sensations of the *opposite* kind: that is, pains, if it be a pleasure: pleasures, if it be a pain.

These two last, however, are in strictness scarcely to be deemed properties of the pleasure or the pain itself;

they are not, therefore, in strictness to be taken into the account of the value of that pleasure or that pain. They are in strictness to be deemed properties only of the act, or other event, by which such pleasure or pain has been produced; and accordingly are only to be taken into the account of the tendency of such act or such event.

IV. To a *number* of persons, with reference to each of whom the value of a pleasure or a pain is considered, it will be greater or less, according to seven circumstances: to wit, the six preceding ones; viz.

1. Its *intensity*.
2. Its *duration*.
3. Its *certainty* or *uncertainty*.
4. Its *propinquity* or *remoteness*.
5. Its *fecundity*.
6. Its *purity*.

And one other; to wit:

7. Its *extent*; that is, the number of persons to whom it *extends*; or (in other words) who are affected by it.

V. To take an exact account then of the general tendency of any act, by which the interests of a community are affected, proceed as follows. Begin with any one person of those whose interests seem most immediately to be affected by it: and take an account.

1. Of the value of each distinguishable *pleasure* which appears to be produced by it in the *first* instance.

2. Of the value of each *pain* which appears to be produced by it in the *first* instance.

3. Of the value of each pleasure which appears to be produced by it *after* the first. This constitutes the *fecundity* of the first *pleasure* and the *impurity* of the first *pain*.

4. Of the value of each *pain* which appears to be produced by it after the first. This constitutes the *fecundity* of the first *pain*, and the *impurity* of the first pleasure.

5. Sum up all the values of all the *pleasures* on the one side, and those of all the pains on the other. The balance, if it be on the side of pleasure, will give the *good* tendency of the act upon the whole, with respect to the interests of that *individual* person; if on the side of pain, the *bad* tendency of it upon the whole.

6. Take an account of the *number* of persons whose interests appear to be concerned; and repeat the above process with respect to each. *Sum up* the numbers expressive of the degrees of *good* tendency, which the act has, with respect to each individual, in regard to whom the tendency of it is *good* upon the whole: do this again with respect to each individual, in regard to whom the tendency of it is *bad* upon the whole. Take the *balance*; which, if on the side of *pleasure*, will give the general *good tendency* of the act, with respect to the total number or community of individuals concerned; if on the side of pain, the general *evil tendency*, with respect to the same community.

VI. It is not to be expected that this process should be strictly pursued previously to every moral judgment, or to every legislative or judicial operation. It may, however, be always kept in view: and as near as the process actually pursued on these occasions approaches to it, so near will such process approach to the character of an exact one.

VII. The same process is alike applicable to pleasure and pain, in whatever shape they appear: and by whatever denomination they are distinguished: to pleasure, whether it be called *good* (which is properly the cause or instrument of pleasure) or *profit* (which is distant pleasure, or the cause or instrument of distant pleasure) or *convenience*, or *advantage, benefit, emolument, happiness*, and so forth; to pain, whether it be called *evil*, (which

corresponds to *good*) or *mischief*, or *inconvenience*, or *disadvantage*, or *loss*, or *unhappiness*, and so forth.

KEY TERM

Principle of utility

STUDY QUESTIONS

1. At the beginning of this selection, Bentham says that pain and pleasure "govern us in all we do, in all we say, in all we think." Does this seem right? How important a role do pain and pleasure play in human life?
2. Bentham repeatedly asserts that increasing the sum of pleasure is the same thing as diminishing the sum of pains. Do you agree? Why or why not?
3. Can you think of any other aspects of pleasure and pain besides those that Bentham lists (intensity, duration, certainty, and propinquity) that add or subtract from the value of the pleasure or pain?
4. How might someone who believed in the principle of utility recommend that we go about "summing up" the values of pleasures and pains? Does it even make sense to talk about pleasures and pains having numerical values?

Utilitarianism

JOHN STUART MILL

John Stuart Mill (1806–1873) was a leading exponent of utilitarianism and empiricist philosophy. In addition to *Utilitarianism*, his works include *A System of Logic, Examination of Sir William Hamilton's Philosophy, Principles of Political Economy*, and *On Liberty*.

· ·

Chapter 1 General Remarks

There are few circumstances among those which make up the present condition of human knowledge,

From *The English Utilitarians*. Copyright © 1949 by Basil Blackwell, Ltd. Reprinted by permission of the publisher.

more unlike what might have been expected, or more significant of the backward state in which speculation on the most important subjects still lingers, than the little progress which has been made in the decision of the controversy respecting the criterion of right and wrong. From the dawn of philosophy, the question concerning the *summum bonum*, or, what is the same thing, concerning the foundation of morality, has been accounted the main problem in speculative thought, has occupied the most gifted intellects, and divided them into sects and schools, carrying on a vigorous warfare against one another. And after more than two thousand years the same discussions continue, philosophers are still ranged under the same contending banners, and neither thinkers nor mankind at large seem nearer to being unanimous on the subject, than when the youth Socrates listened to the old Protagoras, and asserted (if Plato's dialogue be grounded on a real conversation) the theory of **utilitarianism** against the popular morality of the so-called sophist.

. . . .

On the present occasion, I shall, without further discussion of the other theories, attempt to contribute something towards the understanding and appreciation of the Utilitarian or Happiness theory, and towards such proof as it is susceptible of. It is evident that this cannot be proof in the ordinary and popular meaning of the term. Questions of ultimate ends are not amenable to direct proof. Whatever can be proved to be good, must be so by being shown to be a means to something admitted to be good without proof. The medical art is proved to be good by its conducing to health; but how is it possible to prove that health is good? The art of music is good, for the reason, among others, that it produces pleasure; but what proof is it possible to give that pleasure is good? If, then, it is asserted that there is a comprehensive formula, including all things which are in themselves good, and that whatever else is good, is not so as an end, but as a mean, the formula may be accepted or rejected, but is not a subject of what is commonly understood by proof. We are not, however, to infer that its acceptance or rejection must depend on blind impulse, or arbitrary choice. There is a larger meaning of the word proof, in which this question is as amenable to it as any other of the disputed questions of philosophy. The subject is within the cognisance of the rational faculty; and neither does that faculty deal with it solely in the way of intuition. Considerations may be presented capable of determining the intellect either to give or withhold its assent to the doctrine; and this is equivalent to proof.

We shall examine presently of what nature are these considerations; in what manner they apply to

the case, and what rational grounds, therefore, can be given for accepting or rejecting the utilitarian formula. But it is a preliminary condition of rational acceptance or rejection, that the formula should be correctly understood. I believe that the very imperfect notion ordinarily formed of its meaning, is the chief obstacle which impedes its reception; and that could it be cleared, even from only the grosser misconceptions, the question would be greatly simplified, and a large proportion of its difficulties removed. Before, therefore, I attempt to enter into the philosophical grounds which can be given for assenting to the utilitarian standard, I shall offer some illustrations of the doctrine itself; with the view of showing more clearly what it is, distinguishing it from what it is not, and disposing of such of the practical objections to it as either originate in, or are closely connected with, mistaken interpretations of its meaning. Having thus prepared the ground, I shall afterwards endeavour to throw such light as I can upon the question, considered as one of philosophical theory.

Chapter 2 What Utilitarianism Is

. . . The creed which accepts as the foundation of morals, Utility, or the **Greatest Happiness Principle**, holds that actions are right in proportion as they tend to promote happiness, wrong as they tend to produce the reverse of happiness. By happiness is intended pleasure, and the absence of pain; by unhappiness, pain, and the privation of pleasure. To give a clear view of the moral standard set up by the theory, much more requires to be said; in particular, what things it includes in the ideas of pain and pleasure; and to what extent this is left an open question. But these supplementary explanations do not affect the theory of life on which this theory of morality is grounded—namely, that pleasure, and freedom from pain, are the only things desirable as ends; and that all desirable things (which are as numerous in the utilitarian as in any other scheme) are desirable either for the pleasure inherent in themselves, or as means to the promotion of pleasure and the prevention of pain.

Now, such a theory of life excites in many minds, and among them in some of the most estimable in feeling and purpose, inveterate dislike. To suppose that life has (as they express it) no higher end than pleasure—no better and nobler object of desire and pursuit—they designate as utterly mean and grovelling; as a doctrine worthy only of swine, to whom the followers of Epicurus were, at a very early period, contemptuously likened; and modern holders of the doctrine are occasionally made the subject of equally polite comparisons by its German, French, and English assailants.

When thus attacked, the Epicureans have always answered, that it is not they, but their accusers, who represent human nature in a degrading light; since the accusation supposes human beings to be capable of no pleasures except those of which swine are capable. If this supposition were true, the charge could not be gainsaid, but would then be no longer an imputation; for if the sources of pleasure were precisely the same to human beings and to swine, the rule of life which is good enough for the one would be good enough for the other. The comparison of the Epicurean life to that of beasts is felt as degrading, precisely because a beast's pleasures do not satisfy a human being's conceptions of happiness. Human beings have faculties more elevated than the animal appetites, and when once made conscious of them, do not regard anything as happiness which does not include their gratification. I do not, indeed, consider the Epicureans to have been by any means faultless in drawing out their scheme of consequences from the utilitarian principle. To do this in any sufficient manner, many Stoic, as well as Christian elements require to be included. But there is no known Epicurean theory of life which does not assign to the pleasures of the intellect, of the feelings and imagination, and of the moral sentiments, a much higher value as pleasures than to those of mere sensation. It must be admitted, however, that utilitarian writers in general have placed the superiority of mental over bodily pleasures chiefly in the greater permanency, safety, uncostliness, etc., of the former—that is, in their circumstantial advantages rather than in their **intrinsic** nature. And on all these points utilitarians have fully proved their case; but they might have taken the other, and, as it may be called, higher ground, with entire consistency. It is quite compatible with the principle of utility to recognise the fact,

that some *kinds* of pleasure are more desirable and more valuable than others. It would be absurd that while, in estimating all other things, quality is considered as well as quantity, the estimation of pleasures should be supposed to depend on quantity alone.

If I am asked, what I mean by difference of quality in pleasures, or what makes one pleasure more valuable than another, merely as a pleasure, except its being greater in amount, there is but one possible answer. Of two pleasures, if there be one to which all or almost all who have experience of both give a decided preference, irrespective of any feeling of moral obligation to prefer it, that is the more desirable pleasure. If one of the two is, by those who are competently acquainted with both, placed so far above the other that they prefer it, even though knowing it to be attended with a greater amount of discontent, and would not resign it for any quantity of the other pleasure which their nature is capable of, we are justified in ascribing to the preferred enjoyment a superiority in quality, so far outweighing quantity as to render it, in comparison, of small account.

Now it is an unquestionable fact that those who are equally acquainted with, and equally capable of appreciating and enjoying, both, do give a most marked preference to the manner of existence which employs their higher faculties. Few human creatures would consent to be changed into any of the lower animals, for a promise of the fullest allowance of a beast's pleasures; no intelligent human being would consent to be a fool, no instructed person would be an ignoramus, no person of feeling and conscience would be selfish and base, even though they should be persuaded that the fool, the dunce, or the rascal is better satisfied with his lot than they are with theirs. They would not resign what they possess more than he for the most complete satisfaction of all the desires which they have in common with him. If they ever fancy they would, it is only in cases of unhappiness so extreme, that to escape from it they would exchange their lot for almost any other, however undesirable in their own eyes. A being of higher faculties requires more to make him happy, is capable probably of more acute suffering, and certainly accessible to it at more points, than one of an inferior type; but in spite of these liabilities, he can never really wish to sink into what he feels to be a lower grade of existence. We may give what explanation we please of this unwillingness; we may attribute to it pride, a name which is given indiscriminately to some of the most and to some of the least estimable feelings of which mankind are capable: we may refer it to the love of liberty and personal independence, an appeal to which was with the Stoics one of the most effective means for the inculcation of it; to the love of power, or to the love of excitement, both of which do really enter into and contribute to it: but its most appropriate appellation is a sense of dignity, which all human beings possess in one form or other, and in some, though by no means in exact, proportion to their higher faculties, and which is so essential a part of the happiness of those in whom it is strong, that nothing which conflicts with it could be, otherwise than momentarily, an object of desire to them. Whoever supposes that this preference takes place at a sacrifice of happiness—that the superior being, in anything like equal circumstances, is not happier than the inferior—confounds the two very different ideas, of happiness, and content. It is indisputable that the being whose capacities of enjoyment are low, has the greatest chance of having them fully satisfied; and a highly endowed being will always feel that any happiness which he can look for, as the world is constituted, is imperfect. But he can learn to bear its imperfections, if they are at all bearable; and they will not make him envy the being who is indeed unconscious of the imperfections, but only because he feels not at all the good which those imperfections qualify. It is better to be a human being dissatisfied than a pig satisfied; better to be Socrates dissatisfied than a fool satisfied. And if the fool, or the pig, are of a different opinion, it is because they only know their own side of the question. The other party to the comparison knows both sides.

It may be objected, that many who are capable of the higher pleasures, occasionally, under the influence of temptation, postpone them to the lower. But this is quite compatible with a full appreciation of the intrinsic superiority of the higher. Men often, from infirmity of character, make their election for the nearer good, though they know it to be the less valuable; and this no less when the choice is between two bodily pleasures, than when it is between bodily

and mental. They pursue sensual indulgences to the injury of health, though perfectly aware that health is the greater good. It may be further objected, that many who begin with youthful enthusiasm for everything noble, as they advance in years sink into indolence and selfishness. But I do not believe that those who undergo this very common change, voluntarily choose the lower description of pleasures in preference to the higher. I believe that before they devote themselves exclusively to the one, they have already become incapable of the other. Capacity for the nobler feelings is in most natures a very tender plant, easily killed, not only by hostile influences, but by mere want of sustenance; and in the majority of young persons it speedily dies away if the occupations to which their position in life has devoted them, and the society into which it has thrown them, are not favourable to keeping that higher capacity in exercise. Men lose their high aspirations as they lose their intellectual tastes, because they have not time or opportunity for indulging them; and they addict themselves to inferior pleasures, not because they deliberately prefer them, but because they are either the only ones to which they have access, or the only ones which they are any longer capable of enjoying. It may be questioned whether any one who has remained equally susceptible to both classes of pleasures, ever knowingly and calmly preferred the lower; though many, in all ages, have broken down in an ineffectual attempt to combine both.

From this verdict of the only competent judges, I apprehend there can be no appeal. On a question which is the best worth having of two pleasures, or which of two modes of existence is the most grateful to the feelings, apart from its moral attributes and from its consequences, the judgment of those who are qualified by knowledge of both, or, if they differ, that of the majority among them, must be admitted as final. And there needs be the less hesitation to accept this judgment respecting the quality of pleasures, since there is no other tribunal to be referred to even on the question of quantity. What means are there of determining which is the acutest of two pains, or the intensest of two pleasurable sensations, except the general suffrage of those who are familiar with both? Neither pains nor pleasures are homogeneous, and pain is always heterogeneous with pleasure. What is there to decide whether a particular pleasure is worth purchasing at the cost of a particular pain, except the feelings and judgment of the experienced? When, therefore, those feelings and judgment declare the pleasures derived from the higher faculties to be preferable *in kind*, apart from the question of intensity, to those of which the animal nature, disjoined from the higher faculties, is susceptible, they are entitled on this subject to the same regard.

I have dwelt on this point, as being a necessary part of a perfectly just conception of Utility or Happiness, considered as the directive rule of human conduct. But it is by no means an indispensable condition to the acceptance of the utilitarian standard; for that standard is not the agent's own greatest happiness, but the greatest amount of happiness altogether; and if it may possibly be doubted whether a noble character is always the happier for its nobleness, there can be no doubt that it makes other people happier, and that the world in general is immensely a gainer by it. Utilitarianism, therefore, could only attain its end by the general cultivation of nobleness of character, even if each individual were only benefited by the nobleness of others, and his own, so far as happiness is concerned, were a sheer deduction from the benefit. But the bare enunciation of such an absurdity as this last, renders refutation superfluous.

According to the Greatest Happiness Principle, as above explained, the ultimate end, with reference to and for the sake of which all other things are desirable (whether we are considering our own good or that of other people), is an existence exempt as far as possible from pain, and as rich as possible in enjoyments, both in point of quantity and quality; the test of quality, and the rule for measuring it against quantity, being the preference felt by those who in their opportunities of experience, to which must be added their habits of self-consciousness and self-observation, are best furnished with the means of comparison. This, being, according to the utilitarian opinion, the end of human action, is necessarily also the standard of morality; which may accordingly be defined, the rules and precepts for human conduct, by the observance of which an existence such as has been described might be, to the greatest extent possible, secured to all mankind; and not to them only, but, so far as the nature of things admits, to the whole sentient creation.

. . . .

I must again repeat, what the assailants of utilitarianism seldom have the justice to acknowledge, that the happiness which forms the utilitarian standard of what is right in conduct, is not the agent's own happiness, but that of all concerned. As between his own happiness and that of others, utilitarianism requires him to be as strictly impartial as a disinterested and benevolent spectator. In the golden rule of Jesus of Nazareth, we read the complete spirit of the ethics of utility. To do as you would be done by, and to love your neighbour as yourself, constitute the ideal perfection of utilitarian morality. As the means of making the nearest approach to this ideal, utility would enjoin, first, that laws and social arrangements should place the happiness, or (as speaking practically it may be called) the interest, of every individual, as nearly as possible in harmony with the interest of the whole; and secondly, that education and opinion, which have so vast a power over human character, should so use that power as to establish in the mind of every individual an indissoluble association between his own happiness and the good of the whole; especially between his own happiness and the practice of such modes of conduct, negative and positive, as regard for the universal happiness prescribes; so that not only he may be unable to conceive the possibility of happiness to himself, consistently with conduct opposed to the general good, but also that a direct impulse to promote the general good may be in every individual one of the habitual motives of action, and the sentiments connected therewith may fill a large and prominent place in every human being's sentient existence. If the impugners of the utilitarian morality represented it to their own minds in this its true character, I know not what recommendation possessed by any other morality they could possibly affirm to be wanting to it; what more beautiful or more exalted developments of human nature any other ethical system can be supposed to foster, or what springs of action, not accessible to the utilitarian, such systems rely on for giving effect to their mandates.

The objectors to utilitarianism cannot always be charged with representing it in a discreditable light.

On the contrary, those among them who entertain anything like a just idea of its disinterested character, sometimes find fault with its standard as being too high for humanity. They say it is exacting too much to require that people shall always act from the inducement of promoting the general interests of society. But this is to mistake the very meaning of a standard of morals, and confound the rule of action with the motive of it. It is the business of ethics to tell us what are our duties, or by what test we may know them; but no system of ethics requires that the sole motive of all we do shall be a feeling of duty; on the contrary, ninety-nine hundredths of all our actions are done from other motives, and rightly so done, if the rule of duty does not condemn them. It is the most unjust to utilitarianism that this particular misapprehension should be made a ground of objection to it, inasmuch as utilitarian moralists have gone beyond almost all others in affirming that the motive has nothing to do with the morality of the action, though much with the worth of the agent. He who saves a fellow creature from drowning does what is morally right, whether his motive be duty, or the hope of being paid for his trouble; he who betrays the friend that trusts him, is guilty of a crime, even if his object be to serve another friend to whom he is under greater obligations. But to speak only of actions done from the motive of duty, and in direct obedience to principle: it is a misapprehension of the utilitarian mode of thought, to conceive it as implying that people should fix their minds upon so wide a generality as the world, or society at large. The great majority of good actions are intended not for the benefit of the world, but for that of individuals, of which the good of the world is made up; and the thoughts of the most virtuous man need not on these occasions travel beyond the particular persons concerned, except so far as is necessary to assure himself that in benefiting them he is not violating the rights, that is, the legitimate and authorised expectations, of any one else. The multiplication of happiness is, according to the utilitarian ethics, the object of virtue: the occasions on which any person (except one in a thousand) has it in his power to do this on an extended scale, in other words to be a public benefactor, are but exceptional; and on these occasions alone is he called on to consider public utility; in every other case, private utility, the interest or happiness of some few persons, is all he has to attend to. Those alone the influence of whose actions extends to society in general, need concern themselves habitually about so large an object. In the case of abstinences indeed—of things which people forbear to do from moral considerations, though the consequences in the particular case might be beneficial— it would be unworthy of an intelligent agent not to be consciously aware that the action is of a class which, if practised generally, would be generally injurious, and that this is the ground of the obligation to abstain from it. The amount of regard for the public interest implied in this recognition, is no greater than is demanded by every system of morals, for they all enjoin to abstain from whatever is manifestly pernicious to society.

The same considerations dispose of another reproach against the doctrine of utility, founded on a still grosser misconception of the purpose of a standard of morality, and of the very meaning of the words right and wrong. It is often affirmed that utilitarianism renders men cold and unsympathising; that it chills their moral feelings towards individuals; that it makes them regard only the dry and hard consideration of the consequences of actions, not taking into their moral estimate the qualities from which those actions emanate. If the assertion means that they do not allow their judgment respecting the rightness or wrongness of an action to be influenced by their opinion of the qualities of the person who does it, this is a complaint not against utilitarianism, but against having any standard of morality at all; for certainly no known ethical standard decides an action to be good or bad because it is done by a good or a bad man, still less because done by an amiable, a brave, or a benevolent man, or the contrary. These considerations are relevant, not to the estimation of actions, but of persons; and there is nothing in the utilitarian theory inconsistent with the fact that there are other things which interest us in persons besides the rightness and wrongness of their actions. The Stoics, indeed, with the paradoxical misuse of language which was part of their system, and by which they strove to raise themselves above all concern about anything but virtue, were fond of saying, that he who has that has everything; that he, and only he, is rich, is beautiful, is a king. But no claim of this description is made for the virtuous man by the utilitarian doctrine. Utilitarians are quite aware that there are other desirable possessions and qualities besides virtue, and are perfectly willing to allow to all of them their full worth. They are also aware that a right action does not necessarily indicate a virtuous character, and that actions which are blamable, often proceed from qualities entitled to praise. When this is apparent in any particular case, it modifies their estimation, not certainly of the act, but of the agent. I grant that they are, notwithstanding, of opinion, that in the long run the best proof of a good character is good actions; and resolutely refuse to consider any mental disposition as good, of which the predominant tendency is to produce bad conduct. This makes them unpopular with many people; but it is an unpopularity which they must share with every one who regards the distinction between right and wrong in a serious light; and the reproach is not one which a conscientious utilitarian need be anxious to repel.

If no more be meant by the objection than that many utilitarians look on the morality of actions, as measured by the utilitarian standard, with too exclusive a regard, and do not lay sufficient stress upon the other beauties of character which go toward making a human being lovable or admirable, this may be admitted. Utilitarians who have cultivated their moral feelings, but not their sympathies nor their artistic perceptions, do fall into this mistake; and so do all other moralists under the same conditions. What can be said in excuse for other moralists is equally available for them, namely, that, if there is to be any error, it is better that it should be on that side. As a matter of fact, we may affirm that among utilitarians as among adherents of other systems, there is every imaginable degree of rigidity and of laxity in the application of their standard: some are even puritanically rigorous, while others are as indulgent as can possibly be desired by sinner or by sentimentalist. But on the whole, a doctrine which brings prominently forward the interest that mankind have in the repression and prevention of conduct which violates the moral law, is likely to be inferior to no other in turning the sanctions of opinion against such violations. It is true, the question,

What does violate the moral law? is one on which those who recognise different standards of morality are likely now and then to differ. But difference of opinion on moral questions was not first introduced into the world by utilitarianism, while that doctrine does supply, if not always an easy, at all events a tangible and intelligible mode of deciding such differences.

It may not be superfluous to notice a few more of the common misapprehensions of utilitarian ethics, even those which are so obvious and gross that it might appear impossible for any person of candour and intelligence to fall into them; since persons, even of considerable mental endowments, often give themselves so little trouble to understand the bearings of any opinion against which they entertain a prejudice, and men are in general so little conscious of this voluntary ignorance as a defect, that the vulgarest misunderstandings of ethical doctrines are continually met with in the deliberate writings of persons of the greatest pretensions both to high principle and to philosophy. We not uncommonly hear the doctrine of utility inveighed against as a *godless* doctrine. If it be necessary to say anything at all against so mere an assumption, we may say that the question depends upon what idea we have formed of the moral character of the Deity. If it be a true belief that God desires, above all things, the happiness of his creatures, and that this was his purpose in their creation, utility is not only not a godless doctrine, but more profoundly religious than any other. If it be meant that utilitarianism does not recognise the revealed will of God as the supreme law of morals, I answer, that a utilitarian who believes in the perfect goodness and wisdom of God, necessarily believes that whatever God has thought fit to reveal on the subject of morals, must fulfil the requirements of utility in a supreme degree. But others besides utilitarians have been of opinion that the Christian revelation was intended, and is fitted, to inform the hearts and minds of mankind with a spirit which should enable them to find for themselves what is right, and incline them to do it when found, rather than to tell them, except in a very general way, what it is; and that we need a doctrine of ethics, carefully followed out, to *interpret* to us the will of God. Whether this opinion is correct or not, it is superfluous here to discuss; since whatever aid religion, either natural or revealed, can afford to ethical investigation, is as open to the utilitarian moralist as to any other. He can use it as the testimony of God to the usefulness or hurtfulness of any given course of action, by as good a right as others can use it for the indication of a transcendental law, having no connexion with usefulness or with happiness.

Again, Utility is often summarily stigmatised as an immoral doctrine by giving it the name of Expediency, and taking advantage of the popular use of that term to contrast it with Principle. But the Expedient, in the sense in which it is opposed to the Right, generally means that which is expedient for the particular interest of the agent himself; as when a minister sacrifices the interests of his country to keep himself in place. When it means anything better than this, it means that which is expedient for some immediate object, some temporary purpose, but which violates a rule whose observance is expedient in a much higher degree. The Expedient, in this sense, instead of being the same thing with the useful, is a branch of the hurtful. Thus, it would often be expedient, for the purpose of getting over some momentary embarrassment, or attaining some object immediately useful to ourselves or others, to tell a lie. But inasmuch as the cultivation in ourselves of a sensitive feeling on the subject of veracity, is one of the most useful, and the enfeeblement of that feeling one of the most hurtful, things to which our conduct can be instrumental; and inasmuch as any, even unintentional, deviation from truth, does that much towards weakening the trustworthiness of human assertion, which is not only the principal support of all present social well-being, but the insufficiency of which does more than any one thing that can be named to keep back civilisation, virtue, everything on which human happiness on the largest scale depends: we feel that the violation, for a present advantage, of a rule of such transcendent expediency, is not expedient, and that he who, for the sake of a convenience to himself or to some other individual, does what depends on him to deprive mankind of the good, and inflict upon them the evil, involved in the greater or less reliance which they can place in each other's word, acts the part of one of their worst enemies. Yet that even this rule, sacred as it is,

admits of possible exceptions, is acknowledged by all moralists; the chief of which is when the withholding of some fact (as of information from a malefactor, or of bad news from a person dangerously ill) would save an individual (especially an individual other than oneself) from great and unmerited evil, and when the withholding can only be effected by denial. But in order that the exception may not extend itself beyond the need, and may have the least possible effect in weakening reliance on veracity, it ought to be recognised, and, if possible, its limits defined; and if the principle of utility is good for anything, it must be good for weighing these conflicting utilities against one another, and marking out the region within which one or the other preponderates.

Again, defenders of utility often find themselves called upon to reply to such objections as this—that there is not time, previous to action, for calculating and weighing the effects of any line of conduct on the general happiness. This is exactly as if any one were to say that it is impossible to guide our conduct by Christianity, because there is not time, on every occasion on which anything has to be done, to read through the Old and New Testaments. The answer to the objection is, that there has been ample time, namely, the whole past duration of the human species. During all that time, mankind have been learning by experience the tendencies of actions; on which experience all the prudence, as well as all the morality of life, are dependent. People talk as if the commencement of this course of experience had hitherto been put off, and as if, at the moment when some man feels tempted to meddle with the property or life of another, he had to begin considering for the first time whether murder and theft are injurious to human happiness. Even then I do not think that he would find the question very puzzling; but, at all events, the matter is now done to his hand. It is truly a whimsical supposition that, if mankind were agreed in considering utility to be the test of morality, they would remain without any agreement as to what *is* useful, and would take no measures for having their notions on the subject taught to the young, and enforced by law and opinion. There is no difficulty in proving any ethical standard whatever to work ill, if we suppose universal idiocy to be conjoined with it; but on any hypothesis short of that, mankind must by this time have acquired positive beliefs as to the effects of some actions on their happiness; and the beliefs which have thus come down are the rules of morality for the multitude, and for the philosopher until he has succeeded in finding better. That philosophers might easily do this, even now, on many subjects; that the received code of ethics is by no means of divine right; and that mankind have still much to learn as to the effects of actions on the general happiness, I admit, or rather, earnestly maintain. The corollaries from the principle of utility, like the precepts of every practical art, admit of indefinite improvement, and, in a progressive state of the human mind, their improvement is perpetually going on. But to consider the rules of morality as improvable, is one thing; to pass over the intermediate generalisations entirely, and endeavour to test each individual action directly by the first principle, is another. It is a strange notion that the acknowledgment of a first principle is inconsistent with the admission of secondary ones. To inform a traveller respecting the place of his ultimate destination, is not to forbid the use of landmarks and direction-posts on the way. The proposition that happiness is the end and aim of morality does not mean that no road ought to be laid down to that goal, or that persons going thither should not be advised to take one direction rather than another. Men really ought to leave off talking a kind of nonsense on this subject, which they would neither talk nor listen to on other matters of practical concernment. Nobody argues that the art of navigation is not founded on astronomy, because sailors cannot wait to calculate the Nautical Almanack. Being rational creatures, they go to sea with it ready calculated; and all rational creatures go out upon the sea of life with their minds made up on the common questions of right and wrong, as well as on many of the far more difficult questions of wise and foolish. And this, as long as foresight is a human quality, it is to be presumed they will continue to do. Whatever we adopt as the fundamental principle of morality, we require subordinate principles to apply it by; the impossibility of doing without them, being common to all systems, can afford no argument against any one in particular; but gravely to argue as if no such secondary principles could be had, and as if mankind had remained till now, and always must

remain, without drawing any general conclusions from the experience of human life, is as high a pitch, I think, as absurdity has ever reached in philosophical controversy.

The remainder of the stock arguments against utilitarianism mostly consist in laying to its charge the common infirmities of human nature, and the general difficulties which embarrass conscientious persons in shaping their course through life. We are told that a utilitarian will be apt to make his own particular case an exception to moral rules, and, when under temptation, will see a utility in the breach of a rule, greater than he will see in its observance. But is utility the only creed which is able to furnish us with excuses for evil doing, and means of cheating our own conscience? They are afforded in abundance by all doctrines which recognise as a fact in morals the existence of conflicting considerations; which all doctrines do, that have been believed by sane persons. It is not the fault of any creed, but of the complicated nature of human affairs, that rules of conduct cannot be so framed as to require no exceptions, and that hardly any kind of action can safely be laid down as either always obligatory or always condemnable. There is no ethical creed which does not temper the rigidity of its laws, by giving a certain latitude, under the moral responsibility of the agent, for accommodation to peculiarities of circumstances; and under every creed, at the opening thus made, self-deception and dishonest casuistry get in. There exists no moral system under which there do not arise unequivocal cases of conflicting obligations. These are the real difficulties, the knotty points both in the theory of ethics, and in the conscientious guidance of personal conduct. They are overcome practically, with greater or with less success, according to the intellect and virtue of the individual; but it can hardly be pretended that any one will be the less qualified for dealing with them, from possessing an ultimate standard to which conflicting rights and duties can be referred. If utility is the ultimate source of moral obligations, utility may be invoked to decide between them when their demands are incompatible. Though the application of the standard may be difficult, it is better than none at all; while in other systems, the moral laws all claiming independent authority, there is no common umpire entitled to interfere between them; their claims to precedence one over another rest on little better than sophistry, and unless determined, as they generally are, by the unacknowledged influence of considerations of utility, afford a free scope for the action of personal desires and partialities. We must remember that only in these cases of conflict between secondary principles is it requisite that first principles should be appealed to. There is no case of moral obligation in which some secondary principle is not involved; and if only one, there can seldom be any real doubt which one it is, in the mind of any person by whom the principle itself is recognised.

Chapter 3 Of the Ultimate Sanction of the Principle of Utility

The question is often asked, and properly so, in regard to any supposed moral standard—What is its sanction? what are the motives to obey it? or more specifically, what is the source of its obligation? whence does it derive its binding force? It is a necessary part of moral philosophy to provide the answer to this question; which, though frequently assuming the shape of an objection to the utilitarian morality, as if it had some special applicability to that above others, really arises in regard to all standards. It arises, in fact, whenever a person is called on to *adopt* a standard, or refer morality to any basis on which he has not been accustomed to rest it. For the customary morality, that which education and opinion have consecrated, is the only one which presents itself to the mind with the feeling of being *in itself* obligatory; and when a person is asked to believe that this morality *derives* its obligation from some general principle round which custom has not thrown the same halo, the assertion is to him a paradox; the supposed corollaries seem to have a more binding force than the original theorem; the superstructure seems to stand better without, than with, what is represented as its foundation. He says to himself, I feel that I am bound not to rob or murder, betray or deceive; but why am I bound to promote the general happiness? If my own happiness lies in something else, why may I not give that the preference?

If the view adopted by the utilitarian philosophy of the nature of the moral sense be correct, this difficulty will always present itself, until the influences which form moral character have taken the same hold of the principle which they have taken of some of the consequences—until, by the improvement of education, the feeling of unity with our fellow-creatures shall be (what it cannot be denied that Christ intended it to be) as deeply rooted in our character, and to our own consciousness as completely a part of our nature, as the horror of crime is in an ordinarily well brought up young person. In the meantime, however, the difficulty has no peculiar application to the doctrine of utility, but is inherent in every attempt to analyse morality and reduce it to principles; which, unless the principle is already in men's minds invested with as much sacredness as any of its applications, always seems to divest them of a part of their sanctity.

The principle of utility either has, or there is no reason why it might not have, all the sanctions which belong to any other system of morals. Those sanctions are either external or internal. Of the external sanctions it is not necessary to speak at any length. They are, the hope of favour and the fear of displeasure, from our fellow-creatures or from the Ruler of the Universe along with whatever we may have of sympathy or affection for them, or of love and awe of Him, inclining us to do His will independently of selfish consequences. There is evidently no reason why all these motives for observance should not attach themselves to the utilitarian morality, as completely and as powerfully as to any other. Indeed, those of them which refer to our fellow-creatures are sure to do so, in proportion to the amount of general intelligence; for whether there be any other ground of moral obligation than the general happiness or not, men do desire happiness; and however imperfect may be their own practice, they desire and commend all conduct in others towards themselves, by which they think their happiness is promoted. With regard to the religious motive, if men believe, as most profess to do, in the goodness of God, those who think that conduciveness to the general happiness is the essence, or even only the criterion of good, must necessarily believe that it is also that which God approves. The whole force therefore of external reward and punishment, whether physical or moral, and whether proceeding from God or from our fellow men, together with all that the capacities of human nature admit of disinterested devotion to either, become available to enforce the utilitarian morality, in proportion as that morality is recognised; and the more powerfully, the more the appliances of education and general cultivation are bent to the purpose.

So far as to external sanctions. The internal sanction of duty, whatever our standard of duty may be, is one and the same—a feeling in our own mind; a pain, more or less intense, attendant on violation of duty, which in properly cultivated moral natures rises, in the more serious cases, into shrinking from it as an impossibility. This feeling, when disinterested, and connecting itself with the pure idea of duty, and not with some particular form of it, or with any of the merely accessory circumstances, is the essence of Conscience; though in that complex phenomenon as it actually exists, the simple fact is in general all encrusted over with collateral associations, derived from sympathy, from love, and still more from fear; from all the forms of religious feeling; from the recollections of childhood and of all our past life; from self-esteem, desire of the esteem of others, and occasionally even self-abasement. This extreme complication is, I apprehend, the origin of the sort of mystical character which, by a tendency of the human mind of which there are many other examples, is apt to be attributed to the idea of moral obligation, and which leads people to believe that the idea cannot possibly attach itself to any other objects than those which, by a supposed mysterious law, are found in our present experience to excite it. Its binding force, however, consists in the existence of a mass of feeling which must be broken through in order to do what violates our standard of right, and which, if we do nevertheless violate that standard, will probably have to be encountered afterwards in the form of remorse. Whatever theory we have of the nature of origin of conscience, this is what essentially constitutes it.

The ultimate sanction, therefore, of all morality (external motives apart) being a subjective feeling in our own minds, I see nothing embarrassing to those whose standard is utility, in the question, what is the sanction of that particular standard? We may answer, the same as of all other moral standards—the conscientious feelings of mankind. Undoubtedly this sanction has no binding efficacy on those who do not possess the feelings it appeals to; but neither will these persons be more obedient to any other moral principle than to the utilitarian one. On them morality of any kind has no hold but through the external sanctions. Meanwhile the feelings exist, a fact in human nature, the reality of which, and the great power with which they are capable of acting on those in whom they have been duly cultivated, are proved by experience. No reason has ever been shown why they may not be cultivated to as great intensity in connexion with the utilitarian, as with any other rule of morals.

There is, I am aware, a disposition to believe that a person who sees in moral obligation a transcendental fact, an objective reality belonging to the province of "Things in themselves," is likely to be more obedient to it than one who believes it to be entirely subjective, having its seat in human consciousness only. But whatever a person's opinion may be on this point of Ontology, the force he is really urged by is his own subjective feeling, and is exactly measured by its strength. No one's belief that duty is an objective reality is stronger than the belief that God is so; yet the belief in God, apart from the expectation of actual reward and punishment, only operates on conduct through, and in proportion to, the subjective religious feeling. The sanction, so far as it is disinterested, is always in the mind itself; and the notion therefore of the transcendental moralists must be, that this sanction will not exist *in* the mind unless it is believed to have its root out of the mind; and that if a person is able to say to himself, This which is restraining me, and which is called my conscience, is only a feeling in my own mind, he may possibly draw the conclusion that when the feeling ceases the obligation ceases, and that if he find the feeling inconvenient, he may disregard it, and endeavour to get rid of it. But is this danger confined to the utilitarian morality? Does the belief that moral obligation has its seat outside the mind make the feeling of it too strong to be got rid of? The fact is so far otherwise, that all moralists admit and lament the ease with which, in the generality of minds, conscience can be silenced or stifled. The question, Need I obey my conscience? is quite as often put to themselves by persons who never heard of the principle of utility, as by its adherents. Those whose conscientious feelings are so weak as to allow of their asking this question, if they answer it affirmatively, will not do so because they believe in the transcendental theory, but because of the external sanctions.

It is not necessary, for the present purpose, to decide whether the feeling of duty is innate or implanted. Assuming it to be innate, it is an open question to what objects it naturally attaches itself; for the philosophic supporters of that theory are now agreed that the intuitive perception is of principles of morality and not of the details. If there be anything innate in the matter, I see no reason why the feeling which is innate should not be that of regard to the pleasures and pains of others. If there is any principle of morals which is intuitively obligatory, I should say it must be that. If so, the intuitive ethics would coincide with the utilitarian, and there would be no further quarrel between them. Even as it is, the intuitive moralists, though they believe that there are other intuitive moral obligations, do already believe this to be one; for they unanimously hold that a large *portion* of morality turns upon the consideration due to the interests of our fellow-creatures. Therefore, if the belief in the transcendental origin of moral obligation gives any additional efficacy to the internal sanction, it appears to me that the utilitarian principle has already the benefit of it.

On the other hand, if, as is my own belief, the moral feelings are not innate, but acquired, they are not for that reason the less natural. It is natural to man to speak, to reason, to build cities, to cultivate the ground, though these are acquired faculties. The moral feelings are not indeed a part of our nature, in the sense of being in any perceptible degree present in all of us; but this, unhappily, is a fact admitted by those who believe the most strenuously in their transcendental origin. Like the other acquired capacities above referred to, the moral faculty, if not a part of our nature, is a natural outgrowth from it; capable, like them, in a certain small degree, of springing up spontaneously; and susceptible of being brought by

cultivation to a high degree of development. Unhappily it is also susceptible, by a sufficient use of the external sanctions and of the force of early impressions, of being cultivated in almost any direction: so that there is hardly anything so absurd or so mischievous that it may not, by means of these influences, be made to act on the human mind with all the authority of conscience. To doubt that the same potency might be given by the same means to the principle of utility, even if it had no foundation in human nature, would be flying in the face of all experience.

But moral associations which are wholly of artificial creation, when intellectual culture goes on, yield by degrees to the dissolving force of analysis: and if the feeling of duty, when associated with utility, would appear equally arbitrary; if there were no leading department of our nature, no powerful class of sentiments, with which that association would harmonise, which would make us feel it congenial, and incline us not only to foster it in others (for which we have abundant interested motives), but also to cherish it in ourselves; if there were not, in short, a natural basis of sentiment for utilitarian morality, it might well happen that this association also, even after it had been implanted by education, might be analysed away.

But there *is* this basis of powerful natural sentiment; and this it is which, when once the general happiness is recognised as the ethical standard, will constitute the strength of the utilitarian morality. This firm foundation is that of the social feelings of mankind; the desire to be in unity with our fellow creatures, which is already a powerful principle in human nature, and happily one of those which tend to become stronger, even without express inculcation, from the influences of advancing civilisation. The social state is at once so natural, so necessary, and so habitual to man, that, except in some unusual circumstances or by an effort of voluntary abstraction, he never conceives himself otherwise than as a member of a body; and this association is riveted more and more, as mankind are further removed from the stage of savage independence. Any condition, therefore, which is essential to a state of society, becomes more and more an inseparable part of every person's conception of the state of things which he is born into, and which is the destiny of a human being. Now, society between human beings, except in the relation of master and slave, is manifestly impossible on any other footing than that the interests of all are to be consulted. Society between equals can only exist on the understanding that the interests of all are to be regarded equally. And since in all states of civilisation, every person, except an absolute monarch, has equals, every one is obliged to live on these terms with somebody; and in every age some advance is made towards a state in which it will be impossible to live permanently on other terms with anybody. In this way people grow up unable to conceive as possible to them a state of total disregard of other people's interests. They are under a necessity of conceiving themselves as at least abstaining from all the grosser injuries, and (if only for their own protection) living in a state of constant protest against them. They are also familiar with the fact of co-operating with others, and proposing to themselves a collective, not an individual interest as the aim (at least for the time being) of their actions. So long as they are co-operating, their ends are identified with those of others; there is at least a temporary feeling that the interests of others are their own interests. Not only does all strengthening of social ties, and all healthy growth of society, give to each individual a stronger personal interest in practically consulting the welfare of others; it also leads him to identify his *feelings* more and more with their good, or at least with an even greater degree of practical consideration for it. He comes, as though instinctively, to be conscious of himself as a being who *of course* pays regard to others. The good of others becomes to him a thing naturally and necessarily to be attended to, like any of the physical conditions of our existence. Now, whatever amount of this feeling a person has, he is urged by the strongest motives both of interest and of sympathy to demonstrate it, and to the utmost of his power encourage it in others; and even if he has none of it himself, he is as greatly interested as any one else that others should have it. Consequently the smallest germs of the feeling are laid hold of and nourished by the contagion of sympathy and the influences of education; and a complete web of corroborative association is woven round it, by the powerful agency of the external

sanctions. This mode of conceiving ourselves and human life, as civilisation goes on, is felt to be more and more natural. Every step in political improvement renders it more so, by removing the sources of opposition of interest, and levelling those inequalities of legal privilege between individuals or classes, owing to which there are large portions of mankind whose happiness it is still practicable to disregard. In an improving state of the human mind, the influences are constantly on the increase, which tend to generate in each individual a feeling of unity with all the rest; which, if perfect, would make him never think of, or desire, any beneficial condition for himself, in the benefits of which they are not included. If we now suppose this feeling of unity to be taught as a religion, and the whole force of education, of institutions, and of opinion, directed, as it once was in the case of religion, to make every person grow up from infancy surrounded on all sides both by the profession and the practice of it, I think that no one, who can realise this conception, will feel any misgiving about the sufficiency of the ultimate sanction for the Happiness morality. To any ethical student who finds the realisation difficult, I recommend, as a means of facilitating it, the second of M. Comte's two principal works, the *Traité de politique positive*. I entertain the strongest objections to the system of politics and morals set forth in that treatise; but I think it has superabundantly shown the possibility of giving to the service of humanity, even without the aid of belief in a Providence, both the psychological power and the social efficacy of a religion; making it take hold of human life, and colour all thought, feeling, and action, in a manner of which the greatest ascendancy ever exercised by any religion may be but a type and foretaste; and of which the danger is, not that it should be insufficient, but that it should be so excessive as to interfere unduly with human freedom and individuality.

Neither is it necessary to the feeling which constitutes the binding force of the utilitarian morality on those who recognise it, to wait for those social influences which would make its obligation felt by mankind at large. In the comparatively early state of human advancement in which we now live, a person cannot indeed feel that entireness of sympathy with all others, which would make any real discordance in the general direction of their conduct in life impossible; but already a person in whom the social feeling is at all developed, cannot bring himself to think of the rest of his fellow-creatures as struggling rivals with him for the means of happiness, whom he must desire to see defeated in their object in order that he may succeed in his. The deeply rooted conception which every individual even now has of himself as a social being, tends to make him feel it one of his natural wants that there should be harmony between his feelings and aims and those of his fellow-creatures. If differences of opinion and of mental culture make it impossible for him to share many of their actual feelings—perhaps make him denounce and defy those feelings—he still needs to be conscious that his real aim and theirs do not conflict; that he is not opposing himself to what they really wish for, namely their own good, but is, on the contrary, promoting it. This feeling in most individuals is much inferior in strength to their selfish feelings, and is often wanting altogether. But to those who have it, it possesses all the characters of a natural feeling. It does not present itself to their minds as a superstition of education, or a law despotically imposed by the power of society, but as an attribute which it would not be well for them to be without. This conviction is the ultimate sanction of the greatest happiness morality. This it is which makes any mind, of well-developed feelings, work with, and not against, the outward motives to care for others, afforded by what I have called the external sanctions; and when those sanctions are wanting, or act in an opposite direction, constitutes in itself a powerful internal binding force, in proportion to the sensitiveness and thoughtfulness of the character; since few but those whose mind is a moral blank, could bear to lay out their course of life on the plan of paying no regard to others except so far as their own private interest compels.

Chapter 4 Of What Sort of Proof the Principle of Utility is Susceptible

It has already been remarked, that questions of ultimate ends do not admit of proof, in the ordinary acceptation of the term. To be incapable of proof by reasoning is common to all first principles; to the first premises of our knowledge, as well as to those of our conduct. But the former, being matters of fact, may be the subject of a direct appeal to the faculties which judge of fact—namely, our senses, and our internal consciousness. Can an appeal be made to the same faculties on questions of practical ends? Or by what other faculty is cognisance taken of them?

Questions about ends are, in other words questions about what things are desirable. The utilitarian doctrine is, that happiness is desirable, and the only thing desirable, as an end; all other things being only desirable as means to that end. What ought to be required of this doctrine—what conditions is it requisite that the doctrine should fulfil—to make good its claim to be believed?

The only proof capable of being given that an object is visible, is that people actually see it. The only proof that a sound is audible, is that people hear it: and so of the other sources of our experience. In like manner, I apprehend, the sole evidence it is possible to produce that anything is desirable, is that people do actually desire it. If the end which the utilitarian doctrine proposes to itself were not, in theory and in practice, acknowledged to be an end, nothing could ever convince any person that it was so. No reason can be given why the general happiness is desirable, except that each person, so far as he believes it to be attainable, desires his own happiness. This, however, being a fact, we have not only all the proof which the case admits of, but all which it is possible to require, that happiness is a good: that each person's happiness is a good to that person, and the general happiness, therefore, a good to the aggregate of all persons. Happiness has made out its title as *one* of the ends of conduct, and consequently one of the criteria of morality.

But it has not, by this alone, proved itself to be the sole criterion. To do that, it would seem, by the same rule, necessary to show, not only that people desire happiness, but that they never desire anything else. Now it is palpable that they do desire things which, in common language, are decidedly distinguished from happiness. They desire, for example, virtue, and the absence of vice, no less really than pleasure and the absence of pain. The desire of virtue is not as universal, but it is as authentic a fact, as the desire of happiness. And hence the opponents of the utilitarian standard deem that they have a right to infer that there are other ends of human action besides happiness, and that happiness is not the standard of approbation and disapprobation.

But does the utilitarian doctrine deny that people desire virtue, or maintain that virtue is not a thing to be desired? The very reverse. It maintains not only that virtue is to be desired, but that it is to be desired disinterestedly, for itself. Whatever may be the opinion of utilitarian moralists as to the original conditions by which virtue is made virtue; however they may believe (as they do) that actions and dispositions are only virtuous because they promote another end than virtue; yet this being granted, and it having been decided, from considerations of this description, what *is* virtuous, they not only place virtue at the very head of the things which are good as means to the ultimate end, but they also recognize as a psychological fact the possibility of its being, to the individual, a good in itself, without looking to any end beyond it; and, hold, that the mind is not in a right state, not a state conformable to Utility, not in the state most conducive to the general happiness, unless it does love virtue in this manner—as a thing desirable in itself, even although, in the individual instance, it should not produce those other desirable consequences which it tends to produce, and on account of which it is held to be virtue. This opinion is not, in the smallest degree, a departure from the Happiness principle. The ingredients of happiness are very various, and each of them is desirable in itself, and not merely when considered as swelling an aggregate. The principle of utility does not mean that any given pleasure, as music, for instance, or any given exemption from pain, as for example health, is to be looked upon as means to a collective something termed happiness, and to be desired on that account. They are desired and desirable in and for themselves; besides being means, they are a part of the end. Virtue, according to the utilitarian doctrine, is not naturally and originally part of the end, but it is capable of becoming so; and in those who love it disinterestedly it has become so, and is desired and cherished, not as a means to happiness, but as a part of their happiness.

To illustrate this farther, we may remember that virtue is not the only thing, originally a means, and which if it were not a means to anything else, would be and remain indifferent, but which by association with what it is a means to, comes to be desired for itself, and that too with the utmost intensity. What, for example, shall we say of the love of money? There is nothing originally more desirable about money than about any heap of glittering pebbles. Its worth is solely that of the things which it will buy; the desires for other things than itself, which it is a means of gratifying. Yet the love of money is not only one of the strongest moving forces of human life, but money is, in many cases, desired in and for itself; the desire to possess it is often stronger than the desire to use it, and goes on increasing when all the desires which point to ends beyond it, to be compassed by it, are falling off. It may, then, be said truly, that money is desired not for the sake of an end, but as part of the end. From being a means to happiness, it has come to be itself a principal ingredient of the individual's conception of happiness. The same may be said of the majority of the great objects of human life—power, for example, or fame; except that to each of these there is a certain amount of immediate pleasure annexed, which has at least the semblance of being naturally inherent in them; a thing which cannot be said of money. Still, however, the strongest natural attraction, both of power and of fame, is the immense aid they give to the attainment of our other wishes; and it is the strong association thus generated between them and all our objects of desire, which gives to the direct desire of them the intensity it often assumes, so as in some characters to surpass in strength all other desires. In these cases the means have become a part of the end, and a more important part of it than any of the things which they are means to. What was once desired as an instrument for the attainment of happiness, has come to be desired for its own sake. In being desired for its own sake it is, however, desired as *part* of happiness. The person is made, or thinks he would be made, happy by its mere possession; and is made unhappy by failure to obtain it. The desire of it is not a different thing from the desire of happiness, any more than the love of music, or the desire of health. They are included in happiness. They are some of the elements of which the desire of happiness is made up. Happiness is not an abstract idea, but a concrete whole; and these are some of its parts. And the utilitarian standard sanctions and approves their being so. Life would be a poor thing, very ill provided with sources of happiness, if there were not this provision of nature, by which things originally indifferent, but conducive to, or otherwise associated with, the satisfaction of our primitive desires, become in themselves sources of pleasure more valuable than the primitive pleasures, both in permanency, in the space of human existence that they are capable of covering, and even in intensity.

Virtue, according to the utilitarian conception, is a good of this description. There was no original desire of it, or motive to it, save its conduciveness to pleasure, and especially to protection from pain. But through the association thus formed, it may be felt a good in itself, and desired as such with as great intensity as any other good; and with this difference between it and the love of money, of power, or of fame, that all of these may, and often do, render the individual noxious to the other members of society to which he belongs, whereas there is nothing which makes him so much a blessing to them as the cultivation of the disinterested love of virtue. And consequently, the utilitarian standard, while it tolerates and approves those other acquired desires, up to the point beyond which they would be more injurious to the general happiness than promotive of it, enjoins and requires the cultivation of the love of virtue up to the greatest strength possible, as being above all things important to the general happiness.

It results from the preceding considerations, that there is in reality nothing desired except happiness. Whatever is desired otherwise than as a means to some end beyond itself, and ultimately to happiness, is desired as itself a part of happiness, and is not desired for itself until it has become so. Those who desire virtue for its own sake, desire it either because the consciousness of it is a pleasure, or because the consciousness of being without it is a pain, or for both reasons united; as in truth the pleasure and pain seldom exist separately, but almost always together, the same person feeling pleasure in degree of virtue attained, and pain in not having attained more. If one of these give him no pleasure, and the other no pain, he would not love or desire virtue, or would desire it only for the other benefits which it might produce to himself or to persons whom he cared for.

We have now, then, an answer to the question, of what sort of proof the principle of utility is susceptible. If the opinion which I have now stated is psychologically true—if human nature is so constituted as to desire nothing which is not either a part of happiness or a means of happiness, we can have no other proof, and we require no other, that these are the only things desirable. If so, happiness is the sole end of human action, and the promotion of it the test by which to judge of all human conduct; from whence it necessarily follows that it must be the criterion of morality, since a part is included in the whole.

And now to decide whether this is really so; whether mankind do desire nothing for itself but that which is a pleasure to them or of which the absence is a pain; we have evidently arrived at a question of fact and experience, dependent, like all similar questions, upon evidence. It can only be determined by practised self-consciousness and self-observation, assisted by observation of others. I believe that these sources of evidence, impartially consulted, will declare that desiring a thing and finding it pleasant, aversion to it and thinking of it as painful, are phenomena entirely inseparable, or rather two parts of the same phenomenon; in strictness of language, two different modes of naming the same psychological fact: that to think of an object as desirable (unless for the sake of its consequences), and to think of it as pleasant, are one and the same thing; and that to desire anything, except in proportion as the idea of it is pleasant, is a physical and metaphysical impossibility.

So obvious does this appear to me, that I expect it will hardly be disputed: and the objection made will be, not that desire can possibly be directed to anything ultimately except pleasure and exemption from pain, but that the will is a different thing from desire; that a person of confirmed virtue, or any other person whose purposes are fixed, carries out his purposes without any thought of the pleasure he has in contemplating them, or expects to derive from their fulfilment; and persists in acting on them, enough though these pleasures are much diminished, by changes in his character or decay of his passive sensibilities, or are outweighed by the pains which the pursuit of the purposes may bring upon him. All this I fully admit, and have stated it elsewhere, as positively and emphatically as any one. Will, the active phenomenon, is a different thing from desire, the state of passive sensibility, and though originally an offshoot from it, may in time take root and detach itself from the parent stock; so much so, that in the case of an habitual purpose, instead of willing the thing because we desire it, we often desire it only because we will it. This, however, is but an instance of that familiar fact, the power of habit, and is nowise confined to the case of virtuous actions. Many indifferent things, which men originally did from a motive of some sort, they continue to do from habit. Sometimes this is done unconsciously, the consciousness coming only after the action; at other times with conscious volition, but volition which has become habitual, and is put in operation by the force of habit, in opposition perhaps to the deliberate preference, as often happens with those who have contracted habits of vicious or hurtful indulgence. Third and last comes the case in which the habitual act of will in the individual instance is not in contradiction to the general intention prevailing at other times, but in fulfilment of it; as in the case of the person of confirmed virtue, and of all who pursue deliberately and consistently any determinate end. The distinction between will and desire thus understood is an authentic and highly important psychological fact; but the fact consists solely in this—that will, like all other parts of our constitution, is amenable to habit, and that we may will from habit what we no longer desire for itself, or desire only because we will it. It is not the less true that will, in the beginning, is entirely produced by desire; including in that term the repelling influence of pain as well as the attractive one of pleasure. Let us take into consideration, no longer the person who has a confirmed will to do right, but him in whom that virtuous will is still feeble, conquerable by temptation, and not to be fully relied on; by what means can it be strengthened? How can the will to be virtuous, where it does not exist in sufficient force, be implanted or awakened? Only by making the person *desire* virtue—by making him think of it in a pleasurable light, or of its absence in a painful one. It is by associating the doing right with pleasure, or the doing wrong with pain, or by eliciting and impressing and bringing home to the person's experience the pleasure naturally involved in the one or the pain in the other, that it is possible to call forth that will to be virtuous, which, when confirmed, acts without any thought of either pleasure or pain. Will is the child of desire, and passes out of the dominion of its parent only to come under that of habit. That which is the result of habit affords no presumption of being intrinsically good; and there would be no reason for wishing that the purpose of virtue should become independent of pleasure and pain, were it not that the influence of the pleasurable and painful associations which prompt to virtue is not sufficiently to be depended on for unerring constancy of action until it has acquired the support of habit. Both in feeling and in conduct, habit is the only thing which imparts certainty; and it is because of the importance to others of being able to rely absolutely on one's feelings and conduct, and to oneself of being able to rely on one's own, that the will to do right ought to be cultivated into this habitual independence. In other words, this state of the will is a means to good, not intrinsically a good; and does not contradict the doctrine that nothing is a good to human beings but in so far as it is either itself pleasurable, or a means of attaining pleasure or averting pain.

But if this doctrine be true, the principle of utility is proved. Whether it is so or not, must now be left to the consideration of the thoughtful reader.

KEY TERMS

Utilitarianism
Greatest Happiness Principle
Intrinsic

STUDY QUESTIONS

1. What does Mill mean when he says that "questions of ultimate ends are not amenable to direct proof"?
2. According to Mill, what grounds the theory of utilitarianism is the view that "pleasure, and freedom from pain, are the only things desirable as ends; and that all desirable things . . . are desirable either for the pleasure inherent in themselves, or as means to the promotion of pleasure and the prevention of pain." Do you agree with this view? Can you think of anything else that might be desirable as an end?
3. Mill distinguishes the *quantity* of pleasures from their *quality*. What sorts of pleasures are of a higher quality? What about them makes them more worthwhile?
4. According to Mill, what is the ultimate sanction of all morality? Do you think he is right about this? Why doesn't this pose a problem for utilitarianism?
5. What sort of "proof" does Mill offer in favor of utilitarianism? Do you find it convincing?

Criticisms of Utilitarianism

E. F. CARRITT

E. F. Carritt (1876–1964) was a Fellow of University College, Oxford. His publications include The Theory of Morals: An Introduction to Ethical Philosophy.

· ·

1. One criticism frequently brought against **utilitarianism** seems to me invalid. It is said that pleasures and pains cannot be measured or weighed like proteins or money and therefore cannot be compared, so that I can never tell whether I shall produce an overbalance of pleasure in this way or in that. I cannot weigh the pleasure of a starving man whom I feed on bread against my own in eating strawberries and say that his is twice as great as mine. Such an argument might seem hardly worth serious discussion had it not been used in defence of applying to conduct a theory of abstract economics: "There is no scientific criterion which would enable us to compare or assess the relative importance of needs of different persons . . . illegitimate interpersonal comparison,"[1] and "There is no means of testing the magnitude of A's satisfaction as compared with B's."[2]

But this argument, though those who use it are not ready to admit so much, really should apply against any comparison of my own desires and needs. I cannot say that two glasses of beer will give me twice as much pleasure as one, and still less that hearing a concert will give me three times or half as much: yet I may know very well indeed which will give me *more*, and may act upon the knowledge, since the two things though not measurable are comparable. It is true that, not being measurable, they are less easy to discriminate precisely, where the difference is not great, than physical objects; I may be unable to say whether the smell of roasting coffee or of bacon fried gives me the greater pleasure (mixed with some pain of appetite) even at two

successive moments. It is no doubt often easier to read off the luminosity of two very similar surfaces on a pointer than to say which looks brighter, though in the end I have to trust my eyes for the pointer. As we have admitted, the mere existence of other minds is not demonstrable, still less is the intensity of their desires. But if in self-regarding acts I am sometimes prepared to spend my money in the belief that I shall desire to-morrow's bread more than to-morrow's jam, the utilitarian is justified, on his principles, in believing that it is his duty to provide bread for the starving sooner than jam for the well fed.

In fact it would be no commendation of an ethical theory if, on its showing, moral or even beneficent choice were always clear, since in practice we know that it is not. We often wonder if we can do more for the happiness, even the immediate happiness, of our parents or of our children; the former seem more in need of enjoyments, the latter have a keener capacity but a quicker recovery from disappointment. Utilitarianism has no need to stake its case on the possibility of an accurate "**hedonistic** (or agathistic) calculus." We have a well-founded belief that starvation hurts most people more than a shortage of grapefruit, and *no knowledge how much* more it will hurt even ourselves to-morrow; and it is on such beliefs that we have to act; we can never know either our objective duty or our objective long-run interest.

2. The second objection to the utilitarians is serious and indeed fatal. They make no room for justice. Most of them readily admitted this when they found it hard on their principle to allow for the admitted obligation to distribute happiness "fairly," that is either equally or in proportion to desert. This led them to qualify their definition of duty as "promoting the greatest amount of happiness," by adding "of the greatest number," and to emphasize this by the proviso "every one count for one and no more."

They can hardly have meant by this merely that it did not matter to whom I gave the happiness so long as I produced the most possible, for this they had already implied. They must at least have meant that if I could produce the same amount either in equal shares or in unequal I ought to prefer the former; and this means that I ought to be just as well as generous. The other demand of justice, that we should take account of past merit in our distribution, I think they would have denied, or rather explained away by the argument that to reward beneficence was to encourage such behaviour by example, and therefore a likely way to increase the total of happiness.

3. A third criticism, incurred by some utilitarians[3] in the attempt to accommodate their theory to our moral judgements, was that of inconsistency in considering differences of quality or kind, as well as of amount, among pleasures when determining what we ought to do. It seems clear that people do not feel the same obligation to endow the art of cookery or pot-boiling as that of poetry or music, and this not because they are convinced that the one causes keener and more constant pleasure to a greater number than the other. Yet the recognition of a stronger obligation to promote "higher" or "better" pleasures implies that we think something good, say musical or poetic experience, not merely in proportion to its general pleasantness but by its own nature. The attempt to unite this "qualification of pleasures" with hedonistic utilitarianism is like saying 'I care about nothing but money, but I would not come by it dishonestly.' The fundamental fact is that we do not think some pleasures, such as that of cruelty, good at all.

4. Though the inconsistency of modifying their theory in these two ways seems to have escaped the notice of most utilitarians, they could not help seeing that they were bound to meet a fourth criticism by giving some account of the universal belief that we have obligations to keep our promises. It is obvious that the payment of money to a rich creditor may not immediately result in so much satisfaction as the keeping of it by a poor debtor or the giving of it to a useful charity, and that yet it may, under most circumstances, be judged a duty and always an obligation. The argument of utilitarians to explain this has usually been as follows: It is true that a particular instance of justice may not directly increase the sum of human happiness but quite the contrary, and yet we often approve such an instance. This is because the *general* practice of such good faith, with the consequent possibility of credit and contract, is supremely conducive to happiness, and therefore so far as any violation of a bargain impairs this confidence, it is, indirectly and in the long run, pernicious.

Such an attempt to bring promise-keeping under the utilitarian formula breaks down because it only applies where the promise and its performance or neglect would be public and therefore serve as an example to others.

Suppose the two explorers in the Arctic have only enough food to keep one alive till he can reach the base, and one offers to die if the other will promise to educate his children. No other person can know that such a promise was made, and the breaking or keeping of it cannot influence the future keeping of promises. On the utilitarian theory, then, its the duty of the returned traveller to act precisely as he ought to have acted if no bargain had been made: to consider how he can spend his money most expediently for the happiness of mankind, and, if he thinks his own child is a genius, to spend it upon him.

Or, to take a different kind of justice, the utilitarian must hold that we are justified in inflicting pain always and only in order to prevent worse pain or bring about greater happiness. This, then, is all we need consider in so-called punishment, which must be purely preventive. But if some kind of very cruel crime becomes common, and none of the criminals can be caught, it might be highly expedient, as an example, to hang an innocent man, if a charge against him could be so framed that he were universally thought guilty; indeed this would only fail to be an ideal instance of utilitarian "punishment" because the victim himself would not have been so likely as a real felon to commit such a crime in the future, in all other respects it would be perfectly deterrent and therefore felicific.

In short, utilitarianism has forgotten rights; it allows no right to a man because he is innocent or because he has worked hard or has been promised or injured, or because he stands in any other special relation to us. It thinks only of duties or rather of a single duty, to dump happiness wherever we most conveniently can. If it speaks of rights at all it could only say all men have one and the same right, namely that all men should try to increase the total happiness. And this is a manifest misuse of language.

NOTES

1. Hayek, *Collectivist Economic Planning*, p. 25.
2. Robbins, *Nature and Significance of Economic Science*, pp. 122–4. Cf. Jay, *The Socialist Case*, ch. 2.
3. E.g., J. S. Mill. Bentham more consistently held that "the pleasure of push-pin is as good as the pleasure of poetry."

KEY TERMS

Utilitarianism
Hedonistic

STUDY QUESTIONS

1. How does Carritt use the terms "measurable" and "comparable" to respond to the first objection against utilitarianism? Do you find his response satisfactory?
2. Why does Carritt think that the utilitarian cannot account for justice?
3. Does the utilitarian's appeal to higher and lower pleasures show that something more than just pleasure is desirable as an end (against what Mill claims)?
4. Can you think of a circumstance (besides the ones mentioned by Carritt) in which someone would be forced to do something morally wrong by attempting to follow the dictates of utilitarianism? How might a utilitarian respond to such scenarios?

Extreme and Restricted Utilitarianism

J. J. C. SMART

J. J. C. Smart (1920–2012) wrote *Philosophy and Scientific Realism*, *Between Science and Philosophy*, and *Ethics, Persuasion and Truth*. He was a Professor of Philosophy at the University of Adelaide and at Australian National University.

. .

I

Utilitarianism is the doctrine that the rightness of actions is to be judged by their consequences. What do we mean by "actions" here? Do we mean particular actions or do we mean classes of actions? According to which way we interpret the word

From *Theories of Ethics*, ed. Philippa Foot (Oxford: Oxford University Press, 1967), pp. 171–83.

Based on a paper read to the Victorian Branch of the Australasian Association of Psychology and Philosophy, October 1955. [The article is discussed in J. H. McCloskey, "An Examination of Restricted Utilitarianism" *Philosophical Review* (1957); also by D. Lyons, *Forms and Limits of Utilitarianism* (Clarendon Press, Oxford, 1965). Ed. *(in original)*]

"actions" we get two different theories, both of which merit the appellation "utilitarian."

1. If by "actions" we mean particular individual actions we get the sort of doctrine held by Bentham, Sidgwick, and Moore. According to this doctrine we test individual actions by their consequences, and general rules, like "keep promises," are mere rules of thumb which we use only to avoid the necessity of estimating the probable consequences of our actions at every step. The rightness or wrongness of keeping a promise on a particular occasion depends only on the goodness or badness of the consequences of keeping or of breaking the promise on that particular occasion. Of course part of the consequences of breaking the promise, and a part to which we will normally ascribe decisive importance, will be the weakening of faith in the institution of promising.

However, if the goodness of the consequences of breaking the rule is *in toto* greater than the goodness of the consequences of keeping it, then we must break the rule, irrespective of whether the goodness of the consequences of *everybody's* obeying the rule is or is not greater than the consequences of *everybody's* breaking it. To put it shortly, rules do not matter, save *per accidens* as rules of thumb and as *de facto* social institutions with which the utilitarian has to reckon when estimating consequences. I shall call this doctrine "extreme utilitarianism."

2. A more modest form of utilitarianism has recently become fashionable. The doctrine is to be found in Toulmin's book *The Place of Reason in Ethics*, in Nowell-Smith's *Ethics* (though I think Nowell-Smith has qualms), in John Austin's *Lectures on Jurisprudence* (Lecture II), and even in J. S. Mill, if Urmson's interpretation of him is correct (*Philosophical Quarterly*, Vol. 3, pp. 3–39, 1953). Part of its charm is that it appears to resolve the dispute in moral philosophy between intuitionists and utilitarians in a way which is very neat. The above philosophers hold, or seem to hold, that moral rules are more than rules of thumb. In general the rightness of an action is *not* to be tested by evaluating its consequences but only by considering whether or not it falls under a certain rule. Whether the rule is to be considered an acceptable moral rule, is, however, to be decided by considering the consequences of adopting the rule. Broadly, then, actions are to be tested by rules and rules by consequences. The only cases in which we must test an individual action directly by its consequences are (*a*) when the action comes under two different rules, one of which enjoins it and one of which forbids it, and (*b*) when there is no rule whatever that governs the given case. I shall call this doctrine "restricted utilitarianism."

It should be noticed that the distinction I am making cuts across, and is quite different from, the distinction commonly made between **hedonistic** and ideal utilitarianism. Bentham was an extreme hedonistic utilitarian and Moore an extreme ideal utilitarian, and Toulmin (perhaps) could be classified as a restricted ideal utilitarian. A hedonistic utilitarian holds that the goodness of the consequences of an action is a function only of their pleasurableness and an ideal utilitarian, like Moore, holds that pleasurableness is not even a necessary condition of goodness. Mill seems, if we are to take his remarks about higher and lower pleasures seriously, to be neither a pure hedonistic nor a pure ideal utilitarian. He seems to hold that pleasurableness is a necessary condition for goodness, but that goodness is a function of other qualities of mind as well. Perhaps we can call him a quasi-ideal utilitarian. When we say that a state of mind is good I take it that we are expressing some sort of *rational preference*. When we say that it is pleasurable I take it that we are saying that it is enjoyable, and when we say that something is a higher pleasure I take it that we are saying that it is more truly, or more deeply, enjoyable. I am doubtful whether "more deeply enjoyable" does not just mean "more enjoyable, even though not more enjoyable on a first look," and so I am doubtful whether quasi-ideal utilitarianism, and possibly ideal utilitarianism too, would not collapse into hedonistic utilitarianism on a closer scrutiny of the logic of words like "preference," "pleasure," "enjoy," "deeply enjoy," and so on. However, it is beside the point of the present paper to go into these questions. I am here concerned only with the issue between extreme and restricted utilitarianism and am ready to concede that both forms of utilitarianism can be either hedonistic or non-hedonistic.

The issue between extreme and restricted utilitarianism can be illustrated by considering the remark "But suppose everyone did the same." (Cf. A. K. Stout's article in *The Australasian Journal of Philosophy*, Vol. 32, pp. 1–29.) Stout distinguishes two forms of the universalization principle, the causal form and the hypothetical form. To say that you ought not to do an action A because it would have bad results if everyone (or many people) did action A may be merely to point out that while the action A would otherwise be the optimific one, nevertheless when you take into account that doing A will probably cause other people to do A too, you can see that A is not, on a broad view, really optimific. If this causal influence could be avoided (as may happen in the case of a secret desert island promise) then we would disregard the universalization principle. This is the causal form of the principle. A person who accepted the universalization principle in its hypothetical form would be one who was concerned only with what would happen *if* everyone did the action A: he would be totally unconcerned with the question of whether in fact everyone would do the action A. That is, he might say that it would be wrong not to vote because it would have bad results if everyone took this attitude, and he would be totally unmoved by arguments purporting to show that my refusing to vote has no effect whatever on other people's propensity to vote. Making use of Stout's distinction, we can say that an extreme utilitarian would apply the universalization principle in the causal form, while a restricted utilitarian would apply it in the hypothetical form.

How are we to decide the issue between extreme and restricted utilitarianism? I wish to repudiate at the outset that milk and water approach which describes itself sometimes as "investigating what is implicit in the common moral consciousness" and sometimes as "investigating how people ordinarily talk about morality." We have only to read the newspaper correspondence about capital punishment or about what should be done with Formosa to realize that the common moral consciousness is in part made up of superstitious elements, of morally bad elements, and of logically confused elements. I address myself to good hearted and benevolent people and so I hope that if we rid ourselves of the logical confusion the superstitious and morally bad elements will largely fall away. For even among good hearted and benevolent people it is possible to find superstitious and morally bad reasons for moral beliefs. These superstitious and morally bad reasons hide behind the protective screen of logical confusion. With people who are not logically confused but who are openly superstitious or morally bad I can of course do nothing. That is, our ultimate pro-attitudes may be different. Nevertheless I propose to rely on *my own* moral consciousness and to appeal to *your* moral consciousness and to forget about what people ordinarily say. "The obligation to obey a rule," says Nowell-Smith (*Ethics*, p. 239), "does not, *in the opinion of ordinary men*," (my italics), "rest on the beneficial consequences of obeying it in a particular case." What does this prove? Surely it is more than likely that ordinary men are confused here. Philosophers should be able to examine the question more rationally.

II

For an extreme utilitarian moral rules are rules of thumb. In practice the extreme utilitarian will mostly guide his conduct by appealing to the rules ("do not lie," "do not break promises," etc.) of common-sense morality. This is not because there is anything sacrosanct in the rules themselves but because he can argue that probably he will most often act in an extreme utilitarian way if he does not think as a utilitarian. For one thing, actions have frequently to be done in a hurry. Imagine a man seeing a person drowning. He jumps in and rescues him. There is no time to reason the matter out, but usually this will be the course of action which an extreme utilitarian would recommend if he did reason the matter out. If, however, the man drowning had been drowning in a river near Berchtesgaden in 1938, and if he had had the well-known black forelock and moustache of Adolf Hitler, an extreme utilitarian would, if he had time, work out the probability of the man's being the villainous dictator, and if the probability were high enough he would, on extreme utilitarian grounds, leave him to drown. The rescuer, however, has not time. He trusts to his instincts and dives in and rescues the man. And this trusting to instincts and to moral rules can be justified on extreme utilitarian grounds. Furthermore, an extreme utilitarian who knew that the drowning man was Hitler would nevertheless praise the rescuer, not condemn him. For by praising the man he is strengthening a courageous and benevolent disposition of mind, and in general this disposition has great positive utility. (Next time, perhaps, it will be Winston Churchill that the man saves!) We must never forget that an extreme utilitarian may praise actions which he knows to be wrong. Saving Hitler was wrong, but it was a member of a class of actions which are generally right, and the motive to do actions of this class is in general an optimific one. In considering questions of praise and blame it is not the expediency of the praised or blamed action that is at issue, but the expediency of the praise. It can be expedient to praise an inexpedient action and inexpedient to praise an expedient one.

Lack of time is not the only reason why an extreme utilitarian may, on extreme utilitarian principles, trust to rules of common-sense morality. He knows that in particular cases where his own interests are involved his calculations are likely to be biased in his own favour. Suppose that he is unhappily married and is deciding whether to get divorced. He will in all probability greatly exaggerate his own unhappiness (and possibly his wife's) and greatly underestimate the harm done to his children by the break up of the family. He will probably also underestimate the likely harm done by the weakening of the general faith in marriage vows. So probably he will come to the correct extreme utilitarian conclusion if he does not in this instance think as an extreme utilitarian but trusts to common-sense morality.

There are many more and subtle points that could be made in connexion with the relation between extreme utilitarianism and the morality of common sense. All those that I have just made and many more will be found in Book IV Chapters 3–5 of Sidgwick's *Methods of Ethics*. I think that this book is the best book ever written on ethics, and that these chapters are the best chapters of the book. As they occur so near the end of a very long book they are unduly neglected. I refer the reader, then, to Sidgwick for the classical exposition of the relation between (extreme) utilitarianism and the morality of common sense. One further point raised by Sidgwick in this connexion is whether an (extreme) utilitarian ought on (extreme) utilitarian principles to propagate (extreme) utilitarianism among the public. As most people are not very philosophical and not good at empirical calculations, it is probable that they will most often act in an extreme utilitarian way if they do not try to think as extreme utilitarians. We have seen how easy it would be to misapply the extreme utilitarian criterion in the case of divorce. Sidgwick seems to think it quite probable that an extreme utilitarian should not propagate his doctrine too widely. However, the great danger to humanity comes nowadays on the plane of public morality—not private morality. There is a greater danger to humanity from the hydrogen bomb than from an increase of the divorce rate, regrettable though that might be, and there seems no doubt that extreme utilitarianism makes for good sense in international relations. When France walked out of the United Nations because she did not wish

Morocco discussed, she said that she was within her rights because Morocco and Algiers are part of her metropolitan territory and nothing to do with U.N. This was clearly a legalistic if not superstitious argument. We should not be concerned with the so-called "rights" of France or any other country but with whether the cause of humanity would best be served by discussing Morocco in U.N. (I am not saying that the answer to this is "Yes." There are good grounds for supposing that more harm than good would have come by such a discussion.) I myself have no hesitation in saying that on extreme utilitarian principles we ought to propagate extreme utilitarianism as widely as possible. But Sidgwick had respectable reasons for suspecting the opposite.

The extreme utilitarian, then, regards moral rules as rules of thumb and as sociological facts that have to be taken into account when deciding what to do, just as facts of any other sort have to be taken into account. But in themselves they do not justify any action.

III

The restricted utilitarian regards moral rules as more than rules of thumb for short-circuiting calculations of consequences. Generally, he argues, consequences are not relevant at all when we are deciding what to do in a particular case. In general, they are relevant only to deciding what rules are good reasons for acting in a certain way in particular cases. This doctrine is possibly a good account of how the modern unreflective twentieth century Englishman often thinks about morality, but surely it is monstrous as an account of how it is most rational to think about morality. Suppose that there is a rule R and that in 99 percent of cases the best possible results are obtained by acting in accordance with R. Then clearly R is a useful rule of thumb; if we have not time or are not impartial enough to assess the consequences of an action it is an extremely good bet that the thing to do is to act in accordance with R. But is it not monstrous to suppose that if we *have* worked out the consequences and if we have perfect faith in the impartiality of our calculations, and if we *know* that in this instance to break R will have better results than to keep it, we should nevertheless obey the rule? Is it not to erect R into a sort of idol if we keep it when breaking it will prevent, say, some avoidable misery? Is not this a form of superstitious rule-worship (easily explicable psychologically) and not the rational thought of a philosopher?

The point may be made more clearly if we consider Mill's comparison of moral rules to the tables in the nautical almanack. (*Utilitarianism*, Everyman Edition, pp. 22–23). This comparison of Mill's is adduced by Urmson as evidence that Mill was a restricted utilitarian, but I do not think that it will bear this interpretation at all. (Though I quite agree with Urmson that many other things said by Mill are in harmony with restricted rather than extreme utilitarianism. Probably Mill had never thought very much about the distinction and was arguing for utilitarianism, restricted or extreme, against other and quite non-utilitarian forms of moral argument.) Mill says: "Nobody argues that the art of navigation is not founded on astronomy, because sailors cannot wait to calculate the Nautical Almanack. Being rational creatures, they go out upon the sea of life with their minds made up on the common questions of right and wrong, as well as on many of the far more difficult questions of wise and foolish. . . . Whatever we adopt as the fundamental principle of morality, we require subordinate principles to apply it." Notice that this is, as it stands, only an argument for subordinate principles as rules of thumb. The example of the nautical almanack is misleading because the information given in the almanack is in all cases the same as the information one would get if one made a long and laborious calculation from the original astronomical data on which the almanack is founded. Suppose, however, that astronomy were different. Suppose that the behaviour of the sun, moon and planets was very nearly as it is now, but that on rare occasions there were peculiar irregularities and discontinuities, so that the almanack gave us rules of the form "in 99 percent of cases where the observations are such and such you can deduce that your position is so and so." Furthermore, let us suppose that there were methods which enabled us, by direct and laborious calculation from the original astronomical data, not using the rough and ready tables of the almanack, to get our correct position in 100 percent of cases. Seafarers might use the almanack because they never had time for the long calculations and they were content with the 99 percent chance of success in calculating their positions. Would it not be absurd, however, if they *did* make the direct calculation, and finding that it disagreed with the almanack calculation, nevertheless they ignored it and stuck to the almanack conclusion? Of course the case would be altered if there were a high enough probability of making slips in the direct calculation: then we might stick to the almanack result, liable to error though we knew it to be, simply because the direct calculation would be open to error for a different reason, the fallibility of the computer. This would be analogous to the case of the extreme utilitarian who abides by the conventional rule against the dictates of his utilitarian calculations simply because he thinks that his calculations are probably affected by personal bias. But if the navigator were sure of his direct calculations would he not be foolish to abide by his almanack? I conclude, then, that if we change our suppositions about astronomy and the almanack (to which there are no exceptions) to bring the case into line with that of morality (to whose rules there are exceptions), Mill's example loses its appearance of supporting the restricted form of utilitarianism. Let me say once more that I am not here concerned with how ordinary men think about morality but with how they ought to think. We could quite well imagine a race of sailors who acquired a superstitious reverence for their almanack, even though it was only right in 99 percent of cases, and who indignantly threw overboard any man who mentioned the possibility of a direct calculation. But would this behaviour of the sailors be rational?

Let us consider a much discussed sort of case in which the extreme utilitarian might go against the conventional moral rule. I have promised to a friend, dying on a desert island from which I am subsequently rescued, that I will see that his fortune (over which I have control) is given to a jockey club. However, when I am rescued I decide that it would be better to give the money to a hospital, which can do more good with it. It may be argued that I am wrong to give the money to the hospital. But why? (*a*) The hospital can do more good with the money than the jockey club can. (*b*) The present case is unlike most cases of promising in that no one except me knows about the promise. In breaking the promise I am doing so with complete secrecy and am doing nothing to weaken the general faith in promises. That is, a factor, which would normally keep the extreme utilitarian from promise breaking even in otherwise unoptimific cases, does not at present operate. (*c*) There is no doubt a slight weakening in my own character as an habitual promise keeper, and moreover psychological tensions will be set up in me every time I am asked what the man made me promise him to do. For clearly I shall have to say that he made me promise to give the money to the hospital, and, since I am an habitual truth teller, this will go very much against the grain with me. Indeed I am pretty sure that in practice I myself would keep the promise. But we are not discussing what my moral habits would probably make me do; we are discussing what I ought to do. Moreover, we must not forget that even if it would be most rational of me to give the money to the hospital it would also be most rational of you to punish or condemn me if you did, most improbably, find out the truth (e.g. by finding a note washed ashore in a bottle). Furthermore, I would agree that though it was most rational of me to give the money to the hospital it would be most rational of you to condemn me for it. We revert again to Sidgwick's distinction between the utility of the action and the utility of the praise of it.

Many such issues are discussed by A. K. Stout in the article to which I have already referred. I do not wish to go over the same ground again, especially as I think that Stout's arguments support my own point of view. It will be useful, however, to consider one other example that he gives. Suppose that during hot weather there is an edict that no water must be used for watering gardens. I have a garden and I reason that most people are sure to obey the edict, and that as the amount of water that I use will be by itself negligible no harm will be done if I use the water secretly. So I do use the water, thus producing some lovely flowers which give happiness to various people. Still, you may say, though the action was perhaps optimific, it was unfair and wrong.

There are several matters to consider. Certainly my action should be condemned. We revert once

more to Sidgwick's distinction. A right action may be rationally condemned. Furthermore, this sort of offence is normally found out. If I have a wonderful garden when everybody else's is dry and brown there is only one explanation. So if I water my garden I am weakening my respect for law and order, and as this leads to bad results an extreme utilitarian would agree that I was wrong to water the garden. Suppose now that the case is altered and that I can keep the thing secret: there is a secluded part of the garden where I grow flowers which I give away anonymously to a home for old ladies. Are you still so sure that I did the wrong thing by watering my garden? However, this is still a weaker case than that of the hospital and the jockey club. There will be tensions set up within myself: my secret knowledge that I have broken the rule will make it hard for me to exhort others to keep the rule. These psychological ill effects in myself may not be inconsiderable: directly and indirectly they may lead to harm which is at least of the same order as the happiness that the old ladies get from the flowers. You can see that on an extreme utilitarian view there are two sides to the question.

So far I have been considering the duty of an extreme utilitarian in a predominantly non-utilitarian society. The case is altered if we consider the extreme utilitarian who lives in a society every member, or most members, of which can be expected to reason as he does. Should he water his flowers now? (Granting, what is doubtful, that in the case already considered he would have been right to water his flowers.) As a first approximation, the answer is that he should not do so. For since the situation is a completely symmetrical one, what is rational for him is rational for others. Hence, by a ***reductio ad absurdum*** argument, it would seem that watering his garden would be rational for none. Nevertheless, a more refined analysis shows that the above argument is not quite correct, though it is correct enough for practical purposes. The argument considers each person as confronted with the choice either of watering his garden or of not watering it. However there is a third possibility, which is that each person should, with the aid of a suitable randomizing device, such as throwing dice, give himself a certain probability of watering his garden.

This would be to adopt what in the theory of games is called "a mixed strategy." If we could give numerical values to the private benefit of garden watering and to the public harm done by 1, 2, 3, etc., persons using the water in this way, we could work out a value of the probability of watering his garden that each extreme utilitarian should give himself. Let a be the value which each extreme utilitarian gets from watering his garden, and let $f(1), f(2), f(3)$, etc., be the public harm done by exactly 1, 2, 3, etc., persons respectively watering their gardens. Suppose that p is the probability that each person gives himself of watering his garden. Then we can easily calculate, as functions of p, the probabilities that exactly 1, 2, 3, etc., persons will water their gardens. Let these probabilities be $p_1, p_2, \ldots p_n$. Then the total net probable benefit can be expressed as

$$V = p_1(a - f(1)) + p_2(2a - f(2)) \\ + \ldots p_n(na - f(n))$$

Then if we know the function of $f(x)$ we can calculate the value of p for which $(dV/dp) = 0$. This gives the value of p which it would be rational for each extreme utilitarian to adopt. The present argument does not of course depend on a perhaps unjustified assumption that the values in question are measurable, and in a practical case such as that of the garden watering we can doubtless assume that p will be so small that we can take it near enough as equal to zero. However the argument is of interest for the theoretical underpinning of extreme utilitarianism, since the possibility of a mixed strategy is usually neglected by critics of utilitarianism, who wrongly assume that the only relevant and symmetrical alternatives are of the form "everybody does X" and "nobody does X."[1]

I now pass on to a type of case which may be thought to be the trump card of restricted utilitarianism. Consider the rule of the road. It may be said that since all that matters is that everyone should do the same it is indifferent which rule we have, "go on the left-hand side" or "go on the right-hand side." Hence the only *reason* for going on the left-hand side in British countries is that this is the rule. Here the rule does seem to be a reason, in itself, for acting in a certain way. I wish to argue against this. The rule in itself is not a reason for our actions. We would be perfectly justified in going on the right-hand side if (*a*) we knew that the rule was to go on the left-hand side, and (*b*) we were in a country peopled by superanarchists who always on principle did the opposite of what they were told. This shows that the rule does not give us a reason for acting so much as an indication of the probable actions of others, which helps us to find out what would be our own most rational course of action. If we are in a country not peopled by anarchists, but by nonanarchist extreme utilitarians, we expect, other things being equal, that they will keep rules laid down for them. Knowledge of the rule enables us to predict their behaviour and to harmonize our own actions with theirs. The rule "keep to the left-hand side," then, is not a logical *reason* for action but an anthropological *datum* for planning actions.

I conclude that in every case if there is a rule R the keeping of which is in general optimific, but such that in a special sort of circumstances the optimific behaviour is to break R, then in these circumstances we should break R. Of course we must consider all the less obvious effects of breaking R, such as reducing people's faith in the moral order, before coming to the conclusion that to break R is right: in fact we shall rarely come to such a conclusion. Moral rules, on the extreme utilitarian view, are rules of thumb only, but they are not bad rules of thumb. But if we *do* come to the conclusion that we should break the rule and if we have weighed in the balance of our own fallibility and liability to personal bias, what good reason remains for keeping the rule? I can understand "it is optimific" as a reason for action, but why should "it is a member of a class of actions which are usually optimific" or "it is a member of a class of actions which as a class are more optimific than any alternative general class" be a good reason? You might as well say that a person ought to be picked to play for Australia just because all his brothers have been, or that the Australian team should be composed entirely of the Harvey family because this would be better than composing it entirely of any other family. The extreme utilitarian does not appeal to artificial feelings, but only to our feelings of benevolence, and what better feelings can there be to appeal to? Admittedly we can have a pro-attitude to anything, even to rules, but such artificially begotten pro-attitudes smack of superstition. Let us get down to realities, human happiness and misery, and make these the objects of our pro-attitudes and anti-attitudes.

The restricted utilitarian might say that he is talking only of *morality*, not of such things as rules of the road. I am not sure how far this objection, if valid, would affect my argument, but in any case I would reply that as a philosopher I conceive of ethics as the study of how it would be *most rational* to act. If my opponent wishes to restrict the word "morality" to a narrower use he can have the word. The fundamental question is the question of rationality of action *in general*. Similarly if the restricted utilitarian were to appeal to ordinary usage and say "it might be most rational to leave Hitler to drown but it would surely not be *wrong* to rescue him," I should again let him have the words "right" and "wrong" and should stick to "rational" and "irrational." We already saw that it would be rational to praise Hitler's rescuer, even though it would have been most rational not to have rescued Hitler. In ordinary language, no doubt, "right" and "wrong" have not only the meaning "most rational to do" and "not most rational to do" but also have the meaning "praiseworthy" and "not praiseworthy." Usually to the utility of an action corresponds utility of praise of it, but as we saw, this is not always so. Moral language could thus do with tidying up, for example by reserving "right" for "most rational" and "good" as an epithet of praise for the motive from which the action sprang. It would be more becoming in a philosopher to try to iron out illogicalities in moral language and to make suggestions for its reform than to use it as a court of appeal whereby to perpetuate confusions.

One last defence of restricted utilitarianism might be as follows. "Act optimifically" might be regarded as itself one of the rules of our system (though it would be odd to say that this rule was justified by its optimificality). According to Toulmin (*The Place of Reason in Ethics*, pp. 146–8) if "keep promises," say, conflicts with another rule we are allowed to argue the case on its merits, as if we were extreme utilitarians. If "act optimifically" is itself one of our rules then there will always be a conflict of rules whenever to keep a rule is not itself optimific. If this is so, restricted utilitarianism collapses into extreme utilitarianism. And no one could read Toulmin's book or Urmson's article on Mill without thinking that Toulmin and Urmson are of the opinion that they have thought of a doctrine which does *not* collapse into extreme utilitarianism, but which is, on the contrary, an improvement on it.

NOTE

1. [This paragraph has been substantially emended by the author. Ed. *(in original)*]

KEY TERMS

Utilitarianism
Hedonistic
Reductio ad absurdum

STUDY QUESTIONS

1. What is extreme about the position that Smart labels "extreme utilitarianism"?
2. What advantage is restricted utilitarianism supposed to have over extreme utilitarianism?
3. According to extreme utilitarianism, what is the purpose of following commonsense rules? Do you think following commonsense rules is a good way to achieve this purpose?
4. How does Smart argue that restricted utilitarianism either fails or else collapses into extreme utilitarianism?

Utilitarianism and Integrity

BERNARD WILLIAMS

..

L ET us look more concretely at two examples, to see what **utilitarianism** might say about them, what we might say about utilitarianism and, most importantly of all, what would be implied by certain ways of thinking about the situations. The examples are inevitably schematized, and they are open to the objection that they beg as many questions as they illuminate. There are two ways in particular in which examples in moral philosophy tend to beg important questions. One is that, as presented, they arbitrarily cut off and restrict the range of alternative courses of action—this objection might particularly be made against the first of my two examples. The second is that they inevitably present one with the situation as a going concern, and cut off questions about how the agent got into it, and correspondingly about moral considerations which might flow from that: this objection might perhaps specially arise with regard to the second of my two situations. These difficulties, however, just have to be accepted, and if anyone finds these examples cripplingly defective in this sort of respect, then he must in his own thought rework them in richer and less question-begging form. If he feels that no presentation of any imagined situation can ever be other than misleading in morality, and that there can never be any substitute for the concrete experienced complexity of actual moral situations, then this discussion, with him, must certainly grind to a halt: but then one may legitimately wonder whether every discussion with him about conduct will not grind to a halt, including any discussion about the actual situations, since discussion about how one would think and feel about situations somewhat different from the actual

(that is to say, situations to that extent imaginary) plays an important role in discussion of the actual.

I. George, who has just taken his Ph.D. in chemistry, finds it extremely difficult to get a job. He is not very robust in health, which cuts down the number of jobs he might be able to do satisfactorily. His wife has to go out to work to keep them, which itself causes a great deal of strain, since they have small children and there are severe problems about looking after them. The results of all this, especially on the children, are damaging. An older chemist, who knows about this situation, says that he can get George a decently paid job in a certain laboratory, which pursues research into chemical and biological warfare. George says that he cannot accept this, since he is opposed to chemical and biological warfare. The older man replies that he is not too keen on it himself, come to that, but after all George's refusal is not going to make the job or the laboratory go away; what is more, he happens to know that if George refuses the job, it will certainly go to a contemporary of George's who is not inhibited by any such scruples and is likely if appointed to push along the research with greater zeal than George would. Indeed, it is not merely concern for George and his family, but (to speak frankly and in confidence) some alarm about this other man's excess of zeal, which had led the older man to offer to use his influence to get George the job. . . . George's wife, to whom he is deeply attached, has views (the details of which need not concern us) from which it follows that at least there is nothing particularly wrong with research into CBW. What should he do?

II. Jim finds himself in the central square of a small South American town. Tied up against the wall are a row of twenty Indians, most terrified, a few defiant, in front of them several armed men in uniform. A heavy man in a sweat-stained khaki shirt turns out to be the captain in charge and, after a good deal of questioning of Jim which establishes that he got there by accident while on a botanical expedition, explains that the Indians are a random group of the inhabitants who, after recent acts of protest against the government, are just about to be killed to remind other possible protestors of the advantages of not protesting. However, since Jim is an honoured visitor from another land, the captain is happy to offer him a guest's privilege of killing one of the Indians himself. If Jim accepts, then as a special mark of the occasion, the other Indians will be let off. Of course, if Jim refuses, then there is no special occasion, and Pedro here will do what he was about to do when Jim arrived, and kill them all. Jim, with some desperate recollection of schoolboy fiction, wonders whether if he got hold of a gun, he could hold the captain, Pedro and the rest of the soldiers to threat, but it is quite clear from the set-up that nothing of that kind is going to work: any attempt at that sort of thing will mean that all the Indians will be killed, and himself. The men against the wall, and the other villagers, understand the situation, and are obviously begging him to accept. What should he do?

To these dilemmas, it seems to me that utilitarianism replies, in the first case, that George should accept the job, and in the second, that Jim should kill the Indian. Not only does utilitarianism give these answers but, if the situations are essentially as described and there are no further special factors, it regards them, it seems to me, as *obviously* the right answers. But many of us would certainly wonder whether, in (I), that could possibly be the right answer at all; and in the case of (II), even one who came to think that perhaps that was the answer, might well wonder whether it was obviously the answer. Nor is it just a question of the rightness or obviousness of these answers. It is also a question of what sort of considerations come into finding the answer. A feature of utilitarianism is that it cuts out a kind of consideration which for some others makes a difference to what they feel about such cases: a consideration involving the idea, as we might first and very simply put it, that each of us is specially responsible for what *he* does, rather than for what other people do. This is an idea closely connected with the value of integrity. It is often suspected that utilitarianism, at least in its direct forms, makes integrity as a value more or less unintelligible. I shall

try to show that this suspicion is correct. Of course, even if that is correct, it would not necessarily follow that we should reject utilitarianism; perhaps, as utilitarians sometimes suggest, we should just forget about integrity, in favour of such things as a concern for the general good. However, if I am right, we cannot merely do that, since the reason why utilitarianism cannot understand integrity is that it cannot coherently describe the relations between a man's projects and his actions.

Two Kinds of Remoter Effect

A lot of what we have to say about this question will be about the relations between my projects and other people's projects. But before we get on to that, we should ask first whether we are assuming too hastily what the utilitarian answers to the dilemmas will be. In terms of more direct effects of the possible decisions, there does not indeed seem much doubt about the answer in either case; but it might be said that in terms of more remote or less evident effects counterweights might be found to enter the utilitarian scales. Thus the effect on George of a decision to take the job might be invoked, or its effect on others who might know of his decision. The possibility of there being more beneficent labours in the future from which he might be barred or disqualified, might be mentioned; and so forth. Such effects—in particular, possible effects on the agent's character, and effects on the public at large—are often invoked by utilitarian writers dealing with problems about lying or promise-breaking, and some similar considerations might be invoked here.

There is one very general remark that is worth making about arguments of this sort. The certainty that attaches to these hypotheses about possible effects is usually pretty low; in some cases, indeed, the hypothesis invoked is so implausible that it would scarcely pass if it were not being used to deliver the respectable moral answer, as in the standard fantasy that one of the effects of one's telling a particular lie is to weaken the disposition of the world at large to tell the truth. The demands on the certainty or probability of these beliefs as beliefs about particular actions are much milder than they would be on beliefs favouring the unconventional course. It may be said that this is as it should be, since the presumption must be in favour of the conventional course: but that scarcely seems a *utilitarian* answer, unless utilitarianism has already taken off in the direction of not applying the consequences to the particular act at all.

Leaving aside that very general point, I want to consider now two types of effect that are often invoked by utilitarians, and which might be invoked in connexion with these imaginary cases. The attitude or tone involved in invoking these effects may sometimes seem peculiar; but that sort of peculiarity soon becomes familiar in utilitarian discussions, and indeed it can be something of an achievement to retain a sense of it.

First, there is the psychological effect on the agent. Our descriptions of these situations have not so far taken account of how George or Jim will be after they have taken the one course or the other; and it might be said that if they take the course which seemed at first the utilitarian one, the effects on them will be in fact bad enough and extensive enough to cancel out the initial utilitarian advantages of that course. Now there is one version of this effect in which, for a utilitarian, some confusion must be involved, namely that in which the agent feels bad, his subsequent conduct and relations are crippled and so on, *because he thinks that he has done the wrong thing*—for if the balance of outcomes was as it appeared to be *before* invoking this effect, then he has not (from the utilitarian point of view) done the wrong thing. So that version of the effect, for a rational and utilitarian agent, could not possibly make any difference to the assessment of right and wrong. However, perhaps he is not a thoroughly rational agent, and is disposed to have bad feelings, whichever he decided to do. Now such feelings, which are from a strictly utilitarian point of view irrational—nothing, a utilitarian can point out, is advanced by having them—cannot, consistently, have any great weight in a utilitarian calculation. I shall consider in a moment an argument to suggest that they should have no weight at all in it. But short of that, the utilitarian could reasonably say that such feelings should not be encouraged, even if we accept their existence, and that to give them a lot of weight is to encourage them. Or, at the very best, even if

they are straightforwardly and without any discount to be put into the calculation, their weight must be small: they are after all (and at best) one man's feelings.

That consideration might seem to have particular force in Jim's case. In George's case, his feelings represent a larger proportion of what is to be weighed, and are more commensurate in character with other items in the calculation. In Jim's case, however, his feelings might seem to be of very little weight compared with other things that are at stake. There is a powerful and recognizable appeal that can be made on this point: as that a refusal by Jim to do what he has been invited to do would be a kind of self-indulgent squeamishness. That is an appeal which can be made by other than utilitarians—indeed, there are some uses of it which cannot be consistently made by utilitarians, as when it essentially involves the idea that there is something dishonourable about such self-indulgence. But in some versions it is a familiar, and it must be said a powerful, weapon of utilitarianism. One must be clear, though, about what it can and cannot accomplish. The most it can do, so far as I can see, is to invite one to consider how seriously, and for what reasons, one feels that what one is invited to do is (in these circumstances) wrong, and in particular, to consider that question from the utilitarian point of view. When the agent is not seeing the situation from a utilitarian point of view, the appeal cannot force him to do so; and if he does come round to seeing it from a utilitarian point of view, there is virtually nothing left for the appeal to do. If he does not see it from a utilitarian point of view, he will not see his resistance to the invitation, and the unpleasant feelings he associates with accepting it, *just* as disagreeable experiences of his; they figure rather as emotional expressions of a thought that to accept would be wrong. He may be asked, as by the appeal, to consider whether he is right, and indeed whether he is fully serious, in thinking that. But the assertion of the appeal, that he is being self-indulgently squeamish, will not itself answer that question, or even help to answer it, since it essentially tells him to regard his feelings just as unpleasant experiences of his, and he cannot, by doing that, answer the question they pose when they are precisely not so regarded, but are regarded as indications of what he thinks is right and wrong. If he does come round fully to the utilitarian point of view then of course he will regard these feelings just as unpleasant experiences of his. And once Jim—at least—has come to see them in that light, there is nothing left for the appeal to do, since *of course* his feelings so regarded, are of virtually no weight at all in relation to the other things at stake. The "squeamishness" appeal is not an argument which adds in a hitherto neglected consideration. Rather, it is an invitation to consider the situation, and one's own feelings, from a utilitarian point of view.

The reason why the squeamishness appeal can be very unsettling, and one can be unnerved by the suggestion of self-indulgence in going against utilitarian considerations, is not that we are utilitarians who are uncertain what utilitarian value to attach to our moral feelings, but that we are partially at least not utilitarians, and cannot regard our moral feelings merely as objects of utilitarian value. Because our moral relation to the world is partly given by such feelings, and by a sense of what we can or cannot "live with," to come to regard those feelings from a purely utilitarian point of view, that is to say, as happenings outside one's moral self, is to lose a sense of one's moral identity; to lose, in the most literal way, one's integrity. At this point utilitarianism alienates one from one's moral feelings; we shall see a little later how, more basically, it alienates one from one's actions as well.

If, then, one is really going to regard one's feelings from a strictly utilitarian point of view, Jim should give very little weight at all to this; it seems almost indecent, in fact, once one has taken that point of view, to suppose that he should give any at all. In George's case one might feel that things were slightly different. It is interesting, though, that one reason why one might think that—namely that one person principally affected is his wife—is very dubiously available to a utilitarian. George's wife has some reason to be interested in George's integrity and his sense of it; the Indians, quite properly, have no interest in Jim's. But it is not at all clear how utilitarianism would describe that difference.

There is an argument, and a strong one, that a strict utilitarian should give not merely small extra weight, in calculations of right and wrong, to

feelings of this kind, but that he should give absolutely no weight to them at all. This is based on the point, which we have already seen, that if a course of action is, before taking these sorts of feelings into account, utilitarianly preferable, then bad feelings about that kind of action will be from a utilitarian point of view irrational. Now it might be thought that even if that is so, it would not mean that in a utilitarian calculation such feelings should not be taken into account; it is after all a well-known boast of utilitarianism that it is a realistic outlook which seeks the best in the world as it is, and takes any form of happiness or unhappiness into account. While a utilitarian will no doubt seek to diminish the incidence of feelings which are utilitarianly irrational—or at least of disagreeable feelings which are so—he might be expected to take them into account while they exist. This is without doubt classical utilitarian doctrine, but there is good reason to think that utilitarianism cannot stick to it without embracing results which are startlingly unacceptable and perhaps self-defeating.

Suppose that there is in a certain society a racial minority. Considering merely the ordinary interests of the other citizens, as opposed to their sentiments, this minority does no particular harm; we may suppose that it does not confer any very great benefits either. Its presence is in those terms neutral or mildly beneficial. However, the other citizens have such prejudices that they find the sight of this group, even the knowledge of its presence, very disagreeable. Proposals are made for removing in some way this minority. If we assume various quite plausible things (as that programmes to change the majority sentiment are likely to be protracted and ineffective) then even if the removal would be unpleasant for the minority, a utilitarian calculation might well end up favouring this step, especially if the minority were a rather small minority and the majority were very severely prejudiced, that is to say, were made very severely uncomfortable by the presence of the minority.

A utilitarian might find that conclusion embarrassing; and not merely because of its nature, but because of the grounds on which it is reached. While a utilitarian might be expected to take into account certain other sorts of consequences of the prejudice, as that a majority prejudice is likely to be displayed in conduct disagreeable to the minority, and so forth, he might be made to wonder whether the unpleasant experiences of the prejudiced people should be allowed, *merely as such*, to count. If he does count them, merely as such, then he has once more separated himself from a body of ordinary moral thought which he might have hoped to accommodate; he may also have started on the path of defeating his own view of things. For one feature of these sentiments is that they are from the utilitarian point of view itself irrational, and a thoroughly utilitarian person would either not have them, or if he found that he did tend to have them, would himself seek to discount them. Since the sentiments in question are such that a rational utilitarian would discount them in himself, it is reasonable to suppose that he should discount them in his calculations about society; it does seem quite unreasonable for him to give just as much weight to feelings—considered just in themselves, one must recall, as experiences of those that have them—which are essentially based on views which are from a utilitarian point of view irrational, as to those which accord with utilitarian principles. Granted this idea, it seems reasonable for him to rejoin a body of moral thought in other respects congenial to him, and discount those sentiments, just considered in themselves, totally, on the principle that no pains or discomforts are to count in the utilitarian sum which their subjects have just because they hold views which are by utilitarian standards irrational. But if he accepts that, then in the cases we are at present considering no extra weight at all can be put in for bad feelings of George or Jim about their choices, if those choices are, leaving out those feelings, on the first round utilitarianly rational.

The psychological effect on the agent was the first of two general effects considered by utilitarians, which had to be discussed. The second is in general a more substantial item, but it need not take so long, since it is both clearer and has little application to the present cases. This is the *precedent effect*. As Burke rightly emphasized, this effect can be important: that one morally *can* do what someone has actually done, is a psychologically effective principle, if not a deontically valid one. For the effect to operate, obviously some conditions must hold on the publicity of the act and on such things as the status of the agent (such considerations weighed importantly with Sir Thomas More); what these may be will vary evidently with circumstances.

In order for the precedent effect to make a difference to a utilitarian calculation, it must be based upon a confusion. For suppose that there is an act which would be the best in the circumstances, except that doing it will encourage by precedent other people to do things which will not be the best things to do. Then the situation of those other people must be relevantly different from that of the original agent; if it were not, then in doing the same as what would be the best course for the original agent, they would necessarily do the best thing themselves. But if the situations are in this way relevantly different, it must be a confused perception which takes the first situation, and the agent's course in it, as an adequate precedent for the second.

However, the fact that the precedent effect, if it really makes a difference, is in this sense based on a confusion, does not mean that it is not perfectly real, nor that it is to be discounted: social effects are by their nature confused in this sort of way. What it does emphasize is that calculations of the precedent effect have got to be realistic, involving considerations of how people are actually likely to be influenced. In the present examples, however, it is very implausible to think that the precedent effect could be invoked to make any difference to the calculation. Jim's case is extraordinary enough, and it is hard to imagine who the recipients of the effect might be supposed to be; while George is not in a sufficiently public situation or role for the question to arise in that form, and in any case one might suppose that the motivations of others on such an issue were quite likely to be fixed one way or another already.

No appeal, then, to these other effects is going to make a difference to what the utilitarian will decide about our examples. Let us now look more closely at the structure of those decisions.

Integrity

The situations have in common that if the agent does not do a certain disagreeable thing, someone else will, and in Jim's situation at least the result, the state of affairs after the other man has acted, if he does, will be worse than after Jim has acted, if Jim does. The same, on a smaller scale, is true of George's case. I have already suggested that it is inherent in consequentialism that it offers a strong doctrine of negative responsibility: if I know that if I do X, O_1 will eventuate, and if I refrain from doing X, O_2 will, and that O_2 is worse than O_1, then I am responsible for O_2 if I refrain voluntarily from doing X. "You could have prevented it," as will be said, and truly, to Jim, if he refuses, by the relatives of the other Indians. . . .

In the present cases, the situation of O_2 includes another agent bringing about results worse than O_1. So far as O_2 has been identified up to this point—merely as the worse outcome which will eventuate if I refrain from doing X—we might equally have said that what that other brings about is O_2; but that would be to underdescribe the situation. For what occurs if Jim refrains from action is not solely twenty Indians dead, but *Pedro's killing twenty Indians*, and that is not a result which Pedro brings about, though the death of the Indians is. We can say: what one does is not included in the outcome of what one does, while what another does can be included in the outcome of what one does. For that to be so, as the terms are now being used, only a very weak condition has to be satisfied: for Pedro's killing the Indians to be the outcome of Jim's refusal, it only has to be causally true that if Jim had not refused, Pedro would not have done it.

That may be enough for us to speak, in some sense, of Jim's responsibility for that outcome, if it occurs; but it is certainly not enough, it is worth noticing, for us to speak of Jim's *making* those things happen. For granted this way of their coming about, he could have made them happen only by making Pedro shoot, and there is no acceptable sense in which his refusal makes Pedro shoot. If the captain had said on Jim's refusal, "you leave me with no alternative," he would have been lying, like most who use that phrase. While the deaths, and the killing, may be the outcome of Jim's refusal, it is misleading to think, in such a case, of Jim having an *effect* on the world through the medium (as it happens) of Pedro's acts; for this is to leave Pedro out of the picture in his essential role of one who has intentions

and projects, projects for realizing which Jim's refusal would leave an opportunity. Instead of thinking in terms of supposed effects of Jim's projects on Pedro, it is more revealing to think in terms of the effects of Pedro's projects on Jim's decision. This is the direction from which I want to criticize the notion of negative responsibility.

. . . .

What projects does a utilitarian agent have? As a utilitarian, he has the general project of bringing about maximally desirable outcomes; how he is to do this at any given moment is a question of what causal levers, so to speak, are at that moment within reach. The desirable outcomes, however, do not just consist of agents carrying out *that* project; there must be other more basic or lower-order projects which he and other agents have, and the desirable outcomes are going to consist, in part, of the maximally harmonious realization of those projects ("in part," because one component of a utilitarianly desirable outcome may be the occurrence of agreeable experiences which are not the satisfaction of anybody's projects). Unless there were first-order projects, the general utilitarian project would have nothing to work on, and would be vacuous. What do the more basic or lower-order projects comprise? Many will be the obvious kinds of desires for things for oneself, one's family, one's friends, including basic necessities of life, and in more relaxed circumstances, objects of taste. Or there may be pursuits and interests of an intellectual, cultural or creative character. I introduce those as a separate class not because the objects of them lie in a separate class, and provide—as some utilitarians, in their churchy way, are fond of saying—"higher" pleasures. I introduce them separately because the agent's identification with them may be of a different order. It does not have to be: cultural and aesthetic interests just belong, for many, along with any other taste; but some people's commitment to these kinds of interests just is at once more thoroughgoing and serious than their pursuit of various objects of taste, while it is more individual and permeated with character than the desire for the necessities of life.

Beyond these, someone may have projects connected with his support of some cause: Zionism, for instance, or the abolition of chemical and biological warfare. Or there may be projects which flow from some more general disposition toward human conduct and character, such as a hatred of injustice, or of cruelty, or of killing.

It may be said that this last sort of disposition and its associated project do not count as (logically) "lower-order" relative to the higher-order project of maximizing desirable outcomes; rather, it may be said, it is itself a "higher-order" project. The vital question is not, however, how it is to be classified, but whether it and similar projects are to count among the projects whose satisfaction is to be included in the maximizing sum, and, correspondingly, as contributing to the agent's happiness. If the utilitarian says "no" to that, then he is almost certainly committed to a version of utilitarianism as absurdly superficial and shallow as Benthamite versions have often been accused of being. For this project will be discounted, presumably, on the ground that it involves, in the specification of its object, the mention of other people's happiness or interests: thus it is the kind of project which (unlike the pursuit of food for myself) presupposes a reference to other people's projects. But that criterion would eliminate any desire at all which was not blankly and in the most straightforward sense egoistic.[1] Thus we should be reduced to frankly egoistic first-order projects, and—for all essential purposes—the one second-order utilitarian project of maximally satisfying first-order projects. Utilitarianism has a tendency to slide in this direction, and to leave a vast hole in the range of human desires, between egoistic inclinations and necessities at one end, and impersonally benevolent happiness-management at the other. But the utilitarianism which has to leave this hole is the most primitive form, which offers a quite rudimentary account of desire. Modern versions of the theory are supposed to be neutral with regard to what sorts of things make people happy or what their projects are. Utilitarianism would do well then to acknowledge the evident fact that among the things that make people happy is not only making other people happy, but being taken up or involved in any of a vast range of projects, or—if we waive the evangelical and moralizing associations of the word—commitments. One can be committed to such things as a person, a cause, an institution, a career, one's own genius, or the pursuit of danger.

Now none of these is itself the *pursuit of happiness*: by an exceedingly ancient platitude, it is not at all clear that there could be anything which was just that, or at least anything that had the slightest chance of being successful. Happiness, rather, requires being involved in, or at least content with, something else.[2] It is not impossible for utilitarianism to accept that point: it does not have to be saddled with a naïve and absurd philosophy of mind about the relation between desire and happiness. What it does have to say is that if such commitments are worth while, then pursuing the projects that flow from them, and realizing some of those projects, will make the person for whom they are worthwhile, happy. It may be that to claim that is still wrong: it may well be that a commitment can make sense to a man (can make sense of his life) without his supposing that it will make him *happy*. But that is not the present point; let us grant to utilitarianism that all worthwhile human projects must conduce, one way or another, to happiness. The point is that even if that is true, it does not follow, nor could it possibly be true, that those projects are themselves projects of pursuing happiness. One has to believe in, or at least want, or quite minimally, be content with, other things, for there to be anywhere that happiness can come from.

Utilitarianism, then, should be willing to agree that its general aim of maximizing happiness does not imply that what everyone is doing is just pursuing happiness. On the contrary, people have to be pursuing other things. What those other things may be, utilitarianism, sticking to its professed empirical stance, should be prepared just to find out. No doubt some possible projects it will want to discourage, on the grounds that their being pursued involves a negative balance of happiness to others: though even there, the unblinking accountant's eye of the strict utilitarian will have something to put in the positive column, the satisfactions of the destructive agent. Beyond that, there will be a vast variety of generally beneficent or at least harmless projects; and some no doubt, will take the form not just of tastes or fancies, but of what I have called "commitments." It may even be that the utilitarian researcher will find that many of those with commitments, who have really identified themselves with objects outside themselves, who are thoroughly involved with other persons, or institutions, or activities or causes, are actually happier than those whose projects and wants are not like that. If so, that is an important piece of utilitarian empirical lore.

· · · · · · · ·

Let us now go back to the agent as utilitarian, and his higher-order project of maximizing desirable outcomes. At this level, he is committed only to that: what the outcome will actually consist of will depend entirely on the facts, on what persons with what projects and what potential satisfactions there are within calculable reach of the causal levers near which he finds himself. His own substantial projects and commitments come into it, but only as one lot among others—they potentially provide one set of satisfactions among those which he may be able to assist from where he happens to be. He is the agent of the satisfaction system who happens to be at a particular point at a particular time: in Jim's case, our man in South America. His own decisions as a utilitarian agent are a function of all the satisfactions which he can affect from where he is: and this means that the projects of others, to an indeterminately great extent, determine his decision.

This may be so either positively or negatively. It will be so positively if agents within the causal field of his decision have projects which are at any rate harmless, and so should be assisted. It will equally be so, but negatively, if there is an agent within the causal field whose projects are harmful, and have to be frustrated to maximize desirable outcomes. So it is with Jim and the soldier Pedro. On the utilitarian view, the undesirable projects of other people as much determine, in this negative way, one's decisions as the desirable ones do positively: if those people were not there, or had different projects, the causal nexus would be different, and it is the actual state of the causal nexus which determines the decision. The determination to an indefinite degree of my decisions by other people's projects is just another aspect of my unlimited responsibility to act for the best in a causal framework formed to a considerable extent by their projects.

The decision so determined is, for utilitarianism, the right decision. But what if it conflicts with some project of mine? This, the utilitarian will say, has already been dealt with: the satisfaction to you of fulfilling your project, and any satisfactions to others of your

so doing, have already been through the calculating device and have been found inadequate. Now in the case of many sorts of projects, that is a perfectly reasonable sort of answer. But in the case of projects of the sort I have called "commitments," those with which one is more deeply and extensively involved and identified, this cannot just by itself be an adequate answer, and there may be no adequate answer at all. For, to take the extreme sort of case, how can a man, as a utilitarian agent, come to regard as one satisfaction among others, and a dispensable one, a project or attitude round which he has built his life, just because someone else's projects have so structured the causal scene that that is how the utilitarian sum comes out?

The point here is not, as utilitarians may hasten to say, that if the project or attitude is that central to his life, then to abandon it will be very disagreeable to him and great loss of utility will be involved. I have already argued [earlier] that it is not like that; on the contrary, once he is prepared to look at it like that, the argument in any serious case is over anyway. The point is that he is identified with his actions as flowing from projects and attitudes which in some cases he takes seriously at the deepest level, as what his life is about (or, in some cases, this section of his life—seriousness is not necessarily the same as persistence). It is absurd to demand of such a man, when the sums come in from the utility network which the projects of others have in part determined, that he should just step aside from his own project and decision and acknowledge the decision which utilitarian calculation requires. It is to alienate him in a real sense from his actions and the source of his action in his own convictions. It is to make him into a channel between the input of everyone's projects, including his own, and an output of optimific decision; but this is to neglect the extent to which *his* actions and *his* decisions have to be seen as the actions and decisions which flow from the projects and attitudes with which he is most closely identified. It is thus, in the most literal sense, an attack on his integrity.

NOTES

1. On the subject of egoistic and non-egoistic desires, see 'Egoism and altruism', in *Problems of the Self* (Cambridge University Press, London, 1973).

2. This does not imply that there is no such thing as the project of pursuing pleasure. Some writers who have correctly resisted the view that all desires are desires for pleasure, have given an account of pleasure so thoroughly adverbial as to leave it quite unclear how there could be a distinctively hedonist way of life at all. Some room has to be left for that, though there are important difficulties both in defining it and living it. Thus (particularly in the case of the very rich) it often has highly ritual aspects, apparently part of a strategy to counter boredom.

KEY TERM

Utilitarianism

STUDY QUESTIONS

1. What were your initial reactions to the cases of George and Jim that Williams offers at the beginning of his article? Do your initial reactions differ from what Williams thinks the utilitarian ought to say? If so, how come?
2. Do you agree with Williams that a consideration of remoter effects will not change what the utilitarian should say about the cases of George and Jim? Why or why not?
3. What is *integrity*, as Williams is using the term, and why should we think it is valuable?
4. How much weight should we give to our own projects, just because they are *our* projects, when deciding what we ought to do?

Famine, Affluence, and Morality

PETER SINGER

Peter Singer (1946–) is a Professor of Bioethics at Princeton University, where he is in the Center for Human Values. His publications include *Democracy and Disobedience*, *Animal Liberation*, and *Practical Ethics*.

. .

As I write this, in November 1971, people are dying in East Bengal from lack of food, shelter, and medical care. The suffering and death that are occurring there now are not inevitable, not unavoidable in any fatalistic sense of the term. Constant poverty, a cyclone, a civil war have turned at least nine million people into destitute refugees; nevertheless, it is not beyond the capacity of the richer nations to give enough assistance to reduce any further suffering to very small proportions. The decisions and actions of human beings can prevent this kind of suffering. Unfortunately, human beings have

From *Philosophy and Public Affairs* 1, no. 3. Copyright © 1972 Princeton University Press. Reprinted by permission of the publisher.

not made the necessary decisions. At the individual level, people have, with very few exceptions, not responded to the situation in any significant way. Generally speaking, people have not given large sums to relief funds; they have not written to their parliamentary representatives demanding increased government assistance; they have not demonstrated in the streets, held symbolic fasts, or done anything else directed toward providing the refugees with the means to satisfy their essential needs. At the government level, no government has given the sort of massive aid that would enable the refugees to survive for more than a few days. Britain, for instance, has given rather more than most countries. It has, to date, given £14,750,000. For comparative purposes, Britain's share of the nonrecoverable development costs of the Anglo-French Concorde project is already in excess of £275,000,000, and on present estimates will reach £440,000,000. The implication is that the British government values a supersonic transport more than thirty times as highly as it values the lives of the nine million refugees. Australia is another country which, on a per capita basis, is well up in the "aid to Bengal" table. Australia's aid, however, amounts to less than one-twelfth of the cost of Sydney's new opera house. The total amount given, from all sources, now stands at about £65,000,000. The estimated cost of keeping the refugees alive for one year is £464,000,000. Most of the refugees have now been in the camps for more than six months. The World Bank has said that India needs a minimum of £300,000,000 in assistance from other countries before the end of the year. It seems obvious that assistance on this scale will not be forthcoming. India will be forced to choose between letting the refugees starve or diverting funds from her own development program, which will mean that more of her own people will starve in the future.[1]

These are the essential facts about the present situation in Bengal. So far as it concerns us here, there is nothing unique about this situation except its magnitude. The Bengal emergency is just the latest and most acute of a series of major emergencies in various parts of the world, arising both from natural and from man-made causes. There are also many parts of the world in which people die from malnutrition and lack of food independent of any special emergency. I take Bengal as my example only because it is the present concern, and because the size of the problem has ensured that it has been given adequate publicity. Neither individuals nor governments can claim to be unaware of what is happening there.

What are the moral implications of a situation like this? In what follows, I shall argue that the way people in relatively affluent countries react to a situation like that in Bengal cannot be justified; indeed, the whole way we look at moral issues—our moral conceptual scheme—needs to be altered, and with it, the way of life that has come to be taken for granted in our society.

In arguing for this conclusion I will not, of course, claim to be morally neutral. I shall, however, try to argue for the moral position that I take, so that anyone who accepts certain assumptions, to be made explicit, will, I hope, accept my conclusion.

I begin with the assumption that suffering and death from lack of food, shelter, and medical care are bad. I think most people will agree about this, although one may reach the same view by different routes. I shall not argue for this view. People can hold all sorts of eccentric positions, and perhaps from some of them it would not follow that death by starvation is in itself bad. It is difficult, perhaps impossible, to refute such positions, and so for brevity I will henceforth take this assumption as accepted. Those who disagree need read no further.

My next point is this: if it is in our power to prevent something bad from happening, without thereby sacrificing anything of comparable moral importance, we ought, morally, to do it. By "without sacrificing anything of comparable moral importance" I mean without causing anything else comparably bad to happen, or doing something that is wrong in itself, or failing to promote some moral good, comparable in significance to the bad thing that we can prevent. This principle seems almost as uncontroversial as the last one. It requires us only to prevent what is bad, and not to promote what is good, and it requires this of us only when we can do it without sacrificing anything that is, from the moral point of view, comparably important. I could even, as far as the application of my argument to the Bengal emergency is concerned, qualify the point so as to make it: if it is in our power to prevent something very bad from happening, without thereby sacrificing anything morally significant, we ought, morally, to do it. An application of this principle would be as follows: if I am walking past a shallow pond and see a child drowning in it, I ought to wade in and pull the child out. This will mean getting my clothes muddy, but this is insignificant, while the death of the child would presumably be a very bad thing.

The uncontroversial appearance of the principle just stated is deceptive. If it were acted upon, even in its qualified form, our lives, our society, and our world would be fundamentally changed. For the principle takes, firstly, no account of proximity or distance. It makes no moral difference whether the person I can help is a neighbor's child ten yards from me or a Bengali whose name I shall never know, ten thousand miles away. Secondly, the principle makes no distinction between cases in which I am the only person who could possibly do anything and cases in which I am just one among millions in the same position.

I do not think I need to say much in defense of the refusal to take proximity and distance into account. The fact that a person is physically near to us, so that we have personal contact with him, may make it more likely that we *shall* assist him, but this does not show that we *ought* to help him rather than another who happens to be further away. If we accept any principle of impartiality, universalizability, equality, or whatever, we cannot discriminate against someone merely because he is far away from us (or we are far away from him). Admittedly, it is possible that we are in a better position to judge what needs to be done to help a person near to us than one far away, and perhaps also to provide the assistance we judge to be necessary. If this were the case, it would be a reason for helping those near to us first. This may once have been a justification for being more concerned with the poor in one's own town than with famine victims in India. Unfortunately for those who like to keep their moral responsibilities limited, instant communication and swift transportation have changed the situation. From the moral point of view, the development of the world into a "global village" has made an important, though still unrecognized, difference to our moral situation. Expert observers and supervisors, sent out by famine relief organizations or permanently stationed in famine-prone areas, can direct our aid to a refugee in Bengal almost as effectively as we could get it to someone in our own block. There would seem, therefore, to be no possible justification for discriminating on geographical grounds.

There may be a greater need to defend the second implication of my principle—that the fact there are millions of other people in the same position, in respect to the Bengali refugees, as I am, does not make the situation significantly different from a situation in which I am the only person who can prevent something very bad from occurring. Again, of course, I admit that there is a psychological difference between the cases; one feels less guilty about doing nothing if one can point to others, similarly placed, who have also done nothing. Yet this can make no real difference to our moral obligations.[2] Should I consider that I am less obliged to pull the drowning child out of the pond if on looking around I see other people, no further away than I am, who have also noticed the child but are doing nothing? One has only to ask this question to see the absurdity of the view that numbers lessen obligation. It is a view that is an ideal excuse for inactivity; unfortunately most of the major evils—poverty, overpopulation, pollution—are problems in which everyone is almost equally involved.

The view that numbers do make a difference can be made plausible if stated in this way: if everyone in circumstances like mine gave £5 to the Bengal Relief Fund, there would be enough to provide food, shelter, and medical care for the refugees; there is no reason why I should give more than anyone else in the same circumstances as I am; therefore I have no obligation to give more than £5. Each premise in this argument is true, and the argument looks sound. It may convince us, unless we notice that it is based on a hypothetical premise, although the conclusion is not stated hypothetically. The argument would be sound if the conclusion were: if everyone in circumstances like mine were to give £5, I would have no obligation to give more than £5. If the conclusion were so stated, however, it would be obvious that the argument has no bearing on a situation in which it is not the case that everyone else gives £5. This, of course, is the actual situation. It is more or less certain that not everyone in circumstances like mine will give £5. So there will not be enough to provide the needed food, shelter, and medical care. Therefore by giving more than £5 I will prevent more suffering than I would if I gave just £5.

It might be thought that this argument has an absurd consequence. Since the situation appears to be that very few people are likely to give substantial amounts, it follows that I and everyone else in similar circumstances ought to give as much as possible, that is, at least up to the point at which by giving more one would begin to cause serious suffering for oneself and one's dependents—perhaps even beyond this point to the point of marginal utility, at which by giving more one would cause oneself and one's dependents as much suffering as one would prevent in Bengal. If everyone does this, however, there will be more than can be used for the benefit of the refugees, and some of the sacrifice will have been unnecessary. Thus, if everyone does what he ought to do, the result will not be as good as it would be if everyone did a little less than he ought to do, or if only some do all that they ought to do.

The paradox here arises only if we assume that the actions in question—sending money to the relief funds—are performed more or less simultaneously, and are also unexpected. For if it is to be expected that everyone is going to contribute something, then clearly each is not obliged to give as much as he would have been obliged to had others not been giving too. And if everyone is not acting more or less simultaneously, then those giving later will know how much more is needed, and will have no obligation to give more than is necessary to reach this amount. To say this is not to deny the principle that people in the same circumstances have the same obligations, but to point out that the fact that others have given, or may be expected to give, is a relevant circumstance: those giving after it has become known that many others are giving and those giving before are not in the same circumstances. So the seemingly absurd consequence of the principle I have put forward can occur only if people are in error about the actual circumstances—that is, if they think they are giving when others are not, but in fact they are giving when others are. The result of everyone doing what he really ought to do cannot be worse than the result of everyone doing less than he ought to do, although the result of everyone doing what he reasonably believes he ought to do could be.

If my argument so far has been sound, neither our distance from a preventable evil nor the number of other people who, in respect to that evil, are in the same situation as we are, lessens our obligation to mitigate or prevent that evil. I shall therefore take as established the principle I asserted earlier. As I have already said, I need to assert it only in its qualified form: if it is in our power to prevent something very bad from happening, without thereby sacrificing anything else morally significant, we ought, morally, to do it.

The outcome of this argument is that our traditional moral categories are upset. The traditional distinction between duty and charity cannot be drawn, or at least, not in the place we normally draw it. Giving money to the Bengal Relief Fund is regarded as an act of charity in our society. The bodies which collect money are known as "charities." These organizations see themselves in this way—if you send them a check, you will be thanked for your "generosity." Because giving money is regarded as an act of charity, it is not thought that there is anything wrong with not giving. The charitable man may be praised, but the man who is not charitable is not condemned. People do not feel in any way ashamed or guilty about spending money on new clothes or a new car instead of giving it to famine relief. (Indeed, the alternative does not occur to them.) This way of looking at the matter cannot be justified. When we buy new clothes not to keep ourselves warm but to look "well-dressed" we are not providing for any important need. We would not be sacrificing anything significant if we were to continue to wear our old clothes, and give the money to famine relief. By doing so, we would be preventing another person from starving. It follows from what I have said earlier that we ought to give money away, rather than spend it on clothes which we do not need to keep us warm. To do so is not charitable, or generous. Nor is it the kind of act which philosophers and theologians have called "**supererogatory**"—an act which it would be good to do, but not wrong not to do. On the contrary, we ought to give the money away, and it is wrong not to do so.

I am not maintaining that there are no acts which are charitable, or that there are no acts which it would be good to do but not wrong not to do. It may be possible to redraw the distinction between duty and charity in some other place. All I am arguing here is that the present way of drawing the distinction, which makes it an act of charity for a man living at the level of affluence which most people in the "developed nations" enjoy to give money to save someone else from starvation, cannot be supported. It is beyond the scope of my argument to consider whether the distinction should be redrawn or abolished altogether. There would be many other possible ways of drawing the distinction—for instance, one might decide that it is good to make other people as happy as possible, but not wrong not to do so.

Despite the limited nature of the revision in our moral conceptual scheme which I am proposing, the revision would, given the extent of both affluence and famine in the world today, have radical implications. These implications may lead to further objections, distinct from those I have already considered. I shall discuss two of these.

One objection to the position I have taken might be simply that it is too drastic a revision of our moral scheme. People do not ordinarily judge in the way I have suggested they should. Most people reserve their moral condemnation for those who violate some moral norm, such as the norm against taking another person's property. They do not condemn those who indulge in luxury instead of giving to famine relief. But given that I did not set out to present a morally neutral description of the way people make moral judgments, the way people do in fact judge has nothing to do with the validity of my conclusion. My conclusion follows from the principle which I advanced earlier, and unless that principle is rejected, or the arguments shown to be unsound, I think the conclusion must stand, however strange it appears.

It might, nevertheless, be interesting to consider why our society, and most other societies, do judge differently from the way I have suggested they should. In a well-known article, J. O. Urmson suggests that the imperatives of duty, which tell us what we must do, as distinct from what it would be good to do but not wrong not to do, function so as to prohibit behavior that is intolerable if men are to live together in society.[3] This may explain the origin and continued existence of the present division between acts of duty and acts of charity. Moral attitudes are shaped by the needs of society, and no doubt society needs people who will observe the rules that make social existence tolerable. From the point of view of a particular society, it is essential to prevent violations of norms against killing, stealing, and so on. It is quite inessential, however, to help people outside one's own society.

If this is an explanation of our common distinction between duty and supererogation, however, it is not a justification of it. The moral point of view requires us to look beyond the interests of our own society. Previously, as I have already mentioned, this may hardly have been feasible, but it is quite feasible now. From the moral point of view, the prevention of the starvation of millions of people outside our society must be considered at least as pressing as the upholding of property norms within our society.

It has been argued by some writers, among them Sidgwick and Urmson, that we need to have a basic moral code which is not too far beyond the capacities of the ordinary man, for otherwise there will be a general breakdown of compliance with the moral code. Crudely stated, this argument suggests that if we tell people that they ought to refrain from murder and give everything they do not really need to famine relief, they will do neither, whereas if we tell them that they ought to refrain from murder and that it is good to give to famine relief but not wrong not to do so, they will at least refrain from murder. The issue here is: Where should we draw the line between conduct that is required and conduct that is good although not required, so as to get the best possible result? This would seem to be an empirical question, although a very difficult one. One objection to the Sidgwick–Urmson line of argument is that it takes insufficient account of the effect that moral standards can have on the decisions we make. Given a society in which a wealthy man who gives five percent of his income to famine relief is regarded as most generous, it is not surprising that a proposal that we all ought to give away half our incomes will be thought to be absurdly unrealistic. In a society which held that no man should have more than enough while others have less than they need, such a proposal might seem narrow-minded. What it is possible for a man to do and what he is likely to do are both, I think, very greatly influenced by what people around him are doing and expecting him to do. In any case, the possibility that by spreading the idea that we ought to be doing very much more than we are to relieve famine we shall bring about a general breakdown of moral behavior seems remote. If the stakes are an end to widespread starvation, it is worth the risk. Finally, it should be emphasized that these considerations are relevant only to the issue of what we should require from others, and not to what we ourselves ought to do.

The second objection to my attack on the present distinction between duty and charity is one which has from time to time been made against utilitarianism. It follows from some forms of **utilitarian** theory that we all ought, morally, to be working full time to increase the balance of happiness over misery. The position I have taken here would not lead to this conclusion in all circumstances, for if there were no bad occurrences that we could prevent without sacrificing something of comparable moral importance, my argument would have no application. Given the present conditions in many parts of the world, however, it does follow from my argument that we ought, morally, to be working full time to relieve great suffering of the sort that occurs as a result of famine or other disasters. Of course, mitigating circumstances can be adduced—for instance, that if we wear ourselves out through overwork, we shall be less effective than we would otherwise have been. Nevertheless, when all considerations of this sort have been taken into account, the conclusion remains: we ought to be preventing as much suffering as we can without sacrificing something else of comparable moral importance. This conclusion is one which we may be reluctant to face. I cannot see, though, why it should be regarded as a criticism of the position for which I have argued, rather than a criticism of our ordinary standards of behavior. Since most people are self-interested to some degree, very few of us are likely to do everything that we ought to do. It would, however, hardly be honest to take this as evidence that it is not the case that we ought to do it.

It may still be thought that my conclusions are so wildly out of line with what everyone else thinks and has always thought that there must be something wrong with the argument somewhere. In order to show that my conclusions, while certainly contrary to contemporary Western moral standards, would not have seemed so extraordinary at other times and in other places, I would like to quote a passage from a writer not normally thought of as a way-out radical, Thomas Aquinas.

Now, according to the natural order instituted by divine providence, material goods are provided for the satisfaction of human needs. Therefore the division and appropriation of property, which proceeds from human law, must not hinder the satisfaction of man's necessity from such goods. Equally, whatever a man has in superabundance is owed, of natural right, to the poor for their sustenance. So Ambrosius says, and it is also to be found in the *Decretum Gratiani*: "The bread which you withhold belongs to the hungry; the clothing you shut away, to the naked; and the money you bury in the earth is the redemption and freedom of the penniless."[4]

I now want to consider a number of points, more practical than philosophical, which are relevant to the application of the moral conclusion we have reached. These points challenge not the idea that we ought to be doing all we can to prevent starvation, but the idea that giving away a great deal of money is the best means to this end.

It is sometimes said that overseas aid should be a government responsibility, and that therefore one ought not to give to privately run charities. Giving privately, it is said, allows the government and the noncontributing members of society to escape their responsibilities.

This argument seems to assume that the more people there are who give to privately organized famine relief funds, the less likely it is that the government will take over full responsibility for such aid. This assumption is unsupported, and does not strike me as at all plausible. The opposite view—that if no one gives voluntarily, a government will assume that its citizens are uninterested in famine relief and would not wish to be forced into giving aid—seems more plausible. In any case, unless there were a definite probability that by refusing to give one would be helping to bring about massive government assistance, people who do refuse to make voluntary contributions are refusing to prevent a certain amount of suffering without being able to point to any tangible beneficial consequence of their refusal. So the onus of showing how their refusal will bring about government action is on those who refuse to give.

I do not, of course, want to dispute the contention that governments of affluent nations should be giving many times the amount of genuine, no-strings-attached aid that they are giving now. I agree, too, that giving privately is not enough, and that we ought to be campaigning actively for entirely new standards for both public and private contributions to famine relief. Indeed, I would sympathize with someone who thought that campaigning was more important than giving oneself, although I doubt whether preaching what one does not practice would be very effective. Unfortunately, for many people the idea that "it's the government's responsibility" is a reason for not giving which does not appear to entail any political action either.

Another, more serious reason for not giving to famine relief funds is that until there is effective population control, relieving famine merely postpones starvation. If we save the Bengal refugees now, others, perhaps the children of these refugees, will face starvation in a few years' time. In support of this, one may cite the now well-known facts about the population explosion and the relatively limited scope for expanded production.

This point, like the previous one, is an argument against relieving suffering that is happening now, because of a belief about what might happen in the future; it is unlike the previous point in that very good evidence can be adduced in support of this belief about the future. I will not go into the evidence here. I accept that the earth cannot support indefinitely a population rising at the present rate. This certainly poses a problem for anyone who thinks it important to prevent famine. Again, however, one could accept the argument without drawing the conclusion that it absolves one from any obligation to do anything to prevent famine. The conclusion that should be drawn is that the best means of preventing famine, in the long run, is population control. It would then follow from the position reached earlier that one ought to be doing all one can to promote population control (unless one held that all forms of population control were wrong in themselves, or would have significantly bad consequences). Since there are organizations working specifically for population control, one would then support them rather than more orthodox methods of preventing famine.

A third point raised by the conclusion reached earlier relates to the question of just how much we all ought to be giving away. One possibility, which has already been mentioned, is that we ought to give until we reach the level of marginal utility—that is, the level at which, by giving more, I would cause as much suffering to myself or my dependents as I would relieve by my gift. This would mean, of course, that one would reduce oneself to very near the material circumstances of a Bengali refugee. It will be recalled that earlier I put forward both a strong and a moderate version of the principle of preventing bad occurrences. The strong version, which required us to prevent bad things from happening unless in doing so we would be sacrificing something of comparable moral significance, does seem to require reducing ourselves to the level of marginal utility. I should also say that the strong version seems to me to be the correct one. I proposed the more moderate version—that we should prevent bad occurrences unless, to do so, we had to sacrifice something morally significant—only in order to show that even on this surely undeniable principle a great change in our way of life is required. On the more moderate principle, it may not follow that we ought to reduce ourselves to the level of marginal utility, for one might hold that to reduce oneself and one's family to this level is to cause something significantly bad to happen. Whether this is so I shall not discuss, since, as I have said, I can see no good reason for holding the moderate version of the principle rather than the strong version. Even if we accepted the principle only in its moderate form, however, it should be clear that we would have to give away enough to ensure that the consumer society, dependent as it is on people spending on trivia rather than giving to famine relief, would slow down and perhaps disappear entirely. There are several reasons why this would be desirable in itself. The value and necessity of economic growth are now being questioned not only by conservationists, but by economists as well.[5] There is no doubt, too, that the consumer society has had a distorting effect on the goals and purposes of its members. Yet looking at the matter purely from the point of view of overseas aid, there must be a limit to the extent to which we should deliberately slow down our economy; for it might be the case that if we gave away, say, forty percent of our Gross National Product, we would slow down the economy so much that in absolute terms we would be giving less than if we gave twenty-five percent of the much larger GNP that we would have if we limited our contribution to this smaller percentage.

I mention this only as an indication of the sort of factor that one would have to take into account in working out an ideal. Since Western societies generally consider one percent of the GNP an acceptable level for overseas aid, the matter is entirely academic. Nor does it affect the question of how much an individual should give in a society in which very few are giving substantial amounts.

It is sometimes said, though less often now than it used to be, that philosophers have no special role to play in public affairs, since most public issues depend primarily on an assessment of facts. On questions of fact, it is said, philosophers as such have no special expertise, and so it has been possible to engage in philosophy without committing oneself to any position on major public issues. No doubt there are some issues of social policy and foreign policy about which it can truly be said that a really expert assessment of the facts is required before taking sides or acting, but the issue of famine is surely not one of these. The facts about the existence of suffering are beyond dispute. Nor, I think, is it disputed that we can do something about it, either through orthodox methods of famine relief or through population control or both. This is therefore an issue on which philosophers are competent to take a position. The issue is one which faces everyone who has more money than he needs to support himself and his dependents, or who is in a position to take some sort of political action. These categories must include practically every teacher and student of philosophy in the universities of the Western world. If philosophy is to deal with matters that are relevant to both teachers and students, this is an issue that philosophers should discuss.

Discussion, though, is not enough. What is the point of relating philosophy to public (and personal) affairs if we do not take our conclusions seriously? In this instance, taking our conclusion seriously means acting upon it. The philosopher will not find it any easier than anyone else to alter his attitudes and way of life to the extent that, if I am right, is involved in doing everything that we ought to be doing. At the very least, though, one can make a start. The philosopher who does so will have to sacrifice some of the benefits of the consumer society, but he can find compensation in the satisfaction of a way of life in which theory and practice, if not yet in harmony, are at least coming together.

NOTES

1. There was also a third possibility: that India would go to war to enable the refugees to return to their lands. Since I wrote this paper, India has taken this way out. The situation is no longer that described above, but this does not affect my argument, as the next paragraph indicates.

2. In view of the special sense philosophers often give to the term, I should say that I use "obligation" simply as the abstract noun derived from "ought," so that "I have an obligation to" means no more, and no less, than "I ought to." This usage is in accordance with the definition of "ought" given by the *Shorter Oxford English Dictionary*: "the general verb to express duty or obligation." I do not think any issue of substance hangs on the way the term is used; sentences in which I use "obligation" could all be rewritten, although somewhat clumsily, as sentences in which a clause containing "ought" replaces the term "obligation."

3. J. O. Urmson, "Saints and Heroes," in *Essays in Moral Philosophy*, ed. Abraham I. Melden (Seattle and London, 1958), p. 214. For a related but significantly different view see also Henry Sidgwick, *The Methods of Ethics*, 7th ed. (London, 1907), pp. 220–1, 492–3.

4. *Summa Theologica*, II–II, Question 66, Article 7, in *Aquinas, Selected Political Writings*, ed. A. P. d'Entreves, trans. J. G. Dawson (Oxford, 1948), p. 171.

5. See, for instance, John Kenneth Galbraith, *The New Industrial State* (Boston, 1967); and E. J. Mishan, *The Costs of Economic Growth* (London, 1967).

KEY TERMS

Supererogatory
Utilitarian

STUDY QUESTIONS

1. On what grounds might someone reject Singer's principle that "if it is in our power to prevent something bad from happening, without thereby sacrificing anything of comparable moral importance, we ought, morally, to do it"? Do you think the principle ought to be rejected? Why or why not?

2. Can you think of any reasons why the fact that there are many other people equally able to give to charities might make a difference to what your particular obligation is?

3. Should you feel guilty about spending money on new clothes, rather than giving it to famine relief? Why or why not?

4. Is there something special about the citizens of our own country that gives us more of an obligation to prevent poverty here rather than abroad?

5. What do you think is the best response to Singer's seemingly "radical" conclusion about how we should all change our way of life?

B. KANTIAN ETHICS

⋈
Groundwork of the Metaphysics of Morals

IMMANUEL KANT

With the exception of Plato and Aristotle, Immanuel Kant (1724–1804) is widely thought of as the most influential thinker in the history of Western philosophy. His most important works came during his "Critical" period, and they include *The Critique of Pure Reason* (1781), *Groundwork of the Metaphysics of Morals* (1785), *The Critique of Practical Reason* (1788), and *The Critique of the Power of Judgment* (1790).

. .

Chapter 1 Passage from Ordinary Rational Knowledge of Morality to Philosophical

The Good Will

It is impossible to conceive anything at all in the world, or even out of it, which can be taken as good without qualification, except a **good will**. Intelligence, wit, judgement, and any other *talents* of the mind we may care to name, or courage, resolution, and constancy of

From *Groundwork of the Metaphysics of Morals*, selections from chapters 1 and 2, translated by H. J. Paton. Copyright © by Hutchinson Publishing Group Limited. Reprinted by permission of the publisher.

All the bolding in this article is found in the original selection, so to prevent confusion, we did not add any bolding. However, there are four key terms that appear in this article that are defined in the glossary: "imperative," "analytic," "synthetic," and "freedom of the will."

purpose, as qualities of *temperament*, are without doubt good and desirable in many respects; but they can also be extremely bad and hurtful when the will is not good which has to make use of these gifts of nature, and which for this reason has the term "*character*" applied to its peculiar quality. It is exactly the same with *gifts of fortune*. Power, wealth, honour, even health and that complete well-being and contentment with one's state which goes by the name of "*happiness*," produce boldness, and as a consequence often over-boldness as well, unless a good will is present by which their influence on the mind—and so too the whole principle of action—may be corrected and adjusted to universal ends; not to mention that a rational and impartial spectator can never feel approval in contemplating the uninterrupted prosperity of a being graced by no touch of a pure and good will, and that consequently a good will seems to constitute the indispensable condition of our very worthiness to be happy.

Some qualities are even helpful to this good will itself and can make its task very much easier. They have none the less no inner unconditioned worth, but rather presuppose a good will which sets a limit to the esteem in which they are rightly held and does not permit us to regard them as absolutely good. Moderation in affections and passions, self-control, and sober reflexion are not only good in many respects: they may even seem to constitute part of the *inner* worth of a person. Yet they are far from being properly described as good without qualification (however unconditionally they have been commended by the ancients). For without the principles of a good will they may become exceedingly bad; and the very coolness of a scoundrel makes him, not merely more dangerous, but also immediately more abominable in our eyes than we should have taken him to be without it.

The Good Will and Its Results

A good will is not good because of what it effects or accomplishes—because of its fitness for attaining some proposed end: it is good through its willing alone—that is, good in itself. Considered in itself it is to be esteemed beyond comparison as far higher than anything it could ever bring about merely in order to favour some inclination or, if you like, the sum total of inclinations. Even if, by some special disfavour of destiny or by the niggardly endowment of stepmotherly nature, this will is entirely lacking in power to carry out its intentions; if by its utmost effort it still accomplishes nothing, and only good will is left (not, admittedly, as a mere wish, but as the straining of every means so far as they are in our control); even then it would still shine like a jewel for its own sake as something which has its full value in itself. Its usefulness or fruitlessness can neither add to, nor subtract from, this value. Its usefulness would be merely, as it were, the setting which enables us to handle it better in our ordinary dealings or to attract the attention of those not yet sufficiently expert, but not to commend it to experts or to determine its value.

· · · · · · · ·

The Good Will and Duty

We have now to elucidate the concept of a will estimable in itself and good apart from any further end. This concept, which is already present in a naturally

sound understanding and requires not so much to be taught as merely to be clarified, always holds the highest place in estimating the total worth of our actions and constitutes the condition of all the rest. We will therefore take up the concept of **duty**, which includes that of a good will, exposed, however, to certain subjective limitations and obstacles. These, so far from hiding a good will or disguising it, rather bring it out by contrast and make it shine forth more brightly.

The Motive of Duty

I will here pass over all actions already recognized as contrary to duty, however useful they may be with a view to this or that end; for about these the question does not even arise whether they could have been done *for the sake of duty* inasmuch as they are directly opposed to it. I will also set aside actions which in fact accord with duty, yet for which men have *no immediate inclination*, but perform them because impelled to do so by some other inclination. For there it is easy to decide whether the action which accords with duty has been done *from duty* or from some purpose of self-interest. This distinction is far more difficult to perceive when the action accords with duty and the subject has in addition an *immediate* inclination to the action. For example, it certainly accords with duty that a grocer should not overcharge his inexperienced customer; and where there is much competition a sensible shopkeeper refrains from so doing and keeps to a fixed and general price for everybody so that a child can buy from him just as well as anyone else. Thus people are served *honestly*; but this is not nearly enough to justify us in believing that the shopkeeper has acted in this way from duty or from principles of fair dealing; his interests required him to do so. We cannot assume him to have in addition an immediate inclination towards his customers, leading him, as it were out of love, to give no man preference over another in the matter of price. Thus the action was done neither from duty nor from immediate inclination, but solely from purposes of self-interest.

On the other hand, to preserve one's life is a duty, and besides this every one has also an immediate inclination to do so. But on account of this the often anxious precautions taken by the greater part of mankind for this purpose have no inner worth, and the maxim of their action is without moral content. They do protect their lives *in conformity with duty*, but not *from the motive of duty*. When, on the contrary, disappointments and hopeless misery have quite taken away the taste for life; when a wretched man, strong in soul and more angered at his fate than faint-hearted or cast down, longs for death and still preserves his life without loving it—not from inclination or fear but from duty; then indeed his maxim has a moral content.

To help others where one can is a duty, and besides this there are many spirits of so sympathetic a temper that, without any further motive of vanity or self interest, they find an inner pleasure in spreading happiness around them and can take delight in the contentment of others as their own work. Yet I maintain that in such a case an action of this kind, however right and however amiable it may be, has still no genuinely moral worth. It stands on the same footing as other inclinations—for example, the inclination for honour, which if fortunate enough to hit on something beneficial and right and consequently honourable, deserves praise and encouragement, but not esteem; for its maxim lacks moral content, namely, the performance of such actions, not from inclination, but *from duty*. Suppose then that the mind of this friend of man was overclouded by sorrows of his own which extinguished all sympathy with the fate of others, but that he still had power to help those in distress, though no longer stirred by the need of others because sufficiently occupied with his own; and suppose that, when no longer moved by any inclination, he tears himself out of this deadly insensibility and does the action without any inclination for the sake of duty alone; then for the first time his action has its genuine moral worth. Still further: if nature had implanted little sympathy in this or that man's heart; if (being in other respects an honest fellow) he were cold in temperament and indifferent to the sufferings of others—perhaps because, being endowed with the special gift of patience and robust endurance in his own sufferings, he assumed the like in others or even demanded it; if such a man (who would in truth not be the worst product of nature) were not exactly fashioned by her to be a philanthropist, would he not still find in himself a source from which he might draw a worth far higher than any

that a good-natured temperament can have? Assuredly he would. It is precisely in this that the worth of character begins to show—a moral worth and beyond all comparison the highest—namely that he does good, not from inclination, but from duty.

To assure one's own happiness is a duty (at least indirectly); for discontent with one's state, in a press of cares and amidst unsatisfied wants, might easily become a great *temptation to the transgression of duty*. But here also, apart from regard to duty, all men have already of themselves the strongest and deepest inclination toward happiness, because precisely in this Idea of happiness there is combined the sum total of inclinations. The prescription for happiness is, however, often so constituted as greatly to interfere with some inclinations, and yet men cannot form under the name of "happiness" any determinate and assured conception of the satisfaction of all inclinations as a sum. Hence it is not to be wondered at that a single inclination which is determinate as to what it promises and as to the time of its satisfaction may outweigh a wavering Idea; and that a man, for example, a sufferer from gout, may choose to enjoy what he fancies and put up with what he can—on the ground that on balance he has here at least not killed the enjoyment of the present moment because of some possibly groundless expectations of the good fortune supposed to attach to soundness of health. But in this case also, when the universal inclination towards happiness has failed to determine his will, when good health, at least for him, has not entered into his calculations as so necessary, what remains over, here as in other cases, is a law—the law of furthering his happiness, not from inclination, but from duty—and in this for the first time his conduct has a real moral worth.

It is doubtless in this sense that we should understand too the passages from Scripture in which we are commanded to love our neighbor and even our enemy. For love out of inclination cannot be commanded; but kindness done from duty—although no inclination impels us, and even although natural and unconquerable disinclination stands in our way—is *practical*, and not *pathological*, love, residing in the will and not in the propensions of feeling, in principles of action and not of melting compassion; and it is this practical love alone which can be an object of command.

. . . .

Chapter II
Passage from Popular
Moral Philosophy to a
Metaphysics of Morals

. . . .

Imperatives in General

Everything in nature works in accordance with laws. Only a rational being has the power to act *in accordance with his idea* of laws—that is, in accordance with principles—and only so has he a *will*. Since *reason* is required in order to derive actions from laws, the will is nothing but practical reason. If reason infallibly determines the will, then in a being of this kind the actions which are recognized to be objectively necessary are also subjectively necessary—that is to say, the will is then a power to choose *only that* which reason independently of inclination recognizes to be practically necessary, that is, to be good. But if reason solely by itself is not sufficient to determine the will; if the will is exposed also to subjective conditions (certain impulsions) which do not always harmonize with the objective ones; if, in a word, the will is not *in itself* completely in accord with reason (as actually happens in the case of men); then actions which are recognized to be objectively necessary are subjectively contingent, and the determining of such a will in accordance with objective laws is *necessitation*. That is to say, the relation of objective laws to a will not good through and through is conceived as one in which the will of a rational being, although it is determined by principles of reason, does not necessarily follow these principles in virtue of its own nature.

The conception of an objective principle so far as this principle is necessitating for a will is called a command (of reason), and the formula of this command is called an **Imperative**.

All imperatives are expressed by an "*ought*" (*Sollen*). By this they mark the relation of an objective law of reason to a will which is not necessarily determined by this law in virtue of its subjective constitution (the relation of necessitation). They say that something would be good to do or to leave undone; only they say it to a will which does not always do a thing because it has been informed that this is a good thing to do. The practically *good* is that which determines the will by concepts of reason, and therefore not by subjective causes, but objectively—that is, on grounds valid for every

rational being as such. It is distinguished from the *pleasant* as that which influences the will, not as a principle of reason valid for every one, but solely through the medium of sensation by purely subjective causes valid only for the senses of this person or that.[1]

A perfectly good will would thus stand quite as much under objective laws (laws of the good), but it could not on this account be conceived as *necessitated* to act in conformity with law, since of itself, in accordance with its subjective constitution, it can be determined only by the concept of the good. Hence for the *divine* will, and in general for a *holy* will, there are no imperatives: "*I ought*" is here out of place, because "*I will*" is already of itself necessarily in harmony with the law. Imperatives are in consequence only formulae for expressing the relation of objective laws of willing to the subjective imperfection of the will of this or that rational being—for example, of the human will.

Classification of Imperatives

All *imperatives* command either *hypothetically* or *categorically*. Hypothetical imperatives declare a possible action to be practically necessary as a means to the attainment of something else that one wills (or that one may will). A categorical imperative would be one which represented an action as objectively necessary in itself apart from its relation to a further end.

Every practical law represents a possible action as good and therefore as necessary for a subject whose actions are determined by reason. Hence all imperatives are formulae for determining an action which is necessary in accordance with the principle of a will in some sense good. If the action would be good solely as a means *to something else*, the imperative is *hypothetical*; if the action is represented as good *in itself* and therefore as necessary, in virtue of its principle, for a will which of itself accords with reason, then the imperative is *categorical*.

An imperative therefore tells me which of my possible actions would be good; and it formulates a practical rule for a will that does not perform an action straight away because the action is good—whether because the subject does not always know that it is good or because, even if he did know this, he might still act on maxims contrary to the objective principles of practical reason.

A hypothetical imperative thus says only that an action is good for some purpose or other, either *possible* or *actual*. In the first case it is a **problematic** practical principle; in the second case an **assertoric** practical principle. A categorical imperative, which declares an action to be objectively necessary in itself without reference to some purpose—that is, even without any further end—ranks as an **apodeictic** practical principle.

Everything that is possible only through the efforts of some rational being can be conceived as a possible purpose of some will; and consequently there are in fact innumerable principles of action so far as action is thought necessary in order to achieve some possible purpose which can be effected by it. All sciences have a practical part consisting of problems which suppose that some end is possible for us and of imperatives which tell us how it is to be attained. Hence the latter can in general be called imperatives of **skill**. Here there is absolutely no question about the rationality or goodness of the end, but only about what must be done to attain it. A prescription required by a doctor in order to cure his man completely and one required by a poisoner in order to make sure of killing him are of equal value so far as each serves to effect its purpose perfectly. Since in early youth we do not know what ends may present themselves to us in the course of life, parents seek above all to make their children learn things *of many kinds*; they provide carefully for *skill* in the use of means to all sorts of *arbitrary* ends, of none of which can they be certain that it could not in the future become an actual purpose of their ward, while it is always *possible* that he might adopt it. Their care in this matter is so great that they commonly neglect on this account to form and correct the judgement of their children about the worth of things which they might possibly adopt as ends.

There is, however, *one* end that can be presupposed as actual in all rational beings (so far as they are dependent beings to whom imperatives apply); and thus there is one purpose which they not only *can* have, but which we can assume with certainty that they all *do* have by a natural necessity—the purpose, namely, of *happiness*. A hypothetical imperative which affirms the practical necessity of an action as a means to the furtherance of happiness is **assertoric**. We may represent it, not simply as necessary to an uncertain, merely possible purpose, but as necessary

to a purpose which we can presuppose a priori and with certainty to be present in every man because it belongs to his very being. Now skill in the choice of means to one's own greatest well-being can be called *prudence*[2] in the narrowest sense. Thus an imperative concerned with the choice of means to one's own happiness—that is, a precept of prudence—still remains *hypothetical*: an action is commanded, not absolutely, but only as a means to a further purpose.

Finally, there is an imperative which, without being based on, and conditioned by, any further purpose to be attained by a certain line of conduct, enjoins this conduct immediately. This imperative is **categorical**. It is concerned, not with the matter of the action and its presumed results, but with its form and with the principle from which it follows; and what is essentially good in the action consists in the mental disposition, let the consequences be what they may. This imperative may be called the imperative of **morality**.

Willing in accordance with these three kinds of principle is also sharply distinguished by a *dissimilarity* in the necessitation of the will. To make this dissimilarity obvious we should, I think, name these kinds of principle most appropriately in their order if we said they were either *rules* of skill or *counsels* of prudence or *commands* (*laws*) of morality. For only *law* carries with it the concept of an *unconditioned*, and yet objective and so universally valid, *necessity*; and commands are laws which must be obeyed—that is, must be followed even against inclination. *Counsel* does indeed involve necessity, but necessity valid only under a subjective and contingent condition—namely, if this or that man counts this or that as belonging to his happiness. As against this, a categorical imperative is limited by no condition and can quite precisely be called a command, as being absolutely, although practically, necessary. We could also call imperatives of the first kind *technical* (concerned with art); of the second kind *pragmatic*[3] (concerned with well-being); of the third kind *moral* (concerned with free conduct as such—that is—with morals).

How Are Imperatives Possible?

The question now arises "How are all these imperatives possible?" This question does not ask how we can conceive the execution of an action commanded by the imperative, but merely how we can conceive the necessitation of the will expressed by the imperative in setting us a task. How an imperative of skill is possible requires no special discussion. Who wills the end, wills (so far as reason has decisive influence on his actions) also the means which are indispensably necessary and in his power. So far as willing is concerned, this proposition is analytic: for in my willing of an object as an effect there is already conceived the causality of myself as an acting cause—that is, the use of means; and from the concept of willing an end the imperative merely extracts the concept of actions necessary to this end. (Synthetic propositions are required in order to determine the means to a proposed end, but these are concerned, not with the reason for performing the act of will, but with the cause which produces the object.) That in order to divide a line into two equal parts on a sure principle I must from its ends describe two intersecting arcs—this is admittedly taught by mathematics only in synthetic propositions; but when I know that the aforesaid effect can be produced only by such an action, the proposition "If I fully will the effect, I also will the action required for it" is analytic; for it is one and the same thing to conceive something as an effect possible in a certain way through me and to conceive myself as acting in the same way with respect to it.

If it were only as easy to find a determinate concept of happiness, the imperatives of prudence would agree entirely with those of skill and would be equally analytic. For here as there it could alike be said "Who wills the end, wills also (necessarily, if he accords with reason) the sole means which are in his power." Unfortunately, however, the concept of happiness is so indeterminate a concept that although every man wants to attain happiness, he can never say definitely and in unison with himself what it really is that he wants and wills. The reason for this is that all the elements which belong to the concept of happiness are without exception empirical—that is, they must be borrowed from experience; but that none the less there is required for the Idea of happiness an absolute whole, a maximum of well-being in my present, and in every future, state. Now it is impossible for the most intelligent, and at the same time most powerful, but nevertheless finite, being to form here a determinate concept of what he really wills. Is it riches that he wants? How much anxiety, envy, and pestering might he not bring in this way on his own head! Is it knowledge and insight? This might perhaps merely give him an eye so sharp that it would make evils at present hidden from him and yet unavoidable seem all the more frightful, or would add a load of still further needs to the desires which already give him trouble enough. Is it long life? Who will guarantee that it would not be a long misery? Is it at least health? How often has infirmity of body kept a man from excesses into which perfect health would have let him fall!—and so on. In short, he has no principle by which he is able to decide with complete certainty what will make him truly happy, since for this he would require omniscience. Thus we cannot act on determinate principles in order to be happy, but only on empirical counsels, for example, of diet, frugality, politeness, reserve, and so on—things which experience shows contribute most to well-being on the average. From this it follows that imperatives of prudence, speaking strictly, do not command at all—that is, cannot exhibit actions objectively as practically *necessary*; that they are rather to be taken as recommendations (*consilia*), than as commands (*praecepta*), of reason; that the problem of determining certainly and universally what action will promote the happiness of a rational being is completely insoluble; and consequently that in regard to this there is no imperative possible which in the strictest sense could command us to do what will make us happy, since happiness is an Ideal, not of reason, but of imagination—an Ideal resting merely on empirical grounds, of which it is vain to expect that they should determine an action by which we could attain the totality of a series of consequences which is in fact infinite. Nevertheless, if we assume that the means to happiness could be discovered with certainty, this imperative of prudence would be an analytic practical proposition; for it differs from the imperative of skill only in this—that in the latter the end is merely possible, while in the former the end is given. In spite of this difference, since both command solely the means to something assumed to be willed as an end, the imperative which commands him who wills the end to will the means is in both cases analytic. Thus there is likewise no difficulty in regard to the possibility of an imperative of prudence.

As against this, the question "How is the imperative of *morality* possible?" is the only one in need of a solution; for it is in no way hypothetical, and consequently we cannot base the objective necessity which it affirms on any presupposition, as we can with hypothetical imperatives. Only we must never forget here that it is impossible to settle *by an example*, and so empirically, whether there is any imperative of this kind at all: we must rather suspect that all imperatives which seem to be categorical may none the less be covertly hypothetical. Take, for example, the saying "Thou shalt make no false promises." Let us assume that the necessity for this abstention is no mere advice for the avoidance of some further evil—as it might be said "You ought not to make a lying promise lest, when this comes to light, you destroy your credit." Let us hold, on the contrary, that an action of this kind must be considered as bad in itself, and that the imperative of prohibition is therefore categorical. Even so, we cannot with any certainty show by an example that the will is determined here solely by the law without any further motive, although it may appear to be so; for it is always possible that fear of disgrace, perhaps also hidden dread of other risks, may unconsciously influence the will. Who can prove by experience that a cause is not present? Experience shows only that it is not perceived. In such a case, however, the so-called moral imperative, which as such appears to be categorical and unconditioned, would in fact be only a pragmatic prescription calling attention to our advantage and merely bidding us take this into account.

We shall thus have to investigate the possibility of a *categorical* imperative entirely a priori, since here we do not enjoy the advantage of having its reality given in experience and so of being obliged merely to explain, and not to establish, its possibility. So much, however, can be seen provisionally—that the categorical imperative alone purports to be a practical **law**, while all the rest may be called *principles* of the will but not laws; for an action necessary merely in order to achieve an arbitrary purpose can be considered as in itself contingent, and we can

always escape from the precept if we abandon the purpose; whereas an unconditioned command does not leave it open to the will to do the opposite at its discretion and therefore alone carries with it that necessity which we demand from a law.

In the second place, with this categorical imperative or law of morality the reason for our difficulty (in comprehending its possibility) is a very serious one. We have here a synthetic a priori practical proposition;[4] and since in theoretical knowledge there is so much difficulty in comprehending the possibility of propositions of this kind, it may readily be gathered that in practical knowledge the difficulty will be no less.

The Formula of Universal Law

In this task we wish first to enquire whether perhaps the mere concept of a categorical imperative may not also provide us with the formula containing the only proposition that can be a categorical imperative; for even when we know the purport of such an absolute command, the question of its possibility will still require a special and troublesome effort, which we postpone to the final chapter.

When I conceive a *hypothetical* imperative in general, I do not know beforehand what it will contain—until its condition is given. But if I conceive a *categorical* imperative, I know at once what it contains. For since besides the law this imperative contains only the necessity that our maxim[5] should conform to this law, while the law, as we have seen, contains no condition to limit it, there remains nothing over to which the maxim has to conform except the universality of a law as such; and it is this conformity alone that the imperative properly asserts to be necessary.

There is therefore only a single categorical imperative and it is this: "*Act only on that maxim through which you can at the same time will that it should become a universal law.*"

Now if all imperatives of duty can be derived from this one imperative as their principle, then even although we leave it unsettled whether what we call duty may not be an empty concept, we shall still be able to show at least what we understand by it and what the concept means.

The Formula of the Law of Nature

Since the universality of the law governing the production of effects constitutes what is properly called *nature* in its most general sense (nature as regards its form)—that is, the existence of things so far as determined by universal laws—the universal imperative of duty may also run as follows: "*Act as if the maxim of your action were to become through your will a* UNIVERSAL LAW OF NATURE."

Illustrations

We will now enumerate a few duties, following their customary division into duties towards self and duties towards others and into perfect and imperfect duties.[6]

1. A man feels sick of life as the result of a series of misfortunes that has mounted to the point of despair, but he is still so far in possession of his reason as to ask himself whether taking his own life may not be contrary to his duty to himself. He now applies the test "Can the maxim of my action really become a universal law of nature?" His maxim is "From self-love I make it my principle to shorten my life if its continuance threatens more evil than it promises pleasure." The only further question to ask is whether this principle of self-love can become a universal law of nature. It is then seen at once that a system of nature by whose law the very same feeling whose function (*Bestimmung*) is to stimulate the furtherance of life should actually destroy life would contradict itself and consequently could not subsist as a system of nature. Hence this maxim cannot possibly hold as a universal law of nature and is therefore entirely opposed to the supreme principle of all duty.

2. Another finds himself driven to borrowing money because of need. He well knows that he will not be able to pay it back; but he sees too that he will get no loan unless he gives a firm promise to pay it back within a fixed time. He is inclined to make such a promise; but he has still enough conscience to ask "Is it not unlawful and contrary to duty to get out of difficulties in this way?" Supposing, however, he did resolve to do so, the maxim of his action would run thus: "Whenever I believe myself short of money, I will borrow money and promise to pay it back, though I know that this will never be done." Now this principle of self-love or personal advantage is perhaps quite compatible with my own entire future welfare; only there remains the question "Is it right?" I therefore transform the demand of self-love into a universal law and frame my question thus: "How would things stand if my maxim became a universal law?" I then see straight away that this maxim can never rank as a universal law and be self-consistent, but must necessarily contradict itself. For the universality of a law that every one believing himself to be in need may make any promise he pleases with the intention not to keep it would make promising, and the very purpose of promising, itself impossible, since no one would believe he was being promised anything, but would laugh at utterances of this kind as empty shams.

3. A third finds in himself a talent whose cultivation would make him a useful man for all sorts of purposes. But he sees himself in comfortable circumstances, and he prefers to give himself up to pleasure rather than to bother about increasing and improving his fortunate natural aptitudes. Yet he asks himself further "Does my maxim of neglecting my natural gifts, besides agreeing in itself with my tendency to indulgence, agree also with what is called duty?" He then sees that a system of nature could indeed always subsist under such a universal law, although (like the South Sea Islanders) every man should let his talents rust and should be bent on devoting his life solely to idleness, indulgence, procreation, and, in a word, to enjoyment. Only he cannot possibly **will** that this should become a universal law of nature or should be implanted in us as such a law by a natural instinct. For as a rational being he necessarily wills that all his powers should be developed, since they serve him, and are given him, for all sorts of possible ends.

4. Yet a *fourth* is himself flourishing, but he sees others who have to struggle with great hardships (and whom he could easily help); and he thinks "What does it matter to me? Let every one be as happy as Heaven wills or as he can make himself; I won't deprive him of anything; I won't even envy him; only I have no wish to contribute anything to his well-being or to his support in distress!" Now admittedly if such an attitude were a universal law of nature, mankind could get on perfectly well—better no doubt than if everybody prates about sympathy and good will, and even takes pains, on occasion, to practise them, but on the other hand cheats where he can, traffics in human rights, or violates them in other ways. But although it is possible that a universal law of nature could subsist in harmony with this maxim, yet it is impossible to **will** that such a principle should hold everywhere as a law of nature. For a will which decided in this way would be at variance with itself, since many a situation might arise in which the man needed love and sympathy from others, and in which, by such a law of nature sprung from his own will, he would rob himself of all hope of the help he wants for himself.

The Canon of Moral Judgment

These are some of the many actual duties—or at least of what we take to be such—whose derivation from the single principle cited above leaps to the eye. We must *be able to will* that a maxim of our action should become a universal law—this is the general canon for all moral judgement of action. Some actions are so constituted that their maxim cannot even be *conceived* as a universal law of nature without contradiction, let alone be *willed* as what *ought* to become one. In the case of others we do not find this inner impossibility, but it is still impossible to *will* that their maxim should be raised to the universality of a law of nature, because such a will would contradict itself. It is easily seen that the first kind of action is opposed to strict or narrow (rigorous) duty, the second only to wider (meritorious) duty; and thus that by these examples all duties—so far as the type of obligation is concerned (not the object of dutiful action)—are fully set out in their dependence on our single principle.

If we now attend to ourselves whenever we transgress a duty, we find that we in fact do not will that our maxim should become a universal law—since this is impossible for us—but rather that its opposite should remain a law universally: we only take the liberty of making an *exception* to it for ourselves (or even just for this once) to the advantage of our inclination. Consequently if we weighed it all up from one and the same point of view—that of reason—we should find a contradiction in our own will, the contradiction that a certain principle should be objectively

necessary as a universal law and yet subjectively should not hold universally but should admit of exceptions. Since, however, we first consider our action from the point of view of a will wholly in accord with reason, and then consider precisely the same action from the point of view of a will affected by inclination, there is here actually no contradiction, but rather an opposition of inclination to the precept of reason (*antagonismus*), whereby the universality of the principle (*universalitas*) is turned into a mere generality (*generalitas*) so that the practical principle of reason may meet our maxim half-way. This procedure, though in our own impartial judgement it cannot be justified, proves none the less that we in fact recognize the validity of the categorical imperative and (with all respect for it) merely permit ourselves a few exceptions which are, as we pretend, inconsiderable and apparently forced upon us.

We have thus at least shown this much—that if duty is a concept which is to have meaning and real legislative authority for our actions, this can be expressed only in categorical imperatives and by no means in hypothetical ones. At the same time—and this is already a great deal—we have set forth distinctly, and determinately for every type of application, the content of the categorical imperative, which must contain the principle of all duty (if there is to be such a thing at all). But we are still not so far advanced as to prove a priori that there actually is an imperative of this kind—that there is a practical law which by itself commands absolutely and without any further motives, and that the following of this law is duty.

. . . .

The Formula of the End in Itself

The will is conceived as a power of determining oneself to action *in accordance with the idea of certain laws*. And such a power can be found only in rational beings. Now what serves the will as a subjective ground of its self-determination is an *end*; and this, if it is given by reason alone, must be equally valid for all rational beings. What, on the other hand, contains merely the ground of the possibility of an action whose effect is an end is called a *means*. The subjective ground of a desire is an *impulsion* (*Triebfeder*);

the objective ground of a volition is a *motive* (*Bewegungsgrund*). Hence the difference between subjective ends, which are based on impulsions, and objective ends, which depend on motives valid for every rational being. Practical principles are *formal* if they abstract from all subjective ends; they are *material*, on the other hand, if they are based on such ends and consequently on certain impulsions. Ends that a rational being adopts arbitrarily as *effects* of his action (material ends) are in every case only relative; for it is solely their relation to special characteristics in the subject's power of appetition which gives them their value. Hence this value can provide no universal principles, no principles valid and necessary for all rational beings and also for every volition—that is, no practical laws. Consequently all these relative ends can be the ground only of hypothetical imperatives.

Suppose, however, there were something *whose existence* has *in itself* an absolute value, something which as *an end in itself* could be a ground of determinate laws; then in it, and in it alone, would there be the ground of a possible categorical imperative—that is, of a practical law.

Now I say that man, and in general every rational being, *exists* as an end in himself, *not merely as a means* for arbitrary use by this or that will: he must in all his actions, whether they are directed to himself or to other rational beings, always be viewed *at the same time as an end*. All the objects of inclination have only a conditioned value; for if there were not these inclinations and the needs grounded on them, their object would be valueless. Inclinations themselves, as sources of needs, are so far from having an absolute value to make them desirable for their own sake that it must rather be the universal wish of every rational being to be wholly free from them. Thus the value of all objects that can *be produced* by our action is always conditioned. Beings whose existence depends, not on our will, but on nature, have none the less, if they are non-rational beings, only a relative value as means and are consequently called *things*. Rational beings, on the other hand, are called *persons* because their nature already marks them out as ends in themselves—that is, as something which ought not to be used merely as a means—and consequently imposes to that extent a limit on all arbitrary treatment of them (and is an object of reverence). Persons, therefore, are not merely subjective ends whose existence as an effect

of our actions has a value *for us*: they are *objective ends*—that is, things whose existence is in itself an end, and indeed an end such that in its place we can put no other end to which they should serve *simply* as means; for unless this is so, nothing at all of *absolute* value would be found anywhere. But if all value were conditioned—that is, contingent—then no supreme principle could be found for reason at all.

If then there is to be a supreme practical principle and—so far as the human will is concerned—a categorical imperative, it must be such that from the idea of something which is necessarily an end for every one because it is an *end in itself* it forms an *objective* principle of the will and consequently can serve as a practical law. The ground of this principle is: *Rational nature exists as an end in itself.* This is the way in which a man necessarily conceives his own existence: it is therefore so far a *subjective* principle of human actions. But it is also the way in which every other rational being conceives his existence on the same rational ground which is valid also for me;[7] hence it is at the same time an *objective* principle, from which, as a supreme practical ground, it must be possible to derive all laws for the will. The practical imperative will therefore be as follows: *Act in such a way that you always treat humanity*, *whether in your own person or in the person of any other*, *never simply as a means*, *but always at the same time as an end.* We will now consider whether this can be carried out in practice.

Illustrations

Let us keep to our previous examples.

First, as regards the concept of necessary duty to oneself, the man who contemplates suicide will ask "Can my action be compatible with the Idea of humanity *as an end in itself*?" If he does away with himself in order to escape from a painful situation, he is making use of a person merely as a *means* to maintain a tolerable state of affairs till the end of his life. But man is not a thing—not something to be used *merely* as a means: he must always in all his actions be regarded as an end in himself. Hence I cannot dispose of man in my person by maiming, spoiling, or killing. (A more precise determination of this principle in order to avoid all misunderstanding—for example, about having limbs amputated to save myself or about exposing my life to danger in order to preserve it, and so on—I must here forego: this question belongs to morals proper.)

Secondly, so far as necessary or strict duty to others is concerned, the man who has a mind to make a false promise to others will see at once that he is intending to make use of another man *merely as a means* to an end he does not share. For the man whom I seek to use for my own purposes by such a promise cannot possibly agree with my way of behaving to him, and so cannot himself share the end of the action. This incompatibility with the principle of duty to others leaps to the eye more obviously when we bring in examples of attempts on the freedom and property of others. For then it is manifest that a violator of the rights of man intends to use the person of others merely as a means without taking into consideration that, as rational beings, they ought always at the same time to be rated as ends—that is, only as beings who must themselves be able to share in the end of the very same action.[8]

Thirdly, in regard to contingent (meritorious) duty to oneself, it is not enough that an action should refrain from conflicting with humanity in our own person as an end in itself: it must also *harmonize with this end*. Now there are in humanity capacities for greater perfection which form part of nature's purpose for humanity in our person. To neglect these can admittedly be compatible with the *maintenance* of humanity as an end in itself, but not with the *promotion* of this end.

Fourthly, as regards meritorious duties to others, the natural end which all men seek is their own happiness. Now humanity could no doubt subsist if everybody contributed nothing to the happiness of others but at the same time refrained from deliberately impairing their happiness. This is, however, merely to agree negatively and not positively with *humanity as an end in itself* unless every one endeavours also, so far as in him lies, to further the ends of others. For the ends of a subject who is an end in himself must, if this conception is to have its *full* effect in me, be also, as far as possible, *my* ends.

The Formula of Autonomy

This principle of humanity, and in general of every rational agent, *as an end in itself* (a principle which is the supreme limiting condition of every man's freedom of action) is not borrowed from experience; firstly, because it is universal, applying as it does to all rational beings as such, and no experience is adequate to determine universality; secondly, because in it humanity is conceived, not as an end of man (subjectively)—that is, as an object which, as a matter of fact, happens to be made an end—but as an objective end—one which, be our ends what they may, must, as a law, constitute the supreme limiting condition of all subjective ends and so must spring from pure reason. That is to say, the ground for every enactment of practical law lies *objectively in the rule* and in the form of universality which (according to our first principle) makes the rule capable of being a law (and indeed a law of nature); *subjectively*, however, it lies in the *end*; but (according to our second principle) the subject of all ends is to be found in every rational being as an end in himself. From this there now follows our third practical principle for the will—as the supreme condition of the will's conformity with universal practical reason—namely, the Idea *of the will of every rational being as a will which makes universal law*.

By this principle all maxims are repudiated which cannot accord with the will's own enactment of universal law. The will is therefore not merely subject to the law, but is so subject that it must be considered as also *making the law* for itself and precisely on this account as first of all subject to the law (of which it can regard itself as the author).

The Exclusion of Interest

Imperatives as formulated above—namely, the imperative enjoining conformity of actions to universal law on the analogy of a *natural order* and that enjoining the universal *supremacy* of rational beings in themselves *as ends*—did, by the mere fact that they were represented as categorical, exclude from their sovereign authority every admixture of interest as a motive. They were, however, merely *assumed* to be categorical because we were bound to make this assumption if we wished to explain the concept of duty. That there were practical propositions which commanded categorically could not itself be proved, any more than it can be proved in this chapter generally; but one thing could have been done—namely, to show that in willing for the sake of duty renunciation of all interest, as the specific mark distinguishing a categorical from a hypothetical imperative, was expressed in the very imperative itself by means of some determination inherent in it. This is what is done in the present third formulation of the principle—namely, in the Idea of the will of every rational being as *a will which makes universal law*.

Once we conceive a will of this kind, it becomes clear that while a will *which is subject to law* may be bound to this law by some interest, nevertheless a will which is itself a supreme law-giver cannot possibly as such depend on any interest; for a will which is dependent in this way would itself require yet a further law in order to restrict the interest of self-love to the condition that this interest should itself be valid as a universal law.

Thus the *principle* that every human will is *a will which by all its maxims enacts universal law*[9]—provided only that it were right in other ways—would be *well suited* to be a categorical imperative in this respect: that precisely because of the Idea of making universal law it is *based on no interest* and consequently can alone among all possible imperatives be *unconditioned*. Or better still—to convert the proposition—if there is a categorical imperative (that is, a law for the will of every rational being), it can command us only to act always on the maxim of such a will in us as can at the same time look upon itself as making universal law; for only then is the practical principle and the imperative which we obey unconditioned, since it is wholly impossible for it to be based on any interest.

We need not now wonder, when we look back upon all the previous efforts that have been made to discover the principle of morality, why they have one and all been bound to fail. Their authors saw man as tied to laws by his duty, but it never occurred to them that he is subject only to *laws which are made by himself* and yet are *universal*, and that he is bound only to act in accordance with a will which is his own but has for its natural purpose the function of making universal law. For when they thought of man merely as subject to a law (whatever it might be), the law had to carry with it some interest in order to attract or compel, because it did not spring as a law from *his own* will: in order to conform with the law his will

had to be necessitated by *something else* to act in a certain way. This absolutely inevitable conclusion meant that all the labour spent in trying to find a supreme principle of duty was lost beyond recall; for what they discovered was never duty, but only the necessity of acting from a certain interest. This interest might be one's own or another's; but on such a view the imperative was bound to be always a conditioned one and could not possibly serve as a moral law. I will therefore call my principle the principle of the **Autonomy** of the will in contrast with all others, which I consequently class under **Heteronomy**.

The Formula of the Kingdom of Ends

The concept of every rational being as one who must regard himself as making universal law by all the maxims of his will, and must seek to judge himself and his actions from this point of view, leads to a closely connected and very fruitful concept—namely, that of *a kingdom of ends*.

I understand by a "*kingdom*" a systematic union of different rational beings under common laws. Now since laws determine ends as regards their universal validity, we shall be able—if we abstract from the personal differences between rational beings, and also from all the content of their private ends—to conceive a whole of all ends in systematic conjunction (a whole both of rational beings as ends in themselves and also of the personal ends which each may set before himself); that is, we shall be able to concieve a kingdom of ends which is possible in accordance with the above principles.

For rational beings all stand under the *law* that each of them should treat himself and all others, *never merely as a means*, but always *at the same time as an end in himself*. But by so doing there arises a systematic union of rational beings under common objective laws—that is, a kingdom. Since these laws are directed precisely to the relation of such beings to one another as ends and means, this kingdom can be called a kingdom of ends (which is admittedly only an Ideal).

A rational being belongs to the kingdom of ends as a *member*, when, although he makes its universal laws, he is also himself subject to these laws. He belongs to it as its *head*, when as the maker of laws he is himself subject to the will of no other.

A rational being must always regard himself as making laws in a kingdom of ends which is possible through freedom of the will—whether it be as member or as head. The position of the latter he can maintain, not in virtue of the maxim of his will alone, but only if he is a completely independent being, without needs and with an unlimited power adequate to his will.

Thus morality consists in the relation of all action to the making of laws whereby alone a kingdom of ends is possible. This making of laws must be found in every rational being himself and must be able to spring from his will. The principle of his will is therefore never to perform an action except on a maxim such as can also be a universal law, and consequently such *that the will can regard itself as at the same time making universal law by means of its maxim.* Where maxims are not already by their very nature in harmony with this objective principle of rational beings as makers of universal law, the necessity of acting on this principle is practical necessitation—that is, *duty.* Duty does not apply to the head in a kingdom of ends, but it does apply to every member and to all members in equal measure.

The practical necessity of acting on this principle—that is, duty—is in no way based on feelings, impulses, and inclinations, but only on the relation of rational beings to one another, a relation in which the will of a rational being must always be regarded as *making universal law*, because otherwise he could not be conceived as *an end in himself.* Reason thus relates every maxim of the will, considered as making universal law, to every other will and also to every action towards oneself: it does so, not because of any further motive or future advantage, but from the Idea of the *dignity* of a rational being who obeys no law other than that which he at the same time enacts himself.

The Dignity of Virtue

In the kingdom of ends everything has either a *price* or a *dignity.* If it has a price, something else can be put in its place as an *equivalent*: if it is exalted above all price and so admits of no equivalent, then it has a dignity.

What is relative to universal human inclinations and needs has a *market price*; what, even without presupposing a need, accords with a certain taste—that is, with satisfaction in the mere purposeless play of our mental powers—has a *fancy price* (*Affektionspreis*); but that which constitutes the sole condition under which anything can be an end in itself has not merely a relative value—that is, a price—but has an intrinsic value—that is, *dignity.*

Now morality is the only condition under which a rational being can be an end in himself; for only through this is it possible to be a law-making member in a kingdom of ends. Therefore morality, and humanity so far as it is capable of morality, is the only thing which has dignity. Skill and diligence in work have a market price; wit, lively imagination, and humour have a fancy price; but fidelity to promises and kindness based on principle (not on instinct) have an intrinsic worth. In default of these, nature and art alike contain nothing to put in their place; for their worth consists, not in the effects which result from them, not in the advantage or profit they produce, but in the attitudes of mind—that is, in the maxims of the will—which are ready in this way to manifest themselves in action even if they are not favoured by success. Such actions too need no recommendation from any subjective disposition or taste in order to meet with immediate favour and approval; they need no immediate propensity or feeling for themselves; they exhibit the will which performs them as an object of immediate reverence; nor is anything other than reason required to *impose* them upon the will, not to *coax* them from the will—which last would anyhow be a contradiction in the case of duties. This assessment reveals as dignity the value of such a mental attitude and puts it infinitely above all price, with which it cannot be brought into reckoning or comparison without, as it were, a profanation of its sanctity.

What is it then that entitles a morally good attitude of mind—or virtue—to make claims so high? It is nothing less than the *share* which it affords to a rational being *in the making of universal law*, and which therefore fits him to be a member in a possible kingdom of ends. For this he was already marked out in virtue of his own proper nature as an end in himself and consequently as a maker of laws in the kingdom of ends—as free in respect of all laws of nature, obeying only those laws which he makes himself and in virtue of which his maxims can have their part in the making of universal law (to which he at the same time subjects himself). For nothing can have a value other than that determined for it by the law. But the law-making which determines all value must for this reason have a dignity—that is, an unconditioned and incomparable worth—for the appreciation of which, as necessarily given by a rational being, the word "*reverence*" is the only becoming expression. *Autonomy* is therefore the ground of the dignity of human nature and of every rational nature.

Review of the Formulae

The aforesaid three ways of representing the principle of morality are at bottom merely so many formulations of precisely the same law, one of them by itself containing a combination of the other two. There is nevertheless a difference between them, which, however, is subjectively rather than objectively practical: that is to say, its purpose is to bring an Idea of reason nearer to intuition (in accordance with a certain analogy) and so nearer to feeling. All maxims have, in short,

1. a *form*, which consists in their universality; and in this respect the formula of the moral imperative is expressed thus: "Maxims must be chosen as if they had to hold as universal laws of nature";

2. a *matter*—that is, an end; and in this respect the formula says: "A rational being, as by his very nature an end and consequently an end in himself, must serve for every maxim as a condition limiting all merely relative and arbitrary ends";

3. a *complete determination* of all maxims by the following formula, namely: "All maxims as proceeding from our own making of law ought to harmonize with a possible kingdom of ends as a kingdom of nature."[10] This progression may be said to take place through the categories of the *unity* of the form of will (its universality); of the *multiplicity* of its matter (its objects—that is, its ends); and of the *totality* or completeness of its systems of ends. It is,

however, better if in moral *judgement* we proceed always in accordance with the strictest method and take as our basis the universal formula of the categorical imperative: "*Act on the maxim which can at the same time be made a universal law.*" If, however, we wish also to secure acceptance for the moral law, it is very useful to bring one and the same action under the above-mentioned three concepts and so, as far as we can, to bring the universal formula nearer to intuition.

Review of the Whole Argument

We can now end at the point from which we started out at the beginning—namely, the concept of an unconditionally good will. The *will* is *absolutely good* if it cannot be evil—that is, if its maxim, when made into a universal law, can never be at variance with itself. This principle is therefore also its supreme law: "Act always on that maxim whose universality as a law you can at the same time will." This is the one principle on which a will can never be at variance with itself, and such an imperative is categorical. Because the validity of the will as a universal law for possible actions is analogous to the universal interconnexion of existent things in accordance with universal laws—which constitutes the formal aspect of nature as such—we can also express the categorical imperative as follows: "*Act on that maxim which can at the same time have for its object itself as a universal law of nature.*" In this way we provide the formula for an absolutely good will.

Rational nature separates itself out from all other things by the fact that it sets itself an end. An end would thus be the matter of every good will. But in the Idea of a will which is absolutely good—good without any qualifying condition (namely, that it should attain this or that end)—there must be complete abstraction from every end that has to be *produced* (as something which would make every will only relatively good). Hence the end must here be conceived, not as an end to be produced, *but as a self-existent* end. It must therefore be conceived only negatively—that is, as an end against which we should never act, and consequently as one which in all our willing we must never rate *merely* as a means, but always at the same time as an end. Now this end can be nothing other than the subject of all possible ends himself, because this subject is also the subject of a will that may be absolutely good; for such a will cannot without contradiction be subordinated to any other object. The principle "So act in relation to every rational being (both to yourself and to others) that he may at the same time count in your maxim as an end in himself" is thus at bottom the same as the principle "Act on a maxim which at the same time contains in itself its own universal validity for every rational being." For to say that in using means to every end I ought to restrict my maxim by the condition that it should also be universally valid as a law for every subject is just the same as to say this— that a subject of ends, namely, a rational being himself, must be made the ground for all maxims of action, never *merely* as a means, but as a supreme condition restricting the use of every means—that is, always also as an end.

Now from this it unquestionably follows that every rational being, as an end in himself, must be able to regard himself as also the maker of universal law in respect of any law whatever to which he may be subjected; for it is precisely the fitness of his maxims to make universal law that marks him out as an end in himself. It follows equally that this dignity (or prerogative) of his above all the mere things of nature carries with it the necessity of always choosing his maxims from the point of view of himself—and also of every other rational being—as a maker of law (and this is why they are called persons). It is in this way that a world of rational beings (*mundus intelligibilis*) is possible as a kingdom of ends— possible, that is, through the making of their own laws by all persons as its members. Accordingly every rational being must so act as if he were through his maxims always a law-making member in the universal kingdom of ends. The formal principle of such maxims is "So act as if your maxims had to serve at the same time as a universal law (for all rational beings)." Thus a kingdom of ends is possible only on the analogy of a kingdom of nature; yet the kingdom of ends is possible only through maxims—that is, self-imposed rules—while nature is possible only through laws concerned with causes whose action is necessitated from without. In spite of this difference, we give to nature as a whole, even although it is

regarded as a machine, the name of a "kingdom of nature" so far as—and for the reason that—it stands in a relation to rational beings as its ends. Now a kingdom of ends would actually come into existence through maxims which the categorical imperative prescribes as a rule for all rational beings, *if these maxims were universally followed*. Yet even if a rational being were himself to follow such a maxim strictly, he cannot count on everybody else being faithful to it on this ground, nor can he be confident that the kingdom of nature and its purposive order will work in harmony with him, as a fitting member, towards a kingdom of ends made possible by himself—or, in other words, that it will favour his expectation of happiness. But in spite of this the law "Act on the maxims of a member who makes universal laws for a merely possible kingdom of ends" remains in full force, since its command is categorical. And precisely here we encounter the paradox that without any further end or advantage to be attained the mere dignity of humanity, that is, of rational nature in man—and consequently that reverence for a mere Idea—should function as an inflexible precept for the will; and that it is just this freedom from dependence on interested motives which constitutes the sublimity of a maxim and the worthiness of every rational subject to be a law-making member in the kingdom of ends; for otherwise he would have to be regarded as subject only to the law of nature—the law of his own needs. Even if it were thought that both the kingdom of nature and the kingdom of ends were united under one head and that thus the latter kingdom ceased to be a mere Idea and achieved genuine reality, the Idea would indeed gain by this the addition of a strong motive, but never any increase in its intrinsic worth; for, even if this were so, it would still be necessary to conceive the unique and absolute lawgiver himself as judging the worth of rational beings solely by the disinterested behaviour they prescribed to themselves in virtue of this Idea alone. The essence of things does not vary with their external relations; and where there is something which, without regard to such relations, constitutes by itself the absolute worth of man, it is by this that man must also be judged by everyone whatsoever—even by the Supreme Being. Thus *morality* lies in the relation of actions to the autonomy of the will—that is, to a possible making of universal law by means of its maxims. An action which is compatible with the autonomy of the will is *permitted*; one which does not harmonize with it is *forbidden*. A will whose maxims necessarily accord with the laws of autonomy is a *holy*, or absolutely good, will. The dependence of a will not absolutely good on the principle of autonomy (that is, moral necessitation) is *obligation*. Obligation can thus have no reference to a holy being. The objective necessity to act from obligation is called *duty*.

From what was said a little time ago we can now easily explain how it comes about that, although in the concept of duty we think of subjection to the law, yet we also at the same time attribute to the person who fulfils all his duties a certain sublimity and *dignity*. For it is not in so far as he is *subject* to the law that he has sublimity, but rather in so far as, in regard to this very same law, he is at the same time its *author* and is subordinated to it only on this ground. We have also shown above how neither fear nor inclination, but solely reverence for the law, is the motive which can give an action moral worth. Our own will, provided it were to act only under the condition of being able to make universal law by means of its maxims—this ideal will which can be ours is the proper object of reverence; and the dignity of man consists precisely in his capacity to make universal law, although only on condition of being himself also subject to the law he makes.

NOTES

1. The dependence of the power of appetition on sensations is called an inclination, and thus an inclination always indicates a *need*. The dependence of a contingently determinable will on principles of reason is called an *interest*. Hence an interest is found only where there is a dependent will which in itself is not always in accord with reason: to a divine will we cannot ascribe any interest. But even the human will can *take an interest* in something without therefore *acting from interest*. The first expression signifies *practical* interest in the action; the second *pathological* interest in the object of the action. The first indicates only dependence of the will on principles of reason by itself; the second its dependence on principles of reason at the service of inclination—that is to say, where reason merely supplies a practical rule for meeting the need of inclination. In the first case what interests me is the action; in the second case what interests me is the object of the action (so far as this object is pleasant to me). We have seen in Chapter 1 that in an action done for the sake of duty we must have regard, not to interest in the object, but to interest in the action itself and in its rational principle (namely, the law).

2. The word "prudence" (*Klugheit*) is used in a double sense: in one sense it can have the name of "worldly wisdom" (*Weltklugheit*): in a second sense that of "personal wisdom" (*Privatklugheit*). The first is the skill of a man in influencing others in order to use them for his own ends. The second is sagacity in combining all these ends to his own lasting advantage. The latter is properly that to which the value of the former can itself be traced; and of him who is prudent in the first sense, but not in the second, we might better say that he is clever and astute, but on the whole imprudent.

3. It seems to me that the proper meaning of the word "*pragmatic*" can be defined most accurately in this way. For those *Sanctions* are called Pragmatic which, properly speaking, do not spring as necessary laws from the Natural Right of States, but from *forethought* in regard to the general welfare. A *history* is written pragmatically when it teaches *prudence*—that is, when it instructs the world of to-day how to provide for its own advantage better than, or at least as well as, the world of other times.

4. Without presupposing a condition taken from some inclination I connect an action with the will a priori and therefore necessarily (although only objectively so—that is, only subject to the Idea of a reason having full power over all subjective impulses to action). Here we have a practical proposition in which the willing of an action is not derived analytically from some other willing already presupposed (for we do not possess any such perfect will), but is on the contrary connected immediately with the concept of the will of a rational being as something which is not contained in this concept.

5. A *maxim* is a subjective principle of action and must be distinguished from an *objective principle*—namely, a practical law. The former contains a practical rule determined by reason in accordance with the conditions of the subject (often his ignorance or again his inclinations): it is thus a principle on which the subject *acts*. A law, on the other hand, is an objective principle valid for every rational being; and

it is a principle on which he *ought to act*—that is, an imperative.

6. It should be noted that I reserve my division of duties entirely for a future *Metaphysics of Morals* and that my present division is therefore put forward as arbitrary (merely for the purpose of arranging my examples). Further, I understand here by a perfect duty one which allows no exception in the interests of inclination, and so I recognize among *perfect duties*, not only outer ones, but also inner. This is contrary to the accepted usage of the schools, but I do not intend to justify it here, since for my purpose it is all one whether this point is conceded or not.

7. This proposition I put forward here as a postulate. The grounds for it will be found in the final chapter. [Editors' note: This final chapter is omitted here.]

8. Let no one think that here the trivial "*quod tibi non vis fieri, etc.*" can serve as a standard or principle. For it is merely derivative from our principle, although subject to various qualifications: it cannot be a universal law since it contains the ground neither of duties to oneself nor of duties of kindness to others (for many a man would readily agree that others should not help him if only he could be dispensed from affording help to them), nor finally of strict duties towards others; for on this basis the criminal would be able to dispute with the judges who punish him, and so on.

9. I may be excused from bringing forward examples to illustrate this principle, since those which were first used as illustrations of the categorical imperative and its formula can all serve this purpose here.

10. Teleology views nature as a kingdom of ends; ethics views a possible kingdom of ends as a kingdom of nature. In the first case the kingdom of ends is a theoretical Idea used to explain what exists. In the second case it is a practical Idea used to bring into existence what does not exist but can be made actual by our conduct—and indeed to bring it into existence in conformity with this Idea.

KEY TERMS

Imperative
Analytic
Synthetic
Freedom of the will

STUDY QUESTIONS

1. What does Kant mean when he says, "Even if . . . this will is entirely lacking in power to carry out its intentions; if by its utmost effort it still accomplishes nothing, and only good will is left; even then it would still shine like a jewel for its own sake as something which has its full value in itself"?

2. What is the distinction between an action that is done merely *in accordance* with duty and one that is done *from* duty?

3. Why does Kant think that the only actions that have moral worth are those that are performed because of "reverence for the law"?

4. Briefly explain the distinction between a *hypothetical* and a *categorical* imperative.

5. Kant gives several different formulations of the categorical imperative. Do you think each formulation is equivalent, in that each will always yield the same results as far as what maxims we should and should not act on?

A Brief Introduction to Kantian Ethics

J. DAVID VELLEMAN

· ·

The Overall Strategy

The overall strategy of Kant's moral theory is to derive the content of our obligations from the very concept of an obligation. Kant thought that we can figure out what we are obligated to do by analyzing the very idea of being obligated to do something. Where I am using the word 'obligation,' Kant used the German word *Pflicht*, which is usually translated into English as "duty." In Kant's vocabulary, then, the strategy of his moral theory is to figure out *what our duties are* by analyzing *what duty is*.

A duty, to begin with, is a practical requirement— a requirement to do something or not to do something. But there are many practical requirements that aren't duties. If you want to read Kant in the original, you have to learn German: there's a practical requirement. Federal law requires you to make yourself available to serve on a jury: there's another practical requirement. But these two requirements have features that clearly distinguish them from moral obligations or duties.

The first requires you to learn German only if you want to read Kant in the original. This requirement is consequently escapable: you can gain exemption from it by giving up the relevant desire. Give up wanting to read Kant in the original and you can forget about this requirement, since it will no longer apply to you. The second requirement is also escapable, but it doesn't point to an escape hatch so clearly, since it doesn't contain an "if" clause stating a condition by which its application is limited.

Nevertheless, its force as a requirement depends on the authority of a particular body—namely, the U.S. Government. Only if you are subject to the authority of the U.S. Government does this requirement apply to you. Hence you can escape the force of this requirement by escaping the authority of the Government: immunity to the authority of the body entails immunity to its requirements.

Now, Kant claimed—plausibly, I think—that our moral duties are inescapable in both of these senses. If we are morally obligated to do something, then we are obligated to do it no matter what our desires, interests, or aims may be. We cannot escape the force of the obligation by giving up some particular desires, interests, or aims. Nor can we escape the force of an obligation by escaping from the jurisdiction of some authority such as the Government. Kant expressed the inescapability of our duties by calling them **categorical** as opposed to **hypothetical**.

According to Kant, the force of moral requirements does not even depend on the authority of God. There is a simple argument for denying this dependence. If we were subject to moral requirements because they were imposed on us by God, the reason would have to be that we are subject to a requirement to do what God requires of us; and the force of this latter requirement, of obedience to

---

"A Brief Introduction to Kantian Ethics" from *Self to Self* by J. David Velleman. (2006). pp. 16–44. Reprinted with the permission of Cambridge University Press.

All the bolding in this article is found in the orginal selection, and none of the bolded terms indicate key terms defined in the glossary.

This essay is an attempt to reconstruct Kantian moral theory in terms intelligible to undergraduates who have not yet read Kant. In the interest of commending to students those parts of Kant's theory which seem right to me, I have changed parts that seem wrong, usually with an explanation of my reasons for doing so. I have also chosen not to complicate the essay with references either to the Kantian texts or to the secondary literature, although my debts to others are numerous and not always obvious. I am especially indebted to the work of Elizabeth Anderson, Michael Bratman, Stephen Darwall, Edward Hinchman, Christine Korsgaard, and Nishi Shah.

God, could not itself depend on God's authority. (To require obedience to God on the grounds that God requires it would be viciously circular.) The requirement to obey God's requirements would therefore have to constitute a fundamental duty, on which all other duties depended; and so God's authority would not account for the force of our duties, after all. Since this argument will apply to any figure or body conceived as issuing requirements, we can conclude that the force of moral requirements must not depend on the authority of any figure or body by which they are conceived to have been issued.

The notion of authority is also relevant to requirements that are conditional on wants or desires. These requirements turn out to depend, not only on the presence of the relevant want or desire, but also on its authority.

Consider the hypothetical requirement "If you want to punch someone in the nose, you have to make a fist." One way in which you might escape the force of this requirement is by not wanting to punch anyone in the nose. But there is also another way. Even if you find yourself wanting to punch someone in the nose, you may regard that desire as nothing more than a passing fit of temper and hence as providing no reason for you to throw a punch. You will then regard your desire as lacking authority over you, in the sense that it shouldn't influence your choice of what to do. The mere psychological fact that you want to punch someone in the nose doesn't give application to the requirement that if you want to punch someone in the nose, you have to make a fist. You *do* want to punch someone in the nose, but you *don't* have to make a fist, because the relevant desire has no authority.

All of the requirements that Kant called hypothetical thus depend for their force on some external source of authority—on a desire to which they refer, for example, or an agency by which they have been issued. And these requirements lack the inescapability of morality because the authority behind them is always open to question. We can always ask why we should obey a particular source of authority, whether it be a desire, the U.S. Government, or even God. But the requirements of morality, being categorical, leave no room for questions about why we

ought to obey them. Kant therefore concluded that moral requirements must not depend for their force on any external source of authority.

Kant reasoned that if moral requirements don't derive their force from any external authority, then they must carry their authority with them, simply by virtue of what they require. That's why Kant thought that he could derive the content of our obligations from the very concept of an obligation. The concept of an obligation, he argued, is the concept of an intrinsically authoritative requirement—a requirement that, simply by virtue of what it requires, forestalls any question as to its authority. So if we want to know what we're morally required to do, we must find something such that a requirement to do *it* would not be open to question. We must find something such that a requirement would carry authority simply by virtue of requiring that thing.

Thus far I have followed Kant fairly closely, but now I am going to depart from his line of argument. When Kant derives what's morally required of us from the authority that must inhere in that requirement, his derivation depends on various technicalities that I would prefer to skip. I shall therefore take a shortcut to Kant's ultimate conclusion.

As we have seen, requirements that depend for their force on some external source of authority turn out to be escapable because the authority behind them can be questioned. We can ask, "Why should I act on this desire?" or "Why should I obey the U.S. Government?" or even "Why should I obey God?" And as we observed in the case of the desire to punch someone in the nose, this question demands a reason for acting. The authority we are questioning would be vindicated, in each case, by the production of a sufficient reason.

What this observation suggests is that any purported source of practical authority depends on reasons for obeying it—and hence on the authority of reasons. Suppose, then, that we attempted to question the authority of reasons themselves, as we earlier questioned other authorities. Where we previously asked "Why should I act on my desire?" let us now ask "Why should I act for reasons?" Shouldn't this question open up a route of escape from *all* requirements?

As soon as we ask why we should act for reasons, however, we can hear something odd in our question. To ask "Why should I?" is to demand a reason; and so to ask "Why should I act for reasons?" is to demand a reason for acting for reasons. This demand implicitly concedes the very authority that it purports to question—namely, the authority of reasons. Why would we demand a reason if we didn't envision acting for it? If we really didn't feel required to act for reasons, then a reason for doing so certainly wouldn't help. So there is something self-defeating about asking for a reason to act for reasons.

The foregoing argument doesn't show that the requirement to act for reasons is inescapable. All it shows is that this requirement cannot be escaped in a particular way: we cannot escape the requirement to act for reasons by insisting on reasons for obeying it. For all that, we still may not be required to act for reasons.

Yet the argument does more than close off one avenue of escape from the requirement to act for reasons. It shows that we are subject to this requirement if we are subject to any requirements at all. The requirement to act for reasons is the fundamental requirement, from which the authority of all other requirements is derived, since the authority of other requirements just consists in there being reasons for us to obey them. There may be nothing that is required of us; but if anything is required of us, then acting for reasons is required.

Hence the foregoing argument, though possibly unable to foreclose escape from the requirement to act for reasons, does succeed in raising the stakes. It shows that we cannot escape the requirement to act for reasons without escaping the force of requirements altogether. Either we think of ourselves as under the requirement to act for reasons, or we think of ourselves as under no requirements at all. And we cannot stand outside both ways of thinking and ask for reasons to enter into one or the other, since to ask for reasons is already to think of ourselves as subject to requirements.

The requirement to act for reasons thus seems to come as close as any requirement can to having intrinsic authority, in the sense of being authoritative by virtue of what it requires. This requirement therefore comes as close as any requirement can to being inescapable. But remember that inescapability was supposed to be the hallmark of a moral obligation or duty: it was the essential element in our *concept* of a duty, from which we hoped that the *content* of our duty could be deduced. What we have now deduced is that the requirement that bears this mark of morality is the requirement to act for reasons; and so we seem to have arrived at the conclusion that "Act for reasons" is the content of our duty. How can this be?

At this point, I can only sketch the roughest outline of an answer; I won't be able to supply any details until the end of this essay. Roughly, the answer is that to act for reasons is to act on the basis of considerations that would be valid for anyone in similar circumstances; whereas immoral behavior always involves acting on considerations whose validity for others we aren't willing to acknowledge. If we steal, for example, we take our own desire for someone else's property as a reason for making it our property instead—as if his desire for the thing weren't a reason for its being his property instead of ours. We thus take our desire as grounds for awarding ownership to ourselves, while denying that his desire is grounds for awarding ownership to him. Similarly, if we lie, we hope that others will believe what we say even though we don't believe it, as if what we say should count as a reason for them but not for us. Once again, we attempt to separate reasons for us from reasons for others. In doing so, we violate the very concept of a reason, which requires that a reason for one be a reason for all. Hence we violate the requirement, "Act for reasons."

So much for a rough outline of Kant's answer. Before I can supply the details, I'll need to explore further what we feel ourselves required to do in being required to act for reasons. And in order to explore this requirement, I'll turn to an example that will seem far removed from morality.

Reasons that are Temporally Constant

Suppose that you stay in shape by swimming laps two mornings a week, when the pool is open to recreational swimmers. But suppose that when your alarm goes off this morning, you just don't feel like facing the sweaty locker room, the dank showers, the stink of chlorine, and the shock of diving into the chilly pool. You consider skipping your morning swim just this once.

(If you don't exercise regularly, you may have to substitute another example for mine. Maybe the exceptions that you consider making "just for this once" are exceptions to your diet, your drinking limit, or your schedule for finishing your schoolwork.)

When you are tempted to make an exception to your program of exercise, you are likely to search for an excuse—some reason for staying in bed rather than going off to the pool. You sniffle a few times, hoping for some signs of congestion; you lift your head to look out the window, hoping for a blizzard; you try to remember your calendar as showing some special commitment for later in the day. Excuse-making of this sort seems perfectly natural, but it ought to seem odd. Why do you need a reason for not doing something that you don't feel like doing?

This question can be understood in several different ways. It may ask why you don't already have a good enough reason for not swimming, consisting in the fact that you just don't feel like it. To this version of the question, the answer is clear. If not feeling like it were a good enough reason for not swimming, then you'd almost never manage to get yourself into the pool, since the mornings on which you're supposed to swim almost always find you not feeling like it. Given that you want to stay in shape by swimming, you can't accept "I don't feel like it" as a valid reason, since it would completely undermine your program of exercise. Similarly, you can't accept "That would taste good" as a reason for going over your limit of drinks, or you wouldn't really have a limit, after all.

Why not accept "I don't feel like it" as a reason on this occasion while resolving to reject it on all others? Again the answer is clear. If a consideration counts as a reason for acting, then it counts as a reason whenever it is true. And on almost any morning, it's true that you don't feel like swimming.

Yet if a reason is a consideration that counts as a reason whenever it's true, then why not dispense with reasons so defined? Why do you feel compelled to act for *that* sort of consideration? Since you don't feel like swimming, you might just roll over and go back to sleep, without bothering to find some fact about the present occasion from which you're willing to draw similar implications whenever it is true. How odd, to skip exercise in order to sleep and then to lose sleep anyway over finding a reason not to exercise!

Kant offered an explanation for this oddity. His explanation was that acting for reasons is essential to being a person, something to which you unavoidably aspire. In order to be a person, you must have an approach to the world that is sufficiently coherent and constant to qualify as a single, continuing point-of-view. And part of what gives you a single, continuing point-of-view is your acceptance of particular considerations as having the force of reasons whenever they are true.

We might be tempted to make this point by saying that you *are* a unified, persisting person and hence that you *do* approach practical questions from a point-of-view framed by constant reasons. But this way of making the point wouldn't explain why you feel compelled to act for reasons; it would simply locate acting for reasons in a broader context, as part of what makes you a person. One of Kant's greatest insights, however, is that a unified, persisting person is something that you *are* because it is something that you *aspire to be*. Antecedently to this aspiration, you are merely aware that you are *capable* of being a person. But any creature aware that it is capable of being a person, in Kant's view, is *ipso facto* capable of appreciating the value of being a person and is therefore ineluctably drawn toward personhood.

The value of being a person in the present context is precisely that of attaining a perspective that transcends that of your current, momentary self. Right now, you would rather sleep than swim, but you also know that if you roll over and sleep, you will wake up wishing that you had swum instead. Your impulse to decide on the basis of reasons is, at bottom, an impulse to transcend these momentary points-of-view, by attaining a single, constant perspective that can subsume both of them. It's like the impulse to attain a higher vantage point that overlooks the restricted standpoints on the ground below. This higher vantage point is neither your current perspective of wanting to sleep, nor your later perspective of wishing you had swum, but a timeless perspective from which you can reflect on now-wanting-this and later-wishing-that, a perspective from which you can attach constant practical implications to these considerations and come to a stable, all-things-considered judgment.

If you want to imagine what it would be like never to attain a continuing point-of-view, imagine being a cat. A cat feels like going out and meows to go out; feels like coming in and meows to come in; feels like going out again and meows to go out; and so on, all day long. The cat cannot think, "I have things to do outside and things to do inside, so how should I organize my day?" But when you, a person, find yourself to-ing and fro-ing in this manner, you feel an impulse to find a constant perspective on the question when you should "to" and when you should "fro."

This impulse is unavoidable as soon as the availability of the more encompassing vantage point appears. As soon as you glimpse the possibility of attaining a constant perspective from which to reflect on and adjudicate among your shifting preferences, you are drawn toward that perspective, as you would be drawn toward the top of a hill that commanded a terrain through which you had been wandering. To attain that standpoint, in this case, would be to attain the single, continuing point-of-view that would constitute the identity of a person. To see the possibility of attaining it is therefore to see the possibility of being a person; and seeing that possibility unavoidably leads you to aspire toward it.

Of course, there is a sense of the word 'person' that applies to any creature capable of grasping the possibility of attaining the single, continuing perspective of a fully unified person. One must already be a person in the former, minimal sense in order to aspire toward personhood in the latter. I interpret Kant as having used words like 'person' in both senses, to denote what we already are and what we consequently aspire to become.

This Kantian thought is well expressed—believe it or not—by a word in Yiddish. In Yiddish, to call someone a *Mensch* is to say that he or she is a good person—solid, centered, true-blue.[1] But *Mensch* is just the German word for "person" or "human being," like the English "man" in its gender-neutral usage. Thus, a *Mensch* in the German sense is merely a creature capable of being a *Mensch* in the Yiddish.

To be a solid, centered human being of the sort that Yiddishers call a *Mensch* entails occupying a unified, persisting point-of-view defined by a constant framework of reasons. But to be a human being at all, according to Kant, is to grasp and hence aspire toward the possibility of attaining personhood in this sense. Hence the imperative that compels you to look for generally valid reasons is an imperative that is naturally felt by all *Menschen*: the imperative "Be a *Mensch*."

The requirement "Be a *Mensch*" already sounds like a moral requirement, but I have introduced it by way of an example about exercise, which we don't usually regard as a moral obligation. My example may therefore seem ill suited to illustrate a requirement that's supposedly fundamental to morality. On second thought, however, we may have to reconsider what sort of a requirement we are dealing with.

If you do roll over and go back to sleep, in my example, you will be left with an emotion that we normally associate with morality—namely, guilt. You feel guilty when you shirk exercise, go over your drinking limit, put off working, or otherwise make an exception "just for this once." Indeed, your motives for seeking a reason on such occasions include the desire to avoid the sense of guilt, by avoiding the sense of having made a singular exception.

There is the possibility that the word 'guilt' is ambiguous, and that self-reproaches about shirking exercise do not manifest the same emotion as self-reproaches about lying or cheating. Alternatively, there is the possibility that the guilt you feel about shirking exercise is genuine but unwarranted. I would reject both of these hypotheses, however. If you go for your usual swim but stop a few laps short of your usual distance, you might well accuse yourself of cheating; if asked whom you were cheating, you would probably say that you were cheating yourself. Insofar as you owe it to yourself to swim the full distance, your sense of guilt may be not only genuine but perfectly appropriate.

Kant believed that moral obligations can be owed not only to others but also to oneself. Defenders of Kant's moral theory often seem embarrassed by his notion of having obligations to oneself, which is said to be odd or even incoherent. But I think that Kant's concept of an obligation is the concept of something that can be owed to oneself, and that any interpretation under which obligations to self seem odd must be a misinterpretation. That's why I have begun my account of Kantian ethics with self-regarding obligations.

Thus far, I have explained how the natural aspiration toward a stable point-of-view is both an aspiration to be a person, in the fullest sense, and a motive to act on considerations that have the same practical implications whenever they are true— that is, to act for reasons. I have thus explained how the felt requirement to be a person can deter you from cheating on your drinking limit or program of exercise and; in that minor respect, impel you to be a *Mensch*. What remains to be explained is how the same requirement can impel you to be a *Mensch* by eschewing other, interpersonal forms of cheating.

Reasons that are Universally Shared[2]

In Kant's view, being a person consists in being a rational creature, both cognitively and practically. And Kant thought that our rationality gives us a glimpse of—and hence an aspiration toward—a perspective even more inclusive than that of our persisting individual selves. Rational creatures have access to a shared perspective, from which they not only see the same things but can also see the visibility of those things to all rational creatures.

Consider, for example, our capacity for arithmetic reasoning. Anyone who adds 2 and 2 sees, not just that the sum is 4, but also that anyone who added 2 and 2 would see that it's 4, and that such a person would see this, too, and so on. The facts of elementary arithmetic are thus common knowledge among all possible reasoners, in the sense that every reasoner knows them, and knows that every reasoner knows them, and knows that every reasoner knows that every reasoner knows them, and so on.

As arithmetic reasoners, then, we have access to a perspective that is constant not only across time but also between persons. We can compute the sum of 2 and 2 *once and for all*, in the sense that we would only get the same answer on any other occasion; and each of us can compute the sum of 2 and 2 *one for all*, in the sense that the others would only get the same answer. What's more, the universality of our perspective on the sum of 2 and 2 is evident to each of us from within that very perspective. In computing the sum of 2 and 2, we are aware of computing it *for all*, from a perspective that's shared by all arithmetic reasoners. In this sense, our judgment of the sum is authoritative, because it speaks for the judgment of all.

This shared perspective is like a vantage point overlooking the individual perspectives of reasoners, a standpoint from which we not only see what everyone sees but also see everyone seeing it. And once we glimpse the availability of this vantage point, we cannot help but aspire to attain it. We are no longer satisfied with estimating or guessing the sum of two numbers, given the possibility of computing it once for all: we are ineluctably drawn to the perspective of arithmetic reason.

Note that the aspect of arithmetic judgments to which we are drawn in this case resembles the authority that we initially regarded as definitive of moral requirements: it's the authority of being inescapable. We can compute the sum of 2 and 2 once for all because the answer we reach is the answer that would be reached from any perspective and is therefore inescapable. We can approach the sum of 2 and 2 from wherever we like, and we will always arrive at the same answer. The case of arithmetic reasoning shows that inescapability can in fact appeal to us, because it is the feature in virtue of which judgments constitute a stable and all-encompassing point-of-view. Perhaps, then, the authority of moral judgments, which consists in their inescapability, can appeal to us in similar fashion, by offering an attractive vantage point of some kind.

But what does arithmetic reasoning have to do with acting for reasons? Well, suppose that the validity of reasons for acting were also visible from a perspective shared by all reasoners—by all practical reasoners, that is. In that case, our aspirations toward personhood would draw us toward the perspective of practical reason as well.

Indeed, that may be the perspective toward which you were being drawn when you felt compelled to find a reason for not exercising. Your immediate concern was to find a set of considerations whose validity as reasons would remain constant through fluctuations in your preferences; but you would also have regarded those considerations as constituting reasons for other people as well, insofar as they were true of those people. In accepting an incipient cold as a reason to skip swimming, you would have regarded it as something that would count as a reason for anyone to skip swimming, in circumstances like yours. What you were seeking may thus have been considerations that could count as reasons not only for you, whenever they were true of you, but for other agents as well.

There is one important difference between practical and arithmetic reasoning, however. When you searched for reasons not to exercise this morning, no considerations just struck you as the ones that would strike any practical reasoner, in the way that 4 strikes you as being the answer that would strike any reasoner adding 2 and 2. Rather, you had to try out different considerations as reasons; and you tried them out by testing whether you would be willing to have them strike you as reasons whenever they were true. That's how you tested and then rejected "I don't feel like it" as a reason for not exercising.

This feature of the case suggests that you may not have access to a pre-existing perspective shared by all reasoners in practical matters as you do in arithmetic. Apparently, however, you were trying to *construct* such a perspective, by asking whether you would be willing for various considerations to count as reasons whenever they were true, as if their reason-giving force, or validity, were accessible from a shared perspective. You asked, "What if 'I don't feel like it' were generally valid as a reason for not exercising?"—as if you could choose whether or not to enshrine the validity of this consideration in a constant perspective of practical reasoning.

There is a sense in which you could indeed enshrine the validity of this consideration in a constant *individual* perspective. For if you had taken something as a sufficient reason for not exercising on this occasion, you would later have remembered doing so, and your deliberations on subsequent occasions might then have been guided by the precedent. Having once accepted a consideration as a reason for not exercising, you might later have felt obliged to accept it again, in other situations where it was true. Even so, however, you aren't capable of enshrining the validity of a consideration in a perspective that would be shared by all practical reasoners, since your taking something as a reason would not influence the deliberations of others as it would the deliberations of your future selves. Although you can construct a *temporally constant* perspective from which to conduct your own practical reasoning, you cannot construct a *universally shared* perspective.

And yet constructing a universally shared perspective of practical reasoning is precisely what Kant said that you must regard yourself as doing when you decide how to act. Kant expressed this requirement as follows: "Act only on a maxim that you can at the same time will to be universal law."

The clearest example of willing a maxim to be universal law—the clearest example that I know of, at least—is the train of thought that you undertake when considering whether to make an exception "just for this once," such as an exception to your diet or program of exercise. You think of potential reasons, in the form of true considerations such as "That would taste good" or "I don't feel like it," but then you realize that you aren't willing to grant these considerations validity as reasons whenever they are true, since doing so would completely undermine your regimen. Having found that you cannot consistently will these considerations to be generally valid as reasons, you refuse to act on them, as if in obedience to Kant's requirement.

According to Kant, however, you are required to act on considerations whose validity as reasons you can consistently will to be evident, not just to yourself on other occasions when they are true, but to other practical reasoners of whom they may be true as well. You are thus required to act only on considerations whose validity you could willingly enshrine in a universally accessible perspective of practical reasoning. That's what Kant meant by acting only on a maxim that you could will to be universal law.

Yet the force of Kant's proposed requirement remains elusive. Even if I have managed to direct your attention to your own sense of being required to construct a temporally constant perspective of practical reasoning, that requirement presupposes the possibility of your constructing such a perspective— a possibility that depends, in turn, on ties of memory between your current decision-making and your decision-making in the future. As we have seen, however, you aren't capable of constructing a perspective of practical reasoning that would be universally accessible to all reasoners. So how can you feel required to construct one?

I'm going to skip over this question for the moment, in order to describe how Kant's moral theory reaches its conclusions. I'll return to the question later, eventually offering two alternative answers to it. First, however, I want to show how substantive moral conclusions can issue from Kant's theory.

Two Examples

Suppose that we were required to act only on considerations whose validity as reasons we could willingly enshrine in a universally accessible perspective of practical reasoning, just as we feel required to act only on considerations whose validity we could enshrine in a temporally constant perspective. This requirement would decisively rule out some considerations. Here is an example from Kant's *Critique of Practical Reason*:

> Suppose, for example, that I have made it my maxim to increase my fortune by every safe means. Now, I have a deposit in my hands, the owner of which is dead and has left no writing about it. This is just the case for my maxim. I desire then to know whether that maxim can also hold good as a universal practical law. I apply it, therefore, to the present case, and ask whether it could take the form of a law, and consequently whether I can by my maxim at the same time give such a law as this, that everyone may deny a deposit of which no one can produce a proof. I at once become aware that such a principle, viewed as a law, would annihilate itself, because the result would be that there would be no deposits.[3]

In this passage, Kant imagines considering whether a consideration such as "I want the money" can count as a reason for denying the receipt of a deposit from someone who has died without leaving any record of it.

Much as you asked whether you were willing to make "I don't feel like it" valid as a reason for not exercising on all occasions when it is true, Kant asks whether he is willing to make "I want the money" valid as a reason for all trustees of whom it is true. Kant says, "The result would be that there would be no deposits." Why not?

The answer is that the validity of reasons for denying unrecorded deposits would have to be common knowledge among all practical reasoners. If a trustee's desire to keep a depositor's money were a valid reason for denying its receipt, then the validity of that reason would have to be known to prospective depositors, who have access to the common knowledge of practical reasoners, and who would then be deterred from making any deposits, in the first place. A trustee can therefore see that he would never receive a single deposit if wanting to keep it would be a valid reason for him to deny its receipt, just as the drinker sees that he wouldn't have a limit if his thirst were a valid reason for exceeding it.

A trustee can therefore see that if "I want the money" were a valid reason for denying the receipt of deposits, there would be no deposits whose receipt he could deny. And a consideration can hardly be a reason for an action that would be rendered unavailable by the validity of that very reason. "I want the money" couldn't be a universally accessible reason for defaulting because, if it were, there would be no opportunities for defaulting. And since it couldn't be a universally accessible reason, it isn't valid as a reason for defaulting, after all.

Actually, this example is an instance of a larger class, since defaulting on the return of a deposit would unavoidably involve lying, and lying also violates the fundamental requirement "Act for reasons." So let's examine this larger class of examples.

To lie is intentionally to tell someone a falsehood. When we tell something to someone, we act with a particular kind of communicative intention: we say or write it to him with the intention of giving him grounds for believing it. Indeed, we intend to give him grounds for belief precisely by manifesting this very communicative intention in our speech or writing. We intend that the person acquire grounds for believing what we say by recognizing that we are acting with the intention of conveying those grounds.

Now, suppose that our wanting to give someone grounds for believing something constituted sufficient reason for telling it to him, whether or not we believed it ourselves. In that case, the validity of this reason would be common knowledge among all reasoners, including him. He would therefore be able to see that, in wanting to give him grounds for believing the thing, as was manifest in our communicative action, we already had sufficient reason for telling it to him, whether or not we believed it. And if he could see that we had sufficient reason for telling it even if we ourselves didn't believe it, then our telling it would give him no grounds for believing it, either. Why should he believe what we tell him if we need no more reason for telling him than the desire, already manifest in the telling, to give him grounds for believing it? So if our wanting to give him grounds for believing something were sufficient reason for telling it to him, then telling him wouldn't accomplish the result that we wanted, and wanting that result wouldn't be a reason for telling him, after all. Wanting to convey grounds for belief can't be a sufficient reason for telling, then, because if it were, it would not be a reason at all.

I introduced these examples by asking you to imagine that you could construct a universally accessible perspective of practical reasoning, so that you could be required to act only on considerations whose validity you could enshrine in such a perspective. Yet it has now turned out that there already *is* such a perspective—or, at least, the beginnings of one—and it hasn't been constructed by anyone. For we have stumbled on one kind of practical result that anyone can see, and can see that anyone can see, and so on.

The kind of practical result that we have found to be universally accessible has the following form: that the validity of some putative reason for acting could not be universally accessible. The validity of "I want the money" as a reason for denying receipt of a deposit, or the validity of "I want him to believe it" as a reason for telling something to someone, could not be universally accessible, any more than the validity of "That would taste good" as a reason for going over your limit of drinks. The fact that the validity of these reasons could not be universally accessible—*this* fact is already universally accessible to practical reasoners, any of whom can perform the reasoning by which it has come to light.

Thus, the notion of sharing a perspective with all practical reasoners is not a pipedream, after all. You already share a perspective with all practical reasoners to this extent: *that it is common knowledge among all reasoners that the validity of certain reasons for acting could not be common knowledge among all reasoners.* This item of common knowledge constitutes a universally accessible constraint on what can count as a reason for acting and hence what can satisfy a requirement to act for reasons. A requirement to act for reasons would forbid acting on the basis of considerations whose validity as reasons could not be common knowledge among all reasoners, and in the case of some considerations, this impossibility is itself common knowledge.

Let me review the argument to this point, which can now be seen to implement the overall strategy of deriving the content of our duties from the very concept of a duty. We began with the idea that moral requirements must be inescapable, which led to the idea that they must be intrinsically authoritative, in the sense of having authority over us simply by virtue of what they require. We then found a requirement that came as close as possible to having such authority—the requirement to act for reasons, which cannot coherently be questioned and must be presupposed by all other practical requirements.

Next we saw how the requirement to act for reasons is experienced in ordinary life, when one looks for an exemption from some regular regimen or policy. In this example, the requirement to act for reasons is experienced as an impulse to act on a consideration from which one is willing to draw the same consequences whenever it is true, an impulse that militates against cheating oneself. And we found such an impulse intelligible as part of one's aspiration toward the unified, persisting point-of-view that makes for a fully integrated person.

Our next step was to observe that rational creatures can attain not only unified individual perspectives but a single perspective that is shared, in the sense that its deliverances are common knowledge among them. And with the help of examples drawn from Kant, we saw that a requirement to act on considerations whose validity was common knowledge would amount to a ban on cheating others. What remains to be explained is how the requirement to act for reasons in this sense is experienced in ordinary life and whether it, too, can be understood as part of the aspiration to be a person.

The Idea of Freedom[4]

In order to answer this remaining question, we must return to a problem that we considered earlier and set aside—the question why we feel compelled to think of ourselves as constructing a universally accessible framework of reasons for acting. We can't actually build a universally accessible framework of reasons, although we do enjoy universal access to the fact that some reasons, in particular, couldn't be built into such a framework. The question is why we feel compelled not to act on reasons that couldn't be built into something that isn't for us to build, in the first place.

Kant's answer to this question was that in order to act, we must conceive of ourselves as free; and that in order to conceive of ourselves as free, we must conceive of ourselves as acting on reasons that owe their authority to us. Considerations have authority as reasons only if they have the sort of validity that is universally accessible to all reasoners; but we won't be free in acting on them, Kant believed, if they have

simply been dictated to us from a universal perspective in which we have no say. We must think of them as reasons on which we ourselves confer authority, by introducing them into that perspective.

I think that Kant was simply wrong about the idea of freedom, insofar as he thinks that it requires us to be the source of the authority in our own reasons for acting. Roughly speaking, I think that we cannot be guided by reasons whose only authority is that with which we ourselves have endowed them.

To endow reasons with authority, as I have now conceived it, would be to *make* their status as reasons common knowledge among all reasoners—a feat that is simply beyond our power. More importantly, it's a feat that we cannot help but *think* is beyond our power. If we thought that something's being a reason could become common knowledge among all reasoners only by dint of our making it so, then we would have no hope of its ever being so. Hence if we thought that reasons owed their authority to us, we would have no hope of their ever having authority.

Why can't reasons owe their authority to us? The answer is that endowing reasons with authority would entail making their validity common knowledge among all reasoners. And if we could promote reasons to the status of being common knowledge among all reasoners, then we should equally be able to demote them from that status—in which case, the status wouldn't amount to rational authority. The point of a reason's being common knowledge among all reasoners, remember, is that there is then no way of evading it, no matter how we shift our point-of-view. No amount of rethinking will make such a reason irrelevant, because its validity as a reason is evident from every perspective. But if we could decide what is to be common knowledge among all thinkers, then a reason's being common knowledge would not entail its being inescapable, since we could also decide that it wasn't to be common knowledge, after all. Our power to construct a universally accessible framework of reasons would therefore undermine the whole point of having one.

I think that Kant's mistake was to claim that we must act under the idea of freedom; what he should have said, I think, is that we must act under the idea of **autonomy**. Let me explain the difference between these concepts.

'Autonomy' is derived from the Greek word for self-rule or self-governance. Our behavior is autonomous when it is self-governed, in the sense that we ourselves are in control of it; it is not autonomous—or, as Kant would say, it is **heteronomous**—when it is controlled by something other than ourselves. To say that behavior is controlled by something other than ourselves is not to say that it is controlled from outside our bodies or our minds. A sneeze or a hiccup is not under our control; neither is a startle or an impulsive cry of pain; but all of these heteronomous behaviors originate within us. What makes them heteronomous is that, while originating *within*, they don't originate *with us*: they aren't fully our doing. Only the behaviors that are fully our doing qualify as autonomous actions.

The fact that we act autonomously doesn't necessarily entail that we have free will—not, at least, in the sense that Kant had in mind. In Kant's view, our having free will would require not only that we sit behind the wheel of our behavior, so to speak, but also that we face more than one direction in which it would be causally possible that we steer it, so that our future course is not pre-determined. One might suspect that if our future course *were* pre-determined, then we wouldn't really be in control of our behavior, and hence that autonomy really does require freedom. Yet there is a way for us to follow a pre-determined course and yet steer that course in a meaningful sense. Our course might be pre-determined by the fact that there are reasons for us to do particular things and that we are rationally responsive to reasons. So long as we are responding to reasons, we remain autonomous, whether or not those reasons predetermine what we do.

Consider here our autonomy with respect to our beliefs. When we consider the sum of 2 and 2, we ourselves draw the conclusion that it is 4. The thought $2 + 2 = 4$ is not dictated to us by anyone else; it is not due to an involuntary mental association, not forced on our minds by an obsession or fixed in our minds by a mental block; in short, it isn't the intellectual equivalent of a sneeze or a hiccup. When we consider the sum of 2 and 2, we make our own

way to the answer 4. And yet there is no other answer that we could arrive at, given that we are arithmetically competent and that, as any reasoner can see, the sum of 2 and 2 is 4. So when we consider the sum of 2 and 2, we are pre-determined to arrive at the answer 4, but to arrive there autonomously, under our own intellectual steam. We aren't free to conclude that $2 + 2$ is 5, and yet we are autonomous in concluding that it is 4.

Perhaps, then, we can steer our behavior as we steer our thoughts, in directions that are pre-determined, not by exogenous forces, but by our rational ability to do what there is reason for doing, just as we think what there is reason for thinking. In that case, we could have autonomy without necessarily having free will.

Kant himself identified what is special about behavior that is rationally necessitated. Whereas heteronomous behavior is determined by antecedent events under a law of nature, he observed, autonomous behavior is determined by *our conception* of a law. A law, in this context, is just a practical requirement of the sort with which this analysis of duty began, a requirement specifying something that we must do. What makes our behavior autonomous is that we do it, not just because our doing it is necessitated by prior events, but because we realize that doing it is required—a realization that constitutes our conception of a law, in Kant's terms. Our recognition of a practical requirement, and our responsiveness to that recognition, is what makes the resulting action attributable to us, as our doing: it's what gets us into the act.

Kant thus explained why acting for reasons makes us autonomous. Acting for reasons makes us autonomous because "Act for reasons" is the ultimate requirement lying behind all other practical requirements, whose authority depends on there being reasons to obey them. Whenever our behavior is determined by our conception of law—that is, by our realization that some action is required—we are being governed at bottom by a recognition of reasons, either constituting or backing up that requirement.

Kant thought that being determined by our recognition of a practical requirement, on the one hand, and being determined by prior events under a law of nature, on the other, are mutually exclusive alternatives, at least in the sense that we cannot conceive of ourselves as being determined in both ways at once. (In fact, he thought that we can perhaps *be* determined in both ways at once but that we can't *conceive* of being so, because we can't reconcile these two modes of determination in our minds.) But I think that being determined by our recognition of a practical requirement can itself be conceived as a causal process, governed by natural laws. I express this possibility by saying that we can conceive of ourselves as autonomous without having to conceive of ourselves as free.

Because Kant thought that we cannot conceive of ourselves as autonomous without also conceiving of ourselves as free, he insisted that we must not conceive of practical requirements as externally dictated. That is, we must not find ourselves confronted with inexorable reasons for doing things, in the way that we find ourselves confronted with an inexorable answer to the calculation of 2 + 2; for if we did, our action would be predetermined, and we wouldn't be free to choose it, just as we aren't free to choose a sum for 2 + 2. Kant thought that we must regard the balance of reasons for acting as being up to us in a way that the sum of 2 and 2 is not.

Kant's insistence that we act under the idea of freedom thus led him to insist that we conceive of ourselves as constructing rather than merely finding a universally accessible framework of reasons for acting. As I have explained, I think that our constructing reasons would deprive them of the authority that universal accessibility is meant to provide. But as I have also explained, I think that Kant's insistence on our constructing them is unnecessary, because we can act under the idea of autonomy, without any pretensions of being free.

Even if we need only think of ourselves as autonomous when we act, we will still be required to act for reasons, since autonomy consists in being determined by authoritative considerations. The requirement to act for reasons can thus be felt to arise from the aspiration to be a person in a more profound form. Our earlier discussion directed our attention toward the general region of experience where the requirement to act for reasons can be found, but it didn't identify the fundamental manifestation of that requirement. We saw that the requirement to act for reasons can be felt to arise from our aspiration to be a person, but we traced it to a fairly specific instance of that aspiration, consisting in our aspiration toward a temporally constant point-of-view. And then we found that this specific aspiration cannot account for the moral force of the requirement in interpersonal cases. The present discussion suggests that the fundamental manifestation of the requirement to act for reasons is a different form of the aspiration to be a person: it's the aspiration toward autonomy. We feel required to act for reasons insofar as we aspire to be persons by being the originators of our own behavior.

Contradictions in the Will

Replacing Kant's references to freedom with references to autonomy needn't alter our analysis of the foregoing examples. The aspiration toward autonomy yields a requirement to act for reasons, and this requirement will forbid us to act on considerations whose practical implications couldn't be common knowledge, as in the cases of cheating analyzed earlier.

Yet there are other cases in which Kant derived moral conclusions in a way that depends on the very aspect of freedom by which it differs from what I have called autonomy. In these examples, what rules out some considerations as reasons for acting, according to Kant, is not that they couldn't be universally accessible, as in the case of our grounds for stealing or lying, but rather that we couldn't consistently *make* them universally accessible. It is precisely our inability to build these considerations into a universally accessible framework of reasons that prevents them from being reasons, according to Kant. Yet our inability to build some considerations into a universally accessible framework of reasons would prevent them from being reasons only if such a framework depended on us for its construction—which is what I have just been denying, in contesting Kant's view of freedom. My disagreement with Kant on the subject of freedom therefore threatens to escalate into a disagreement about which considerations can be reasons and, from there, into a disagreement about what is morally required.

The clearest cases of this kind have the form of prisoners' dilemmas.[5] Prisoners' dilemmas get their name from a philosophical fiction in which two people—say, you and I—are arrested on suspicion of having committed a crime together. The police separate us for interrogation and offer us similar plea bargains: if either gives evidence against the other, his sentence (whatever it otherwise would have been) will be shortened by one year, and the other's sentence will be lengthened by two. The expected benefits give each of us reason to testify against the other. The unfortunate result is that each sees his sentence shortened by one year in payment for his own testimony, but lengthened by two because of the other's testimony; and so we both spend one more year in jail than we would have if both had kept silent.

Let me pause to apologize for a misleading feature of this story. Because the characters in the story are criminals, and the choice confronting them is whether to tell the whole truth and nothing but the truth, turning state's evidence may seem to be the option that's favored by morality. But this story serves as a model for every case in which the choice is whether to join some beneficial scheme of cooperation, such as rendering aid or keeping commitments to one another. There are parts of morality whose basic point is to enjoin cooperation in cases of this kind, and philosophers use the prisoners' dilemma as a model for those parts of morality. In order to understand philosophical uses of the prisoners' dilemma, then, we have to remember that cooperating with one's fellow prisoner represents the moral course in this philosophical fiction, because it is the course of mutual aid and commitment.

Prisoners' dilemmas are ripe for Kantian moral reasoning because the two participants are in exactly similar situations, which provide them with exactly similar reasons. When each of us sees the prospect of a reduced sentence as a reason to testify against the other, he must also see that the corresponding prospect is visible to the other as a reason for doing likewise, and indeed that the validity of these reasons is common knowledge between us.

Given that our reasons must be common knowledge, however, I ought to wish that the incentives offered to me were insufficient reason for testifying against you, since the incentives offered to you would then be insufficient reason for testifying against me, and both of us would remain silent, to our mutual advantage. And you must also wish that the incentives were insufficient reason for testifying against me, so that I would likewise find them insufficient for testifying against you. Furthermore, each of us must realize that the other shares the wish that the incentives were insufficient reason for turning against the other. The following is therefore common knowledge between us: we agree in wishing that what was common knowledge between us was that our reasons for turning against one another were insufficient.

Here, the power to construct a shared framework of reasons would certainly come in handy, since you and I would naturally converge on which reasons to incorporate into that framework and which reasons to exclude. The power to construct a shared framework of reasons would thus transform our predicament, in a way that it would not have transformed the cases considered earlier.

In the case of lying, for example, we found that it was not just undesirable but downright impossible that our desire for someone to believe something should be a sufficient reason for telling it to him. This desire couldn't possibly be such a reason, we concluded, because its being a reason would entail common knowledge of its being one, which in turn would ensure that it wasn't a reason, after all. This conclusion did not depend on the assumption that we could in any way affect the rational import of wanting someone to believe something—that we could elevate it to the status of a reason or demote it from that status. Even if reasons were handed down to us from a universally accessible perspective that we took no part in constructing, we would know in advance that the deliverances of that perspective would not include, as a sufficient reason for telling something to someone, the mere desire that he believe it.

Hence our conclusion about lying is not at all threatened by the doubts outlined earlier about the Kantian doctrine of freedom. But those doubts do threaten the prospect of drawing any Kantian conclusions about the prisoners' dilemma. For whereas some reasons for lying are rendered impossible by the necessity of their being common knowledge, our reasons for turning against one another in the prisoners' dilemma are rendered merely undesirable. And if reasons are indeed handed down to us from a universally accessible perspective that we take no part in constructing, then we have no guarantee against being handed undesirable reasons, even if they were universally undesirable. Only if we construct the shared framework of reasons can we expect it to exclude undesirable reasons, such as our reasons for turning against one another in the prisoners' dilemma.

Our proposed reasons for lying are ruled out by what Kant called a **contradiction in conception**. This contradiction prevents us from conceiving that the desire for someone to believe something should be a sufficient reason for telling it to him. Kant thought that our proposed reasons for turning against one another in the prisoners' dilemma can also be ruled out, not because a contradiction would be involved in their *conception*, but rather because a contradiction would be involved in their *construction*—a contradiction of the sort that Kant called a **contradiction in the will**. Specifically, building these reasons into the universally accessible framework would contradict our desire that what was common knowledge between us were reasons for cooperating instead. But if the framework of reasons is not for us to construct, then contradictions in the will are no obstacle to anything's being a reason, and half of Kantian ethics is in danger of failure. Securing Kantian ethics against this failure requires a substantial revision in the theory, in my opinion. I'll briefly outline one possible revision.

The prisoners' dilemma places you and me at odds not only with one another but also with ourselves. If you find that the incentives are a sufficient reason for turning state's evidence, you will wish that they weren't, given that their status as a reason must be common knowledge between us, which will persuade me to turn state's evidence as well. You therefore find yourself in possession of reasons that you wish you didn't have. Of course, you may often

find yourself in such a position. As you drag yourself out of bed and head for the pool, for example, you may wish that you didn't have such good reasons for sticking to your regimen of exercise. These cases may not involve any contradiction in your will, strictly speaking, but they do involve a conflict, which complicates your decision-making and compromises the intelligibility of your decisions. Think of the way that you vacillate when confronted with unwelcome reasons for acting, and the way that you subsequently doubt your decision, whatever it is.

I have argued that you cannot simply will away unwelcome reasons for acting, but the fact remains that you can gradually bring about changes in yourself and your circumstances that mitigate or even eliminate the conflict. You can learn to relish early-morning swims, you can switch to a more enticing form of exercise, or you can find some other way to lower your cholesterol. You can also cultivate a disdain for advantages that you wouldn't wish to be generally available, such as the advantages to be gained in the prisoners' dilemma by turning against a confederate. You might even learn to regard an additional year in prison as a badge of honor, when it is incurred for refusing to turn against a confederate, and a shortened sentence as a mark of shame under these circumstances—in which case, the plea bargain offered to you would no longer be a bargain from your point-of-view, and the prisoners' dilemma would no longer be a dilemma. This attitude toward incarceration can't be called up at a moment's notice, of course; it may take years to cultivate. But when you adopted a life of crime, you could have foreseen being placed in precisely the position represented by the prisoners' dilemma, and you could already have begun to develop attitudes that would clarify such a position for you. (Surely, that's what lifetime criminals do, and rationally so—however irrational they may be to choose a life of crime, in the first place.)

Thus, if you find yourself confronted with unwelcome reasons for acting, you have probably failed at some earlier time to arrange your circumstances or your attitudes so as to head off conflicts of this kind. You can't change your personality or your circumstances on the spot; nor can you change their status as reasons for acting here and now. But with a bit of foresight and self-command, you could have avoided the predicament of acting on reasons that you wished you didn't have. Since you had reason for taking steps to avoid such a conflict, you have somewhere failed to act for reasons—not here and now, as you act on your unwelcome reasons, but at some earlier time, when you allowed yourself to get into that predicament.

Hence the requirement "Act for reasons" can favor morality in two distinct ways. First, it can rule out various actions, such as lying, that are based on considerations whose validity as reasons is inconceivable. Second, it can rule out acquiring reasons whose validity, though conceivable, is unwelcome. In the latter case, it doesn't rule out performing any particular actions; rather, it rules out becoming a particular kind of person, whose reasons for acting are regrettable, even from his own point-of-view.

Before I turn from the current line of thought, I should reiterate that it cannot be traced to the works of Kant himself. Kant would reject the suggestion that contradictions in the will are always such as to have occurred long before the time of action, and hence to be beyond correction on the spot. The resulting moral theory is therefore kantian with a small k.

Respect for Persons[6]

There is one more way in which the requirement to act for reasons constrains us to be moral, in Kant's view. Kant actually thought that this constraint is equivalent to the ones that I've already discussed—that it is one of the aforementioned contradictions viewed from a different angle or described in different terms. I disagree with Kant on this point, and so I'll present this constraint as independent of the others, thus departing again from Kant.

Many people take up a regimen of diet or exercise as a means of staying healthy, but some overdo it, so that they ruin their health instead. Most people accumulate money as a means of buying useful or enjoyable things, but some overdo it, grubbing for money so hard that they have no time to spend it. In either case, the overdoers are making a fundamental mistake about reasons for acting: they are exchanging an end for the means to that end, thus exchanging something valuable for something else that is valuable only for its sake. Exercise is not valuable in itself but only for the sake of health (or so I am assuming for the moment); money is not valuable in itself but only for the sake of happiness. To sacrifice health for the sake of exercise, or to sacrifice happiness for the sake of money, is to stand these values on their heads. The prospect of gains in exercise or income can't provide reason for accepting a net loss in the ends for whose sake alone they are valuable.

Kant's greatest insight, in my view, was that we can commit the same mistake in practical reasoning with respect to persons and their interests. The basis of this insight is that the relation between a person and his interests is similar to, though not exactly the same as, the relation between an end, such as happiness, and the means to it, such as money. Kant believed that persons themselves are ends, and that they consequently must not be exchanged for the things that stand to them in the capacity analogous to that of means.

Some commentators interpret Kant as meaning that persons are ends in the same sense as health or happiness—that is, in the sense that we have reason to promote or preserve their existence. What Kant really meant, however, is that persons are things *for the sake of which* other things can have value.

The phrase 'for the sake of' indicates the subordination of one concern to another. To want money for the sake of happiness is to want money because, and insofar as, you want to be happy; to pursue exercise for the sake of health is to pursue it because, and insofar as, you want to be healthy. You may also care about things for the sake of a person. You may want professional success for your own sake, but you may also want it for the sake of your parents, who love you and made sacrifices to give you a good start. In the latter case, your concern for your happiness depends upon your concern for others; in the former, it depends upon your concern for yourself.

The dependence between these concerns is evident in the familiar connection between how you feel about yourself and how you feel about your happiness. Sometimes when you realize that you have done something mean-spirited, you come to feel worthless as a person. You may even hate yourself; and one symptom of self-hatred is a loss of concern for your own happiness. It no longer seems to matter whether life is good to you, because you yourself seem to be no good. Your happiness matters only insofar as *you* matter, because it is primarily for your sake that your happiness matters at all.

Now, to want money for the sake of happiness is to want the one as a means of promoting or preserving the existence of the other; but to want happiness for your own sake is not to want it as a means of promoting or preserving your existence. Happiness is not a means of self-preservation, and the instinct of self-preservation is not the attitude that underlies your concern for it. The underlying self-concern is a sense of your value as a person, a sense of self-worth, which is not at all the same as the urge to survive. Hence, wanting happiness for your own sake is both like and unlike wanting money for the sake of happiness. The cases are alike in that they involve the subordination of one concern to another; but they are unlike with respect to whether the objects of concern are related as instruments and outcomes.

When Kant referred to persons as ends, he was not saying that they lend value to anything that stands to them as instruments, or means. He was saying merely that they are things for the sake of which other things can have value, as your happiness is valuable for your sake. The dependence between these values, however, is enough to yield a rational constraint similar to the constraint on exchanging ends for means.

If your happiness is valuable for your sake, and matters only insofar as you matter, then you cannot have reason to sacrifice yourself for the sake of happiness, just as you cannot have reason to sacrifice happiness for the sake of money. Just as your concern for money is subordinate to your concern for happiness, so your concern for happiness is subordinate to self-concern, and the former concerns must not take precedence over the latter, as would happen if you pursued money at the sacrifice of your happiness, or happiness at the sacrifice of yourself.

Sacrificing yourself for the sake of happiness may sound impossible, but it isn't. People make this exchange whenever they kill themselves in order to end their unhappiness, or ask to be killed for that purpose. The requirement to act for reasons rules out such mercy killing, which exchanges a person for something that's valuable only for his sake. Because a person's happiness is valuable for his sake, it cannot provide a reason for sacrificing the person himself.

(Before I go further, I should point out that Kantian ethics does not, in my view, rule out suicide or euthanasia in every case. As we have seen, Kantian ethics rules out actions only insofar as they are performed for particular reasons. For example, it doesn't rule out false utterances in general but only those which are made for the sake of getting someone to believe a falsehood. Similarly, it doesn't rule out suicide and euthanasia in general but only when they are performed for the sake of ending unhappiness. With that qualification in place, let me return to my explanation of persons as ends.)

Kant thought that the status of persons as ends rules out more than sacrificing them for their interests; he thought that it rules out treating them in any way that would amount to using them merely as means to other ends. In his view, persons shed value on other things, by making them valuable for a person's sake; whereas means merely reflect the value shed on them by the ends for whose sake they are valuable. To treat a person as a means is to treat him as a mere reflector of value rather than a value-source, which is a confusion on the order of mistaking the sun for the moon. Indeed, Kant thought that a universe without persons would be pitch dark with respect to value.

Here let me remind you of the aspiration in which the requirement to act for reasons is manifested in our experience. Reasons for acting are considerations that are authoritative in the sense that their practical import is common knowledge among all reasoners, including not only other people but also ourselves at other times. Having access to such considerations enables us to act autonomously, as the originators of our own behavior. And being autonomous is essential to—perhaps definitive of—being a person. Hence the requirement to act for reasons expresses our aspiration to realize a central aspect of personhood—or, as I put it, the aspiration to "be a *Mensch*."

This alternative formulation of the requirement to act for reasons has implications for the current discussion of persons as ends-in-themselves. What it implies is that the felt authority of reasons is due, in part, to our appreciation of ourselves as persons. In acting for reasons, we live up to our status as persons, and we act for reasons partly as a way of living up to that status. The motivational grip that reasons have on us is subordinate to our appreciation for the value of being a *Mensch*.

If you think back to our initial search for an intrinsically inescapable requirement, you will recall that "Act for reasons," though close to being inescapable, was not perfectly so. We settled for it after reflecting that we are required to act for reasons if we are subject to any requirements at all. What we have subsequently discovered is that seeing ourselves as subject to practical requirements is essential to seeing ourselves as autonomous and, in that respect, as persons. Thus, although we are required to act for reasons only insofar as we are subject to practical requirements at all, we are obliged to conceive of ourselves as subject to requirements, and hence required to act for reasons, by our aspiration toward personhood.

The value of persons now emerges as paramount, not only over the value of what we do for someone's sake, but over the value of acting for any reason whatsoever. Acting for reasons matters because being a person matters.

What's more, the value of our individual personhood here and now is inseparable from the value of participating in personhood as a status shared with our selves at other times and with other people, whose access to the same framework of reasons is what lends those reasons authority. Only by sharing in the common knowledge of reasoners do we find ourselves subject to authoritative requirements, recognition of which must determine our behavior if we are to be autonomous persons. Being an autonomous person is thus impossible without belonging to the community of those with access to the same sources of autonomy. Insofar as being a person matters, belonging to the community of persons must matter, and the importance of both is what makes it important to act for reasons.

That's why it's irrational to treat any person merely as a means, for any reason whatsoever. No reason for acting can justify treating a person as a mere reflector of value, because the importance of acting for reasons depends on the importance of personhood in general as a source of value. Reasons matter because persons matter, and so we cannot show our regard for reasons by showing disregard for persons.

NOTES

1. I say more about what it is to be a *Mensch* in "The Centered Self," (Chapter 11).
2. For further elaboration on the material in this section and the next, see "The Voice of Conscience," (Chapter 5).
3. Immanuel Kant, *Critique of Practical Reason*, trans. by Lewis White Beck (Indianapolis: Bobbs Merrill, 1956), 27.
4. The material in this section and the next is developed further in "Willing the Law," (Chapter 12).
5. I discuss prisoners' dilemmas further in "The Centered Self," (Chapter 11). See note 2 of that chapter for an explanation of how to coordinate it with what I say about prisoners' dilemmas here.
6. The material in this section is developed further in "Love as a Moral Emotion" (Chapter 4) and in "A Right of Self-Termination?" *Ethics* 109 (1999): 606–28.

STUDY QUESTIONS

1. According to Velleman, Kant believed we have duties to ourselves. Explain the reasoning behind Kant's position. Is Kant right?
2. On Velleman's view, what does Kant mean when he says that we should "act only on a maxim that you can at the same time will to be universal law"? In what way, according to Kant, must the maxims on which we act be "universal"? Why does Kant hold this view? Is he right?
3. What does Velleman believe is the difference between autonomy and free will (or freedom)? In what way did Kant think freedom was required for morality? Explain why Velleman disagrees with Kant on this matter.
4. Kant thought that we morally should not treat persons as "mere means to an end." Why? Give an example of what it would be for someone to treat another as a "mere means."

Kantian Approaches to Some Famine Problems

ONORA O'NEILL

Onora O'Neill (1941–) was the Chair of the Nuffield Foundation (1998–2010) and is a Professor of Philosophy at the University of Cambridge. She is well known for her important contributions to ethics and political philosophy, specifically her development of a Kantian approach to ethics. Her books include *Constructions of Reason: Exploration of Kant's Practical Philosophy*, *Towards Justice and Virtue*, and *Bounds of Justice*.

. .

§22 A Simplified Account of Kant's Ethics

Kant's moral theory has acquired the reputation of being forbiddingly difficult to understand and, once understood, excessively demanding in its requirements. I don't believe that this reputation has been wholly earned, and I am going to try to undermine it. In §§23–26 I shall try to reduce some of the difficulties, and in §§27–29 I shall try to show the implications of a Kantian moral theory for action toward those who do or may suffer famine. Finally, I shall compare Kantian and **utilitarian** approaches and assess their strengths and weaknesses.

The main method by which I propose to avoid some of the difficulties of Kant's moral theory is by explaining only one part of the theory. This does not seem to me to be an irresponsible approach in this case. One of the things that makes Kant's moral theory hard to understand is that he gives a number of different versions of the principle that he calls the Supreme Principle of Morality, and these different versions don't look at all like one another. They also don't look at all like the utilitarians' **Greatest Happiness Principle**. But the Kantian principle is supposed to play a similar role in arguments about what to do.

Kant calls his Supreme Principle the *Categorical Imperative*: its various versions also have sonorous names. One is called the Formula of Universal Law;

another is the Formula of the Kingdom of Ends. The one on which I shall concentrate is known as the *Formula of the End in Itself*. To understand why Kant thinks that these picturesquely named principles are equivalent to one another takes quite a lot of close and detailed analysis of Kant's philosophy. I shall avoid this and concentrate on showing the implications of this version of the Categorical Imperative.

§23 The Formula of the End in Itself

Kant states the Formula of the End in Itself as follows:

> Act in such a way that you always treat humanity, whether in your own person or in the person of any other, never simply as a means but always at the same time as an end.[1]

To understand this we need to know what it is to treat a person as a means or as an end. According to Kant, each of our acts reflects one or more *maxims*. The maxim of the act is the principle on which one sees oneself as acting. A maxim expresses a person's policy, or if he or she has no settled policy, the principle underlying the particular intention or decision on which he or she acts. Thus, a person who decides "This year I'll give 10 percent of my income to famine relief" has as a maxim the principle of tithing his or her income for famine relief. In practice, the difference between intentions and maxims is of little importance, for given any intention, we can formulate the corresponding maxim by deleting references to particular times, places, and persons. In what follows I shall take the terms "maxim" and "intention" as equivalent.

Whenever we act intentionally, we have at least one maxim and can, if we reflect, state what it is. (There is of course room for self-deception here—"I'm only keeping the wolf from the door" we may claim as we wolf down enough to keep ourselves overweight, or, more to the point, enough to feed someone else who hasn't enough food.)

When we want to work out whether an act we propose to do is right or wrong, according to Kant, we should look at our maxims and not at how much misery or happiness the act is likely to produce, and whether it does better at increasing happiness than other available acts. We just have to check that the act we have in mind will not use anyone as a mere means, and, if possible, that it will treat other persons as ends in themselves.

§24 Using Persons as Mere Means

To use someone as a *mere means* is to involve them in a scheme of action *to which they could not in principle consent*. Kant does not say that there is anything wrong about using someone as a means. Evidently we have to do so in any cooperative scheme of action. If I cash a check I use the teller as a means, without whom I could not lay my hands on the cash; the teller in turn uses me as a means to earn his or her living. But in this case, each party consents to her or his part in the transaction. Kant would say that though they use one another as means, they do not use one another as *mere* means. Each person assumes that the other has maxims of his or her own and is not just a thing or a prop to be manipulated.

But there are other situations where one person uses another in a way to which the other could not in principle consent. For example, one person may make a promise to another with every intention of breaking it. If the promise is accepted, then the person to whom it was given must be ignorant of what the promisor's intention (maxim) really is. If one knew that the promisor did not intend to do what he or she was promising, one would, after all, not accept or rely on the promise. It would be as though there had been no promise made. Successful false promising depends on deceiving the person to whom the promise is made about what one's real maxim is. And since the person who is deceived doesn't know that real maxim, he or she can't in principle consent to his or her part in the proposed scheme of action. The person who is deceived is, as it were, a prop or a tool—a mere means—in the false promisor's scheme. A person who promises falsely treats the acceptor of the promise as a prop or a thing and not as a person. In Kant's view, it is this that makes false promising wrong.

One standard way of using others as mere means is by deceiving them. By getting someone involved in a business scheme or a criminal activity on false pretenses, or by giving a misleading account of what one is about, or by making a false promise or a fraudulent contract, one involves another in something to which he or she in principle cannot consent, since the scheme requires that he or she doesn't know what is going on. Another standard way of using others as mere means is by coercing them. If a rich or powerful person threatens a debtor with bankruptcy unless he or she joins in some scheme, then the creditor's intention is to coerce; and the debtor, if coerced, cannot consent to his or her part in the creditor's scheme. To make the example more specific: If a moneylender in an Indian village threatens not to renew a vital loan unless he is given the debtor's land, then he uses the debtor as a mere means. He coerces the debtor, who cannot truly consent to this "offer he can't refuse." (Of course the outward form of such transactions may look like ordinary commercial dealings, but we know very well that some offers and demands couched in that form are coercive.)

In Kant's view, acts that are done on maxims that require deception or coercion of others, and so cannot have the consent of those others (for consent precludes both deception and coercion), are wrong. When we act on such maxims, we treat others as mere means, as things rather than as ends in themselves. If we act on such maxims, our acts are not only wrong but unjust: such acts wrong the particular others who are deceived or coerced.

§25 Treating Persons
as Ends in Themselves

Duties of justice are, in Kant's view (as in many others'), the most important of our duties. When we fail in these duties, we have used some other or others as mere means. But there are also cases where, though we do not use others as mere means, still we fail to use them as ends in themselves in the fullest possible way. To treat someone as an end in him or herself requires in the first place that one not use him or her as mere means, that one respect each as a rational person with his or her own maxims. But beyond that, one may also seek to foster others' plans and maxims by sharing some of their ends. To act beneficently is to seek others' happiness, therefore to intend to achieve some of the things that those others aim at with their maxims. If I want to make others happy, I will adopt maxims that not merely do not manipulate them but that foster some of their plans and activities. Beneficent acts try to achieve what others want. However, we cannot seek everything that others want; their wants are too numerous and diverse, and, of course, sometimes incompatible. It follows that beneficence has to be selective.

There is then quite a sharp distinction between the requirements of justice and of beneficence in Kantian ethics. Justice requires that we act on *no* maxims that use others as mere means. Beneficence requires that we act on *some* maxims that foster others' ends, though it is a matter for judgment and discretion which of their ends we foster. Some maxims no doubt ought not to be fostered because it would be unjust to do so. Kantians are not committed to working interminably through a list of happiness-producing and misery-reducing acts; but there are some acts whose obligatoriness utilitarians may need to debate as they try to compare total outcomes of different choices, to which Kantians are stringently bound. Kantians will claim that they have done nothing wrong if none of their acts is unjust, and that their duty is complete if in addition their life plans have in the circumstances been reasonably beneficent.

In making sure that they meet all the demands of justice, Kantians do not try to compare all available acts and see which has the best effects. They consider only the proposals for action that occur to them and check that these proposals use no other as mere means.

If they do not, the act is permissible; if omitting the act would use another as mere means, the act is obligatory. Kant's theory has less scope than utilitarianism. Kantians do not claim to discover whether acts whose maxims they don't know fully are just. They may be reluctant to judge others' acts or policies that cannot be regarded as the maxim of any person or institution. They cannot rank acts in order of merit. Yet, the theory offers more precision than utilitarianism when data are scarce. One can usually tell whether one's act would use others as mere means, even when its impact on human happiness is thoroughly obscure.

§26 Kantian Deliberations
on Famine Problems

The theory I have just sketched may seem to have little to say about famine problems. For it is a theory that forbids us to use others as mere means but does not require us to direct our benevolence first to those who suffer most. A conscientious Kantian, it seems, has only to avoid being unjust to those who suffer famine and can then be beneficent to those nearer home. He or she would not be obliged to help the starving, even if no others were equally distressed.

Kant's moral theory does make less massive demands on moral agents than utilitarian moral theory. On the other hand, it is somewhat clearer just what the more stringent demands are, and they are not negligible. We have here a contrast between a theory that makes massive but often indeterminate demands and a theory that makes fewer but less unambiguous demands and leaves other questions, in particular the allocation of beneficence, unresolved. We have also a contrast between a theory whose scope is comprehensive and one that is applicable only to persons acting intentionally and to those institutions that adopt policies, and so maxims. Kantian ethics is silent about the moral status of unintentional action; utilitarians seek to assess all consequences regardless of the intentions that led to them.

§27 Kantian Duties of Justice
in Times of Famine

In famine situations, Kantian moral theory requires unambiguously that we do no injustice. We should not act on any maxim that uses another as mere means, so we should neither deceive nor coerce others. Such a requirement can become quite exacting when the means of life are scarce, when persons can more easily be coerced, and when the advantage of gaining more than what is justly due to one is great. I shall give a list of acts that on Kantian principles it would be unjust to do, but that one might be strongly tempted to do in famine conditions.

I will begin with a list of acts that one might be tempted to do as a member of a famine-stricken population. First, where there is a rationing scheme, one ought not to cheat and seek to get more than one's share—any scheme of cheating will use someone as mere means. Nor may one take advantage of others' desperation to profiteer or divert goods onto the black market or to accumulate a fortune out of others' misfortunes. Transactions that are outwardly sales and purchases can be coercive when one party is desperate. All the forms of corruption that deceive or put pressure on others are also wrong: hoarding unallocated food, diverting relief supplies for private use, corruptly using one's influence to others' disadvantage. Such requirements are far from trivial and frequently violated in hard times. In severe famines, refraining from coercing and deceiving may risk one's own life and require the greatest courage.

Second, justice requires that in famine situations one still try to fulfill one's duties to particular others. For example, even in times of famine, a person has duties to try to provide for dependents. These duties may, tragically, be unfulfillable. If they are, Kantian ethical theory would not judge wrong the acts of a person who had done her or his best. There have no doubt been times in human history where there was nothing to be done except abandon the weak and old or to leave children to fend for themselves as best they might. But providing the supporter of dependents acts on maxims of attempting to meet their claims, he or she uses no others as mere means to his or her own survival and is not unjust. A conscientious attempt to meet the particular obligations one has undertaken may also require of one many further maxims of self-restraint and of endeavor—for example, it may require a conscientious attempt to avoid having (further) children; it may require contributing one's time and effort to programs of economic development. Where there is no other means

to fulfill particular obligations, Kantian principles may require a generation of sacrifice. They will not, however, require one to seek to maximize the happiness of later generations but only to establish the modest security and prosperity needed for meeting present obligations.

The obligations of those who live with or near famine are undoubtedly stringent and exacting; for those who live further off it is rather harder to see what a Kantian moral theory demands. Might it not, for example, be permissible to do nothing at all about those suffering famine? Might one not ensure that one does nothing unjust to the victims of famine by adopting no maxims whatsoever that mention them? To do so would, at the least, require one to refrain from certain deceptive and coercive practices frequently employed during the European exploration and economic penetration of the now underdeveloped world and still not unknown. For example, it would be unjust to "purchase" valuable lands and resources from persons who don't understand commercial transactions or exclusive property rights or mineral rights, so do not understand that their acceptance of trinkets destroys their traditional economic pattern and way of life. The old adage "trade follows the flag" reminds us to how great an extent the economic penetration of the less-developed countries involved elements of coercion and deception, so was on Kantian principles unjust (regardless of whether or not the net effect has benefited the citizens of those countries).

Few persons in the developed world today find themselves faced with the possibility of adopting on a grand scale maxims of deceiving or coercing persons living in poverty. But at least some people find that their jobs require them to make decisions about investment and aid policies that enormously affect the lives of those nearest to famine. What does a commitment to Kantian moral theory demand of such persons?

It has become common in writings in ethics and social policy to distinguish between one's *personal responsibilities* and one's *role responsibilities*. So a person may say, "As an individual I sympathize, but in my official capacity I can do nothing"; or we may excuse persons' acts of coercion because they are acting in some particular capacity—e.g., as a soldier or a jailer. On the other hand, this distinction isn't made or accepted by everyone. At the Nuremberg trials of war criminals, the defense "I was only doing my job" was disallowed, at least for those whose command position meant that they had some discretion in what they did. Kantians generally would play down any distinction between a person's own responsibilities and his or her role responsibilities. They would not deny that in any capacity one is accountable for certain things for which as a private person one is not accountable. For example, the treasurer of an organization is accountable to the board and has to present periodic reports and to keep specified records. But if she fails to do one of these things for which she is held accountable she will be held responsible for that failure—it will be imputable to her as an individual. When we take on positions, we *add* to our responsibilities those that the job requires; but we do not lose those that are already required of us. Our social role or job gives us, on Kant's view, no license to use others as mere means; even business executives and aid officials and social revolutionaries will act unjustly, so wrongly, if they deceive or coerce—however benevolent their motives.

If persons are responsible for all their acts, it follows that it would be unjust for aid officials to coerce persons into accepting sterilization, wrong for them to use coercive power to achieve political advantages (such as military bases) or commercial advantages (such as trade agreements that will harm the other country). It would be wrong for the executives of large corporations to extort too high a price for continued operation employment and normal trading. Where a less-developed country is pushed to exempt a multinational corporation from tax laws, or to construct out of its meager tax revenues the infrastructure of roads, harbors, or airports (not to mention executive mansions) that the corporation—but perhaps not the country—needs, then one suspects that some coercion has been involved.

The problem with such judgments—and it is an immense problem—is that it is hard to identify coercion and deception in complicated institutional settings. It is not hard to understand what is coercive about one person threatening another with serious injury if he won't comply with the first person's suggestion. But it is not at all easy to tell where the outward forms of political and commercial negotiation—which often involve an element of threat—have become coercive. I can't here explore this fascinating question. But I think it is at least fairly clear that the preservation of the outward forms of negotiation, bargaining, and voluntary consent do *not* demonstrate that there is no coercion, especially when one party is vastly more powerful or the other in dire need. Just as our judiciary has a long tradition of voiding contracts and agreements on grounds of duress or incompetence of one of the parties, so one can imagine a tribunal of an analogous sort rejecting at least some treaties and agreements as coercive, despite the fact that they were negotiated between "sovereign" powers or their representatives. In particular, where such agreements were negotiated with some of the cruder deceptions and coercion of the early days of European economic expansion or the subtler coercions and deceptions of contemporary superpowers, it seems doubtful that the justice of the agreement could be sustained.

Justice, of course, is not everything, even for Kantians. But its demands are ones that they can reasonably strive to fulfill. They may have some uncertain moments—for example, does advocating cheap raw materials mean advocating an international trade system in which the less developed will continue to suffer the pressures of the developed world—or is it a benevolent policy that will maximize world trade and benefit all parties, while doing no one an injustice? But for Kantians, the important moral choices are above all those in which one acts directly, not those in which one decides which patterns of actions to encourage in others or in those institutions that one can influence. And such moral decisions include decisions about the benevolent acts that one will or will not do.

§28 Kantian Duties of Beneficence in Times of Famine

The grounds of duties of beneficence are that such acts not merely don't use others as mere means but are acts that develop or promote others' ends and that, in particular, foster others' capacities to pursue ends, to be autonomous beings.

Clearly there are many opportunities for beneficence. But one area in which the *primary* task of developing others' capacity to pursue their own ends is particularly needed is in the parts of the world where extreme poverty and hunger leave people unable to pursue *any* of their other ends. Beneficence directed at putting people in a position to pursue whatever ends they may have has, for Kant, a stronger claim on us than beneficence directed at sharing ends with those who are already in a position to pursue varieties of ends. It would be nice if I bought a tennis racquet to play with my friend who is tennis mad and never has enough partners; but it is more important to make people able to plan their own lives to a minimal extent. It is nice to walk a second mile with someone who requests one's company; better to share a cloak with someone who may otherwise be too cold to make any journey. Though these suggestions are not a detailed set of instructions for the allocation of beneficence by Kantians, they show that relief of famine must stand very high among duties of beneficence.

§29 The Limits of Kantian Ethics: Intentions and Results

Kantian ethics differs from utilitarian ethics both in its scope and in the precision with which it guides action. Every action, whether of a person or of an agency, can be assessed by utilitarian methods, provided only that information is available about all the consequences of the act. The theory has unlimited scope, but, owing to a lack of data, often lacks precision. Kantian ethics has a more restricted scope. Since it assesses actions by looking at the maxims of agents, it can only assess intentional acts. This means that it is most at home in assessing individuals' acts; but it can be extended to assess acts of agencies that (like corporations and governments and student unions) have decision-making procedures. It can do nothing to assess patterns of action that reflect no intention or policy, hence it cannot assess the acts of groups lacking decision-making procedures, such as the student movement, the women's movement, or the consumer movement.

It may seem a great limitation of Kantian ethics that it concentrates on intentions to the neglect of results. It might seem that all conscientious Kantians

have to do is to make sure that they never intend to use others as mere means, and that they sometimes intend to foster others' ends. And, as we all know, good intentions sometimes lead to bad results, and correspondingly, bad intentions sometimes do no harm, or even produce good. If Hardin is right, the good intentions of those who feed the starving lead to dreadful results in the long run. If some traditional arguments in favor of capitalism are right, the greed and selfishness of the profit motive have produced unparalleled prosperity for many.

But such discrepancies between intentions and results are the exception and not the rule. For we cannot just *claim* that our intentions are good and do what we will. Our intentions reflect what we expect the immediate results of our action to be. Nobody credits the "intentions" of a couple who practice neither celibacy nor contraception but still insist "we never meant to have (more) children." Conception is likely (and known to be likely) in such cases. Where people's expressed intentions ignore the normal and predictable results of what they do, we infer that (if they are not amazingly ignorant) their words do not express their true intentions. The Formula of the End in Itself applies to the intentions on which one acts—not to some prettified version that one may avow. Provided this intention—the agent's real intention—uses no other as mere means, he or she does nothing unjust. If some of his or her intentions foster others' ends, then he or she is sometimes beneficent. It is therefore possible for people to test their proposals by Kantian arguments even when they lack the comprehensive causal knowledge that utilitarianism requires. Conscientious Kantians can work out whether they will be doing wrong by some act even though they know that their foresight is limited and that they may cause some harm or fail to cause some benefit. But they will not cause harms that they can foresee without this being reflected in their intentions.

NOTE

1. I. Kant, *Groundwork of the Metaphysics of Morals*, trans. H. J. Paton (New York: Harper Torchbooks, 1964), p. 96.

KEY TERMS

Utilitarian
Greatest Happiness Principle

STUDY QUESTIONS

1. Describe one scenario that might well arise in ordinary life that involves someone being treated as a mere means, in the Kantian sense.

2. What does it mean to share another person's ends?

3. Is there any reason to think that our Kantian duty of beneficence doesn't extend to those who are suffering from famine in other countries?

4. How does O'Neill argue that Kantian morality does take the consequences of action into consideration to a great extent, despite what some critics say?

5. Do you think the intention with which someone acted is more morally important than the consequences of someone's action? Why or why not?

C. ARISTOTELIAN ETHICS

✗

Nicomachean Ethics

ARISTOTLE

Aristotle (384–322 B.C.) is unquestionably one of the most important philosophers in the Western philosophical tradition. He was a student of Plato, but in many important ways his views diverge from those of his teacher. His work has been highly influential, from early Arabic and Islamic philosophy (where he was known as "The First Teacher") to the Scholastic philosophy of the Middle Ages to contemporary work in virtue ethics. He is considered the author of as many as two hundred treatises, and is best known for his *Metaphysics* and the *Nicomachean Ethics*.

· ·

Book I

1 Every art and every inquiry, and similarly every action
1094ᵃ and pursuit, is thought to aim at some good; and for this reason the good has rightly been declared to be that at which all things aim. But a certain difference is found among ends; some are activities, others are products apart from the activities that produce them. Where there are ends apart from the actions, it is the nature of the products to be better than the activities. Now, as there are many actions, arts, and sciences, their ends also are many; the end of the medical art is health, that of shipbuilding a vessel, that of strategy victory, that of economics wealth. But where such arts fall under a single capacity—as bridlemaking and the

other arts concerned with the equipment of horses fall under the art of riding, and this and every military action under strategy, in the same way other arts fall under yet others—in all of these the ends of the master arts are to be preferred to all the subordinate ends; for it is for the sake of the former that the latter are pursued. It makes no difference whether the activities themselves are the ends of the actions, or something else apart from the activities, as in the case of the sciences just mentioned.

2 If, then, there is some end of the things we do, which we desire for its own sake (everything else being desired for the sake of this), and if we do not choose everything for the sake of something else (for at that rate the process would go on to infinity, so that our desire would be empty and vain), clearly this must be the good and the chief good. Will not the knowledge of it, then, have a great influence on life? Shall we not, like archers who have a mark to aim at, be more

likely to hit upon what is right? If so, we must try, in outline at least, to determine what it is, and of which of the sciences or capacities it is the object. It would seem to belong to the most authoritative art and that which is most truly the master art. And politics appears to be of this nature; for it is this that ordains 1094ᵇ which of the sciences should be studied in a state, and which each class of citizens should learn and up to what point they should learn them; and we see even the most highly esteemed of capacities to fall under this, e.g. strategy, economics, rhetoric; now, since politics uses the rest of the sciences, and since, again, it legislates as to what we are to do and what we are to abstain from, the end of this science must include those of the others, so that this end must be the good for man. For even if the end is the same for a single man and for a state, that of the state seems at all events something greater and more complete whether to attain or to preserve; though it is worth while to attain the end merely for one man, it is finer and more godlike to attain it for a nation or for city-states. These, then, are the ends at which our inquiry aims, since it is political science, in one sense of that term.

3   Our discussion will be adequate if it has as much clearness as the subject-matter admits of, for precision is not to be sought for alike in all discussions, any more than in all the products of the crafts. Now fine and just actions, which political science investigates, admit of much variety and fluctuation of opinion, so that they may be thought to exist only by convention, and not by nature. And goods also give rise to a similar fluctuation because they bring harm to many people; for before now men have been undone by reason of their wealth, and others by reason of their courage. We must be content, then, in speaking of such subjects and with such premisses to indicate the truth roughly and in outline, and in speaking about things which are only for the most part true and with premisses of the same kind to reach conclusions that are no better. In the same spirit, therefore, should each type of statement be *received*; for it is the mark of an educated man to look for precision in each class of things just so far as the nature of the subject admits; it is evidently equally foolish to accept probable reasoning from a mathematician and to demand from a rhetorician scientific proofs.

Now each man judges well the things he knows, 1095ᵃ and of these he is a good judge. And so the man who has been educated in a subject is a good judge of that subject, and the man who has received an all-round education is a good judge in general. Hence a young man is not a proper hearer of lectures on political science; for he is inexperienced in the actions that occur in life, but its discussions start from these and are about these; and, further, since he tends to follow his passions, his study will be vain and unprofitable, because the end aimed at is not knowledge but action. And it makes no difference whether he is young in years or youthful in character; the defect does not depend on time, but on his living, and pursuing each successive object, as passion directs. For to such persons, as to the incontinent, knowledge brings no profit; but to those who desire and act in accordance with a rational principle knowledge about such matters will be of great benefit.

These remarks about the student, the sort of treatment to be expected, and the purpose of the inquiry, may be taken as our preface.

Let us resume our inquiry and state, in view of the 4 fact that all knowledge and every pursuit aims at some good, what it is that we say political science aims at and what is the highest of all goods achievable by action. Verbally there is very general agreement; for both the general run of men and people of superior refinement say that it is happiness, and identify living well and doing well with being happy; but with regard to what happiness is they differ, and the many do not give the same account as the wise. For the former think it is some plain and obvious thing, like pleasure, wealth, or honour; they differ, however, from one another—and often even the same man identifies it with different things, with health when he is ill, with wealth when he is poor; but, conscious of their ignorance, they admire those who proclaim some great ideal that is above their comprehension. Now some thought that apart from these many goods there is another which is self-subsistent and causes the goodness of all these as well. To examine all the opinions that have been held were perhaps somewhat fruitless; enough to examine those that are most prevalent or that seem to be arguable.

Let us not fail to notice, however, that there is a difference between arguments from and those to the first principles. For Plato, too, was right in raising this question and asking, as he used to do, "are we on the way from or to the first principles?" There is a difference, as there is in a racecourse between the course from the judges to the turning-point and the way back. For, while we must begin with what is known, things are objects of knowledge in two senses—some to us, some without qualification. Presumably, then, *we* must begin with things known to *us*. Hence any one who is to listen intelligently to lectures about what is noble and just and, generally, about the subjects of political science must have been brought up in good habits. For the fact is the starting-point, and if this is sufficiently plain to him, he will not at the start need the reason as well; and the man who has been well brought up has or can easily get starting-points. And as for him who neither has nor can get them, let him hear the words of Hesiod:

> Far best is he who knows all things himself;
> Good, he that hearkens when men counsel right;
> But he who neither knows, nor lays to heart
> Another's wisdom, is a useless wight.

5   Let us, however, resume our discussion from the point at which we digressed. To judge from the lives that men lead, most men, and men of the most vulgar type, seem (not without some ground) to identify the good, or happiness, with pleasure; which is the reason why they love the life of enjoyment. For there are, we may say, three prominent types of life—that just mentioned, the political, and thirdly the contemplative life. Now the mass of mankind are evidently quite slavish in their tastes, preferring a life suitable to beasts, but they get some ground for their view from the fact that many of those in high places share the tastes of Sardanapallus. A consideration of the prominent types of life shows that people of superior refinement and of active disposition identify happiness with honour; for this is, roughly speaking, the end of the political life. But it seems too superficial to be what we are looking for, since it is thought to depend on those who bestow honour rather than on him who receives it, but the good we divine to be something proper to a man and not easily taken from him. Further, men seem to pursue honour in order that they may be assured of their goodness; at least it is by men of practical wisdom that they seek to be honoured,

and among those who know them, and on the ground of their virtue; clearly, then, according to them, at any rate, virtue is better. And perhaps one might even suppose this to be, rather than honour, the end of the political life. But even this appears somewhat incomplete; for possession of virtue seems actually compatible with being asleep, or with lifelong inactivity, and, further, with the greatest sufferings and misfortunes; but a man who was living so no one would call happy, unless he were maintaining a thesis at all costs. Third comes the contemplative life, which we shall consider later. But enough of this; for the subject has been sufficiently treated even in the current discussions.

The life of money-making is one undertaken under compulsion, and wealth is evidently not the good we are seeking; for it is merely useful and for the sake of something else. And so one might rather take the aforenamed objects to be ends; for they are loved for themselves. But it is evident that not even these are ends; yet many arguments have been thrown away in support of them. Let us leave this subject, then.

. . . .

7   Let us again return to the good we are seeking, and ask what it can be. It seems different in different actions and arts; it is different in medicine, in strategy, and in the other arts likewise. What then is the good of each? Surely that for whose sake everything else is done. In medicine this is health, in strategy victory, in architecture a house, in any other sphere something else, and in every action and pursuit the end; for it is for the sake of this that all men do whatever else they do. Therefore, if there is an end for all that we do, this will be the good achievable by action, and if there are more than one, these will be the goods achievable by action.

So the argument has by a different course reached the same point; but we must try to state this even more clearly. Since there are evidently more than one end, and we choose some of these (e.g. wealth, flutes, and in general instruments) for the sake of something else, clearly not all ends are final ends; but the chief good is evidently something final. Therefore, if there is only one final end, this will be what we are seeking, and if there are more than one, the most final of these will be what we are seeking. Now we call that which is in itself worthy of pursuit more final than that which is worthy of pursuit for the sake of something else, and that which is never desirable for the sake of something else more final than the things that are desirable both in themselves and for the sake of that other thing, and therefore we call final without qualification that which is always desirable in itself and never for the sake of something else.

1097ᵇ Now such a thing happiness, above all else, is held to be; for this we choose always for itself and never for the sake of something else, but honour, pleasure, reason, and every virtue we choose indeed for themselves (for if nothing resulted from them we should still choose each of them), but we choose them also for the sake of happiness, judging that by means of them we shall be happy. Happiness, on the other hand, no one chooses for the sake of these, nor, in general, for anything other than itself.

From the point of view of self-sufficiency the same result seems to follow; for the final good is thought to be self-sufficient. Now by self-sufficient we do not mean that which is sufficient for a man by himself, for one who lives a solitary life, but also for parents, children, wife, and in general for his friends and fellow citizens, since man is born for citizenship. But some limit must be set to this; for if we extend our requirement to ancestors and descendants and friends' friends we are in for an infinite series. Let us examine this question, however, on another occasion; the self-sufficient we now define as that which when isolated makes life desirable and lacking in nothing; and such we think happiness to be; and further we think it most desirable of all things, without being counted as one good thing among others—if it were so counted it would clearly be made more desirable by the addition of even the least of goods; for that which is added becomes an excess of goods, and of goods the greater is always more desirable. Happiness, then, is something final and self-sufficient, and is the end of action.

Presumably, however, to say that happiness is the chief good seems a platitude, and a clearer account of what it is is still desired. This might perhaps be given, if we could first ascertain the function of man. For just as for a flute-player, a sculptor, or any artist, and, in general, for all things that have a function or activity, the good and the "well" is thought to reside in the function, so would it seem to be for man, if he has a function. Have the carpenter, then, and the tanner certain functions or activities, and has man none? Is he born without a function? Or as eye, hand, foot, and in general each of

the parts evidently has a function, may one lay it down that man similarly has a function apart from all these? What then can this be? Life seems to be common even to plants, but we are seeking what is peculiar to man. Let us exclude, therefore, the life of nutrition and growth. 1098ᵃ Next there would be a life of perception, but it also seems to be common even to the horse, the ox, and every animal. There remains, then, an active life of the element that has a rational principle; of this, one part has such a principle in the sense of being obedient to one, the other in the sense of possessing one and exercising thought. And, as "life of the rational element" also has two meanings, we must state that life in the sense of activity is what we mean; for this seems to be the more proper sense of the term. Now if the function of man is an activity of soul which follows or implies a rational principle, and if we say "a so-and-so" and "a good so-and-so" have a function which is the same in kind, e.g. a lyre-player and a good lyre-player, and so without qualification in all cases, eminence in respect of goodness being added to the name of the function (for the function of a lyre-player is to play the lyre, and that of a good lyre-player is to do so well): if this is the case, [and we state the function of man to be a certain kind of life, and this to be an activity or actions of the soul implying a rational principle, and the function of a good man to be the good and noble performance of these, and if any action is well performed when it is performed in accordance with the appropriate excellence: if this is the case,] human good turns out to be activity of soul in accordance with virtue, and if there are more than one virtue, in accordance with the best and most complete.

But we must add "in a complete life." For one swallow does not make a summer, nor does one day; and so too one day, or a short time, does not make a man blessed and happy.

Let this serve as an outline of the good; for we must presumably first sketch it roughly, and then later fill in the details. But it would seem that any one is capable of carrying on and articulating what has once been well outlined, and that time is a good discoverer or partner in such a work; to which facts the advances of the arts are due; for any one can add what is lacking. And we must also remember what has been said before, and not look for precision in all things alike, but in each class of things such precision as accords with the subject-matter, and so much as is appropriate to the inquiry. For a carpenter and a geometer investigate the right angle in different ways; the former does so in so far as the right angle is useful for his work, while the latter inquires what it is or what sort of thing it is; for he is a spectator of the truth. We must act in the same way, then, in all other matters as well, that our main task may not be subordinated to minor questions. Nor must we demand the cause in all matters alike; it is enough in some cases that the *fact* be well established, as in the case of the first principles; the fact is the primary thing or first principle. Now of first principles we see some by induction, some by perception, some by a certain habituation, and others too in other ways. But each set of principles we must try to investigate in the natural way, and we must take pains to state them definitely, since they have a great influence on what follows. For the beginning is thought to be more than half of the whole, and many of the questions we ask are cleared up by it.

8   We must consider it, however, in the light not only of our conclusion and our premises, but also of what is commonly said about it; for with a true view all the data harmonize, but with a false one the facts soon clash. Now goods have been divided into three classes, and some are described as external, others as relating to soul or to body; we call those that relate to soul most properly and truly goods, and psychical actions and activities we class as relating to soul. Therefore our account must be sound, at least according to this view, which is an old one and agreed on by philosophers. It is correct also in that we identify the end with certain actions and activities; for thus it falls among goods of the soul and not among external goods. Another belief which harmonizes with our account is that the happy man lives well and does well; for we have practically defined happiness as a sort of good life and good action. The characteristics that are looked for in happiness seem also, all of them, to belong to what we have defined happiness as being. For some identify happiness with virtue, some with practical wisdom, others with a kind of philosophic wisdom, others with these, or one of these, accompanied by pleasure or not without pleasure; while others include also external prosperity. Now some of these views have been held by many men and men of old, others by a few eminent persons; and it is not probable that

either of these should be entirely mistaken, but rather that they should be right in at least some one respect or even in most respects.

With those who identify happiness with virtue or some one virtue our account is in harmony; for to virtue belongs virtuous activity. But it makes, perhaps, no small difference whether we place the chief good in possession or in use, in state of mind or in activity. For the state of mind may exist without producing any good result, as in a man who is asleep or in some other way quite inactive, but the activity cannot; for one who has the activity will of necessity be acting, and acting well. And as in the Olympic Games it is not the most beautiful and the strongest that are crowned but those who compete (for it is some of these that are victorious), so those who act win, and rightly win, the noble and good things in life.

Their life is also in itself pleasant. For pleasure is a state of *soul*, and to each man that which he is said to be a lover of is pleasant; e.g. not only is a horse pleasant to the lover of horses, and a spectacle to the lover of sights, but also in the same way just acts are pleasant to the lover of justice and in general virtuous acts to the lover of virtue. Now for most men their pleasures are in conflict with one another because these are not by nature pleasant, but the lovers of what is noble find pleasant the things that are by nature pleasant; and virtuous actions are such, so that these are pleasant for such men as well as in their own nature. Their life, therefore, has no further need of pleasure as a sort of adventitious charm, but has its pleasure in itself. For, besides what we have said, the man who does not rejoice in noble actions is not even good; since no one would call a man just who did not enjoy acting justly, nor any man liberal who did not enjoy liberal actions; and similarly in all other cases. If this is so, virtuous actions must be in themselves pleasant. But they are also *good* and *noble*, and have each of these attributes in the highest degree, since the good man judges well about these attributes; his judgement is such as we have described. Happiness then is the best, noblest, and most pleasant thing in the world, and these attributes are not severed as in the inscription at Delos—

Most noble is that which is justest, and best is health;
But pleasantest is it to win what we love.

For all these properties belong to the best activities; and these, or one—the best—of these, we identify with happiness.

1099ᵇ   Yet evidently, as we said, it needs the external goods as well; for it is impossible, or not easy, to do noble acts without the proper equipment. In many actions we use friends and riches and political power as instruments; and there are some things the lack of which takes the lustre from happiness, as good birth, goodly children, beauty; for the man who is very ugly in appearance or ill-born or solitary and child-less is not very likely to be happy, and perhaps a man would be still less likely if he had thoroughly bad children or friends or had lost good children or friends by death. As we said, then, happiness seems to need this sort of prosperity in addition; for which reason some identify happiness with good fortune, though others identify it with virtue.

. . . .

13   Since happiness is an activity of soul in accordance with perfect virtue, we must consider the nature of virtue; for perhaps we shall thus see better the na-ture of happiness. The true student of politics, too, is thought to have studied virtue above all things; for he wishes to make his fellow citizens good and obedient to the laws. As an example of this we have the law-givers of the Cretans and the Spartans, and any oth-ers of the kind that there may have been. And if this inquiry belongs to political science, clearly the pur-suit of it will be in accordance with our original plan. But clearly the virtue we must study is human virtue; for the good we were seeking was human good and the happiness human happiness. By human virtue we mean not that of the body but that of the soul; and happiness also we call an activity of soul. But if this is so, clearly the student of politics must know somehow the facts about soul, as the man who is to heal the eyes or the body as a whole must know about the eyes or the body; and all the more since politics is more prized and better than medicine; but even among doctors the best educated spend much labour on acquiring knowledge of the body. The student of politics, then, must study the soul, and must study it with these objects in view, and do so just to the extent which is sufficient for the questions we are discuss-ing; for further precision is perhaps something more laborious than our purposes require.

Some things are said about it, adequately enough, even in the discussions outside our school, and we must use these; e.g. that one element in the soul is irrational and one has a rational principle. Whether these are separated as the parts of the body or of anything divisible are, or are distinct by definition but by nature inseparable, like convex and concave in the circumference of a circle, does not affect the present question.

Of the irrational element one division seems to be widely distributed, and vegetative in its nature, I mean that which causes nutrition and growth; for it is this kind of power of the soul that one must assign to all nurslings and to embryos, and this same power 1102ᵇ to full-grown creatures; this is more reasonable than to assign some different power to them. Now the excel-lence of this seems to be common to all species and not specifically human; for this part or faculty seems to function most in sleep, while goodness and bad-ness are least manifest in sleep (whence comes the saying that the happy are no better off than the wretched for half their lives; and this happens natu-rally enough, since sleep is an inactivity of the soul in that respect in which it is called good or bad), unless perhaps to a small extent some of the movements ac-tually penetrate to the soul, and in this respect the dreams of good men are better than those of ordi-nary people. Enough of this subject, however; let us leave the nutritive faculty, alone, since it has by its nature no share in human excellence.

There seems to be also another irrational element in the soul—one which in a sense, however, shares in a rational principle. For we praise the rational principle of the continent man and of the inconti-nent, and the part of their soul that has such a prin-ciple, since it urges them aright and towards the best objects; but there is found in them also another element naturally opposed to the rational principle, which fights against and resists that principle. For exactly as paralysed limbs when we intend to move them to the right turn on the contrary to the left, so is it with the soul; the impulses of incontinent people move in contrary directions. But while in the body we see that which moves astray, in the soul we do not. No doubt, however, we must none the less sup-pose that in the soul too there is something contrary to the rational principle, resisting and opposing it. In what sense it is distinct from the other elements does not concern us. Now even this seems to have a share in a rational principle, as we said; at any rate in the continent man it obeys the rational principle—and presumably in the temperate and brave man it is still more obedient; for in him it speaks, on all matters, with the same voice as the rational principle.

Therefore the irrational element also appears to be twofold. For the vegetative element in no way shares in a rational principle, but the appetitive and in general the desiring element in a sense shares in it, in so far as it listens to and obeys it; this is the sense in which we speak of "taking account" of one's father or one's friends, not that in which we speak of "accounting" for a mathematical property. That the irrational element is in some sense persuaded by a rational principle is indicated also by the giving of advice and by all reproof and exhortation. And if this element also must be said to have a rational principle, that which has a rational principle (as well as that which has not) will be twofold, one subdivision having it in the strict sense and in itself, and the other having a tendency to obey as one does one's father.

Virtue too is distinguished into kinds in accordance with this difference; for we say that some of the virtues are intellectual and others moral, philosophic wisdom and understanding and practical wisdom being intellectual, liberality and temperance moral. For in speaking about a man's character we do not say that he is wise or has understanding but that he is good-tempered or temperate; yet we praise the wise man also with respect to his state of mind; and of states of mind we call those which merit praise virtues.

Book II

1 Virtue, then, being of two kinds, intellectual and moral, intellectual virtue in the main owes both its birth and its growth to teaching (for which reason it requires experience and time), while moral virtue comes about as a result of habit, whence also its name (ἠθική) is one that is formed by a slight variation from the word ἔθος (habit). From this it is also plain that none of the moral virtues arises in us by nature; for nothing that exists by nature can form a habit contrary to its nature. For instance the stone which by nature moves downwards cannot be habituated to move upwards, not even if one tries to train it by throwing it up ten thousand times; nor can fire be habituated to move downwards, nor can anything else that by nature behaves in one way be trained to behave in another. Neither by nature, then, nor contrary to nature do the virtues arise in us; rather we are adapted by nature to receive them, and are made perfect by habit.

Again, of all the things that come to us by nature we first acquire the potentiality and later exhibit the activity (this is plain in the case of the senses; for it was not by often seeing or often hearing that we got these senses, but on the contrary we had them before we used them, and did not come to have them by using them); but the virtues we get by first exercising them, as also happens in the case of the arts as well. For the things we have to learn before we can do them, we learn by doing them, e.g. men become builders by building and lyre-players by playing the lyre; so too we become just by doing just acts, temperate by doing temperate acts, brave by doing brave acts.

This is confirmed by what happens in states; for legislators make the citizens good by forming habits in them, and this is the wish of every legislator, and those who do not effect it miss their mark, and it is in this that a good constitution differs from a bad one.

Again, it is from the same causes and by the same means that every virtue is both produced and destroyed, and similarly every art; for it is from playing the lyre that both good and bad lyre-players are produced. And the corresponding statement is true of builders and of all the rest; men will be good or bad builders as a result of building well or badly. For if this were not so, there would have been no need of a teacher, but all men would have been born good or bad at their craft. This, then, is the case with the virtues also; by doing the acts that we do in our transactions with other men we become just or unjust, and by doing the acts that we do in the presence of danger, and being habituated to feel fear or confidence, we become brave or cowardly. The same is true of appetites and feelings of anger; some men become temperate and good-tempered, others self-indulgent and irascible, by behaving in one way or the other in the appropriate circumstances. Thus, in one word, states of character arise out of like activities. This is why the activities we exhibit must be of a certain kind; it is because the states of character correspond to the differences between these. It makes no small difference, then, whether we form habits of one kind or of another from our very youth; it makes a very great difference, or rather *all* the difference.

2   Since, then, the present inquiry does not aim at theoretical knowledge like the others (for we are inquiring not in order to know what virtue is, but in order to become good, since otherwise our inquiry would have been of no use), we must examine the nature of actions, namely how we ought to do them; for these determine also the nature of the states of character that are produced, as we have said. Now, that we must act according to the right rule is a common principle and must be assumed—it will be discussed later, i.e. both what the right rule is, and how 1104ᵃ it is related to the other virtues. But this must be agreed upon beforehand, that the whole account of matters of conduct must be given in outline and not precisely, as we said at the very beginning that the accounts we demand must be in accordance with the subject-matter; matters concerned with conduct and questions of what is good for us have no fixity, any more than matters of health. The general account being of this nature, the account of particular cases is yet more lacking in exactness; for they do not fall under any art or precept but the agents themselves must in each case consider what is appropriate to the occasion, as happens also in the art of medicine or of navigation.

But though our present account is of this nature we must give what help we can. First, then, let us consider this, that it is the nature of such things to be destroyed by defect and excess, as we see in the case of strength and of health (for to gain light on things imperceptible we must use the evidence of sensible things); both excessive and defective exercise destroys the strength, and similarly drink or food which is above or below a certain amount destroys the health, while that which is proportionate both produces and increases and preserves it. So too is it, then, in the case of temperance and courage and the other virtues. For the man who flies from and

fears everything and does not stand his ground against anything becomes a coward, and the man who fears nothing at all but goes to meet every danger becomes rash; and similarly the man who indulges in every pleasure and abstains from none becomes self-indulgent, while the man who shuns every pleasure, as boors do, becomes in a way insensible; temperance and courage, then, are destroyed by excess and defect, and preserved by the mean.

But not only are the sources and causes of their origination and growth the same as those of their destruction, but also the sphere of their actualization will be the same; for this is also true of the things which are more evident to sense, e.g. of strength; it is produced by taking much food and undergoing much exertion, and it is the strong man that will be most able to do these things. So too is it with the virtues; by abstaining from pleasures we become temperate, and it is when we have become so that we are most able to abstain from them; and similarly too in the case of courage; for by being habituated to 1104ᵇ despise things that are terrible and to stand our ground against them we become brave, and it is when we have become so that we shall be most able to stand our ground against them.

We must take as a sign of states of character the pleasure or pain that ensues on acts; for the man who abstains from bodily pleasures and delights in this very fact is temperate, while the man who is annoyed at it is self-indulgent, and he who stands his ground against things that are terrible and delights in this or at least is not pained is brave, while the man who is pained is a coward. For moral excellence is concerned with pleasures and pains; it is on account of the pain that we abstain from noble ones. Hence we ought to have been brought up in a particular way from our very youth, as Plato says, so as both to delight in and to be pained by the things that we ought; for this is the right education.

Again, if the virtues are concerned with actions and passions, every passion and every action is accompanied by pleasure and pain, for this reason also virtue will be concerned with pleasures and pains. This is indicated also by the fact that punishment is inflicted by these means; for it is a kind of cure, and it is the nature of cures to be effected by contraries.

Again, as we said but lately, every state of soul has a nature relative to and concerned with the kind of things by which it tends to be made worse or better; but it is by reason of pleasures and pains that men become bad, by pursuing and avoiding these—either the pleasures and pains they ought not or when they ought not or as they ought not, or by going wrong in one of the other similar ways that may be distinguished. Hence men even define the virtues as certain states of impassivity and rest; not well, however, because they speak absolutely, and do not say "as one ought" and "as one ought not" and "when one ought or ought not," and the other things that may be added. We assume, then, that this kind of excellence tends to do what is best with regard to pleasures and pains, and vice does the contrary.

The following facts also may show us that virtue and vice are concerned with these same things. There being three objects of choice and three of avoidance, the noble, the advantageous, the pleasant, and their contraries, the base, the injurious, the painful, about all of these the good man tends to go right and the bad man to go wrong, and especially about pleasure; for this is common to the animals, and also it accompanies all objects of choice; for even the noble and the advantageous appear pleasant.

1105ª   Again, it has grown up with us all from our infancy; this is why it is difficult to rub off this passion, engrained as it is in our life. And we measure even our actions, some of us more and others less, by the rule of pleasure and pain. For this reason, then, our whole inquiry must be about these; for to feel delight and pain rightly or wrongly has no small effect on our actions.

Again, it is harder to fight with pleasure than with anger, to use Heraclitus' phrase, but both art and virtue are always concerned with what is harder; for even the good is better when it is harder. Therefore for this reason also the whole concern both of virtue and of political science is with pleasures and pains; for the man who uses these well will be good, he who uses them badly bad.

That virtue, then, is concerned with pleasures and pains, and that by the acts from which it arises it is both increased and, if they are done differently, destroyed, and that the acts from which it arose are those in which it actualizes itself—let this be taken as said.

The question might be asked, what we mean by saying that we must become just by doing just acts, and temperate by doing temperate acts; for if men do just and temperate acts, they are already just and temperate, exactly as, if they do what is in accordance with the laws of grammar and of music, they are grammarians and musicians.

Or is this not true even of the arts? It is possible to do something that is in accordance with the laws of grammar, either by chance or at the suggestion of another. A man will be a grammarian, then, only when he has both done something grammatical and done it grammatically; and this means doing it in accordance with the grammatical knowledge in himself.

Again, the case of the arts and that of the virtues are not similar; for the products of the arts have their goodness in themselves, so that it is enough that they should have a certain character, but if the acts that are in accordance with the virtues have themselves a certain character it does not follow that they are done justly or temperately. The agent also must be in a certain condition when he does them; in the first place he must have knowledge, secondly he must choose the acts, and choose them for their own sakes, and thirdly his action must proceed from a firm and unchangeable character. These are not reckoned in   1105ᵇ as conditions of the possession of the arts, except the bare knowledge; but as a condition on the possession of the virtues knowledge has little or no weight, while the other conditions count not for a little but for everything, i.e. the very conditions which result from often doing just and temperate acts.

Actions, then, are called just and temperate when they are such as the just or the temperate man would do; but it is not the man who does these that is just and temperate, but the man who also does them *as* just and temperate men do them. It is well said, then, that it is by doing just acts that the just man is produced, and by doing temperate acts the temperate man; without doing these no one would have even a prospect of becoming good.

But most people do not do these, but take refuge in theory and think they are being philosophers and will become good in this way, behaving somewhat like patients who listen attentively to their doctors, but do none of the things they are ordered to do. As the latter will not be made well in body by such a course of treatment, the former will not be made well in soul by such a course of philosophy.

5   Next we must consider what virtue is. Since things that are found in the soul are of three kinds—passions, faculties, states of character, virtue must be one of these. By passions I mean appetite, anger, fear, confidence, envy, joy, friendly feeling, hatred, longing, emulation, pity, and in general the feelings that are accompanied by pleasure or pain; by faculties the things in virtue of which we are said to be capable of feeling these, e.g. of becoming angry or being pained or feeling pity; by states of character the things in virtue of which we stand well or badly with reference to the passions, e.g. with reference to anger we stand badly if we feel it violently or too weakly, and well if we feel it moderately; and similarly with reference to the other passions.

Now neither the virtues nor the vices are *passions*, because we are not called good or bad on the ground of our passions, but are so called on the ground of our virtues and our vices, and because we are neither praised nor blamed for our passions (for the man who feels fear or anger is not praised, nor is the man who simply feels anger blamed, but the man who feels it in a certain way), but for our virtues and our vices we *are* praised or blamed.

1106ᵃ   Again, we feel anger and fear without choice, but the virtues are modes of choice or involve choice. Further, in respect of the passions we are said to be moved, but in respect of the virtues and the vices we are said not to be moved but to be disposed in a particular way.

For these reasons also they are not *faculties*: for we are neither called good nor bad, nor praised nor blamed, for the simple capacity of feeling the passions; again, we have the faculties by nature, but we are not made good or bad by nature; we have spoken of this before.

If, then, the virtues are neither passions nor faculties, all that remains is that they should be *states of character*.

Thus we have stated what virtue is in respect of its genus.

6   We must, however, not only describe virtue as a state of character, but also say what sort of state it is. We may remark, then, that every virtue or excellence both brings into good condition the thing of which it is the excellence and makes the work of that thing be done well; e.g. the excellence of the eye makes both the eye and its work good; for it is by the excellence of the eye that we see well. Similarly the excellence of the horse makes a horse both good in itself and good at running and at carrying its rider and at awaiting the attack of the enemy. Therefore, if this is true in every case, the virtue of man also will be the state of character which makes a man good and which makes him do his own work well.

How this is to happen we have stated already, but it will be made plain also by the following consideration of the specific nature of virtue. In everything that is continuous and divisible it is possible to take more, less, or an equal amount, and that either in terms of the thing itself or relatively to us; and the equal is an intermediate between excess and defect. By the intermediate in the object I mean that which is equidistant from each of the extremes, which is one and the same for all men; by the intermediate relatively to us that which is neither too much nor too little—and this is not one, nor the same for all. For instance, if ten is many and two is few, six is the intermediate, taken in terms of the object; for it exceeds and is exceeded by an equal amount; this is intermediate according to arithmetical proportion. But the intermediate relatively to us is not to be taken so; if ten pounds are too much for a particular person to eat   1106ᵇ and two too little, it does not follow that the trainer will order six pounds; for this also is perhaps too much for the person who is to take it, or too little—too little for Milo, too much for the beginner in athletic exercises. The same is true of running and wrestling. Thus a master of any art avoids excess and defect, but seeks the intermediate and chooses this—the intermediate not in the object but relatively to us.

If it is thus, then, that every art does its work well—by looking to the intermediate and judging its works by this standard (so that we often say of good works of art that it is not possible either to take away or to add anything, implying that excess and defect destroy the goodness of works of art, while the mean preserves it; and good artists, as we say, look to this in their work), and if, further, virtue is more exact and better than any art, as nature also is, then virtue must have the quality of aiming at the intermediate. I mean moral virtue; for it is this that is concerned with passions and actions, and in these there is excess, defect, and the intermediate. For instance, both fear and confidence and appetite and anger and pity and in general pleasure and pain may be felt both too much and too little, and in both cases not well; but to feel them at the right times, with reference to the right objects, towards the right people, with the right motive, and in the right way, is what is both intermediate and best, and this is characteristic of virtue. Similarly with regard to actions also there is excess, defect, and the intermediate. Now virtue is concerned with passions and actions, in which excess is a form of failure, and so is defect, while the intermediate is praised and is a form of success; and being praised and being successful are both characteristics of virtue. Therefore virtue is a kind of mean, since, as we have seen, it aims at what is intermediate.

Again, it is possible to fail in many ways (for evil belongs to the class of the unlimited, as the Pythagoreans conjectured, and good to that of the limited), while to succeed is possible only in one way (for which reason also one is easy and the other difficult—to miss the mark easy, to hit it difficult); for these reasons also, then, excess and defect are characteristic of vice, and the mean of virtue;

For men are good in but one way, but bad in many.

1107ª Virtue, then, is a state of character concerned with choice, lying in a mean, i.e., the mean relative to us, this being determined by a rational principle, and by that principle by which the man of practical wisdom would determine it. Now it is a mean between two vices, that which depends on excess and that which depends on defect; and again it is a mean because the vices respectively fall short of or exceed what is right in both passions and actions, while virtue both finds and chooses that which is intermediate. Hence in respect of its substance and the definition which states its essence virtue is a mean, with regard to what is best and right an extreme.

But not every action nor every passion admits of a mean; for some have names that already imply badness, e.g. spite, shamelessness, envy, and in the case of actions adultery, theft, murder; for all of these and suchlike things imply by their names that they are themselves bad, and not the excesses or deficiencies of them. It is not possible, then, ever to be right

with regard to them; one must always be wrong. Nor does goodness or badness with regard to such things depend on committing adultery with the right woman, at the right time, and in the right way, but simply to do any of them is to go wrong. It would be equally absurd, then, to expect that in unjust, cowardly, and voluptuous action there should be a mean, an excess, and a deficiency; for at that rate there would be a mean of excess and of deficiency, an excess of excess, and a deficiency of deficiency. But as there is no excess and deficiency of temperance and courage because what is intermediate is in a sense an extreme, so too of the actions we have mentioned there is no mean nor any excess and deficiency, but however they are done they are wrong; for in general there is neither a mean of excess and deficiency, nor excess and deficiency of a mean.

We must, however, not only make this general statement, but also apply it to the individual facts. For among statements about conduct those which are general apply more widely, but those which are particular are more genuine, since conduct has to do with individual cases, and our statements must harmonize with the facts in these cases. We may take these cases from our table. With regard to feelings of 1107ᵇ fear and confidence courage is the mean; of the people who exceed, he who exceeds in fearlessness has no name (many of the states have no name), while the man who exceeds in confidence is rash, and he who exceeds in fear and falls short in confidence is a coward. With regard to pleasures and pains—not all of them, and not so much with regard to the pains— the mean is temperance, the excess self-indulgence. Persons deficient with regard to the pleasures are not often found; hence such persons also have received no name. But let us call them "insensible."

With regard to giving and taking of money the mean is liberality, the excess and the defect prodigality and meanness. In these actions people exceed and fall short in contrary ways; the prodigal exceeds in spending and falls short in taking, while the mean man exceeds in taking and falls short in spending. . . . With regard to money there are also other dispositions—a mean, magnificence (for the magnificent man differs from the liberal man; the former deals with large sums, the latter with small ones), an excess, tastelessness and vulgarity, and a deficiency, niggardliness; these differ from the states opposed to liberality. . . .

With regard to honour and dishonor the mean is proper pride, the excess is known as a sort of "empty vanity," and the deficiency is undue humility; and as we said liberality was related to magnificence, differing from it by dealing with small sums, so there is a state similarly related to proper pride, being concerned with small honours while that is concerned with great. For it is possible to desire honour as one ought, and more than one ought, and less, and the man who exceeds in his desires is called ambitious, the man who falls short unambitious, while the intermediate person has no name. The dispositions also are nameless, except that that of the ambitious man is called ambition. Hence the people who are at the extremes lay claim to the middle place; and we ourselves sometimes call the intermediate person ambitious and sometimes unambitious, and sometimes praise the ambitious man and sometimes the unambitious. . . . [N]ow let us speak of the remaining states according to the method which has been indicated.

1108ᵃ   With regard to anger also there is an excess, a deficiency, and a mean. Although they can scarcely be said to have names, yet since we call the intermediate person good-tempered let us call the mean good temper; of the persons at the extremes let the one who exceeds be called irascible, and his vice irascibility, and the man who falls short an inirascible sort of person, and the deficiency inirascibility.

There are also three other means, which have a certain likeness to one another, but differ from one another: for they are all concerned with intercourse in words and actions, but differ in that one is concerned with truth in this sphere, the other two with pleasantness; and of this one kind is exhibited in giving amusement, the other in all the circumstances of life. We must therefore speak of these too, that we may the better see that in all things the mean is praiseworthy, and the extremes neither praiseworthy nor right, but worthy of blame. Now most of these states also have no names, but we must try, as in the other cases, to invent names ourselves so that we may be clear and easy to follow. With regard to truth, then, the intermediate is a truthful sort of

person and the mean may be called truthfulness, while the pretence which exaggerates is boastfulness and the person characterized by it a boaster, and that which understates is mock modesty and the person characterized by it mock-modest. With regard to pleasantness in the giving of amusement the intermediate person is ready-witted and the disposition ready wit, the excess is buffoonery and the person characterized by it a buffoon, while the man who falls short is a sort of boor and his state is boorishness. With regard to the remaining kind of pleasantness, that which is exhibited in life in general, the man who is pleasant in the right way is friendly and the mean is friendliness, while the man who exceeds is an obsequious person if he has no end in view, a flatterer if he is aiming at his own advantage, and the man who falls short and is unpleasant in all circumstances is a quarrelsome and surly sort of person.

There are also means in the passions and concerned with the passions; since shame is not a virtue, and yet praise is extended to the modest man. For even in these matters one man is said to be intermediate, and another to exceed, as for instance the bashful man who is ashamed of everything; while he who falls short or is not ashamed of anything at all is shameless, and the intermediate person is modest. Righteous indignation is a mean between envy and spite, and these states are concerned with the pain 1108ᵇ and pleasure that are felt at the fortunes of our neighbours; the man who is characterized by righteous indignation is pained at undeserved good fortune, the envious man, going beyond him, is pained at all good fortune, and the spiteful man falls so far short of being pained that he even rejoices. . . .

There are three kinds of disposition, then, two of 8 them vices, involving excess and deficiency respectively, and one a virtue, viz. the mean, and all are in a sense opposed to all; for the extreme states are contrary both to the intermediate state and to each other, and the intermediate to the extremes; as the equal is greater relatively to the less, less relatively to the greater, so the middle states are excessive relatively to the deficiencies, deficient relatively to the excesses, both in passions and in actions. For the brave man appears rash relatively to the coward, and cowardly relatively to the rash man; and similarly the temperate man appears self-indulgent relatively to the insensible man, insensible relatively to the self-indulgent, and the liberal man prodigal relatively to the mean man, mean relatively to the prodigal. Hence also the people at the extremes push the intermediate man each over to the other, and the brave man is called rash by the coward, cowardly by the rash man, and correspondingly in the other cases.

These states being thus opposed to one another, the greatest contrariety is that of the extremes to each other, rather than to the intermediate; for these are further from each other than from the intermediate, as the great is further from the small and the small from the great than both are from the equal. Again, to the intermediate some extremes show a certain likeness, as that of rashness to courage and that of prodigality to liberality; but the extremes show the greatest unlikeness to each other; now contraries are defined as the things that are furthest from each other, so that things that are further apart are more contrary.

1109ᵃ   To the mean in some cases the deficiency, in some the excess is more opposed; e.g. it is not rashness, which is an excess, but cowardice, which is a deficiency, that is more opposed to courage, and not insensibility, which is a deficiency, but self-indulgence, which is an excess, that is more opposed to temperance. This happens from two reasons, one being drawn from the thing itself; for because one extreme is nearer and liker to the intermediate, we oppose not this but rather its contrary to the intermediate. E.g., since rashness is thought liker and nearer to courage, and cowardice more unlike, we oppose rather the latter to courage; for things that are further from the intermediate are thought more contrary to it. This, then, is one cause, drawn from the thing itself; another is drawn from ourselves; for the things to which we ourselves more naturally tend seem more contrary to the intermediate. For instance, we ourselves tend more naturally to pleasures, and hence are more easily carried away towards self-indulgence than toward propriety. We describe as contrary to the mean, then, rather the directions in which we more often go to great lengths; and therefore self-indulgence, which is an excess, is the more contrary to temperance.

That moral virtue is a mean, then, and in what sense it is so, and that it is a mean between two vices, the one involving excess, the other deficiency, and that it is such because its character is to aim at what is intermediate in passions and in actions, has been sufficiently stated. Hence also it is no easy task to be good. For in everything it is no easy task to find the middle, e.g. to find the middle of a circle is not for every one but for him who knows; so, too, any one can get angry—that is easy—or to give or spend money; but to do this to the right person, to the right extent, at the right time, with the right motive, and in the right way, *that* is not for every one, nor is it easy; wherefore goodness is both rare and laudable and noble.

Hence he who aims at the intermediate must first depart from what is the more contrary to it, as Calypso advises—

Hold the ship out beyond that surf and spray.

For of the extremes one is more erroneous, one less so; therefore, since to hit the mean is hard in the extreme, we must as a second best, as people say, take the least of the evils; and this will be done best in the way we describe.

But we must consider the things towards which   1109ᵇ we ourselves also are easily carried away; for some of us tend to one thing, some to another; and this will be recognizable from the pleasure and the pain we feel. We must drag ourselves away to the contrary extreme; for we shall get into the intermediate state by drawing well away from error, as people do in straightening sticks that are bent.

Now in everything the pleasant or pleasure is most to be guarded against; for we do not judge it impartially. We ought, then, to feel towards pleasure as the elders of the people felt towards Helen, and in all circumstances repeat their saying; for if we dismiss pleasure thus we are less likely to go astray. It is by doing this, then, (to sum the matter up) that we shall best be able to hit the mean.

But this is no doubt difficult, and especially in individual cases; for it is not easy to determine both how and with whom and on what provocation and how long one should be angry; for we too sometimes praise those who fall short and call them good-tempered, but sometimes we praise those who get angry and call them manly. The man, however, who deviates little from goodness is not blamed, whether he do so in the direction of the more or of the less, but only the man who deviates more widely; for *he* does not fail to be noticed. But up to what point and to what extent a man must deviate before he becomes blameworthy it is not easy to determine by reasoning, any more than anything else that is perceived by the senses; such things depend on particular facts, and the decision rests with perception. So much, then, is plain, that the intermediate state is in all things to be praised, but that we must incline sometimes towards the excess, sometimes towards the deficiency; for so shall we most easily hit the mean and what is right.

. . . .

Book X

7   If happiness is activity in accordance with virtue, it is reasonable that it should be in accordance with the highest virtue; and this will be that of the best thing in us. Whether it be reason or something else that is this element which is thought to be our natural ruler and guide and to take thought of things noble and divine, whether it be itself also divine or only the most divine element in us, the activity of this in accordance with its proper virtue will be perfect happiness. That this activity is contemplative we have already said.

Now this would seem to be in agreement both with what we said before and with the truth. For, firstly, this activity is the best (since not only is reason the best thing in us, but the objects of reason are the best of knowable objects); and, secondly, it is the most continuous, since we can contemplate truth more continuously than we can *do* anything. And we think happiness has pleasure mingled with it, but the activity of philosophic wisdom is admittedly the pleasantest of virtuous activities; at all events the pursuit of it is thought to offer pleasures marvellous for their purity and their enduringness, and it is to be expected that those who know will pass their time more pleasantly than those who inquire. And the self-sufficiency that is spoken of must belong most to

the contemplative activity. For while a philosopher, as well as a just man or one possessing any other virtue, needs the necessaries of life, when they are sufficiently equipped with things of that sort the just man needs people towards whom and with whom he shall act justly, and the temperate man, the brave man, and each of the others is in the same case, but the philosopher, even when by himself, can contemplate truth, and the better the wiser he is; he can perhaps do so better if he has fellow-workers, but still he is the most self-sufficient. And this activity alone would seem to be loved for its own sake; for nothing arises from it apart from the contemplating, while from practical activities we gain more or less apart from the action. And happiness is thought to depend on leisure; for we are busy that we may have leisure, and make war that we may live in peace. Now the activity of the practical virtues is exhibited in political or military affairs, but the actions concerned with these seem to be unleisurely. Warlike actions are completely so (for no one chooses to be at war, or provokes war, for the sake of being at war; any one would seem absolutely murderous if he were to make enemies of his friends in order to bring about battle and slaughter); but the action of the statesman is also unleisurely, and—apart from the political action itself—aims at despotic power and honours, or at all events happiness, for him and his fellow citizens—a happiness different from political action, and evidently sought as being different. So if among virtuous actions political and military actions are distinguished by nobility and greatness, and these are unleisurely and aim at an end and are not desirable for their own sake, but the activity of reason, which is contemplative, seems both to be superior in serious worth and to aim at no end beyond itself, and to have its pleasure proper to itself (and this augments the activity), and the self-sufficiency, leisureliness, unweariedness (so far as this is possible for man), and all the other attributes ascribed to the supremely happy man are evidently those connected with this activity, it follows that this will be the complete happiness of man, if it be allowed a complete term of life (for none of the attributes of happiness is *in*complete).

But such a life would be too high for man; for it is not in so far as he is man that he will live so, but in so far as something divine is present in him; and by so much as this is superior to our composite nature is its activity superior to that which is the exercise of the other kind of virtue. If reason is divine, then, in comparison with man, the life according to it is divine in comparison with human life. But we must not follow those who advise us, being men, to think of human things, and, being mortal, of mortal things, but must, so far as we can, make ourselves immortal, and strain every nerve to live in accordance with the best thing in us; for even if it be small 1178ᵃ in bulk, much more does it in power and worth surpass everything. This would seem, too, to be each man himself, since it is the authoritative and better part of him. It would be strange, then, if he were to choose not the life of his self but that of something else . . . [T]hat which is proper to each thing is by nature best and most pleasant for each thing; for man, therefore, the life according to reason is best and pleasantest, since reason more than anything else *is* man. This life therefore is also the happiest.

8   But in a secondary degree the life in accordance with the other kind of virtue is happy; for the activities in accordance with this befit our human estate. Just and brave acts, and other virtuous acts, we do in relation to each other, observing our respective duties with regard to contracts and services and all manner of actions and with regard to passions; and all of these seem to be typically human. Some of them seem even to arise from the body, and virtue of character to be in many ways bound up with the passions. Practical wisdom, too, is linked to virtue of character, and this to practical wisdom, since the principles of practical wisdom are in accordance with the moral virtues and rightness in morals is in accordance with practical wisdom. Being connected with the passions also, the moral virtues must belong to our composite nature; and the virtues of our composite nature are human; so, therefore, are the life and the happiness which correspond to these. The excellence of the reason is a thing apart; we must be content to say this much about it, for to describe it precisely is a task greater than our purpose requires. It would seem, however, also to need external equipment but little, or less than moral virtue does. Grant that both need the necessaries, and do so equally, even if the statesman's work is the more concerned with the body and

things of that sort; for there will be little difference there; but in what they need for the exercise of their activities there will be much difference. The liberal man will need money for the doing of his liberal deeds, and the just man too will need it for the returning of services (for wishes are hard to discern, and even people who are not just pretend to wish to act justly); and the brave man will need power if he is to accomplish any of the acts that correspond to his virtue, and the temperate man will need opportunity; for how else is either he or any of the others to be recognized? It is debated, too, whether the will or the deed is more essential to virtue, which is assumed to involve both; it is surely clear that its perfection involves both; but for deeds many things are 1178ᵇ needed, and more, the greater and nobler the deeds are. But the man who is contemplating the truth needs no such thing, at least with a view to the exercise of his activity; indeed they are, one may say, even hindrances, at all events to his contemplation; but in so far as he is a man and lives with a number of people, he chooses to do virtuous acts; he will therefore need such aids to living a human life.

But that perfect happiness is a contemplative activity will appear from the following consideration as well. We assume the gods to be above all other beings blessed and happy; but what sort of actions must we assign to them? Acts of justice? Will not the gods seem absurd if they make contracts and return deposits, and so on? Acts of a brave man, then, confronting dangers and running risks because it is noble to do so? Or liberal acts? To whom will they give? It will be strange if they are really to have money or anything of the kind. And what would their temperate acts be? Is not such praise tasteless, since they have no bad appetites? If we were to run through them all, the circumstances of action would be found trivial and unworthy of gods. Still, every one supposes that they *live* and therefore that they are active; we cannot suppose them to sleep like Endymion. Now if you take away from a living being action, and still more production, what is left but contemplation? Therefore the activity of God, which surpasses all others in blessedness, must be contemplative; and of human activities, therefore, that which is most akin to this must be most of the nature of happiness.

This is indicated, too, by the fact that the other animals have no share in happiness, being completely deprived of such activity. For while the whole life of the gods is blessed, and that of men too in so far as some likeness of such activity belongs to them, none of the other animals is happy, since they in no way share in contemplation. Happiness extends, then, just so far as contemplation does, and those to whom contemplation more fully belongs are more truly happy, not as a mere concomitant but in virtue of the contemplation; for this is in itself precious. Happiness, therefore, must be some form of contemplation.

1179a   But, being a man, one will also need external prosperity; for our nature is not self-sufficient for the purpose of contemplation, but our body also must be healthy and must have food and other attention. Still, we must not think that the man who is to be happy will need many things or great things, merely because he cannot be supremely happy without external goods; for self-sufficiency and action do not involve excess, and we can do noble acts without ruling earth and sea; for even with moderate advantages one can act virtuously (this is manifest enough; for private persons are thought to do worthy acts no less than despots—indeed even more); and it is enough that we should have so much as that; for the life of the man who is active in accordance with virtue will be happy. Solon, too, was perhaps sketching well the happy man when he described him as moderately furnished with externals but as having done (as Solon thought) the noblest acts, and lived temperately; for one can with but moderate possessions do what one ought. Anaxagoras also seems to have supposed the happy man not to be rich nor a despot, when he said that he would not be surprised if the happy man were to seem to most people a strange person; for they judge by externals, since these are all they perceive. The opinions of the wise seem, then, to harmonize with our arguments. But while even such things carry some conviction, the truth in practical matters is discerned from the facts of life; for these are the decisive factor. We must therefore survey what we have already said, bringing it to the test of the facts of life, and if it harmonizes with the facts we must accept it, but if it clashes with them we must suppose it to be mere theory. Now he who exercises his reason and cultivates it seems to be both in the best state of mind and most dear to the gods. For if the gods have any care for human affairs, as they are thought to have, it would be reasonable both that they should delight in that which was best and most akin to them (i.e. reason) and that they should reward those who love and honour this most, as caring for the things that are dear to them and acting both rightly and nobly. And that all these attributes belong most of all to the philosopher is manifest. He, therefore, is the dearest to the gods. And he who is that will presumably be also the happiest; so that in this way too the philosopher will more than any other be happy.

STUDY QUESTIONS

1. Do you think, as Aristotle suggests, that "there is some end of the things we do, which we desire for its own sake"? What could it be?
2. What do you think Aristotle means when he talks about the possibility that human beings have a "function"? What could this function be?
3. When discussing a person's character, Aristotle says that "states of character arise out of like activities." Do you think he is right about this? What would this tell us about how we should live?
4. If someone does the right thing out of habit, can we really praise this person for his action? Why or why not?
5. How does Aristotle argue that "perfect happiness is a contemplative activity"? Are you convinced?

Right Action

ROSALIND HURSTHOUSE

Rosalind Hursthouse is a Professor of Philosophy at the University of Auckland, New Zealand. She is best known for her development of virtue ethics, basing her account of morality on that of Aristotle. She is the author of *On Virtue Ethics* and *Ethics, Humans, and Other Animals*.

. .

VIRTUE ethics has been characterized in a number of ways. It is described (1) as an ethics which is "agent-centred" rather than "act-centred"; (2) as concerned with Being rather than Doing; (3) as addressing itself to the question, "What sort of person should I be?" rather than to the question, "What sorts of action should I do?"; (4) as taking certain areteic concepts (*good, excellence, virtue*) as basic rather than deontic ones (*right, duty, obligation*); (5) as rejecting the idea that ethics is codifiable in rules or principles that can provide specific action guidance.

I give this list because these descriptions of **virtue ethics** are so commonly encountered, not because I think they are good ones. On the contrary, I think that all of them, in their crude brevity, are seriously misleading. Of course, there is some truth in each of them, which is why they are so common, and I shall return to them as we proceed, to note what truth, with what qualifications, they may be seen as containing. Readers familiar with the recent literature I mentioned in the Introduction, which has blurred the lines of demarcation between the three approaches in normative ethics, will no doubt have discarded or qualified them long since. But here, at the outset, it seems best to begin at a simple level, with the descriptions most readers will recognize, and work our way through to some of the complications and subtleties that are not so well known.

"Right Action," from *On Virtue Ethics*, pp. 22–42. Oxford University Press.

Right Action

The descriptions, especially when encountered for the first time, can easily be read as all making roughly the same point, and one way in which they are all misleading is that they encourage the thought that virtue ethics cannot be a genuine rival to utilitarianism and deontology. The thought goes like this:

> If virtue ethics is 'agent-centred rather than act-centred', concerned with 'What sort of person should I be?' rather than 'What sorts of action should I do?' (with 'Being rather than Doing'), if it concentrates on the *good* or *virtuous* agent rather than on *right* action and on what anyone, virtuous or not, has an *obligation* to do; how can it be a genuine rival to utilitarianism and deontology? Surely ethical theories are supposed to tell us about right action, i.e. about what sorts of act we should do. Utilitarianism and deontology certainly do that; if virtue ethics does not, it cannot be a genuine rival to them.

Now the descriptions do not actually say that virtue ethics does not concern itself at all with right action, or what we should do; it is in so far as it is easy to take them that way they are misleading. For virtue ethics can provide action guidance. The way it does this can most helpfully be shown by comparing it with the guidance given by some versions of utilitarianism and deontology, all laid out in a similar way.

Suppose an act utilitarian began her account of right action as follows:

P.1. An action is right iff it promotes the best consequences.

This premise provides a specification of right action, forging the familiar act-utilitarian link between the concepts of right action and *best consequences*, but gives one no guidance about how to act until one knows what to count as the best consequences. So these must be specified in a second premise, for example:

P.2. The best consequences are those in which happiness is maximized—which forges the familiar utilitarian link between the concepts of *best consequences* and *happiness*.

Many simple versions of **deontology** can be laid out in a way that displays the same basic structure. They begin with a premise providing a specification of right action:

P.1. An action is right iff it is in accordance with a correct moral rule or principle.

Like the first premise of act utilitarianism, this gives one no guidance about how to act until, in this case, one knows what to count as a correct moral rule (or principle). So this must be specified in a second premise, which begins

P.2. A correct moral rule (principle) is one that . . .

and this may be completed in a variety of ways, for example,

(1) . . . is on the following list—(and then a list follows, perhaps completed with an 'etc.'), or
(2) . . . is laid down for us by God, or
(3) . . . is universalizable/a categorical imperative, or
(4) . . . would be the object of choice of all rational beings,

and so on.

Although this way of laying out fairly familiar versions of **utilitarianism** and deontology is hardly controversial, it shows that there is something wrong with an over-used description of them, namely the slogan, "Utilitarianism begins with" (or "takes as its fundamental concept" etc.) "the Good, whereas deontology begins with the Right."[1] If the concept a normative ethics "begins with" is the one it uses to specify right action, then utilitarianism might indeed be said to begin with the Good (taking this to be the same concept as that of the best), but we should surely hasten to add, "but only in relation to consequences or states of affairs, not, for instance, in relation to *good* agents, or living *well*." And even then, we shall not be able to go on to say that most versions of deontology "begin with" the Right, for they use the concept of moral rule or principle to specify right action. The only versions which, in this sense, "begin with" the Right would have to be versions of what Frankena calls "extreme act-deontology"[2] which (I suppose) specify a right action as one which just *is* right.

And if the slogan is supposed to single out, rather vaguely, the concept which is "most important," then the concepts of *consequences* or *happiness* seem as deserving of mention as the concept of the Good for utilitarianism, and what counts as most important for deontologists (if any one concept does) would surely vary from case to case. For some it would be God, for others universalizability, for others the Categorical Imperative, for others rational acceptance, and so on. (Should we say that for Kant it is the good will, or the Categorical Imperative, or both?)

It is possible that too slavish a reliance on this slogan contributes to the belief that virtue ethics cannot provide its own specification of right action. For many who rely on it go on to say, "Utilitarianism derives the concept of the Right from that of the Good, and deontology derives the Good from the Right; but how can virtue ethics possibly derive the Good and the Right from the concept of the Virtuous Agent, which it begins with?" Now indeed, with no answer forthcoming to the questions "Good *what*? Right *what*?," I have no idea. But if the question is, "How can virtue ethics give an account of right action in such a way as to provide action guidance?" the answer is easy. Here is its first premise.

P.1. An action is right iff it is what a virtuous agent would characteristically (i.e. acting in character) do in the circumstances.

This specification rarely, if ever, silences those who maintain that virtue ethics cannot tell us what we should do. On the contrary, it tends to provoke irritable laughter and scorn. "That's no use," the objectors say. "It gives us no guidance whatsoever. Who are the virtuous agents?"

But if the failure of the first premise of an account of right action, the premise which forges a link between the concept of right action and a concept distinctive of a particular normative ethics, may provoke scorn because it provides no practical guidance, why not direct similar scorn at the first premises of act utilitarianism and deontology in the form in which I have given them? Of each of them I remarked, apparently in passing, but really with a view to this point, that they gave us no guidance. Act utilitarianism must specify what are to count as the best consequences, and deontology what is to count as a correct moral rule, producing a second premise, before any guidance is given. And, similarly, virtue ethics must specify who is to count as a virtuous agent. So far, the three are all in the same position.

Of course, if the virtuous agent can be specified only as an agent disposed to act in accordance with correct moral rules, as is sometimes assumed, then virtue ethics collapses back into deontology and is no rival to it. So let us add a subsidiary premise to this skeletal outline, intended to show that virtue ethics aims to provide a non-deontological specification of the virtuous agent *via* a specification of the virtues, which will be given in its second premise.

P.1a. A virtuous agent is one who has, and exercises, certain character traits, namely, the virtues.

P.2. A virtue is a character trait that...

This second premise of virtue ethics, like the second premise of some versions of deontology, might be completed simply by enumeration—"is on the following list"—and then a list is given, perhaps completed with "etc." Or we might interpret the Hume of the second *Enquiry* as espousing virtue ethics. According to Hume, we might say, a virtue is a character trait (of human beings) that is useful or agreeable to its possessor or to others (inclusive "or" both times). Or we might give the standard neo-Aristotelian completion, which claims that a virtue is a character trait a human being needs for *eudaimonia*, to flourish or live well.

Here, then, we have a specification of right action, whose structure closely resembles those of act utilitarianism and many simple forms of deontology. Comparing the three, we see that we could say, "Virtue ethics (in its account of right action) is agent-centred rather than consequences- or rules-centred. It is agent-centred in that it introduces the concept of the virtuous *agent* in the first premise of its account of right action, where utilitarianism and deontology introduce the concepts of *consequences* and *moral rule* respectively." That's true; it does. But note that it is not thereby "agent-centred *rather than* act-centred." It has an aswer to "How shall I decide what to do?"

So there is the first misunderstanding cleared away. Virtue ethics does have something to say about right action. But this is only a first step in dealing with the misunderstanding, for many people find what it has to say unsatisfactory. The reasons for their dissatisfaction are so varied that they will occupy us for several chapters; in this one, I shall concentrate on some that are naturally expressed in the complaint that virtue ethics does not and cannot tell us what to do; the complaint that it does not and cannot provide moral guidance.

"Virtue ethics does not provide us with moral guidance"—how can it fail to, when it has provided a specification of right action? Sometimes people suspect that it has provided only a circular specification, not a specification that we could use to guide us. "It has told us that the right action is what a virtuous agent would do. But that's a truism. Of course the virtuous agent 'does what is right'; if she didn't, she wouldn't be virtuous; we are just going round in circles."

Now it is true that the first premise of virtue ethics' account of right action has the air of being a truism. For although act utilitarians will want to deny the deontologists' first premise ("No! We should break the rule if the consequences of doing so would be better than those of keeping it"), and deontologists will deny the utilitarian one ("No! We must stick to the rules regardless of the consequences"), it is quite likely that both of them would accept what virtue ethics says: "An action is right iff it is what a virtuous agent would do." But, if they did, they would each be assuming that they had settled what right action was already, using their first and second premises, and were then using the truism to specify what, for them, counted as a virtuous agent. "A virtuous agent is one who does what is right (in my sense of 'right')."[3]

What I need to emphasize is that the apparent truism, "An action is right iff it is what a virtuous agent would characteristically do in the circumstances," is not figuring as a truism in virtue ethics' account of right action. It is figuring as the first premise of that account, a premise that, like the first premises of the other two accounts, awaits filling out in the second premise. Perhaps I could make this clearer by restating the first premise, and its supplement, in a way that made the necessity for filling them out glaringly obvious, thus:

P.1. An action is right iff it is what an X agent would characteristically do in the circumstances, and

P.1a. An X agent is one who has and exercises certain character traits, namely the Xs.

And put that way, P.1 does not look at all like a truism.

Unfortunately, it now looks uninformative, once again, apparently, contrasting unfavourably with the first premises of act utilitarianism and deontology: "We all have some idea about what best consequences might be and of what correct moral rules or principles are, but what on earth is an X agent?" But now I must repeat the point made earlier. The other first premises, taken strictly, are equally uninformative. We overlook this point because the utilitarian specifications of best consequences are so familiar, and all the deontologists we know cite familiar moral rules. But, for all that is said in the first premise of either, strange things might emerge in the second.

Someone might specify the "best consequences" as those in which the number of Roman Catholics was maximized (and the number of non-Catholics minimized). It would be a very odd view to hold; no proper Catholic could hold it, but some madman brought up in the Catholic faith might. Or someone might specify the "best consequences" as those in which certain moral rules were adhered to. "We all have some idea of what best consequences might be," not because this is *given* in the first premise of the act utilitarian account, but because we are all familiar with the idea that, by and large, if an action has, as a consequence, that many people are made happy, or much suffering is relieved, this counts as a good consequence.

Similarly, when we read the deontologist's first premise, we suppose that "we all have some idea of what correct moral rules or principles are." We expect (something like) "Do not kill" and "Keep promises." We do not expect "Purify the Aryan race," "Keep women in their proper place, subordinate to men," "Kill the infidel." But we know only too well that these not only might be specified, but have been specified, as correct moral rules. As far as the first premise of the deontological account of right action goes, we do not, in fact, have any idea, given by that premise, of what correct moral rules or principles are; we bring our own ideas to it.

So, understood as a first premise comparable to those of act utilitarianism and deontology, "An action is right iff it is what a virtuous agent would, characteristically, do in the circumstances," far from being a truism, is, *like* the first premises of the others, uninformative. All three start to be informative only when the second premise is added.

Epistemological Problems

At this stage we may notice an interesting division in the three accounts, a division which puts act utilitarianism on one side, and deontology and virtue ethics on the other. As soon as act utilitarianism produces its second premise, saying that the best consequences are those in which happiness is maximized, we seem to know where the act utilitarian stands. (I shall question below whether we really do, but we certainly seem to.) We can work out that the act utilitarian will say, for example, that it is right to tell a lie when telling the truth would make no one happy and someone very unhappy. But whether we know what a deontologist and a virtue ethicist will say about such a case after they have produced their second premises depends on the form they take.

If a list of correct moral rules or virtues is given, we have something fairly concrete. If one list contains "Do not lie" and the other "Honesty," we can work out that the deontologist and virtue ethicist are probably not going to agree with the act utilitarian about the rightness of telling the lie. But what if the deontologist's second premise is one of the others I gave? We all know that there has been, and is, much dispute about what God has laid down, and about what it is rational to accept, and so on—in short, much dispute about which moral rules or principles are the correct ones. When a deontologist produces one of her abstract tests for the correctness of a moral rule, we may be sure that she will defend and justify the rules she believes are correct in terms of it—but what these will be we do not know. Will she defend rules prohibiting suicide or abortion or rules permitting them? Will she turn out to be a pacifist or a supporter of killing in self-defence? We do not know.

Virtue ethics is similarly non-committal. We all know, it is said, that there has been, and is, much dispute about which character traits are the virtues. When a virtue ethicist produces one of her abstract tests, we may be sure that she will defend the character traits she believes are the virtues in terms of it, and dismiss the ones she does not accept—but what these will be we do not know. Will she defend humility, modesty, and compassion or (like Hume, Aristotle, and Nietzsche, respectively) will she dismiss them? Will she defend impartiality or friendship? We do not know.

So here we have an interesting contrast between act utilitarianism on the one hand, and deontology and virtue ethics on the other. The latter look as though they are bound to land us with a huge problem about how we can *know* that a particular action is right, for whatever either says, we can ask "But how do we know *which* moral rules or principles are the correct ones, *which* character traits are the virtues?" If they each just produce their list we can worry whether it is the right list. If they produce one of their abstract tests we can worry about the fact that, with sufficient ingenuity, or different further premises, these can be got to yield different results. So both lay themselves open to the threat of moral cultural relativism or, even worse, moral scepticism. Maybe we can do no more than list the rules, or character traits, accepted by our own culture or society and just have to accept that all we can know is what is right according to us, which might be wrong according to some other culture. Or, even worse, when we remember how much moral disagreement there is between "us," maybe we cannot even do that. Maybe we have to accept that there isn't anything that counts as knowing that a particular action is right; all there is, is feeling convinced that it is because it is in accordance with a certain rule one personally wants to adhere to, or because it is what would be done by the sort of person one personally wants to be.

Act utilitarianism is not, or not immediately, open to the same threat. True, it may be hard, on occasion, to predict the consequences of an action, but this is a practical problem in life which all three accounts have to take on board. Though it is sometimes said that deontologists "take no account of consequences," this is manifestly false, for many actions we deliberate about only fall under rules or principles when we bring in their predicted consequences. A deontological surgeon wondering whether she should perform a particular operation on a patient may be in doubt, not because she has any doubts about the correctness of her principles, but because it is so hard for her to predict whether the consequences of the operation will be that the patient enjoys several more years of life or is finished off. A surgeon who subscribes to virtue ethics has the same problem: she may not doubt that charity, which is concerned with others' good, is a virtue; her doubt is over whether the consequences of the operation will be that her patient is benefited or harmed.

The difficulty of being able to predict the consequences of one's actions does not bring with it the threat of moral relativism or moral scepticism; it is just a general problem in life. However, if the consequences concern *happiness*, as in the utilitarian account, doesn't the threat come in there? Different cultures, different individuals, have different ideas of happiness. How can we know that a particular action is right if we cannot define precisely and correctly that "happiness" we are supposed to be maximizing?

I think that one might well press something along these lines as a problem for utilitarianism, and this is a point to which I shall return below. But it is hardly plausible to say it shows that act utilitarianism is *immediately* open to the threat of moral relativism and scepticism. Suppose people's ideas of happiness do vary; why should that matter, for practical purposes? This person will be happy if I give her a book on religious contemplation and upset if I give her a sexy novel, someone else will delight in the novel but be bored to tears by the other. If I can afford both books, act utilitarianism makes it perfectly clear what I should do, without having to define happiness or worry about the fact that these two people doubtless have very different ideas of it. As Jonathan Glover robustly remarks, "most of us, whether utilitarians or not, take some account of the likely effects of our actions on people's happiness, and we should all be in a mess if there was no correspondence between trying to make someone happier and succeeding."[4]

So let us say, for the moment, that act utilitarianism is not immediately threatened by the spectre of moral relativism or scepticism, but that virtue ethics, in company with deontology, is. And, having said it and acknowledged the problem, let us put it to one side for later chapters.[5] For the moment I shall assume that both deontology and virtue ethics give an open-ended, and familiar, list in their second premises. Deontology, we may suppose, lists such familiar rules as "Do not kill," "Tell the truth," "Keep promises," "Do no evil or harm to others," "Help others/promote their well-being," etc.; virtue ethics lists such familiar character traits as justice, honesty, charity, courage, practical wisdom, generosity, loyalty, etc. And, having assumed that, we can return to the question of whether virtue ethics, even given such a list, somehow fails to provide guidance in the way that act utilitarianism and deontology do.

Moral Rules

A common objection goes as follows.

> Deontology gives a set of clear prescriptions which are readily applicable. But virtue ethics yields only the prescription, 'Do what the virtuous agent—the one who is just, honest, charitable etc.—would do in these circumstances.' And this gives me no guidance unless I am (and know I am) a virtuous agent myself—in which case I am hardly in need of it. If I am less than fully virtuous, I shall have no idea what a virtuous agent would do, and hence cannot apply the only prescription virtue ethics has given me. True, act utilitarianism also yields only a single prescription ('Do what maximizes happiness'), but there are no parallel difficulties in applying that; it too is readily applicable. So there is the way in which virtue ethics' account of right action fails to be action guiding where deontology and utilitarianism succeed.

In response, it is worth pointing out that, if I know that I am far from perfect, and am quite unclear what a virtuous agent would do in the circumstances in which I find myself, the obvious thing to do is to go and ask one, should this be possible. This is far from being a trivial point, for it gives a straightforward explanation of an important aspect of our moral life, namely the fact that we do not always act as "autonomous," utterly self-determining agents, but quite often seek moral guidance from people we think are morally better than ourselves. When I am looking for an excuse to do something I have a horrid suspicion is wrong, I ask my moral inferiors (or peers if I am bad enough), 'Wouldn't you do such-and-such if you were in my shoes?' But when I am anxious to do what is right, and do not see my way clear, I go to people I respect and admire: people who I think are kinder, more honest, more just, wiser, than I am myself, and ask them what they would do in my circumstances. How, or indeed whether, utilitarianism and deontology can explain this fact, I do not know, but, as I said, the explanation within the terms of virtue ethics is straightforward. If you want to do what is right, and doing what is right is doing what the virtuous agent would do in the circumstances, then you should find out what she would do if you do not already know.

Moreover, seeking advice from virtuous people is not the only thing an imperfect agent trying to apply the "single prescription" of virtue ethics can do. For it is simply false that, in general, "if I am less than fully virtuous, then I shall have no idea what a virtuous agent would do," as the objection claims. Recall that we are assuming that the virtues have been enumerated as, say, honesty, charity, fidelity, etc. So, *ex hypothesi*, a virtuous agent is one who is honest, charitable, true to her word, etc. So what she characteristically does is what is honest, charitable, true to her word, etc. and not what would be dishonest, uncharitable, untrue to her word. So, given such an enumeration of the virtues, I may well have a perfectly good idea of what the virtuous person would do in my circumstances, despite my own imperfection. Would she lie in her teeth to acquire an unmerited advantage? No, for that would be both dishonest and unjust. Would she help the wounded stranger by the roadside even though he had no right to her help, or pass by on the other side? The former, for that is charitable and the latter callous. Might she keep a death-bed promise even though living people would benefit from its being broken? Yes, for she is true to her word. And so on.[6]

This second response to the objection that virtue ethics' account of right action fails to be action guiding amounts to a denial of the oft-repeated claim that "virtue ethics does not come up with any rules," (which is another version of the thought that it is concerned with Being rather than Doing), and needs to be supplemented with rules. We can now see that it comes up with a large number of rules. Not only does each virtue generate a prescription—do what is honest, charitable, generous—but each vice a prohibition—do not do what is dishonest, uncharitable, mean.[7]

Once this point about virtue ethics is grasped (and it is remarkable how often it is overlooked), can there remain any reason for thinking that virtue ethics cannot tell us what we should do? Yes, there is one. The reason given is, roughly, that rules such as "Do what is honest, do not do what is uncharitable," are, like the rule "Do what the virtuous agent would do," still the wrong sort of rule, still somehow doomed to fail to provide the action guidance supplied by the rules (or rule) of deontology and act utilitarianism.

But how so? It is true that these rules of virtue ethics (henceforth "v-rules") are couched in terms, or concepts, that are certainly "evaluative" in *some* sense, or senses, of that difficult word. Is it this which dooms them to failure? Surely not, unless many forms of utilitarianism and deontology fail for this reason too.

There are, indeed, some forms of utilitarianism which aim to be entirely "value-free" or empirical, such as those which define happiness in terms of the satisfaction of actual desires or preferences, regardless of their content, or as a mental state whose presence is definitively established by introspection. Such forms run into well-known problems, and have always seemed to me the least plausible, but I accept that anyone who embraces them may consistently complain that v-rules give inferior action guidance in virtue of containing "evaluative" terms. But a utilitarian who wishes to employ any distinction between the higher and lower pleasures, or pronounce on what rational preferences would be, or rely on some list of goods (such as autonomy, friendship, or knowledge of important matters) in defining happiness, must grant that even her single rule is implicitly "evaluative." (This is why, briefly, I think that utilitarianism is not generally immune to the threat of moral relativism or scepticism, as I mentioned above.)

What about deontology? If we concentrate on the single example of lying, defining lying to be "asserting what you believe to be untrue, with the intention of deceiving your hearer(s)," then we might, for a moment, preserve the illusion that a deontologist's rules do not contain "evaluative" terms. But as soon as we remember that few deontologists will want to forego principles of non-maleficence and (or) beneficence, the illusion vanishes. For these principles, and their corresponding rules (do no evil or harm to others, help others, promote their well-being), rely on terms or concepts which are at least as "evaluative" as those employed in the v-rules.

We see revealed here a further inadequacy in the slogan "Utilitarianism begins with the Good, deontology with the Right" when this is taken as committing deontology to making the concept of the Good (and, presumably, the Bad or Evil) somehow derivative from the concept of the Right (and Wrong). A "utilitarian" who relied on the concept of right, or virtuous, action in specifying his concept of happiness would find it hard to shrug off the scare quotes, but no one expects a deontologist to be able to state each of her rules without ever employing a concept of *good* which is not simply the concept of *right action for its own sake*, or without any mention of *evil* or *harm*.

We might also note that few deontologists will rest content with the simple, quasi-biological "Do not kill," but more refined versions of that rule such as "Do not murder," or "Do not kill the innocent," once again employ "evaluative" terms, and "Do not kill unjustly" is itself a particular instantiation of a v-rule.

Supposing this point were granted, a deontologist might still claim that the v-rules are markedly inferior to deontological rules as far as providing guidance for children is concerned. Granted, adult deontologists must think hard about what really constitutes harming someone, or promoting their well-being, or respecting their autonomy, or murder, but surely the simple rules we learnt at our mother's knee are indispensable. How could virtue ethics plausibly seek to dispense with these and expect toddlers to grasp "act charitably, honestly, and kindly, don't act unjustly," and so on? Rightly are these concepts described as "thick"! Far too thick for a child to grasp.

Strictly speaking, this objection is rather different from the *general* objection that v-rules fail to provide action guidance, but it arises naturally in the context of the general one and I am more than happy to address it. For it pinpoints a condition of adequacy that any normative ethics must meet, namely that such an ethics must not only come up with action guidance for a clever rational adult, but also generate some account of moral education, of how one generation teaches the next what they should do. But an ethics inspired by Aristotle is unlikely to have forgotten the question of moral education, and the objection fails to hit home. Firstly, the implicit empirical claim that toddlers are taught only the deontologist's rules, not the "thick" concepts, is surely false. Sentences such as "Don't do that, it hurts the cat, you mustn't be cruel," "Be kind to your brother, he's only little," "Don't be so mean, so greedy," are commonly addressed to toddlers. For some reason, we do not seem to teach "just" and "unjust" early on, but we certainly teach "fair" and "unfair."

Secondly, why should a proponent of virtue ethics deny the significance of such mother's-knee rules as "Don't lie," "Keep promises," "Help others"? Although it is a mistake (I have claimed) to define a virtuous agent simply as one disposed to act in accordance with deontologists' moral rules, it is a very understandable mistake, given the obvious connection between, for example, the exercise of the virtue of honesty and refraining from lying. Virtue ethicists want to emphasize the fact that, if children are to be taught to be honest, they must be taught to love and prize the truth, and that *merely* teaching them not to lie will not achieve this end. But they need not deny that, to achieve this end, teaching them not to lie is useful, or even indispensable.

So we can see that virtue ethics not only comes up with rules (the v-rules, couched in terms derived from the virtues and vices) but, further, does not exclude the more familiar deontologists' rules. The theoretical distinction between the two is that the familiar rules, and their applications in particular cases, are given entirely different backings. According to deontology, I must not tell this lie because, applying the (correct) rule "Do not lie" to this case, I find that lying is prohibited. According to virtue ethics, I must not tell this lie because it would be dishonest to do so, and dishonesty is a vice.[8]

Uncodifiability

What then of the claim that virtue ethics, typically, rejects the idea that ethics is codifiable in rules or principles that can provide specific action guidance? It now stands revealed as a claim that invites the rather tiresome response, "Well, it all depends on what you mean by 'codifiable.'"

It used to be quite commonly held that the task of normative ethics was to come up with a set (possibly one-membered, as in the case of act utilitarianism) of universal rules or principles which would have two significant features: (a) they would amount to a decision procedure for determining what the right action was in any particular case; (b) they would be stated in such terms that any nonvirtuous person could understand and apply them correctly.[9] Call this the "strong codifiability thesis." And it was, and is, indeed typical of virtue ethicists to reject that thesis.[10] But, for at least two, no doubt related, reasons, the idea is now much less common.

One reason has been the increasing sense that the enterprise of coming up with such a set of rules or principles has failed. In the early, heady days of applied ethics, it looked feasible, but as more philosophers relying on the same abstract principles applied them in such a way as to produce different conclusions, as different modifications or exclusion clauses were put on the general principles to yield different conclusions, as more philosophers trying to resolve real-life hard cases in medical ethics found themselves compelled to say that there were good arguments on both sides—as, quite generally, the gap between the abstract principles and the complex particularity of concrete moral situations became more obvious, so the idea that the rules should have both the features mentioned began to lose its appeal.

The concurrent emergence of virtue ethics articulated at least one way in which the original idea needed to be modified. It became increasingly obvious, when one considered whether doctors needed to be virtuous, that arrogant, uncaring, dishonest, and self-centred ones could not be guaranteed to do what they should merely by requiring that they acted in accordance with certain rules. The Devil, after all, can quote scripture to serve his own purposes; one can conform to the letter of a rule while violating its spirit. Hence it was recognized that a certain amount of virtue and corresponding moral or **practical wisdom** (*phronesis*) might be required both to interpret the rules and to determine *which* rule was most appropriately to be applied in a particular case.[11]

Of course, I am not claiming that this is now universally recognized, only that it is much more common than it used to be, particularly in books *of* applied ethics as opposed to books about what normative ethics is or should be. So should we say that those who have given up the original idea "reject the idea that ethics is codifiable" as, it is said, virtue ethicists do? Clearly, they share with virtue ethicists the view that ethics is not *as* codifiable as used to be commonly supposed, but there is still, I think, a lingering view that it is, or ought to be, more codifiable than virtue ethics makes it out to be.

Sometimes this amounts to no more than the mistake I noted earlier, namely the view that virtue ethics does not come up with any rules or principles, combined, I suspect, with a gut unwillingness to join the virtue ethics camp. Beauchamp and Childress, whose *Principles of Medical Ethics*, from being initially dismissive, has become increasingly friendly to virtue ethics in its successive editions, are still to be found insisting that virtue ethics needs to be *supplemented* by a list of principles, which they give. They do not say, but they might well, that it doesn't *codify* enough. But the list looks like this:

Principles	*Corresponding Virtues*
Respect for autonomy	Respectfulness
Nonmaleficence	Nonmalevolence
Beneficence	Benevolence
Justice	Justice or fairness

Rules	
Veracity	Truthfulness
etc.[12]	

Now if this is all that is at issue, let us by all means say that virtue ethics does *not* reject the idea that ethics is codifiable. It does not need to be supplemented by such principles; it embodies them already—and many many more besides. (It is a noteworthy feature of our virtue and vice vocabulary that, although our list of generally recognized virtue terms is, I think, quite short, our list of vice terms is remarkably—and usefully—long, far exceeding anything that anyone who thinks in terms of standard deontological rules has ever come up with. Much invaluable action guidance comes from avoiding courses of action that are irresponsible, feckless, lazy, inconsiderate, uncooperative, harsh, intolerant, indiscreet, incautious, unenterprising, pusillanimous, feeble, hypocritical, self-indulgent, materialistic, grasping, short-sighted, ... and on and on.)[13]

What else might still be at issue? A prevailing criticism of virtue ethics, related to the idea that it gives up on codifiability too soon, that it does not codify enough, is that it fails to provide action guidance when we come to hard cases or dilemmas. So it is to a consideration of virtue ethics in relation to hard cases—a surprisingly large topic—that we now turn.

NOTES

1. For a particularly illuminating critique of Rawls's distinction, see G. Watson, "On the Primacy of Character" (1990). See also Hudson, "What is Morality all About?", (1990) and Herman, *The Practice of Moral Judgement*, ch. 10, who both challenge the slogan in relation to Kant's deontology.
2. W. Frankena, *Ethics* (1973).
3. Cf. Watson's opening paragraphs in "On the Primacy of Character".
4. J. Glover, *Causing Death and Saving Lives*, 3.
5. Indeed, given the size of the problem, one might say "for a later book".
6. Cf. Anscombe: "It would be a great improvement if, instead of 'morally wrong' one always named a genus such as 'untruthful', 'unchaste', 'unjust'

... the answer would sometimes be clear at once." "Modern Moral Philosophy" (1958, repr. 1981), 33.
7. Making this point in earlier articles, I expressed the generated rules adverbially—act honestly, charitably, generously; do not act dishonestly, etc. But the adverbs connote not only doing what the virtuous agent would do, but also doing it "in the way" she would do it, which includes "for the same sort(s) of reason(s)", and it has seemed to me better here to separate out the issue of the virtuous agent's reasons for a later chapter.
8. This clear distinction (between deontology and virtue ethics) is just one of the many things that has been blurred by the recent happy convergence of Kantians and virtue ethicists.
9. E. Pincoffs, "Quandary Ethics" (1971), identified this as the dominant view of the task of normative ethics at the time, beginning his article with a number of illustrative quotes from contemporary authors.
10. Most notably, J. McDowell in "Virtue and Reason" (1979).
11. "It is true that principles underdetermine decisions. This is hardly news for those who have advocated ethical theories that make principles or rules central. Kant, for example, insisted that we can have no algorithm for judgement, since every application of a rule would itself need supplementing by further rules." O'Neill, "Abstraction, Idealization and Ideology in Ethics," (1987), 58.
12. T. L. Beauchamp and J. F. Childress, (eds.). *Principles of Biomedical Ethics*, 4th edn. (1994), 67.
13. Some virtue ethicists might want to insist on a strong correspondence between the virtues and the vices; not only that to each virtue there corresponds at least one particular vice but also that every vice is opposed to some particular virtue. Of course one can, formally, insist that to laziness there corresponds the virtue of being the opposite of lazy, which happens to lack a word in English ("industriousness" doesn't really work); more plausibly one could claim that describing someone as "responsible" in a character reference describes them as having a particular virtue for which we have the adjective but not the noun. But I do not myself believe that things are that tidy.

KEY TERMS

Virtue ethics
Deontology
Utilitarianism
Practical wisdom

STUDY QUESTIONS

1. Why does Hursthouse think that it is a mistake to characterize virtue ethics as "agent-centred rather than act-centred"?

2. Explain why many think that virtue ethics gives no moral guidance. How does Hursthouse's P.1. help with this problem? What needs to be added to P.1. to answer the critic's challenge?

3. What is the "strong codifiability thesis"? Why does Hursthouse think that we should reject it?

D. JUSTICE AND EQUALITY

A Theory of Justice

JOHN RAWLS

John Rawls (1921–2002) was the James Bryant Conant University Professor at Harvard University. He is primarily known for his contributions to political and moral philosophy, but he was also an important historian of moral philosophy. His *magnum opus*, *A Theory of Justice*, is widely regarded as one of the most important pieces of political philosophy in the liberal tradition. There, Rawls argues for a conception of justice as fairness and presents what he takes to be the two principles of justice. In addition to *A Theory of Justice*, Rawls was also the author of *Political Liberalism*, *The Law of Peoples*, *Justice as Fairness: A Restatement*, and *Lectures on the History of Moral Philosophy*.

· ·

Chapter I. Justice as Fairness

· · · · · · · ·

1. The Role of Justice

Justice is the first virtue of social institutions, as truth is of systems of thought. A theory however elegant and economical must be rejected or revised if it is untrue; likewise laws and institutions no matter how efficient and well arranged must be reformed or abolished if they are unjust. Each person possesses an inviolability founded on justice that even the welfare of society as a whole cannot override. For this reason

justice denies that the loss of freedom for some is made right by a greater good shared by others. It does not allow that the sacrifices imposed on a few are outweighed by the larger sum of advantages enjoyed by many. Therefore in a just society, the liberties of equal citizenship are taken as settled; the rights secured by justice are not subject to political bargaining or to the calculus of social interests. The only thing that permits us to acquiesce in an erroneous theory is the lack of a better one; analogously, an injustice is tolerable only when it is necessary to avoid an even greater injustice. Being first virtues of human activities, truth and justice are uncompromising.

These propositions seem to express our intuitive conviction of the primacy of justice. No doubt they are expressed too strongly. In any event I wish to inquire whether these contentions or others similar to them are sound, and if so how they can be accounted for. To this end it is necessary to work out a theory of justice in the light of which these assertions can be interpreted and assessed. I shall begin by considering the role of the principles of justice. Let us assume, to fix ideas, that a society is a more or less self-sufficient association of persons who in their relations to one another recognize certain rules of conduct as binding and who for the most part act in accordance with them. Suppose further that these rules specify a system of cooperation designed to advance the good of those taking part in it. Then, although a society is a cooperative venture for mutual advantage, it is typically marked by a conflict as well as by an identity of interests. There is an identity of interests since social cooperation makes possible a better life for all than any would have if each were to live solely by his own efforts. There is a conflict of interests since persons are not indifferent as to how the greater benefits produced by their collaboration are distributed, for in order to pursue their ends they each prefer a larger to a lesser share. A set of principles is required for choosing among the various social arrangements which determine this division of advantages and for underwriting an agreement on the proper distributive shares. These principles are the principles of social justice: they provide a way of assigning rights and duties in the basic institutions of society and they define the appropriate distribution of the benefits and burdens of social cooperation.

Now let us say that a society is well ordered when it is not only designed to advance the good of its members but when it is also effectively regulated by a public conception of justice. That is, it is a society in which (1) everyone accepts and knows that the others accept the same principles of justice, and (2) the basic social institutions generally satisfy and are generally known to satisfy these principles. In this case while men may put forth excessive demands on one another, they nevertheless acknowledge a common point of view from which their claims may be adjudicated. If men's inclination to self-interest makes their vigilance against one another necessary, their public sense of justice makes their secure association together possible. Among individuals with disparate aims and purposes a shared conception of justice establishes the bonds of civic friendship; the general desire for justice limits the pursuit of other ends. One may think of a public conception of justice as constituting the fundamental charter of a well-ordered human association.

. . . .

2. The Subject of Justice

Many different kinds of things are said to be just and unjust: not only laws, institutions, and social systems, but also particular actions of many kinds, including decisions, judgments, and imputations. We also call the attitudes and dispositions of persons, and persons themselves, just and unjust. Our topic, however, is that of social justice. For us the primary subject of justice is the basic structure of society, or more exactly, the way in which the major social institutions distribute fundamental rights and duties and determine the division of advantages from social cooperation. By major institutions I understand the political constitution and the principal economic and social arrangements. Thus the legal protection of freedom of thought and liberty of conscience, competitive markets, private property in the means of production, and the monogamous family are examples of major social institutions. Taken together as one scheme, the major institutions define men's rights and duties and influence their life-prospects, what they can expect to be and how well they can hope to do. The basic structure is the primary subject of justice because its effects are so profound and present from the start. The intuitive notion here is that this structure contains various social positions and that men born into different positions have different expectations of life determined, in part, by the political system as well as by economic and social circumstances. In this way the institutions of society favor certain starting places over others. These are especially deep inequalities. Not only are they pervasive, but they affect men's initial chances in life; yet they cannot possibly be justified by an appeal to the notions of merit or desert. It is these inequalities, presumably inevitable in the basic structure of any society, to which the principles of social justice must in the first instance apply. These principles, then regulate the choice of a political constitution and the main elements of the economic and social system. The justice of a social scheme depends essentially on how fundamental rights and duties are assigned and on the economic opportunities and social conditions in the various sectors of society.

. . . .

3. The Main Idea of the Theory of Justice

My aim is to present a conception of justice which generalizes and carries to a higher level of abstraction the familiar theory of the social contract as found, say, in Locke, Rousseau, and Kant. In order to do this we are not to think of the original contract as one to enter a particular society or to set up a particular form of government. Rather, the guiding idea is that the principles of justice for the basic structure of society are the object of the original agreement. They are the principles that free and rational persons concerned to further their own interests would accept in an initial position of equality as defining the fundamental terms of their association. These principles are to regulate all further agreements; they specify the kinds of social cooperation that can be entered into and the forms of government that can be established. This way of regarding the principles of justice I shall call justice as fairness.

Thus we are to imagine that those who engage in social cooperation choose together, in one joint act, the principles which are to assign basic rights and duties and to determine the division of social benefits. Men are to decide in advance how they are to regulate their claims against one another and what is to be the foundation charter of their society. Just as each person must decide by rational reflection what constitutes his good, that is, the system of ends which it is rational for him to pursue, so a group of persons must decide once and for all what is to count among them as just and unjust. The choice which rational men would make in this hypothetical situation of equal liberty, assuming for the present that this choice problem has a solution, determines the principles of justice.

In justice as fairness **the original position** of equality corresponds to the state of nature in the traditional theory of the social contract. This original position is not, of course, thought of as an actual historical state of affairs, much less as a primitive condition of culture. It is understood as a purely hypothetical situation characterized so as to lead to a certain conception of justice.

Among the essential features of this situation is that no one knows his place in society, his class position or social status, nor does any one know his fortune in the distribution of natural assets and abilities, his intelligence, strength, and the like. I shall even assume that the parties do not know their conceptions of the good or their special psychological propensities. The principles of justice are chosen behind a **veil of ignorance**. This ensures that no one is advantaged or disadvantaged in the choice of principles by the outcome of natural chance or the contingency of social circumstances. Since all are similarly situated and no one is able to design principles to favor his particular condition, the principles of justice are the result of a fair agreement or bargain. For given the circumstances of the original position, the symmetry of everyone's relations to each other, this initial situation is fair between individuals as moral persons, that is, as rational beings with their own ends and capable, I shall assume, of a sense of justice. The original position is, one might say, the appropriate initial status quo, and thus the fundamental agreements reached in it are fair. This explains the propriety of the name "justice as fairness"; it conveys the idea that the principles of justice are agreed to in an initial situation that is fair. The name does not mean that the concepts of justice and fairness are the same, any more than the phrase "poetry as metaphor" means that the concepts of poetry and metaphor are the same.

Justice as fairness begins, as I have said, with one of the most general of all choices which persons might make together, namely, with the choice of the first principles of a conception of justice which is to regulate all subsequent criticism and reform of institutions. Then, having chosen a conception of justice, we can suppose that they are to choose a constitution and a legislature to enact laws, and so on, all in accordance with the principles of justice initially agreed upon. Our social situation is just if it is such that by this sequence of hypothetical agreements we would have contracted into the general system of rules which defines it. Moreover, assuming that the original position does determine a set of principles (that is, that a particular conception of justice would be chosen), it will then be true that whenever social institutions satisfy these principles those engaged in them can say to one another that they are cooperating on terms to which they would agree if they were free and equal persons whose relations with respect to one another were fair. They could all view their arrangements as meeting the stipulations which they would acknowledge in an initial situation that embodies widely accepted and reasonable constraints on the choice of principles. The general recognition of this fact would provide the basis for a public acceptance of the corresponding principles of justice. No society can, of course, be a scheme of cooperation which men enter voluntarily in a literal sense; each person finds himself placed at birth in some particular position in some particular society, and the nature of this position materially affects his life prospects. Yet a society satisfying the principles of justice as fairness comes as close as a society can to being a voluntary scheme, for it meets the principles which free and equal persons would assent to under circumstances that are fair. In this sense its members are autonomous and the obligations they recognize self-imposed.

One feature of justice as fairness is to think of the parties in the initial situation as rational and mutually disinterested. This does not mean that the parties are egoists, that is, individuals with only certain kinds of interests, say in wealth, prestige, and domination. But they are conceived as not taking an interest in one another's interests. They are to presume that even their spiritual aims may be opposed, in the way that the aims of those of different religions may be opposed. Moreover, the concept of rationality must be interpreted as far as possible in the narrow sense, standard in economic theory, of taking the most effective means to given ends. . . . [O]ne must try to avoid introducing into it any controversial ethical elements. The initial situation must be characterized by stipulations that are widely accepted.

In working out the conception of justice as fairness one main task clearly is to determine which principles of justice would be chosen in the original position. To do this we must describe this situation in some detail and formulate with care the problem of choice which it presents. . . . It may be observed, however, that once the principles of justice are thought of as arising from an original agreement in a situation of equality, it is an open question whether the principle of utility would be acknowledged. Offhand it hardly seems likely that persons who view themselves as equals, entitled to press their claims upon one another, would agree to a principle which may require lesser life prospects for

some simply for the sake of a greater sum of advantages enjoyed by others. Since each desires to protect his interests, his capacity to advance his conception of the good, no one has a reason to acquiesce in an enduring loss for himself in order to bring about a greater net balance of satisfaction. In the absence of strong and lasting benevolent impulses, a rational man would not accept a basic structure merely because it maximized the algebraic sum of advantages irrespective of its permanent effects on his own basic rights and interests. Thus it seems that the **principle of utility** is incompatible with the conception of social cooperation among equals for mutual advantage. It appears to be inconsistent with the idea of reciprocity implicit in the notion of a well-ordered society. Or, at any rate, so I shall argue.

I shall maintain instead that the persons in the initial situation would choose two rather different principles: the first requires equality in the assignment of basic rights and duties, while the second holds that social and economic inequalities, for example inequalities of wealth and authority, are just only if they result in compensating benefits for everyone, and in particular for the least advantaged members of society. These principles rule out justifying institutions on the grounds that the hardships of some are offset by a greater good in the aggregate. It may be expedient but it is not just that some should have less in order that others may prosper. But there is no injustice in the greater benefits earned by a few provided that the situation of persons not so fortunate is thereby improved. The intuitive idea is that since everyone's well-being depends upon a scheme of cooperation without which no one could have a satisfactory life, the division of advantages should be such as to draw forth the willing cooperation of everyone taking part in it, including those less well situated. Yet this can be expected only if reasonable terms are proposed. The two principles mentioned seem to be a fair agreement on the basis of which those better endowed, or more fortunate in their social position, neither of which we can be said to deserve, could expect the willing cooperation of others when some workable scheme is a necessary condition of the welfare of all. Once we decide to look for a conception of justice that nullifies the accidents of natural endowment and the contingencies of social circumstance as counters in quest for political and economic advantage, we are led to these principles. They express the result of leaving aside those aspects of the social world that seem arbitrary from a moral point of view.

. . . .

4. The Original Position and Justification

I have said that the original position is the appropriate initial status quo which insures that the fundamental agreements reached in it are fair. This fact yields the name "justice as fairness." It is clear, then, that I want to say that one conception of justice is more reasonable than another, or justifiable with respect to it, if rational persons in the initial situation would choose its principles over those of the other for the role of justice. Conceptions of justice are to be ranked by their acceptability to persons so circumstanced. Understood in this way the question of justification is settled by working out a problem of deliberation: we have to ascertain which principles it would be rational to adopt given the contractual situation. This connects the theory of justice with the theory of rational choice.

If this view of the problem of justification is to succeed, we must, of course, describe in some detail the nature of this choice problem. A problem of rational decision has a definite answer only if we know the beliefs and interests of the parties, their relations with respect to one another, the alternatives between which they are to choose, the procedure whereby they make up their minds, and so on. As the circumstances are presented in different ways, correspondingly different principles are accepted. The concept of the original position, as I shall refer to it, is that of the most philosophically favored interpretation of this initial choice situation for the purposes of a theory of justice.

But how are we to decide what is the most favored interpretation? I assume, for one thing, that there is a broad measure of agreement that principles of justice should be chosen under certain conditions. To justify a particular description of the initial situation one shows that it incorporates these commonly shared presumptions. One argues from widely accepted but weak premises to more specific conclusions. Each of the presumptions should by

itself be natural and plausible; some of them may seem innocuous or even trivial. The aim of the contract approach is to establish that taken together they impose significant bounds on acceptable principles of justice. The ideal outcome would be that these conditions determine a unique set of principles; but I shall be satisfied if they suffice to rank the main traditional conceptions of social justice.

One should not be misled, then, by the somewhat unusual conditions which characterize the original position. The idea here is simply to make vivid to ourselves the restrictions that it seems reasonable to impose on arguments for principles of justice, and therefore on these principles themselves. Thus it seems reasonable and generally acceptable that no one should be advantaged or disadvantaged by natural fortune or social circumstances in the choice of principles. It also seems widely agreed that it should be impossible to tailor principles to the circumstances of one's own case. We should insure further that particular inclinations and aspirations, and persons' conceptions of their good do not affect the principles adopted. The aim is to rule out those principles that it would be rational to propose for acceptance, however little the chance of success, only if one knew certain things that are irrelevant from the standpoint of justice. For example, if a man knew that he was wealthy, he might find it rational to advance the principle that various taxes for welfare measures be counted unjust; if he knew that he was poor, he would most likely propose the contrary principle. To represent the desired restrictions one imagines a situation in which everyone is deprived of this sort of information. One excludes the knowledge of those contingencies which sets men at odds and allows them to be guided by their prejudices. In this manner the veil of ignorance is arrived at in a natural way. This concept should cause no difficulty if we keep in mind the constraints on arguments that it is meant to express. At any time we can enter the original position, so to speak, simply by following a certain procedure, namely, by arguing for principles of justice in accordance with these restrictions.

It seems reasonable to suppose that the parties in the original position are equal. That is, all have the same rights in the procedure for choosing principles; each can make proposals, submit reasons for their acceptance, and so on. Obviously the purpose of these conditions is to represent equality between human beings as moral persons, as creatures having a conception of their good and capable of a sense of justice. The basis of equality is taken to be similarity in these two respects. Systems of ends are not ranked in value; and each man is presumed to have the requisite ability to understand and to act upon whatever principles are adopted. Together with the veil of ignorance, these conditions define the principles of justice as those which rational persons concerned to advance their interests would consent to as equals when none are known to be advantaged or disadvantaged by social and natural contingencies.

There is, however, another side to justifying a particular description of the original position. This is to see if the principles which would be chosen match our considered convictions of justice or extend them in an acceptable way. We can note whether applying these principles would lead us to make the same judgments about the basic structure of society which we now make intuitively and in which we have the greatest confidence; or whether, in cases where our present judgments are in doubt and given with hesitation, these principles offer a resolution which we can affirm on reflection. There are questions which we feel sure must be answered in a certain way. For example, we are confident that religious intolerance and racial discrimination are unjust. We think that we have examined these things with care and have reached what we believe is an impartial judgment not likely to be distorted by an excessive attention to our own interests. These convictions are provisional fixed points which we presume any conception of justice must fit. But we have much less assurance as to what is the correct distribution of wealth and authority. Here we may be looking for a way to remove our doubts. We can check an interpretation of the initial situation, then, by the capacity of its principles to accommodate our firmest convictions and to provide guidance where guidance is needed.

In searching for the most favored description of this situation we work from both ends. We begin by describing it so that it represents generally shared and preferably weak conditions. We then see if these conditions are strong enough to yield a significant set of principles. If not, we look for further premises equally reasonable. But if so, and these principles match our considered convictions of justice, then so far well and good. But presumably there will be discrepancies. In this case we have a choice. We can either modify the account of the initial situation or we can revise our existing judgments, for even the judgments we take provisionally as fixed points are liable to revision. By going back and forth, sometimes altering the conditions of the contractual circumstances, at others withdrawing our judgments and conforming them to principle, I assume that eventually we shall find a description of the initial situation that both expresses reasonable conditions and yields principles which match our considered judgments duly pruned and adjusted. This state of affairs I refer to as **reflective equilibrium**.[1] It is an equilibrium because at last our principles and judgments coincide; and it is reflective since we know to what principles our judgments conform and the premises of their derivation. At the moment everything is in order. But this equilibrium is not necessarily stable. It is liable to be upset by further examination of the conditions which should be imposed on the contractual situation and by particular cases which may lead us to revise our judgments. Yet for the time being we have done what we can to render coherent and to justify our convictions of social justice. We have reached a conception of the original position.

I shall not, of course, actually work through this process. Still, we may think of the interpretation of the original position that I shall present as the result of such a hypothetical course of reflection. It represents the attempt to accommodate within one scheme both reasonable philosophical conditions on principles as well as our considered judgments of justice. In arriving at the favored interpretation of the initial situation there is no point at which an appeal is made to self-evidence in the traditional sense either of general conceptions or particular convictions. I do not claim for the principles of justice proposed that they are necessary truths or derivable from such truths. A conception of justice cannot be deduced from self-evident premises or conditions or principles; instead, its justification is a matter of the mutual support of many considerations, of everything fitting together into one coherent view.

A final comment. We shall want to say that certain principles of justice are justified because they would be agreed to in an initial situation of equality. I have emphasized that this original position is purely hypothetical. It is natural to ask why, if this agreement is never actually entered into, we should take any interest in these principles, moral or otherwise. The answer is that the conditions embodied in the description of the original position are ones that we do in fact accept. Or if we do not, then perhaps we can be persuaded to do so by philosophical reflection. Each aspect of the contractual situation can be given supporting grounds. Thus what we shall do is to collect together into one conception a number of conditions on principles that we are ready upon due consideration to recognize as reasonable. These constraints express what we are prepared to regard as limits on fair terms of social cooperation. One way to look at the idea of the original position, therefore, is to see it as an expository device which sums up the meaning of these conditions and helps us to extract their consequences. On the other hand, this conception is also an intuitive notion that suggests its own elaboration, so that led on by it we are drawn to define more clearly the standpoint from which we can best interpret moral relationships. We need a conception that enables us to envision our objective from afar: the intuitive notion of the original position is to do this for us.

5. Classical Utilitarianism

. . . [T]he kind of utilitarianism I shall describe here is the strict classical doctrine which receives perhaps its clearest and most accessible formulation in Sidgwick. The main idea is that society is rightly ordered, and therefore just, when its major institutions are arranged so as to achieve the greatest net balance of satisfaction summed over all the individuals belonging to it.

We may note first that there is, indeed, a way of thinking of society which makes it easy to suppose that the most rational conception of justice is utilitarian. For consider: each man in realizing his own interests is certainly free to balance his own losses against his own gains. We may impose a sacrifice on ourselves now for the sake of a greater advantage later. A person quite properly acts, at least when others are not affected, to achieve his own greatest good, to advance his rational ends as far as possible. Now why should not a society act on precisely the same principle applied to the group and therefore regard that which is rational for one man as right for an association of men? Just as the well-being of a person is constructed from the series of satisfactions that are experienced at different moments in the course of his life, so in very much the same way the well-being of society is to be constructed from the fulfillment of the systems of desires of the many individuals who belong to it. Since the principle for an individual is to advance as far as possible his own welfare, his own system of desires, the principle for society is to advance as far as possible the welfare of the group, to realize to the greatest extent the comprehensive system of desire arrived at from the desires of its members. Just as an individual balances present and future gains against present and future losses, so a society may balance satisfactions and dissatisfactions between different individuals. And so by these reflections one reaches the principle of utility in a natural way: a society is properly arranged when its institutions maximize the net balance of satisfaction. The principle of choice for an association of men is interpreted as an extension of the principle of choice for one man. Social justice is the principle of rational prudence applied to an aggregative conception of the welfare of the group. . . .

This idea is made all the more attractive by a further consideration. The two main concepts of ethics are those of the right and the good; the concept of a morally worthy person is, I believe, derived from them. The structure of an ethical theory is, then, largely determined by how it defines and connects these two basic notions. Now it seems that the simplest way of relating them is taken by teleological theories: the good is defined independently from the right, and then the right is defined as that which maximizes the good. More precisely, those institutions and acts are right which of the available alternatives produce the most good, or at least as much good as any of the other institutions and acts open as real possibilities (a rider needed when the maximal class is not a singleton). Teleological theories have a deep intuitive appeal since they seem to embody the idea of rationality. It is natural to think that rationality is maximizing something and that in morals it must be maximizing the good. Indeed, it is tempting to suppose that it is self-evident that things should be arranged so as to lead to the most good.

It is essential to keep in mind that in a teleological theory the good is defined independently from the right. This means two things. First, the theory accounts for our considered judgments as to which things are good (our judgments of value) as a separate class of judgments intuitively distinguishable by common sense, and then proposes the hypothesis that the right is maximizing the good as already specified. Second, the theory enables one to judge the goodness of things without referring to what is right. For example, if pleasure is said to be the sole good, then presumably pleasures can be recognized and ranked in value by criteria that do not presuppose any standards of right, or what we would normally think of as such. Whereas if the distribution of goods is also counted as a good, perhaps a higher order one, and the theory directs us to produce the most good (including the good of distribution among others), we no longer have a teleological view in the classical sense. The problem of distribution falls under the concept of right as one intuitively understands it, and so the theory lacks an independent definition of the good. The clarity and simplicity of classical teleological theories derives largely from the fact that they factor our moral judgments into two classes, the one being characterized separately while the other is then connected with it by a maximizing principle.

Teleological doctrines differ, pretty clearly, according to how the conception of the good is specified. If it is taken as the realization of human excellence in the various forms of culture, we have what may be called perfectionism. This notion is found in Aristotle and Nietzsche, among others. If the good is defined as pleasure, we have hedonism; if as happiness, eudaimonism, and so on. I shall understand the principle of utility in its classical form as defining the good as the satisfaction of desire, or perhaps better, as the satisfaction of rational desire. This accords with the view in all essentials and provides, I believe, a fair interpretation of it. The appropriate terms of social cooperation are settled by whatever in the circumstances will achieve the greatest sum of satisfaction of the rational desires of individuals. It is impossible to deny the initial plausibility and attractiveness of this conception.

The striking feature of the utilitarian view of justice is that it does not matter, except indirectly, how this sum of satisfactions is distributed among individuals any more than it matters, except indirectly, how one man distributes his satisfactions over time. The correct distribution in either case is that which yields the maximum fulfillment. Society must allocate its means of satisfaction whatever these are, rights and duties, opportunities and privileges, and various forms of wealth, so as to achieve this maximum if it can. But in itself no distribution of satisfaction is better than another except that the more equal distribution is to be preferred to break ties. It is true that certain common-sense precepts of justice, particularly those which concern the protection of liberties and rights, or which express the claims of desert, seem to contradict this contention. But from a utilitarian standpoint the explanation of these precepts and of their seemingly stringent character is that they are those precepts which experience shows should be strictly respected and departed from only under exceptional circumstances if the sum of advantages is to be maximized. Yet, as with all other precepts, those of justice are derivative from the one end of attaining the greatest balance of satisfaction. Thus there is no reason in principle why the greater gains of some should not compensate for the lesser losses of others; or more importantly, why the violation of the liberty of a few might not be made right by the greater good shared by many. It simply happens that under most conditions, at least in a reasonably advanced stage of civilization, the greatest sum of advantages is not attained in this way. No doubt the strictness of common-sense precepts of justice has a certain usefulness in limiting men's propensities to injustice and to socially injurious actions, but the utilitarian believes that to affirm this strictness as a first principle of morals is a mistake. For just as it is rational for one man to maximize the fulfillment of his system of desires, it is right for a society to maximize the net balance of satisfaction taken over all of its members.

The most natural way, then, of arriving at utilitarianism (although not, of course, the only way of doing so) is to adopt for society as a whole the principle of rational choice for one man. Once this is recognized, the place of the impartial spectator and the emphasis on sympathy in the history of utilitarian thought is readily understood. For it is by the conception of the impartial spectator and the use of sympathetic identification in guiding our imagination that the principle for one man is applied to society. It is this spectator who is conceived as carrying out the required organization of the desires of all persons into one coherent system of desire; it is by this construction that many persons are fused into one. Endowed with ideal powers of sympathy and imagination, the impartial spectator is the perfectly rational individual who identifies with and experiences the desires of others as if these desires were his own. In this way he ascertains the intensity of these desires and assigns them their appropriate weight in the one system of desire the satisfaction of which the ideal legislator then tries to maximize by adjusting the rules of the social system. On this conception of society separate individuals are thought of as so many different lines along which rights and duties are to be assigned and scarce means of satisfaction allocated in accordance with rules so as to give the greatest fulfillment of wants. The nature of the decision made by the ideal legislator is not, therefore, materially different from that of an entrepreneur deciding how to maximize his profit by producing this or that commodity, or that of a consumer deciding how to maximize his satisfaction by the purchase of this or that collection of goods. In each case there is a single person whose system of desires determines the best allocation of limited means. The correct decision is essentially a question of efficient administration. This view of social cooperation is the consequence of extending to society the principle of choice for one man, and then, to make this extension work, conflating all persons into one through the imaginative acts of the impartial sympathetic spectator. Utilitarianism does not take seriously the distinction between persons.

. . . .

11. Two Principles of Justice

I shall now state in a provisional form the two principles of justice that I believe would be chosen in the original position. . . .

The first statement of the two principles reads as follows.

First: each person is to have an equal right to the most extensive basic liberty compatible with a similar liberty for others.

Second: social and economic inequalities are to be arranged so that they are both (a) reasonably expected to be to everyone's advantage, and (b) attached to positions and offices open to all.

. . . .

By way of general comment, these principles primarily apply, as I have said, to the basic structure of society. They are to govern the assignment of rights and duties and to regulate the distribution of social and economic advantages. As their formulation suggests, these principles presuppose that the social structure can be divided into two more or less distinct parts, the first principle applying to the one, the second to the other. They distinguish between those aspects of the social system that define and secure the equal liberties of citizenship and those that specify and establish social and economic inequalities. The basic liberties of citizens are, roughly speaking, political liberty (the right to vote and to be eligible for public office) together with freedom of speech and assembly; liberty of conscience and freedom of thought; freedom of the person along with the right to hold (personal) property; and freedom from arbitrary arrest and seizure as defined by the concept of the rule of law. These liberties are all required to be equal by the first principle, since citizens of a just society are to have the same basic rights.

The second principle applies, in the first approximation, to the distribution of income and wealth and to the design of organizations that make use of differences in authority and responsibility, or chains of command. While the distribution of wealth and income need not be equal, it must be to everyone's advantage, and at the same time, positions of authority and offices of command must be accessible to all. One applies the second principle by holding positions open, and then, subject to this constraint, arranges social and economic inequalities so that everyone benefits.

These principles are to be arranged in a serial order with the first principle prior to the second. This ordering means that a departure from the institutions of equal liberty required by the first principle cannot be justified by, or compensated for, by greater social and economic advantages. The distribution of wealth and income, and the hierarchies of authority, must be consistent with both the liberties of equal citizenship and equality of opportunity.

It is clear that these principles are rather specific in their content, and their acceptance rests on certain assumptions that I must eventually try to explain and justify. A theory of justice depends upon a theory of society in ways that will become evident as we proceed. For the present, it should be observed that the two principles (and this holds for all formulations) are a special case of a more general conception of justice that can be expressed as follows.

> All social values—liberty and opportunity, income and wealth, and the bases of self-respect—are to be distributed equally unless an unequal distribution of any, or all, of these values is to everyone's advantage.

Injustice, then, is simply inequalities that are not to the benefit of all. Of course, this conception is extremely vague and requires interpretation.

As a first step, suppose that the basic structure of society distributes certain primary goods, that is, things that every rational man is presumed to want. These goods normally have a use whatever a person's rational plan of life. For simplicity, assume that the chief primary goods at the disposition of society are rights and liberties, powers and opportunities, income and wealth. (Later on in Part Three the primary good of self-respect has a central place.) These are the social primary goods. Other primary goods such as health and vigor, intelligence and imagination, are natural goods; although their possession is influenced by the basic structure, they are not so directly under its control. Imagine, then, a hypothetical initial arrangement in which all the social primary goods are equally distributed: everyone has similar rights and duties, and income and wealth are evenly shared. This state of affairs provides a benchmark for judging improvements. If certain inequalities of wealth and organizational powers would make everyone better off than in this hypothetical starting situation, then they accord with the general conception.

Now it is possible, at least theoretically, that by giving up some of their fundamental liberties men are sufficiently compensated by the resulting social and economic gains. The general conception of justice imposes no restrictions on what sort of inequalities are permissible; it only requires that everyone's position be improved. We need not suppose anything so drastic as consenting to a condition of slavery. Imagine instead that men forego certain political rights when the economic returns are significant and their capacity to influence the course of policy by the exercise of these rights would be marginal in any case. It is this kind of exchange which the two principles as stated rule out; being arranged in serial order they do not permit exchanges between basic liberties and economic and social gains. The serial ordering of principles expresses an underlying preference among primary social goods. When this preference is rational so likewise is the choice of these principles in this order.

. . . .

Now the second principle insists that each person benefit from permissible inequalities in the basic structure. This means that it must be reasonable for each relevant representative man defined by this structure, when he views it as a going concern, to prefer his prospects with the inequality to his prospects without it. One is not allowed to justify differences in income or organizational powers on the ground that the disadvantages of those in one position are outweighed by the greater advantages of those in another. Much less can infringements of liberty be counterbalanced in this way. Applied to the basic structure, the principle of utility would have us maximize the sum of expectations of representative men (weighted by the number of persons they represent, on the classical view); and this would permit us to compensate for the losses of some by the gains of others. Instead, the two principles require that everyone benefit from economic and social inequalities.

. . . .

26. The Reasoning Leading to the Two Principles of Justice

In this [section] I take up the choice between the two principles of justice and the principle of average utility. Determining the rational preference between these two options is perhaps the central problem in developing the conception of justice as fairness as a viable alternative to the utilitarian tradition. I shall begin in this section by presenting some intuitive remarks favoring the two principles. I shall also discuss briefly the qualitative structure of the argument that needs to be made if the case for these principles is to be conclusive.

It will be recalled that the general conception of justice as fairness requires that all primary social goods be distributed equally unless an unequal distribution would be to everyone's advantage. No restrictions are placed on exchanges of these goods and therefore a lesser liberty can be compensated for by greater social and economic benefits. Now looking at the situation from the standpoint of one person selected arbitrarily, there is no way for him to win special advantages for himself. Nor, on the other hand, are there grounds for his acquiescing in special disadvantages. Since it is not reasonable for him to expect more than an equal share in the division of social goods, and since it is not rational for him to agree to less, the sensible thing for him to do is to acknowledge as the first principle of justice one requiring an equal distribution. Indeed, this principle is so obvious that we would expect it to occur to anyone immediately.

Thus, the parties start with a principle establishing equal liberty for all, including equality of opportunity, as well as an equal distribution of income and wealth. But there is no reason why this acknowledgment should be final. If there are inequalities in the basic structure that work to make everyone better off in comparison with the benchmark of initial equality, why not permit them? The immediate gain which a greater equality might allow can be regarded as intelligently invested in view of its future return. If, for example, these inequalities set up various incentives which succeed in eliciting more productive efforts, a person in the original position may look upon them as necessary to cover the costs of training and to encourage effective performance. One might think that ideally individuals should want to serve one another. But since the parties are assumed not to take an interest in one another's interests, their acceptance of these inequalities is only the acceptance of the relations in which men stand in the circumstances of justice. They have no grounds for complaining of one another's motives. A person in the original position would, therefore, concede

the justice of these inequalities. Indeed, it would be shortsighted of him not to do so. He would hesitate to agree to these regularities only if he would be dejected by the bare knowledge or perception that others were better situated; and I have assumed that the parties decide as if they are not moved by envy. In order to make the principle regulating inequalities determinate, one looks at the system from the standpoint of the least advantaged representative man. Inequalities are permissible when they maximize, or at least all contribute to, the long-term expectations of the least fortunate group in society.

Now this general conception imposes no constraints on what sorts of inequalities are allowed, whereas the special conception, by putting the two principles in serial order (with the necessary adjustments in meaning) forbids exchanges between basic liberties and economic and social benefits. I shall not try to justify this ordering here. . . . But roughly, the idea underlying this ordering is that if the parties assume that their basic liberties can be effectively exercised, they will not exchange a lesser liberty for an improvement in economic well-being. It is only when social conditions do not allow the effective establishment of these rights that one can concede their limitation; and these restrictions can be granted only to the extent that they are necessary to prepare the way for a free society. The denial of equal liberty can be defended only if it is necessary to raise the level of civilization so that in due course these freedoms can be enjoyed. Thus in adopting a serial order we are in effect making a special assumption in the original position, namely, that the parties know that the conditions of their society, whatever they are, admit the effective realization of the equal liberties. The serial ordering of the two principles of justice eventually comes to be reasonable if the general conception is consistently followed. This lexical ranking is the long-run tendency of the general view. For the most part I shall assume that the requisite circumstances for the serial order obtain.

It seems clear from these remarks that the two principles are at least a plausible conception of justice. The question, though, is how one is to argue for them more systematically. Now there are several things to do. One can work out their consequences for institutions and note their implications for fundamental social policy. In this way they are tested by a comparison with our considered judgments of justice. . . . But one can also try to find arguments in their favor that are decisive from the standpoint of the original position. In order to see how this might be done, it is useful as a heuristic device to think of the two principles as the maximin solution to the problem of social justice. There is an analogy between the two principles and the maximin rule for choice under uncertainty. This is evident from the fact that the two principles are those a person would choose for the design of a society in which his enemy is to assign him his place. The maximin rule tells us to rank alternatives by their worst possible outcomes: we are to adopt the alternative the worst outcome of which is superior to the worst outcomes of the others. The persons in the original position do not, of course, assume that their initial place in society is decided by a malevolent opponent. As I note below, they should not reason from false premises. The veil of ignorance does not violate this idea, since an absence of information is not misinformation. But that the two principles of justice would be chosen if the parties were forced to protect themselves against such a contingency explains the sense in which this conception is the maximin solution. And this analogy suggests that if the original position has been described so that it is rational for the parties to adopt the conservative attitude expressed by this rule, a conclusive argument can indeed be constructed for these principles. Clearly the maximin rule is not, in general, a suitable guide for choices under uncertainty. But it is attractive in situations marked by certain special features. My aim, then, is to show that a good case can be made for the two principles based on the fact that the original position manifests these features to the fullest possible degree, carrying them to the limit, so to speak.

Consider the gain-and-loss table below. It represents the gains and losses for a situation which is not a game of strategy. There is no one playing against the person making the decision; instead he is faced with several possible circumstances which may or may not obtain. Which circumstances happen to exist does not depend upon what the person choosing decides or whether he announces his moves in

advance. The numbers in the table are monetary values (in hundreds of dollars) in comparison with some initial situation. The gain (g) depends upon the individual's decision (d) and the circumstances (c). Thus $g = f(d, c)$. Assuming that there are three possible decisions and three possible circumstances, we might have this gain-and-loss table.

Decisions	Circumstances		
	C_1	C_2	C_3
d_1	−7	8	12
d_2	−8	7	14
d_3	5	6	8

The maximin rule requires that we make the third decision. For in this case the worst that can happen is that one gains five hundred dollars, which is better than the worst for the other actions. If we adopt one of these we may lose either eight or seven hundred dollars. Thus, the choice of d_3 maximizes $f(d,c)$ for that value of c, which for a given d, minimizes f. The term "maximin" means the *maximum minimorum*; and the rule directs our attention to the worst that can happen under any proposed course of action, and to decide in the light of that.

Now there appear to be three chief features of situations that give plausibility to this unusual rule. First, since the rule takes no account of the likelihoods of the possible circumstances, there must be some reason for sharply discounting estimates of these probabilities. Offhand, the most natural rule of choice would seem to be to compute the expectation of monetary gain for each decision and then to adopt the course of action with the highest prospect. (This expectation is defined as follows: let us suppose that g_{ij} represent the numbers in the gain-and-loss table, where i is the row index and j is the column index; and let p_j, $j = 1, 2, 3$, be the likelihoods of the circumstances, with $\Sigma p_j = 1$. Then the expectation for the ith decision is equal to $\Sigma p_j g_{ij}$.) Thus it must be, for example, that the situation is one in which a knowledge of likelihoods is impossible, or at best extremely insecure. In this case it is unreasonable not to be skeptical of probabilistic calculations unless there is no other way out, particularly if the decision is a fundamental one that needs to be justified to others.

The second feature that suggests the maximin rule is the following: the person choosing has a conception of the good such that he cares very little, if anything, for what he might gain above the minimum stipend that he can, in fact, be sure of by following the maximin rule. It is not worthwhile for him to take a chance for the sake of a further advantage, especially when it may turn out that he loses much that is important to him. This last provision brings in the third feature, namely, that the rejected alternatives have outcomes that one can hardly accept. The situation involves grave risks. Of course these features work most effectively in combination. The paradigm situation for following the maximin rule is when all three features are realized to the highest degree. This rule does not, then, generally apply, nor of course is it self-evident. Rather, it is a maxim, a rule of thumb, that comes into its own in special circumstances. Its application depends upon the qualitative structure of the possible gains and losses in relation to one's conception of the good, all this against a background in which it is reasonable to discount conjectural estimates of likelihoods.

It should be noted, as the comments on the gain-and-loss table say, that the entries in the table represent monetary values and not utilities. This difference is significant since for one thing computing expectations on the basis of such objective values is not the same thing as computing expected utility and may lead to different results. The essential point though is that in justice as fairness the parties do not know their conception of the good and cannot estimate their utility in the ordinary sense. In any case, we want to go behind de facto preferences generated by given conditions. Therefore expectations are based upon an index of primary goods and the parties make their choice accordingly. The entries in the example are in terms of money and not utility to indicate this aspect of the contract doctrine.

Now, as I have suggested, the original position has been defined so that it is a situation in which the maximin rule applies. In order to see this, let us review briefly the nature of this situation with these three special features in mind. To begin with, the veil of ignorance excludes all but the vaguest

knowledge of likelihoods. The parties have no basis for determining the probable nature of their society, or their place in it. Thus they have strong reasons for being wary of probability calculations if any other course is open to them. They must also take in account the fact that their choice of principles should seem reasonable to others, in particular their descendants, whose rights will be deeply affected by it. There are further grounds for discounting that I shall mention as we go along. For the present it suffices to note that these considerations are strengthened by the fact that the parties know very little about the gain-and-loss table. Not only are they unable to conjecture the likelihoods of the various possible circumstances, they cannot say much about what the possible circumstances are, much less enumerate them and foresee the outcome of each alternative available. Those deciding are much more in the dark than the illustration by a numerical table suggests. It is for this reason that I have spoken of an analogy with the maximin rule.

Several kinds of arguments for the two principles of justice illustrate the second feature. Thus, if we can maintain that these principles provide a workable theory of social justice, and that they are compatible with reasonable demands of efficiency, then this conception guarantees a satisfactory minimum. There may be, on reflection, little reason for trying to do better. . . .

Finally, the third feature holds if we can assume that other conceptions of justice may lead to institutions that the parties would find intolerable. For example, it has sometimes been held that under some conditions the utility principle (in either form) justifies, if not slavery or serfdom, at any rate serious infractions of liberty for the sake of greater social benefits. We need not consider here the truth of this claim, or the likelihood that the requisite conditions obtain. For the moment, this contention is only to illustrate the way in which conceptions of justice may allow for outcomes which the parties may not be able to accept. And having the ready alternative of the two principles of justice which secure a satisfactory minimum, it seems unwise, if not irrational, for them to take a chance that these outcomes are not realized.

NOTE

1. The process of mutual adjustment of principles and considered judgments is not peculiar to moral philosophy. See Nelson Goodman, *Fact, Fiction, and Forecast* (Cambridge, Mass.: Harvard University Press, 1955), pp. 65–68, for parallel remarks concerning the justification of the principles of deductive and inductive inference.

KEY TERMS

Justice
The original position
Veil of ignorance
Principle of utility
Reflective equilibrium

STUDY QUESTIONS

1. How does Rawls compare justice in social institutions to truth in systems of thought? Do you think this comparison is apt? Why or why not?
2. Explain, in your own words, Rawls's idea of "justice as fairness."
3. What role does the idea of the "veil of ignorance" play in Rawls's theory?
4. What's the idea behind "reflective equilibrium"? Do you think it is a worthy ideal? Why or why not?
5. Rawls puts forth two principles of justice that he thinks "would be chosen in the original position." Do you agree with him that these principles would be chosen? Can you think of other principles that might fare better?

Justice and Entitlement

ROBERT NOZICK

· ·

Chapter 7
Distributive Justice

· · · · · · · ·

The term "**distributive justice**" is not a neutral one. Hearing the term "distribution," most people presume that some thing or mechanism uses some principle or criterion to give out a supply of things. Into this process of distributing shares some error may have crept. So it is an open question, at least, whether *re*distribution should take place; whether we should do again what has already been done once, though poorly. However, we are not in the position of children who have been given portions of pie by someone who now makes last minute adjustments to rectify careless cutting. There is no *central* distribution, no person or group entitled to control all the resources,

jointly deciding how they are to be doled out. What each person gets, he gets from others who give to him in exchange for something, or as a gift. In a free society, diverse persons control different resources, and new holdings arise out of the voluntary exchanges and actions of persons. There is no more a distributing or distribution of shares than there is a distributing of mates in a society in which persons choose whom they shall marry. The total result is the product of many individual decisions which the different individuals involved are entitled to make. . . . We shall speak of people's holdings; a principle of justice in holdings describes (part of) what justice tells us (requires) about holdings. I shall state first what I take to be the correct view about justice in holdings, and then turn to the discussion of alternate views.

The Entitlement Theory

The subject of justice in holdings consists of three major topics. The first is the *original acquisition of holdings*, the appropriation of unheld things. This includes the issues of how unheld things may come to be held, the process, or processes, by which unheld things may come to be held, the things that may come to be held by these processes, the extent of what comes to be held by a particular process, and so on. We shall refer to the complicated truth about this topic, which we shall not formulate here, as the principle of justice in acquisition. The second topic concerns the *transfer of holdings* from one person to another. By what processes may a person transfer holdings to another? How may a person acquire a holding from another who holds it? Under this topic come general descriptions of voluntary exchange, and gift and (on the other hand) fraud, as well as reference to particular conventional details fixed upon in a given society. The complicated truth about this subject (with placeholders for conventional details) we shall call the principle of justice in transfer. (And we shall suppose it also includes principles governing how a person may divest himself of a holding, passing it into an unheld state.)

If the world were wholly just, the following inductive definition would exhaustively cover the subject of justice in holdings.

1. A person who acquires a holding in accordance with the principle of justice in acquisition is entitled to that holding.
2. A person who acquires a holding in accordance with the principle of justice in transfer, from someone else entitled to the holding, is entitled to the holding.
3. No one is entitled to a holding except by (repeated) applications of 1 and 2.

The complete principle of distributive justice would say simply that a distribution is just if everyone is entitled to the holdings they possess under the distribution.

A distribution is just if it arises from another just distribution by legitimate means. The legitimate means of moving from one distribution to another are specified by the principle of justice in transfer. The legitimate first "moves" are specified by the principle of justice in acquisition.[1] Whatever arises from a just situation by just steps is itself just. The means of change

specified by the principle of justice in transfer preserve justice. As correct rules of inference are truth preserving, and any conclusion deduced via repeated application of such rules from only true premises is itself true, so the means of transition from one situation to another specified by the principle of justice in transfer are justice preserving, and any situation actually arising from repeated transitions in accordance with the principle from a just situation is itself just. The parallel between justice-preserving transformations and truth-preserving transformations illuminates where it fails as well as where it holds. That a conclusion could have been deduced by truth-preserving means from premises that are true suffices to show its truth. That from a just situation a situation *could* have arisen via justice-preserving means does *not* suffice to show its justice. The fact that a thief's victims voluntarily *could* have presented him with gifts does not entitle the thief to his ill-gotten gains. Justice in holdings is historical; it depends upon what actually has happened. We shall return to this point later.

Not all actual situations are generated in accordance with the two principles of justice in holdings: the principle of justice in acquisition and the principle of justice in transfer. Some people steal from others, or defraud them, or enslave them, seizing their product and preventing them from living as they choose, or forcibly exclude others from competing in exchanges. None of these are permissible modes of transition from one situation to another. And some persons acquire holdings by means not sanctioned by the principle of justice in acquisition. The existence of past injustice (previous violations of the first two principles of justice in holdings) raises the third major topic under justice in holdings: the rectification of injustice in holdings. If past injustice has shaped present holdings in various ways, some identifiable and some not, what now, if anything, ought to be done to rectify these injustices? What obligations do the performers of injustice have toward those whose position is worse than it would have been had the injustice not been done? Or, than it would have been had compensation been paid promptly? How, if at all, do things change if the beneficiaries and those made worse off are not the direct parties in the act of injustice, but, for example, their descendants? Is an injustice done to someone whose holding was itself based upon an unrectified injustice? How far back must one go in wiping clean the historical slate of injustices? What may victims of injustice permissibly do in order to rectify the injustices being done to them, including the many injustices done by persons acting through their government? I do not know of a thorough or theoretically sophisticated treatment of such issues. Idealizing greatly, let us suppose theoretical investigation will produce a principle of rectification. This principle uses historical information about previous situations and injustices done in them (as defined by the first two principles of justice and rights against interference), and information about the actual course of events that flowed from these injustices, until the present, and it yields a description (or descriptions) of holdings in the society. The principle of rectification presumably will make use of its best estimate of subjunctive information about what would have occurred (or a probability distribution over what might have occurred, using the expected value) if the injustice had not taken place. If the actual description of holdings turns out not to be one of the descriptions yielded by the principle, then one of the descriptions yielded must be realized.[2]

The general outlines of the theory of justice in holdings are that the holdings of a person are just if he is entitled to them by the principles of justice in acquisition and transfer, or by the principle of rectification of injustice (as specified by the first two principles). If each person's holdings are just, then the total set (distribution) of holdings is just. To turn these general outlines into a specific theory we would have to specify the details of each of the three principles of justice in holdings: the principle of acquisition of holdings, the principle of transfer of holdings, and the principle of rectification of violations of the first two principles. I shall not attempt that task here. (Locke's principle of justice in acquisition is discussed below.)

Historical Principles and End-result Principles

The general outlines of the entitlement theory illuminate the nature and defects of other conceptions of distributive justice. The entitlement theory of justice in distribution is *historical*; whether a distribution is just depends upon how it came about. In contrast, *current time-slice principles* of justice hold that the justice of a distribution is determined by how things are distributed (who has what) as judged by some *structural* principle(s) of just distribution. A utilitarian who judges between any two distributions by seeing which has the greater sum of utility and, if the sums tie, applies some fixed equality criterion to choose the more equal distribution, would hold a current time-slice principle of justice. As would someone who had a fixed schedule of trade-offs between the sum of happiness and equality. According to a current time-slice principle, all that needs to be looked at, in judging the justice of a distribution, is who ends up with what; in comparing any two distributions one need look only at the matrix presenting the distributions. No further information need be fed into a principle of justice. It is a consequence of such principles of justice that any two structurally identical distributions are equally just. (Two distributions are structurally identical if they present the same profile, but perhaps have different persons occupying the particular slots. My having ten and your having five, and my having five and your having ten are structurally identical distributions.) Welfare economics is the theory of current time-slice principles of justice. The subject is conceived as operating on matrices representing only current information about distribution. This, as well as some of the usual conditions (for example, the choice of distribution is invariant under relabeling of columns), guarantees that welfare economics will be a current time-slice theory, with all of its inadequacies.

Most persons do not accept current time-slice principles as constituting the whole story about distributive shares. They think it relevant in assessing the justice of a situation to consider not only the distribution it embodies, but also how that distribution came about. If some persons are in prison for murder or war crimes, we do not say that to assess the justice of the distribution in the society we must look only at what this person has, and that person has, and that person has, . . . at the current time. We think it relevant to ask whether someone did something so that he *deserved* to be punished, deserved to have a lower share. Most will agree to the relevance of further information with regard to punishments and penalties. Consider also desired things. One traditional socialist view is that workers are entitled to the product and full fruits of their labor; they have earned it; a distribution is unjust if it does not give the workers what they are entitled to. Such entitlements are based upon some past history. No socialist holding this view would find it comforting to be told that because the actual distribution *A* happens to coincide structurally with the one he desires *D, A* therefore is no less just than *D*; it differs only in that the "parasitic" owners of capital receive under *A* what the workers are entitled to under *D*, and the workers receive under *A* what the owners are entitled to under *D*, namely very little. This socialist rightly, in my view, holds onto the notions of earning, producing, entitlement, desert, and so forth, and he rejects current time-slice principles that look only to the structure of the resulting set of holdings. (The set of holdings resulting from what? Isn't it implausible that how holdings are produced and come to exist has no effect at all on who should hold what?) His mistake lies in his view of what entitlements arise out of what sorts of productive processes.

We construe the position we discuss too narrowly by speaking of *current* time-slice principles. Nothing is changed if structural principles operate upon a time sequence of current time-slice profiles and, for example, give someone more now to counterbalance the less he has had earlier. A utilitarian or an egalitarian or any mixture of the two over time will inherit the difficulties of his more myopic comrades. He is not helped by the fact that *some* of the information others consider relevant in assessing a distribution is reflected, unrecoverably, in past matrices. Henceforth, we shall refer to such unhistorical principles of distributive justice, including the current time-slice principles, as *end-result principles* or *end-state principles*.

In contrast to end-result principles of justice, *historical principles* of justice hold that past circumstances or actions of people can create differential entitlement or differential deserts to things. An injustice can be worked by moving from one distribution to another structurally identical one, for the second, in profile the same, may violate people's entitlements or deserts; it may not fit the actual history.

Patterning

The entitlement principles of justice in holdings that we have sketched are historical principles of justice. To better understand their precise character, we shall distinguish them from another subclass of the historical principles. Consider, as an example, the principle of distribution according to moral merit. This principle requires that total distributive shares vary directly with moral merit; no person should have a greater share than anyone whose moral merit is greater. (If moral merit could be not merely ordered but measured on an interval or ratio scale, stronger principles could be formulated.) Or consider the principle that results by substituting "usefulness to society" for "moral merit" in the previous principle. Or instead of "distribute according to moral merit," or "distribute according to usefulness to society," we might consider "distribute according to the weighted sum of moral merit, usefulness to society, and need," with the weights of the different dimensions equal. Let us call a principle of distribution *patterned* if it specifies that a distribution is to vary along with some natural dimension, weighted sum of natural dimensions, or lexicographic ordering of natural dimensions. And let us say a distribution is patterned if it accords with some patterned principle. (I speak of natural dimensions, admittedly without a general criterion for them, because for any set of holdings some artificial dimensions can be gimmicked up to vary along with the distribution of the set.) The principle of distribution in accordance with moral merit is a patterned historical principle, which specifies a patterned distribution. "Distribute according to I.Q." is a patterned principle that looks to information not contained in distributional matrices. It is not historical, however, in that it does not look to any past actions creating differential entitlements to evaluate a distribution; it requires only distributional matrices whose columns are labeled by I.Q. scores. The distribution in a society, however, may be composed of such simple patterned distributions, without itself being simply patterned. Different sectors may operate different patterns, or some combination of patterns may operate in different proportions across a society. A distribution composed in this manner, from a small number of patterned distributions, we also shall term "patterned." And we extend the use of "pattern" to include the overall designs put forth by combinations of end-state principles.

Almost every suggested principle of distributive justice is patterned: to each according to his moral merit, or needs, or marginal product, or how hard he tries, or the weighted sum of the foregoing, and so on. The principle of entitlement we have sketched is *not* patterned. There is no one natural dimension or weighted sum or combination of a small number of natural dimensions that yields the distributions generated in accordance with the principle of entitlement. The set of holdings that results when some persons receive their marginal products, others win at gambling, others receive a share of their mate's income, others receive gifts from foundations, others receive interest on loans, others receive gifts from admirers, others receive returns on investment, others make for themselves much of what they have, others find things, and so on, will not be patterned.

. . . .

How Liberty Upsets Patterns

It is not clear how those holding alternative conceptions of distributive justice can reject the entitlement conception of justice in holdings. For suppose a distribution favored by one of these nonentitlement conceptions is realized. Let us suppose it is your favorite one and let us call this distribution D_1; perhaps everyone has an equal share, perhaps shares vary in accordance with some dimension you treasure. Now suppose that Wilt Chamberlain is greatly in demand by basketball teams, being a great gate attraction. (Also suppose contracts run only for a year, with players being free agents.) He signs the following sort of contract with a team: In each home game, twenty-five cents from the price of each ticket of admission goes to him. (We ignore the question of whether this is "gouging" the owners, letting them look out for themselves.) The season starts, and people cheerfully attend his team's games; they buy their tickets, each time dropping a separate

twenty-five cents of their admission price into a special box with Chamberlain's name on it. They are excited about seeing him play; it is worth the total admission price to them. Let us suppose that in one season one million persons attend his home games, and Wilt Chamberlain winds up with $250,000, a much larger sum than the average income and larger even than anyone else has. Is he entitled to this income? Is this new distribution D_2, unjust? If so, why? There is *no* question about whether each of the people was entitled to the control over the resources they held in D_1; because that was the distribution (your favorite) that (for the purposes of argument) we assumed was acceptable. Each of these persons *chose* to give twenty-five cents of their money to Chamberlain. They could have spent it on going to the movies, or on candy bars, or on copies of *Dissent* magazine, or of *Monthly Review*. But they all, at least one million of them, converged on giving it to Wilt Chamberlain in exchange for watching him play basketball. If D_1 was a just distribution, and people voluntarily moved from it to D_2, transferring parts of their shares they were given under D_1 (what was it for if not to do something with?), isn't D_2 also just? If the people were entitled to dispose of the resources to which they were entitled (under D_1), didn't this include their being entitled to give it to, or exchange it with, Wilt Chamberlain? Can anyone else complain on grounds of justice? Each other person already has his legitimate share under D_1. Under D_1, there is nothing that anyone has that anyone else has a claim of justice against. After someone transfers something to Wilt Chamberlain, third parties *still* have their legitimate shares; *their* shares are not changed. By what process could such a transfer among two persons give rise to a legitimate claim of distributive justice on a portion of what was transferred, by a third party who had no claim of justice on any holding of the others *before* the transfer?

. . . .

The general point illustrated by the Wilt Chamberlain example . . . is that no end-state principle or distributional-patterned principle of justice can be continuously realized without continuous interference with people's lives. Any favored pattern would be transformed into one unfavored by the principle, by people choosing to act in various ways; for example, by people exchanging goods and services with other people, or giving things to other people, things the transferrers are entitled to under the favored distributional pattern. To maintain a pattern one must either continually interfere to stop people from transferring resources as they wish to, or continually (or periodically) interfere to take from some persons resources that others for some reason chose to transfer to them.

. . . .

Locke's Theory of Acquisition

. . . [W]e must introduce an additional bit of complexity into the structure of the entitlement theory. This is best approached by considering Locke's attempt to specify a principle of justice in acquisition. Locke views property rights in an unowned object as originating through someone's mixing his labor with it. This gives rise to many questions. What are the boundaries of what labor is mixed with? If a private astronaut clears a place on Mars, has he mixed his labor with (so that he comes to own) the whole planet, the whole uninhabited universe, or just a particular plot? Which plot does an act bring under ownership? The minimal (possibly disconnected) area such that an act decreases entropy in that area, and not elsewhere? Can virgin land (for the purposes of ecological investigation by high-flying airplane) come under ownership by a Lockean process? Building a fence around a territory presumably would make one the owner of only the fence (and the land immediately underneath it).

Why does mixing one's labor with something make one the owner of it? Perhaps because one owns one's labor, and so one comes to own a previously unowned thing that becomes permeated with what one owns. Ownership seeps over into the rest. But why isn't mixing what I own with what I don't own a way of losing what I own rather than a way of gaining what I don't? If I own a can of tomato juice and spill it in the sea so that its molecules (made radioactive, so I can check this) mingle evenly throughout the sea, do I thereby come to own the sea, or have I foolishly dissipated my tomato juice? Perhaps the idea, instead, is that laboring on something improves it and makes it more valuable; and anyone is entitled to own a thing whose value he has created. (Reinforcing this, perhaps, is the view

that laboring is unpleasant. If some people made things effortlessly, as the cartoon characters in *The Yellow Submarine* trail flowers in their wake, would they have lesser claim to their own products whose making didn't *cost* them anything?) Ignore the fact that laboring on something may make it less valuable (spraying pink enamel paint on a piece of driftwood that you have found). Why should one's entitlement extend to the whole object rather than just to the *added value* one's labor has produced? (Such reference to value might also serve to delimit the extent of ownership; for example, substitute "increases the value of" for "decreases entropy in" in the above entropy criterion.) No workable or coherent value-added property scheme has yet been devised, and any such scheme presumably would fall to objections (similar to those) that fell the theory of Henry George.

It will be implausible to view improving an object as giving full ownership to it, if the stock of unowned objects that might be improved is limited. For an object's coming under one person's ownership changes the situation of all others. Whereas previously they were at liberty (in Hohfeld's sense) to use the object, they now no longer are. This change in the situation of others (by removing their liberty to act on a previously unowned object) need not worsen their situation. If I appropriate a grain of sand from Coney Island, no one else may now do as they will with *that* grain of sand. But there are plenty of other grains of sand left for them to do the same with. Or if not grains of sand, then other things. Alternatively, the things I do with the grain of sand I appropriate might improve the position of others, counterbalancing their loss of the liberty to use that grain. The crucial point is whether appropriation of an unowned object worsens the situation of others.

Locke's proviso that there be "enough and as good left in common for others" (sect. 27) is meant to ensure that the situation of others is not worsened.

. . . .

Is the situation of persons who are unable to appropriate (there being no more accessible and useful unowned objects) worsened by a system allowing appropriation and permanent property? Here enter the various familiar social considerations favoring private property: it increases the social product by putting means of production in the hands of those who can use them most efficiently (profitably); experimentation is encouraged, because with separate persons controlling resources, there is no one person or small group whom someone with a new idea must convince to try it out; private property enables people to decide on the pattern and types of risks they wish to bear, leading to specialized types of risk bearing; private property protects future persons by leading some to hold back resources from current consumption for future markets; it provides alternate sources of employment for unpopular persons who don't have to convince any one person or small group to hire them, and so on. These considerations enter a Lockean theory to support the claim that appropriation of private property satisfies the intent behind the "enough and as good left over" proviso, *not* as a utilitarian justification of property. They enter to rebut the claim that because the proviso is violated no natural right to private property can arise by a Lockean process. The difficulty in working such an argument to show that the proviso is satisfied is in fixing the appropriate baseline for comparison. Lockean appropriation makes people no worse off than they would be *how?* This question of fixing the baseline needs more detailed investigation than we are able to give it here.

. . . .

The Proviso

Whether or not Locke's particular theory of appropriation can be spelled out so as to handle various difficulties, I assume that any adequate theory of justice in acquisition will contain a proviso similar to the weaker of the ones we have attributed to Locke. A process normally giving rise to a permanent bequeathable property right in a previously unowned thing will not do so if the position of others no longer at liberty to use the thing is thereby worsened. It is important to specify *this* particular mode of worsening the situation of others, for the proviso does not encompass other modes. It does not include the worsening due to more limited opportunities to appropriate . . . , and it does not include how I "worsen" a seller's position if I appropriate materials to make some of what he is selling, and then enter into competition with him. Someone whose appropriation otherwise would violate the proviso still may

appropriate provided he compensates the others so that their situation is not thereby worsened; unless he does compensate the others, his appropriation will violate the proviso of the principle of justice in acquisition and will be an illegitimate one. A theory of appropriation incorporating this Lockean proviso will handle correctly the cases (objections to the theory lacking the proviso) where someone appropriates the total supply of something necessary for life.

A theory which includes this proviso in its principle of justice in acquisition must also contain a more complex principle of justice in transfer. Some reflection of the proviso about appropriation constrains later actions. If my appropriating all of a certain substance violates the Lockean proviso, then so does my appropriating some and purchasing all the rest from others who obtained it without otherwise violating the Lockean proviso. If the proviso excludes someone's appropriating all the drinkable water in the world, it also excludes his purchasing it all. (More weakly, and messily, it may exclude his charging certain prices for some of his supply.) This proviso (almost?) never will come into effect; the more someone acquires of a scarce substance which others want, the higher the price of the rest will go, and the more difficult it will become for him to acquire it all. But still, we can imagine, at least, that something like this occurs: someone makes simultaneous secret bids to the separate owners of a substance, each of whom sells assuming he can easily purchase more from the other owners; or some natural catastrophe destroys all of the supply of something except that in one person's possession. The total supply could not be permissibly appropriated by one person at the beginning. His later acquisition of it all does not show that the original appropriation violated the proviso. . . . Rather, it is the combination of the original appropriation *plus* all the later transfers and actions that violates the Lockean proviso.

Each owner's title to his holding includes the historical shadow of the Lockean proviso on appropriation. This excludes his transferring it into an agglomeration that does violate the Lockean proviso and excludes his using it in a way, in coordination with others or independently of them, so as to violate the proviso by making the situation of others worse than their baseline situation. Once it is known that someone's ownership runs afoul of the Lockean proviso, there are stringent limits on what he may do with (what it is difficult any longer unreservedly to call) "his property." Thus a person may not appropriate the only water hole in a desert and charge what he will. Nor may he charge what he will if he possesses one, and unfortunately it happens that all the water holes in the desert dry up, except for his. This unfortunate circumstance, admittedly no fault of his, brings into operation the Lockean proviso and limits his property rights. Similarly, an owner's property right in the only island in an area does not allow him to order a castaway from a shipwreck off his island as a trespasser, for this would violate the Lockean proviso.

....

The fact that someone owns the total supply of something necessary for others to stay alive does *not* entail that his (or anyone's) appropriation of anything left some people (immediately or later) in a situation worse than the baseline one. A medical researcher who synthesizes a new substance that effectively treats a certain disease and who refuses to sell except on his terms does not worsen the situation of others by depriving them of whatever he has appropriated. The others easily can possess the same materials he appropriated; the researcher's appropriation or purchase of chemicals didn't make those chemicals scarce in a way so as to violate the Lockean proviso. Nor would someone else's purchasing the total supply of the synthesized substance from the medical researcher. The fact that the medical researcher uses easily available chemicals to synthesize the drug no more violates the Lockean proviso than does the fact that the only surgeon able to perform a particular operation eats easily obtainable food in order to stay alive and to have the energy to work. This shows that the Lockean proviso is not an "end-state principle"; it focuses on a particular way that appropriative actions affect others, and not on the structure of the situation that results.

Intermediate between someone who takes all of the public supply and someone who makes the total supply out of easily obtainable substances is someone who appropriates the total supply of something in a way that does not deprive the others of it. For example, someone finds a new substance in an out-of-the-way place. He discovers that it effectively treats a certain disease and appropriates the total supply. He does not worsen the situation of others; if he did not stumble upon the substance no one else would have, and the others would remain without it. However, as time passes, the likelihood increases that others would have come across the substance; upon this fact might be based a limit to his property right in the substance so that others are not below their baseline position; for example, its bequest might be limited. The theme of someone worsening another's situation by depriving him of something he otherwise would possess may also illuminate the example of patents. An inventor's patent does not deprive others of an object which would not exist if not for the inventor. Yet patents would have this effect on others who independently invent the object. Therefore, these independent inventors, upon whom the burden of proving independent discovery may rest, should not be excluded from utilizing their own invention as they wish (including selling it to others). Furthermore, a known inventor drastically lessens the chances of actual independent invention. For persons who know of an invention usually will not try to reinvent it, and the notion of independent discovery here would be murky at best. Yet we may assume that in the absence of the original invention, sometime later someone else would have come up with it. This suggests placing a time limit on patents, as a rough rule of thumb to approximate how long it would have taken, in the absence of knowledge of the invention, for independent discovery.

I believe that the free operation of a market system will not actually run afoul of the Lockean proviso. . . .

NOTES

1. Applications of the principle of justice in acquisition may also occur as part of the move from one distribution to another. You may find an unheld thing now and appropriate it. Acquisitions also are to be understood as included when, to simplify, I speak only of transitions by transfers.
2. If the principle of rectification of violations of the first two principles yields more than one description of holdings, then some choice must be made as to which of these is to be realized. Perhaps the sort of considerations about distributive justice and equality that I argue against play a legitimate role in *this* subsidiary choice. Similarly, there may be room for such considerations in deciding which otherwise arbitrary features a statute will embody, when such features

are unavoidable because other considerations do not specify a precise line; yet a line must be drawn.

KEY TERM

Distributive justice

STUDY QUESTIONS

1. What are the three different "topics" under the heading *justice in holdings*? How do they relate to one another? Do you think that these three principles of justice exhaust what we need to know about holdings in order to know whether a certain distribution is just?
2. What does Nozick mean when he says that the entitlement theory of justice is *historical*? How does he argue for this claim?
3. Why isn't the principle of entitlement *patterned*?
4. What is the upshot of Nozick's Wilt Chamberlain example? What does the example tell us about patterning?
5. What is the "Lockean proviso" that Nozick thinks must be a part of any adequate theory of justice in acquisition? Why does he think it is necessary?

Where the Action Is:
On the Site of Distributive Justice

G. A. COHEN

G. A. Cohen (1941–2009) was the Chichele Professor of Social and Political Philosophy at All Souls College, Oxford. Cohen is best known for his defense of Marxism, but he was also an important critic of the liberal tradition within political philosophy. He was the author of *Karl Marx's Theory of History: A Defence*; *If You're an Egalitarian, How Come You're So Rich?*; and *Rescuing Justice and Equality*.

. .

I

In this paper I defend a claim which can be expressed in the words of a now familiar slogan: the personal is political. That slogan, as it stands, is vague, but I shall mean something reasonably precise by it here, to wit, that principles of distributive

From *Philosophy and Public Affairs*, 26. Copyright © 1997 by Princeton University Press. Reprinted by permission of the publisher.

For comments that influenced the final version of this paper, I thank Gerald Barnes, Diemut Bubeck, Joshua Cohen, Margaret Gilbert, Susan Hurley, John McMurtry, Derek Parfit, Thomas Pogge, John Roemer, Amelie Rorty, Hillel Steiner, Andrew Williams, Erik Wright, and Arnold Zuboff.

justice, principles, that is, about the just distribution of benefits and burdens in society, apply, wherever else they do, to people's legally unconstrained choices. Those principles, so I claim, apply to the choices that people make *within* the legally coercive structures to which, so everyone would agree, principles of justice (also) apply. In speaking of the choices that people make *within* coercive structures, I do not include the choice whether or not to comply with the rules of such structures (to which choice, once again, so everyone would agree, principles of justice [also] apply), but the choices left open by those rules because neither enjoined nor forbidden by them.

The slogan that I have appropriated here is widely used by **feminists**.[1] More importantly, however, the idea itself, which I have here used the slogan to formulate, and which I have tried to explicate above, is a feminist idea. Notice, however, that, in briefly explaining the idea that I shall defend, I have not mentioned relations between men and women in particular, or the issue of sexism. We can distinguish between the substance and the form of the feminist critique of standard ideas about justice, and it is the form of it which is of prime concern to me here,[2] even though I also endorse its substance.

The substance of the feminist critique is that standard liberal theory of justice, and the theory of Rawls in particular, unjustifiably ignore an unjust division of labor, and unjust power relations, within families (whose legal structure *may* show no sexism at all). That is the key point of the feminist critique, from a political point of view. But the (often merely implicit) form of the feminist critique, which we get when we abstract from its gender-centered content, is that choices not regulated by the law fall within the primary purview of justice, and that is the key lesson of the critique, from a theoretical point of view.

In defending the claim that the personal is political, the view that I oppose is the Rawlsian one that principles of justice apply only to what Rawls calls the "basic structure" of society. Feminists have noticed that Rawls wobbles, across the course of his writings, on the matter of whether or not the family belongs to the basic structure and is therefore, in his view, a site at which principles of justice apply. I shall argue that Rawls's wobble on this matter is not a case of mere indecision, which could readily be resolved in favor of inclusion of the family within the basic structure: that is the view of Susan Okin,[3] and, in my opinion, she is wrong about that. I shall show (in Section V below) that Rawls cannot admit the family into the basic structure of society without abandoning his insistence that it is to the basic structure only that principles of distributive justice apply. In supposing that he could include family relations, Okin shows failure to grasp the *form* of the feminist critique of Rawls.

II

I reach the conclusion announced above at the end of a trail of argument that runs as follows. Here, in Section II, I restate a criticism that I have made elsewhere of John Rawls's application of his difference principle,[4] to wit, that he does not apply it in censure of the self-seeking choices of high-flying marketeers, which induce an inequality that, so I claim, is harmful to the badly off. In Section III, I present an objection to my criticism of Rawls. The objection says that the difference principle is, by stipulation and design, a principle that applies only to social institutions (to those, in particular, which compose the basic structure of society), and, therefore, not one that applies to the choices, such as those of self-seeking high fliers, that people make *within* such institutions. Sections IV and V offer independent replies to that *basic structure objection*. I show, in Section IV, that the objection is inconsistent with many statements by Rawls about the role of principles of justice in a just society. I then allow that the discordant statements may be dropped from the Rawlsian canon, and, in Section V, I reply afresh to the basic structure objection, by showing that no defensible account of what the basic structure *is* allows Rawls to insist that the principles which apply to it do not apply to choices within it. I conclude that my original criticism of Rawls rests vindicated, against the particular objection in issue here. (Section VI comments on the implications of my position for the moral blamability of individuals whose choices violate principles of justice. The Endnote explores the distinction between coercive and noncoercive institutions, which plays a key role in the argument of Section V.)

My criticism of Rawls is of his application of **the difference principle**. That principle says, in one of its formulations,[5] that inequalities are just if and only if they are necessary to make the worst off people in society better off than they would otherwise be. I have no quarrel here with the difference principle itself,[6] but I disagree sharply with Rawls on the matter of *which* inequalities pass the test for justifying inequality that it sets and, therefore, about how *much* inequality passes that test. In my view, there is hardly any serious inequality that satisfies the requirement set by the difference principle, when it is conceived, as Rawls himself proposes to conceive it,[7] as regulating the affairs of a society whose members themselves accept that principle. If I am right, affirmation of the difference principle implies that justice requires (virtually) unqualified equality itself, as opposed to the "deep inequalities" in initial life chances with which Rawls thinks justice to be consistent.[8]

It is commonly thought, for example by Rawls, that the difference principle licenses an argument for inequality which centers on the device of material incentives. The idea is that talented people will produce more than they otherwise would if, and only if, they are paid more than an ordinary wage, and some of the extra which they will then produce can be recruited on behalf of the worse off.[9] The inequality consequent on differential material incentives is said to be justified within the terms of the difference principle, for, so it is said, that inequality benefits the worst off people: the inequality is necessary for them to be positioned as well as they are, however paltry their position may nevertheless be.

Now, before I mount my criticism of this argument, a *caveat* is necessary with respect to the terms in which it is expressed. The argument focuses on a *choice* enjoyed by well-placed people who command a high salary in a market economy: they can choose to work more or less hard, and also to work at this occupation rather than that one, and for this employer rather than that one, in accordance with how well they are remunerated. These well-placed people, in the foregoing standard presentation of the argument, are designated as "the talented," and, for reasons to be given presently, I shall so designate them throughout my criticism of the argument. Even so, these fortunate people need not be thought to be talented, in any sense of that word which implies something more than a capacity for high market earnings, for the argument to possess whatever force it has. All that need be true of them is that *they are so positioned that, happily, for them, they do command a high salary and they can vary their productivity according to exactly how high it is.* But, as far as the incentives argument is concerned, their happy position could be due to circumstances that are entirely accidental, relative to whatever kind of natural or even socially induced endowment they possess. One need not think that the average dishwasher's endowment of strength, flair, ingenuity, and so forth falls below that of the average chief executive to accept the argument's message.

One no doubt does need to think some such thing to agree with the different argument which justifies rewards to well-placed people in whole or in part as a fair return to exercise of unusual ability, but Rawls's theory is built around his rejection of such desert considerations. Nor are the enhanced rewards justified because extra contribution warrants extra reward on grounds of proper reciprocity. They are justified purely because they elicit more productive performance.

I nevertheless persist in designating the relevant individuals as "the talented," because to object that they are not actually especially talented *anyway* is to enter an empirical claim which is both contentious and, in context, misleading, since it would give the impression that it should matter to our assessment of the incentives argument whether or not well-placed people merit the contestable designation. The particular criticism of the incentives argument that I shall develop is best understood in its specificity when the apparently concessive word "talented" is used: it does not indicate a concession on the factual question of how top people in a market society get to be where they are. My use of the argument's own terms shows the strength of my critique of it: that critique stands even if we make generous assumptions about how well-placed people secured their powerful market positions. It is, moreover, especially appropriate to make such assumptions here, since the Rawlsian difference principle is lexically secondary to his principle that fair equality of opportunity has been enforced with respect to the attainment of desired positions: if anything ensures that those who occupy them possess superior creative endowment, that does. (Which is not to say that it indeed ensures that: it is consistent with fair equality of opportunity that what principally distinguishes top people is superior cunning and/or prodigious aggressivity, and nothing more admirable.)

Now, for the following reasons, I believe that the incentives argument for inequality represents a distorted application of the difference principle, even though it is its most familiar and perhaps even its most persuasive application. Either the relevant talented people themselves affirm the difference principle or they do not. That is: either they themselves believe that inequalities are unjust if they are not necessary to make the badly off better off, or they do not believe that to be a dictate of justice. If they do not believe it, then their society is not just in the appropriate Rawlsian sense, for a society is just, according to Rawls, only if its members themselves affirm and uphold the correct principles of justice. The difference principle might be appealed to in justification of a government's toleration, or promotion, of inequality in a society in which the talented do not themselves accept it, but it then justifies a public policy of inequality in a society some members of which—the talented—do not share community with the rest:[10] their behavior is then taken as fixed or parametric, a datum vis-à-vis a principle applied to it from without, rather than as itself answerable to that principle. That is not how principles of justice operate in a just society, as Rawls specifies that concept: within his terms, one may distinguish between a just society and a just government, one, that is, which applies just principles to a society whose members may not themselves accept those principles.

So we turn to the second and only remaining possibility, which is that the talented people do affirm the difference principle, that, as Rawls says, they apply the principles of justice *in their daily life* and achieve a sense of their own justice in doing so.[11] But they can then be asked why, in the light of their own belief in the principle, they require more pay than the untalented get, for work that may indeed demand special talent, but which is not specially unpleasant (for no such consideration enters the Rawlsian justification of incentives-derived inequality). The talented can be asked whether the extra they get is *necessary* to enhance the position of the worst off, which is the only thing, according to the difference principle, that could justify it. Is it necessary *tout court*, that is, independently of human will, so that, with all the will in the world removal of inequality would make everyone worse off? Or is it necessary only insofar as the talented would *decide* to produce less than they now do, or not to take up posts where they are in special demand, if inequality were removed (by, for example, income taxation which redistributes to fully egalitarian effect)?[12]

Talented people who affirm the difference principle would find those questions hard to handle. For

they could not claim, *in self-justification*, at the bar of the difference principle, that their high rewards are necessary to enhance the position of the worst off, since, in the standard case,[13] it is they themselves who *make* those rewards necessary, through their own unwillingness to work for ordinary rewards as productively as they do for exceptionally high ones, an unwillingness which ensures that the untalented get less than they otherwise would. Those rewards are, therefore, necessary only because the choices of talented people are not appropriately informed by the difference principle.

Apart, then, from the very special cases in which the talented literally *could* not, as opposed to the normal case where they (merely) would not, perform as productively as they do without superior remuneration, the difference principle can justify inequality only in a society where not everyone accepts that very principle. It therefore cannot justify inequality in the appropriate Rawlsian way.

Now, this conclusion about what it means to accept and implement the difference principle implies that the justice of a society is not exclusively a function of its legislative structure, of its legally imperative rules, but also of the choices people make within those rules. The standard (and, in my view, misguided) Rawlsian application of the difference principle can be modeled as follows. There is a market economy all agents in which seek to maximize their own gains, and there is a Rawlsian state that selects a tax function on income that maximizes the income return to the worst off people, within the constraint that, because of the self-seeking motivation of the talented, a fully equalizing taxation system would make everyone worse off than one which is less than fully equalizing. But this double-minded modeling of the implementation of the difference principle, with citizens inspired by justice endorsing a state policy which plays a tax game against (some of) them in their manifestation as self-seeking economic agents, is wholly out of accord with the (sound) Rawlsian requirement on a just society that its citizens themselves willingly submit to the standard of justice embodied in the difference principle. A society that is just within the terms of the difference principle, so we may conclude, requires not simply just coercive *rules*, but also an *ethos* of justice that informs individual choices. In the absence of such an ethos, inequalities will obtain that are not necessary to enhance the condition of the worst off: the required ethos promotes a distribution more than what the rules of the economic game by themselves can secure.

To be sure, one might imagine, in the abstract, a set of coercive rules so finely tuned that universally self-interested choices within them would raise the worst off to as high a position as any other pattern of choices would produce. Where coercive rules had and were known to have such a character, agents could choose self-interestedly in confidence that the results of their choices would satisfy an appropriately uncompromising interpretation of the difference principle. In that (imaginary) case, the only ethos necessary for difference principle justice would be willing obedience to the relevant rules, an ethos which Rawls expressly requires. But the vast economics literature on incentive compatibility teaches that rules of the contemplated perfect kind cannot be designed. Accordingly, as things actually are, the required ethos must, as I have argued, guide choice within the rules, and not merely direct agents to obey them. (I should emphasize that this is not so because it is *in general* true that the point of the rules governing an activity must be aimed at when agents pursue that activity in good faith: every competitive sport represents a counterexample to that generalization. But my argument for the conclusion stated above did not rest on that false generalization.)

III

There is an objection which friends of Rawls's *Theory of Justice* would press against my argument in criticism of his application of the difference principle. The objection is that my focus on the posture of talented producers in daily economic life is inappropriate, since their behavior occurs within, and does not determine, *the basic structure* of society, and it is only to the latter that the difference principle applies.[14] Whatever people's choices within it may be, the basic structure is just provided that it satisfies the two principles of justice. To be sure, so Rawls acknowledges, people's choices can themselves be

assessed as just or unjust, from a number of points of view. Thus, for example, appointment to a given job of candidate A rather than candidate B might be judged unjust, even though it occurs within the rules of a just basic structure.[15] But injustice in such a choice is not the sort of injustice that the Rawlsian principles are designed to condemn. For, *ex hypothesi*, that choice occurs within an established basic structure: it therefore cannot affect the justice of the basic structure itself, which is what, according to Rawls, the two principles govern. Nor, similarly, should the choices with respect to work and remuneration that talented people make be submitted for judgment at the bar of the difference principle. So to judge those choices is to apply that principle at the wrong point. The difference principle is a "principle of justice for institutions."[16] It governs the choice of institutions, not the choices made within them. The development of the second horn of the dilemma argument misconstrues the Rawlsian requirement that citizens in a just society uphold the principles that make it just: by virtue of the stipulated scope of the difference principle, talented people do count as faithfully upholding it, as long as they conform to the prevailing economic rules *because* that principle requires those rules.

Call that "the basic structure objection." Now, before I develop it further, and then reply to it, I want to point out that there is an important ambiguity in the concept of the basic structure, as that is wielded by Rawlsians. The ambiguity turns on whether the Rawlsian basic structure includes only coercive aspects of the social order or, also, conventions and usages that are deeply entrenched but not legally or literally coercive. I shall return to that ambiguity in Section V below, and I shall show that it shipwrecks not only the basic structure objection but also the whole approach to justice that Rawls has taught so many to pursue. But, for the time being, I shall ignore the fatal ambiguity, and I shall take the phrase "basic structure," as it appears in the basic structure objection, as denoting *some* sort of structure, be it legally coercive or not, but whose key feature, for the purposes of the objection, is that it is indeed a structure, that is, a framework of rules within which choices are made, as opposed to a set of choices and/or actions.[17] Accordingly, my Rawlsian critic would say, whatever structure, precisely, the basic structure is, the objection stands that my criticism of the incentives argument misapplies principles devised for a structure to individual choices and actions.

In further clarification of the polemical position, let me make a background point about the difference between Rawls and me with respect to the site or sites at which principles of justice apply. My own fundamental concern is neither the basic structure of society, in any sense, nor people's individual choices, but the pattern of benefits and burdens in society: that is neither a structure in which choice occurs nor a set of choices, but the upshot of structure and choices alike. My concern is *distributive justice*, by which I uneccentrically mean justice (and its lack) in the distribution of benefits and burdens to individuals. My root belief is that there is injustice in distribution when inequality of goods reflects not such things as differences in the arduousness of different people's labors, or people's different preferences and choices with respect to income and leisure, but myriad forms of lucky and unlucky circumstance. Such differences of advantage are a function of the structure *and* of people's choices within it, so I am concerned, secondarily, with *both* of those.

Now Rawls could say that his concern, too, is distributive justice, in the specified sense, but that, for him, distributive justice obtains just in case the allocation of benefits and burdens in society results from actions which display full conformity with the rules of a just basic structure.[18] When full compliance with the rules of a just basic structure obtains, it follows, on Rawls's view, that there is no scope for (further) personal justice and injustice which affects *distributive* justice, whether it be by enhancing it or by reducing it. There is, Rawls would, of course, readily agree, scope, within a just structure, for distribution-affecting meanness and generosity,[19] but generosity, though it would alter the distribution, and might make it more equal than it would otherwise be, could not make it more *just* than it would otherwise be, for it would then be doing the impossible, to wit, enhancing the justice of what is already established as a (perfectly) just distribution by virtue merely of the just structure in conformity with which it is produced. But, as I have indicated, I believe that there is scope for relevant (relevant, that is, because it affects justice in distribution) personal justice and injustice *within* a just structure, and, indeed, that it is not possible to achieve distributive justice by purely structural means.

In discussion of my claim that social justice requires a social *ethos* that inspires uncoerced equality-supporting choice, Ronald Dworkin suggested[20] that a Rawlsian government might be thought to be charged with a duty, under the difference principle, of promoting such an ethos. Dworkin's suggestion was intended to support Rawls, against me, by diminishing the difference between Rawls's position and my own, and thereby reducing the reach of my criticism of him. I do not know what Rawls's response to Dworkin's proposal would be, but one thing is clear: Rawls could not say that, to the extent that the indicated policy failed, society would, as a result, be less just than if the policy had been more successful. Accordingly, if Dworkin is right that Rawlsian justice requires government to promote an ethos friendly to equality, it could not be for the sake of making society more distributively just that it was doing so, *even* though it would be for the sake of making its distribution more *equal*. The following threefold conjunction, which is an inescapable consequence of Rawls's position, on Dworkin's not unnatural interpretation of it, is strikingly incongruous: (1) the difference principle is an egalitarian principle of distributive justice; (2) it imposes on government a duty to promote an egalitarian ethos; (3) it is not for the sake of enhancing distributive justice in society that it is required to promote that ethos. Dworkin's attempt to reduce the distance between Rawls's position and my own threatens to render the former incoherent.

Now, before I mount my two replies to the basic structure objection, a brief conceptual digression is required, in clarification of the relationship between a just *society*, in Rawls's (and my own) understanding of that idea and a just *distribution*, in my (non-Rawlsian) understanding of that different idea. A just society, here, is one whose citizens affirm and act upon the correct principles of justice, but justice in distribution, as here defined, consists in a certain egalitarian profile of rewards. It follows that, as a matter of logical possibility, a just distribution might obtain in a society that is not itself just.

To illustrate this possibility, imagine a society whose ethos, though not inspired by a belief in equality, nevertheless induces an equal distribution. An example of such an ethos would be an intense Protestant ethic, which is indifferent to equality (on earth) as such, but whose stress on self-denial, hard work, and investment of assets surplus to needs somehow (despite the asceticism in it) makes the worst off as well off as is possible. Such an ethos achieves difference principle justice in distribution, but agents informed by it would not be motivated by the difference principle, and they could not, therefore, themselves be accounted just, within the terms of that principle. Under the specifications that were introduced here, this Protestant society would not be just, despite the fact that it displays a just distribution. We might say of the society that it is accidentally, but not constitutively, just. But, whatever phrasings we may prefer, the important thing is to distinguish "society" and "distribution" as candidate subjects of the predicate "just." (And it bears mentioning that, in contemporary practice, an ethos that achieves difference principle equality would almost certainly have to be equality-inspired: the accident of a non-equality-inspired ethos producing the right result is, at least in modern times, highly unlikely. The Protestantism described here is utterly fantastic, at least for our day.)

Less arresting is the opposite case, in which people strive to govern their behavior by (what are in fact) just principles, but ignorance, or the obduracy of wholly external circumstance, or collective action problems, or self-defeatingness of the kinds studied by Derek Parfit,[21] or something else which I have not thought of, frustrates their intention, so that the distribution remains unjust. It would perhaps be peculiar to call such a society *just*, and neither Rawls nor I need do so: justice in citizens was put, above, as a *necessary* condition of a just society.

However we resolve the secondary, and largely verbal, complications raised in this digression, the point will stand[22] that an ethos informing choice within just rules is necessary in a society that is committed to the difference principle. My argument for that conclusion did not rely on aspects of my conception of justice which distinguish it from Rawls's, but on our shared conception of what a just society is.

The fact that distributive justice, as I conceive it, causally requires an ethos (be it merely equality-promoting, such as our imaginary Protestantism, or also equality-inspired) that goes beyond conformity to just rules, was not a premise in my argument against Rawls. The argument of Section II turned essentially on my understanding of Rawls's well-considered requirement that the citizens of a just society are themselves just. The basic structure objection challenges that understanding.

IV

I now present a preliminary reply to the basic structure objection. It is preliminary in that it precedes my interrogation, in Section V, of what the phrase "basic structure" denotes, and also in that, by contrast with the fundamental reply that will follow that interrogation, there is a certain way out for Rawls, in face of the preliminary reply. That way out is not costless for him, but it does exist.

Although Rawls says often enough that the two principles of justice govern only justice in basic structure, he also says three things that tell against that restriction. This means that, in each case, he must either uphold the restriction and repudiate the comment in question, or maintain the comment and drop the restriction.[23]

First, Rawls says that, when the difference principle is satisfied, society displays *fraternity*, in a particularly strong sense: its citizens do not want

> to have greater advantages unless this is to the benefit of others who are less well off. . . . Members of a family commonly do not wish to gain unless they can do so in ways that further the interests of the rest. Now wanting to act on the difference principle has precisely this consequence.[24]

But fraternity of that strong kind is not realized when all the justice delivered by that principle comes from the basic structure, and, therefore, whatever people's motivations may be. Wanting not "to gain unless they can do so in ways that further the interests of the rest" is incompatible with the self-interested motivation of market maximizers, which the difference principle, in its purely structural interpretation, does not condemn.[25]

Second, Rawls says that the worst off in a society governed by the difference principle can bear their inferior position with dignity, since they know that no improvement of it is possible, that they would lose under any less unequal dispensation. Yet that is false, if justice relates to structure alone, since it might then be necessary for the worst off to occupy their relatively low place only because the choices of the better off tend strongly against equality. Why should the fact that no purely structurally induced improvement in their position is possible suffice to guarantee the dignity of the worst off, when their position might be very inferior indeed, because of unlimited self-seekingness in the economic choices of well-placed people?[26] Suppose, for example, that, as many politicians claim, raising rates of income taxation with a view to enhancing benefits for the badly off would be counterproductive, since the higher rates would induce severe disincentive effects on the productivity of the better off. Would awareness of that truth contribute to a sense of dignity on the part of the badly off?

Third, Rawls says that people in a just society act with a sense of justice *from* the principles of justice in their daily lives: they strive to apply those principles in their own choices. And they do so because they

> have a desire to express their nature as free and equal moral persons, and this they do most adequately by acting *from* the principles that they would acknowledge in the original position. When all strive to comply with these principles and each succeeds, then individually and collectively their nature as moral persons is most fully realized, and with it their individual and collective good.[27]

But why do they have to act *from* the principles of justice, and "apply" them "as their circumstances require"[28] if just behavior consists in choosing as one pleases within, and without disturbing, a structure designed to effect an implementation of those principles? And how can they, without a redolence of hypocrisy, celebrate the full realization of their natures as moral persons, when they know that they are out for the most that they can get in the market?

Now, as I said, these inconsistencies are not decisive against Rawls. For, in each case, he could stand pat on his restriction of justice to basic structure, and give up, or weaken, the remark that produces the inconsistency. And that is indeed what he is disposed to do at least with respect to the third inconsistency that I have noted. He said[29] that *A Theory of Justice* erred by in some respects treating the two principles as defining a *comprehensive* conception of justice:[30] he would, accordingly, now drop the high-pitched homily which constitutes the text to footnote 27. But this accommodation carries a cost: it means that the ideals of dignity, fraternity, and full realization of people's moral natures can no longer be said to be delivered by Rawlsian justice.[31]

V

I now provide a more fundamental reply to the basic structure objection. It is more fundamental in that it shows, decisively, that justice requires an ethos governing daily choice that goes beyond one of obedience to just rules,[32] on grounds which do not, as the preliminary reply did, exploit things that Rawls says in apparent contradiction of his stipulation that justice applies to the basic structure of society alone. The fundamental reply interrogates, and refutes, that stipulation itself.

A major fault line in the Rawlsian architectonic not only wrecks the basic structure objection but also produces a dilemma for Rawls's view of the subject[33] of justice from which I can imagine no way out. The fault line exposes itself when we ask the apparently simple question: what (exactly) *is* the basic structure? For there is a fatal ambiguity in Rawls's specification of the basic structure, and an associated discrepancy between his criterion for what justice judges and his desire to exclude the effects of structure-consistent personal choice from the purview of its judgment.

The basic structure, the primary subject of justice, is always said by Rawls to be a set of institutions, and, so he infers, the principles of justice do not judge the actions of people within (just) institutions whose rules they observe. But it is seriously unclear *which* institutions are supposed to qualify as part of the basic structure. Sometimes it appears that coercive (in the legal sense) institutions exhaust it, or, better, that institutions belong to it only insofar as they are (legally) coercive.[34] In this widespread interpretation of what Rawls intends by the "basic structure" of a society, that structure is legible in the provisions of its constitution, in such specific legislation as may be required to implement those provisions, and in further legislation and policy which are of central importance but which resist formulation in the constitution itself.[35] The basic structure, in this first understanding of it, is, so one might say, the *broad coercive outline* of society, which determines in a relatively fixed and general way what people may and must do, in advance of legislation that is optional, relative to the principles of justice, and irrespective of the constraints and opportunities created and destroyed by the choices that people make within the given basic structure, so understood.

Yet it is quite unclear that the basic structure is *always* thus defined, in exclusively coercive terms, within the Rawlsian text. For Rawls often says that the basic structure consists of the *major* social institutions, and he does not put a particular accent on coercion when he announces *that* specification of the basic structure.[36] In this second reading of what it is, institutions belong to the basic structure whose structuring can depend far less on law than on convention, usage, and expectation: a signal example is the family, which Rawls sometimes includes in the basic structure and sometimes does not.[37] But once the line is crossed, from coercive ordering to the non-coercive ordering of society by rules and conventions of accepted practice, then the ambit of justice can no longer exclude chosen behavior, since the usages which constitute informal structure (think, again, of the family) are bound up with the customary actions of people.

"Bound up with" is vague, so let me explain how I mean it, here. One can certainly speak of the structure of the family, and it is not identical with the choices that people customarily make within it; but it is nevertheless impossible to claim that the principles of justice which apply to family structure do not apply to day-to-day choices within it. For consider the following contrast. The *coercive* structure arises independently of people's quotidian choices:

it is formed by those specialized choices which legislate the law of the land. By contrast, the non-coercive structure of the family has the character it does only because of the choices that its members routinely make. The constraints and pressures that sustain the non-coercive structure reside in the dispositions of agents which are actualized as and when those agents choose to act in a constraining or pressuring way. With respect to coercive structure, one may fairly readily distinguish the choices which institute and sustain a structure from the choices that occur within it.[38] But with respect to informal structure, that distinction, though conceptually intelligible, collapses extensionally: when A chooses to conform to the prevailing usages, the pressure on B to do so is reinforced, and no such pressure exists, the very usages themselves do not exist, in the absence of conformity to them.

Now, since that is so, since behavior is *constitutive* of *non*-coercive structure, it follows that the only way of protecting the basic structure objection against my claim that the difference principle condemns maximizing economic behavior (and, more generally, of protecting the restriction of justice to the basic structure against the insistence that the personal, too, is political) is by holding fast to a purely coercive specification of the basic structure. But that way out is not open to Rawls, because of a further characterization that he offers of the basic structure: this is where the discrepancy adverted to in the second paragraph of this section appears. For Rawls says that "the basic structure is the primary subject of justice because its effects are so profound and present from the start."[39] Nor is that further characterization of the basic structure optional: it is needed to explain why it *is* primary, as far as justice is concerned. Yet it is false that only the *coercive* structure causes profound effects, as the example of the family once again reminds us.[40] Accordingly, if Rawls retreats to coercive structure, he contradicts his own criterion for what justice judges, and he lands himself with an arbitrarily narrow definition of his subject matter. So he must let other structure in, and that means, as we have seen, letting chosen behavior in. What is more, even if behavior were not, as I claim it is, constitutive of non-coercive structure, it will come in by direct appeal to the profundity-of-effect criterion for what justice governs. So, for example, we need not decide whether or not a regular practice of favoring sons over daughters in the matter of providing higher education forms part of the *structure* of the family to condemn it as unjust, under that criterion.[41]

Given, then, his stated rationale[42] for exclusive focus on the basic structure—and what *other* rationale could there be for calling it the *primary* subject of justice?—Rawls is in a dilemma. For he must either admit application of the principles of justice to (legally optional) social practices, and, indeed, to patterns of personal choice that are not legally prescribed, *both* because they are the substance of those practices, *and* because they are similarly profound in effect, in which case the restriction of justice to structure, in any sense, collapses; or, if he restricts his concern to the coercive structure only, then he saddles himself with a purely arbitrary delineation of his subject matter. I now illustrate this dilemma by reference to the two contexts that have figured most in this paper: the family, and the market economy.

Family structure is fateful for the benefits and burdens that redound to different people, and, in particular, to people of different sexes, where "family structure" includes the socially constructed expectations which lie on husband and wife. And such expectations are sexist and unjust if, for example, they direct the woman in a family where both spouses work outside the home to carry a greater burden of domestic tasks. Yet such expectations need not be supported by the law for them to possess informal coercive force: sexist family structure is consistent with sex-neutral family law. Here, then, is a circumstance, outwith the basic structure, as that would be coercively defined, which profoundly affects people's life-chances, *through the choices people make in response to the stated expectations, which are, in turn, sustained by those choices.*[43] Yet Rawls must say, on pain of giving up the basic structure objection, that (legally uncoerced) family structure and behavior have no implications for justice in the sense of "justice" in which the basic structure has implications for justice, since they are not a consequence of the formal coercive order. But that implication of the stated position is perfectly incredible: no such differentiating sense is available.

John Stuart Mill taught us to recognize that informal social pressure can restrict liberty as much as formal coercive law does. And the family example shows that informal pressure is as relevant to distributive justice as it is to liberty. One reason why the rules of the basic structure, when it is coercively defined, do not by themselves determine the justice of the distributive upshot is that, by virtue of circumstances that are relevantly independent of coercive rules, some people have much more power than others to determine what happens *within* those rules.

The second illustration of discrepancy between what coercive structure commands and what profoundly affects the distribution of benefits and burdens is my own point about incentives. Maximizing legislation,[44] and, hence, a coercive basic structure that is just as far as the difference principle is concerned, are consistent with a maximizing ethos across society which, under many conditions, will produce severe inequalities and a meager level of provision for the worst off, yet both have to be declared just by Rawls, if he stays with a coercive conception of what justice judges. And that implication is, surely, perfectly incredible.

Rawls cannot deny the difference between the coercively defined basic structure and that which produces major distributive consequences: the coercively defined basic structure is only an instance of the latter. Yet he must, to retain his position on justice and personal choice, restrict the ambit of justice to what a coercive basic structure produces. But, so I have (by implication) asked: why should we *care* so disproportionately about the coercive basic structure, when the major reason for caring about it, its impact on people's lives, is *also* a reason for caring about informal structure and patterns of personal choice? To the extent that we care about coercive structure because it is fateful with regard to benefits and burdens, we must care equally about the ethi that sustain gender inequality, and inegalitarian incentives. And the similarity of our reasons for caring about these matters will make it lame to say: ah, but only the caring about coercive structure is a caring about *justice*, in a certain distinguishable sense. That thought is, I submit, incapable of coherent elaboration.

My response to the basic structure objection is now fully laid out, but before proceeding, in the sections that remain, to matters arising, it will be useful to rehearse, in compressed form, the arguments that were presented in Sections II through V.

My original criticism of the incentives argument ran, in brief, as follows:

1. Citizens in a just society adhere to its principles of justice.

But

2. They do not adhere to the difference principle if they are acquisitive maximizers in daily life.
∴3. In a society that is governed by the difference principle, citizens lack the acquisitiveness that the incentives argument attributes to them.

The basic structure objection to that criticism is of this form:

4. The principles of justice govern only the basic structure of a just society.
∴5. Citizens in a just society may adhere to the difference principle whatever their choices may be within the structure it determines, and, in particular, even if their economic choices are entirely acquisitive.
∴6. Proposition 2. lacks justification.

My preliminary reply to the basic structure objection says:

7. Proposition 5. is inconsistent with many Rawlsian statements about the relationship between citizens and principles of justice in a just society.

And my fundamental reply to the basic structure objection says:

8. Proposition 4. is unsustainable.

VI

So the personal is indeed political: personal choices to which the writ of the law is indifferent are fateful for social justice.

But that raises a huge question, with respect to *blame*. The injustice in distribution that reflects personal choices within a just coercive structure can plainly not be blamed on that structure itself, nor, therefore, on whoever legislated that structure. Must it, then, be blamed, in our two examples, on men[45] and on acquisitive people, respectively?

I shall presently address, and answer, that question about blame, but, before I do so, I wish to explain why I could remain silent in the face of it, why, that is, my argument in criticism of Rawls's restricted application of the principles of justice requires no judgment about blaming individual choosers. The conclusion of my argument is that the principles of justice apply not only to coercive rules but also to the pattern in people's (legally) uncoerced choices. Now, if we judge a certain set of rules to be just or unjust, we need not add, as pendant to that judgment, that those who legislated the rules in question should be praised or blamed for what they did.[46] And something analogous applies when we come to see that the ambit of justice covers the pattern of choices in a society. We can believe whatever we are inclined to do about how responsible and/or culpable people are for their choices, and that includes believing that they are not responsible and/or culpable for them at all, while holding that on which I insist: that the pattern in such choices is relevant to how just or unjust a society is.

That said, I return to the question of how blamable individuals are. It would be inappropriate to answer it, here, by first declaring my position, if, indeed, I have one, on the philosophical problem of the freedom of the will. Instead, I shall answer the question about blame on the prephilosophical assumptions which inform our ordinary judgments about when, and how much, blame is appropriate. On such assumptions, we should avoid two opposite mistakes about how culpable chauvinistic men and self-seeking high fliers are. One is the mistake of saying: there is no ground for blaming these people as *individuals*, for they simply participate in an accepted social practice, however tawdry or awful that practice may be. That is a mistake, since people do have choices: it is, indeed, *only* their choices that reproduce social practices; and some, moreover, choose *against* the grain of nurture, habit, and self-interest. But one also must not say: look how each of these people shamefully decides to behave so badly. That, too, is unbalanced, since, although there exists personal choice, there is heavy social conditioning behind it and there can be heavy costs in deviating from the prescribed and/or permitted ways. If we care about social justice, we have to look at four things: the coercive structure, other structures, the social ethos, and the choices of individuals, and judgment on the last of those must be informed by awareness of the power of the others. So, for example, a properly sensitive appreciation of these matters allows one to hold that an acquisitive ethos is profoundly unjust in its effects, without holding that those who are gripped by it are commensurately unjust. It is essential to apply principles of justice to dominant patterns in social behavior—that, as it were, is where the action is—but it doesn't follow that we should have a persecuting attitude to the people who emit that behavior. We might have good reason to exonerate the perpetrators of injustice, but we should not deny, or apologize for, the injustice itself.[47]

On an extreme view, which I do not accept but need not reject, a typical husband in a thoroughly sexist society, one, that is, in which families in their overwhelming majority display an unjust division of domestic labor, is literally incapable of revising his behavior, or capable of revising it only at the cost of cracking up, to nobody's benefit. But even if that is true of typical husbands, we know it to be false of husbands in general. It is a plain empirical fact that some husbands are capable of revising their behavior, since some husbands have done so, in response to feminist criticism. These husbands, we could say, were moral pioneers. They made a path which becomes easier and easier to follow as more and more people follow it, until social pressures are so altered that it becomes harder to stick to sexist ways than to abandon them. That is a central way in which a social ethos changes. Or, for another example, consider the recent rise in ecological consciousness. At first, only people that appear to be freaky because they do so bother to save and recycle their paper, plastic, and so forth. Then, more do that, and, finally, it becomes not only difficult not to do it but easy to do it. It is pretty easy to discharge burdens that have become part of

the normal round of everybody's life. Expectations determine behavior, behavior determines expectations, which determine behavior, and so on.

Are there circumstances in which a similar incremental process could occur with respect to economic behavior? I do not know. But I do know that universal maximizing is by no means a necessary feature of a market economy. For all that much of its industry was state-owned, the United Kingdom from 1945 to 1951 had a market economy. But salary differentials were nothing like as great as they were to become, or as they were then in the United States. Yet, so I hazard, when British executives making five times what their workers did met American counterparts making fifteen times what their (anyhow better paid) workers did, many of the British executives would *not* have felt: *we* should press for more. For there was a social ethos of reconstruction after war, an ethos of common project, that restrained desire for personal gain. It is not for a philosopher to delimit the conditions under which such, and even more egalitarian ethi, can prevail. But a philosopher can say that a maximizing ethos is not a necessary feature of society, even of market society, and that, to the extent that such an ethos prevails, satisfaction of the difference principle is prejudiced.

In 1988, the ratio of top executive salaries to production worker wages was 6.5 to 1 in West Germany and 17.5 to 1 in the United States.[48] Since it is not plausible to think that Germany's lesser inequality was a disincentive to productivity, since it is plausible to think that an ethos that was relatively friendly to equality[49] protected German productivity in the face of relatively modest material incentives, we can conclude that the said ethos caused the worst paid to be better paid than they would have been under a different culture of reward. It follows, on my view of things, that the difference principle was better realized in Germany in 1988 than it would have been if its culture of reward had been more similar to that of the United States. But Rawls cannot say that, since the smaller inequality that benefited the less well off in Germany was not a matter of law but of ethos. I think that Rawls's inability to regard Germany as having done comparatively well with respect to the difference principle is a grave defect in his conception of the site of distributive justice.

Endnote on Coercive and Other Structure

The legally coercive structure of society functions in two ways. It *prevents* people from doing things by erecting insurmountable barriers (fences, police lines, prison walls, etc.), and it *deters* people from doing things by ensuring that certain forms of unprevented behavior carry an (appreciable risk of) penalty.[50] The second (deterrent) aspect of coercive structure may be described counterfactually, in terms of what would or might happen to someone who elects the forbidden behavior: knowledge of the relevant counterfactual truths motivates the complying citizen's choices.

Not much pure prevention goes on within the informal structure of society: not none, but not much. (Locking an errant teenager in her room would represent an instance of pure prevention, which, if predictable for determinate behavior, would count as part of a society's informal structure: it would be a rule in accordance with which that society operates.) That being set aside, informal structure manifests itself in predictable sanctions such as criticism, disapproval, anger, refusal of future cooperation, ostracism, beating (of, for example, wives who refuse sexual service) and so on.

Finally, to complete this conceptual review, the ethos of a society is the set of sentiments and attitudes in virtue of which its normal practices, and informal pressures, are what they are.

Now, the pressures that sustain the informal structure lack force save insofar as there is a normal practice of compliance with the rules they enforce. That is especially true of that great majority of those pressures (beating does not belong to that majority) which carry a moral coloring: criticism and disapproval are ineffective when they come from the mouths of those who ask others not to do what they do themselves. To be sure, that is not a conceptual truth, but a social-psychological one. Even so, it enables us to say that what people ordinarily do supports and partly constitutes (again, not conceptually,

but in effect) the informal structure of society, in such a way that it makes no sense to pass judgments of justice on that structure while withholding such judgment from the behavior that supports and constitutes it: that point is crucial to the anti-Rawlsian inference above.[51] Informal structure is not a behavior pattern, but a set of rules, yet the two are so closely related that, so one might say, they are *merely* categorially different. Accordingly, so I argued, to include (as one must) informal structure within the basic structure is to countenance behavior, too, as a primary subject of judgments of justice.

Now, two truths about legally coercive structure might be thought to cast doubt on the contrast I drew between it and informal structure in Section V above. First, although the legally coercive structure of society is indeed discernible in the ordinances of its constitution and law, those ordinances count as delineating it only on condition that they enjoy a broad measure of compliance.[52] And, second, legally coercive structure achieves its intended social effect only in and through the actions which constitute compliance with its rules. To be more accurate, those propositions are true provided that we exclude from consideration "1984" states in which centralized brute force prevails against nonconformity even, if necessary, at the cost of half the population being in jail. But it is appropriate to ignore 1984 scenarios here.[53]

In light of those truths, it might be objected that the dilemma that I posed for Rawls and by means of which I sought to defeat his claim that justice judges structure *as opposed to* the actions of agents, was critically misframed. For I said, against that claim, that the required opposition between structure and actions works for coercive structure only, with respect to which a relevantly strong distinction can be drawn between structure-sustaining and structure-conforming action, but that coercive structure could not reasonably be thought to exhaust the structure falling within the purview of justice: accordingly, so I concluded, justice must also judge everyday actions.

The truths rehearsed two paragraphs back challenge my articulation of the distinction between coercive structure and action within it. They thereby also challenge the contrast that I drew between two relationships, that between coercive structure and action, and that between informal structure and action.

This problem needs more thought than I have to date spent on it. For the moment I shall say this: even if coercive structure counts as such only if appropriate compliance obtains, that structure may nevertheless be *identified* with a set of laws which are not themselves patterns of behavior. And one can distinguish sharply between behavior forbidden and directed by those laws, and behavior that is optional under them, however systematic and widespread it may be. By contrast, the identity of informal structure is less separable from practice: no distinction is sustainable between widespread practices which do not.

If the would-be saving contrast which I there essay is an unrealistic idealization, then the distinction, vis-à-vis action, between coercive and informal structure, may be more blurred than I have been disposed to allow. Yet that would not be because informal structure is more separable from action than I claimed, but because coercive structure is less separable from it. Therefore, even if the dilemma constructed above was for the stated reasons misframed, the upshot would hardly be congenial to Rawls's position, that justice judges structure rather than actions, but, if anything, congenial to my own rejection of it, if not, indeed, to the terms in which some of the argument for that rejection was cast.

NOTES

1. But it was, apparently, used by Christian liberation theologians before it was used by feminists: see Denys Turner, "Religion: Illusions and Liberation," in Terrel Carver, ed., *The Cambridge Companion to Marx* (Cambridge: Cambridge University Press, 1991), p. 334.

2. Or, more precisely, that which *distinguishes* its form. (Insofar as the feminist critique targets government legislation and policy, there is nothing distinctive about its form.)

3. Okin is singularly alive to Rawls's ambivalence about admitting or excluding the family from the basic structure: see, e.g. her "*Political Liberalism*, Justice and Gender," *Ethics* 105, no. 1 (Oct. 1994): 23–24, and, more generally, her *Justice, Gender and the Family* (New York: Basic Books, 1989), Chapter 5. But, so far as I can tell, she is unaware of

the wider consequences, for Rawls's view of justice in general, of the set of ambiguities of which this one is an instance.

4. See "Incentives, Inequality, and Community," in Grethe Peterson, ed., *The Tanner Lectures on Human Values*, Vol. 13 (Salt Lake City: University of Utah Press, 1992), and "The Pareto Argument for Inequality," *Social Philosophy and Policy*, 12 (Winter 1995). These articles are henceforth referred to as "Incentives" and "Pareto," respectively.

5. See "Incentives," p. 266, n. 6, for four possible formulations of the difference principle, all of which, arguably, find support in *A Theory of Justice* (Cambridge, Mass.: Harvard University Press, 1971). The argument of the present paper is, I believe, robust across those variant formulations of the principle.

6. I do have some reservations about the principle, but they are irrelevant to this paper. I agree, for example, with Ronald Dworkin's criticism of the "ambition-insensitivity" of the difference principle: see his "What Is Equality? Part 2: Equality of Resources," *Philosophy & Public Affairs*, 10, no. 4 (Fall 1981): 343.

7. "Proposes to conceive it": I use that somewhat precious phrase because part of the present criticism of Rawls is that he does not succeed in so conceiving it—he does not, that is, recognize the implications of so conceiving it.

8. *A Theory of Justice*, p. 7.

9. This is just the crudest causal story connecting superior payment to the better off with benefit to the worst off. I adopt it here for simplicity of exposition.

10. They do not, more precisely, share *justificatory community* with the rest, in the sense of the italicized phrase that I specified at p. 282 of "Incentives."

11. "Citizens in everyday life affirm and act from the first principles of justice." They act "from these principles as their sense of justice dictates" and thereby "their nature as moral persons is most fully realized." (Quotations drawn from, respectively, "Kantian Constructivism in Moral Theory," *The Journal of Philosophy*, 77, no. 9 (Sept. 1980): 521, 528, and *A Theory of Justice*, p. 528.)

12. That way of achieving equality preserves the information function of the market while extinguishing its motivational function: see Joseph Carens, *Equality, Moral Incentives, and the Market* (Chicago: University of Chicago Press, 1981).

13. See "Incentives," p. 298 *et circa*, for precisely what I mean by "the standard case."

14. For a typical statement of this restriction, see John Rawls, *Political Liberalism* (New York: Columbia University Press, 1993), pp. 282–83.

15. See the first sentence of Sec. 2 of *A Theory of Justice* ("The Subject of Justice"): "Many different kinds of things are said to be just and unjust: not only laws, institutions, and social systems, but also particular actions of many kinds, including decisions, judgments, and imputations" (*ibid.*, p. 7). But Rawls excludes examples such as the one given in the text above from his purview, because "our topic . . . is that of social justice. For us the primary subject of justice is the basic structure of society" (*ibid.*).

16. *A Theory of Justice*, p. 303.

17. The contrast between structure and action is further explained, though also, as it were, put in its place, in the Endnote to this article.

18. *A Theory of Justice*, pp. 274–75: "The principles of justice apply to the basic structure. . . . The social system is to be designed so that the resulting distribution is just however things turn out." Cf. *ibid.*, p. 545: ". . . the distribution of material means is left to take care of itself in accordance with the idea of pure procedural justice."

19. This is a different point from the one made at p. 632 above, to wit, that there is scope within a just structure for justice and injustice in choice in a "nonprimary" sense of "justice."

20. At a seminar in Oxford, in Hilary Term of 1994.

21. See his *Reasons and Persons* (Oxford: Oxford University Press, 1984), Chapter 4.

22. If, that is, my argument survives the basic structure objection, to which I reply in Secs. IV and V.

23. Because of these tensions in Rawls, people have resisted my incentives critique of him in two opposite ways. Those convinced that his primary concern is the basic structure object in the fashion set out in Sec. III. But others do not realize how important that commitment is to him: they accept my (as I see it, anti-Rawlsian) view that the difference principle should condemn incentives, but they believe that Rawls would also accept it, since they think his commitment to that principle is relevantly uncompromising. They therefore do not regard what I say about incentives as a *criticism* of Rawls.

  Those who respond in that second fashion seem not to realize that Rawls's liberalism is jeopardized if he takes the route that they think open to him. He then becomes a radical egalitarian socialist, whose outlook is very different from that of a liberal who holds that "deep inequalities" are

"inevitable in the basic structure of any society" (*A Theory of Justice*, p. 7).

24. *A Theory of Justice*, p. 105.

25. See, further, "Incentives," pp. 321–22, "Pareto," pp. 178–79.

26. See, further, "Incentives," pp. 320–21.

27. *A Theory of Justice*, p. 528, my emphasis. See, further, footnote 11 above, and "Incentives," pp. 316–20.

28. John Rawls, "Justice as Fairness: A Briefer Restatement," Harvard University, 1989, typescript, p. 154.

29. In reply to a lecture that I gave at Harvard in March of 1993.

30. That is, as (part of) a complete moral theory, as opposed to a purely political one: see, for explication of that distinction, *Political Liberalism*, *passim*, and, in particular, pp. xv–xvii.

31. See "Incentives," p. 322.

32. Though not necessarily an ethos embodying the very principles that the rules formulate: see the last four paragraphs of Sec. III above. Justice will be shown to require an ethos, and the basic structure objection will thereby be refuted, but it will be a contingent question whether the ethos required by justice can be read off the content of the just rules themselves. Still, the answer to that question is almost certainly "Yes."

33. That is, the subject matter that principles of justice judge. I follow Rawls's usage here (e.g. in the title of Lecture VII of *Political Liberalism*: "The Basic Structure as Subject"; and cf. n. 15 above).

34. Henceforth, unless I indicate otherwise, I shall use "coercive," "coercion," etc. to mean "legally coercive," etc.

35. Thus, the difference principle, though pursued through (coercively sustained) state policy, cannot, so Rawls thinks, be aptly inscribed in a society's constitution: see *Political Liberalism*, pp. 227–30.

36. Consider, for example, the passage at pp. 7–8 of *A Theory of Justice* in which the concept of the basic structure is introduced:

Our topic . . . is that of social justice. For us the primary subject of justice is the basic structure of society, or more exactly, the way in which the major social institutions distribute fundamental rights and duties and determine the division of advantages from social cooperation. By major institutions I understand the political constitution and the principal economic and social arrangements. Thus the legal protection of freedom of thought and liberty of conscience, competitive markets, private property in the means of production, and the monogamous family are examples of major social institutions. . . . I shall not consider the justice of institutions and social practices generally. . . . [The two principles of justice] may not work for the rules and practices of private associations or for those of less comprehensive social groups. They may be irrelevant for the various informal conventions and customs of everyday life; they may not elucidate the justice, or perhaps better, the fairness of voluntary cooperative arrangements or procedures for making contractual agreements.

I cannot tell, from those statements, what is to be included in, and what excluded from, the basic structure, nor, more particularly, whether coercion is the touchstone of inclusion. Take, for example, the case of the monogamous family. Is it simply its "legal protection" that is a major social institution, in line with a coercive definition of the basic structure (if not, perhaps, with the syntax of the relevant sentence)? Or is the monogamous family itself part of that structure? And, in that case, are its typical usages part of it? They certainly constitute a "principal social arrangement," yet they may also count as "practices of private associations or ... of less comprehensive social groups," and they are heavily informed by the "conventions and customs of everyday life."

Puzzlement with respect to the bounds of the basic structure is not relieved by examination of the relevant pages of *Political Liberalism*, to wit, 11, 68, 201–202, 229, 258, 268, 271–72, 282–83, and 301. Some formulations on those pages lean toward a coercive specification of the basic structure. Others do not.

37. See the final paragraph of Sec. I of this paper.
38. For more on structure and choice, see the Endnote to this article. Among other things, I there entertain a doubt about the strength of the distinction drawn in the above sentence, but, as I indicate, if that doubt is sound, then my case against Rawls is not weakened.
39. *A Theory of Justice*, p. 7.
40. Or consider access to that primary good which Rawls calls "the social basis of self-respect." While the law may play a large role in securing that good to people vulnerable to racism, legally unregulable racist attitudes also have an enormous negative impact on how much of that primary good they get.

But are the profound effects of the family, or of racism, "present from the start" (see the text to n. 39)? I am not sure how to answer that question, because I am unclear about the intended import, here, of the quoted phrase. Rawls probably means "present from the start of each person's life": the surrounding text at *Theory*, p. 7 supports this interpretation. If so, the family, and racial attitudes, certainly qualify. If not, then I do not know how to construe the phrase. But what matters, surely, is the asserted profundity of effect, not whether it

is "present from the start," whatever may be the sense which attaches, here, to that phrase.

41. Note that one can condemn the said practice without condemning those who engage in it. For there might be a collective action problem here, which weighs heavily on poor families in particular. If, in addition to discrimination in education, there is discrimination in employment, then a poor family might sacrifice a great deal through choosing evenhandedly across the sexes with whatever resources it can devote to its children's education. This illustrates the important distinction between condemning injustice and condemning the people whose actions perpetuate it: see, further, Sec. VI below.
42. See the text to n. 39 above.
43. Hugo Adam Bedau noticed that the family falls outside the basic structure, under the coercive specification of it often favored by Rawls, though he did not notice the connection between non-coercive structure and choice that I emphasize in the above sentence: see his "Social Justice and Social Institutions," *Midwest Studies in Philosophy*, 3 (1978):171.
44. That is, legislation which maximizes the size of the primary goods bundle held by the worst off people, given whatever is correctly expected to be the pattern in the choices made by economic agents.
45. We can here set aside the fact that women often subscribe to, and inculcate, male-dominative practices.
46. We can distinguish between how unjust past practices (e.g. slavery) were and how unjust those who protected and benefited from those unjust practices were. Most of us (rightly) do not condemn Lincoln for his (conditional) willingness to tolerate slavery as strongly as we would a statesman who did the same in 1997, but the institution of slavery itself was as unjust in Lincoln's time as it would be today.

What made slavery unjust in, say, Greece, is exactly what would make slavery (with, of course, the very same rules of subordination) unjust today, to wit, the content of its rules. But sound judgments about the justice and injustice of people are much more contextual: they must take into account the institutions under which they live, the prevailing level of intellectual and oral development, collective action problems such as the one delineated in n. 41 above, and so forth. The morally best slaveholder might deserve admiration. The morally best form of slavery would not.

47. See the preceding note.
48. See Lawrence Mishel and David M. Frankel, *The State of Working America, 1990–1991* (Armonk, N.Y.: M. E. Sharpe, 1991), p. 122.

49. That ethos need not have been an egalitarian one. For present purposes, it could have been an ethos which disendorses acquisitiveness as such (see n. 32, and the digression at the end of Sec. III), other than on behalf of the worst off.

50. The distinction given above corresponds to that between the difficulty and the cost of actions: see my *Karl Marx's Theory of History* (Oxford: Oxford University Press, and Princeton: Princeton University Press, 1978), pp. 238–39.

51. See the sentence beginning "But once" on the bottom of that page.

52. It does not follow that they are not *laws* unless they enjoy such compliance: perhaps they are nevertheless laws, if they "satisfy a test set out in a Hartian rule of recognition, even if they are themselves neither complied with nor accepted" (Joshua Cohen, in comment on an earlier draft of this paper). But such laws (or "laws") are not plausibly represented as part of the basic structure of society, so the statement in the text can stand as it is.

53. That is because of Rawls's reasonable stipulation that, in a just society, the threat of coercion is necessary for assurance game reasons only: each is disposed to comply provided that others do, and coercion is needed not because, in the absence of its threat *to me*, I might not comply, but because in the absence of its threat to others I cannot be sure that *they* will comply (see *A Theory of Justice*, p. 315). This stipulation makes formal law less *essentially* coercive than one might otherwise suppose and therefore less contrastable with custom than I have supposed.

KEY TERMS

Distributive justice
Feminists
The difference principle

STUDY QUESTIONS

1. According to Cohen, what is the "key lesson" of the feminist critique of Rawls's theory of justice? How is it supposed to be an objection to the Rawlsian account?

2. How does Cohen spell out Rawls's *difference principle*, and what is Cohen's critique of the principle?

3. What is the "basic structure objection" and how does Cohen reply to it? Do you think Cohen's reply is successful?

4. What is the ambiguity that Cohen claims to find in Rawls's concept of the basic structure? Why does Cohen think that the ambiguity is "fatal"? Do you agree?

5. After reading the article, what do you think is the best way to explain Cohen's slogan that "the personal is political"?

The Subjection of Women

JOHN STUART MILL

· ·

THE object of this Essay is to explain as clearly as I am able, the grounds of an opinion which I have held from the very earliest period when I had formed any opinions at all on social or political matters, and which, instead of being weakened or modified, has been constantly growing stronger by the progress of reflection and the experience of life: That the principle which regulates the existing social relations between the two sexes—the legal subordination of one sex to the other—is wrong in itself, and now one of the chief hindrances to human improvement; and that it ought to be replaced by a principle of perfect equality, admitting no power or privilege on the one side, nor disability on the other.

From *The Subjection of Women* (Indianapolis: Hackett, 1988). pp. 1, 17–24.

...

The preceding considerations are amply sufficient to show that custom, however universal it may be, affords in this case no presumption and ought not to create any prejudice, in favour of the arrangements which place women in social and political subjection to men. But I may go farther, and maintain that the course of history, and the tendencies of progressive human society, afford not only no presumption in favour of this system of inequality of rights, but a strong one against it; and that, so far as the whole course of human improvement up to this time, the whole stream of modern tendencies, warrants any inference on the subject, it is, that this relic of the past is discordant with the future, and must necessarily disappear.

For, what is the peculiar character of the modern world—the difference which chiefly distinguishes modern institutions, modern social ideas, modern life itself, from those of times long past? It is, that human beings are no longer born to their place in life, and chained down by an inexorable bond to the place they are born to, but are free to employ their faculties, and such favourable chances as offer, to achieve the lot which may appear to them most desirable. Human society of old was constituted on a very different principle. All were born to a fixed social position, and were mostly kept in it by law, or interdicted from any means by which they could emerge from it. As some men are born white and others black, so some were born slaves and others freemen and citizens; some were born patricians, other plebeians; some were born feudal nobles, others commoners and *roturiers*. A slave or serf could never make himself free, nor, except by the will of his master, become so. In most European countries it was not till towards the close of the middle ages, and as a consequence of the growth of regal power, that commoners could be ennobled. Even among nobles, the eldest son was born the exclusive heir to the paternal possessions, and a long time elapsed before it was fully established that the father could disinherit him. Among the industrious classes, only those who were born members of a guild, or were admitted into it by its members, could lawfully practise their calling within its local limits; and nobody could practise any calling deemed important, in any but the legal manner—by processes authoritatively prescribed. Manufacturers have stood in the pillory for presuming to carry on their business by new and improved methods. In modern Europe, and most in those parts of it which have participated most largely in all other modern improvements, diametrically opposite doctrines now prevail. Law and government do not undertake to prescribe by whom any social or industrial operation shall or shall not be conducted, or what modes of conducting them shall be lawful. These things are left to the unfettered choice of individuals. Even the laws which required that workmen should serve an apprenticeship, have in this country been repealed: there being ample assurance that in all cases in which an apprenticeship is necessary, its necessity will suffice to enforce it. The old theory was, that the least possible should be left to the choice of the individual agent; that all he had to do should, as far as practicable, be laid down for him by superior wisdom. Left to himself he was sure to go wrong. The modern conviction, the fruit of a thousand years of experience, is, that things in which the individual is the person directly interested, never go right but as they are left to his own discretion; and that any regulation of them by authority, except to protect the rights of others, is sure to be mischievous. This conclusion, slowly arrived at, and not adopted until almost every possible application of the contrary theory had been made with disastrous result, now (in the industrial department) prevails universally in the most advanced countries, almost universally in all that have pretensions to any sort of advancement. It is not that all processes are supposed to be equally good, or all persons to be equally qualified for everything; but that freedom of individual choice is now known to be the only thing which procures the adoption of the best processes, and throws each operation into the hands of those who are best qualified for it. Nobody thinks it necessary to make a law that only a strong-armed man shall be a blacksmith. Freedom and competition suffice to make blacksmiths strong-armed men, because the weak-armed can earn more by engaging in occupations for which they are more fit. In consonance with this doctrine, it is felt to be an overstepping of the proper bounds of authority to fix beforehand, on some general presumption, that certain persons are not fit to do certain things. It is now thoroughly known and admitted that if some such presumptions exist, no such presumption is infallible. Even if it be well grounded in a majority of cases, which it is very likely not to be, there will be a minority of exceptional cases in which it does not hold: and in those it is both an injustice to the individuals, and a detriment to society, to place barriers in the way of their using their faculties for their own benefit and for that of others. In the cases, on the other hand, in which the unfitness is real, the ordinary motives of human conduct will on the whole suffice to prevent the incompetent person from making, or from persisting in, the attempt.

If this general principle of social and economical science is not true; if individuals, with such help as they can derive from the opinion of those who know them, are not better judges than the law and the government, of their own capacities and vocation; the world cannot too soon abandon this principle, and return to the old system of regulations and disabilities. But if the principle is true, we ought to act as if we believed it, and not to ordain that to be born a girl instead of a boy, any more than to be born black instead of white, or a commoner instead of a nobleman, shall decide the person's position through all life—shall interdict people from all the more elevated social positions, and from all, except a few, respectable occupations. Even were we to admit the utmost that is ever pretended as to the superior fitness of men for all the functions now reserved to them, the same argument applies which forbids a legal qualification for members of Parliament. If only once in a dozen years the conditions of eligibility exclude a fit person, there is a real loss, while the exclusion of thousands of unfit persons is no gain; for if the constitution of the electoral body disposes them to choose unfit persons, there are always plenty of such persons to choose from. In all things of any difficulty and importance, those who can do them well are fewer than the need, even with the most unrestricted latitude of choice: and any limitation of the field of selection deprives society of some chances of being served by the competent, without ever saving it from the incompetent.

At present, in the more improved countries, the disabilities of women are the only case, save one, in which laws and institutions take persons at their birth, and ordain that they shall never in all their lives be allowed to compete for certain things. The one exception is that of royalty. Persons still are born to the throne; no one, not of the reigning family, can ever occupy it, and no one even of that family can, by any means but the course of hereditary succession, attain it. All other dignities and social advantages are open to the whole male sex: many indeed are only attainable by wealth, but wealth may be striven for by any one, and is actually obtained by many men of the very humblest origin. The difficulties, to the majority, are indeed insuperable without the aid of fortunate accidents; but no male human being is under any legal ban: neither law nor opinion superadd artificial obstacles to the natural ones. Royalty, as I have said, is excepted: but in this case every one feels it to be an exception—an anomaly in the modern world, in marked opposition to its customs and principles, and to be justified only by extraordinary special expediencies, which, though individuals and nations differ in estimating their weight, unquestionably do in fact exist. But in this exceptional case, in which a high social function is, for important reasons, bestowed on birth instead of being put up to competition, all free nations contrive to adhere in substance to the principle from which they nominally derogate; for they circumscribe this high function by conditions avowedly intended to prevent the person to whom it ostensibly belongs from really performing it; while the person by whom it is performed, the responsible minister, does obtain the post by a competition from which no full-grown citizen of the male sex is legally excluded. The disabilities, therefore, to which women are subject from the mere fact of their birth, are the solitary examples of the kind in modern legislation. In no instance except this, which comprehends half the human race, are the higher social functions closed against any one by a fatality of birth which no exertions, and no change of circumstances, can overcome; for even religious disabilities (besides that in England and in Europe they have practically almost ceased to exist) do not close any career to the disqualified person in case of conversion.

The social subordination of women thus stands out an isolated fact in modern social institutions; a solitary breach of what has become their fundamental law; a single relic of an old world of thought and practice exploded in everything else, but retained in the one thing of most universal interest; as if a gigantic dolmen, or a vast temple of Jupiter Olympius, occupied the site of St. Paul's and received daily worship, while the surrounding Christian churches were only resorted to on fasts and festivals. This entire discrepancy between one social fact and all those which accompany it, and the radical opposition between its nature and the progressive movement which is the boast of the modern world, and which has successively swept away everything else of an analogous character, surely affords, to a conscientious observer of human tendencies, serious matter for reflection. It raises a prima facie presumption on the unfavourable side, far outweighing any which custom and usage could in such circumstances create on the favourable; and should at least suffice to make this, like the choice between republicanism and royalty, a balanced question.

The least that can be demanded is, that the question should not be considered as prejudged by existing act and existing opinion, but open to discussion on its merits, as a question of justice and expediency: the decision on this, as on any of the other social arrangements of mankind, depending on what an enlightened estimate of tendencies and consequences may show to be most advantageous to humanity in general, without distinction of sex. And the discussion must be a real discussion, descending to foundations, and not resting satisfied with vague and general assertions. It will not do, for instance, to assert in general terms, that the experience of mankind has pronounced in favour of the existing system. Experience cannot possibly have decided between two courses, so long as there has only been experience of one. If it be said that the doctrine of the equality of the sexes rests only on theory, it must be remembered that the contrary doctrine also has only theory to rest upon. All that is proved in its favour by direct experience, is that mankind have been able to exist under it, and to attain the degree of improvement and prosperity which we now see; but whether that prosperity has been attained sooner, or is now greater, than it would have been under the other system, experience does not say. On the other hand, experience does say, that every step in improvement has been so invariably accompanied by a step made

in raising the social position of women, that historians and philosophers have been led to adopt their elevation or debasement as on the whole the surest test and most correct measure of the civilization of a people or an age.[1] Through all the progessive period of human history, the condition of women has been approaching nearer to equality with men. This does not of itself prove that the assimilation must go on to complete equality; but it assuredly affords some presumption that such is the case.

Neither does it avail anything to say that the *nature* of the two sexes adapts them to their present functions and position, and renders these appropriate to them. Standing on the ground of common sense and the constitution of the human mind, I deny that any one knows, or can know, the nature of the two sexes, as long as they have only been seen in their present relation to one another. If men had ever been found in society without women, or women without men, or if there had been a society of men and women in which the women were not under the control of the men, something might have been positively known about the mental and moral differences which may be inherent in the nature of each. What is now called the nature of women is an eminently artificial thing—the result of forced repression in some directions, unnatural stimulation in others. It may be asserted without scruple, that no other class of dependents have had their character so entirely distorted from its natural proportions by their relation with their masters; for, if conquered and slave races have been, in some respects, more forcibly repressed, whatever in them has not been crushed down by an iron heel has generally been let alone, and if left with any liberty of development, it has developed itself according to its own laws; but in the case of women, a hot-house and stove cultivation has always been carried on of some of the capabilities of their nature, for the benefit and pleasure of their masters. Then, because certain products of the general vital force sprout luxuriantly and reach a great development in this heated atmosphere and under this active nurture and watering, while other shoots from the same root, which are left outside in the wintry air, with ice purposely heaped all around them, have a stunted growth, and some are burnt off with fire and disappear; men, with that inability to recognise their own work which distinguishes the unanalytic mind, indolently believe that the tree grows of itself in the way they have made it grow, and that it would die if one half of it were not kept in a vapour bath and the other half in the snow.

Of all difficulties which impede the progress of thought, and the formation of well-grounded opinions on life and social arrangements, the greatest is now the unspeakable ignorance and inattention of mankind in respect to the influences which form human character. Whatever any portion of the human species now are, or seem to be, such, it is supposed, they have a natural tendency to be: even when the most elementary knowledge of the circumstances in which they have been placed, clearly points out the causes that made them what they are. Because a cottier deeply in arrears to his landlord is not industrious, there are people who think that the Irish are naturally idle. Because constitutions can be overthrown when the authorities appointed to execute them turn their arms against them, there are people who think the French incapable of free government. Because the Greeks cheated the Turks, and the Turks only plundered the Greeks, there are persons who think that the Turks are naturally more sincere: and because women, as is often said, care nothing about politics except their personalities, it is supposed that the general good is naturally less interesting to women than to men. History, which is now so much better understood than formerly, teaches another lesson: if only by showing the extraordinary susceptibility of human nature to external influences, and the extreme variableness of those of its manifestations which are supposed to be most universal and uniform. But in history, as in travelling, men usually see only what they already had in their own minds; and few learn much from history, who do not bring much with them to its study.

Hence, in regard to that most difficult question, what are the natural differences between the two sexes—a subject on which it is impossible in the present state of society to obtain complete and correct knowledge—while almost everybody dogmatizes upon it, almost all neglect and make light of the only means by which any partial insight can be obtained into it. This is, an analytic study of the most important department of psychology, the laws of the influence of circumstances on character. For, however great and apparently ineradicable the moral and intellectual differences between men and women might be, the evidence of their being natural differences could only be negative. Those only could be inferred to be natural which could not possibly be artificial—the residuum, after deducting every characteristic of either sex which can admit of being explained from education or external circumstances. The profoundest knowledge of the laws of the formation of character is indispensable to entitle any one to affirm even that there is any difference, much more what the difference is, between the two sexes considered as moral and rational beings; and since no one, as yet, has that knowledge, (for there is hardly any subject which, in proportion to its importance, has been so little studied), no one is thus far entitled to any positive opinion on the subject. Conjectures are all that can at present be made; conjectures more or less probable, according as more or less authorized by such knowledge as we yet have of the laws of psychology, as applied to the formation of character.

NOTE

1. Charles Fourier and Karl Marx were two such philosophers.

STUDY QUESTIONS

1. Why does Mill think that "freedom of individual choice is now known to be the only thing which procures adoption of the best processes"? Do you agree?
2. Mill appears to argue that the fact that "the condition of women has been approaching nearer to equality with men" gives us some reason to think that it should go on to complete equality. Is this a convincing argument? Why or why not?
3. Why does Mill think that "it is impossible in the present state of society to obtain complete and correct knowledge" of the natural differences between the two sexes? Do you think it is just as impossible today as Mill thought it was in his day?
4. In what arenas of today's society do you still see the social subordination of women?

The Need for More Than Justice

ANNETTE C. BAIER

Annette Baier (1929–2012) was a distinguished philosopher. She made important contributions in many areas, including moral philosophy, philosophy of mind, and feminist philosophy. She was also an important Hume scholar. Her works include *Reflections on How We Live* (2009), *Death and Character: Further Reflections on Hume* (2008), and *The Commons of Mind* (1997), a published version of her Paul Carus Lectures.

· ·

In recent decades in North American social and moral philosophy, alongside the development and discussion of widely influential theories of **justice**, taken as Rawls takes it as the 'first virtue of social institutions,'[1] there has been a countermovement gathering strength, one coming from some interesting sources. For some of the most outspoken of the diverse group who have in a variety of ways been challenging the assumed supremacy of justice among the moral and social virtues are members of those sections of society whom one might have expected to be especially aware of the supreme importance of justice, namely blacks and women. Those who have only recently won recognition of their equal rights, who have only recently seen the correction or partial correction of longstanding racist and sexist injustices to their race and sex, are among the philosophers now suggesting that justice is only one virtue among many, and one that may need the presence of the others in order to deliver its own undenied value. Among these philosophers of the philosophical counterculture, as it were—but an increasingly large counterculture—I include Alasdair MacIntyre,[2] Michael Stocker,[3] Lawrence Blum,[4] Michael Slote,[5] Laurence Thomas,[6] Claudia Card,[7] Alison Jaggar,[8] Susan Wolf[9] and a whole group of men and women, myself included, who have been influenced by the writings of Harvard educational psychologist Carol Gilligan, whose book *In a Different Voice* (Harvard 1982; hereafter D.V.) caused a considerable stir both in the popular press and, more slowly, in the philosophical journals.[10]

Let me say quite clearly at this early point that there is little disagreement that justice is *a* social value of very great importance, and injustice an evil. Nor would those who have worked on theories of justice want to deny that other things matter besides justice. Rawls, for example, incorporates the value of freedom into his account of justice, so that denial of basic freedoms counts as injustice. Rawls also leaves room for a wider theory of the right, of which the theory of justice is just a part. Still, he does claim that justice is the 'first' virtue of social institutions, and it is only that claim about priority that I think has been challenged. It is easy to exaggerate the differences of view that exist, and I want to avoid that. The differences are as much in emphasis as in substance, or we can say that they are differences in tone of voice. But these differences do tend to make a difference in approaches to a wide range of topics not just in moral theory but in areas like medical ethics, where the discussion used to be conducted in terms of patients' rights, of informed consent, and so on, but now tends to get conducted in an enlarged moral vocabulary, which draws on what Gilligan calls the **ethics of *care*** as well as that of *justice*.

For 'care' is the new buzz-word. It is not, as Shakespeare's Portia demanded, mercy that is to season justice, but a less authoritarian humanitarian supplement, a felt concern for the good of others and for community with them. The 'cold jealous virtue of justice' (Hume) is found to be too cold, and it is

From "The Need for More Than Justice" in *Canadian Journal of Philosophy Supp. Vol.* 13, pp. 41–56. © 1987 by Taylor and Francis Group. Reprinted with permission.

'warmer' more communitarian virtues and social ideals that are being called in to supplement it. One might say that liberty and equality are being found inadequate without fraternity, except that 'fraternity' will be quite the wrong word, if as Gilligan initially suggested, it is *women* who perceive this value most easily. ('Sorority' will do no better, since it is too exclusive, and English has no gender-neuter word for the mutual concern of siblings.) She has since modified this claim, allowing that there are two perspectives on moral and social issues that we all tend to alternate between, and which are not always easy to combine, one of them what she called the justice perspective, the other the care perspective. It is increasingly obvious that there are many male philosophical spokespersons for the care perspective (Laurence Thomas, Lawrence Blum, Michael Stocker) so that it cannot be the prerogative of women. Nevertheless Gilligan still wants to claim that women are most unlikely to take *only* the justice perspective, as some men are claimed to, at least until some mid-life crisis jolts them into 'bifocal' moral vision (see D.V., ch. 6).

Gilligan in her book did not offer any explanatory theory of why there should be any difference between female and male moral outlook, but she did tend to link the naturalness to women of the care perspective with their role as primary care-takers of young children, that is with their parental and specifically maternal role. She avoided the question of whether it is their biological or their social role that is relevant, and some of those who dislike her book are worried precisely by this uncertainty. Some find it retrograde to hail as a special sort of moral wisdom an outlook that may be the product of the socially enforced restriction of women to domestic roles (and the reservation of such roles for them alone). For that might seem to play into the hands of those who still favor such restriction. (Marxists, presumably, will not find it so surprising that moral truths might depend for their initial clear voicing on the social oppression, and memory of it, of those who voice the truths.) Gilligan did in the first chapter of D.V. cite the theory of Nancy Chodorow (as presented in *The Reproduction of Mothering* [Berkeley 1978]) which traces what appears as gender differences in personality to early social development, in particular to the effects of the child's primary care-taker being or not being of the same gender as the child. Later, both in "The Conquistador and the Dark Continent: Reflections on the Nature of Love" (*Daedalus* [Summer 1984]), and "The Origins of Morality in Early Childhood" (in press), she develops this explanation. She postulates two evils that any infant may become aware of, the evil of detachment or isolation from others whose love one needs, and the evil of relative powerlessness and weakness. Two dimensions of moral development are thereby set—one aimed at achieving satisfying community with others, the other aiming at autonomy or equality of power. The relative predominance of one over the other development will depend both upon the relative salience of the two evils in early childhood, and on early and later reinforcement or discouragement in attempts made to guard against these two evils. This provides the germs of a theory about *why*, given current customs of childrearing, it should be mainly women who are not content with only the moral outlook that she calls the justice perspective, necessary though that was and is seen by them to have been to their hard won liberation from sexist oppression. They, like the blacks, used the language of rights and justice to change their own social position, but nevertheless see limitations in that language, according to Gilligan's findings as a moral psychologist. She reports their discontent with the individualist more or less Kantian moral framework that dominates Western moral theory and which influenced moral psychologists such as Lawrence Kohlberg, to whose conception of moral maturity she seeks an alternative. Since the target of Gilligan's criticism is the dominant Kantian tradition, and since that has been the target also of moral philosophers as diverse in their own views as Bernard Williams, Alasdair MacIntyre, Philippa Foot, Susan Wolf, Claudia Card, her book is of interest as much for its attempt to articulate an alternative to the Kantian justice perspective as for its implicit raising of the question of male bias in Western moral theory, especially liberal-democratic theory. For whether the supposed blind spots of that outlook are due to male bias, or to non-parental bias, or to early traumas of powerlessness or to early resignation to "detachment" from others, we need first to be persuaded that they *are* blind spots before we will have any interest in their cause and cure. Is justice blind to important social values, or at least only one-eyed? What is it that comes into view from the "care perspective" that is not seen from the "justice perspective"?

Gilligan's position here is mostly easily described by contrasting it with that of Kohlberg, against which she developed it. Kohlberg, influenced by Piaget and the Kantian philosophical tradition as developed by John Rawls, developed a theory about typical moral development which saw it to progress from a pre-conventional level, where what is seen to matter is pleasing or not offending parental authority-figures, through a conventional level in which the child tries to fit in with a group, such as a school community, and conform to its standards and rules, to a post-con-ventional critical level, in which such conventional rules are subjected to tests, and where those tests are of a Utilitarian, or, eventually, a Kantian sort—namely ones that require respect for each person's in-dividual rational will, or autonomy, and conformity to any implicit social contract such wills are deemed to have made, or to any hypothetical ones they would make if thinking clearly. What was found when Kohlberg's questionnaires (mostly by verbal response to verbally sketched moral dilemmas) were applied to female as well as male subjects, Gilligan reports, is that the girls and women not only scored generally lower than the boys and men, but tended to *revert* to the lower stage of the conventional level even after briefly (usually in adolescence) attaining the post con-ventional level. Piaget's finding that girls were defi-cient in 'the legal sense' was confirmed.

These results led Gilligan to wonder if there might not be a quite different pattern of development to be discerned, at least in female subjects. She there-fore conducted interviews designed to elicit not just how far advanced the subjects were towards an ap-preciation of the nature and importance of Kantian **autonomy**, but also to find out what the subjects themselves saw as progress or lack of it, what concep-tions of moral maturity they came to possess by the time they were adults. She found that although the Kohlberg version of **moral maturity** as respect for fellow persons, and for their rights as equals (rights including that of free association), did seem shared by many young men, the women tended to speak in a different voice about morality itself and about moral maturity. To quote Gilligan, 'Since the reality of

interconnexion is experienced by women as given rather than freely contracted, they arrive at an under-standing of life that reflects the limits of autonomy and control. As a result, women's development delin-eates the path not only to a less violent life but also to a maturity realized by interdependence and taking care' (D.V., 172). She writes that there is evidence that 'women perceive and construe social reality differ-ently from men, and that these differences center around experiences of attachment and separation . . . because women's sense of integrity appears to be in-tertwined with an ethics of care, so that to see them-selves as women is to see themselves in a relationship of connexion, the major changes in women's lives would seem to involve changes in the understanding and activities of care' (D.V., 171). She contrasts this progressive understanding of care, from merely pleasing others to helping and nurturing, with the sort of progression that is involved in Kohlberg's stages, a progression in the understanding, not of mutual care, but of mutual *respect*, where this has its Kantian overtones of distance, even of some fear for the respected, and where personal autonomy and *in*-dependence, rather than more satisfactory interde-pendence, are the paramount values.

This contrast, one cannot but feel, is one which Gilligan might have used the Marxist language of al-ienation to make. For the main complaint about the Kantian version of a society with its first virtue justice, construed as respect for equal rights to formal goods such as having contracts kept, due process, equal op-portunity including opportunity to participate in po-litical activities leading to policy and law-making, to basic liberties of speech, free association and assembly, religious worship, is that none of these goods do much to ensure that the people who have and mutually re-spect such rights will have any other relationships to one another than the minimal relationship needed to keep such a 'civil society' going. They may well be lonely, driven to suicide, apathetic about their work and about participation in political processes, find their lives meaningless and have no wish to leave off-spring to face the same meaningless existence. Their rights, and respect for rights, are quite compatible with very great misery, and misery whose causes are not just individual misfortunes and psychic sickness, but social and moral impoverishment.

What Gilligan's older male subjects complain of is precisely this sort of alienation from some dimly glimpsed better possibility for human beings, some richer sort of network of relationships. As one of Gilligan's male subjects put it, 'People have real emotional needs to be attached to something, and equality does not give you attachment. Equality fractures society and places on every person the burden of standing on his own two feet' (D.V., 167). It is not just the difficulty of self reliance which is complained of, but its socially 'fracturing' effect. Whereas the younger men, in their college years, had seen morality as a matter of reciprocal non-interference, this older man begins to see it as reciprocal attachment. 'Morality is . . . essential . . . for creating the kind of environment, interaction between people, that is a prerequisite to the fulfillment of individual goals. If you want other people not to interfere with your pursuit of whatever you are into, you have to play the game,' says the spokesman for traditional liberalism (D.V. 98). But if what one is 'into' is interconnexion, interdependence rather than an individual autonomy that may involve 'detachment,' such a version of morality will come to seem inadequate. And Gilligan stresses that the interconnexion that her mature women subjects, and some men, wanted to sustain was not merely freely chosen interconnexion, nor interconnexion between equals, but also the sort of interconnexion that can obtain between a child and her unchosen mother and father, or between a child and her unchosen older and younger siblings, or indeed between most workers and their unchosen fellow workers, or most citizens and their unchosen fellow citizens.

A model of a decent community different from the liberal one is involved in the version of moral maturity that Gilligan voices. It has in many ways more in common with the older religion-linked versions of morality and a good society than with the modern Western liberal ideal. That perhaps is why some find it so dangerous and retrograde. Yet it seems clear that it also has much in common with what we can call Hegelian versions of moral maturity and of social health and malaise, both with Marxist versions and with so-called right-Hegelian views.

Let me try to summarize the main differences, as I see them, between on the one hand Gilligan's version of moral maturity and the sort of social

structures that would encourage, express and protect it, and on the other the orthodoxy she sees herself to be challenging. I shall from now on be giving my own interpretation of the significance of her challenges, not merely reporting them.[11] The most obvious point is the challenge to the **individualism** of the Western tradition, to the fairly entrenched belief in the possibility and desirability of each person pursuing his own good in his own way, constrained only by a minimal formal common good, namely a working legal apparatus that enforces contracts and protects individuals from undue interference by others. Gilligan reminds us that noninterference can, especially for the relatively powerless, such as the very young, amount to neglect, and even between equals can be isolating and alienating. On her less individualist version of individuality, it becomes defined by responses to dependency and to patterns of interconnexion, both chosen and unchosen. It is not something a person *has*, and which she then chooses relationships to suit, but something that develops out of a series of dependencies and interdependencies, and responses to them. This conception of individuality is not flatly at odds with, say, Rawls' Kantian one, but there is at least a difference of tone of voice between speaking as Rawls does of each of us having our own rational life plan, which a just society's moral traffic rules will allow us to follow, and which may or may not include close association with other persons, and speaking as Gilligan does of a satisfactory life as involving 'progress of affiliative relationship' (D.V., 170) where 'the concept of identity expands to include the experience of interconnexion' (D.V., 173). Rawls can allow that progress to Gilligan-style moral maturity may be *a* rational life plan, but not a moral constraint on every life-pattern. The trouble is that it will not do just to say 'let this version of morality be an optional extra. Let us agree on the essential minimum, that is on justice and rights, and let whoever wants to go further and cultivate this more demanding ideal of responsibility and care.' For, first, it cannot be satisfactorily cultivated without closer cooperation from others than respect for rights and justice will ensure, and, second, the encouragement of some to cultivate it while others do not could easily lead to exploitation of those who do. It obviously *has* suited some in most societies well enough that others take on the responsibilities of care (for the sick, the helpless, the young) leaving them free to pursue their own less altruistic goods. Volunteer forces of those who accept an ethic of care, operating within a society where the power is exercised and the institutions designed, redesigned, or maintained by those who accept a less communal ethic of minimally constrained self-advancement, will not be the solution. The liberal individualists may be able to 'tolerate' the more communally minded, if they keep the liberals' rules, but it is not so clear that the more communally minded can be content with just those rules, nor be content to be tolerated and possibly exploited.

For the moral tradition which developed the concept of rights, autonomy and justice is the same tradition that provided 'justifications' of the oppression of those whom the primary right-holders depended on to do the sort of work they themselves preferred not to do. The domestic work was left to women and slaves, and the liberal morality for right-holders was surreptitiously supplemented by a different set of demands made on domestic workers. As long as women could be got to assume responsibility for the care of home and children, and to train their children to continue the sexist system, the liberal morality could continue to be the official morality, by turning its eyes away from the contribution made by those it excluded. The long unnoticed moral proletariat were the domestic workers, mostly female. Rights have usually been for the privileged. Talking about laws, and the rights those laws recognize and protect, does not in itself ensure that the group of legislators and rights-holders will not be restricted to some elite. Bills of rights have usually been proclamations of the rights of some in-group, barons, land-owners, males, whites, non-foreigners. The 'justice perspective,' and the legal sense that goes with it, are shadowed by their patriarchal past. What did Kant, the great prophet of autonomy, say in his moral theory about women? He said they were incapable of legislation, not fit to vote, that they needed the guidance of more 'rational' males.[12] Autonomy was not for them, only for first class, really rational, persons. It is ironic that Gilligan's original findings in a way confirm Kant's views—it seems that autonomy really may not be for women. Many of them reject that ideal (D.V., 48), and have been found not as good at making rules as are

men. But where Kant concludes—'so much the worse for women,' we can conclude—'so much the worse for the male fixation on the special skill of drafting legislation, for the bureaucratic mentality of rule worship, and for the male exaggeration of the importance of independence over mutual interdependence.'

It is however also true that the moral theories that made the concept of a person's rights central were not just the instruments for excluding some persons, but also the instruments used by those who demanded that more and more persons be included in the favored group. Abolitionists, reformers, women, used the language of rights to assert their claims to inclusion in the group of full members of a community. The tradition of liberal moral theory has in fact developed so as to include the women it had for so long excluded, to include the poor as well as rich, blacks and whites, and so on. Women like Mary Wollstonecraft used the male moral theories to good purpose. So we should not be wholly ungrateful for those male moral theories, for all their objectionable earlier content. They were undoubtedly patriarchal, but they also contained the seeds of the challenge, or antidote, to this patriarchal poison.

But when we transcend the values of the Kantians, we should not forget the facts of history—that those values were the values of the oppressors of women. The Christian church, whose version of the moral law Aquinas codified, in his very legalistic moral theory, still insists on the maleness of the God it worships, and jealously reserves for males all the most powerful positions in its hierarchy. Its patriarchical prejudice is open and avowed. In the secular moral theories of men, the sexist patriarchal prejudice is today often less open, not as blatant as it is in Aquinas, in the later natural law tradition, and in Kant and Hegel, but is often still there. No moral theorist today would say that women are unfit to vote, to make laws, or to rule a nation without powerful male advisors (as most queens had), but the old doctrines die hard. In one of the best male theories we have, John Rawls's theory, a key role is played by the idea of the 'head of a household.' It is heads of households who are to deliberate behind a 'veil of ignorance' of historical details, and of details of their own special situation, to arrive at the 'just' constitution for a society. Now of course Rawls does not think or say that these 'heads' are fathers rather than mothers. But if we have really given up the age-old myth of women needing, as Grotius put it, to be under the 'eye' of a more 'rational' male protector and master, then how do families come to have any one 'head,' except by the death or desertion of one parent? They will either be two-headed, or headless. Traces of the old patriarchal poison still remain in even the best contemporary moral theorizing. Few may actually say that women's place is in the home, but there is much muttering, when unemployment figures rise, about how the relatively recent flood of women into the work force complicates the problem, as if it would be a good thing if women just went back home whenever unemployment rises, to leave the available jobs for the men. We still do not really have a wide acceptance of the equal right of women to employment outside the home. Nor do we have wide acceptance of the equal duty of men to perform those domestic tasks which in no way depend on special female anatomy, namely cooking, cleaning, and the care of weaned children. All sorts of stories (maybe true stories), about children's need for one 'primary' parent, who must be the mother if the mother breast feeds the child, shore up the unequal division of domestic responsibility between mothers and fathers, wives and husbands. If we are really to transvalue the values of our patriarchal past, we need to rethink all of those assumptions, really test those psychological theories. And how will men ever develop an understanding of the 'ethics of care' if they continue to be shielded or kept from that experience of caring for a dependent child, which complements the experience we all have had of being cared for as dependent children? These experiences form the natural background for the development of moral maturity as Gilligan's women saw it.

Exploitation aside, why would women, once liberated, not be content to have their version of morality merely tolerated? Why should they not see themselves as voluntarily, for their own reasons, taking on *more* than the liberal rules demand, while having no quarrel with the content of those rules themselves, nor with their remaining the only ones that are expected to be generally obeyed? To see why, we need to move on to three more differences between the Kantian liberals (usually contractarians) and their

critics. These concern the relative weight put on relationships between equals, and the relative weight put on freedom of choice, and on the authority of intellect over emotions. It is a typical feature of the dominant moral theories and traditions, since Kant, or perhaps since Hobbes, that relationships between equals or those who are deemed equal in some important sense, have been the relations that morality is concerned primarily to regulate. Relationships between those who are clearly unequal in power, such as parents and children, earlier and later generations in relation to one another, states and citizens, doctors and patients, the well and the ill, large states and small states, have had to be shunted to the bottom of the agenda, and then dealt with by some sort of 'promotion' of the weaker so that an appearance of virtual equality is achieved. Citizens collectively become equal to states, children are treated as adults-to-be, the ill and dying are treated as continuers of their earlier more potent selves, so that their 'rights' could be seen as the rights of equals. This pretence of an equality that is in fact absent may often lead to desirable protection of the weaker, or more dependent. But it somewhat masks the question of what our moral relationships *are* to those who are our superiors or our inferiors in power. A more realistic acceptance of the fact that we begin as helpless children, that at almost every point of our lives we deal with both the more and the less helpless, that equality of power and interdependency, between two persons or groups, is rare and hard to recognize when it does occur, might lead us to a more direct approach to questions concerning the design of institutions structuring these relationships between unequals (families, schools, hospitals, armies) and of the morality of our dealings with the more and the less powerful. One reason why those who agree with the Gilligan version of what morality is about will not want to agree that the liberals' rules are a good minimal set, the only ones we need pressure *everyone* to obey, is that these rules do little to protect the young or the dying or the starving or any of the relatively powerless against neglect, or to ensure an education that will form persons to be *capable* of conforming to an ethics of care and responsibility. Put baldly, and in a way Gilligan certainly has not put it, the liberal morality, if unsupplemented, may *unfit* people to be anything other than what its justifying theories suppose them to be, ones who have no interest in each others' interests. Yet some must take an interest in the next generation's interests. Women's traditional work, of caring for the less powerful, especially for the young, is obviously socially vital. One cannot regard any version of morality that does not ensure that it gets well done as an adequate 'minimal morality,' any more than we could so regard one that left any concern for more distant future generations an optional extra. A moral theory, it can plausibly be claimed, cannot regard concern for new and future persons as an optional charity left for those with a taste for it. If the morality the theory endorses is to sustain itself, it must provide for its own continuers, not just take out a loan on a carefully encouraged maternal instinct or on the enthusiasm of a self-selected group of environmentalists, who make it their business or hobby to be concerned with what we are doing to mother earth.

The recognition of the importance for all parties of relations between those who are and cannot but be unequal, both of these relations in themselves and for their effect on personality formation and so on other relationships, goes along with a recognition of the plain fact that not all morally important relationships can or should be freely chosen. So far I have discussed three reasons women have not to be content to pursue their own values within the framework of the liberal morality. The first was its dubious record. The second was its inattention to relations of inequality or its pretence of equality. The third reason is its exaggeration of the scope of choice, or its inattention to unchosen relations. Showing up the partial myth of equality among actual members of a community, and of the undesirability of trying to pretend that we are treating all of them as equals, tends to go along with an exposure of the companion myth that moral obligations arise from freely *chosen* associations between such equals. Vulnerable future generations do not choose their dependence on earlier generations. The unequal infant does not choose its place in a family or nation, nor is it treated as free to do as it likes until some association is freely entered into. Nor do its parents always choose their parental role, or freely assume their parental responsibilities any more

than we choose our power to affect the conditions in which later generations will live. Gilligan's attention to the version of morality and moral maturity found in women, many of whom had faced a choice of whether or not to have an abortion, and who had at some point become mothers, is attention to the perceived inadequacy of the language of rights to help in such choices or to guide them in their parental role. It would not be much of an exaggeration to call the Gilligan 'different voice' the voice of the potential parents. The emphasis on care goes with a recognition of the often unchosen nature of the responsibilities of those who give care, both of children who care for their aged or infirm parents, and of parents who care for the children they in fact have. Contract soon ceases to seem the paradigm source of moral obligation once we attend to parental responsibility, and justice as a virtue of social institutions will come to seem at best only first equal with the virtue, whatever its name, that ensures that each new generation is made appropriately welcome and prepared for their adult lives.

This all constitutes a belated reminder to Western moral theorists of a fact they have always known, that as Adam Ferguson, and David Hume before him emphasized, we are born into families, and the first society we belong to, one that fits or misfits us for later ones, is the small society of parents (or some sort of child-attendants) and children, exhibiting as it may both relationships of near equality and of inequality in power. This simple reminder, with the fairly considerable implications it can have for the plausibility of contractarian moral theory, is at the same time a reminder of the role of human emotions as much as human reason and will in moral development as it actually comes about. The fourth feature of the Gilligan challenge to liberal orthodoxy is a challenge to its typical *rationalism*, or intellectualism, to its assumption that we need not worry what passions persons have, as long as their rational wills can control them. This Kantian picture of a controlling reason dictating to possibly unruly passions also tends to seem less useful when we are led to consider what sort of person we need to fill the role of parent, or indeed want in any close relationship. It might be important for father figures to have rational control over their violent urges to beat to death the children whose screams enrage them, but more than control of such nasty passions seems needed in the mother or primary parent, or parent-substitute, by most psychological theories. They need to love their children, not just to control their irritation. So the emphasis in Kantian theories on rational control of emotions, rather than on cultivating desirable forms of emotion, is challenged by Gilligan, along with the challenge to the assumption of the centrality of autonomy, or relations between equals, and of freely chosen relations.

The same set of challenges to 'orthodox' liberal moral theory has come not just from Gilligan and other women, who are reminding other moral theorists of the role of the family as a social institution and as an influence on the other relationships people want to or are capable of sustaining, but also, as I noted at the start, from an otherwise fairly diverse group of men, ranging from those influenced by both Hegelian and Christian traditions (MacIntyre) to all varieties of other backgrounds. From this group I want to draw attention to the work of one philosopher in particular, namely Laurence Thomas, the author of a fairly remarkable article[13] in which he finds sexism to be a more intractable social evil than racism. In a series of articles, and a forthcoming book,[14] Thomas makes a strong case for the importance of supplementing a concern for justice and respect for rights with an emphasis on equally needed virtues, and on virtues seen as appropriate *emotional* as well as rational capacities. Like Gilligan (and unlike MacIntyre) Thomas gives a lot of attention to the childhood beginnings of moral and social capacities, to the role of parental love in making that possible, and to the emotional as well as the cognitive development we have reason to think both possible and desirable in human persons.

It is clear, I think, that the best moral theory has to be a cooperative product of women and men, has to harmonize justice and care. The morality it theorizes about is after all for all persons, for men and for women, and will need their combined insights. As Gilligan said (D.V., 174), what we need now is a 'marriage' of the old male and the newly articulated female insights. If she is right about the special moral aptitudes of women, it will most likely be the women who propose the marriage, since they are the ones with more natural empathy, with the better diplomatic skills, the ones more likely to shoulder responsibility and take moral initiative, and the ones who find it easiest to empathize and care about how the other party feels. Then, once there is this union of male and female moral wisdom, we maybe can teach each other the moral skills each gender currently lacks, so that the gender difference in moral outlook that Gilligan found will slowly become less marked.

NOTES

1. John Rawls, *A Theory of Justice* (Harvard University Press).
2. Alasdair MacIntyre, *After Virtue* (Notre Dame: Notre Dame University Press).
3. Michael Stocker, "The Schizophrenia of Modern Ethical Theories," *Journal of Philosophy* 73, 14, 453–66 and "Agent and Other: Against Ethical Universalism," *Australasian Journal of Philosophy* 54, 206–220.
4. Lawrence Blum, *Friendship, Altruism and Morality* (London: Routledge & Kegan Paul, 1980).
5. Michael Slote, *Goods and Virtues* (Oxford: Oxford University Press, 1983).
6. Laurence Thomas, "Love and Morality," in *Epistemology and Sociobiology*, James Fetzer, ed. (1985); and "Justice, Happiness and Self Knowledge," *Canadian Journal of Philosophy* (March, 1986). Also "Beliefs and the Motivation to Be Just," *American Philosophical Quarterly* 22 (4), 347–52.
7. Claudia Card, "Mercy," *Philosophical Review* 81, 1, and "Gender and Moral Luck," forthcoming.
8. Alison Jaggar, *Feminist Politics and Human Nature* (London: Rowman and Allenheld, 1983).
9. Susan Wolf, "Moral Saints," *Journal of Philosophy* 79 (August, 1982), 419–439.
10. For a helpful survey article see Owen Flanagan and Kathryn Jackson, "Justice, Care & Gender: The Kohlberg-Gilligan Debate Revisited," *Ethics*.
11. I have previously written about the significance of her findings for moral philosophy in "What Do Women Want in a Moral Theory?" *Nous* 19 (March 1985), "Trust and Antitrust," *Ethics* 96

(1986), and in "Hume the Women's Theorist?" in *Women and Moral Theory*, Kittay and Meyers, ed., forthcoming.

12. Immanuel Kant, *Metaphysics of Morals*, sec. 46.

13. Laurence Thomas, "Sexism and Racism: Some Conceptual Differences," *Ethics* 90 (1980), 239–250; republished in *Philosophy, Sex and Language*, Vetterling-Braggin, ed. (Totowa, NJ: Littlefield Adams 1980).

14. See articles listed in note 6, above. The forthcoming book has the title *A Psychology of Moral Character.*

KEY TERMS

Justice
Ethics of care
Autonomy
Moral maturity
Individualism
Rationalism

STUDY QUESTIONS

1. What does Baier mean by an ethics of justice? An ethics of care?

2. Drawing from the work of Carol Gilligan, Baier suggests a difference between the moral maturity men arrive at and the moral maturity women typically arrive at. Why is there a difference, according to Baier, and what is it?

3. How does Baier characterize the Kantian conception of society that puts justice at its center? What is problematic about this conception of society? What sorts of people might it leave out?

4. How does a focus on justice affect the way one views individualism? Compare this to how a focus on care might affect the way one conceives of individualism.

5. Baier describes four differences between a society that makes justice its first principle and a society that puts care at its center. Briefly describe these four differences. Can you think of any other possible differences? Do you agree with Baier about the differences she suggests?

E. CONTEMPORARY MORAL PROBLEMS

✕

A Defense of Abortion[1]

JUDITH JARVIS THOMSON

Judith Jarvis Thomson (1921–) is Professor Emeritus at MIT. She has made very significant contributions to various areas of philosophy, especially in ethics and metaphysics. Among her many influential works are *Normativity* (2008), a published version of her Paul Carus Lectures, and *Realm of Rights* (1990), a study of what it is to have a right and which ones we have.

. .

MOST opposition to abortion relies on the premise that the fetus is a human being, a person, from the moment of conception. The premise is argued for, but, as I think, not well. Take, for example, the most common argument. We are asked to notice that the development of a human being from conception through birth into childhood is continuous; then it is said that to draw a line, to choose a point in this development and say "before this point the thing is not a person, after this point it is a person" is to make an arbitrary choice, a choice for which in the nature of things no good reason can be given. It is concluded that the fetus is, or anyway that we had better say it is, a person from the moment of conception. But this conclusion does not follow. Similar things might be said about the development

of an acorn into an oak tree, and it does not follow that acorns are oak trees, or that we had better say they are. Arguments of this form are sometimes called "**slippery slope arguments**"—the phrase is perhaps self-explanatory—and it is dismaying that opponents of abortion rely on them so heavily and uncritically.

I am inclined to agree, however, that the prospects for "drawing a line" in the development of the fetus look dim. I am inclined to think also that we shall probably have to agree that the fetus has already become a human person well before birth. Indeed, it comes as a surprise when one first learns how early in its life it begins to acquire human characteristics. By the tenth week, for example, it already has a face, arms and legs, fingers and toes; it has internal organs, and brain activity is detectable.[2] On the other hand, I think that the premise is false, that the fetus is not a person from the moment of conception. A newly fertilized ovum, a newly implanted clump of cells, is

From "A Defense of Abortion" in *Philosophy and Public Affairs* 1.1, pp. 47–66. © 1971 by Wiley. Reprinted with permission.

no more a person than an acorn is an oak tree. But I shall not discuss any of this. For it seems to me to be of great interest to ask what happens if, for the sake of argument, we allow the premise. How, precisely, are we supposed to get from there to the conclusion that abortion is morally impermissible? Opponents of abortion commonly spend most of their time establishing that the fetus is a person, and hardly any time explaining the step from there to the impermissibility of abortion. Perhaps they think the step too simple and obvious to require much comment. Or perhaps instead they are simply being economical in argument. Many of those who defend abortion rely on the premise that the fetus is not a person, but only a bit of tissue that will become a person at birth; and why pay out more arguments than you have to? Whatever the explanation, I suggest that the step they take is neither easy nor obvious, that it calls for closer examination than it is commonly given, and that when we do give it this closer examination we shall feel inclined to reject it.

I propose, then, that we grant that the fetus is a person from the moment of conception. How does the argument go from here? Something like this, I take it. Every person has a **right to life**. So the fetus has a right to life. No doubt the mother has a **right to decide** what shall happen in and to her body; everyone would grant that. But surely a person's right to life is stronger and more stringent than the mother's right to decide what happens in and to her body, and so outweighs it. So the fetus may not be killed; an abortion may not be performed.

It sounds plausible. But now let me ask you to imagine this. You wake up in the morning and find yourself back to back in bed with an unconscious violinist. A famous unconscious violinist. He has been found to have a fatal kidney ailment, and the Society of Music Lovers has canvassed all the available medical records and found that you alone have the right blood type to help. They have therefore kidnapped you, and last night the violinist's circulatory system was plugged into yours, so that your kidneys can be used to extract poisons from his blood as well as your own. The director of the hospital now tells you, "Look, we're sorry the Society of Music Lovers did this to you—we would never have permitted it if we had known. But still, they did it, and the violinist now is plugged into you. To unplug you would be to kill him. But never mind, it's only for nine months. By then he will have recovered from his ailment, and can safely be unplugged from you." Is it morally incumbent on you to accede to this situation? No doubt it would be very nice of you if you did, a great kindness. But do you *have* to accede to it? What if it were not nine months, but nine years? Or longer still? What if the director of the hospital says, "Tough luck, I agree, but you've now got to stay in bed, with the violinist plugged into you, for the rest of your life. Because remember this. All persons have a right to life, and violinists are persons. Granted you have a right to decide what happens in and to your body, but a person's right to life outweighs your right to decide what happens in and to your body. So you cannot ever be unplugged from him." I imagine you would regard this as outrageous, which suggests that something really is wrong with that plausible-sounding argument I mentioned a moment ago.

In this case, of course, you were kidnapped; you didn't volunteer for the operation that plugged the violinist into your kidneys. Can those who oppose abortion on the ground I mentioned make an exception for a pregnancy due to rape? Certainly. They can say that persons have a right to life only if they didn't come into existence because of rape; or they can say that all persons have a right to life, but that some have less of a right to life than others, in particular, that those who came into existence because of rape have less. But these statements have a rather unpleasant sound. Surely the question of whether you have a right to life at all, or how much of it you have, shouldn't turn on the question of whether or not you are the product of a rape. And in fact the people who oppose abortion on the ground I mentioned do not make this distinction, and hence do not make an exception in case of rape.

Nor do they make an exception for a case in which the mother has to spend the nine months of her pregnancy in bed. They would agree that would be a great pity, and hard on the mother; but all the same, all persons have a right to life, the fetus is a person, and so on. I suspect, in fact, that they would not make an exception for a case in which, miraculously enough, the pregnancy went on for nine years, or even the rest of the mother's life.

Some won't even make an exception for a case in which continuation of the pregnancy is likely to shorten the mother's life; they regard abortion as impermissible even to save the mother's life. Such cases are nowadays very rare, and many opponents of abortion do not accept this extreme view. All the same, it is a good place to begin: a number of points of interest come out in respect to it.

1. Let us call the view that abortion is impermissible even to save the mother's life "the extreme view." I want to suggest first that it does not issue from the argument I mentioned earlier without the addition of some fairly powerful premises. Suppose a woman has become pregnant, and now learns that she has a cardiac condition such that she will die if she carries the baby to term. What may be done for her? The fetus, being a person, has a right to life, but as the mother is a person too, so has she a right to life. Presumably they have an equal right to life. How is it supposed to come out that an abortion may not be performed? If mother and child have an equal right to life, shouldn't we perhaps flip a coin? Or should we add to the mother's right to life her right to decide what happens in and to her body, which everybody seems to be ready to grant—the sum of her rights now outweighing the fetus' right to life?

The most familiar argument here is the following. We are told that performing the abortion would be **directly killing**[3] the child, whereas doing nothing would not be killing the mother, but only letting her die. Moreover, in killing the child, one would be killing an innocent person, for the child has committed no crime, and is not aiming at his mother's death. And then there are a variety of ways in which this might be continued. (1) But as directly killing an innocent person is always and absolutely impermissible, an abortion may not be performed. Or, (2) as directly killing an innocent person is murder, and murder is always and absolutely impermissible, an abortion may not be performed.[4] Or, (3) as one's duty to refrain from directly killing an innocent person is more stringent than one's duty to keep a person from dying, an abortion may not be performed. Or, (4) if one's only options are directly killing an innocent person or letting a person die, one must prefer letting the person die, and thus an abortion may not be performed.[5]

Some people seem to have thought that these are not further premises which must be added if the conclusion is to be reached, but that they follow from the very fact that an innocent person has a right to life.[6] But this seems to me to be a mistake, and perhaps the simplest way to show this is to bring out that while we must certainly grant that innocent persons have a right to life, the theses in (1) through (4) are all false. Take (2), for example. If directly killing an innocent person is murder, and thus is impermissible, then the mother's directly killing the innocent person inside her is murder, and thus is impermissible. But it cannot seriously be thought to be murder if the mother performs an abortion on herself to save her life. It cannot seriously be said that she *must* refrain, that she *must* sit passively by and wait for her death. Let us look again at the case of you and the violinist. There you are, in bed with the violinist, and the director of the hospital says to you, "It's all most distressing, and I deeply sympathize, but you see this is putting an additional strain on your kidneys, and you'll be dead within the month. But you *have* to stay where you are all the same. Because unplugging you would be directly killing an innocent violinist, and that's murder, and that's impermissible." If anything in the world is true, it is that you do not commit murder, you do not do what is impermissible, if you reach around to your back and unplug yourself from that violinist to save your life.

The main focus of attention in writings on abortion has been on what a third party may or may not do in answer to a request from a woman for an abortion. This is in a way understandable. Things being as they are, there isn't much a woman can safely do to abort herself. So the question asked is what a third party may do, and what the mother may do, if it is mentioned at all, is deduced, almost as an afterthought, from what it is concluded that third parties may do. But it seems to me that to treat the matter in this way is to refuse to grant to the mother that very status of person which is so firmly insisted on for the fetus. For we cannot simply read off what a person may do from what a third party may do. Suppose you find yourself trapped in a tiny house with a growing child. I mean a very tiny house, and a rapidly growing child—you are already up against the wall of the house and in a few minutes you'll be crushed to death. The child on the other hand won't be crushed to death; if nothing is done to stop him from growing he'll be hurt, but in the end he'll simply burst open the house and walk out a free man. Now I could well understand it if a bystander were to say, "There's nothing we can do for you. We cannot choose between your life and his, we cannot be the ones to decide who is to live, we cannot intervene." But it cannot be concluded that you too can do nothing, that you cannot attack it to save your life. However innocent the child may be, you do not have to wait passively while it crushes you to death. Perhaps a pregnant woman is vaguely felt to have the status of house, to which we don't allow the **right of self-defense**. But if the woman houses the child, it should be remembered that she is a person who houses it.

I should perhaps stop to say explicitly that I am not claiming that people have a right to do anything whatever to save their lives. I think, rather, that there are drastic limits to the right of self-defense. If someone threatens you with death unless you torture someone else to death, I think you have not the right, even to save your life, to do so. But the case under consideration here is very different. In our case there are only two people involved, one whose life is threatened, and one who threatens it. Both are innocent: the one who is threatened is not threatened because of any fault, the one who threatens does not threaten because of any fault. For this reason we may feel that we bystanders cannot intervene. But the person threatened can.

In sum, a woman surely can defend her life against the threat to it posed by the unborn child, even if doing so involves its death. And this shows not merely that the theses in (1) through (4) are false; it shows also that the extreme view of abortion is false, and so we need not canvass any other possible ways of arriving at it from the argument I mentioned at the outset.

2. The extreme view could of course be weakened to say that while abortion is permissible to save the mother's life, it may not be performed by a third party, but only by the mother herself. But this cannot be right either. For what we have to keep in mind is that the mother and the unborn child are not like two tenants in a small house which has, by an unfortunate mistake, been rented to both: the mother *owns* the house. The fact that she does adds to the offensiveness of deducing that the mother can do nothing from the supposition that third parties can do nothing. But it does more than this: it casts a bright light on the supposition that third parties can do nothing. Certainly it lets us see that a third party who says "I cannot choose between you" is fooling himself if he thinks this is impartiality. If Jones has found and fastened on a certain coat, which he needs to keep him from freezing, but which Smith also needs to keep him from freezing, then it is not impartiality that says "I cannot choose between you" when Smith owns the coat. Women have said again and again "This body is *my* body!" and they have reason to feel angry, reason to feel that it has been like shouting into the wind. Smith, after all, is hardly likely to bless us if we say to him, "Of course it's your coat, anybody would grant that it is. But no one may choose between you and Jones who is to have it."

We should really ask what it is that says "no one may choose" in the face of the fact that the body that houses the child is the mother's body. It may be simply a failure to appreciate this fact. But it may be something more interesting, namely the sense that one has a right to refuse to lay hands on people, even where it would be just and fair to do so, even where justice seems to require that somebody do so. Thus justice might call for somebody to get Smith's coat back from Jones, and yet you have a right to refuse to be the one to lay hands on Jones, a right to refuse to do physical violence to him. This, I think, must be granted. But then what should be said is not "no one may choose," but only "*I* cannot choose," and indeed not even this, but "*I* will not *act*," leaving it open that somebody else can or should, and in particular that anyone in a position of authority, with the job of securing people's rights, both can and should. So this is no difficulty. I have not been arguing that any given third party must accede to the mother's request that he perform an abortion to save her life, but only that he may.

I suppose that in some views of human life the mother's body is only on loan to her, the loan not being one which gives her any prior claim to it. One who held this view might well think it impartiality to say "I cannot choose." But I shall simply ignore this possibility. My own view is that if a human being has any just, prior claim to anything at all, he has a just, prior claim to his own body. And perhaps this needn't be argued for here anyway, since, as I mentioned, the arguments against abortion we are looking at do grant that the woman has a right to decide what happens in and to her body.

But although they do grant it, I have tried to show that they do not take seriously what is done in granting it. I suggest the same thing will reappear even more clearly when we turn away from cases in which the mother's life is at stake, and attend, as I propose we now do, to the vastly more common cases in which a woman wants an abortion for some less weighty reason than preserving her own life.

3. Where the mother's life is not at stake, the argument I mentioned at the outset seems to have a much stronger pull. "Everyone has a right to life, so the unborn person has a right to life." And isn't the child's right to life weightier than anything other than the mother's own right to life, which she might put forward as ground for an abortion?

This argument treats the right to life as if it were unproblematic. It is not, and this seems to me to be precisely the source of the mistake.

For we should now, at long last, ask what it comes to, to have a right to life. In some views having a right to life includes having a right to be given at least the bare minimum one needs for continued life. But suppose that what in fact *is* the bare minimum a man needs for continued life is something he has no right at all to be given? If I am sick unto death, and the only thing that will save my life is the touch of Henry Fonda's cool hand on my fevered brow, then all the same, I have no right to be given the touch of Henry Fonda's cool hand on my fevered brow. It would be frightfully nice of him to fly in from the West Coast to provide it. It would be less nice, though no doubt well meant, if my friends flew out to the West Coast and carried Henry Fonda back with them. But I have no right at all against anybody that he should do this for me. Or again, to return to the story I told earlier, the fact that for continued life that violinist needs the continued use of your kidneys does not establish that he has a right to be given the continued use of your kidneys. He certainly has no right against you that *you* should give him continued use of your kidneys. For nobody has any right to use your kidneys unless you give him such a right; and nobody

has the right against you that you shall give him this right—if you do allow him to go on using your kidneys, this is a kindness on your part, and not something he can claim from you as his due. Nor has he any right against anybody else that *they* should give him continued use of your kidneys. Certainly he had no right against the Society of Music Lovers that they should plug him into you in the first place. And if you now start to unplug yourself, having learned that you will otherwise have to spend nine years in bed with him, there is nobody in the world who must try to prevent you, in order to see to it that he is given something he has a right to be given.

Some people are rather stricter about the right to life. In their view, it does not include the right to be given anything, but amounts to, and only to, the right not to be killed by anybody. But here a related difficulty arises. If everybody is to refrain from killing that violinist, then everybody must refrain from doing a great many different sorts of things. Everybody must refrain from slitting his throat, everybody must refrain from shooting him—and everybody must refrain from unplugging you from him. But does he have a right against everybody that they shall refrain from unplugging you from him? To refrain from doing this is to allow him to continue to use your kidneys. It could be argued that he has a right against us that *we* should allow him to continue to use your kidneys. That is, while he had no right against us that we should give him the use of your kidneys, it might be argued that he anyway has a right against us that we shall not now intervene and deprive him of the use of your kidneys. I shall come back to third-party interventions later. But certainly the violinist has no right against you that *you* shall allow him to continue to use your kidneys. As I said, if you do allow him to use them, it is a kindness on your part, and not something you owe him.

The difficulty I point to here is not peculiar to the right to life. It reappears in connection with all the other natural rights; and it is something which an adequate account of rights must deal with. For present purposes it is enough just to draw attention to it. But I would stress that I am not arguing that people do not have a right to life—quite to the contrary, it seems to me that the primary control we must place on the acceptability of an account of rights is that it should turn out in that account to be a truth that all persons have a right to life. I am arguing only that having a right to life does not guarantee having either a right to be given the use of or a right to be allowed continued use of another person's body—even if one needs it for life itself. So the right to life will not serve the opponents of abortion in the very simple and clear way in which they seem to have thought it would.

4. There is another way to bring out the difficulty. In the most ordinary sort of case, to deprive someone of what he has a right to is to treat him unjustly. Suppose a boy and his small brother are jointly given a box of chocolates for Christmas. If the older boy takes the box and refuses to give his brother any of the chocolates, he is unjust to him, for the brother has been given a right to half of them. But suppose that, having learned that otherwise it means nine years in bed with that violinist, you unplug yourself from him. You surely are not being unjust to him, for you gave him no right to use your kidneys, and no one else can have given him any such right. But we have to notice that in unplugging yourself, you are killing him; and violinists, like everybody else, have a right to life, and thus in the view we were considering just now, the right not to be killed. So here you do what he supposedly has a right you shall not do, but you do not act unjustly to him in doing it.

The emendation which may be made at this point is this: the right to life consists not in the right not to be killed, but rather in the right not to be killed unjustly. This runs a risk of circularity, but never mind: it would enable us to square the fact that the violinist has a right to life with the fact that you do not act unjustly toward him in unplugging yourself, thereby killing him. For if you do not kill him unjustly, you do not violate his right to life, and so it is no wonder you do him no injustice.

But if this emendation is accepted, the gap in the argument against abortion stares us plainly in the face: it is by no means enough to show that the fetus is a person, and to remind us that all persons have a right to life—we need to be shown also that killing the fetus violates its right to life, i.e., that abortion is unjust killing. And is it?

I suppose we may take it as a datum that in a case of pregnancy due to rape the mother has not given

the unborn person a right to the use of her body for food and shelter. Indeed, in what pregnancy could it be supposed that the mother has given the unborn person such a right? It is not as if there were unborn persons drifting about the world, to whom a woman who wants a child says "I invite you in."

But it might be argued that there are other ways one can have acquired a right to the use of another person's body than by having been invited to use it by that person. Suppose a woman voluntarily indulges in intercourse, knowing of the chance it will issue in pregnancy, and then she does become pregnant; is she not in part responsible for the presence, in fact the very existence, of the unborn person inside her? No doubt she did not invite it in. But doesn't her partial responsibility for its being there itself give it a right to the use of her body?[7] If so, then her aborting it would be more like the boy's taking away the chocolates, and less like your unplugging yourself from the violinist—doing so would be depriving it of what it does have a right to, and thus would be doing it an injustice.

And then, too, it might be asked whether or not she can kill it even to save her own life: If she voluntarily called it into existence, how can she now kill it, even in self-defense?

The first thing to be said about this is that it is something new. Opponents of abortion have been so concerned to make out the independence of the fetus, in order to establish that it has a right to life, just as its mother does, that they have tended to overlook the possible support they might gain from making out that the fetus is *dependent* on the mother, in order to establish that she has a special kind of responsibility for it, a responsibility that gives it rights against her which are not possessed by any independent person—such as an ailing violinist who is a stranger to her.

On the other hand, this argument would give the unborn person a right to its mother's body only if her pregnancy resulted from a voluntary act, undertaken in full knowledge of the chance a pregnancy might result from it. It would leave out entirely the unborn person whose existence is due to rape. Pending the availability of some further argument, then, we would be left with the conclusion that unborn persons whose existence is due to rape have no right to the use of their mothers' bodies, and thus that aborting them is not depriving them of anything they have a right to and hence is not unjust killing.

And we should also notice that it is not at all plain that this argument really does go even as far as it purports to. For there are cases and cases, and the details make a difference. If the room is stuffy, and I therefore open a window to air it, and a burglar climbs in, it would be absurd to say, "Ah, now he can stay, she's given him a right to the use of her house—for she is partially responsible for his presence there, having voluntarily done what enabled him to get in, in full knowledge that there are such things as burglars, and that burglars burgle." It would be still more absurd to say this if I had had bars installed outside my windows, precisely to prevent burglars from getting in, and a burglar got in only because of a defect in the bars. It remains equally absurd if we imagine it is not a burglar who climbs in, but an innocent person who blunders or falls in. Again, suppose it were like this: people-seeds drift about in the air like pollen, and if you open your windows, one may drift in and take root in your carpets or upholstery. You don't want children, so you fix up your windows with fine mesh screens, the very best you can buy. As can happen, however, and on very, very rare occasions does happen, one of the screens is defective; and a seed drifts in and takes root. Does the person-plant who now develops have a right to the use of your house? Surely not—despite the fact that you voluntarily opened your windows, you knowingly kept carpets and upholstered furniture, and you knew that screens were sometimes defective. Someone may argue that you are responsible for its rooting, that it does have a right to your house, because after all you *could* have lived out your life with bare floors and furniture, or with sealed windows and doors. But this won't do—for by the same token anyone can avoid a pregnancy due to rape by having a hysterectomy, or anyway by never leaving home without a (reliable!) army.

It seems to me that the argument we are looking at can establish at most that there are *some* cases in which the unborn person has a right to the use of its mother's body, and therefore *some* cases in which abortion is unjust killing. There is room for much discussion and argument as to precisely which, if any. But I think we should sidestep this issue and leave it open, for at any rate the argument certainly does not establish that all abortion is unjust killing.

5. There is room for yet another argument here, however. We surely must all grant that there may be cases in which it would be morally indecent to detach a person from your body at the cost of his life. Suppose you learn that what the violinist needs is not nine years of your life, but only one hour: all you need do to save his life is to spend one hour in that bed with him. Suppose also that letting him use your kidneys for that one hour would not affect your health in the slightest. Admittedly you were kidnapped. Admittedly you did not give anyone permission to plug him into you. Nevertheless it seems to me plain you *ought* to allow him to use your kidneys for that hour—it would be indecent to refuse.

Again, suppose pregnancy lasted only an hour, and constituted no threat to life or health. And suppose that a woman becomes pregnant as a result of rape. Admittedly she did not voluntarily do anything to bring about the existence of a child. Admittedly she did nothing at all which would give the unborn person a right to the use of her body. All the same it might well be said, as in the newly emended violinist story, that she *ought* to allow it to remain for that hour—that it would be indecent in her to refuse.

Now some people are inclined to use the term "right" in such a way that it follows from the fact that you ought to allow a person to use your body for the hour he needs, that he has a right to use your body for the hour he needs, even though he has not been given that right by any person or act. They may say that it follows also that if you refuse, you act unjustly toward him. This use of the term is perhaps so common that it cannot be called wrong; nevertheless it seems to me to be an unfortunate loosening of what we would do better to keep a tight rein on. Suppose that box of chocolates I mentioned earlier had not been given to both boys jointly, but was given only to the older boy. There he sits, stolidly eating his way through the box, his small brother watching enviously. Here we are likely to say "You ought not to be so mean. You ought to give your brother some of those chocolates." My own view is that it just does not follow from the truth of this that the brother has any right to any of the chocolates. If the boy refuses to give his brother any, he is greedy, stingy, callous—but not unjust.

I suppose that the people I have in mind will say it does follow that the brother has a right to some of the chocolates, and thus that the boy does act unjustly if he refuses to give his brother any. But the effect of saying this is to obscure what we should keep distinct, namely the difference between the boy's refusal in this case and the boy's refusal in the earlier case, in which the box was given to both boys jointly, and in which the small brother thus had what was from any point of view clear title to half.

A further objection to so using the term "right" that from the fact that A ought to do a thing for B, it follows that B has a right against A that A do it for him, is that it is going to make the question of whether or not a man has a right to a thing turn on how easy it is to provide him with it; and this seems not merely unfortunate, but morally unacceptable. Take the case of Henry Fonda again. I said earlier that I had no right to the touch of his cool hand on my fevered brow, even though I needed it to save my life. I said it would be frightfully nice of him to fly in from the West Coast to provide me with it, but that I had no right against him that he should do so. But suppose he isn't on the West Coast. Suppose he has only to walk across the room, place a hand briefly on my brow—and lo, my life is saved. Then surely he ought to do it, it would be indecent to refuse. Is it to be said "Ah, well, it follows that in this case she has a right to the touch of his hand on her brow, and so it would be an injustice in him to refuse"? So that I have a right to it when it is easy for him to provide it, though no right when it's hard? It's rather a shocking idea that anyone's rights should fade away and disappear as it gets harder and harder to accord them to him.

So my own view is that even though you ought to let the violinist use your kidneys for the one hour he needs, we should not conclude that he has a right to do so—we should say that if you refuse, you are, like the boy who owns all the chocolates and will give none away, self-centered and callous, indecent in fact, but not unjust. And similarly, that even supposing a case in which a woman pregnant due to rape ought to allow the unborn person to use her body for the hour he needs, we should not conclude that he has a right to do so; we should conclude that she is self-centered, callous, indecent, but not unjust, if she refuses. The

complaints are no less grave; they are just different. However, there is no need to insist on this point. If anyone does wish to deduce "he has a right" from "you ought," then all the same he must surely grant that there are cases in which it is not morally required of you that you allow that violinist to use your kidneys, and in which he does not have a right to use them, and in which you do not do him an injustice if you refuse. And so also for mother and unborn child. Except in such cases as the unborn person has a right to demand it—and we were leaving open the possibility that there may be such cases—nobody is morally *required* to make large sacrifices, of health, of all other interests and concerns, of all other duties and commitments, for nine years, or even for nine months, in order to keep another person alive.

6. We have in fact to distinguish between two kinds of Samaritan: the **Good Samaritan** and what we might call the **Minimally Decent Samaritan**. The story of the Good Samaritan, you will remember, goes like this:

A certain man went down from Jerusalem to Jericho, and fell among thieves, which stripped him of his raiment, and wounded him, and departed, leaving him half dead.

And by chance there came down a certain priest that way; and when he saw him, he passed by on the other side.

And likewise a Levite, when he was at the place, came and looked on him, and passed by on the other side.

But a certain Samaritan, as he journeyed, came where he was; and when he saw him he had compassion on him.

And went to him, and bound up his wounds, pouring in oil and wine, and set him on his own beast, and brought him to an inn, and took care of him.

And on the morrow, when he departed, he took out two pence, and gave them to the host, and said unto him, "Take care of him; and whatsoever thou spendest more, when I come again, I will repay thee." 　　　　　　　　　　(Luke 10:30–35)

The Good Samaritan went out of his way, at some cost to himself, to help one in need of it. We are not told what the options were, that is, whether or not the priest and the Levite could have helped by doing less than the Good Samaritan did, but assuming they could have, then the fact they did nothing at all shows they were not even Minimally Decent Samaritans, not because they were not Samaritans, but because they were not even minimally decent.

These things are a matter of degree, of course, but there is a difference, and it comes out perhaps most clearly in the story of Kitty Genovese, who, as you will remember, was murdered while thirty-eight people watched or listened, and did nothing at all to help her. A Good Samaritan would have rushed out to give direct assistance against the murderer. Or perhaps we had better allow that it would have been a Splendid Samaritan who did this, on the ground that it would have involved a risk of death for himself. But the thirty-eight not only did not do this, they did not even trouble to pick up a phone to call the police. Minimally Decent Samaritanism would call for doing at least that, and their not having done it was monstrous.

After telling the story of the Good Samaritan, Jesus said "Go, and do thou likewise." Perhaps he meant that we are morally required to act as the Good Samaritan did. Perhaps he was urging people to do more than is morally required of them. At all events it seems plain that it was not morally required of any of the thirty-eight that he rush out to give direct assistance at the risk of his own life, and that it is not morally required of anyone that he give long stretches of his life—nine years or nine months—to sustaining the life of a person who has no special right (we were leaving open the possibility of this) to demand it.

Indeed, with one rather striking class of exceptions, no one in any country in the world is *legally* required to do anywhere near as much as this for anyone else. The class of exceptions is obvious. My main concern here is not the state of the law in respect to abortion, but it is worth drawing attention to the fact that in no state in this country is any man compelled by law to be even a Minimally Decent Samaritan to any person; there is no law under which charges could be brought against the thirty-eight who stood by while Kitty Genovese died. By contrast, in most states in this country women are compelled by law to be not merely Minimally Decent Samaritans, but Good Samaritans to unborn persons

inside them. This doesn't by itself settle anything one way or the other, because it may well be argued that there should be laws in this country—as there are in many European countries—compelling at least Minimally Decent Samaritanism.[8] But it does show that there is a gross injustice in the existing state of the law. And it shows also that the groups currently working against liberalization of abortion laws, in fact working toward having it declared unconstitutional for a state to permit abortion, had better start working for the adoption of Good Samaritan laws generally, or earn the charge that they are acting in bad faith.

I should think, myself, that Minimally Decent Samaritan laws would be one thing, Good Samaritan laws quite another, and in fact highly improper. But we are not here concerned with the law. What we should ask is not whether anybody should be compelled by law to be a Good Samaritan, but whether we must accede to a situation in which somebody is being compelled—by nature, perhaps—to be a Good Samaritan. We have, in other words, to look now at third-party interventions. I have been arguing that no person is morally required to make large sacrifices to sustain the life of another who has no right to demand them, and this even where the sacrifices do not include life itself; we are not morally required to be Good Samaritans or anyway Very Good Samaritans to one another. But what if a man cannot extricate himself from such a situation? What if he appeals to us to extricate him? It seems to me plain that there are cases in which we can, cases in which a Good Samaritan would extricate him. There you are, you were kidnapped, and nine years in bed with that violinist lie ahead of you. You have your own life to lead. You are sorry, but you simply cannot see giving up so much of your life to the sustaining of his. You cannot extricate yourself, and ask us to do so. I should have thought that—in light of his having no right to the use of your body—it was obvious that we do not have to accede to your being forced to give up so much. We can do what you ask. There is no injustice to the violinist in our doing so.

7. Following the lead of the opponents of abortion, I have throughout been speaking of the fetus merely as a person, and what I have been asking is whether or not the argument we began with, which

proceeds only from the fetus' being a person, really does establish its conclusion. I have argued that it does not.

But of course there are arguments and arguments, and it may be said that I have simply fastened on the wrong one. It may be said that what is important is not merely the fact that the fetus is a person, but that it is a person for whom the woman has a special kind of responsibility issuing from the fact that she is its mother. And it might be argued that all my analogies are therefore irrelevant—for you do not have that special kind of responsibility for that violinist, Henry Fonda does not have that special kind of responsibility for me. And our attention might be drawn to the fact that men and women both *are* compelled by law to provide support for their children.

I have in effect dealt (briefly) with this argument in section 4 above; but a (still briefer) recapitulation now may be in order. Surely we do not have any such "special responsibility" for a person unless we have assumed it, explicitly or implicitly. If a set of parents do not try to prevent pregnancy, do not obtain an abortion, and then at the time of birth of the child do not put it out for adoption, but rather take it home with them, then they have assumed responsibility for it, they have given it rights, and they cannot *now* withdraw support from it at the cost of its life because they now find it difficult to go on providing for it. But if they have taken all reasonable precautions against having a child, they do not simply by virtue of their biological relationship to the child who comes into existence have a special responsibility for it. They may wish to assume responsibility for it, or they may not wish to. And I am suggesting that if assuming responsibility for it would require large sacrifices, then they may refuse. A Good Samaritan would not refuse—or anyway, a Splendid Samaritan, if the sacrifices that had to be made were enormous. But then so would a Good Samaritan assume responsibility for that violinist; so would Henry Fonda, if he is a Good Samaritan, fly in from the West Coast and assume responsibility for me.

8. My argument will be found unsatisfactory on two counts by many of those who want to regard abortion as morally permissible. First, while I do argue that abortion is not impermissible, I do not argue that it is always permissible. There may well be

cases in which carrying the child to term requires only Minimally Decent Samaritanism of the mother, and this is a standard we must not fall below. I am inclined to think it a merit of my account precisely that it does *not* give a general yes or a general no. It allows for and supports our sense that, for example, a sick and desperately frightened fourteen-year-old schoolgirl, pregnant due to rape, may *of course* choose abortion, and that any law which rules this out is an insane law. And it also allows for and supports our sense that in other cases resort to abortion is even positively indecent. It would be indecent in the woman to request an abortion, and indecent in a doctor to perform it, if she is in her seventh month, and wants the abortion just to avoid the nuisance of postponing a trip abroad. The very fact that the arguments I have been drawing attention to treat all cases of abortion, or even all cases of abortion in which the mother's life is not at stake, as morally on a par ought to have made them suspect at the outset.

Secondly, while I am arguing for the permissibility of abortion in some cases, I am not arguing for the right to secure the death of the unborn child. It is easy to confuse these two things in that up to a certain point in the life of the fetus it is not able to survive outside the mother's body; hence removing it from her body guarantees its death. But they are importantly different. I have argued that you are not morally required to spend nine months in bed, sustaining the life of that violinist; but to say this is by no means to say that if, when you unplug yourself, there is a miracle and he survives, you then have a right to turn round and slit his throat. You may detach yourself even if this costs him his life; you have no right to be guaranteed his death, by some other means, if unplugging yourself does not kill him. There are some people who will feel dissatisfied by this feature of my argument. A woman may be utterly devastated by the thought of a child, a bit of herself, put out for adoption and never seen or heard of again. She may therefore want not merely that the child be detached from her, but more, that it die. Some opponents of abortion are inclined to regard this as beneath contempt—thereby showing insensitivity to what is surely a powerful source of despair. All the same, I agree that the desire for the child's death is not one which anybody may gratify, should it turn out to be possible to detach the child alive.

At this place, however, it should be remembered that we have only been pretending throughout that the fetus is a human being from the moment of conception. A very early abortion is surely not the killing of a person, and so is not dealt with by anything I have said here.

NOTES

1. I am very much indebted to James Thomson for discussion, criticism, and many helpful suggestions.
2. Daniel Callahan, *Abortion: Law, Choice and Morality* (New York, 1970), p. 373. This book gives a fascinating survey of the available information on abortion. The Jewish tradition is surveyed in David M. Feldman, *Birth Control in Jewish Law* (New York, 1968), Part 5, the Catholic tradition in John T. Noonan, Jr., "An Almost Absolute Value in History," in *The Morality of Abortion*, ed. John T. Noonan, Jr. (Cambridge, Mass., 1970).
3. The term "direct" in the arguments I refer to is a technical one. Roughly, what is meant by "direct killing" is either killing as an end in itself, or killing as a means to some end, for example, the end of saving someone else's life. See note 6, below, for an example of its use.
4. Cf. *Encyclical Letter of Pope Pius XI on Christian Marriage*, St. Paul Editions (Boston, n.d.), p. 32: "however much we may pity the mother whose health and even life is gravely imperiled in the performance of the duty allotted to her by nature, nevertheless what could ever be a sufficient reason for excusing in any way the direct murder of the innocent? This is precisely what we are dealing with here." Noonan (*The Morality of Abortion*, p. 43) reads this as follows: "What cause can ever avail to excuse in any way the direct killing of the innocent? For it is a question of that."
5. The thesis in (4) is in an interesting way weaker than those in (1), (2), and (3): they rule out abortion even in cases in which both mother *and* child will die if the abortion is not performed. By contrast, one who held the view expressed in (4) could consistently say that one needn't prefer letting two persons die to killing one.
6. Cf. the following passage from Pius XII, *Address to the Italian Catholic Society of Midwives*: "The baby in the maternal breast has the right to life immediately from God.—Hence there is no man,

no human authority, no science, no medical, eugenic, social, economic or moral 'indication' which can establish or grant a valid juridical ground for a direct deliberate disposition of an innocent human life, that is a disposition which looks to its destruction either as an end or as a means to another end perhaps in itself not illicit.—The baby, still not born, is a man in the same degree and for the same reason as the mother" (quoted in Noonan, *The Morality of Abortion*, p. 45).
7. The need for a discussion of this argument was brought home to me by members of the Society for Ethical and Legal Philosophy, to whom this paper was originally presented.
8. For a discussion of the difficulties involved, and a survey of the European experience with such laws, see *The Good Samaritan and the Law*, ed. James M. Ratcliffe (New York, 1966).

KEY TERMS

Slippery slope arguments
Right to life
Right to decide
Right of self-defense
Direct killing
Good Samaritan
Minimally Decent Samaritan

STUDY QUESTIONS

1. What has the debate about abortion traditionally been about? What is the slippery slope argument Thomson discusses at the beginning of her essay?
2. What is the argument against abortion, which centers on the right to life, that Thomson is arguing against in her piece? Do you find this argument convincing?
3. Describe Thomson's violinist case. What role does it play in her argument?
4. What is the "extreme view" and how does Thomson argue against it?
5. What is Thomson's preferred conception of the right to life? What does it imply about the morality of abortion?
6. Consider Thomson's burglar example. What is its relevance for her argument?

Thomson's Arguments

ROSALIND HURSTHOUSE

Rosalind Hursthouse is a Professor of Philosophy at the University of Auckland, New Zealand. She is best known for her development of virtue ethics, basing her account of morality on that of Aristotle. She is the author of On Virtue Ethics *and* Ethics, Humans, and Other Animals.

· ·

I shall here consider the well-known article, 'A Defense of Abortion',[1] by Judith Jarvis Thomson. She explicitly takes account of the fact that abortion is the termination of a pregnancy by discussing it in terms of the exercise of one's **right to determine what happens in or to one's own body**—the aspect of abortion which feminists have always emphasized. No other real case of killing involves the exercise of this right (though Thomson considers some imaginary ones); abortion does and is thereby unique.

One particularly important consequence of actually bringing in the fact that abortion arises in relation to pregnancy and is thereby unique is that quite a lot can be said in defence of abortion *without* wholesale commitment to other sorts of killing. Although Thomson allows, for the sake of the argument, the most conservative premise about the moral status of the fœtus (that it is morally on a par with an adult human being or a person), and argues for a fairly permissive position on abortion, she does not thereby commit herself to any correspondingly permissive line on infanticide, or murder, in general, as supporters of utilitarianism and the person view do.

This is not to say that she entirely avoids committal to, what I would say are, unacceptable consequences, nor, as I shall try to show, does she entirely avoid the fault of inappropriate black and white deliverances. She still has not brought in a large enough range of considerations as relevant. Nevertheless, her arguments represent a 'quantum jump' in their level

of sophistication when compared to those we have been considering, and for this reason I take the article as worth going through very carefully.

Before embarking on this detailed discussion, I should mention the article's most salient characteristics.

(1) Without herself believing it, Thomson allows the conservative opponents of abortion their premise that the fœtus is a human being or a person[2] from the moment of conception. She argues that, even granting this premise, abortion is permissible in a large number of cases.

(2) She explicitly does not attempt to argue that abortion is always permissible. On the contrary, she maintains that abortion is sometimes permissible, sometimes not—not 'according to the consequences' as utilitarianism says, but 'according to the circumstances' as all but the most 'conservative' opponent of abortion say. (Few non-Catholics subscribe to the view that abortion to save the mother's life is impermissible even when, without the abortion, both mother and child will die. In those circumstances, at least, abortion is justifiable.)

(3) As I mentioned above, she takes account of what is special about, or peculiar to, abortion as a form of killing, by discussing it in terms of the exercise of a right over one's own body.

(4) She allows that actions can be wrong *in different ways*. They can be wrong in being unjust, when they violate a right, but they can also be wrong because they are callous, cruel, selfish and so on.

From *Beginning Lives*, by Rosalind Hursthouse. © 1987 Blackwell Publishers.

2 Thomson's Arguments

Thomson begins by laying out what she takes the conservative argument against abortion to be.

> Every person has a **right to life**. So the fœtus has a right to life. No doubt the mother has a right to decide what shall happen in and to her body; everyone would grant that. But surely a person's right to life is stronger and more stringent than the mother's right to decide what happens in and to her body, and so outweighs it. So the fœtus may not be killed; an abortion may not be performed.[3]

Agreeing that it sounds plausible, she goes on to describe an imaginary case which, she says, 'suggests that something really is wrong with that plausible-sounding argument'. The imaginary case is one in which I wake up one morning to find that a kidney patient has been attached to my kidneys. If we stay thus attached then in nine months he will be cured of his fatal ailment and able to survive independently. But he will die if I detach myself before then, because, until he is cured he needs to be attached to someone else's kidneys and I alone have the right blood group to help. This case makes Thomson suspect something is wrong with the plausible-sounding argument for the following reason. Like the fœtus case, it is a conflict between the right to life and the right to decide what happens to and in your body. But in this case it is not obvious that the right to life completely overrides the right to decide what happens to one's body—that, morally speaking, I simply have to put up with it and stay plugged in to this man. After all, what if he needs not nine months, but nine years? Or the rest of my life?

Thomson concludes that it would be 'outrageous' to suppose that I would be morally obliged to spend the rest of my life attached to this man. (For no relevant reason, he is a violinist, so the example is always referred to as '**the violinist case**'.) But if I am not morally obliged to do so, something must be wrong—there must at least be some premises missing—in the plausible-sounding conservative argument.

To some people this sort of far-fetched example (which is but the first of many in Thomson's article) seems simply irrelevant. It may be that this reaction, though ill-grounded as it stands, can eventually be argued for (see below, p. [669]). But until it is argued for, we should accept the relevance of the role such examples play in argument—if I say such and such in one case (that the right to life overrides), I must agree that the same is true in another case *or* point to the morally relevant difference between the two cases. Of course, many morally relevant differences between pregnancy and finding that someone has attached my kidneys to a kidney patient immediately leap to mind, but many of these are discussed by Thomson later in the article. So far, all the example is supposed to have shown is that it is not obvious that the conservative premise about the fœtus's right to life is going to guarantee, without further assumptions, that abortion is impermissible in many cases. It suggests that the standard liberal premise about the woman's right to decide what happens to her body might, with some further assumptions, guarantee that abortion was permissible in many cases.

Conflicts Between Rights to Life

Thomson opens her attack by discussing, not the generality of cases, but the small number where what is at issue is the conflict between the fœtus's and the mother's right to life, and she justifies a woman's performing an abortion on herself in such cases by appeal to the right of self defence.

In discussing this justification in Chapter Two (Section 2) I claimed that it was not clear that 'if my choice lies between my life or an infant's it is straightforwardly permissible for me to kill the infant'. But according to Thomson this *is* clear; if I kill an innocent person to save my life, whether this be by infanticide or abortion or unplugging myself from the violinist, it is clear if anything is that I do *not* do what is impermissible. This is close to being a rock-bottom disagreement (though see below p. [666]) between Thomson and me so I shall leave it aside for the moment.

Suppose Thomson is right on this point, and hence that, even supposing the fœtus to have as much right to life as any child or adult, abortion by the mother to save her life is permissible. Does it follow that abortion to save the mother's life is permissible when performed by a third party? It clearly does not *follow*, for the reasons I gave in Chapter Two: the third party is not killing the foetus in *self* defence but in defence of the mother, and nothing said so far has justified a third party's supporting the mother's right to life rather than the foetus's. Indeed, it might be said that no third party is justified in taking it upon themselves to choose who will live and who will die when two lives are in conflict.

But Thomson argues that choosing, as a third party, between the mother's life and the foetus's (or the mother's right to life and the foetus's) is not a case of choosing between people with equal rights. The foetus and the mother have an equal right to life, that is true, but the mother also has a right to decide what happens to her body, because she owns it, it is hers, not the foetus's.

Criticizing this argument, Glover remarks (a) that it is inappropriate to describe someone's body as their property, as if it were their house or coat and (b) that even if this were allowed, property rights do not have the moral weight that Thomson is giving them here.[4] If I am on a river bank and see two drowning people reaching for the only life-belt, it is surely not true that I ought to intervene and make sure its owner is the one who survives. Actually, Thomson cautiously says that she is arguing only that a doctor *may* perform an abortion (when the mother's life is at stake) not that the doctor ought to. But the criticism still applies. Is it even morally permissible to intervene and choose which life to secure solely on grounds of property? Is it morally permissible for me to choose to take the life support machine from one person and attach it to someone else who will die without it, solely on the grounds that she is very rich and owns it? I do not think so.

However, although Thomson herself uses the analogy of the house and coat, I think that these examples are neither necessary nor appropriate, and betray a misunderstanding of the concept of the right over one's own body. This is a 'property right' in the old sense of 'property' according to which it covers not only external goods, but anything which is one's own, and which one has a right to or in. When the concept of a natural right was really flourishing (in

the seventeenth and eighteenth centuries) the favoured examples of things that were one's own 'property' were one's life, limbs, body and actions and it would have been odder to describe something morally insignificant, like a coat or life-belt, as someone's property. So what we need, as the parallel case, is one in which two people with an equal right to life differ in that if a third party intervenes to save one he or she will also be protecting some further serious natural right of that person. Perhaps while they are both alive, one is, innocently, causing the other one great agony. To kill the first is both to protect the right to life of the second and also, say, to protect that person's right not to be subjected to unnecessary suffering (supposing that that is a natural right). This is not an ideal parallel case, because, at the opposite extreme from coats, preventable great agony is perhaps too morally significant. It may have much more weight than the right to decide what happens to one's body in the case of abortion. But—and this is probably significant—I cannot think of any other.

Violating the Right to Life

The opening moves in Thomson's argument are fairly self-contained; they could indeed be regarded as a mini-article about 'Conflicts between rights to life'. But from now on the argument takes a much more radical turn, to consider cases in which the mother's life is not at risk. Since 'the right to life' is, in such cases, not something that weighs on both sides and cancels out, it becomes necessary to consider what it amounts to, and hence what counts as violating it.

Does it, for instance, include the right to be given the bare minimum one needs to survive? One might think it was bound to (and traditionally it has been taken to include the basic necessities of food, drink and shelter). But Thomson argues that it does not, since something an individual needs to survive might not be anything that he had a right to be given by anyone. Suppose that what I need in order to get over an operation is a pint of your blood. Do I have a right to it? Thomson thinks not—it would be kind of you to give it to me but you are not obliged by justice to do so. In terms of the virtues, it would be an act of charity (of loving kindness or benevolence) to do so, but you would not act unjustly in refusing. Thomson's reason for saying that I do not have a right to a pint of your blood would be, once again, that it is *yours* not mine.

The point of this argument is to show that the fœtus's right to life does not include the right to be given the use of the mother's body, despite needing this to survive. And since depriving the fœtus of the use of the mother's body is, as things are, killing it, it turns out the fœtus's right to life does not include the right not to be killed—or at least, it does not include the right not to be killed by the mother. So she does not violate its right to life by killing it.

One might think that if the right to life did not amount at least to the right not to be killed then it did not amount to anything at all. But in the next move in her argument Thomson suggests that the right to life consists in the right not to be killed *unjustly*. What she means by this in general is left unspecified, but she does give us one sort of example. I would be killing someone unjustly (a) trivially, if I killed them without their actual or presumed consent, and (b) by depriving them of something they had a right to. The clause (b) gives the backing to the killing's being unjust—it is unjust because it is a violation of a right.

So let us take a case in which someone does have a right to the use of my body to survive precisely because I have given them that right; I say, 'It's yours, to use as you need for the next (say) nine months.' If, having given them the right to use my body in this way, I then deprive them of its use and thereby kill them, this, in Thomson's view, is an unjust killing, and thereby a violation of the right to life.

Thomson already holds that the fœtus does not have a right to the use of the mother's body *which follows from*, or is included in, its right to life. But now the question arises, does it have the right, or could it acquire it, in some other way? It might for instance be said that a woman gives the fœtus that right by becoming pregnant. If that were so then abortions would turn out to be unjust killings and hence violations of the right to life after all.

Against this Thomson asserts it as a premise that a woman cannot be said to have given the fœtus the right to use her body if she is pregnant because of rape. Plausibly the pregnancy must result from voluntary intercourse. (Plausibly too, though Thomson does not mention this, the woman—or perhaps girl in this context—must know that intercourse may result in pregnancy: the innocent or mentally deficient who have intercourse without realizing that this is how pregnancy comes about cannot be regarded as having given the fœtus the right to use their bodies.) However, this still leaves a very large number of cases; does Thomson agree that in all cases of pregnancy due to voluntary intercourse in full knowledge of the facts of life the mother could be said to have given the fœtus the right to use her body—that the intercourse as it were amounts to an offer to have one's body thus used?

She clearly does not, but her argument at this point depends on two rather unsatisfactory analogies. In one she imagines that children come about by people-seeds taking root in one's carpet; this may happen even if one has gone to great trouble to try to prevent it by putting fine mesh screens over one's windows. In the other analogy, she does not consider children, but how people might acquire a right to use my house, and says it would be absurd to suppose that someone had acquired it by just blundering in, through a window I had happened to open, behind bars I had installed to keep people out which happened to have a defect. In each case I go to some trouble to try to keep people-seeds or people out; in each case there is supposed to be a way that would guarantee keeping them out, say with sealed windows, but it cannot be said that I am responsible for their being in my house and that hence they have a right to it simply because I do not go in for this extreme measure.

These analogies are obviously supposed to be with contraception; despite the woman's efforts not to become pregnant, she does. Given that she was trying not to, her voluntary intercourse cannot count as an offer, conferring a right, to have her body used by the fœtus. But the difficulty with the people-seed analogy is that, because it is so far-fetched, it lacks all the background that enables one (sometimes) to make up one's mind. Do these people-seeds just root for nine months? What are the available alternatives to uprooting and killing them—can they be transplanted, can you swap your house for nine months with someone who wants children . . .? The difficulty with the other analogy is that it misses out the crucial aspect of the fœtus being dependent on the use of the woman's body for its survival. The analogy that is needed would be a case in which, somehow, by opening the window I ran a (small but recognizable) risk of someone's coming in whose survival depended on his staying.

Suppose I am living in a house in France in 1944. As I happen to know, its earlier occupiers had run it as a link in a chain smuggling Jews out of Germany, and—as I happen to know—the simple signal they use to show that the hiding places were free was to leave a window open. If all the windows were shut it meant 'Danger, keep away'. The chain was broken years ago; I kept all the windows shut throughout the first summer just in case but heard not even a rumour of any Jew trying to hide anywhere in the village. By the second summer, the risk seemed negligible, so I allowed myself to open the occasional window when it was very hot. Suppose one night a Jewish refugee climbs in, not having heard the chain was broken, and interpreting the open window in the way I knew there was the possibility someone might. His survival depends on my sheltering him, as I knew the survival of anyone who interpreted the open window in the old way would. Can I now say that I am not responsible for his being in my house and dependent for his survival on me? If not, then it may well be that Thomson's analogy lacks the very feature which is relevant, *viz.* that someone's survival hangs on what is done. (If someone thinks it is essential that this case should provide some parallel with care about contraception, which I in fact do not, it can be read in. This case can be seen as analogous to one in which a woman becomes pregnant after she had good reason to suppose she was past the age of conceiving. For the first year she uses contraception, by the second year, the risk seems negligible, so she stops.)

The point of this section of the argument is to show that the fœtus may be killed without its right to life being violated in all those cases in which the woman has not given the fœtus the right to use her body. It is taken as a premise that the woman has obviously not given the fœtus such a right in the case of pregnancy due to rape, and argued that she has not done so in (any?) cases in which she has become

pregnant despite practising contraception. So, Thomson concludes, the best that the conservative argument can establish is that there are *some* cases in which abortions are unjust killings and hence violations of the right to life—say, when a woman tries to get pregnant, and succeeds and then changes her mind for some reason—and this is a far weaker position than the conservative view is standardly content with.

There is a regrettably loose use of the term 'right', Thomson says, according to which it is said to follow from the fact that I ought to do something to or for someone that they have a right that I do so. Someone who used the term in this loose way might argue against Thomson in the following way. 'Rights do not arise only because someone has voluntarily assumed responsibility. Take pregnancy arising from rape. I agree that the woman has not *given* the fœtus the right to use her body. Nevertheless, as things have unfortunately turned out, the fœtus (who, remember, we are assuming is to be regarded as morally on a par with any other person) is dependent for its survival on the use of her body. So obviously she ought to allow it to use her body. So in that sense, the fœtus has a right to the use of her body.'

Thomson's major objection to this use of the term 'right' is that it obliterates the real distinctions there are to be drawn between acting unjustly (violating someone's right) and acting wrongly in other ways—greedily, callously, cruelly and so on. Acting in the latter ways is no less wrong than acting unjustly, but the ways are different. These distinctions have already been prefigured in the discussion above. To give a pint of blood when this involves trouble and perhaps serious risk on my part would be an act of charity or kindness; to refuse to give a pint of blood when I am on the spot and can thereby save someone's life, without trouble or risk, would be callous. But it would not be unjust.

However, in the context of this particular argument about abortion, Thomson sees no need to insist on this point—as long as the people who are using 'right' in the loose way do not get confused about what is 'morally required'. They may say that I 'have a right to' everything that you ought to do for me, as long as they grant that, even in this sense of 'right', I do *not* have a right that anyone should 'make large sacrifices, of health, of all other interests and concerns, of all other duties and commitments, for nine years, or even for nine months' in order to keep me alive. That is, no one is morally required to keep me alive at such a cost—unless someone has given me a (real) right, and then *he* is morally required even at such a cost.

The point of this section of the argument is twofold. It identifies a muddleheaded way in which someone might object to Thomson's argument so far (by relying, without realizing it, on the loose sense of 'have a right'). Once it is clear that what is really at issue, whether described in terms of 'having a right' or not, is whether one person is *morally required* to do or undergo certain things in order to save another's life, we are ready to go on to recognize the difference between the **Minimally Decent Samaritan** and the **Good Samaritan**.

The Samaritans

In the Bible story of the Good Samaritan (Luke 10: 30–5) there are at least two people, the priest and the Levite, who act wrongly or 'indecently' in Thomson's terminology; they see a naked wounded man lying half dead by the side of the road, and, turning a blind eye on this person who obviously is in desperate need of help, each one 'passed by on the other side'. These two, in Thomson's terminology, fail to act as even Minimally Decent Samaritans. The third man, the Good Samaritan, acts very well—kindly, compassionately, generously; he stops, binds up the man's wounds, puts him on his own beast and takes him to an inn, and further, takes care of him until the next day, and further, before he leaves, he asks the innkeeper to go on looking after the man, and further, he pays for some of this care in advance and further he promises to pay whatever else the care costs next time he comes.

If that is the sort of thing that a Good Samaritan does, what would a Minimally Decent Samaritan do? Well, not as much as the Good Samaritan and not as little as the two people who act so callously and selfishly. The Minimally Decent Samaritan at least stops to see if there is something fairly trouble-free he could do to help; he can surely spare something to put on the worst of the wounds and the time to take the wounded man to the nearest inn even if at that point he seizes the opportunity to shift the responsibility on to someone else and hurry away. There is room for some disagreement here; some people might say that all that decency required was stopping and doing what one could in a few minutes before hurrying on. On the other side, some people might say decency requires not just shuffling the responsibility off when you get to the inn, but making sure someone else, e.g. the innkeeper, has taken over. Still, these are disagreements within a framework of agreement—that there is acting as a Minimally Decent Samaritan and there is acting better than that, as a Good Samaritan.

The point of this distinction is that we are, Thomson thinks, morally required to be Minimally Decent Samaritans, but we are not morally required to be Good Samaritans. And the point of claiming this in the context of abortion is that Thomson thinks that in many cases of carrying a child to term, the woman is being, not just a Minimally Decent but a Good Samaritan to the unborn person inside her.

She then returns again to the question of third party intervention. Earlier, she had concluded that the fœtus's right to life did not include the right not to be killed *by the mother*, for *she* might refuse the fœtus the use of her body, and be within her rights to do so. But this left open the question of whether a third party, i.e. the doctor who performs the abortion, was entitled to intervene and protect her right in this way. But now we can consider the question in a new version. Suppose that someone has somehow got themselves into a situation in which they are being compelled to act as a Good Samaritan would, but against their own wishes. Since they are not morally required to act as a Good Samaritan, it seems that, without being indecent, they can try to extricate themselves from this predicament, and one way of trying would be to ask a third party to get them out. Can a third person do so with minimal decency? According to Thomson, intervention in some cases would not simply be an act of minimal decency, but what a Good Samaritan would do. (I must confess I cannot see why she says it is what a Good Samaritan would do.) So where a woman, in being pregnant, is being compelled to act as a Good Samaritan, a doctor may extricate her from this situation by performing an abortion for her, and herself act as a Good Samaritan in so doing.

Conclusions

Of course, all this is consistent with there being some cases in which carrying the child to term calls for only minimal decency. Thomson leaves unspecified what these might be, but she does assert that it would be positively indecent for a woman to request (and for a doctor to perform) an abortion at seven months for a trivial reason, such as to avoid the nuisance of postponing a leisure trip abroad. She claims it as a merit of her account that it does not yield a general yes or a general no on the question of whether abortion is permissible or impermissible, but rather supports the view that some abortions are and some are not. Moreover (though she does not mention this point), this view that some abortions are impermissible (e.g. the sort just mentioned) whereas others are obviously permissible (e.g. a sick and terrified fourteen-year-old, pregnant due to rape) is not essentially dependent upon an appeal to the varying status of the foetus, as in the mixed strategy, for the argument throughout has been allowing the conservative premise that the foetus is a person from the moment of conception. Late abortions due to changes of mind for trivial reasons will be indecent not essentially because the foetus has become a person, but rather because, assuming it to have been a person from the moment of conception, the mother assumes responsibility for it and thereby gives it rights if she knowingly allows it to use her body to survive for several months. Once she has done this, she cannot (with minimal decency) change her mind for trivial reasons. We may compare this with another example Thomson gives: a couple might decide to have a child they have conceived adopted, simply because they do not want children. If they had taken all reasonable precautions against conception, and had nontrivial reasons against having an abortion, then, Thomson thinks, this would be all right, because the child does not have a right to them as (acting) parents just in virtue of their biological relationships.

But if they try to conceive the child, and then do not put it out for adoption but take it home with them—then they have given the child rights, and they cannot now (with minimal decency) arrange to have the child adopted because they have changed their minds and decided they do not want children at the moment after all.

3 Discussion and Further Criticisms

Thomson's article raises a number of particularly interesting and difficult issues. I shall concentrate on one central criticism, namely that her concentration on the single consideration of *rights* leads her to overlook the force of the other considerations which she has, very properly, introduced. Briefly, I shall argue that the most her arguments could hope to establish is that abortion (assuming the foetus is a human being or a person) is frequently not unjust (the violation of a right), leaving it open whether abortion is usually, in her own words, 'self-centred, callous [or] indecent' and hence impermissible for these reasons. It is to her credit that, instead of restricting herself to the blanket descriptions 'right/wrong' or 'permissible/impermissible/required', she has introduced into the discussion the more complex considerations of justice, callousness and self-centredness, and indeed the distinction between the minimally decent and the very good. But she mostly overlooks the force of these, concentrating almost exclusively instead on justice, in the form of questions about rights.

The preoccupation with rights shows up in two ways:

(1) In relation to the only form of the conservative argument that she considers seriously.
(2) In relation to two assumptions which dominate much of her discussion.

The Conservative Argument

John Finnis,[5] in an article written in response to Thomson's, criticized her concentration on rights, and in her reply Thomson said:

. . . his main complaint against me in the part of his paper which deals with rights is that I was wrong to discuss them at all—my doing so 'needlessly complicates and confuses the issue.' I find this puzzling. My aim was to raise doubts about the argument that abortion is impermissible because the fœtus is a person and all persons have a right to life; and how is one to do that without attending to rights?[6]

Now it is true that Thomson does begin the original article by saying that she is going to raise doubts about this argument:

> Opponents of abortion commonly spend most of their time establishing that the fœtus is a person, and hardly any time explaining the step from there to the impermissibility of abortion . . . I suggest that the step they take is neither easy nor obvious, that it calls for closer examination than it is commonly given, and that when we do give it this closer examination we shall feel inclined to reject it. I propose, then, that we grant that the fœtus is a person from the moment of conception. How does the argument go from here? Something like this, I take it. Every person has a right to life. So the fœtus has a right to life. No doubt the mother has a right to decide what shall happen in and to her body; everyone would grant that. But surely a person's right to life is stronger and more stringent than the mother's right to decide what happens in and to her body, and so outweighs it. So the fœtus may not be killed; an abortion may not be performed.[7]

And that argument is indeed the one she goes on to 'raise doubts about' in some detail, as we have seen.

But, having raised these doubts, she is entitled to conclude only that *this* version of the argument does not establish that, if the fœtus is a person, abortion is impermissible. If what you have done is show that a particular argument does not work, then that is *all* you have shown—you have not shown that its conclusion is false. But by the end of the article she is claiming that this is what she has argued: 'I *do* argue that abortion is not impermissible', 'I *am* arguing for the permissibility of abortion in some cases' (my italics).

The end of the article would be, if not justified, at least not a *non sequitur* if she had maintained that *the*

argument had to take the form she imposes on it. But it would have been most implausible of her to maintain this, for the following reason. As she herself notes there are other versions of 'the' argument which do not mention the right to life; for example, the fœtus is a person, the fœtus is an innocent person, 'directly' killing an innocent person is impermissible, so abortion is impermissible. One may read Thomson as dismissing this, and similar versions of 'the' argument on the grounds (a) that they all make killing in self defence impermissible (and indeed they do), and (b) that this is plainly false—killing in self defence is not impermissible. Now I would not criticize her for simply assuming (b) with no argument— she has to be allowed some premises. But as versions of a conservative argument against most abortions, these cannot be dismissed so readily. Suppose they were each amended—as some people do amend them—to rule out all direct killing of the innocent *except* in self defence. Then they are still arguments against a third party saving the mother's life at the expense of the fœtus (which she discusses only in terms of the right to life version) and they are still arguments against abortion on any other grounds[8]— which she also discusses only in terms of her version.

Two Assumptions

It may be that Thomson overlooks the possibility that other versions of the conservative argument might prove challenging because of her reliance on the first of the two assumptions I mentioned above. These, as I said, reflect her obsession with rights, and shape much of her discussion. They are:

> *Assumption 1* The only thing I am morally required to do is *not violate other people's rights.*
> *Assumption 2* Other people have a right 'against' me (i.e. I have a moral duty or requirement in relation to them) only if I have voluntarily assumed a special responsibility for them.

These two assumptions (or something remarkably close to them) can be seen at work on the several occasions on which Thomson argues that I may (I am not morally required not to) deprive someone of, or deny them, something they need for survival *because* they do not have a right to it (Assumption 1); where the reason why they don't have a right to it is that I have not given them that right by voluntarily assuming a special responsibility for them (Assumption 2). Someone might summarize her article as follows:

'Even supposing the fœtus to be a person from the moment of conception, it is in only a few cases that a woman has a duty, or is morally required, to carry a child to term rather than have an abortion. For she is morally required to do this only if having an abortion would be violating a right of the fœtus and hence an unjust killing (Assumption 1). But the fœtus has a right to the continued use of her body only if she has voluntarily assumed a special responsibility for it (Assumption 2).

'This is clearly shown by the case of the violinist, who (by Assumption 2) has no right to the use of my body. I would be being a Good rather than a Minimally Decent Samaritan if I stayed hooked up to him, because I am not morally required to stay hooked up; and I am not required to stay hooked up because he does not have that right (Assumption 1).'

It was within the assumptions of this argument that I produced the example about living in the house which used to be a refuge for Jews escaping from the Nazis. Leaving the argument itself uncriticized I produced the example to suggest that contrary to the implication of Thomson's analogies, a woman who had voluntary intercourse, even with contraception, could be regarded as thereby assuming a special responsibility towards any fœtus that resulted.

But now let us criticize the assumptions themselves. Consider Assumption 2: why should it be so confidently assumed that I can land myself with responsibilities only through my own voluntary actions, rather than get saddled with them by accident? Suppose someone abandons a baby on my doorstep. If I do not realize this has happened, and the baby dies of exposure during the night, this could not in any way be said to be my fault. The baby is not my responsibility—I did not even know it was there. But suppose I find the baby there when I am putting the milk out. Can I just shut the door again, saying

'No responsibility of mine'? It seems to me that I cannot. By sheer bad luck I have been saddled with the responsibility of this baby simply because whoever abandoned it picked my doorstep and I happened to open the door. And it will remain my responsibility until I can find someone else, or some institution, to take it on. (In many countries this will not be too difficult; I can take it to the police and then it becomes their responsibility.)

'But', it might be said, 'even if you can acquire a special responsibility for this baby just through the accident of its being on your doorstep and your opening the door, that doesn't mean it has thereby acquired a right in relation to you. To assume it has a right that you take it in just because you ought to take it in is to use "has a right" in exactly the loose extended sense that Thomson discusses.'

This response is justified with respect to the question of *what establishes rights*. But in connection with Thomson, all it does is direct one's attention to the first assumption. Let us accept that the baby does not have a right 'against' me that I bring it in. But if it is also granted that I cannot just shut the door on it, that it is morally incumbent on me to bring it in, then here is something that I am morally required to do for someone which is not a case of their having the right against me that I do it. So the first assumption is false.

Although it is, I think, clear that much of what Thomson says involves Assumptions 1 and 2, other things she says seem obviously inconsistent with them. For one thing, she could hardly make Assumption 2 without making the so-called 'right to life' no right at all. But (although she severely limits what the right to life involves) she agreed that everyone has the right to life; and this cannot possibly be because each one of us has voluntarily assumed a special responsibility to everyone else.

But the really interesting inconsistency lies in the fact that the baby on the doorstep example I used above to disprove Assumption 1 is simply a variation on the Samaritan story. It is indecent simply to turn a blind eye on someone who is in need of help you can give if they are not to die; a minimally decent person does not simply shut the door or pass by on the other side. And though we are not morally required to act as Good

Samaritans, we are morally required to act as minimally decent ones. And if Thomson herself says this,
how can she be supposed to make Assumption 1?

I think this is a point on which she is confused,
and the confusion occurs at a pivotal point in the argument. Assumption 1 (that the only moral requirement is not to be unjust, i.e. we are not, in effect,
morally required to act as Minimally Decent Samaritans) is operating until the distinction between the
two sorts of Samaritan is implicitly introduced. That
is, the earlier moves fail to anticipate what a big difference the introduction of considerations about callousness, self-centredness, or indecency, is going to
make. Up until this point, the only question allowed
is 'Would it be unjust of me to unhook myself from
the violinist?'

Once these considerations *are* introduced, the all-
important question becomes 'Would it be callous,
self-centred or indecent of me in some other way, to
unhook myself from the violinist?' But Thomson
does not explicitly address herself to that question.
Instead she says that 'nobody is morally *required*' to
stay hooked up 'for nine years or even nine months'
in order to keep another person alive—except that is,
in the cases where the other person has a right to
demand it.

But this is a fatal equivocation. If by 'nobody is
morally required to', Thomson means 'no one would
be unjust who refused to' then she has indeed argued
for this—but its (putative) truth has nothing to do
with the question 'Would someone be callous, etc. if
they refused to?' If, on the other hand, by 'nobody is
morally required to' she really does mean 'no one
would be callous, self-centred or indecent who refused to' then she has indeed answered the all-im-
portant question—but she has answered it with only
the barest unargued assertion.

That 'Would it be callous, etc.?' is the 'all-impor-
tant question', and hence the one for which argument
rather than bare assertion is crucial, can easily be
shown.

According to Thomson herself, being callous,
self-centred or indecent is 'no less grave' than being
unjust; we are morally required not to do it. And
although not being indecent is a far cry from being
a Good Samaritan, it is frequently being a minimally decent one. So we are morally required to be

Minimally Decent Samaritans. Now let us take this
point back to the beginning of the article and 'the'
conservative argument against abortion.

The claim that we are all morally required to act
as Minimally Decent Samaritans immediately yields
a new version of the argument. Something like this:
there are ways of treating people which are morally
indecent (for instance, arranging their death when
they need only nine months effort from you to survive), the foetus is a person and needs its mother's
body for only nine months to survive, so most abortions are morally indecent. So no Minimally Decent
Samaritan would have one (in most cases). So they
are impermissible (one is morally required not to
have them, or perform them) in most cases.

Of course, Thomson could, and undoubtedly
would, reject *this* instance of what is morally indecent, since she takes it as an assumption that someone
who stays hooked up to the violinist for nine months
is not just a Minimally Decent but a Good Samaritan. But *that* is the very assumption which has not
been argued for at all.

Refusing to Sustain

Now that we are clear about the way in which the
violinist case is central, let us look at it again. The
fundamental claim is that, in the violinist case, I am
not morally required to stay hooked up to him for
nine months—it would not be callous, or selfish, or
self-centred, or indecent in some other way of me to
unhook myself and let him die.

My difficulty here really is over allowing the argument to get started. I agreed with Thomson that the
violinist does not *have a right* that I stay hooked up to
him. I also agree with her that I would not be acting
indecently if I refused to stay hooked up to him, in
bed, for the rest of my life; and that I would be acting
indecently if all he needed was one hour's use of my
kidneys to survive and I refused him that. But I do
not share her confidence that, between this great
spread of a lifetime, or even nine years, which cannot
be required of one, and an hour, which can, the nine
months so certainly belongs on the nine years/life-
time side. I wonder how far Thomson is prepared to
extend the one hour side. Suppose he needs a day? A
week? A month? Would it still be callous to refuse?

In the attempt to get clearer about what to think about the violinist case we might turn to consider what we would say about other cases in which sheer chance lands one in the position of choosing between letting a stranger die or giving up some substantial amount of one's time and effort to enable them to survive. There are not, I think, many such cases. One, which was standard fare in fiction until the establishment of the telephone, is that of the wanderer who arrives sick unto death on my doorstep and has to be very carefully nursed for weeks or even months until he recovers. At least traditionally it is always assumed in such cases, I think, that the stranger *cannot* be left to die, that we are morally required to take him in, even in the full knowledge that he will, say, be on our hands for the next four months or so (because of the snows or the rains). Closely related examples still occur at sea: if we find someone adrift we are morally required to pick him up and not leave him to die, even in the full knowledge that he will make life in the boat physically miserable (because of shortage of food and space) and that we shall not be able to contact another boat to take him on board for months.

A different sort of case has resulted from recent developments in information processing. Leukaemia victims can sometimes be saved by bone-marrow transplants, but at present it is often difficult if not impossible to find suitable bone-marrow. A patient's closest relatives are the best bet, but if their marrow is not suitable, or if the patient has no close relatives then usually there is nothing further that can be done. But in the United States they have started putting information about people's marrow type on computer and centralizing all this information. Recently a search through the listings yielded just one person whose marrow could save the life of a particular young man dying of leukaemia. The hospital wrote to the person telling them about this and asking for their help (of course all the expenses were to be paid). And the person refused.

The hospital did not divulge the reasons for refusing—perhaps indeed they were not given— and perhaps the person had reasons which would justify the refusal. But, personally, reading about it, I was shocked. I agree it is quite something suddenly to drop everything one is doing, fly from one side of America to the other, have an operation surrounded by strangers, and be in some pain. I can see how someone might find the prospect frightening and upsetting and want to put it off, or, failing that, avoid it completely. But—to save someone's life? You cannot refuse to do something just because it is frightening and unpleasant and a bit painful when it is a matter of someone else's life, can you? As I say, I thought not, and that, though it was indeed 'tough luck' in Thomson's words on the person to find themselves landed in this position, there was only one morally decent way out of it—to try to save the patient's life.

These cases lead me to conclude that a significant amount of time and trouble, worry and risk, may be morally required of one, to save someone's life even when only chance has brought about a circumstance in which one's choice lies between giving that time and trouble, or letting someone die.

It is true that the preceding cases are not just like Thomson's violinist case. But then it in turn is not just like pregnancy. In her case I am (a) bed-ridden, (b) in enforced communicating company with a stranger, and (c) like that for a whole nine months. It is presumably the fact that I am bed-ridden which licenses her describing the case (by implication) as one in which I have to sacrifice my other duties and commitments and that fact plus the presence of this stranger which makes it one in which I have to sacrifice many of my other interests and concerns. I cannot do my job, I cannot visit my sick mother, I cannot go to my sister's wedding, I cannot go to the films, I cannot go swimming, I cannot read (well, perhaps the violinist is a great talker), I cannot have a confidential conversation with anyone and I cannot make love. And all of this for a whole nine months. But the usual pregnancy does not make one bed-ridden, and even when it does, very rarely for nine months; nor is the fœtus, even assuming it to be a person, someone whose presence rules out reading, private conversations, and sex.

Now *if* what I had to do to save someone's life was spend nine whole months bed-ridden, in their constant company, with all that that entailed, then that, one might say, demands a great deal more than either nine months of nursing (when I still have some time to myself, and I am on my feet and have some private life) or a day or so bed-ridden, surrounded by strangers, preparing for and recovering from an operation (which is only a day or so, not nine months). So someone might agree with my judgement about the other cases, but agree with Thomson's about the violinist. But then most cases of pregnancy are more like the other cases than they are like that of the violinist. I am not sure what I think about the violinist case, but I am sure that the more I make it akin to the average pregnancy (I am not bed-ridden, can lead my normal life for a lot of the nine months, etc.) the more certain I become that anyone who finds themselves in the violinist situation *is* morally required to put up with it; that it would be callous, or cowardly, or self-indulgent or self-centred to refuse cold-bloodedly. (I say 'cold-bloodedly' because if you had to decide quickly whether to put up with it or not you might panic about the responsibility and refuse or pull out the plug without really thinking. And then it would not be true that, in full knowledge of what you were doing, you had deliberately chosen to let someone die rather than endure whatever was needed, and hence not true that you had made a callous or cowardly or self-indulgent or whatever choice.)

So I conclude that Thomson does not manage to establish that abortion is, in many cases, permissible, while granting that the fœtus is a person. *If* it were granted that the fœtus is a person most pregnancies would be most similar to cases in which someone faced with a choice between letting someone die and putting up with what was needed to save them would be morally required to endure it; to refuse would be callous or cowardly or self-indulgent, etc. So, *if* the fœtus is a person many abortions would be callous or cowardly or self-indulgent, etc.—and impermissible.

4 Abortion as Special

Three Features

That Thomson should fail to establish the permissibility of abortion, in almost any case but self defence, is not particularly surprising, given that she began by conceding to the conservatives their premise that the fœtus is a person, even in the earliest stages of pregnancy. In doing so, one might say, she set herself an impossible task, and can hardly be criticized for failing to achieve it.

But one might well criticize her for believing that she could succeed. Believing she could succeed amounts to believing that the feminists' appeal to the right over one's own body is enough to meet head on the most conservative position over the status of the fœtus, without the need to appeal to anything that is special about abortion. And that, I would maintain, is a mistake.

At the beginning of this chapter, I criticized the exponents of the person view and utilitarianism for failing to take account of the important uniqueness of abortion as a case of killing. Thomson's article, I said, avoids this fault 'to a certain extent', by discussing abortion in terms of the right to determine what happens in or to one's own body. No other real case of killing involves the exercise of this right; abortion does and is thereby unique. However, that abortion, as a case of killing, uniquely involves the exercise of the right is far from being its only special feature, and I would maintain that the fundamental flaw in Thomson's article is that this is the only special feature she clearly recognizes. This flaw underlies her singular concentration on rights which I criticized in the preceding section, but it shows up in many other ways too.

As I said above, it shows up in the very task the article sets itself. The very idea that one could show that in many cases of abortion, other than abortion to save the mother's life, the only relevant consideration was the woman's right to do as she chose with her own body—that the status of the fœtus and whether or not it was a person was not relevant—is a mistake.

Abortion has not just one, but several special features, and it is a mistake to ignore any of them. One is indeed the one Thomson brings out—that it is the exercise of one's (putative) right to determine what happens in and to one's own body. But another is that the fœtus is not a person—not like the violinist or any ordinary average adult one might find oneself involved with. Notwithstanding my wholesale attack on the person view, I have never attempted to deny that obvious truth, and it is noteworthy that Thomson's article becomes particularly implausible at just the point at which she has to maintain that unhooking oneself from the violinist, when one's own life is not at stake, is morally permissible. Cold-bloodedly causing the death of another adult, communicating, conscious human being with, it is reasonable to suppose, his own family and friends, interests, hopes and plans, just because you have a (putative) right to do so, is bound to be shockingly callous, and it is important that causing the death of a foetus, particularly in its early stages, is not *just* like that. As I indicated in the second chapter, my own view on the moral status of the foetus is that, as a potential human being, it is morally unique, and hence that abortion is, as it were, especially special, in being the killing of such a being. But whatever view one holds about the status of the foetus, it remains true that abortion is not *just* like killing an average adult human, with his own complicated involvement in an ongoing life.

But these two features (that abortion is the exercise of one's right over one's body, and that it is not just like the killing of an ordinary adult) are not the only two ways in which abortion is special as a form of killing. Its third extremely important feature is that it is the termination of a pregnancy and there are many morally relevant differences between pregnancy and the violinist case. These, put at their simplest, are (a) that their effects or upshots are very different, and (b) that their causes are very different.

The difference between the effects of staying hooked up to the violinist on the one hand, and going through with a pregnancy on the other, is huge. The issue, in the violinist case, is always, and only, my present physical condition. Putting aside again the self defence case, the only question is, can I stand remaining in this condition for the next nine months for his sake? I do not have any worries at all about the future beyond these nine months. But (putting aside again the case of abortion to save the woman's life) very few abortions are sought because the pregnant woman is concerned solely about her present physical condition in itself, with no worries about the future beyond the next nine (or rather, eight or seven) months. If I do not unhook myself from the violinist then the upshot after nine months is that some adult human being, with whom I can shake hands and bid goodbye, survives. If I do not have an abortion, then after nine

months the upshot is that there will be a *child*, a new person in the world, and moreover, that child will be mine—I shall have become a mother, and in one sense will remain one for the rest of my life.

Such a child will be, not only my child, but the child of its father. The fact that pregnancy is (standardly) caused by a single act of sexual intercourse and that the male partner in that act is the father of any child that results, once again makes for a huge difference between pregnancy and the violinist case.

A critic of Thomson's has said that in the case of rape, the woman's situation is 'adequately analogous to the violinist case for our intuitions about the latter to transfer convincingly' but that in all other cases this is not so since

> in the normal case [of unwanted pregnancy] we cannot claim that the woman is in no way responsible for her predicament; she could have remained chaste, or taken her pills more faithfully, or abstained on dangerous days and so on. If, on the other hand you are kidnapped by strangers and hooked up to a strange violinist, then you are free of any shred of responsibility for the situation, on the basis of which it could be argued that you are obligated to keep the violinist alive.[9]

This criticism of Thomson is stated within the terms of accepting that I cannot acquire responsibilities through sheer bad luck. But, putting any criticism of that point to one side, we should still be struck by how very unlike the violinist situation and even pregnancy due to rape are. For wanting to terminate a pregnancy caused by rape is particularly a response to its cause, to the knowledge that what is growing inside one is in some sense *his*, the rapist's, and will become a child which is one's own and *his*, if one does not have an abortion. But the knowledge that one has been kidnapped to sustain the violinist does not make him a constant reminder of something terrifying and disgusting, nor invest one's present situation with any particular horror, nor give one reason to dread the future.

That pregnancy is utterly unlike the violinist situation in these different ways is, of course, perfectly obvious, though all too easily forgotten in the context of abstract philosophy. What is not so obvious is why they are morally relevant. They are relevant because abortions are sought for reasons which connect with these facts.

It is a notable aspect of Thomson's article that very little is said about women's reasons for wanting abortions. The only two cases that are mentioned (apart from abortion to preserve one's own life) are the desperately frightened fourteen-year-old girl pregnant due to rape and the woman who, for once, *is* concerned only with her present physical condition and wants to terminate her seven-month pregnancy so that she can have a holiday abroad. Now this is once again the result of the preoccupation with rights and hence with acts which are unjust; for the injustice of an act is largely determined by whether or not it violates rights, independently of the agent's reasons for acting so. But Thomson herself has introduced callousness, self-centredness and other moral faults onto the board, and once this is done, we must consider the particular sorts of reasons women have for wanting abortions. For it is the reasons people have for doing things that reveal them as callous, self-centred and so on, or not. But as soon as we do discuss the reasons women have for wanting and seeking abortions and the sorts of considerations that come up, the many ways in which abortion is utterly unlike the violinist case immediately become apparent.

Reminding ourselves of how varied the reasons can be makes particularly vivid two points of Thomson's which we may rather have lost sight of. I noted, at the beginning of this chapter, that she maintains (a) not that abortion is always permissible, but that it is sometimes permissible, sometimes not, according to the circumstances, and (b) that, when it is wrong, it can be wrong in different ways—sometimes unjust, sometimes callous and so on. Precisely which circumstances make a relevant difference, and precisely how many different ways there are for abortion to be wrong, is probably impossible to determine. But in the remainder of this chapter I shall discuss briefly some of the considerations that come up when one is trying to determine whether it would be wrong for *this* woman (or girl) to have an abortion in *these* circumstances, and what sort of person would do so for *those* reasons, by way of illustration of how various the decisions can be.

My discussion will be limited by the premise that, since abortion is the killing of something, and something human at that, it is, contrary to utilitarianism and the person view, intrinsically a morally serious matter. Naturally, I do not pretend to have proved that abortion, as the killing of something human, is thereby a morally serious matter. I have done my best to undermine the arguments purporting to show that it is not, and would claim that these suffice to shift the burden of proof, but I can do more.

Reasons for Abortions

Let us begin by briefly considering the cases which are most akin to the violinist one, in that the woman wants an abortion for reasons that are at least mostly connected with the physical condition of pregnancy and the prospect of the seven or eight months to come. When women are in very poor physical health, or worn out by child-bearing, or forced to do physically very demanding jobs, then they cannot be described as self-indulgent, or callous or irresponsible, if they seek abortions. To go through with a pregnancy when one is utterly exhausted, or when one's job consists of crawling along tunnels hauling coal, as many women in the nineteenth century did perforce, is heroic but people are not to be blamed for not achieving heroism. That they can view the pregnancy only as eight months of misery, followed by hours if not days of agony and exhaustion, and abortion only as the blessed escape from this prospect is entirely understandable, and does not manifest any lack of serious respect for human life.

These cases contrast sharply with others which are connected with the physical condition of pregnancy, such as Thomson's paradigm example of an indecent reason for seeking an abortion. To regard pregnancy, especially in its more advanced stages, as nothing but a tiresome and pleasure-inhibiting physical condition, as an adolescent regards a pimple before a date, is startlingly self-centred, callous, insensitive, and does manifest a lack of serious respect for life. Indeed, it could truly be described *as* childish or adolescent, though this sounds like an understatement. It may be taken as less of an understatement if we remember that a degree of absorption in one's own pleasures and pursuits, and lack of thought for others, which is quite natural in children, amounts to cruelty, callousness and wickedness in adults. A twelve-year-old who hits her baby brother because he will not stop crying and puts him in the bottom drawer and goes out to play is one thing; a twenty-five-year-old who does the same is quite different. We do not expect children to 'know what life's about', to appreciate what is serious. But adults are supposed to, and when they do not, and continue to live as though all that mattered in life were their own immediate pleasures, they tend to do particularly frightful things.

Abortions are more usually sought for reasons that connect with the fact that pregnancy produces, not just *a* child but, the woman's child. She does not want to have any more children, or she does not want to have children at all, or she does not want to have one now; and so she wants to terminate the pregnancy.

But the 'and so' is too swift. For if what she wants is not to increase her family, or not have a family at all, or not start a family now, then *those* wants could be satisfied by continuing with the pregnancy and having the baby adopted. Utilitarianism apparently commits healthy women of child-bearing age to the self-sacrificial duty of producing babies for couples who want them, and though one can reject this as an outrageous demand, it usefully serves to remind us of how desperately unhappy childless couples can be, and how their whole lives can be transformed by being able to adopt. In countries where there is a shortage of babies for adoption, this seems to be a consideration which a generous and thoughtful woman would take into account. To throw away the opportunity to bring so much happiness into other people's lives, to destroy the very thing they value so much because you don't value it, described that way, abortion to avoid having to bring up a child seems self-centred, callous and wanton.

However, this judgement would, in its turn, be too swift. It is not clear that we would admire a woman, who went through a pregnancy with a view to having the baby adopted by strangers, as particularly generous and thoughtful. She might, on the contrary, seem rather cold-blooded. This, I take it, is a reflection of the fact that we expect women to become deeply emotionally involved with the children they bear; a woman who can contemplate the idea of giving her child to strangers without pain seems oddly detached in a way that is not admirable.

Indeed, it seems that many woman who opt for abortion rather than pregnancy followed by adoption, despite believing that abortion is wrong, do so because they cannot contemplate the idea without pain. Some say that if they had the baby they know they could not bring themselves to have it adopted, so their choice has to lie between abortion and having a child that they bring up. Others say that if they had the baby and had it adopted they would always worry about how it was getting on, and what had become of it. But at the end of her article Thomson raises a telling point in relation to this:

> . . . while I am arguing for the permissibility of abortion in some cases, I am not arguing for the right to secure the death of the unborn child. It is easy to confuse these two things in that up to a certain point in the life of the foetus it is not able to survive outside the mother's body; hence removing it from her body guarantees its death. But they are importantly different. I have argued that you are not morally required to spend nine months in bed, sustaining the life of that violinist; but to say this is by no means to say that if, when you unplug yourself, there is a miracle and he survives, you then have a right to turn round and slit his throat. You may detach yourself even if this costs him his life; you have no right to be guaranteed his death, by some other means, if unplugging yourself does not kill him. There are some people who will feel dissatisfied by this feature of my argument. A woman may be utterly devastated by the thought of a child, a bit of herself put out for adoption and never seen or heard of again. She may therefore want not merely that the child be detached from her, but more, that it die. Some opponents of abortion are inclined to regard this as beneath contempt—thereby showing insensitivity to what is surely a powerful source of despair. All the same, I agree that the desire for the child's death is not one that anybody may gratify, should it turn out to be possible to detach the child alive.[10]

Having said this much, Thomson reminds us that she has been talking throughout *as if* the fœtus is a human being, like the violinist, but that it is not. 'A very early abortion', she says, 'is surely not the killing of a person, and so is not dealt with by anything I have said here.' But this at best leaves it as an open question what Thomson thinks about 'the right' or the decency of securing the death of the fœtus, as an alternative to suffering with the knowledge that one's child is somewhere out in the world, unseen and unheard of. Suppose that medical technology had advanced to the point where fœtuses, or even embryos, could be extracted from the womb alive and undamaged, and develop into normal healthy babies in laboratory conditions. Would we think then that a woman had a right to say whether her fœtus was to be aborted dead or live, on the grounds that she would be devastated by feeling responsible for it for the rest of her life? And if she had such a right, that it was all right for her to exercise it?

One possible case might be conception due to rape, where the woman could not face the thought of a child who literally embodies a combination of herself and the man who did this terrible thing to her. But in any other case, for a woman, who has successfully terminated her pregnancy, and who is not prepared to bring up the child herself, to insist that the fœtus be killed, because she cannot bear the thought of *her* child growing up somewhere unseen and unheard of, does seem selfish, self-indulgent and even greedy in some way. What would childless couples desperate to take the fœtus over say about her decision? She has something they want terribly; she does not want it, but she does not want them to have it either.

As things are at present, a woman who opted for adoption despite the devastation she expected it to cause her, would also have to be someone who opted for carrying the child to term and bearing it. And refusing to do that, one might say, is nothing like as selfish or self-indulgent as simply insisting that an extracted fœtus or embryo be killed. Nevertheless, there may be something selfish and self-indulgent in taking abortion as the easy way out of avoiding either the guilt of adoption or the responsibility of bringing up the child oneself. It may also be simply thoughtless—if the woman does not even get round

to considering adoption as a possibility—or cowardly. For another salient feature of pregnancy is that, in its later stages, it *shows*. If one carries a child to term, everyone will know, and lots of people will say things to one in the expectation that (of course) you are going to keep it—and to many of them you will have to say blatantly, 'Oh no, I've arranged to have it adopted'. And one might simply cringe at the thought of having to go through that, especially if one's reasons for not wanting to bring the child up oneself were rather selfish or self-indulgent.

I have not yet mentioned one of the distinguishing features of pregnancy, namely the fact that, outside of cases of rape, pregnancy is standardly caused by voluntary intercourse with some man, who is thereby the father of the child. This brings him and his rights, interests and feelings into the picture in a way that no third party with whom *I* have some special connection is bound to be brought into the picture in the violinist case. In a decision to terminate a pregnancy which resulted from a casual night with a stranger, consideration of his rights and feelings is not called for. But if the decision amounts to killing what would be not only *my* child, but the child of someone with whom I have bonds of respect and trust, friendship if not love, then what *he* thinks and wants must be a consideration to be taken into account if I am not to be callous, irresponsible, arrogant and insensitive.

This would be particularly so if he were the father of a child conceived within a marriage, or similar partnership. For marriage seriously thought of, as a partnership of mutual love, involves at least a mutual interest in the results of sexual intercourse within that marriage, and commitment to a shared future. If I do not want us to have children, or not yet, and my partner does want us to have children, right now, I can expect him to consider my wishes with sympathy and respect but must consider his the same way.

Finally, I must briefly mention the reason for seeking abortion which connects not so much with the fact that a woman's pregnancy results in her, and the father's, child, as with the fact that it results in *a* child, a new life. It is particularly in connection with this fact that abortions are sought to avoid bringing a disabled child into the world. For many women, and couples, who wonder whether to opt for abortion this decision is by far the most painful and difficult, and in probably most cases, it is agonized over in entirely unselfish terms. No doubt some women or couples think 'I can't face how much *I* shall suffer' but it is, I think, unduly cynical to suppose that this is common. What is usually dreaded is how much the child might suffer or how narrow its life might be.

Since it is a decision that usually involves such unhappiness I am unwilling to devote much abstract discussion to it. People who are philosophers by profession can often bring their philosophy to bear on the most painful episodes in their lives, or indeed on its end, with no sense of oddity or strain, but it is at best pretentious and at worst cruel to thrust it at most people who are suffering or have suffered. So I should like even the brief discussion below to be taken as addressed to those of us who have been fortunate enough not to be faced with such decisions, not as criticizing anyone who is or has been.

My criticism is directed against those who describe or think of the decision to have an abortion in such cases in a certain way. It is often described as though disabled people ought not to be born or allowed to live; indeed in an intemperate article in the *Guardian*, Polly Toynbee maintained that it was a 'scandal' that so many disabled babies were born, when 'almost all these births are now preventable'. The outraged response that her article, and similar articles and TV programmes, provoke from disabled people themselves, and from their parents, shows immediately what is wrong with this way of talking. The decision to have an abortion in the case of actual or suspected disability cannot be justified in terms of its being better that such people are not born or by saying that it is 'more humane' to kill them, or that their lives would not be worth living, without manifesting the most callous insensitivity to the obvious value of the lives of many already existing people.

No doubt this callousness is usually the result of people not thinking carefully enough about what their words mean; they do not really intend to say, of various people with various disabilities, that all these people would be better off dead, and that it would be 'more humane' to kill them *now*. But one rather wonders about the woman who wrote to *The Times* saying that she considers it 'anti-social' for pictures of thalidomide children laughing to be shown in newspapers or on television. And even if those who say that the lives of the disabled are not worth living do not really mean it, many disabled people, and parents of disabled children, find its being said, understandably, enraging, insulting, hurtful, devastating—and threatening. A blind woman who is actually pro 'abortion on demand' reported being in a group listening to other women discussing disablement as a justification for late abortions; she said, 'Their relationship to me and the way they were talking about it was really very bad. It actually negates my whole purpose in this life. I felt totally intimidated. I just sat and sort of cried inside.' Another blind woman followed up this remark by saying, 'The really awful thing is that they talk about abortion and disabled children as if you weren't there . . . I do feel sometimes they are talking about *me*. I think that generally people do think disabled people shouldn't be allowed to exist.'

One would hope that very few people really do think that disabled people should be killed against their will. But it is true that, when discussing the killing of new-born babies with disabilities, or even more, the aborting of babies with actual or possible disabilities, people without disabilities do talk as though people with them did not exist. And I think disabled people, and indeed any people who care about the morality of our society, are right to see this as threatening and dangerous.

One way in which it is dangerous is that it fosters a lot of false beliefs. Until I read a letter from a woman with severe spina bifida (in response to a 'put them out of their misery' article on infanticide) I had been conned by the media into believing that the lives of spina bifida babies were entirely wretched and that in any case they never survived to grow up. I also for many years had a set of entirely inadequate beliefs about babies born with Down's syndrome (Mongolism), thinking that they rarely if ever developed beyond the mental age of a toddler. This lamentable ignorance on my part, which I assume is not rare, is in part the result of a sort of conspiracy of silence that exists in our society about the disabled, a silence which makes their lives and the lives of their families even more difficult in many ways.

The way in which their lives are actually coming under threat is, I think, as follows. It is said that in many cases, abortion or infanticide is the only humane thing to do, since the alternative is a miserable life neglected in an unfeeling and understaffed institution. Now in an individual case this will, not invariably but usually, be simply false. Unless the mother or parents are literally unable to look after a child with the anticipated disability, and everyone is unwilling to adopt a baby with disabilities, it is simply false that *'the* alternative' to being killed is a miserable life in an institution and correspondingly false that 'the *only*' humane thing to do is to abort the fœtus or kill the baby.

Conclusion

The above brief review, schematic as it has been, should serve to remind us of how very complicated an issue 'the' abortion issue is. A variety of women, ranging from twelve-year-olds to fifty-year-olds, seek a variety of abortions, from early to late, in a variety of circumstances, from the most comfortable or fortunate to the most exacting or difficult, for a variety of reasons, from the callous and selfish to the sensitive and unselfish. Small wonder that people say 'every woman's experience of abortion is different'. Small wonder if moral philosophy cannot come up with the cut and dried answer to the question of whether abortion is always wrong or not. And small wonder if people think that moral philosophy could not offer any systematic or theoretical way of thinking about this rich complexity.

But in fact, the terms in which the last part of the discussion has been couched form the iceberg tip of a large system in moral philosophy, to an exposition of which I now turn.

NOTES

1. Thomson, Judith Jarvis (1971) 'A Defense of Abortion', *Philosophy and Public Affairs*, vol. 1, no. 1. Reprinted in many places, including Singer, Peter (1986) *Applied Ethics*ʲ Oxford University Press.

2. We shall not now be drawing any distinction between these two.
3. Thomson, *ibid.*
4. Glover, *op. cit.*, pp. 131–2, quoting Warren (1973) *op. cit.*
5. Finnis, John (1973) 'The Rights and Wrongs of Abortion', *Philosophy and Public Affairs*, vol. 2, no. 2.
6. Thomson, Judith Jarvis (1973), 'Rights and Deaths', *Philosophy and Public Affairs*, vol. 2, no. 2.
7. Thomson, 'A Defense of Abortion'.
8. See Chapter Two, Section 2, 'The conservative view', p. 41.
9. Warren, *op. cit.*
10. Thompson, *op. cit.*

KEY TERMS

Right to determine what happens in or to
  one's own body
Right to life
Violinist case
Good Samaritan
Minimally Decent Samaritan

STUDY QUESTIONS

1. What is the argument against abortion that Thomson is responding to? How does Hursthouse reformulate this argument?
2. What is Thomson's "violinist case"? Why is it a problem for the anti-abortion argument she considers?
3. Thomson distinguishes between a Good Samaritan and a Minimally Decent Samaritan. What is the difference? What problems does this distinction raise for her argument, according to Hursthouse?
4. How is the violinist case different from pregnancy and abortion, according to Hursthouse? Why is this problematic for Thomson?
5. According to Hursthouse, what makes abortion unique? Why is this relevant to thinking about its morality?

Markets in Women's Reproductive Labor

DEBRA SATZ

Debra Satz is the Martha Sutton Weeks Professor of Ethics in Society and Associate Dean of the Humanities at Stanford University. Satz's work has focused on the ethics of markets, equality, decision theory, feminist philosophy, and international justice. She is the author of *Why Some Things Should Not Be for Sale: The Moral Limits of Markets.*

. .

MUCH of the evolution of social policy in the twentieth century has occurred around conflicts over the scope of markets. To what extent, under what conditions, and for what reasons should we limit the use of markets?[1] Recently, American society has begun to experiment with markets in women's reproductive labor. Many people believe that markets in women's reproductive labor, as exemplified by contract pregnancy,[2] are more problematic than other currently accepted labor markets. I will call this the asymmetry thesis because its proponents believe that there ought to be an asymmetry between our treatment of reproductive labor and our treatment of other forms of labor. Advocates of the asymmetry thesis hold that treating reproductive labor as a commodity, as something subject to the supply-and-demand principles that govern economic markets, is worse than treating other types of human labor as commodities. Is the asymmetry thesis true? And, if so, what are the reasons for thinking that it is true?

My aims in this article are to criticize several popular ways of defending the asymmetry thesis[3] and to offer an alternative defense. Other foundations for an argument against contract pregnancy are, of course, possible. For example, several of the arguments that I examine in this article have sometimes been raised in the context of more general anticommodification arguments. I do not examine such general arguments here. Instead, I focus my discussion on those arguments against contract pregnancy that *depend* on the asymmetry thesis. I believe that the asymmetry thesis both captures strong intuitions that exist in our society and provides a plausible argument against contract pregnancy.

Many feminists hold that the asymmetry thesis is true because women's reproductive labor is a special kind of labor that should not be treated according to market norms. They draw a sharp dividing line between women's reproductive labor and human labor in general: while human labor may be bought and sold, women's reproductive labor is intrinsically not a commodity. According to these views, contract pregnancy allows for the extension of the market into the "private" sphere of sexuality and reproduction. This intrusion of the economic into the personal is seen as improper: it fails to respect the intrinsic, special nature of reproductive labor. As one writer has put it, "When women's labor is treated as a commodity, the women who perform it are degraded."[4]

Below, I argue that this is the wrong way to defend the asymmetry thesis. While I agree with the intuition that markets in women's reproductive labor are more troubling than other labor markets, in this article I develop an alternative account of why this should be so. My analysis has four parts. In the first part, I criticize the arguments against the **commodification** of women's reproductive labor

From *Philosophy and Public Affairs*, 21. Copyright © 1992 by Princeton University Press. Reprinted by permission of the publisher.

Many people were helpful during the "gestation" of this essay. I especially wish to thank Elizabeth Anderson, Richard Arneson, Michael Bratman, Jiwei Ci, Rachel Cohon, John Dupre, Howard Eilberg-Schwartz, John Ferejohn, Geoff Garrett, Margo Horn, Andrew Levine, Susan Okin, Margaret Jane Radin, Richard Terdiman, Mark Tunick, Jacob Weiner, Elisabeth Wood, and the Editors of Philosophy & Public Affairs for their detailed comments. Versions of this article were read at a Stanford Political Theory Seminar and the Stanford Feminist Theory Seminar; I am grateful for discussions with all of the participants. Research on this article was supported by a Stanford University Humanities Center Fellowship and an NEH Summer Grant.

that turn on the assumption that reproductive labor is a special form of labor, part of a separate realm of sexuality. I argue that there is no distinction between women's reproductive labor and human labor generally, which is relevant to the debate about contract pregnancy. Moreover, I argue that the sale of women's reproductive labor is not *ipso facto* degrading. Rather, it becomes "degrading" only in a particular political and social context.[5] In the second part, I criticize arguments in support of the asymmetry thesis that appeal to norms of parental love. Here, the asymmetry between reproductive labor and labor in general is taken to derive from a special bond between mothers and children: the bond between a mother and her child is different from the bond between a worker and his product. In response, I argue that the bond between mothers and children is more complicated than critics of contract pregnancy have assumed and that, moreover, contract pregnancy does not cause parents to view children as commodities. The third part of the article examines an argument that stresses the potential negative consequences of contract pregnancy for children. While this argument has some merit, I argue that it is unpersuasive.

The first three parts of the article argue that the various reasons given in the literature for banning contract pregnancy on the basis of its asymmetry with other forms of labor are inadequate. Nonetheless, most people think that there should be some limits to commodification, and there does seem to be something more problematic about pregnancy contracts than other types of labor contract. The question is, what is the basis for and the significance of these intuitions? And what, apart from its agreement with these particular intuitions, can be said in favor of the asymmetry thesis?

In the fourth part of my article, I argue that the asymmetry thesis is true, but that the reason it is true has not been properly understood. The asymmetry thesis should be defended on external and not intrinsic or essentialist grounds. The conditions of pervasive gender inequality in our society are primary to the explanation of what is wrong with contract pregnancy. I claim that the most compelling objection to contract pregnancy concerns the background conditions of gender inequality that characterize our

society. Markets in women's reproductive labor are especially troubling because they reinforce gender hierarchies in a way that other accepted labor markets do not. My defense of the asymmetry thesis thus rests on the way that contract pregnancy reinforces asymmetrical social relations of gender domination in American society. However, not all of the features of contract pregnancy that make it troubling concern gender inequality. Contract pregnancy may also heighten racial inequalities[6] and have harmful effects on the other children of the gestational mother.[7] In addition, the background conditions of economic inequality that characterize our society raise questions about the equal status of the contracting parties. I do not address these points in detail here. However, these latter considerations would have to be addressed in order to generate a complete argument against contract pregnancy.

I. The Special Nature of Reproductive Labor

A wide range of attacks on contract pregnancy turn out to share a single premise, viz., that the intrinsic nature of reproductive labor is different from that of other kinds of labor. Critics claim that reproductive labor is not just another kind of work; they argue that unlike other forms of labor, reproductive labor is not properly regarded as a commodity. I will refer to this thesis as the essentialist thesis, since it holds that reproductive labor is *essentially* something that should not be bought and sold.

In contrast to the essentialist thesis, modern economic theories tend to treat the market as "theoretically all encompassing."[8] Such theories tend to treat all goods and capacities as exchangeable commodities, at least in principle.[9] Economists generally base their defense of markets as distributive mechanisms on three distinct ideas.

First, there is the idea that markets are good for social welfare. Indeed, the fundamental theorem of welfare economics states that every competitive (market) equilibrium is Pareto optimal.[10] A Pareto optimum is a distribution point at which, given the initial distribution of resources, no individual can become better off (in view of her preferences) without at least one other individual becoming worse off. The so-called converse theorem of welfare economics states that every Pareto optimum is a competitive equilibrium.

Second, there is the idea that markets promote freedom. The agent of economic theory is a free, autonomous chooser.[11] Markets enhance her capacities for choosing by decentralizing decision-making, decentralizing information, and providing opportunities for experimentation. Markets also place limits on the viability of unjust social relationships by providing avenues for individual exit, thereby making the threat of defection a credible bargaining device.

Third, there is the idea that excluding a free exchange of some good, as a matter of principle, is incompatible with liberal neutrality. Liberalism requires state neutrality among conceptions of value. This neutrality constrains liberals from banning free exchanges: liberals cannot mandate that individuals accept certain values as having "**intrinsic**" or ultimate worth.[12] Liberals can, of course, seek to regulate exchanges so that they fall within the bounds of justice. But any argument prohibiting rather than regulating market activity is claimed to violate liberal neutrality.[13]

If we accept the logic of the economic approach to human behavior, we seem led to endorse a world in which everything is potentially for sale: body parts, reproductive labor, children, even persons.[14] Many people are repulsed by such a world. But what exactly is the problem with it? Defenders of the essentialist thesis provide the starting point for a counterattack: not all human goods are commodities. In particular, human reproductive labor is improperly treated as a commodity. When reproductive labor is purchased on the market, it is inappropriately valued.

The essentialist thesis provides support for the asymmetry thesis. The nature of reproductive labor is taken to be fundamentally different from that of labor in general. In particular, proponents of the essentialist thesis hold that women's reproductive labor should be respected and not used.[15] What is it about women's reproductive labor that singles it out for a type of respect that precludes market use?

Some versions of the essentialist thesis focus on the biological or naturalistic features of women's reproductive labor: (1) Women's reproductive labor has both a genetic and a gestational component.[16] Other forms of labor do not involve a genetic relationship between the worker and her product. (2) While much human labor is voluntary at virtually every step, many of the phases of the reproductive process are involuntary. Ovulation, conception, gestation, and birth occur without the conscious direction of the mother. (3) Reproductive labor extends over a period of approximately nine months; other types of labor do not typically necessitate a long-term commitment. (4) Reproductive labor involves significant restrictions of a woman's behavior during pregnancy; other forms of labor are less invasive with respect to the worker's body.

These characteristics of reproductive labor do not, however, establish the asymmetry thesis: (1) With respect to the genetic relationship between the reproductive worker and her product, most critics object to contract pregnancy even where the "surrogate" is not the genetic mother. In fact, many critics consider "gestational surrogacy"—in which a woman is implanted with a preembryo formed in vitro from donated gametes—more pernicious than those cases in which the "surrogate" is also the genetic mother.[17] In addition, men also have a genetic tie to their offspring, yet many proponents of the asymmetry thesis would not oppose the selling of sperm. (2) With respect to the degree to which reproductive labor is involuntary, there are many forms of work in which workers do not have control over the work process; for example, mass-production workers cannot generally control the speed of the assembly line, and they have no involvement in the overall purpose of their activity. (3) With regard to the length of the contract's duration, some forms of labor involve contracts of even longer duration, for example, book contracts. Like pregnancy contracts, these are not contracts in which one can quit at the end of the day. Yet, presumably, most proponents of the essentialist thesis would not find commercial publishing contracts objectionable. (4) With regard to invasions into the woman's body, nonreproductive labor can also involve incursions into the body of the worker. To take an obvious example, athletes sign contracts that give team owners considerable control over their diet and behavior, allowing owners to conduct periodic tests for drug use. Yet there is little controversy over the sale of athletic capacities.[18] Sales of blood also run afoul of a noninvasiveness condition. In fact, leaving aside the genetic component of reproductive labor, voluntary military service involves features 2 through 4; do we really want to object to such military service on *essentialist* grounds?

Carole Pateman suggests a different way of defending the asymmetry thesis as the basis for an argument against contract pregnancy. Rather than focusing on the naturalistic, biological properties of reproductive labor, she argues that a woman's reproductive labor is more "integral" to her identity than her other productive capacities. Pateman first sketches this argument with respect to prostitution: "Womanhood, too, is confirmed in sexual activity, and when a prostitute contracts out use of her body she is thus selling herself in a very real sense. Women's selves are involved in prostitution in a different manner from the involvement of the self in other occupations. Workers of all kinds may be more or less 'bound up in their work,' but the integral connection between sexuality and sense of the self means that, for self-protection, a prostitute must distance herself from her sexual use."[19]

Pateman's objection to prostitution rests on a claim about the intimate relation between a woman's sexuality and her identity. It is by virtue of this tie, Pateman believes, that sex should not be treated as an alienable commodity. Is her claim true? How do we decide which of a woman's attributes or capacities are essential to her identity and which are not? In particular, why should we consider sexuality more integral to self than friendship, family, religion, nationality, and work?[20] Yet we allow commodification in each of these spheres. For example, rabbis or priests may view their religion as central to their identity, but they often accept payment for performing religious services, and hardly anyone objects to their doing so. Does Pateman think that *all* activities that fall within these spheres and that bear an intimate relationship to a person's identity should be inalienable?

Pateman's argument in the above passage appears to support the asymmetry thesis, by suggesting that a woman's sexuality is *more* intimately related to her identity than her other capacities. Yet she provides no explicit argument for this suggestion. Indeed, at times, her argument seems intended not so much to support the asymmetry thesis as to support a more general thesis against alienating those activities that are closely tied to the identity of persons. But this more general argument is implausible. It would not allow individuals to sell their homes or their paintings or their book manuscripts or their copyrights.

A similar argument about the close connection between sexuality and identity underlies the objection to contract pregnancy raised by the British government–commissioned Warnock Report on Human Fertilisation and Embryology. The Warnock Report links reproductive labor to a person's dignity, claiming that "it is inconsistent with human dignity that a woman should use her uterus for financial profit."[21] But why is selling the use of a woman's uterus "undignified" while selling the use of images of her body in a television commercial is not?

The Warnock Report's argument implicitly rests on the assumption that women's sexuality and reproduction belong to a sacred, special realm. In the words of another author, it is a realm "worthy of respect."[22] Even if this is so, however, the idea of respect alone cannot guarantee the conclusion that reproductive labor should not be treated as a commodity. We sometimes sell things that we also respect. As Margaret Radin puts it, "we can both know the price of something and know that it is priceless."[23] For example, I think that my teaching talents should be respected, but I don't object to being paid for teaching on such grounds. Giving my teaching a price does not diminish the other ways in which my teaching has value.

This point undermines Pateman's argument as well. For although Pateman would not endorse the idea that sexuality is part of a private realm, she does believe that it bears a special relationship to our identities and that by virtue of that relationship it should be inalienable. But we sometimes sell things intimately tied to our identities, without ceasing to be the people that we are. For example, as I suggested above, a person's home may be intimately tied to her identity, but she can also sell it without losing her sense of self.[24]

Finally, I believe that it is a mistake to focus, as does the Warnock Report, on maintaining certain cultural values without examining critically the specific social circumstances from which those values emerge. Thus, the view that selling sexual or reproductive capacities is "degrading" may reflect society's attempts to control women and their sexuality. At the very least, the relations between particular views of sexuality and the maintenance of gender inequality must be taken into account. This is especially important insofar as one powerful defense of contract pregnancy rests on its alleged consequence of empowering poor women.[25] Indeed, there is something hypocritical in the objection to contract pregnancy as "degrading," when the fundamental background conditions of social inequality—many of which are at least "degrading"—are ignored.

II. The Special Bonds of Motherhood

Sometimes what critics of pregnancy contracts have in mind is not the effect of such contracts on the relationship between reproductive labor and a woman's sense of self or her dignity, but its effect on her views (and ours) of the mother-fetus and mother-child bond. On this view, what is wrong with commodifying reproductive labor is that by relying on a mistaken picture of the nature of these relationships, it degrades them. Further, it leads to a view of children as fungible objects. In part 1 of this section I examine arguments against contract pregnancy based on its portrayal of the mother-fetus bond; in part 2 I examine arguments based on contract pregnancy's portrayal of the mother-child bond.

1. Mothers and Fetuses

Some critics of contract pregnancy contend that the relationship between a mother and a fetus is not simply a biochemical relationship or a matter of contingent physical connection. They claim that the relationship between a mother and a fetus is essentially different from that between a worker and her material product. The long months of pregnancy and the experience of childbirth are part of forming a relationship with the child-to-be. Elizabeth Anderson

makes an argument along these lines. She suggests that the commodification of reproductive labor makes pregnancy an alienated form of labor for the women who perform it: selling her reproductive labor alienates a woman from her "normal" and justified emotions.[26] Rather than viewing pregnancy as an evolving relationship with a child-to-be, contract pregnancy reinforces a vision of the pregnant woman as a mere "home" or an "environment."[27] The commodification of reproductive labor thus distorts the nature of the bond between the mother and fetus by misrepresenting the nature of a woman's reproductive labor. What should we make of this argument?

Surely there is truth in the claim that pregnancy contracts may reinforce a vision of women as baby machines or mere "wombs." Recent court rulings with respect to contract pregnancy have tended to acknowledge women's contribution to reproduction only insofar as it is identical to men's: the donation of genetic material. The gestational labor involved in reproduction is explicitly ignored in such rulings. Thus, Mary Beth Whitehead won back her parental rights in the "Baby M" case because the New Jersey Supreme Court acknowledged her genetic contribution.[28]

However, as I will argue in Section IV below, the concern about the discounting of women's reproductive labor is best posed in terms of the principle of equal treatment. By treating women's reproductive labor as identical to men's when it is not, women are not in fact being treated equally. But those who conceptualize the problem with pregnancy contracts in terms of the degradation of the mother-fetus relationship rather than in terms of the equality of men and women tend to interpret the social practice of pregnancy in terms of a maternal "instinct," a sacrosanct bonding that takes place between a mother and her child-to-be. However, not all women "bond" with their fetuses. Some women abort them.

Indeed, there is a dilemma for those who wish to use the mother-fetus bond to condemn pregnancy contracts while endorsing a woman's right to choose abortion. They must hold that it is acceptable to abort a fetus, but not to sell it. While the Warnock Report takes no stand on the issue of abortion, it uses present abortion law as a term of reference in considering contract pregnancy. Since abortion is currently legal in England, the Report's position has this paradoxical consequence: one can kill a fetus, but one cannot contract to sell it.[29] One possible response to this objection would be to claim that women do not bond with their fetuses in the first trimester. But the fact remains that some women never bond with their fetuses; some women even fail to bond with their babies after they deliver them.

Additionally, are we really sure that we know which emotions pregnancy "normally" involves? While married women are portrayed as nurturing and altruistic, society has historically stigmatized the unwed mother as selfish, neurotic, and unconcerned with the welfare of her child. Until quite recently, social pressure was directed at unwed mothers to surrender their children after birth. Thus, married women who gave up their children were seen as "abnormal" and unfeeling, while unwed mothers who failed to surrender their children were seen as selfish.[30] Such views of the mother-fetus bonding relationship reinforce this traditional view of the family and a woman's proper role within it.

2. Mothers and Children

A somewhat different argument against contract pregnancy contends that the commodification of women's reproductive labor entails the commodification of children. Once again, the special nature of reproduction is used to support the asymmetry thesis: the special nature of maternal love is held to be incompatible with market relations. Children should be loved by their mothers, yet commercial surrogacy responds to and promotes other motivations. Critics argue that markets in reproductive labor give people the opportunity to "shop" for children. Prospective womb-infertile couples will seek out arrangements that "maximize" the value of their babies: sex, eye color, and race will be assessed in terms of market considerations.[31] Having children on the basis of such preferences reflects an inferior conception of persons. It brings commercial attitudes into a sphere that is thought to be properly governed by love.

What are the reasons that people seek to enter into contract pregnancy arrangements? Most couples or single people who make use of "surrogates"

want simply to have a child that is "theirs," that is, genetically related to them. In fact, given the clogged adoption system, some of them may simply want to have a child. Furthermore, the adoption system itself is responsive to people's individual preferences: it is much easier, for example, to adopt an older black child than a white infant. Such preferences may be objectionable, but no one seriously argues that parents should have no choice in the child they adopt nor that adoption be prohibited because it gives rein to such preferences. Instead, we regulate adoption to forbid the differential payment of fees to agencies on the basis of a child's ascribed characteristics. Why couldn't contract pregnancy be regulated in the same way?

Critics who wish to make an argument for the asymmetry thesis based on the nature of maternal love must defend a strong claim about the relationship between markets and love. In particular, they must claim that even regulated markets in reproductive services will lead parents to love their children for the wrong reasons: love will be conditional on the child's having the "right" set of physical characteristics. While I share the view that there is something wrong with the "shopping" attitude in the sphere of personal relations, I wonder if it has the adverse effects that the critics imagine. Individuals in our society seek partners with attributes ranging from a specified race and height to a musical taste for Chopin. Should such singles' advertisements in magazines be illegal? Should we ban dating services that cater to such preferences? Isn't it true that people who meet on such problematic grounds may grow to love each other? I suspect that most parents who receive their child through a contract pregnancy arrangement will love their child as well.

Even if contract pregnancy does not distort our conception of personhood per se, critics can still associate contract pregnancy with baby-selling. One popular argument runs: In contract pregnancy women not only sell their reproductive services, but also their babies. Because baby-selling is taken to be intrinsically wrong, this type of argument attempts to use an analogy to support the following syllogism: If baby-selling is wrong, and contract pregnancy is a form of baby-selling, then contract pregnancy is wrong. The Warnock Report, for example, makes this charge.[32] Suppose that we grant, as seems plausible, that—baby-selling is wrong (perhaps on essentialist grounds). Is this argument successful?

It is important to keep in mind that pregnancy contracts do not enable fathers (or prospective "mothers," women who are infertile or otherwise unable to conceive) to acquire children as property. Even where there has been a financial motivation for conceiving a child, and whatever the status of the labor that produced it, the *child* cannot be treated as a commodity. The father cannot, for example, destroy, transfer, or abandon the child. He is bound by the same norms and laws that govern the behavior of a child's biological or adoptive parents. Allowing women to contract for their reproductive services does not entail baby-selling, if we mean by that a proxy for slavery.

Anderson has argued that what makes contract pregnancy a form of baby-selling is the way such contracts treat the "mother's rights over her child."[33] Such contracts mandate that the mother relinquish her parental rights to the child. Furthermore, such contracts can be enforced against the mother's wishes. Anderson argues that forcing a woman to part with her child and to cede her parental rights by sale entails treating the child as a mere commodity, as something that can be sold. Even if this is true, it does not necessarily lead to the conclusion that pregnancy contracts should be banned. There are many similarities between contract pregnancy and adoption. Like adoption, pregnancy contracts could be regulated to respect a change of mind of the "surrogate" within some specified time period; to accord more with an "open" model in which all the parties to the contract retain contact with the child; or by making pregnancy contracts analogous to contracts that require informed consent, as in the case of medical experiments. Pregnancy contracts could be required to provide detailed information about the emotional risks and costs associated with giving up a child.[34]

Finally, some writers have objected to pregnancy contracts on the ground that they must, by their nature, exploit women. They point to the fact that the compensation is very low, and that many of the women who agree to sell their reproductive labor have altruistic motivations. Anderson writes,

"A kind of exploitation occurs when one party to a transaction is oriented toward the exchange of 'gift' values, while the other party operates in accordance with the norms of the market exchange of commodities."[35]

Two responses are possible to this line of argument. First, even if it is the case that all or most of the women who sell their reproductive labor are altruistically motivated,[36] it is unfair to argue that the other parties to the contract are motivated solely in accord with market values. The couples who use contract pregnancy are not seeking to make a profit, but to have a child. Some of them might even be willing to maintain an "extended family" relationship with the "surrogate" after the child's birth. Second, even if an asymmetry in motivation is established, it is also present in many types of service work: teaching, health care, and social work are all liable to result in "exploitation" of this sort. In all of these areas, the problem is at least partially addressed by regulating compensation. Why is contract pregnancy different?

III. The Consequences of Contract Pregnancy for Children

Susan Okin makes an argument against contract pregnancy that is based on its direct consequences for children, and not on the intrinsic features of reproductive labor or the bonds of motherhood. She argues that the problem with pregnancy contracts is that they do not consider the interests of the child.[37] Okin thus focuses on a different aspect of the concern that contract pregnancy leads us to adopt an inferior understanding of children. She points not to the conception itself, but to its consequences for children. The asymmetry, then, between reproductive labor and other forms of labor is based on the fact that only in the former are the child's interests directly at stake.

Putting aside the difficult question of what actually constitutes the child's best interests,[38] it is not certain that such interests will always be served by the child's remaining with its biological parents. Some children may be better off separated from their biological parents when such parents are abusive. No one would claim that children should always remain with their biological parents. Nevertheless, I agree with Okin that one problem with pregnancy contracts lies in their potential for weakening the biological ties that give children a secure place in the world.[39] If it can be shown that pregnancy contracts make children more vulnerable, for example, by encouraging parental exit, then such a consideration might contribute to calls for restricting or prohibiting such contracts.[40] Such an argument will have nothing to do with the special nature of reproductive labor, nor will it have to do with the special biological relationship between a parent and a child. It will remain valid even where the child bears no genetic relation to its parents. Children are vulnerable and dependent, and this vulnerability justifies the moral obligations parents have toward them. While this objection can be used to support the asymmetry thesis, it is important to note that asymmetrical vulnerabilities are found throughout the social world; they are not unique to the spheres of the family, sex, and reproduction. The same principles that will mandate against pregnancy contracts will also mandate against the use of child labor and argue for helping the disabled and the aged.

Nonetheless, this objection does point out an asymmetry between reproductive labor and other forms of labor. Can it be used to justify prohibiting contract pregnancy? One of the difficulties with evaluating pregnancy contracts in terms of their effects on children is that we have very little empirical evidence of these effects. The first reported case of a pregnancy contract in the United States occurred in 1976.[41] Even with the more established practice of artificial insemination, no research is available on the effects of donor anonymity on the child. Nor do we know how different family structures, including single-parent and alternative families and adoption, affect children. We should be wary of prematurely making abstract arguments based on the child's best interests without any empirical evidence. Moreover, in the case of families whose life situation may be disapproved of by their community, we may have moral reasons for overriding the best interests of an individual child.[42] For example, if the child of a single or lesbian mother

were to suffer discrimination, I do not think that this would justify removal of the child from the mother. Thus, while pregnancy contracts may threaten the interests of children, this is not yet established; nor is this consideration by itself a sufficient reason for forbidding such contracts.

IV. Reproductive Labor and Equality

In the preceding three sections I have argued that the asymmetry thesis cannot be defended by claiming that there is something "essential" about reproductive labor that singles it out for different treatment from other forms of labor; nor by arguing that contract pregnancy distorts the nature of the bonds of motherhood; nor by the appeal to the best interests of the child. The arguments I have examined ignore the existing background conditions that underlie pregnancy contracts, many of which are objectionable. In addition, some of the arguments tend to accept uncritically the traditional picture of the family. Such arguments take current views of the maternal bond and the institution of motherhood as the baseline for judging pregnancy contracts—as if such views were not contested.

If we reject these arguments for the asymmetry thesis, are we forced back to the view that the market is indeed theoretically all-encompassing? Can we reject contract pregnancy, and defend the asymmetry thesis, without claiming either that reproductive labor is essentially not a commodity, or that it necessarily degrades the bonds between mothers and children, or that it is harmful to children?

I think that the strongest argument against contract pregnancy that depends upon the asymmetry thesis is derived from considerations of gender equality. It is this consideration that I believe is tacitly driving many of the arguments; for example, it is the background gender inequality that makes the commodification of women's and children's attributes especially objectionable. My criticism of contract pregnancy centers on the hypothesis that in our society such contracts will turn women's labor into something that is used and controlled by others[43] and will reinforce gender stereotypes that have been used to justify the unequal treatment of women.

Contrary to the democratic ideal, gender inequality is pervasive in our society. This inequality includes the unequal distribution of housework and child care that considerably restricts married women's opportunities in the work force; the fact that the ratio between an average full-time working woman's earnings and those of her average male counterpart is 59.3:100,[44] and the fact that divorce is an economically devastating experience for women (during the 1970s, the standard of living of young divorced mothers fell 73%, while men's standard of living following divorce rose 42%).[45] These circumstances constitute the baseline from which women form their preferences and make their "choices." Thus, even a woman's choice to engage in commercial surrogacy must be viewed against a background of unequal opportunity. Most work done by women in our society remains in a "female ghetto": service and clerical work, secretarial work, cleaning, domestic labor, nursing, elementary school teaching, and waitressing.

I assume that there is something deeply objectionable about gender inequality. My argument is that contract pregnancy's reinforcing of this inequality lies at the heart of what is wrong with it. In particular, reproduction is a sphere that historically has been marked by inequality: women and men have not had equal influence over the institutions and practices involved in human reproduction. In its current form and context, contract pregnancy contributes to gender inequality in three ways:

1. Contract pregnancy gives others increased access to and control over women's bodies and sexuality. In a provocative book, Carmel Shalev argues that it is wrong to forbid a woman to sell her reproductive capacities when we already allow men to sell their sperm.[46] But Shalev ignores a crucial difference between artificial insemination by donor (AID) and a pregnancy contract. AID does not give anyone control over men's bodies and sexuality. A man who elects AID simply sells a product of his body or his sexuality; he does not sell control over his body itself. The current practices of AID and pregnancy contracts are remarkably different in the scope of intervention and control they allow the "buyer." Pregnancy contracts involve substantial control over women's bodies.[47]

What makes this control objectionable, however, is not the intrinsic features of women's reproductive labor, but rather the ways in which such control reinforces a long history of unequal treatment. Consider an analogous case that has no such consequence: voluntary (paid) military service, where men sell their fighting capacities. Military service, like contract pregnancy, involves significant invasions into the body of the seller; soldiers' bodies are controlled to a large extent by their commanding officers under conditions in which the stakes are often life and death. But military service does not *directly* serve to perpetuate traditional gender inequalities.[48] The fact that pregnancy contracts, like military contracts, give someone control over someone else's body is not the issue. Rather, the issue is that in contract pregnancy the body that is controlled belongs to a woman, in a society that historically has subordinated women's interests to those of men, primarily through its control over her sexuality and reproduction.

Market theorists might retort that contract pregnancy could be regulated to protect women's autonomy, in the same way that we regulate other labor contracts. However, it will be difficult, given the nature of the interests involved, for such contracts not to be very intrusive with respect to women's bodies in spite of formal agreements. The purpose of such contracts is, after all, to produce a healthy child. In order to help guarantee a healthy baby, a woman's behavior must be highly controlled.[49]

Moreover, if the pregnancy contract is a contract for reproductive labor, then, as in other types of labor contracts, compliance—what the law terms "specific performance"—cannot be enforced. For example, if I contract to paint your house, and I default on my agreement, you can sue me for breaking the contract, but even if you win, the courts will not require me to paint your house. Indeed, this is the salient difference between even poorly paid wage labor and indentured servitude. Thus, by analogy, if the woman in a pregnancy contract defaults on her agreement and decides to keep the child, the other parties should not be able to demand performance (that is, surrender of the child); rather, they can demand monetary compensation.[50]

This inability to enforce performance in pregnancy contracts may have consequences for the *content* of such contracts that will make them especially objectionable. Recall that such contracts occur over a long period of time, during which a woman may undergo fundamental changes in her willingness to give up the child. The other parties will need some mechanism to ensure her compliance. There are two mechanisms that are likely to produce compliance, but both are objectionable: (a) The contract could be set up so that payment is delivered to the woman only after the child is born. But this structure of compensation closely resembles baby-selling; it now looks as if what is being bought is not the woman's services, but the child itself. Thus, if baby-selling is wrong, then we should be very troubled by the fact that, in order to be self-enforcing, contract pregnancy must use incentives that make it resemble baby-selling. (b) The contract could mandate legal and psychological counseling for a woman who is tempted to change her mind. Given that it is hard to imagine in advance what it means to surrender a child, such counseling could involve a great deal of manipulation and coercion of the woman's emotions.[51]

2. Contract pregnancy reinforces stereotypes about the proper role of women in the reproductive division of labor. At a time when women have made strides in labor force participation, moving out of the family into other social spheres, pregnancy contracts provide a monetary incentive for women to remain in the home.[52] And, while some women may "prefer" to stay at home, we need to pay attention to the limited range of economic opportunities available to these women, and to the ways in which these opportunities have shaped their preferences. Under present conditions, pregnancy contracts entrench a traditional division of labor—men at work, women in the home—based on gender.

Additionally, pregnancy contracts will affect the way society views women: they will tend to reinforce the view of women as "baby machines."[53] It is also likely that they will affect the way women see themselves. Insofar as the sale of women's reproductive capacities contributes to the social subordination of women, and only of women, there are antidiscrimination grounds for banning it.

3. Contract pregnancy raises the danger, manifested in several recent court rulings, that "motherhood" will be defined in terms of genetic material, in the same way as "fatherhood." Mary Beth Whitehead won back parental rights to Baby M on the basis of her being the genetic "mother." On the other hand, Anna Johnson, a "gestational" surrogate, lost such rights because she bore no genetic relationship to the child.[54] These court rulings establish the principle of motherhood on the basis of genetic contribution. In such cases, women's contribution to reproduction is recognized only insofar as it is identical to that of men. Genes alone are taken to define natural and biological motherhood. By not taking women's actual gestational contributions into account, the courts reinforce an old stereotype of women as merely the incubators of men's seeds.[55] In fact, the court's inattention to women's unique labor contribution is itself a form of unequal treatment. By defining women's rights and contributions in terms of those of men, when they are different, the courts fail to recognize an adequate basis for women's rights and needs. These rulings place an additional burden on women.[56]

Given its consequences for gender inequality, I think that the asymmetry thesis is true, and that pregnancy contracts are especially troubling. Current gender inequality lies at the heart of what is wrong with pregnancy contracts. The problem with commodifying women's reproductive labor is not that it "degrades" the special nature of reproductive labor, or "alienates" women from a core part of their identities, but that it reinforces a traditional gender-hierarchical division of labor. A consequence of my argument is that under very different background conditions, in which men and women had equal power and had an equal range of choices, such contracts would be less objectionable.[57] For example, in a society in which women's work was valued as much as men's and in which child care was shared equally, pregnancy contracts might serve primarily as a way for single persons, disabled persons, and same-sex families to have children. Indeed, pregnancy contracts and similar practices have the potential to transform the nuclear family. We know too little about possible new forms of family life to restrict such experiments on a priori grounds; but in our society, I have argued that there are consequentialist reasons for making this restriction.

At the same time, there are potential caveats to the acceptability of a regulated form of pregnancy contract even under conditions of gender equality: (1) the importance of background economic inequality;[58] (2) the effect of the practice on race equality; (3) the need to ensure the woman's participation in the overall purpose of the activity; (4) the need to ensure that the vulnerable—children—are protected. We know very little about the prerequisites for psychologically healthy children. We know very little about the effects of pregnancy contracts on parental exit or on the other children of the birth mother.[59] For this reason, even under more ideal circumstances, there is reason to be cautious about the potential use of such contracts. For the time being, I believe that pregnancy contracts should be discouraged. This can be done by making such contracts unenforceable in the courts. Furthermore, in contested cases, the courts should recognize no distinction between genetic and gestational "surrogates" with respect to parental rights. Finally, brokerage of pregnancy contracts should be illegal. These proposals aim to discourage contract pregnancy and to strengthen the position of the "surrogate," who is the most economically and emotionally vulnerable party in any such arrangement.

V. Conclusion: Wage Labor, Reproductive Labor, and Equality

In this article, I have analyzed various grounds for forbidding markets in women's reproductive labor. While I rejected most of these grounds, including the essentialist thesis, the opposing approach of market theorists misses the point that there are noneconomic values that should constrain social policy. Market theorists, in representing all of human behavior as if it were a product of voluntary choice, ignore the fact of unequal power in the family and in the wider society.

While market theorists often defend their approach in terms of the values of liberty, welfare, and neutrality, they abstract away from the inegalitarian social context in which an individual's preferences are formed. But how preferences are formed, and in the light of what range of choices,[60] has a great deal

to do with whether or not acting on those preferences is liberty- and welfare-enhancing.[61] Under some circumstances, for example, it could be welfare-enhancing to sell oneself into slavery.[62]

What about liberal neutrality? Market theorists may claim that the asymmetry thesis is a violation of liberal neutrality: it imposes a standard of gender equality on free exchanges. Furthermore, it may seem biased—distinguishing activities that harm women from those that harm everyone. The issue of neutrality is a difficult matter to assess, for there are many interpretations of neutrality. At the very least, however, two considerations seem relevant. First, why should existing distributions serve as the standard against which neutrality is measured? I have argued that it is a mistake to assume that the realm of reproduction and sexuality is "neutral"; it is a product (at least in part) of the unequal social, political, and economic power of men and women. Second, most liberals draw the line at social practices such as slavery, indentured servitude, labor at slave wages, and the selling of votes or political liberties. Each of these practices undermines a framework of free deliberation among equals. If such restrictions violate viewpoint "neutrality," then the mere violation of neutrality does not seem objectionable.

Contract pregnancy places women's bodies under the control of others and serves to perpetuate gender inequality. The asymmetries of gender—the fact of social relations of gender domination—provide the best foundation for the asymmetry thesis. However, not all of the negative consequences of contract pregnancy involve its effects on gender inequality. I have also referred to its possible effects on children, and to the problematic form that such contracts will have to take to be self-enforcing. In addition, a full assessment of the practice would have to consider both its potential for deepening racial inequality and the unequal bargaining power of the parties to the contract. Some of these features of pregnancy contracts are shared with other labor contracts. Indeed, there is an important tradition in social philosophy that argues that it is precisely these shared features that make wage labor itself unacceptable. This tradition emphasizes that wage labor, like contract pregnancy, places the productive capacities of one group of citizens at the service and under the control of another. Unfortunately, there has been little attention in political philosophy to the effects of gender and class inequality on the development of women's and workers' deliberative capacities or on the formation of their preferences. We have to ask: What kinds of work and family relations and environments best promote the development of the deliberative capacities needed to support democratic institutions?

NOTES

1. See Karl Polanyi, *The Great Transformation* (Boston: Beacon Press, 1970); Gosta Esping-Anderson, *Politics Against Markets: The Social Democratic Road to Power* (Princeton: Princeton University Press, 1985); Michael Walzer, *Spheres of Justice: A Defense of Pluralism and Equality* (New York: Basic Books, 1983); Richard M. Titmuss, *The Gift Relationship: From Human Blood to Social Policy* (New York: Pantheon Books, 1971); Margaret Jane Radin, "Market-Inalienability," *Harvard Law Review* 100 (1987): 1849–1937; Viviana A. Zelizer, "Human Values and the Market: The Case of Life Insurance and Death in Nineteenth Century America," *American Journal of Sociology* 84 (1978): 591–610.

2. I will use the terms *contract pregnancy* and *pregnancy contract* in place of the misleading term *surrogacy*. The so-called surrogate mother is not a surrogate; she is the biological and/or gestational mother. In this article, I do not make any assumptions about who is and who is not a "real" mother.

3. See Elizabeth S. Anderson, "Is Women's Labor a Commodity?" *Philosophy & Public Affairs* 19, no. 1 (Winter 1990): 71–92; Christine Overall, *Ethics and Human Reproduction: A Feminist Analysis* (Boston: Allen and Unwin, 1987); Mary Warnock, *A Question of Life: The Warnock Report on Human Fertilisation and Embryology* (Oxford: Basil Blackwell, 1985); Martha Field, *Surrogate Motherhood: The Legal and Human Issues* (Cambridge, Mass.: Harvard University Press, 1988); Gena Corea, *The Mother Machine* (New York: Harper and Row, 1985); Carole Pateman, *The Sexual Contract* (Stanford: Stanford University Press, 1988). Not all of the arguments against contract pregnancy in these texts depend on the asymmetry thesis.

4. Anderson, "Women's Labor," p. 75.

5. I believe that my argument can also be applied to the case of prostitution, but I do not pursue that point in this article.

6. See Anita Allen, "Surrogacy, Slavery and the Ownership of Life," *Harvard Journal of Law and Public Policy* 13 (1990): 139–49.

7. See Amy Z. Overvold, *Surrogate Parenting* (New York: Pharos, 1988); Elizabeth Kane, *Birth Mother* (San Diego: Harcourt Brace Jovanovich, 1988).

8. Radin, "Market-Inalienability," p. 1859. Radin refers to this view as "universal commodification."

9. The theoretical assumption that everything is commodifiable characterizes a range of modern economic theories. It is found in both liberal welfare economics and in the conservative economics of the Chicago School. In welfare economics, there are technical reasons for this assumption: Walrasian equilibrium theory, as generalized by Arrow and Debreu, depends on there being markets in everything, including futures, uncertainty, and public goods. In order to demonstrate the existence of a general equilibrium, all goods must be included in the equations.

The economists of the Chicago School argue that most things should be treated as commodities. They start with the assumption that rational human beings make their choices according to economic principles. Gary Becker, for example, has claimed that all human behavior can be understood in terms of maximizing efficiency, market equilibrium, and stable preferences. Becker's work uses these assumptions to explain criminal punishment, marriage, childbearing, education, and racial discrimination. See Becker, *The Economic Approach to Human Behavior* (Chicago: University of Chicago Press, 1976). (For criticisms of the application of Walrasian equilibrium theory to certain domains, see Joseph Stiglitz, "The Causes and Consequences of the Dependence of Quality on Price," *Journal of Economic Literature* 25 [1987]: 1-48; Louis Putterman, "On Some Recent Explanations of Why Capital Hires Wage Labor," in *The Economic Nature of the Firm*, ed. Putterman [Cambridge: Cambridge University Press, 1986]; Samuel Bowles and Herbert Gintis, "Contested Exchange: New Microfoundations for the Political Economy of Capitalism," *Politics and Society* 18 [1990]: 165–222.)

10. The first welfare theorem holds only under specific conditions, for example, where external economies and diseconomies are absent.

11. See Milton Friedman, *Capitalism and Freedom* (Chicago: University of Chicago Press, 1962).

12. See Will Kymlicka, "Rethinking the Family," *Philosophy & Public Affairs* 20, no. 1 (Winter 1991): 95–96.

13. In *Birthpower* (New Haven: Yale University Press, 1989) Carmel Shalev develops a powerful defense of contract pregnancy that draws on considerations of liberty, welfare, and liberal neutrality. She argues that it is a matter of the "constitutional privacy" of individuals to define legal parenthood in terms of their prior-to-conception intentions; that contract pregnancy will empower women and improve their welfare by unleashing a new source of economic wealth; and that the market is neutral between competing conceptions of human relationships.

14. See Robert Nozick, *Anarchy, State and Utopia* (New York: Basic Books, 1974), p. 331.

15. See Anderson, "Women's Labor," p. 72.

16. In cases of in vitro fertilization, reproductive labor is divided between two women.

17. See Katha Pollitt, "When Is a Mother Not a Mother?" *The Nation*, 31 December 1990, p. 843.

18. See Orlando Patterson, *Slavery and Social Death* (Cambridge, Mass.: Harvard University Press, 1982) for comparisons between slaves and athletes.

19. Pateman, *The Sexual Contract*, p. 207.

20. Freudian theory, with its emphasis on "natural" drives, might give us such reasons, but Pateman does not explicitly endorse such a theory.

21. Warnock, *A Question of Life*, p. 45.

22. See Anderson, "Women's Labor," p. 72.

23. Margaret Jane Radin, "Justice and the Market Domain," in *Markets and Justice*, ed. John W. Chapman and J. R. Pennock (New York: New York University Press, 1989), p. 175.

24. However, I believe that there should be limits on the sale of housing: poor people should not be displaced from their homes for someone else's profit. But in this case, as in contract pregnancy, I think that markets should be limited by considerations of equality. For an interesting alternative approach, see Margaret Jane Radin, "Residential Rent Control," *Philosophy & Public Affairs* 15, no. 4 (Fall 1986): 350–80.

25. Radin calls our attention to the problem of the "double bind": under current conditions of inequality, there are negative external effects of both banning and allowing pregnancy contracts. See Radin, "Market-Inalienability," p. 1917.

26. Anderson, "Women's Labor," p. 81.

27. See Orange County Superior Court Judge Richard Parslow's ruling in which he referred to birth mother Anna Johnson as a "home" for an embryo and not a "mother," *New York Times*, 23 October 1990.

28. *In the Matter of Baby M*, 537 A.2d 1227 (N.J. 1988).

29. Michael Bratman has suggested that the analogy between abortion and contract pregnancy breaks down in the following way. In contract pregnancy, a woman gets pregnant with the intention of giving up the child. There is presumably no analogous intention in the case of abortion: few women, if any, intentionally get pregnant in order to have an abortion. Critics of contract pregnancy might claim that intentionally conceiving a child either to give it up for money or to abort it is immoral. I am not persuaded by such arguments. If abortion is murder, then it is so regardless of the intentions involved. My own view is that the best argument in favor of the right to abortion makes no reference to intentions, but concerns the consequences of abortion restrictions for women, restrictions that, moreover, directly burden only women.

30. See Adrienne Rich, *Of Women Born: Motherhood as Experience and Institution* (New York: Norton, 1976).

31. See Radin, "Market-Inalienability," p. 1927.

32. Warnock, *A Question of Life*, p. 45.

33. Anderson, "Women's Labor," p. 78.

34. I owe this suggestion to Rachel Cohon.

35. Anderson, "Women's Labor," p. 84.

36. Philip Parker, "Motivation of Surrogate Mothers: Initial Findings," *American Journal of Psychiatry* 140 (1983): 117–18. I am grateful to Elizabeth Anderson for bringing this article to my attention.

37. Susan Okin, "A Critique of Pregnancy Contracts: Comments on Articles by Hill, Merrick, Shevory, and Woliver," *Politics and the Life Sciences* 8 (1990): 205–10.

38. See Jon Elster, *Solomonic Judgements* (Cambridge: Cambridge University Press, 1989) for a discussion of the difficulties of ascertaining the best interests of the child. Elster is also skeptical of the idea that the best interests of the child should necessarily prevail in custody disputes.

39. Anderson raises this point as well. See "Women's Labor," p. 80.

40. We must be careful in considering the scope of this argument. Divorce and adoption, for example, may

weaken the ties between children and parents, but very few people would be willing to give the state the right to forbid divorce or adoption on such grounds.

41. D. Gelman and E. Shapiro, "Infertility: Babies by Contract," *Newsweek*, 4 November 1985.

42. See Elster, *Solomonic Judgements*, pp. 148ff.

43. Of course, pregnancy contracts also give another woman, the adoptive mother, control over the body of the surrogate mother. The important point here is that in a society characterized by gender inequalities, such contracts put women's bodies at the disposal of others.

44. This figure compares the earnings of white women and white men. In 1980, black and Hispanic women earned, respectively, 55.3% and 40.1% of white men's earnings. See Sara M. Evans and Barbara Nelson, *Wage Justice: Comparable Worth and the Paradox of Technocratic Reform* (Chicago: University of Chicago Press, 1989).

45. Lenore J. Weitzman, *The Divorce Revolution: The Unexpected Social and Economic Consequences for Women and Children in America* (New York: The Free Press, 1985), p. 323.

46. Shalev, *Birthpower.*

47. A man who buys women's reproductive labor can choose his "surrogate"; he does not legally require his wife's permission; pregnancy contracts include substantial provisions regulating the surrogate's behavior. Such provisions include agreements concerning medical treatment, the conditions under which the surrogate agrees to undergo an abortion, and regulation of the surrogate's emotions. Thus, in the case of Baby M, Mary Beth Whitehead consented to refrain from forming or attempting to form any relationship with the child she would conceive. She agreed not to smoke cigarettes, drink alcoholic beverages, or take medications without written consent from her physician. She also agreed to undergo amniocentesis and to abort the fetus "upon demand of William Stern, natural father" if tests found genetic or congenital defects. See "Appendix: Baby M Contract," *Beyond Baby M*, ed. Dianne Bartels (Clifton, N.J.: Humana Press, 1990).

48. This is not to imply that voluntary military service is not objectionable on other grounds, a question that I cannot discuss here.

49. There is already legal precedent for regulating women's behavior in the "best interests" of the fetus. A Massachusetts woman was charged with vehicular homicide when her fetus was delivered stillborn following a car accident. See Eileen McNamara, "Fetal Endangerment Cases on the Rise," *Boston Globe*, 3 October 1989; cited in Lawrence Tribe, *Abortion: The Clash of Absolutes* (New York: Norton, 1990).

50. This analogy may be complicated by the fact that the other parties to the contract may have at least some biological relationship to the child.

51. Anderson also makes this point. See "Women's Labor," pp. 84ff.

52. This is not to imply that the current sexual division of labor, in which women are disproportionately involved in unpaid domestic work, is just.

53. See Corea, *The Mother Machine.*

54. Anita Allen, in "Ownership of Life," has pointed to the disturbing possibilities contract pregnancy poses for racial equality. In cases like *Johnson v. Calvert*, where the gestator (surrogate), Johnson, was a black woman and the Calverts were white and Filipina, it is difficult to imagine a judge awarding the baby to Johnson. For example, there are almost no adoption cases in which a healthy white infant is placed with black parents. In his ruling in *Johnson v. Calvert*, Judge Parslow referred to Johnson as the baby's "wet nurse." Any full assessment of contract pregnancy must consider the implications of the practice for women of color.

55. The medieval church held that the male implanted into the female body a fully formed homunculus (complete with a soul). See Barbara Ehrenreich and Deidre English, *Witches, Midwives and Nurses: A History of Women Healers* (Old Westbury, N.Y.: Feminist Press, 1973).

56. For a perceptive discussion of the ways in which the social treatment of difference has been used to perpetuate inequalities, see Martha Minow, *Making All the Difference* (Ithaca, N.Y.: Cornell University Press, 1990).

57. Of course, under different conditions, the importance of genetically based ties between parents and children might decline.

58. According to a 1987 study by the U.S. Office of Technology Assessment, the typical clients of surrogate parenting agencies are white: 64% have annual incomes of over $50,000. By contrast, 66% of the "surrogates" reported annual incomes of less than $30,000.

59. See n. 7 above.

60. I am indebted to Elisabeth Wood for many discussions about the importance of the "range of choice" in evaluating social practices.

61. Cass Sunstein has criticized the tendency of a wide range of political views to take preferences as given, without attention to the background conditions

that shaped them. See his "Preferences and Politics," *Philosophy & Public Affairs* 20, no. 1 (Winter 1991): 3–34.

62. See Patterson, *Slavery and Social Death*, for a discussion of such circumstances.

KEY TERMS

Commodification
Intrinsic

STUDY QUESTIONS

1. What is the "asymmetry thesis" that Satz argues for? Before you read her arguments for the asymmetry thesis, did you find it plausible? Why or why not?

2. What would you say is wrong with a world, if anything, in which the sale of children is allowed? Are children *essentially* things that ought not to be sold? Or are there independent reasons for thinking that they ought not to be sold?

3. If someone accepts that abortion in the first trimester is morally permissible, should he or she thereby accept that the sale of a first-trimester fetus is morally permissible as well? If not, what is the morally relevant difference?

4. How does Satz think contract pregnancy reinforces gender equality? Is this a good reason for thinking that contract pregnancy is problematic?

Racisms

KWAME ANTHONY APPIAH

Kwame Anthony Appiah (1954–   ) is Professor of Philosophy at Princeton University, where he is also in the Center for Human Values. He is the author of *Assertions and Conditionals* and, with Amy Gutmann, *Color Conscious: The Political Morality of Race*, among other works.

· ·

IF the people I talk to and the newspapers I read are representative and reliable, there is a good deal of racism about. People and policies in the United States, in Eastern and Western Europe, in Asia and Africa and Latin America are regularly described as "racist." Australia had, until recently, a racist immigration policy; Britain still has one; racism is on the rise in France; many Israelis support Meir Kahane, an anti-Arab racist; many Arabs, according to a leading authority, are anti-Semitic racists;[1] and the movement to establish English as the "official language" of the United States is motivated by racism. Or, at least, so many of the people I talk to and many of the journalists with the newspapers I read believe.

But visitors from Mars—or from Malawi—unfamiliar with the Western concept of racism could be excused if they had some difficulty in identifying what exactly racism was. We see it everywhere, but rarely does anyone stop to say what it is, or to explain what is wrong with it. Our visitors from Mars would soon grasp that it had become at least conventional in recent years to express abhorrence for racism. They might even notice that those most often accused of it—members of the South African Nationalist party, for example—may officially abhor it also. But if they sought in the popular media of our day—in newspapers and magazines, on television or radio, in novels or films—for an explicit definition of this thing "we" all abhor, they would very likely be disappointed.

Now, of course, this would be true of many of our most familiar concepts. *Sister, chair, tomato*—none of these gets defined in the course of our daily business. But the concept of racism is in worse shape than these. For much of what we say about it is, on the face of it, inconsistent.

It is, for example, held by many to be racist to refuse entry to a university to an otherwise qualified "Negro" candidate, but not to be so to refuse entry to an equally qualified "Caucasian" one. But "Negro" and "Caucasian" are both alleged to be names of races, and invidious discrimination on the basis of race is usually held to be a paradigm case of racism. Or, to take another example, it is widely believed to be evidence of unacceptable racism to exclude people from clubs on the basis of race; yet most people, even those who think of "Jewish" as a racial term, seem to think that there is nothing wrong with Jewish clubs, whose members do not share any particular religious beliefs, or Afro-American societies, whose members share the juridical characteristic of American citizenship and the "racial" characteristic of being black.

I say that these are inconsistencies "on the face of it," because, for example, affirmative action in university admissions is importantly different from the earlier refusal to admit blacks or Jews (or other "Others") that it is meant, in part, to correct. Deep enough analysis may reveal it to be quite consistent with the abhorrence of racism; even a shallow analysis suggests that it is intended to be so. Similarly, justifications can be offered for "racial" associations in a plural society that are not available for the racial exclusivisms of the country club. But if we take racism seriously we ought to be concerned about the adequacy of these justifications.

In this essay, then, I propose to take our ordinary ways of thinking about race and racism and point up some of their presuppositions. And since popular concepts are, of course, usually fairly fuzzily and untheoretically conceived, much of what I have to say will seem to be both more theoretically and more precisely committed than the talk of racism and racists in our newspapers and on television. My claim is that these theoretical claims are required to make sense of racism as the practice of reasoning human beings. If anyone were to suggest that much,

perhaps most, of what goes under the name "racism" in our world cannot be given such a rationalized foundation, I should not disagree: but to the extent that a practice cannot be rationally reconstructed it ought, surely, to be given up by reasonable people. The right tactic with racism, if you really want to oppose it, is to object to it rationally in the form in which it stands the best chance of meeting objections. The doctrines I want to discuss can be rationally articulated: and they are worth articulating rationally in order that we can rationally say what we object to in them.

Racist Propositions

There are at least three distinct doctrines that might be held to express the theoretical content of what we call "racism." One is the view—which I shall call *racialism*[2]—that there are heritable characteristics, possessed by members of our species, that allow us to divide them into a small set of races, in such a way that all the members of these races share certain traits and tendencies with each other that they do not share with members of any other race. These traits and tendencies characteristic of a race constitute, on the racialist view, a sort of racial essence; and it is part of the content of racialism that the essential heritable characteristics of what the nineteenth century called the "Races of Man" account for more than the visible morphological characteristics—skin color, hair type, facial features—on the basis of which we make our informal classifications. Racialism is at the heart of nineteenth-century Western attempts to develop a science of racial difference; but it appears to have been believed by others—for example, Hegel, before then, and many in other parts of the non-Western world since—who have had no interest in developing scientific theories.

Racialism is not, in itself, a doctrine that must be dangerous, even if the racial essence is thought to entail moral and intellectual dispositions. Provided positive moral qualities are distributed across the races, each can be respected, can have its "separate but equal" place. Unlike most Western-educated people, I believe—and I have argued elsewhere[3]—that racialism is false; but by itself, it seems to be a cognitive rather than a moral problem. The issue is how the world is, not how we would want it to be.

Racialism is, however, a presupposition of other doctrines that have been called "racism," and these other doctrines have been, in the last few centuries, the basis of a great deal of human suffering and the source of a great deal of moral error.

One such doctrine we might call "extrinsic racism": extrinsic racists make moral distinctions between members of different races because they believe that the racial essence entails certain morally relevant qualities. The basis for the extrinsic racists' discrimination between people is their belief that members of different races differ in respects that *warrant* the differential treatment, respects—such as honesty or courage or intelligence—that are uncontroversially held (at least in most contemporary cultures) to be acceptable as a basis for treating people differently. Evidence that there are no such differences in morally relevant characteristics—that Negroes do not necessarily lack intellectual capacities, that Jews are not especially avaricious—should thus lead people out of their racism if it is purely extrinsic. As we know, such evidence often fails to change an extrinsic racist's attitudes substantially, for some of the extrinsic racist's best friends have always been Jewish. But at this point—if the racist is sincere—what we have is no longer a false doctrine but a cognitive incapacity, one whose significance I shall discuss later in this essay.

I say that the *sincere* extrinsic racist may suffer from a cognitive incapacity. But some who espouse extrinsic racist doctrines are simply insincere intrinsic racists. For *intrinsic racists*, on my definition, are people who differentiate morally between members of different races because they believe that each race has a different moral status, quite independent of the moral characteristics entailed by its racial essence. Just as, for example, many people assume that the fact that they are biologically related to another person—a brother, an aunt, a cousin—gives them a moral interest in that person,[4] so an intrinsic racist holds that the bare fact of being of the same race is a reason for preferring one person to another. (I shall return to this parallel later as well.)

For an intrinsic racist, no amount of evidence that a member of another race is capable of great moral, intellectual, or cultural achievements, or has

characteristics that, in members of one's own race, would make them admirable or attractive, offers any ground for treating that person as he or she would treat similarly endowed members of his or her own race. Just so, some sexists are "intrinsic sexists," holding that the bare fact that someone is a woman (or man) is a reason for treating her (or him) in certain ways.

There are interesting possibilities for complicating these distinctions: some racists, for example, claim, as the Mormons once did, that they discriminate between people because they believe that God requires them to do so. Is this an extrinsic racism, predicated on the combination of God's being an intrinsic racist and the belief that it is right to do what God wills? Or is it intrinsic racism because it is based on the belief that God requires these discriminations because they are right? (Is an act pious because the gods love it, or do they love it because it is pious?) Nevertheless, the distinctions between racialism and racism and between two potentially overlapping kinds of racism provide us with the skeleton of an anatomy of the propositional contents of racial attitudes.

Racist Dispositions

Most people will want to object already that this discussion of the propositional content of racist moral and factual beliefs misses something absolutely crucial to the character of the psychological and sociological reality of racism, something I touched on when I mentioned that extrinsic racist utterances are often made by people who suffer from what I called a "cognitive incapacity." Part of the standard force of accusations of racism is that their objects are in some way *irrational*. The objection to Professor Shockley's claims about the intelligence of blacks is not just that they are false; it is rather that Professor Shockley seems, like many people we call "racist," to be unable to see that the evidence does not support his factual claims and that the connection between his factual claims and his policy prescriptions involves a series of non sequiturs.

What makes these cognitive incapacities especially troubling—something we should respond to with more than a recommendation that the individual, Professor Shockley, be offered psycho-therapy—is that they conform to a certain pattern: namely, that it is especially where beliefs and policies are to the disadvantage of nonwhite people that he shows the sorts of disturbing failure that have made his views both notorious and notoriously unreliable. Indeed, Professor Shockley's reasoning works extremely well in some other areas: that he is a Nobel Laureate in physics is part of what makes him so interesting an example.

This cognitive incapacity is not, of course, a rare one. Many of us are unable to give up beliefs that play a part in justifying the special advantages we gain (or hope to gain) from our positions in the social order—in particular, beliefs about the positive characters of the class of people who share that position. Many people who express extrinsic racist beliefs—many white South Africans, for example—are beneficiaries of social orders that deliver advantages to them by virtue of their "race," so that their disinclination to accept evidence that would deprive them of a justification for those advantages is just an instance of this general phenomenon.

So too, evidence that access to higher education is as largely determined by the quality of our earlier educations as by our own innate talents, does not, on the whole, undermine the confidence of college entrants from private schools in England or the United States or Ghana. Many of them continue to believe in the face of this evidence that their acceptance at "good" universities shows them to be intellectually better endowed (and not just better prepared) than those who are rejected. It is facts such as these that give sense to the notion of false consciousness, the idea that an ideology can prevent us from acknowledging facts that would threaten our position.

The most interesting cases of this sort of ideological resistance to the truth are not, perhaps, the ones I have just mentioned. On the whole, it is less surprising, once we accept the admittedly problematic notion of self-deception, that people who think that certain attitudes or beliefs advantage them or those they care about should be able, as we say, to "persuade" themselves to ignore evidence that undermines those beliefs or attitudes. What is more interesting is the existence of people who resist the truth of a proposition while thinking that its wider

acceptance would in no way disadvantage them or those individuals about whom they care—this might be thought to describe Professor Shockley; or who resist the truth when they recognize that its acceptance would actually advantage them—this might be the case with some black people who have internalized negative racist stereotypes; or who fail, by virtue of their ideological attachments, to recognize what is in their own best interests at all.

My business here is not with the psychological or social processes by which these forms of ideological resistance operate, but it is important, I think, to see the refusal on the part of some extrinsic racists to accept evidence against the beliefs as an instance of a widespread phenomenon in human affairs. It is a plain fact, to which theories of ideology must address themselves, that our species is prone both morally and intellectually to such distortions of judgment, in particular to distortions of judgment that reflect partiality. An inability to change your mind in the face of appropriate[5] evidence is a cognitive incapacity; but it is one that all of us surely suffer from in some areas of belief; especially in areas where our own interests or self-images are (or seem to be) at stake.

It is not, however, as some have held, a tendency that we are powerless to resist. No one, no doubt, can be impartial about everything—even about everything to which the notion of partiality applies; but there is no subject matter about which most sane people cannot, in the end, be persuaded to avoid partiality in judgment. And it may help to shake the convictions of those whose incapacity derives from this sort of ideological defense if we show them how their reaction fits into this general pattern. It is, indeed, because it generally *does* fit this pattern that we call such views "racism"—the suffix "-ism" indicating that what we have in mind is not simply a theory but an ideology. It would be odd to call someone brought up in a remote corner of the world with false and demeaning views about white people a "racist" if that person gave up these beliefs quite easily in the face of appropriate evidence.

Real live racists, then, exhibit a systematically distorted rationality, the kind of systematically distorted rationality that we are likely to call "ideological." And it is a distortion that is especially striking in the cognitive domain: extrinsic racists, as

I said earlier, however intelligent or otherwise well informed, often fail to treat evidence against the theoretical propositions of extrinsic racism dispassionately. Like extrinsic racism, intrinsic racism can also often be seen as ideological; but since scientific evidence is not going to settle the issue, a failure to see that it is wrong represents a cognitive incapacity only on controversially realist views about morality. What makes intrinsic racism similarly ideological is not so much the failure of inductive or deductive rationality that is so striking in someone like Professor Shockley but rather the connection that it, like extrinsic racism, has with the interests—real or perceived—of the dominant group.[6] Shockley's racism is in a certain sense directed *against* nonwhite people: many believe that his views would, if accepted, operate against their objective interests, and he certainly presents the black "race" in a less than flattering light.

I propose to use the old-fashioned term "racial prejudice" in the rest of this essay to refer to the deformation of rationality in judgment that characterizes those whose racism is more than a theoretical attachment to certain propositions about race.

Racial Prejudice

It is hardly necessary to raise objections to what I am calling "racial prejudice"; someone who exhibits such deformations of rationality is plainly in trouble. But it is important to remember that propositional racists in a racist culture have false moral beliefs but may not suffer from racial prejudice. Once we show them how society has enforced extrinsic racist stereotypes, once we ask them whether they really believe that race in itself, independently of those extrinsic racist beliefs, justifies differential treatment, many will come to give up racist propositions, although we must remember how powerful a weight of authority our arguments have to overcome. Reasonable people may insist on substantial evidence if they are to give up beliefs that are central to their cultures.

Still, in the end, many will resist such reasoning; and to the extent that their prejudices are really not subject to any kind of rational control, we may wonder whether it is right to treat such people as morally responsible for the acts their racial prejudice motivates, or morally reprehensible for holding the views to which their prejudice leads them. It is a bad thing that such people exist; they are, in a certain sense, bad people. But it is not clear to me that they are responsible for the fact that they are bad. Racial prejudice, like prejudice generally, may threaten an agent's autonomy, making it appropriate to treat or train rather than to reason with them.

But once someone has been offered evidence both (1) that their reasoning in a certain domain is distorted by prejudice, and (2) that the distortions conform to a pattern that suggests a lack of impartiality, they ought to take special care in articulating views and proposing policies in that domain. They ought to do so because, as I have already said, the phenomenon of partiality in judgment is well attested in human affairs. Even if you are not immediately persuaded that you are yourself a victim of such a distorted rationality in a certain domain, you should keep in mind always that this is the usual position of those who suffer from such prejudices. To the extent that this line of thought is not one that itself falls within the domain in question, one can be held responsible for not subjecting judgments that *are* within that domain to an especially extended scrutiny; and this is a fortiori true if the policies one is recommending are plainly of enormous consequence.

If it is clear that racial prejudice is regrettable, it is also clear in the nature of the case that providing even a superabundance of reasons and evidence will often not be a successful way of removing it. Nevertheless, the racist's prejudice will be articulated through the sorts of theoretical propositions I dubbed extrinsic and intrinsic racism. And we should certainly be able to say something reasonable about why these theoretical propositions should be rejected.

Part of the reason that this is worth doing is precisely the fact that many of those who assent to the propositional content of racism do not suffer from racial prejudice. In a country like the United States, where racist propositions were once part of the national ideology, there will be many who assent to racist propositions simply because they were raised to do so. Rational objection to racist propositions has a fair chance of changing such people's beliefs.

Extrinsic and Intrinsic Racism

It is not always clear whether someone's theoretical racism is intrinsic or extrinsic, and there is certainly no reason why we should expect to be able to settle the question. Since the issue probably never occurs to most people in these terms, we cannot suppose that they must have an answer. In fact, given the definition of the terms I offered, there is nothing barring someone from being both an intrinsic and an extrinsic racist, holding both that the bare fact of race provides a basis for treating members of his or her own race differently from others and that there are morally relevant characteristics that are differentially distributed among the races. Indeed, for reasons I shall discuss in a moment, *most* intrinsic racists are likely to express extrinsic racist beliefs, so that we should not be surprised that many people seem, in fact, to be committed to both forms of racism.

The Holocaust made unreservedly clear the threat that racism poses to human decency. But it also blurred our thinking because in focusing our attention on the racist character of the Nazi atrocities, it obscured their character as atrocities. What is appalling about Nazi racism is not just that it presupposes, as all racism does, false (racialist) beliefs—not simply that it involves a moral incapacity (the inability to extend our moral sentiments to all our fellow creatures) and a moral failing (the making of moral distinctions without moral differences)—but that it leads, first, to oppression and then to mass slaughter. In recent years, South African racism has had a similar distorting effect. For although South African racism has not led to killings on the scale of the Holocaust—even if it has both left South Africa judicially executing more (mostly black) people per head of population than most other countries and led to massive differences between the life chances of white and nonwhite South Africans—it *has* led to the systematic oppression and economic exploitation of people who are not classified as "white," and to the infliction of suffering on citizens of all racial classifications, not least by the police state that is required to maintain that exploitation and oppression.

Part of our resistance, therefore, to calling the racial ideas of those, such as the Black Nationalists of the 1960s, who advocate racial solidarity, by the same term that we use to describe the attitudes of Nazis or of members of the South African Nationalist party, surely resides in the fact that they largely did not contemplate using race as a basis for inflicting harm. Indeed, it seems to me that there is a significant pattern in the modern rhetoric of race, such that the discourse of racial solidarity is usually expressed through the language of *intrinsic* racism, while those who have used race as the basis for oppression and hatred have appealed to *extrinsic* racist ideas. This point is important for understanding the character of contemporary racial attitudes.

The two major uses of race as a basis for moral solidarity that are most familiar in the West are varieties of Pan-Africanism and Zionism. In each case it is presupposed that a "people," Negroes or Jews, has the basis for shared political life in the fact of being of the same race. There are varieties of each form of "nationalism" that make the basis lie in shared traditions; but however plausible this may be in the case of Zionism, which has in Judaism, the religion, a realistic candidate for a common and nonracial focus for nationality, the peoples of Africa have a good deal less in common culturally than is usually assumed. I discuss this issue at length in *In My Father's House: Essays in the Philosophy of African Culture*, but let me say here that I believe the central fact is this: what blacks in the West, like secularized Jews, have mostly in common is that they are perceived—both by themselves and by others—as belonging to the same race, and that this common race is used by others as the basis for discriminating against them. "If you ever forget you're a Jew, a goy will remind you." The Black Nationalists, like some Zionists, responded to their experience of racial discrimination by accepting the racialism it presupposed.[7]

Although race is indeed at the heart of Black Nationalism, however, it seems that it is the fact of a shared race, not the fact of a shared racial character, that provides the basis for solidarity. Where racism is implicated in the basis for national solidarity, it is intrinsic, not (or not only) extrinsic. It is this that makes the idea of fraternity one that is naturally applied in nationalist discourse. For, as I have already observed, the moral status of close family members is not normally thought of in most cultures as depending on qualities of character; we are supposed to love our brothers and sisters in spite of their faults and not because of their virtues. Alexander Crummell, one of the founding fathers of Black Nationalism, literalizes the metaphor of family in these startling words:

Races, like families, are the organisms and ordinances of God; and race feeling, like family feeling, is of divine origin. The extinction of race feeling is just as possible as the extinction of family feeling. Indeed, a race *is* a family.[8]

It is the assimilation of "race feeling" to "family feeling" that makes intrinsic racism seem so much less objectionable than extrinsic racism. For this metaphorical identification reflects the fact that, in the modern world (unlike the nineteenth century), intrinsic racism is acknowledged almost exclusively as the basis of feelings of community. We can surely, then, share a sense of what Crummell's friend and co-worker Edward Blyden called "the poetry of politics," that is, "the feeling of race," the feeling of "people with whom we are connected."[9] The racism here is the basis of acts of supererogation, the treatment of others better than we otherwise might, better than moral duty demands of us.

This is a contingent fact. There is no logical impossibility in the idea of racialists whose moral beliefs lead them to feelings of hatred for other races while leaving no room for love of members of their own. Nevertheless most racial hatred is in fact expressed through extrinsic racism: most people who have used race as the basis for causing harm to others have felt the need to see the others as independently morally flawed. It is one thing to espouse fraternity without claiming that your brothers and sisters have any special qualities that deserve recognition, and another to espouse hatred of others who have done nothing to deserve it.[10]

Many Afrikaners—like many in the American South until recently—have a long list of extrinsic racist answers to the question why blacks should not have full civil rights. Extrinsic racism has usually been the basis for treating people worse than we otherwise might, for giving them less than their humanity entitles them to. But this too is a contingent fact. Indeed, Crummell's guarded respect for white people derived from a belief in the superior moral qualities of the Anglo-Saxon race.

Intrinsic racism is, in my view, a moral error. Even if racialism were correct, the bare fact that someone was of another race would be no reason to treat them worse—or better—than someone of my race. In our public lives, people are owed treatment independently of their biological characters: if they are to be differently treated there must be some morally relevant difference between them. In our private lives, we are morally free to have aesthetic preferences between people, but once our treatment of people raises moral issues, we may not make arbitrary distinctions. Using race in itself as a morally relevant distinction strikes most of us as obviously arbitrary. Without associated moral characteristics, why should race provide a better basis than hair color or height or timbre of voice? And if two people share all the properties morally relevant to some action we ought to do, it will be an error—a failure to apply the Kantian injunction to universalize our moral judgments—to use the bare facts of race as the basis for treating them differently. No one should deny that a common ancestry might, in particular cases, account for similarities in moral character. But then it would be the moral similarities that justified the different treatment.

It is presumably because most people—outside the South African Nationalist party and the Ku Klux Klan—share the sense that intrinsic racism requires arbitrary distinctions that they are largely unwilling to express it in situations that invite moral criticism. But I do not know how I would argue with someone who was willing to announce an intrinsic racism as a basic moral idea; the best one can do, perhaps, is to provide objections to possible lines of defense of it.

De Gustibus

It might be thought that intrinsic racism should be regarded not so much as an adherence to a (moral) proposition as the expression of a taste, analogous, say, to the food prejudice that makes most English people unwilling to eat horse meat, and most Westerners unwilling to eat the insect grubs that the

Kung people find so appetizing. The analogy does at least this much for us, namely, to provide a model of the way the *extrinsic* racist propositions can be a reflection of an underlying prejudice. For, of course, in most cultures food prejudices are rationalized: we say insects are unhygienic and cats taste horrible. Yet a cooked insect is no more health-threatening than a cooked carrot, and the unpleasant taste of cat meat, far from justifying our prejudice against it, probably derives from that prejudice.

But there the usefulness of the analogy ends. For intrinsic racism, as I have defined it, is not simply a taste for the company of one's "own kind," but a moral doctrine, one that is supposed to underlie differences in the treatment of people in contexts where moral evaluation is appropriate. And for moral distinctions we cannot accept that "de gustibus non est disputandum." We do not need the full apparatus of Kantian ethics to require that public morality be constrained by reason.

A proper analogy would be with someone who thought that we could continue to kill cattle for beef, even if cattle exercised all the complex cultural skills of human beings. I think it is obvious that creatures that shared our capacity for understanding as well as our capacity for pain should not be treated the way we actually treat cattle—that "intrinsic speciesism" would be as wrong as racism. And the fact that most people think it is worse to be cruel to chimpanzees than to frogs suggests that they may agree with me. The distinction in attitudes surely reflects a belief in the greater richness of the mental life of chimps. Still, I do not know how I would *argue* against someone who could not see this; someone who continued to act on the contrary belief might, in the end, simply have to be locked up.

The Family Model

I have suggested that intrinsic racism is, at least sometimes, a metaphorical extension of the moral priority of one's family; it might, therefore, be suggested that a defense of intrinsic racism could proceed along the same lines as a defense of the family as a center of moral interest. The possibility of a defense of family relations as morally relevant—or,

more precisely, of the claim that one may be morally entitled (or even obliged) to make distinctions between two otherwise morally indistinguishable people because one is related to one and not to the other—is theoretically important for the prospects of a philosophical defense of intrinsic racism. This is because such a defense of the family involves—like intrinsic racism—a denial of the basic claim, expressed so clearly by Kant, that from the perspective of morality, it is as rational agents *simpliciter* that we are to assess and be assessed. For anyone who follows Kant in this, what matters, as we might say, is not who you are but how you try to live. Intrinsic racism denies this fundamental claim also. And, in so doing, as I have argued elsewhere, it runs against the mainstream of the history of Western moral theory.[11]

The importance of drawing attention to the similarities between the defense of the family and the defense of the race, then, is not merely that the metaphor of family is often invoked by racism; it is that each of them offers the same general challenge to the Kantian stream of our moral thought. And the parallel with the defense of the family should be especially appealing to an intrinsic racist, since many of us who have little time for racism would hope that the family is susceptible to some such defense.

The problem in generalizing the defense of the family, however, is that such defenses standardly begin at a point that makes the argument for intrinsic racism immediately implausible: namely, with the family as the unit through which we live what is most intimate, as the center of private life. If we distinguish, with Bernard Williams, between ethical thought, which takes seriously "the demands, needs, claims, desires, and generally, the lives of other people,"[12] and morality, which focuses more narrowly on obligation, it may well be that private life matters to us precisely because it is altogether unsuited to the universalizing tendencies of morality.

The functioning family unit has contracted substantially with industrialization, the disappearance of the family as the unit of production, and the increasing mobility of labor, but there remains that irreducible minimum: the parent or parents with the child or children. In this "nuclear" family, there is, of course, a substantial body of shared experience, shared attitudes, shared knowledge and beliefs; and the mutual psychological investment that exists within this group is, for most of us, one of the things that gives meaning to our lives. It is a natural enough confusion—which we find again and again in discussions of adoption in the popular media—that identifies the relevant group with the biological unit of *genitor*, *genetrix*, and *offspring* rather than with the social unit of those who share a common domestic life.

The relations of parents and their biological children are of moral importance, of course, in part because children are standardly the product of behavior voluntarily undertaken by their biological parents. But the moral relations between biological siblings and half-siblings cannot, as I have already pointed out, be accounted for in such terms. A rational defense of the family ought to appeal to the causal responsibility of the biological parent and the common life of the domestic unit, and not to the brute fact of biological relatedness, even if the former pair of considerations defines groups that are often coextensive with the groups generated by the latter. For brute biological relatedness bears no necessary connection to the sorts of human purposes that seem likely to be relevant at the most basic level of ethical thought.

An argument that such a central group is bound to be crucially important in the lives of most human beings in societies like ours is not, of course, an argument for any specific mode of organization of the "family": feminism and the gay liberation movement have offered candidate groups that could (and sometimes do) occupy the same sort of role in the lives of those whose sexualities or whose dispositions otherwise make the nuclear family uncongenial; and these candidates have been offered specifically in the course of defenses of a move toward societies that are agreeably beyond patriarchy and homophobia. The central thought of these feminist and gay critiques of the nuclear family is that we cannot continue to view any one organization of private life as "natural," once we have seen even the broadest outlines of the archaeology of the family concept.

If that is right, then the argument for the family must be an argument for a mode of organization of life and feeling that subserves certain positive functions; and however the details of such an argument would proceed it is highly unlikely that the same functions could be served by groups on the scale of races, simply because, as I say, the family is attractive in part exactly for reasons of its personal scale.

I need hardly say that rational defenses of intrinsic racism along the lines I have been considering are not easily found. In the absence of detailed defenses to consider, I can only offer these general reasons for doubting that they can succeed: the generally Kantian tenor of much of our moral thought threatens the project from the start; and the essentially unintimate nature of relations within "races" suggests that there is little prospect that the defense of the family—which seems an attractive and plausible project that extends ethical life beyond the narrow range of a universalizing morality—can be applied to a defense of races.

Conclusions

I have suggested that what we call "racism" involves both propositions and dispositions.

The propositions were, first, that there are races (this was *racialism*) and, second, that these races are morally significant either (a) because they are contingently correlated with morally relevant properties (this was *extrinsic racism*) or (b) because they are intrinsically morally significant (this was *intrinsic racism*).

The disposition was a tendency to assent to false propositions, both moral and theoretical, about races—propositions that support policies or beliefs that are to the disadvantage of some race (or races) as opposed to others, and to do so even in the face of evidence and argument that should appropriately lead to giving those propositions up. This disposition I called "racial prejudice."

I suggested that intrinsic racism had tended in our own time to be the natural expression of feelings of community, and this is, of course, one of the reasons why we are not inclined to call it racist. For, to the extent that a theoretical position is not associated with irrationally held beliefs that tend to the *dis*advantage of some group, it fails to display the *directedness* of the distortions of rationality characteristic of racial prejudice. Intrinsic racism may be as irrationally held as any other view, but it does not *have* to be directed *against* anyone.

So far as theory is concerned I believe racialism to be false: since theoretical racism of both kinds presupposes racialism, I could not logically support racism of either variety. But even if racialism were true, both forms of theoretical racism would be incorrect. Extrinsic racism is false because the genes that account for the gross morphological differences that underlie our standard racial categories are not linked to those genes that determine, to whatever degree such matters are determined genetically, our moral and intellectual characters. Intrinsic racism is mistaken because it breaches the Kantian imperative to make moral distinctions only on morally relevant grounds—granted that there is no reason to believe that race, *in se*, is morally relevant, and also no reason to suppose that races are like families in providing a sphere of ethical life that legitimately escapes the demands of a universalizing morality.

NOTES

1. Bernard Lewis, *Semites and Anti-Semites* (New York: Norton, 1986).
2. I shall be using the words "racism" and "racialism" with the meanings I stipulate: in some dialects of English they are synonyms, and in most dialects their definition is less than precise. For discussion of recent biological evidence see M. Nei and A. K. Roychoudhury, "Genetic Relationship and Evolution of Human Races," *Evolutionary Biology*, vol. 14 (New York: Plenum, 1983), pp. 1–59; for useful background see also M. Nei and A. K. Roychoudhury, "Gene Differences between Caucasian, Negro, and Japanese Populations," *Science*, 177 (August 1972), pp. 434–35.
3. See my "The Uncompleted Argument: Du Bois and the Illusion of Race," *Critical Inquiry*, 12 (Autumn 1985); reprinted in Henry Louis Gates (ed.), *Race, Writing, and Difference* (Chicago: University of Chicago Press, 1986), pp. 21–37.
4. This fact shows up most obviously in the assumption that adopted children intelligibly make claims against their natural siblings: natural parents are, of course, causally responsible for their child's existence and that could be the basis of moral claims, without any sense that biological relatedness

entailed rights or responsibilities. But no such basis exists for an interest in natural *siblings*; my sisters are not causally responsible for my existence. See "The Family Model," later in this essay.
5. Obviously what evidence should *appropriately* change your beliefs is not independent of your social or historical situation. In mid-nineteenth-century America, in New England quite as much as in the heart of Dixie, the pervasiveness of the institutional support for the prevailing system of racist belief—the fact that it was reinforced by religion and state, and defended by people in the universities and colleges, who had the greatest cognitive authority—meant that it would have been appropriate to insist on a substantial body of evidence and argument before giving up assent to racist propositions. In California in the 1980s, of course, matters stand rather differently. To acknowledge this is not to admit to a cognitive relativism; rather, it is to hold that, at least in some domains, the fact that a belief is widely held—and especially by people in positions of cognitive authority—may be a good prima facie reason for believing it.
6. Ideologies, as most theorists of ideology have admitted, standardly outlive the period in which they conform to the objective interests of the dominant group in a society; so even someone who thinks the dominant group in our society no longer needs racism to buttress its position can see racism as the persisting ideology of an earlier phase of society. (I say "group" to keep the claim appropriately general; it seems to me a substantial further claim that the dominant group whose interests an ideology serves is always a class.) I have argued, however, in "The Conservation of 'Race'" that racism continues to serve the interests of the ruling classes in the West; in *Black American Literature Forum*, 23 (Spring 1989), pp. 37–60.
7. As I argued in "The Uncompleted Argument: Du Bois and the Illusion of Race." The reactive (or dialectical) character of this move explains why Sartre calls its manifestations in Négritude an "antiracist racism"; see "Orphée Noir," his preface to Senghor's *Anthologie de la nouvelle poésie nègre et malgache de langue française* (Paris: PUF, 1948). Sartre believed, of course, that the synthesis of this dialectic would be the transcendence of racism; and it was his view of it as a stage—the antithesis—in that process that allowed him to see it as a positive advance over the original "thesis" of European racism. I suspect that the reactive character of

antiracist racism accounts for the tolerance that is regularly extended to it in liberal circles; but this tolerance is surely hard to justify unless one shares Sartre's optimistic interpretation of it as a stage in a process that leads to the end of all racisms. (And unless your view of this dialectic is deterministic, you should in any case want to play an argumentative role in moving to this next stage.)

For a similar Zionist response see Horace Kallen's "The Ethics of Zionism," *Maccabaean*, August 1906.

8. "The Race Problem in America," in Brotz's *Negro Social and Political Thought* (New York: Basic Books, 1966), p. 184.

9. *Christianity, Islam and the Negro Race* (1887; reprinted Edinburgh: Edinburgh University Press, 1967), p. 197.

10. This is in part a reflection of an important asymmetry: loathing, unlike love, needs justifying; and this, I would argue, is because loathing usually leads to acts that are *in se* undesirable, whereas love leads to acts that are largely *in se* desirable—indeed, supererogatorily so.

11. See my "Racism and Moral Pollution," *Philosophical Forum*, 18 (Winter-Spring 1986–87), pp. 185–202.

12. *Ethics and the Limits of Philosophy* (Cambridge, Mass.: Harvard University Press, 1985), p. 12. I do not, as is obvious, share Williams's skepticism about morality.

STUDY QUESTIONS

1. Do you think that private clubs that restrict membership to people of a certain race should be considered racist organizations? What if membership is restricted to people of a minority race? Does this change your previous judgment? Why or why not?

2. What is the difference between what Appiah calls "racialism," "extrinsic racism," and "intrinsic racism"? Which form of racism do you encounter most often?

3. What reasons does Appiah give for thinking that racists "exhibit a systematically distorted rationality"? Do you agree?

4. Do you agree that "brute biological relatedness" should not make an ethical difference in our deliberations about how to treat others?

Racism and Visible Race

LINDA MARTIN ALCOFF

Linda Martin Alcoff is Professor of Philosophy at Hunter College and the CUNY Graduate Center. She has written extensively on many subjects, including social identity and race, epistemology and politics, sexual violence, and many historical figures, such as Michel Foucault and Enrique Dussel. Among her many works are two authored books: *Real Knowing: New Versions of the Coherence Theory* (1996) and *Visible Identities: Race, Gender, and the Self* (2006).

. .

When the critical legal theorist Gary Peller was growing up during the period of school desegregation in Atlanta, he was chosen among a select group of high school students to participate in a citywide project of "unlearning racism." The students were brought together in a large room, the lights were turned off, and they were then invited to touch each other's faces in the dark. The administrators hoped that, in the dark, the students would realize that race makes no difference. Peller persuasively critiques this exercise as a sham

From *Visible Identities: Race, Gender, and the Self.* © 2006 by Oxford Univ. Press.

because, when the lights were turned back on, the economic and political disparities between the black and white communities in Atlanta were still in place, and a serious attempt to address racism would have had to address those disparities. But in one sense, the school administrators understood correctly the importance of racialized visible differences in student interaction. By eliminating visibility, they hoped the usual distrust, discomfort, and hostility would be absent and new forms of interaction might surface. Unfortunately, the lights had to be turned back on, and things were then indeed, as Peller says, just the same.

In this chapter I want to think through the relationship between racism and the visibility of racialized identity. If one believes that the very existence of racialized identity entails racism, this question will be a nonstarter, but this issue turns on the way in which we understand what racialized identities are. I have argued in earlier chapters that social identities are **hermeneutic locations** attached to historical experiences that are also concrete sites of interpretation and understanding. On this account, racial identity is not a product of "race"—as if this were a natural phenomena or meaningful biological category—but is historically evolving and culturally contextual, and thus it is not clear to me that racist hierarchies are necessarily entailed. The historical legacy of racial identities will always carry as a central feature the history of racism, and in this way there is an association of race with racism, but *future* meanings of racial identity itself are open-ended. Nonetheless, to identify social groups through their visible racialized features (that is, features in which race is thought to inhere) seems arbitrary and, at the very least, inherently dangerous. If the viability of race as a nonracist category of identity depends on its cultural horizon rather than physical manifestations, shouldn't the whole process of *seeing* race come to an end? This is the topic that I want to focus on in this chapter: the visibility of race. Peller is surely right that eliminating the visible practices of racialization is not *sufficient* for the elimination of racism, but we might still ask: is it perhaps *necessary*?

It is easy to imagine a situation, such as Danzy Senna describes in her autobiographical novel, *Caucasia*, in which two sisters share the same two parents, grow up in the same house, but are assigned different racial identities (Senna 1998). If their parents differ in racial background, or if even just one parent comes from a "mixed" background, this scenario is all too common in social contexts, such as North America, where gradations of skin color or alterations in hair texture signify differences of type. In other words, though siblings are genetically closer than any other human relationship, racial identity can be assigned differentially without regard to ancestry, background experiences, or biology.

It is easy for me to imagine such a scenario because it is close to the one I experienced in childhood. As very young girls, my older sister and I came from Panama to the Jim Crow South, lived with our white mother's family in their home, and attended white schools. Through the accidents of birth, I could generally pass, but my sister was not so "lucky," and some of our white relatives had Klan-like sensibilities. The fact that she spoke only Spanish at first compounded the problem. She was consequently shunned at home, and she failed in school. As siblings, my sister and I shared close genetic ties, but our visible difference ensured a social disparity. I raise this to underscore the complete idiocy of practices of racial seeing that ground identity in such a way that family, experience, and background are trumped by trivial physical features. But one might then wonder the following: would I prefer that the two sisters Senna writes about share a racial identity, on one side or the other? Am I suggesting that though their "visible" race is thought to differ, their "real" race, based on genetic inheritance, is the same? This is equally absurd. It would seem then that neither biological nor morphological features should have the power of designating race.

However, it is an indisputable fact about the social reality of mainstream North America that racial consciousness works through learned practices and habits of visual discrimination and visible marks on the body. In this way, race operates differently from ethnic or cultural identities, which can be transcended, with enough effort. Inherent to the concept of race is the idea that it exists there on the body itself, not simply on its ornaments or in its behaviors. Races may have indeterminate borders, and some individuals may appear ambiguous, but many people believe that (a) there exists a fact of the matter about one's racial identity, usually determined by ancestry, and (b) that identity is discernible if one peers long enough at, or observes carefully enough, the person's physical features and practiced mannerisms. Though the commonly accepted definition of race explains it by ancestry, the ideology of race asserts its impervious visibility, despite the fact that the two are not always in sync.

Knowing how to pin down those of ambiguous lineage is crucial in this society because racializing perceptual practices are used to produce a visual registry of any given social field, as was argued in the last chapter. This field is organized differently to distribute the likelihood of intersubjective trust, the extension of epistemic credence, and empathy. A body that is racialized, then, is overdetermined through racial classifications and their associated attributions. This was what Fanon was getting at when he wrote that he was a "slave not of the 'idea' others have of me but of my own appearance" (1967, 116).

Should We Unlearn Racial Seeing?

There are several reasons, one might argue, that we must unlearn racial seeing. Most simply, we could argue that without racial seeing, there could be no races, and thus no racism. Even if we want to hold onto the cultural or ethnic identities that race is sometimes used to signify, we could hold that it is the visible feature of *race*, as opposed to culture and ethnicity, that is inherently pernicious and that this is because the visualization of raced attributes works to naturalize the constructions of racial types. There is no doubt that visual differences are "real" differences, in the sense that the visual markers of race are manifest in real features even if those features are made to stand out in relief and are treated as type distinctions rather than gradations. Still, it is the very fact of visibility itself that makes such markers especially valuable for the naturalizing ideologies of race. All the more reason to disentangle social identity from visible bodily attributes.

Moreover, perception has the added attribute of being, as Merleau-Ponty said, "not presumed true, but defined as access to truth" (1962, xvi). As we saw in the previous chapter, this means that perception cannot readily or easily become the object of analysis itself. Recall Merleau-Ponty's description of how perceptual processes involved in cognition can become organized, like bodily movements used to perform various everyday operations, into integrated units that become attenuated to such a degree that they are experienced as simple, uninterpreted perception. This is surely how racial profiling is experienced most of the time: the profiler does not understand him or herself to be using judgment at all but simply perceiving danger. The development of the concept of racial profiling is an attempt to make such perceptual practices manifest and thus open to critique.

A vision-centric approach to cognition would seem to lend itself especially easily to a **positivist** ideology, as if the act of seeing were not an act of interpretation, and as if what is visible and thus what is seen were thus indubitable. In a series of recent studies on the effect of **ocularcentrism** in the history of philosophy, collected by David Michael Levin, a number of other problems with vision as a source of knowledge are explored (Levin 1993, 1997). According to Nietzsche, the will wants everything to be totally visible and totally clear, since unclarity produces anxiety. Thus we desire a form of knowing that is analogous to the certain reliability of clear sight, which explains the human tendency toward a metaphysics of presence. As Gary Shapiro points out, however, this indicates that for Nietzsche it is not that the organ of sight itself tends toward transcendental metaphysics, since here it is merely doing the bidding of the will (Shapiro 1993). But Nietzsche's observations do suggest that vision is especially useful in perpetrating the illusion of transparent cognition. Ocularcentric **epistemologies** also have the reverse effect, of not only characterizing the nature of the known but also defining with absolute finality the unknowable. What cannot be "made totally visible and clear" may disappear altogether from consciousness, as Herman Rapaport argues in regard to atrocities beyond our field of immediate vision or comprehension (1993). If knowing is seeing, then what cannot be seen cannot be known or considered.

A further danger of an ocularcentric epistemology follows from the fact that vision itself is all too often thought to operate as a *solitary* means to knowledge. Against claims from another, one demands to "see for oneself," as if sight is an individual operation that passes judgment on the claims that others make without also always relying on them. By contrast, knowledge based on the auditory sense, some have argued, is inherently dialogic, and encourages us to listen to what the other says, rather than merely confirming their claims or judging how they appear. And from Foucault we have developed a sensibility to the disciplining potential of visibility. Ours is an era where surveillance is the preferred route of power; where power expands itself through an expansion of visibility in work places, public spaces, and even private ones. On this point Foucault is in agreement with his nemesis, Sartre, for whom the look of the other is a source of domination.

Racism makes productive use of this look, using learned visual cues to demarcate and organize human kinds. Recall the suggestion from Goldberg and West that the genealogy of race itself emerged simultaneously to the ocularcentric tendencies of the Western episteme, in which the criterion for knowledge was classifiability, which in turn required visible difference. Without the operation through sight, then, perhaps race would truly wither away, or mutate into less oppressive forms of social identity such as ethnicity and culture, which make reference to the histories, experiences, and productions of a people, to their subjective lives, in other words, and not merely to objective and arbitrary bodily features.

Without too much effort, one can imagine a distant future in which human differences are not organized in terms of race; as I argued earlier, one can imagine this much more easily than, by contrast, one might imagine a future without gender. Unless we abolish the biological division of labor in the reproduction of the human species, there will continue to be a profound difference between the males and females of our species, even if the meanings, the implications, the boundaries, and the intensity of that difference continue to transform. Still, the bodily and visible differences that exist between most males and females is **supervenient** on the biological division of labor. Alternatively, the visible markers of race have no biological correlates, as Gould, Marshall, Washburn, Livingstone, and others have shown (see Harding 1993). Conventional race categories have no correspondence to genotype, genetic variability, or clinal variations. And the phenotypical features used to differentiate the races are underdetermined by genetic inheritance in any case. The claim that there is a behavioral or intellectual correlation to current race categories would require (a) a genetic frequency that conforms to race categories, but that in fact does not

obtain, and (b) proof that genes determine phenotype, morphology, and behavior, but that also does not obtain (and could not given everything we know about genes). Thus, using racial categories to direct biological research has been described as focusing the microscope on the box the slides came in (see, esp., Livingstone 1993; Marshall 1993).

The physical features conventionally used to differentiate the races are almost laughably insignificant: skin tone, hair texture, shape of facial features. These markers do have *some* practical effects, in the effects of sun exposure on the skin, for example. But such facts are much less significant than one's role in reproduction. Thus, it is easier to imagine a future without race than without gender: if the complete elimination of gender would require a radical rehaul of biological reproduction, the elimination of race would seem to require only a retooling of our perceptual apparatuses. But here, I want to insert a worry: some white folks have declared, no doubt prematurely, that they have already reached utopia. While the rest of us continue to see in color, they declare themselves to be color-blind, to not notice whether people are "black, white, green or purple."

Color Blindness

Bernita Berry and Patricia Williams have both noted and analyzed the phenomenon of **racial color blindness** (Berry 1995; P. Williams 1997). Williams recounts that in her son's nursery school, color blindness had been pressed upon the children by well-meaning teachers, with the result of leaving "those in my son's position pulled between the clarity of their own experience and the often alienating terms in which they must seek social acceptance" (4). Despite the teachers' attempts to deny the relevance of color, racism was still active on the playground as the children fought over whether "black people could play 'good guys'" (3). Williams argues that although she embraces "color-blindness as a legitimate hope for the future," in our contemporary context "the very notion of blindness about color constitutes an ideological confusion at best, and denial at its very worst" (4). Berry similarly argues that such statements as "I just see people; I don't see color" reflect "a deeply hidden effect of racism. This statement reduces socially significant human differences to invisibleness and meaningless hype whereby one does not have to acknowledge what one does not see" (46). Ultimately, she explains, the statement is meant to impart that racism "may be a reality for those other people—'those minorities'—but they do not exist for the speaker" (46). I found growing up in the post–civil rights South that color blindness was regularly claimed by white folks and regularly repudiated by folks of color. There seemed to be an anxiety about the perception of race on the part of some whites, a fear of acknowledging that one sees it.

The interesting independent and avant garde film *Suture* has been talked about as the best visual representation of postmodernism in the past decade, but I think it also evidences a revealing anxiety about seeing race. The film offers an intriguing narrative about a case of fratricide in which a white man (Vincent) attempts to murder his black brother (Clay) and stage it as his own suicide. The attempted murder fails, but Clay is severely burned and injured, and only after much surgery does Clay regain his body intact. The twist is that, although Vincent's attempt to murder Clay fails, his identity switch succeeds. As Clay recuperates, with his dark skin quite visible, we expect the hospital staff and Vincent's friend who visits him in the hospital to notice that the survivor of the accident is a different man, not the white Vincent as the identification papers on his body at the time of the accident led people to believe. But they all mistake him as Vincent. And Clay's amnesia eventually results in his own belief that he is his white brother, despite the fact that he looks at pictures and even a videotape of the "original" Vincent.

Suture thus provides an effective dramatization of the way in which the self is constituted by the other: Clay becomes Vincent because everyone around him treats him as Vincent. And because Vincent is white and Clay is black, when Clay becomes Vincent his life takes a 180-degree turn, which is played to comic effect in, for example, his sudden development of a taste in classical music. Clay becomes Vincent in social position, sensibilities, and even memory. He assumes ownership of all of Vincent's possessions, and Vincent's friends and the police impose memories of Vincent's past on Clay. Thus, it is not simply that Clay has been mistaken for Vincent, but that Clay is transformed into Vincent when he is interpellated as white; his subjectivity and characteristics change so radically that, by the end, it is clear that Clay is, indeed, dead.

The term "**suture**" itself is, of course, a key concept from Lacan. Kalpana Seshadri-Crooks, who has developed a very interesting Lacanian reading of the film, explains Lacan's concept of suture as "the process by which the subject comes to find a place for itself in a signifying chain by inserting itself in what is perceived as a gap, a place-holder for it" (2000, 105). Clay becomes Vincent by such a process in which he, or his body, is inserted into the place-holder for Vincent. Seshadri-Crooks's reading of the film develops several different themes, but she shares my view that it foregrounds for the audience our own racial seeing, that is, the importance we attach to racial identity. The new Vincent's skin tone is not explained in reference to skin grafting or surgery; his friends and family all look at the old Vincent's photographs, then back to the new Vincent, and exclaim that there is an exact match. The movie ends with none of the characters noticing that the man who survived the car bombing has dark skin while the man they think him to be had light skin. As Seshadri-Crooks puts it, "By requiring us to suspend our *belief* [that is, that no one in the film recognizes the visible difference between Clay and Vincent], the film . . . puts pressure on our suturing into the narration and forces a purchase of our visual pleasure at the price of our own raced subjectivities" (104). The suturing we are made to be aware of, the filmmakers must have hoped, is ultimately not Clay's into his brother's life but our own suturing into racist society.

While I can appreciate the efficacy of the film toward this end, I also believe it manifests a (white) anxiety about seeing race. The coherence of the narrative depends on all the characters being, in effect, color blind, in the colloquial sense of the phrase that Williams and Berry critique. Yet if the audience is made to feel that their own racial seeing is racist, they must then aspire to become like the whites in the movie who apparently cannot see skin color. It is true that by the end of the movie, Clay no longer exists in any significant sense, and thus Clay *is* Vincent. But the audience is also privy to the knowledge that even if Clay no longer exists, the man who has assumed

Vincent's life is not Vincent. By the logic of the film, however, anyone, of any body type, could be sutured into anyone else's life. On this view, the "true" self that exists below the surface can cast aside its racialized identity as an animal might shed its skin. Even if we can imagine a distant future without race, I would argue that today racial identity cannot be shed this easily and is not fully reducible to its visible markers such that without them, an individual would simply drop his racial identity.

In order to consider the viability and desirability of the view that *Suture* seems to endorse, let me start by raising again the question of whether the hope for an eradication of visible racial identity is in collusion with the color-blind declaration that Williams and Berry critique. Williams and Berry leave open the possibility of a future beyond race, but their critique of the color-blind position is, as I said, based not simply on skepticism of its likely reality but also on their insistence that race needs to be seen. As Berry puts it, the refusal to see race has the effect of reducing "socially significant human difference to invisibleness and meaningless hype." This argument could be interpreted in two possible ways: (1) race needs to be seen because only then will racism and the ways in which race has distorted human identity be seen, or (2) race needs to be seen in order to see racism and the ways in which race has distorted human identity, but also in order to acknowledge the positive sense of racial identity that has been carved from histories of oppression. Racial identity may have begun in oppression, but the experience of even these sorts of collective identities (i.e., racialized identities) is not always expressed as trauma or manifested as an antagonistic tribalism.

In *Black Orpheus* Sartre perceptively addressed some aspects of racism in Western literature but assumed that the future we all want would be not reformulation and redemption of racial identity, but its disappearance. He seemed incapable of imagining social identities generally as anything but constraints on individual freedom. But social identities can take numerous forms, and collective differences can be articulated through historical experience, religion, cultural coherence, even geographical location, any of which is surely better than the arbitrary and insignificant phenotypic differences by which race is assigned. What is unique about race is this necessary marking of the body itself. Gender also operates in this way

socially, but as I've said it bears a deeper relation to truly significant human difference than race has or can, and thus its visible markers have less of an air of arbitrary unfairness. Isn't it the visibility itself that gives race what Toni Morrison called its "lethal cling"?

If this is so, we might then want to ask: what are the real possibilities of reducing race visibility?

What's Possible?

Despite the fact that, since Locke, philosophers have characterized color as a secondary rather than primary quality, color perception is the result of external stimulation just as with all other forms of perception. In particular, as C. L. Hardin, a philosopher of color, explains, color perception is "the detection of electromagnetic radiation in the wavelength band extending from 380 to 760 nm (one nanometer = one millimicron = one billionth of a meter)" (1984, 125). The immediate source of visual stimulation is "light which has been reflected from the surface of physical objects. Such surfaces normally reflect incident light selectively; the pattern of wavelength selectivity determines the color which we see the object as having" (125). Variations in color perception are explained generally by "the state of adaptation of the eye, the character of the illuminant, and the color and brightness of surrounding objects" (125). There is disagreement among scientists who study color perception about why our vision is restricted to the color spectrum that runs from red to blue, and why the mix of hues is limited, but the facts about our perceptual limits are indisputable. For human beings, as the old example goes, "nothing can be red all over and green all over."

Such naturalized accounts of color perception may well create anxiety when linked to practices of racial identification, given that naturalized accounts of race and racism have been such an important part of racial ideology. And in fact, naturalized explanations of the creation of racial categories are still popular. Psychologist Lawrence Hirschfeld reports that "the prevalent point of view in psychology is that racialized thought is a by-product of the way information is organized and processed" (1996, 8). Here's how the argument goes: The propensity to classify facilitates thought by "reducing the sheer amount of information to which people need to attend" (8). Moreover, classifications can "extend our knowledge by capturing nonobvious similarities between their members" (8). We need only see that a given creature is a cat to be able to infer its food preferences, sleeping habits, and likely aversion to dogs without having to learn these facts from an extended observation of the individual animal. Psychologists then surmise that (a) because of the human propensity to classify on the basis of "conspicuous physical similarities" and (b) because gender and race have "prominent physical correlates," it follows that the categorization of humans by gender and race is natural to human cognition.

But would such a process be functional in the way that, say, the classification "cat" is functional? In regard to gender, the physical capacities for reproduction of males and females is certainly a fact that will at times be useful to know, but what do we learn when we classify people by race? What hair salon they might go to? What is pernicious about race classifications, which of course has also been pernicious about the history of gender classifications, is the host of attributes purportedly correlating to physical racial features. Here is where we clearly need more explanatory resources than the basic wiring of the human eye and the functional orientation of human cognition.

There is good evidence that the practice of othering those who are different in skin tone is historically and culturally particular rather than universal. In *The Black Notebooks*, Toi Derricotte describes what her life has been like as a black woman who is light enough to often pass as white. She recounts the following experience:

A black boy in the fourth grade says to me, "I'd like to be your son."

A white boy sitting near him responds, "You could *never* be her son."

"Why not?" I ask.

"Because he's black."

[And then Toi says,] "But I'm black, too."

He looks at me, his eyes swimming with confusion and pain.

Derricotte offers an explanation of this incident as follows:

White children might have a more difficult time forming a concept of kinship with people of different colors. Black children grow up in families where there is every conceivable color, texture of hair, thickness of feature. In white families there is much less difference. I decide to test this.

"How many in the room have people in their families that are all different colors, some people as light as I am, some people as dark as Sheldon?"

All the black kids raise their hands.

"How many have people in their family that are all just about the same color?"

All the white kids raise their hands. (1995, 105)

The propensity to identify those of different colors as potential family members is commonplace in Caribbean cultures as well, where families often include people who are of different "races," at least races by North American standards, and these are not just in-laws. This does not make racism or the preference for whiteness disappear, but it does shift the locus of othering such that skin tone is not sufficient for classification.

Lawrence Hirschfeld's work on children's construction of human kinds provides evidence that children come to know which visible features are relevant to human classifications only after they "integrate their perceptual knowledge with **ontological** knowledge" (1996, 137). This is not to say that the **perceptual competences** are irrelevant or secondary, but that they become operable in cognition only when children adapt to what Hirschfeld calls **domain-specific competence**, or the ability to gain, organize, and use "knowledge about a particular content area" (12). In other words, the mind is not, as previous psychologists typically imagined, like a general all-purpose problem solver but more like a "collection of . . . special-purpose tools, each targeting a specific problem or content."[1] Domain-specific competences direct attention "to certain sorts of data" and posit ontological organizations of perceptible phenomena. Hirschfeld's experiments provide an empirical confirmation of the claims of philosophers from Mead to Heidegger to Merleau-Ponty that the results of perception represent sedimented contextual knowledges, that "our individual sensibilities and perceptions are never purely individual, but are the result of our upbringing, heritage and identity" (137).

Previous researchers on race classification have generally hypothesized the construction of racial categories as building from perception in a linear causal sequence. In contrast, Hirschfeld hypothesized two types of cognitive competence: perceptual and domain-specific, which can work in tandem or sequentially in either order. For example, a child may learn the relevant conceptual domain of color in her culture, by which color is used to organize human kinds, and only then "begin to attend in earnest to the physical correlates that adults believe are important in racial classification" (137). To show this he devised a set of experiments to test the following prediction: that the ability to recall the racial identity of a person should be higher on "verbal rather than visual tasks," given his hypothesis that social ontologies are initially derived from discursive information rather than visual information alone. "The standard view," that is, the view that he put to empirical test, "predicts that racial cognition should be better evoked by visual than by verbal stimuli" (140). Hirschfeld's method was as follows: "Sixty-four 3- and 4-year-old French pre-schoolers" were read a series of simple stories in which the characters were each described in terms of race, occupation, gender, behavior, and a nonracial physical feature (such as body type or age).[2] The children's recall was then tested. In every case, occupation was remembered far better than any other attribute. However, four-year-olds showed a marked improvement over three-year-olds in their ability to remember race. These results were then compared to a similar study in which visual narratives rather than spoken narratives were used with a different group of children. Here, gender outranked occupation in the number of times it was recalled, and race dropped significantly down. In a further visual narrative experiment adding in more variables, children remembered clothing, gender, and behavior about equally, with race dropping to less than half and even to a quarter of the other markers. The fact that race was less well remembered when the narrative was visual rather than verbal strongly suggests that the visual cues of race become operable only after a child has developed a cognitive competence specific to the domain of race in his or her cultural context.

These results do not suggest that human beings might be led to confuse light with dark skin tone, as in the *Suture* example, or that we would become color-blind, but that color could certainly become less salient, less memorable, and that we could come to perceive skin tone in the way it more exactly is presented to consciousness: as a continuously varying attribute rather than a set of discrete categories.

The attempts to explain racial classifications by natural facts of human cognition are surely inadequate. Sight does not lead in a direct line to race. However, we still have the arguments of the philosophers that relying on vision for knowledge is itself a dangerous practice: it obscures its interpretive operations through a veneer of pure perception, and thus can lend itself to a metaphysics of presence where the perception of "sexual licentiousness" or "dull wittedness" appears as a fact in the world. But is sight really worse than other avenues in this regard? Differences of diction and accent can get as easily marked as the sign of innate inferiority as differences of appearance. The olfactory senses have also been used to legitimize discrimination. Racism is an equal-opportunity interpreter across the five senses.

One might well think that we should turn away from the senses altogether as too unreliable. But sometimes sight is our best chance for human communication, if we can only learn to be attentive enough. Adorno reminds us, against Levinas, that "the mechanism of 'pathic projection' determines that those in power perceive as human only their own reflected image" (Adorno 1988, 105; quoted in Levin 1993, 19). We are not always moved to ethical responsiveness by the face of the Other. Nonetheless, if our visual faculty did not by itself lead us to this depravity, then eliminating its role in cognition cannot be either necessary or sufficient if we wish to unlearn racism. Rather, we need new domain-specific competences within which to practice our sight. In the movie *My Dinner with Andre*, the egotistical Andre recounts to his dull-witted friend Wallace that he has suddenly seen anew the picture of his wife that he has carried in his wallet for twenty years. Before, he had always seen his wife in the picture as sensuous and beautiful; only much later did he look hard at the photograph and notice how sad she looked, how profoundly unhappy. It took maturity perhaps for Andre to see the truth that the picture held for him, to learn the competences by which he could notice what was right before his eyes all along. I suspect that we, like Andre, simply need to learn to see better.

NOTES

1. This is Georgia Warnke's helpful gloss on the view of vision held by Mead and Habermas. See Warnke 1993, 305.
2. Hirschfeld describes his experiments and reports their results in chapters 4, 5, and 6 of *Race in the Making*.

BIBLIOGRAPHY

Adorno, Theodor. 1988. *Minima Moralia: Reflections from Damaged Life*. London: New Left Books.

Berry, Bernita. 1995. "'I Just See People': Exercises in Learning the Effects of Racism and Sexism." In *Overcoming Racism and Sexism*, edited by Linda A. Bell and David Blumenfeld, 45–51. Lanham, Md.: Rowman and Littlefield.

Derricotte, Toi. 1997. *The Black Notebooks: An Interior Journey*. New York: W. W. Norton.

Fanon, Frantz. 1967. *Black Skin, White Masks*. Translated by Charles Lam Markmann. New York: Grove Press.

Hardin, C. L. 1984. "A New Look at Color." *American Philosophical Quarterly* 21, no. 2 (April): 125–34.

Harding, Sandra, ed. 1993. *The Racial Economy of Science: Toward a Democratic Future*. Bloomington: Indiana University Press.

Hirschfeld, Lawrence. 1996. *Race in the Making: Cognition, Culture, and the Child's Construction of Human Kinds*. Cambridge, Mass.: MIT Press.

Levin, David Michael, ed. 1993. *Modernity and the Hegemony of Vision*. Berkeley: University of California Press.

———. 1997. *Sites of Vision: The Discursive Construction of Sight in the History of Philosophy*. Cambridge, Mass.: MIT Press.

Livingstone, Frank B. 1993. "On the Nonexistence of Human Races." In *The Racial Economy of Science: Toward a Democratic Future*, edited by Sandra Harding, 131–41. Bloomington: Indiana University Press.

Marshall, Gloria. 1993. "Racial Classifications: Popular and Scientific." In *The Racial Economy of Science: Toward a Democratic Future*, edited by Sandra Harding, 116–27. Bloomington: Indiana University.

Merleau-Ponty, Maurice. 1962. *Phenomenology of Perception*. Translated by Colin Smith. London: Routledge and Kegan Paul.

Rapaport, Herman. 1993. "Time's Cinders." In *Modernity and the Hegemony of Vision*, edited by David Michael Levin, 218–33. Berkeley: University of California Press.

Senna, Danzy. 1998. *Caucasia*. New York: Penguin.

Seshadri-Crooks, Kalpana. 2000. *Desiring Whiteness: A Lacanian Analysis of Race*. New York: Routledge.

Shapiro, Gary. 1993. "In the Shadows of Philosophy: Nietzsche and the Question of Vision." In *Modernity and the Hegemony of Vision*, edited by David Michael Levin, 124–42. Berkeley: University of California Press.

Warnke, Georgia. 1993. "Ocularcentrism and Social Criticism." In *Modernity and the Hegemony of Vision*, edited by David Michael Levin, 287–308. Berkley: University of California Press.

Williams, Patricia J. 1997. *Seeing a Color-Blind Future: The Paradox of Race*. New York: Farrar, Straus, and Giroux.

KEY TERMS

Hermeneutic location
Positivist
Ocularcentrism
Epistemology
Supervenient
Racial color blindness
Suture
Ontological
Perceptual competence
Domain-specific competence

STUDY QUESTIONS

1. What does Alcoff mean when she says that racial identity is not a product of "race"?
2. What is meant by "racial color blindness"? What does Alcoff think is problematic about this idea?
3. What happens in the film *Suture*? What worry does Alcoff raise about this movie?
4. Describe Toi Derricotte's experience. Why is this significant for Alcoff?
5. What is meant by the terms "domain-specific competence" and "perceptual competence"? Why is recognizing these two competences important for Alcoff?
6. Does Alcoff think we must stop seeing race in order to be rid of racism? Why or why not?

F. CHALLENGES TO MORALITY

1. MORALITY AND SELF–INTEREST

The Republic

PLATO

· ·

Part I
(Book I)
Some Current Views of Justice

Chapter I (I. 327–331 d)
Cephalus: Justice as Honesty
in Word and Deed

The whole imaginary conversation is narrated by Socrates to an unspecified audience. The company who will take part in it assemble at the house of Cephalus, a retired manufacturer living at the Piraeus, the harbour town about five miles from Athens. It includes, besides Plato's elder brothers, Glaucon and Adeimantus, Cephalus' sons, Polemarchus, Lysias, well known as a writer of speeches, and Euthydemus; Thrasymachus of Chalcedon, a noted teacher of rhetoric, who may have formulated the definition of justice as 'the interest of the stronger,' though hardly any evidence about his opinions exists outside the Republic; and a number of Socrates' young friends.

The occasion is the festival of Bendis, a goddess whose cult had been imported from Thrace. Cephalus embodies the wisdom of a long life honourably spent in business. He is well-to-do, but values money as a means to that peace of mind which comes of honesty and the ability to render to gods and men their due. This is what he understands by 'right' conduct or justice.

SOCRATES. I walked down to the Piraeus yesterday with Glaucon, the son of Ariston, to make my prayers to the goddess. As this was the first celebration of her festival, I wished also to see how the ceremony would be conducted. The Thracians, I thought, made as fine a show in the procession as our own people, though they did well enough. The prayers and the spectacle were over, and we were leaving to go back to the city, when from some way off Polemarchus, the son of Cephalus, caught sight of us starting homewards and sent his slave running to ask us to wait for him. The boy caught my garment from behind and gave me the message.

I turned round and asked where his master was. There, he answered; coming up behind. Please wait.

Very well, said Glaucon; we will.

A minute later Polemarchus joined us, with Glaucon's brother, Adeimantus, and Niceratus, the son of Nicias, and some others who must have been at the procession.

Socrates, said Polemarchus, I do believe you are starting back to town and leaving us.

You have guessed right, I answered.

Well, he said, you see what a large party we are?

I do.

Unless you are more than a match for us, then, you must stay here.

Isn't there another alternative? said I; we might convince you that you must let us go.

How will you convince us, if we refuse to listen?

We cannot, said Glaucon.

Well, we shall refuse; make up your minds to that.

Here Adeimantus interposed: Don't you even know that in the evening there is going to be a torch-race on horseback in honour of the goddess?

On horseback! I exclaimed; that is something new. How will they do it? Are the riders going to race with torches and hand them on to one another?

Just so, said Polemarchus. Besides, there will be a festival lasting all night, which will be worth seeing. We will go out after dinner and look on. We shall find plenty of young men there and we can have a talk. So please stay, and don't disappoint us.

It looks as if we had better stay, said Glaucon.

Well, said I, if you think so, we will.

Accordingly, we went home with Polemarchus; and there we found his brothers, Lysias and Euthydemus, as well as Thrasymachus of Chalcedon, Charmantides of Paeania, and Cleitophon, the son of Aristonymus. Polemarchus' father, Cephalus, was at home too. I had not seen him for some time, and it struck me that he had aged a good deal. He was sitting in a cushioned chair, wearing a garland, as he had just been conducting a sacrifice in the courtyard. There were some chairs standing round, and we sat down beside him.

As soon as he saw me, Cephalus greeted me. You don't often come down to the Piraeus to visit us, Socrates, he said. But you ought to. If I still had the strength to walk to town easily, you would not have to come here; we would come to you. But, as things are, you really ought to come here oftener. I find, I can assure you, that in proportion as bodily pleasures lose their savour, my appetite for the things of the mind grows keener and I enjoy discussing them

more than ever. So you must not disappoint me. Treat us like old friends, and come here often to have a talk with these young men.

To tell the truth, Cephalus, I answered, I enjoy talking with very old people. They have gone before us on a road by which we too may have to travel, and I think we do well to learn from them what it is like, easy or difficult, rough or smooth. And now that you have reached an age when your foot, as the poets say, is on the threshold, I should like to hear what report you can give and whether you find it a painful time of life.

I will tell you by all means what it seems like to me, Socrates. Some of us old men often meet, true to the old saying that people of the same age like to be together. Most of our company are very sorry for themselves, looking back with regret to the pleasures of their young days, all the delights connected with love affairs and merry-making. They are vexed at being deprived of what seems to them so important; life was good in those days, they think, and now they have no life at all. Some complain that their families have no respect for their years, and make that a reason for harping on all the miseries old age has brought. But to my mind, Socrates, they are laying the blame on the wrong shoulders. If the fault were in old age, so far as that goes, I and all who have ever reached my time of life would have the same experience; but in point of fact, I have met many who felt quite differently. For instance, I remember someone asking Sophocles, the poet, whether he was still capable of enjoying a woman. "Don't talk that way," he answered; "I am only too glad to be free of all that; it is like escaping from bondage to a raging madman." I thought that a good answer at the time, and I still think so; for certainly a great peace comes when age sets us free from passions of that sort. When they weaken and relax their hold, most certainly it means, as Sophocles said, a release from servitude to many forms of madness. All these troubles, Socrates, including the complaints about not being respected, have only one cause; and that is not old age, but a man's character. If you have a contented mind at peace with itself, age is no intolerable burden; without that, Socrates, age and youth will be equally painful.

I was charmed with these words and wanted him to go on talking; so I tried to draw him out. I fancy, Cephalus, said I, most people will not accept that account; they imagine that it is not character that makes your burden light, but your wealth. The rich, they say, have many consolations.

That is true, he replied; they do not believe me; and there is something in their suggestion, though not so much as they suppose. When a man from Seriphus taunted Themistocles and told him that his fame was due not to himself but to his country, Themistocles made a good retort: "Certainly, if I had been born a Seriphian, I should not be famous; but no more would you, if you had been born at Athens." And so one might say to men who are not rich and feel old age burdensome: If it is true that a good man will not find it easy to bear old age and poverty combined, no more will riches ever make a bad man contented and cheerful.

And was your wealth, Cephalus, mostly inherited or have you made your own fortune?

Made my fortune, Socrates? As a man of business I stand somewhere between my grandfather and my father. My grandfather, who was my namesake, inherited about as much property as I have now and more than doubled it; whereas my father Lysanias reduced it below its present level. I shall be content if I can leave these sons of mine not less than I inherited, and perhaps a little more.

I asked, said I, because you strike me as not caring overmuch about money; and that is generally so with men who have not made their own fortune. Those who have are twice as fond of their possessions as other people. They have the same affection for the money they have earned that poets have for their poems, or fathers for their children: they not merely find it useful, as we all do, but it means much to them as being of their own creation. That makes them disagreeable company; they have not a good word for anything but riches.

That is quite true.

It is indeed, I said; but one more question: what do you take to be the greatest advantage you have got from being wealthy?

One that perhaps not many people would take my word for. I can tell you, Socrates, that, when the prospect of dying is near at hand, a man begins to feel some alarm about things that never troubled him before. He may have laughed at those stories they tell of another world and of punishments there for wrongdoing in this life; but now the soul is tormented by a doubt whether they may not be true. Maybe from the weakness of old age, or perhaps because, now that he is nearer to what lies beyond, he begins to get some glimpse of it himself—at any rate he is beset with fear and misgiving; he begins thinking over the past: is there anyone he has wronged? If he finds that his life has been full of wrongdoing, he starts up from his sleep in terror like a child, and his life is haunted by dark forebodings; whereas, if his conscience is clear, that "sweet Hope" that Pindar speaks of is always with him to tend his age. Indeed, Socrates, there is great charm in those lines describing the man who has led a life of righteousness:

> Hope is his sweet companion, she who guides
> Man's wandering purpose, warms his heart
> And nurses tenderly his age.

That is admirably expressed, admirably. Now in this, as I believe, lies the chief value of wealth, not for everyone, perhaps, but for the right-thinking man. It can do much to save us from going to that other world in fear of having cheated or deceived anyone even unintentionally or of being in debt to some god for sacrifice or to some man for money. Wealth has many other uses, of course; but, taking one with another, I should regard this as the best use that can be made of it by a man of sense.

You put your case admirably, Cephalus, said I. But take this matter of doing right: can we say that it really consists in nothing more nor less than telling the truth and paying back anything we may have received? Are not these very actions sometimes right and sometimes wrong? Suppose, for example, a friend who had lent us a weapon were to go mad and then ask for it back, surely anyone would say we ought not to return it. It would not be "right" to do so; nor yet to tell the truth without reserve to a madman.

No, it would not.

Right conduct, then, cannot be defined as telling the truth and restoring anything we have been trusted with.

Yes, it can, Polemarchus broke in, at least if we are to believe Simonides.

Well, well, said Cephalus, I will bequeath the argument to you. It is time for me to attend to the sacrifice.

Your part, then, said Polemarchus, will fall to me as your heir.

By all means, said Cephalus with a smile; and with that he left us, to see to the sacrifice.

Chapter II (I. 331 E–336 A)
Polemarchus: Justice as Helping
Friends and Harming Enemies

. . . .

Then, said I, if you are to inherit this discussion, tell me, what is this saying of Simonides about right conduct which you approve?

That is just to render every man his due. That seems to me a fair statement.

It is certainly hard to question the inspired wisdom of a poet like Simonides; but what this saying means you may know, Polemarchus, but I do not. Obviously it does not mean what we were speaking of just now—returning something we have been entrusted with to the owner even when he has gone out of his mind. And yet surely it is his due, if he asks for it back?

Yes.

But it is out of the question to give it back when he has gone mad?

True.

Simonides, then, must have meant something different from that when he said it was just to render a man his due.

Certainly he did; his idea was that, as between friends, what one owes to another is to do him good, not harm.

I see, said I; to repay money entrusted to one is not to render what is due, if the two parties are friends and the repayment proves harmful to the lender. That is what you say Simonides meant?

Yes, certainly.

And what about enemies? Are we to render whatever is their due to them?

Yes certainly, what really is due to them; which means, I suppose, what is appropriate to an enemy—some sort of injury.

It seems, then, that Simonides was using words with a hidden meaning, as poets will. He really meant to define justice as rendering to everyone what is appropriate to him; only he called that his "due."

Well, why not?

But look here, said I. Suppose we could question Simonides about the art of medicine—whether a physician can be described as rendering to some object what is due or appropriate to it; how do you think he would answer?

That the physician administers the appropriate diet or remedies to the body.

And the art of cookery—can that be described in the same way?

Yes; the cook gives the appropriate seasoning to his dishes.

Good. And the practice of justice?

If we are to follow those analogies, Socrates, justice would be rendering services or injuries to friends or enemies.

So Simonides means by justice doing good to friends and harm to enemies?

I think so.

And in matters of health who would be the most competent to treat friends and enemies in that way?

A physician.

And on a voyage, as regards the dangers of the sea?

A ship's captain.

In what sphere of action, then, will the just man be the most competent to do good or harm?

In war, I should imagine; when he is fighting on the side of his friends and against his enemies.

I see. But when we are well and staying on shore, the doctor and the ship's captain are of no use to us.

True.

Is it also true that the just man is useless when we are not at war?

I should not say that.

So justice has its uses in peace-time too?

Yes.

Like farming, which is useful for producing crops, or shoemaking, which is useful for providing us with shoes. Can you tell me for what purposes justice is useful or profitable in time of peace?

For matters of business, Socrates.

In a partnership, you mean?

Yes.

But if we are playing draughts, or laying bricks, or making music, will the just man be as good and helpful a partner as an expert draught-player, or a builder, or a musician?

No.

Then in what kind of partnership will he be more helpful?

Where money is involved, I suppose.

Except, perhaps, Polemarchus, when we are putting our money to some use. If we are buying or selling a horse, a judge of horses would be a better partner; or if we are dealing in ships, a shipwright or a sea-captain.

I suppose so.

Well, when will the just man be especially useful in handling our money?

When we want to deposit it for safe-keeping.

When the money is to lie idle, in fact?

Yes.

So justice begins to be useful only when our money is out of use?

Perhaps so.

And in the same way, I suppose, if a pruning-knife is to be used, or a shield, or a lyre, then a vine-dresser, or a soldier, or a musician will be of service; but justice is helpful only when these things are to be kept safe. In fact justice is never of any use in using things; it becomes useful when they are useless.

That seems to follow.

If that is so, my friend, justice can hardly be a thing of much value. And here is another point. In boxing or fighting of any sort skill in dealing blows goes with skill in keeping them off; and the same doctor that can keep us from disease would also be clever at producing it by stealth; or again, a general will be good at keeping his army safe, if he can also cheat the enemy and steal his plans and dispositions. So a man who is expert in keeping things will always make an expert thief.

Apparently.

The just man, then, being good at keeping money safe, will also be good at stealing it.

That seems to be the conclusion, at any rate.

So the just man turns out to be a kind of thief. You must have learnt that from Homer, who showed his predilection for Odysseus' grandfather Autolycus by remarking that he surpassed all men in cheating and perjury. Justice, according to you and Homer and Simonides, turns out to be a form of skill in cheating, provided it be to help a friend or harm an enemy. That was what you meant?

Good God, no, he protested; but I have forgotten now what I did mean. All the same, I do still believe that justice consists in helping one's friends and harming one's enemies.

. . . .

Which do you mean by a man's friends and enemies—those whom he believes to be good honest people and the reverse, or those who really are, though they may not seem so?

Naturally, his loves and hates depend on what he believes.

But don't people often mistake an honest man for a rogue, or a rogue for an honest man; in which case they regard good people as enemies and bad people as friends?

No doubt.

But all the same, it will then be right for them to help the rogue and to injure the good man?

Apparently.

And yet a good man is one who is not given to doing wrong.

True.

According to your account, then, it is right to ill-treat a man who does no wrong.

No, no, Socrates; that can't be sound doctrine.

It must be the wrongdoers, then, that it is right to injure, and the honest that are to be helped.

That sounds better.

Then, Polemarchus, the conclusion will be that for a bad judge of character it will often be right to injure his friends, when they really are rogues, and to help his enemies, when they really are honest men—the exact opposite of what we took Simonides to mean.

That certainly does follow, he said. We must shift our ground. Perhaps our definition of friend and enemy was wrong.

What definition, Polemarchus?

We said a friend was one whom we believe to be an honest man.

And how are we to define him now?

As one who really is honest as well as seeming so. If he merely seems so, he will be only a seeming friend. And the same will apply to enemies.

On this showing, then, it is the good people that will be our friends, the wicked our enemies.

Yes.

You would have us, in fact, add something to our original definition of justice: it will not mean merely doing good to friends and harm to enemies, but doing good to friends who are good, and harm to enemies who are wicked.

Yes, I think that is all right.

Can it really be a just man's business to harm any human being?

Certainly; it is right for him to harm bad men who are his enemies.

But does not harming a horse or a dog mean making it a worse horse or dog, so that each will be a less perfect creature in its own special way?

Yes.

Isn't that also true of human beings—that to harm them means making them worse men by the standard of human excellence?

Yes.

And is not justice a peculiarly human excellence?

Undoubtedly.

To harm a man, then, must mean making him less just.

I suppose so.

But a musician or a riding-master cannot be exercising his special skill, if he makes his pupils unmusical or bad riders.

No.

Whereas the just man is to exercise his justice by making men unjust? Or, in more general terms, the good are to make men bad by exercising their virtue? Can that be so?

No, it cannot.

It can no more be the function of goodness to do harm than of heat to cool or of drought to produce moisture. So if the just man is good, the business of harming people, whether friends or not, must belong to his opposite, the unjust.

I think that is perfectly true, Socrates.

So it was not a wise saying that justice is giving every man his due, if that means that harm is due from the just man to his enemies, as well as help to his friends. That is not true; because we have found that it is never right to harm anyone.

I agree.

Then you and I will make common cause against anyone who attributes that doctrine to Simonides or to any of the old canonical sages, like Bias or Pittacus.

Yes, he said, I am prepared to support you.

Do you know, I think that account of justice, as helping friends and harming enemies, must be due to some despot, so rich and powerful that he thought he could do as he liked—someone like Periander, or Perdiccas, or Xerxes, or Ismenias of Thebes.

That is extremely probable.

Very good, said I; and now that we have disposed of that definition of justice, can anyone suggest another?

Chapter III (I. 336 B–347 E)
Thrasymachus: Justice as the
Interest of the Stronger

. . . .

All this time Thrasymachus had been trying more than once to break in upon our conversation; but his neighbours had restrained him, wishing to hear the argument to the end. In the pause after my last words he could keep quiet no longer; but gathering himself up like a wild beast he sprang at us as if he would tear us in pieces. Polemarchus and I were frightened out of our wits, when he burst out to the whole company:

What is the matter with you two, Socrates? Why do you go on in this imbecile way, politely deferring to each other's nonsense? If you really want to know what justice means, stop asking questions and scoring off the answers you get. You know very well it is easier to ask questions than to answer them. Answer yourself, and tell us what you think justice means. I won't have you telling us it is the same as what is obligatory or useful or advantageous or profitable or expedient; I want a clear and precise statement; I won't put up with that sort of verbiage.

I was amazed by this onslaught and looked at him in terror. If I had not seen this wolf before he saw me, I really believe I should have been struck dumb; but fortunately I had looked at him earlier, when he was beginning to get exasperated with our argument; so I was able to reply, though rather tremulously:

Don't be hard on us, Thrasymachus. If Polemarchus and I have gone astray in our search, you may be quite sure the mistake was not intentional. If we had been looking for a piece of gold, we should never have deliberately allowed politeness to spoil our chance of finding it; and now when we are looking for justice, a thing much more precious than gold, you cannot imagine we should defer to each other in that foolish way and not do our best to bring it to light. You must believe we are in earnest, my friend; but I am afraid the task is beyond our powers, and we might expect a man of your ability to pity us instead of being so severe.

Thrasymachus replied with a burst of sardonic laughter.

Good Lord, he said; Socrates at his old trick of shamming ignorance! I knew it; I told the others you would refuse to commit yourself and do anything sooner than answer a question.

Yes, Thrasymachus, I replied; because you are clever enough to know that if you asked someone what are the factors of the number twelve, and at the same time warned him: "Look here, you are not to tell me that 12 is twice 6, or 3 times 4, or 6 times 2, or 4 times 3; I won't put up with any such nonsense"—you must surely see that no one would answer a question put like that. He would say: "What do you mean, Thrasymachus? Am I forbidden to give any of these answers, even if one happens to be right? Do you want me to give a wrong one?" What would you say to that?

Humph! said he. As if that were a fair analogy!

I don't see why it is not, said I; but in any case, do you suppose our barring a certain answer would prevent the man from giving it, if he thought it was the truth?

Do you mean that you are going to give me one of those answers I barred?

I should not be surprised, if it seemed to me true, on reflection.

And what if I give you another definition of justice, better than any of those? What penalty are you prepared to pay?[1]

The penalty deserved by ignorance, which must surely be to receive instruction from the wise. So I would suggest that as a suitable punishment.

I like your notion of a penalty! he said; but you must pay the costs as well.

I will, when I have any money.

That will be all right, said Glaucon; we will all subscribe for Socrates. So let us have your definition, Thrasymachus.

Oh yes, he said; so that Socrates may play the old game of questioning and refuting someone else, instead of giving an answer himself!

But really, I protested, what can you expect from a man who does not know the answer or profess to know it, and, besides that, has been forbidden by no mean authority to put forward any notions he may have? Surely the definition should naturally come from you, who say you do know the answer and can tell it us. Please do not disappoint us. I should take it as a kindness, and I hope you will not be chary of giving Glaucon and the rest of us the advantage of your instruction.

Glaucon and the others added their entreaties to mine. Thrasymachus was evidently longing to win credit, for he was sure he had an admirable answer ready, though he made a show of insisting that I should be the one to reply. In the end he gave way and exclaimed:

So this is what Socrates' wisdom comes to! He refuses to teach, and goes about learning from others without offering so much as thanks in return.

I do learn from others, Thrasymachus; that is quite true; but you are wrong to call me ungrateful. I give in return all I can—praise; for I have no money. And how ready I am to applaud any idea that seems to me sound, you will see in a moment, when you have stated your own; for I am sure that will be sound.

Listen then, Thrasymachus began. What I say is that "just" or "right" means nothing but what is to the interest of the stronger party. Well, where is your applause? You don't mean to give it me.

I will, as soon as I understand, I said. I don't see yet what you mean by right being the interest of the stronger party. For instance, Polydamas, the athlete, is stronger than we are, and it is to his interest to eat beef for the sake of his muscles; but surely you don't mean that the same diet would be good for weaker men and therefore be right for us?

You are trying to be funny, Socrates. It's a low trick to take my words in the sense you think will be most damaging.

No, no, I protested; but you must explain.

Don't you know, then, that a state may be ruled by a despot, or a democracy, or an aristocracy?

Of course.

And that the ruling element is always the strongest?

Yes.

Well then, in every case the laws are made by the ruling party in its own interest; a democracy makes democratic laws, a despot autocratic ones, and so on. By making these laws they define as "right" for their subjects whatever is for their own interest, and they call anyone who breaks them a "wrongdoer" and punish him accordingly. That is what I mean: in all states alike "right" has the same meaning, namely what is for the interest of the party established in power, and that is the strongest. So the sound conclusion is that what is "right" is the same everywhere: the interest of the stronger party.

Now I see what you mean, said I; whether it is true or not, I must try to make out. When you define right in terms of interest, you are yourself giving one of those answers you forbade to me; though, to be sure, you add "to the stronger party."

An insignificant addition, perhaps!

Its importance is not clear yet; what is clear is that we must find out whether your definition is true. I agree myself that right is in a sense a matter of interest; but when you add "to the stronger party," I don't know about that. I must consider.

Go ahead, then.

I will. Tell me this. No doubt you also think it is right to obey the men in power?

I do.

Are they infallible in every type of state, or can they sometimes make a mistake?

Of course they can make a mistake.

In framing laws, then, they may do their work well or badly?

No doubt.

Well, that is to say, when the laws they make are to their own interest; badly, when they are not?

Yes.

But the subjects are to obey any law they lay down, and they will then be doing right?

Of course.

If so, by your account, it will be right to do what is not to the interest of the stronger party, as well as what is so.

What's that you are saying?

Just what you said, I believe; but let us look again. Haven't you admitted that the rulers, when they enjoin certain acts on their subjects, sometimes mistake their own best interests, and at the same time that it is right for the subjects to obey, whatever they may enjoin?

Yes, I suppose so.

Well, that amounts to admitting that it is right to do what is not to the interest of the rulers or the stronger party. They may unwittingly enjoin what is to their own disadvantage; and you say it is right for the others to do as they are told. In that case, their duty must be the opposite of what you said, because the weaker will have been ordered to do what is against the interest of the stronger. You with your intelligence must see how that follows.

Yes, Socrates, said Polemarchus, that is undeniable.

No doubt, Cleitophon broke in, if you are to be a witness on Socrates' side.

No witness is needed, replied Polemarchus; Thrasymachus himself admits that rulers sometimes ordain acts that are to their own disadvantage, and that it is the subjects' duty to do them.

That is because Thrasymachus said it was right to do what you are told by the men in power.

Yes, but he also said that what is to the interest of the stronger party is right; and, after making both these assertions, he admitted that the stronger sometimes command the weaker subjects to act against their interests. From all which it follows that what is in the stronger's interest is no more right than what is not.

No, said Cleitophon; he meant whatever the stronger *believes* to be in his own interest. That is what the subject must do, and what Thrasymachus meant to define as right.

That was not what he said, rejoined Polemarchus.

No matter, Polemarchus, said I; if Thrasymachus says so now, let us take him in that sense. Now, Thrasymachus, tell me, was that what you intended to say—that right means what the stronger thinks is to his interest, whether it really is so or not?

Most certainly not, he replied. Do you suppose I should speak of a man as "stronger" or "superior" at the very moment when he is making a mistake?

I did think you said as much when you admitted that rulers are not always infallible.

That is because you are a quibbler, Socrates. Would you say a man deserves to be called a physician at the moment when he makes a mistake in treating his patient and just in respect of that mistake; or a mathematician, when he does a sum wrong and just in so far as he gets a wrong result? Of course we do commonly speak of a physician or a mathematician or a scholar having made a mistake; but really none of these, I should say, is ever mistaken, in so far as he is worthy of the name we give him. So strictly speaking—and you are all for being precise—no one who practices a craft makes mistakes. A man is mistaken when his knowledge fails him; and at that moment he is no craftsman. And what is true of craftsmanship or any sort of skill is true of the ruler; though anyone might speak of a ruler making a mistake, just as he might of a physician. You must understand that I was talking in that loose way when I answered your question just now; but the precise statement is this. The ruler, in so far as he is acting as a ruler, makes no mistakes and consequently enjoins what is best for himself; and that is what the subject is to do. So, as I said at first, "right" means doing what is to the interest of the stronger.

Very well, Thrasymachus, said I. So you think I am quibbling?

I am sure you are.

You believe my questions were maliciously designed to damage your position?

I know it. But you will gain nothing by that. You cannot outwit me by cunning, and you are not the man to crush me in the open.

Bless your soul, I answered, I should not think of trying. But, to prevent any more misunderstanding, when you speak of that ruler or stronger party whose interest the weaker ought to serve, please make it clear whether you are using the words in the ordinary way or in that strict sense you have just defined.

I mean a ruler in the strictest possible sense. Now quibble away and be as malicious as you can. I want no mercy. But you are no match for me.

Do you think me mad enough to beard a lion or try to outwit a Thrasymachus?

You did try just now, he retorted, but it wasn't a success.

. . . .

Enough of this, said I. Now tell me about the physician in that strict sense you spoke of: is it his business to earn money or to treat his patients? Remember, I mean your physician who is worthy of the name.

To treat his patients.

And what of the ship's captain in the true sense? Is he a mere seaman or the commander of the crew?

The commander.

Yes, we shall not speak of him as a seaman just because he is on board a ship. That is not the point. He is called captain because of his skill and authority over the crew.

Quite true.

And each of these people has some special interest?[2]

No doubt.

And the craft in question exists for the very purpose of discovering that interest and providing for it?

Yes.

Can it equally be said of any craft that it has an interest, other than its own greatest possible perfection?

What do you mean by that?

Here is an illustration. If you ask me whether it is sufficient for the human body just to be itself, with no need of help from without, I should say, Certainly not; it has weaknesses and defects, and its condition is not all that it might be. That is precisely why the art of medicine was invented: it was designed to help the body and provide for its interests. Would not that be true?

It would.

But now take the art of medicine itself. Has that any defects or weaknesses? Does any art stand in need of some further perfection, as the eye would be imperfect without the power of vision or the ear without hearing, so that in their case an art is required that will study their interests and provide for their carrying out those functions? Has the art itself any corresponding need of some further art to remedy its defects and look after its interests; and will that further art require yet another, and so on for ever? Or will every art look after its own interests? Or, finally, is it not true that no art needs to have its weaknesses remedied or its interests studied either by another art or by itself, because no art has in itself any weakness or fault, and the only interest it is required to serve is that of its subject-matter? In itself, an art is sound and flawless, so long as it is entirely true to its own nature as an art in the strictest sense—and it is the strict sense that I want you to keep in view. Is not that true?

So it appears.

Then, said I, the art of medicine does not study its own interest, but the needs of the body, just as a groom shows his skill by caring for horses, not for the art of grooming. And so every art seeks, not its own advantage—for it has no deficiencies—but the interest of the subject on which it is exercised.

It appears so.

But surely, Thrasymachus, every art has authority and superior power over its subject.

To this he agreed, though very reluctantly.

So far as arts are concerned, then, no art ever studies or enjoins the interest of the superior or stronger party, but always that of the weaker over which it has authority.

Thrasymachus assented to this at last, though he tried to put up a fight. I then went on:

So the physician, as such, studies only the patient's interest, not his own. For as we agreed, the business of the physician, in the strict sense, is not to make money for himself, but to exercise his power over the patient's body; and the ship's captain, again, considered strictly as no mere sailor, but in command of the crew, will study and enjoin the interest of his subordinates, not his own.

He agreed reluctantly.

And so with government of any kind: no ruler, in so far as he is acting as ruler, will study or enjoin what is for his own interest. All that he says and does will be said and done with a view to what is good and proper for the subject for whom he practises his art.

. . . .

At this point, when everyone could see that Thrasymachus' definition of justice had been turned inside out, instead of making any reply, he said:

Socrates, have you a nurse?

Why do you ask such a question as that? I said. Wouldn't it be better to answer mine?

Because she lets you go about sniffling like a child whose nose wants wiping. She hasn't even taught you to know a shepherd when you see one, or his sheep either.

What makes you say that?

Why, you imagine that a herdsman studies the interests of his flocks or cattle, tending and fattening them up with some other end in view than his master's profit or his own; and so you don't see that, in politics, the genuine ruler regards his subjects exactly like sheep, and thinks of nothing else, night and day, but the good he can get out of them for himself. You are so far out in your notions of right and wrong, justice and injustice, as not to know that "right" actually means what is good for someone else, and to be "just" means serving the interest of the stronger who rules, at the cost of the subject who obeys; whereas injustice is just the reverse, asserting its authority over those innocents who are called just, so that they minister solely to their master's advantage and happiness, and not in the least degree to their own. Innocent as you are yourself, Socrates, you must see that a just man always has the worst of it. Take a private business: when a partnership is wound up, you will never find that the more honest of two partners comes off with the larger share; and in their relations to the state, when there are taxes to be paid, the honest man will pay more than the other on the same amount of property; or if there is money to be distributed, the dishonest will get it all. When either of them hold some public office, even if the just man loses in no other way, his private affairs at any rate will suffer from neglect, while his principles will not allow him to help himself from the public funds; not to mention the offence he will give to his friends and relations by refusing to sacrifice those principles to do them a good turn. Injustice has all the opposite advantages. I am speaking of the type I described just now, the man who can get the better of other people on a large scale: you must fix your eye on him, if you want to judge how much it is to one's own interest not to be just. You can see that best in the most consummate form of injustice, which rewards wrongdoing with supreme welfare and happiness and reduces its victims, if they won't retaliate in kind, to misery. That form is despotism, which uses force or fraud to plunder the goods of others, public or private, sacred or profane, and to do it in a wholesale way. If you are caught committing any one of these crimes on a small scale, you are punished and disgraced: they call it sacrilege, kidnapping, burglary, theft and brigandage. But if, besides taking their property, you turn all your countrymen into slaves, you will hear no more of those ugly names; your countrymen themselves will call you the happiest of men and bless your name, and so will everyone who hears of such a complete triumph of injustice; for when people denounce injustice, it is because they are afraid of suffering wrong, not of doing it. So true is it, Socrates, that injustice, on a grand enough scale, is superior to justice in strength and freedom and autocratic power; and "right," as I said at first, means simply what serves the interest of the stronger party; "wrong" means what is for the interest and profit of oneself.

Having deluged our ears with this torrent of words, as the man at the baths might empty a bucket over one's head, Thrasymachus meant to take himself off; but the company obliged him to stay and defend his position. I was specially urgent in my entreaties.

My good Thrasymachus, said I, do you propose to fling a doctrine like that at our heads and then go away without explaining it properly or letting us point out to you whether it is true or not? Is it so small a matter in your eyes to determine the whole course of conduct which every one of us must follow to get the best out of life?

Don't I realize it is a serious matter? he retorted.

Apparently not, said I; or else you have no consideration for us, and do not care whether we shall lead better or worse lives for being ignorant of this truth you profess to know. Do take the trouble to let us into your secret; if you treat us handsomely, you may be sure it will be a good investment; there are so many of us to show our gratitude. I will make no secret of my own conviction, which is that injustice is not more profitable than justice, even when left free to work its will unchecked. No; let your unjust man have full power to do wrong, whether by successful violence or by escaping detection; all the same he will

not convince me that he will gain more than he would by being just. There may be others here who feel as I do, and set justice above injustice. It is for you to convince us that we are not well advised.

How can I? he replied. If you are not convinced by what I have just said, what more can I do for you? Do you want to be fed with my ideas out of a spoon?

God forbid! I exclaimed; not that. But I do want you to stand by your own words; or, if you shift your ground, shift it openly and stop trying to hoodwink us as you are doing now. You see, Thrasymachus, to go back to your earlier argument, in speaking of the shepherd you did not think it necessary to keep to that strict sense you laid down when you defined the genuine physician. You represent him, in his character of shepherd, as feeding up his flock, not for their own sake but for the table or the market, as if he were out to make money as a caterer or a cattle-dealer, rather than a shepherd. Surely the sole concern of the shepherd's art is to do the best for the charges put under its care; its own best interest is sufficiently provided for, so long as it does not fall short of all that shepherding should imply. On that principle it followed, I thought, that any kind of authority, in the state or in private life, must, in its character of authority, consider solely what is best for those under its care. Now what is your opinion? Do you think that the men who govern states—I mean rulers in the strict sense—have no reluctance to hold office?

I don't think so, he replied; I know it.

Well, but haven't you noticed, Thrasymachus, that in other positions of authority no one is willing to act unless he is paid wages, which he demands on the assumption that all the benefit of his action will go to his charges? Tell me: Don't we always distinguish one form of skill from another by its power to effect some particular result? Do say what you really think, so that we may get on.

Yes, that is the distinction.

And also each brings us some benefit that is peculiar to it: medicine gives health, for example; the art of navigation, safety at sea; and so on.

Yes.

And wage-earning brings us wages; that is its distinctive product. Now, speaking with that precision which you proposed, you would not say that the art of navigation is the same as the art of medicine, merely on the ground that a ship's captain regained his health on a voyage, because the sea air was good for him. No more would you identify the practice of medicine with wage-earning because a man may keep his health while earning wages, or a physician attending a case may receive a fee.

No.

And, since we agreed that the benefit obtained by each form of skill is peculiar to it, any common benefit enjoyed alike by all these practitioners must come from some further practice common to them all?

It would seem so.

Yes, we must say that if they all earn wages, they get that benefit in so far as they are engaged in wage-earning as well as in practising their several arts.

He agreed reluctantly.

This benefit, then—the receipt of wages—does not come to a man from his special art. If we are to speak strictly, the physician, as such, produces health; the builder, a house; and then each, in his further capacity of wage-earner, gets his pay. Thus every art has its own function and benefits its proper subject. But suppose the practitioner is not paid; does he then get any benefit from his art?

Clearly not.

And is he doing no good to anyone either, when he works for nothing?

No, I suppose he does some good.

Well then, Thrasymachus, it is now clear that no form of skill or authority provides for its own benefit. As we were saying some time ago, it always studies and prescribes what is good for its subject—the interest of the weaker party, not of the stronger. And that, my friend, is why I said that no one is willing to be in a position of authority and undertake to set straight other men's troubles, without demanding to be paid; because, if he is to do his work well, he will never, in his capacity of ruler, do, or command others to do, what is best for himself, but only what is best for the subject. For that reason, if he is to consent, he must have his recompense, in the shape of money or honour, or of punishment in case of refusal.

What do you mean, Socrates? asked Glaucon. I recognize two of your three kinds of reward; but I don't understand what you mean by speaking of punishment as a recompense.

Then you don't understand the recompense required by the best type of men, or their motive for accepting authority when they do consent. You surely know that a passion for honours or for money is rightly regarded as something to be ashamed of.

Yes, I do.

For that reason, I said, good men are unwilling to rule, either for money's sake or for honour. They have no wish to be called mercenary for demanding to be paid, or thieves for making a secret profit out of their office; nor yet will honours tempt them, for they are not ambitious. So they must be forced to consent under threat of penalty; that may be why a readiness to accept power under no such constraint is thought discreditable. And the heaviest penalty for declining to rule is to be ruled by someone inferior to yourself. That is the fear, I believe, that makes decent people accept power; and when they do so, they face the prospect of authority with no idea that they are coming into the enjoyment of a comfortable berth; it is forced upon them because they can find no one better than themselves, or even as good, to be entrusted with power. If there could ever be a society of perfect men, there might well be as much competition to evade office as there now is to gain it; and it would then be clearly seen that the genuine ruler's nature is to seek only the advantage of the subject, with the consequence that any man of understanding would sooner have another to do the best for him than be at the pains to do the best for that other himself. On this point, then, I entirely disagree with Thrasymachus' doctrine that right means what is to the interest of the stronger.

Chapter IV (I. 347 E–354 C)
Thrasymachus: Is Injustice More
Profitable Than Justice?

. . . .

However, I continued, we may return to that question later. Much more important is the position Thrasymachus is asserting now: that a life of injustice is to be preferred to a life of justice. Which side do you take, Glaucon? Where do you think the truth lies?

I should say that the just life is the better worth having.

You heard Thrasymachus' catalogue of all the good things in store for injustice?

I did, but I am not convinced.

Shall we try to convert him, then, supposing we can find some way to prove him wrong?

By all means.

We might answer Thrasymachus' case in a set speech of our own, drawing up a corresponding list of the advantages of justice; he would then have the right to reply, and we should make our final rejoinder; but after that we should have to count up and measure the advantages on each list, and we should need a jury to decide between us. Whereas, if we go on as before, each securing the agreement of the other side, we can combine the functions of advocate and judge. We will take whichever course you prefer.

I prefer the second, said Glaucon.

Come then, Thrasymachus, said I, let us start afresh with our questions. You say that injustice pays better than justice, when both are carried to the furthest point?

I do, he replied; and I have told you why.

And how would you describe them? I suppose you would call one of them an excellence and the other a defect?

Of course.

Justice an excellence, and injustice a defect?

Now is that likely, when I am telling you that injustice pays, and justice does not?

Then what do you say?

The opposite.

That justice is a defect?

No; rather the mark of a good-natured simpleton.

Injustice, then, implies being ill-natured?

No; I should call it good policy.

Do you think the unjust are positively superior in character and intelligence, Thrasymachus?

Yes, if they are the sort that can carry injustice to perfection and make themselves masters of whole cities and nations. Perhaps you think I was talking of pickpockets. There is profit even in that trade, if you can escape detection; but it doesn't come to much as compared with the gains I was describing.

I understand you now on that point, I replied. What astonished me was that you should class injustice with superior character and intelligence and justice with the reverse.

Well, I do, he rejoined.

That is a much more stubborn position, my friend; and it is not so easy to see how to assail it. If you would admit that injustice, however well it pays, is nevertheless, as some people think, a defect and a discreditable thing, then we could argue on generally accepted principles. But now that you have gone so far as to rank it with superior character and intelligence, obviously you will say it is an admirable thing as well as a source of strength, and has all the other qualities we have attributed to justice.

You read my thoughts like a book, he replied.

However, I went on, it is no good shirking; I must go through with the argument, so long as I can be sure you are really speaking your mind. I do believe you are not playing with us now, Thrasymachus, but stating the truth as you conceive it.

Why not refute the doctrine? he said. What does it matter to you whether I believe it or not?

It does not matter, I replied.

. . . .

Thrasymachus' assent was dragged out of him with a reluctance of which my account gives no idea. He was sweating at every pore, for the weather was hot; and I saw then what I had never seen before—Thrasymachus blushing. However, now that we had agreed that justice implies superior character and intelligence, injustice a deficiency in both respects, I went on:

Good; let us take that as settled. But we were also saying that injustice was a source of strength. Do you remember, Thrasymachus?

I do remember; only your last argument does not satisfy me, and I could say a good deal about that. But if I did, you would tell me I was haranguing you like a public meeting. So either let me speak my mind at length, or else, if you want to ask questions, ask them, and I will nod or shake my head, and say "Hm?" as we do to encourage an old woman telling us a story.

No, please, said I; don't give your assent against your real opinion.

Anything to please you, he rejoined, since you won't let me have my say. What more do you want?

Nothing, I replied. If that is what you mean to do, I will go on with my questions.

Go on, then.

Well, to continue where we left off, I will repeat my question: What is the nature and quality of justice as compared with injustice? It was suggested, I believe, that injustice is the stronger and more effective of the two; but now we have seen that justice implies superior character and intelligence, it will not be hard to show that it will also be superior in power to injustice, which implies ignorance and stupidity; that must be obvious to anyone. However, I would rather look deeper into this matter than take it as settled offhand. Would you agree that a state may be unjust and may try to enslave other states or to hold a number of others in subjection unjustly?

Of course it may, he said; above all if it is the best sort of state, which carries injustice to perfection.

I understand, said I; that was your view. But I am wondering whether a state can do without justice when it is asserting its superior power over another in that way.

Not if you are right, that justice implies intelligence; but if I am right, injustice will be needed.

I am delighted with your answer, Thrasymachus; this is much better than just nodding and shaking your head.

It is all to oblige you.

Thank you. Please add to your kindness by telling me whether any set of men—a state or an army or a band of robbers or thieves—who were acting together for some unjust purpose would be likely to succeed, if they were always trying to injure one another. Wouldn't they do better, if they did not?

Yes, they would.

Because, of course, such injuries must set them quarrelling and hating each other. Only fair treatment can make men friendly and of one mind.

Be it so, he said; I don't want to differ from you.

Thank you once more, I replied. But don't you agree that, if injustice has this effect of implanting hatred wherever it exists, it must make any set of people, whether freemen or slaves, split into factions, at feud with one another and incapable of any joint action?

Yes.

And so with any two individuals: injustice will set them at variance and make them enemies to each other as well as to everyone who is just.

It will.

And will it not keep its character and have the same effect, if it exists in a single person?

Let us suppose so.

The effect being, apparently, wherever it occurs—in a state or a family or an army or anywhere else—to make united action impossible because of factions and quarrels, and moreover to set whatever it resides in at enmity with itself as well as with any opponent and with all who are just.

Yes, certainly.

Then I suppose it will produce the same natural results in an individual. He will have a divided mind and be incapable of action, for lack of singleness of purpose; and he will be at enmity with all who are just as well as with himself?

Yes.

And "all who are just" surely includes the gods?

Let us suppose so.

The unjust man, then, will be a god-forsaken creature; the good-will of heaven will be for the just.

Enjoy your triumph, said Thrasymachus. You need not fear my contradicting you. I have no wish to give offence to the company.

. . . .

You will make my enjoyment complete, I replied, if you will answer my further questions in the same way. We have made out so far that just men are superior in character and intelligence and more effective in action. Indeed without justice men cannot act together at all; it is not strictly true to speak of such people as ever having effected any strong action in common. Had they been thoroughly unjust, they could not have kept their hands off one another; they must have had some justice in them, enough to keep them from injuring one another at the same time with their victims. This it was that enabled them to achieve what they did achieve: their injustice only partially incapacitated them for their career of wrong-doing; if perfect, it would have disabled them for any action whatsoever. I can see that all this is true, as against your original position. But there is a further question which we postponed: Is the life of justice the better and happier life? What we have said already leaves no doubt in my mind; but we ought to consider more carefully, for this is no light matter: it is the question, what is the right way to live?

Go on, then.

I will, said I. Some things have a function;[3] a horse, for instance, is useful for certain kinds of work. Would you agree to define a thing's function in general as the work for which that thing is the only instrument or the best one?

I don't understand.

Take an example. We can see only with the eyes, hear only with the ears; and seeing and hearing might be called the functions of those organs.

Yes.

Or again, you might cut vine-shoots with a carving-knife or a chisel or many other tools, but with none so well as with a pruning-knife made for the purpose; and we may call that its function.

True.

Now, I expect, you see better what I meant by suggesting that a thing's function is the work that it alone can do, or can do better than anything else.

Yes, I will accept that definition.

Good, said I; and to take the same examples, the eye and the ear, which we said have each its particular function: have they not also a specific excellence or virtue? Is not that always the case with things that have some appointed work to do?

Yes.

Now consider: is the eye likely to do its work well, if you take away its peculiar virtue and substitute the corresponding defect?

Of course not, if you mean substituting blindness for the power of sight.

I mean whatever its virtue may be; I have not come to that yet. I am only asking, whether it is true of things with a function—eyes or ears or anything else—that there is always some specific virtue which enables them to work well; and if they are deprived of that virtue, they work badly.

I think that is true.

Then the next point is this. Has the soul a function that can be performed by nothing else? Take for example such actions as deliberating or taking charge and exercising control: is not the soul the only thing of which you can say that these are its proper and peculiar work?

That is so.

And again, living—is not that above all the function of the soul?

No doubt.

And we also speak of the soul as having a certain specific excellence or virtue?

Yes.

Then, Thrasymachus, if the soul is robbed of its peculiar virtue, it cannot possibly do its work well. It must exercise its power of controlling and taking charge well or ill according as it is itself in a good or a bad state.

That follows.

And did we not agree that the virtue of the soul is justice, and injustice its defect?

We did.

So it follows that a just soul, or in other words a just man, will live well; the unjust will not.

Apparently, according to your argument.

But living well involves well-being and happiness.

Naturally.

Then only the just man is happy; injustice will involve unhappiness.

Be it so.

But you cannot say it pays better to be unhappy.

Of course not.

Injustice then, my dear Thrasymachus, can never pay better than justice.

Well, he replied, this is a feast-day, and you may take all this as your share of the entertainment.

For which I have to thank you, Thrasymachus; you have been so gentle with me since you recovered your temper. It is my own fault if the entertainment has not been satisfactory. I have been behaving like a greedy guest, snatching a taste of every new dish that comes round before he has properly enjoyed the last. We began by looking for a definition of justice: but before we had found one, I dropped that question and hurried on to ask whether or not it involved superior character and intelligence; and then, as soon as another idea cropped up, that injustice pays better, I could not refrain from pursuing that.

So now the whole conversation has left me completely in the dark; for so long as I do not know what justice is, I am hardly likely to know whether or not it is a virtue, or whether it makes a man happy or unhappy.

Part II
(Books II–IV, 445 B)
Justice in the State and in the Individual

Chapter V (II. 357 A–367 E)
The Problem Stated

. . . .

I thought that, with these words, I was quit of the discussion; but it seems this was only a prelude. Glaucon, undaunted as ever, was not content to let Thrasymachus abandon the field.

Socrates, he broke out, you have made a show of proving that justice is better than injustice in every way. Is that enough, or do you want us to be really convinced?

Certainly I do, if it rests with me.

Then you are not going the right way about it. I want to know how you classify the things we call good. Are there not some which we should wish to have, not for their consequences, but just for their own sake, such as harmless pleasures and enjoyments that have no further result beyond the satisfaction of the moment?

Yes, I think there are good things of that description.

And also some that we value both for their own sake and for their consequences—things like knowledge and health and the use of our eyes?

Yes.

And a third class which would include physical training, medical treatment, earning one's bread as a doctor or otherwise—useful, but burdensome things, which we want only for the sake of the profit or other benefit they bring.

Yes, there is that third class. What then?

In which class do you place justice?

I should say, in the highest, as a thing which anyone who is to gain happiness must value both for itself and for its results.

Well, that is not the common opinion. Most people would say it was one of those things, tiresome and disagreeable in themselves, which we cannot avoid practising for the sake of reward or a good reputation.

I know, said I; that is why Thrasymachus has been finding fault with it all this time and praising injustice. But I seem to be slow in seeing his point.

Listen to me, then, and see if you agree with mine. There was no need, I think, for Thrasymachus to yield so readily, like a snake you had charmed into submission; and nothing so far said about justice and injustice has been established to my satisfaction. I want to be told what each of them really is, and what effect each has, in itself, on the soul that harbours it, when all rewards and consequences are left out of account. So here is my plan, if you approve. I shall revive Thrasymachus' theory. First, I will state what is commonly held about the nature of justice and its origin; secondly, I shall maintain that it is always practised with reluctance, not as good in itself, but as a thing one cannot do without; and thirdly, that this reluctance is reasonable, because the life of injustice is much the better life of the two—so people say. That is not what I think myself, Socrates; only I am bewildered by all that Thrasymachus and ever so many others have dinned into my ears; and I have never yet heard the case for justice stated as I wish to hear it. You, I believe, if anyone, can tell me what is to be said in praise of justice in and for itself; that is what I want. Accordingly, I shall set you an example by glorifying the life of injustice with all the energy that I hope you will show later in denouncing it and exalting justice in its stead. Will that plan suit you?

Nothing could be better, I replied. Of all subjects this is one on which a sensible man must always be glad to exchange ideas.

Good, said Glaucon. Listen then, and I will begin with my first point: the nature and origin of justice.

What people say is that to do wrong is, in itself, a desirable thing; on the other hand, it is not at all desirable to suffer wrong, and the harm to the sufferer outweighs the advantage to the doer. Consequently, when men have had a taste of both, those who have not the power to seize the advantage and escape the harm decide that they would be better off if they made a compact neither to do wrong nor to suffer it. Hence they began to make laws and covenants with one another; and whatever the law prescribed they called lawful and right. That is what right or justice is and how it came into existence; it stands half-way between the best thing of all—to do wrong with impunity—and the worst, which is to suffer wrong without the power to retaliate. So justice is accepted as a compromise, and valued, not as good in itself, but for lack of power to do wrong; no man worthy of the name, who had that power, would ever enter into such a compact with anyone; he would be mad if he did. That, Socrates, is the nature of justice according to this account, and such the circumstances in which it arose.

The next point is that men practice it against the grain, for lack of power to do wrong. How true that is, we shall best see if we imagine two men, one just, the other unjust, given full license to do whatever they like, and then follow them to observe where each will be led by his desires. We shall catch the just man taking the same road as the unjust; he will be moved by self-interest, the end which it is natural to every creature to pursue as good, until forcibly turned aside by law and custom to respect the principle of equality.

Now, the easiest way to give them that complete liberty of action would be to imagine them possessed of the talisman found by Gyges, the ancestor of the famous Lydian. The story tells how he was a shepherd in the king's service. One day there was a great storm, and the ground where his flock was feeding was rent by an earthquake. Astonished at the sight, he went down into the chasm and saw, among other wonders of which the story tells, a brazen horse, hollow, with windows in its sides. Peering in, he saw a dead body, which seemed to be of more than human size. It was naked save for a gold ring, which he took from the finger and made his way out. When the shepherds met, as they did every month, to send an account to the King of the state of his flocks, Gyges came wearing the ring. As he was sitting with the others, he happened to turn the bezel of the ring inside his hand. At once he became invisible, and his companions, to his surprise, began to speak of him as if he had left them. Then, as he was fingering the ring, he turned the bezel outwards and

became visible again. With that, he set about testing the ring to see if it really had this power, and always with the same result: according as he turned the bezel inside or out he vanished and reappeared. After this discovery he contrived to be one of the messengers sent to the court. There he seduced the Queen, and with her help murdered the King and seized the throne.

Now suppose there were two such magic rings, and one were given to the just man, the other to the unjust. No one, it is commonly believed, would have such iron strength of mind as to stand fast in doing right or keep his hands off other men's goods, when he could go to the marketplace and fearlessly help himself to anything he wanted, enter houses and sleep with any woman he chose, set prisoners free and kill men at his pleasure, and in a word go about among men with the powers of a god. He would behave no better than the other; both would take the same course. Surely this would be strong proof that men do right only under compulsion; no individual thinks of it as good for him personally, since he does wrong whenever he finds he has the power. Every man believes that wrongdoing pays him personally much better, and, according to this theory, that is the truth. Granted full licence to do as he liked, people would think him a miserable fool if they found him refusing to wrong his neighbours or to touch their belongings, though in public they would keep up a pretence of praising his conduct, for fear of being wronged themselves. So much for that.

Finally, if we are really to judge between the two lives, the only way is to contrast the extremes of justice and injustice. We can best do that by imagining our two men to be perfect types, and crediting both to the full with the qualities they need for their respective ways of life. To begin with the unjust man: he must be like any consummate master of a craft, a physician or a captain, who, knowing just what his art can do, never tries to do more, and can always retrieve a false step. The unjust man, if he is to reach perfection, must be equally discreet in his criminal attempts, and he must not be found out, or we shall think him a bungler; for the highest pitch of injustice is to seem just when you are not. So we must endow our man with the full complement of injustice; we must allow him to have secured a spotless reputation for virtue while committing the blackest crimes; he must be able to retrieve any mistake, to defend himself with convincing eloquence if his misdeeds are denounced, and, when force is required, to bear down all opposition by his courage and strength and by his command of friends and money.

Now set beside this paragon the just man in his simplicity and nobleness, one who, in Aeschylus' words, "would be, not seem, the best." There must, indeed, be no such seeming; for if his character were apparent, his reputation would bring him honours and rewards, and then we should not know whether it was for their sake that he was just or for justice's sake alone. He must be stripped of everything but justice, and denied every advantage the other enjoyed. Doing no wrong, he must have the worst reputation for wrong-doing, to test whether his virtue is proof against all that comes of having a bad name; and under this lifelong imputation of wickedness, let him hold on his course of justice unwavering to the point of death. And so, when the two men have carried their justice and injustice to the last extreme, we may judge which is the happier.

My dear Glaucon, I exclaimed, how vigorously you scour these two characters clean for inspection, as if you were burnishing a couple of statues!

I am doing my best, he answered. Well, given two such characters, it is not hard, I fancy, to describe the sort of life that each of them may expect; and if the description sounds rather coarse, take it as coming from those who cry up the merits of injustice rather than from me. They will tell you that our just man will be thrown into prison, scourged and racked, will have his eyes burnt out, and, after every kind of torment, be impaled. That will teach him how much better it is to seem virtuous than to be so. In fact those lines of Aeschylus I quoted are more fitly applied to the unjust man, who, they say, is a realist and does not live for appearances: "he would be, not seem" unjust,

reaping the harvest sown
In those deep furrows of the thoughtful heart
Whence wisdom springs.

With his reputation for virtue, he will hold offices of state, ally himself by marriage to any family he may choose, become a partner in any business, and, having no scruples about being dishonest, turn all these advantages to profit. If he is involved in a lawsuit, public or private, he will get the better of his opponents, grow rich on the proceeds, and be able to help his friends and harm his enemies. Finally, he can make sacrifices to the gods and dedicate offerings with due magnificence, and, being in a much better position than the just man to serve the gods as well as his chosen friends, he may reasonably hope to stand higher in the favour of heaven. So much better, they say, Socrates, is the life prepared for the unjust by gods and men.

Here Glaucon ended, and I was meditating a reply, when his brother Adeimantus exclaimed:

Surely, Socrates, you cannot suppose that that is all there is to be said.

Why, isn't it? said I.

The most essential part of the case has not been mentioned, he replied.

Well, I answered, there is a proverb about a brother's aid. If Glaucon has failed, it is for you to make good his shortcomings; though, so far as I am concerned, he has said quite enough to put me out of the running and leave me powerless to rescue the cause of justice.

Nonsense, said Adeimantus; there is more to be said, and you must listen to me. If we want a clear view of what I take to be Glaucon's meaning, we must study the opposite side of the case, the arguments used when justice is praised and injustice condemned. When children are told by their fathers and all their pastors and masters that it is a good thing to be just, what is commended is not justice in itself but the respectability it brings. They are to let men see how just they are, in order to gain high positions and marry well and win all the other advantages which Glaucon mentioned, since the just man owes all these to his good reputation.

In this matter of having a good name, they go farther still: they throw in the favourable opinion of heaven, and can tell us of no end of good things with which they say the gods reward piety. There is the good old Hesiod, who says the gods make the just man's oak-trees "bear acorns at the top and bees in the middle; and their sheep's fleeces are heavy with wool," and a great many other blessings of that sort. And Homer speaks in the same strain:

> As when a blameless king fears the gods and upholds right judgment; then the dark earth yields wheat and barley, and the trees are laden with fruit; the young of his flocks are strong, and the sea gives abundance of fish.

Musaeus and his son Eumolpus enlarge in still more spirited terms upon the rewards from heaven they promise to the righteous. They take them to the other world and provide them with a banquet of the Blest, where they sit for all time carousing with garlands on their heads, as if virtue could not be more nobly recompensed than by an eternity of intoxication. Others, again, carry the rewards of heaven yet a stage farther: the pious man who keeps his oaths is to have children's children and to leave a posterity after him. When they have sung the praises of justice in that strain, with more to same effect, they proceed to plunge the sinners and unrighteous men into a pool of mud in the world below, and set them to fetch water in a sieve. Even in this life, too, they give them a bad name, and make out that the unjust suffer all those penalties which Glaucon described as falling upon the good man who has a bad reputation: they can think of no others. That is how justice is recommended and injustice denounced.

Besides all this, think of the way in which justice and injustice are spoken of, not only in ordinary life, but by the poets. All with one voice reiterate that self-control and justice, admirable as they may be, are difficult and irksome, whereas vice and injustice are pleasant and very easily to be had; it is mere convention to regard them as discreditable. They tell us that dishonesty generally pays better than honesty. They will cheerfully speak of a bad man as happy and load him with honours and social esteem, provided he be rich and otherwise powerful; while they despise and disregard one who has neither power nor wealth, though all the while they acknowledge that he is the better man of the two.

Most surprising of all is what they say about the gods and virtue: that heaven itself often allots misfortunes and a hard life to the good man, and gives prosperity to the wicked. Mendicant priests and soothsayers come to the rich man's door with a story of a power they possess by the gift of heaven to atone for any offence that he or his ancestors have committed with incantations and sacrifice, agreeably accompanied by feasting. If he wishes to injure an enemy, he can, at a trifling expense, do him a hurt with equal case, whether he be an honest man or not, by means of certain invocations and spells which, as they profess, prevail upon the gods to do their bidding. In support of all these claims they call the poets to witness. Some, by way of advertising the easiness of vice, quote the words: "Unto wickedness men attain easily and in multitudes; smooth is the way and her dwelling is very near at hand. But the gods have ordained much sweat upon the path to virtue" and a long road that is rough and steep.

Others, to show that men can turn the gods from their purpose, cite Homer: "Even the gods themselves listen to entreaty. Their hearts are turned by the entreaties of men with sacrifice and humble prayers and libation and burnt offering, whensoever anyone transgresses and does amiss." They produce a whole farrago of books in which Musaeus and Orpheus, described as descendants of the Muses and the Moon, prescribe their ritual; and they persuade entire communities, as well as individuals, that, both in this life and after death, wrongdoing may be absolved and purged away by means of sacrifices and agreeable performances which they are pleased to call rites of initiation. These deliver us from punishment in the other world, where awful things are in store for all who neglect to sacrifice.

Now, my dear Socrates, when all this stuff is talked about the estimation in which virtue and vice are held by heaven and by mankind, what effect can we suppose it has upon the mind of a young man quick-witted enough to gather honey from all these flowers of popular wisdom and to draw his own conclusions as to the sort of person he should be and the way he should go in order to lead the best possible life? In all likelihood he would ask himself, in Pindar's words: "Will the way of right or the by-paths of deceit lead me to the higher fortress," where I may entrench myself for the rest of my life? For, according to what they tell me, I have nothing to gain but trouble and manifest loss from being honest, unless I also get a name for being so; whereas, if I am dishonest and provide myself with a reputation for honesty, they promise me a marvellous career. Very well, then; since "outward seeming," as wise men inform me, "overpowers the truth" and decides the question of happiness, I had better go in for appearances wholeheartedly. I must ensconce myself behind an imposing facade designed to look like virtue, and trail the fox behind me, "the cunning shifty fox"—Archilochus knew the world as well as any man. You may say it is not so easy to be wicked without ever being found out. Perhaps not; but great things are never easy. Anyhow, if we are to reach happiness, everything we have been told points to this as the road to be followed. We will form secret societies to save us from exposure; besides, there are men who teach the art of winning over popular assemblies and courts of law; so that, one way or another, by persuasion or violence, we shall get the better of our neighbours without being punished. You might object that the gods are not to be deceived and are beyond the reach of violence. But suppose that there are no gods, or that they do not concern themselves with the doings of men; why should we concern ourselves to deceive them? Or, if the gods do exist and care for mankind, all we know or have ever heard about them comes from current tradition and from the poets who recount their family history, and these same authorities also assure us that they can be won over and turned from their purpose "by sacrifice and humble prayers" and votive offerings. We must either accept both these statements or neither. If we are to accept both, we had better do wrong and use part of the proceeds to offer sacrifice. By being just we may escape the punishment of heaven, but we shall be renouncing the profits of injustice; whereas by doing wrong we shall make our profit and escape punishment into the bargain, by means of those entreaties which win over the gods when we transgress and do amiss. But then, you will say, in the other world the penalty for our misdeeds on earth will fall either upon us or upon our children's children. We can counter that objection by reckoning on the great efficacy of mystic rites and the divinities of absolution, vouched for by the most advanced societies and by the descendants of the gods who have appeared as poets and spokesmen of heavenly inspiration.

What reason, then, remains for preferring justice to the extreme of injustice, when common belief and the best authorities promise us the fulfilment of our desires in this life and the next, if only we conceal our ill-doing under a veneer of decent behaviour? The upshot is, Socrates, that no man possessed of superior powers of mind or person or rank or wealth will set any value on justice; he is more likely to laugh when he hears it praised. So, even one who could prove my case false and were quite sure that justice is best, far from being indignant with the unjust, will be very ready to excuse them. He will know that, here and there, a man may refrain from wrong because it revolts some instinct he is graced with or because he has come to know the truth; no one else is virtuous of his own will; it is only lack of spirit or the infirmity of age or some other weakness that makes men condemn the iniquities they have not the strength to practise. This is easily seen: give such a man the power, and he will be the first to use it to the utmost.

What lies at the bottom of all this is nothing but the fact from which Glaucon, as well as I, started upon this long discourse. We put it to you, Socrates, with all respect, in this way. All you who profess to sing the praises of right conduct, from the ancient heroes whose legends have survived down to the men of the present day, have never denounced injustice or praised justice apart from the reputation, honours, and rewards they bring; but what effect either of them in itself has upon its possessor when it dwells in his soul unseen of gods or men, no poet or ordinary man has ever yet explained. No one has proved that a soul can harbour no worse evil than injustice, no greater good than justice. Had all of you said that from the first and tried to convince us from our youth up, we should not be keeping watch upon our neighbours to prevent them from doing wrong to us, but everyone would keep a far more effectual watch over himself, for fear lest by wronging others he should open his doors to the worst of all evils.

That, Socrates, is the view of justice and injustice which Thrasymachus and, no doubt, others would state, perhaps in even stronger words. For myself, I believe it to be a gross perversion of their true worth and effect; but, as I must frankly confess, I have put the case with all the force I could muster because I want to hear the other side from you. You must not be content with proving that justice is superior to injustice; you must make clear what good or what harm each of them does to its possessor, taking it simply in itself and, as Glaucon required, leaving out of account the reputation it bears. For unless you deprive each of its true reputation and attach to it the false one, we shall say that you are praising or denouncing nothing more than the appearances in either case, and recommending us to do wrong without being found out; and that you hold with Thrasymachus that right means what is good for someone else, being the interest of the stronger, and wrong is what really pays, serving one's own interest at the expense of the weaker. You have agreed that justice belongs to that highest class of good things which are worth having not only for their consequences, but much more for their own sakes—things like sight and hearing, knowledge, and health, whose value is genuine and intrinsic, not dependent on opinion. So I want you, in commending justice, to consider only how justice, in itself, benefits a man who has it in him, and how injustice harms him, leaving rewards and reputation out of account. I might put up with others dwelling on those outward effects as a reason for praising the one and condemning the other; but from you, who have spent your life in the study of this question, I must beg leave to demand something better. You must not be content merely to prove that justice is superior to injustice, but explain how one is good, the other evil, in virtue of the intrinsic effect each has on its possessor, whether gods or men see it or not.

Chapter VI (II. 367 E–372 A)
The Rudiments of Social
Organization

....

I was delighted with these speeches from Glaucon and Adeimantus, whose gifts I had always admired. How right, I exclaimed, was Glaucon's lover to begin that poem of his on your exploits at the battle of Megara by describing you two as the

sons divine
Of Ariston's noble line!

Like father, like sons: there must indeed be some divine quality in your nature, if you can plead the cause of injustice so eloquently and still not be convinced yourselves that it is better than justice. That you are not really convinced I am sure from all I know of your dispositions, though your words might well have left me in doubt. But the more I trust you, the harder I find it to reply. How can I come to the rescue? I have no faith in my own powers, when I remember that you were not satisfied with the proof I thought I had given to Thrasymachus that it is better to be just. And yet I cannot stand by and hear justice reviled without lifting a finger. I am afraid to commit a sin by holding aloof while I have breath and strength to say a word in its defence. So there is nothing for it but to do the best I can.

Glaucon and the others begged me to step into the breach and carry through our inquiry into the real nature of justice and injustice, and the truth about their respective advantages. So I told them what I thought. This is a very obscure question, I said, and we shall need keen sight to see our way. Now, as we are not remarkably clever, I will make a suggestion as to how we should proceed. Imagine a rather short-sighted person told to read an inscription in small letters from some way off. He would think it a godsend if someone pointed out that the same inscription was written up elsewhere on a bigger scale, so that he could first read the larger characters and then make out whether the smaller ones were the same.

No doubt, said Adeimantus; but what analogy do you see in that to our inquiry?

I will tell you. We think of justice as a quality that may exist in a whole community as well as in an individual, and the community is the bigger of the two. Possibly, then, we may find justice there in larger proportions, easier to make out. So I suggest that we should begin by inquiring what justice means in a state. Then we can go on to look for its counterpart on a smaller scale in the individual.

That seems a good plan, he agreed.

Well then, I continued, suppose we imagine a state coming into being before our eyes. We might then be able to watch the growth of justice or of injustice within it. When that is done, we may hope it will be easier to find what we are looking for.

Much easier.

Shall we try, then, to carry out this scheme? I fancy it will be no light undertaking; so you had better think twice.

No need for that, said Adeimantus. Don't waste any more time.

My notion is, said I, that a state comes into existence because no individual is self-sufficing; we all have many needs. But perhaps you can suggest some different origin for the foundation of a community?

No, I agree with you.

So, having all these needs, we call in one another's help to satisfy our various requirements; and when we have collected a number of helpers and associates to live together in one place, we call that settlement a state.

Yes.

So if one man gives another what he has to give in exchange for what he can get, it is because each finds that to do so is for his own advantage.

Certainly.

Very well, said I. Now let us build up our imaginary state from the beginning. Apparently, it will owe its existence to our needs, the first and greatest need being the provision of food to keep us alive. Next we shall want a house; and thirdly, such things as clothing.

True.

How will our state be able to supply all these demands? We shall need at least one man to be a farmer, another a builder, and a third a weaver. Will that do, or shall we add a shoemaker and one or two more to provide for our personal wants?

By all means.

The minimum state, then, will consist of four or five men.

Apparently.

Now here is a further point. Is each one of them to bring the product of his work into a common stock? Should our one farmer, for example, provide food enough for four people and spend the whole of his working time in producing corn, so as to share with the rest; or should he take no notice of them and spend only a quarter of his time on growing just enough corn for himself, and divide the other three-quarters between building his house, weaving his clothes, and making his shoes, so as to save the trouble of sharing with others and attend himself to all his own concerns?

The first plan might be the easier, replied Adeimantus.

That may very well be so, said I; for, as you spoke, it occurred to me, for one thing, that no two people are born exactly alike. There are innate differences which fit them for different occupations.

I agree.

And will a man do better working at many trades, or keeping to only one?

Keeping to one.

And there is another point: obviously work may be ruined, if you let the right time go by. The workman must wait upon the work; it will not wait upon his leisure and allow itself to be done in a spare moment. So the conclusion is that more things will be produced and the work be more easily and better done, when every man is set free from all other occupations to do, at the right time, the one thing for which he is naturally fitted.

That is certainly true.

We shall need more than four citizens, then, to supply all those necessaries we mentioned. You see, Adeimantus, if the farmer is to have a good plough and spade and other tools, he will not make them himself. No more will the builder and weaver and shoemaker make all the many implements they need. So quite a number of carpenters and smiths and other craftsmen must be enlisted. Our miniature state is beginning to grow.

It is.

Still, it will not be very large, even when we have added cowherds and shepherds to provide the farmers with oxen for the plough, and the builders as well as the farmers with draught-animals, and the weavers and shoemakers with wool and leather.

No; but it will not be so very small either.

And yet, again, it will be next to impossible to plant our city in a territory where it will need no imports. So there will have to be still another set of people, to fetch what it needs from other countries.

There will.

Moreover, if these agents take with them nothing that those other countries require in exchange, they will return as empty-handed as they went. So, besides everything wanted for consumption at home, we must produce enough goods of the right kind for the foreigners whom we depend on to supply us. That will mean increasing the number of farmers and craftsmen.

Yes.

And then, there are these agents who are to import and export all kinds of goods—merchants, as we call them. We must have them; and if they are to do business overseas, we shall need quite a number of ship-owners and others who know about that branch of trading.

We shall.

Again, in the city itself how are the various sets of producers to exchange their products? That was our object, you will remember, in forming a community and so laying the foundation of our state.

Obviously, they must buy and sell.

That will mean having a market-place, and a currency to serve as a token for purposes of exchange.

Certainly.

Now suppose a farmer, or an artisan, brings some of his produce to market at a time when no one is there who wants to exchange with him. Is he to sit there idle, when he might be at work?

No, he replied; there are people who have seen an opening here for their services. In well-ordered communities they are generally men not strong enough to be of use in any other occupation. They have to stay where they are in the market-place and take goods for money from those who want to sell, and money for goods from those who want to buy.

That, then, is the reason why our city must include a class of shopkeepers—so we call these people who sit still in the market-place to buy and sell, in contrast with merchants who travel to other countries.

Quite so.

There are also the services of yet another class, who have the physical strength for heavy work, though on intellectual grounds they are hardly worth including in our society—hired labourers, as we call them, because they sell the use of their strength for wages. They will go to make up our population.

Yes.

Well, Adeimantus, has our state now grown to its full size?

Perhaps.

Then, where in it shall we find justice or injustice? If they have come in with one of the elements we have been considering, can you say with which one?

I have no idea, Socrates; unless it be somewhere in their dealings with one another.

You may be right, I answered. Anyhow, it is a question which we shall have to face.

Chapter VII (II 372 A–374 E)
The Luxurious State

. . . .

Let us begin, then, with a picture of our citizens' manner of life, with the provision we have made for them. They will be producing corn and wine, and making clothes and shoes. When they have built their houses, they will mostly work without their coats or shoes in summer, and in winter be well shod and clothed. For their food, they will prepare flour and barley-meal for kneading and baking, and set out a grand spread of loaves and cakes on rushes or fresh leaves. Then they will lie on beds of myrtle-boughs and bryony and make merry with their children, drinking their wine after the feast with garlands on their heads and singing the praises of the gods. So they will live pleasantly together; and a prudent fear of poverty or war will keep them from begetting children beyond their means.

Here Glaucon interrupted me: You seem to expect your citizens to feast on dry bread.

True, I said; I forgot that they will have something to give it a relish, salt, no doubt, and olives, and cheese, and country stews of roots and vegetables. And for dessert we will give them figs and peas and beans; and they shall roast myrtle-berries and acorns at the fire, while they sip their wine. Leading such a healthy life in peace, they will naturally come to a good old age, and leave their children to live after them in the same manner.

That is just the sort of provender you would supply, Socrates, if you were founding a community of pigs.

Well, how are they to live, then, Glaucon?

With the ordinary comforts. Let them lie on couches and dine off tables on such dishes and sweets as we have nowadays.

Ah, I see, said I; we are to study the growth, not just of a state, but of a luxurious one. Well, there may be no harm in that; the consideration of luxury may help us to discover how justice and injustice take root in society. The community I have described seems to me the ideal one, in sound health as it were: but if you want to see one suffering from inflammation, there is nothing to hinder us. So some people, it seems, will not be satisfied to live in this simple way; they must have couches and tables and furniture of all sorts; and delicacies too, perfumes, unguents, courtesans, sweetmeats, all in plentiful variety. And besides, we must not limit ourselves now to those bare necessaries of house and clothes and shoes; we shall have to set going the arts of embroidery and painting, and collect rich materials, like gold and ivory.

Yes.

Then we must once more enlarge our community. The healthy one will not be big enough now; it must be swollen up with a whole multitude of callings not ministering to any bare necessity: hunters and fishermen, for instance; artists in sculpture, painting, and music; poets with their attendant train of professional reciters, actors, dancers, producers; and makers of all sorts of household gear, including everything for women's adornment. And we shall want more servants: children's nurses and attendants, lady's maids, barbers, cooks and confectioners. And then swineherds—there was no need for them in our original state, but we shall want them now; and a great quantity of sheep and cattle too, if people are going to live on meat.

Of course.

And with this manner of life physicians will be in much greater request.

No doubt.

The country, too, which was large enough to support the original inhabitants, will now be too small. If we are to have enough pasture and plough land, we shall have to cut off a slice of our neighbours' territory; and if they too are not content with necessaries, but give themselves up to getting unlimited wealth, they will want a slice of ours.

That is inevitable, Socrates.

So the next thing will be, Glaucon, that we shall be at war.

No doubt.

We need not say yet whether war does good or harm, but only that we have discovered its origin in desires which are the most fruitful source of evils both to individuals and to states.

Quite true.

This will mean a considerable addition to our community—a whole army, to go out to battle with any invader, in defence of all this property and of the citizens we have been describing.

Why so? Can't they defend themselves?

Not if the principle was right, which we all accepted in framing our society. You remember we agreed that no one man can practise many trades or arts satisfactorily.

True.

Well, is not the conduct of war an art, quite as important as shoemaking?

Yes.

But we would not allow our shoemaker to try to be also a farmer or weaver or builder, because we wanted our shoes well made. We gave each man one trade, for which he was naturally fitted; he would do good work, if he confined himself to that all his life, never letting the right moment slip by. Now in no form of work is efficiency so important as in war; and fighting is not so easy a business that a man can follow another trade, such as farming or shoemaking, and also be an efficient soldier. Why, even a game like draughts or dice must be studied from childhood; no one can become a fine player in his spare moments. Just taking up a shield or other weapon will not make a man capable of fighting that very day in any sort of warfare, any more than taking up a tool or implement of some kind will make a man a craftsman or an athlete, if he does not understand its use and has never been properly trained to handle it.

No; if that were so, tools would indeed be worth having.

These guardians of our state, then, inasmuch as their work is the most important of all, will need the most complete freedom from other occupations and the greatest amount of skill and practice.

I quite agree.

And also a native aptitude for their calling.

Certainly.

So it is our business to define, if we can, the natural gifts that fit men to be guardians of a commonwealth, and to select them accordingly. It will certainly be a formidable task; but we must grapple with it to the best of our power.

Yes.

Chapter VIII (II. 375 A–376 E)
The Guardian's Temperament

. . . .

Don't you think then, said I, that, for the purpose of keeping guard, a young man should have much the same temperament and qualities as a well-bred watch-dog? I mean, for instance, that both must have quick senses to detect an enemy, swiftness in pursuing him, and strength, if they have to fight when they have caught him.

Yes, they will need all those qualities.

And also courage, if they are to fight well.

Of course.

And courage, in dog or horse or any other creature, implies a spirited disposition. You must have noticed that a high spirit is unconquerable. Every soul possessed of it is fearless and indomitable in the face of any danger.

Yes, I have noticed that.

So now we know what physical qualities our Guardian must have, and also that he must be of a spirited temper.

Yes.

Then, Glaucon, how are men of that natural disposition to be kept from behaving pugnaciously to one another and to the rest of their countrymen?

It is not at all easy to see.

And yet they must be gentle to their own people and dangerous only to enemies; otherwise they will destroy themselves without waiting till others destroy them.

True.

What are we to do, then? If gentleness and a high temper are contraries, where shall we find a character to combine them? Both are necessary to make a good Guardian, but it seems they are incompatible. So we shall never have a good Guardian.

It looks like it.

Here I was perplexed, but on thinking over what we had been saying, I remarked that we deserved to be puzzled, because we had not followed up the comparison we had just drawn.

What do you mean? he asked.

We never noticed that, after all, there are natures in which these contraries are combined. They are to be found in animals, and not least in the kind we compared to our Guardian. Well-bred dogs, as you know, are by instinct perfectly gentle to people whom they know and are accustomed to, and fierce to strangers. So the combination of qualities we require for our Guardian is, after all, possible and not against nature.

Evidently.

Do you further agree that, besides this spirited temper, he must have a philosophical element in his nature?

I don't see what you mean.

This is another trait you will see in the dog. It is really remarkable how the creature gets angry at the mere sight of a stranger and welcomes anyone he knows, though he may never have been treated unkindly by the one or kindly by the other. Did that never strike you as curious?

I had not thought of it before; but that certainly is how a dog behaves.

Well, but that shows a fine instinct, which is philosophic in the true sense.

How so?

Because the only mark by which he distinguishes a friendly and an unfriendly face is that he knows the one and does not know the other; and if a creature makes that the test of what it finds congenial or otherwise, how can you deny that it has a passion for knowledge and understanding?

Of course, I cannot.

And that passion is the same thing as philosophy—the love of wisdom.

Yes.

Shall we boldly say, then, that the same is true of human beings? If a man is to be gentle towards his own people whom he knows, he must have an instinctive love of wisdom and understanding.

Agreed.

So the nature required to make a really noble Guardian of our commonwealth will be swift and strong, spirited, and philosophic.

Quite so. . . .

. . . .

Chapter X (III. 412 B–IV. 414 C)
Selection of Rulers: The Guardians' Manner of Living

. . . .

What is the next point to be settled? Is it not the question, which of these Guardians are to be rulers and which are to obey?

No doubt.

Well, it is obvious that the elder must have authority over the young, and that the rulers must be the best.

Yes.

And as among farmers the best are those with a natural turn for farming, so, if we want the best among our Guardians, we must take those naturally fitted to watch over a commonwealth. They must have the right sort of intelligence and ability; and also they must look upon the commonwealth as their special concern—the sort of concern that is felt for something so closely bound up with oneself that its interests and fortunes, for good or ill, are held to be identical with one's own.

Exactly.

So the kind of men we must choose from among the Guardians will be those who, when we look at the whole course of their lives, are found to be full of zeal to do whatever they believe is for the good of the commonwealth and never willing to act against its interest.

Yes, they will be the men we want.

We must watch them, I think, at every age and see whether they are capable of preserving this conviction that they must do what is best for the community, never forgetting it or allowing themselves to be either forced or bewitched into throwing it over.

How does this throwing over come about?

I will explain. When a belief passes out of the mind, a man may be willing to part with it, if it is false and he has learnt better, or unwilling, if it is true.

I see how he might be willing to let it go; but you must explain how he can be unwilling.

Where is your difficulty? Don't you agree that men are unwilling to be deprived of good, though ready enough to part with evil? Or that to be deceived about the truth is evil, to possess it good? Or don't you think that possessing truth means thinking of things as they really are?

You are right. I do agree that men are unwilling to be robbed of a true belief.

When that happens to them, then, it must be by theft, or violence, or bewitchment.

Again I do not understand.

Perhaps my metaphors are too high-flown. I call it theft when one is persuaded out of one's belief or forgets it. Argument in the one case, and time in the other, steal it away without one's knowing what is happening. You understand now?

Yes.

And by violence I mean being driven to change one's mind by pain or suffering.

That too I understand, and you are right.

And bewitchment, as I think you would agree, occurs when a man is beguiled out of his opinion by the allurements of pleasure or scared out of it under the spell of panic.

Yes, all delusions are like a sort of bewitchment.

As I said just now, then, we must find out who are the best guardians of this inward conviction that they must always do what they believe to be best for the commonwealth. We shall have to watch them from earliest childhood and set them tasks in which they would be most likely to forget or to be beguiled out of this duty. We shall then choose only those whose memory holds firm and who are proof against delusion.

Yes.

We must also subject them to ordeals of toil and pain and watch for the same qualities there. And we must observe them when exposed to the test of yet a third kind of bewitchment. As people lead colts up to alarming noises to see whether they are timid, so these young men must be brought into terrifying situations and then into scenes of pleasure, which will put them to severer proof than gold tried in the furnace. If we find one bearing himself well in all these trials and resisting every enchantment, a true guardian of himself, preserving always that perfect rhythm and harmony of being which he has acquired from his training in music and poetry, such a one will be of the greatest service to the commonwealth as well as to himself. Whenever we find one who has come unscathed through every test in childhood, youth, and manhood, we shall set him as a Ruler to watch over the commonwealth; he will be honoured in life, and after death receive the highest tribute of funeral rites and other memorials. All who do not reach this standard we must reject. And that, I think, my dear Glaucon, may be taken as an outline of the way in which we shall select Guardians to be set in authority as Rulers.

I am very much of your mind.

These, then, may properly be called Guardians in the fullest sense, who will ensure that neither foes without shall have the power, nor friends within the wish, to do harm. Those young men whom up to now we have been speaking of as Guardians, will be better described as Auxiliaries, who will enforce the decisions of the Rulers.

I agree.

. . . .

Chapter XII (IV. 427 c–434 d)
The Virtues in the State

. . . .

So now at last, son of Ariston, said I, your commonwealth is established. The next thing is to bring to bear upon it all the light you can get from any quarter, with the help of your brother and Polemarchus and all the rest, in the hope that we may see where justice is to be found in it and where injustice, how they differ, and which of the two will bring happiness to its possessor, no matter whether gods and men see that he has it or not.

Nonsense, said Glaucon; you promised to conduct the search yourself, because it would be a sin not to uphold justice by every means in your power.

That is true; I must do as you say, but you must all help.

We will.

I suspect, then, we may find what we are looking for in this way. I take it that our state, having been founded and built up on the right lines, is good in the complete sense of the word.

It must be.

Obviously, then, it is wise, brave, temperate, and just.

Obviously.

Then if we find some of these qualities in it, the remainder will be the one we have not found. It is as if we were looking somewhere for one of any four things: if we detected that one immediately, we should be satisfied; whereas if we recognized the other three first, that would be enough to indicate the thing we wanted; it could only be the remaining one. So here we have four qualities. Had we not better follow that method in looking for the one we want?

Surely.

To begin then: the first quality to come into view in our state seems to be its wisdom; and there appears to be something odd about this quality.[4]

What is there odd about it?

I think the state we have described really has wisdom; for it will be prudent in counsel, won't it?

Yes.

And prudence in counsel is clearly a form of knowledge; good counsel cannot be due to ignorance and stupidity.

Clearly.

But there are many and various kinds of knowledge in our commonwealth. There is the knowledge possessed by the carpenters or the smiths, and the knowledge how to raise crops. Are we to call the state wise and prudent on the strength of these forms of skill?

No; they would only make it good at furniture-making or working in copper or agriculture.

Well then, is there any form of knowledge, possessed by some among the citizens of our new-founded commonwealth, which will enable it to take thought, not for some particular interest, but for the best possible conduct of the state as a whole in its internal and external relations?

Yes, there is.

What is it, and where does it reside?

It is precisely that art of guardianship which resides in those Rulers whom we just now called Guardians in the full sense.

And what would you call the state on the strength of that knowledge?

Prudent and truly wise.

And do you think there will be more or fewer of these genuine Guardians in our state than there will be smiths?

Far fewer.

Fewer, in fact, than any of those other groups who are called after the kind of skill they possess?

Much fewer.

So, if a state is constituted on natural principles, the wisdom it possesses as a whole will be due to the knowledge residing in the smallest part, the one which takes the lead and governs the rest. Such knowledge is the only kind that deserves the name of wisdom, and it appears to be ordained by nature that the class privileged to possess it should be the smallest of all.

Quite true.

Here then we have more or less made out one of our four qualities and its seat in the structure of the commonwealth.

To my satisfaction, at any rate.

Next there is courage. It is not hard to discern that quality or the part of the community in which it resides so as to entitle the whole to be called brave.

Why do you say so?

Because anyone who speaks of a state as either brave or cowardly can only be thinking of that part of it which takes the field and fights in its defence; the reason being, I imagine, that the character of the state is not determined by the bravery or cowardice of the other parts.

No.

Courage, then, is another quality which a community owes to a certain part of itself. And its being brave will mean that, in this part, it possesses the power of preserving, in all circumstances, a conviction about the sort of things that it is right to be afraid of—the conviction implanted by the education which the law-giver has established. Is not that what you mean by courage?

I do not quite understand. Will you say it again?

I am saying that courage means preserving something.

Yes, but what?

The conviction, inculcated by lawfully established education, about the sort of things which may rightly be feared. When I added "in all circumstances," I meant preserving it always and never abandoning it, whether under the influence of pain or of pleasure, of desire or of fear. If you like, I will give an illustration.

Please do.

You know how dyers who want wool to take a purple dye, first select the white wool from among all the other colours, next treat it very carefully to make it take the dye in its full brilliance, and only then dip it in the vat. Dyed in that way, wool gets a fast colour, which no washing, even with soap, will rob of its brilliance; whereas if they choose wool of any colour but white, or if they neglect to prepare it, you know what happens.

Yes, it looks washed-out and ridiculous.

That illustrates the result we were doing our best to achieve when we were choosing our fighting men and training their minds and bodies. Our only purpose was to contrive influences whereby they might take the colour of our institutions like a dye, so that, in virtue of having both the right temperament and the right education, their convictions about what ought to be feared and on all other subjects might be indelibly fixed, never to be washed out by pleasure and pain, desire and fear, solvents more terribly effective than all the soap and fuller's earth in the world. Such a power of constantly preserving, in accordance with our institutions, the right conviction about the things which ought, or ought not, to be feared, is what I call courage. That is my position, unless you have some objection to make.

None at all, he replied; if the belief were such as might be found in a slave or an animal—correct, but not produced by education—you would hardly describe it as in accordance with our institutions, and you would give it some other name than courage.

Quite true.

Then I accept your account of courage.

You will do well to accept it, at any rate as applying to the courage of the ordinary citizen; if you like we will go into it more fully some other time. At present we are in search of justice, rather than of courage; and for that purpose we have said enough.

I quite agree.

Two qualities, I went on, still remain to be made out in our state, temperance and the object of our whole inquiry, justice. Can we discover justice without troubling ourselves further about temperance?

I do not know, and I would rather not have justice come to light first, if that means that we should not go on to consider temperance. So if you want to please me, take temperance first.

Of course I have every wish to please you.

Do go on then.

I will. At first sight, temperance seems more like some sort of concord or harmony than the other qualities did.

How so?

Temperance surely means a kind of orderliness, a control of certain pleasures and appetites. People use the expression, "master of oneself," whatever that means, and various other phrases that point the same way.

Quite true.

Is not "master of oneself" an absurd expression? A man who was master of himself would presumably be also subject to himself, and the subject would be master; for all these terms apply to the same person.

No doubt.

I think, however, the phrase means that within the man himself, in his soul, there is a better part and a worse; and that he is his own master when the part which is better by nature has the worse under its control. It is certainly a term of praise; whereas it is considered a disgrace, when, through bad breeding or bad company, the better part is overwhelmed by the worse, like a small force outnumbered by a multitude. A man in that condition is called a slave to himself and intemperate.

Probably that is what is meant.

Then now look at our newly founded state and you will find one of these two conditions realized there. You will agree that it deserves to be called master of itself, if temperance and self-mastery exist where the better part rules the worse.

Yes, I can see that is true.

It is also true that the great mass of multifarious appetites and pleasures and pains will be found to occur chiefly in children and women and slaves, and, among free men so called, in the inferior multitude; whereas the simple and moderate desires which, with the aid of reason and right belief, are guided by reflection, you will find only in a few, and those with the best inborn dispositions and the best educated.

Yes, certainly.

Do you see that this state of things will exist in your commonwealth, where the desires of the inferior multitude will be controlled by the desires and wisdom of the superior few? Hence, if any society can be called master of itself and in control of pleasures and desires, it will be ours.

Quite so.

On these grounds, then, we may describe it as temperate. Furthermore, in our state, if anywhere, the governors and the governed will share the same conviction on the question who ought to rule. Don't you think so?

I am quite sure of it.

Then, if that is their state of mind, in which of the two classes of citizens will temperance reside— in the governors or in the governed?

In both, I suppose.

So we were not wrong in divining a resemblance between temperance and some kind of harmony. Temperance is not like courage and wisdom, which made the state wise and brave by residing each in one particular part. Temperance works in a different way; it extends throughout the whole gamut of the state, producing a consonance of all its elements from the weakest to the strongest as measured by any standard you like to take—wisdom, bodily strength, numbers, or wealth. So we are entirely justified in identifying with temperance this unanimity or harmonious agreement between the naturally superior and inferior elements on the question which of the two should govern, whether in the state or in the individual.

I fully agree.

Good, said I. We have discovered in our commonwealth three out of our four qualities, to the best of our present judgment. What is the remaining one, required to make up its full complement of goodness? For clearly this will be justice.

Clearly.

Now is the moment, then, Glaucon, for us to keep the closest watch, like huntsmen standing round a covert, to make sure that justice does not slip through and vanish undetected. It must certainly be somewhere hereabouts; so keep your eyes open for a view of the quarry, and if you see it first, give me the alert.

I wish I could, he answered; but you will do better to give me a lead and not count on me for more than eyes to see what you show me.

Pray for luck, then, and follow me.

I will, if you will lead on.

The thicket looks rather impenetrable, said I; too dark for it to be easy to start up the game. However, we must push on.

Of course we must.

Here I gave the view halloo. Glaucon, I exclaimed, I believe we are on the track and the quarry is not going to escape us altogether.

That is good news.

Really, I said, we have been extremely stupid. All this time the thing has been under our very noses from the start, and we never saw it. We have been as absurd as a person who hunts for something he has all the time got in his hand. Instead of looking at the thing, we have been staring into the distance. No doubt that is why it escaped us.

What do you mean?

I believe we have been talking about the thing all this while without ever understanding that we were giving some sort of account of it.

Do come to the point. I am all ears.

Listen, then, and judge whether I am right. You remember how, when we first began to establish our commonwealth and several times since, we have laid down, as a universal principle, that everyone ought to perform the one function in the community for which his nature best suited him. Well, I believe that that principle, or some form of it, is justice.

We certainly laid that down.

Yes, and surely we have often heard people say that justice means minding one's own business and not meddling with other men's concerns; and we have often said so ourselves.

We have.

Well, my friend, it may be that this minding of one's own business, when it takes a certain form, is acutally the same thing as justice. Do you know what makes me think so?

No, tell me.

I think that this quality which makes it possible for the three we have already considered, wisdom, courage, and temperance, to take their place in the commonwealth, and so long as it remains present secures their continuance, must be the remaining one. And we said that, when three of the four were found, the one left over would be justice.

It must be so.

Well now, if we had to decide which of these qualities will contribute most to the excellence of our commonwealth, it would be hard to say whether it was the unanimity of rulers and subjects or the soldier's fidelity to the established conviction about what is, or is not, to be feared, or the watchful intelligence of the Rulers; or whether its excellence were not above all due to the observance by everyone, child or woman, slave or freeman or artisan, ruler or ruled, of this principle that each one should do his own proper work without interfering with others.

It would be hard to decide, no doubt.

It seems, then that this principle can at any rate claim to rival wisdom, temperance, and courage as conducing to the excellence of a state. And would you not say that the only possible competitor of these qualities must be justice?

Yes, undoubtedly.

Here is another thing which points to the same conclusion. The judging of law-suits is a duty that you will lay upon your Rulers, isn't it?

Of course.

And the chief aim of their decisions will be that neither party shall have what belongs to another or be deprived of what is his own.

Yes.

Because that is just?

Yes.

So here again justice admittedly means that a man should possess and concern himself with what properly belongs to him.

True.

Again, do you agree with me that no great harm would be done to the community by a general interchange of most forms of work, the carpenter and the cobbler exchanging their positions and their tools and taking on each other's jobs, or even the same man undertaking both?

Yes, there would not be much harm in that.

But I think you will also agree that another kind of interchange would be disastrous. Suppose, for instance, someone whom nature designed to be an artisan or tradesman should be emboldened by some advantage, such as wealth or command of votes or bodily strength, to try to enter the order of fighting men; or some member of that order should aspire, beyond his merits, to a seat in the council-chamber of the Guardians. Such interference and exchange of social positions and tools, or the attempt to combine all these forms of work in the same person, would be fatal to the commonwealth.

Most certainly.

Where there are three orders, then, any plurality of functions or shifting from one order to another is not merely utterly harmful to the community, but one might fairly call it the extreme of wrongdoing. And you will agree that to do the greatest of wrongs to one's own community is injustice.

Surely.

This, then, is injustice. And, conversely, let us repeat that when each order—tradesman, Auxiliary, Guardian—keeps to its own proper business in the commonwealth and does its own work, that is justice and what makes a just society.

I entirely agree.

Chapter XIII (IV. 434 D–441 C)
The Three Parts of the Soul

. . . .

We must not be too positive yet, said I. If we find that this same quality when it exists in the individual can equally be identified with justice, then we can at once give our assent; there will be no more to be said; otherwise, we shall have to look further. For the moment, we had better finish the inquiry which we began with the idea that it would be easier to make out the nature of justice in the individual if we first tried to study it in something on a larger scale. That larger thing we took to be a state, and so we set about constructing the best one we

could, being sure of finding justice in a state that was good. The discovery we made there must now be applied to the individual. If it is confirmed, all will be well; but if we find that justice in the individual is something different, we must go back to the state and test our new result. Perhaps if we brought the two cases into contact like flint and steel, we might strike out between them the spark of justice, and in its light confirm the conception in our own minds.

A good method. Let us follow it.

Now, I continued, if two things, one large, the other small, are called by the same name, they will be alike in that respect to which the common name applies. Accordingly, in so far as the quality of justice is concerned, there will be no difference between a just man and a just society.

No.

Well, but we decided that a society was just when each of the three types of human character it contained performed its own function; and again, it was temperate and brave and wise by virtue of certain other affections and states of mind of those same types.

True.

Accordingly, my friend, if we are to be justified in attributing those same virtues to the individual, we shall expect to find that the individual soul contains the same three elements and that they are affected in the same way as are the corresponding types in society.

That follows.

Here, then, we have stumbled upon another little problem: Does the soul contain these three elements or not?

Not such a very little one, I think. It may be a true saying, Socrates, that what is worth while is seldom easy.

Apparently; and let me tell you, Glaucon, it is my belief that we shall never reach the exact truth in this matter by following our present methods of discussion; the road leading to that goal is longer and more laborious. However, perhaps we can find an answer that will be up to the standard we have so far maintained in our speculations.

Is not that enough? I should be satisfied for the moment.

Well, it will more than satisfy me, I replied.

Don't be disheartened, then, but go on.

Surely, I began, we must admit that the same elements and characters that appear in the state must exist in every one of us; where else could they have come from? It would be absurd to imagine that among peoples with a reputation for a high-spirited character, like the Thracians and Scythians and northerners generally, the states have not derived that character from their individual members; or that it is otherwise with the love of knowledge, which would be ascribed chiefly to our own part of the world, or with the love of money, which one would specially connect with Phoenicia and Egypt.

Certainly.

So far, then, we have a fact which is easily recognized. But here the difficulty begins. Are we using the same part of ourselves in all these three experiences, or a different part in each? Do we gain knowledge with one part, feel anger with another, and with yet a third desire the pleasures of food, sex, and so on? Or is the whole soul at work in every impulse and in all these forms of behaviour? The difficulty is to answer that question satisfactorily.

I quite agree.

Let us approach the problem whether these elements are distinct or identical in this way. It is clear that the same thing cannot act in two opposite ways or be in two opposite states at the same time, with respect to the same part of itself, and in relation to the same object. So if we find such contradictory actions or states among the elements concerned, we shall know that more than one must have been involved.

Very well.

Consider this proposition of mine, then. Can the same thing, at the same time and with respect to the same part of itself, be at rest and in motion?

Certainly not.

We had better state this principle in still more precise terms, to guard against misunderstanding later on. Suppose a man is standing still, but moving his head and arms. We should not allow anyone to say that the same man was both at rest and in motion at the same time, but only that part of him was at rest, part in motion. Isn't that so?

Yes.

An ingenious objector might refine still further and argue that a peg-top, spinning with its peg fixed at the same spot, or indeed any body that revolves in the same place, is both at rest and in motion as a whole, but we should not agree, because the parts in respect of which such a body is moving and at rest are not the same. It contains an axis and a circumference; and in respect of the axis it is at rest inasmuch as the axis is not inclined in any direction, while in respect of the circumference it revolves; and if, while it is spinning, the axis does lean out of the perpendicular in all directions, then it is in no way at rest.

That is true.

No objection of that sort, then, will disconcert us or make us believe that the same thing can ever act or be acted upon in two opposite ways, or be two opposite things, at the same time, in respect of the same part of itself, and in relation to the same object.

I can answer for myself at any rate.

Well, anyhow, as we do not want to spend time in reviewing all such objections to make sure that they are unsound, let us proceed on this assumption, with the understanding that, if we ever come to think otherwise, all the consequences based upon it will fall to the ground.

Yes, that is a good plan.

Now, would you class such things as assent and dissent, striving after something and refusing it, attraction and repulsion, as pairs of opposite actions or states of mind—no matter which?

Yes, they are opposites.

And would you not class all appetites such as hunger and thirst, and again willing and wishing, with the affirmative members of those pairs I have just mentioned? For instance, you would say that the soul of a man who desires something is striving after it, or trying to draw to itself the thing it wishes to possess, or again, in so far as it is willing to have its want satisfied, it is giving its assent to its own longing, as if to an inward question.

Yes.

And, on the other hand, disinclination, unwillingness, and dislike, we should class on the negative side with acts of rejection or repulsion.

Of course.

That being so, shall we say that appetites form one class, the most conspicuous being those we call thirst and hunger?

Yes.

Thirst being desire for drink, hunger for food?
Yes.

Now, is thirst, just in so far as it is thirst, a desire in the soul for anything more than simply drink? Is it, for instance, thirst for hot drink or for cold, for much drink or for little, or in a word for drink of any particular kind? Is it not rather true that you will have a desire for cold drink only if you are feeling hot as well as thirsty, and for hot drink only if you are feeling cold; and if you want much drink or little, that will be because your thirst is a great thirst or a little one? But, just in itself, thirst or hunger is a desire for nothing more than its natural object, drink or food, pure and simple.

Yes, he agreed, each desire, just in itself, is simply for its own natural object. When the object is of such and such a particular kind, the desire will be correspondingly qualified.[5]

We must be careful here, or we might be troubled by the objection that no one desires mere food and drink, but always wholesome food and drink. We shall be told that what we desire is always something that is good; so if thirst is a desire, its object must be, like that of any other desire, something—drink or whatever it may be—that will be good for one.[6]

Yes, there might seem to be something in that objection.

But surely, wherever you have two correlative terms, if one is qualified, the other must always be qualified too; whereas if one is unqualified, so is the other.

I don't understand.

Well, "greater" is a relative term; and the greater is greater than the less; if it is much greater, then the less is much less; if it is greater at some moment, past or future, then the less is less at that same moment. The same principle applies to all such correlatives, like "more" and "fewer," "double" and "half"; and again to terms like "heavier" and "lighter," "quicker" and "slower," and to things like hot and cold.

Yes.

Or take the various branches of knowledge: is it not the same there? The object of knowledge pure and simple is the knowable—if that is the right word—without any qualification; whereas a particular kind of knowledge has an object of a particular kind. For example, as soon as men learnt how to build houses, their craft was distinguished from others under the name of architecture, because it had a unique character, which was itself due to the character of its object; and all other branches of craft and knowledge were distinguished in the same way.

True.

This, then, if you understand me now, is what I meant by saying that, where there are two correlatives, the one is qualified if, and only if, the other is so. I am not saying that the one must have the same quality as the other—that the science of health and disease is itself healthy and diseased, or the knowledge of good and evil is itself good and evil—but only that, as soon as you have a knowledge that is restricted to a particular kind of object, namely health and disease, the knowledge itself becomes a particular kind of knowledge. Hence we no longer call it merely knowledge, which would have for its object whatever can be known, but we add the qualification and call it medical science.

I understand now and I agree.

Now, to go back to thirst: is not that one of these relative terms? It is essentially thirst for something.

Yes, for drink.

And if the drink desired is of a certain kind, the thirst will be correspondingly qualified. But thirst which is just simply thirst is not for drink of any particular sort—much or little, good or bad—but for drink pure and simple.

Quite so.

We conclude, then, that the soul of a thirsty man, just in so far as he is thirsty, has no other wish than to drink. That is the object of its craving, and towards that it is impelled.

That is clear.

Now if there is ever something which at the same time pulls it the opposite way, that something must be an element in the soul other than the one which is thirsting and driving it like a beast to drink; in accordance with our principle that the same thing cannot behave in two opposite ways at the same time and towards the same object with the same part of itself. It is like an archer drawing the bow: it is not accurate to say that his hands are at the same time both pushing and pulling it. One hand does the pushing, the other the pulling.

Exactly.

Now, is it sometimes true that people are thirsty and yet unwilling to drink?

Yes, often.

What, then, can one say of them, if not that their soul contains something which urges them to drink and something which holds them back, and that this latter is a distinct thing and overpowers the other?

I agree.

And is it not true that the intervention of this inhibiting principle in such cases always has its origin in reflection; whereas the impulses driving and dragging the soul are engendered by external influences and abnormal conditions?

Evidently.

We shall have good reason, then, to assert that they are two distinct principles. We may call that part of the soul whereby it reflects, rational; and the other, with which it feels hunger and thirst and is distracted by sexual passion and all the other desires, we will call irrational appetite, associated with pleasure in the replenishment of certain wants.

Yes, there is good ground for that view.

Let us take it, then, that we have now distinguished two elements in the soul. What of that passionate element which makes us feel angry and indignant? Is that a third, or identical in nature with one of those two?

It might perhaps be identified with appetite.

I am more inclined to put my faith in a story I once heard about Leontius, son of Aglaion. On his way up from the Piraeus outside the north wall, he noticed the bodies of some criminals lying on the ground, with the executioner standing by them. He wanted to go and look at them, but at the same time he was disgusted and tried to turn away. He struggled for some time and covered his eyes, but at last the desire was too much for him. Opening his eyes wide, he ran up to the bodies and cried, 'There you are, curse you; feast yourselves on this lovely sight!'

Yes, I have heard that story too.

The point of it surely is that anger is sometimes in conflict with appetite, as if they were two distinct principles. Do we not often find a man whose desires would force him to go against his reason, reviling himself and indignant with this part of his nature which is trying to put constraint on him? It is like a struggle between two factions, in which indignation takes the side of reason. But I believe you have never observed, in yourself or anyone else, indignation make common cause with appetite in behaviour which reason decides to be wrong.

No, I am sure I have not.

Again, take a man who feels he is in the wrong. The more generous his nature, the less can he be indignant at any suffering, such as hunger and cold, inflicted by the man he has injured. He recognizes such treatment as just, and, as I say, his spirit refuses to be roused against it.

That is true.

But now contrast one who thinks it is he that is being wronged. His spirit boils with resentment and sides with the right as he conceives it. Persevering all the more for the hunger and cold and other pains he suffers, it triumphs and will not give in until its gallant struggle has ended in success or death; or until the restraining voice of reason, like a shepherd calling off his dog, makes it relent.

An apt comparison, he said; and in fact it fits the relation of our Auxiliaries to the Rulers: they were to be like watch-dogs obeying the shepherds of the commonwealth.

Yes, you understand very well what I have in mind. But do you see how we have changed our view? A moment ago we were supposing this spirited element to be something of the nature of appetite; but now it appears that, when the soul is divided into factions, it is far more ready to be up in arms on the side of reason.

Quite true.

Is it, then, distinct from the rational element or only a particular form of it, so that the soul will contain no more than two elements, reason and appetite? Or is the soul like the state, which had three orders to hold it together, traders, Auxiliaries, and counsellors? Does the spirited element make a third, the natural auxiliary of reason, when not corrupted by bad upbringing?

It must be a third.

Yes, I said, provided it can be shown to be distinct from reason, as we saw it was from appetite.

That is easily proved. You can see that much in children: they are full of passionate feelings from their very birth; but some, I should say, never become rational, and most of them only late in life.

A very sound observation, said I, the truth of which may also be seen in animals. And besides, there is the witness of Homer in that line I quoted before: "He smote his breast and spoke, chiding his heart." The poet is plainly thinking of the two elements as distinct, when he makes the one which has chosen the better course after reflection rebuke the other for its unreasoning passion.

I entirely agree.

Chapter XIV (IV. 441 C–445 B)
The Virtues in the Individual

. . . .

And so, after a stormy passage, we have reached the land. We are fairly agreed that the same three elements exist alike in the state and in the individual soul.

That is so.

Does it not follow at once that state and individual will be wise or brave by virtue of the same element in each and in the same way? Both will possess in the same manner any quality that makes for excellence.

That must be true.

Then it applies to justice: we shall conclude that a man is just in the same way that a state was just. And we have surely not forgotten that justice in the state meant that each of the three orders in it was doing its own proper work. So we may henceforth bear in mind that each one of us likewise will be a just person, fulfilling his proper function, only if the several parts of our nature fulfil theirs.

Certainly.

And it will be the business of reason to rule with wisdom and forethought on behalf of the entire soul; while the spirited element ought to act as its subordinate and ally. The two will be brought into accord, as we said earlier, by that combination of mental and bodily training which will tune up one string of the instrument and relax the other, nourishing the reasoning part on the study of noble literature and allaying the other's wildness by harmony and rhythm. When both have been thus nurtured and trained to know their own true functions, they must be set in command over the appetites, which form the greater part of each man's soul and are by nature insatiably covetous. They must keep watch lest this part, by battening on the pleasures that are called bodily, should grow so great and powerful that it will no longer keep to its own work, but will try to enslave the others and usurp a dominion to which it has no right, thus turning the whole of life upside down. At the same time, those two together will be the best of guardians for the entire soul and for the body against all enemies from without: the one will take counsel, while the other will do battle, following its ruler's commands and by its own bravery giving effect to the ruler's designs.

Yes, that is all true.

And so we call an individual brave in virtue of this spirited part of his nature, when, in spite of pain or pleasure, it holds fast to the injunctions of reason about what he ought or ought not to be afraid of.

True.

And wise in virtue of that small part which rules and issues these injunctions, possessing as it does the knowledge of what is good for each of the three elements and for all of them in common.

Certainly.

And, again, temperate by reason of the unanimity and concord of all three, when there is no internal conflict between the ruling element and its two subjects, but all are agreed that reason should be ruler.

Yes, that is an exact account of temperance, whether in the state or in the individual.

Finally, a man will be just by observing the principle we have so often stated.

Necessarily.

Now is there any indistinctness in our vision of justice, that might make it seem somehow different from what we found it to be in the state?

I don't think so.

Because, if we have any lingering doubt, we might make sure by comparing it with some commonplace notions. Suppose, for instance, that a sum of money were entrusted to our state or to an individual of corresponding character and training, would anyone imagine that such a person would be specially likely to embezzle it?

No.

And would he not be incapable of sacrilege and theft, or of treachery to friend or country; never false to an oath or any other compact; the last to be guilty of adultery or of neglecting parents or the due service of the gods?

Yes.

And the reason for all this is that each part of his nature is exercising its proper function, of ruling or of being ruled.

Yes, exactly.

Are you satisfied, then, that justice is the power which produces states or individuals of whom that is true, or must we look further?

There is no need; I am quite satisfied.

And so our dream has come true—I mean the inkling we had that, by some happy chance, we had lighted upon a rudimentary form of justice from the very moment when we set about founding our commonwealth. Our principle that the born shoemaker or carpenter had better stick to his trade turns out to have been an adumbration of justice; and that is why it has helped us. But in reality justice, though evidently analogous to this principle, is not a matter of external behaviour, but of the inward self and of attending to all that is, in the fullest sense, a man's proper concern. The just man does not allow the several elements in his soul to usurp one another's functions; he is indeed one who sets his house in order, by self-mastery and discipline coming to be at peace with himself, and bringing into tune those three parts, like the terms in the proportion of a musical scale, the highest and lowest notes and the mean between them, with all the intermediate intervals. Only when he has linked these parts together in well-tempered harmony and has made himself one man instead of many, will he be ready to go about whatever he may have to do, whether it be making money and satisfying bodily wants, or business transactions, or the affairs of state. In all these fields, when he speaks of just and honourable conduct, he will mean the behaviour that helps to produce and to preserve this habit of mind; and by wisdom he will mean the knowledge which presides over such conduct. Any action which tends to break down this habit will be for him unjust; and the notions governing it he will call ignorance and folly.

This is perfectly true, Socrates.

Good, said I. I believe we should not be thought altogether mistaken, if we claimed to have discovered the just man and the just state, and wherein their justice consists.

Indeed we should not.

Shall we make that claim, then?

Yes, we will.

So be it, said I. Next, I suppose, we have to consider injustice.

Evidently.

This must surely be a sort of civil strife among the three elements, whereby they usurp and encroach upon one another's functions and some one part of the soul rises up in rebellion against the whole, claiming a supremacy to which it has no right because its nature fits it only to be the servant of the ruling principle. Such turmoil and aberration we shall, I think, identify with injustice, intemperance, cowardice, ignorance, and in a word with all wickedness.

Exactly.

And now that we know the nature of justice and injustice, we can be equally clear about what is meant by acting justly and again by unjust action and wrongdoing.

How do you mean?

Plainly, they are exactly analogous to those wholesome and unwholesome activities which respectively produce a healthy or unhealthy condition in the body; in the same way just and unjust conduct produce a just or unjust character. Justice is produced in the soul, like health in the body, by establishing the elements concerned in their natural relations of control and subordination, whereas injustice is like disease and means that this natural order is inverted.

Quite so.

It appears, then, that virtue is as it were the health and comeliness and well-being of the soul, as wickedness is disease, deformity, and weakness.

True.

And also that virtue and wickedness are brought about by one's way of life, honourable or disgraceful.

That follows.

So now it only remains to consider which is the more profitable course: to do right and live honourably and be just, whether or not anyone knows what manner of man you are, or to do wrong and be unjust, provided that you can escape the chastisement which might make you a better man.

But really, Socrates, it seems to me ridiculous to ask that question now that the nature of justice and injustice has been brought to light. People think that all the luxury and wealth and power in the world cannot make life worth living when the bodily constitution is going to rack and ruin; and are we to believe that, when the very principle whereby we live is deranged and corrupted, life will be worth living so long as a man can do as he will, and wills to do anything rather than to free himself from vice and wrongdoing and to win justice and virtue?

Yes, I replied, it is a ridiculous question.

NOTES

1. In certain lawsuits the defendant, if found guilty, was allowed to propose a penalty alternative to that demanded by the prosecution. The judges then decided which should be inflicted. The "costs" here means the fee which the sophist, unlike Socrates, expected from his pupils.

2. All the persons mentioned have some interest. The craftsman *qua* craftsman has an interest in doing his work as well as possible, which is the same thing as serving the interest of the subjects on whom his craft is exercised; and the subjects have their interest, which the craftsman is there to promote.

3. The word translated "function" is the common word for "work." Hence the need for illustrations to confine it to the narrower sense of "function," here defined for the first time.

4. Because the wisdom of the whole resides in the smallest part, as explained below.

5. The object of the following subtle argument about relative terms is to distinguish thirst as a mere blind craving for drink from a more complex desire whose object includes the pleasure or health expected to result from drinking. We thus forestall the objection that all desires have "the good" (apparent or real) for their object and include an intellectual or rational element, so that the conflict of motives might be reduced to an intellectual debate, in the same "part" of the soul, on the comparative values of two incompatible ends.

6. If this objection were admitted, it would follow that the desire would always be correspondingly qualified. It is necessary to insist that we do experience blind cravings which can be isolated from any judgement about the goodness of their object.

STUDY QUESTIONS

1. Why does Socrates think that right conduct cannot be defined as "telling the truth and restoring anything we have been trusted with"?

2. Do you agree with Thrasymachus that a life of injustice is more profitable than a life of justice? If so, then why should we be just?

3. In your opinion, does justice belong in the category of things that we value both for themselves and for their results? What reasons does Glaucon give to think that it belongs in a different category?

4. If you had a ring that made you invisible, which of the two characters that Glaucon describes do you think you'd end up like? Do you think Glaucon's case of the ring tells us anything important about the nature of justice?

5. What are the three parts of the soul, according to Socrates? What is the relationship between the three parts of the soul and the state?

An Enquiry Concerning the Principles of Morals

DAVID HUME

· ·

Section I
Of the General Principles
of Morals

Disputes with men, pertinaciously obstinate in their principles, are, of all others, the most irksome; except, perhaps, those with persons, entirely disingenuous, who really do not believe the opinions they defend, but engage in the controversy, from affectation, from a spirit of opposition, or from a desire of showing wit and ingenuity, superior to the rest of mankind. The same blind adherence to their own arguments is to be expected in both; the same contempt of their antagonists; and the same passionate vehemence, in inforcing sophistry and falsehood. And as reasoning is not the source, whence either disputant derives his tenets; it is in vain to expect, that any logic, which speaks not to the affections, will ever engage him to embrace sounder principles.

Those who have denied the reality of moral distinctions, may be ranked among the disingenuous disputants; nor is it conceivable, that any human creature could ever seriously believe, that all characters and actions were alike entitled to the affection and regard of everyone. The difference, which nature has placed between one man and another, is so wide, and this difference is still so much farther widened, by education, example, and habit, that, where the opposite extremes come at once under our apprehension, there is no scepticism so scrupulous, and scarce any assurance so determined, as absolutely to deny all distinction between them. Let a man's insensibility be ever so great, he must often be touched with the images of Right and Wrong; and let his prejudices be

From *Enquiries Concerning Human Understanding and Concerning the Principles of Morals*, edited by L. A. Selby-Bigge, 3rd edition, revised by P. H. Nidditch. Copyright © 1975 by Oxford University Press. Reprinted by permission of the publisher.

ever so obstinate, he must observe, that others are susceptible of like impressions. The only way, therefore, of converting an antagonist of this kind, is to leave him to himself. For, finding that nobody keeps up the controversy with him, it is probable he will, at last, of himself, from mere weariness, come over to the side of common sense and reason.

There has been a controversy started of late, much better worth examination, concerning the general foundation of Morals; whether they be derived from Reason, or from Sentiment; whether we attain the knowledge of them by a chain of argument and induction, or by an immediate feeling and finer internal sense; whether, like all sound judgement of truth and falsehood, they should be the same to every rational intelligent being; or whether, like the perception of beauty and deformity, they be founded entirely on the particular fabric and constitution of the human species.

The ancient philosophers, though they often affirm, that virtue is nothing but conformity to reason, yet, in general, seem to consider morals as deriving their existence from taste and sentiment. On the other hand, our modern enquirers, though they also talk much of the beauty of virtue, and deformity of vice, yet have commonly endeavoured to account for these distinctions by metaphysical reasonings, and by deductions from the most abstract principles of the understanding. Such confusion reigned in these subjects, that an opposition of the greatest consequence could prevail between one system and another, and even in the parts of almost each individual system; and yet nobody, till very lately, was ever sensible of it. The elegant Lord Shaftesbury, who first gave occasion to remark this distinction, and who, in general, adhered to the principles of the ancients, is not, himself, entirely free from the same confusion.

It must be acknowledged, that both sides of the question are susceptible of specious arguments.

Moral distinctions, it may be said, are discernible by pure *reason*: else, whence the many disputes that reign in common life, as well as in philosophy, with regard to this subject: the long chain of proofs often produced on both sides; the examples cited, the authorities appealed to, the analogies employed, the fallacies detected, the inferences drawn, and the several conclusions adjusted to their proper principles. Truth is disputable; not taste: what exists in the nature of things is the standard of our judgement; what each man feels within himself is the standard of sentiment. Propositions in geometry may be proved, systems in physics may be controverted; but the harmony of verse, the tenderness of passion, the brilliancy of wit, must give immediate pleasure. No man reasons concerning another's beauty; but frequently concerning the justice or injustice of his actions. In every criminal trial the first object of the prisoner is to disprove the facts alleged, and deny the actions imputed to him: the second to prove, that, even if these actions were real, they might be justified, as innocent and lawful. It is confessedly by deductions of the understanding, that the first point is ascertained: how can we suppose that a different faculty of the mind is employed in fixing the other?

On the other hand, those who would resolve all moral determinations into *sentiment*, may endeavour to show, that it is impossible for reason ever to draw conclusions of this nature. To virtue, say they, it belongs to be *amiable*, and vice *odious*. This forms their very nature or essence. But can reason or argumentation distribute these different epithets to any subjects, and pronounce beforehand, that this must produce love, and that hatred? Or what other reason can we ever assign for these affections, but the original fabric and formation of the human mind, which is naturally adapted to receive them?

The end of all moral speculations is to teach us our duty; and, by proper representations of the deformity of vice and beauty of virtue, beget correspondent habits, and engage us to avoid the one, and embrace the other. But is this ever to be expected from inferences and conclusions of the understanding, which of themselves have no hold of the affections nor set in motion the active powers of men? They discover truths: but where the truths which they discover are indifferent, and beget no desire or aversion, they can have no influence on conduct and behaviour. What is honourable, what is fair, what is becoming, what is noble, what is generous, takes possession of the heart, and animates us to embrace and maintain it. What is intelligible, what is evident, what is probable, what is true, procures only the cool assent of the understanding; and gratifying a speculative curiosity, puts an end to our researches.

Extinguish all the warm feelings and prepossessions in favour of virtue, and all disgust or aversion to vice; render men totally indifferent towards these distinctions; and morality is no longer a practical study, nor has any tendency to regulate our lives and actions.

These arguments on each side (and many more might be produced) are so plausible, that I am apt to suspect, they may, the one as well as the other, be solid and satisfactory, and that *reason* and *sentiment* concur in almost all moral determinations and conclusions. The final sentence, it is probable, which pronounces characters and actions amiable or odious, praise-worthy or blameable; that which stamps on them the mark of honour or infamy, approbation or censure; that which renders morality an active principle and constitutes virtue our happiness, and vice our misery: it is probable, I say, that this final sentence depends on some internal sense or feeling, which nature has made universal in the whole species. For what else can have an influence of this nature? But in order to pave the way for such a sentiment, and give a proper discernment of its object, it is often necessary, we find, that much reasoning should precede, that nice distinctions be made, just conclusions drawn, distant comparisons formed, complicated relations examined, and general facts fixed and ascertained. Some species of beauty, especially the natural kinds, on their first appearance, command our affection and approbation; and where they fail of this effect, it is impossible for any reasoning to redress their influence, or adapt them better to our taste and sentiment. But in many orders of beauty, particularly those of the finer arts, it is requisite to employ much reasoning, in order to feel the proper sentiment; and a false relish may frequently be corrected by argument and reflection. There are just grounds to conclude, that moral beauty partakes much of this latter species, and demands the assistance of our intellectual faculties, in order to give it a suitable influence on the human mind.

But though this question, concerning the general principles of morals, be curious and important, it is needless for us, at present, to employ further care in our researches concerning it. For if we can be so happy, in the course of this enquiry, as to discover the true origin of morals, it will then easily appear how far either sentiment or reason enters into all determinations of this nature.[1] In order to attain this purpose, we shall endeavour to follow a very simple method; we shall analyse that complication of mental qualities, which form what, in common life, we call Personal Merit: we shall consider every attribute of the mind, which renders a man an object either of esteem and affection, or of hatred and contempt; every habit or sentiment or faculty, which, if ascribed to any person, implies either praise or blame, and may enter into any panegyric or satire of his character and manners. The quick sensibility, which, on this head, is so universal among mankind, gives a philosopher sufficient assurance, that he can never be considerably mistaken in framing the catalogue, or incur any danger of misplacing the objects of his contemplation: he needs only enter into his own breast for a moment, and consider whether or not he should desire to have this or that quality ascribed to him, and whether such or such an imputation would proceed from a friend or an enemy. The very nature of language guides us almost infallibly in forming a judgement of this nature; and as every tongue possesses one set of words which are taken in a good sense, and another in the opposite, the least acquaintance with the idiom suffices, without any reasoning, to direct us in collecting and arranging the estimable or blameable qualities of men. The only object of reasoning is to discover the circumstances on both sides, which are common to these qualities; to observe that particular in which the estimable qualities agree on the one hand, and the blameable on the other; and thence to reach the foundation of ethics, and find those universal principles, from which all censure or approbation is ultimately derived. As this is a question of fact, not of abstract science, we can only expect success, by following the experimental method, and deducing general maxims from a comparison of particular instances. The other scientific method, where a general abstract principle is first established, and is afterwards branched out into a variety of inferences and conclusions, may be more perfect in itself, but suits less the imperfection of human nature, and is a common source of illusion and mistake in this as well as in other subjects. Men are now cured of their passion for hypotheses and systems in natural philosophy, and will hearken to no arguments but those which are derived from experience. It is full time they should attempt a like reformation in all moral disquisitions; and reject every system of ethics, however subtle or ingenious, which is not founded on fact and observation.

We shall begin our enquiry on this head by the consideration of the social virtues, Benevolence and Justice. The explication of them will probably give us an opening by which the others may be accounted for.

Section II
Of Benevolence

Part I

It may be esteemed, perhaps, a superfluous task to prove, that the benevolent or softer affections are estimable; and wherever they appear, engage the approbation and good-will of mankind. The epithets *sociable*, *good-natured*, *humane*, *merciful*, *grateful*, *friendly*, *generous*, *beneficent*, or their equivalents, are known in all languages, and universally express the highest merit, which *human nature* is capable of attaining. Where these amiable qualities are attended with birth and power and eminent abilities, and display themselves in the good government or useful instruction of mankind, they seem even to raise the possessors of them above the rank of *human nature*, and make them approach in some measure to the divine. Exalted capacity, undaunted courage, prosperous success; these may only expose a hero or politician to the envy and ill-will of the public: but as soon as the praises are added of humane and beneficent; when instances are displayed of lenity, tenderness or friendship; envy itself is silent, or joins the general voice of approbation and applause.

. . . .

Part II

We may observe that, in displaying the praises of any humane, beneficent man, there is one circumstance which never fails to be amply insisted on, namely, the happiness and satisfaction, derived to society from his intercourse and good offices. To his parents, we are apt to say, he endears himself by his pious attachment and duteous care still more than by the connexions of nature. His children never feel his authority, but when employed for their advantage. With him, the ties of love are consolidated by beneficence and friendship. The ties of friendship approach, in a fond observance of each obliging office, to those of love and inclination. His domestics and dependants have in him a sure resource; and no longer dread the power of fortune, but so far as she exercises it over him. From him the hungry receive food, the naked clothing, the ignorant and slothful skill and industry. Like the sun, an inferior minister of providence he cheers, invigorates, and sustains the surrounding world.

If confined to private life, the sphere of his activity is narrower; but his influence is all benign and gentle. If exalted into a higher station, mankind and posterity reap the fruit of his labours.

As these topics of praise never fail to be employed, and with success, where we would inspire esteem for any one; may it not thence be concluded, that the utility, resulting from the social virtues, forms, at least, a *part* of their merit, and is one source of that approbation and regard so universally paid to them?

. . . .

In all determinations of morality, this circumstance of public utility is ever principally in view; and wherever disputes arise, either in philosophy or common life, concerning the bounds of duty, the question cannot, by any means, be decided with greater certainty, than by ascertaining, on any side, the true interests of mankind. If any false opinion, embraced from appearances, has been found to prevail; as soon as farther experience and sounder reasoning have given us juster notions of human affairs, we retract our first sentiment, and adjust anew the boundaries of moral good and evil.

Giving alms to common beggars is naturally praised; because it seems to carry relief to the distressed and indigent: but when we observe the encouragement thence arising to idleness and debauchery, we regard that species of charity rather as a weakness than a virtue.

Tyrannicide, or the assassination of usurpers and oppressive princes, was highly extolled in ancient times; because it both freed mankind from many of these monsters, and seemed to keep the others in awe, whom the sword or poinard could not reach. But history and experience having since convinced us, that this practice increases the jealousy and cruelty of princes, a Timoleon and a Brutus, though treated with indulgence on account of prejudices of their times, are now considered as very improper models for imitation.

Liberality in princes is regarded as a mark of beneficence, but when it occurs, that the homely bread of the honest and industrious is often thereby converted into delicious cates for the idle and the prodigal, we soon retract our heedless praises. The regrets of a prince, for having lost a day, were noble and generous; but had he intended to have spent it in acts of generosity to his greedy courtiers, it was better lost than misemployed after that manner.

Luxury, or a refinement on the pleasures and conveniencies of life, had long been supposed the source of every corruption in government, and the immediate cause of faction, sedition, civil wars, and the total loss of liberty. It was, therefore, universally regarded as a vice, and was an object of declamation to all satirists, and severe moralists. Those, who prove, or attempt to prove, that such refinements rather tend to the increase of industry, civility, and arts regulate anew our *moral* as well as *political* sentiments, and represent, as laudable or innocent, what had formerly been regarded as pernicious and blameable.

Upon the whole, then, it seems undeniable, *that* nothing can bestow more merit on any human creature than the sentiment of benevolence in an eminent degree; and *that* a *part*, at least, of its merit arises from its tendency to promote the interests of our species, and bestow happiness on human society. We carry our view into the salutary consequences of such a character and disposition; and whatever has so benign an influence, and forwards so desirable an end, is beheld with complacency and pleasure. The social virtues are never regarded without their beneficial tendencies, nor viewed as barren and unfruitful. The happiness of mankind, the order of society, and harmony of families, the mutual support of friends, are always considered as the result of their gentle dominion over the breasts of men.

How considerable a *part* of their merit we ought to ascribe to their utility, will better appear from future disquisitions[2]; as well as the reason, why this circumstance has such a command over our esteem and approbation.[3]

Section III
Of Justice

Part I

That Justice is useful to society, and consequently that *part* of its merit, at least, must arise from that consideration, it would be a superfluous undertaking to prove. That public utility is the *sole* origin of justice, and that reflections on the beneficial consequences of this virtue are the *sole* foundation of its merit; this proposition, being more curious and important, will better deserve our examination and enquiry.

Let us suppose that nature has bestowed on the human race such profuse *abundance* of all *external* conveniencies, that, without any uncertainty in the event, without any care or industry on our part, every individual finds himself fully provided with whatever his most voracious appetites can want, or luxurious imagination wish or desire. His natural beauty, we shall suppose, surpasses all acquired ornaments; the perpetual clemency of the seasons renders useless all clothes or covering: the raw herbage affords him the most delicious fare; the clear fountain, the richest beverage. No laborious occupation required: no tillage: no navigation. Music, poetry, and contemplation form his sole business: conversation, mirth, and friendship his sole amusement.

It seems evident that, in such a happy state, every other social virtue would flourish, and receive tenfold increase; but the cautious, jealous virtue of justice would never once have been dreamed of. For what purpose make a partition of goods, where every one has already more than enough? Why give rise to property, where there cannot possibly be any injury? Why call this object *mine*, when upon the seizing of it by another, I need but stretch out my hand to possess myself of what is equally valuable? Justice, in that case, being totally useless, would be an idle ceremonial, and could never possibly have place in the catalogue of virtues.

We see, even in the present necessitous condition of mankind, that, wherever any benefit is bestowed by nature in an unlimited abundance, we leave it always in common among the whole human race, and make no subdivisions of right and property. Water and air, though the most necessary of all objects, are not challenged as the property of individuals; nor can any man commit injustice by the most lavish use and enjoyment of these blessings. In fertile extensive countries, with few inhabitants, land is regarded on the same footing. And no topic is so much insisted on by those, who defend the liberty of the seas, as the unexhausted use of them in navigation. Were the advantages, procured by navigation, as inexhaustible, these reasoners had never had any adversaries to refute; nor had any claims ever been advanced of a separate, exclusive dominion over the ocean.

It may happen, in some countries, at some periods, that there be established a property in water, none in land; if the latter be in greater abundance than can be used by the inhabitants, and the former be found, with difficulty, and in very small quantities.

Again; suppose, that, though the necessities of the human race continue the same as the present, yet the mind is so enlarged, and so replete with friendship and generosity, that every man has the utmost tenderness for every man, and feels no more concern for his own interest than for that of his fellows; it seems evident, that the use of justice would, in this case, be suspended by such an extensive benevolence, nor would the divisions and barriers of property and obligation have ever been thought of. Why should I bind another, by a deed or promise, to do me any good office, when I know that he is already prompted, by the strongest inclination, to seek my happiness, and would, of himself, perform the desired service; except the hurt, he thereby receives, be greater than the benefit accruing to me? in which case, he knows, that, from my innate humanity and friendship, I should be the first to oppose myself to his imprudent generosity. Why raise land-marks between my neighbour's field and mine, when my heart has made no division between our interests; but shares all his joys and sorrows with the same force and vivacity as if originally my own? Every man, upon this supposition, being a second self to another, would trust all his interests to the discretion of every man; without jealousy, without partition, without distinction. And the whole human race would form only one family; where all would lie in common, and be used freely, without regard to property; but cautiously too, with as entire regard to the necessities of each individual, as if our own interests were most intimately concerned.

In the present disposition of the human heart, it would, perhaps, be difficult to find complete instances of such enlarged affections; but still we may observe, that the case of families approaches towards it; and the stronger the mutual benevolence is among the individuals, the nearer it approaches; till all distinction of property be, in a great measure, lost and confounded among them. Between married persons, the cement of friendship is by the laws supposed so strong as to abolish all division of possessions; and has often, in reality, the force ascribed to it. And it is observable, that, during the ardour of new enthusiasms, when every principle is inflamed into extravagance, the community of goods has frequently been attempted; and nothing but experience of its inconveniencies, from the returning or disguised selfishness of men, could make the imprudent fanatics adopt anew the ideas of justice and of separate property. So true is it, that this virtue derives its existence entirely from its necessary *use* to the intercourse and social state of mankind.

To make this truth more evident, let us reverse the foregoing suppositions; and carrying everything to the opposite extreme, consider what would be the effect of these new situations. Suppose a society to fall into such want of all common necessaries, that the utmost frugality and industry cannot preserve the greater number from perishing, and the whole

from extreme misery; it will readily, I believe, be admitted, that the strict laws of justice are suspended, in such a pressing emergence, and give place to the stronger motives of necessity and self-preservation. Is it any crime, after a shipwreck, to seize whatever means or instrument of safety one can lay hold of, without regard to former limitations of property? Or if a city besieged were perishing with hunger; can we imagine, that men will see any means of preservation before them, and lose their lives, from a scrupulous regard to what, in other situations, would be the rules of equity and justice? The use and tendency of that virtue is to procure happiness and security, by preserving order in society: but where the society is ready to perish from extreme necessity, no greater evil can be dreaded from violence and injustice; and every man may now provide for himself by all the means which prudence can dictate, or humanity permit. The public, even in less urgent necessities, opens granaries, without the consent of proprietors; as justly supposing, that the authority of magistracy may, consistent with equity, extend so far: but were any number of men to assemble, without the tie of laws or civil jurisdiction; would an equal partition of bread in a famine, though effected by power and even violence, be regarded as criminal or injurious?

Suppose likewise, that it should be a virtuous man's fate to fall into the society of ruffians, remote from the protection of laws and government; what conduct must he embrace in that melancholy situation? He sees such a desperate rapaciousness prevail; such a disregard to equity, such contempt of order, such stupid blindness to future consequences, as must immediately have the most tragical conclusion, and must terminate in destruction to the greater number, and in a total dissolution of society to the rest. He, meanwhile, can have no other expedient than to arm himself, to whomever the sword he seizes, or the buckler, may belong: To make provision of all means of defence and security: And his particular regard to justice being no longer of use to his own safety or that of others, he must consult the dictates of self-preservation alone, without concern for those who no longer merit his care and attention.

When any man, even in political society, renders himself by his crimes, obnoxious to the public, he is punished by the laws in his goods and person; that is, the ordinary rules of justice are, with regard to him, suspended for a moment, and it becomes equitable to inflict on him, for the *benefit* of society, what otherwise he could not suffer without wrong or injury.

The rage and violence of public war; what is it but a suspension of justice among the warring parties, who perceive, that this virtue is now no longer of any *use* or advantage to them? The laws of war, which then succeed to those of equity and justice, are rules calculated for the *advantage* and *utility* of that particular state, in which men are now placed. And were a civilized nation engaged with barbarians, who observed no rules even of war, the former must also suspend their observance of them, where they no longer serve to any purpose; and must render every action or rencounter as bloody and pernicious as possible to the first aggressors.

Thus, the rules of equity or justice depend entirely on the particular state and condition in which men are placed, and owe their origin and existence to that utility, which results to the public from their strict and regular observance. Reverse, in any considerable circumstance, the condition of men: Produce extreme abundance or extreme necessity: Implant in the human breast perfect moderation and humanity, or perfect rapaciousness and malice: By rendering justice totally *useless*, you thereby totally destroy its essence, and suspend its obligation upon mankind.

The common situation of society is a medium amidst all these extremes. We are naturally partial to ourselves, and to our friends; but are capable of learning the advantage resulting from a more equitable conduct. Few enjoyments are given us from the open and liberal hand of nature; but by art, labour, and industry, we can extract them in great abundance. Hence the ideas of property become necessary in all civil society: Hence justice derives its usefulness to the public: And hence alone arises its merit and moral obligation.

. . . .

The more we vary our views of human life, and the newer and more unusual the lights are in which we survey it, the more shall we be convinced, that the origin here assigned for the virtue of justice is real and satisfactory.

Were there a species of creatures intermingled with men, which, though rational, were possessed of such inferior strength, both of body and mind, that they were incapable of all resistance, and could never, upon the highest provocation, make us feel the effects of their resentment; the necessary consequence, I think, is that we should be bound by the laws of humanity to give gentle usage to these creatures, but should not, properly speaking, lie under any restraint of justice with regard to them, nor could they possess any right or property, exclusive of such arbitrary lords. Our intercourse with them could not be called society, which supposes a degree of equality; but absolute command on the one side, and servile obedience on the other. Whatever we covet, they must instantly resign: Our permission is the only tenure, by which they hold their possessions: Our compassion and kindness the only check, by which they curb our lawless will: And as no inconvenience ever results from the exercise of a power, so firmly established in nature, the restraints of justice and property, being totally *useless*, would never have place in so unequal a confederacy.

This is plainly the situation of men, with regard to animals; and how far these may be said to possess reason, I leave it to others to determine. The great superiority of civilized Europeans above barbarous Indians, tempted us to imagine ourselves on the same footing with regard to them, and made us throw off all restraints of justice, and even of humanity, in our treatment of them. In many nations, the female sex are reduced to like slavery, and are rendered incapable for all property, in opposition to their lordly masters. But though the males, when united, have in all countries bodily force sufficient to maintain this severe tyranny, yet such are the insinuation, address, and charms of their fair companions, that women are commonly able to break the confederacy, and share with the other sex in all the rights and privileges of society.

Were the human species so framed by nature as that each individual possessed within himself every faculty, requisite both for his own preservation and for the propagation of his kind: Were all society and intercourse cut off between man and man, by the primary intention of the supreme Creator: It seems evident, that so solitary a being would be as much incapable of justice, as of social discourse and conversation. Where mutual regards and forbearance serve to no manner of purpose, they would never direct the conduct of any reasonable man. The headlong course of the passions would be checked by no reflection on future consequences. And as each man is here supposed to love himself alone, and to depend only on himself and his own activity for safety and happiness, he would, on every occasion, to the utmost of his power, challenge the preference above every other being, to none of which he is bound by any ties, either of nature or of interest.

But suppose the conjunction of the sexes to be established in nature, a family immediately arises; and particular rules being found requisite for its subsistence, these are immediately embraced; though without comprehending the rest of mankind within their prescriptions. Suppose that several families unite together into one society, which is totally disjoined from all others, the rules, which preserve peace and order, enlarge themselves to the utmost extent of that society; but becoming then entirely useless, lose their force when carried one step farther. But again suppose, that several distinct societies maintain a kind of intercourse for mutual convenience and advantage, the boundaries of justice still grow larger, in proportion to the largeness of men's views, and the force of their mutual connexions. History, experience, reason sufficiently instruct us in this natural progress of human sentiments, and in the gradual enlargement of our regards to justice, in proportion as we become acquainted with the extensive utility of that virtue.

. . . .

Section V
Why Utility Pleases

Part I

It seems so natural a thought to ascribe to their utility the praise, which we bestow on the social virtues, that one would expect to meet with this principle everywhere in moral writers, as the chief foundation of their reasoning and enquiry. In common life, we may observe, that the circumstance of utility is always appealed to; nor is it supposed, that a greater eulogy can be given to any man, than to display his usefulness to the public, and enumerate the services, which he has performed to mankind and society. What praise, even of an inanimate form, if the regularity and elegance of its parts destroy not its fitness for any useful purpose! And how satisfactory an apology for any disproportion or seeming deformity, if we can show the necessity of that particular construction for the use intended! A ship appears more beautiful to an artist, or one moderately skilled in navigation, where its prow is wide and swelling beyond its poop, than if it were framed with a precise geometrical regularity, in contradiction to all the laws of mechanics. A building, whose doors and windows were exact squares, would hurt the eye by that very proportion; as ill adapted to the figure of a human creature, for whose service the fabric was intended. What wonder then, that a man, whose habits and conduct are hurtful to society, and dangerous or pernicious to every one who has an intercourse with him, should, on that account, be an object of disapprobation, and communicate to every spectator the strongest sentiment of disgust and hatred.

But perhaps the difficulty of accounting for these effects of usefulness, or its contrary, has kept philosophers from admitting them into their systems of ethics, and has induced them rather to employ any other principle, in explaining the origin of moral good and evil. But it is no just reason for rejecting any principle, confirmed by experience, that we cannot give a satisfactory account of its origin, nor are able to resolve it into other more general principles. And if we would employ a little thought on the present subject, we need be at no loss to account for the influence of utility, and to deduce it from principles, the most known and avowed in human nature.

From the apparent usefulness of the social virtues, it has readily been inferred by sceptics, both ancient and modern, that all moral distinctions arise from education, and were, at first, invented, and afterwards encouraged, by the art of politicians, in order to render men tractable, and subdue their natural ferocity and selfishness, which incapacitated them for society. This principle, indeed, of precept and education, must so far be owned to have a powerful influence, that it may frequently increase or diminish, beyond their natural standard, the sentiments of approbation or dislike; and may even, in particular instances, create, without any natural principle, a new sentiment of this kind; as is evident in all superstitious practices and observances: But that *all* moral affection or dislike arises from this origin, will never surely be allowed by any judicious enquirer. Had nature made no such distinction, founded on the original constitution of the mind, the words, *honourable* and *shameful*, *lovely* and *odious*, *noble* and *despicable*, had never had place in any language; nor could politicians, had they invented these terms, ever have been able to render them intelligible, or make them convey any idea to the audience. So that nothing can be more superficial than this paradox of the sceptics; and it were well, if, in the abstruser studies of logic and metaphysics, we could as easily obviate the cavils of that sect, as in the practical and more intelligible sciences of politics and morals.

The social virtues must, therefore, be allowed to have a natural beauty and amiableness, which, at first, antecedent to all precept or education, recommends them to the esteem of uninstructed mankind, and engages their affections. And as the public utility of these virtues is the chief circumstance, whence they derive their merit, it follows, that the end, which they have a tendency to promote, must be some way agreeable to us, and take hold of some natural affection. It must please, either from considerations of self-interest, or from more generous motives and regards.

It has often been asserted, that, as every man has a strong connexion with society, and perceives the impossibility of his solitary subsistence, he becomes, on that account, favourable to all those habits or principles, which promote order in society, and insure to him the quiet possession of so inestimable a blessing. As much as we value our own happiness and welfare, as much must we applaud the practice of justice and humanity, by which alone the social confederacy can be maintained, and every man reap the fruits of mutual protection and assistance.

This deduction of morals from self-love, or a regard to private interest, is an obvious thought, and has not arisen wholly from the wanton sallies and sportive assaults of the sceptics. To mention no others, Polybius, one of the gravest and most judicious, as well as most moral writers of antiquity, has assigned this selfish origin to all our sentiments of virtue. But though the solid practical sense of that author, and his aversion to all vain subtilties, render his authority on the present subject very considerable; yet is not this an affair to be decided by authority, and the voice of nature and experience seems plainly to oppose the selfish theory.

We frequently bestow praise on virtuous actions, performed in very distant ages and remote countries; where the utmost subtilty of imagination would not discover any appearance of self-interest, or find any connexion of our present happiness and security with events so widely separated from us.

A generous, a brave, a noble deed, performed by an adversary, commands our approbation; while in its consequences it may be acknowledged prejudicial to our particular interest.

Where private advantage concurs with general affection for virtue, we readily perceive and avow the mixture of these distinct sentiments, which have a very different feeling and influence on the mind. We praise, perhaps, with more alacrity, where the generous humane action contributes to our particular interest: But the topics of praise, which we insist on, are very wide of this circumstance. And we may attempt to bring over others to our sentiments, without endeavouring to convince them, that they reap any advantage from the actions which we recommend to their approbation and applause.

Frame the model of a praiseworthy character, consisting of all the most amiable moral virtues: Give instances, in which these display themselves after an eminent and extraordinary manner: You readily engage the esteem and approbation of all your audience, who never so much as enquire in what age and country the person lived, who possessed these noble qualities: A circumstance, however, of all others, the most material to self-love, or a concern for our own individual happiness.

Once on a time, a statesman, in the shock and contest of parties, prevailed so far as to procure, by his eloquence, the banishment of an able adversary; whom he secretly followed, offering him money for his support during his exile, and soothing him with topics of consolation in his misfortunes. *Alas!* cries the banished statesman, *with what regret must I leave my friends in this city, where even enemies are so generous*! Virtue, though in an enemy, here pleased him: And we also give it the just tribute of praise and approbation; nor do we retract these sentiments, when we hear, that the action passed at Athens, about two thousand years ago, and that the persons names were Eschines and Demosthenes.

What is that to me? There are few occasions, when this question is not pertinent: And had it that universal, infallible influence supposed, it would turn into ridicule every composition, and almost every conversation, which contain any praise or censure of men and manners.

It is but a weak subterfuge, when pressed by these facts and arguments, to say, that we transport ourselves, by the force of imagination, into distant ages and countries, and consider the advantage, which we should have reaped from these characters, had we been contemporaries, and had any commerce with the persons. It is not conceivable, how a *real* sentiment or passion can ever arise from a known *imaginary* interest; especially when our *real* interest is still kept in view, and is often acknowledged to be entirely distinct from the imaginary, and even sometimes opposite to it.

A man, brought to the brink of a precipice, cannot look down without trembling; and the sentiment of *imaginary* danger actuates him, in opposition to the opinion and belief of *real* safety. But the imagination is here assisted by the presence of a striking object; and yet prevails not, except to be also aided by novelty, and the unusual appearance of the object. Custom soon reconciles us to heights and precipices, and wears off these false and delusive terrors. The reverse is observable in the estimates which we form of characters and manners; and the more we habituate ourselves to an accurate scrutiny of morals, the more delicate feeling do we acquire of the most minute distinctions between vice and virtue. Such frequent occasion, indeed, have we, in common life, to pronounce all kinds of moral determinations, that no object of this kind can be new or unusual to us; nor could any *false* views or prepossessions maintain their ground against an experience, so common and familiar. Experience being chiefly what forms the associations of ideas, it is impossible that any association could establish and support itself, in direct opposition to that principle.

Usefulness is agreeable, and engages our approbation. This is a matter of fact, confirmed by daily observation. But, *useful?* For what? For somebody's interest, surely. Whose interest then? Not our own only: For our approbation frequently extends farther. It must, therefore, be the interest of those, who are served by the character or action approved of; and these we may conclude, however remote, are not totally indifferent to us. By opening up this principle, we shall discover one great source of moral distinctions.

Part II

Self-love is a principle in human nature of such extensive energy, and the interest of each individual is, in general, so closely connected with that of the community, that those philosophers were excusable, who fancied that all our concern for the public might be resolved into a concern for our own happiness and preservation. They saw every moment, instances of approbation or blame, satisfaction or displeasure towards characters and actions; they denominated the objects of these sentiments, *virtues*, or *vices*; they observed, that the former had a tendency to increase the happiness, and the latter the misery of mankind; they asked, whether it were possible that we could have any general concern for society, or any disinterested resentment of the welfare or injury of others; they found it simpler to consider all these sentiments as modifications of self-love; and they discovered a pretence, at least, for this unity of principle, in that close union of interest, which is so observable between the public and each individual.

But notwithstanding this frequent confusion of interests, it is easy to attain what natural philosophers, after Lord Bacon, have affected to call the *experimentum crucis*, or that experiment which points out the right way in any doubt or ambiguity. We have found instances, in which private interest was separate from public; in which it was even contrary: And yet we observed the moral sentiment to continue, notwithstanding this disjunction of interests. And whenever these distinct interests sensibly concurred, we always found a sensible increase of the sentiment, and a more warm affection to virtue, and detestation of vice, or what we properly call, *gratitude* and *revenge*. Compelled by these instances, we must renounce the theory, which accounts for every moral sentiment by the principle of self-love. We must adopt a more public affection, and allow, that the interests of society are not, even on their own account, entirely indifferent to us. Usefulness is only a tendency to a certain end; and it is a contradiction in terms, that anything pleases as means to an end, where the end itself no wise affects us. If usefulness, therefore, be a source of moral sentiment, and if this usefulness be not always considered with a reference to self; it follows, that everything, which contributes to the happiness of society, recommends itself directly to our approbation and good-will. Here is a principle, which accounts, in great part, for the origin of morality: And what need we seek for abstruse and remote systems, when there occurs one so obvious and natural?[4]

Have we any difficulty to comprehend the force of humanity and benevolence? Or to conceive, that the very aspect of happiness, joy, prosperity, gives pleasure; that of pain, suffering, sorrow, communicates uneasiness? The human countenance, says Horace, borrows smiles or tears from the human countenance. Reduce a person to solitude, and he loses all enjoyment, except either of the sensual or speculative kind; and that because the movements of his heart are not forwarded by correspondent movements in his fellow-creatures. The signs of sorrow and mourning, though arbitrary, affect us with melancholy; but the natural symptoms, tears and cries and groans, never fail to infuse compassion and uneasiness. And if the effects of misery touch us in so lively a manner; can we be supposed altogether insensible or indifferent towards its causes; when a malicious or treacherous character and behaviour are presented to us?

We enter, I shall suppose, into a convenient, warm, well-contrived apartment: We necessarily receive a pleasure from its very survey; because it presents us with the pleasing ideas of ease, satisfaction, and enjoyment. The hospitable, good-humoured, humane landlord appears. This circumstance surely must embellish the whole; nor can we easily forbear reflecting, with pleasure, on the satisfaction which results to every one from his intercourse and good-offices.

His whole family, by the freedom, ease, confidence, and calm enjoyment, diffused over their countenances, sufficiently express their happiness. I have a pleasing sympathy in the prospect of so much joy, and can never consider the source of it, without the most agreeable emotions.

He tells me, that an oppressive and powerful neighbour had attempted to dispossess him of his inheritance, and had long disturbed all his innocent and social pleasures. I feel an immediate indignation arise in me against such violence and injury.

But it is no wonder, he adds, that a private wrong should proceed from a man, who had enslaved provinces, depopulated cities, and made the field and scaffold stream with human blood. I am struck with horror at the prospect of so much misery, and am actuated by the strongest antipathy against its author.

In general, it is certain, that, wherever we go, whatever we reflect on or converse about, everything still presents us with the view of human happiness or misery, and excites in our breast a sympathetic movement of pleasure or uneasiness. In our serious occupations, in our careless amusements, this principle still exerts its active energy.

. . . .

If any man from a cold insensibility, or narrow selfishness of temper, is unaffected with the images of human happiness or misery, he must be equally indifferent to the images of vice and virtue: As, on the other hand, it is always found, that a warm concern for the interests of our species is attended with a delicate feeling of all moral distinctions; a strong resentment of injury done to men; a lively approbation of their welfare. In this particular, though great superiority is observable of one man above another; yet none are so entirely indifferent to the interest of their fellow-creatures, as to perceive no distinctions of moral good and evil, in consequence of the different tendencies of actions and principles. How, indeed, can we suppose it possible in any one, who wears a human heart, that if there be subjected to his censure, one character or system of conduct, which is beneficial, and another which is pernicious, to his species or community, he will not so much as give a cool preference to the former, or ascribe to it the smallest merit or regard? Let us suppose such a person ever so selfish; let private interest have ingrossed ever so much his attention; yet in instances, where that is not concerned, he must unavoidably feel *some* propensity to the good of mankind, and make it an object of choice, if everything else be equal. Would any man, who is walking along, tread as willingly on another's gouty toes, whom he has no quarrel with, as on the hard flint and pavement? There is here surely a difference in the case. We surely take into consideration the happiness and misery of others, in weighing the several motives of action, and incline to the former, where no private regards draw us to seek our own promotion or advantage by the injury of our fellow-creatures. And if the principles of humanity are capable, in many instances, of influencing our actions, they must, at all times, have *some* authority over our sentiments, and give us a general approbation of what is useful to society, and blame of what is dangerous or pernicious. The degrees of these sentiments may be the subject of controversy; but the reality of their existence, one should think, must be admitted in every theory or system.

. . . .

A statesman or patriot, who serves our own country in our own time, has always a more passionate regard paid to him, than one whose beneficial influence operated on distant ages or remote nations; where the good, resulting from his generous humanity, being less connected with us, seems more obscure, and affects us with a less lively sympathy. We may own the merit to be equally great, though our sentiments are not raised to an equal height, in both cases. The judgment here corrects the inequalities of our internal emotions and perceptions; in like manner, as it preserves us from error, in the several variations of images, presented to our external senses. The same object, at a double distance, really throws on the eye a picture of but half the bulk; yet we imagine that it appears of the same size in both situations; because we know that on our approach to it, its image would expand on the eye, and that the difference consists not in the object itself, but in our position with regard to it. And, indeed, without such a correction of appearances, both in internal and external sentiment, men could never think or talk steadily on any subject; while their fluctuating situations produce a continual variation on objects, and throw them into such different and contrary lights and positions.[5]

The more we converse with mankind, and the greater social intercourse we maintain, the more shall we be familiarized to these general preferences and distinctions, without which our conversation and discourse could scarcely be rendered intelligible to each other. Every man's interest is peculiar to himself, and the aversions and desires, which result from it, cannot be supposed to affect others in a like degree. General language, therefore, being formed for general use, must be moulded on some more general views, and must affix the epithets of praise or blame, in conformity to sentiments, which arise from the general interests of the community. And if these sentiments, in most men, be not so strong as those, which have a reference to private good; yet still they must make some distinction, even in persons the most depraved and selfish; and must attach the notion of good to a beneficent conduct, and of evil to the contrary. Sympathy, we shall allow, is much fainter than our concern for ourselves, and sympathy with persons remote from us much fainter than that with persons near and contiguous; but for this very reason it is necessary for us, in our calm judgements and discourse concerning the characters of men, to neglect all these differences, and render our sentiments more public and social. Besides, that we ourselves often change our situation in this particular, we every day meet with persons who are in a situation different from us, and who could never converse with us were we to remain constantly in that position and point of view, which is peculiar to ourselves. The intercourse of sentiments, therefore, in society and conversation, makes us form some general unalterable standard, by which we may approve or disapprove of characters and manners. And though the heart takes not part entirely with those general notions, nor regulates all its love and hatred, by the universal abstract differences of vice and virtue, without regard to self, or the persons with whom we are more intimately connected; yet have these moral differences a considerable influence, and being sufficient, at least, for discourse, serve all our purposes in company, in the pulpit, on the theatre, and in the schools.

Thus, in whatever light we take this subject, the merit, ascribed to the social virtues, appears still uniform, and arises chiefly from that regard, which the natural sentiment of benevolence engages us to pay to the interests of mankind and society. If we consider the principles of the human make, such as they appear to daily experience and observation, we must, a priori, conclude it impossible for such a creature as man to be totally indifferent to the well or ill-being of his fellow-creatures, and not readily, of himself, to pronounce, where nothing gives him any particular bias, that what promotes their happiness is good, what tends to their misery is evil, without any farther regard to consideration. Here then are the faint rudiments, at least, or outlines, of a *general* distinction between actions; and in proportion as the humanity of the person is supposed to encrease, his connexion with those who are injured or benefited, and his lively conception of their misery or happiness; his consequent censure or approbation acquires proportionable vigour. There is no necessity, that a generous action, barely mentioned in an old history or remote gazette, should communicate any strong feelings of applause and admiration. Virtue, placed at such a distance, is like a fixed star, which, though to the eye of reason it may appear as luminous as the sun in his meridian, is so infinitely removed as to affect the senses, neither with light nor heat. Bring this virtue nearer, by our acquaintance or connexion with the persons, or even by an eloquent recital of the case; our hearts are immediately caught, our sympathy enlivened, and our cool approbation converted into the warmest sentiments of friendship and regard. These seem necessary and infallible consequences of the general principles of human nature, as discovered in common life and practice.

Again; reverse these views and reasonings: Consider the matter a posteriori; and weighing the consequences, enquire if the merit of social virtue be not, in a great measure, derived from the feelings of humanity, with which it affects the spectators. It appears to be matter of fact, that the circumstance of *utility*, in all subjects, is a source of praise and approbation: That it is constantly appealed to in all moral decisions concerning the merit and demerit of actions: That it is the *sole* source of that high regard paid to justice, fidelity, honour, allegiance, and chastity: That it is inseparable from all the other social virtues, humanity, generosity, charity, affability, lenity, mercy, and moderation: And, in a word, that it is a foundation of the chief part of morals, which has a reference to mankind and our fellow-creatures.

It appears also, that, in our general approbation of characters and manners, the useful tendency of the social virtues moves us not by any regards to self-interest, but has an influence much more universal and extensive. It appears that a tendency to public good, and to the promoting of peace, harmony, and order in society, does always, by affecting the benevolent principles of our frame, engage us on the side of social virtues. And it appears, as an additional confirmation, that these principles of humanity and sympathy enter so deeply into all our sentiments, and have so powerful an influence, as may enable them to excite the strongest censure and applause. The present theory is the simple result of all these influences, each of which seems founded on uniform experience and observation.

Were it doubtful, whether there were any such principle in our nature as humanity or a concern for others, yet when we see, in numberless instances, that whatever has a tendency to promote the interests of society, is so highly approved of, we ought thence to learn the force of the benevolent principle; since it is impossible for anything to please as means to an end, where the end is totally indifferent. On the other hand, were it doubtful, whether there were, implanted in our nature, any general principle of moral blame and approbation, yet when we see, in numberless instances, the influence of humanity, we ought thence to conclude, that it is impossible, but that everything which promotes the interest of society must communicate pleasure, and what is pernicious give uneasiness. But when these different reflections and observations concur in establishing the same conclusion, must they not bestow an undisputed evidence upon it?

. . . .

Section IX
Conclusion

Part I

It may justly appear surprising that any man in so late an age, should find it requisite to prove, by elaborate reasoning, that Personal Merit consists altogether in the possession of mental qualities, *useful* or *agreeable* to the *person himself* or to *others*. It might be expected that this principle would have occurred even to the first rude, unpractised enquirers concerning morals, and been received from its own evidence, without any argument or disputation. Whatever is valuable in any kind, so naturally classes itself under the division of *useful* or *agreeable*, the *utile* or the *dulce*, that it is not easy to imagine why we should ever seek further, or consider the question as a matter of nice research or inquiry. And as every thing useful or agreeable must possess these qualities with regard either to the *person himself* or to *others*, the complete delineation or description of merit seems to be performed as naturally as a shadow is cast by the sun, or an image is reflected upon water.

. . . .

And as every quality which is useful or agreeable to ourselves or others is, in common life, allowed to be a part of personal merit; so no other will ever be received, where men judge of things by their natural, unprejudiced reason, without the delusive glosses of superstition and false religion. Celibacy, fasting, penance, mortification, self-denial, humility, silence, solitude, and the whole train of monkish virtues; for what reason are they everywhere rejected by men of sense, but because they serve to no manner of purpose; neither advance a man's fortune in the world, nor render him a more valuable member of society; neither qualify him for the entertainment of company, nor increase his power of self-enjoyment? We observe, on the contrary, that they cross all these desirable ends; stupify the understanding and harden the heart, obscure the fancy and sour the temper. We justly, therefore, transfer them to the opposite column, and place them in the catalogue of vices; nor has any superstition force sufficient among men of the world, to pervert entirely these natural sentiments. A gloomy, hair-brained enthusiast, after his death, may have a place in the calendar; but will scarcely ever be admitted, when alive, into intimacy and society, except by those who are as delirious and dismal as himself.

It seems a happiness in the present theory, that it enters not into that vulgar dispute concerning the *degrees* of benevolence or self-love, which prevail in human nature; a dispute which is never likely to have any issue, both because men, who have taken part, are not easily convinced, and because the phenomena, which can be produced on either side, are so dispersed, so uncertain, and subject to so many interpretations, that it is scarcely possible accurately to compare them, or draw from them any determinate inference or conclusion. It is sufficient for our present purpose, if it be allowed, what surely, without the greatest absurdity cannot be disputed, that there is some benevolence, however small, infused into our bosom; some spark of friendship for human kind; some particle of the dove kneaded into our frame, along with the elements of the wolf and serpent. Let these generous sentiments be supposed ever so weak; let them be insufficient to move even a hand or finger of our body, they must still direct the determinations of our mind, and where everything else is equal, produce a cool preference of what is useful and serviceable to mankind, above what is pernicious and dangerous. A *moral distinction*, therefore, immediately arises; a general sentiment of blame and approbation; a tendency, however faint, to the objects of the one, and a proportionable aversion to those of the other. Nor will those reasoners, who so earnestly maintain the predominant selfishness of human kind, be any wise scandalized at hearing of the weak sentiments of virtue implanted in our nature. On the contrary, they are found as ready to maintain the one tenet as the other; and their spirit of satire (for such it appears, rather than of corruption) naturally gives rise to both opinions; which have, indeed, a great and almost an indissoluble connexion together.

Avarice, ambition, vanity, and all passions vulgarly, though improperly, comprised under the denomination of *self-love*, are here excluded from our theory concerning the origin of morals, not because they are too weak, but because they have not a proper direction for that purpose. The notion of morals implies some sentiment common to all mankind, which recommends the same object to general approbation, and makes every man, or most men, agree in the same opinion or decision concerning it. It also implies some sentiment, so universal and comprehensive as to extend to all mankind, and render the actions and conduct, even of the persons the most remote, an object of applause or censure, according as they agree or disagree with that rule of right which is established. These two requisite circumstances belong alone to the sentiment of humanity here insisted on. The other passions produce in every breast, many strong sentiments of desire and aversion, affection and hatred; but these neither are felt so much in common, nor are so comprehensive, as to be the foundation of any general system and established theory of blame or approbation.

When a man denominates another his *enemy*, his *rival*, his *antagonist*, his *adversary*, he is understood to speak the language of self-love, and to express sentiments, peculiar to himself, and arising from his particular circumstances and situation. But when he bestows on any man the epithets of *vicious* or *odious* or *depraved*, he then speaks another language, and expresses sentiments, in which he expects all his audience are to concur with him. He must here, therefore, depart from his private and particular situation, and must choose a point of view, common to him with others; he must move some universal principle of the human frame, and touch a string to which all mankind have an accord and symphony. If he mean, therefore, to express that this man possesses qualities, whose tendency is pernicious to society, he has chosen this common point of view, and has touched the principle of humanity, in which every man, in some degree, concurs. While the human heart is compounded of the same elements as at present, it will never be wholly indifferent to public good, nor entirely unaffected with the tendency of characters and manners. And though this affection of humanity may not generally be esteemed so strong as vanity or ambition, yet, being common to all men, it can alone be the foundation of morals, or of any general system of blame or praise. One man's ambition is not another's ambition, nor will the same event or object satisfy both; but the humanity of one man is the humanity of every one, and the same object touches this passion in all human creatures.

But the sentiments, which arise from humanity, are not only the same in all human creatures, and produce the same approbation or censure; but they also comprehend all human creatures; nor is there any one whose conduct or character is not, by their means, an object to every one of censure or approbation. On the contrary, those other passions, commonly denominated selfish, both produce different sentiments in each individual, according to his particular situation; and also contemplate the greater part of mankind with the utmost indifference and unconcern. Whoever has a high regard and esteem for me flatters my vanity; whoever expresses contempt mortifies and displeases me; but as my name is known but to a small part of mankind, there are few who come within the sphere of this passion, or excite, on its account, either my affection or disgust. But if you represent a tyrannical, insolent, or barbarous behaviour, in any country or in any age of the world, I soon carry my eye to the pernicious tendency of such a conduct, and feel the sentiment of repugnance and displeasure towards it. No character can be so remote as to be, in this light, wholly indifferent to me. What is beneficial to society or to the person himself must still be preferred. And every quality or action, of every human being, must, by this means, be ranked under some class or denomination, expressive of general censure or applause.

What more, therefore, can we ask to distinguish the sentiments, dependent on humanity, from those connected with any other passion, or to satisfy us, why the former are the origin of morals, not the latter? Whatever conduct gains my approbation, by touching my humanity, procures also the applause of all mankind, by affecting the same principle in them; but what serves my avarice or ambition pleases these passions in me alone, and affects not the avarice and ambition of the rest of mankind. There is no circumstance of conduct in any man, provided it have a beneficial tendency, that is not agreeable to my humanity, however remote the person; but every man, so far removed as neither to cross nor serve my avarice and ambition, is regarded as wholly indifferent by those passions. The distinction, therefore, between these species of sentiment being so great and evident, language must soon be moulded upon it, and must invent a peculiar set of terms, in order to express those universal sentiments of censure or approbation, which arise from humanity, or from views of general usefulness and its contrary. Virtue and Vice become then known; morals are recognized; certain general ideas are framed of human conduct and behaviour; such measures are expected from men in such situations. This action is determined to be conformable to our abstract rule; that other, contrary. And by such universal principles are the particular sentiments of self-love frequently controlled and limited.

From instances of popular tumults, seditions, factions, panics, and of all passions, which are shared with a multitude, we may learn the influence of society in exciting and supporting any emotion; while the most ungovernable disorders are raised, we find, by that means, from the slightest and most frivolous occasions. Solon was no very cruel, though, perhaps, an unjust legislator, who punished neuters in civil wars; and few, I believe, would, in such cases, incur the penalty, were their affection and discourse allowed sufficient to absolve them. No selfishness, and scarce any philosophy, have there force sufficient to support a total coolness and indifference; and he must be more or less than man, who kindles not in the common blaze. What wonder then, that moral sentiments are found of such influence in life; though springing from principles, which may appear, at first sight, somewhat small and delicate? But these principles, we must remark, are social and universal; they form, in a manner, the *party* of humankind against vice or disorder, its common enemy. And as the benevolent concern for others is diffused, in a greater or less degree, over all men, and is the same in all, it occurs more frequently in discourse, is cherished by society and conversation, and the blame and approbation, consequent on it, are thereby roused from that lethargy into which they are probably lulled, in solitary and uncultivated nature. Other passions though perhaps originally stronger, yet being selfish and private, are often overpowered by its force, and yield the dominion of our breast to those social and public principles.

. . . .

Part II

Having explained the moral *approbation* attending merit or virtue, there remains nothing but briefly to consider our interested *obligation* to it, and to inquire whether every man, who has any regard to his own happiness and welfare, will not best find his account in the practice of every moral duty. If this can

be clearly ascertained from the foregoing theory, we shall have the satisfaction to reflect, that we have advanced principles, which not only, it is hoped, will stand the test of reasoning and inquiry, but may contribute to the amendment of men's lives, and their improvement in morality and social virtue. And though the philosophical truth of any proposition by no means depends on its tendency to promote the interests of society; yet a man has but a bad grace, who delivers a theory, however true, which, he must confess, leads to a practice dangerous and pernicious. Why rake into those corners of nature which spread a nuisance all around? Why dig up the pestilence from the pit in which it is buried? The ingenuity of your researches may be admired, but your systems will be detested; and mankind will agree, if they cannot refute them, to sink them, at least, in eternal silence and oblivion. Truths which are *pernicious* to society, if any such there be, will yield to errors which are salutary and *advantageous*.

But what philosophical truths can be more advantageous to society, than those here delivered, which represent virtue in all her genuine and most engaging charms, and make us approach her with ease, familiarity, and affection? The dismal dress falls off, with which many divines, and some philosophers, have covered her; and nothing appears but gentleness, humanity, beneficence, affability; nay, even at proper intervals, play, frolic, and gaiety. She talks not of useless austerities and rigours, suffering and self-denial. She declares that her sole purpose is to make her votaries and all mankind, during every instant of their existence, if possible, cheerful and happy; nor does she ever willingly part with any pleasure but in hopes of ample compensation in some other period of their lives. The sole trouble which she demands, is that of just calculation, and a steady preference of the greater happiness. And if any austere pretenders approach her, enemies to joy and pleasure, she either rejects them as hypocrites and deceivers; or, if she admit them in her train, they are ranked, however, among the least favoured of her votaries.

And, indeed, to drop all figurative expression, what hopes can we ever have of engaging mankind to a practice which we confess full of austerity and rigour? Or what theory of morals can ever serve any useful purpose, unless it can show, by a particular detail, that all the duties which it recommends, are also the true interest of each individual? The peculiar advantage of the foregoing system seems to be, that it furnishes proper mediums for that purpose.

That the virtues which are immediately *useful* or *agreeable* to the person possessed of them, are desirable in a view of self-interest, it would surely be superfluous to prove. Moralists, indeed, may spare themselves all the pains which they often take in recommending these duties. To what purpose collect arguments to evince that temperance is advantageous, and the excesses of pleasure hurtful. When it appears that these excesses are only denominated such, because they are hurtful; and that, if the unlimited use of strong liquors, for instance, no more impaired health or the faculties of mind and body than the use of air or water, it would not be a whit more vicious or blameable.

It seems equally superfluous to prove, that the *companionable* virtues of good manners and wit, decency and genteelness, are more desirable than the contrary qualities. Vanity alone, without any other consideration, is a sufficient motive to make us wish for the possession of these accomplishments. No man was ever willingly deficient in this particular. All our failures here proceed from bad education, want of capacity, or a perverse and unpliable disposition. Would you have your company coveted, admired, followed; rather than hated, despised, avoided? Can any one seriously deliberate in the case? As no enjoyment is sincere, without some reference to company and society; so no society can be agreeable, or even tolerable, where a man feels his presence unwelcome, and discovers all around him symptoms of disgust and aversion.

But why, in the greater society or confederacy of mankind, should not the case be the same as in particular clubs and companies? Why is it more doubtful, that the enlarged virtues of humanity, generosity, beneficence, are desirable with a view to happiness and self-interest, than the limited endowments of ingenuity and politeness? Are we apprehensive lest those social affections interfere, in a greater and more immediate degree than any other pursuits, with private utility, and cannot be gratified, without some important sacrifice of honour and advantage?

If so, we are but ill-instructed in the nature of the human passions, and are more influenced by verbal distinctions than by real differences.

Whatever contradiction may vulgarly be supposed between the *selfish* and *social* sentiments or dispositions, they are really no more opposite than selfish and ambitious, selfish and revengeful, selfish and vain. It is requisite that there be an original propensity of some kind, in order to be a basis to self-love, by giving a relish to the objects of its pursuit; and none more fit for this purpose than benevolence or humanity. The goods of fortune are spent in one gratification or another; the miser who accumulates his annual income, and lends it out at interest, has really spent it in the gratification of his avarice. And it would be difficult to show why a man is more a loser by a generous action, than by any other method of expense; since the utmost which he can attain by the most elaborate selfishness, is the indulgence of some affection.

Now if life, without passion, must be altogether insipid and tiresome; let a man suppose that he has full power of modelling his own disposition, and let him deliberate what appetite or desire he would choose for the foundation of his happiness and enjoyment. Every affection, he would observe, when gratified by success, gives a satisfaction proportioned to its force and violence; but besides this advantage, common to all, the immediate feeling of benevolence and friendship, humanity and kindness, is sweet, smooth, tender, and agreeable, independent of all fortune and accidents. These virtues are besides attended with a pleasing consciousness or remembrance, and keep us in humour with ourselves as well as others; while we retain the agreeable reflection of having done our part towards mankind and society. And though all men show a jealousy of our success in the pursuits of avarice and ambition; yet are we almost sure of their good-will and good wishes, so long as we persevere in the paths of virtue, and employ ourselves in the execution of generous plans and purposes. What other passion is there where we shall find so many advantages united; an agreeable sentiment, a pleasing consciousness, a good reputation? But of these truths, we may observe, men are, of themselves, pretty much convinced; nor are they deficient in their duty to society, because they would not wish to be generous, friendly, and humane; but because they do not feel themselves such.

Treating vice with the greatest candour, and making it all possible concessions, we must acknowledge that there is not, in any instance, the smallest pretext for giving it the preference above virtue, with a view to self-interest; except, perhaps, in the case of justice, where a man, taking things in a certain light, may often seem to be a loser by his integrity. And though it is allowed that, without a regard to property, no society could subsist; yet according to the imperfect way in which human affairs are conducted, a sensible knave, in particular incidents, may think that an act of iniquity or infidelity will make a considerable addition to his fortune, without causing any considerable breach in the social union and confederacy. That *honesty is the best policy*, may be a good general rule, but is liable to many exceptions; and he, it may perhaps be thought, conducts himself with most wisdom, who observes the general rule, and takes advantage of all the exceptions.

I must confess that, if a man think that this reasoning much requires an answer, it will be a little difficult to find any which will to him appear satisfactory and convincing. If his heart rebel not against such pernicious maxims, if he feel no reluctance to the thoughts of villainy or baseness, he has indeed lost a considerable motive to virtue; and we may expect that his practice will be answerable to his speculation. But in all ingenuous natures, the antipathy to treachery and roguery is too strong to be counter-balanced by any views of profit or pecuniary advantage. Inward peace of mind, consciousness of integrity, a satisfactory review of our own conduct; these are circumstances, very requisite to happiness, and will be cherished and cultivated by every honest man, who feels the importance of them.

Such a one has, besides, the frequent satisfaction of seeing knaves, with all their pretended cunning and abilities, betrayed by their own maxims; and while they purpose to cheat with moderation and secrecy, a tempting incident occurs, nature is frail, and they give into the snare; whence they can never extricate themselves, without a total loss of reputation, and the forfeiture of all future trust and confidence with mankind.

But were they ever so secret and successful, the honest man, if he has any tincture of philosophy, or even common observation and reflection, will discover that they themselves are, in the end, the greatest dupes, and have sacrificed the invaluable enjoyment of a character, with themselves at least, for the acquisition of worthless toys and gewgaws. How little is requisite to supply the *necessities* of nature? And in a view to *pleasure*, what comparison between the unbought satisfaction of conversation, society, study, even health and the common beauties of nature, but above all the peaceful reflection on one's own conduct; what comparison, I say, between these and the feverish, empty amusements of luxury and expense? These natural pleasures, indeed, are really without price; both because they are below all price in their attainment, and above it in their enjoyment.

Appendix I

Concerning Moral Sentiment

If the foregoing hypothesis be received, it will now be easy for us to determine the question first started,[6] concerning the general principles of morals; and though we postponed the decision of that question, lest it should then involve us in intricate speculations, which are unfit for moral discourses, we may resume it at present, and examine how far either *reason* or *sentiment* enters into all decisions of praise or censure.

One principal foundation of moral praise being supposed to lie in the usefulness of any quality or action, it is evident that *reason* must enter for a considerable share in all decisions of this kind; since nothing but that faculty can instruct us in the tendency of qualities and actions, and point out their beneficial consequences to society and to their possessor. In many cases this is an affair liable to great controversy; doubts may arise; opposite interests may occur; and a preference must be given to one side, from very nice views, and a small overbalance of utility. This is particularly remarkable in questions with regard to justice; as is, indeed, natural to suppose, from that species of utility which attends this virtue. Were every single instance of justice, like that of benevolence, useful to society;

this would be a more simple state of the case, and seldom liable to great controversy. But as single instances of justice are often pernicious in their first and immediate tendency, and as the advantage to society results only from the observance of the general rule, and from the concurrence and combination of several persons in the same equitable conduct; the case here becomes more intricate and involved. The various circumstances of society; the various consequences of any practice; the various interests which may be proposed; these, on many occasions, are doubtful, and subject to great discussion and inquiry. The object of municipal laws is to fix all the questions with regard to justice; the debates of civilians; the reflections of politicians; the precedents of history and public records, are all directed to the same purpose. And a very accurate *reason* or *judgement* is often requisite, to give the true determination, amidst such intricate doubts arising from obscure or opposite utilities.

But though reason, when fully assisted and improved, be sufficient to instruct us in the pernicious or useful tendency of qualities and actions; it is not alone sufficient to produce any moral blame or approbation. Utility is only a tendency to a certain end; and were the end totally indifferent to us, we should feel the same indifference towards the means. It is requisite a *sentiment* should here display itself, in order to give a preference to the useful above the pernicious tendencies. This sentiment can be no other than a feeling for the happiness of mankind, and a resentment of their misery; since these are the different ends which virtue and vice have a tendency to promote. Here therefore *reason* instructs us in the several tendencies of actions, and *humanity* makes a distinction in favour of those which are useful and beneficial.

This partition between the faculties of understanding and sentiment, in all moral decisions, seems clear from the preceding hypothesis. But I shall suppose that hypothesis false; it will then be requisite to look out for some other theory that may be satisfactory; and I dare venture to affirm that none such will ever be found, so long as we suppose reason to be the sole source of morals. To prove this, it will be proper to weigh the . . . following considerations.

I. It is easy for a false hypothesis to maintain some appearance of truth, while it keeps wholly in generals, makes use of undefined terms, and employs comparisons, instead of instances. This is particularly remarkable in that philosophy, which ascribes the discernment of all moral distinctions to reason alone, without the concurrence of sentiment. It is impossible that, in any particular instance, this hypothesis can so much as be rendered intelligible, whatever specious figure it may make in general declamations and discourses. Examine the crime of *ingratitude*, for instance; which has place, wherever we observe good-will, expressed and known, together with good-offices performed, on the one side, and a return of ill-will or indifference, with ill-offices or neglect on the other; anatomize all these circumstances, and examine, by your reason alone, in what consists the demerit or blame. You never will come to any issue or conclusion.

Reason judges either of *matter of fact* or of *relations*. Enquire then, *first*, where is that matter of fact which we here call *crime*; point it out; determine the time of its existence; describe its essence of nature; explain the sense or faculty to which it discovers itself. It resides in the mind of the person who is ungrateful. He must, therefore, feel it, and be conscious of it. But nothing is there, except the passion of ill-will or absolute indifference. You cannot say that these, of themselves, always, and in all circumstances, are crimes. No, they are only crimes when directed towards persons who have before expressed and displayed good-will towards us. Consequently, we may infer, that the crime of ingratitude is not any particular individual *fact*; but arises from a complication of circumstances, which, being presented to the spectator, excites the *sentiment* of blame, by the particular structure and fabric of his mind.

This representation, you say, is false. Crime, indeed, consists not in a particular *fact*, of whose reality we are assured by *reason*; but it consists in certain *moral relations*, discovered by reason, in the same manner as we discover by reason the truths of geometry or algebra. But what are the relations, I ask, of which you here talk? In the case stated above, I see first good-will and good-offices in one person; then ill-will and ill-offices in the other. Between these, there is a relation of *contrariety*. Does the crime consist in that relation? But suppose a person bore me ill-will or did me ill-offices; and I, in return, were indifferent towards him, or did him good-offices. Here is the same relation of *contrariety*; and yet my conduct is often highly laudable. Twist and turn this matter as much as you will, you can never rest the morality on relation; but must have recourse to the decisions of sentiment.

When it is affirmed that two and three are equal to the half of ten, this relation of equality I understand perfectly. I conceive, that if ten be divided into two parts, of which one has as many units as the other; and if any of these parts be compared to two added to three, it will contain as many units as that compound number. But when you draw thence a comparison to moral relations, I own that I am altogether at a loss to understand you. A moral action, a crime, such as ingratitude, is a complicated object. Does the morality consist in the relation of its parts to each other? How? After what manner? Specify the relation: be more particular and explicit in your propositions, and you will easily see their falsehood.

No, say you, the morality consists in the relation of actions to the rule of right; and they are denominated good or ill, according as they agree or disagree with it. What then is this rule of right? In what does it consist? How is it determined? By reason, you say, which examines the moral relations of actions. So that moral relations are determined by the comparison of action to a rule. And that rule is determined by considering the moral relations of objects. Is not this fine reasoning?

All this is metaphysics, you cry. That is enough; there needs nothing more to give a strong presumption of falsehood. Yes, reply I, here are metaphysics surely; but they are all on your side, who advance an abstruse hypothesis, which can never be made intelligible, nor quadrate with any particular instance of illustration. The hypothesis which we embrace is plain. It maintains that morality is determined by sentiment. It defines virtue to be *whatever mental action or quality gives to a spectator the pleasing sentiment of approbation*; and vice the contrary. We then proceed to examine a plain matter of fact, to wit, what actions have this influence. We consider all the circumstances in which these actions agree, and thence endeavour to extract some general observations with regard to these sentiments. If you call this metaphysics, and find anything abstruse here, you

need only conclude that your turn of mind is not suited to the moral sciences.

II. When a man, at any time, deliberates concerning his own conduct (as, whether he had better, in a particular emergence, assist a brother or a benefactor), he must consider these separate relations, with all the circumstances and situations of the persons, in order to determine the superior duty and obligation; and in order to determine the proportion of lines in any triangle, it is necessary to examine the nature of that figure, and the relations which its several parts bear to each other. But notwithstanding this appearing similarity in the two cases, there is, at bottom, an extreme difference between them. A speculative reasoner concerning triangles or circles considers the several known and given relations of the parts of these figures, and thence infers some unknown relation, which is dependent on the former. But in moral deliberations we must be acquainted beforehand with all the objects, and all their relations to each other; and from a comparison of the whole, fix our choice or approbation. No new fact to be ascertained; no new relation to be discovered. All the circumstances of the case are supposed to be laid before us, ere we can fix any sentence of blame or approbation. If any material circumstance be yet unknown or doubtful, we must first employ our inquiry or intellectual faculties to assure us of it; and must suspend for a time all moral decision or sentiment. While we are ignorant whether a man were aggressor or not, how can we determine whether the person who killed him be criminal or innocent? But after every circumstance, every relation is known, the understanding has no further room to operate, nor any object on which it could employ itself. The approbation or blame which then ensues, cannot be the work of the judgement, but of the heart; and is not a speculative proposition or affirmation, but an active feeling or sentiment. In the disquisitions of the understanding, from known circumstances and relations, we infer some new and unknown. In moral decisions, all the circumstances and relations must be previously known; and the mind, from the contemplation of the whole, feels some new impression of affection or disgust, esteem or contempt, approbation or blame.

Hence the great difference between a mistake of *fact* and one of *right*; and hence the reason why the one is commonly criminal and not the other. When Oedipus killed Laius, he was ignorant of the relation, and from circumstances, innocent and involuntary, formed erroneous opinions concerning the action which he committed. But when Nero killed Agrippina, all the relations between himself and the person, and all the circumstances of the fact, were previously known to him; but the motive of revenge, or fear, or interest, prevailed in his savage heart over the sentiments of duty and humanity. And when we express that detestation against him to which he himself, in a little time, became insensible, it is not that we see any relations, of which he was ignorant; but that, from the rectitude of our disposition, we feel sentiments against which he was hardened from flattery and a long perseverance in the most enormous crimes. In these sentiments then, not in a discovery of relations of any kind, do all moral determinations consist. Before we can pretend to form any decision of this kind, everything must be known and ascertained on the side of the object or action. Nothing remains but to feel, on our part, some sentiment of blame or approbation; whence we pronounce the action criminal or virtuous.

. . . .

V. It appears evident that the ultimate ends of human actions can never, in any case, be accounted for by *reason*, but recommend themselves entirely to the sentiments and affections of mankind, without any dependence on the intellectual faculties. Ask a man *why he uses exercise*; he will answer, *because he desires to keep his health*. If you then enquire, *why he desires health*, he will readily reply, *because sickness is painful*. If you push your enquiries farther, and desire a reason *why he hates pain*, it is impossible he can ever give any. This is an ultimate end, and is never referred to any other object.

Perhaps to your second question, *why he desires health*, he may also reply, that *it is necessary for the exercise of his calling*. If you ask, *why he is anxious on that head*, he will answer, *because he desires to get money*. If you demand *Why? It is the instrument of pleasure*, says he. And beyond this it is an absurdity to ask for a reason. It is impossible there can be a progress *in infinitum*; and that one thing can always be a reason why another is desired. Something must be desirable on its own account, and because of its

immediate accord or agreement with human sentiment and affection.

Now as virtue is an end, and is desirable on its own account, without fee or reward, merely for the immediate satisfaction which it conveys; it is requisite that there should be some sentiment which it touches, some internal taste or feeling, or whatever you please to call it, which distinguishes moral good and evil, and which embraces the one and rejects the other.

Thus the distinct boundaries and offices of *reason* and of *taste* are easily ascertained. The former conveys the knowledge of truth and falsehood: the latter gives the sentiment of beauty and deformity, vice and virtue. The one discovers objects as they really stand in nature, without addition or diminution: the other has a productive faculty, and gilding or staining all natural objects with the colours, borrowed from internal sentiment, raises in a manner a new creation. Reason being cool and disengaged, is no motive to action, and directs only the impulse received from appetite or inclination, by showing us the means of attaining happiness or avoiding misery: Taste, as it gives pleasure or pain, and thereby constitutes happiness or misery, becomes a motive to action, and is the first spring or impulse to desire and volition. From circumstances and relations, known or supposed, the former leads us to the discovery of the concealed and unknown: after all circumstances and relations are laid before us, the latter makes us feel from the whole a new sentiment of blame or approbation. The standard of the one, being founded on the nature of things, is eternal and inflexible, even by the will of the Supreme Being: the standard of the other, arising from the internal frame and constitution of animals, is ultimately derived from that Supreme Will, which bestowed on each being its peculiar nature, and arranged the several classes and orders of existence.

Appendix II

Of Self-love

There is a principle, supposed to prevail among many, which is utterly incompatible with all virtue or moral sentiment; and as it can proceed from nothing but the most depraved disposition, so in its turn it tends still further to encourage that depravity. This principle is, that all *benevolence* is mere hypocrisy, friendship a cheat, public spirit a farce, fidelity a snare to procure trust and confidence; and that while all of us, at bottom, pursue only our private interest, we wear these fair disguises, in order to put others off their guard, and expose them the more to our wiles and machinations. What heart one must be possessed of who professes such principles, and who feels no internal sentiment that belies so pernicious a theory, it is easy to imagine: and also what degree of affection and benevolence he can bear to a species whom he represents under such odious colours, and supposes so little susceptible of gratitude or any return of affection. Or if we should not ascribe these principles wholly to a corrupted heart, we must at least account for them from the most careless and precipitate examination. Superficial reasoners, indeed, observing many false pretences among mankind, and feeling, perhaps, no very strong restraint in their own disposition, might draw a general and a hasty conclusion that all is equally corrupted, and that men, different from all other animals, and indeed from all other species of existence, admit of no degrees of good or bad, but are, in every instance, the same creatures under different disguises and appearances.

There is another principle, somewhat resembling the former; which has been much insisted on by philosophers, and has been the foundation of many a system; that, whatever affection one may feel, or imagine he feels for others, no passion is, or can be disinterested; that the most generous friendship, however sincere, is a modification of self-love; and that, even unknown to ourselves, we seek only our own gratification, while we appear the most deeply engaged in schemes for the liberty and happiness of mankind. By a turn of imagination, by a refinement of reflection, by an enthusiasm of passion, we seem to take part in the interests of others, and imagine ourselves divested of all selfish considerations: but, at bottom, the most generous patriot and most niggardly miser, the bravest hero and most abject coward, have, in every action, an equal regard to their own happiness and welfare.

Whoever concludes from the seeming tendency of this opinion, that those, who make profession of it, cannot possibly feel the true sentiments of benevolence, or have any regard for genuine virtue, will often find himself, in practice, very much mistaken. Probity and honour were no strangers to Epicurus and his sect. Atticus and Horace seem to have enjoyed from nature, and cultivated by reflection, as generous and friendly dispositions as any disciple of the austerer schools. And among the modern, Hobbes and Locke, who maintained the selfish system of morals, lived irreproachable lives; though the former lay not under any restraint of religion which might supply the defects of his philosophy.

An Epicurean or a Hobbist readily allows, that there is such a thing as friendship in the world, without hypocrisy or disguise; though he may attempt, by a philosophical chymistry, to resolve the elements of this passion, if I may so speak, into those of another, and explain every affection to be self-love, twisted and moulded, by a particular turn of imagination, into a variety of appearances. But as the same turn of imagination prevails not in every man, nor gives the same direction to the original passion; this is sufficient even according to the selfish system to make the widest difference in human characters, and denominate one man virtuous and humane, another vicious and meanly interested. I esteem the man whose self-love, by whatever means, is so directed as to give him a concern for others, and render him serviceable to society: as I hate or despise him, who has no regard to any thing beyond his own gratifications and enjoyments. In vain would you suggest that these characters, though seemingly opposite, are at bottom the same, and that a very inconsiderable turn of thought forms the whole difference between them. Each character, notwithstanding these inconsiderable differences, appears to me, in practice, pretty durable and untransmutable. And I find not in this more than in other subjects, that the natural sentiments arising from the general appearances of things are easily destroyed by subtile reflections concerning the minute origin of these appearances. Does not the lively, cheerful colour of a countenance inspire me with complacency and pleasure; even though I learn from philosophy that all difference of complexion arises from the most minute differences of thickness, in the most minute parts of the skin; by means of which a superficies is qualified to reflect one of the original colours of light, and absorb the others?

But though the question concerning the universal or partial selfishness of man be not so material as is usually imagined to morality and practice, it is certainly of consequence in the speculative science of human nature, and is a proper object of curiosity and enquiry. It may not, therefore, be unsuitable, in this place, to bestow a few reflections upon it.[7]

The most obvious objection to the selfish hypothesis is, that, as it is contrary to common feeling and our most unprejudiced notions, there is required the highest stretch of philosophy to establish so extraordinary a paradox. To the most careless observer there appear to be such dispositions as benevolence and generosity; such affections as love, friendship, compassion, gratitude. These sentiments have their causes, effects, objects, and operations, marked by common language and observation, and plainly distinguished from those of the selfish passions. And as this is the obvious appearance of things, it must be admitted, till some hypothesis be discovered, which by penetrating deeper into human nature, may prove the former affections to be nothing but modifications of the latter. All attempts of this kind have hitherto proved fruitless, and seem to have proceeded entirely from that love of *simplicity* which has been the source of much false reasoning in philosophy. I shall not here enter into any detail on the present subject. Many able philosophers have shown the insufficiency of these systems. And I shall take for granted what, I believe, the smallest reflection will make evident to every impartial enquirer.

. . . .

. . . Tenderness to their offspring, in all sensible beings, is commonly able alone to counter-balance the strongest motives of self-love, and has no manner of dependance on that affection. What interest can a fond mother have in view, who loses her health by assiduous attendance on her sick child, and afterwards languishes and dies of grief, when freed, by its death, from the slavery of that attendance?

Is gratitude no affection of the human breast, or is that a word merely, without any meaning or reality? Have we no satisfaction in one man's company above another's, and no desire of the welfare of our friend, even though absence or death should prevent us from all participation in it? Or what is it commonly, that gives us any participation in it, even while alive and present, but our affection and regard to him?

These and a thousand other instances are marks of a general benevolence in human nature, where no *real* interest binds us to the object. And how an *imaginary* interest known and avowed for such, can be the origin of any passion or emotion, seems difficult to explain. No satisfactory hypothesis of this kind has yet been discovered; nor is there the smallest probability that the future industry of men will ever be attended with more favourable success.

But farther, if we consider rightly of the matter, we shall find that the hypothesis which allows of a disinterested benevolence, distinct from self-love, has really more *simplicity* in it, and is more conformable to the analogy of nature than that which pretends to resolve all friendship and humanity into this latter principle. There are bodily wants or appetites acknowledged by every one, which necessarily precede all sensual enjoyment, and carry us directly to seek possession of the object. Thus, hunger and thirst have eating and drinking for their end; and from the gratification of these primary appetites arises a pleasure, which may become the object of another species of desire or inclination that is secondary and interested. In the same manner there are mental passions by which we are impelled immediately to seek particular objects, such as fame or power, or vengeance without any regard to interest; and when these objects are attained a pleasing enjoyment ensues, as the consequence of our indulged affections. Nature must, by the internal frame and constitution of the mind, give an original propensity to fame, ere we can reap any pleasure from that acquisition, or pursue it from motives of self-love, and a desire of happiness. If I have no vanity, I take no delight in praise: if I be void of ambition, power gives me no enjoyment: if I be not angry, the punishment of an adversary is totally indifferent to me. In all these cases there is a passion which points immediately to the object, and constitutes it our good or happiness; as there are other secondary passions which afterwards arise and pursue it as a part of our happiness, when once it is constituted such by our original affections. Were there no appetite of any kind antecedent to self-love, that propensity could scarcely ever exert itself; because we should, in that case, have felt few and slender pains or pleasures, and have little misery or happiness to avoid or to pursue.

Now where is the difficulty in conceiving, that this may likewise be the case with benevolence and friendship, and that, from the original frame of our temper, we may feel a desire of another's happiness or good, which, by means of that affection, becomes our own good, and is afterwards pursued, from the combined motives of benevolence and self-enjoyment? Who sees not that vengeance, from the force alone of passion, may be so eagerly pursued, as to make us knowingly neglect every consideration of ease, interest, or safety; and, like some vindictive animals, infuse our very souls into the wounds we give an enemy; and what a malignant philosophy must it be, that will not allow to humanity and friendship the same privileges which are undisputably granted to the darker passions of enmity and resentment? Such a philosophy is more like a satyr than a true delineation or description of human nature; and may be a good foundation for paradoxical wit and raillery, but is a very bad one for any serious argument or reasoning.

NOTES

1. See Appendix I.
2. Sect. III and IV.
3. Sect. V.
4. It is needless to push our researches so far as to ask, why we have humanity or a fellow-feeling with others. It is sufficient, that this is experienced to be a principle in human nature. We must stop somewhere in our examination of causes; and there are, in every science, some general principles, beyond which we cannot hope to find any principle more general. No man is absolutely indifferent to the happiness and misery of others. The first has a natural tendency to give pleasure; the second, pain. This every one may find in himself. It is not probable, that these principles can be resolved into principles more simple and universal, whatever attempts may have been made to that purpose. But if it were possible, it belongs not to the present subject; and we may here safely consider these principles as original: happy, if we can render all the consequences sufficiently plain and perspicious!
5. For a like reason, the tendencies of actions and characters, not their real accidental consequences,

are alone regarded in our moral determinations or general judgements; though in our real feeling or sentiment, we cannot help paying greater regard to one whose station, joined to virtue, renders him really useful to society, than to one, who exerts the social virtues only in good intentions and benevolent affections. Separating the character from the fortune, by an easy and necessary effort of thought, we pronounce these persons alike, and give them the same general praise. The judgement corrects or endeavours to correct the appearance: But is not able entirely to prevail over sentiment.

Why is this peach-tree said to be better than that other; but because it produces more or better fruit? And would not the same praise be given it, though snails or vermin had destroyed the peaches, before they came to full maturity? In morals too, is not *the tree known by the fruit?* And cannot we easily distinguish between nature and accident, in the one case as well as in the other?
6. Sect. I.
7. Benevolence naturally divides into two kinds, the *general* and the *particular.* The first is, where we have no friendship or connexion or esteem for the person, but feel only a general sympathy with him or a compassion for his pains, and a congratulation with his pleasures. The other species of benevolence is founded on an opinion of virtue, on services done us, or on some particular connexions. Both these sentiments must be allowed real in human nature: but whether they will resolve into some nice considerations of self-love, is a question more curious than important. The former sentiment, to wit, that of general benevolence, or humanity, or sympathy, we shall have occasion frequently to treat of in the course of this enquiry; and I assume it as real, from general experience, without any other proof.

STUDY QUESTIONS

1. What does Hume mean when he says, "Truth is disputable; not taste"?
2. By what method does Hume propose to "discover the true origin of morals"? Does this seem like a promising method? .
3. What thought-experiments does Hume use to argue that "the rules of equity or justice depend entirely on the particular state and condition in which men are placed, and owe their origin and existence to that

utility, which results to the public from their strict and regular observance"? Do his thought-experiments really support this conclusion? Why or why not?

4. Why does Hume think that "we must renounce the theory, which accounts for every moral sentiment by the principle of self-love"? What is his argument for this claim?

5. Why does Hume think that reason alone is not enough to produce any moral blame or approbation? What else is needed, and why is it needed?

Morality and Advantage

DAVID GAUTHIER

David Gauthier (1932–) is a Professor of Philosophy at the University of Pittsburgh. His publications include *The Logic of Leviathan* and *Morals by Agreement*.

. .

I

Hume asks, rhetorically, "what theory of morals can ever serve any useful purpose, unless it can show, by a particular detail, that all the duties which it recommends, are also the true interest of each individual?"[1] But there are many to whom this question does not seem rhetorical. Why, they ask, do we speak the language of morality, impressing upon our fellows their duties and obligations, urging them with appeals to what is right and good, if we could speak to the same effect in the language of prudence, appealing to considerations of interest and advantage? When the poet, Ogden Nash, is moved by the muse to cry out:

O Duty,
Why hast thou not the visage of a sweetie or a cutie?[2]

we do not anticipate the reply:

O Poet,
I really am a cutie and I think you ought to know it.

The belief that duty cannot be reduced to interest, or that morality may require the agent to subordinate

all considerations of advantage, is one which has withstood the assaults of contrary-minded philosophers from Plato to the present. Indeed, were it not for the conviction that only interest and advantage can motivate human actions, it would be difficult to understand philosophers contending so vigorously for the identity, or at least compatibility, of morality with prudence.

Yet if morality is not true prudence it would be wrong to suppose that those philosophers who have sought some connection between morality and advantage have been merely misguided. For it is a truism that we should all expect to be worse off if men were to substitute prudence, even of the most enlightened kind, for morality in all of their deliberations. And this truism demands not only some connection between morality and advantage, but a seemingly paradoxical connection. For if we should all expect to suffer, were men to be prudent instead of moral, then morality must contribute to advantage in a unique way, a way in which prudence— following reasons of advantage—cannot.

Thomas Hobbes is perhaps the first philosopher who tried to develop this seemingly paradoxical connection between morality and advantage. But since he could not admit that a man might ever reasonably subordinate considerations of advantage to the dictates of obligation, he was led to deny the

From *The Philosophical Review*, 76. Copyright © 1967 by *The Philosophical Review*. Reprinted by permission of the publisher.

possibility of real conflict between morality and prudence. So his argument fails to clarify the distinction between the view that claims of obligation reduce to considerations of interest and the view that claims of obligation promote advantage in a way in which considerations of interest cannot.

More recently, Kurt Baier has argued that "being moral is following rules designed to overrule self-interest whenever it is in the interest of everyone alike that everyone should set aside his interest."[3] Since prudence is following rules of (enlightened) self-interest, Baier is arguing that morality is designed to overrule prudence when it is to everyone's advantage that it do so—or, in other words, that morality contributes to advantage in a way in which prudence cannot.[4]

Baier does not actually demonstrate that morality contributes to advantage in this unique and seemingly paradoxical way. Indeed, he does not ask how it is possible that morality should do this. It is this possibility which I propose to demonstrate.

II

Let us examine the following proposition, which will be referred to as "the thesis": *Morality is a system of principles such that it is advantageous for everyone if everyone accepts and acts on it, yet acting on the system of principles requires that some persons perform disadvantageous acts.*[5]

What I wish to show is that this thesis *could be true*, that morality could possess those characteristics attributed to it by the thesis. I shall not try to show that the thesis is true—indeed, I shall argue in Section V that it presents at best an inadequate conception of morality. But it is plausible to suppose that a modified form of the thesis states a necessary, although not a sufficient, condition for a moral system.

Two phrases in the thesis require elucidation. The first is "advantageous for everyone." I use this phrase to mean that *each* person will do better if the system is accepted and acted on than if *either* no system is accepted and acted on *or* a system is accepted and acted on which is similar, save that it never requires any person to perform disadvantageous acts.

Clearly, then, the claim that it is advantageous for everyone to accept and act on the system is a very strong one; it may be so strong that no system of principles which might be generally adopted could meet it. But I shall consider in Section V one among the possible ways of weakening the claim.

The second phrase requiring elucidation is "disadvantageous acts." I use this phrase to refer to acts which, in the context of their performance, would be less advantageous to the performer than some other act open to him in the same context. The phrase does not refer to acts which merely impose on the performer some short-term disadvantage that is recouped or outweighed in the long run. Rather it refers to acts which impose a disadvantage that is never recouped. It follows that the performer may say to himself, when confronted with the requirement to perform such an act, that it would be better *for him* not to perform it.

It is essential to note that the thesis, as elucidated, does not maintain that morality is advantageous for everyone in the sense that each person will do *best* if the system of principles is accepted and acted on. Each person will do better than if no system is adopted, or than if the one particular alternative mentioned above is adopted, but not than if any alternative is adopted.

Indeed, for each person required by the system to perform some disadvantageous act, it is easy to specify a better alternative—namely, the system modified so that it does not require *him* to perform any act disadvantageous to himself. Of course, there is no reason to expect such an alternative to be better than the moral system for everyone, or in fact for anyone other than the person granted the special exemption.

A second point to note is that each person must gain more from the disadvantageous acts performed by others than he loses from the disadvantageous acts performed by himself. If this were not the case, then some person would do better if a system were adopted exactly like the moral system save that it never requires *any* person to perform disadvantageous acts. This is ruled out by the force of "advantageous for everyone."

This point may be clarified by an example. Suppose that the system contains exactly one principle. Everyone is always to tell the truth. It follows from the thesis that each person gains more from those occasions on which others tell the truth, even though it is disadvantageous to them to do so, than he loses from those occasions on which he tells the truth even though it is disadvantageous to him to do so.

Now this is not to say that each person gains by telling others the truth in order to ensure that in return they tell him the truth. Such gains would merely be the result of accepting certain short-term disadvantages (those associated with truth-telling) in order to reap long-term benefits (those associated with being told the truth). Rather, what is required by the thesis is that those disadvantages which a person incurs in telling the truth, when he can expect neither short-term nor long-term benefits to accrue to him from truth-telling, are outweighed by those advantages he receives when others tell him the truth when they can expect no benefits to accrue to them from truth-telling.

The principle enjoins truth-telling in those cases in which whether one tells the truth or not will have no effect on whether others tell the truth. Such cases include those in which others have no way of knowing whether or not they are being told the truth. The thesis requires that the disadvantages one incurs in telling the truth in these cases are less than the advantages one receives in being told the truth by others in parallel cases; and the thesis requires that this holds for everyone.

Thus we see that although the disadvantages imposed by the system on any person are less than the advantages secured him through the imposition of disadvantages on others, yet the disadvantages are real in that incurring them is *unrelated* to receiving the advantages. The argument of long-term prudence, that I ought to incur some immediate disadvantage *so that* I shall receive compensating advantages later on, is entirely inapplicable here.

III

It will be useful to examine in some detail an example of a system which possesses those characteristics ascribed by the thesis to morality. This example, abstracted from the field of international relations, will enable us more clearly to distinguish, first, conduct based on immediate interest; second, conduct which is truly prudent; and third, conduct which promotes mutual advantage but is not prudent.

A and B are two nations with substantially opposed interests, who find themselves engaged in an arms race against each other. Both possess the latest in weaponry, so that each recognizes that the actual outbreak of full-scale war between them would be mutually disastrous. This recognition leads A and B to agree that each would be better off if they were mutually disarming instead of mutually arming. For mutual disarmament would preserve the balance of power between them while reducing the risk of war.

Hence A and B enter into a disarmament pact. The pact is advantageous for both if both accept and act on it, although clearly it is not advantageous for either to act on it if the other does not.

Let A be considering whether or not to adhere to the pact in some particular situation, whether or not actually to perform some act of disarmament. A will quite likely consider the act to have disadvantageous consequences. A expects to benefit, not by its own acts of disarmament, but by B's acts. Hence if A were to reason simply in terms of immediate interest, A might well decide to violate the pact.

But A's decision need be neither prudent nor reasonable. For suppose first that B is able to determine whether or not A adheres to the pact. If A violates, then B will detect the violation and will then consider what to do in the light of A's behavior. It is not to B's advantage to disarm alone; B expects to gain, not by its own acts of disarmament, but by A's acts. Hence A's violation, if known to B, leads naturally to B's counter-violation. If this continues, the effect of the pact is entirely undone, and A and B return to their mutually disadvantageous arms race. A, foreseeing this when considering whether or not to adhere to the pact in the given situation, must therefore conclude that the truly prudent course of action is to adhere.

Now suppose that B is unable to determine whether or not A adheres to the pact in the particular situation under consideration. If A judges adherence to be in itself disadvantageous, then it will decide, both on the basis of immediate interest and on the basis of prudence, to violate the pact. Since A's decision is unknown to B, it cannot affect whether or not B adheres to the pact, and so the advantage gained by A's violation is not outweighed by any consequent loss.

Therefore if A and B are prudent they will adhere to their disarmament pact whenever violation would be detectable by the other, and violate the pact whenever violation would not be detectable by the other. In other words, they will adhere openly and violate secretly. The disarmament pact between A and B thus possesses two of the characteristics ascribed by the thesis to morality. First, accepting the pact and acting on it is more advantageous for each than making no pact at all. Second, in so far as the pact stipulates that each must disarm even when disarming is undetectable by the other, it requires each to perform disadvantageous acts—acts which run counter to considerations of prudence.

One further condition must be met if the disarmament pact is to possess those characteristics ascribed by the thesis to a system of morality. It must be the case that the requirement that each party perform disadvantageous acts be essential to the advantage conferred by the pact; or, to put the matter in the way in which we expressed it earlier, both A and B must do better to adhere to this pact than to a pact which is similar save that it requires no disadvantageous acts. In terms of the example, A and B must do better to adhere to the pact than to a pact which stipulates that each must disarm only when disarming is detectable by the other.

We may plausibly suppose this condition to be met. Although A will gain by secretly retaining arms itself, it will lose by B's similar acts, and its losses may well outweigh its gains. B may equally lose more by A's secret violations than it gains by its own. So, despite the fact that prudence requires each to violate secretly, each may well do better if both adhere secretly than if both violate secretly. Supposing this to be the case, the disarmament pact is formally analogous to a moral system, as characterized by the thesis. That is, acceptance of and adherence to the pact by A and B is more advantageous for each, either than making no pact at all or than acceptance of and adherence to a pact requiring only open disarmament, and the pact requires each to perform acts of secret disarmament which are disadvantageous.

Some elementary notion, adapted for our purposes from the mathematical theory of games, may make the example even more perspicuous. Given a disarmament pact between A and B, each may pursue two pure strategies—adherence and violation. There are, then, four possible combinations of strategies, each determining a particular outcome. These outcomes can be ranked preferentially for each nation; we shall let the numerals 1 to 4 represent the ranking from first to fourth preference. Thus we construct a simple matrix,[6] in which A's preferences are stated first:

		B	
		adheres	*violates*
	adheres	2, 2	4, 1
A			
	violates	1, 4	3, 3

The matrix does not itself show that agreement is advantageous to both, for it gives only the rankings of outcomes given the agreement. But it is plausible to assume that A and B would rank mutual violation on a par with no agreement. If we assume this, we can then indicate the value to each of making and adhering to the pact by reference to the matrix.

The matrix shows immediately that adherence to the pact is not the most advantageous possibility for either, since each prefers the outcome, if it alone violates, to the outcome of mutual adherence. It shows also that each gains less from its own violations than it loses from the other's, since each ranks mutual adherence above mutual violation.

Let us now use the matrix to show that, as we argued previously, public adherence to the pact is prudent and mutually advantageous, whereas private adherence is not prudent although mutually advantageous. Consider first the case where adherence—and so violation—are open and public.

If adherence and violation are open, then each knows the strategy chosen by the other, and can adjust its own strategy in the light of this knowledge—or, in other words, the strategies are interdependent. Suppose that each initially chooses the strategy of adherence. A notices that if it switches to violation it gains—moving from 2 to 1 in terms of preference ranking. Hence immediate interest dictates such a switch. But it notices further that if it switches, then B can also be expected to switch—moving from 4 to 3 on its preference scale. The eventual outcome would be stable, in that neither could benefit from switching from violation back to adherence. But the eventual outcome would represent not a gain for A but a loss—moving from 2 to 3 on its preference scale. Hence prudence dictates no change from the strategy of adherence. This adherence is mutually advantageous; A and B are in precisely similar positions in terms of their pact.

Consider now the case when adherence and violation are secret and private. Neither nation knows the strategy chosen by the other, so the two strategies are independent. Suppose A is trying to decide which strategy to follow. It does not know B's choice. But it notices that if B adheres, then it pays A to violate, attaining 1 rather than 2 in terms of preference ranking. If B violates, then again it pays A to violate, attaining 3 rather than 4 on its preference scale. Hence, no matter which strategy B chooses, A will do better to violate, and so prudence dictates violation.

B of course reasons in just the same way. Hence each is moved by considerations of prudence to violate the pact, and the outcome assigns each rank 3 on its preference scale. This outcome is mutually disadvantageous to A and B, since mutual adherence would assign each rank 2 on its preference scale.

If A and B are both capable only of rational prudence, they find themselves at an impasse. The advantage of mutual adherence to the agreement when violations would be secret is not available to them, since neither can find it in his own overall interest not to violate secretly. Hence, strictly prudent nations cannot reap the maximum advantage possible from a pact of the type under examination.

Of course, what A and B will no doubt endeavor to do is eliminate the possibility of secret violations of their pact. Indeed, barring additional complications, each must find it to his advantage to make it possible for the other to detect his own violations. In other words, each must find it advantageous to ensure that their choice of strategies is interdependent, so that the pact will always be prudent for each to keep. But it may not be possible for them to ensure this, and to the extent that they cannot, prudence will prevent them from maximizing mutual advantage.

IV

We may now return to the connection of morality with advantage. Morality, if it is a system of principles of the type characterized in the thesis, requires that some persons perform acts genuinely disadvantageous to themselves, as a means to greater mutual advantage. Our example shows sufficiently that such a system is possible, and indicates more precisely its character. In particular, by an argument strictly parallel to that which we have pursued, we may show that men who are merely prudent will not perform the required disadvantageous acts. But in so violating the principles of morality, they will disadvantage themselves. Each will lose more by the violations of others than he will gain by his own violations.

Now this conclusion would be unsurprising if it were only that no man can gain if he alone is moral rather than prudent. Obviously such a man loses, for he adheres to moral principles to his own disadvantage, while others violate them also to his disadvantage. The benefit of the moral system is not one which any individual can secure for himself, since each man gains from the sacrifices of others.

What is surprising in our conclusion is that no man can ever gain if he is moral. Not only does he not gain by being moral if others are prudent, but he also does not gain by being moral if others are moral. For although he now receives the advantage of others' adherence to moral principles, he reaps the disadvantage of his own adherence. As long as his own adherence to morality is independent of what others do (and this is required to distinguish morality from prudence), he must do better to be prudent.

If all men are moral, all will do better than if all are prudent. But any one man will always do better if he is prudent than if he is moral. There is no real paradox in supposing that morality is advantageous, even though it requires the performance of disadvantageous acts.

On the supposition that morality has the characteristics ascribed to it by the thesis, is it possible to answer the question "Why should we be moral?" where "we" is taken distributively, so that the question is a compendious way of asking, for each person, "Why should I be moral?" More simply, is it possible to answer the question "Why should I be moral?"

I take it that this question, if asked seriously, demands a reason for being moral other than moral reasons themselves. It demands that moral reasons be shown to be reasons for acting by a non-circular argument. Those who would answer it, like Baier, endeavor to do so by the introduction of considerations of advantage.

Two such considerations have emerged from our discussion. The first is that if all are moral, all will do better than if all are prudent. This will serve to answer the question "Why should we be moral?" if this question is interpreted rather as "Why should we all be moral—rather than all being something else?" If we must all be the same, then each person has a reason—a prudential reason—to prefer that we all be moral.

But, so interpreted, "Why should we be moral?" is not a compendious way of asking, for each person, "Why should I be moral?" Of course, if everyone is to be whatever I am, then I should be moral. But a general answer to the question "Why should I be moral?" cannot presuppose this.

The second consideration is that any individual always does better to be prudent rather than moral, provided his choice does not determine other choices. But in so far as this answers the question "Why should I be moral?" it leads to the conclusion "I should not be moral." One feels that this is not the answer which is wanted.

We may put the matter otherwise. The individual who needs a reason for being moral which is not itself a moral reason cannot have it. There is nothing surprising about this; it would be much more surprising if such reasons could be found. For it is more than apparently paradoxical to suppose that considerations of advantage could ever of themselves justify accepting a real disadvantage.

V

I suggested in Section II that the thesis, in modified form, might provide a necessary, although not a sufficient, condition for a moral system. I want now to consider how one might characterize the man who would qualify as moral according to the thesis— I shall call him the "moral" man—and then ask what would be lacking from this characterization, in terms of some of our commonplace moral views.

The rationally prudent man is incapable of moral behavior, in even the limited sense defined by the thesis. What difference must there be between the prudent man and the "moral" man? Most simply, the "moral" man is the prudent but trustworthy man. I treat trustworthiness as the capacity which enables its possessor to adhere, and to judge that he ought to adhere, to a commitment which he has made, without regard to considerations of advantage.

The prudent but trustworthy man does not possess this capacity completely. He is capable of trustworthy behavior only in so far as he regards his *commitment* as advantageous. Thus he differs from the prudent man just in the relevant respect; he accepts arguments of the form "If it is advantageous for me to agree[7] to do x, and I do agree to do x, then I ought to do x, whether or not it then proves advantageous for me to do x."

Suppose that A and B, the parties to the disarmament pact, are prudent but trustworthy. A, considering whether or not secretly to violate the agreement, reasons that its advantage in making and keeping the agreement, provided B does so as well, is greater than its advantage in not making it. If it can assume that B reasons in the same way, then it is in a position to conclude that it ought not to violate the pact. Although violation would be advantageous, consideration of this advantage is ruled out by A's trustworthiness, given the advantage in agreeing to the pact.

The prudent but trustworthy man meets the requirements implicitly imposed by the thesis for the "moral" man. But how far does this "moral" man display two characteristics commonly associated with morality—first, a willingness to make sacrifices, and second, a concern with fairness?

Whenever a man ignores his own advantage for reasons other than those of greater advantage, he may be said to make some sacrifice. The "moral" man, in being trustworthy, is thus required to make certain sacrifices. But these are extremely limited. And—not surprisingly, given the general direction of our argument—it is quite possible that they limit the advantages which the "moral" man can secure.

Once more let us turn to our example. A and B have entered into a disarmament agreement and, being prudent but trustworthy, are faithfully carrying it out. The government of A is now informed by its scientists, however, that they have developed an effective missile defense, which will render A invulnerable to attack by any of the weapons actually or potentially at B's disposal, barring unforeseen technological developments. Furthermore, this defense can be installed secretly. The government is now called upon to decide whether to violate its agreement with B, install the new defense, and, with the arms it has retained through its violation, establish its dominance over B.

A is in a type of situation quite different from that previously considered. For it is not just that A will do better by secretly violating its agreement. A reasons not only that it will do better to violate no matter what B does, but that it will do better if both violate than if both continue to adhere to the pact. A is now in a position to gain from abandoning the agreement; it no longer finds mutual adherence advantageous.

We may represent this new situation in another matrix:

		B	
		adheres	*violates*
	adheres	3, 2	4, 1
A			
	violates	1, 4	2, 3

We assume again that the ranking of mutual violation is the same as that of no agreement. Now had this situation obtained at the outset, no agreement would have been made, for A would have had no reason to enter into a disarmament pact. And of course had A expected this situation to come about, no agreement—or only a temporary agreement—would have been made; A would no doubt have risked the short-term dangers of the continuing arms race in the hope of securing the long-run benefit of predominance over B once its missile defense was completed. On the contrary, A expected to benefit from the agreement, but now finds that, because of its unexpected development of a missile defense, the agreement is not in fact advantageous to it.

The prudent but trustworthy man is willing to carry out his agreements, and judges that he ought to carry them out, in so far as he considers them advantageous. A is prudent but trustworthy. But is A willing to carry out its agreement to disarm, now that it no longer considers the agreement advantageous?

If A adheres to its agreement in this situation, it makes a sacrifice greater than any advantage it receives from the similar sacrifices of others. It makes a sacrifice greater in kind than any which can be required by a mutually advantageous agreement. It must, then, possess a capacity for trustworthy behavior greater than that ascribed to the merely prudent but trustworthy man (or nation). This capacity need not be unlimited; it need not extend to a willingness to adhere to any commitment no matter what sacrifice is involved. But it must involve a willingness to adhere to a commitment made in the expectation of advantage, should that expectation be disappointed.

I shall call the man (or nation) who is willing to adhere, and judges that he ought to adhere, to his prudentially undertaken agreements even if they prove disadvantageous to him, the trustworthy man. It is likely that there are advantages available to trustworthy men which are not available to merely prudent but trustworthy men. For there may be situations in which men can make agreements which each expects to be advantageous to him, provided he can count on the others' adhering to it whether or not their expectation of advantage is realized. But each can count on this only if all have the capacity to adhere to commitments regardless of whether the commitment actually proves advantageous. Hence, only trustworthy men who know each other to be such will be able rationally to enter into, and so to benefit from, such agreements.

Baier's view of morality departs from that stated in the thesis in that it requires trustworthy, and not merely prudent but trustworthy, men. Baier admits that "a person might do better for himself by following enlightened self-interest rather than morality."[8] This admission seems to require that morality be a system of principles which each person may expect, initially, to be advantageous to him, if adopted and adhered to by everyone, but not a system which actually is advantageous to everyone.

Our commonplace moral views do, I think support the view that the moral man must be trustworthy. Hence, we have established one modification required in the thesis, if it is to provide a more adequate set of conditions for a moral system.

But there is a much more basic respect in which the "moral" man falls short of our expectations. He is willing to temper his single-minded pursuit of advantage only by accepting the obligation to adhere to prudentially undertaken commitments. He has no real concern for the advantage of others, which would lead him to modify his pursuit of advantage when it conflicted with the similar pursuits of others. Unless he expects to gain, he is unwilling to accept restrictions on the pursuit of advantage which are intended to equalize the opportunities open to all. In other words, he has no concern with fairness.

We tend to think of the moral man as one who does not seek his own well-being by means which would deny equal well-being to his fellows. This marks him off clearly from the "moral" man, who differs from the prudent man only in that he can overcome the apparent paradox of prudence and obtain those advantages which are available only to those who can display real restraint in their pursuit of advantage.

Thus a system of principles might meet the conditions laid down in the thesis without taking any account of considerations of fairness. Such a system would contain principles for ensuring increased advantage (or expectation of advantage) to everyone, but no further principle need be present to determine the distribution of this increase.

It is possible that there are systems of principles which, if adopted and adhered to, provide advantages which strictly prudent men, however rational, cannot attain. These advantages are a function of the sacrifices which the principles impose on their adherents.

Morality may be such a system. If it is, this would explain our expectation that we should all be worse off were we to substitute prudence for morality in our deliberations. But to characterize morality as a system of principles advantageous to all is not to answer the question "Why should I be moral?" nor is it to provide for those considerations of fairness which are equally essential to our moral understanding.

NOTES

1. David Hume, *An Enquiry Concerning the Principles of Morals*, sec. ix, pt. ii.
2. Ogden Nash, "Kind of an Ode to Duty."
3. Kurt Baier, *The Moral Point of View: A Rational Basis of Ethics* (Ithaca, 1958), p. 314.
4. That this, and only this, is what he is entitled to claim may not be clear to Baier, for he supposes his account

of morality to answer the question "Why should we be moral?," interpreting "we" distributively. This, as I shall argue in Sec. IV, is quite mistaken.

5. The thesis is not intended to state Baier's view of morality. I shall suggest in Sec. V that Baier's view would require substituting "everyone can expect to benefit" for "it is advantageous to everyone." The thesis is stronger and easier to discuss.

6. Those familiar with the theory of games will recognize the matrix as a variant of the Prisoner's Dilemma. In a more formal treatment, it would be appropriate to develop the relation between morality and advantage by reference to the Prisoner's Dilemma. This would require reconstructing the disarmament pact and the moral system as proper games. Here I wish only to suggest the bearing of game theory on our enterprise.

7. The word "agree" requires elucidation. It is essential not to confuse an advantage in agreeing to do x with an advantage in saying that one will do x. If it is advantageous for me to agree to do x, then there is some set of actions open to me which includes both saying that I will do x and doing x, and which is more advantageous to me than any set of actions open to me which does not include saying that I will do x. On the other hand, if it is advantageous for me to say that I will do x, then there is some set of actions open to me which includes saying that I will do x, and which is more advantageous to me than any set which does not include saying that I will do x. But this set need not include doing x.

8. Baier, *op. cit.*, p. 314.

STUDY QUESTIONS

1. What is paradoxical about the claim that morality contributes to advantage in a way that prudence cannot?
2. How does Gauthier argue that it is advantageous for nation A to adhere to the disarmament pact, even if A's violations of the pact would go undetected? Can you think of other examples where the prudent action is not the most advantageous?
3. In your own words, explain the following statement: "If all men are moral, all will do better than if all are prudent. But any one man will always do better if he is prudent than if he is moral."
4. Why does Gauthier think that "the individual who needs a reason for being moral which is not itself a moral reason cannot have it"? Do you agree?

2. SUBJECTIVISM, RELATIVISM, AND SKEPTICISM

The Subjectivity of Values

J. L. MACKIE

J. L. Mackie (1917–1981) taught philosophy at University College, Oxford. His writings were influential in a number of areas of philosophy, including ethics and metaphysics. They include *The Cement of the Universe* and *Ethics: Inventing Right and Wrong*.

. .

1. Moral Scepticism

There are no objective values. This is a bald statement of the thesis of this chapter, but before arguing for it I shall try to clarify and restrict it in ways that may meet some objections and prevent some misunderstanding.

The statement of this thesis is liable to provoke one of the three very different reactions. Some will think it not merely false but pernicious; they will see it as a threat to morality and to everything else that is worthwhile, and they will find the presenting of such a thesis in what purports to be a book on ethics paradoxical or even outrageous. Others will regard it as a trivial truth, almost too obvious to be worth mentioning, and certainly too plain to be worth much argument. Others again will say that it is meaningless or empty, that no real issue is raised by the question whether values are or are not part of the fabric of the world. But, precisely because there can be these three different reactions, much more needs to be said.

The claim that values are not objective, are not part of the fabric of the world, is meant to include not only moral goodness, which might be most naturally equated with moral value, but also other things that could be more loosely called moral values or disvalues—rightness and wrongness, duty, obligation, an action's being rotten and contemptible, and so on. It also includes non-moral values, notably aesthetic ones, beauty and various kinds of artistic merit. I shall not discuss these explicitly, but clearly much the same considerations apply to aesthetic and to moral values, and there would be at least some initial implausibility in a view that gave the one a different status from the other.

Since it is with moral values that I am primarily concerned, the view I am adopting may be called moral scepticism. But this name is likely to be misunderstood: "moral scepticism" might also be used as a name for either of two first order views, or perhaps for an incoherent mixture of the two. A moral sceptic might be the sort of person who says "All this talk of morality is tripe," who rejects morality and will take no notice of it. Such a person may be literally rejecting all moral judgments; he is more likely to be making moral judgments of his own, expressing a positive moral condemnation of all that conventionally passes for morality; or he may be confusing these two logically incompatible views, and saying that he rejects all morality, while he is in fact rejecting only a particular morality that is current in that society in which he has grown up. But I am not at present concerned with the merits or faults of such a position. These are first order moral views, positive or negative: the person who adopts either of them is taking a certain practical, normative, stand. By contrast, what I am discussing is a second order view, a view about the status of moral values and the nature of moral valuing, about where and how they fit into the world. These first and second order views are not merely distinct but completely independent: one could be a second order moral sceptic without being a first order one, or again the other way round. A man could hold strong moral views, and indeed ones whose content was thoroughly conventional, while believing that they were simply attitudes and policies with regard to conduct that he and other people held. Conversely, a man could reject all established morality while believing it to be an objective truth that it was evil or corrupt.

With another sort of misunderstanding moral scepticism would seem not so much pernicious as absurd. How could anyone deny that there is a difference between a kind action and a cruel one, or that a coward and a brave man behave differently in the face of danger? Of course, this is undeniable; but it is not to the point. The kinds of behaviour to which moral values and disvalues are ascribed are indeed part of the furniture of the world, and so are the natural, descriptive, differences between them; but, not perhaps, their differences in value. It is a hard fact that cruel actions differ from kind ones, and hence that we can learn, as in fact we all do, to distinguish them fairly well in practice, and to use the words "cruel" and "kind" with fairly clear descriptive meanings; but is it an equally hard fact that actions which are cruel in such a descriptive sense are to be condemned? The present issue is with regard to the objectivity specifically of value, not with regard to the objectivity of those natural, factual, differences on the basis of which differing values are assigned.

2. Subjectivism

Another name often used, as an alternative to "moral scepticism," for the view I am discussing is "subjectivism." But this too has more than one meaning. Moral subjectivism too could be a first order, normative, view, namely that everyone really ought to do whatever he thinks he should. This plainly is a (systematic) first order view; on examination it soon ceases to be plausible, but that is beside the point, for it is quite independent of the second order thesis at present under consideration. What is more confusing is that different second order views compete for the name "subjectivism." Several of these are doctrines about the meaning of moral terms and moral statements. What is often called moral subjectivism is the doctrine that, for example, "This action is right" *means* "I approve of this action," or more generally that moral judgments are equivalent to reports of the speaker's own feelings or attitudes. But the view I am now discussing is to be distinguished in two vital respects from any such doctrine as this. First, what I have called moral scepticism is a negative doctrine, not a positive one: it says what there isn't, not what there is. It says that there do not exist entities or relations of a certain kind, objective values or requirements, which many people have believed to exist. Of course, the moral sceptic cannot leave it at that. If his position is to be at all plausible, he must give some account of how other people have fallen into what he regards as an error, and this account will have to include some positive suggestions about how values fail to be objective, about what has been mistaken for, or has led to false beliefs about, objective values. But this will be a development of his theory, not its core: its core is the negation. Secondly, what I have called moral subjectivism, is an ontological thesis, not a linguistic or conceptual one. It is not, like the other doctrine often called moral subjectivism, a view about the meanings of moral statements.

Again, no doubt, if it is to be at all plausible, it will have to give some account of their meanings, and I shall say something about this in Section 7 of this chapter. . . . But this too will be a development of the theory, not its core.

It is true that those who have accepted the moral subjectivism which is the doctrine that moral judgments are equivalent to reports of the speaker's own feelings or attitudes have usually presupposed what I am calling moral scepticism. It is because they have assumed that there are no objective values that they have looked elsewhere for an analysis of what moral statements might mean, and have settled upon subjective reports. Indeed, if all our moral statements were such subjective reports, it would follow that, at least so far as we are aware, there are no objective moral values. If we were aware of them, we would say something about them. In this sense this sort of subjectivism entails moral scepticism. But the converse entailment does not hold. The denial that there are objective values does not commit one to any particular view about what moral statements mean, and certainly not to the view that they are equivalent to subjective reports. No doubt if moral values are not objective they are in some very broad sense subjective, and for this reason I would accept "moral subjectivism" as an alternative name to "moral scepticism." But subjectivism in this broad sense must be distinguished from the specific doctrine about meaning referred to above. Neither name is altogether satisfactory: we simply have to guard against the (different) misinterpretations which each may suggest.

. . . .

5. Standards of Evaluation

One way of stating the thesis that there are no objective values is to say that value statements cannot be either true or false. But this formulation, too, lends itself to misinterpretation. For there are certain kinds of value statements which undoubtedly can be true or false, even if, in the sense I intend, there are no objective values. Evaluations of many sorts are commonly made in relation to agreed and assumed standards. The classing of wool, the grading of apples, the awarding of prizes at sheepdog trials, flower shows, skating and diving championships, and even the marking of examination papers are carried out in relation to standards of quality or merit which are peculiar to each particular subject-matter or type of contest, which may be explicitly laid down but which, even if they are nowhere explicitly stated, are fairly well understood and agreed by those who are recognized as judges or experts in each particular field. Given any sufficiently determinate standards, it will be an objective issue, a matter of truth and falsehood, how well any particular specimen measures up to those standards. Comparative judgments in particular will be capable of truth and falsehood: it will be a factual question whether this sheepdog has performed better than that one.

The subjectivist about values, then, is not denying that there can be objective evaluations relative to standards, and these are as possible in the aesthetic and moral fields as in any of those just mentioned. More than this, there is an objective distinction which applies in many such fields, and yet would itself be regarded as a peculiarly moral one: the distinction between justice and injustice. In one important sense of the word it is a paradigm case of injustice if a court declares someone to be guilty of an offence of which it knows him to be innocent. More generally, a finding is unjust if it is at variance with what the relevant law and the facts together require, and particularly if it is known by the court to be so. More generally still, any award of marks, prizes, or the like is unjust if it is at variance with the agreed standards for the contest in question: if one diver's performance in fact measures up better to the accepted standards for diving than another's, it will be unjust if the latter is awarded higher marks or the prize. In this way the justice or injustice of decisions relative to standards can be a thoroughly objective matter, though there may still be a subjective element in the interpretation or application of standards. But the statement that a certain decision is thus just or unjust will not be objectively prescriptive: in so far as it can be simply true it leaves open the question whether there is any objective requirement to do what is just and to refrain from what is unjust, and equally leaves open the practical decision to act in either way.

Recognizing the objectivity of justice in relation to standards, and of evaluative judgments relative to standards, then, merely shifts the question of the objectivity of values back to the standards themselves. The subjectivist may try to make his point by insisting that there is no objective validity about the choice of standards. Yet he would clearly be wrong if he said that the choice of even the most basic standards in any field was completely arbitrary. The standards used in sheepdog trials clearly bear some relation to the work that sheepdogs are kept to do, the standards for grading apples bear some relation to what people generally want in or like about apples, and so on. On the other hand, standards are not as a rule strictly validated by such purposes. The appropriateness of standards is neither fully determinate nor totally indeterminate in relation to independently specifiable aims or desires. But however determinate it is, the objective appropriateness of standards in relation to aims or desires is no more of a threat to the denial of objective values than is the objectivity of evaluation relative to standards. In fact it is logically no different from the objectivity of goodness relative to desires. Something may be called good simply in so far as it satisfies or is such as to satisfy a certain desire; but the objectivity of such relations of satisfaction does not constitute in our sense an objective value.

6. Hypothetical and Categorical Imperatives

We may make this issue clearer by referring to Kant's distinction between **hypothetical** and **categorical imperatives**, though what he called imperatives are more naturally expressed as "ought" statements than in the imperative mood. "If you want X, do Y" (or "You ought to do Y") will be a hypothetical imperative if it is based on the supposed fact that Y is, in the circumstances, the only (or the best) available means to X, that is, on a causal relation between Y and X. The reason for doing Y lies in its causal connection with the desired end, X; the oughtness is contingent upon the desire. But "You ought to do Y" will be a categorical imperative if you ought to do Y irrespective of any such desire for any end to which Y would contribute, if the oughtness is not thus contingent upon any desire. But this distinction needs to be handled with some care. An "ought"-statement is not in this sense hypothetical merely because it incorporates a conditional clause. "If you promised to do Y, you ought to do Y" is not a hypothetical imperative merely on account of the stated if-clause; what is meant may be either a hypothetical or

a categorical imperative, depending upon the implied reason for keeping the supposed promise. If this rests upon some such further unstated conditional as "If you want to be trusted another time," then it is a hypothetical imperative; if not, it is categorical. Even a desire of the agent's can figure in the antecedent of what, though conditional in grammatical form, is still in Kant's sense a categorical imperative. "If you are strongly attracted sexually to young children you ought not to go in for school teaching" is not, in virtue of what it explicitly says, a hypothetical imperative: the avoidance of school teaching is not being offered as a means to the satisfaction of the desires in question. Of course, it could still be a hypothetical imperative, if the implied reason were a prudential one; but it could also be a categorical imperative, a moral requirement where the reason for the recommended action (strictly, avoidance) does not rest upon that action's being a means to the satisfaction of any desire that the agent is supposed to have. Not every conditional ought-statement or command, then, is a hypothetical imperative; equally, not every non-conditional one is a categorical imperative. An appropriate if-clause may be left unstated. Indeed, a simple command in the imperative mood, say a parade-ground order, which might seem most literally to qualify for the title of a categorical imperative, will hardly ever be one in the sense we need here. The implied reason for complying with such an order will almost always be some desire of the person addressed, perhaps simply the desire to keep out of the trouble. If so, such an apparently categorical order will be in our sense a hypothetical imperative. Again, an imperative remains hypothetical even if we change the "if" to "since": the fact that the desire for X is actually present does not alter the fact that the reason for doing Y is contingent upon the desire for X by way of Y's being a means to X. In Kant's own treatment, while imperatives of skill relate to desires which an agent may or may not have, imperatives of prudence relate to the desire for happiness which, Kant assumes, everyone has. So construed, imperatives of prudence are no less hypothetical than imperatives of skill, no less contingent upon desires that the agent has at the time the imperatives are addressed to him. But if we think rather of a counsel of prudence as being related to the agent's future welfare, to the satisfaction of desires that he does not yet have—not even to a present desire that his future desires should be satisfied—then a counsel of prudence is a categorical imperative, different indeed from a moral one, but analogous to it.

A categorical imperative, then, would express a reason for acting which was unconditional in the sense of not being contingent upon any present desire of the agent to whose satisfaction the recommended action would contribute as a means—or more directly: "You ought to dance," if the implied reason is just that you want to dance or like dancing, is still a hypothetical imperative. Now Kant himself held that moral judgments are categorical imperatives, or perhaps are all applications of one categorical imperative, and it can plausibly be maintained at least that many moral judgments contain a categorically imperative element. So far as ethics is concerned, my thesis that there are no objective values is specifically the denial that any such categorically imperative element is objectively valid. The objective values which I am denying would be action-directing absolutely, not contingently (in the way indicated) upon the agent's desires and inclinations.

Another way of trying to clarify this issue is to refer to moral reasoning or moral arguments. In practice, of course, such reasoning is seldom fully explicit: but let us suppose that we could make explicit the reasoning that supports some evaluative conclusion, where this conclusion has some action-guiding force that is not contingent upon desires or purposes or chosen ends. Then what I am saying is that somewhere in the input to this argument—perhaps in one or more of the premises, perhaps in some part of the form of the argument—there will be something which cannot be objectively validated—some premiss which is not capable of being simply true, or some form of argument which is not valid as a matter of general logic, whose authority or cogency is not objective, but is constituted by our choosing or deciding to think in a certain way.

7. The Claim to Objectivity

If I have succeeded in specifying precisely enough the moral values whose objectivity I am denying, my thesis may now seem to be trivially true. Of course, some will say, valuing, preferring, choosing, recommending, rejecting, condemning, and so on, are human activities, and there is no need to look for values that are prior to and logically independent of all such activities. There may be widespread agreement in valuing, and particular value-judgments are not in general arbitrary or isolated: they typically cohere with others, or can be criticized if they do not, reasons can be given for them, and so on: but if all that the subjectivist is maintaining is that desires, ends, purposes, and the like figure somewhere in the system of reasons, and that no ends or purposes are objective as opposed to being merely inter-subjective, then this may be conceded without much fuss.

But I do not think that this should be conceded so easily. As I have said, the main tradition of European moral philosophy includes the contrary claim, that there are objective values of just the sort I have denied. I have referred already to Plato, Kant, and Sidgwick. Kant in particular holds that the categorical imperative is not only categorical and imperative but objectively so: though a rational being gives the moral law to himself, the law that he thus makes is determinate and necessary. Aristotle begins the *Nicomachean Ethics* by saying that the good is that at which all things aim, and that ethics is part of a science which he calls "politics," whose goal is not knowledge but practice; yet he does not doubt that there can be *knowledge* of what is the good for man, nor, once he has identified this as well-being or happiness, **eudaimonia**, that it can be known, rationally determined, in what happiness consists; and it is plain that he thinks that this happiness is intrinsically desirable, not good simply because it is desired. The rationalist Samuel Clarke holds that

> these eternal and necessary differences of things make it *fit and reasonable* for creatures so to act . . . even separate from the consideration of these rules being the *positive will* or *command of God*; and also antecedent to any respect or regard, expectation or apprehension, of any *particular private and personal advantage or disadvantage, reward or punishment*, either present or future. . . .

Even the sentimentalist Hutcheson defines moral goodness as "some quality apprehended in actions, which procures approbation . . . ," while saying that the moral sense by which we perceive virtue and vice has been given to us (by the Author of nature) to direct our actions. Hume indeed was on the other side, but he is still a witness to the dominance of the objectivist tradition, since he claims that when we "see that the distinction of vice and virtue is not founded merely on the relations of objects, nor is perceiv'd by reason," this "wou'd subvert all the vulgar systems of morality." And Richard Price insists that right and wrong are "real characters of actions," not "qualities of our minds," and are perceived by the understanding; he criticizes the notion of moral sense on the ground that it would make virtue an affair of taste, and moral right and wrong "nothing in the objects themselves"; he rejects Hutcheson's view because (perhaps mistakenly) he sees it as collapsing into Hume's.

But this objectivism about values is not only a feature of the philosophical tradition. It has also a firm basis in ordinary thought, and even in the meanings of moral terms. No doubt it was an extravagance for Moore to say that "good" is the name of a non-natural quality, but it would not be so far wrong to say that in moral contexts it is used as if it were the name of a supposed non-natural quality, where the description "non-natural" leaves room for the peculiar evaluative, prescriptive, intrinsically action-guiding aspects of this supposed quality. . . . Someone in a state of moral perplexity, wondering whether it would be wrong for him to engage, say, in research related to bacteriological warfare, wants to arrive at some judgment about this concrete case, his doing this work at this time in these actual circumstances; his relevant characteristics will be part of the subject of the judgment, but no relation between him and the proposed action will be part of the predicate. The question is not, for example, whether he really wants to do this work, whether it will satisfy or dissatisfy him, whether he will in the long run have a pro-attitude towards it, or even whether this is an action of a sort that he can happily and sincerely recommend in all relevantly similar cases. Nor is he even wondering just whether to recommend such action in all relevantly similar cases. He wants to know whether this course of action would be wrong in itself. Something like this is the everyday objectivist concept of which talk about non-natural qualities is a philosopher's reconstruction.

The prevalence of this tendency to objectify values—and not only moral ones—is confirmed by a pattern of thinking that we find in existentialists and those influenced by them. The denial of objective values can carry with it an extreme emotional reaction, a feeling that nothing matters at all, that life has lost its purpose. Of course this does not follow; the lack of objective values is not a good reason for abandoning subjective concern or for ceasing to want anything. But the abandonment of a belief in objective values can cause, at least temporarily, a decay of subjective concern and sense of purpose. That it does so is evidence that the people in whom this reaction occurs have been tending to objectify their concerns and purposes, have been giving them a fictitious external authority. A claim to objectivity has been so strongly associated with their subjective concerns and purposes that the collapse of the former seems to undermine the latter as well.

This view, that conceptual analysis would reveal a claim to objectivity, is sometimes dramatically confirmed by philosophers who are officially on the other side. Bertrand Russell, for example, says that "ethical propositions should be expressed in the optative mood, not in the indicative"; he defends himself effectively against the charge of inconsistency in both holding ultimate ethical valuations to be subjective and expressing emphatic opinions on ethical questions. Yet at the end he admits:

> Certainly there *seems* to be something more. Suppose, for example, that some one were to advocate the introduction of bull-fighting in this country. In opposing the proposal, I should *feel*, not only that I was expressing my desires, but that my desires in the matter are *right*, whatever that may mean. As a matter of argument, I can, I think, show that I am not guilty of any logical inconsistency in holding to the above interpretation of ethics and at the same time expressing strong ethical preferences. But in feeling I am not satisfied.

But he concludes, reasonably enough, with the remark: "I can only say that, while my own opinions as to ethics do not satisfy me, other people's satisfy me still less."

I conclude, then, that ordinary moral judgments include a claim to objectivity, an assumption that there are objective values in just the sense in which I am concerned to deny this. And I do not think it is going too far to say that this assumption has been incorporated in the basic, conventional, meanings of moral terms. Any analysis of the meanings of moral terms which omits this claim to objective, intrinsic, prescriptivity is to that extent incomplete. . . .

If second order ethics were confined, then, to linguistic and conceptual analysis, it ought to conclude that moral values at least are objective: that they are so in part of what our ordinary moral statements mean: the traditional moral concepts of the ordinary man as well as of the main line of western philosophers are concepts of objective value. But it is precisely for this reason that linguistic and conceptual analysis is not enough. The claim to objectivity, however ingrained in our language and thought, is not self-validating. It can and should be questioned. But the denial of objective values will have to be put forward not as the result of an analytic approach, but as an "**error theory**," a theory that although most people in making moral judgments implicitly claim, among other things, to be pointing to something objectively prescriptive, these claims are all false. It is this that makes the name "moral scepticism" appropriate.

But since this is an error theory, since it goes against assumptions ingrained in our thought and built into some of the ways in which language is used, since it conflicts with what is sometimes called common sense, it needs very solid support. It is not something we can accept lightly or casually and then quietly pass on. If we are to adopt this view, we must argue explicitly for it. Traditionally it has been supported by arguments of two main kinds, which I shall call the argument from relativity and the argument from queerness, but these can, as I shall show, be supplemented in several ways.

8. The Argument from Relativity

The argument from relativity has as its premiss the well-known variation in moral codes from one society to another and from one period to another, and also the differences in moral beliefs between different groups and classes within a complex community. Such variation is in itself merely a truth of descriptive morality, a fact of anthropology which entails neither first order nor second order ethical views. Yet it may indirectly support second order subjectivism: radical differences

between first order moral judgments make it difficult to treat those judgments as apprehensions of objective truths. But it is not the mere occurrence of disagreements that tells against the objectivity of values. Disagreement on questions in history or biology or cosmology does not show that there are no objective issues in these fields for investigators to disagree about. But such scientific disagreement results from speculative inferences or explanatory hypotheses based on inadequate evidence; and it is hardly plausible to interpret moral disagreement in the same way. Disagreement about moral codes seems to reflect people's adherence to and participation in different ways of life. The causal connection seems to be mainly that way round: it is that people approve of monogamy because they participate in a monogamous way of life rather than that they participate in a monogamous way of life because they approve of monogamy. Of course, the standards may be an idealization of the way of life from which they arise: the monogamy in which people participate may be less complete, less rigid, than that of which it leads them to approve. This is not to say that moral judgments are purely conventional. Of course there have been and are moral heretics and moral reformers, people who have turned against the established rules and practices of their own communities for moral reasons, and often for moral reasons that we would endorse. But this can usually be understood as the extension, in ways which, though new and unconventional, seemed to them to be required for consistency, of rules to which they already adhered as arising out of an existing way of life. In short, the argument from relativity has some force simply because the actual variations in the moral codes are more readily explained by the hypothesis that they reflect ways of life than by the hypothesis that they express perceptions, most of them seriously inadequate and badly distorted, of objective values.

But there is a well-known counter to this argument from relativity, namely to say that the items for which objective validity is in the first place to be claimed are not specific moral rules or codes but very general basic principles which are recognized at least implicitly to some extent in all society—such principles as provide the foundation of what Sidgwick has called different methods of ethics: the principle of universalizability, perhaps, or the rule that one ought to conform to the specific rules of any way of life in which one takes part, from which one profits, and on which one relies, or some utilitarian principle of doing what tends, or seems likely, to promote the general happiness. It is easy to show that such general principles, married with differing concrete circumstances, different existing social patterns or different preferences, will beget different specific moral rules; and there is some plausibility in the claim that the specific rules thus generated will vary from community to community or from group to group in close agreement with the actual variations in accepted codes.

The argument from relativity can be only partly countered in this way. To take this line the moral objectivist has to say that it is only in these principles that the objective moral character attaches immediately to its descriptively specified ground or subject: other moral judgments are objectively valid or true, but only derivatively and contingently—if things had been otherwise, quite different sorts of actions would have been right. And despite the prominence in recent philosophical ethics of universalization, utilitarian principles, and the like, these are very far from constituting the whole of what is actually affirmed as basic in ordinary moral thought. Much of this is concerned rather with what Hare calls "ideals" or, less kindly, "fanaticism." That is, people judge that some things are good or right, and others are bad or wrong, not because—or at any rate not only because—they exemplify some general principle for which widespread implicit acceptance could be claimed, but because something about those things arouses certain responses immediately in them, though they would arouse radically and irresolvably different responses in others. "Moral sense" or "intuition" is an initially more plausible description of what supplies many of our basic moral judgments than "reason." With regard to all these starting points of moral thinking the argument from relativity remains in full force.

9. The Argument from Queerness

Even more important, however, and certainly more generally applicable, is the argument from queerness. This has two parts, one metaphysical, the other

epistemological. If there were objective values, then they would be entities or qualities or relations of a very strange sort, utterly different from anything else in the universe. Correspondingly, if we were aware of them, it would have to be by some special faculty of moral perception or intuition, utterly different from our ordinary ways of knowing everything else. These points were recognized by Moore when he spoke of non-natural qualities, and by the intuitionists in their talk about a "faculty of moral intuition." **Intuitionism** has long been out of favour, and it is indeed easy to point out its implausibilities. What is not so often stressed, but is more important, is that the central thesis of intuitionism is one to which any objectivist view of values is in the end committed: intuitionism merely makes unpalatably plain what other forms of objectivism wrap up. Of course the suggestion that moral judgments are made or moral problems solved by just sitting down and having an ethical intuition is a travesty of actual moral thinking. But, however complex the real process, it will require (if it is to yield authoritatively prescriptive conclusions) some input of this distinctive sort, either premises or forms of argument or both. When we ask the awkward question, how we can be aware of this authoritative prescriptivity, of the truth of these distinctively ethical premises or of the cogency of this distinctively ethical pattern of reasoning, none of our ordinary accounts of sensory perception or introspection or the framing and confirming of explanatory hypotheses or inference or logical construction or conceptual analysis, or any combination of these, will provide a satisfactory answer; "a special sort of intuition" is a lame answer, but it is the one to which the clearheaded objectivist is compelled to resort.

Indeed, the best move for the moral objectivist is not to evade this issue, but to look for companions in guilt. For example, Richard Price argues that it is not moral knowledge alone that such an empiricism as those of Locke and Hume is unable to account for, but also our knowledge and even our ideas of essence, number, identity, diversity, solidity, inertia, substance, the necessary existence and infinite extension of time and space, necessity and possibility in general, power, and causation. If the understanding, which Price defines as the faculty within us that discerns truth, is also a source of new simple ideas of so many other sorts, may it not also be a power of immediately perceiving right and wrong, which yet are real characters of actions?

This is an important counter to the argument from queerness. The only adequate reply to it would be to show how, on empiricist foundations, we can construct an account of the ideas and beliefs and knowledge that we have of all these matters. I cannot even begin to do that here, though I have undertaken some parts of the task elsewhere. I can only state my belief that satisfactory accounts of most of these can be given in empirical terms. If some supposed metaphysical necessities or essences resist such treatment, then they too should be included, along with objective values, among the targets of the argument from queerness.

. . . .

Plato's Forms give a dramatic picture of what objective values would have to be. The Form of the Good is such that knowledge of it provides the knower with both a direction and an overriding motive; something's being good both tells the person who knows this to pursue it and makes him pursue it. An objective good would be sought by anyone who was acquainted with it, not because of any contingent fact that this person, or every person, is so constituted that he desires this end, but just because the end has to-be-pursuedness somehow built into it. Similarly, if there were objective principles of right and wrong, any wrong (possible) course of action would have not-to-be-doneness somehow built into it. Or we should have something like Clarke's necessary relations of fitness between situations and actions, so that a situation would have a demand for such-and-such an action somehow built into it.

The need for an argument of this sort can be brought out by reflection on Hume's argument that "reason"—in which at this stage he includes all sorts of knowing as well as reasoning—can never be an "influencing motive of the will." Someone might object that Hume has argued unfairly from the lack of influencing power (not contingent upon desires) in ordinary objects of knowledge and ordinary reasoning, and might maintain that values differ from natural objects precisely in their power, when known, automatically to influence the will. To this

Hume could, and would need to, reply that this objection involves the postulating of value-entities or value-features of quite a different order from anything else with which we are acquainted, and of a corresponding faculty with which to detect them. That is, he would have to supplement his explicit argument with what I have called the argument from queerness.

Another way of bringing out this queerness is to ask, about anything that is supposed to have some objective moral quality, how this is linked with its natural features. What is the connection between the natural fact that an action is a piece of deliberate cruelty—say, causing pain just for fun—and the moral fact that it is wrong? It cannot be an entailment, a logical or semantic necessity. Yet it is not merely that the two features occur together. The wrongness must somehow be "consequential" or "supervenient"; it is wrong because it is a piece of deliberate cruelty. But just what *in the world* is signified by this "because"? And how do we know the relation that it signifies, if this is something more than such actions being socially condemned, and condemned by us too, perhaps through our having absorbed attitudes from our social environment? It is not even sufficient to postulate a faculty which "sees" the wrongness: something must be postulated which can see at once the natural features that constitute the cruelty, and the wrongness, and the mysterious consequential link between the two. Alternatively, the intuition required might be the perception that wrongness is a higher order property belonging to certain natural properties; but what is this belonging of properties to other properties, and how can we discern it? How much simpler and more comprehensible the situation would be if we could replace the moral quality with some sort of subjective response which could be causally related to the detection of the natural features on which the supposed quality is said to be consequential.

. . . .

10. Patterns of Objectification

Considerations of these kinds suggest that it is in the end less paradoxical to reject than to retain the common-sense belief in the objectivity of moral values, provided that we can explain how this belief, if it is false, has become established and is so resistant to criticisms. This proviso is not difficult to satisfy.

On a subjectivist view, the supposedly objective values will be based in fact upon attitudes which the person has who takes himself to be recognizing and responding to those values. If we admit what Hume calls the mind's "propensity to spread itself on external objects," we can understand the supposed objectivity of moral qualities as arising from what we can call the projection or objectification of moral attitudes. This would be analogous to what is called the "pathetic fallacy," the tendency to read our feelings into their objects. If a fungus, say, fills us with disgust, we may be inclined to ascribe to the fungus itself a non-natural quality of foulness. But in moral contexts there is more than this propensity at work. Moral attitudes themselves are at least partly social in origin: socially established—and socially necessary—patterns of behaviour put pressure on individuals, and each individual tends to internalize these pressures and to join in requiring these patterns of behaviour of himself and of others. The attitudes that are objectified into moral values have indeed an external source, though not the one assigned to them by the belief in their absolute authority. Moreover, there are motives that would support objectification. We need morality to regulate interpersonal relations, to control some of the ways in which people behave towards one another, often in opposition to contrary inclinations. We therefore want our moral judgments to be authoritative for other agents as well as for ourselves: objective validity would give them the authority required. Aesthetic values are logically in the same position as moral ones; much the same metaphysical and epistemological considerations apply to them. But aesthetic values are less strongly objectified than moral ones; their subjective status, and an "error theory" with regard to such claims to objectivity as are incorporated in aesthetic judgments, will be more readily accepted, just because the motives for their objectification are less compelling.

But it would be misleading to think of the objectification of moral values as primarily the projection of feelings, as in the pathetic fallacy. More important are wants and demands. As Hobbes says, "whatsoever is the object of any man's Appetite or Desire, that is it, which he for his part calleth *Good*", and certainly both the adjective "good" and the noun "goods" are used in non-moral contexts of things because they are such as to satisfy desires. We get the notion of something's being objectively good, or having intrinsic value, by reversing the direction of dependence here, by making the desire depend upon the goodness, instead of the goodness on the desire. And this is aided by the fact that the desired thing will indeed have features that make it desired, that enable it to arouse a desire or that make it such as to satisfy some desire that is already there. It is fairly easy to confuse the way in which a thing's desirability is indeed objective with its having in our sense objective value. The fact that the word "good" serves as one of our main moral terms is a trace of this pattern of objectification.

Similarly related uses of words are covered by the distinction between hypothetical and categorical imperatives. The statement that someone "ought to" or, more strongly, "must" do such-and-such may be backed up explicitly or implicitly by reference to what he wants or to what his purposes and objects are. Again, there may be a reference to the purposes of someone else, perhaps the speaker: "You must do this"—"Why?"—"Because I want such-and-such." The moral categorical imperative which could be expressed in the same words can be seen as resulting from the suppression of the conditional clause in a hypothetical imperative without its being replaced by any such reference to the speaker's wants. The action in question is still required in something like the way in which it would be if it were appropriately related to a want, but it is no longer admitted that there is any contingent want upon which its being required depends. Again this move can be understood when we remember that at least our central and basic moral judgments represent social demands, where the source of the demand is indeterminate and diffuse. Whose demands or wants are in question, the agent's, or the speaker's, or those of an indefinite multitude of other people? All of this in a way, but there are advantages in not specifying them precisely. The speaker is expressing demands which he makes as a member of a community, which he has developed in and by participation in a joint way of life; also, what is required of this particular agent would be required of any other in a relevantly similar situation; but the agent too is expected to have internalized the relevant demands, to act as if the ends for which the action is required were his own. By suppressing any explicit reference to demands and making the imperatives categorical we facilitate conceptual moves from one such demand relation to another. The moral uses of such words as "must" and "ought" and "should", all of which are used also to express hypothetical imperatives, are traces of this pattern of objectification.

It may be objected that this explanation links normative ethics too closely with descriptive morality, with the mores or socially enforced patterns of behaviour that anthropologists record. But it can hardly be denied that moral thinking starts from the enforcement of social codes. Of course it is not confined to that. But even when moral judgments are detached from the mores of any actual society they are liable to be framed with reference to an ideal community of moral agents, such as Kant's kingdom of ends, which but for the need to give God a special place in it would have been better called a commonwealth of ends.

Another way of explaining the objectification of moral values is to say that ethics is a system of law from which the legislator has been removed. This might have derived either from the positive law of a state or from a supposed system of divine law. There can be no doubt that some features of modern European moral concepts are traceable to the theological ethics of Christianity. The stress on quasi-imperative notions, on what ought to be done or on what is wrong in a sense that is close to that of "forbidden," are surely relics of divine commands. Admittedly, the central ethical concepts for Plato and Aristotle also are in a broad sense prescriptive or intrinsically action-guiding, but in concentrating rather on "good" than on "ought" they show that their moral thought is an objectification of the desired and the satisfying rather than of the commanded. Elizabeth Anscombe has argued that modern, non-Aristotelian, concepts of *moral* obligation, *moral* duty, of what is *morally* right and wrong, and of the *moral* sense of "ought" are survivals outside the framework of thought that made them really intelligible, namely the belief in divine law. She infers that "ought" has

"become a word of mere mesmeric force," with only a "delusive appearance of content," and that we would do better to discard such terms and concepts altogether, and go back to Aristotelian ones.

There is much to be said for this view. But while we can explain some distinctive features of modern moral philosophy in this way, it would be a mistake to see the whole problem of the claim to objective prescriptivity as merely local and unnecessary, as a post-operative complication of a society from which a dominant system of theistic belief has recently been rather hastily excised. As Cudworth and Clarke and Price, for example, show, even those who still admit divine commands, or the positive law of God, may believe moral values to have an independent objective but still action-guiding authority. Responding to Plato's **Euthyphro** dilemma, they believe that God commands what he commands because it is in itself good or right, not that it is good or right merely because and in that he commands it. Otherwise God himself could not be called good. Price asks, "What can be more preposterous, than to make the Deity nothing but will; and to exalt this on the ruins of all his attributes?" The apparent objectivity of moral value is a widespread phenomenon which has more than one source: the persistence of a belief in something like divine law when the belief in the divine legislator has faded out is only one factor among others. There are several different patterns of the objectification, all of which have left characteristic traces in our actual moral concepts and moral language.

11. The General Goal of Human Life

The argument of the preceding sections is meant to apply quite generally to moral thought, but the terms in which it has been stated are largely those of the Kantian and post-Kantian tradition of English moral philosophy. To those who are more familiar with another tradition, which runs through Aristotle and Aquinas, it may seem wide of the mark. For them, the fundamental notion is that of the good for man, or the general end or goal of human life, or perhaps of a set of basic goods or primary human purposes. Moral reasoning consists partly in achieving a more adequate understanding of this basic goal (or set of goals), partly in working out the best way of pursuing and realizing it. But this approach is open to two radically different interpretations. According to one, to say that something is the good for man or the general goal of human life is just to say that this is what men in fact pursue or will find ultimately satisfying, or perhaps that it is something which, if postulated as an implicit goal, enables us to make sense of actual human strivings and to detect a coherent pattern in what would otherwise seem to be a chaotic jumble of conflicting purposes. According to the other interpretation, to say that something is the good for man or the general goal of human life is to say that this is man's proper end, that this is what he ought to be striving after, whether he in fact is or not. On the first interpretation we have a descriptive statement, on the second a normative or evaluative or prescriptive one. But this approach tends to combine the two interpretations, or to slide from one to the other, and to borrow support for what are in effect claims of the second sort from the plausibility of statements of the first sort.

I have no quarrel with this notion interpreted in the first way, I would only insert a warning that there may well be more diversity even of fundamental purposes, more variation in what different human beings will find ultimately satisfying, than the terminology of "*the* good for man" would suggest. Nor indeed, have I any quarrel with the second, prescriptive, interpretation, provided that it is recognized as subjectively prescriptive, that the speaker is here putting forward his own demands or proposals, or those of some movement that he represents, though no doubt linking these demands or proposals with what he takes to be already in the first, descriptive, sense fundamental human goals. . . . But if it is claimed that something is objectively the right or proper goal of human life, then this is tantamount to the assertion of something that is objectively categorically imperative, and comes fairly within the scope of our previous arguments. Indeed, the running together of what I have here called the two interpretations is yet another pattern of objectification: a claim to objective prescriptivity is constructed by combining the normative element in the second interpretation with the objectivity allowed by the first, by the statement that such and such are fundamentally pursued or ultimately satisfying human goals. The argument from relativity still applies: the radical diversity of the goals that men actually pursue and find satisfying makes it implausible to construe such pursuits as resulting from an imperfect grasp of a unitary true good. So too does the argument from queerness; we can still ask what this objectively prescriptive rightness of the true goal can be, and how this is linked on the one hand with the descriptive features of this goal and on the other with the fact that it is to *some extent* an actual goal of human striving.

To meet these difficulties, the objectivist may have recourse to the purpose of God: the true purpose of human life is fixed by what God intended (or, intends) men to do and to be. Actual human strivings and satisfactions have some relation to this true end because God made men for this end and made them such as to pursue it—but only *some* relation, because of the inevitable imperfection of created beings.

I concede that if the requisite theological doctrine could be defended, a kind of objective ethical prescriptivity could be thus introduced. Since I think that theism cannot be defended, I do not regard this as any threat to my argument. . . . Those who wish to keep theism as a live option can read the arguments of the intervening chapters hypothetically, as a discussion of what we can make of morality without recourse to God, and hence of what we can say about morality if, in the end, we dispense with religious belief.

. . . .

[Editor's note: The quotation on page 781 from Samuel Clarke is from selections in D. D. Raphael ed., *British Moralists 1650–1800* (Oxford, 1969). The quotation from Bertrand Russell on page 782 is from his "Reply to Criticism" in P. A. Schlipp, ed., *The Philosophy of Bertrand Russell* (Evanston, 1944).]

KEY TERMS

Hypothetical imperative
Categorical imperative
Eudaimonia
Error theory
Intuitionism
Euthyphro dilemma

STUDY QUESTIONS

1. What is the distinction that Mackie makes between *first-order* and *second-order* views, and why does his view count as a second-order view?
2. Mackie spends a lot of time telling us what his thesis does *not* say. But what *does* it say?
3. Mackie says that "the lack of objective values is not a good reason for abandoning subjective concern or for ceasing to want anything." Why should we agree with him?
4. Do you think that the fact that many cultures have completely different views of right and wrong is evidence to think that morality is subjective? Why or why not?
5. Suppose that objective values exist. How might we come to know what they are? Do you agree with Mackie that this question is an embarrassment for the believer in objective values? Why or why not?

Ethics and Observation

GILBERT HARMAN

Gilbert Harman (1938–) is the author of a number of important works on epistemology and ethics, including *Thought, Change in View*, and *The Nature of Morality*. He is a Professor of Philosophy at Princeton University.

. .

The Basic Issue

Can moral principles be tested and confirmed in the way scientific principles can? Consider the principle that, if you are given a choice between five people alive and one dead or five people dead and one alive, you should always choose to have five people alive and one dead rather than the other way round. We can easily imagine examples that appear to confirm this principle. Here is one:

You are a doctor in a hospital's emergency room when six accident victims are brought in. All six are in danger of dying but one is much worse off than the others. You can just barely save that person if you devote all of your resources to him and let the others die. Alternatively, you can save the other five if you are willing to ignore the most seriously injured person.

It would seem that in this case you, the doctor, would be right to save the five and let the other person die. So this example, taken by itself, confirms the principle under consideration. Next, consider the following case.

You have five patients in the hospital who are dying, each in need of a separate organ. One needs a kidney, another a lung, a third a heart, and so forth. You can save all five if you take a single healthy person and remove his heart, lungs, kidneys, and so forth, to distribute to these five patients. Just such a healthy person is in room 306. He is in the hospital for routine tests. Having seen his test results, you know that he is perfectly healthy and of the right tissue compatibility. If you do nothing, he will survive without incident; the other patients will die, however. The other five patients can be saved only if the person in Room 306 is cut up and his organs distributed. In that case, there would be one dead but five saved.

The principle in question tells us that you should cut up the patient in Room 306. But in this case, surely you must not sacrifice this innocent bystander, even to save the five other patients. Here a moral principle has been tested and disconfirmed in what may seem to be a surprising way.

This, of course, was a "thought experiment." We did not really compare a hypothesis with the world. We compared an explicit principle with our feelings about certain imagined examples. In the same way, a physicist performs thought experiments in order to compare explicit hypotheses with his "sense" of what should happen in certain situations, a "sense" that he has acquired as a result of his long working familiarity with current theory. But scientific hypotheses can also be tested in real experiments, out in the world.

Can moral principles be tested in the same way, out in the world? You can observe someone do something, but can you ever perceive the rightness or wrongness of what he does? If you round a corner and see a group of young hoodlums pour gasoline on a cat and ignite it, you do not need to *conclude* that what they are doing is wrong; you do not need to figure anything out; you can *see* that it is wrong. But is your reaction due to the actual wrongness of what you see or is it simply a reflection of your moral "sense," a "sense" that you have acquired perhaps as a result of your moral upbringing?

Observation

The issue is complicated. There are no pure observations. Observations are always "theory laden." What you perceive depends to some extent on the theory you hold, consciously or unconsciously. You see some children pour gasoline on a cat and ignite it. To really see that, you have to possess a great deal of knowledge, know about a considerable number of objects, know about people: that people pass through the life stages infant, baby, child, adolescent, adult. You must know what flesh and blood animals are, and in particular, cats. You must have some idea of life. You must know what gasoline is, what burning is, and much more. In one sense, what you "see" is a pattern of light on your retina, a shifting array of splotches, although even that is theory,

and you could never adequately describe what you see in that sense. In another sense, you see what you do because of the theories you hold. Change those theories and you would see something else, given the same pattern of light.

Similarly, if you hold a moral view, whether it is held consciously or unconsciously, you will be able to perceive rightness or wrongness, goodness or badness, justice or injustice. There is no difference in this respect between moral propositions and other theoretical propositions. If there is a difference, it must be found elsewhere.

Observation depends on theory because perception involves forming a belief as a fairly direct result of observing something; you can form a belief only if you understand the relevant concepts and a concept is what it is by virtue of its role in some theory or system of beliefs. To recognize a child as a child is to employ, consciously or unconsciously, a concept that is defined by its place in a framework of the stages of human life. Similarly, burning is an empty concept apart from its theoretical connections to the concepts of heat, destruction, smoke, and fire.

Moral concepts—Right and Wrong, Good and Bad, Justice and Injustice—also have a place in your theory or system of beliefs and are the concepts they are because of their context. If we say that observation has occurred whenever an opinion is a direct result of perception, we must allow that there is moral observation, because such an opinion can be a moral opinion as easily as any other sort. In this sense, observation may be used to confirm or disconfirm moral theories. The observational opinions that, in this sense, you find yourself with can be in either agreement or conflict with your consciously explicit moral principles. When they are in conflict, you must choose between your explicit theory and observation. In ethics, as in science, you sometimes opt for theory, and say that you made an error in observation or were biased or whatever, or you sometimes opt for observation, and modify your theory.

In other words, in both science and ethics, general principles are invoked to explain particular cases and, therefore, in both science and ethics, the general principles you accept can be tested by appealing to particular judgments that certain things are right or wrong, just or unjust, and so forth; and these judgments are analogous to direct perceptual judgments about facts.

Observational Evidence

Nevertheless, observation plays a role in science that it does not seem to play in ethics. The difference is that you need to make assumptions about certain physical facts to explain the occurrence of the observations that support a scientific theory, but you do not seem to need to make assumptions about any moral facts to explain the occurrence of the so-called moral observations I have been talking about. In the moral case, it would seem that you need only make assumptions about the psychology or moral sensibility of the person making the moral observation. In the scientific case, theory is tested against the world.

The point is subtle but important. Consider a physicist making an observation to test a scientific theory. Seeing a vapor trail in a cloud chamber, he thinks, "There goes a proton." Let us suppose that this is an observation in the relevant sense, namely, an immediate judgment made in response to the situation without any conscious reasoning having taken place. Let us also suppose that his observation confirms his theory, a theory that helps give meaning to the very term "proton" as it occurs in his observational judgment. Such a confirmation rests on inferring an explanation. He can count his making the observation as confirming evidence for his theory only to the extent that it is reasonable to explain his making the observation by assuming that, not only is he in a certain psychological "set," given the theory he accepts and his beliefs about the experimental apparatus, but furthermore, there really was a proton going through the cloud chamber, causing the vapor trail, which he saw as a proton. (This is evidence for the theory to the extent that the theory can explain the proton's being there better than competing theories can.) But, if his having made that observation could have been equally well explained by his psychological set alone, without the need for any assumption about a proton, then the observation would not have been evidence for the existence of that proton and therefore would not have been evidence for the theory. His making the

observation supports the theory only because, in order to explain his making the observation, it is reasonable to assume something about the world over and above the assumptions made about the observer's psychology. In particular, it is reasonable to assume that there was a proton going through the cloud chamber, causing the vapor trail.

Compare this case with one in which you make a moral judgment immediately and without conscious reasoning, say, that the children are wrong to set the cat on fire or that the doctor would be wrong to cut up one healthy patient to save five dying patients. In order to explain your making the first of these judgments, it would be reasonable to assume, perhaps, that the children really are pouring gasoline on a cat and you are seeing them do it. But, in neither case is there any obvious reason to assume anything about "moral facts," such as that it really is wrong to set the cat on fire or to cut up the patient in Room 306. Indeed, an assumption about moral facts would seem to be totally irrelevant to the explanation of your making the judgment you make. It would seem that all we need assume is that you have certain more or less well articulated moral principles that are reflected in the judgments you make, based on your moral sensibility. It seems to be completely irrelevant to our explanation whether your intuitive immediate judgment is true or false.

The observation of an event can provide observational evidence for or against a scientific theory in the sense that the truth of that observation can be relevant to a reasonable explanation of why that observation was made. A moral observation does not seem, in the same sense, to be observational evidence for or against any moral theory, since the truth or falsity of the moral observation seems to be completely irrelevant to any reasonable explanation of why that observation was made. The fact that an observation of an event was made at the time it was made is evidence not only about the observer but also about the physical facts. The fact that you made a particular moral observation when you did does not seem to be evidence about moral facts, only evidence about you and your moral sensibility. Facts about protons can affect what you observe, since a proton passing through the cloud chamber can cause a vapor trail that reflects light to your eye in a way that, given your scientific training and psychological set, leads you to judge that what you see is a proton. But there does not seem to be any way in which the actual rightness or wrongness of a given situation can have any effect on your perceptual apparatus. In this respect, ethics seems to differ from science.

In considering whether moral principles can help explain observations, it is therefore important to note an ambiguity in the word "observation." You see the children set the cat on fire and immediately think, "That's wrong." In one sense, your observation is that what the children are doing is wrong. In another sense, your observation is your thinking that thought. Moral observations might explain observations in the first sense but not in the second sense. Certain moral principles might help to explain why it was wrong of the children to set the cat on fire, but moral principles seem to be of no help in explaining your thinking that that is wrong. In the first sense of "observation," moral principles can be tested by observation—"That this act is wrong is evidence that causing unnecessary suffering is wrong." But in the second sense of "observation," moral principles cannot clearly be tested by observation, since they do not appear to help explain observations in this second sense of "observation." Moral principles do not seem to help explain your observing what you observe.

Of course, if you are already given the moral principle that it is wrong to cause unnecessary suffering, you can take your seeing the children setting the cat on fire as observational evidence that they are doing something wrong. Similarly, you can suppose that your seeing the vapor trail is observational evidence that a proton is going through the cloud chamber, if you are given the relevant physical theory. But there is an important apparent difference between the two cases. In the scientific case, your making that observation is itself evidence for the physical theory because the physical theory explains the proton, which explains the trail, which explains your observation. In the moral case, your making your observation does not seem to be evidence for the relevant moral principle because that principle does not seem to help explain your observation. The explanatory chain from principle to observation seems to be broken in morality. The moral principle may "explain" why it is wrong for the children to set the cat on fire. But the

wrongness of that act does not appear to help explain the act, which you observe, itself. The explanatory chain appears to be broken in such a way that neither the moral principle nor the wrongness of the act can help explain why you observe what you observe.

A qualification may seem to be needed here. Perhaps the children perversely set the cat on fire simply "because it is wrong." Here it may seem at first that the actual wrongness of the act does help explain why they do it and therefore indirectly helps explain why you observe what you observe just as a physical theory, by explaining why the proton is producing a vapor trail, indirectly helps explain why the observer observes what he observes. But on reflection we must agree that this is probably an illusion. What explains the children's act is not clearly the actual wrongness of the act but, rather, their belief that the act is wrong. The actual rightness or wrongness of their act seems to have nothing to do with why they do it.

Observational evidence plays a part in science it does not appear to play in ethics, because scientific principles can be justified ultimately by their role in explaining observations, in the second sense of observation—by their explanatory role. Apparently, moral principles cannot be justified in the same way. It appears to be true that there can be no explanatory chain between moral principles and particular observings in the way that there can be such a chain between scientific principles and particular observings. Conceived as an explanatory theory, morality, unlike science, seems to be cut off from observation.

Not that every legitimate scientific hypothesis is susceptible to direct observational testing. Certain hypotheses about "black holes" in space cannot be directly tested, for example, because no signal is emitted from within a black hole. The connection with observation in such a case is indirect. And there are many similar examples. Nevertheless, seen in the large, there is the apparent difference between science and ethics we have noted. The scientific realm is accessible to observation in a way the moral realm is not.

Ethics and Mathematics

Perhaps ethics is to be compared, not with physics, but with mathematics. Perhaps such a moral principle as "You ought to keep your promises" is confirmed or disconfirmed in the way (whatever it is) in which such a mathematical principle as "5 + 7 = 12" is. Observation does not seem to play the role in mathematics it plays in physics. We do not and cannot perceive numbers, for example, since we cannot be in causal contact with them. We do not even understand what it would be like to be in causal contact with the number 12, say. Relations among numbers cannot have any more of an effect on our perceptual apparatus than moral facts can.

Observation, however, *is* relevant to mathematics. In explaining the observations that support a physical theory, scientists typically appeal to mathematical principles. On the other hand, one never seems to need to appeal in this way to moral principles. Since an observation is evidence for what best explains it, and since mathematics often figures in the explanations of scientific observations, there is indirect observational evidence for mathematics. There does not seem to be observational evidence, even indirectly, for basic moral principles. In explaining why certain observations have been made, we never seem to use purely moral assumptions. In this respect, then, ethics appears to differ not only from physics but also from mathematics.

STUDY QUESTIONS

1. Do you think that humans have what Harman calls a "moral sense"? Why or why not?
2. Why does Harman think that "observation depends on theory"? Do you agree?
3. What is the difference, according to Harman, between the role of observation in science and the role of observation in ethics?
4. How similar are ethical "thought-experiments" to actual scientific experiments?

Moral Explanations

NICHOLAS L. STURGEON

Nicholas L. Sturgeon (1942–) is a Professor of Philosophy at Cornell University who writes about ethics and related issues.

· ·

T HERE is one argument for moral skepticism that I respect even though I remain unconvinced. It has sometimes been called the argument from moral diversity or relativity, but that is somewhat misleading, for the problem arises not from the diversity of moral views, but from the apparent difficulty of *settling* moral disagreements, or even of knowing what would be required to settle

From *Morality, Reason, and Truth: New Essays on the Foundation of Ethics*, Rowman and Allanheld, 1984. Reprinted by permission of Rowman and Littlefield. Abridged and slightly revised.

them, a difficulty thought to be noticeably greater than any found in settling disagreements that arise in, for example, the sciences. This provides an argument for moral skepticism because one obviously possible explanation for our difficulty in settling moral disagreements is that they are really unsettleable, that there is no way of justifying one rather than another competing view on these issues; and a possible further explanation for the unsettleability of moral disagreements, in turn, is moral nihilism, the view that on these issues there just is no fact of the matter, that the impossibility of discovering and establishing moral truths is due to there not being any.

I am, as I say, unconvinced: partly because I think this argument exaggerates the difficulty we actually find in settling moral disagreements, partly because there are alternative explanations to be considered for the difficulty we do find. Under the latter heading, for example, it certainly matters to what extent moral disagreements depend on disagreements about other questions which, however, disputed they may be, are nevertheless regarded as having objective answers: questions such as which, if any, religion is true, which account of human psychology, which theory of human society. And it also matters to what extent consideration of moral questions is in practice skewed by distorting factors such as personal interest and social ideology. These are large issues. Although it is possible to say some useful things to put them in perspective,[1] it appears impossible to settle them quickly or in any **a priori** way. Consideration of them is likely to have to be piecemeal and, in the short run at least, frustratingly indecisive.

These large issues are not my topic here. But I mention them, and the difficulty of settling them, to show why it is natural that moral skeptics have hoped to find some quicker way of establishing their thesis. I doubt that any exist, but some have of course been proposed. **Verificationist** attacks on ethics should no doubt be seen in this light, and J. L. Mackie's recent "argument from queerness" is a clear instance. (Mackie, 1977, pp. 38–42). The quicker response on which I shall concentrate, however, is neither of these, but instead an argument by Gilbert Harman designed to bring out the "basic problem" about morality, which in his view is "its apparent immunity from observational testing" and "the seeming irrelevance of observational evidence" (Harman, 1977, pp. vii, viii. Unless otherwise indicated, parenthetical page references are to *Morality, Reason, and Truth: New Essays on the Foundation of Ethics*). The argument is that reference to moral facts appears unnecessary for the *explanation* of our moral observations and beliefs.

Harman's view, I should say at once, is not in the end a skeptical one, and he does not view the argument I shall discuss as a decisive defense of moral skepticism or moral nihilism. Someone else might easily so regard it, however. For Harman himself regards it as creating a strong prima facie case for skepticism and nihilism, strong enough to justify calling it "the problem with ethics."[2] And he believes it shows that the only recourse for someone who wishes to avoid moral skepticism is to find defensible reductive definitions for ethical terms; so skepticism would be the obvious conclusion to draw for anyone who doubted the possibility of such definitions. I believe, however, that Harman is mistaken on both counts. I shall show that his argument for skepticism either rests on claims that most people would find quite implausible (and so cannot be what constitutes, for *them*, the problem with ethics); or else becomes just the application to ethics of a familiar *general* skeptical strategy, one which, if it works for ethics, will work equally well for unobservable theoretical entities, or for other minds, or for an external world (and so, again, can hardly be what constitutes the distinctive problem with *ethics*). I have argued elsewhere,[3] moreover, that one can in any case be a moral realist, and indeed an ethical naturalist, without believing that we are now or ever will be in possession of reductive naturalistic definitions for ethical terms.

The Problem with Ethics

Moral theories are often tested in thought experiments, against imagined examples; and, as Harman notes, trained researchers often test scientific theories in the same way. The problem, though, is that scientific theories can also be tested against the world, by observations or real experiments; and, Harman asks, "can moral principles be tested in the same way, out in the world?" (p. 790 in this book).

This would not be a very interesting or impressive challenge, of course, if it were merely a resurrection of standard verificationist worries about whether moral assertions and theories have any testable empirical implications, implications statable in some relatively austere "observational" vocabulary. One problem with that form of the challenge, as Harman points out, is that there are no "pure" observations, and in consequence no purely observational vocabulary either. But there is also a deeper problem that Harman does not mention, one that remains even if we shelve worries about "pure" observations and, at least for the sake of argument, grant the verificationist his observational language, pretty much as it was usually conceived: that is, as lacking at the very least any obviously theoretical terminology from any recognized science, and of course as lacking any moral terminology. For then the difficulty is that moral principles fare just as well (or just as badly) against the verificationist challenge as do typical scientific principles. For it is by now a familiar point about scientific principles—principles such as Newton's law of universal gravitation or Darwin's theory of evolution—that they are entirely devoid of empirical implications when considered in isolation.[4] We do of course base observational predictions on such theories and so test them against experience, but that is because we do *not* consider them in isolation. For we can derive these predictions only by relying at the same time on a large background of additional assumptions, many of which are equally theoretical and equally incapable of being tested in isolation.

A less familiar point, because less often spelled out, is that the relation of moral principles to observation is similar in *both* these respects. Candidate moral principles—for example, that an action is wrong just in case there is something else the agent could have done that would have produced a greater balance of pleasure over pain—lack empirical implications when considered in isolation. But it is easy to derive empirical consequences from them, and thus to test them against experience, if we allow ourselves, as we do in the scientific case, to rely on a background of other assumptions of comparable status. Thus, if we conjoin the act-utilitarian principle I just cited with the further view, also untestable in isolation, that it is always wrong deliberately to kill a human being, we can deduce from these two premises together the consequence that deliberately killing a human being always produces a lesser balance of pleasure over pain than some available alternative act; and this claim is one any positivist would have conceded we know, in principle at least, how to test. If we found it to be false, moreover, then we would be forced by this empirical test to abandon at least one of the moral claims from which we derived it.

It might be thought a worrisome feature of this example, however, and a further opening for skepticism, that there could be controversy about which moral premise to abandon, and that we have not explained how our empirical test can provide an answer

to *this* question. And this may be a problem. It should be a familiar problem, however, because the Duhemian commentary includes a precisely corresponding point about the scientific case: that if we are at all cautious in characterizing what we observe, then the requirement that our theories merely be *consistent* with observation is a very weak one. There are always many, perhaps indefinitely many, different mutually inconsistent ways to adjust our views to meet this constraint. Of course, in practice we are often confident of how to do it: if you are a freshman chemistry student, you do not conclude from your failure to obtain the predicted value in an experiment that it is all over for the atomic theory of gases. And the decision can be equally easy, one should note, in a moral case. Consider two examples. From the surprising moral thesis that Adolf Hitler was a morally admirable person, together with a modest piece of moral theory to the effect that no morally admirable person would, for example, instigate and oversee the degradation and death of millions of persons, one can derive the testable consequence that Hitler did not do this. But he did, so we must give up one of our premises; and the choice of which to abandon is neither difficult nor controversial.

Or, to take a less monumental example, contrived around one of Harman's own, suppose you have been thinking yourself lucky enough to live in a neighborhood in which no one would do anything wrong, at least not in public; and that the modest piece of theory you accept, this time, is that malicious cruelty, just for the hell of it, is wrong. Then, as in Harman's example, "you round a corner and see a group of young hoodlums pour gasoline on a cat and ignite it." At this point, either your confidence in the neighborhood or your principle about cruelty has got to give way. But the choice is easy, if dispiriting, so easy as hardly to require thought. As Harman says, "You do not need to *conclude* that what they are doing is wrong; you do not need to figure anything out; you can *see* that it is wrong" (p. 790 in this book). But a skeptic can still wonder whether this practical confidence, or this "seeing," rests in either sort of case on anything more than deeply ingrained conventions of thought—respect for scientific experts, say, and for certain moral traditions—as opposed to anything answerable to the facts of the matter, any reliable strategy for getting it right about the world.

Now, Harman's challenge is interesting partly because it does not rest on these verificationist doubts about whether moral beliefs have observational implications, but even more because what it does rest on is a partial answer to the kind of general skepticism to which, as we have seen, reflection on the verificationist picture can lead. Many of our beliefs are justified, in Harman's view, by their providing or helping to provide a reasonable *explanation* of our observing what we do. It would be consistent with your failure, as a beginning student, to obtain the experimental result predicted by the gas laws, that the laws are mistaken. But a better explanation, in light of your inexperience and the general success experts have had in confirming and applying these laws, is that you made some mistake in running the experiment. So our scientific beliefs can be justified by their explanatory role; and so too, in Harman's view, can mathematical beliefs and so many commonsense beliefs about the world.

Not so, however, moral beliefs: they appear to have no such explanatory role. That is "the problem with ethics." Harman spells out his version of this contrast:

> You need to make assumptions about certain physical facts to explain the occurrence of the observations that support a scientific theory, but you do not seem to need to make assumptions about any moral facts to explain the occurrence of the so-called moral observations I have been talking about. In the moral case, it would seem that you need only make assumptions about the psychology or moral sensibility of the person making the moral observation. (p. 791 in this book).

More precisely, and applied to his own example, it might be reasonable, in order to explain your judging that the hoodlums are wrong to set the cat on fire, to assume "that the children really are pouring gasoline on a cat and you are seeing them do it." But there is no

> obvious reason to assume anything about "moral facts," such as that it is really wrong to set the cat on

fire. . . . Indeed, an assumption about moral facts would seem to be totally irrelevant to the explanation of your making the judgment you make. It would seem that all we need assume is that you have certain more or less well articulated moral principles that are reflected in the judgments you make, based on your moral sensibility. (p. 791 in this book).

And Harman thinks that if we accept this conclusion, suitably generalized, then, subject to one possible qualification concerning reduction that I have discussed elsewhere,[5] we must conclude that moral theories cannot be tested against the world as scientific theories can, and that we have no reason to believe that moral facts are part of the order of nature or that there is any moral knowledge (pp. 23, 35).

My own view is that Harman is quite wrong, not in thinking that the explanatory role of our beliefs is important to their justification, but in thinking that moral beliefs play no such role.[6] I shall have to say something about the initial plausibility of Harman's thesis as applied to his own example, but part of my reason for dissenting should be apparent from the other example I just gave. We find it easy (and so does Harman [p. 108]) to conclude from the evidence not just that Hitler was not morally admirable, but that he was morally depraved. But isn't it plausible that Hitler's moral depravity—the fact of his really having been morally depraved—forms part of a reasonable explanation of why we believe he was depraved? I think so, and I shall argue concerning this and other examples that moral beliefs very commonly play the explanatory role Harman denies them. Before I can press my case, however, I need to clear up several preliminary points about just what Harman is claiming and just how his argument is intended to work.

Observation and Explanation

1. For there are several ways in which Harman's argument invites misunderstanding. One results from his focusing at the start on the question of whether there can be moral *observations*.[7] But this question turns out to be a side issue, in no way central to his argument that moral principles cannot be tested against the world. There are a couple of reasons for this, of which the more important[8] by far is that Harman does not really require of moral facts, if belief in them is to be justified, that they figure in the explanation of moral observations. It would be enough, on the one hand, if they were needed for the explanation of moral beliefs that are not in any interesting sense observations. For example, Harman thinks belief in moral facts would be vindicated if they were needed to explain our drawing the moral conclusions we do when we reflect on hypothetical cases, but I think there is no illumination in calling these conclusions observations.[9] It would also be enough, on the other hand, if moral facts were needed for the explanation of what were clearly observations, but not moral observations. Harman thinks mathematical beliefs are justified, but he does not suggest that there are mathematical observations; it is rather that appeal to mathematical truths helps to explain why we make the physical observations we do (pp. 792–793 in this book). Moral beliefs would surely be justified, too, if they played such a role, whether or not there are any moral observations.

So the claim is that moral facts are not needed to explain our having any of the moral beliefs we do, whether or not those beliefs are observations, and are equally unneeded to explain any of the observations we make, whether or not those observations are moral. In fact, Harman's view appears to be that moral facts aren't needed to explain anything at all: though it would perhaps be question-begging for him to begin with this strong a claim, since he grants that if there were any moral facts, then appeal to other moral facts—more general ones, for example— might be needed to explain *them*. But he is certainly claiming, at the very least, that moral facts aren't needed to explain any nonmoral facts we have any reason to believe in.

2. Other possible misunderstandings concern what is meant in asking whether reference to moral facts is *needed* to explain moral beliefs. One warning about this question I have dealt with in my discussion of reduction elsewhere;[10] but another, about what Harman is clearly *not* asking, and about what sort of answer I can attempt to defend to the question he is asking, I can spell out here. For Harman's question is clearly not just whether there is *an* explanation of our moral beliefs that does not mention moral

facts. Almost surely there is. Equally surely, however, there is an explanation of our commonsense nonmoral beliefs that does not mention an external world: one which cites only our sensory experience, for example, together with whatever needs to be said about our psychology to explain why with that history of experience we would form just the beliefs we do. Harman means to be asking a question that will lead to skepticism about moral facts, but not to skepticism about the existence of material bodies or about well-established scientific theories of the world.

Harman illustrates the kind of question he is asking, and the kind of answer he is seeking, with an example from physics that it will be useful to keep in mind. A physicist sees a vapor trail in a cloud chamber and thinks, "There goes a proton." What explains his thinking this? Partly, of course, his psychological set, which largely depends on his beliefs about the apparatus and all the theory he has learned; but partly also, perhaps, the hypothesis that "there really was a proton going through the cloud chamber, causing the vapor trail, which he saw as a proton." We will *not* need this latter assumption, however, "if his having made that observation could have been equally well explained by his psychological set alone, without the need for any assumption about a proton" (p. 791 in this book).[11] So for reference to moral facts to be *needed* in the explanation of our beliefs and observations, is for this reference to be required for an explanation that is somehow *better* than competing explanations. Correspondingly, reference to moral facts will be unnecessary to an explanation, in Harman's view, not just because we can find some explanation that does not appeal to them, but because *no* explanation that appeals to them is any better than some competing explanation that does not.

Now, fine discriminations among competing explanations of almost anything are likely to be difficult, controversial, and provisional. Fortunately, however, my discussion of Harman's argument will not require any fine discriminations. This is because Harman's thesis, as we have seen, is *not* that moral explanations lose out by a small margin; nor is it that moral explanations, though sometimes initially promising, always turn out on further examination to be inferior to nonmoral ones. It is, rather, that reference to moral facts always looks, right from the start, to be "completely irrelevant" to the explanation of any of our observations and beliefs. And my argument will be that this is mistaken: that many moral explanations appear to be good explanations, or components in good explanations, that are not obviously undermined by anything else that we know. My suspicion, in fact, is that moral facts are needed in the sense explained, that they will turn out to belong in our best overall explanatory picture of the world, even in the long run, but I shall not attempt to establish that here. Indeed, it should be clear why I could not pretend to do so. For I have explicitly put to one side the issue (which I regard as incapable in any case of quick resolution) of whether and to what extent actual moral disagreements can be settled satisfactorily; but I assume it would count as a defect in any sort of explanation to rely on claims about which rational agreement proved unattainable. So I concede that it *could* turn out, for anything I say here, that moral explanations are all defective and should be discarded. What I shall try to show is merely that many moral explanations look reasonable enough to be in the running; and, more specifically, that nothing Harman says provides any reason for thinking they are not. This claim is surely strong enough (and controversial enough) to be worth defending.

3. It is implicit in this statement of my project, but worth noting separately, that I take Harman to be proposing an *independent* skeptical argument—independent not merely of the argument from the difficulty of settling disputed moral questions, but also of other standard arguments for moral skepticism. Otherwise his argument is not worth separate discussion. For *any* of these more familiar skeptical arguments will of course imply that moral explanations are defective, on the reasonable assumption that it would be a defect in any explanation to rely on claims as doubtful as these arguments attempt to show all moral claims to be. But if *that* is why there is a problem with moral explanations, one should surely just cite the relevant skeptical argument, rather than this derivative difficulty about moral explanations, as the basic "problem with ethics," and it is that argument we should discuss. So I take Harman's interesting suggestion to be that there is a *different* difficulty that remains even if we put other arguments for moral skepticism aside and *assume*,

for the sake of argument, that there are moral facts (for example, that what the children in his example are doing is really wrong): namely, that these assumed facts *still* seem to play no explanatory role.

This understanding of Harman's thesis crucially affects my argumentative strategy in a way to which I should alert the reader in advance. For it should be clear that assessment of this thesis not merely permits, but *requires*, that we provisionally assume the existence of moral facts. I can see no way of evaluating the claim that *even if* we assumed the existence of moral facts they would still appear explanatorily irrelevant, without assuming the existence of some, to see how they would look. So I do freely assume this in each of the examples I discuss in the next section. (I have tried to choose plausible examples, moreover, moral facts most of us would be inclined to believe in if we did believe in moral facts, since those are the easiest to think about; but the precise examples don't matter, and anyone who would prefer others should feel free to substitute her own.) I grant, furthermore, that if Harman were right about the outcome of this thought experiment—that even after we assumed these facts they still looked irrelevant to the explanation of our moral beliefs and other nonmoral facts—then we might conclude with him that there were, after all, no such facts. But I claim he is wrong: that once we have provisionally assumed the existence of moral facts they *do* appear relevant, by perfectly ordinary standards, to the explanation of moral beliefs and of a good deal else besides. Does this prove that there *are* such facts? Well of course it helps support that view, but here I carefully make no claim to have shown so much. What I *show* is that any remaining reservations about the existence of moral facts must be based on those *other* skeptical arguments, of which Harman's argument is independent. In short, there may still be a "problem with ethics," but it has *nothing* special to do with moral explanations.

Moral Explanations

Now that I have explained how I understand Harman's thesis, I turn to my arguments against it.

I shall first add to my example of Hitler's moral character several more in which it seems plausible to cite moral facts as part of an explanation of non-moral facts, and in particular of people's forming the moral opinions they do. I shall then argue that Harman gives us no plausible reason to reject or ignore these explanations; I shall claim, in fact, that the same is true for his own example of the children igniting the cat. I shall conclude, finally, by attempting to diagnose the source of the disagreement between Harman and me on these issues.

My Hitler example suggests a whole range of extremely common cases that appear not to have occurred to Harman, cases in which we cite someone's moral character as part of an explanation of his or her deeds, and in which that whole story is then available as a plausible further explanation of someone's arriving at a correct assessment of that moral character. Take just one other example. Bernard DeVoto, in *The Year of Decision: 1846*, describes the efforts of American emigrants already in California to rescue another party of emigrants, the Donner Party, trapped by snows in the High Sierras, once their plight became known. At a meeting in Yerba Buena (now San Francisco), the relief efforts were put under the direction of a recent arrival, Passed Midshipman Selim Woodworth, described by a previous acquaintance as "a great busybody and ambitious of taking a command among the emigrants."[12] But Woodworth not only failed to lead rescue parties into the mountains himself, where other rescuers were counting on him (leaving children to be picked up by him, for example), but had to be "shamed, threatened and bullied" even into organizing the efforts of others willing to take the risk; he spent time arranging comforts for himself in camp, preening himself on the importance of his position; and as a predictable result of his cowardice and his exercises in vainglory, many died who might have been saved, including four known still to be alive when he turned back for the last time in mid-March.

DeVoto concludes: "Passed Midshipman Woodworth was just no damned good" (1942, p. 442). I cite this case partly because it has so clearly the structure of an inference to a reasonable explanation. One can think of competing explanations, but the evidence points against them. It isn't, for example,

that Woodworth was a basically decent person who simply proved too weak when thrust into a situation that placed heroic demands on him. He volunteered, he put no serious effort even into tasks that required no heroism, and it seems clear that concern for his own position and reputation played a much larger role in his motivation than did any concern for the people he was expected to save. If DeVoto is right about this evidence, moreover, it seems reasonable that part of the explanation of his believing that Woodworth was no damned good is just that Woodworth *was* no damned good.

DeVoto writes of course with more moral intensity (and with more of a flourish) than academic historians usually permit themselves, but it would be difficult to find a serious work of biography, for example, in which actions are not explained by appeal to moral character: sometimes by appeal to specific virtues and vices, but often enough also by appeal to a more general assessment. A different question, and perhaps a more difficult one, concerns the sort of example on which Harman concentrates, the explanation of judgments of right and wrong. Here again he appears just to have overlooked explanations in terms of moral character: a judge's thinking that it would be wrong to sentence a particular offender to the maximum prison term the law allows, for example, may be due in part to her decency and fair mindedness, which I take to be moral properties if any are. But do moral features of the action or institution being judged ever play an explanatory role? Here is an example in which they appear to. An interesting historical question is why vigorous and reasonably widespread moral opposition to slavery arose for the first time in the eighteenth and nineteenth centuries, even though slavery was a very old institution; and why this opposition arose primarily in Britain, France, and in French- and English-speaking North America, even though slavery existed throughout the New World.[13] There is a standard answer to this question. It is that chattel slavery in British and French America, and then in the United States, was much *worse* than previous forms of slavery, and much worse than slavery in Latin America. This is, I should add, a controversial explanation. But as is often the case with historical explanations, its proponents do not claim it is the whole story, and many of its opponents grant that there may be some truth in these comparisons, and that they may after all form a small part of a larger explanation.[14] This latter concession is all I require for my example. Equally good for my purpose would be the more limited thesis which explains the growth of antislavery sentiment in the United States, between the Revolution and the Civil War, in part by saying that slavery in the United States became a more oppressive institution during that time. The appeal in these standard explanations is straightforwardly to moral facts.

What is supposed to be wrong with all these explanations? Harman says that assumptions about moral facts seem "completely irrelevant" in explaining moral observations and moral beliefs (p. 791 in this book), but on its more natural reading that claim seems pretty obviously mistaken about these examples. For it is natural to think that if a particular assumption is completely irrelevant to the explanation of a certain fact, then that fact would have obtained, and we could have explained it just as well, even if the assumption had been false.[15] But I do not believe that Hitler would have done all he did if he had not been morally depraved, nor, on the assumption that he was not depraved, can I think of any plausible explanation for his doing those things. Nor is it plausible that we would all have believed he was morally depraved even if he hadn't been. Granted, there is a tendency for writers who do not attach much weight to fascism as a social movement to want to blame its evils on a single maniacal leader, so perhaps some of them would have painted Hitler as a moral monster even if he had not been one. But this is only a tendency, and one for which many people know how to discount, so I doubt that our moral belief really is overdetermined in this way. Nor, similarly, do I believe that Woodworth's actions were overdetermined, so that he would have done just as he did even if he had been a more admirable person. I suppose one could have doubts about DeVoto's objectivity and reliability; it is obvious he dislikes Woodworth, so perhaps he would have thought him a moral loss and convinced his readers of this no matter what the man was really like. But it is more plausible that the dislike is mostly based on the same evidence that supports DeVoto's moral view of him,

and that very different evidence, at any rate, would have produced a different verdict. If so, then Woodworth's moral character is part of the explanation of DeVoto's belief about his moral character.

It is more plausible of course that serious moral opposition to slavery would have emerged in Britain, France, and the United States even if slavery hadn't been worse in the modern period than before, and worse in the United States than in Latin America, and that the American antislavery movement would have grown even if slavery had not become more oppressive as the nineteenth century progressed. But that is because these moral facts are offered as at best a partial explanation of these developments in moral opinion. And if they really *are* part of the explanation, as seems plausible, then it is also plausible that whatever effect they produced was not entirely overdetermined; that, for example, the growth of the antislavery movement in the United States would at least have been somewhat slower if slavery had been and remained less bad an institution. Here again it hardly seems "completely irrelevant" to the explanation whether or not these moral facts obtained.

It is more puzzling, I grant, to consider Harman's own example in which you see the children igniting a cat and react immediately with the thought that this is wrong. Is it true, as Harman claims, that the assumption that the children are really doing something wrong is "totally irrelevant" to any reasonable explanation of your making that judgment? Would you, for example, have reacted in just the same way, with the thought that the action is wrong, even if what they were doing *hadn't* been wrong, and could we explain your reaction equally well on this assumption? Now, there is more than one way to understand this counterfactual question, and I shall return below to a reading of it that might appear favorable to Harman's view. What I wish to point out for now is merely that there is a natural way of taking it, parallel to the way in which I have been understanding similar counterfactual questions about my own examples, on which the answer to it has to be simply: it depends. For to answer the question, I take it,[16] we must consider a situation in which what the children are doing is not wrong, but which is otherwise as much like the actual situation as possible, and then decide what your reaction would be in that situation. But since what makes their action wrong, what its wrongness *consists* in, is presumably something like its being an act of gratuitous cruelty (or, perhaps we should add, of intense cruelty, and to a helpless victim), to imagine them not doing something wrong we are going to have to imagine their action different in this respect. More cautiously and more generally, if what they are actually doing is wrong, and if moral properties are, as many writers have held, supervenient on natural ones,[17] then in order to imagine them not doing something wrong we are going to have to suppose their action different from the actual one in some of its natural features as well. So our question becomes: Even if the children had been doing something else, something just different enough not to be wrong, would you have taken them even so to be doing something wrong?

Surely there is no one answer to this question. It depends on a lot about you, including your moral views and how good you are at seeing at a glance what some children are doing. It probably depends also on a debatable moral issue; namely, just *how* different the children's action would have to be in order not to be wrong. (Is unkindness to animals, for example, also wrong?) I believe we can see how, in a case in which the answer was clearly affirmative, we might be tempted to agree with Harman that the wrongness of the action was no part of the explanation of your reaction. For suppose you are like this. You hate children. What you especially hate, moreover, is the sight of children enjoying themselves; so much so that whenever you see children having fun, you immediately assume they are up to no good. The more they seem to be enjoying themselves, furthermore, the readier you are to fasten on any pretext for thinking them engaged in real wickedness. Then it is true that even if the children had been engaged in some robust but innocent fun, you would have thought they were doing something wrong; and Harman is perhaps right[18] about you that the actual wrongness of the action you see is irrelevant to your thinking it wrong. This is because your reaction is due to a feature of the action that coincides only very accidentally with the ones that make it wrong.[19] But, of course, and fortunately, many people aren't like this (nor does Harman

argue that they are). It isn't true of them, in general, that if the children had been doing something similar, although different enough not to be wrong, they would still have thought the children were doing something wrong. And it isn't true either, therefore, that the wrongness of the action is irrelevant to the explanation of why they think it wrong.

Now, one might have the sense from my discussion of all these examples, but perhaps especially from my discussion of this last one, Harman's own, that I have perversely been refusing to understand his claim about the explanatory irrelevance of moral facts in the way he intends. And perhaps I have not been understanding it as he wishes. In any case, I agree, I have certainly not been understanding the crucial counterfactual question, of whether we would have drawn the same moral conclusion even if the moral facts had been different, in the way he must intend. But I am not being perverse. I believe, as I have said, that my way of taking the question is the more natural one. And, more importantly: although there is, I grant, a reading of that question on which it will always yield the answer Harman wants—namely, that a difference in the moral facts would *not* have made a difference in our judgment—I do not believe this reading can support his argument. I must now explain why.

It will help if I contrast my general approach with his. I am approaching questions about the justification of belief in the spirit of what Quine has called "epistemology naturalized" (Quine, 1969a; see also Quine 1969b). I take this to mean that we have in general no a priori way of knowing which strategies for forming and refining our beliefs are likely to take us closer to the truth. The only way we have of proceeding is to assume the approximate truth of what seems to us the best overall theory we already have of what we are like and what the world is like, and to decide in the light of *that* what strategies of research and reasoning are likely to be reliable in producing a more nearly true overall theory. One result of applying these procedures, in turn, is likely to be the refinement or perhaps even the abandonment of parts of the tentative theory with which we began.

I take Harman's approach, too, to be an instance of this one. He says we are justified in believing in those facts that we need to assume to explain why we observe what we do. But he does not think that our knowledge of this principle about justification is a priori. Furthermore, as he knows, we cannot decide whether one explanation is better than another without relying on beliefs we already have about the world. Is it really a better explanation of the vapor trail the physicist sees in the cloud chamber to suppose that a proton caused it, as Harman suggests in his example, rather than some other charged particle? Would there, for example, have been no vapor trail in the absence of that proton? There is obviously no hope of answering such questions without assuming at least the approximate truth of some quite far-reaching microphysical theory, and our knowledge of such theories is not a priori.

But my approach differs from Harman's in one crucial way. For among the beliefs in which I have enough confidence to rely on in evaluating explanations, at least at the outset, are some moral beliefs. And I have been relying on them in the following way.[20] Harman's thesis implies that the supposed moral fact of Hitler's being morally depraved is irrelevant to the explanation of Hitler's doing what he did. (For we may suppose that if it explains his doing what he did, it also helps explain, at greater remove, Harman's belief and mine in his moral depravity.) To assess this claim, we need to conceive a situation in which Hitler was *not* morally depraved and consider the question whether in that situation he would still have done what he did. My answer is that he would not, and this answer relies on a (not very controversial) moral view: that in any world at all like the actual one, only a morally depraved person could have initiated a world war, ordered the "final solution," and done any number of other things Hitler did. That is why I believe that, if Hitler hadn't been morally depraved, he wouldn't have done those things, and hence that the fact of his moral depravity is relevant to an explanation of what he did.

Harman, however, cannot want us to rely on any such moral views in answering this counterfactual question. This comes out most clearly if we return to his example of the children igniting the cat. He claims that the wrongness of this act is irrelevant to an explanation of your thinking it wrong, that you would have *thought* it wrong even if it wasn't. My reply was that in order for the action not to be wrong

it would have had to lack the feature of deliberate, intense, pointless cruelty, and that if it had differed in this way you might very well *not* have thought it wrong. I also suggested a more cautious version of this reply: that since the action is in fact wrong, and since moral properties supervene on more basic natural ones, it would have had to be different in *some* further natural respect in order not to be wrong; and that we do not know whether if it had so differed you would still have thought it wrong. Both of these replies, again, rely on moral views, the latter merely on the view that there is *something* about the natural features of the action of Harman's example that makes it wrong, the former on a more specific view as to which of these features do this.

But Harman, it is fairly clear, intends for us *not* to rely on any such moral views in evaluating his counterfactual claim. His claim is not that if the action had not been one of deliberate cruelty (or had otherwise differed in whatever way would be required to remove its wrongness), you would still have thought it wrong. It is, instead, that if the action were one of deliberate, pointless cruelty, but this *did not make it wrong*, you would still have thought it was wrong. And to return to the example of Hitler's moral character, the counterfactual claim that Harman will need in order to defend a comparable conclusion about that case is not that if Hitler had been, for example, humane and fairminded, free of nationalistic pride and racial hatred, he would still have done exactly as he did. It is, rather, that if Hitler's psychology, and anything else about his situation that could strike us as morally relevant, had been exactly as it in fact was, but this had *not constituted moral depravity*, he would still have done exactly what he did.

Now the antecedents of these two conditionals are puzzling. For one thing, both are, I believe, necessarily false. I am fairly confident, for example, that Hitler really was morally depraved;[21] and since I also accept the view that moral features **supervene** on more basic natural properties,[22] I take this to imply that there is no possible world in which Hitler has just the personality he in fact did, in just the situation he was in, but is not morally depraved. Any attempt to describe such a situation, moreover, will surely run up against the limits of our moral concepts—what Harman calls our "moral sensibility"—and this is no accident. For what Harman is asking us to do, in general, is to consider cases in which absolutely *everything* about the non-moral facts that could seem morally relevant to us, in light of whatever moral theory we accept and of the concepts required for understanding that theory, is held fixed, but in which the moral judgment that our theory yields about the case is nevertheless mistaken. So it is hardly surprising that, using that theory and those concepts, we should find it difficult to conceive in any detail what such a situation would be like. It is especially not surprising when the cases in question are as paradigmatic in light of the moral outlook we in fact have as is Harman's example or, even more so, mine of Hitler's moral character. The only way we could be wrong about this latter case (assuming we have the nonmoral facts right) would be for our whole theory to be hopelessly wrong, so radically mistaken that there could be no hope of straightening it out through adjustments from within.

But I do not believe we should conclude, as we might be tempted to,[23] that we therefore know a priori that this is not so, or that we cannot understand these conditionals that are crucial to Harman's argument. Rather, now that we have seen how we have to understand them, we should grant that they are true: that if our moral theory were somehow hopelessly mistaken, but all the nonmoral facts remained exactly as they in fact are, then, since we do *accept* that moral theory, we would still draw exactly the moral conclusions we in fact do. But we should deny that any skeptical conclusion follows from this. In particular, we should deny that it follows that moral facts play no role in explaining our moral judgments.

For consider what follows from the parallel claim about microphysics, in particular about Harman's example in which a physicist concludes from his observation of a vapor trail in a cloud chamber, and from the microphysical theory he accepts, that a free proton has passed through the chamber. The parallel claim, notice, is *not* just that if the proton had not been there the physicist would still have thought it was. This claim is implausible, for we may assume that the physicist's theory is generally correct, and it follows from that theory that if there hadn't been a proton there, then there wouldn't have been a vapor trail. But in a perfectly similar way it is implausible

that if Hitler hadn't been morally depraved we would still have thought he was: for we may assume that our moral theory also is at least roughly correct, and it follows from the most central features of that theory that if Hitler hadn't been morally depraved, he wouldn't have done what he did. The *parallel* claim about the microphysical example is, instead, that if there hadn't been a proton there, but there *had* been a vapor trail, the physicist would still have concluded that a proton was present. More precisely, to maintain a perfect parallel with Harman's claims about the moral cases, the antecedent must specify that although no proton is present, absolutely *all* the non-microphysical facts that the physicist, in light of his theory, might take to be relevant to the question of whether or not a proton is present, are exactly as in the actual case. (These macrophysical facts, as we may for convenience call them, surely include everything one would normally think of as an observable fact.) Of course, we shall be unable to imagine this without imagining that the physicist's theory is pretty badly mistaken;[24] but I believe we should grant that, if the physicist's theory were somehow this badly mistaken, but all the macrophysical facts (including all the observable facts) were held fixed, then the physicist, since he does accept that theory, would still draw all the same conclusions that he actually does. That is, this conditional claim, like Harman's parallel claim about the moral cases, is true.

But no skeptical conclusions follow; nor can Harman, since he does not intend to be a skeptic about physics, think that they do. It does not follow, in the first place, that we have any reason to think the physicist's theory *is* generally mistaken. Nor does it follow, furthermore, that the hypothesis that a proton really did pass through the cloud chamber is not part of a good explanation of the vapor trail, and hence of the physicist's thinking this has happened. This looks like a reasonable explanation, of course, only on the assumption that the physicist's theory is at least roughly true, for it is this theory that tells us, for example, what happens when charged particles pass through a supersaturated atmosphere, what other causes (if any) there might be for a similar phenomenon, and so on. But, as I say, we have not been provided with any reason for not trusting the theory to this extent.

Similarly, I conclude, we should draw no skeptical conclusions from Harman's claims about the moral cases. It is true that if our moral theory were seriously mistaken, but we still believed it, and the nonmoral facts were held fixed, we would still make just the moral judgments we do. But *this* fact by itself provides us with no reason for thinking that our moral theory is generally mistaken. Nor, again, does it imply that the fact of Hitler's really having been morally depraved forms no part of a good explanation of his doing what he did and hence, at greater remove, of our thinking him depraved. This explanation will appear reasonable, of course, only on the assumption that our accepted moral theory is at least roughly correct, for it is this theory that assures us that only a depraved person could have thought, felt, and acted as Hitler did. But, as I say, Harman's argument has provided us with no reason for not trusting our moral views to this extent, and hence with no reason for doubting that it is sometimes moral facts that explain our moral judgments.

I conclude with three comments about my argument.

1. I have tried to show that Harman's claim—that we would have held the particular moral beliefs we do even if those beliefs were untrue—admits of two readings, one of which makes it implausible, and the other of which reduces it to an application of a general skeptical strategy, a strategy which could as easily be used to produce doubt about microphysical as about moral facts. The general strategy is this. Consider any conclusion C we arrive at by relying both on some distinguishable "theory" T and on some body of evidence not being challenged, and ask whether we would have believed C even if it had been false. The plausible answer, *if* we are allowed to rely on T will often be no: for if C had been false, then (according to T) the evidence would have had to be different, and in that case we wouldn't have believed C. (I have illustrated the plausibility of this sort of reply for all my moral examples, as well as for the microphysical one.) But the skeptic of course intends us *not* to rely on T in this way, and so rephrases the question: Would we have believed C even if it were false but all the evidence had been exactly as it in fact was? Now the answer has to be yes; and the skeptic

concludes that C is doubtful. (It should be obvious how to extend this strategy to belief in other minds, or in an external world.) I am of course not convinced: I do not think answers to the rephrased question show anything interesting about what we know or justifiably believe. But it is enough for my purposes here that no such *general* skeptical strategy could pretend to reveal any problems peculiar to belief in *moral* facts.

2. My conclusion about Harman's argument, although it is not exactly the same, is nevertheless similar to and very much in the spirit of the Duhemian point I invoked earlier against verificationism. There the question was whether typical moral assertions have testable implications, and the answer was that they do, so long as you include additional moral assumptions of the right sort among the background theories on which you rely in evaluating these assertions. Harman's more important question is whether we should ever regard moral facts as relevant to the explanation of nonmoral facts, and in particular of our having the moral beliefs we do. But the answer, again, is that we should, so long as we are willing to hold the right sorts of *other* moral assumptions fixed in answering counterfactual questions. Neither answer shows morality to be on any shakier ground than, say, physics, for typical microphysical hypotheses, too, have testable implications, and appear relevant to explanations, only if we are willing to assume at least the approximate truth of an elaborate microphysical theory and to hold this assumption fixed in answering counterfactual questions.

3. Of course, this picture of how explanations depend on background theories, and moral explanations in particular on moral background theories, does show why someone already tempted toward moral skepticism on other grounds (such as those I mentioned at the beginning of this essay) might find Harman's claim about moral explanations plausible. To the extent that you already have pervasive doubts about moral theories, you will also find moral facts nonexplanatory. So I grant that Harman has located a natural symptom of moral skepticism; but I am sure he has neither traced this skepticism to its roots nor provided any independent argument for it. His claim (p. 22) that we do not *in fact* cite moral facts in explanation of moral beliefs and observations cannot provide such an argument, for that claim is false. So, too, is the claim that assumptions about moral facts seem irrelevant to such explanations, for many do not. The claim that we *should* not rely on such assumptions because they *are* irrelevant, on the other hand, unless it is supported by some independent argument for moral skepticism, will just be question-begging: for the principal test of whether they are relevant, in any situation in which it appears they might be, is a counterfactual question about what would have happened if the moral fact had not obtained, and how we answer that question depends precisely upon whether we *do* rely on moral assumptions in answering it.

My own view I stated at the outset: that the only argument for moral skepticism with any independent weight is the argument from the difficulty of settling disputed moral questions. I have shown that anyone who finds Harman's claim about moral explanations plausible must already have been tempted toward skepticism by some other considerations, and I suspect that the other considerations will typically be the ones I sketched. So that is where discussion should focus. I also suggested that those considerations may provide less support for moral skepticism than is sometimes supposed, but I must reserve a thorough defense of that thesis for another occasion.[25]

NOTES

1. As, for example, in Gewirth (1960), in which there are some useful remarks about the first of them.
2. Harman's title for the entire first section of his book.
3. In the longer article of which this is an abridgement.
4. This point is generally credited to Pierre Duhem (1906, 1954). It is a prominent theme in the influential writings of W. V. O. Quine. For an especially clear application of it, see Putnam (1977).
5. See note 3.
6. Harman is careful always to say only that moral beliefs *appear* to play no such role, and since he eventually concludes that there *are* moral facts (p. 132), this caution may be more than stylistic.

I shall argue that this more cautious claim, too, is mistaken (indeed, that is my central thesis). But to avoid issues about Harman's intent, I shall simply mean by "Harman's argument" the skeptical argument of his first two chapters, whether or not he means to endorse all of it. This argument surely deserves discussion in its own right in either case, especially since Harman never explains what is wrong with it.

7. He asks: "Can moral principles be tested in the same way [as scientific hypotheses can], out in the world? You can observe someone do something, but can you ever perceive the rightness or wrongness of what he does?" (p. 790 in this book).
8. The other is that Harman appears to use "observe" (and "perceive" and "see") in a surprising way. One would normally take observing (or perceiving, or seeing) something to involve *knowing* it was the case. But Harman apparently takes an observation to be *any* opinion arrived at as "a direct result of perception" (p. 5) or, at any rate (see next note), "immediately and without conscious reasoning" (p. 7). This means that observations need not even be true, much less known to be true. A consequence is that the existence of moral observations, in Harman's sense, would not be sufficient to show that there is moral knowledge, although this *would* be sufficient if "observe" were being used in a more standard sense. What I argue in the text is that the existence of moral observations (in either Harman's or the standard sense) is not *necessary* for showing that there is moral knowledge, either.
9. This sort of case does not meet Harman's characterization of an observation as an opinion that is "a direct result of perception" (p. 5), but he is surely right that moral facts would be as well vindicated if they were needed to explain our drawing conclusions about hypothetical cases as they would be if they were needed to explain observations in the narrower sense. To be sure, Harman is still confining his attention to cases in which we draw the moral conclusion from our thought experiment "immediately and without conscious reasoning" (p. 7) and it is no doubt the existence of such cases that gives purchase to talk of a "moral sense." But this feature, again, can hardly matter to the argument: would belief in moral facts be less justified if they were needed only to explain the instances in which we draw the moral conclusion *slowly*? Nor can it make any difference for that matter

whether the case we are reflecting on is hypothetical: so my example in which we, quickly or slowly, draw a moral conclusion about Hitler from what we know of him, is surely relevant.

10. In the longer paper from which this is abridged. The salient point is that there are two very *different* reasons one might have for thinking that no reference to moral facts is needed in the explanation of moral beliefs. One—Harman's reason, and my target in this essay—is that no moral explanations even *seem* plausible, that reference to moral facts always strikes us as "completely irrelevant" to the explanation of moral beliefs. This claim, if true, would tend to support moral skepticism. The other, which might appeal to a "reductive" naturalist in ethics, is that any moral explanations that *do* seem plausible can be paraphrased without explanatory loss in entirely nonmoral terms. I doubt this view, too, and I argue in the longer version of this selection that no ethical naturalist need hold it. But anyone tempted by it should note that it is anyway no version of moral skepticism: for what it says is that we know *so much* about ethics that we are always able to say, in entirely nonmoral terms, exactly which natural properties the moral terms in any plausible moral explanations refer to—that's why the moral expressions are dispensable. These two reasons should not be confused with one another.

11. It is surprising that Harman does not mention the obvious intermediate possibility, which would occur to any instrumentalist: to cite the physicist's psychological set *and* the vapor trail, but say nothing about protons or other unobservables. It is *this* explanation, as I emphasize below, that is most closely parallel to an explanation of beliefs about an external world in terms of sensory experience and psychological makeup, or of moral beliefs in terms of nonmoral facts together with our "moral sensibility."

12. DeVoto (1942), p. 426; a quotation from the notebooks of Francis Parkman. The account of the entire rescue effort is on pp. 424–44.

13. What is being explained, of course is not just why people came to think slavery wrong, but why people who were not themselves slaves or in danger of being enslaved came to think it so seriously wrong as to be intolerable. There is a much larger and longer history of people who thought it wrong but tolerable, and an even longer one of people who appear not to have got past the thought that the world would be a better place without it. See Davis (1966).

14. For a version of what I am calling the standard view of slavery in the Americas, see Tannenbaum (1947). For an argument against both halves of the standard view, see Davis (1966), esp. pp. 60–61, 223–25, 262–63.

15. This counterfactual test requires qualification, but none of the plausible qualifications matters to my examples. See the longer version of this essay, and also my "Harman on Moral Explanations of Natural Facts," *The Southern Journal of Philosophy* 24 (1986), Supplementary Issue.

16. Following, informally, Stalnaker and Lewis on counterfactuals. See Stalnaker (1968) and Lewis (1973).

17. What would be generally granted is just that if there are moral properties they supervene on natural properties. But, remember, we are assuming for the sake of argument that there are.

I think that moral properties are natural properties; and from this view it of course follows trivially that they supervene on natural properties: that, necessarily, nothing could differ in its moral properties without differing in some natural respect. But I also accept the more interesting thesis usually intended by the claim about supervenience—that there are more basic natural features such that, necessarily, once they are fixed, so are the moral properties. (In supervening on more basic natural facts of some sort, moral facts are like most natural facts. Social facts like unemployment, for example, supervene on complex histories of many individuals and their relations; and facts about the existence and properties of macroscopic physical objects—colliding billiard balls, say—clearly supervene on the microphysical constitution of the situations that include them.)

18. Not certainly right, because there is still the possibility that your reaction is to some extent overdetermined, and is to be explained partly by your sympathy for the cat and your dislike of cruelty, as well as by your hatred for children (although this last alone would have been sufficient to produce it).

We could of course rule out this possibility by making you an even less attractive character, indifferent to the suffering of animals and not offended by cruelty. But it may then be hard to imagine that such a person (whom I shall cease calling "you") could retain enough of a grip on moral thought for us to be willing to say he thought the action wrong, as opposed to saying that he merely pretended to do so. This difficulty is perhaps not unsuperable, but it is revealing. Harman says that the actual wrongness of the action is "completely irrelevant" to the explanation of the observer's reaction. Notice that what is in fact true, however, is that it is very hard to imagine someone who reacts in the way Harman describes, but whose reaction is not due, at least in part, to the actual wrongness of the action.

19. Perhaps deliberate cruelty is worse the more one enjoys it (a standard counterexample to hedonism). If so, the fact that the children are enjoying themselves makes their action worse, but presumably isn't what makes it wrong to begin with.

20. Harman of course allows us to assume the moral facts whose explanatory relevance is being assessed: that Hitler was depraved, or that what the children in his example are doing is wrong. But I have been assuming something more—something about what depravity is, and about what makes the children's action wrong. (At a minimum, in the more cautious version of my argument, I have been assuming that something about its more basic features makes it wrong, so that it could not have differed in its moral quality without differing in those other features as well.)

21. And anyway, remember, this is the sort of fact Harman allows us to assume in order to see whether, if we assume it, it will look explanatory.

22. It is about here that I have several times encountered the objection: but surely supervenient properties aren't needed to explain anything. It is a little hard, however, to see just what this objection is supposed to come to. If it includes endorsement of the conditional I here attribute to Harman, then I believe the remainder of my discussion is an adequate reply to it. If it is the claim that, because moral properties are supervenient, we can always exploit the insights in any moral explanations, however plausible, without resort to moral language, then I have already dealt with it in my discussion of reductionism (see note 10, above): the claim is probably false, but even if it is true it is no support for Harman's view, which is not that moral explanations are plausible but reducible, but that they are totally implausible. And doubts about the causal efficacy of supervenient facts seem misplaced in any case, as attention to my earlier examples (note 17) illustrates. High unemployment causes widespread hardship, and can also bring down the rate of inflation. The masses and velocities of two colliding billiard balls causally influence

the subsequent trajectories of the two balls. There is no doubt some sense in which these facts are causally efficacious in virtue of the way they supervene on—that is, are constituted out of, or causally realized by—more basic facts, but this hardly shows them inefficacious. (Nor does Harman appear to think it does: for his favored explanation of your moral belief about the burning cat, recall, appeals to psychological facts (about your moral sensibility), a biological fact (that it's a cat), and macrophysical facts (that it's on fire)—supervenient facts all, on his physicalist view and mine.) If anyone does hold to a general suspicion of causation by supervenient facts and properties, however, as Jaegwon Kim appears to (1979, pp. 47–48), it is enough to note that this suspicion cannot diagnose any special difficulty with *moral* explanations, any distinctive "problem with ethics." The "problem," arguably, will be with every discipline but fundamental physics.

23. And as I take it Philippa Foot (1978), for example, is still prepared to do, at least about paradigmatic cases.

24. If we imagine the physicist *regularly* mistaken in this way, moreover, we will have to imagine his theory not just mistaken but hopelessly so. And we can easily reproduce the other notable feature of Harman's claims about the moral cases, that what we are imagining is *necessarily* false, if we suppose that one of the physicist's (or better, chemist's) conclusions is about the microstructure of some common substance, such as water. For I agree with Saul Kripke that whatever microstructure water has is essential to it, that it has this structure in every possible world in which it exists. (Kripke, 1980, pp. 115–44.) If we are right (as we have every reason to suppose) in thinking that water is actually H_2O, therefore, the conditional, "If water were not H_2O, but all the observable, macrophysical facts were just as they actually are, chemists would still have come to *think* it was H_2O," has a necessarily false antecedent; just as, if we are right (as we also have good reason to suppose) in thinking that Hitler was actually morally depraved, the conditional, "If Hitler were just as he was in all natural respects, but not morally depraved, we would still have *thought* he was depraved," has a necessarily false antecedent. Of course, I am not suggesting that in either case our knowledge that the antecedent is false is a priori.

These counterfactuals, because of their impossible antecedents, will have to be interpreted over worlds that are (at best) only "epistemically" possible; and, as Richard Boyd has pointed out to me, this helps to explain why anyone who accepts a causal theory of knowledge (or any theory according to which the justification of our beliefs depends on what explains our holding them) will find their truth irrelevant to the question of how much we know, either in chemistry or in morals. For although there certainly are counterfactuals that are relevant to questions about what causes what (and, hence, about what explains what), these have to be counterfactuals about real possibilities, not merely epistemic ones.

25. This essay has benefited from helpful discussion of earlier versions read at the University of Virginia, Cornell University, Franklin and Marshall College, Wayne State University, and the University of Michigan. I have been aided by a useful correspondence with Gilbert Harman; and I am grateful also for specific comments from Richard Boyd, David Brink, David Copp, Stephen Darwall, Terence Irwin, Norman Kretzmann, Ronald Nash, Peter Railton, Bruce Russell, Sydney Shoemaker, and Judith Slein.

REFERENCES

Davis, David Brion. 1966. *The Problem of Slavery in Western Culture*. Ithaca, N.Y.: Cornell University Press.

DeVoto, Bernard. 1942. *The Year of Decision: 1846*. Boston: Houghton Mifflin.

Duhem, Pierre. 1906. *The Aim and Structure of Physical Theory*, translated by Philip P. Wiener (1954). Princeton, N.J.: Princeton University Press.

Foot, Philippa. 1978. *Moral Relativism*. The Lindley Lecture, The University of Kansas, Lawrence.

Gewirth, Alan. 1960. "Positive 'Ethics' and Normative 'Science'." *The Philosophical Review* 69, 311–30.

Harman, Gilbert. 1977. *The Nature of Morality: An Introduction to Ethics*. New York: Oxford University Press.

Kim, Jaegwon. 1979. "Causality, Identity and Supervenience in the Mind-Body Problem," in Peter A. French, Theodore E. Uehling, Jr., and Howard K. Wettstein, eds., *Midwest Studies in Philosophy 4, Studies in Metaphysics*, pp. 31–49. Minneapolis: University of Minnesota Press.

Kripke, Saul. 1980. *Naming and Necessity*. Cambridge: Harvard University Press.

Lewis, David. 1973. *Counterfactuals*. Cambridge: Harvard University Press.

Mackie, J. L. 1977. *Ethics: Inventing Right and Wrong*. Harmondsworth, England: Penguin.

Putnam, Hilary. 1977. "The 'Corroboration' of Theories," in *Mathematics, Matter and Method, Philosophical Papers, Volume I*, 2d ed., pp. 250–69. Cambridge: Cambridge University Press.

Quine, W. V. O. 1969a. "Epistemology Naturalized," in *Ontological Relativity and Other Essays*, pp. 69–90. New York: Columbia University Press.

———. 1969b. "Natural Kinds," in *Ontological Relativity and Other Essays*, pp. 114–38. New York: Columbia University Press.

Stalnaker, Robert. 1968. "A Theory of Conditionals," in Nicholas Rescher, ed., *Studies in Logical Theory*. APQ Monograph No. 2. Oxford: Basil Blackwell.

Tannenbaum, Frank. 1947. *Slave and Citizen*. New York: Alfred A. Knopf.

KEY TERMS

A priori
Verificationist
Supervene

STUDY QUESTIONS

1. How does Sturgeon use the case of DeVoto to argue that there are genuine moral explanations? Are you convinced?

2. According to Sturgeon, how do explanations depend on background theories?

3. What does Sturgeon think is wrong with the counterfactual question, "Would you have reacted in just the same way [to seeing the children igniting the cat] with the thought that the action is wrong, even if what they were doing *hadn't* been wrong"?

4. How does Sturgeon argue that if a skeptical conclusion follows in the moral case, one should also follow in the scientific case, and hence that Harman should not think the skeptical conclusion follows in the moral case?

PART VI

EXISTENTIAL ISSUES

INTRODUCTION

From what perspective is it appropriate to view life and to evaluate it? Thomas Nagel invokes a distinction between perspectives to illuminate various phenomena, including central questions about meaning and value. For Nagel, it is crucial to distinguish the "subjective" perspective, from which we actually live our lives, from relatively more "objective" perspectives (involving increasing abstraction from our actual circumstances). Nagel argues that human beings are unique in possessing the capacity to take both a subjective and an objective perspective, and in his philosophy overall he invokes the distinction between subjective and objective perspectives to shed light on such phenomena as the mind, morality, death, free will, and the meaning of life. In "The Absurd," Nagel argues that absurdity issues from our capacity to take both perspectives, together with our inability to reconcile them or reduce one to the other. On Nagel's view, our lives can possess distinctive meaning precisely because we are capable of taking an objective perspective as well as a subjective perspective, but this very capacity also makes our lives absurd. Absurdity, it might be said, is the flip side of meaning. The life of a human being can be meaningful in a way an ant's life cannot be, but our lives can also be absurd in a way in which an ant's life cannot be.

Albert Camus and Richard Taylor discuss the famous Greek myth of Sisyphus, who was condemned by the gods to roll a rock to the top of a mountain endlessly. When the rock gets to the top, it falls to the bottom, ready to be pushed up again. The questions both Camus and Taylor raise are: Exactly what makes Sisyphus's life meaningless, if indeed we agree that it is meaningless? What needs to be *added* to such a life—the life of endlessly rolling a rock up a hill—to make it meaningful in the distinctive way a human life can be meaningful? How exactly is Sisyphus's life relevantly different from our human lives?

In "The Meanings of Lives," Susan Wolf distinguishes the question of "the meaning of life" from questions about the "meaningfulness of lives." Wolf finds the first question either unintelligible or simply not worth dwelling on; in contrast, she focuses on the second question. Her proposal for a general answer to the second question can be crystallized as follows: "A meaningful life is one that is actively and at least somewhat successfully engaged in a project (or projects) of positive value." Wolf builds on Nagel's distinction between the subjective and objective perspectives, but whereas Nagel believes that meaningfulness in life somehow issues from the irreconcilable conflict between the perspectives, Wolf argues that it comes from the *intersection* of the subjective and objective perspectives. On her view, the subjective perspective provides the "engagement," but it is not enough (for the relevant notion of meaningfulness) that an agent is actively engaged in a project; the project must be objectively meaningful. Thus, on Wolf's view, meaningfulness is found at the intersection of subjective and objective value.

Of course, there are many sources of meaning in our lives. In "Love and Death," Dan Moller considers one of these sources: our romantic relationships. Such relationships often add a great deal of meaning to our lives, leading us to feel important, and irreplaceable, and as though we're necessary for another person's going on. Moller gives us reason to doubt these feelings, though. Particularly, Moller adduces evidence from psychology that shows people are surprisingly resilient; though they suffer an initial trauma upon losing a loved one, they "quickly recover from loss and manifest little long-term distress." This raises worries about whether we are in fact as important as we take ourselves to be. Moller's essay explores these worries.

Perhaps Moller's worries wouldn't arise if we didn't die. And perhaps then our lives would be more meaningful. Alas, in the long run this might not make things any better. Many—although certainly not all—philosophers have thought that our lives' being meaningful depends on their being finite, and thus, on death. Thomas Nagel's paper, "Death," raises many of the fundamental questions pertaining to death. (Some of these questions can be traced back to the ancient Greek philosopher Epicurus and his Roman follower, Lucretius). Some of the most puzzling and important questions are as follows: How can death be a bad thing (a misfortune or perhaps a "harm") for the individual who dies, given that the individual no longer exists (and thus, by hypothesis, is not the subject of possible experiences)? Can something be genuinely bad for an individual, if it is not— and cannot be—experienced as bad by the individual? If death is bad for an individual, who exactly is the subject of the misfortune, and when does the misfortune take place? If death is indeed (or can be) bad for the individual who dies, why wouldn't prenatal nonexistence also be bad for the individual, given the apparent symmetry between prenatal and posthumous nonexistence? That is, if it is rational to regret that one dies when one actually dies, rather than later, why wouldn't it be equally rational to regret that one was born when one actually was born, rather than earlier? In their essay "Why Is Death Bad?" Anthony L. Brueckner and John Martin Fischer attempt to answer some of these questions. Specifically, they offer an account of why death, but not prenatal nonexistence, is a bad thing for the agent. And if Brueckner and Fischer are correct in thinking that death is a bad thing for the individual who dies, might immortality (embodied infinitely long life) be desirable?

The Myth of Sisyphus

ALBERT CAMUS

Albert Camus (1913–1960) was a French author and philosopher who was largely concerned with the idea of the Absurd. Camus received the Nobel Prize for Literature in 1957. His works include *The Stranger*, *The Fall*, and *The Myth of Sisyphus*.

. .

THE gods had condemned Sisyphus to cease-lessly rolling a rock to the top of a mountain, whence the stone would fall back of its own weight. They had thought with some reason that there is no more dreadful punishment than futile and hopeless labour.

If one believes Homer, Sisyphus was the wisest and most prudent of mortals. According to another tradition, however, he was disposed to practise the profession of highwayman. I see no contradiction in this. Opinions differ as to the reasons why he became the futile labourer of the underworld. To begin with, he is accused of a certain levity in regard to the gods. He stole their secrets. Aegina, the daughter of Aesopus, was carried off by Jupiter. The father was shocked by that disappearance and complained to Sisyphus. He, who knew of the abduction, offered to tell about it on condition that Aesopus would give water to the citadel of Corinth. To the celestial thunderbolts he preferred the benediction of water. He was punished for this in the underworld. Homer tells us also that Sisyphus had put Death in chains. Pluto could not endure the sight of his deserted, silent empire. He dispatched the god of war who liberated Death from the hands of her conqueror.

It is said also that Sisyphus, being near to death, rashly wanted to test his wife's love. He ordered her to cast his unburied body into the middle of the public square. Sisyphus woke up in the underworld.

And there, annoyed by an obedience so contrary to human love, he obtained from Pluto permission to return to earth in order to chastise his wife. But when he had seen again the face of this world, enjoyed water and sun, warm stones and the sea, he no longer wanted to go back to the infernal darkness. Recalls, signs of anger, warnings were of no avail. Many years more, he lived facing the curve of the gulf, the sparkling sea, and the smiles of earth. A decree of the gods was necessary. Mercury came and seized the impudent man by the collar and, snatching him from his joys, led him forcibly back to the underworld where his rock was ready for him.

You have already grasped that Sisyphus is the absurd hero. He *is*, as much through his passions as through his torture. His scorn of the gods, his hatred of death, and his passion for life won him that unspeakable penalty in which the whole being is exerted towards accomplishing nothing. This is the price that must be paid for the passions of this earth. Nothing is told us about Sisyphus in the underworld. Myths are made for the imagination to breathe life into them. As for this myth, one sees merely the whole effort of a body straining to raise the huge stone, to roll it and push it up a slope a hundred times over; one sees the face screwed up, the cheek tight against the stone, the shoulder bracing the clay-covered mass, the foot wedging it, the fresh start with arms outstretched, the wholly human security of two earth-clotted hands. At the very end of his long effort measured by skyless space and time without depth, the purpose is achieved. Then Sisyphus watches the stone rush down in a few moments towards that lower world whence he will have to push it up again towards the summit. He goes back down to the plain.

It is during that return, that pause, that Sisyphus interests me. A face that toils so close to stones is already stone itself! I see that man going back down with a heavy yet measured step towards the torment of which he will never know the end. That hour like a breathing-space which returns as surely as his suffering, that is the hour of consciousness. At each of those moments when he leaves the heights and gradually sinks towards the lairs of the gods, he is superior to his fate. He is stronger than his rock.

If this myth is tragic, that is because its hero is conscious. Where would his torture be, indeed, if at every step the hope of succeeding upheld him? The workman of to-day works every day in his life at the same tasks and this fate is no less absurd. But it is tragic only at the rare moments when it becomes conscious. Sisyphus, proletarian of the gods, powerless and rebellious, knows the whole extent of his wretched condition; it is what he thinks of during his descent. The lucidity that was to constitute his torture at the same time crowns his victory. There is no fate that cannot be surmounted by scorn.

If the descent is thus sometimes performed in sorrow, it can also take place in joy. This word is not too much. Again I fancy Sisyphus returning towards his rock, and the sorrow was in the beginning. When the images of earth cling too tightly to memory, when the call of happiness becomes too insistent, it happens that melancholy rises in man's heart: this is the rock's victory, this is the rock itself. The boundless grief is too heavy to bear. These are our nights of Gethsemane. But crushing truths perish from being acknowledged. Thus Oedipus at the outset obeys fate without knowing it. But from the moment he knows, his tragedy begins. Yet at the same moment, blind and desperate, he realizes that the only bond linking him to the world is the cool hand of a girl. Then a tremendous remark rings out: 'Despite so many ordeals, my advanced age and the nobility of my soul make me conclude that all is well.' Sophocles' Oedipus, like Dostoievsky's Kirilov, thus gives the recipe for the absurd victory. Ancient wisdom confirms modern heroism.

One does not discover the absurd without being tempted to write a manual of happiness. 'What! by such narrow ways . . . ?' There is but one world, however. Happiness and the absurd are two sons of the same earth. They are inseparable. It would be a mistake to say that happiness necessarily springs from the absurd discovery. It happens as well that the feeling of the absurd springs from happiness. 'I conclude that all is well,' says Oedipus, and that remark is sacred. It echoes in the wild and limited universe of man. It teaches that all is not, has not been, exhausted. It drives out of this world a god who had come into it with dissatisfaction and a preference for futile sufferings. It makes of fate a human matter, which must be settled among men.

All Sisyphus' silent joy is contained therein. His fate belongs to him. His rock is his thing. Likewise, the absurd man, when he contemplates his torment, silences all the idols. In the universe suddenly restored to its silence, the myriad wondering little voices of the earth rise up. Unconscious, secret calls, invitations from all the faces, they are the necessary reverse and price of victory. There is no sun without shadow, and it is essential to know the night. The absurd man says yes and his effort will henceforth be unceasing. If there is a personal fate, there is no higher destiny or at least there is but one which he concludes is inevitable and despicable. For the rest, he knows himself to be the master of his days. At that subtle moment when man glances backward over his life, Sisyphus returning towards his rock, in that slight pivoting, he contemplates that series of unrelated actions which becomes his fate, created by him, combined under his memory's eye and soon sealed by his death. Thus, convinced of the wholly human origin of all that is human, a blind man eager to see who knows that the night has no end, he is still on the go. The rock is still rolling.

I leave Sisyphus at the foot of the mountain! One always finds one's burden again. But Sisyphus teaches the higher fidelity that negates the gods and raises rocks. He, too, concludes that all is well. This universe henceforth without a master seems to him neither sterile nor futile. Each atom of that stone, each mineral flake of that night-filled mountain, in itself forms a world. The struggle itself towards the heights is enough to fill a man's heart. One must imagine Sisyphus happy.

STUDY QUESTIONS

1. What is it about Sisyphus's punishment that makes it seem like such a meaningless task?
2. What importance does Camus place on the fact that Sisyphus is consciously aware of the absurdity of his plight?

3. Do you think that Sisyphus leads a meaningless life? What is the smallest change that one could make to Sisyphus's situation to turn it into a life full of meaning?

The Absurd

THOMAS NAGEL

M OST people feel on occasion that life is absurd, and some feel it vividly and continually. Yet the reasons usually offered in defense of this conviction are patently inadequate: they *could* not really explain why life is absurd. Why then do they provide a natural expression for the sense that it is?

I

Consider some examples. It is often remarked that nothing we do now will matter in a million years. But if that is true, then by the same token, nothing that will be the case in a million years matters now. In particular, it does not matter now that in a million years nothing we do now will matter. Moreover, even if what we did now *were* going to matter in a million years, how could that keep our present concerns from being absurd? If their mattering now is not enough to accomplish that, how would it help if they mattered a million years from now?

Whether what we do now will matter in a million years could make the crucial difference only if its mattering in a million years depended on its mattering, period. But then to deny that whatever happens now will matter in a million years is to beg the question

against its mattering, period; for in that sense one cannot know that it will not matter in a million years whether (for example) someone now is happy or miserable, without knowing that it does not matter, period.

What we say to convey the absurdity of our lives often has to do with space or time: we are tiny specks in the infinite vastness of the universe; our lives are mere instants even on a geological time scale, let alone a cosmic one; we will all be dead any minute. But of course none of these evident facts can be what *makes* life absurd, if it is absurd. For suppose we lived forever; would not a life that is absurd if it lasts seventy years be infinitely absurd if it lasted through eternity? And if our lives are absurd given our present size, why would they be any less absurd if we filled the universe (either because we were larger or because the universe was smaller)? Reflection on our minuteness and brevity appears to be intimately connected with the sense that life is meaningless; but it is not clear what the connection is.

Another inadequate argument is that because we are going to die, all chains of justification must leave off in mid-air: one studies and works to earn money to pay for clothing, housing, entertainment, food, to sustain oneself from year to year, perhaps to support a family and pursue a career—but to what final end? All of it is an elaborate journey leading nowhere. (One will also have some effect on other people's lives, but that simply reproduces the problem, for they will die too.)

There are several replies to this argument. First, life does not consist of a sequence of activities each of which has as its purpose some later member of the sequence. Chains of justification come repeatedly to an end within life, and whether the process as a whole can be justified has no bearing on the finality of these end-points. No further justification is needed to make it reasonable to take aspirin for a headache, attend an exhibition of the work of a painter one admires, or stop a child from putting his hand on a hot stove. No larger context or further purpose is needed to prevent these acts from being pointless.

Even if someone wished to supply a further justification for pursuing all the things in life that are commonly regarded as self-justifying, that justification would have to end somewhere too. If *nothing* can justify unless it is justified in terms of something outside itself, which is also justified, then an infinite regress results, and no chain of justification can be complete. Moreover, if a finite chain of reasons cannot justify anything, what could be accomplished by an infinite chain, each link of which must be justified by something outside itself?

Since justifications must come to an end somewhere, nothing is gained by denying that they end where they appear to, within life—or by trying to subsume the multiple, often trivial ordinary justifications of action under a single, controlling life scheme. We can be satisfied more easily than that. In fact, through its misrepresentation of the process of justification, the argument makes a vacuous demand. It insists that the reasons available within life are incomplete, but suggests thereby that all reasons that come to an end are incomplete. This makes it impossible to supply any reasons at all.

The standard arguments for absurdity appear therefore to fail as arguments. Yet I believe they attempt to express something that is difficult to state, but fundamentally correct.

II

In ordinary life a situation is absurd when it includes a conspicuous discrepancy between pretension or aspiration and reality: someone gives a complicated speech in support of a motion that has already been passed; a notorious criminal is made president of a major philanthropic foundation; you declare your love over the telephone to a recorded announcement; as you are being knighted, your pants fall down.

When a person finds himself in an absurd situation, he will usually attempt to change it, by modifying his aspirations, or by trying to bring reality into better accord with them, or by removing himself from the situation entirely. We are not always willing or able to extricate ourselves from a position whose absurdity has become clear to us. Nevertheless, it is usually possible to imagine some change that would remove the absurdity—whether or not we can or will implement it. The sense that life as a whole is absurd arises when we perceive, perhaps dimly, an inflated pretension or aspiration which is inseparable from the continuation of human life and which makes its absurdity inescapable, short of escape from life itself.

Many people's lives are absurd, temporarily or permanently, for conventional reasons having to do with their particular ambitions, circumstances, and personal relations. If there is a philosophical sense of absurdity, however, it must arise from the perception of something universal—some respect in which pretension and reality inevitably clash for us all. This condition is supplied, I shall argue, by the collision between the seriousness with which we take our lives and the perpetual possibility of regarding everything about which we are serious as arbitrary, or open to doubt.

We cannot live human lives without energy and attention, nor without making choices which show that we take some things more seriously than others. Yet we have always available a point of view outside the particular form of our lives, from which the seriousness appears gratuitous. These two inescapable viewpoints collide in us, and that is what makes life absurd. It is absurd because we ignore the doubts that we know cannot be settled, continuing to live with nearly undiminished seriousness in spite of them.

This analysis requires defense in two respects: first as regards the unavoidability of seriousness; second as regards the inescapability of doubt.

We take ourselves seriously whether we lead serious lives or not and whether we are concerned primarily with fame, pleasure, virtues, luxury, triumph, beauty, justice, knowledge, salvation, or mere survival. If we take other people seriously and devote ourselves to them, that only multiplies the problem. Human life is full of effort, plans, calculation, success and failure: we *pursue* our lives, with varying degrees of sloth and energy.

It would be different if we could not step back and reflect on the process, but were merely led from impulse to impulse without self-consciousness. But human beings do not act solely on impulse. They are prudent, they reflect, they weigh consequences, they ask whether what they are doing is worthwhile. Not only are their lives full of particular choices that hang together in larger activities with temporal structure: they also decide in the broadest terms what to pursue and what to avoid, what the priorities among their various aims should be, and what kind of people they want to be or become. Some men are faced with such choices by the large decisions they make from time to time; some merely by reflection on the course their lives are taking as the product of countless small decisions. They decide whom to marry, what profession to follow, whether to join the Country Club, or the Resistance; or they may just wonder why they go on being salesmen or academics or taxi drivers, and then stop thinking about it after a certain period of inconclusive reflection.

Although they may be motivated from act to act by those immediate needs with which life presents them, they allow the process to continue by adhering to the general system of habits and the form of life in which such motives have their place—or perhaps only by clinging to life itself. They spend enormous quantities of energy, risk, and calculation on the details. Think of how an ordinary individual sweats over his appearance, his health, his sex life, his emotional honesty, his social utility, his self-knowledge, the quality of his ties with family, colleagues, and friends, how well he does his job, whether he understands the world and what is going on in it. Leading a human life is a full-time occupation, to which everyone devotes decades of intense concern.

This fact is so obvious that it is hard to find it extraordinary and important. Each of us lives his own life—lives with himself twenty-four hours a day. What else is he supposed to do—live someone else's life? Yet humans have the special capacity to step back and survey themselves, and the lives to which they are committed, with that detached amazement which comes from watching an ant struggle up a heap of sand. Without developing the illusion that they are able to escape from their highly specific and idiosyncratic position, they can view it **sub specie aeternitatis**—and the view is at once sobering and comical.

The crucial backward step is not taken by asking for still another justification in the chain, and failing to get it. The objections to that line of attack have already been stated; justifications come to an end. But this is precisely what provides universal doubt with its object. We step back to find that the whole system of justification and criticism, which controls our choices and supports our claims to rationality, rests on responses and habits that we never question, that we should not know how to defend without circularity, and to which we shall continue to adhere even after they are called into question.

The things we do or want without reasons, and without requiring reasons—the things that define what is a reason for us and what is not—are the starting points of our skepticism. We see ourselves from outside, and all the contingency and specificity of our aims and pursuits become clear. Yet when we take this view and recognize what we do as arbitrary, it does not disengage us from life, and there lies our absurdity: not in the fact that such an external view can be taken of us, but in the fact that we ourselves can take it, without ceasing to be the persons whose ultimate concerns are so coolly regarded.

III

One may try to escape the position by seeking broader ultimate concerns, from which it is impossible to step back—the idea being that absurdity results because what we take seriously is something small and insignificant and individual. Those seeking to supply their lives with meaning usually envision a role or function in something larger than themselves. They therefore seek fulfillment in service to society, the state, the revolution, the progress of history, the advance of science, or religion and the glory of God.

But a role in some larger enterprise cannot confer significance unless that enterprise is itself significant. And its significance must come back to what we can understand, or it will not even appear to give us what we are seeking. If we learned that we were being raised to provide food for other creatures fond of human flesh, who planned to turn us into cutlets before we got too stringy—even if we learned that the human race had been developed by animal breeders precisely for this purpose—that would still not give our lives meaning, for two reasons. First, we would still be in the dark as to the significance of the lives of those other beings; second, although we might acknowledge that this culinary role would make our lives meaningful to them, it is not clear how it would make them meaningful to us.

Admittedly, the usual form of service to a higher being is different from this. One is supposed to behold and partake of the glory of God, for example, in a way in which chickens do not share in the glory of coq au vin. The same is true of service to a state, a movement, or a revolution. People can come to feel, when they are part of something bigger, that it is part of them too. They worry less about what is peculiar to themselves, but identify enough with the larger enterprise to find their role in it fulfilling.

However, any such larger purpose can be put in doubt in the same way that the aims of an individual life can be, and for the same reasons. It is as legitimate to find ultimate justification there as to find it earlier, among the details of individual life. But this does not alter the fact that justifications come to an end when we are content to have them end—when we do not find it necessary to look any further. If we can step back from the purposes of individual life and doubt their point, we can step back also from the progress of human history, or of science, or the success of a society, or the kingdom, power, and glory of God, and put all these things into question in the same way. What seems to us to confer meaning, justification, significance, does so

in virtue of the fact that we need no more reasons after a certain point.

What makes doubt inescapable with regard to the limited aims of individual life also makes it inescapable with regard to any larger purpose that encourages the sense that life is meaningful. Once the fundamental doubt has begun, it cannot be laid to rest.

Camus maintains in *The Myth of Sisyphus* that the absurd arises because the world fails to meet our demands for meaning. This suggests that the world might satisfy those demands if it were different. But now we can see that this is not the case. There does not appear to be any conceivable world (containing us) about which unsettlable doubts could not arise. Consequently the absurdity of our situation derives not from a collison between our expectations and the world, but from a collision within ourselves.

IV

It may be objected that the standpoint from which these doubts are supposed to be felt does not exist—that if we take the recommended backward step we will land on thin air, without any basis for judgment about the natural responses we are supposed to be surveying. If we retain our usual standards of what is important, then questions about the significance of what we are doing with our lives will be answerable in the usual way. But if we do not, then those questions can mean nothing to us, since there is no longer any content to the idea of what matters, and hence no content to the idea that nothing does.

But this objection misconceives the nature of the backward step. It is not supposed to give us an understanding of what is *really* important, so that we see by contrast that our lives are insignificant. We never, in the course of these reflections, abandon the ordinary standards that guide our lives. We merely observe them in operation, and recognize that if they are called into question we can justify them only by reference to themselves, uselessly. We adhere to them because of the way we are put together; what seems to us important or serious or valuable would not seem so if we were differently constituted.

In ordinary life, to be sure, we do not judge a situation absurd unless we have in mind some standards of seriousness, significance, or harmony with which the absurd can be contrasted. This contrast is not implied by the philosophical judgment of absurdity, and that might be thought to make the concept unsuitable for the expression of such judgments. This is not so, however, for the philosophical judgment depends on another contrast which makes it a natural extension from more ordinary cases. It departs from them only in contrasting the pretensions of life with a larger context in which *no* standards can be discovered, rather than with a context from which alternative, overriding standards may be applied.

V

In this respect, as in others, philosophical perception of the absurd resembles epistemological **skepticism**. In both cases the final, philosophical doubt is not contrasted with any unchallenged certainties, though it is arrived at by extrapolation from examples of doubt within the system of evidence or justification, where a contrast with other certainties *is* implied. In both cases our limitedness joins with a capacity to transcend those limitations in thought (thus seeing them as limitations, and as inescapable).

Skepticism begins when we include ourselves in the world about which we claim knowledge. We notice that certain types of evidence convince us, that we are content to allow justifications of belief to come to an end at certain points, that we feel we know many things even without knowing or having grounds for believing the denial of others which, if true, would make what we claim to know false.

For example, I know that I am looking at a piece of paper, although I have no adequate grounds for claiming I know that I am not dreaming; and if I am dreaming then I am not looking at a piece of paper. Here an ordinary conception of how appearance may diverge from reality is employed to show that we take our world largely for granted; the certainty that we are not dreaming cannot be justified except circularly, in terms of those very appearances which

are being put in doubt. It is somewhat far-fetched to suggest I may be dreaming; but the possibility is only illustrative. It reveals that our claims to knowledge depend on our not feeling it necessary to exclude certain incompatible alternatives, and the dreaming possibility or the total-hallucination possibility are just representatives for limitless possibilities most of which we cannot even conceive.[1]

Once we have taken the backward step to an abstract view of our whole system of beliefs, evidence, and justification, and seen that it works only, despite its pretensions, by taking the world largely for granted, we are *not* in a position to contrast all these appearances with an alternative reality. We cannot shed our ordinary responses, and if we could it would leave us with no means of conceiving a reality of any kind.

It is the same in the practical domain. We do not step outside our lives to a new vantage point from which we see what is really, objectively significant. We continue to take life largely for granted while seeing that all our decisions and certainties are possible only because there is a great deal we do not bother to rule out.

Both epistemological skepticism and a sense of the absurd can be reached via initial doubts posed within systems of evidence and justification that we accept, and can be stated without violence to our ordinary concepts. We can ask not only why we should believe there is a floor under us, but also why we should believe the evidence of our senses at all—and at some point the framable questions will have outlasted the answers. Similarly, we can ask not only why we should take aspirin, but why we should take trouble over our own comfort at all. The fact that we shall take the aspirin without waiting for an answer to this last question does not show that it is an unreal question. We shall also continue to believe there is a floor under us without waiting for an answer to the other question. In both cases it is this unsupported natural confidence that generates skeptical doubts; so it cannot be used to settle them.

Philosophical skepticism does not cause us to abandon our ordinary beliefs, but it lends them a peculiar flavor. After acknowledging that their truth is incompatible with possibilities that we have no grounds for believing do not obtain—apart from grounds in those very beliefs which we have called into question—we return to our familiar convictions with a certain irony and resignation. Unable to abandon the natural responses on which they depend, we take them back, like a spouse who has run off with someone else and then decided to return; but we regard them differently (not that the new attitude is necessarily inferior to the old, in either case).

The same situation obtains after we have put in question the seriousness with which we take our lives and human life in general and have looked at ourselves without presuppositions. We then return to our lives, as we must, but our seriousness is laced with irony. Not that irony enables us to escape the absurd. It is useless to mutter: "Life is meaningless; life is meaningless..." as an accompaniment to everything we do. In continuing to live and work and strive, we take ourselves seriously in action no matter what we say.

What sustains us, in belief as in action, is not reason for justification, but something more basic than these—for we go on in the same way even after we are convinced that the reasons have given out.[2] If we tried to rely entirely on reason, and pressed it hard, our lives and beliefs would collapse—a form of madness that may actually occur if the inertial force of taking the world and life for granted is somehow lost. If we lose our grip on that, reason will not give it back to us.

VI

In viewing ourselves from a perspective broader than we can occupy in the flesh, we become spectators of our own lives. We cannot do very much as pure spectators of our own lives, so we continue to lead them, and devote ourselves to what we are able at the same time to view as no more than a curiosity, like the ritual of an alien religion.

This explains why the sense of absurdity finds its natural expression in those bad arguments with which the discussion began. References to our small size and short lifespan and to the fact that all of mankind will eventually vanish without a trace are metaphors for the backward step which permits us to regard ourselves from without and to find the particular form of our lives curious and slightly surprising. By feigning a nebula's-eye view, we illustrate the capacity to see ourselves without presuppositions, as arbitrary, idiosyncratic, highly specific occupants of the world, one of countless possible forms of life.

Before turning to the question whether the absurdity of our lives is something to be regretted and if possible escaped, let me consider what would have to be given up in order to avoid it.

Why is the life of a mouse not absurd? The orbit of the moon is not absurd either, but that involves no strivings or aims at all. A mouse, however, has to work to stay alive. Yet he is not absurd, because he lacks the capacities for self-consciousness and self-transcendence that would enable him to see that he is only a mouse. If that *did* happen, his life would become absurd, since self-awareness would not make him cease to be a mouse and would not enable him to rise above his mousely strivings. Bringing his new-found self-consciousness with him, he would have to return to his meager yet frantic life, full of doubts that he was unable to answer, but also full of purposes that he was unable to abandon.

Given that the transcendental step is natural to us humans, can we avoid absurdity by refusing to take that step and remaining entirely within our sublunar lives? Well, we cannot refuse consciously, for to do that we would have to be aware of the viewpoint we were refusing to adopt. The only way to avoid the relevant self-consciousness would be either never to attain it or to forget it—neither of which can be achieved by the will.

On the other hand, it is possible to expend effort on an attempt to destroy the other component of the absurd—abandoning one's earthly, individual, human life in order to identify as completely as possible with that universal viewpoint from which human life seems arbitrary and trivial. (This appears to be the ideal of certain Oriental religions.) If one succeeds, then one will not have to drag the superior awareness through a strenuous mundane life, and absurdity will be diminished.

However, insofar as this self-etiolation is the result of effort, will-power, aceticism, and so forth, it requires that one take oneself seriously as an individual—that one be willing to take considerable trouble to avoid being creaturely and absurd. Thus one may undermine the aim of unworldliness by pursuing it too vigorously. Still, if someone simply allowed his individual, animal nature to drift and respond to impulse, without making the pursuit of its needs a central conscious aim, then he might, at considerable dissociative cost, achieve a life that was less absurd than most. It would not be a meaningful life either, of course; but it would not involve the engagement of a transcendent awareness in the assiduous pursuit of mundane goals. And that is the main condition of absurdity—the dragooning of an unconvinced transcendent consciousness into the service of an immanent, limited enterprise like a human life.

The final escape is suicide; but before adopting any hasty solutions, it would be wise to consider carefully whether the absurdity of our existence truly presents us with a problem, to which some solution must be found—a way of dealing with prima facie disaster. That is certainly the attitude with which Camus approaches the issue, and it gains support from the fact that we are all eager to escape from absurd situations on a smaller scale.

Camus—not on uniformly good grounds—rejects suicide and the other solutions he regards as escapist. What he recommends is defiance or scorn. We can salvage our dignity, he appears to believe, by shaking a fist at the world which is deaf to our pleas, and continuing to live in spite of it. This will not make our lives un-absurd, but it will lend them a certain nobility.[3]

This seems to me romantic and slightly self-pitying. Our absurdity warrants neither that much distress nor that much defiance. At the risk of falling into romanticism by a different route, I would argue that absurdity is one of the most human things about us: a manifestation of our most advanced and interesting characteristics. Like skepticism in epistemology, it is possible only because we possess a certain kind of insight—the capacity to transcend ourselves in thought.

If a sense of the absurd is a way of perceiving our true situation (even though the situation is not absurd until the perception arises), then what reason can we have to resent or escape it? Like the capacity for epistemological skepticism, it results from the ability to understand our human limitations. It need not be a matter for agony unless we make it so. Nor need it evoke a defiant contempt of fate that allows us to feel brave or proud. Such dramatics, even if carried on in private, betray a failure to appreciate the cosmic unimportance of the situation. If *sub specie aeternitatis* there is no reason to believe that anything matters, then that does not matter either, and we can approach our absurd lives with irony instead of heroism or despair.

NOTES

1. I am aware that skepticism about the external world is widely thought to have been refuted, but I have remained convinced of its irrefutability since being exposed at Berkeley to Thompson Clarke's largely unpublished ideas on the subject.
2. As Hume says in a famous passage of the *Treatise*: "Most fortunately it happens, that since reason is incapable of dispelling these clouds, nature herself suffices to that purpose, and cures me of this philosophical melancholy and delirium, either by relaxing this bent of mind, or by some avocation, and lively impression of my senses, which obliterate all these chimeras. I dine, I play a game of backgammon, I converse, and am merry with my friends; and when after three or four hours' amusement, I would return to these speculations, they appear so cold, and strain'd, and ridiculous, that I cannot find in my heart to enter into them any farther" (bk. 1, pt. iv, sect. 7; Selby-Bigge edition, p. 269).
3. "Sisyphus, proletarian of the gods, powerless and rebellious, knows the whole extent of his wretched condition: it is what he thinks of during his descent. The lucidity that was to constitute his torture at the same time crowns his victory. There is no fate that cannot be surmounted by scorn" (*The Myth of Sisyphus*, trans. Justin O'Brien [New York: Vintage, 1959], p. 90; first published, Paris: Gallimard, 1942).

KEY TERMS

Sub specie aeternitatis
Skepticism

STUDY QUESTIONS

1. Nagel says that humans have the capacity to view their lives *sub specie aeternitatis*—from the point of view of eternity. When we do so, he says, what we see is both sobering and comical. In what way is the view sobering? In what way is it comical?

2. According to Nagel, many of us search for significance by seeking fulfillment in something larger than ourselves. But he argues that "some larger enterprise cannot confer significance unless that enterprise is itself significant." Is he right about this? Can you think of a counterexample?

3. Nagel argues that while human life is absurd, the life of a mouse is not. What is the difference, according to Nagel? Do you think he is right that the life of a mouse is not absurd? Why should the ability to be reflective about the world make a difference to life's meaning?

4. What would it be to approach one's life with irony, as Nagel suggests we should do?

The Meaning of Human Existence

RICHARD TAYLOR

Richard Taylor (1919–2003) was an influential American philosopher who wrote much in metaphysics and ethics. His books include *Metaphysics*, *Action and Purpose*, and *Freedom, Anarchy, and the Law*.

. .

ARTHUR Schopenhauer, in a comment on human existence that is somber even for this philosopher, wrote

It is really incredible how meaningless and void of significance when looked at from without, how dull and unenlightened by intellect when felt from within, is the course of the life of the great majority of men. It is a weary longing and complaining, a dream-like staggering through the four ages of life to death, accompanied by a series of trivial thoughts. Such men are like clockwork, which is wound up, and goes it knows not why; and every time a man is begotten and born, the clock of human life is wound up anew, to repeat the same old piece it has played innumerable times before, passage after passage, measure after measure, with insignificant variations. Every individual, every human being and his course of life, is but another short dream of the endless spirit of nature, of the persistent will to live; is only another fleeting form, which it carelessly sketches on its infinite page, space and time; allows to remain for a time so short that it vanishes into nothing in comparison with these, and then obliterates to make new room. And yet, and here lies the serious side of life, every one of these fleeting forms, these empty fancies, must be paid for by the whole will to live, in all its activity, with many and deep sufferings, and finally with a bitter death, long feared and coming at last. This is why the sight of a corpse makes us suddenly so serious.

What Schopenhauer was calling attention to here was not, of course, some malady that might be corrected by modifying the structure of government, or by a new economic order, or even by philosophical enlightenment. Nor was he claiming that human existence cannot be, at least in some cases, happy. Nor was he calling attention to the familiar evils that beset life. These themes belong to political and economic theory, or to ethics. Schopenhauer, instead, was suggesting that this meaninglessness of our existence is metaphysical, unavoidable, or part of the very nature of life. He accordingly offered no program for overcoming it.

I am going to pursue this Schopenhauerian claim, but without any special reference to Schopenhauer. I believe that his perception was basically correct, that human life, in spite of its joys and in spite of the tenacity with which we cling to it, does have the character that led Schopenhauer to deem it meaningless. I also believe, however, that this is not the final verdict on life and that, having conceded to pessimism the facts that it claims are there, we can find another, to which both philosophy and religion have hitherto given little attention, that will at least partly redeem the otherwise forlorn description.

Life and Meaning

Life is not self-authenticating, any more in a person than in an animal. That a given thing—a housefly, a horse, a man, whatever—should be living is a fact, but not as such a meaningful one; for a life just considered by itself can be quite devoid of significance. Meaningfulness does not follow automatically on the mere occurrence of a heartbeat.

Thus the efforts, so commonly made, to sustain a fading and flickering life at all costs are entirely misguided. Here the potentiality for meaning has usually evaporated, and the effort at a mere prolongation of bodily processes can only rest upon the absurd idea that life itself, as a mere fact, is something precious. The life of a breathing but comatose and dying person has no more value than does that of an expiring insect. Its meaning is gone, and, more important, its potentiality of achieving meaning is gone.

Nor does the fact that a given life is *human* automatically invest it with meaning. To be a living person may—and, indeed, certainly does—enhance the possibility of meaningfulness; but it is still only a possibility. Being human, as distinct from being

something else, such as canine, ursine, or whatever, is not by itself a quality possessed of worth. Life's meaning for a dying person lies entirely in the life that has been lived, not in anything that exists any longer, even though that person is undeniably still possessed of his or her humanity. And the same, alas, is true of many whose mundane lives are still far from over and even, sometimes, only just beginning. For, while they have the gift of life, and even the quality of personality, that is, of being *persons*, circumstances still will never allow them to give their lives the slightest meaning or, at least, any meaning that is not as easily possessed by any animal. A person's life can be long, quite free from pain, and even enjoyed and clung to, yet bereft of meaning; for the life of any animal can have all these characteristics. Still the extinction of that life can be without the slightest significance anywhere in the world, as meaningless as the autumn withering and falling of a leaf from a tree.

People want to deny this, to claim that the life of every person has exactly the same value as that of any other, as though one needed only to be born and to draw breath from one day to another to have a meaningful existence. There is a challenge in the claim that a person's life can be meaningless—the challenge, namely, to make it otherwise—and not everyone feels that he or she can rise to it. Indeed, rather few persons have a very clear idea of what they would need to do to meet that challenge. They accordingly reject the challenge by declaring, in effect, that it has already been met—met by the simple expedient of being born and continuing to draw breath!

There is, moreover, a threat in what has been said, the threat of discovering, too late, that one's own life is quite meaningless. We can all recognize the utter insignificance in the fact that a leaf withers and falls from a tree, or that a housefly perishes. It is not so easy to view our own existence in the same light, to think of our own decay as the culmination of a life that never had any significance to begin with. Our conceit forbids it.

Thus we are tempted to say, in desperation, that every individual's life is meaningful *to him* or *to her*, quite regardless of any other consideration, thinking that we have thereby made some sort of point. All this actually means, however, is that people normally cling to their lives, no matter what. Which is certainly true. There are exceptions, as in the cases of suicide, or sometimes a weariness with life that comes with very advanced age, but normally, the threat to life is regarded by anyone as supremely terrible. Who can on reflection suppose, however, that one's own or any other life can be made meaningful just by the fact of being clung to? This anxious concern for one's own being might be, and in fact clearly is, quite blind, that is, without any rational conviction of life's worth. Even animals flee from danger and try with their most desperate efforts to ward off every threat to their existence. No one can suppose that this is because they have *chosen* to, after rationally balancing life's good and evils. They still cling to life even when the balance seems clearly tipped in favor of evil, for they do so from blind impulse. And it is no different in the case of a person. One may claim, if one likes, that in our case the blessings of life do greatly outweigh its evils, which certainly seems doubtful, but whether this is true or not, it is irrelevant. For a person normally clings to existence with the same tenacity as an animal even without balancing these things or making any rational choice at all. Like any animal, a person's craving for existence, sometimes called an "instinct" for self-preservation, is the blindest, least enlightened craving there is. The most worthless things are sometimes desperately sought and grasped. Indeed, actual evils, even things destructive of what one cherishes most deeply, are sometimes fervently sought and held—in ignorance of their true nature, perhaps (perhaps not), but clung to none the less. Nothing, accordingly, can be made good or significant just by the fact of its being thus fervently grasped; and to say that every person's life is meaningful *to that person*, meaning only that every person does cling to it, is really to say nothing at all to the point.

The Image of Meaninglessness

We need, then, to get before us some clear idea of meaningfulness, to avoid entanglement in epigrams having to do with human worth and the quality of personality that are nothing more than slogans. And the best way to do this will be by creating a picture of meaninglessness. Thus, if we can portray a kind of existence that is clearly meaningless, and then see just what makes it so, we can certainly give content to the claim that human life is meaningless—for we can say that it is such, to just the extent that it resembles that picture. And then we can proceed to say what a meaningful existence would be; for life will, by these criteria, be meaningful just to the extent that these ingredients of meaninglessness are abolished. By going about things in this way, we will, it is hoped, avoid the kind of banality that characterizes so much of the discussions of questions such as these. We will not, for example, think of meaningful existence in terms of the mere attainment of ambitions and goals; for if those should happen to be of only illusory value, then whatever meaning they would appear to give to one's life would be no less illusory.

Probably no clearer image of meaninglessness can be found in literature than in the ancient myth of Sisyphus. Sisyphus, it will be recalled, was condemned by the gods to this fate: that he should roll a stone to the top of a hill, whereupon it would at once roll back down, and Sisyphus would then have the task of again rolling it to the top, and it would once more roll to the bottom, and so on, and so on throughout eternity.

This myth has always haunted men, like a bad dream that we cannot awaken from. We are moved by pity for the condemned Sisyphus, yet that is not all of it; there is something deeper to it than his suffering. We are struck by both the stupidity of what he is doing—moving a stone, the commonest and least worthwhile object on the face of the earth—and by his inability ever to stop. If it were a jewel that he were moving, or perhaps a lovely picture that he was condemned endlessly to be painting, or the infinite stars that he was to try counting, then his existence would not be quite so pathetic. Then besides this is the element of a rhythmic recurrence of what he does, as though his life were divided into uniform cycles of rising and falling, with nothing ever becoming finally settled, either for good or for bad.

The more important things to note about the picture, however, are that Sisyphus's labors are purposeless and endlessly repetitive. It is this combination that is unique to the picture, and haunting. The pathos of it does not lie in the thought that Sisyphus is condemned to great toil but, rather, that nothing ever comes of his efforts that must, nevertheless, be repeated, forever. Not even the minimal achievement that the picture warrants, the mere coming to rest of the stone, is ever reached. It has always to be moved once again, endlessly, pointlessly, meaninglessly. These elements of pointlessness and repetitiveness would remain even if we were to suppose that the stone was not even heavy, that it could be transported almost effortlessly. Toilsome or not, the work would still fit the pattern of endless pointlessness.

But we need not go to mythology or even to fiction to find exactly the same image. There is, for example, a convent in Quebec in which the following scene is enacted every day: About a dozen nuns enter a barren room and, standing in a circle, chant prayers, in Latin and in perfect unison, for several hours. Having finished, they are replaced by another similar group of nuns who do exactly the same thing for several hours, these to be replaced by still another group. Thus does the chant rise from this bleak and dreary room, without variation, day after day and year after year, unendingly. The nuns who participate in this repetitive ritual have no other life; they are either in their places, chanting in unison, or resting, to resume exactly that behavior when their turn comes around again, very shortly. They go on and off in shifts. Nightfall brings no rest, nor do any holy days, nor does anything whatsoever except ultimately, of course, death. But even then a replacement, trained for the role, steps into it. The prayers chanted, being in Latin and delivered in a fixed and highly ritualized manner, are virtually meaningless to any hearer, aesthetically worthless, and probably without meaning any longer to the nuns who pronounce them.

Here, in the life of such a nun, is precisely the image contained in the myth of Sisyphus. Nothing ever gets completed, for a prayer is uttered, at length and at considerable speed, only to be commenced again, from the same beginning as before. Nor does anything count as bringing the agent of this labor closer to achieving her purpose, for that purpose simply is to repeat, over and over, what has already been done, over and over.

Consider now another picture, an imaginative one this time, but sufficiently like what is common to be recognizable. Imagine, that is, a man, totally innocent of any wrongdoing, who is nevertheless, by an appalling miscarriage of justice, condemned to a lifetime of hard labor. Suppose further that his sentence is beyond appeal and irrevocable, and beyond all hope of mitigation. And suppose further that the labor contrived for him, to engage all his remaining days, is this: that he shall start by digging an immense hole in the barren prison yard, this to occupy him for an entire day. On the next day he will fill it up again, restoring everything to its original condition. Then on the day after that he will dig another huge hole, this one to be filled up again like the first, on the day following. And so on, for every day—he shall be bending his back to the shovel, either in creating a large hole in the ground or in refilling the very such hole that he made the day before, this work to continue without rest or modification through every day of his life. Thus looking back, at the end of his life, to assess his life's work, he will find that it consists either of a large and meaningless hole in the ground or of a hole just filled in, nothing more.

The resemblance of this picture to the image of Sisyphus, or of the chanting nuns, is obvious. The element of meaninglessness is similarly obvious in all three pictures. And that element is not simply that of gross injustice, or onerous toil, or frustration, or pain, or hopes dashed, even though all these things are clearly contained in the pictures. It is not hard, for example, to find instances of injustice that, however evil, do not convert the lives of their victims to meaninglessness. And it is similarly not hard, and in fact very easy, to find in typical life examples of lifelong toil more onerous than what has been portrayed here; yet lives in which such toil is an ingredient are not thereby made meaningless. Indeed, the most seemingly meaningful lives may sometimes be the hardest, in terms of the sheer work that is exacted from their possessors. Similarly, the pictures we have before us, though they are obviously not portrayals of pleasure, are also not strong images of pain, either. If our purpose were to illustrate a life of pain, we could easily do much better than this, by describing almost any slum, for example, or terminal ward of a hospital. Nor again do we have before us the clearest images of frustrated hope. In the case of the nuns, it is even possible to suppose that their strange existence is the fulfillment of their hope, this having been ignited and fueled by a religious conviction.

The meaninglessness in these portrayals is something different from all these things and is perhaps captured by the following supposition. Suppose someone, quite capable of understanding what he was being told, were informed that his whole life would be spent in the manner of those illustrated. It is not hard to imagine the condemned man hearing, and completely believing, such a pronouncement, for example. What, then, exactly, would be the cause of his despair? Simply this: that his life would thus be divested of all purpose, including even the minimal purpose of somehow avoiding total boredom from one hour to the next. That a lifetime should be spent to no purpose is, however common, tragic enough. That it should in addition be deprived even of that minimal sort of variety that enables the hours and the days to pass by one more or less unnoticed, as his attention is drawn to other things, is totally appalling. We have here, in this combination of things, the very essence of meaningless existence.

Meaning and Contentment

Our next undertaking will be to see to what extent life itself resembles the pictures of meaninglessness that have just been sketched. Are those pictures aberrations? Do they express the rare, exceptional, the somewhat bizarre deviations from the normal course of life? Or do they, on the contrary, typify it?

We cannot in a straightforward manner answer this question with respect to human life, for we are too close to it, and we tend, moreover, to interpret it through the reflections of hope and optimism, so that we are in danger of not seeing what is really there. This is sometimes clear enough with respect to certain individual lives. Thus we sometimes see someone whose life so perfectly resembles the pictures just drawn, and is so patently without meaning, that this verdict is forced upon us—yet that very individual may rejoice in his or her meaningless existence. Consider, for example, the employee of the slaughterhouse whose lifelong work is to wield a sledgehammer against the skulls of beef cattle

as they are conveyed before him, hanging terrified by their hind legs. One after another, in a steady procession, for a full working day, day in and day out, through the weeks, years, through the major part of a lifetime, the work goes on, blow after blow after blow, never varying. Of course this portrayal is revolting and filled with horror, but that is not to the point. The agent of this endless infliction of suffering and death has long since ceased to be troubled by the nature of his work. Like anyone else, he delights after the day's work in playing with his dog or his kitten, putting his children to bed, listening to soft music, whatever. And that *is* just the point; namely, that he rejoices in life, in spite of its meaninglessness. And it is especially at this point that one must suppress the impulse to say, "Then how can anyone say that his life is without meaning?" True, the individual rejoices. And true, the slaughterer's work is by normal standards valuable to humanity, possibly even necessary. And true, he does it well. Yet it would be difficult to find a life that more exactly resembles these pictures of meaninglessness. So the lesson that should be drawn is not that a life that is lived with contentment is by virtue of that fact made meaningful but, rather, that even a meaningless life can be filled with contentment. And that is, of course, the great danger—that the inner satisfactions of our lives can blind us to their meaninglessness.

We may all be like the slaughterer, not in the sense that our lives are lived in the ambience of horror and death, but in the sense that they are ultimately without meaning and that we are blinded to this by our inner satisfaction.

The Meaninglessness of Animal Life

Instead, then, of looking directly at human existence at this point, we will have a much better chance of seeing things as they are if we look first upon the life that surrounds us, at the whole of living nature excepting human beings. We shall thereby avoid not only the misrepresentation of things arising from our own contentments, as the life we describe is not our own, but also the kind of fatuous investment of life with such qualities as dignity, nobility, and inherent worth that philosophers so delight in when humanity is the object of their inquiry. Whatever else one might say about insects and rodents, for example, the temptation is never to ascribe to them inherent worth.

Consider, then, the life of any animal whatever, and note its perfect resemblance to the pictures of meaninglessness that have been sketched. We can begin anywhere, with whatever living thing next catches our attention. Consider the ground mole. This pathetic and innocuous little animal has settled into the most forbidding environment imaginable, into the dark and abrasive earth itself, and there each generation lives out its life in unredeeming toil. This animal has vestigial eyes, capable only of distinguishing light from darkness, and it instinctively knows that the moment light appears, it is vulnerable to whatever preying animal is about. Its huge shovel-like claws get it with incredible labor from one point to another, and this is how it spends its life, digging. And to what end? Only that it may find a worm or grub that will nourish it and give it strength to dig farther to yet another worm or grub, and then on to still another, day after day, endlessly. The resemblance to Sisyphus is perfect. And is there no further purpose to all this? There is, of course—but that is where the irony of this animal's existence becomes complete. For its purpose is simply and solely to beget others exactly like itself, and having exactly the same destiny, to inch along through the hard ground in search of a worm, and then another, and another—throughout eternity. Nothing ever comes of this pointless endeavor, except more pointless endeavor that is its exact replication.

This animal epitomizes all animal life. An insect spends its whole existence feeding, for no other end than that another generation of insects may do the same again. Sometimes the preparations for this are staggering, as in the case of the seventeen-year locust. It is so called because this animal spends that great period of time burrowing deep in the darkness of the earth, only then finally to emerge into the light of day, spend a few days in the sun, and lay eggs, just so that this long and meaningless cycle can begin once more, to be repeated again and again, endlessly. The bee that emerges today is no different from the one that took wing ten million years ago, and its destiny is no different. It toils only that others exactly like it may do exactly the same, for another million years, then a million more, and, indeed, forever. The birds that move north and south, back and forth, with the cycles of the seasons, often over unbelievable distances, do so only that the same pointless behavior will be repeated again and again. At no point is a signal ever given to stop. At no point can one find that even the slightest beginning has been made in anything at all, beyond the sheer perpetuation of repetitive toil. What, one wants to ask, is it all *for*? And the answer is perfectly obvious: It is all for nothing, it just goes on and on, to no end whatever.

The Meaninglessness of Human Life

Do we, then, find ourselves at a new level when we move from animal to human existence? Can we accept the obvious meaninglessness of all the life that surrounds us, assured that our lives are essentially different, that there is some unique meaning to human life that is denied to everything else?

Most people simply take for granted that there is, without feeling the least need to support that conviction. They assume that a human life is precious just because it is human and that no matter how closely its pattern may resemble the pictures of meaninglessness we have drawn, we are nevertheless spared the obvious inference. And there have, of course, always been plenty of philosophers and theologians to add their own comforting assurances, as though what is here in question should be perfectly obvious to all. Thus theologians and clergy claim man to be the very image of God, and their hearers nod their automatic assent, without even knowing what might be meant by this, beyond the implication that human life is not without meaning. It is the comfort conveyed by these words, and not their truth, that elicits assent. And philosophers, for their part, speak of the human dignity, absolute worth, and autonomy that are shared by no other living things. Again, the declarations are comforting, however meaningless to the mind. Some have turned with great hope to man's supposed rational nature, even calling this the divine element, after the manner of Plato and Aristotle. Thus are philosophers able to join with the theologians and to speak with one voice of man's kinship with God, utterly oblivious to the obscurity of this fond idea, and equally oblivious to our most manifest kinship with the whole of living nature.

It is all very well to proclaim that human nature has some unique value and meaning, but to give that declaration credibility, one must somehow show that human life is not like the image of meaninglessness that we have before us. And that is not an easy thing to do. For if we actually look at mankind, at human history or at the typical life of an individual, what we find is every ingredient of meaninglessness that was carefully inserted into the pictures of Sisyphus, the nuns, or the hole-digging convict. Schopenhauer's description is apt. Our lives are lived out like clockwork, accompanied by trivial thoughts and impulses. Their whole meaning, by whatever lofty words we may choose to describe it, appears to arise solely from the intensity with which we cling to this clockwork existence, forever vainly supposing that what seems to be of the very essence of life is instead some sort of accident, a temporary aberration, that will surely disappear in another day or so. We are like aging parents who nourish the hope that their child, long since lost, is still living after all and will come back any day, or someone who still lives in the fantasy of a love long dead, imagining that it will now be revived and go on as before, yet inwardly knowing that it really is dead. We hope that the banality of our lives and the speciousness of our satisfactions will at any moment be converted to lasting triumphs and that we will be able to say, finally, that it really was worth it after all. But inwardly we know better. We partially conceal the truth even from ourselves, in order not to overwhelm hope; and in this we are again assisted by philosophers, who declare that our very humanity is enough to make our existence utterly good and meaningful. We need not, they say, in effect, look any further; what we seek has already been conferred.

It is a pleasant notion. It may even be a necessary one, once the alternatives are seriously considered.

Consider the life of any individual person—someone who says, with the utmost sincerity, that he or she is happy, someone filled with the zest for life—for the question is not whether anyone is happy, but rather, whether human existence, in an individual or in the race as a whole, has any meaning. We find that each day simply duplicates the one that went before, with only insignificant variations. The person you meet after a year is the same, doing what he or she was doing then, responding to the same things in the same ways, saying much the same things, and thinking much the same things, most of them unworthy of thought to begin with. Hardly a thing has changed. A child has been born, a business venture undertaken, some purchases made, a trip completed, a few games watched or played—all about the same as the year before, and the year forthcoming. And what, besides the pleasure of the moment or, more likely, the momentary escape from boredom, is the purpose of it all? Rarely is it anything beyond the accumulation of possessions. The similarity to Sisyphus is still inescapable as is the similarity to the nuns, who simply add one meaningless chant to another, the total swelling, but never being anything but more of the same.

The Evil of Inaction

How much of life is spent in the sheer escape from boredom? A person who rises in the morning knowing that his day will be about the same as the one before will nevertheless undertake it with zest, provided that it will deliver him from the otherwise unbearable boredom. Thus he will engage in his familiar routine—corresponding, making decisions of the same sort that he made yesterday and a year ago, realizing a profit here and a loss there, along with the usual breaks for lunch or whatever, relating and hearing anecdotes such as are by now familiar, then finally to dinner and bed, to repeat the same tomorrow. The picture is perfectly familiar, wherever you turn—to the postal worker making the same rounds each day; the truck driver moving hither and thither, filling the long hours, diverted only by such things as he sees along the way though he has already seen them a hundred times; the dentist; the physician; the teacher. Do not ask, "Are they happy?" Very likely they are, for they manage to escape the greatest evil of the world, which is boredom. Ask instead, "Do their lives resemble the image of

Sisyphus?" And then, without shifting the subject to one of happiness, human worth, or other pleasant things, give an honest answer.

When we think of evil, we are likely to think of pain and death, but these are not the greatest evils. The greatest evil that can be inflicted upon anyone is unrelieved boredom, and the escape from it is therefore necessarily good, though only in a negative sense. It is good in the way in which an animal's *not* being caught in a trap, or a child's *not* being hit by a truck, is good. But negative though this good is, it is absolutely essential to have it, for the alternative, boredom, is such an unmitigated evil. It is not hard to see this if one looks closely at the picture of it. Thus suppose that you were told, by someone having the power to carry out this threat, that you were going to be strapped in a fixed position, that henceforth you would not be able to move any muscle, and that you would be sustained like this for years by a means of nourishment and the maintenance of other vital functions without your participation at all. And suppose that what you were thus condemned to look at the rest of your life was sheer nothingness—the blank sky, for instance, or perhaps an illuminated expanse of white. There would, in short, be nothing for you ever to do again, nothing to claim your attention. Surely the most tormented sufferer in the terminal ward of a hospital, struggling against unbearable pain, is lucky in comparison to this. There is a rare affliction, in which the victim is likely to awaken and realize that he or she is unable to move a single muscle, not even to speak or otherwise convey his or her plight to anyone. Suppose one were to thus awaken and then, however painlessly, remain in that state for years! I have seen a man, very young and a few years ago faced with every blessing and good fortune, who as the result of a sudden brain injury was left unable to move anything but his eyes. He languishes in a nursing home, amidst the sick and the old who have been sent there to die, but with this difference: that he, being still young, is condemned to quite a long life. What does he think of all day, week after week? Perhaps his overwhelming boredom has by now deadened his power of thought, so that his mind is slowly becoming as helpless as the rest of him. Surely, one hopes so. For otherwise, no greater evil can be imagined.

Human Animality

We noted that it is the destiny of every animal simply to beget more of its kind, these in turn struggling against all odds to achieve the very same thing again, a succession of identical generations never ceasing. Is mankind different? Superficially, yes. The world changes at our hands and a human history unfolds, the chapters of which are not all exactly alike, as they are in the case of other living things. Yet basically, we are the same. We respond to the urge to beget as blindly as does everything else. And it is, in our case as in theirs, a blind and irrational urge, not a goal. Many living things never see their offspring, and it is not really for them that they copulate and bring them forth. They do this because they are impelled to, by an irrational force.

We are not basically different. At the basis of our own lives is the same mindless urge, though our inventive intellects have imposed variations that distinguish the expression of this urge from that of other creatures and superficially lead us to think that it is something quite different. For we have found ways to avoid the natural outcome of this impulse in its primary expression, namely, the begetting of children, and we have also found numberless ways of diverting it into totally novel modes of expression. That we go through all the motions of begetting children and yet avoid that result by numerous clever means, shows clearly enough that we have no such goal in mind. In fact, we have no goal other than the sheer indulgence of an appetite, imposed on us by nature and never intellectually chosen at all. Moreover, we differ from the animals in that we have a culture. We are not merely the product of external nature; we are also the product of human acculturation. And an enormous part of that acculturation, what in fact seems sometimes to lie at the very basis of it, is the suppression of the sexual impulse. Everywhere it is hedged about by rules, imposed at such a tender age that they seem eventually to be part of our natures. The result is that we seek "other outlets," as it is aptly expressed. That is, people throw themselves into careers, the pursuit of glory, office-seeking, honors. Every bit of this behavior belongs in the same genre as that of a bird, spreading and preening itself before an intended mate, making itself glorious. In the case of the bird, the point of it all is copulation—not to create offspring, for it really cares nothing for these things, perhaps never to be seen anyway, but simply for its own sake—in response to the promptings of nature. We are not that different. What it comes to is simply this: that we feel *alive* when we are doing things, especially when we are preening ourselves and making ourselves, as it seems to us, glorious. The most natural way of doing this, the way that more than anything else makes us feel alive, is in sexual intimacy. It is the only thing for which nothing is too great to sacrifice. With it goes the passion of loving and the total sense of fulfillment that comes from feeling loved, the only thing that the world offers that comes even close to being truly good. But when the barriers erected by culture and custom, reinforced by religion and law and every instrument on which humans can lay their hands, stand in the way of this most obvious expression of *eros*, then we find other things to do, that is, other ways of glorifying ourselves and seeming, even if only for a while, to come alive. Because they are substitutes, we have to hurl ourselves into them with that much more energy, to get anything resembling the intended result. And thereby do we escape boredom. To be barred from sexual intimacy and genuine, deeply felt affection is indeed hard, but not impossible if we are still allowed to come alive otherwise. But to be denied *this*, to be so placed that we have nothing to do, to be placed in unremitting boredom and allowed no hope of escape, is to suffer the ultimate evil. Better to be simply running in circles, which is what the lives of most persons consist in, than languishing in inaction, that is, in utter boredom.

Behold, then, the life of any individual. If you select someone who is happy and by every ordinary measure successful, so much the better, for you will then not need to ask whether he is happy or successful. You can ask instead whether his existence has any meaning. His life, you will find, consists of a perpetual running in circles, with periods of rest that serve only to revitalize him for more of exactly the same running in circles. These circles are defined by things undertaken and done—a business venture consummated here, a love affair there, a trip to this place or that for novel sights and sounds, an occasional victory for some trivial reward, a little applause here, praise there, reassuring words, and bits of self-glorification. And these circles, instead of leading on to something different and perhaps nobler, for the most part overlap, such that the creator of them tends very much to be recreating the same circle over and over. Viewed from within, that is, from the standpoint of the person himself, his existence can quite truly be said to be happy. At least it is not one either of pain or boredom—which is quite enough to satisfy the demands of happiness. But viewed from without it has exactly the pattern of Sisyphus.

The Individual and the Species

Do we, then, move to some new level of meaningfulness when we pass from such an individual to the race as a whole? Other animals, we found, simply replicate in each generation the generations that went before, as exactly as does each journey of Sisyphus up the hill repeat his preceding ones. No variation is introduced at all. What, then, of mankind?

Here we could be reassured if it could be shown that, although the life of each individual may be without ultimate purpose or meaning, the individual is nevertheless part of a greater being, or the whole of humanity, whose existence does have meaning. And there is no doubt that most persons deem their own lives in some sense meaningful if they can view their efforts, or sometimes their life's work, as having made some sort of contribution to mankind. But, if we look at it more closely, that kind of meaning is as specious as the others we have considered. The conditions of life change, to be sure, from one generation to another, and no doubt some of them get better, in some sense, just as others get worse. Life gets longer. For many it becomes less onerous. Disease is in some sense conquered. Changes of this sort are familiar and need no review. We can even say, though it is not obviously true, that life has for most people become happier; in any case, they have become less vulnerable to some of the ancient evils, even though new evils may now threaten. But even granting all this, it can hardly be said that there is any clear meaning to human existence that is lacking in the existence of the individual. On the contrary, the life of the species here resembles exactly the life of the individual, and both resemble the pattern of meaninglessness embodied in the pictures with which we began.

For what do we actually find here? Generation following upon generation, all in response to the all-powerful urge to beget, but to no purpose whatever. No sooner has one generation of men arisen, passed across the stage of life, then sunk into oblivion, than another is seen following in its steps, repeating exactly what went before, with only minor variations in the externals. The spectacle is like a play, in which the lines of each act simply paraphrase the preceding ones and in which there is no real story, no theme, no point. From time to time stage hands appear to rearrange the settings, and the actors themselves, instead of repeating verbatim what was said in the previous acts, find different ways to say the very same things. Otherwise, all goes on as before, and any observer knows ahead of time how things will unfold, the surprises, such as they are, being confined to the stage settings. The thing builds up to no point, no redeeming theme comes across, no meaning is even hinted at, only endless banality. A metaphysician contemplating this, and noting that the players seem sometimes to rejoice, sometimes to suffer, always moving about, mostly in circles, determined above all to lay the conditions for another episode to follow, would be led to wonder: But what is this all about? Why all this trouble, the elaborate preparations, this prodigious expenditure of effort? In what does it all culminate, what is its meaning, what is its point? And certainly he would have to conclude that it has no point, that these things are all done, over and over in about the same way, just because that is the way the thing has been written, and it is the sad lot of the actors to have been cast in that dismal production. Of course someone might point out that each act does, after all, constitute the foundation for the next, that the actors play their parts well, even that they enjoy them, that they are happy in what they are doing, and that it is, in any case, far better than just standing there doing nothing at all, all of which is obvious and true. And all of which is, of course, beside the point.

The Concept of Meaning

So far we have dwelt only on life's meaninglessness, construing this as the repetitive pointlessness that was illustrated at the outset. It is time now to consider the more positive side of life, if there is one, to determine what a positively meaningful existence would be, and whether it is attainable.

To do this we must revert to the pictures of meaninglessness with which we began, to see how they might be modified in order for a conception of meaningful existence to emerge.

Consider once more, then, the nuns, whose whole lives are spent repeating exactly the same chanted prayers and adorations, over and over. That all life, human as well as animal, bears a resemblance to this is, I think, unquestionable. Yet our own lives, as we live them, do not seem to us like that—otherwise we could not declare ourselves to be happy, while at the same time pitying the nuns. There are differences, and we need to see first what these are, and then see whether any of them confer the kind of meaningfulness we are seeking.

With respect, then, to the nuns, we can consider four possibilities, each of which, while leaving the picture exactly what it was insofar as it is a picture, nevertheless alters its significance.

For the first possibility, let us suppose, with rather cruel imagination, that the nuns are in effect enslaved persons and that their vocation was in no way chosen by them. We can imagine, for example, that arrangements have been made with some orphanage to deliver over infant female children from time to time and that these children are then raised up, more or less as animals might be, to perform this strange role throughout their lives, no attempt at explanation or justification being offered to them or to anyone. We are not, in other words, supposing now that the nuns are motivated by religious zeal or by any conviction at all; rather, we are saying that they are virtual automata, simply trained and brainwashed, like so much clockwork, to behave in the way that they do, and never to stop. Their behavior is in no sense voluntary, for they are, due to the conditions of their lives from infancy on, psychologically so degenerate that they have no power of choice, no purposes or goals of their own.

Second, varying this extreme image a bit, we can suppose that these nuns have in fact chosen this vocation but that their choice was essentially irrational. We can suppose, for example, that they were simply subjected to severe and constant indoctrination during childhood, the effect of which was to plant in their minds the conviction that such a life was the finest and noblest that could be offered to anyone. Thus coming to value such a life above any other that they could envisage, they vied with others for the chance to be chosen for it and rejoiced when they were chosen. Eventually, we can imagine, they began to have doubts and misgivings, but by then it was too late, their vows were irrevocable, and in any case they still take pride in having been chosen and in being able to fulfill their deepest wish, born in them at a tender age. We are not, by this second supposition, imagining that these nuns are motivated by faith in any significant way; rather, they are driven by a desire that was implanted in them by others, and their religious faith, which is of course unquestioned by them, is the product, rather than the source, of that desire.

Third, we can significantly modify this last image by supposing that the nuns are in fact moved by religious faith, that they are deeply and unshakably convinced of the reality of God and of the truth of the religion that they have received, and that, they completely believe that by their life of prayer, lived in exactly the way in which it is lived, they glorify God in the noblest way possible. We need not here suppose that these religious convictions are in fact true; what we are supposing is, rather, that they are unshakably held and that it is because of those convictions that the nuns have embarked upon the severe and demanding vocations we have described. Unlike our second supposition, then, we here suppose that the nuns' religious faith is the source, not the mere product, of their behavior.

And finally, for our fourth and final image, let us make exactly the same supposition as we just did, but with the qualification that (we are supposing) the religious beliefs of these nuns are in fact *true*; that is, that God does exist, that He created heaven and earth, that the creed of the nuns is true in every detail, and, most important of all, that the nuns do in fact glorify God by their prayers or, if this is unclear, that they do

without doubt thus carry out His will, and that their lives are accordingly, not just in their eyes but in the eyes of God as well, noble beyond measure.

Meaning and Purpose

Now let us look at this image of the chanting nuns in these four quite different contexts, to see what distinguishes a meaningless from a meaningful existence.

That the picture of the nuns within the first context is a picture of total meaninglessness is obvious. The most fertile imagination could not construct a better image of meaninglessness. Here we have not only the elements of pointlessness and endlessness, but the absence of anything that could in any way redeem the life portrayed. There is no hint that this endless toil either accomplishes anything or is meant to do so, and the nuns themselves are deprived even of the personal satisfaction, however illusory it would be, that they are engaged in a noble or even worthwhile vocation. All they do is chant, meaninglessly, forever, and to no purpose.

Then what of the second image, wherein we suppose that the nuns have, however irrationally, at least chosen this life for themselves? Does the presence of choice confer meaning on their lives? Hardly, for what they have chosen is precisely a meaningless existence, and the choice is irrational in just the sense that no justification can be given for it. Their desire for it was planted in their minds by others, and their choice was nothing more than a response to this desire. If we were to suppose that their desire to chant endlessly, and to do nothing else, were nothing but the effect of some hormonal imbalance in their endocrinal systems, to emphasize its irrational source, then the failure of this to confer meaningfulness on their lives would be perfectly manifest. It is hardly less obvious on the supposition we have made. The lives of the nuns, considered in either of the first two contexts that we have imagined, are as meaningless as the behavior of a clock running on and on, but without hands.

What, then, of our third context? Here we supposed that the nuns have chosen their extraordinary vocations, their choice being not simply the effects of some groundless conditioning but, instead, a deliberate and considered commitment of their faith. Do we finally have here the element that gives their lives meaning?

Not really, for those beliefs that governed their choice might, however firmly held, be illusory. Mere strength of convictions does not convert an illusion to truth, even though the things believed might be lofty and inspiring. To suppose otherwise would be to beg the very question we are raising by saying, in effect, that any life is meaningful given only that it is believed to be so. The plainly meaningless lives of the nuns considered in our first imaginary context could, no doubt, be made to appear meaningful to their possessors, and, while this might make their fate seem less cruel, it would certainly not make it more genuinely meaningful. Similarly, the convict of our other example might somehow be led to believe, quite falsely, that he was gradually achieving some great purpose by his hole digging, but from this it would certainly not follow that he was. His hole digging would still be nothing but pointless hole digging, whatever might be his own distorted conception of it.

Here it is important to avoid a locution that seems almost spontaneously to rise to people's lips considering this kind of example, namely, that the lives described are meaningful "to them." For this only repeats what has been said, that is, that they do have that conviction and that they do, in the light of it, believe their lives to be meaningful. That very belief can be totally false. Human beings are not, to be sure, quite so much an object of pity when governed by such grand illusion, for they are thus made content with their meaningless existence. But that kind of contentment, far from implying that their existence is after all meaningful, certainly entails that it is not. And the ingredients of meaningfulness still elude our search.

What, then, of our fourth context? Here, finally, we have one of the elements of meaningful existence, but only one; for we can at least say that the repetitive labor of the nuns is not utterly lacking in purpose. On the contrary, on the supposition we are making, it achieves a purpose that is the noblest imaginable: the very glorification of God. If one doubts this claim, it is only because one has not really made the supposition required by this fourth context, namely, that the religious conviction of the nuns is in fact *true*. If anyone's labors did in some real and unmistakable sense tend to the glorification of the *earth*, then no one would suggest that they were without purpose, for no one doubts the reality of the earth. But what could this purpose be in comparison with that of glorifying the very creator of the earth, and of everything else, assuming, as we must here, that this creator exists and that these labors do in some perhaps mysterious way achieve this purpose?

This point can perhaps be made more convincingly with reference to the example of Sisyphus. Let us suppose that Sisyphus does not, as the ancient myth presents it, simply roll the same stone over and over, accomplishing nothing. Instead, suppose that he rolls a succession of stones, one after another, and that each, instead of rolling back to the bottom of the hill, remains at the top, as intended. And suppose, further, that this task is unending or, in other words, that no matter how many stones Sisyphus moves to the top of the hill, presumably with dreadful labor, there will always be another that he must move, so that his work is never completed. So far, these modifications in the original story constitute no significant change, for if we actually contemplate what Sisyphus does, his work is virtually indistinguishable from that in the original story—he moves a rock over and over to the top of the hill—except in this case he moves a different rock each time. But now suppose that these rocks, which we said remain on the hill, do not merely accumulate there in a meaningless pile of rubble but instead become the foundation for a vast and beautiful and indestructible temple and then, gradually, the materials for its walls and all its many parts, with this construction going on and on, endlessly, and the temple gradually becoming ever more beautiful and inspiring and capable of enduring to the end of time. Can we still say that Sisyphus's existence is without meaning? Surely not! For one of the two ingredients of meaningfulness now appears in this picture. Namely, his efforts are not purposeless or pointless— something does result from them—and what results is of great and lasting significance.

Subjective Meaningfulness

Here we must be careful to avoid a tempting error. And that is to suppose that the question, whether or not Sisyphus's labors are meaningful, depends on how he feels about them and about their effect—that is, whether he really wants to build this temple badly enough to devote an endless life to it. That does not really matter. For the temple was described as beautiful and everlasting, and if it really is such, then it does not matter whether Sisyphus appreciates that fact or not. Our question was not whether Sisyphus enjoys his existence or approves of the purpose to which it is put but rather, whether his existence has meaning. And in the picture before us, it certainly has an end or purpose, and (we are supposing) a significant one, and that was one of the two elements of meaningfulness. Putting this point otherwise, we can say that just as someone's enjoyment of a meaningless life does not convert that life to meaningfulness, so one's failure to appreciate true meaningfulness does not obliterate that meaningfulness.

The Meaninglessness of Endless Pursuit

But what of the other ingredient? The lives sketched earlier were meaningless, we noted, in two ways, one being the lack of purpose and the other their quality of repetitive toil. And while we have, in our last examples, eliminated the first, by endowing these lives with great purpose, the element of repetitiveness remains. The nuns, we suppose, do indeed glorify God, but in a sense, they never get anywhere. They are on a treadmill that turns a great wheel and performs a great task, but the task is unending, and the purpose is never really fulfilled. So it is with Sisyphus. Even though his mission now is to erect an everlasting temple of great beauty, and he can be said actually to be doing that, he is nevertheless doomed to the frustration of never completing the work, thus never really fulfilling his purpose. Every pursuit of a goal is animated by the hope of achieving it. If the very goal of one's existence is impossible to attain, if the purpose is there but the fulfillment of it always elusive, then life is merely a betrayal—like that of a dog in pursuit of a stuffed rabbit that hangs from a pole in front of it, the pole being fixed to the dog itself, so that the increased frenzy of pursuit only results in the accelerated elusiveness of the dog's

already illusory prey. Our goals, unlike the dog's, may be real enough, but if the hope of attaining them is as illusory as in this simile, if there is no possibility of fulfilling them, then in a very real sense they are false goals after all, and the same falseness is imparted to our lives. At some point it must be possible to rest. Life cannot be *just* a pursuit; and making the thing pursued something real and worthwhile, although it gives the pursuit itself meaning, does not really give meaning to life if the goal is forever unattainable. The resemblance to Sisyphus is still too painfully clear. At some point Sisyphus must be able finally to stop and reflect: There, I *did* it. If his final truth is that he is doing it, will forever be doing it, with no possibility of stopping, then the goal becomes after all a basis for eternal frustration—the very element that is most conspicuous in the story of Sisyphus as it was originally told.

Meaning and Creativity

If, then, a meaningless existence is one spent in pointless and repetitive toil, is a meaningful existence simply one in which these elements are replaced by their opposites? Can we say, in other words, that a fully meaningful life will be one in which some truly worthwhile goal is sought and achieved? Or, in terms of some of our examples, if we suppose that Sisyphus's labors do culminate in the creation of a lasting and beautiful temple, or that the adoration of the nuns does in fact in some real and theologically significant sense tend to the glory of God, then can we pronounce those lives meaningful? And generalizing, can we say that if human existence has or can be given these ingredients, then human existence is to that extent meaningful after all?

Not quite, I think. For even if we suppose these conditions to be fulfilled, the pictures we have drawn can still fall short of meaningfulness. To see this, let us suppose that Sisyphus, for example, by his labors erects a beautiful and lasting temple that he had no part whatever in creating. His only role, by this supposition, was to pile stone upon stone in a preconceived way, as might be done by some mindless machine that had been programmed to such behavior. We can, for example, suppose that Sisyphus is a slave, bereft of any autonomy or power of choice, whose work from moment to moment is entirely under the direction and within the control of someone having complete power over him. The temple he builds is, therefore, really the work of another, even though the building of it is entirely his. We can even suppose that the purpose or goal is his as well, in the sense that he does want to achieve it and sincerely proclaims it to be his life's purpose. Here we have an image wherein the ingredients of meaningfulness elicited before are clearly present. That is, Sisyphus's existence is not without purpose and, of equal significance, that purpose is of genuine significance, and it is finally and lastingly achieved. What is lacking is that the goal of his life is not of his own creation. It is simply imposed upon him from without.

The same conclusion would emerge from our image of the prisoner, condemned to a lifetime of hole digging. We can, with a bit of imagination, suppose that his labor results in something of lasting beauty and worth, and even that he is aware of this and can entirely comprehend it in his own mind. But still, if that goal, whatever it is, was itself conceived by someone else, so that his role is simply to be the instrument for the realization of what someone else has created, then his existence is still significantly lacking in meaningfulness. What he does, and everything that he does, could as well be done by an unthinking engine.

And similarly in the case of the nuns: if they are merely trained to do what they do, and themselves have no hand in the creation of their goal, then their lives are still essentially meaningless, even though we may suppose this goal to be of great or even supreme worth and to be actually attained by them. For whatever else can be said in justification of their existence, they are still automata, the mere tools to the realization of an end, however noble, rather than the creators of that end.

We do then now have, it seems, all the basic ingredients of meaningless existence before us and, by their negation, all the basic ingredients of meaningful existence. Life is meaningless if it is lacking in a real, not merely illusory, purpose—one that is genuinely significant and not merely believed to be so; capable of attainment, and not forever eluding its pursuer; created and chosen by him whose goal is to

achieve it, and not imposed from without. Or, putting the whole matter positively, we can say that life is truly meaningful only if it is directed to goals of one's own creation and choice and if those goals are genuinely noble, beautiful, or otherwise lastingly worthwhile and attained.

The Will to Live

Having said that, however, we must not casually dismiss the dismal portrayal of human existence with which we began and blithely declare life to be meaningful after all. For what still needs to be done is to set human existence, as we find it, against these standards and see whether it is meaningful after all. The conception of meaningfulness at which we have now arrived, is one thing; but the discovery of it in our own lives is something else. And what we might discover instead is the mere illusion of it. That possibility cannot just be waved aside. Even a bright and totally convincing illusion is, after all, an illusion still, and it is all the harder to banish if it is metaphysical in character rather than the mere product of prejudice or ignorance.

What is human existence, typically? What, that is, do we actually find if we look objectively at the expression of life in any ordinary individual? We have already described it. It is what Schopenhauer, in the passage with which we began, described as a clockworklike thing, without purpose or meaning. Looked at from without, the typical life of an ordinary person perfectly resembles each of the images of meaninglessness that we have set forth, the main ingredient of these being repetitive routine that culminates in nothing but more of the same.

Why, then, do people cling to it? Why do people cherish life above everything else, consider the loss of it the ultimate calamity, and ward off any threat to their existence at any cost? And why, above all, do people rejoice in it? For, if you look about you, you will find a strange paradox, namely, that the happiest people, the ones who find least to complain of in their lot, are precisely those whose lives are the most totally meaningless. The people whose days have hardly varied from an accustomed routine through their entire lives, and who now, toward the end, pursue exactly the same routines, with no different results from before, that is to say, no more effect than the enlargement of some senseless objective that they have already reached a thousand times, nevertheless declare with total honesty that they are happy, that life has been good, and that they look with pride upon what they have brought about—some considerable accumulation of possessions, or the notice of their peers, or sometimes nothing more than a great number of years of walking a treadmill. The sheer magnitude of the labor is sometimes a source of deep contentment, even though at the end of it nothing has been changed.

Why is this what we actually find when at the same time the image of Sisyphus, or of the prisoner, filled with the zest of life, laughing and singing as they plod year in and year out at their meaningless labor, would seem to be the height of incongruity and absurdity?

We can find the answer to this if we look once more at the chanting nuns in the context of the second of our four suppositions. Suppose, that is, that these nuns, instead of being reluctantly driven to their task, have been somehow conditioned to embrace it, so that their behavior is the expression of a strong and deep urge. In this case their lives, however meaningless, will be nevertheless joyous. Or consider Sisyphus once more. Suppose that the gods, when they condemned him to an eternity of stone rolling, had at the same time imbued him with an intense and insatiable desire to roll stones. Perhaps we can make this possibility seem more real if we imagine Sisyphus to have had injected into his veins some hormonal substance designed to rouse in him just that kind of intense and irrational urge. In that case, of course, Sisyphus would not have viewed his fate as a condemnation at all, but as a fulfillment, the fulfillment of his deepest and strongest desires. Or varying the image once more, consider a sensualist, whose desire for sexual indulgence is, let us suppose, constant and recurring and, moreover, so strong as to dominate every other desire and to govern his entire activity, so that he is completely undiscriminating in his choice of persons and quite heedless of the effects of his behavior. And now let us place beside it the image of our prisoner, in the earlier example, who was condemned to a lifetime of digging holes. But let

us add to it the supposition that this prisoner has exactly the same kind of intense, insatiable, and overwhelming desire to dig holes as does the sensualist's desire for eroticism. Now the convict, like Sisyphus, will view his life, not as one of hard labor, certainly not one of meaninglessness, but as good! He will be in exactly the same position as the sensualist who is surprised to discover himself "condemned" to a lifetime of erotic stimulus, wherein all his fantasies and dreams find fulfillment.

Or in other words, he will find himself in a position much like that of all of us. For the impulses that govern the lives of most people are no more rational than this and have as little to justify them in their outcome. What is to be said for them is that they are strong, sometimes insatiable, and always recurring. So long, then, as we are free to respond to them, free to pursue our ends and goals as we imagine them, we deem our lives to be good and declare ourselves to be happy. The picture of the person devoted entirely to the accumulation of property, daily enlarging this until by life's end it has assumed grotesque proportions—and the achiever of this result has become the envy of all—this picture resembles exactly that of a prisoner who has spent his entire working life digging one immense hole. If such a prisoner had been conditioned to seek such an end, to regard it as a means of self-glorification, and if the rest of us had similarly been so conditioned, then he would by no means think of himself as a prisoner but rather as the most blessed of men, and we would look upon him with the same envy with which the rich are typically viewed. We can say, if we like, that there is no point to digging a vast hole, but neither is there any point to creating a vast pile of rocks, or anything else. And the point to be made is that such prodigious achievements do not *become* meaningful merely because the agents of them find them fulfilling and declare themselves happy in the pursuit of them. If you were to learn that the rest of your life would be spent digging an enormous hole, then it would perhaps be a reassurance of sorts to be told that you were actually going to enjoy doing it. If, further, you were born with, or at any early age conditioned to, a strong desire to do this, then you would not need to have such a task assigned to you—you would go to great lengths to gain the opportunity and consider yourself lucky if you got it. And you would someday view the great hole you had dug with a deep sense of fulfillment. And therein does each of us find, in varying degrees, the very picture of his or her own life.

Creative Existence

Does it have to be so? The first thing, of course, is to see that it *is* so, that really the main feature of all existence is its meaninglessness, and to see that this meaninglessness does not evaporate under the supposition that we somehow find it fulfilling. Having done that, we have hope of describing a meaningful life, without being blinded by the idea that we need not seek any further, having already found it.

If the ingredients of meaninglessness are what we have described, namely, existence that is repetitive and without purpose, or whose purposes are illusory in the sense described, then we can say what a genuinely meaningful life would be. It would be a life that has a purpose—not just any sort of purpose that we happen to find satisfying, but one that is truly noble and good. And it must be one that is in fact achieved and not just endlessly pursued; and it must be lasting; and finally, it must be our *own* rather than just something imbibed. In short, the only genuinely meaningful existence is one that is *creative*. That one word sums it up, and, if really understood, discloses entirely what is missing, not only in all the animate and inanimate existence that surrounds us but in the lives of the vast majority of human beings. It is also what philosophers have always sought as godlike or what makes man, in the ancient metaphor, the image of God. For what is godlike is not blind power, or aimless knowledge, or unguided reason, but simply creative power. It is the primary attribute in the very conception of God. It is what makes the concept of God awesome.

To see this, let us return one last time to the image of Sisyphus, radically revising it so that it becomes the image, not of meaninglessness, but rather of genuinely meaningful life. It is not enough, as we have seen, merely to make Sisyphus an object of envy rather than of pity, by supposing him to fulfill his deepest desires, as the rest of us desire to fulfill ours. For the desire itself might be worthless.

Suppose, then, that Sisyphus, in rolling stones day after day, is not carrying out a sentence, but rather a plan. Suppose, further, that the plan is his own, totally the fruit of his creative mind rather than something that has been handed to him. And suppose that his plan is to build a great and everlasting temple, not merely beautiful to his eyes, but truly beautiful, in the eyes of every future generation of mortals and, let us suppose, of the gods as well. And let us finally suppose that Sisyphus succeeds in this. Here we have, finally, the perfect image of meaningfulness, albeit an extreme one. Every element of meaninglessness that we inserted into our earlier images has been replaced in this one by its opposite, so that as those conveyed, in extreme and exaggerated form, the idea of meaninglessness, this one conveys, once it is grasped, the idea of meaningfulness, though in similarly exaggerated form.

If we now apply what has been said to life as we actually find it, rather than to extreme and imaginary cases, we can discover the difference between a meaningful and a meaningless life, quite unmistakably. A person who does actually succeed in creating something genuinely good, perhaps even beautiful or noble, has lived meaningfully. And we need not ask whether this person is happy, whether what he or she has done receives any acclaim or is even noticed; for we are not asking what is required to become happy or noteworthy, but rather, what is required for an individual life to have meaning. Some persons might not, to be sure, seek such a meaningful existence, even if it were pointed out to them. Indeed, probably most persons would not. But that, too, is beside the point. We have been concentrating on two quite specific ideas, namely, meaninglessness and its opposite; and this has nothing to do with what the majority of persons happen to seek, or even what they would seek if the world were different.

The Meaning of Creation

Does all this mean, then, that the only meaningful life is one devoted to the creation of some *object*, some great work of art, of whatever kind? It does not. But at the same time, a perfectly clear idea of a meaningful existence is just that. Just as not all of us spend our lives digging holes, rolling rocks, or chanting meaningless words, nevertheless our lives do greatly resemble those pictures. And similarly, just as not everyone's life is that of a genuine creator, one's life *can* resemble that.

For creation is not just the creation of things. Creativity is a state of mind, which sometimes expresses itself in small and otherwise insignificant ways. Great or small, it is precious, and it is the only thing that finally converts life to meaning. No animal, for example, can look at nature, or at any object of nature, creatively, but a person can. A person can contemplate the simplest, and otherwise least significant, thing creatively—can thus consider a blade of grass, a hill, a thunderstorm, a snowflake, virtually anything. Similarly, the creation of such a work as Plato's *Republic* is certainly meaningful. It would be laughable for anyone, from whatever ideology, to suggest that Plato's life had no meaning. Yet meaningful thought need not be thought that has such a result as this or, indeed, any result whatever beyond itself. One's very thoughts can be poems, even if unuttered, in contrast to being trivial or banal or imitative, as most thought is most of the time. Consider two persons looking, say, at a meadow. One sees it for its size, its possible value, the use to which it might be put. He sees it, in short, only in terms of his own conditioned desires, rather as an animal would see it. The other, we can suppose, considers none of these things but is instead drawn to a tiny and insignificant flower at her feet and looks at it in a way that the other person is incapable of viewing it, in a way that no animal can view it. She looks at it creatively, not merely *finding* it meaningful, but investing it with meanings, by her own creative power. This is not the creation of an object, but it is creation just the same.

It is quite possible to go through life this way, more or less—more in the case of true genius, less, but in the same mode, for others, but not at all for the most foresaken of persons, who are totally bereft of creative thought and feeling and simply replicate, as animals do, what others have already thought and felt and done. Thus one can be creative in his or her relationships with other persons, infusing into these much more thought and feeling than would simply be elicited by passive encounter; or one can simply respond, unthinkingly and uncreatively, as he or she feels prompted. Most human relationships are, of course, of this second kind. For some persons they are all that is really possible. But that more is possible is perfectly apparent to anyone of a creative spirit.

And so it is with everything under the sun, with the entire earth and all it contains, and even the heavens too. God, we are taught, did not merely come upon all this and decide to make it his own through sheer power. Instead, he created it all, as we are told, and really is for this reason alone thought to be God. We are not gods, but we are not just animals either. We need not stagger dreamlike through the four stages of life to death, accompanied by a series of trivial thoughts, as Schopenhauer expressed it. We can instead—or, at least, some can—live meaningfully, by creating our own meanings, whether great or small, and then literally glorying in them, caring not in the least what we "get" from it all. We will already have gotten all that is meaningful.

STUDY QUESTIONS

1. Taylor suggests that the best way to figure out what makes a life meaningful is first to get an image of a life that is meaning*less*. Is this an appropriate strategy? Will a life that has none of the things that would make for meaninglessness automatically be meaning*ful*? Or is something more needed? If so, what?

2. Do you agree with Taylor that the mere fact that we are human does not mean that we live meaningful lives?

3. Do you think that the lives of Sisyphus, the chanting nuns, and the hole-digging convict are all equally meaningless and for the same reasons? Or are there distinctions among these scenarios that Taylor is overlooking?

4. Taylor proposes three characteristics that are necessary for a meaningful life. What is his motivation for proposing each? Do you think that a life that satisfied only two of these three would be automatically meaningless?

5. Are you inclined to agree that most humans don't choose their ends freely, but rather because of social conditioning? What effect, if any, would this have on the meaningfulness of our lives?

The Meanings of Lives

SUSAN WOLF

..

THIS question, "What is the meaning of life?" was once taken to be a paradigm of philosophical inquiry. Perhaps, outside of the academy, it still is. In philosophy classrooms and academic journals, however, the question has nearly disappeared, and when the question is brought up, by a naïve student, for example, or a prospective donor to the cause of a liberal arts education, it is apt to be greeted with uncomfortable embarrassment.

What is so wrong with the question? One answer is that it is extremely obscure, if not downright unintelligible. It is unclear what exactly the question is supposed to be asking. Talk of meaning in other contexts does not offer ready analogies for understanding the phrase "the meaning of life." When we ask the meaning of a word, for example, we want to know what the word stands for, what it represents. But life is not part of a language, or of any other sort of symbolic system. It is not clear how it could "stand for" anything, nor to whom. We sometimes use "meaning" in nonlinguistic contexts: "Those dots mean measles." "Those footprints mean that someone was here since it rained." In these cases, talk of meaning seems to be equivalent to talk of evidence, but the contexts in which such claims are made tend to specify what hypotheses are in question within relatively fixed bounds. To ask what life means without a similarly specified context, leaves us at sea.

Still, when people do ask about the meaning of life, they are evidently expressing some concern or other, and it would be disingenuous to insist that the rest of us haven't the faintest idea what that is. The question at least gestures toward a certain set of concerns with which most of us are at least somewhat familiar. Rather than dismiss a question with which many people have been passionately occupied as pure and simple nonsense, it seems more appropriate to try

to interpret it and reformulate it in a way that can be more clearly and unambiguously understood. Though there may well be many things going on when people ask, "What is the meaning of life?", the most central among them seems to be a search to find a purpose or a point to human existence. It is a request to find out why we are here (that is, why we exist at all), with the hope that an answer to this question will also tell us something about what we should be doing with our lives.

If understanding the question in this way, however, makes the question intelligible, it might not give reason to reopen it as a live philosophical problem. Indeed, if some of professional philosophy's discomfort with discussion of the meaning of life comes from a desire to banish ambiguity and obscurity from the field, as much comes, I think, from the thought that the question, when made clearer, has already been answered, and that the answer is depressing. Specifically, if the question of the Meaning of Life is to be identified with the question of the purpose of life, then the standard view, at least among professional philosophers, would seem to be that it all depends on the existence of God. In other words, the going opinion seems to be that if there is a God, then there is at least a chance that there is a purpose, and so a meaning to life. God may have created us for a reason, with a plan in mind. But to go any further along this branch of thinking is not in the purview of secular philosophers.[1] If, on the other hand, there is no God, then there can be no meaning, in the sense of a point or a purpose to our existence. We are simply a product of physical processes—there are no reasons for our existence, just causes.

At the same time that talk of Life having a Meaning is banished from philosophy, however, the talk of lives being more or less *meaningful* seems to be on the rise. Newspapers, magazines, self-help manuals[2] are filled with essays on how to find meaning in your life;

From "The Meanings of Lives," by Susan Wolf, reprinted with permission of the author.

sermons and therapies are built on the truism that happiness is not just a matter of material comfort, or sensual pleasure, but also of a deeper kind of fulfillment. Though philosophers to date have had relatively little to say about what gives meaning to individual lives, passing references can be found throughout the literature; it is generally acknowledged as an intelligible and appropriate thing to want in one's life. Indeed, it would be crass to think otherwise.

But how can individual lives have meaning if life as a whole has none? Are those of us who suspect there is no meaning *to* life deluding ourselves in continuing to talk about the possibility of finding meaning *in* life? (Are we being short-sighted, failing to see the implications of one part of our thought on another?) Alternatively, are these expressions mere homonyms, with no conceptual or logical connections between them? Are there simply two wholly unconnected topics here?

Many of you will be relieved to hear that I do not wish to revive the question of whether there is a meaning to life. I am inclined to accept the standard view that there is no plausible interpretation of that question that offers a positive answer in the absence of a fairly specific religious metaphysics. An understanding of meaningfulness in life, however, does seem to me to merit more philosophical attention than it has so far received, and I will have some things to say about it here. Here, too, I am inclined to accept the standard view—or a part of the standard view—viz., that meaningfulness is an intelligible feature to be sought in a life, and that it is, at least sometimes attainable but not everywhere assured. But what that feature is—what we are looking for—is controversial and unclear, and so the task of analyzing or interpreting that feature will take up a large portion of my remarks today. With an analysis proposed, I shall return to the question of how a positive view about the possibility of meaning in lives can fit with a negative or agnostic view about the meaning of life. The topics are not, I think, as unconnected as might at first seem necessary for their respectively optimistic and pessimistic answers to coexist. Though my discussion will offer nothing new in the way of an answer to the question of the meaning of life, therefore, it may offer a somewhat different perspective on that question's significance.

Let us begin, however, with the other question, that of understanding what it is to seek meaning in life. What do we want when we want a meaningful life? What is it that makes some lives meaningful, others less so?

If we focus on the agent's, or the subject's, perspective—on a person wanting meaning in her life, her feeling the need for more meaning—we might incline toward a subjective interpretation of the feature being sought. When a person self-consciously looks for something to give her life meaning, it signals a kind of unhappiness. One imagines, for example, the alienated housewife, whose life seems to her to be a series of endless chores. What she wants, it might appear, is something that she can find more subjectively rewarding.

This impression is reinforced if we consider references to "meaningful experiences." (The phrase might be applied, for example, to a certain kind of wedding or funeral.) The most salient feature of an event that is described as meaningful seems to be its "meaning a lot" *to* the participants. To say that a ceremony, or, for that matter, a job, is meaningful seems at the very least to include the idea that it is emotionally satisfying. An absence of meaning is usually marked by a feeling of emptiness and dissatisfaction; in contrast, a meaningful life, or meaningful part of life, is necessarily at least somewhat rewarding or fulfilling. It is noteworthy, however, that meaningful experiences are not necessarily particularly happy. A trip to one's birthplace may well be meaningful; a visit to an amusement park is unlikely to be so.

If we step back, however, and ask ourselves, as observers, what lives strike us as especially meaningful, if we ask what sorts of lives exemplify meaningfulness, subjective criteria do not seem to be in the forefront. Who comes to mind? Perhaps, Gandhi, or Albert Schweitzer, or Mother Teresa; perhaps Einstein or Jonas Salk. Cezanne, or Manet, Beethoven, Charlie Parker. Tolstoy is an interesting case to which I shall return. Alternatively, we can look to our neighbors, our colleagues, our relatives— some of whom, it seems to me, live more meaningful lives than others. Some, indeed, of my acquaintance seem to me to live lives that are paradigms of meaning—right up there with the famous names on the earlier lists; while others (perhaps despite their modicum of fame) would score quite low on the meaningfulness scale. If those in the latter category feel a lack of meaning in their lives—well, they are right to feel it, and it is a step in the right direction that they notice that there is something about their lives that they should try to change.

What is it to live a meaningful life, then? What does meaningfulness in life amount to? It may be easier to make progress by focusing on what we want to avoid. In that spirit, let me offer some paradigms, not of meaning*ful*, but of meaning*less* lives.

For me, the idea of a meaningless life is most clearly and effectively embodied in the image of a person who spends day after day, or night after night, in front of a television set, drinking beer and watching situation comedies. Not that I have anything against television or beer. Still the image, understood as an image of a person whose life is lived in hazy passivity, a life lived at a not unpleasant level of consciousness, but unconnected to anyone or anything, going nowhere, achieving nothing—is, I submit, as strong an image of a meaningless life as there can be. Call this case The Blob.

If any life, any human life, is meaningless, the Blob's life is. But this doesn't mean that any meaningless life must be, in all important respects, like the Blob's. There are other paradigms that highlight by their absences other elements of meaningfulness.

In contrast to the Blob's passivity, for example, we may imagine a life full of activity, but silly or decadent or useless activity. (And again, I have nothing against silly activity, but only against a life that is wholly occupied with it.) We may imagine, for example, one of the idle rich who flits about, fighting off boredom, moving from one amusement to another. She shops, she travels, she eats at expensive restaurants, she works out with her personal trainer.

Curiously, one might also take a very un-idle rich person to epitomize a meaningless life in a slightly different way. Consider, for example, the corporate executive who works twelve-hour, seven-day weeks, suffering great stress, for the sole purpose of the accumulation of personal wealth. Related to this perhaps is David Wiggins' example of the pig farmer who buys more land to grow more corn to feed more

pigs to buy more land to grow more corn to feed more pigs.[3]

These last three cases of the idle rich, the corporate executive and the pig farmer are in some ways very different, but they all share at least this feature: they can all be characterized as lives whose dominant activities seem pointless, useless, or empty. Classify these cases under the heading Useless.

A somewhat different and I think more controversial sort of case to consider involves someone who is engaged, even dedicated, to a project that is ultimately revealed as bankrupt, not because the person's values are shallow or misguided, but because the project fails. The person may go literally bankrupt: for example, a man may devote his life to creating and building up a company to hand over to his children, but the item his company manufactures is rendered obsolete by technology shortly before his planned retirement. Or consider a scientist whose life's work is rendered useless by the announcement of a medical breakthrough just weeks before his own research would have yielded the same results. Perhaps more poignantly, imagine a woman whose life is centered around a relationship that turns out to be a fraud. Cases that fit this mold we may categorize under the heading Bankrupt.

The classification of this third sort of case as an exemplification of meaninglessness may meet more resistance than the classification of the earlier two. Perhaps these lives should not be considered meaningless after all. Nonetheless, these are cases in which it is not surprising that an argument of some sort is needed—it is not unnatural or silly that the subjects of these lives should entertain the thought that their lives have been meaningless. Even if they are wrong, the fact that their thoughts are not, so to speak, out of order, is a useful datum. So, of course, would be the sort of thing one would say to convince them, or ourselves, that these thoughts are ultimately mistaken.

If the cases I have sketched capture our images of meaninglessness more or less accurately, they provide clues to what a positive case of a meaningful life must contain. In contrast to the Blob's passivity, a person who lives a meaningful life must be actively engaged. But, as the Useless cases teach us, it will not do to be engaged in just anything, for any reason or with any goal—one must be engaged in a project or projects that have some positive value, and in some way that is nonaccidentally related to what gives them value. Finally, in order to avoid Bankruptcy, it seems necessary that one's activities be at least to some degree successful (though it may not be easy to determine what counts as the right kind or degree of success). Putting these criteria together, we get a proposal for what it is to live a meaningful life: viz., a meaningful life is one that is actively and at least somewhat successfully engaged in a project (or projects) of positive value.

Several remarks are needed to qualify and refine this proposal. First, the use of the word "project" is not ideal: it is too suggestive of a finite, determinate task, something one takes on, and, if all goes well, completes. Among the things that come to mind as projects are certain kinds of hobbies or careers, or rather, specific tasks that fall within the sphere of such hobbies or careers: things that can be seen as accomplishments, like the producing of a proof or a poem or a pudding, the organizing of a union or a high school band. Although such activities are among the things that seem intuitively to contribute to the meaningfulness of people's lives, there are other forms of meaningfulness that are less directed, and less oriented to demonstrable achievement, and we should not let the use of the word "project" distort or deny the potential of these things to give meaningfulness to life. Relationships, in particular, seem at best awkwardly described as projects. Rarely does one deliberately take them on and, in some cases, one doesn't even have to work at them—one may just have them and live, as it were, within them. Moreover, many of the activities that are naturally described as projects—coaching a school soccer team, planning a surprise party, reviewing an article for a journal—have the meaning they do for us only because of their place in the nonprojectlike relationships in which we are enmeshed and with which we identify. In proposing that a meaningful life is a life actively engaged in projects, then, I mean to use "projects" in an unusually broad sense, to encompass not only goal-directed tasks but other sorts of ongoing activities and involvements as well.

Second, the suggestion that a meaningful life should be "actively engaged" in projects should be understood in a way that recognizes and embraces the connotations of "engagement." Although the idea that a meaningful life requires activity was introduced by contrast to the life of the ultra-passive Blob, we should note that meaning involves more than mere, literal activity. The alienated housewife, presumably, is active all the time—she buys groceries and fixes meals, cleans the house, does the laundry, chauffeurs the children from school to soccer to ballet, arranges doctors' appointments and babysitters. What makes her life insufficiently meaningful is that her heart, so to speak, isn't in these activities. She does not identify with what she is doing—she does not embrace her roles as wife, mother, and homemaker as expressive of who she is and wants to be. We may capture her alienated condition by saying that though she is active, she is not actively engaged. (She is, one might say, just going through the motions.) In characterizing a meaningful life, then, it is worth stressing that living such a life is not just a matter of having projects (broadly construed) and actively and somewhat successfully getting through them. The projects must engage the person whose life it is. Ideally, she would proudly and happily embrace them, as constituting at least part of what her life is about.[4]

Finally, we must say more about the proposal's most blatantly problematic condition—viz, that the projects engagement with which can contribute to a meaningful life must be projects "of positive value." The claim is that meaningful lives must be engaged in projects of positive value—but who is to decide which projects have positive value, or even to guarantee that there is such a thing?

I would urge that we leave the phrase as unspecific as possible in all but one respect. We do not want to build a theory of positive value into our conception of meaningfulness. As a proposal that aims to capture what most people mean by a meaningful life, what we want is a concept that "tracks" whatever we think of as having positive value. This allows us to explain at least some divergent intuitions about meaningfulness in terms of divergent intuitions or beliefs about what has positive value, with the implication that if one is wrong about what has positive value, one will also be wrong about what contributes to a meaningful life. (Thus, a person who finds little to admire in sports—who finds ridiculous, for example, the sight of grown men trying to knock a little ball into a hole with a club, will find relatively little potential for meaning in the life of an avid golfer; a person who places little stock in esoteric intellectual pursuits will be puzzled by someone who strains to write, much less read, a lot of books on supervenience.)

The exception I would make to this otherwise maximally tolerant interpretation of the idea of positive value is that we exclude merely subjective value as a suitable interpretation of the phrase.

It will not do to allow that a meaningful life is a life involved in projects that seem to have positive value from the perspective of the one who lives it. Allowing this would have the effect of erasing the distinctiveness of our interest in meaningfulness; it would blur or remove the difference between an interest in living a meaningful life and an interest in living a life that feels or seems meaningful. That these interests are distinct, and that the former is not merely instrumental to the latter can be seen by reflecting on a certain way the wish or the need for meaning in one's life may make itself felt. What I have in mind is the possibility of a kind of epiphany, in which one wakes up—literally or figuratively—to the recognition that one's life to date has been meaningless. Such an experience would be nearly unintelligible if a lack of meaning were to be understood as a lack of a certain kind of subjective impression. One can hardly understand the idea of waking up to the thought that one's life to date has seemed meaningless. To the contrary, it may be precisely because one did not realize the emptiness of one's projects or the shallowness of one's values until that moment that the experience I am imagining has the poignancy it does. It is the sort of experience that one might describe in terms of scales falling from one's eyes. And the yearning for meaningfulness, the impulse to do something about it, will not be satisfied (though it may be eliminated) by putting the scales back on, so to speak. If one suspects that the life one has been living is meaningless, one will not bring meaning to it by getting therapy or taking a pill that, without changing one's life in any other way, makes one believe that one's life has meaning.

To care that one's life is meaningful, then, is, according to my proposal, to care that one's life is actively and at least somewhat successfully engaged in projects (understanding this term broadly) that not just seem to have positive value, but that really do have it. To care that one's life be meaningful, in other words, is in part to care that what one does with one's life is, to pardon the expression, at least somewhat objectively good. We should be careful, however, not to equate objective goodness with moral goodness, at least not if we understand moral value as essentially involving benefiting or honoring humanity. The concern for meaning in one's life does not seem to be the same as the concern for moral worth, nor do our judgments about what sorts of lives are meaningful seem to track judgments of moral character or accomplishment.

To be sure, some of the paradigms of meaningful lives are lives of great moral virtue or accomplishment—I mentioned Gandhi and Mother Teresa, for example. Others, however, are not. Consider Gauguin, Wittgenstein, Tchaikovsky—morally unsavory figures all, whose lives nonetheless seem chock full of meaning. If one thinks that even they deserve moral credit, for their achievements made the world a better place, consider instead Olympic athletes and world chess champions, whose accomplishments leave nothing behind but their world records. Even more important, consider the artists, scholars, musicians, athletes of our more ordinary sort. For us, too, the activities of artistic creation and research, the development of our skills and our understanding of the world give meaning to our lives—but they do not give moral value to them.

It seems then that meaning in life may not be especially moral, and that indeed lives can be richly meaningful even if they are, on the whole, judged to be immoral. Conversely, that one's life is at least moderately moral, that it is lived, as it were, above reproach, is no assurance of its being moderately meaningful. The alienated housewife, for example, may be in no way subject to moral criticism. (And it is debatable whether even the Blob deserves specifically moral censure.)

That people do want meaning in their lives, I take it, is an observable, empirical fact. We have already noted the evidence of self-help manuals, and therapy groups. What I have offered so far is an analysis of what that desire or concern amounts to. I want now to turn to the question of whether the desire is one that it is good that people have, whether, that is, there is some positive reason why they *should* want this.

At a minimum, we may acknowledge that it is at least not bad to want meaning in one's life. There is, after all, no harm in it. Since people do want this, and since there are no moral objections to it, we should recognize the concern for meaning as a legitimate concern, at least in the weak sense that people should be allowed to pursue it. Indeed, insofar as meaningfulness in one's life is a significant factor in a life's overall well-being, we should do more than merely allow its pursuit: we should positively try to increase opportunities for people to live lives of meaning.

Most of us, however, seem to have a stronger positive attitude toward the value of meaningfulness than this minimum concession admits. We do not think it is merely all right for people to want meaning in their lives—as it is all right for people to like country music, or to take an interest in figure-skating. We think people positively ought to care that their lives be meaningful. It is disturbing, or at least regrettable, to find someone who doesn't care about this. Yet this positive assessment ought to strike us, at least initially, as somewhat mysterious. What is the good, after all, of living a meaningful life, and to whom?

Since a meaningful life is not necessarily a *morally* better life than a meaningless one (the Olympic athlete may do no more good nor harm than the idly rich socialite), it is not necessarily better *for the world* that people try to live or even succeed in living meaningful lives. Neither is a meaningful life assured of being an especially happy one, however. Many of the things that give meaning to our lives (relationships to loved ones, aspirations to achieve) make us vulnerable to pain, disappointment and stress. From the inside, the Blob's hazy passivity may be preferable to the experience of the tortured artist or political crusader. By conventional standards, therefore, it is not clear that caring about or even succeeding in living a meaningful life is better *for the person herself.*

Yet, as I have already mentioned, those of us who do care that our lives be meaningful tend to think that it is a positively good thing that we do. We not only want to live meaningful lives, we want to want this—we approve of this desire, and think it is better for others if they have this desire, too. If, for example, you see a person you care about conducting her life in a way that you find devoid of worth—she is addicted to drugs, perhaps, or just to television, or she is overly enthusiastic in her career as a corporate lawyer—you are apt to encourage her to change, or at least hope that she will find a new direction on her own. Your most prominent worry may well be that she is heading for a fall. You fear that at some point she will wake up to the fact that she has been wasting or misdirecting her life, a point that may come too late for easy remedy and will, in any case, involve a lot of pain and self-criticism. But the fear that she will wake up to the fact that she has been wasting her life (and have difficulty turning her life around) may not be as terrible as the fear that she won't wake up to it. If you came to feel secure that no painful moment of awakening would ever come because your friend (or sister or daughter) simply does not care whether her life is meaningful, you might well think that this situation is not better but worse. We seem to think there is something regrettable about a person living a meaningless life, even if the person herself does not mind that she is. We seem to think she *should* want meaning in her life, even if she doesn't realize it.

What, though, is the status of this "should," the nature or source of the regret? The mystery that I earlier suggested we should feel about our value in meaningfulness is reflected in the uneasy location of this judgment. If my own reaction to the woman who doesn't care whether her life is meaningful is typical, the thought that she should, or ought to care is closer to a prudential judgment than it is to a moral one. (If there is a moral objection to a person who lives a meaningless life and is content with that, it is not, in my opinion, a very strong one. The Blob, after all, is not hurting anyone, nor is the idle rich jet-setter. She may, for example, give money to environmental causes to offset the damage she is doing in her SUV, and write generous checks to Oxfam and UNICEF on a regular basis.) The thought that it is too bad if a person does not live a meaningful life (even if she doesn't mind) seems rather to be the thought that it is too bad *for her.*

The closest analogue to this thought in the history of ethics of which I am aware is Aristotle's conception of **eudaimonia.** His conception of the virtuous life as the happiest life is offered as a conclusion of an enlightened self-interest. According to standard conceptions of self-interest, however (either hedonistic or preference-based), it is not obvious why this should be so, and, unfortunately, Aristotle himself does not address the question explicitly. Rather, he seems to think that if you do not just see that the virtuous life, in which one aims for and achieves what is "fine," is a better, more desirable life for yourself, that just shows that you were not well brought up, and in that case, there is no point trying to educate you.

Our question, the question of whether and what kind of reason there is for a person to strive for a meaningful life, is not quite the same as the question of whether and what kind of reason there is to aspire to virtue,—though, when one is careful to interpret "virtue" in the broad and not specifically moral way that Aristotle uses the term, it is closer than it might seem. Still, as I say, Aristotle does not really address the question, and so, though I take my line of thought to be Aristotelian in spirit, a scholarly study of Aristotle's texts is not likely to be an efficient way of finding an answer to the question ourselves.

What reason is there, then, if any, for a person to want to live a meaningful life? I have said that we seem to think it would be better for her, that it is, at least roughly, in her self-interest. At the same time, the thought that she should care about meaning seems to depend on claims from outside herself. Even if there are no desires latent in her psychology which meaningfulness would satisfy, we seem to think, there is reason why she should have such desires. She seems to be making some kind of mistake.

If my analysis of what is involved in living a meaningful life is right, then the question of why one should care about living a meaningful life is equivalent to the question of why one should care that one's life be actively and somewhat successfully engaged in projects of positive value. The source of perplexity seems, in particular, to be about the reason to care that one's projects be positively valuable. As long as

you are engaged by your activities, and they make you happy, why should one care that one's activities be objectively worthwhile?

The answer, I believe, is that to devote one's life entirely to activities whose value is merely subjective, to devote oneself to activities whose sole justification is that it is good for you, is, in a sense I shall try to explain, practically solipsistic. It flies in the face of one's status as, if you will, a tiny speck in a vast universe, a universe with countless perspectives of equal status with one's own, from which one's life might be assessed. Living a life that is engaged with and so at least partially focussed on projects whose value has a nonsubjective source is a way of acknowledging one's non-privileged position. It harmonizes, in a way that a purely egocentric life does not, with the fact that one is not the center of the universe.

The basic idea is this: The recognition of one's place in the universe, of one's smallness, one might say, or one's insignificance, and of the independent existence of the universe in which one is a part involves, among other things, the recognition of "the mereness" of one's subjective point of view. To think of one's place in the universe is to recognize the possibility of a perspective, of infinitely many perspectives, really, from which one's life is merely gratuitous; it is to recognize the possibility of a perspective, or rather of infinitely many perspectives, that are indifferent to whether one exists at all, and so to whether one is happy or sad, satisfied or unsatisfied, fulfilled or unfulfilled.

In the face of this recognition, a life that is directed solely to its subject's own fulfillment, or, to its mere survival or towards the pursuit of goals that are grounded in nothing but the subject's own psychology, appears either solipsistic or silly.

A person who lives a largely egocentric life—who devotes, in other words, lots of energy and attention and care toward himself, who occupies himself more specifically with satisfying and gratifying himself, expresses and reveals a belief that his happiness matters. Even if it doesn't express the view that his happiness matters objectively, it at least expresses the idea that it matters to him. To be solely devoted to his own gratification, then, would express and reveal the fact that his happiness is *all* that matters, at least all that matters to him. If, however, one accepts a framework that recognizes distinctions in nonsubjective value, (and if one believes, as seems only reasonable, that what has nonsubjective value has no special concentration in or connection to oneself) this attitude seems hard to justify.

To accept that framework is, after all, to accept the view that some things are better than others. To me, it makes sense partially to understand this literally: Some *things*, it seems to me, are better than others: people, for example, are better than rocks or mosquitoes, and a Vermeer painting is better than the scraps on my compost heap.[5] What is essential, though, is that accepting a framework that recognizes distinctions in nonsubjective value involves seeing the world as value-filled, as containing with it distinctions of better and worse, of more and less worthwhile, if not of better and worse objects per se, then of better and worse features of the world, or activities, or opportunities to be realized. Against this background, a life solely devoted to one's own gratification or to the satisfaction of one's whims seems gratuitous and hard to defend. For, as I have said, to live such a life expresses the view that one's happiness is all that matters, at least to oneself. But why should this be the only thing that matters, when there is so much else worth caring about?

Those familiar with Thomas Nagel's book, *The Possibility of Altruism*, may have recognized an allusion to it in my suggestion that a life indifferent to meaning was practically solipsistic. The allusion is significant, for the argument I am making here, though it is directed to a different conclusion, bears a strong resemblance to the argument of that book. Nagel's argument invites us to see a person who, while evidently trying to avoid or minimize pain to himself, shows total indifference to the pain of others, as a practical solipsist in the sense that he fails, in his practical outlook, to recognize and appreciate that he is one person among others, equally real. Roughly, the suggestion seems to be that if you appreciate the reality of others, then you realize that their pains are just as painful as yours. If the painfulness of your pain is a reason to take steps to avoid it, then, the painfulness of their pain should provide reasons, too. To be totally indifferent to the pain of others, then, bespeaks a failure to recognize their pain (to recognize it, that is, as *really* painful, in the same way that yours is painful to you).

This is not the occasion to discuss the plausibility of Nagel's interpretation of the pure egoist as a practical solipsist, nor even to describe Nagel's complex and subtle position in enough detail to be able fairly to evaluate it. What I want to call attention to has to do not with the substance of the argument but with the type of argument it is: specifically, Nagel's argument suggests that appreciation of a certain fact—in this case, the fact that you are just one person among others, equally real—is a source of practical reason—in this case, it gives you reason to take the pains of others to constitute reasons for action. If Nagel is right, we have reason to care about the pain of others that is grounded, not in our own psychologies (and more specifically, not in any of our own desires), but in a fact about the world. His suggestion is that a person who fails to see the pain of others as a source of reason acts "as if" the pain of others is not real, or not painful. But of course the pain of others *is* real and *is* painful. Such a person thus exhibits a failure not just of morality or sympathy, but of practical reason, in the sense that his practical stance fails to accord with a very significant fact about the world.

My suggestion that we have reason to care about and to try to live meaningful rather than meaningless lives resembles Nagel's in form. Like him, I am suggesting that we can have a reason to do something or to care about something that is grounded not in our own psychologies, nor specifically in our own desires, but in a fact about the world. The fact in question in this case is the fact that we are, each of us, specks in a vast and value-filled universe, and that as such we have no privileged position as a source of or possessor of objective value. To devote oneself wholly to one's own satisfaction seems to me to fly in the face of this truth, to act "as if" one is the only thing that matters, or perhaps, more, that one's own psychology is the only source of (determining) what matters. By focusing one's attention and one's energies at least in part on things, activities, aspects of the world that have value independent of you, you implicitly acknowledge your place and your status in the world. Your behavior, and your practical stance is thus more in accord with the facts.

Admittedly, this is not the sort of reason that one must accept on pain of inconsistency or any other failure of logic. Just as a person may simply not care whether her life is meaningful, so she may also simply not care whether her life is in accord with, or harmonizes with the facts. (It is one thing to say we should live in accord with the facts of physics, geography, and the other sciences. Living in accordance with these facts has evident instrumental value—it helps us get around in the world. But living in a way that practically acknowledges, or harmonizes with the fact that we are tiny specks in a value-filled world will not make our lives go better that way.) Such a person cannot be accused in any strict sense of irrationality. Like noninstrumental reasons to be moral, the reason to care about living a worthwhile life is not one that narrow rationality requires one to accept. At the same time, it seems appropriate to characterize my suggestion (and Nagel's) as one that appeals to reason in a broader sense. For my suggestion is that an interest in living a meaningful life is an appropriate response to a fundamental truth, and that failure to have such a concern constitutes a failure to acknowledge that truth.

As we have already seen, the truth to which I am proposing a meaningful life provides a response is the truth that we are, each of us, tiny specks in a vast and value-filled universe. Like the truth that we are, each of us, one person among others, equally real, it opposes what children and many adults may have a tendency to assume—namely, that they are the center of the universe, either the possessor or the source of all value. (It is because both Nagel's truth and mine are opposites of that assumption that both might plausibly be understood as alternatives to practical solipsism.) Unlike Nagel's truth, mine is not specifically addressed to our relation to other people. A person may, therefore, appreciate and practically express one of these truths and not the other. Whereas an appropriate response to the equal reality of other people may be, if Nagel is right, an embrace of morality or something relating to morality, my proposal is that an appropriate response to our status as specks in a vast universe is a concern and aspiration to have one's life wrapped up with projects of positive value.

Perhaps, however, I have not made it clear why this is an appropriate response. The question

may seem especially pressing because the thought that we are tiny specks in a vast universe, and the sense that it calls for or demands a response has, in the past, tended to move philosophers in a different direction. Specifically, the thought that we are tiny specks in a vast universe was in the past closely associated with that murky and ponderous question to which I referred at the beginning of my [paper]—the question of The Meaning of Life. The thought that we are tiny specks in a vast universe has indeed often evoked that question, and, to those who either do not believe in or do not want to rest their answers in the existence of a benevolent God, it has more or less immediately seemed also to indicate an answer. Considering their answer to the question of the Meaning of Life and contrasting it with my response to the fact of our smallness, may clarify the substance of my proposal.

The train of thought I have in mind is one that has, with variations, been expressed by many distinguished philosophers, including Camus, Tolstoy, Richard Taylor, and, curiously, Nagel himself. For them, the recognition of our place in the universe—our smallness, or our speckness, if you will—seems to warrant the conclusion not only that there is no meaning to life as such but also that each individual life is necessarily absurd.

On the view of these philosophers, a life can be meaningful only if it can mean something *to* someone, and not just to *someone*, but to someone other than oneself and indeed someone of more intrinsic or ultimate value than oneself. Of course, anyone can live in such a way as to make her life meaningful to *someone* other than herself. She can maintain her relationship with parents and siblings, establish friendships with neighbors and colleagues. She can fall in love. If all else fails, she can have a child who will love her, or two children, or six. She can open up an entire clinic for God's sake. But if a life that is devoted solely to yourself, a life that is good to no one other than yourself lacks meaning, these philosophers not implausibly think, so will a life that is devoted to any other poor creature, for he or she will have no more objective importance than you have, and so will be no more fit a stopping place by which to ground the claim of meaningfulness than you. Nor, according to this train of thought, will it help to expand your circle, to be of use or to have an effect on a larger segment of humankind. If each life is individually lacking in meaning, then the collective is meaningless as well. If each life has but an infinitesimal amount of value, then although one's meaning will increase in proportion to one's effect, the total quantity of meaning relative to the cosmos will remain so small as to make the effort pathetic.

From the perspective of these philosophers, if there is no God, then human life, each human life, must be objectively meaningless, because if there is no God, there is no appropriate being *for whom* we could have meaning.

From this perspective, my suggestion that the living of a worthwhile life constitutes a response to a recognition of our place in the universe might seem ridiculously nearsighted, as if, having acknowledged the mereness of my own subjectivity, I then failed to acknowledge the equal mereness of the subjectivity of others. But I think this misunderstands the point in my proposal of living a life that realizes nonsubjective value, a misunderstanding that derives from too narrow a view about what an appropriate and satisfactory response to the fact of our place in the universe must be.

The philosophers I have been speaking about— we can call them the pessimists—take the fundamental lesson to be learned from the contemplation of our place in the universe to be that we are cosmically insignificant, a fact that clashes with our desire to be very significant indeed. If God existed, such philosophers might note, we would have a chance at being significant. For God himself, is presumably very significant and so we could be significant by being or by making ourselves significant to Him. In the absence of a God, however, it appears that we can only be significant to each other, to beings, that is, as pathetically small as ourselves. We want to be important, but we cannot be important, and so our lives are absurd.

The pessimists are right about the futility of trying to make ourselves important. Insofar as contemplation of the cosmos makes us aware of our smallness, whether as individuals or as a species, we simply must accept it and come to terms with it. Some people do undoubtedly get very upset, even despondent when they start to think about their cosmic insignificance. They want to be important, to have an impact on the world, to make a mark that will last forever. When they realize that they cannot achieve this, they are very disappointed. The only advice one can give to such people is: Get Over It.

Rather than fight the fact of our insignificance, however, and of the mereness of our subjectivity, my proposal is that we live in a way that acknowledges the fact, or, at any rate, that harmonizes with it. Living in a way that is significantly focussed on, engaged with, and concerned to promote or realize value whose source comes from outside of oneself, does seem to harmonize with this, whereas living purely egocentrically does not. Living lives that attain or realize some nonsubjective value may not make us meaningful, much less important, to anyone other than ourselves, but it will give us something to say, to think, in response to the recognition of perspectives that we ourselves imaginatively adopt that are indifferent to our existence and to our well-being.

At the beginning of this paper, I raised the question of how the meaning of life—or the absence of such meaning—was related to the meaningfulness of particular lives. As I might have put it, does it really make sense to think that there can be meaningful lives in a meaningless world? In light of this discussion, we can see how the answer to that question might be "yes" while still holding on to the idea that the similar wording of the two phrases is not merely coincidental.

If I am right about what is involved in living a meaningful life—if, that is, living a meaningful life is a matter of at least partly successful engagement in projects of positive value—then the possibility of living meaningful lives despite the absence of an overall meaning *to* life can be seen to depend on the fact that distinctions of value (that is, of objective value) do not rely on the existence of God or of any overarching purpose to the human race as a whole. Whether or not God exists, the fact remains that some objects, activities and ideas are better than others. Whether or not God exists, some ways of living are more worthwhile than others. Some activities are a waste of time.

People are sometimes tempted to think that if God doesn't exist, then nothing matters. They are tempted to think that if we will all die, and eventually all traces of our existence will fade from all consciousness, there is no point to doing anything; nothing makes any difference. Tolstoy evidently thought this sometimes, and gave eloquent voice to that view. But the reasoning is ridiculous. If one activity is worthwhile and another is a waste, then one has reason to prefer the former, even if there is no God to look down on us and approve. More generally, we seem to have reason to engage ourselves with projects of value whether God exists and gives life a purpose or not.

Putting things this way, however, fails to explain why we use the language of meaning to describe lives engaged in activities of worth. Putting things this way there seems to be no connection at all between the question of whether there is a meaning to life and the question of whether individual lives can be meaningful. I believe, however, that there is a connection, that shows itself, or perhaps that consists in the fact that the wish for both kinds of meaning are evoked by the same thought, and that, perhaps, either kind of meaning would be an appropriate and satisfying response to that thought. The thought in question is the thought (the true thought) that we are tiny specks in a vast universe. It is a thought that is apt to be upsetting when it first hits you—at least in part because, looking back from that position, it may seem that one had until then lived "as if" something opposite were true. One had lived perhaps until then as if one were the center of the universe, the sole possessor or source of all value. One had all along assumed one had a special and very important place in the world, and now one's assumption is undermined. One can see how, in this context, one might wish for a meaning to life. For if there were a meaning—a purpose, that is, to human existence that can be presumed to be of great importance, then, by playing a role, by contributing to that purpose, one can recover some of the significance one thought one's life had. Like the pessimistic philosophers I talked about a few minutes ago, I doubt that that path is open to us. But there seems another way one can respond to the thought, or to the recognition of our relatively insignificant place in the universe, that is more promising, and that can, and sometimes does, provide a different kind of comfort. If one lived one's life, prior to the recognition of our smallness, as if one was the center of the universe, the appropriate response to that recognition is simply *to stop living that way*. If one turns one's attention to other parts of the universe—even to other specks like oneself—in a way that appreciates and engages with the values or valuable objects that come from outside oneself, then one corrects one's practical stance. If, in addition, one is partly successful in producing, preserving, or promoting value—if one does some good, or realizes value, then one has something to say, or to think in response to the worry that one's life has no point.

Only if some suggestion like mine is right can we make sense of the intuitions about meaningfulness to which I called attention in the earlier part of this paper. According to those intuitions the difference between a meaningful and a meaningless life is not a difference between a life that does a lot of good, and a life that does a little. (Nor is it a difference between a life that makes a big splash and one that, so to speak, sprays only a few drops.) It is rather a difference between a life that does good or is good or realizes value and a life that is essentially a waste. According to these intuitions, there is as sharp a contrast between the Blob and a life devoted to the care of a single needy individual as there is between the Blob and someone who manages to change the world for the better on a grand scale. Indeed, there may be an equally sharp contrast between the Blob and the monk of a contemplative order whose existence confers no benefit or change on anyone else's life at all. Ironically, along this dimension, Tolstoy fares exceptionally well.

Thus it seems to me that even if there is no meaning to life, even if, that is, life as a whole has no purpose, no direction, no point, that is no reason to doubt the possibility of finding and making meaning in life—that is no reason, in other words, to doubt the possibility of people living meaningful lives. In coming to terms with our place and our status in the universe, it is natural and appropriate that people should want to explore the possibility of both types of meaning. Even if philosophers have nothing new or encouraging to say about the possibility of meaning of the first sort, there may be some point to elaborating the different meanings of the idea of finding meaning in life, and in pointing out the different forms that coming to terms with the human condition can take.

NOTES

1. Thomas Nagel has what might be thought to be an even more pessimistic view—viz, that even if there is a God, there is no reason God's purpose should be our purpose, no reason, therefore, to think that God's existence could give meaning, in the right sense, to our lives.

2. E.g., the day I sat down to begin notes on this article, a review of a book by Monique Greenwood, *Having What Matters: The Black Woman's Guide to Creating the Life You Really Want* was in the paper (*Baltimore Sun*, January 16, 2002). The book is offered as a guide to replace Helen Gurley Brown's 1980s manifesto about having it all. Instead of "she who has the most toys wins," Greenwood says "she who has the most joy wins." She is focused on how to "achieve a life with value and meaning."

3. David Wiggins, "Truth, Invention, and the Meaning of Life," in *Proceedings of the British Academy*, LXII, 1976.

4. It seems to me there is a further condition or qualification on what constitutes a meaningful life, though it does not fit gracefully into the definition I have proposed, and is somewhat peripheral to the focus of this essay: namely, that the projects that contribute to a meaningful life must be of significant duration, and contribute to the unity of the life or of a significant stage of it. A person who is always engaged in some valuable project or other, but whose projects don't express any underlying core of interest and value is not, at least, a paradigm of someone whose *life* is meaningful. Here perhaps there is something illuminating in making analogies to other uses of "meaning," for what is at issue here has to do with their being a basis for "making sense" of the life, of being able to see it as a narrative.

5. *Pace* the creepy scene in the movie *American Beauty* of the garbage bag blowing in the wind.

KEY TERM

Eudaimonia

STUDY QUESTIONS

1. What is the importance of the distinction that Wolf draws between asking about the Meaning of Life and asking about the meaningfulness of a particular life? Are you as pessimistic as Wolf is about a satisfactory answer to the first sort of question?

2. Do you think that the lives of the Blob, Useless, and Bankrupt are all equally meaningless? With respect to Bankrupt, in particular, should it really matter to the meaningfulness of someone's life whether the person's colleagues always beat him or her to the new idea? How important is Wolf's notion of *success*?

3. Do you agree with Wolf that people who really want to make a lasting impact on the world really just need to "get over it"? Or is there something to be said in favor of the idea?

4. What is your reaction to the thought that we are just tiny specks in an infinite universe? Do you think that thought can tell us anything about whether and how we can lead meaningful lives?

Death

THOMAS NAGEL

..

"The syllogism he had learnt from Kiesewetter's Logic: 'Caius is a man, men are mortal, therefore Caius is mortal,' had always seemed to him correct as applied to Caius, but certainly not as applied to himself ... What did Caius know of the smell of that striped leather ball Vanya had been so fond of?"

Tolstoy
The Death of Ivan Ilych

I f, as many people believe, death is the unequivocal and permanent end of our existence, the question arises whether it is a bad thing to die. There is conspicuous disagreement about the matter: some people think death is dreadful; others have no objection to death *per se*, though they may hope their own will be neither premature nor painful.

Those in the former category tend to think those in the latter are blind to the obvious, while the latter suppose the former to be prey to some sort of confusion. On the one hand it can be said that life is all one has, and the loss of it is the greatest loss one can sustain. On the other hand it may be objected that death deprives this supposed loss of its subject, and that if one realizes that death is not an unimaginable condition of the persisting person, but a mere blank, one will see that it can have no value whatever, positive or negative.

Since I want to leave aside the question whether we are, or might be, immortal in some form, I shall simply use the word 'death' and its cognates in this discussion to mean *permanent* death, unsupplemented by any form of conscious survival. I wish to consider whether death is in itself an evil; and how great an evil, and of what kind, it might be. This question should be of interest even to those who

believe that we do not die permanently, for one's attitude towards immortality must depend in part on one's attitude towards death.

Clearly if death is an evil at all, it cannot be because of its positive features, but only because of what it deprives us of. I shall try to deal with the difficulties surrounding the natural view that death is an evil because it brings to an end all the goods that life contains. An account of these goods need not occupy us here, except to observe that some of them, like perception, desire, activity, and thought, are so general as to be constitutive of human life. They are widely regarded as formidable benefits in themselves, despite the fact that they are conditions of misery as well as happiness, and that a sufficient quantity of more particular evils can perhaps outweigh them.

I wish to add only two observations. First, the value of life and its contents does not attach to mere organic survival: almost everyone would be indifferent (other things equal) between immediate death and immediate coma followed by death twenty years later without reawakening. And secondly, like most goods, this one can be multiplied by time: more is better than less. (It should be remarked that the added quantities need not be temporally continuous. People are attracted to the possibility of long-term suspended animation or freezing, followed by the resumption of conscious life, because they can regard it from within simply as a *continuation* of their present life. If these techniques are ever perfected, what from outside

"Death" from *Mortal Questions*, by Thomas Nagel. (1979). pp. 1–10. Reprinted with the permission of Cambridge University Press.

appeared as a dormant interval of three hundred years could be experienced by the subject as nothing more than a sharp discontinuity in the character of his experiences.)

If we turn from what is good about life to what is bad about death, the case is completely different. Essentially, though there may be problems about their specification, what we find desirable in life are certain states, conditions, or types of activity. It is *being* alive, *doing* certain things, having certain experiences, that we consider good. But if death is an evil, it is the *loss of life*, rather than the state of being dead, or non-existent, or unconscious, that is objectionable.[1] This asymmetry is important. If it is good to be alive, that advantage can be attributed to a person at each point of his life. It is a good of which Bach had more than Schubert, simply because he lived longer. Death, however, is not an evil of which Shakespeare has so far received a larger portion than Proust. If death is a disadvantage, it is not easy to say when a man suffers it.

Two other facts indicate that we do not object to death merely because it involves long periods of nonexistence. First, as has been mentioned, most of us would not regard the *temporary* suspension of life, even for substantial intervals, as in itself a misfortune. If it develops that people can be frozen without reduction of the conscious lifespan, it will be inappropriate to pity those who are temporarily out of circulation. Secondly, none of us existed before we were born (or conceived), but few regard that as a misfortune. I shall have more to say about this later.

The point that death is not regarded as an unfortunate *state* enables us to refute a curious but very common suggestion about the origin of the fear of death. It is often said that those who object to death have made the mistake of trying to imagine what it is like to *be* dead. It is alleged that the failure to realize that this task is logically impossible (for the banal reason that there is nothing to imagine) leads to the conviction that death is a mysterious and therefore terrifying prospective *state*. But this diagnosis is evidently false, for it is just as impossible to imagine being totally unconscious as to imagine being dead, (though it is easy enough to imagine oneself, from the outside, in either of those conditions). Yet people

who are averse to death are not usually averse to unconsciousness (so long as it does not entail a substantial cut in the total duration of waking life).

If we are to make sense of the view that to die is bad, it must be on the ground that life is a good and death is the corresponding deprivation or loss, bad not because of any positive features but because of the desirability of what it removes. We must now turn to the serious difficulties which this hypothesis raises, difficulties about loss and privation in general, and about death in particular.

Essentially there are three types of problem. First, doubt may be raised whether *anything* can be bad for a man without being positively unpleasant to him: specifically, it may be doubted that there are any evils which consist merely in the deprivation or absence of possible goods, and which do not depend on someone's *minding* that deprivation. Secondly, there are special difficulties, in the case of death, about how the supposed misfortune is to be assigned to a subject at all. There is doubt both as to *who* its subject is, and as to *when* he undergoes it. So long as a person exists, he has not yet died, and once he has died, he no longer exists; so there seems to be no time when death, if it is a misfortune, can be ascribed to its unfortunate subject. The third type of difficulty concerns the asymmetry, mentioned above, between our attitudes to posthumous and prenatal nonexistence. How can the former be bad if the latter is not?

It should be recognized that if these are valid objections to counting death as an evil, they will apply to many other supposed evils as well. The first type of objection is expressed in general form by the common remark that what you don't know can't hurt you. It means that even if a man is betrayed by his friends, ridiculed behind his back, and despised by people who treat him politely to his face, none of it can be counted as a misfortune for him so long as he does not suffer as a result. It means that a man is not injured if his wishes are ignored by the executor of his will, or if, after his death, the belief becomes current that all the literary works on which his fame rests were really written by his brother, who died in Mexico at the age of twenty-eight. It seems to me worth asking what assumptions about good and evil lead to these drastic restrictions.

All the questions have something to do with time. There certainly are goods and evils of a simple kind (including some pleasures and pains) which a person possesses at a given time simply in virtue of his condition at that time. But this is not true of all the things we regard as good or bad for a man. Often we need to know his history to tell whether something is a misfortune or not; this applies to ills like deterioration, deprivation, and damage. Sometimes his experiential *state* is relatively unimportant—as in the case of a man who wastes his life in the cheerful pursuit of a method of communicating with asparagus plants. Someone who holds that all goods and evils must be temporally assignable states of the person may of course try to bring difficult cases into line by pointing to the pleasure or pain that more complicated goods and evils cause. Loss, betrayal, deception, and ridicule are on this view bad because people suffer when they learn of them. But it should be asked how our ideas of human value would have to be constituted to accommodate these cases directly instead. (This would enable us to explain *why* their discovery causes suffering.) One possible account is that most good and ill fortune has as its subject a person identified by his history and his possibilities, rather than merely by his categorical state of the moment—and that while this subject can be exactly located in a sequence of places and times, the same is not necessarily true of the goods and ills that befall him.[2]

These ideas can be illustrated by an example of deprivation whose severity approaches that of death. Suppose an intelligent person receives a brain injury that reduces him to the mental condition of a contented infant, and that such desires as remain to him are satisfied by a custodian, so that he is free from care. Such a development would be widely regarded as a severe misfortune, not only for his friends and relations, or for society, but also, and primarily, for the person himself. This does not mean that a contented infant is unfortunate. The intelligent adult who has been *reduced* to this condition is the subject of the misfortune. He is the one we pity, though of course he does not mind his condition—there is some doubt, in fact, whether he can be said to exist any longer.

The view that such a man has suffered a misfortune is open to the same objections which have been raised in regard to death. He does not mind his condition. It is in fact the same condition he

was in at the age of three months, except that he is bigger. If we did not pity him then, why pity him now; in any case, who is there to pity? The intelligent adult has disappeared, and for a creature like the one before us, happiness consists in a full stomach and a dry diaper.

If these objections are invalid, it must be because they rest on a mistaken assumption about the temporal relation between the subject of a misfortune and the circumstances which constitute it. If, instead of concentrating exclusively on the oversized baby before us, we consider the person he was, and the person he *could* be now, then his reduction to this state and the cancellation of his natural adult development constitute a perfectly intelligible catastrophe.

This case should convince us that it is arbitrary to restrict the goods and evils that can befall a man to nonrelational properties ascribable to him at particular times. As it stands, that restriction excludes not only such cases of gross degeneration, but also a good deal of what is important about success and failure, and other features of a life that have the character of processes. I believe we can go further, however. There are goods and evils which are irreducibly relational; they are features of the relations between a person, with spatial and temporal boundaries of the usual sort, and circumstances which may not coincide with him either in space or in time. A man's life includes much that does not transpire within the boundaries of his body and his mind, and what happens to him can include much that does not take place within the boundaries of his life. These boundaries are commonly crossed by the misfortunes of being deceived, or despised, or betrayed. (If this is correct, there is a simple account of what is wrong with breaking a deathbed promise. It is an injury to the dead man. For certain purposes it is possible to regard time as just another type of distance.) The case of mental degeneration shows us an evil that depends on a contrast between the reality and the possible alternatives. A man is the subject of good and evil as much because he has hopes which may or may not be fulfilled, or possibilities which may or may not be realized, as because of his capacity to suffer and enjoy. If death is an evil, it must be accounted for in these terms, and the impossibility of locating it within life should not trouble us.

When a man dies we are left with his corpse, and while a corpse can suffer the kind of mishap that may occur to an article of furniture, it is not a suitable object for pity. The man, however, is. He has lost his life, and if he had not died, he would have continued to live it, and to possess whatever good there is in living. If we apply to death the account suggested for the case of dementia, we shall say that although the spatial and temporal locations of the individual who suffered the loss are clear enough, the misfortune itself cannot be so easily located. One must be content just to state that his life is over and there will never be any more of it. That *fact*, rather than his past or present condition, constitutes his misfortune, if it is one. Nevertheless if there is a loss, someone must suffer it, and *he* must have existence and specific spatial and temporal location even if the loss itself does not. The fact that Beethoven had no children may have been a cause of regret to him, or a sad thing for the world, but it cannot be described as a misfortune for the children that he never had. All of us, I believe, are fortunate to have been born. But unless good and ill can be assigned to an embryo, or even to an unconnected pair of gametes, it cannot be said that not to be born is a misfortune. (That is a factor to be considered in deciding whether abortion and contraception are akin to murder.)

This approach also provides a solution to the problem of temporal asymmetry, pointed out by Lucretius. He observed that no one finds it disturbing to contemplate the eternity preceding his own birth, and he took this to show that it must be irrational to fear death, since death is simply the mirror image of the prior abyss. That is not true, however, and the difference between the two explains why it is reasonable to regard them differently. It is true that both the time before a man's birth and the time after his death are times when he does not exist. But the time after his death is time of which his death deprives him. It is time in which, had he not died then, he would be alive. Therefore any death entails the loss of *some* life that its victim would have led had he not died at that or any earlier point. We know perfectly well what it would be for him to have had it instead of losing it, and there is no difficulty in identifying the loser.

But we cannot say that the time prior to a man's birth is time in which he would have lived had he been born not then but earlier. For aside from the brief margin permitted by premature labor, he *could* not have been born earlier: anyone born substantially earlier than he was would have been someone else. Therefore the time prior to his birth is not time in which his subsequent birth prevents him from living. His birth, when it occurs, does not entail the loss to him of any life whatever.

The direction of time is crucial in assigning possibilities to people or other individuals. Distinct possible lives of a single person can diverge from a common beginning, but they cannot converge to a common conclusion from diverse beginnings. (The latter would represent not a set of different possible lives of one individual, but a set of distinct possible individuals, whose lives have identical conclusions.) Given an identifiable individual, countless possibilities for his continued existence are imaginable, and we can clearly conceive of what it would be for him to go on existing indefinitely. However inevitable it is that this will not come about, its possibility is still that of the continuation of a good for him, if life is the good we take it to be.[3]

We are left, therefore, with the question whether the nonrealization of this possibility is in every case a misfortune, or whether it depends on what can naturally be hoped for. This seems to me the most serious difficulty with the view that death is always an evil. Even if we can dispose of the objections against admitting misfortune that is not experienced, or cannot be assigned to a definite time in the person's life, we still have to set some limits on *how* possible a possibility must be for its nonrealization to be a misfortune, (or good fortune, should the possibility be a bad one). The death of Keats at 24 is generally regarded as tragic; that of Tolstoy at 82 is not. Although they will both be dead forever, Keats's death deprived him of many years of life which were allowed to Tolstoy; so in a clear sense Keats's loss was greater, (though not in the sense standardly employed in mathematical comparison between infinite quantities). However, this does not prove that Tolstoy's loss was insignificant. Perhaps we record an objection only to evils which are gratuitously added to the inevitable; the fact that it is worse to die at 24 than at 82 does not imply that it is not a terrible thing to die at 82, or even at 806. The question is whether we can regard as a misfortune any limitation, like mortality, that is normal to the species. Blindness is not a misfortune for a mole, nor would it be for a man, if that were the natural condition of the human race.

The trouble is that life familiarizes us with the goods of which death deprives us. If we put aside doubts about their status as goods and grant that their quantity is in part a function of their duration, the question remains whether death, no matter when it occurs, can be said to deprive its victim of what is in the relevant sense a possible continuation of life. The situation is an ambiguous one. Observed from without, human beings obviously have a natural lifespan and cannot live much longer than a hundred years. A man's sense of his own experience, on the other hand, does not embody this idea of a natural limit. His existence defines for him an essentially open-ended possible future, containing the usual mixture of goods and evils that he has found so tolerable in the past. Having been gratuitously introduced to the world by a collection of natural, historical, and social accidents, he finds himself the subject of a *life*, with an indeterminate and not essentially limited future. Viewed in this way, death, no matter how inevitable, is an abrupt cancellation of indefinitely extensive possible goods. Normality seems to have nothing to do with it, for the fact that we will all inevitably die in a few score years cannot by itself imply that it would not be good to live longer. If there is no limit to the amount of life that it would be good to have, then it may be that a bad end is in store for us all.

NOTES

1. It is sometimes suggested that what we really mind is the process of *dying*. But I should not really object to dying if it were not followed by death.
2. It is certainly not true in general of the things that can be said of him. For example, Abraham Lincoln was taller than Louis XIV. But when?
3. I confess to being troubled by the above argument, on the grounds that it is too sophisticated to explain the simple difference between our attitudes to prenatal and posthumous nonexistence. For this

reason I suspect that something essential is omitted from the account of the badness of death by an analysis that treats it as a deprivation of possibilities. My suspicion is supported by the following suggestion of Robert Nozick. We could imagine discovering that people developed from individual spores that had existed indefinitely far in advance of their birth. In this fantasy, birth never occurs naturally more than a hundred years before the permanent end of the spore's existence. But then we discover a way to trigger the premature hatching of these spores, and people are born who have thousands of years of active life before them. Given such a situation, it would be possible to imagine *oneself* having come into existence thousands of years previously. If we put aside the question whether this would really be the same person, even given the identity of the spore, then the consequence appears to be that a person's birth at a given time *could* deprive him of many earlier years of possible life. Now while it would be cause for regret that one had been deprived of all those possible years of life by being born too late, the feeling would differ from that which many people have about death. I conclude that something about the future *prospect* of permanent nothingness is not captured by the analysis in terms of denied possibilities. If so, then Lucretius's argument still awaits an answer. I suspect that it requires a general treatment of the difference between past and future in our attitudes toward our own lives. Our attitudes toward past and future pain are very different, for example. Derek Parfit's writings on this topic have revealed its difficulty to me.

STUDY QUESTIONS

1. In your own words, what does Nagel think is meant by the claim that "it is good simply to be alive"?
2. What does Nagel mean when he says that "there are goods and evils which are irreducibly relational"? How does he argue for this conclusion?
3. How does Nagel explain the asymmetry in our attitudes toward the time after we die and the time before we were born? Do you think that this explanation is adequate? What other explanations for the asymmetry can you think of?
4. According to Nagel, what is "the most serious difficulty with the view that death is always an evil"? Why does he consider it a difficulty?

Why Is Death Bad?

ANTHONY L. BRUECKNER AND JOHN MARTIN FISCHER

Anthony L. Brueckner (1953–2014) was a Professor of Philosophy at the University of California, Santa Barbara. He is best known for his contributions in epistemology, but he also contributed to the philosophy of language and metaphysics. He is the author of *Essays on Skepticism*.

> I find this in my diary, written twenty and more years ago:
> People say of death, 'There's nothing to be frightened of.
> 'They say it quickly, casually. Now let's say it again, slowly,
> with re-emphasis. 'There's NOTHING to be frightened
> of. 'Jules Renard. 'The word that is most true, most exact,
> most filled with meaning, is the word "nothing."'
>
> Julian Barnes,
> *Nothing To Be Frightened Of*

. .

I. Why Is Death Bad?

It seems that, whereas a person's death needn't be a bad thing for him, it *can* be. In some circumstances, death isn't a "bad thing" or an "evil" for a person. For instance, if a person has a terminal and very painful disease, he might rationally regard his own death as a good thing for him, or at least, he may regard it as something whose prospective occurrence shouldn't be regretted. But the attitude of a "normal" and healthy human being—adult or child—toward the prospect of his death is different; it is *not* unreasonable in certain cases to regard one's own death as a bad thing for oneself.[1] If this is so, then the question arises as to *why* death is bad, in those cases in which it is bad.

If one believes in an afterlife, one could explain how death (conceived of roughly as the cessation of bodily functioning) can be bad insofar as it can involve eternal torment—an indefinitely long sequence of (highly) unpleasant experiences. Of course, on this sort of account, death *needn't* be bad,

even for a normal and healthy human being, since he may experience eternal bliss in the afterlife. If there is an afterlife, and for some it includes unpleasant experiences, then this would explain how death can be a bad thing, but it is controversial whether there is an afterlife. Since it is quite possible to deny the controversial assumption that there is an afterlife and yet regard death as a bad thing, it would be desirable to produce an explanation of death's badness which doesn't presuppose that there are experiences after death. Many have thought that such an explanation can be given.

If death can be a bad thing for a person, though not in virtue of including unpleasant experiences of that person, then death is a bad thing for a person in a way that is different from the way in which, say, *pain* is a bad thing for a person. That is, some things which are bad (or evil) for a person (such as pain) are "experienced as bad by the person," whereas other things which are bad for a person (such as death) are not (ever) experienced as bad by the person.[2] Death, then, is assimilated to such bads as betrayal by a friend behind one's back, which, though never experienced as bad (one never finds out and suffers no bad consequences), are nevertheless bad for a person.[3]

"Why Is Death Bad?" from *Philosophical Studies*, Vol. 50, No. 2. Reprinted with permission.

Let's suppose that some things which are never experienced as bad by a person are nevertheless bad for the person. **Death** could then be an *experiential blank* and still be a bad thing for an individual. And one plausible explanation of why this is so is that death (though an experiential blank) is a *deprivation* of the good things of life. That is, when life is, on balance, good, then death is bad insofar as it robs one of this good: if one had died later than one actually did, then one would have had more of the good things in life. This is the sort of explanation of death's badness which is adopted by Thomas Nagel.[4]

But a problem emerges. We intuitively think that it is appropriate to have **asymmetric** attitudes toward prenatal nonexistence and death. We think that it is reasonable to regard death as a bad thing in a way in which prenatal nonexistence is not. If death involves bad experiences in an afterlife, then this asymmetry could be explained. But we are assuming here that death's badness is *not* experienced as bad by the individual who dies. If this is so, how can we explain the intuitive asymmetry between prenatal and posthumous nonexistence? Both periods are, after all, experiential blanks. And it seems that prenatal nonexistence constitutes a deprivation in a sense analogous to that in which death is a deprivation: if a person had been born earlier than he actually was born, then he would have had more of the good things in life. (When it is supposed that one is born earlier here, we hold fixed the date of one's death. Similarly, when it is supposed above that one dies later, we hold fixed the date of one's birth.) Being born at the time at which one was born (rather than earlier) is a deprivation in the same sense as dying at the time when one dies (rather than later). Both Epicurus and Lucretius argued that our ordinary asymmetric attitudes are irrational and since we don't regret prenatal nonexistence, we ought not regard death as a bad thing. If death is a bad insofar as it is a deprivation, the challenge posed by Epicurus and Lucretius is pressing: why should we treat prenatal and posthumous nonexistence asymmetrically?

One way to respond to the challenge (and thus defend the Nagelian explanation of death's badness) is to say that, whereas one could (logically) have lived longer, it is logically impossible that one should have

been born much earlier. Further, the claim is that it is irrational (or impossible) to regret that a proposition which is necessarily false isn't true.[5] This response is unsatisfying. It is not clear that it is logically impossible that an individual should have been born substantially earlier than he actually was. It is not at all clear, for instance, that Socrates—the very same Socrates—couldn't (logically) have come into being ten years earlier than he in fact did. Why exactly should (roughly) the actual time of one's birth be an essential property of a person? Given that the essentiality of the actual time of birth is a *controversial* metaphysical claim, it is unsatisfying to use it as part of an explanation of the intuitive asymmetry.[6] The explanation will not be acceptable to anyone who denies the assumption.[7] If it is at least logically possible that one should have been born much earlier (and no reason has been offered to rule this out), then we still need to develop a response to the challenge raised by Epicurus and Lucretius (insofar as we cling to the explanation of death's badness in terms of deprivation).

Recently, Derek Parfit has suggested another response.[8] His position could be put as follows:

> We have a (not irrational) bias toward the future to the extent that there are cases where we are indifferent toward (or care substantially less about) our own past suffering but *not* indifferent toward our own future suffering. Since there are such cases, and the attitudes therein seem rational, the general principle that it is always rational to have symmetric attitudes toward (comparable) past and future bads is false, and so it might be true that it isn't irrational to have asymmetric attitudes toward our own past and future nonexistence (where such periods of nonexistence are taken to be *bads*). Thus, death could be considered a bad thing for us, and yet we needn't assume symmetric attitudes toward death and prenatal nonexistence.

Consider Parfit's example:

> I am in some hospital, to have some kind of surgery. This kind of surgery is completely safe, and always successful. Since I know this, I have no fears about the effects. The surgery may be brief, or it may instead take a long time. Because I have to co-operate

with the surgeon, I cannot have anaesthetics. I have had this surgery once before, and I can remember how painful it is. Under a new policy, because the operation is so painful, patients are now afterwards made to forget it. Some drug removes their memories of the last few hours.

I have just woken up. I cannot remember going to sleep. I ask my nurse if it has been decided when my operation is to be, and how long it must take. She says that she knows the facts about both me and another patient, but that she cannot remember which facts apply to whom. She can tell me only that the following is true. I may be the patient who had his operation yesterday. In that case, my operation was the longest ever performed, lasting ten hours. I may instead be the patient who is to have a short operation later today. It is either true that I did suffer for ten hours, or true that I shall suffer for one hour.

I ask the nurse to find out which is true. While she is away, it is clear to me which I prefer to be true. If I learn that the first is true, I shall be greatly relieved.[9]

Parfit's claim is that it seems to be a deep-seated feature of us that we regard our own past and future sufferings asymmetrically. He doesn't explicitly defend the rationality of this sort of asymmetry, but he has pointed to a class of examples involving bads *other than death* in which it doesn't appear obviously unreasonable to hold asymmetric attitudes.[10]

Let us grant, for the sake of argument, that Parfit is correct about his example. The problem is that it cannot be extended to the case of death. The reason is that Parfit's case involves a bad for a person which is *experienced as bad by the person*. One's own pain is perhaps paradigmatic of such bads. But death is not a bad of this kind; indeed, the entire problem of justifying our intuitive asymmetric attitudes arises precisely because death is a bad for a person which is *not* experienced as bad by the person. Further, it seems that it is plausible to suppose that Parfit's conclusion will *only* apply to cases involving bads experienced as bad by the person. Cases which are structurally similar to Parfit's except involving bads *not* experienced as bad by the person yield *symmetric* attitudes.

Suppose, for instance, that you know that either some friends of yours have betrayed you behind your back nine times in the past or some friend will betray you behind your back once in the future. Here, it seems that you should prefer the one betrayal in the future (given that the betrayals are comparable, etc.). It also appears that, given a choice between being mocked once behind your back in the past and being similarly treated once in the future, you should be *indifferent*. (Of course, we assume here that you know that you can have no effect on the future events).[11] These cases suggest that Parfit's point only applies to the class of bads experienced as bad by the person, and *not* to the class of bads (like death) which are *not* experienced as bad by the person.

Note that there are two different kinds of cases within the class of things which a particular person might reasonably regret (or wish wouldn't happen or take to be bad), but which he himself doesn't experience as bad. One kind contains things which no person experiences as bad (such as death). Another kind contains things which are experienced as bad by *another* person (such as another's pain). If it is reasonable to take temporally symmetric attitudes toward regrettable things which we don't experience as bad and which *no one* experiences as bad, then it shouldn't be surprising that we take temporally symmetric attitudes toward regrettable things which are experienced as bad *by others*. And Parfit has produced just such an example:

I am an exile from some country, where I have left my widowed mother. Though I am deeply concerned about her, I very seldom get news. I have known for some time that she is fatally ill, and cannot live long. I am now told something new. My mother's illness has become very painful, in a way that drugs cannot relieve. For the next few months, before she dies, she faces a terrible ordeal. That she will soon die I already knew. But I am deeply distressed to learn of the suffering that she must endure.

A day later I am told that I had been partly misinformed. The facts were right, but not the timing. My mother did have many months of suffering, but she is now dead.[12]

Parfit claims, about this example, that the new piece of information—that my mother's suffering is in the past—should *not* have a crucial impact on my attitude. Concerning the suffering of others it is rational to have temporally symmetric attitudes. This is precisely what one should expect in the light of the foregoing discussion of the appropriateness of temporally symmetric attitudes toward certain bads not experienced as bad by the person—those not experienced by *anyone*. The difference between our symmetric attitudes toward another's past and future suffering and our asymmetric attitudes toward our own past and future suffering is a special case of the difference between our attitudes toward bads not experienced by us and bads experienced by us. If this is correct, it is appropriate to have temporally symmetric attitudes toward the class of regrettable things experienced by others, even if it is appropriate to have temporally asymmetric attitudes toward the class of regrettable things experienced by us.[13] Thus Parfit's own example highlights the inadequacy of the present response to the challenge posed by Epicurus and Lucretius, namely the response suggested by Parfit's examples of temporally asymmetric attitudes toward experienced bads.

It might seem appealing to suggest that what makes death a bad thing for a person is that it is the deprivation of good things *already had* by the person. On this account, the asymmetry between our attitudes toward prenatal and posthumous nonexistence is due to the fact that the time before our birth cannot be conceived as a deprivation of good things we have *already had*, whereas the time after our death clearly can be so conceived. But why exactly should we care especially about the lack of good things we already have had, in comparison with the lack of good things which we could have had, had we been born earlier?

The plausibility of the suggestion may come from a psychological truth which says that, in general, if a person has experienced a good thing and then been deprived of it, he tends to lament its absence (to "miss it") in a way in which a person who has never experienced the good *doesn't*. If a person has regularly drunk fine wines with dinner, he regrets the lack of a fine wine at tonight's dinner more than someone who has never had a fine wine with dinner.

But why would one regret the absence of something good to which one has grown accustomed? Presumably, because one tends to be *frustrated* by the lack

of such goods—their absence causes *unpleasant experiences*. When a person accustomed to fine wines must do without, he is likely to have unpleasant experiences caused by the (partially involuntary) comparison of his present quite ordinary wine with his past delightful wines. In general, it *is* true that, when one is accustomed to a good thing, its absence causes unpleasant experiences and is therefore especially regrettable.

But clearly this principle is not applicable to death, since death deprives a person of goods *without* causing *any* experiences at all (according to our supposition). The psychological principle may apply to bads which are experienced as bad by a person (or which *cause* unpleasant experiences had by the person), but it doesn't apply to death, since it is *not* such a bad. So this explanation of our asymmetric attitudes suffers from the same problem as the above strategy. Suppose, on the other hand, that we do not appeal to the psychological principle and instead conceive of death as a bad which is *not* experienced. Then, insofar as it is held that in regretting the prospect of death we regret the future deprivation of goods we have already had, it would be equally reasonable to regret the prenatal deprivation of such goods, goods which, we *now* know, could have graced our life had it begun earlier.

If death is taken to be a bad thing for a person, and it is appropriate to take symmetric attitudes toward past and future bads that are not experienced as bad by the person, then either we ought radically to revise our attitudes toward prenatal nonexistence, or we haven't explained why death is a bad thing for a person. In *Annie Hall*, Woody Allen says, "We have two complaints about life. First, life is terrible. And second, life is too short." If life is terrible, it is—in the typical case—because of bad experiences. But if life is too short, why?

II. Why Death Is Bad

Imagine that you are in some hospital to test a drug. The drug induces intense pleasure for an hour followed by amnesia. You awaken and ask the nurse about your situation. She says that either you tried the drug yesterday (and had an hour of pleasure) or you will try the drug tomorrow (and will have an hour of pleasure). While she checks on your status, it is clear that you prefer to have the pleasure tomorrow. There is a temporal asymmetry in our attitudes to "experienced goods" which is parallel to the asymmetry in our attitudes to experienced bads: we are indifferent to past pleasures and look forward to future pleasures.

Perhaps it is this temporal asymmetry in our attitudes toward certain goods, and not the asymmetry in our attitudes toward bads, which explains our asymmetric attitudes toward prenatal and posthumous nonexistence. Death is a bad insofar as it is a deprivation of the good things in life (some of which, let us suppose, are "experienced as good" by the individual). If death occurs in the future, then it is a deprivation of something to which we look forward and about which we care—*future* experienced goods. But prenatal nonexistence is a deprivation of *past* experienced goods, goods to which we are indifferent. Death deprives us of something we care about, whereas prenatal nonexistence deprives us of something to which we are indifferent.

Thus we can defend Nagel's account of the badness of death by explaining the asymmetry in our attitudes toward prenatal and posthumous nonexistence. This explanation makes use of a principle clearly related to (but different from) Parfit's principle concerning the asymmetry in our attitudes toward past and future experienced bads. If we have asymmetric attitudes toward past and future experienced goods, then death is a bad thing in a way in which prenatal nonexistence is not.[14]

Let us end with a fanciful example that illustrates the present point. It is now 1985 and you will live eighty years in any case. Suppose you are given the following choice. Either you were born in 1915 and will die in 1995, or you were born in 1925 and will die in 2005. In each case, we will suppose, your life contains the same amount of pleasure and pain, distributed evenly through time. It is quite clear that you would prefer the second option—you want your good experiences in the future. Note that the periods before 1915 and after 2005 involve "experiential blanks" *in any case*. However, on the first option there is an "extra" blank between 1995 and 2005, and on the second option this extra blank is placed between 1915 and 1925. If one focuses simply on this experiential blank of ten years and asks whether it would be better to have the blank in the past or the future, it seems that one shouldn't care. That is, as argued above, it is rational for a person to have temporally symmetric attitudes toward bads not experienced by him. Thus, our preference for the second option—living more in the future—cannot be explained directly by an alleged asymmetry in our attitudes toward experiential blanks. Rather, it is crucial that the placement of the "extra" experiential blank of ten years *determines* the temporal distribution of experienced goods, since we do have temporally asymmetric attitudes toward experienced goods.

Nagel is correct to assimilate death to a bad such as betrayal by a friend behind one's back—both bads do not involve unpleasant experiences. But the two sorts of bads are interestingly different. If death occurs later than it actually does, we will have a stream of good experiences in the future. The alternative to death is good experiences, whereas (in the typical case, at least) the alternative to a future betrayal behind one's back is not good experiences. Thus prenatal and posthumous nonexistence deprives us of things to which we have temporally asymmetric attitudes, whereas past and future betrayals do not. Death's badness is similar to the badness of betrayal behind one's back, but different in a way which explains why death is rationally regarded as worse than prenatal nonexistence.[15]

NOTES

1. This does not imply that it is rational to *preoccupy* oneself with one's own death or to focus one's attention upon it constantly, etc.
2. Something is "experienced as bad by a person" roughly speaking insofar as that thing causes unpleasant experiential episodes in the person (and perhaps, the person believes that the thing is causing such experiences).
3. Thomas Nagel discusses such bads in: "Death," reprinted in Thomas Nagel, *Mortal Questions* (Cambridge: Cambridge University Press, 1979), pp. 1–10.

Also, Robert Nozick discusses similar examples in: "On the Randian Argument," in Jeffrey Paul (ed.), *Reading Nozick* (Totowa, N.J.: Rowman & Littlefield, 1981), pp. 218–222.

4. Nagel, *Ibid.*

5. *Ibid.*, pp. 7–8.

6. Even if one—controversially—held that generation from such and such gametes is an essential property of an individual, this would not commit one to the further essentialist claim in the text.

7. Nagel himself is unsatisfied with this response. (Nagel, *Ibid.* fn. 3, pp. 8–9). He points out that "it is too sophisticated to explain the simple difference between our attitudes toward prenatal and posthumous nonexistence." (*Ibid.*) To explain his doubts, he presents an example (attributed to Robert Nozick) in which it is granted that it is logically possible that an individual be born years before he is actually born (by prematurely "hatching" the spore from which one develops), and yet it seems that even here the intuitive asymmetry is justified. Thus, the logical impossibility of being born earlier cannot *explain* the asymmetry in our attitudes.

8. Derek Parfit, *Reasons and Persons* (Oxford: Oxford University Press, 1984), pp. 165–185, esp. p. 175.

9. *Ibid.*, pp. 165–166.

10. Nagel seems to have been aware of some version of Parfit's claim. Given his worries about the view that it is logically impossible that one should have been born much earlier than one actually was, Nagel admits that "Lucretius' argument still awaits an answer." He continues (*Ibid.*, fn. 3, p. 9): "I suspect that it might require a general treatment of the difference between past and future in our attitudes toward our own lives. Our attitudes toward past and future pain are very different, for example. Derek Parfit's unpublished writings on this topic have revealed its difficulty to me."

11. So a *symmetric* attitude towards past and future betrayals involves *preference* for one betrayal over several comparable ones regardless of when they occur and *indifference* between two comparable betrayals regardless of when they occur.

12. *Ibid.*, p. 181.

13. Parfit (*Ibid.*, p. 182), says: "My own examples reveal a surprising asymmetry in our concern about our own and other people's pasts. I would not be distressed at all if I was reminded that I myself once had to endure several months of suffering. But I would be greatly distressed if I learnt that, before she died, my mother had to endure such an ordeal."

This asymmetry is not the same as the asymmetry between my attitudes toward my own past and my own future, yet the two asymmetries are connected as follows. The first asymmetry consists in my indifference to my own past suffering paired with my concern for another's past suffering. Given my concern for my own future suffering, it follows that I have asymmetric attitudes toward my own past suffering and my own future suffering. Given my concern for another's future suffering, it follows that I have symmetric attitudes toward another's past suffering and another's future suffering. Thus the contrast between temporally asymmetric attitudes regarding my own suffering and temporally symmetric attitudes regarding another's suffering stems from the "surprising" asymmetry Parfit notes in the above-quoted passage. But the contrast in question, which arises from the "surprising" asymmetry, is precisely what one should expect given the discussion in the text: the contrast matches up with the contrast between bads which one experiences and bads which one does not.

14. Though Parfit focuses upon examples involving temporally asymmetric attitudes towards pain, he speaks of our "bias toward the future" with respect to experienced goods such as pleasure as well. So he would endorse the principle about temporally asymmetric attitudes toward experienced goods, which grounds the foregoing explanation of the asymmetry in our attitudes toward prenatal and posthumous nonexistence. Though this explanation is *consistent* with Parfit's remarks in the passages surrounding his discussion of Epicurus on death, that discussion itself does not indicate that he had the explanation in mind: "Epicurus's argument fails for a different reason: we are biased towards the future. Because we have this bias, the bare knowledge that we once suffered may not now disturb us. But our equanimity does not show that our past suffering was not bad. The same could be true of our past nonexistence. Epicurus's argument therefore has force only for those people who lack the bias towards the future, and do not regret their past non-existence. There are no such people. So the argument has force for no one." (*Ibid.*, p. 175)

In any case, it is crucial to see that only the principle about temporally asymmetric attitudes toward experienced *goods* such as pleasure will afford an explanation of why death is bad. The principle about experienced *bads* which is suggested by Parfit's examples, it has been argued, will not generate such an explanation.

15. We would like to thank Phillip Bricker for helping us to arrive at the foregoing explanation of why death is bad.

KEY TERMS

Death
Experiential blank
Asymmetric attitudes

STUDY QUESTIONS

1. Explain the asymmetric attitudes we have towards our prenatal nonexistence and death. What did Lucretius think of these attitudes? Explain his position.
2. Explain one of the possible solutions to the problem of asymmetric attitudes that Brueckner and Fischer consider.
3. What is Brueckner and Fischer's solution to the problem? Why do they think that it is rational to have symmetric attitudes toward prenatal and posthumous nonexistence?

Love and Death

DAN MOLLER

Dan Moller is Associate Professor of Philosophy at the University of Maryland. He specializes in moral and political philosophy and often uses psychology and economics to inform his philosophy. Some of his works include "Wealth, Disability and Happiness," published in *Philosophy and Public Affairs*, "Anticipated Emotions and Emotional Valence," published in *Philosophers Imprint*, and the following selection, published in *The Journal of Philosophy*.

. .

THE Ecclesiast, purveyor of dyspeptic wisdom, reflects on the misfortunes of the dead: "The dead know nothing; they have no more reward and even the memory of them is lost" (9:5). If at least the memory lingered on—that would be something. But the Ecclesiast uncharacteristically misses an opportunity to rub it in, for it can actually seem much worse: it is not just that we are forgotten in the vast eternities of time, it is that even those we love[1] and who love us the most display an astonishing facility for "moving on," for adapting to their loss and

so avoiding significant distress over our demise. Moreover, wives and husbands remarry, often at depressingly brief intervals, further diminishing the significance of the loss to them; we retain photographs and other trinkets of remembrance, but all of the emotions that were once insurmountable barriers to similar relationships with others are irrecoverably lost. All of this occurs because of adaptive processes that may be in the self-interest of the survivor since they facilitate a rapid return to a healthy emotional baseline, but they involve profound reasons for regret as well, both because of what these processes say about the bereaved and, more generally, what they say about the significance of our relationships with one another. At least, that is one interpretation of love and death. I find this gloomy view both compelling and

From "Love and Death" in *Journal of Philosophy* 104, pp. 301–316. © 2007 by *The Journal of Philosophy*. Reprinted with permission.

depressing, and it is worth expounding it in more detail for the light it sheds on our lives and our deaths.

I

How *do* spouses or partners in a long-term, committed relationship react when the person they love dies? In answering this question, we may be tempted to form an estimate by focusing on what we imagine we might feel immediately after hearing the news that our husband or wife had died. But this and other armchair estimates of emotional responses are notoriously unreliable, and fortunately there exists a large empirical literature on the psychology of bereavement that can serve as a fixed point. The most important finding of this body of work is summarized by a leading researcher:

> [M]any, and sometimes the majority, of bereaved individuals exhibit only short-lived grief-reactions and a relatively rapid return to baseline functioning. . . . Bereavement theorists have tended to assume that the normative responses to loss involve either chronic suffering or gradual recovery lasting at least several years; the relative absence of distress during bereavement is thought [to] be both rare and psychopathological. . . . [But] recent research has provided a strong challenge to these views: The relative absence of grief symptoms and the continued ability to function adequately following the death of a close relation do not appear to reflect denial or pathology but rather an inherent and adaptive resilience in the face of loss.[2]

The results of empirical investigation thus seem to conflict with a widely held view in our culture that the loss of a partner or spouse is invariably or at least usually an agonizing blow with long-lasting and significant impact. Contrary to this folk view (and certain nonempirical bereavement theories), empirical research seems to show that most people manifest what the author above refers to as **resilience** in the face of loss: although they are initially traumatized, they quickly recover and manifest little long-term distress. And, again contrary to folk wisdom, this does not seem to be the result of repression or of having had an unfulfilling relationship; most people

simply adapt far better to their loss than we tend to believe.

Nor is this finding at all unusual; indeed, it represents the consensus of nearly all of the empirical research dedicated to testing how people actually react to the loss of a spouse. The author cites another study in which nearly half of the participants did not show even mild depression following a spousal loss.[3] Another researcher who carried out a long-term investigation reports that, compared to a control group, "The effect of bereavement on symptoms of depression and general psychopathology . . . was significant only at 2 months following loss."[4] Still another expert sums up his work, "A general conclusion of this study is that the death of a spouse in later life does impact the surviving spouse's subjective well-being but not to the extent that many would expect."[5] If these results are surprising, it gets stranger still: research indicates that not only do half or more of bereaved spouses tend to be resilient or muted in their reaction to their loss, but a consistent 10% or so of the bereaved experience a dramatic *increase* in subjective well-being following the loss.[6] And prospective studies that allow the tracking of well-being before as well as after a loss reveal that a large proportion of those who *do* report being deeply unhappy several months after their loss were deeply unhappy before the loss as well; in other words, it is unclear that their distress is caused by their loss rather than standing features of personality or circumstance.[7] Moreover, with some minor differences these results appear to apply cross-culturally.[8] Finally, given this muted reaction, it is no surprise that the bereaved often find it fairly easy to remarry within a fairly short period of time. Although there are somewhat different figures given in the literature, owing perhaps to different investigative methods, it is clear that those who are young and therefore find it relatively easy to secure new partners remarry quite soon after their loss.[9] And of course we must bear in mind that even among the elderly who remarry far less often, the *desire* to remarry or date is much higher than the actual rate, both for generic reasons and because of an increasing gender imbalance with age increase.[10]

It is important to concede the other side of the story and not to exaggerate these findings, summarized in extreme brevity just now. Obviously a large number of people in absolute terms are completely devastated by their loss, and some never recover. Loss of a spouse is in fact associated with a sharp rise in risk of death, especially shortly after the loss, indicating that the consequences are anything but trivial.[11] Even when subjects report relatively little psychic trauma, they do sometimes report grieving for a substantial length of time, though this reported grieving appears to have little connection with measures of happiness or subjective well-being (and thus does not correspond, perhaps, to grief in the way it is usually understood).[12] Nevertheless, the cumulative evidence seems to show quite clearly that most people do not experience significant long-term distress when they lose the person they have committed their lives to. It is important to note, also, that the investigations cited for the most part rely on self-reports of grief, either in response to in-person interviews or more usually responses to paper-and-pencil surveys. The direction of exaggeration is thus very likely to be in the direction of overreporting grief and distress since this is what we culturally expect of those experiencing such a loss. In fact, this expectation is so strong that increased grief display is positively correlated with likeability ratings.[13]

Like all empirical findings, these results are subject to revision and refutation. I will assume that they are roughly accurate, but even if they turn out not to be, if we like we can simply stipulate that the discussion applies to the (majority) group whose reaction to the loss ranges from muted or resilient to ebullient. This provides a certain immunity to future revision, since presumably only the size but not the existence of this group is likely to be challenged. In any case, later on I will try and show that these empirical findings, while useful for motivating the discussion, are not essential to my claims.

II

Some may find these results encouraging and only encouraging: a large class of people whose lives we thought were shattered by a major loss turn out to be affected only to a fairly low degree. There is less misery in the world than we thought. If this response is unadulterated by qualms or hedges, it may be rooted in a general view about how to evaluate reactions to losses: the best reaction to a loss is the one that most promotes the interests of the one suffering the loss. Call this the *Adaptive Theory*. This theory may in turn find some support in a still more general conception of human behavior—one that says that the way to evaluate the rationality of *any* human activity is in terms of its propensity to promote the person's interests. (The self-interest theory of rationality is one manifestation of this normative attitude toward behavior.[14]) Since many people suppose that unpleasant experiences of grief and psychological distress are contrary to our interests, they might infer from the Adaptive Theory that the response most people actually seem to have is close to the best response; in failing to be significantly distressed, the bereaved are coping in a near-maximally adaptive fashion. Since the evidence indicates that there is no penalty to be paid for failing to suffer from a loss, the best response to grief may thus seem to be little or none at all.

However, many people are not only surprised but shocked and dismayed by these results, as the tendency toward greater dislike for those who display comparatively little grief brings out. Why is that? What is it that might make us uncomfortable about resilience? One reason we should consider is that insufficient grief following a loss may indicate that the one suffering the loss never valued the object sufficiently in the first place. We may imagine dying and infer from the subjunctive truth that those we love would probably not be deeply affected by our absence that we are not valued very highly even now. To the extent that responses to losses and valuing of the thing lost go together, it can seem tempting to move from disappointment with the one to suspicion about the other. If this were right, we would need to think harder about the use of "best" in the Adaptive Theory. Perhaps resilience is best for promoting the person's own self-interest, but that may only show that in this domain, as in so many others, there are considerations counting against having the attitudes that best promote our interests.

There is, however, a powerful objection to this line of thought. For what is true of reactions to the loss of a spouse turns out to be true of our reactions to other major losses as well. We are systematically mistaken in what is sometime called our "*affective forecasting*":[15] what we imagine to be catastrophes for us routinely turn out to be only minor blips that we quickly overcome. Being denied tenure, for instance, has very little effect on long-term happiness.[16] Contrary to what most academics imagine, whether or not they are denied tenure is unlikely to make much of a difference in their subjective well-being after an initial and short-lived dip. Similarly, dissolving a romantic relationship, losing a child,[17] sustaining a debilitating spinal-cord injury,[18] or other major medical problems[19] may produce differences compared to control groups, but these are often surprisingly small and tend to diminish or even disappear after a short while. (Conversely, we are also wrong about things like gaining tenure or winning the lottery, which tend not to produce as much happiness as we predict.) The reasons for these rapid recoveries are not fully understood and seem to be heterogeneous.[20] However, some of the mechanisms at work are fairly obvious, particularly various contrast effects. Recent improvements or declines in well-being contrast with still-vivid memories of previous states and affect us strongly, but after a short while this contrast effect wears off and we get used to what we now regard as the new baseline. Also, sudden changes can reduce the significance of previously important-seeming events, so that, say, simple pleasures like going to the movies suddenly seem less exciting once we have won the lottery. For these and other sorts of reasons, it appears to be difficult permanently to raise or lower people's levels of happiness provided there are not continual "shocks," and provided a certain threshold has been reached. This view is supported by the finding that, when it comes to events (as opposed to persistent states, like being clinically depressed), almost nothing that happens to us has a significant impact on happiness beyond three months or so.[21]

What this shows is that even when it comes to paradigm cases of things we care very deeply about (for example, our spinal cords) our reaction to loss is muted and far less than we tend to imagine it would be. This seems to suggest that we cannot explain dissatisfaction with resilience to the loss of a spouse by claiming that resilience indicates apathy. Moreover, these findings imply that any plausible attack on the Adaptive Theory must account for the fact that our

reactions to bereavement form part of a general pattern of resilience toward even extreme and disastrous changes. The Adaptive Theorist can now point out that resilience to losing those we love is part of a disposition that plays a deep and systematic role in making us the kinds of creatures that can overcome the frequent and inevitable setbacks that we must suffer over a lifetime.

Of course, the point about our not caring enough about what we lose could be broadened to take this larger pattern into account. An embittered cynic might say, "I used to think that reactions to the loss of a spouse were especially objectionable. These new facts show that not to be the case. But now things are worse. Apparently we do not care very much about *anything*. The facts about our reactions to losses show that evolution has endowed us with a deplorably superficial capacity for valuing things in general. My sorrow at learning that lovers don't care enough about each other to be significantly distressed by the loss of the other isn't mitigated by learning that they don't care that much about their spinal cords either." This extreme position might be buttressed by claiming that part of what it *is* to care deeply about something is to be disposed to suffer deeply following losses: "A person who cares about something is, as it were, invested in it. He *identifies* himself with what he cares about in the sense that he makes himself vulnerable to losses."[22] If we prove *in*vulnerable or insufficiently vulnerable, that may ground suspicion that we did not deeply care to begin with. To put it another way, facts about caring have conditional implications involving responses to losses, and we can reason from the failure of these conditionals to be satisfied to the absence of concern. This may be reflected, for instance, in the difficulty we have in accepting statements like this: "You are the love and light of my life; but naturally, were you to die, it would have little significant impact on me beyond a few months, and I would probably fall in love with someone else shortly thereafter."[23]

Apart from being implausibly extreme in implying that none of us cares about much of anything, this view overlooks the massive evidence that we do care deeply about people before they die. This concern is manifested in our willingness to make sacrifices for them, our pain in the face of even their minor misfortunes, and our general disposition to protect and advance the interests of those we love. The extreme view also overlooks different reasons for failing to be devastated by loss, only one of which is failing to care about something to begin with. Take denial of tenure. The reason people are so wrong about their predicted response to this event is not that they care less about tenure than they think, but rather that they overlook the elaborate psychological apparatus we possess for dealing with such events.[24] After their initial horror, unfortunate junior professors soon begin to rationalize their failure by appealing to baroque conspiracy theories, departmental politics, and so on (never the inadequacy of their work), and within a few months the contrast between a lousy present and better immediate past is lost in any case. Given the prima facie evidence in favor of the antecedent high concern for tenure, the best explanation for lack of distress over denial of tenure is thus likely to be the engaging of various adaptive mechanisms, not a prior absence of concern. Although the bereaved are different to the extent that rationalization and other coping mechanisms of junior professors probably do not apply to them, they too can say that their lack of distress merely indicates that concern for a person or object can be severed from distress over its loss by adaptive mechanisms. It is these mechanisms that explain how someone could be willing to risk her life for her husband while failing to be significantly traumatized by his death. It just turns out to be a remarkable trait of our species that caring very deeply about someone is compatible with a strongly muted reaction to their death. Friends of the Adaptive Theory can thus not only claim that our response to loss is best, but that so far no ground for genuine ill-ease with that response has been located.

The extreme response is a dead end; resilience is evidence of a post-factum ability to adapt to loss, not an antecedent lack of concern. Nonetheless, there is something right about the extreme response. Resilience does tell us something important and distressing about our relationships with those we love, even if the precise feature at issue has been misidentified by the extremist. One source of anxiety concerning our adaptive capabilities lies, I believe, in what they imply about our **importance** for those we love. The problem is that because our deaths make a comparatively minor impact on their lives, we may feel forced to conclude that we do not possess the kind of importance for them that we thought we had. The notion of "importance" that is relevant here, or what we might in some contexts call "significance" or "value" notwithstanding subtle differences between the three, is a hard one to pin down, but a few simple examples will make clear what is at issue. Our importance to an organization like a baseball team or Congress is great when we make an enormous difference to its operations, when our absence wreaks havoc, and when we are unique and irreplaceable in what we do. Conversely, claims of importance or significance are inflated when it turns out that nothing we do really matters or that a year's leave of absence would go unnoticed and we could be easily replaced. Similarly, in the personal sphere we need and therefore value relationships with some people more than others. Friends who add greatly to our lives seem important to us, while the pizza delivery boy is insignificant to us since he does not do anything we need all that much and even the little he does is easily done by someone else. (As this example shows, the insignificance of something *for us*—relative to certain aims and preferences—need not imply anything about the value of the object as such. Nothing I say here is incompatible with the infinite Kantian worth of rational pizza boys.)

An important feature of *importance* is thus that the concept has a counterfactual dimension; my supposed importance to a baseball team can be undercut by what happens after I leave it. It is for this reason that worries about our significance in the face of resilience cannot be quelled by the point made earlier against the extremist: evidence that we care for our lovers while they live is not undermined by facts about what happens after they die, but the same is not true of importance. A muted response to our death *is* relevant to our importance while we still live, since counterfactuals in part determine the importance or value of something. We like to believe that we are *needed* by our husband or wife and that consequently losing us should have a profound and lasting effect on them, just as the sudden injury of a key baseball player should have a disruptive and debilitating effect on the team. Most of us tend to assume that our relationship with the ones we love is so important to them that severing that relationship would make a deep impact on their ability to continue to lead happy worthwhile lives. The fact that our beliefs about these matters are false and that our loved ones are resilient to the loss of us seems to show that we do not have the significance that we thought we did.

We can explain what is distressing about the high probability of and brief interval before remarriage along similar lines. Not being *needed* is one way to fail to be important, but of course not the only way, since even people performing essential functions can be *replaced*, and fungibility is antithetical to importance or value. (That is part of the reason for the well-known tendency of leaders such as founders of businesses or Roman emperors to fail to institute succession plans: the existence of such a plan immediately reduces the leader's own importance.) Of course, it would be not only crass but inaccurate to think of remarriage as replacing the deceased *in toto*. Both people and the specific contours of their relationships are unique and will never be wholly mimicked by successor-relationships. But the same is true of baseball players and Congressmen: a team will function somewhat differently once it loses a wily southpaw, and Congress will never be quite the same without Preston Brooks and his cane. The reason the operations of these organizations are not substantially impeded by such losses is that the differences that matter to organizations are determined by their overall goals and functioning (winning ball games and legislating effectively), and these are not much affected by mere idiosyncrasies. Contrary to the suggestion made earlier, at least some spouses and lovers may need us very much. But the tendency toward remarriage combined with the comparatively low rates of distress among the bereaved suggest that the ways in which we are needed are functional rather than idiosyncratic; we play an important role in the lives of those we love, but not a role that others cannot with relative ease fill once we are gone, since our unique traits do make much of a difference to our success in those roles. We may be desperately needed as companions, friends, sex partners and intimates, but these roles endow us with much less significance than we imagine, given that we can be functionally replaced in these respects, and—so the evidence indicates—upon our deaths very often are. This is not to say that those who remarry do not have a special place in their heart for their previous spouse that will never be touched by his or her successor; it is only to explain why the adaptive responses of those we love can give us reason for regret, since they seem to show that we do not have the importance for our husbands and wives that we thought.

But it is not only those contemplating their own demise and the lack of impact that event will have on those they love who have reason to be uneasy about resilience; for despite the obvious advantages the Adaptive Theory draws our attention to, even those who have *lost* their spouse, and so directly benefit from adaptation, may have reason to regret the benefits resilience confers. Our "emotional immune system," while promoting our interests by allowing us to continue functioning in the face of trauma, also renders us unable to take in and register fully the significance of our losses. Part of what being the vulnerable creatures of flesh and blood that we are means is that we are subject to staggering losses in the form of the deaths of those we love, and yet our reaction to those losses is utterly incommensurate with their value, especially after the first month or two have passed. The good of a happy relationship with a lover is one that we value more highly than almost any other, and yet when we lose that good, our response over time does not seem to reflect its preciousness to us. Resilience thus seems to deprive us of our ability to care about those we love to their full measure after they are gone, and so deprives us of insight into our own condition.

This claim may seem peculiar. Assuming we are not in some pathological state of denial and are thus in possession of the appropriate beliefs, how can we possibly fail to register our losses? The answer to this lies in the difference between the superficial discrimination of some fact and what we sometimes describe by saying that someone has really "absorbed" or "taken in" something—a difference that typically involves having certain emotions in connection with what has been registered. Explaining what exactly the relationship between having emotional responses is to digesting fully various goods and bads that befall us is admittedly difficult, since on reflection it is far from clear why there should be an affective component to processing certain experiences. Why need feelings accompany the purely cognitive processes of discrimination in order for us to believe that someone has really "gotten it" when, say, she gets word of a death or an amputation or a (welcome) marriage proposal? Perhaps part of it is that emotions sometimes seem to have a role analogous to sense organs for us: the emotions are part of the means by which we perceive value.[25] Of course, emotions also do other things, and cognitive processes like practical reasoning can play a role in perceiving value as well, but it is nonetheless hard to envision someone being fully capable of recognizing a good or a bad without the appropriate emotional responses. In fact, there is powerful empirical evidence to suggest that without emotional responses we find it so difficult to recognize value that we cannot make even elementary decisions that require us to see one option as better than another.[26] Similarly, psychopaths seem unable to grasp the moral significance of their victims despite possessing normal cognitive abilities, and the best evidence is that this is due to their inability to experience certain emotions.[27] Those with affective disorders thus seem unable to grasp whether certain things really *matter.* If these remarks are on track, then our adaptive but muted responses prevent us from forming a correct picture of how things really are, value-wise. In a sense, resilience is a form of benign—or at least adaptive—blindness.[28]

But even if this were right, it may not seem obvious that such a blindness or inability fully to comprehend the loss of a good is a bad thing. The loss itself is one bad, and experiencing intense psychological distress in response to it simply adds a second; how can suffering one but not the second bad be *worse* than suffering both? The oddity comes out especially well in Proust's statement of the view I am defending:

> Our dread of a future in which we must forego the sight of faces and the sound of voices which we love and from which today we derive our dearest joy, this dread, far from being dissipated, is intensified, if to the pain of such a privation we feel that there will be added what seems to us now in anticipation more painful still: not to feel it as a pain at all—to remain indifferent.[29]

We can explicate the feeling Proust refers to by noting that failing to recognize how great a good we have irretrievably lost means that we are to some extent deluded about our own condition. That seems undesirable for the same reason other forms of pleasant delusion are often undesirable. To the extent that we care about being aware of our general condition, we have grounds to regret even adaptive syndromes which impede that awareness. (Notice that such a lack of emotional awareness can seem equally disturbing when it involves something good, as in an autobiography that refers to "unaccountably streaming eyes" at a wedding that is wedged somewhere between treatises in logic and lessons in Chinese.[30]) There may even be implications for how we conceive of ourselves: the fact that what ought (in virtue of its disvalue) to make a massive and traumatic impact on us leaves only a comparatively minor dent, while obviously advantageous, suggests that most of us lack the kind of emotional depth that accompanies deep insight into one's condition and which concomitantly enables deep suffering. We may thus begin to think of ourselves as less substantial, more superficial beings for our inability to hold on to our concern for great goods once we have lost them.

Against all this, it might be said that our current pattern of resilience or at least something close to it is inescapable. "What on earth is the *alternative* to an emotional immune system that allows us to overcome trauma?" someone might demand. The point here is not (I hope) the trivial one that we might not be able to overcome entrenched features of human nature, but the deeper one that any imaginable alternative to resilience would make life unbearable. To modulate from the metaphor of immunity to clotting, the alternative simply sounds like a kind of emotional hemophilia. However, this objection involves a dialectical mistake. The goal here is not to advocate practical changes or even to show that resilience is bad *all things considered.* Perhaps the Adaptive Theory is true: the best (overall) response to grief is the one that promotes our interests the most, and perhaps our actual response is close to optimal in that respect. What I have been concerned to show, rather, is that there are *reasons* for regret; there are subtle and easily overlooked drawbacks to our partial immunity. Our embrace of the Adaptive Theory should be an uneasy one at best. That being the goal, there is no need to provide an alternative to resilience.

III

Not everyone yearns to be important to others or for supposedly profound insight into their life situation. Some readers may remain unmoved. For them I offer a different kind of argument, designed to show that something like the concerns I have described *must* be valid. Consider a species of alien persons (or modified humans) who are like us except that members have *no* grief reactions at all to what would strike us as great tragedies. These are the *Super-resilient*. When their spouses drop dead in front of them, they shrug their shoulders and check what is on television. They remarry as soon as they are able to find another mate, often within weeks. They too deny not caring for their loved ones; in fact, investigation reveals that they are willing to walk through fire for their husbands and wives, and generally show tremendous concern before their loss. It is just that afterwards adaptive mechanisms operate so as immediately to extinguish any feelings of distress. The Super-resilient pity us for our insufficiently muted response to loss and wonder how we manage to endure through entire weeks of deep grief. Is there anything to be said against this extreme response to loss? Most people seem to think so. If that is right, this shows that the reasons for regretting resilience that I have been developing—or else others to the same effect—must at the very least get a grip on us, even if we insist that the Super-resilient merely embody a good thing taken too far. We cannot insist that there cannot be anything to regret about resilience if we find the Super-resilient troubling, though we might of course reject the particular reasons that were sketched above.

However, this argument may prompt a counter-argument. The Super-resilient are at one extreme, but now consider the *Sub-resilient* at the other extreme. The Sub-resilient are like us except that they *never* cease caring as deeply for their spouses as at the moment of death; the loss of that relationship is as deeply felt at half a century as it is at half an hour. The bereaved Sub-resilient are consequently extremely unhappy people who feel they suffer from a

kind of never-healing open wound. The undiminished depth of feeling for the deceased prevents them from remarrying. On the other hand, they have a profound sense of mutual importance since the loss of a spouse is so devastating. And they view us with a certain contempt; we seem to them incredibly shallow in our inability to realize the extent of our loss. The point now is not the recently discredited one that this alternative to resilience is unappealing—no one says otherwise—it is rather that the two extremes formed by the Sub- and Super-resilient bookend a continuum that includes a mean, and that we are at least roughly positioned as the proverbial healthy mean between the extremes. What is there to regret, what even counts against having a system of attitudes and emotional dispositions that avoids the pitfalls of either extreme and leaves us at the most livable point on the continuum, or at least reasonably close to it? Evolution may not be sensitive to factors like "mutual importance" or "insight" that were discussed earlier, but for whatever reason we nonetheless find ourselves endowed with a level of resilience that reflects these concerns to or close to the extent that we could endure before skirting the other extreme.

This seems to me the best response to the gloomy approach to love and death that I have been articulating. But alas, it too is unconvincing. Continua flanked by undesirable extremes are not all alike; sometimes what makes a center-value appealing is that it altogether avoids what bothers us about the extremes, but not always. Courage is the mean between cowardice and a kind of rash, wild disposition,[31] and objections to cowardice (or the other extreme) do not really apply to courage—it is not as if we reluctantly settle for courage while ruing our inability to access the benefits of cowardice. But take a more complex disposition not as easily assimilated to the Aristotelian model, say the beneficent treatment of people increasingly peripheral to us. On one extreme is the egalitarian disposition to treat total strangers and our children on an equal footing (either by elevating the former or demoting the latter or both). On the other side lies the tendency to narrow the scope of our beneficent concern to include only our spouse and children, say, and to treat even grandchildren, neighbors, and colleagues as we now do total strangers. Our actual disposition lies somewhere in between, though no doubt very far toward the latter end. Perhaps we are better off with our middle value than we would be under the egalitarian extreme, since we would then lack such goods as being special to our family members. But even if that is true all things considered, we still might think that there is something deeply troubling and unfortunate about our inability to recognize strangers as equally worthy objects of beneficence. We might even find the stance we are endowed with to be inconsistent with our considered moral beliefs.[32] And the same seems true of resilience. Quite apart from the question of whether evolution has instilled in us a level of resilience that is optimum relative to our various concerns, *any* deviation from the Sub-resilient raises difficult and painful questions. The kind of importance we have for one another, our irreplaceability or lack thereof, and our inability to appreciate fully our own condition as vulnerable victims of loss are issues that should concern us no matter how powerful the countervailing reasons are for accepting a mean (or more-nearly mean) position on the continuum. The values embraced by the Sub-resilient are much harder to dismiss than those associated with cowardice.

We can now see why the sensationalist empirical findings we started out with are useful for motivating the discussion but ultimately inessential. Even if it turned out that we undergo intense distress for a few years rather than a few months, the question of whether we have reason to regret the attitudes toward a lost spouse that resilience instills would remain. (Though naturally as we begin to approach sub-resilience the issue begins to seem less pressing.) And, as I have argued, there are such reasons, though these reasons may be outweighed by other considerations; all things considered most of us might not wish to be significantly less resilient than we are.

For a philosopher to say any of this to the bereaved is a little like a spectator giving cheerful advice at a crucifixion. But the marketplace of ideas is already full of such effronteries. On the one hand, there is a widespread self-help approach to loss, which counsels therapeutic grief in order to begin what is called "the healing process,"[33] and on the other hand there is a technical literature, cited earlier, which emphasizes that many (though by no means all) victims of loss neither suffer much distress nor benefit in the long

term from going through the supposed healing process. But at this point it should be clear that there is something deeply wrong about both of these stances. The first is invested in empirical assumptions that have simply proven false, and the second fails to register any of the profound complications we have seen resilience to involve. Perhaps these complications I have reviewed should not be allowed to have the last word, given certain assumptions about the relative value of things like psychological well-being versus depth of insight into one's own condition, but that does not mean we should ignore them altogether.

NOTES

1. The focus here will be on "romantic" love, though much of what I say applies to other forms as well.
2. G. Bonanno et al., "Resilience to Loss in Bereaved Spouses, Bereaved Parents, and Bereaved Gay Men," *The Journal of Personality and Social Psychology*, lxxxviii (2005): 827–43; quoted from p. 827, citations omitted.
3. The study is S. Zisook et al., "The Many Faces of Depression Following Spousal Bereavement," *Journal of Affective Disorders*, xlv (1997): 85–94.
4. A. Futterman, J. Peterson, and M. Gilewski, "The Effects of Late-Life Spousal Bereavement over a 30-Month Interval," *Psychology and Aging*, vi (1991): 434–41, on p. 438.
5. Dale Lund, "Impact of Spousal Bereavement on the Subjective Well-Being of Older Adults," in Lund et al., eds., *Older Bereaved Spouses* (New York: Hemisphere, 1989), pp. 3–15, on p. 12; cited in Jeremy Blumenthal, "Law and the Emotions: The Problems of Affective Forecasting," *Indiana Law Journal*, lxxx (2004): 1–95.
6. Bonanno, R. Nesse, and C. Wortman, "Prospective Patterns of Resilience and Maladjustment during Widowhood," *Psychology and Aging*, xix (2004): 260–71.
7. Bonanno et al., "Resilience to Loss and Chronic Grief: A Prospective Study from Preloss to 18 Months," *The Journal of Personality and Social Psychology*, lxxxiii (2002): 1150–64.
8. Bonanno et al., "Grief Processing and Deliberate Grief Avoidance: A Prospective Comparison of Bereaved Spouses and Parents in the United States and the People's Republic of China," *Journal of Consulting and Clinical Psychology*, lxxiii (2005): 86–98.

9. The median interval for remarriage among whites is 1.7 years for men and 3.5 for women. About 90% of white widows under 45 remarry, with a similar pattern holding for women as well until the mid 30s, at which point there is a steep drop-off in probability of remarriage. Interestingly, these figures are respectively higher and lower among blacks. See W. Cleveland and D. Gianturco, "Remarriage Probability after Widowhood," *Journal of Gerontology*, xxxi (1976): 99–103. Naturally, remarriage looks very different among the aged. For a recent study, see K. Smith, C. Zick, and G. Duncan, "Remarriage Patterns among Recent Widows and Widowers," *Demographics*, xxviii (1991): 361–74.

10. D. Carr, "The Desire to Date and Remarry among Older Widows and Widowers," *The Journal of Marriage and Family*, lxvi (2004): 1051–68.

11. N. Christakis and P. Allison, "Mortality after the Hospitalization of a Spouse," *New England Journal of Medicine*, cccliv (2006): 719–30. It is important to note that the subjects of this study were quite old—the average age was over 70—and also that the same effect was observed in nonlethal hospitalizations. For example, the spousal risk to men whose wives have been hospitalized with a hip injury is comparable to the risk associated with a wife's death, especially after the first few months. This indicates that what is at issue is probably not extreme grief or depression but more mundane problems arising from interdependence.

12. Bonanno et al., "Resilience to Loss in Bereaved Spouses."

13. Bonanno et al., "Resilience to Loss in Bereaved Spouses."

14. See Derek Parfit's *Reasons and Persons* (New York: Oxford, 1984) for an extended discussion and critique of the self-interest theory.

15. See the account and further references given in D. Gilbert and J. Ebert, "Decisions and Revisions: The Affective Forecasting of Changeable Outcomes," *Journal of Personality and Social Psychology*, lxxxii (2002): 503–14.

16. D. Gilbert et al., "Immune Neglect: A Source of Durability Bias in Affective Forecasting," *The Journal of Personality and Social Psychology*, lxxv (1998): 617–38.

17. Bonanno et al., "Resilience to Loss in Bereaved Spouses."

18. P. Brickman, D. Coates, and R. Janoff-Bulman, "Lottery Winners and Accident Victims: Is Happiness Relative?" *The Journal of Personality and Social Psychology*, xxxvi (1978): 917–27.

19. For an important study and further references, see J. Riis et al., "Ignorance of Hedonic Adaptation to Hemodialysis," *Journal of Experimental Psychology: General*, cxxxiv, 1 (2005): 3–9.

20. Bonanno, "Resilience in the Face of Potential Trauma," *Current Directions in Psychological Science*, xiv, 3(2005): 135–38.

21. E. Suh, E. Diener, and F. Fujita, "Events and Subjective Well-Being: Only Recent Events Matter," *The Journal of Personality and Social Psychology*, lxx (1996): 1091–102.

22. Harry Frankfurt, "The Importance of What We Care About," in *The Importance of What We Care About* (New York: Cambridge, 1988), pp. 80–94, on p. 83.

23. Since I go on to rebut this view on other grounds, I will not tarry over the possibility that the inconsistency involves mere conversational pragmatics.

24. That is, we neglect our "affective immune system." See Gilbert et al., "Immune Neglect."

25. Some will want to follow Hume in saying that the emotions are the means by which we project value (for example, second Enquiry, Appendix I). But Humeans can and should lament the inability to project in roughly the same way anti-Humeans lament the inability to perceive value; it is not as if Humeans are less appalled by those afflicted with affective disorders which prevent them from reacting to important changes in well being. Their explanation will simply take a different form. For discussion, see Simon Blackburn's *Ruling Passions* (New York: Oxford, 1998), especially chapter 9. For a defense of the view that emotions can represent things like losses and that emotions involve perceptions of our relation to the world, see Jesse Prinz, *Gut Reactions: A Perceptual Theory of Emotion* (New York: Oxford, 2004), chapters 3 (especially pp. 60–66) and 10. Prinz also defends the assumption I make here that emotions involve feelings and are not purely cognitive.

26. For instance, subjects with affective disorders often fail at certain games of chance because they do not see bad outcomes as bad anymore. See Antonio Damasio, *Descartes' Error* (New York: Avon, 1994), especially chapters 3 and 9.

27. See the interesting discussion by Shaun Nichols, "How Psychopaths Threaten Moral Rationalism," *The Monist*, lxxxv (2002): 285–304.

28. There are many further issues here that I cannot pursue, for example, whether value judgments do

not give rise to emotions rather than vice versa. My proposal should be viewed as a tentative attempt to identify the core issues, not to settle them. Some of these matters are explored at greater length in Michael Stocker's *Valuing Emotions* (New York: Cambridge, 1996), especially chapters 2–7, and Ronald de Sousa's *The Rationality of Emotion* (Cambridge: MIT, 1987).

29. Proust, *In Search of Lost Time: Within a Budding Grove*, translated by C.K. Moncrieff et al. (New York: Modern Library), p. 340. Proust goes on rather implausibly to suggest that the reason we fear our prospective indifference is that this would indicate a "death of the self."

30. W. V. Quine, *The Time of My Life* (Cambridge: MIT, 1985), p. 201.

31. For which we do not really have a name, as Aristotle points out (*Nicomachean Ethics*, 1115b25).

32. Of course, we might also take this stance as grounds for altering our considered moral beliefs, one man's *modus tollens* being another man's *modus ponens*.

33. Though he would despise being associated with the self-helpers, C. S. Lewis's record of bereavement is perhaps the most impressive exemplar of their view, which emphasizes (a) initial anguish that (b) results in a certain catharsis or insight, followed (c) by a successful recovery and return to baseline that could not have been achieved without (a) and (b). See *A Grief Observed* (New York: Harper Collins, 1961).

KEY TERMS

Resilience
Adaptive theory
Affective forecasting
Importance

STUDY QUESTIONS

1. What does Moller mean by "resilience"? What worries does the research about resilience raise for him?

2. Do you think we should be worried about resilience?

3. Does Moller think our resilience in the face of loss means we don't care about anything? Do you agree with him?

4. Why does Moller take our resilience after loss to indicate that we aren't as important as we might hope we are?

5. What does Moller mean by the "adaptive theory"? Does the person suffering a loss have reason to regret her resilience, according to this theory? Is there any reason for such a person to feel regret about her resilience, according to Moller?

PART VII

PUZZLES AND PARADOXES

INTRODUCTION

Puzzles and paradoxes have played an important role in the history of philosophy and are both challenging and fun to think about. Of course, any philosophical problem can be considered a puzzle. But we have in mind problems expressed in relatively few words that immediately reveal some puzzling aspect of things to which there is no obvious and clearly satisfactory solution. Most of these puzzles can be stated in the form of *paradoxes*. A paradox is an argument that *appears* to derive self-contradictory or otherwise absurd conclusions by valid reasoning from acceptable premises.

When a paradox becomes well-enough understood, whether as the result of a few moments' work by an individual or the insights of successive generations of thinkers, the appearance of a valid derivation of an absurdity should disappear. In some cases, when properly understood the conclusion will cease to seem absurd. In other cases the premises will no longer seem acceptable or the reasoning will no longer seem valid. W. V. Quine calls paradoxes of the first sort *veridical*, those of the second sort *falsidical*, and those for which we can neither accept the conclusion nor spot the mistake *antinomies*. All three kinds are represented here.

Some of the puzzles are presented as paradoxes, whereas others are simply set forth as problems or puzzles. In deciding what to say about these latter problems or puzzles, students will usually find they can state their reasoning in the form of a paradox.

There is extensive literature on each of these puzzles, and we cite some of it. But we think puzzles are most interesting if students approach them, at least at first, as occasions for unfettered thought rather than as scholarly projects. For example, in the case of Newcomb's problem we urge students to first decide what they would do in the imagined circumstances, to construct arguments justifying their choice, and, then, to try to find flaws or loopholes in their arguments—perhaps with the aid of students who support the opposite strategy. This approach is more rewarding than going to the library and looking up what the experts have said about the problem.

A. ZENO'S PARADOXES

Ж

Zeno of Elea was born around 490 B.C. He was a supporter of the philosopher Parmenides, founder of the Eleatic School of Greek philosophy, who held that the particularity of individual things is an illusion. Zeno supported this view by producing arguments to show that plurality and change are really self-contradictory notions. Because most philosophers have regarded the conclusions of Zeno's arguments as absurd, they are known as paradoxes. Some fragments of Zeno's writings that contain arguments against plurality survive; the arguments against motion are known almost entirely through Aristotle's account of them in his *Physics*.

There is an excellent discussion of Zeno and his paradoxes by Gregory Vlastos in Paul Edwards's *Encyclopedia of Philosophy*. This article also contains a good bibliography. Max Black's treatment of Zeno's arguments in his *Problems of Analysis* (Ithaca, N.Y., 1954) and Adolf Grünbaum's *Modern Science and Zeno's Paradoxes* (Middletown, Conn., 1967) might be particularly useful to the student wishing to learn about these paradoxes. Here, we give versions of two of the paradoxes of motion and one of plurality. The statement of the plurality puzzle is that of Carl Ginet, Professor of Philosophy at Cornell University.

Achilles and the Tortoise

. .

SUPPOSE that Achilles and the tortoise are having a race. Because Achilles is faster, we give the tortoise a head start of 10 yards. We suppose that the tortoise can run 1 yard in a second and that Achilles can run 10 yards in a second. It seems that Achilles will certainly catch and pass the tortoise. However, in order to pass the tortoise, Achilles must perform an endless sequence of tasks, one after the other. But it is easily seen that this is impossible.

The first task Achilles must perform is to reach the point where the tortoise starts. Call this Point 1. This takes one second. But, after Achilles does this, the tortoise is still 1 yard ahead, at what we will call Point 2.

The second task Achilles must perform is to reach Point 2, the point that the tortoise is at after Achilles completes the first task. When Achilles completes this second task, though, the tortoise is still ahead by 0.1 yard, at Point 3.

The third task Achilles must perform is to reach Point 3. After Achilles does this, though, the tortoise will still be ahead by 0.01 yard at Point 4.

We can see that after each task of this sort that Achilles performs, the tortoise will still be ahead, and there will be another task of the same sort still facing Achilles. That is, for any n (no matter how large), after Achilles has completed n tasks of this sort, he still won't have caught up with the tortoise, who will still be ahead by $\frac{1}{10}^{n-1}$ yards. But Achilles can never complete more tasks than there are numbers because we never run out of numbers. So Achilles will never catch the tortoise.

The Racecourse

It seems embarrassing enough for the advocates of motion and change that a runner so fast as Achilles can never catch a runner so slow as the tortoise. But things are worse. Achilles cannot even win a one-man race, for wherever the finish line is, he will never reach it.

· ·

SUPPOSE Achilles is to run from the starting point S to the goal G. To do this, he must do all of the following:

1. Run to the point halfway from S to G.
2. Run from that point to the point halfway between it and G.
3. Run from that point to the point halfway between it and G.
4. Run from that point to the point halfway between it and G, etc.

The "etc." clearly goes on forever. That is, the first point is only halfway to G, the second point only three-fourths of the way to G, the third point only seven-eighths of the way to G, the fourth point only fifteen-sixteenths of the way to G, and, in general, the nth point will be only $2^n - 1/2^n$ of the way to G. Hence, Achilles will never make it to G.

The Argument Against Plurality

· ·

A. The Main Argument:

1. If a finite spatial interval is divisible (i.e., composed of a plurality of parts), then it can be endlessly divided into ever-larger numbers of ever-smaller distinct and equal parts.

2. Therefore, any such interval is composed of infinitely many distinct and equal parts.

3. Each of these parts either (a) has some length or (b) has no length.

4. If (a), then the whole finite interval must be infinitely long.

5. If (b), then the whole finite interval must have no length.

6. Therefore, if a finite spatial interval is divisible, then either it is infinitely long or it has no length.

7. But every finite interval has a non-zero finite length.

8. Therefore, a finite spatial interval is not divisible.

B. An Argument for A.5:

1. If a finite spatial interval is composed of length-less points, then its length must be the sum of the lengths of those points.

2. The length of any such point is zero.

3. The sum of any number of zeros (even infinitely many) is zero.

4. Therefore, if a finite spatial interval is composed of lengthless points, then its length is zero.

B. METAPHYSICAL AND EPISTEMOLOGICAL PUZZLES AND PARADOXES

X

The Paradox of Identity

Problems about the notion of identity through change have played a long and important role in philosophy. Heraclitus, a Greek philosopher of the fifth century B.C., claimed that one could not step in the same river twice because new waters were always rushing in. This supported his general view of things, which was the opposite of that of Parmenides and Zeno. They thought that Being was one thing that didn't change; he thought that Being was an incredible plurality in constant flux. Many centuries later, David Hume argued that all attributions of identity over time were based on confusion. The following argument for the absurd conclusion that nothing persists through time, although perhaps cruder than either of these great philosophers would accept, captures some of the spirit of their line of thinking about identity.

· ·

B Y *identity*, we mean that relation that obtains between each thing and itself and that never obtains between a thing and anything else. So if *A* is identical with *B*, there is just one thing that is both *A* and *B*. For example, the man who coached the Stanford football team to Bowl victories in the mid-1970s is identical with the man who coached the San Francisco Forty-Niners to a Super Bowl victory in 1982. Thus, there is one man (Bill Walsh) who did both things. That is, there is one man who is the man who coached the Stanford football team to Bowl victories in the mid-1970s and who is the man who coached the San Francisco Forty-Niners to a Super Bowl victory in 1982.

Note that *identity* is not always used in ordinary English with this precise meaning. Sometimes, it is used to mean something like *exactly similar* or *exactly similar with respect to some important property*. Given *our* use of *identity*, for example, the term *identical twins* is self-contradictory. If *A* and *B* are twins, *A* and *B* are two individuals who are not identical in *our* official sense.

Now, given this sense of identity, there is one important principle that should be completely noncontroversial:

> If *A* is identical with *B*, then *A* and *B* have exactly the same properties.

We can call this principle *the indiscernibility of the identical*. It should not be confused with Leibniz's principle of the identity of the indiscernible:

> If *A* and *B* have exactly the same properties, then *A* is identical with *B*.

This latter principle is controversial. But the first should not be. For, if *A* and *B* are identical, then there is just one thing that is both *A* and *B*, and the principle just requires that it has the properties it has, which is utterly trivial.

But, given this principle, it follows that no individual persists through time.

First, note that our principle has the consequence that no individual persists through change and that the very example we used to illustrate the concept of identity makes no sense. For,

The coach of the Stanford football team has the property of being the coach of the Stanford football team. (Obviously)

The coach of the San Francisco Forty-Niners does not have the property of being the coach of the Stanford football team. (It would be a violation of NCAA rules.)

But then it is obvious that, contrary to our example, the first cannot be identical with the second.

But, note that any individual who is alive at a certain time moment *(t)* has a certain exact age *(n)*—where *n* is the number of moments the individual has been alive, up to and including *t*. But a moment later, at *t'*, this individual will no longer have this exact age. But, then, we see that the whole idea of persistence makes no sense, for to persist from moment to moment an individual has to change in respect to his or her exact age, but we have seen that change is ruled out.

So there is no persistence through change; no individual existing at any given time *t* is identical with any individual existing at any earlier or later time *t'*. Not only is there no individual who coached Stanford at one time and the Forty-Niners at some later time, there is not even an individual who coached Stanford to Bowl victories in different years, nor even one who coached them on successive days, nor even through a single practice.

The Paradox of the Heap

This is an ancient paradox that is very flexible. Here, we first use it to "show" that there is no such thing as a heap. Then, we use the same sort of reasoning to "show" that there is no such thing as baldness and that if it is wrong to have an abortion toward the end of a pregnancy, it is always wrong. This paradox can be used to "show" many other things. When versions of this paradox are set out as a chain of syllogisms, they have the form known in Aristotelian logic as the Sorites; the paradox is often just called by that name.

· ·

ONE grain of sand is not a heap of sand. If something is not a heap of sand, addition (or dimunition) by one grain will not make it a heap. But, then, nothing is a heap. For, by starting with one grain of sand and adding to it a grain at a time, we will never have a heap. If something arrived at by such a method is not a heap, then nothing just like it, arrived at by some other method, is a heap either. So there are no heaps of sand and the whole idea is incoherent.

Given a person who is not bald, plucking one hair never makes that person bald. For the person is already bald before the last hair is plucked. Plucking one hair from a person who is not bald will never make that person bald. So, if we started with a man or woman with a full head of hair and plucked his or her hairs one at a time, we would never make that person bald. Thus, the whole idea of baldness is incoherent.

Everyone agrees that it is wrong to have an abortion on the last day of a normal pregnancy. But, surely, if it is wrong to have an abortion on a given day (or at a certain minute of a pregnancy or at a certain second of a pregnancy), it is equally wrong to have it the day (minute, second) before. But, then, it is equally wrong to have an abortion at each point in a pregnancy, and so, by our opening assumption, always wrong.

The Surprise Examination

W. V. Quine reports that this puzzle has been around since 1943. He discusses it in his essay "On a Supposed Antinomy" in *The Ways of Paradox* (New York, 1966). Richard Montague and David Kaplan discuss it in "A Paradox Regained" in Montague's *Formal Philosophy*, edited by R. H. Thomason (New Haven, Conn., 1974). Both of these discussions contain bibliographies. The student who consults the literature will find it quickly gets intricate. Yet the problem is easily grasped. Note that it is easy to generate analogous puzzles involving hangings (the version Quine discusses), air-raid drills, and other events whose unpleasantness is enhanced when they are a surprise. The version involving an examination seems most relevant to the philosophy student.

. .

PROFESSOR X announces at the end of class on Friday that there will be a surprise hour-examination the following week. Student Y contemplates spending the weekend in study, but she hits on an argument that shows there can be no such examination. Here is her argument.

The exam cannot be on Friday. For, then, I would know Thursday after class that it was going to be on Friday, for it would not have been on Monday, Tuesday, Wednesday, or Thursday. But, then, it would not be a surprise, for I would know in advance when it was.

But, because it cannot be on Friday, it cannot be given on Thursday either. For, given that it cannot be on Friday, if it is not given Monday, Tuesday, or Wednesday, it has to be given on Thursday. So I would know after Wednesday's class that it was going to be given on Thursday, and it would not be a surprise.

But, because it cannot be given on Thursday or Friday, by similar reasoning it cannot be given on Wednesday either. And, indeed, the same reasoning works for Tuesday and Monday, too. So there will be no surprise examination, and I can relax this weekend.

Student Y does not study. The following Wednesday Professor X hands out an exam. Student Y is surprised, and she does quite poorly.

Goodman's New Riddle of Induction

This paradox is based on a problem introduced by Nelson Goodman in his book *Fact, Fiction and Forecast*, 2nd ed. (Indianapolis, Ind., 1965). He explains his own approach in this book, and his discussion has given rise to a voluminous literature.

. .

WE ordinarily assume that we can confirm a general hypothesis by examination of instances and that this process of induction is useful in conducting our lives. For example, we assume that repeated observations of green emeralds and failure to observe any that are not green supports the hypothesis that all emeralds are green. Thus, it is reasonable to expect the next emerald we examine to be green if we have no other evidence to go on. But, actually, such confirmation provides no basis for forming expectations at all, and induction is quite useless.

Suppose that it is January 1, 1987, and that all emeralds examined have been green. This seems to support the hypothesis that all emeralds are green and to make it rational, other things being equal, to expect the next emerald we examine to also be green.

But, let the word *grue* apply to things just in case:

1. They are examined before January 1, 1987, and are green.
2. They have not been examined before January 1, 1987, and are blue.

All of the emeralds examined before January 1, 1987, are grue as well as green. Hence, our observations up to that time support the hypothesis that all emeralds are grue every bit as much as the hypothesis that all emeralds are green. Hence, our observations give us as much reason to expect the next emerald we examine to be grue as to expect it to be green. But, if the next emerald we examine is grue, it is also blue, and not green. So our observations give us as much reason to expect the next emerald we examine to be blue as they do to expect that it will be green. But, obviously, we could repeat the same argument to show that we have as much reason to expect the next emerald we examine to be any color other than green. E.g., we could repeat the argument by using the predicate *gred*, which applies to things examined before January 1, 1987, if they are green and to other things if they are red. So our observations give us no more reason to expect the next emerald we examine to be green than they do to expect it to be blue or red or any other color. So, contrary to what we assumed to be plausible, induction is totally useless.

C. PUZZLES OF RATIONAL CHOICE

The Prisoner's Dilemma

This problem has been discussed in the literature on rational action for many years. The following statement is that of Carl Ginet.

· ·

Two men suspected of committing a crime together are arrested and placed in separate cells. They are not permitted to communicate with one another. Each of them is told the following:

1. You may either confess to the crime or refuse to confess.
2. If one of you confesses but the other does not, then the one who confesses will go free and the other one will go to jail for four years.
3. If both of you confess, then you will both go to jail for three years.
4. If neither of you confesses, then you will both go to jail for one year.

5. The other one of you is being told these same things.

Assume that each prisoner is concerned solely with his own welfare and knows that the fewer years he spends in jail the better off he will be. Assume also that each knows that the other is likewise concerned only with minimizing his own jail term.

In these circumstances, which alternative, to confess or to refuse to confess, should each prisoner choose? That is, given what each prisoner knows, which alternative would it be more rational for him to choose?

Newcomb's Problem

This problem was posed by William Newcomb, a physicist. The philosophical world first heard of it from Robert Nozick in his "Newcomb's Problem and Two Principles of Choice," which appeared in *Essays in Honor of Carl G. Hempel*, edited by Nicholas Rescher (Dordrecht, The Netherlands: Reidel, 1970).

· ·

A psychology professor at your school has a reputation for being brilliant as well as possessed of an enormous fortune she has dedicated to her research. One day you get a request to report to her office at a certain hour. On a table are two boxes. One of them, labeled *A*, is transparent; in it you can see an enormous pile of $100 bills. The other, labeled *B*, is opaque. She tells you that there is $10,000 in transparent box *A* and that in box *B* there is either $1,000,000 or nothing.

She tells you that she is going to give you a choice between:

1. Taking just what is in box *B*.
2. Taking what is in both boxes.

(Think about what you would choose given this much information.)

Then she tells you that this is part of an experiment. During registration at the beginning of the quarter, you walked under a peculiar device that reminded you of the machines at airports that are used to prevent hijacking. You didn't think much about it at the time. But she now informs you that this machine was something she designed and that it recorded an instant profile of your basic personality and character traits. On the basis of your profile, she made a prediction

about what choice you would make, and she decided what to put in Box *B* on the basis of this prediction:

1. If she predicted you would take both, she put nothing in Box *B*.
2. If she predicted you would take only Box *B*, she put $1,000,000 in it.

(Now, think about what you would do given this much information.)

At this point you ask her how accurate her predictions have been. She says that 1,000 students have been given the choice, and she has only been wrong once. In all the other cases, students who chose both boxes got only $10,000, whereas those who chose only box *B* got $1,000,000. Then she tells you to choose. What do you do?

Kavka's Toxin Puzzle

This puzzle was introduced by Gregory S. Kavka in his paper, "The Toxin Puzzle," *Analysis* 43 (1983): 33–36. In that paper Kavka also notes relations between this puzzle and puzzles about deterrent intentions—for example, an intention, adopted in order to deter an attack, to retaliate if attacked.

. .

A psychology professor at your school—perhaps the one also described in the discussion of Newcomb's Problem—has both a large fortune and an uncanny ability to detect intentions. In the interest of science she makes the following offer to you: "Here is this toxin. It is vile stuff. It will make you very sick for a day if you drink it—though it would not harm you in any lasting way. If tonight, at the stroke of midnight, you fully intend to drink it tomorrow at noon I will irrevocably put $1,000,000 into your bank account. To get the money it is not necessary that you actually drink the toxin; it is only necessary that you really do intend to drink it. However, you may not make any bets or promises that you will drink it, or

otherwise arrange for bad effects of not drinking it. Nor may you in any way cause yourself to become irrational. To win the money what you must do, without violating such constraints, is fully to intend tonight to drink the toxin tomorrow."

Suppose you are confident that the psychologist is sincere and is a reliable detector of intentions. You think $1,000,000 is worth a day's sickness: you would gladly drink the toxin to get the money. So you are more than willing, in order to get the money, simply to intend to drink it. After all, merely intending to drink it won't even make you sick! But it occurs to you that if at midnight you expect yourself not to drink the stuff the next day you will not really intend at midnight to drink it. And then you note that even if you do intend at midnight to drink the toxin the next day, and even if you thereby get rich, you will have no reason at all actually to drink the stuff come tomorrow noon: the money will already be in the bank and all that drinking would do would be to make you sick. So

you would, at midnight, fully expect yourself not to drink the toxin; but then you would not really intend to drink it. Still, you very much want to intend to drink the toxin, for you very much want the money.

Can you win the money?

Quinn's Puzzle of the Self-Torturer

Suppose that you prefer option A to option B, and also prefer option B to option C. If your preferences are *transitive* it will follow that you also prefer option A to option C. We normally expect people's preferences to be transitive: if you prefer studying tonight to going to the movies, and prefer going to the movies to washing the car, then we would normally assume you prefer studying tonight to washing the car. But there are cases in which people seem to have intransitive preferences, and such cases can be puzzling in various ways. In his paper, "The Puzzle of the Self-Torturer," *Philosophical Studies* 59 (1990): 79–90, Warren Quinn posed a particularly striking puzzle raised by a case of intransitive preferences.

· ·

You have agreed to be permanently hooked up to a very tiny machine that administers electric shocks. (If you are wondering why you would agree to this, see below.) The machine can be set at any level from 0 to 1000: at 0 there is no shock at 1000 the voltage is very high and the pain is terrible. Once the machine is set at a certain level it cannot be set lower, but it can be set higher. In general, at setting $n+1$ the voltage is very slightly higher than at setting n, but the difference in voltage is small enough that you cannot tell the difference between the two settings. Of course, you can easily tell the difference between setting 0 and setting 1000! (Compare: just by looking you cannot tell the difference between two very, very close shades of red but you can certainly tell the difference between red and violet.)

You have allowed yourself to be hooked up to this machine because the experimenter has agreed

to give you $10,000 simply for getting hooked up, and has also agreed to give you an additional $10,000 for each self-imposed increment in level of voltage. It is clear to you that the pain induced at level 1000 is so severe you would not choose it for any amount of money. But now that you are at level 0 you can see that you can get another $10,000 by going up to level 1, and that you will not notice the difference between level 0 and level 1. So you seem to have a very good reason to move up to level 1. And so you do. But now that you are at level 1 you can see that you can get another $10,000 by going up to level 2, and that you will not notice the difference between level 1 and level 2. So you seem to have a very good reason to move up to level 2. And so you do. But now that you are at level 2 . . .

Will a rational person end up at level 1000?

D. PARADOXES OF LOGIC, SET THEORY, AND SEMANTICS

The Paradox of the Liar

Here are two basic principles of logic:

NC—THE PRINCIPLE OF NONCONTRA-DICTION: No statement is both true and false.

EM—THE PRINCIPLE OF THE EXCLUD-ED MIDDLE: Every statement is either true or false.

But now consider this statement:
(1) Statement (1) is false.
By EM (1) is either true or false. Suppose (1) is true. Then (1) is false, for this is what (1) says. But then (1) is both true and false, contrary to NC. Thus, the supposition that (1) is true leads to a contradiction and must be denied. So we must suppose that (1) is false. But if (1) is false, then what (1) says is so, for what (1) says is that (1) is false. But then (1) is true. But then (1) is both false and true, contrary to NC. So the supposition that (1) is false leads to a contradiction and must be denied. But now we have a contradiction. For by EM (1) is either true or false; but by our argument (1) is neither true nor false.

Other Versions of the Liar

There are many different versions of the liar paradox, which the student may wish to think about after coming up with some hypotheses about what to say about the first version. Here are some of them.

****
(1) Statement (2) is true.
(2) Statement (1) is false.
****
(1) Statement (1) is not true.
****

> The Statement in Box *A*
> is not true

Box *A*

****
"yields a falsehood when appended to its own quotation" yields a falsehood when appended to its own quotation.

(Quine, "The Ways of Paradox")

Russell's Paradox

This paradox, which Quine calls the most celebrated of all antinomies, was discovered by Bertrand Russell in 1901. Here is Quine's statement:

..

SOME classes are members of themselves; some are not. For example, the class of all classes that have more than five members clearly has more than five classes as members; therefore the class is a member of itself. On the other hand, the class of all men is not a member of itself, not being a man. What of the class of all classes that are not members of themselves? Since its members are the non-self-members, it qualifies as a member of itself if and only if it is not.

Grelling's Paradox

..

CONSIDER the relation of describing between adjectives and objects. *Red* describes an object *x* if and only if *x* is red, *Tall* describes an object if and only if *X* is tall, and so forth.

Among adjectives are those that describe words. For example, *7-lettered* describes the word *example*, and *ambiguous* describes the word *bank*. This raises the possibility of adjectives that describe themselves, and there are many of them. For example, *14-charactered* describes itself, as do *English*, *short*, *ambiguous*, and *polysyllabic*. Let us call these words *autological*.

There are also lots of adjectives that do not apply to themselves. Among these are *long*, *German*, *monosyllabic*, and *50-lettered*. Let us call such adjectives *heterological*. That is, an adjective *A* is heterological if and only if *A* does not describe *A*.

Is *heterological* heterological?

E. PUZZLES OF ETHICS

✕

The Trolley Problem

This puzzle was originally presented in Philippa Foot, "The Problem of Abortion and the Doctrine of the Double Effect," *Oxford Review* 5 (1967): 5–15; and Judith Jarvis Thomson, "Killing, Letting Die, and the Trolley Problem," *The Monist* 59 (1976): 204–17. The version presented here is based on part of the introductory essay in John Martin Fischer and Mark Ravizza, eds., *Ethics: Problems and Principles* (Fort Worth, Texas: Harcourt Brace Jovanovich, 1992).

. .

START with Bystander. A trolley is hurtling down the tracks. There is an innocent person on the track ahead of the trolley, and he will be killed if the trolley continues going straight ahead. There is a spur of track leading to the right. Unfortunately, there are five innocent persons on that spur of track. The brakes of the trolley have failed, and you are strolling by the track. You see that you could throw a switch that would cause the trolley to go onto the right spur. You are an "innocent bystander," in the sense that you are not an employee of the railroad or a member of any public safety agency. You can throw the switch, saving the one person, but causing the five to die, or you can do nothing, allowing the one to die. Unfortunately, the only way in which you can save the one person is by causing the five to die. What should you do?

It seems that (barring any special information distinguishing the persons at risk) it would at least be permissible for you to omit the option of shunting the train to the right and thus allow it to continue going straight ahead. Perhaps it is also obligatory to do this, but it seems at least reasonable that you may allow the trolley to continue. You fail to save the one, but you preserve the lives of the five.

Consider now a second case, Transplant. You are a great surgeon—a remarkably great surgeon.

There are five persons in the hospital, each of whom needs an organ in order to survive. It just so happens that an innocent visitor has arrived in the hospital, and you know that he is tissue-compatible with all the people who need organs, and that you could cut him up and distribute his parts among the five who need them. Would it be permissible for you to perform the operation with his consent?

Surely, it is uncontroversial that you may not proceed. It is impermissible for you to perform the operation, and it seems that this is so even if you could conceal what you had done. Why is it permissible for you to save the five in Bystander, but not in Transplant? In both cases the numbers are the same: you can either act so that one lives or act so that five live.

Consider a third case, Drug. You own a bottle of medicine. Five persons are dying, and each needs one-fifth of the medicine in order to survive. Another person is dying, but he needs all of the medicine in order to survive. What should you do? Given that you have not promised the medicine to the one person, it is at least permissible for you to give the medicine to the five. Perhaps it is also morally required that you give the medicine to the five (supposing that you do not need it), but it is evidently at least permissible to do so.

Imagine now a fourth case, Fat Man. You are standing on a bridge, watching a trolley hurtling down the tracks below you toward five innocent persons. The brakes have failed, and the only way you can stop the train is to impede its progress by throwing a heavy object in its path. There is a fat man standing on the bridge next to you, and you could push him over the railing and onto the tracks below. If you do, the fat man will die, but the five will be saved. (You can even imagine that you wouldn't need to push the fat man to get him to topple. Perhaps he is peering over the handrailing

watching the lamentable scenario below, and you can simply wobble the handrail . . .)

What should you do? What is morally permissible? It may seem, upon first thinking about the case, that it is quite clear that you may not push the fat man over the railing. This conclusion, however, raises the question, "Why is it permissible to save the five in Drug but not in Fat Man? More generally, why is it permissible to save the five in Bystander and Drug, but not in Transplant and Fat Man?"

Ducking Harm and Sacrificing Others

This puzzle was originally presented in Christopher Boorse and Roy A. Sorensen, "Ducking Harm," *Journal of Philosophy* 85 (1988): 115–134. Boorse and Sorenson start with the following story:

. .

. . . two campers, Alex and Bruce, meet a ravenous bear. As Alex grabs his running shoes, Bruce points out that no one can outrun a bear. "I don't have to outrun him," Alex replies. "I only have to outrun you." (p. 115)

Boorse and Sorenson present the following three case-pairs to illustrate the distinction between ducking harm and sacrificing others:

Mall Gunman

(a1) Angela, at the end of a movie ticket line, sees X about to shoot a .22 automatic at her. Angela knows that a .22 bullet will kill one person but not two. Angela leaps aside; the bullet kills Brenda, who is next in line.

(a2) Same as (a1), but Angela grabs Brenda and moves her in front as a shield and the bullet kills Brenda.

Speeding Truck

(b1) Arthur, at the end of a line of stopped traffic, sees a runaway truck in his rearview mirror.

Arthur changes lanes; the truck crashes into Brian's car, injuring him.

(b2) Same as (b1), but Arthur beckons to a new driver, Brian, to join the line behind him; Brian does so and is injured by the truck.

Terrorists

(c1) Alison is one of 25 United States government officials on an airplane, each with a briefcase bearing an official seal. Terrorist hijackers announce they will kill one American per hour until their demands are met. Surreptitiously Alison covers her seal with a Libya Air sticker. The terrorists pass her briefcase and shoot Beatrice, the next American.

(c2) Same as (c1), but Alison has no Libyan sticker. Instead, she switches briefcases with Babette, a French novelist, while she is in the bathroom. The terrorists shoot Babette. (p. 116)

The puzzle is to invoke a general moral principle (or set of such principles) that satisfactorily explains the putative difference between ducking harm and sacrificing others. Upon reflection, is there really a moral difference?

GLOSSARY OF PHILOSOPHICAL TERMS

Some of the bolded words in the text are mere cognates to the words that appear in this glossary, so if you are unable to find the precise word that was bolded in the text, try looking for cognate words.

accidental and **essential**   A property is essential for an object if the object must have the property to exist and be the kind of thing that it is. A property is accidental if the object has the property, but doesn't have to have it to exist or be the kind of thing that it is.

Suppose Fred has short hair. That is an accidental property of his. He would still be Fred, and still be a human being, if he let his hair grow long or shaved it off completely. An essential property is one that a thing has to have to be the thing that it is, or to be the kind of thing it fundamentally is. As a human being, Fred wouldn't exist unless he had a human body, so having a human body is an essential property of his.

Statements about which properties are essential tend to be controversial. A *dualist* might disagree about our last example, arguing that Fred is fundamentally a mind that might exist without any body at all, so having a body isn't one of his essential properties. Someone who has been reading Kafka's *Metamorphoses* might argue that Fred could turn into a cockroach, so having a *human* body isn't one of his essential properties. Some philosophers argue that the metaphysical idea that underlies the accidental–essential distinction is wrong. Things belong to many kinds, which are more or less important for various classificatory purposes, but there is no kind that is more fundamental than all others apart from such purposes. Quine, a leading skeptic, gives the example of a bicyclist: If Fred is a bicyclist, is he necessarily two-legged?

affirming the consequent   Affirming the consequent is the logical fallacy committed by arguments of the following form:

> *If P, then Q.*
> *Q.*
> *Therefore, P.*

This is an invalid argument form. Consider this argument, which affirms the consequent:

> If Jones is 20 years old, then Jones is younger than 50 years old.
> Jones is younger than 50 years old.
> Therefore, Jones is 20 years old.

Clearly, this argument is a bad one: Jones could be any age younger than 50.

When someone affirms the consequent, often he or she is mistaking his or her inference as a harmless instance of *modus ponens*.

agent-causation   Agent-causation is a (putative) type of causation that can best be understood by contrasting it with *event-causation*. When a ball hits and breaks a window, one may think of the causal relationship here in terms of one event causing another, namely, *the ball's hitting the window* causing *the window's being broken*. In an instance of *agent*-causation, it is not one *event* that causes another. Rather, an agent—a persisting substance—causes an event. Some philosophers, such as Roderick Chisholm (see Chisholm, "Human Freedom and the Self") have argued that agent-causation is required for genuine free will. Agent-causation is also (see Chisholm) sometimes referred to as *immanent causation*, and event-causation is sometimes referred to as *transeunt causation*.

ampliative/nonampliative inference   *See* **deductive argument.**

analogy   An analogy is a similarity between things. In an argument from analogy, one argues from known similarities to further similarities. Such arguments often occur in philosophy. In his *Dialogues Concerning Natural Religion*, David Hume considers an argument from analogy that purports to show that the universe was created by an intelligent being. The character Cleanthes claims that the world as a whole is similar to things like clocks. A clock has a variety of interrelated parts that function together in ways that serve ends. The world is also a complex of interrelated parts that function in ways that serve ends, such as providing food for human consumption. Clocks are the result of intelligent design, so, Cleanthes concludes, probably the world as a whole is also the product of intelligent design. Hume's character Philo criticizes the argument. In "The Argument from Analogy for Other Minds," Bertrand Russell uses an argument from analogy to try to justify his belief that other conscious beings exist.

Arguments from analogy are seldom airtight. It is possible for things to be very similar in some respects, but quite different in others. A loaf of bread might be about the same size and shape as a rock. But it differs considerably in weight, texture, taste, and nutritive value. A successful argument from analogy needs to defend the relevance of the known analogies to the argued for analogies.

analytic and **synthetic**   Analytic statements are those that are true (or false) in virtue of the way the ideas or meanings in them fit together. A standard example is "No bachelor is married." This is true simply in virtue of the meanings of the words. "No bachelor is happy," on the other hand, is synthetic. It isn't true or false just in virtue of the meanings of the words. It is true or false in virtue of the experiences of bachelors, and these can't be determined just by thinking about the meanings of the words.

The analytic/synthetic distinction is closely related to the *necessary–contingent* distinction and the *a priori–a posteriori* distinction; indeed, these three distinctions are often confused with one another. But they are not the same. The last one has to do with knowledge, the middle one with possibility, and the first one with meaning. Although some philosophers think that the three distinctions amount to the same thing, others do not. Kant maintains that truths of arithmetic are a priori and necessary but not analytic. Kripke maintains that some identity statements are necessary, but not analytic or a priori.

analytical philosophy   The term *analytical philosophy* is often used for a style of doing philosophy that was dominant throughout most of the twentieth century in Great Britain, North America, Australia, and New Zealand. This way of doing philosophy puts great emphasis on clarity, and it usually sees philosophy as a matter of clarifying important concepts in the sciences, the humanities, politics, and everyday life, rather than providing an independent source of knowledge. Analytical philosophy is often contrasted with *continental philosophy*, the sort of philosophy that has been more dominant in France, Germany, Spain, Italy, and some other European countries.

The term was first associated with the movement initiated by Bertrand Russell and G. E. Moore early in the twentieth century to reject the idealistic philosophy of F. H. Bradley, which had been influenced by the German idealism of Hegel and others. Moore saw philosophy as the analysis of concepts. Analytical philosophy grew out of the approach and concerns of Moore and Russell, combined with the logical positivist movement and certain elements of pragmatism in America. However, the term *analytical philosophy* now refers to many philosophers who do not subscribe to the exact conceptions of philosophy held by the analysts, logical positivists, or pragmatists.

Indeed, there are really no precise conceptual or geographic boundaries separating analytical and continental philosophy. There are many analytical philosophers on the continent of Europe and many who identify themselves with continental philosophy in English-speaking countries. And there are important subgroups within each group. Within analytical philosophy, some philosophers take logic as their model, and others emphasize ordinary language. Both analytical and continental philosophers draw inspiration from the great philosophers of history, from the pre-Socratics, Plato, and Aristotle to Hume, Kant, Hegel, Marx, Mill, Frege, Husserl, James, and Dewey.

antecedent *See* **conditionals**.

anthropomorphism Anthropomorphism is the practice of ascribing to nonhuman beings properties and characteristics of human beings. In philosophy of religion, there is a general concern whether and to what extent our thought about God is problematically *anthropomorphic*. For instance, it is commonly held that depictions of God as having a body are mere anthropomorphisms. But what about depictions of God as becoming angry or frustrated? Whether such depictions ought to be taken literally or treated as merely anthropomorphic is a matter of some controversy.

a posteriori and **a priori** A posteriori knowledge is based on experience, on observation of how things are in the world of changing things. A priori knowledge is based on reasoning rather than observation.

Your knowledge that it is raining outside is a posteriori knowledge. It is based on your experience, your observation of what is happening outside. One couldn't figure out whether it was raining or not by just reasoning about it. Now consider the following questions: (1) Are there any married bachelors? (2) What is the sum of 38 and 27? After a bit of thought, you should conclude that there are no married bachelors, and 38 + 27 = 65. You know these things a priori. You didn't need to make any observations about what was happening. You just needed to reason.

One important question about a priori truths is whether they are all analytic, or whether there are some synthetic a priori truths. The philosopher Kant thought that (1) above was a priori and

analytic, whereas (2) was a priori and synthetic. *See* **analytic** and **synthetic** for further discussion.

An *a priori argument* is one that uses no empirical premises. An *a priori concept* is one that is innate or could be acquired just by using one's reason.

See also **analytic** and **synthetic; contingent** and **necessary; matters of fact** and **relations of ideas**.

a priori *See* **a posteriori** and **a priori**.

argument from analogy *See* **analogy**.

asymmetric attitudes To say that our attitudes toward two things are asymmetrical is simply to say that they are different. The asymmetric attitudes arise as a particular puzzle when the things toward which we hold asymmetric attitudes are apparently the same in relevant ways.

A prime example of this is the asymmetric attitudes we hold toward the time before birth and the time after death. Both are long periods of time in which we do not exist. It would seem, then, that our attitudes toward them should be symmetric. Intuitively, though, it seems reasonable to regard death as a bad thing, and unreasonable to regard the period of prenatal nonexistence as comparably bad. That is, we hold asymmetric attitudes toward death and prenatal nonexistence.

atheism Atheism is disbelief in a god. Strictly speaking, atheists are those who don't believe in any god or gods, but often writers will describe someone who does not believe in the god or gods in which they believe as an atheist.

basic structure In "A Theory of Justice," John Rawls says that his theory of justice concerns a society's major social, political, and economic institutions. His examples include the existence of competitive markets, basic political liberties, and the structure of the family. Rawls calls this the *basic structure* of a society. G. A. Cohen, in "Where the Action Is," argues that there is an important ambiguity in this idea.

behaviorism Behaviorism is used in somewhat different senses in psychology and philosophy. In psychology, behaviorism was a twentieth-century movement that maintained that the study of behavior is the best or even the only way to study mental phenomena scientifically. It is opposed to the introspective methods for the study of the mind emphasized in much psychology of the nineteenth century. This is *methodological behaviorism*. A methodological behaviorist might even believe in an immaterial mind (*see* **dualism**), but maintain nevertheless that there was no scientific way to study the immaterial mind except through its effects on observable, bodily behavior.

In philosophy, however, behaviorism opposes dualism; the term means some form of the view that the mind is nothing above and beyond behavior. *Logical behaviorists* maintain that talk about the mind can be reduced without remainder to talk about behavior. *Criteriological behaviorists* maintain that mental terms may not be completely reducible to behavioral terms, but they can only be given meaning through ties to behavioral criteria.

Behaviorism is closely related to *functionalism*.

British Empiricism   *See* **empiricism**.

Cartesian dualism   *See* **dualism**.

category-mistake   According to Gilbert Ryle (see "Descartes's Myth") a *category-mistake* is committed (roughly) when one thinks of or represents things of a certain kind as being or belonging to a category or logical type to which they do not belong. Ryle's examples illustrate this sort of mistake nicely. Suppose someone visits your university, and you take him on a tour of the campus, showing him the student commons, the library, and so on. At the end of the tour he says, "This is all very well, but what I'd like to see is the *university*." Your friend would here be making a category-mistake. He apparently thinks that the university is yet another building in addition to the library, and so on, whereas in reality it is more like the sum total of such buildings and their relationships.

causal determinism   *See* **determinism**.

cause and **effect**   We think of the world as more than just things happening; the things that happen are connected to one another, and what happens later depends on what happens earlier. We suppose that some things cause others, their effects. The notion of cause connects with other important notions, such as responsibility. We blame people for the harm they cause, not for things that just happened when they were in the vicinity. We assume that there is a cause when things go wrong—when airliners crash, or the climate changes, or the electricity goes off—and we search for an explanation that discloses the cause or causes.

Causation is intuitively a relation of dependence between events. The event that is caused, the effect, depends for its occurrence on the cause. It wouldn't have happened without it. The occurrence of the cause explains the effect. Once we see that the cause happened, we understand why the effect did.

Most philosophers agree that causal connections are *contingent* rather than *necessary*. Suppose the blowout caused the accident. Still, it was possible for the blowout to happen and the accident not to occur. After all, the world might have worked in such a way that a blowout was followed not by an accident but by the car's gradually slowing to a halt.

On one common view, however, causation implies laws of nature in the sense that causal connections are instances of such laws. So causal relations are "relatively necessary": they are contingent only insofar as the laws of nature are contingent. It may be a contingent fact that the laws of physics are what they are. But, on this view, *given* the contingent fact that the laws of nature are as they are, the accident had to happen once the blowout did.

Hume holds such a view. He claims that, at least as far as humans can comprehend things, *A* causing *B* amounts, at bottom, to the fact that events like *A* are always followed by events like *B*. Causation requires universal succession. (Such universal succession is sometimes called *customary* or *constant conjunction*.) At first this doesn't seem very plausible. After all, many blowouts don't lead to accidents. It seems more plausible if we assume that Hume is thinking of the total cause, the blowout plus all the other relevant factors that in this case led to the accident, including the design of the car and the skill of the driver. Taken this way, the universal succession analysis implies that if the blowout caused the accident, then if all of these relevant conditions were duplicated in another case, and there is a blowout, an accident would happen. If not, and if the blowout really caused the accident in the original case, there must be some relevant difference. This version of universal succession seems more plausible, but perhaps not totally convincing.

Even if we grant the Humean relevant difference principle, there are difficulties with the idea that causation simply is universal succession. Consider what it means about the case of the blowout causing the accident. What is the real connection, according to the universal succession theory, between this particular blowout and this particular accident? It just seems to be that the blowout occurred, and then the accident occurred. That's all there really is to causation, as it pertains to these two events. All the rest that is required, on the universal succession analysis, has to do with other events—events *like* the blowout and events *like* the accident. It seems that there is more to causation than this.

Hume offers a candidate for this additional something involved in causation. He says it is really just a certain feeling we have when we have experienced many cases of events of one type being followed by events of another. When we have had this experience, our minds pass from the perception of an event of the first kind to an expectation of one of the second kind. Hume challenges us, if we are not satisfied that causation is just universal succession together with the feeling of the mind passing from perception to expectation, to identify what else there is.

commodification   We treat some goods as subject to norms of a market: They can be bought and sold for prices that are subject to pressures of supply and demand. This is how we see, for example, cars and computers: We treat cars and computers as *commodities*. Are there moral limits to such commodification—moral limits to the appropriate scope of markets? If so, what are they

and what is their justification? These are questions Debra Satz explores in her "Markets in Women's Reproductive Labor."

compatibilism and **incompatibilism**   In philosophy, the term *compatibilism* usually refers to a position in the issue of *freedom* versus *determinism*. Intuitively it seems that freedom excludes determinism, and vice versa. But this has been denied by some philosophers; they claim that acts can be *both* free *and* determined, usually adding that the traditional problem is the product of confused thinking abetted by too little attention to the meaning of words.

Hume held this position. In Section VIII of his *An Inquiry Concerning Human Understanding*, he describes his project as one of "reconciling" *liberty* with *necessity*, these being his terms for freedom and determinism. Hume said that liberty consists of acting according to the determinations of your will; that is, doing as you decide to do. A free act is not one that is *uncaused*, but one that is caused by the wants, desires, and decisions of the person who performs it. Hence an act can be both free and an instance of a universal causal principle. On this conception, an unfree act is one that one must do *in spite of* one's own desires and decisions, rather than because of them.

Some compatibilists go further and maintain that freedom requires determinism. The idea is that for our own will to determine what we do, our decisions must cause our actions, and causation in turn requires determinism.

Given this distinction, the views of most philosophers on the issue of freedom and determinism can be located among the following possible positions:

1. Incompatibilism: Freedom and determinism are incompatible. This view leaves open two main theoretical options:
    a. *Libertarianism*: There are some free acts, so determinism is false.
    b. *Hard determinism*: Determinism is true, so there are no free acts.
2. Compatibilism: Freedom and determinism are compatible. This view is typically part of a view called *soft determinism*, according

to which there are free acts and determinism is also true. This view in turn comes in two varieties:

   a. There are free acts. Determinism is as a matter of fact true, but there would be free acts whether or not determinism were true.

   b. There are free acts. Determinism is true and its truth is required for freedom.

3. Freedom is incoherent: Freedom both requires and is incompatible with determinism, and hence makes no sense.

Some philosophers distinguish between freedom of action and free will. Free will involves more than having one's actions determined by one's decisions and desires. It involves having control over those desires and decisions themselves. Someone might have freedom, as the compatibilist understands it, without having free will. For example, a person addicted to smoking might be free in the sense that whether or not he or she smokes on a given occasion is determined by personal desire. But what if this person doesn't want to have or be controlled by that desire? Does he or she have the power to get rid of the desire, or weaken its hold? This is the question of free will. The issue of whether free will is compatible or incompatible with determinism can then be raised.

conclusion　*See* **deductive argument.**

conditionals　A conditional is a kind of statement that is made out of two others. The normal form of the statements is "If *P* then *Q*." *P* is the *antecedent* and *Q* the *consequent*. "If *P*, *Q*" and "*Q*, if *P*" are stylistic variations of "If *P* then *Q*."

Conditionals can be in various tenses and in the indicative or subjunctive:

Indicative: *If Susan comes to the party, then Michael brings the salad. If Susan came to the party, then Michael brought the salad. If Susan will come to the party, Michael will bring the salad.*

Subjunctive: *If Susan were to come to the party, Michael would bring the salad. If Susan had come to the party, Michael would have brought the salad.*

A *counterfactual* conditional, one in which the antecedent is false, will usually be in the subjunctive if the speaker realizes that the antecedent is false.

One thing seems quite clear about conditionals: *If the antecedent is true, and the consequent false, then the conditional as a whole is false.* If Susan comes to the party, and Michael doesn't bring the salad, then all of the examples preceding are false. This is the basis for two clearly valid rules of inference:

Modus ponens: From *If P, then Q* and *P*, infer *Q*.
Modus tollens: From *If P, then Q* and *not-Q*, infer *not-P*.

In symbolic logic a defined symbol (often "R") is called the conditional. The conditions under which conditional statements that involve this symbol are true are stipulated by logicians as follows:

1. Antecedent true, consequent true, conditional true
2. Antecedent true, consequent false, conditional false
3. Antecedent false, consequent true, conditional true
4. Antecedent false, consequent false, conditional true

This defined symbol, then, agrees with the ordinary language conditional on the clear case, number 2, the case that is crucial for the validity of *modus ponens* and *modus tollens*. But what about the other cases? Suppose Susan doesn't come to the party, but Michael brings that salad (antecedent false, consequent true). The symbolic logic statement,

Susan comes to the party $\longrightarrow$
                            Michael brings the
                            salad

is true in this case, because of part 3 of the definition. It isn't so clear that the ordinary language conditionals are true. Suppose that Michael says, "I brought the salad because Susan couldn't make it. If she had come, she would have brought it." Are any or all of the ordinary language conditionals listed true in this case? False? What of Michael's second sentence, which is also a conditional?

See **necessary** and **sufficient conditions.**

consequent   *See* **conditionals.**

consequentialism   Consequentialism is a view about what makes it right or wrong to do something. It maintains that the rightness of an action is determined by the goodness or badness of relevant consequences. *Utilitarianism* is a consequentialist theory that holds that what makes consequences better or worse is, at bottom, the welfare or happiness of sentient beings. A *deontological* ethics rejects consequentialism and holds that the rightness of action depends at least in part on things other than the goodness of relevant consequences. For example, someone who rejects consequentialism might hold that the principle under which an act is done determines whether it is right or wrong. Kant held a version of this view; *see* the Introduction to Part V.

continental philosophy   *See* **analytical philosophy.**

continental rationalism   *See* **rationalism.**

contingent and **necessary**   Some things are facts, but would not have been facts if things had happened differently. These are contingent facts. Consider, for example, the fact that Columbus reached America in 1492. Things could have turned out differently. If he had gotten a later start, he might not have reached America until 1493. So the fact that he arrived in 1492 is contingent. Necessary facts are those that could not have failed to be facts. The year 1492 would have occurred before the year 1493 no matter how long it took Columbus to get his act together. It is a necessary fact. Mathematical facts are a particularly clear example of necessary facts. The fact that 2 + 2 = 4 doesn't depend on one thing happening rather than another.

Philosophers sometimes use the idea of a possible world to explain this distinction. Necessary truths are true in every possible world. Contingent truths are true in the actual world but false in some other possible worlds. Necessary

falsehoods are false in the actual world and false in every other possible world, too. If one thinks of the distinction this way, one must be careful to distinguish between the truth of a sentence and the truth of what it says. It is easy to imagine a possible world in which the sentence "2 + 2 = 4" is false. Just imagine that the numeral "2" stood for the number three, but "4" still stands for four. But imagining the sentence to have a meaning that makes it false is not the same as imagining what it says, given its actual meaning, to be false. It is the latter that is important when we ask if it is necessary or contingent that 2 + 2 = 4.

The distinction between the necessary and contingent is a *metaphysical* distinction. It has to do with facts or propositions and truth. It is closely related to the epistemological distinction between *a priori* and *a posteriori* and the distinction between *analytic* and *synthetic* statements. These three similar distinctions shouldn't be confused. Some philosophers claim that they are *coextensional*. But they are not *cointensional*, so this is a substantive philosophical claim. For example, some philosophers claim that there are mathematical facts that have nothing to do with the meanings of words, and may never be known at all, and are hence not knowable a priori, but are still necessary.

corroboration   *See* **deductivism.**

cosmogony   *See* **cosmos.**

cosmological argument   *See* **cosmos.**

cosmology   *See* **cosmos.**

cosmos   The cosmos is the universe considered as an integrated orderly system. Sometimes the cosmos is the orderly part of a larger whole, the other part being *chaos*. Any account of the origin of the universe as a whole, whether based on myth, religion, philosophy, or science, is a *cosmogony*. An account of the nature and origin of the universe that is systematic is a *cosmology*. This term is used for the particular branch of physics that considers this question, and also for inquiries of a more philosophical nature. Cosmological arguments for the existence of God begin with very general facts about the known universe, such as causation, movement, and contingency, and then argue that God must exist, as first cause, or unmoved mover, or necessary being, to account for these facts. The first two ways of proving the existence of God listed by St. Thomas Aquinas are cosmological arguments.

customary/constant conjunction *See* **cause** and **effect.**

death The end of life; the cessation of the biological functioning of the body. All known living things eventually die.

deductive argument Arguments have premises and a conclusion. The truth of the premises should provide grounds for the truth of the conclusion, so that the argument gives one who believes the premises a good reason for believing the conclusion.

In a valid argument, the truth of the premises entails the truth of the conclusion. This means that it is impossible for the premises to be true and the conclusion false. A valid argument may have a false conclusion because the validity of an argument does not imply the truth of the premises. If the premises of a valid argument are true, then the argument is sound. Clearly the conclusion of any sound argument will be true.

An argument that aims at validity is *deductive*, or *demonstrative*. Such arguments are *nonampliative* in the following sense: The conclusion does not contain anything not already found in the premises. In other words, the conclusion is simply "drawn out of" the premises. They are thus *necessarily truth preserving*: If the premises are true, the conclusion (because, logically, it says no more than the premises) must also be true. *Deductive logic* provides rules of inference that exhibit valid patterns of reasoning.

An argument can provide those who believe its premises good reason for accepting its conclusion even if it is not valid. Among arguments that are not valid, we can distinguish between those that are strong and weak. A *strong* nondemonstrative or nondeductive argument makes the truth of the conclusion very probable. *Analogical arguments*, for example, are nondeductive but can be quite strong.

Inductive arguments involve generalizing from instances. Having noticed that a certain radio station plays rock music on a number of occasions, you may infer that it always does so, or that it is at least very likely that it will do so next time you tune in. This process is called *induction by enumeration*. Inductive arguments are *ampliative* in character: The conclusion of these arguments "goes beyond" what is contained in the premises. Such inferences are not valid, but it seems that they can be quite strong, and in fact the whole idea of using past experiences to guide our conduct depends on them. *See* **induction, problem of.**

deductivism Deductivism is the thesis that science should focus solely on *deductive arguments* rather than *inductive arguments* because there is no good response to the *problem of induction*. Deductivism is most closely associated with the twentieth-century philosopher of science Karl Popper. Popper advocated the *hypothetico-deductive model* of science, which held that science should make *falsifiable* hypotheses about the world and then test them. Hypotheses that are not falsified despite severe tests are *corroborated* (although not *confirmed*). According to this model of science, the difference between scientific and (say) *metaphysical* claims is that scientific claims are *falsifiable*. For discussion, see Salmon, "The Problem of Induction."

demonstrative/nondemonstrative inference *See* **deductive argument.**

deontological ethics *See* **consequentialism.**

deontology Deontology is the study of ethical concepts having to do with permissibility and impermissibility, e.g., rights, duties, and obligations. *See* deontological ethics.

determinism Determinism is the doctrine that every event, including every intentional action of a human being, is determined by prior causes. This is usually thought to imply that there are universal, nonstatistical laws of nature covering every aspect of everything that happens. *See* **cause** and **effect.**

Given the state of the universe at any time, these laws determine everything else that will ever happen. Some philosophers oppose determinism, because they think that the ultimate laws of nature are statistical. Others oppose it because they believe there are free actions, and that no actions can be both free and determined. *See* **freedom, compatibilism** and **incompatibilism, fatalism.**

difference principle   A central idea of John Rawls's theory of justice, referred to as *the difference principle*, is that inequalities in the distribution of relevant goods are just if and only if these inequalities are needed to improve the plight of everyone, in particular of those who are the worst off. (*See* Rawls's second principle of justice, "A Theory of Justice," p. 595, and G. A. Cohen's formulation, "Where the Action Is," p. 616.)

distributive justice   *See* **justice.**

double effect, doctrine of   An act typically has both intended and unintended effects. For example, swatting a fly may have the intended effect of killing a fly, and the unintended effects of making a noise and waking up your brother. The latter effect may be unintended even though it is foreseen. You knew that swatting the fly would or at least might wake your brother. That's not why you were doing it; you were doing it to get rid of the fly. Perhaps you didn't much care whether or not your brother slept. Perhaps you hated to wake him, but it was very important to you to swat the fly. In these cases, swatting the fly is the intended effect of your act, and waking your brother is merely foreseen.

According to the doctrine (or principle) of double effect, the moral status of intended effects differs from those that are merely foreseen. This principle is sometimes appealed to as a part of a *deontological* moral theory. According to this principle, it might be wrong to swat the fly with the intention of waking up your brother, but permissible to swat the fly with the intention of killing it, knowing it would wake up your brother. A more interesting example is abortion. Some people maintain that it is wrong to act with the intention of aborting a fetus, but that nevertheless certain operations may be permissible, even though abortion of the fetus is a foreseeable result, so long as they are done for some other purpose, such as preventing the injury to a mother that continued pregnancy might involve. Some philosophers maintain the distinction makes no sense. Others believe there is a coherent distinction between intended and merely expected consequences, but doubt that it has the moral significance it is given by the doctrine of double effect.

doxastic/doxically   Doxastic states are states having to do with beliefs. If I have the belief that *p*, I am in the doxastic state of believing that *p*. A consideration is *doxically* relevant if it is relevant to one's beliefs.

dualism   The term *dualism* has a number of uses in philosophy, but perhaps the most common is to describe positions on the mind-body problem that hold that the mind cannot be identified with the body or part of the body, or that mental properties are not physical properties.

The form of dualism Descartes advocated is called *Cartesian dualism* or *interactive dualism*. The mind is that which is responsible for mental states of all kinds, including sensation, perception, thought, emotion, deliberation, decision, and intentional action. Some philosophers maintain that this role is played by the brain, but Descartes argued that this could not be so. His view was that the mind was a separate thing, or substance, that causally interacted with the brain, and through it with the rest of the body and the rest of the world. Sensation and perception involve states of the world affecting states of sense organs, which in turn affect the brain, which causes the mind to be in certain states. Action involves states of mind affecting the brain, which in turn affects the body, which may interact with other things in the world.

Other forms of dualism include *epiphenomenalism*, *parallelism*, and *property dualism*. The epiphenomenalist holds that the body affects the mind, but not vice versa. The mind only appears to affect the body, because the apparent mental causes of bodily changes (like the decision to lift my arm) coincide with the true bodily causes (some change in my brain). Parallelists hold that mind and body are two substances that do not interact at all. Property dualism maintains that the mind can be identified with the brain (or with the body as a whole), but mental properties cannot be reduced to physical ones. On this view, it is my brain that is responsible for sensation, perception, and other mental phenomena. But the fact that my brain is thinking a certain thought, for example, is an additional fact about it, one that cannot be reduced to any of its physical properties.

effect   *See* **cause** and **effect**.

efficient causation   Efficient causation is one of the four types of causation that Aristotle distinguished. Of these four types, efficient causation is the sort of causation that best fits contemporary usage of the word *causation*. The efficient cause of an event is (roughly) the agent or event that brings the effect about. If a ball breaks a window, the efficient cause of this event is roughly the ball's hitting the window. If Jones raises his hand, the efficient cause of this event is, according to some, Jones himself. When (as in this last example) an agent is supposed to be the efficient cause of some event, this is a (putative) instance of *agent-causation* (*see* **agent-causation**). For another type of causation distinguished by Aristotle, *see* **final causation**.

egoism   *Egoism* has many usages in philosophical discourse. On one usage, it refers to the view that human beings *ought* to pursue their own self-interest. On another usage, it refers simply to the view that human beings *do* (perhaps exclusively) pursue their own self-interest.

eliminative materialism   *See* **materialism** and **physicalism**.

embodiment   An embodied thing has taken physical, tangible form. That which has been embodied has, literally, been put into a body. Embodiment can mean either the process of taking form in this way, or the state of having been embodied. Philosophers are most concerned with the embodiment of *consciousness*, that is, with the way in which thinking, conscious things inhabit physical forms, and how a conscious being relates to its embodiment.

empiricism   Empiricism is an epistemological position that emphasizes the importance of experience and denies or is very skeptical of claims to a priori knowledge or concepts. The empirical tradition in seventeenth-, eighteenth-, and nineteenth-century philosophy was centered in Britain, and Bacon, Locke, Berkeley, Hume, and Mill are often referred to as *British Empiricists*. *See also* **rationalism**.

endurance   *See* **perdurance** and **endurance**.

en-soi   According to the existentialist philosopher Jean-Paul Sartre, the world is divided between two sorts of beings: beings-in-themselves (en-soi) and beings-for-themselves (pour-soi). Beings-in-themselves are inanimate things like rocks, whereas beings-for-themselves are beings that exhibit feeling and agency.

entails   *See* **deductive argument**.

epiphenomenalism   *See* **dualism**.

epistemology   Epistemology is the theory of knowledge, the inquiry into its possibility, nature, and structure.

ergon   This is the Greek word for *function*, which is a concept that plays an important role in Aristotle's moral theory. For Aristotle, the *ergon* of an object is more than just what we may use that object for—rather, it is whatever activity makes that object the sort of thing that it is. For example, although we can use a knife to hammer a nail into a wall if we wish, this is not the knife's *ergon*. Rather, a knife's *ergon* is to cut.

error theory   Some philosophical views have the implication that we regularly but unknowingly fall into error when we make claims about some particular domain of inquiry. For instance, it is a consequence of J. L. Mackie's view in "The Subjectivity of Values" that although we regularly think that at least some of our moral judgments are true, they are in fact systematically false. Mackie thus provides an error theory about moral judgments. As Mackie points out, such theories require strong support because of the challenge they pose to common sense.

essential   *See* **accidental** and **essential**.

eternalism and **presentism**   Of course dinosaurs don't exist *right now*, but do they just plain exist? Again, of course my great-great-grandson doesn't exist *at this moment*, but does he exist nevertheless? According to eternalism, which is a view about past and future objects, the answer to these questions is "Yes." Just as the Eiffel Tower exists even though it doesn't exist *over here*, so dinosaurs exist even though they don't exist *right now*. This view is often contrasted with a view called *presentism*, according to which the only objects that exist are those that exist *right now*. According to presentism, when dinosaurs went extinct, they didn't just cease to exist *from then on*—rather, they ceased to exist altogether.

eudaimonia   Eudaimonia—sometimes translated "happiness" or "flourishing"—is a central concept in Aristotle's ethics. *See* "Aristotelian Ethics" in Part V.

Euthyphro dilemma   The original Euthyphro dilemma is found in one of Plato's dialogues in which Socrates is questioning an Athenian named Euthyphro about the nature of piety. When Euthyphro attempts to explain piety by saying that pious actions are those actions that the gods love, Socrates responds by asking whether the gods love pious actions because they are pious or whether pious actions are pious because the gods love them. This is a dilemma because either response is to some degree unsatisfactory. If Euthyphro says that the gods love pious actions because they are pious, then this seems to imply that there is something out of the control of the gods—namely what actions count as pious. But, on the other hand, if we say that pious actions are pious because the gods love them, then presumably the gods could have loved morally despicable actions, in which case it would follow that some morally despicable actions would be pious.

More recently, the term *Euthyphro dilemma* has come to refer to the structurally parallel problem about moral rightness and wrongness, rather than piety. For example, are wrong actions wrong because God forbids them or does God forbid them because they are wrong? In general, the dilemma demands an order of explanation—is an action's being wrong explained by its being forbidden, or is God's act of forbidding the action explained by the action's being wrong?—and so any order of explanation dilemma, whether about God or not, may be considered a version of the Euthyphro dilemma.

event-causation   *See* **agent-causation**.

evil, problem of   Many philosophers have thought that the existence of evil poses a problem for those who believe that there is a perfect God. A perfect God, it seems, would be able to do anything (*omnipotence*), would know everything (*omniscience*), and would have all the moral virtues, such as benevolence. If such a God created the world, why is there any evil? Does God not care if we suffer? Then God is not benevolent. Is this world the best God could make? Then God is not omnipotent. Or perhaps God wanted to do better, and had the power, but didn't quite know what to do. Then God is not omniscient. A perfect God would have made the best of all possible worlds. So, the argument goes, the existence of our imperfect world, full of sin and suffering, shows that God does not exist, or is not perfect.

The problem of evil is pressed by Philo, a main character in Hume's *Dialogues Concerning Natural Religion*. Both Philo and his main adversary, Cleanthes, give up the idea that God is perfect. Philo concludes that while the world was probably created by an intelligent being or beings, there is no reason to attribute benevolence to that being or those beings. Cleanthes allows that God may be only finitely powerful.

Other philosophers have thought, however, that our problems with evil simply show how difficult it is for finite beings to grasp the plan of an infinitely perfect being. This is, contrary to first impressions, the best of all possible worlds. This is Leibniz's position in "God, Evil and the Best of All Possible Worlds."

experiential blank   The complete absence of experience. This is to be distinguished from the sort of "experience of nothing" that results from sensory deprivation. An experiential blank is a complete absence of consciousness and awareness. It is typically assumed (in secular discussions) that both the time before our birth (or, perhaps better, conception) and the time after our death are experiential blanks.

extension   (alternate) Things that occupy space have *extension*. Some things that (apparently) exist lack extension, including numbers, properties, and—according to *dualism*—minds or souls. This usage of *extension* should be distinguished from the usage that concerns the application of predicates; *see* **extension** and **intension.**

extension and **intension**   Consider a *predicate* like "human being." It applies to or is true of a number of individuals, those who are human beings. The set of these individuals is the extension of the predicate. The members of this set have the property of being a human being in common. This property (or, for some philosophers, the concept of this property) is the intension of the predicate.

Terms that have the same extension are *co-extensional*; terms that have the same intension are *co-intensional*. It seems that terms can be co-extensional without being co-intensional. Russell's example is "human being" and "featherless biped that is not a plucked chicken." These terms are not *co-intensional*, as the property of being a human being is not the same as the property of being a featherless biped that is not a plucked chicken. But they are *co-extensional*. If you set aside the plucked chickens, humans are the only bipeds without feathers. (Probably their extensions are not *quite* the same; after all there are plucked turkeys, too, but Russell thought the example was close enough to being correct to make the point.)

The term *extension* is often used in an extended sense in which names and sentences have extensions as well as terms or predicates. (The terminology is due to Rudolf Carnap, and the idea it incorporates goes back to Gottlob Frege.) The extension of a name is the thing it names; the extension of a sentence is its truth value, true or false. This brings out the systematic connection among name, predicate, and sentence. The sentence "Fido is barking" will have the extension True (i.e., be true), just in case the extension of "Fido" (i.e., Fido) is a member of the extension of "is barking." That is, the extension of the parts (the name "Fido" and the predicate "is barking") determines the extension of the whole sentence. Sentences like this, their truth-value being determined by the extension of their parts, are *extensional*.

If a sentence is extensional, substitution of a name in it for another co-extensional name (or a predicate for another co-extensional predicate) won't affect the truth value. Suppose Fido is also called "Bad-breath." Then the substitution of "Bad-breath" for "Fido" will preserve the truth value of our sentence. If "Fido is barking" is true, so too will be "Bad-breath is barking."

Not all sentences are extensional. Consider the true sentence "Bad-breath is so called because of his smell." If we substitute the co-extensional name "Fido" for "Bad-breath" the result is "Fido is so called because of his smell." This sentence isn't true. So our original sentence, "Bad-breath is so called because of his smell," isn't extensional, but *nonextensional*.

We can generalize and say that any expression is extensional if its extension is determined by the extensions of its parts. Consider the predicate "is portrayed as a human being." Suppose this is true of Donald Duck, because he is portrayed in cartoons as having so many human characteristics. If we substitute "featherless biped" for "human being" we get the predicate "is portrayed as a featherless biped." This doesn't seem to be true of Donald, as he is always portrayed as a feathered biped.

In these examples, it seems possible to pick out the expressions that lead to the nonextensionality. In the first example it is "so called"; in the second it is "portrayed as." Expressions like these that give rise to nonextensionality are often called *nonextensional contexts*.

Some concepts that are very important in philosophy seem to generate nonextensional sentences. Consider "Harold believes that Cicero was a great Roman." Because "Tully" is another name for Cicero, if this sentence is extensional, it seems we should be able to substitute "Tully" for "Cicero" without changing the truth value of the whole. But it seems that if Harold has never heard Cicero called "Tully," "Harold believes that Tully was a great Roman" would *not* be true.

The term *intensional* is used in three ways, one strict and comparatively rare, one loose and very common, and one incorrect. Strictly speaking, an expression is intensional if its intension is determined by the intensions of its parts. This is the way Carnap used the term. It is common to use it loosely, however, simply to mean "nonextensional," so that an "intensional context" means a form of words, like "so called" and "portrayed as" and "believes," that leads to nonextensional predicates and sentences. *Intensional* is often confused with *intentional* in the broad sense that is sometimes taken to be the mark of the mental. This is understandable, because many words that describe intentional phenomena, such as *believes*, seem to be intensional, in the loose sense.

In *possible worlds semantics*, names, predicates, and sentences are said to have extensions *at* possible worlds—the set of things that the predicate applies to in the world. Sentences are also said to have extensions at worlds: their truth values in the worlds. The intension of a predicate is a function from worlds to extensions, and the intension of a sentence is a function from worlds to truth values.

extensional   *See* **extension.**

extrinsic   An extrinsic property is one that an object has partly in virtue of its relations to other things and their properties. A thing could lose such a property without really changing at all. For example, Omaha has the property of being the largest city in Nebraska. It could lose this property by virtue of Grand Island growing a great deal. Omaha wouldn't have to lose population to lose this property, or change in any other way. Being the largest city in Nebraska is thus an extrinsic property of Omaha. An *intrinsic* property, by contrast, is one that an object has because of the way it is in itself, independently of its relations to other things and their properties.

The distinction is often useful, because a property that we might have thought to be intrinsic turns out to be extrinsic on closer examination.

It is very difficult, however, to give a really clear and precise explanation, or unchallengeable list, of intrinsic properties of ordinary, spatiotemporally extended objects.

falsifiability   *See* **deductivism.**

fatalism   Fatalism is the doctrine that certain events are fated to happen, no matter what. This might mean that an event is fated to take place at a specific time, or that someone is going to do some deed, no matter what anyone does to try to prevent it. Fatalism differs from *determinism*. One way they differ is that a fatalistic view about the occurrence of a certain event does not depend on the laws of nature determining only a single course of events. There may be many possible futures that differ in many ways, but they all will include the fated event. Oedipus, for example, was (allegedly) fated to marry his mother and kill his father. This didn't mean that there was only one course of action open to him after hearing the prophecy, but that no matter which course he took, he would eventually end up doing that which he wanted most to avoid. A second way they differ is that an event may be determined by prior causes even though it was not fated to occur; for among those prior causes may be the decisions and efforts of human agents. So determinism does not entail fatalism about all events.

feminism   Feminism is an intellectual, social, and political movement. The movement is very diverse, but one strand that runs through all varieties is the conviction that important intellectual, social, and political structures have been based on the assumption, sometimes implicit, sometimes quite explicit, that being fully human means being male. Reexamination of these structures from a perspective that appreciates the interests, values, styles, ideas, roles, methods, and emotions of women as well as men can lead to fruitful and in some cases radical reform.

final causation   According to the Aristotelian doctrine of final causes, the final cause (or *telos*) of a thing's existence is the purpose or end for which it exists. For instance, the final cause of a chair is sitting, and so on. *Teleology* is the branch of knowledge having to do with purposes and design. A fact is *teleological* if it is of or related to teleology or final causes. Some arguments for the existence of God are teleological in nature; such arguments appeal to the apparent design or purpose of human beings or the universe to argue for the existence of a cosmic designer.

first cause argument   The first cause argument purports to prove the existence of God as the first cause. In the world we know, everything has a cause and nothing causes itself. The series of causes cannot go back to infinity, so there must be a first cause, and this is God. St. Thomas Aquinas's second way of proving the existence of God is a version of the first cause argument. Philosophers have challenged each step of the argument.

first-order desires   *See* **second-order volitions.**

formal   The formal properties of representations are distinguished from their *content* properties. "All cows are animals" and "all houses are buildings" have different contents, but the same form: *All Fs are Gs*. *Formal logic* seeks to classify inferences in terms of their formal properties. Where *P* and *Q* are sentences, any inference of the following form, known as *modus ponens*, is valid, no matter what the content is.

> If *P* then *Q*
> *P*
> Therefore, *Q*.

Some philosophers have argued that philosophical confusion can sometimes be avoided by putting claims into the *formal mode* rather than the *material mode*. To put a claim in the formal mode is to express it, as nearly as possible, as a claim about words or other symbols, rather than about the things the words purport to stand for. "Santa Claus doesn't exist" is a claim in the material mode, which may be confused or confusing because it looks as if we are saying something about a thing, Santa Claus, who isn't really there to say anything about. Better to say "'Santa Claus' doesn't refer to anything."

formal logic   *See* **formal.**

formal mode   *See* **formal.**

freedom   In ordinary conversation we call people free who aren't prevented from doing what they want to do and conducting their life as they see fit. In politics and political philosophy, freedom usually means having civil or political liberty, having certain basic rights or freedoms, such as those codified in the American Bill of Rights, the Rights of Man, or the Charter of the United Nations.

In the realm of metaphysics and the philosophy of mind, the term *freedom* refers to a very basic feature of decisions or actions. When we perform an ordinary act, like drinking a cup of coffee, or going to a movie, or helping a friend, we have a feeling that our action results from our own decision and *that we could have done otherwise*. It seems that only when this is the case do we take full responsibility (blame or credit) for our actions. A person might be free in this sense, although not enjoying freedom in the sense of political liberties. A writer under house arrest, and prevented from publishing, would not enjoy basic civil liberties. But many of her actions would still be free in this metaphysical sense. She has coffee in the morning; she could have had tea. Perhaps she writes her essays even though she can't publish them. This is a free act, in that she could have gardened or stayed in bed instead; if she had chosen to do those things, no one would have forced her to write.

One fundamental question about freedom in this sense concerns its relation to *determinism*. If determinism is true, are any of our actions *really* free, or is freedom simply an illusion? This debate often turns on the exact definition of freedom. *Compatibilists* are likely to think of freedom as being able to act in accord with one's desires and decisions, even if those desires and decisions are themselves the influences of more remote causes, outside the agent. This is compatible with determinism, in that one's own desires and decisions might be the causes of one's actions, even though those desires and decisions were themselves caused by other things, and lie at the end of a chain of causes and effects that goes back to the time before the agent was born. An *incompatibilist* typically thinks of a free decision or act as one that is not caused by anything else, or is caused by the agent, independent of external causes.

The term *free will* is sometimes used to contrast with *freedom of action*. One's *will* in this sense is one's decision, choice, or dominating desire. Even if one is free to follow one's strongest desire, and hence has freedom of action in the compatibilist sense, does one have any control over those desires and choices themselves? Can one influence the strength of one's desires, or are they determined by external influences? One might be a compatibilist with respect to free action and determinism, but an incompatibilist with respect to free will and determinism.

In theological contexts, the question of free will is whether humans can have any choice if there is a god who has foreknowledge of what they will do.

free will   *See* **freedom.**

functionalism   The function of a thing is its operation within a system. It is the role the thing has, when the system is operating properly. For example, the function of a carburetor is to supply an atomized and vaporized mixture of fuel and air to the intake manifold of an internal combustion engine. One can contrast the function of a thing with its structure and the material from which it is made. The structure of a carburetor differs from that of a fuel injection system, although both have the same function and are made of the same types of materials.

Functionalism in the philosophy of mind is the view that mental states are real states definable by their functions, specifically by their causal role with respect to stimuli, other mental states, and behavior. Functionalism can be contrasted with Cartesian dualism and behaviorism. Functionalism agrees with Cartesian dualism in holding that mental states are real, but differs in that the latter maintains that the mental states are essentially states of an immaterial mind, defined by their basic nature, rather than their function. Functionalism agrees with *logical behaviorism* in seeing a definitional connection between mental states and behavior. They differ in that the logical behaviorist maintains that mental states are

not real at all; the terms that seem to stand for them are just misleading ways of describing behavior. For the behaviorist, the definitions that connect stimuli, behavior, and mental states are reductive; they show how to eliminate reference to mental states in favor of reference to stimuli and behavior. For this reason, a behaviorist definition of a mental state cannot allow ineliminable reference to other mental states. The selection from Armstrong explains and defends versions of functionalism.

Good Samaritan   The Good Samaritan is a well-known parable from the New Testament. In it, a traveler is lying injured on a road, having just been robbed. A priest and then a Levite see the man and continue walking, failing to help him in his need. Finally, a Samaritan stops and helps him, taking him to a nearby inn and tending to his wounds. The term *Good Samaritan* is now often used to refer to people who go out of their way, who go over and above their duties, to help others in need. In her essay "A Defense of Abortion," Judith Jarvis Thomson distinguishes the Good Samaritan from the Minimally Decent Samaritan. The latter is meant to refer to a person who does what is required of him or her but doesn't go over and above to help others in need.

Greatest Happiness Principle   *See* **utilitarianism.**

hallucination, argument from   *See* **illusion, argument from.**

hard determinism   *See* **compatibilism** and **incompatibilism.**

hedonism   *See* the discussion of utilitarianism in the Introduction to Part V.

hedonistic utilitarianism   *See* **utilitarianism.**

hierarchical model of moral responsibility   According to a hierarchical model of moral responsibility, a person is morally responsible for her actions only if there is a "mesh" between her *higher-order preferences* and the *first-order preferences* on which she acts. First-order preferences are our preferences about things—like a desire to have sushi for lunch or to go on a date with your significant other. Higher-order preferences concern *other* preferences. I may, for instance prefer that my first-order desire for a cigarette not move me to action, or I might hope my actions will be guided by my desire to meet my deadline, leading me to stay home and work rather than go out with my friends. When my higher-order preferences prevail and I am moved by the first-order preferences they designate, there is a mesh between my higher-order and first-order preferences. At the most basic level of analysis, a hierarchical model of the mind posits mental states of different orders (first-, second-, and so forth), and a hierarchical model of moral responsibility exploits this sort of model of the mind to give an account of moral responsibility.

hypothetico-deductive method   *See* **deductivism.**

ideas   There are two quite different uses of the term *idea* in philosophy. The term *idea* is used for the denizens of Plato's heaven. Sometimes *form* is used as a less misleading translation of *eidos*. Plato's ideas or forms are not parts of our minds, but objective, unchanging, immaterial entities that our minds somehow grasp and use for the classification of things in the changing world, which Plato held to be their pale imitations.

John Locke uses the term *idea* for that which the mind is immediately aware of, as distinguished from the qualities or *objects* in the external world the ideas are of. This use for the term leaves it rather vague. Idea can be the images involved in perception, or the constituents of thought. Hume calls the first *impressions*, the latter *ideas*, and the whole class *perceptions*. For Hume, the class of impressions includes passions (emotions) as well as sensations. A feeling of anger would be an impression, as would the sensation of red brought about by looking at a fire truck. Later memory of the feeling of anger or the fire truck would involve the ideas of anger and red.

The conception of ideas as immediate objects of perception and thought, intervening between our minds and the ordinary objects we perceive and think about, was part of a philosophical movement, sometimes called "the way of ideas," greatly influenced by Descartes's *Meditations.*

Descartes there uses a form of the *argument from illusion* to motivate the distinction between the mental phenomena we are certain of and the external reality that is represented by them.

identity   A thing is *identical* with itself and no other. If *a* is identical with *b*, then there is just one thing that is both *a* and *b*; "*a*" and "*b*" are two names for that one thing. It follows from this that the relation of identity is *transitive* (if *a* is identical with *b*, and *b* is identical with *c*, then *a* is identical with *c*), symmetrical (if *a* is identical with *b*, then *b* is identical with *a*), and confers indiscernibility (if *a* is identical with *b*, and *a* has property P, *b* has property P).

The term *identity* is not always used in this strict sense. For example, in this sense, "identical twins" are not identical—they couldn't be twins if they were, as there would be only one of them. We sometimes use identity to mean close resemblance in one respect or another. It is best, in philosophical contexts, to use identity in the way previously explained and some other word, like *similar* or *resembles*, when that is what is meant.

The terms *numerical identity* and *qualitative identity* are sometimes used, but are best avoided. One needs to distinguish between the identity of qualities (red is one and the same color as rouge) and similarity with respect to a quality (the couch and the chair are both red; they are similar in respect of color), and this terminology obscures the distinction.

Some issues about identity are raised in the section on personal identity and in "The Paradox of Identity."

identity theory   David Armstrong in "The Nature of Mind" maintains that mental states are quite literally identical with physical states. Our concept of a mental state is of a state that occupies a certain causal role; it turns out that physical states do occupy those roles; hence, mental states are physical states. This *identity theory* is a species of *materialism*. It is also, strictly speaking, a form of *functionalism*, because it maintains that mental states are definable by their function or causal role. Many functionalists, however, think that mental states cannot be identified with physical states.

They maintain that the relation is a less stringent one, *supervenience*. Functionalism in this narrower sense is often contrasted with the identity theory.

illusion, argument from Philosophers use the term *argument from illusion* for a general type of argument and for a specific version of it. These arguments are intended to show that what we are directly aware of when we perceive ordinary things are not those ordinary things themselves. We can distinguish three such arguments: the argument from perceptual relativity, the argument from illusion, and the argument from hallucination.

The argument from perceptual relativity starts with the fact that perceptions of the same object in different circumstances involve different perceptual experiences. For example, a building seen from a great distance casts a different-sized image on your retina, and creates quite a different experience, than the same building seen from a few yards away. Consider seeing a quarter held at a ninety-degree angle to your line of sight, and the same quarter held at a forty-five-degree angle. In the first case a round image is cast on your retina; in the second an elliptical image. The perceptual experience is different, although the object seen, the quarter, is the same. The conclusion drawn is that there is something involved in the experience besides the agent and the quarter, which are the same in both, that accounts for the difference. This is the *immediate* object of perception. Some philosophers take these objects to be ideas in the mind of the perceiver that represent the external object; *see* **representative ideas, theory of.** Others have taken them to be nonmental sense data. Some philosophers have taken the ideas or sense data to be materials out of which external objects are constructed, rather than representations of them.

The argument from illusion itself starts with the fact that two different objects can create the same experience. For example, a quarter held at an angle and an elliptical disk held at ninety degrees might cast exactly the same image on the retina and create the same experience. What is it that is the same? Not the objects seen, which are different. The answer again is an intervening object, which may be taken to be a subjective idea or something objective.

The argument from hallucination considers the case in which it is to one as if one were seeing an object, although there is in fact nothing at all there. This sort of case, a true hallucination, is much more unusual than those noted for the earlier two arguments. What is it that is present in our perception when there is nothing seen? It is, again, the subjective idea or the objective sense datum.

immanent causation   *See* **agent-causation.**

immutability   Immutability is a property often, and traditionally, attributed to God. Roughly, a being is immutable if and only if that being cannot change. However, it is a matter of some controversy whether and to what extent God is immutable. Some theists have thought that saying that God is immutable is theologically undesirable. According to these theists, God does things like creating the world and performing miracles, and (it is argued) an absolutely immutable being could not do such things, because doing them involves changing from doing one thing at one time to doing another at another time. Such theists typically argue that God's immutability should be restricted to God's character: God's character (or what God is like) cannot change.

imperatives, categorical and **hypothetical**   *See* the discussion of Kantian ethics in the Introduction to Part V.

impressions   *See* **ideas.**

incompatibilism   *See* **compatibilism** and **incompatibilism.**

induction   *See* **induction, problem of** and **deductive argument.**

induction by enumeration   *See* **deductive argument.**

induction, problem of   The problem of induction, sometimes known as *Hume's problem*, has to do with justifying a very basic sort of *nondeductive* inference. We often seem to infer from observation that some sample of a population has a certain attribute to the conclusion that the next members of the population we encounter will also have that attribute. When you eat a piece of bread, for example, you are concluding from the many times in the past that bread has nourished you, that it will also do so this time. But it is conceivable that bread should have nourished in the past, but not this time. It isn't a *necessary, analytic,* or *a priori* truth that the next piece of bread you eat will be like the ones you have eaten before. How does your inference bridge the gap? It is natural to appeal to various general principles that one has discovered to hold. But, as Hume points out, the future application of principles found reliable in the past presents exactly the same problem. For example, consider the most general principle of all, that the future will be like the past. All one has really observed was that, in the past, the future was like the past. How does one know that in the future it will be? The problem of induction is stated in Hume's *An Enquiry Concerning Human Understanding*, Section III, and discussed by Salmon, "The Problem of Induction."

inductive argument   *See* **deductive argument.**

infinity   The concept of infinity is a fascinating, tricky, and complex one. It has been used in a number of philosophical arguments, such as Zeno's arguments about motion, and in some of St. Thomas Aquinas's arguments for the existence of God. In the last two hundred years mathematicians have given us a clearer framework for thinking about infinity than earlier philosophers had, but this doesn't mean all of the puzzles and problems are easy to resolve.

Infinite means without end. Let's say that to count a collection of objects is to assign the natural numbers (1, 2, 3 . . .) in order to its members, so that every member is assigned a number and no number gets assigned twice. Let's say that *to finish counting a collection of objects* is to assign numbers in this way to every object in the collection. A finite collection of things is one that one could finish counting, at least theoretically, and say "it has n members" where n is some natural number. An infinite collection is one for which one could not finish counting. One can see from this that the set of natural numbers is itself infinite, for one would never finish counting it.

Assigning objects from one set to those in another, so that each object is assigned to only one object and has only one object assigned to it, is called putting the sets in a one-to-one correspondence. Sets that can be correlated in this way are the same size—they have the same number of elements. Using this idea, modern mathematics has shown that not all infinite sets are the same size, so that one needs to distinguish among different infinite or *transcendental* numbers. The number of natural numbers is called aleph$_0$.

Somewhat surprisingly, this is also the number of even numbers, as there is a one-to-one correlation between numbers and even numbers (assign $2n$ to n). But it is not the number of points in a line for there is not a one-to-one correlation between the set of such points and the natural numbers. This is shown by a variation of Zeno's Racecourse Argument. Let the line be of length m. If we assign 1 to the point $m/2$, 2 to $m/4, \ldots n$ to $m/2n$, we will have paired a point from the continuum with each natural number, but no matter how long we go on, we will never assign a natural number to any of the points beyond $m/2$.

In thinking about infinity, it is important to keep certain distinctions in mind. One might have two quite different things in mind when calling a magnitude "infinite": that it goes on forever, or that the process of dividing it could go on forever. A finite distance like ten feet is not infinite in the first sense, but seems to be in the second: One could take the first half, half of what's left, and so on without end. Intuitively, one can traverse a finite, but infinitely divisible, distance in a finite amount of time, but not an infinite distance. Zeno's Racecourse Argument seems to show that one cannot even traverse a finite distance. But keeping this distinction in mind, what exactly does it show?

Aristotle distinguished between the potential and actual infinite. When we say that a distance of ten feet is infinitely divisible, we don't mean one could actually divide it into an infinite number of parts, but only that there are an infinite number of points in which one could divide it. Aristotle thought that this distinction took care of Zeno's arguments.

intension, intensional   *See* **extension.**

intentionality   An intentional act or state is one that is directed at objects and characterized by the objects at which it is directed. Intentionality in this sense is a feature not only of intentions, but of many other mental phenomena. Some philosophers take it to be the essence of mentality and consciousness. Think about how you would describe your intentions. You don't say what they look like or feel like or sound like, or what material they are made of. You say something like, "I have an intention to paint my room." You say what your intention is as an intention *to do*. This essential characteristic of your intention is its *object*, the event or state of affairs it is aimed at bringing about. Similarly, if you are asked to describe your wants, you would describe *what you want*—a new car, say, or world peace. The *object* of the want or desire, the thing or state of affairs that would satisfy it, seems essential to it.

Beliefs and other *propositional attitudes* are also considered intentional. We describe our beliefs by giving the circumstances under which they are true: "Fred believes that San Francisco is the capital of California." The object of the belief is the *proposition, that San Francisco is the capital of California*. This proposition may be the object of the belief even if it is not true.

The term *intentional* should not be confused with the term *intensional*, although they are related. Many of the concepts used to describe intentional phenomena are nonextensional, which is one meaning of intensional. For example, "Oedipus intended to marry Jocasta" is a true description of an intention of Oedipus. If we substitute "his mother" for "Jocasta," we change this truth into a falsehood. So the sentence is intensional.

interactive dualism   *See* **dualism.**

intrinsic   *See* **extrinsic.**

intuitionism   Moral or ethical intuitionism is the view that we can have some knowledge about right and wrong that is not acquired through inference. Rather, there are some moral truths that we can "just see" or "just know," perhaps through some faculty of moral intuition. J. L. Mackie criticizes this view in "The Subjectivity of Values."

justice   Issues about justice are traditionally divided into issues about justice in the distribution of benefits and burdens to different individuals and groups in a society (*distributive justice*) and issues about the justice of various forms of punishment (*retributive justice*).

laws of nature   Many scientists take themselves to be engaged in the project of figuring out what rules and guidelines describe the universe and its inhabitants at the most general level. That is, they are attempting to figure out the laws of nature that govern our world. For instance, Einstein discovered the law of nature that nothing travels faster than the speed of light. Presumably there is some set of statements like this that is complete in the sense that these statements would completely describe the behavior of the physical universe. These statements would be all the laws of nature (sometimes also called the laws of physics). For a discussion of how the laws of nature relate to determinism and freedom of the will, see Peter van Inwagen's piece, "The Powers of Rational Beings: Freedom of the Will."

libertarianism   *See* **compatibilism** and **incompatibilism.**

logical behaviorism   *See* **behaviorism.**

logical positivism   Also called "logical empiricism," logical positivism was a philosophical movement in the first half of the twentieth century. It was characterized by a concern for scientific methodology. Logical positivists were particularly interested in developing an understanding of philosophy as fitting into this scientific enterprise.

manichean/manichaeism   Manicheanism was a gnostic religion that originated in Persia in the third century A.D. In philosophy, manicheanism primarily arises in connection with its interesting approach to the problem of evil. According to manicheans, there are two co-eternal powers of Light and Darkness that are in perpetual conflict.

We find ourselves in the midst of this struggle. Because the manicheans, unlike traditional theists, give equal priority to Light and Darkness, they do not have the problem of explaining how evil came to exist in a world created by a perfectly good being (such as God).

materialism and **physicalism**   Materialism is the doctrine that reality consists of material objects and their material, spatial, and temporal properties and relations. Narrowly construed, materialism refers to material substances and properties as conceived in eighteenth-century physics and philosophy, so that material properties are confined to the primary qualities then recognized, including figure (shape), extension (size), number, motion, and solidity. A more general term is *physicalism*, where *physical properties* are taken to be whatever properties physics postulates in the best account of the physical world. The physicalist leaves open the possibility that the fundamental properties needed by physics will not be much like the primary qualities of the materialist. A chief obstacle to materialism or physicalism is the mind. *Cartesian dualists* claim that the mind is an immaterial or nonphysical object; other kinds of dualists claim that at least mental properties are above and beyond the physical properties. The physicalist response has taken the form of identity theories (the mind is the brain; mental properties are physical properties), behaviorist theories (mental terms are ways of talking about behavior), and eliminative materialism (there are no minds or mental properties; the terms that seem to refer to them are just parts of a discredited theory of how people work). *Functionalism* is hard to categorize; perhaps it maintains the letter of property dualism but the spirit of physicalism.

matters of fact and **relations of ideas**   This is Hume's terminology for the *analytic–synthetic* distinction, which Hume didn't distinguish from the *a priori–a posteriori* distinction and the *necessary–contingent* distinction. Hume thought our thinking is conducted with simple ideas that are copied from impressions of external objects and complex ideas that result from combining the simple ones. The mind can put ideas together in new ways not derived from perception, so complex ideas need not correspond to external objects. These ideas also serve as the meanings of words. *Relations of ideas* are truths that simply reflect the way these ideas are related to each other and don't depend on whether the ideas actually apply to anything. Hume's examples are "that three times five is equal to the half of thirty" and "that the square of hypotenuse is equal to the square of the two sides." Such truths "are discoverable by the mere operation of thought, without dependence on what is anywhere existent in the universe." The contrary of a relation of ideas will imply a contradiction and is impossible.

In contrast, matters of fact have to do with what the world is like, and not just how ideas are related. The contrary of a matter of fact is possible and doesn't imply a contradiction. Hume's example is "that the sun will rise tomorrow." This is true, and we are quite certain of it, at least most of the time. But it is true because of what happens tomorrow, not because of the way ideas are related. Its contrary, "that the sun will not rise tomorrow," is not a contradiction.

Hume maintained that only relations of ideas can be discovered a priori, and that no matter of fact can be demonstrated with only relations of ideas as premises. He argued that many principles philosophers had claimed to know a priori, such as that nothing happens without a cause, were matters of fact and could not be known that way.

Most philosophers agree that mathematical truths, like Hume's examples cited earlier, are necessary and knowable a priori. But many do think that they are not analytic—are not simply a matter of relations of ideas, in Hume's sense.

means-end analysis   To give a means-end analysis of some concept is to define it as a particular way of achieving some goal or purpose. Thus giving a means-end analysis involves two parts: a description of the goal to be achieved (the end), and a description of the way of achieving that goal (the means). For instance, we might give a means-end analysis of the concept of *intimidation*. We could specify the goal or end by saying that intimidation is a way of bringing it about that another acts in accord with one's wishes. We can then specify the means by saying that intimidation achieves this goal by making threats of one kind or another. On this means-ends analysis, then, intimidation is bringing it about that another acts in accord with one's wishes by making threats of one kind or another.

mechanisms   On the account of moral responsibility suggested by J. M. Fischer, one is morally responsible insofar as one acts from one's own, appropriately reasons-responsible mechanism. A mechanism here is not thought of as a "thing," but, intuitively, as a "way" of acting or "process" that issues in a choice and action.

metaphysics   Metaphysics considers very general questions about the nature of reality. It includes the study of the basic categories of things (*ontology*). Questions such as whether there are universals, events, substances, individuals, necessary beings, possible worlds, numbers, ideal objects, abstract objects, and the like arise here. Metaphysics also includes questions about space, time, identity and change, mind and body, personal identity, causation, determinism, freedom, and the structure of action.

methodological behaviorism   *See* **behaviorism.**

mind-body problem   The mind-body problem is the problem of accounting for the way in which our minds interact with or are related to our bodies. The mind-body problem thus comprises a central area of the subfield of philosophy called *philosophy of mind.*

modus ponens   *See* **conditionals.**

modus tollens   *See* **conditionals.**

moral responsibility   If an agent is morally responsible for her actions then those actions can make her the appropriate target of certain attitudes and practices. A morally responsible agent can be an appropriate target for what Peter Strawson dubbed the *reactive attitudes.* These include resentment, indignation, gratitude, and approval. She can also be the appropriate target for our practices of praise, blame, reward, and punishment.

We should distinguish moral responsibility from *causal* responsibility. One can be causally responsible for something, but not morally responsible for it. For instance, if you spill a glass of water on my computer, then you are causally responsible

for the damage that ensues. You are also morally responsible—it could be appropriate for me to resent you for not being more careful. If, however, it is my cat that spills the water, then the cat, though just as causally responsible for the damage as you would be, is not morally responsible. It makes no sense for me to resent my cat: cats just are not an appropriate target for the reactive attitudes.

It is fairly easy to see why the cat is not morally responsible: the cat is not a person, and only persons can be morally responsible for their actions. However, not all persons are morally responsible for their actions. For instance, children are persons, but are not generally taken to be fully responsible for their actions. Philosophers disagree about the conditions under which persons are morally responsible—about just what makes someone an appropriate target for reactive attitudes and practices of praise and blame.

naive realism   *See* **realism.**

natural evil   In discussions about the philosophical *problem of evil*, a distinction is commonly made between *moral evil* and *natural evil*. Moral evil is (roughly) evil that is brought about by the bad actions of human beings (or other created beings), whereas natural evil is evil that is (seemingly) brought about by nonagential forces (e.g., hurricanes, tornados, drought, and so on). A deer's being badly burned in a naturally caused forest fire is a paradigmatic instance of natural evil. It is important to see that responses to the problem of moral evil are not necessarily good responses to the problem of natural evil.

naturalism   Naturalism is a powerful if somewhat vague philosophical view, with both epistemological and metaphysical sides. All knowledge derives from the methods we use to study the natural world, sense-perception extended by the methods of the natural sciences. The only objects and properties that we should countenance are those that we perceive in the natural world, and those that are required to explain natural phenomena by our best theories. Thus, in the title of his *Dialogues on Natural Religion*, the word *natural* tells us that Hume will consider whether basically scientific methods of inquiry and argument can lead us to a belief in an intelligent creator.

Naturalism in ethics maintains that good and bad, right and wrong are definable in terms of natural properties, such as pleasure and pain, and that there are no special methods of knowledge for moral facts.

natural religion   The term *natural religion* occurs in Hume's *Dialogues*. It is basically opposed to *revealed religion*. Natural religion is religious belief based on the same sorts of evidence that we use in everyday life and science: observation and inference to the most plausible explanations for what is observed by principles based on experience. It is in this spirit that Cleanthes puts forward his analogical argument for the existence of an intelligent creator. In contrast, revealed religion relies on sacred texts and the authority of tradition and church.

necessary   *See* **contingent** and **necessary**.

necessary and **sufficient conditions**   In the phrases *necessary condition* and *sufficient condition*, the term *condition* may be used for properties, statements, propositions, events, or actions. The basic idea is always that:

A *is sufficent for* B. Having (being, doing) A is one way of having (being, doing) B; nothing more is needed. You may not need to have A to have B, for there may be other ways of having B. But A is one way.

A *is necessary for* B. Every way of having (being, doing) B involves having (being, doing) A. A may not be all you need; it may be that every way of having B involves not only having A but also something more. But you've got to have A to have B.

For example: Having a car is sufficient, but not necessary for having a vehicle. One could have a bicycle instead. But having a car is certainly enough.

Having blood is necessary for being alive, but not sufficient. A dead man can have blood; more than blood is required to be alive. But you can't do without it.

Being in England is necessary, but not sufficient, for being in London. Being in London is sufficient, but not necessary, for being in England.

Given these explanations, there is a symmetry to necessary and sufficient conditions:

If A is necessary for B, B is sufficient for A.

Indeed, if we take conditions to be statements we can say:

When: If P, then Q,

P is sufficient for Q, and Q is necessary for P.

Philosophers are often interested in finding an *analysis* of some interesting condition. This involves finding a set of conditions that are *individually necessary and jointly sufficient*. If A, B, C are individually necessary and jointly sufficient for D, then each of A, B, and C are necessary, and the conjunctive condition A & B & C is sufficient. For example, being a male, being unmarried, and being an adult are (arguably) individually necessary and jointly sufficient for being a bachelor.

It is necessary, finally, to distinguish different kinds of necessity and sufficiency. Is the relationship a matter of logic, metaphysics, the laws of nature, or something else? The necessity of blood for human life, for example, seems a matter of natural or causal necessity, not logic or metaphysics.

necessarily truth preserving   *See* **deductive argument.**

normative/normativity   Normative judgments or statements concern how things should or ought to be, rather than simply how things as a matter of fact are.

object   The term *object* is used in different ways by different philosophers, and one has to be careful when one encounters it. Sometimes it means any sort of things at all, whether abstract or concrete, universal or particular. On this usage numbers, people, rocks, properties, moods, propositions, and facts are all objects. Sometimes it is used for objects of thought. Sometimes it has the connotation of an ordinary material thing.

omnipotence   Omnipotence is one of the traditional attributes of God. In common usage, to say that God is omnipotent is to say that God is "all powerful" or that God can (in some sense) "do anything." However, it has been notoriously difficult to analyze satisfactorily the concept of omnipotence. For instance, it is commonly held that omnipotence must be restricted to what is *logically possible to bring about*. That is, one might think that although God can do anything that is *logically possible*, he cannot do that which is logically impossible; he cannot, say, create a square circle or bring it about that 2 and 2 equals 5. Descartes, however, apparently denied this thesis, holding that God's omnipotence is unrestrained by logical possibility. Other problems associated with the thesis that God is omnipotent involve the question of whether God can sin. If God cannot sin, as has been traditionally held, it appears that there is something that God cannot do, and thus God is not omnipotent. This problem has led various philosophers and theologians to maintain that omnipotence should not be thought to entail the ability to sin, or to deny that omnipotence is a property that ought to belong to the greatest possible being.

omniscience   Omniscience is one of the traditional attributes of God. In common usage, to say that God is omniscient is to say that God is "all-knowing" or that God "knows everything." More carefully, a common analysis of omniscience is that a being is omniscient if and only if that being knows all true propositions and believes no false propositions. However, some philosophers have sought to analyze the concept of omniscience in terms of what is *possible* to know. These philosophers argue that a being is omniscient if and only if that being knows all that is *possible* to know.

ontology   *See* **metaphysics**.

original position   *See* **veil of ignorance**.

paradox   A paradox is an argument that appears to derive absurd conclusions from acceptable premises by valid reasoning. Quine distinguishes veridical paradoxes from falsidical paradoxes and antinomies. In the case of a veridical paradox, the premises are acceptable and the reasoning valid, and we must accept the conclusion, which turns out not to be absurd under close analysis. A falsidical paradox really does have an absurd conclusion, but upon close analysis the premises turn out to be unacceptable or the reasoning invalid. An antinomy defies resolution by close analysis, for the paradox brings to the surface a real problem with part of our conceptual scheme that only revision can eliminate.

parallelism   *See* **dualism**.

particulars   *See* **universals** and **particulars**.

perceptual relativity, argument from   *See* **illusion, argument from**.

perdurance and **endurance**   It certainly seems that objects can lose parts over time without ceasing to exist. In fact, we gain and lose cells at such a rate that we are made up of completely new cells perhaps as quickly as every decade. But this simple fact gives rise to a philosophical puzzle: If I don't right now still have any of the same atoms in my body as those that were there when I was 5 years old, then how can the person writing these words be the same person as that little 5-year-old? What is it for a person to persist through time and change? According to the view called endurance, the relationship between my 15-year-old self and my 5-year-old self is identity. On this view, a single object—me—moves from one instant of time to the next as time passes, leaving nothing behind. According to another answer to this question, which has come to be known as perdurance, I am actually a four-dimensional object, extended not only in the three dimensions of space but in the one dimension of time, as well. Thus I have not only spatial parts—like my right hand and my left hand—but I also have distinct temporal parts—like my 5-year-old self and my 15-year-old self, and so on. According to perdurance, a single object "moves" through time by having a distinct temporal part at each moment of that object's existence.

personal identity   Problems concerning personal identity are about what makes us persons. What are the essential properties of persons, or those properties without which a person would not be a person? What makes one person the same person from one moment to the next? What sorts of changes can a person undergo while still being the same person? Such questions are questions of personal identity. *See also* **perdurance** and **endurance.**

petitio principii   The petitio principii is the Latin name for the fallacy of "begging the question." One has committed the fallacy of petitio principii or has "begged the question" (roughly) when one assumes in one's argument what one ought to be (or is trying) to prove. This fallacy is often called the fallacy of *circular argument*: When one assumes what one ought to be (or is) trying to prove, one is relying on the truth of one's conclusion when making one's argument, and is thus arguing "in a circle."

phenomenal character/qualia   *See* **qualia.**

phenomenology   Phenomenology is an approach to some philosophical issues developed by Edmund Husserl and his followers. It conceives of philosophy as the study of phenomena as revealed to consciousness, "bracketing" the assumptions of an orderly external world that are made by science and common sense. Phenomenology emphasizes the intentionality of consciousness. The term *phenomenology* is also used more loosely, to indicate a survey of experience connected with some topic conducted as a preliminary to theorizing. The phenomenology of an experience, in this sense, refers to how an experience seems to the person experiencing it.

physicalism   *See* **materialism.**

Platonism and **platonism**   Platonism refers to the philosophy of Plato (428–348 B.C.) and the movements specifically inspired by it. Uncapitalized, platonism has become a technical term in *ontology* for those who countenance abstract entities that are not merely abstractions from or constructions out of particulars, and specifically, in the philosophy of mathematics, for those who maintain that numbers are such objects. Although Plato was a platonist in this sense, most modern platonists do not hold many of Plato's most important doctrines in metaphysics, epistemology, and ethics.

possible world   *See* **contingent** and **necessary.**

Pour-soi   *See* **En-soi.**

practical wisdom (phronesis)   Practical wisdom is a virtue—a quality of character—that allows for the proper application of a general, theoretical understanding of morality to particular, concrete cases. Someone has practical wisdom inasmuch as they are able to make competent judgments about ethical matters.

predicate   The term *predicate* traditionally refers to the part of a sentence that characterizes the subject. In "Sally kissed Fred," "Sally" is the subject and "kissed Fred" is the predicate. Philosophers and logicians extend this notion, so that a sentence with one or more *singular terms* removed is a predicate. Predicates are 1-place, 2-place, and so forth, depending on the number of singular terms needed to make a sentence. A predicate is said to be *true of* an object or sequence of objects if a true sentence would result if terms referring to that object or those objects were inserted. From our example, we can get these predicates:

1. (1) kissed Fred.
2. (1) kissed (2)
3. Sally kissed (2)
4. (1) kissed (1).

(1) is a 1-place predicate, true of Sally and whoever else has kissed Fred. Predicate (2) is a 2-place predicate, true of the pair of Sally and Fred, and any other pair, the first of which has kissed the second. Number (3) is a 1-place predicate, true of Fred and others Sally has kissed. And (4) is a 1-place predicate, because it only takes one referring expression to complete the sentence, although it must be inserted twice. It is true of people who have kissed themselves.

The notion of a predicate does not necessarily fit very well with the categories linguists use to describe the structure of sentences. For example, the words *Sally kissed*, which remain after *Fred* is removed from our sentence, giving predicate (3), are not usually considered a syntactic part of the original sentence.

premise   *See* **deductive argument.**

presentism   *See* **eternalism** and **presentism.**

principle of alternate possibilities   In Harry Frankfurt's article, "Alternate Possibilities and Moral Responsibility," he formulates this principle as the claim that a person is morally responsible for what he or she has done only if he or she could have done otherwise. The idea that this principle attempts to capture is related to the "garden of forking paths" picture described in Peter van Inwagen's article, "The Powers of Rational Beings: Freedom of the Will."

Principle of Utility   *See* **utilitarianism**.

problem of other minds   The problem of how (and whether) one can know that other minds exist besides one's own. For discussion, see Russell's "The Argument from Analogy for Other Minds."

properties and **relations**   Consider these three facts:

1. Nixon was born in California.
2. Carter was born in Georgia.
3. Nixon was older than Carter.

These facts have different things in common with one another. Facts 1 and 3 are about the same people, Nixon and Carter, but involve different relations. Facts 1 and 2 are about different *individuals*, but involve the same relation.

The relation involved in 1 and 2 is *being born in*. This is a relation between people and places. Philosophers might say that 1 states that the relation *being born in* obtains between Nixon and California, 2 states that it obtains between Carter and Georgia, and 3 states that the relation *older than* obtains between Nixon and Carter.

Being born in and being older than are both binary or 2-ary relations: relations that obtain between two objects. Three important properties of 2-ary relations are *transitivity*, *symmetry*, and *reflexivity*. Suppose that R is a 2-ary relation. Then:

- R is *transitive* if it follows from the fact that a has R to b and b has R to c that a has R to c. For example, *being longer than* is a transitive relation: If a is longer than b and b is longer than c, then a is longer than c. However, *liking* is not transitive: From the fact that Bob likes Mary, and Mary likes Carol, it does not follow that Bob likes Carol.

- R is *symmetrical* if it follows from the fact that a has R to b that b has R to a. *Being a sibling of* is symmetrical; *being a brother of* is not.

- R is *reflexive* if it follows from the fact that a has R to b that a has R to a. If Bob is the same height as anyone at all—if he is the sort of thing that has height at all—then he is the same height as himself.

Relations that are transitive, symmetrical, and reflexive are *equivalence relations*. There are also 3-ary relations, and in principle there are n-ary relations for any n. When we say, "Nebraska City is between Omaha and Topeka," we are stating that a 3-place relation obtains among three cities. It is often useful to use variables to indicate the places of relations, so the relation here is *x is between y and z*.

It is sometimes useful to talk about the *arguments* or *parameters* of a relation. Thus one could say that the place argument (or parameter) of the relation of being born in was filled in 1 by California and in 2 by Georgia. In the example in the last paragraph, we might say that Topeka filled the *z* argument of the relation of *x is between y and z*.

When we say that a person is old, or tired, or silly, we are not saying something about a relation he or she stands in to someone or something else, but stating a property that he or she has or doesn't have by himself or herself. Properties are 1-ary relations.

So far we have been ignoring time. Consider 4:

4. Carter lives in Georgia.

Number 4 is true now, but wasn't true when Carter was president and lived in Washington, D.C. It seems that living in is really a 3-ary relation, among people, places, and times, even though it looks like a 2-ary relation. Similarly, because people can be old, tired, or silly at one time, while being young, energetic, and serious at others, these are all really 2-ary rather than 1-ary relations. When we take time into account, we need to think of most properties as 2-ary relations between individuals and times.

property dualism   *See* **dualism**.

proposition   Consider the report, "Russell said that Hegel was confused." The phrase "that Hegel was confused" identifies a proposition, which was *what Russell said*. Others could assert the same proposition, and it could also be believed, doubted, denied, and the like. We could say, "Taylor doubted that Hegel was confused," "Moore believed that Hegel was confused," and so forth. It seems that the same proposition could be expressed in other languages, so a proposition is not just a particular sentence type. A proposition is an abstract object that has conditions of truth, and it is true or false depending on whether those conditions are met. Propositions are identified by statements and are referred to by "that-clauses," like "that Hegel was confused."

The existence and ontological status of propositions are matters of controversy. Some philosophers believe that propositions are mysterious entities that should be avoided; we should get by just talking about sentences that are true, without bringing in propositions. Among philosophers who accept the need for propositions, some think they should be defined in terms of properties, facts, possible worlds, and other more basic categories, whereas others think they are primitive.

propositional attitude   The propositional attitudes are those mental acts and states, such as belief, knowledge, and desire, that have truth or satisfaction conditions, so that they may be characterized by the propositions that capture those conditions. We say, for example, "Russell believed *that Hegel was confused*," characterizing Russell's belief by a proposition that captures its truth conditions. And we say that Russell desired that *there would be no more wars*, thereby characterizing Russell's desire by a proposition that captures its satisfaction conditions.

Pyrrhonism   Unless used in specialized historical contexts, Pyrrhonism is synonymous with *skepticism. See* **sceptic, skeptic.**

qualia   Consider what it is like to have a headache and how it feels. It is somewhat different from what it is like to have a toothache, and vastly different from what it is like to taste a chocolate chip cookie. We try to avoid headaches because of what it is like to have them, and we try to find and eat chocolate chip cookies, because of what it is like to taste them.

What it is like to have a certain kind of experience is one aspect of that experience. Philosophers call such aspects *qualia*. Other terms that are used more or less similarly are *subjective characters* and *phenomenal characters*.

Philosophers such as Frank Jackson in "What Mary Didn't Know" claim that the qualia or subjective characters of mental events and states cannot be identified with or reduced to physical aspects of those events and states. Thus even if we suppose that headaches *are* brain states, we have to admit that these brain states have nonphysical properties, their qualia. If we accept the arguments of Jackson, we seem to have to accept some form of *dualism*. Minds may not be immaterial *things*, but at least they have immaterial *properties*, such as being in states with certain conscious aspects or qualia.

qualities   *See* **primary** and **secondary qualities**.

rationalism   Rationalism is an epistemological position that emphasizes reason as a source of knowledge itself, not merely a way of organizing and drawing further hypotheses from knowledge gotten by sense perception. *Continental rationalism* is a term sometimes applied to Descartes, Spinoza, Leibniz, and other seventeenth- and eighteenth-century philosophers. *See also* **empiricism**.

realism   In philosophy the term *realism* is used in a context of controversy in which the reality of objects of some category has been denied in some way, usually by claiming that the objects in question are creations or constructions of the human mind. The realist in the controversy is one who defends the status of the controversial objects. A philosopher can be a realist about one issue, while denying realism with respect to some other. The two most common contexts in which the term is used are universals and the objects of sense perception. A realist about universals holds that they are real, in the sense of not being mere names or concepts.

A realist about the objects of sense perception holds that they are real, in the sense of enjoying an existence independent of the perceiving mind.

Naive realism is the view that the objects of perception not only exist, but exist just as they seem to be. This position is often taken to be refuted by the various forms of the argument from illusion. *See* **illusion, argument from; representative ideas, theory of.**

reason   Reason is the ability or faculty to engage in theoretical and practical reasoning. A number of philosophical issues are concerned with the role of reason in various spheres of human life. *Rationalists* and *empiricists* disagree about the role of reason in the formation of concepts and the development of knowledge, the latter seeing it only as an aid to experience. Kant supposed that there were fundamental principles of conduct provided by practical reason, whereas Hume argued that in the practical sphere reason "is, and ought only to be the slave of the passions." *See* **reasoning, practical** and **theoretical.**

reasoning, practical and **theoretical**   Theoretical reasoning is aimed at assessing evidence and drawing conclusions about what is true. Practical reasoning is aimed at making decisions about what to do.

reasons-responsiveness   This is a family of ideas that specify that an agent (or an agent acting on a particular mechanism) has (or exhibits) a capacity to identify and act in accordance with reasons for action. Reasons are typically thought to be considerations that count in favor of actions. So a reasons-responsive agent (or mechanism) is capable of identifying and acting in accordance with considerations that count in favor of actions. Some philosophers (including J. M. Fischer, S. Wolf, and R. J. Wallace) have given accounts of moral responsibility in terms of reasons-responsiveness.

reciprocity   Engaging in reciprocity involves, as it were, "returning the favor." When we help others as we have been helped we are engaging in a reciprocal relationship.

reductio ad absurdum   Literally translated from Latin, this phrase means "reduction to the absurd." It is a form of argument in which some statement is shown to be true because its denial has obviously false consequences. For instance, suppose we are trying to establish that p is true. To argue for p by reductio ad absurdum would be to argue that the denial of p leads to the obviously false statement q. But because q is obviously false, it must have been wrong to deny p in the first place—so, p must be true.

reductionism   In philosophy the term *reductionism* occurs in the context of a controversy about the status of some kind of object. The reductionist maintains that talk and knowledge about such objects really amount to talk and knowledge about some class of objects that is usually thought to be quite different. Talk and knowledge about the first kind of object are *reduced* to talk and knowledge about the second kind. For example, Berkeley thought that talk and knowledge about ordinary objects were really just talk and knowledge about ideas. A philosopher can be a reductionist about some categories of objects while being a nonreductionist about others.

refers   Philosophers use a number of terms for the relationship that holds between singular terms and the objects they designate or stand for. *Refers* is used both for the relation between singular terms and what they stand for, and for the act of using a singular term to stand for something ("'That piece of furniture' refers to the chair" vs. "Jane used 'that piece of furniture' to refer to the chair.") The thing referred to is often called the *referent*. *Denotes* is most properly used for the relation between a definite description and the object that uniquely meets the descriptive part, as in "'The author of *Waverley*' denotes Sir Walter Scott." But *denotes* is often simply used as a synonym of *refers*. The thing denoted is sometimes called the *denotation* and, less often, the *denotatum*. *Names* is used for the relation between a name and its *bearer* (or *nominatum*), as in "'Fred' names that man." *Designate* and *stands for* are used in a very general way, as the latter has been in this discussion. *See also* **extension** and **intension; singular term.**

reflective equilibrium   In the course of theorizing, one often has to make some sort of compromise between general principles and considered judgments about particular cases. Sometimes general principles will need to be amended in the light of conflicting considered judgments, and sometimes judgments will need to be revised in the light of otherwise successful general principles. To arrive at a balance between the two is to achieve reflective equilibrium. For more details and further discussion, see John Rawls, "A Theory of Justice."

relation of ideas   *See* **matters of fact** and **relations of ideas**.

relativism   The term *relativism* is used with reference to a body of statements or alleged truths about some sort of phenomena. The relativist maintains that these statements (1) are only true (or false) *relative* to some further factor or parameter, not explicitly mentioned in the statements themselves; (2) that this parameter is a person or group of people making the judgment, or something corresponding to a group of people such as a culture or a language; (3) hence there is no *objective* truth or falsity; that is, no truth or falsity merely concerning the objects involved in the phenomena independently of the subjects making those judgments. (In the terms explained in *properties* and *relations*, the relativist is claiming that an *n*-ary property is being treated as an $(n-1)$-ary property.)

Here is an example where relativism is pretty plausible. Consider the comparative merits of the taste of food. Does the issue of whether carrots taste better or worse than cucumbers have an answer? The relativist, with regard to this issue, would say that there is an answer only *relative* to a particular taster. Carrots may taste better than cucumbers *to* Mary, whereas cucumbers taste better than carrots *to* Fred. The relativist would say that there is no *further* question of who is right. The question whether carrots taste better than cucumbers *simpliciter*, without further reference to a person who does the tasting, makes no sense. On the relativist view, the judgments of Fred and Mary are misconstrued if they are taken to be opinions about some nonrelative truth. Because taste is relative, there should be no room for such a dispute.

There are many types of relativism that are more controversial and so more interesting than relativism about the taste of food. *Ontological relativists* claim that existence is relative: that different languages, cultures, or conceptual schemes recognize different classes of objects and properties, and questions of existence make no sense considered outside of such *conceptual schemes*. Perhaps the most interesting example is *ethical relativism*. Ethical relativists claim that judgments of right and wrong are relative to individuals, societies, or cultures.

representative ideas, theory of   The theory of representative ideas maintains that knowledge of external things is mediated by ideas in the mind of the knower that represent those things in virtue of a twofold relation they have to them. The ideas are *caused by* the external things, and *depict* those external things as having certain properties. Suppose, for example, one perceives a chair in front of one. The chair causes light to fall on the retina in a certain pattern, which causes other events in the visual system, which ultimately cause ideas of a certain sort in the mind. These ideas have certain features, which depict the object causing it to be a chair of a certain sort.

This theory allows an account of error and a treatment of the *argument from perceptual relativity* and the *argument from illusion*. The argument from perceptual relativity shows that which thing an idea represents and how it depicts that object to be do not depend just on the features of the idea, but also on auxiliary beliefs. The same visual image might represent an object as elliptical or circular, depending on whether it was taken to be held at a right angle or an acute angle to the line of vision. Normal errors and illusions occur when the idea caused by a thing does not accurately depict it, either because the auxiliary beliefs are wrong, or something unusual in the perceiving conditions or the perceiver's state leads to a wrong idea being produced. The more radical types of error involved in certain kinds of delusions, such as hallucinations, involve having an idea that is not caused by an external thing at all, but by some disorder in the perceiver.

Fairly explicit versions of the theory of representative ideas may be found in Descartes and Locke. Berkeley, Hume, and others have criticized the theory for various reasons, including that it leads to *skepticism*, as it seems to provide no direct means of knowing the external objects, that the notion of depiction makes no sense, and that the whole picture of "double existence" is incoherent.

revealed religion   *See* **natural religion**.

sceptic, skeptic   *Skeptic* is an American spelling, *sceptic* the British. When a view is labeled *skeptical*, there are two things that must be ascertained, the type of skepticism and its topic. The skeptic can be advocating suspension of claims of knowledge or certainty, suspension of belief, or positive disbelief. Hume, for example, thinks that we cannot *know* through reason that the future will be like the past, but does not claim we should refrain from believing it; indeed, he thinks it is both natural to do so and impossible not to do so except for brief periods while doing philosophy. He describes this position as skeptical. Whatever type of skepticism is being advocated, a philosopher can be skeptical about some things and not others. For example, a philosopher might be skeptical about the existence of God, but not about the external world.

second-order desires   *See* **second-order volitions**.

second-order volitions   The theory of freedom that Harry Frankfurt constructs in his "Freedom of the Will and the Concept of a Person" relies on the idea that our desires are structured hierarchically. On the first order, we desire objects or states of affairs in the world. For instance, my desire to have another cup of coffee is a first-order desire. But humans have enough psychological complexity to have second-order desires as well, which are preferences in favor of or against having certain first-order desires. So perhaps the only reason I desire another cup of coffee is that I'm addicted to caffeine, but I would rather not be addicted. In this situation, although I may have a first-order desire for another cup of coffee, I have a second-order desire not to have the desire for another cup of coffee.

Roughly, to figure out what your first-order desires are, ask yourself, "What do I want?" To figure out what your second-order desires are, ask yourself, "What do I want to want?" In theory, the hierarchy of desires has no end (there can be third- and fourth-order desires as well), but after two or three the structure is quite difficult to think about clearly.

Second-order volitions, as Frankfurt uses the term, are special sorts of second-order desires. Some second-order desires are simply desires to have a particular first-order desire. But others are desires that some particular first-order desire effectively move the agent to action. In other words, whereas sometimes we merely want to have certain first-order desires, other times we want those first-order desires actually to move us to act. These latter sorts of second-order desires are what Frankfurt calls second-order volitions. Frankfurt dubs creatures who lack second-order volitions *wantons*.

secondary qualities   *See* **primary** and **secondary qualities**.

semicompatibilism   Semicompatibilism is the doctrine that causal determinism is compatible with moral responsibility, quite apart from the issue of whether causal determinism is compatible with freedom to do otherwise. The view presupposes that moral responsibility does not require freedom to do otherwise. (The term was introduced by J. M. Fischer.)

sense-data   Some philosophers who accept that the various forms of the argument from illusion show that we do not directly perceive material objects use the terms *sense-datum* and *sense-data* for what we do directly perceive. Unlike the terms *idea* or *sensation*, the term *sense-data* does not imply that the direct objects of perception are mental, but leaves that question open. Sense-data are objects of some sort, distinguished from the act of being aware of them. Sense-data are usually supposed to have all of the properties they seem to have. Suppose, for example, you see a blue tie in a store with fluorescent lighting, it looks green, and you take it to be so. A philosopher who believes in sense-data would say that you are directly aware of a sense-datum that is green; your mistake is in your inference from the fact about the sense-datum's color to the tie's color.

sex   Sex can refer to various forms of intimate, erotic activity. Exactly which activities of this sort are, properly speaking, sex is a matter of controversy, both in philosophy and elsewhere.

simplicity   Simplicity is a property traditionally attributed to God. Roughly, a being is simple if and only if that being lacks parts or composition. The doctrine of divine simplicity is very controversial; philosophers not only do not agree about whether God is simple, but do not agree about what the doctrine of divine simplicity means or entails. Classical theists such as Augustine, Anselm, and Aquinas have defended the doctrine of divine simplicity. Of course, simplicity (lacking parts or internal structure) is a property that can be possessed by entities other than God.

singular term   Singular terms include proper names (John, Fred), singular definite descriptions (the author of *Waverley*, the present king of France, the square root of two), singular pronouns (I, you, she, he, it), and singular demonstrative phrases (that man, this ship). These terms all identify or purport to identify a particular object, about which something further is said.

The category *singular term* is found in philosophy and philosophical logic more than in linguistics. The category includes expressions that are syntactically quite different, like definite descriptions and names, and separates things that syntactically seem closely related, like singular and plural definite descriptions ("the governor of Maryland," "the senators from Maryland").

solipsism   Solipsism is the thesis that only the self exists, or (alternatively) that only the self can be known to exist. Solipsism is one radical solution to the "problem of other minds," the problem of how it is that one can know that any minds besides one's own exist. According to the solipsist, one can't know that the (apparent) persons one interacts with actually have mental lives like one's own.

sophism   A sophism is a bad argument presented as if it were a good one to deceive, mislead, or cheat someone; *sophistry* is the practice of doing this.

In ancient Greece, the sophists were itinerant teachers of the fourth and fifth centuries B.C., some of whom, such as Protagoras and Gorgias, Socrates criticized vigorously. His negative view was based on the empiricism, relativism, and skepticism of their teachings; on the fact that they took a fee; and on the fact that they taught argument for the sake of persuasion and manipulation of others, rather than for the pursuit of truth.

sound   *See* **deductive argument**.

state of nature   The state of nature is the hypothetical situation in which human beings would find themselves without the existence of any government or state that could exercise coercive force over them.

subjective character   *See* **qualia**.

Sub specie aeternitatis   Literally, this phrase is translated as "under the aspect of eternity." It is used in roughly the same way as the phrase "from a God's-eye point of view" and is meant to indicate an impersonal, detached, and objective view of the world and its goings-on. Thomas Nagel invokes this notion while discussing the meaning of life in "The Absurd."

substance   The term *substance* has been used in a variety of ways in philosophy. In modern philosophy, a substance is a thing capable of independent existence. Substances are contrasted with qualities and relations, on the one hand, and complexes, on the other. These are all merely ways that substances are. Philosophers have had dramatically different opinions about what meets these conditions. Descartes thought that there were two basically different kinds of substance, material and immaterial, and there were many of each, and that no way of being material was a way of being mental and vice versa. Spinoza thought that there was but one substance, and material and mental reality were aspects of it. (He called this thing *God*, although many of his opponents thought his view amounted to atheism.) In "Of Scepticism with Regard to the Senses," Hume treats our perceptions as substances—the ultimate, independent constituents of reality.

supererogation   If you ought to do some action, then it is *obligatory*. If some action is not obligatory but would nevertheless be good to do, then it is super-erogatory. Many think that to give money to famine relief, for instance, is to go "above and beyond" one's obligations and hence is to perform an action that is supererogatory. For a challenge to this view of giving money to famine relief, however, see Peter Singer's "Famine, Affluence, and Morality."

supervenience   A set of properties *A* supervenes on another set of properties *B* if all objects with the same *B*-properties have the same *A*-properties. Many advocates of *functionalism* maintain that although mental properties cannot be identified with physical properties (as the *identity theory* holds), they nevertheless *supervene* on them. Both the identity theorist and the supervenience theorist maintain that beings that are physically indiscernible will have the same mental properties. But the superve-nience theorist allows that beings that are mentally alike may be quite different physically. For example, a philosopher might think that agents built out of silicon-based computers, humans, and individuals from outer space with a completely different biology than ours could all have beliefs, desires, and inten-tions, in spite of the difference of their physical con-stitution and organization.

syllogism   A syllogism is a valid deductive argu-ment or argument form with two premises and a conclusion, that involves universal and existential statements involving three terms. For example:

> All *As* are *Bs*.
> All *Bs* are *Cs*.
> Therefore, all *As* are *Cs*.

> Some *As* are *Bs*.
> No *Bs* are *Cs*.
> Therefore some *As* are not *Cs*.

In these examples, *B* is the *middle term*; it ap-pears in the premises to connect the terms in the conclusion, but does not itself appear in the conclusion. *A* is the *minor term* because it is the subject of the conclusion and *C* is the *major term* because it is the predicate of the conclusion. Much of the theory of syllogism was worked out by Ar-istotle. The class of valid deductive arguments studied in modern logic is much larger.

synthetic   *See* **analytic** and **synthetic**.

teleological ethics   *See* **consequentialism**.

teleology/teleological   *See* **final causation**.

theodicy   A philosophical response on the part of a believer to the *problem of evil*.

transeunt causation   *See* **agent-causation**.

transitive   *See* **properties** and **relations**.

Turing machine   A Turing machine is not a real ma-chine one can go out and buy, but an abstract con-ception invented by A. M. Turing to help think about computing and computers. The machine scans a square on a tape, erases what it finds there, prints something new, moves to a new square, and goes into a new state. What it prints, where it moves, and into what state it goes are all determined by the state in which it was in the beginning and what it found on the square. Computer scientists and logi-cians have shown that Turing machines—given enough time and tape—can compute any function that any computer can compute.

types and **tokens**   How many words are in this statement?

> An argument is an argument,
> but a good cigar is a smoke.

There are twelve word tokens, but only eight word types. There are two tokens each of the word types "an," "argument," "is," and "a" and one each of "but," "good," "cigar," and "smoke." The types are *universals*, whereas the tokens are *particulars*.

uniformity of nature   The principle of the unifor-mity of nature maintains that the same basic pat-terns or laws are found throughout nature; the future will be like the past, at least in terms of the basic operations of nature; and more generally the unexamined parts of nature will be like the parts that have been examined up to a certain point. This principle seems to underlie the use of past ex-perience to form expectations about the future, but, according to Hume, it isn't itself susceptible of proof. The principle is discussed by Hume and Hempel; Goodman's new riddle of induction poses a puzzle about how this principle is to be understood.

universal causation, principle of   The principle of universal causation holds that all events have causes, though not necessarily deterministic causes. *See also* **determinism**.

universals and **particulars**   A particular is what we would ordinarily think of as a thing, with a particular position in space at any one time. A universal is that which particulars have in common, or may have in common. The kind, *human*, is a universal; individual people are particulars. *Types* are universals, *tokens* are particulars. Properties such as being red are universals; philosophers disagree about whether it is red things (roses, barns) that have them in common, or particular cases of the property (the redness of the rose, the redness of the barn). Not all philosophers agree that there are universals. *Nominalists* maintain that universals are just names that we apply to different objects that resemble one another; metaphysics should recognize particulars that resemble each other in various ways, but not universals above and beyond those particulars. A nominalist might claim that the type–token distinction really amounts to providing two ways of counting tokens, not two kinds of object to be counted.

use and **mention**   Ordinarily when a word appears in a statement, it is being used to talk about something else. If one wants to talk about the word itself, one has to mention it. In the statement,

> The word "four" has four letters,

"four" is mentioned the first time it occurs and used the second time it occurs. When a word is mentioned, one may be talking about the *token* or the *type*.

utilitarianism   Utilitarianism is a *consequentialist* ethical theory. Utilitarianism is usually connected with the more specific doctrines of Bentham and Mill, who took the goodness of consequences to be measured by their effect on the happiness or welfare of sentient creatures. (This is sometimes referred to as the principle of Utility or the Greatest Happiness Principle.) Bentham focused on pleasure, Mill on a more abstract notion of happiness that allowed him to maintain that "it is better to be a human being dissatisfied than a pig satisfied; better to be Socrates dissatisfied than a pig satisfied." For further discussion, see the Introduction to Part V.

valid   *See* **deductive argument**.

veil of ignorance   The term *veil of ignorance* is sometimes used to characterize the skeptical consequences of the *theory of representative ideas*. According to this theory, we only directly know the contents of our own mind; these then form a sort of veil between us and the external world. This term is also often used in religion to suggest a fundamental feature of the human condition: All of experience is simply a veil of ignorance between us and what is most real, or matters most.

The term was given a new use in ethics by John Rawls, as an important part of his characterization of the *original position*. The original position is a hypothetical state of affairs in which members of a society choose the principles of justice that will govern them. This choice is to be made behind a veil of ignorance in the sense that the persons making this choice are not to know their class, position, social class, intelligence, strength, and so forth. The underlying intuition is that by being ignorant of these specifics, these individuals will be led to make an impartial and fair choice.

verificationism   Although it comes in many varieties, verificationism is characterized by a general distrust of claims that cannot be shown to be true, or verified, using only empirical methods like those available to the natural sciences. Many have held that because the claims of ethics, metaphysics, and religion cannot be empirically verified, they are meaningless. Although this view of meaning is largely discredited today, it was highly influential in the early twentieth century.

virtue ethics   *See* **virtue theory**.

virtue theory (virtue ethics)   This is an approach to ethical theory that is frequently traced to Aristotle and contrasted with approaches drawn from, for example, Kant and Mill. A virtue theory highlights questions about the nature of those character traits that are virtues—for example, courage. Such questions are seen as in some way fundamental to the theory.

wanton   *See* **second-order volitions**.